6. Learn the music business.

7. Build local and regional success.

8. Visit music centers and make personal contacts.

9. Continue researching and studying.

10. Write, rewrite, write.

Read Pat Luboff's article on page 4 for complete information on how to start your songwriting career.

1992
Songwriter's Market

Where & How to Market Your Songs

Edited by
Brian C. Rushing

Assisted by
Anne M. Bowling

Writer's Digest Books

Cincinnati, Ohio

Distributed in Canada by McGraw-Hill,
300 Water Street,
Whitby Ontario L1N 9B6.
Also distributed in Australia by Kirby Books, Private Bag No. 19, P.O. Alexandria NSW2015.

Managing Editor, Market Books Department: Constance J. Achabal; Assistant Managing Editor: Glenda Tennant Neff

International Standard Serial Number 0161-5971
International Standard Book Number 0-89879-474-9

Contents

Resources

From the Editor

What does it take to become a successful songwriter? This question has been asked so many times by so many different people that you'd think there would be a concrete, definitive answer. Wrong! In such a highly volatile, ever-changing industry, songwriters have always grappled with the processes of successful songwriting. As every songwriter and publisher knows, there are no absolutes. But, there are proven ways to prepare yourself, both creatively and in a business sense, to upgrade the quality of your songs and improve your chances of success. That's the major idea behind *1992 Songwriter's Market*: to give you, the songwriter, the nuts-and-bolts approaches to the music industry, and to show you the things you can do to fulfill your goals.

Two articles in this edition will give you the information you need to get started. The first is Pat Luboff's Bloom Where You're Planted: Start Songwriting in Your Hometown. Luboff goes into detail about the steps you can take in building a local and regional base before branching out nationally. It's a grass roots look at being a songwriter outside of a music center. She stresses research and business education as precursors to success. The second major piece, The Business of Songwriting, is a trove of helpful information on how the music business works (even how earnings are distributed) and how the songwriter who's ready to push his songs should work within the industry.

A new feature this year is the Songwriters' Roundtable, which questions three recently commercially successful songwriters about their struggles to "break through" song markets. Even if you're not interested in hitting the *Billboard* charts, it will be helpful for you to read what Dyna Brein, Jud Friedman and Catesby Jones have learned along the way. The Roundtable is a good "reality check," as it touches on some important topics for songwriters at any level.

We've also rounded up a diverse group of Close-up personalities, all with different outlooks and functions in the music industry. They represent many types of music, including pop, country, jazz, blues, commercial music for advertising, children's and fine arts. Read and study what these successful people have to say—and I think you'll find good, solid advice.

Of course, to put all this information to use, you need contacts. This year we boast over 2,000 listings of music publishers, record companies, producers and others interested in original music. *Songwriter's Market* is a celebration of markets for music of any kind. It's the perfect guide for those who want to turn that magical moment we call a song into a marketable product. Whatever your musical style, there's a place for your songs. Just browsing the myriad of exploitable markets indicates that. So take your time, read and study the upfront articles, section introductions, Close-ups and listings, and I'm sure you'll find this newest edition of *Songwriter's Market* an invaluable asset to your songwriting endeavors.

Brian C Rushing

How to Use Your Songwriter's Market

Before studying the listings and making your marketing plans, read these suggestions for the most productive use of all the features in *Songwriter's Market*. Especially note the explanations of the information given in the sample listing.

Read the section introductions *first*. Each gives a brief overview of the market area and can help you decide if it's a facet of the music industry appropriate for your style of writing and your personal goals.

Keep in mind that the information you are reading in the listings came directly from representatives of the companies listed. It is reported exactly as they gave it to us.

The Glossary in the back of this book will explain unfamiliar terms you might encounter while reading the listings.

For an explanation of the information given in the listings, match the numbered phrases in the sample listing with the corresponding numbers in the copy that follows.

(1) *CREATIVE ENTERTAINMENT MUSIC, Suite 700, 6290 Sunset Blvd., Los Angeles CA 90028. **(2)** Professional Manager: Mark Savage. **(3)** Music publisher and management firm. **(4)** BMI, ASCAP. Member NMPA. **(5)** Estab. 1982. **(6)** Publishes 35 songs/year; publishes 10 new songwriters/year. **(7)** Receives 100 submissions/month. **(8)** Teams collaborators. **(9)** Pays standard royalty.
Affiliates: (10) Creative Entertainment Music (BMI), Weezy Music (ASCAP).
How to Contact: (11) Submit a demo tape—unsolicited submissions are OK. Prefers cassette with 1-3 songs and lyric sheet. **(12)** "No telephone calls please!" **(13)** SASE. **(14)** Reports in 1 month.
Music: (15) R&B and dance. **(16)** Published "Lead Me Into Love" (by Lane/Prentiss), recorded by Anita Baker on Elektra Records (R&B); "Ground Zero" (by Lauren Wood), recorded by Animotion on PolyGram Records (rock); "So Happy" (by David Jones), recorded by Eddie Murphy on CBS Records (R&B); and "More Love" (by Steve Lane, Rodney Saulsberry, Peter Brown), recorded by Jasmine Guy on WB Records (R&B).
Tips: (17) "Smart, crafty lyrics and the most up-to-date grooves and record quality demos aren't enough. You also need surprises."

(1) New listing. An asterisk appears before the names of companies new to this edition.
(2) Contact. The name of the contact person(s) is supplied by the company listed. Address all submissions to this person unless otherwise indicated in the submission instructions.
(3) Type of company. Each listing provides a description of the company's function(s).
(4) Performing rights. If a company indicated which performing rights societies it is affiliated with, we can include this information. ASCAP, BMI and SESAC are the major U.S. societies. SOCAN (Canada), PRS (U.K.) and GEMA (Germany) are examples of societies from other countries. If the company is involved with membership organizations, that information is included here as well.
(5) Establishment date. The year the company was established is given for each company that responded to that question.
(6) Size of market. Figures given (e.g., number of songs published, released or produced per year or number of new songwriters published per year) are approximations to help you determine a market's activity and its openness to material from new songwriters.
(7) Submissions received. States the average number of musical submissions the company receives in a given period (either monthly or annually).

(8) Additional services/activities. If applicable, the listing specifies that the company hires staff writers, works with composers and/or lyricists, and helps to team collaborators. Some markets list additional services offered to songwriters.

(9) Payment. Most companies indicate their payment policy. "Standard" royalty means music publishers split royalties received with the songwriter 50-50. Some markets (advertising agencies, audiovisual firms) pay by the job or per hour rather than by royalty. Some markets (play producers, fine arts) are nonprofit and do not pay at all but offer valuable exposure for songs. Some listings in Record Producers and Managers and Booking Agents indicate that they charge a legitimate fee (negotiated in advance) for their services rendered rather than pay money to songwriters. They are still considered "markets" because they are in a position to shop songs to artists and companies for you, and they may be seeking writer/artists to represent.

(10) Affiliates. If a publisher has affiliated companies, they are listed in this special subhead. The affiliates are usually members of a different performing rights society than the main company listed, so they can work with writers who are members of either organization.

(11) How to submit. The types of music, the number of songs you may include in the submission, and the way you should submit your songs are stated in each listing. Failure to follow these instructions could result in your submission being refused or returned. Your close attention to the exact specifications of a particular listing will help assure your success. "Query" means to contact the company by phone or mail *before* submitting anything. "Does not accept unsolicited material" means you should never submit anything before you request and receive permission to submit. For more on submission procedure, turn to The Business of Songwriting on page 21.

(12) Additional instructions. Many listings give additional submission instructions. Following these requests increases the chance of your demo being reviewed quickly.

(13) Return envelope. All mail should contain a stamped, self-addressed envelope (SASE); submissions to listings in countries other than your own should include a self-addressed envelope (SAE) and International Reply Coupons (IRC) available at most major post offices. Some companies will not even answer a query letter unless you include a reply card or an SASE for their response. Those companies with "SASE" printed in their listing have indicated that they will return submissions if a large enough SASE with sufficient postage is included.

(14) Reporting time. The length of time markets say that they need to report back to songwriters on submissions is approximate. Music professionals go through periods of unbelievably heavy loads of submissions, and sometimes fall behind. Allow extra time for international submissions.

(15) Musical styles. The companies listed indicate which types of music they are most interested in. Some of the terminology is standard (for instance, R&B = rhythm and blues) but some of the descriptions are worded exactly the way the company reported it to us. Remember, do not bother to send inappropriate material. And it is certainly improper to "shotgun" your demo tapes—that is, sending your demos blindly without regard to the company's musical interests.

(16) Examples of work. The published works, releases and productions given within the Music subhead of each listing represent examples of the companies' accomplishments and not a complete list. In many instances they are not necessarily the companies' most current releases but the ones they feel best represent the kind of music they want to see.

(17) Tips. Many listings share additional information to help you further evaluate their needs and goals. Don't overlook this unique information!

Bloom Where You're Planted: Start Songwriting in Your Hometown

by Pat Luboff

Being a songwriter is a lot like being a flying trapeze artist. When you're in the audience, it seems as though it's all glamour and magic. It looks so easy to do. Suppose the circus came through your town and you fell in love with the idea of flying through the air with the greatest of ease. Can you imagine what it would take to get your dreams off the ground and into the air? You would have years of grueling physical work and repetitive practice, accompanied by painful mistakes, under your sequined belt before the ringmaster announced your appearance high above the center ring.

It takes the same kind of behind-the-scenes, sweaty, hard work to get songs on the air. I have found in teaching hundreds of songwriters in workshops around the country that most songwriters aren't aware of this harsh reality. Maybe because music is magical, they think that it leaps from their guitars, keyboards and throats onto hit records. This kind of thinking leads to frustration and disappointment.

Songwriting is not magic. It's a life-growing process consisting of realistic steps you can take anywhere you live. You can study songwriting in your own home and in your local songwriting community. You can connect with local outlets for your songs and reach commercial success on this level. You can and you must. The level of writing and the competition in the music center cities is unbelievably high. You will need the strength of your successes on the local level to turn the ears of the people who can help you make larger-scale connections for your songs.

Here are some steps you can take right where you're standing that will prepare you for taking the leap into songwriting in the three music center cities: Los Angeles, Nashville and New York.

Step 1: The songwriter in the mirror

One of the hardest but most important things you have to do as a songwriter is to take an honest look at yourself and your songs and see the truth of where you stand. You must not lie to yourself about your strengths and weaknesses. Pretending that you are good at everything will only hold you back. The songwriter who can write lyrics and melodies equally well is a rare one. Most of us have been gifted with talents in specific areas.

Consider your lyrics. Are they clear, concise and charged with emotional images? Do they express feelings that strike at the heart of the human experience? Are they unique, fresh, interesting? Do the rhymes flow naturally, or do they feel forced? When you sing your lyrics to people, do they know without question what your message is? How do your lyrics compare with the lyrics of the successful songs that you admire most? Do you really

Pat Luboff and her husband, Pete, have taught songwriting workshops around the country for 12 years. They are the editors of The L.A. Record, the newsletter of the L.A. Chapter of the Recording Academy, and the California Copyright Conference newsletter. They co-wrote 88 Songwriting Wrongs and How to Right Them (Writer's Digest Books). Their songs have been recorded by Patti LaBelle, Bobby Womack, the Ray Charles Singers and the Norman Luboff Choir.

love words and the process of searching for just the right one to fit the situation?

If your answers to all of these questions are solidly positive, you have a talent that is much in demand. Strong lyricists are harder to find than good composers. If your answers to all but the last question are negative, you still have what it takes to become a strong lyricist. Your love of words will keep you going through the long learning process ahead.

Next, take an objective listen to your melody writing. Do your melodies have emotional highs and lows that keep them interesting throughout? Does the title melody line stand out as the most intense and memorable part of the melody? If your song has a verse/chorus structure, does the melody build to the chorus and take off in the chorus? When you play your songs to people, can they remember the melodies and sing them back to you? Are your melodies easy and fun to sing? How do your melodies compare to those of the songs you admire the most? Do you love to fiddle around with notes and chords until you get just the right one for the occasion?

Again, strong positive answers to all of these questions will confirm your strength as a composer. One lone "yes" on the last question means you're ready and able to learn. And negative replies to the questions will help you to avoid struggling to compose melodies that never quite satisfy you or your listeners.

If this is the first time you've asked yourself these questions and, to your surprise, you realize you have some weak points, a career in songwriting is not over. You have made a step in the direction of a new start that can really take you places.

Collaboration is the road that will lead you to bigger and better songs than you can do on your own. You do not have to write all alone. One of the biggest benefits of a serious self-evaluation is the identification of the talents you need to look for in potential collaborators. If you know now that your lyric writing or composing is weak, there's no shame in it. You just need to look for a collaborator whose work complements yours. The idea is to maximize your strengths and minimize your weaknesses.

The process of finding and working with a collaborator is an adventure in itself. Collaborators can be found in your school or college, your church or synagogue, local clubs, in up-and-coming local bands, your songwriting organization and even across the seas on the PAN computer network, if you're electronically inclined.

Now that you know where you stand, you can take your next step.

Step 2: Seeing your songs

It is crucial that you develop the ability to evaluate your songs objectively. You waste money and the professional listener's time if you don't get your act together before you take it on the road. Of course, you love your songs. They are your very own creations, your babies. But are they ready to stand on their own feet and walk into the big world of the music business? How do you develop an objective, professional way of looking at your songs? Ideally, take your songs to a songwriting workshop where you get feedback from the workshop leader and the other writers. Don't invest money in a demo until you've heard and considered the suggestions made by such groups.

Read the introduction to the Organizations section in this book (page 459) for information on national songwriting organizations and some of the regional groups. There may be a songwriter organization near you. If you do not have one locally, now is the time to start one. It's not just that you don't *have to* do this alone, you *can't* do it alone. You must connect with other people and the best people to start with are other songwriters. We need each other's support, encouragement and shared resources. (To get help starting your own organization, call National Academy of Songwriters at 1-800-826-7287 outside of California or (213)473-7178 in California.)

Feedback can begin at home if you have someone in your family or circle of friends whose judgment and honesty you trust. Play your song for that person and ask them questions such as: What is the message of the song? Was there anything that confused you in the song? What is the title? Do you remember the melody? Sometimes you'll see that things you thought were perfectly clear are *not* to the listener.

Eventually, you can develop an attitude which we call "being a stranger to your own song." You will be able to look at it as if never seeing it before. And you'll see what is *really* there, not what you *think* is there. Once you develop a discerning attitude toward your songs, you will know when they are ready for an investment in a demo. Too many songwriters spend too much money on demos, duplication, stationery and postage to pitch songs that either need lots more work or should be chalked up as learning experiences and abandoned.

If you must spend money, spend it on making yourself a better songwriter. Buy tapes and CDs of songs you love. Then, don't just listen to them, pick them apart and study what makes the songs great. Imitating good songs is an excellent learning tool. For instance, you could write an entirely new lyric to an existing song, then write a new melody to your new lyric. This exercise will teach you all kinds of things about rhyme scheme, song structure, title placement and melody lines. You can study with the masters of songwriting right in your own bedroom! Ultimately, you will develop your own unique voice which will incorporate the knowledge you have absorbed from your studies.

After exercising your songwriting muscles by writing, writing and more writing, you have some strong material to show for all your work. But ask yourself the all-important question: Are you ready to do business with your music?

Step 3: Doing business as a songwriter

The music business is a business like any other business. There is a special language, a jargon in which words take on special meanings. There is a body of rules and regulations on an international scale. There are forms to fill out and contracts to sign. There are sales charts, statistics and trends in a variety of marketplaces. But most of all there are people who do business on a person-to-person level.

When you are on the outside looking in, the music business can seem imposing and unapproachable. Arming yourself with a basic working knowledge of how things work in the music business can go a long way to making you feel more comfortable. You can learn a lot about the legal and business aspects of songwriting without having to move from your own easy chair. Today's songwriters are lucky to have a wonderful selection of books to choose from that explain the business side of music in user-friendly language. *Billboard* magazine is a treasure trove of information for songwriters. The careful reader can discover: who has just been promoted to the A&R position at your target artist's record company; who has just started his own independent publishing company; which songs are on the charts in every style of music and who wrote, produced and published them; and everything of importance that has anything to do with the music business.

Unfortunately, a subscription to *Billboard* is around $200 per year. This is another problem that a local songwriting organization can help you solve. If you can gather just 10 songwriters together, you can all benefit from a year of *Billboard* for only $20 each. (To order a subscription, call 1-800-247-2160 or, if you live in Iowa, 1-800-362-2860.) Reading an issue of *Billboard* is an education in what the music business really boils down to: big bucks on an international scale.

One of the first things to look at in *Billboard* is the charts: Adult Contemporary; Contemporary Christian; Country; Dance; Gospel; Hot 100; Latin; Modern Rock Tracks; New Age; Pop; R&B; Rap; Rock Tracks; Top 40 Radio Monitor and World Music are listed in each issue. Charts for jazz and classical categories are published less regularly.

What does this mean to you? It means that when it comes down to selling records, the people who sell them need to categorize them. Radio stations play a certain style of music to appeal to a certain group of listeners who will buy the products their advertisers are selling. Radio is the main promotional tool for most music, rap being a notable exception.

Therefore, the wise songwriter will examine closely what songs are on the radio.

Ask yourself: Which kind of music do I love the most? It's a good idea to sample the various kinds of music. You may find an unexpected affinity for country music or another style that you normally don't listen to. Write the kind of songs you love—pop, country, R&B, rock or gospel—and you will do your best work.

Your challenge as a songwriter is to be true to your own unique creativity while maintaining an awareness that you will have to please dozens of people in the music business chain (each with his own separate priorities) if your song is to get on the air and into the world. Among these people are the publisher, producer, artist, A&R executive at the record label, label president and assorted vice presidents, promoters, distributors, record store personnel, radio station program directors and disc jockeys.

Why should all these people take a chance on spending their time and money on your song? The music business is a gamble, with record labels betting a half a million dollars that a new artist's album will make money. Most of them don't meet the outlay for the first few albums. Bruce Springsteen took three albums to earn more money than the label spent on developing and promoting his albums. With such high stakes, you can't blame the record labels for upping their odds a little. There's no such thing as a sure thing but, as horse racing fans know, a strong track record makes it feel like there's less risk involved.

"Track record" is a phrase used in the music business to describe the past successes of a writer or an artist. If your track record is very strong, it translates into something called "clout." Clout gets you the best deals when you are negotiating with publishers and record companies. We've gone far afield into the realm of worldwide recognition here, but it's a journey that must start in your own hometown. How do you get there from here? And is that really where you want to go?

Step 4: Building a track record

Whether you happen to live in a music center or "in the sticks," there are ways to gain exposure for your songs to build that track record you need. My husband (Pete Luboff) and I taught a songwriting workshop in Marshall, Minnesota, a town of about 10,000 people surrounded by miles and miles of corn, soy beans and hogs. During the workshop, we invited a local disc jockey, the lead singer of a local touring band, and the owner of a local record label to come in for interviews. We like to show the workshop participants that there are people making a living in the music business right in their own hometown. The workshop culminated in a concert that was given at the town's bandshell and became a front-page news story, complete with a large photograph of several of the workshop participants. Can these songwriters use this experience and exposure as a stepping stone to something bigger? As they say in Minnesota, you bet!

What one songwriter can do, a group of songwriters can do better. Another good reason to discover and cultivate your local songwriting community is to create learning opportunities you can share. As a group, you can appeal to your local community college, adult education system or arts funding source to finance a songwriting workshop in your hometown. In a smaller town, this kind of an activity can be big news. When these workshops are publicized, they attract more songwriters to your community, which in turn gives you more resources and power to create opportunities for your songs.

After a workshop at Santa Fe Community College in New Mexico, workshop participants formed the Santa Fe Songwriter's Guild. One of the members happened to own a club where the group could meet to share information, get feedback from the others on their songs, connect with collaborators, seek and find help with playing and singing on demos and plan for public performances of their songs.

For the past couple of years, The Arizona Songwriter's Association has provided the live entertainment for the Annual Hot Air Balloon Race, which attracts tens of thousands of people. They sponsor and publicize visits by music business professionals, mainly from

Los Angeles. Their newsletter also announces Open Mic Nights at a local club and the successes of their members. The New Mexico Musicians and Songwriters Association (now defunct) connected up with the Marines' "Toys for Tots" drive and presented a concert of their original material to thousands of people. The Rocky Mountain Music Association in Denver presents an annual MusicFest, featuring several days of educational seminars, showcases and a trade show. The Northern California Songwriters Association, near San Francisco, produces an annual conference which attracts upwards of 500 songwriters. The Alaska Songwriters Association has more than 100 members!

All of these songwriters' groups have been visited by membership representatives from the performance rights organizations (ASCAP, SESAC and BMI). There is a great competition for writer members between these three organizations, whose job it is to collect money from users of music (such as TV, radio, dance clubs, stadiums and stores), and distribute it to the publishers and writers of the songs. So, they are always on the lookout for new talent and will help their members with connections to collaborators and publishers. These organizations deal in millions of dollars, so they can afford to send representatives to your group if you are organized enough to create an event to attract them.

The track record that begins in your friendly local songwriter organization can be built upon to stack up local songwriting successes. Your local radio station may be willing to play music by the songwriters in its listening area. There is no money in this because the performances would probably not be picked up in the performance rights organizations' surveys, but a positive reaction from the station's audience could be parlayed into airplay at another, perhaps bigger radio station. Or, the leaders of your group could meet with the radio station's program director to ask about instituting a special weekly half-hour show that features songs by local songwriters. There will be a lot of work in the collection and selection of what goes on the air. Your group could offer to help in that process. When we bring local radio station personnel into our workshops to share their knowledge, we have found they are quite receptive to the songwriters in their community. Songwriters in the big market cities do not have this advantage. You can capitalize on the community pride people feel in smaller towns when their neighbors do something special.

Another outlet for your music is local advertisers. Radio stations often have terrible music or no music at all in their ads. Businesses which advertise might be persuaded to use a catchy jingle. If your hometown is large enough, you probably have advertising agencies you can approach with a pitch for writing jingles as well.

Check out your local colleges and universities. Do they have a film or television studies program? Students who are creating film projects need music. Local cable television stations have an obligation to provide community access. Perhaps your songwriter group can put together a regular show, or a series of spots for broadcast. Are there any film production companies in your area that are in the business of making industrial, travel, educational or other types of short films? They could use music to add excitement to their information delivery.

Songwriting competitions, such as the ones listed in this book, can be helpful. Go easy on this one; don't enter 20 songs and empty your bank account. And always check first with a national songwriters' organization to verify contest legitimacy. If there has been any trouble with a particular contest, you can bet that songwriters have let them know.

If you want to build your track record by selling records and you are a songwriter who does not aspire to being an artist, you need to connect with an artist to have an outlet for your songs. You may find your outlet in a songwriter in your group who is also an artist and needs a collaborator. Local clubs are good places to look for groups who could use good material. A band that plays Top 40 songs may dream of doing something more creative. You can play a very important part in that dream. Record labels want to have as little work to do as possible. They love it when the band arrives complete with great original material. Get to know some great singers. Your relationship may start out as songwriter hiring a demo singer and end up as the songwriter/producer in the artist's deal with a label.

If you are a writer/artist or a writer who has made a solid connection with an artist/band, it is a tremendous learning process and a common calling card to produce your own cassette album. When you put your money where your songs are, you give the publishing or record companies what they want—an easy job. If you manage to sell a substantial number of these cassettes on your own, you not only make money, you give yourself clout when it comes to making a deal with a company that can promote your tape on a larger scale.

Pursuing local and regional publishers

This book is filled with thousands of connections, many of them not in the big three music centers. It would be wise to scan the listings and identify which ones are within 100 miles of home. Try to set up appointments with a few that seem appropriate to you and have some face-to-face encounters. Look at these as learning exercises. Knowing that you are doing this for your own education empowers you and relieves you of the delusion that somebody else is going to "make you a star." You can take the confidence you develop in these encounters into larger-scale meetings later.

What can regional publishers and record labels do for you that you cannot do for yourself? That depends entirely on the individual company. In fact, it may come down to the individual company owner. Remember to always research the past activities of your potential business partners.

If you find a local or regional record company willing to produce a record with you, they will pay for the recording project and deduct the expenses later from artist royalties. If a regional record of your song is released, it may not get beyond your state or the surrounding states, but it is another notch on your track record belt. You may never see any money for your efforts. But then again, it may take off and get bigger than regional, thus increasing the odds of being heard at a major record label.

There are many songwriters/artists who produce their own tapes and sell them at their live performances. They are content to have a regional circle of fans. They work at creating a mailing list to keep their fans informed about performances and new recordings as they come available. They sell their tapes directly through mail order to their fans and by leaving them on consignment in unusual retail situations for music, such as book stores, gift shops and stores that sell plants and flowers. These writers lead happy and fulfilling lives at the grass roots level and do not aspire to hit the big time. This is definitely a choice to be considered.

Step 5: To market, to market, to pitch a hit song

Suppose you sent songs to the song evaluation services of a national songwriter organization and the response to every one of them was, "This is a hit song! Don't change one word or one note!" It's time to pack your bags. You could buy a ticket for one of the big three: Nashville, New York or Los Angeles, but they're not the only cities that are home to music makers. There are smaller, but active music scenes in Atlanta, Austin, Boston, Chicago, Dallas, Detroit, Houston, Memphis, Miami, Minneapolis, Muscle Shoals (Alabama), Philadelphia, Portland, San Francisco and Seattle.

Where there are recording studios, there is music being recorded. *The International Recording Equipment & Studio Directory* (a *Billboard* publication) lists studios in every state but North Dakota. It might suit you better to move into one of these medium-size music markets closer to home to build even further on your track record of local appearances, airplay, jingles, cassette releases and/or contest-winning songs. Use the same techniques you used in your hometown to pitch your songwriting in these markets.

Try a testing-the-waters visit before you make a permanent move to one of the big three. Call ahead to your songwriter organization to find out when the next big event is coming up and time your visit to coincide with it. Autumn is the best time to come to Los Angeles. The LASS Songwriters EXPO is held in October and you will be among 1,000 or more songwriters enjoying a weekend of nonstop education and connections. NSAI holds one of its big songwriter weekends in the spring. Don't worry if you can't come during those particular events because workshops, song evaluations and pitching sessions are going on constantly in all three cities.

Also ask your songwriter organization about events given by other organizations. The Recording Academy (the organization that gives the Grammy® Awards) has chapters in seven cities that often hold educational and social events. In New York, check out the National Academy of Popular Music and its Songwriters' Hall of Fame. In Los Angeles, the California Copyright Conference's monthly dinner meetings are a great place to meet people and learn about the latest developments affecting copyrights. Seek out situations where you will have an opportunity to schmooze with potential music business contacts. Music is a person-to-person business and you need to make personal contacts to succeed.

Call before your trip to make an appointment with a membership representative at ASCAP, BMI, SESAC or all three. They can open some publisher's doors for you if they feel your songs are strong enough. Make as many connections as possible in person. The relationships you start on this trip can be continued and built up by phone and mail from your home base, should you decide not to move.

You will probably be amazed at the number of songwriters you will meet and at the high quality of their songs. All songwriting roads eventually lead to these three cities and the competition is intense. It's not that the songwriters are trying to do each other out of anything, it's just that they're all trying to get their songs into the same few openings at the top. Since only 10 percent of pop artists record songs written by someone other than themselves or their producers, the supply of great songs far exceeds the demand.

Whenever there is a recording project, all the top songwriters hear about it and try to get their songs on the album. When you want to have Whitney Houston sing one of your songs, you are in competition with the top songwriters in the country, the writers who have stacks of No. 1 hits on their track records. If your song is to be considered, it has to be an absolute killer song. And if it is to be recorded, it must get to the right person with the right connections to the right artist at the right time.

Brace yourself. If you're going to make it as a professional songwriter, you have to remain standing through a tidal wave of rejection. Many of today's top songwriters went through years and years of living in a music center and pitching their songs with no success before getting their first break. Allan Rich, co-writer of the No. 1 hit for James Ingram, "I Don't Have the Heart," was a serious, hard-working songwriter for 16 years before that song hit. Don't set yourself up to be crushed if the songs you are so sure of get rejected. Many songs that made it to No. 1 on the charts were rejected many times before an artist recorded them. For example, Randy Goodrum's "You Needed Me" was rejected more than 100 times before Anne Murray took it to the top of the charts.

Home is where you make it

Whether you are in a small town or in the big time, the steps you take are the same. You identify and develop your talent; study and write, write, write to improve your writing; make person-to-person contacts; and keep learning every step of the way. The difference in the big cities is that you are swinging with the top-of-the-line triple somersault songwriters.

You may decide after your trial visit that you are not ready for the altitude or you just don't like the noise, crime and pollution. This is the time to remember that you are a music center in yourself. If you really want to be a songwriter, you can find a way to do it anywhere.

Songwriters' Roundtable: Breaking Through

Everyone involved with the music business knows how difficult it is to succeed as a songwriter. Only a fortunate few are able to break through and achieve a hit on the charts. Even so, with enough perseverance, initiative, hard work and talent, it can be done, as this Roundtable suggests.

We've gathered three tunesmiths with recent commercial breakthroughs to share their thoughts and advice on making it in the music business on a creative and business level. Dyna Brein, Jud Friedman and Catesby Jones—each scored her/his first hit in the past year and a half. Between the three of them, they have more than 30 years experience in the music business.

Dyna Brein *is a staff writer for Famous Music in Burbank, California. In 1990 she got her first hit with "Comfort of a Man," recorded by Stephanie Mills. Brein's tune broke the Top 10 on the R&B charts.*

Jud Friedman, *a songwriter/producer living in North Hollywood, California, co-wrote "I Don't Have the Heart," a No. 1 Pop hit for James Ingram. The same song was also recorded by Stacy Lattisaw. Jud is a staff writer for Peer Music.*

Catesby Jones *is the Nashville contingent on the Roundtable. His "Country Club" single for Travis Tritt reached the Country Top 10 and has helped fuel Tritt's Gold debut LP.*

Briefly describe your background in music (or other fields if applicable) and how you arrived at the decision to pursue songwriting as a career.

Dyna: Actually, music was something I always did but for some reason I never thought I could be a songwriter to make money. Then one day (in 1978) a light clicked on and I decided to do it. For the next 12-13 years I stayed pretty tunnel-vision with it and it was surprising because as a general rule I think human beings need constant reinforcement, whether it's in a relationship or a job. And I had never done anything for such a length of time while getting rejected so often and so much. But I think that when you decide in your heart that you want to do something and it feels like the only thing you want to do, then you go for it.

Up until about a year ago I was a publicist for eight years, doing PR for everybody from Ozzy Osbourne to Sheena Easton to Paul Anka, and it was a pretty grueling profession. I also did legal secretary work. But right now, since I have my publishing deal, I can pretty much write music fulltime. I'm not living high on the hog, but it allows me to do that.

Jud: I bounced around to quite a lot of schools—went to college, actually got a law degree, practiced law a little bit. But all along I was writing and recording, just kind of enjoying it. The more I did it, the more I realized I wanted to do it for real. After law school I started working part-time as a lawyer and playing in bands in New York. On the side I began to put together some tapes of my songs, to see if anybody else liked them. I sent them out and got some good attention from people out here on the West Coast. I felt with the kind of response I was getting from my songs, the best way to get to make records was to start out as a songwriter, then become a producer and produce myself as an artist at some point down the road. But I wanted to get the songs out there to start. I wasn't very impressed with publishers. For the most part the relationships that songwriters seem to have with their publishers are "banking" types of relationships, and they weren't interesting to me. Before I was willing to give up a percentage of my publishing income from my songs, I wanted to feel that the publisher was going to be a real partner in the endeavor of making my career happen—not just a bank that's going to give me money and that's it. Eventually, though, I found a company I liked—Peer Music. I started doing one-off deals with them. They were very into my stuff, and they worked my songs. Our relationship evolved into a staff writing and production deal.

Catesby: I started writing songs after I graduated from Transylvania University and made a living as a performer for 15 years. I no longer travel or play the clubs and other than an occasional carpentry project for friends and family, I am a fulltime staff songwriter. It goes nicely with raising preschool children. I have been active in the music scenes in Boston, New York, Lexington, Cleveland, St. Thomas, South Texas and Memphis, but things have really clicked since we moved to Nashville. This is a wonderful school and a great place to share your love for songwriting.

What is the story behind your first hit song? Not necessarily how you wrote it (but you may include this), but how it was pitched, how it fell into the right hands, and how the artist came to record it.

Dyna: I was on the freeway and heard an artist (Miki Howard) on the radio singing a great song. I went to a record store and looked up the producer on the album and found out his name, Lamel Humes. I was working at the time where a lot of people know producers. I asked around, but only one person knew of him, and that person was reluctant to give out the number. I ended up in that person's office around eight o'clock that night finding my fingers suddenly, mystically, appearing in her Rolodex. I scrambled it down, ran home . . . and I finally called and left a message for him. I said something incoherent like "You don't know me. I stole your phone number, but if you believe in God and you believe a good song can come from anywhere, call me. What do you have to lose?" Four days later the phone rang and it was him. We talked for awhile and at the end of the time I said, "It's my birthday tomorrow," (which it was, but I would have lied even if it wasn't) "let me send you a tape." He got it and ended up loving "Comfort of a Man," and proceeded to find the right artist for it. At the time, both Patti LaBelle and Stephanie Mills wanted to record it, but we went with Stephanie.

Jud: Bernadette O'Reilly (former Peer Music A&R in New York) got "I Don't Have the Heart" cut by Stacy Lattisaw. Out here, my co-writer (Allan Rich) sent James Ingram a demo tape, and also Warner Bros. had gotten it. Basically, James heard it and fell in love with it. He called and said "I don't care what happens with this song—I don't care what anyone else says, but I'm going to cut it." And he never wavered once.

Catesby: I wrote "Country Club" with my dear friend Dennis Ford. The song came fast and easy. We rewrote the story line several times, but the chorus is a first write. My publisher at the time, Sue Patton, was instrumental in the decision to make our "tongue-in-cheek" song about rich people into a funny song about an unlikely couple. Mike Sebastian, our song plugger, gave the demo to Greg Brown (his college friend, who works at Warner Bros.), who happened to be producing Travis Tritt. This was Tritt's first record and his first release. The song went to No. 9, but for all the response it has received, I suspect it really got No. 1 airplay. Whatever the arithmetic, it adds up to a career song for Travis as well as for Dennis and myself.

How has this hit affected your songwriting? Is there increased pressure on you to write more hit songs?

Dyna: Every time a song comes out and it does well, you feel a pressure to top it. I think also it's kind of drug-like. When your song is on the charts and it's going up, it's very exciting every week to open *Billboard* and see where it is. But it's not JUST for that. There's a certain satisfaction of someone validating your work by saying, "I like this song and I'm going to put it on an album."

One hit, even if it's a relatively good one on the R&B charts, doesn't secure you in the Hall of Fame. But what it did for me was allow me to parlay that into a deal. When you live in California, you realize that there are thousands of people doing exactly what you're doing. So, if you get one break, you must capitalize on it. As the song was climbing the charts, I started making the rounds at publishing companies. This song opened that door for me.

Jud: It's been very positive. There has been more pressure in some ways, mostly self-imposed. I realize that I'm at a career-turning point and I have to seize the moment. When you have a song that's successful, you start to get some credibility and recognition. Suddenly the door opens just that little bit, and I want to charge through. However, having a No. 1 song doesn't mean your phone is going to be ringing off the hook by any means. People are a little more interested in taking your calls. By the same token, there are dangers in trying to pursue all the opportunities that arise. For example, you find yourself sitting in a room with an artist churning out some little ditty just to get on a record. That's OK, but I don't think you should fool yourself. I'm trying to keep up the integrity in my writing. I want to write stuff that has a little bit of inspiration, that will really make people happy.

Catesby: The success of "Country Club" has given me a great deal of professional and personal satisfaction and credibility in an industry that thrives on perceived importance. Since that hit, I have had one more cut by Josh Logan and several songs have been on hold right up to the wire, so I know I'm on the right track. As far as the networking goes, I find it much easier to approach the more successful writers for advice, conversation and for co-writing possibilities. I don't personally feel any pressure to outdo my recent success, but I am more aware of the type of song that country radio likes to play. I am a multi-faceted writer, and I enjoy at least half-a-dozen musical styles. I think it would be a shame to limit my creativity to just writing radio hits, although it would be nice to have that choice. All in all I try to judge my songs according to how they please me and my immediate musical family. I trust the response I get at writers' night performances and I can get a good idea whether a song is a hit by balancing these three factors.

Comment on making contacts in the music industry—how important it is and the BEST way to go about making contacts on the grass roots level.

Dyna: Become a caterer—threaten to flambé somebody if they don't sign you. Whatever you can do, be it going to mixers or fundraisers or places where musicians hang out. Go to clubs, listen to the radio constantly, see what's popular, call up publishers and ask what you need to do to get a meeting. If they say "send a tape," never let it go at that. Say, "Well, I'm sure you get tons of tapes, is there anything I can put on my tape particularly that will remind you of this conversation?" Make contacts on the grass roots level—go to any type of music outlet—like LASS here in California. If there isn't one in your community, I would put something in the local newspaper and start a chapter of a songwriter's club or workshop. If worse comes to worst and you're stuck in Podunk, but songwriting is what you want to do, you've got to move to the hub. That's the bottom line.

Jud: This is the most non-linear business that I know of. If you're a doctor, lawyer or plumber, there's a method. Trying to become a successful songwriter—the processes are undefined. However, in any area, even in something as disorganized and nuts as the music business, you need some type of plan to follow. When I came out here I already had some contacts with Kenny Rogers and his organization. From there, I branched out. I did my rounds with the music publishers and record companies around town, I read *Billboard* and other publications, and tried to keep on top of who was in the studio and who was looking for material.

Catesby: This is a business of friends helping friends and the more people you know and like, the better your chances. That's why making it outside of town is hard—you need to know the people making the machine work. There are several professional organizations which hold a host of meetings and seminars that are helpful to the songwriter.

When negotiating publishing deals early on in a songwriter's career, is it OK to give up publishing, or should you ALWAYS retain publishing rights?

Dyna: I've got a feeling that when you give in too easily, the value of the worth of the song is usually not held so high. If it were a situation where the song would be cut by a good artist and the question is do you give it up or do you stand on principle—I'd say give it up. Sometimes, too, when you're starting out and you hook up with a publisher who maybe wants to groom you, then that's something to consider. It's always best to try to get a copublishing agreement, because if it doesn't work out with that one guy, then you have somewhere else to go with it. A lot of times, the artists want to have publishing as well. So if you give it all up, you lose your negotiating power.

Do you ALWAYS retain publishing rights? There is never going to be an always . . . sometimes it's just not viable. My situation with "Comfort of a Man" is very much like that. When we did the song I wasn't signed, and we gave up half of it to the producer. Everybody has their paws in the pie and in a situation like that you have to be smart—and it's best to remember at that point lawyers are paid to handle it.

Jud: It's the one bargaining tool that a songwriter has, and you should use it. But, if you are going to give part of your publishing away, give it to someone who will give you something in return. Be very aware that you're giving up something that may be extremely valuable in the future. As a young songwriter you don't tend to think of the actual dollar amounts that are involved.

Catesby: The writer-publisher split can be a great business deal or a big heartache, depending on the players and the shared understanding of what each expects from the other. If you are looking for advance monies you have less chance of retaining part of your publishing, especially if you haven't had any chart success. I personally don't mind giving up my publishing at this stage because I don't want to pay for demos or pitch the songs when I could be writing. Maybe if I become a big success I'll see this differently, but for now I believe a bigger carrot will make my publisher plow the music now a lot harder and, ultimately, give me more hay at harvest time.

What have you learned about the process of becoming successful? Is there anything you would have done differently along the way?

Dyna: I would love to say there is a way to have shortened the 13 years of getting doors slammed in my face before I was able to get a song out there. But I worked my butt off. I networked and schmoozed, and I did everything right. Sometimes it's just timing. Really the only thing I can say is be persistent. A lot of people get weeded out in New York, California and Nashville by not being persistent. You lose people and others forge ahead. So there's really nothing I would've done differently, except maybe had a father who owned Warner Bros.—that would be nice.

Jud: I think I would've worked even harder at the outset. The difficult thing for someone who believes in himself/herself to accept, is how difficult and competitive it is.

Catesby: My only regret is that I wasn't more aggressive about writing with some potential artists who have since become successful. At one point they were as green as I, and I should have been more receptive to offers to cowrite.

In your eyes, what separates a successful songwriter from those who fall short of success?

Dyna: I think a successful songwriter is the one who listens to exactly what's going on in the marketplace, is versatile enough to write not just one style of music, but can switch from country to rock to pop to R&B—you must be versatile in that way. Because it's nepotism all the way. Everybody's got a friend or a friend of a friend, so in order to break through you've got to write in several different styles and you have to be pretty damned good at it. You've got to have that strong desire to withstand all the negativity and rejection that's going to come your way.

Jud: Most people who go into the arts in general—songwriting, film, theater, whatever—

do so because they feel they don't want to be business people. They don't want a 9-to-5 office job. But the big joke on songwriters is that you have to be the ultimate business person. As a songwriter, you not only have to be the manufacturer of the product, but also the salesperson, the advertiser, the designer, everything. I think there are two main components of success: ability on a musical level to write special songs; and having a good business sense. It took me years of really working hard to break through. A lot of people write songs. Anyone who can play guitar or piano or invest in a decent sequencer and synthesizer can put little demos together. But putting down a groove or coming up with a fun idea for a song or even writing an entire song—it's a different thing from trying to become a professional songwriter. It's different in terms of the commitment. You have to come up with a lot of ideas—and you must take those ideas and make them into something commercial. Then, getting the song to the right people—that's the key, and it's very difficult.

Catesby: There is a delicate balance between sticking by your guns and shooting yourself in the foot. You have to learn how to keep your musical integrity while, at the same time, learn how to file the rough edges so that others can relate to your songs. I have found it essential to determine whether I am writing a song for my own satisfaction or for commercial acceptance. This frees me to make the necessary changes or to stand for my artistic expression. I think successful writers have found this balance and have learned to enjoy the process of writing and not just the paycheck.

As a beginning songwriter, do you think it's necessary to collaborate? Or is it best to, early on, delve into your own songwriting talents and see what evolves?

Dyna: Collaboration is a wonderful thing—especially in the beginning. There are very few of us who are prodigies. I remember when I was writing stuff about feelings and prayers and birds and glistening lights. Sometimes you can bounce this stuff off of a collaborator and it helps hone your craft. Now, you can both be like Stevie Wonder on the freeway and be bad together. But for the most part it gives you a sounding board, and you can improve. It broadens your base, it broadens your knowledge and it's a great idea.

Jud: However you feel. There are no rules, as I said before. I think collaboration can be very helpful. I love to write songs by myself, and, as a matter of fact, I used to write by myself almost exclusively. It's very useful to collaborate on a creative level and business level—it challenges you. It's great to find someone who you click with creatively who has contacts also, so both of you can pool your contacts. There's nothing wrong with a writer developing a personal vision and wanting to develop that. If you work hard enough at it, there's nothing that says you *must* write with someone else.

Catesby: It's a blessing to be able to write alone and it's a virtue to be able to cooperate with another creative soul who feels as strongly about his direction for a song as you do about yours. When I started writing, I had never even heard about co-writing and I came to town with 300 songs of my own invention. I now have 300 co-written songs and I enjoy both for different reasons. My solo songs are more personal and introspective; the co-written songs are more commercial. I need both and wish I had collaborated earlier in my career.

When you write today, do you write with a particular artist in mind or do you write what comes naturally, in hopes that an artist will hear the song, share your sentiments and decide to use the song?

Dyna: The songs that I love to write, the pop and rock songs, are written by the Holly Knights and the Desmond Childs and the Dianne Warrens, and unless you're personal friends with Richard Marx or Winger or Huey Lewis (or whoever), it's very rare you'll get a song on those albums. It seems like the best outlets right now are the R&B markets. On occasion, when an artist is looking, you tailor-make something for them. I did a song that was perfect for Tina Turner, and in fact, I got a girl to sing the song who sounds like Tina. I thought it was a sure thing, and her management company loved it. But, when it came down to it, she went with one of her friends. So now I have this demo that cost $700 and if I play it for someone else they say, "Well, it sounds like a Tina Turner song." When you shoot for one specific artist too much, you may box yourself into a corner. The best thing to do sometimes (if you can afford it) is to do two versions. If not, keep it more generic.

Jud: "I Don't Have the Heart" certainly was not written just for James Ingram. Most of my best songs haven't been written with a particular artist in mind. To me, the inspiration is a very important part of the song—that spark of magic. I find that is not something controllable. I can't turn on my Whitney Houston spark or my Pointer Sisters spark. I sit down at the keyboard and something happens sometimes, and I have to go with it from there. That's *not* to say that I'm not very aware of what's out there. I keep close tabs on who's looking for what.

Catesby: I sometimes write a song with a particular artist in mind, but more often than not that song belongs on the artist's last record. Today's young competitive artists are always pushing their boundaries, trying to stay fresh. I write what I know and feel in hopes that someone will honestly fall in love with my reflections on life and love. Great songs will find a home.

I've heard several hit songwriters and composers mention that it's important to have a "mentor" early in one's songwriting career. Is this true for you?

Dyna: I did not have a mentor. It would've been nice, but it didn't happen.

Jud: Not exactly a mentor—no godfather figure. However, my publisher has really helped me. Although it hasn't been a mentoring process, it's very much an active partnership. Steve Rosen and Kathy Spanberger have really been behind me and had faith in me, and that makes all the difference. It's great to have someone you really trust to help you along the way. Sometimes it's very lonely writing songs and trying to meet people and pitch your stuff. You're pretty much a one-man organization and there are times when you really need help. When I got involved with Peer Music, that's what they gave me—a support group.

Catesby: In my early songwriting days, I did not have a mentor, who is by definition "a wise and trusted counselor," because I didn't really care what anyone else thought of my music. Today I turn to my publisher and my family for advice.

What is your strategy for dealing with creative block?

Dyna: Everybody says, "Go out and take a walk"; "Go to a movie" . . . those are OK ideas. I think sometimes you have to stop writing totally. Almost like a punishment. Music is in the air; it's always there. Sometimes you overload. So I've found if you stop writing for a couple weeks until you get that itch—until you want to do it so badly. But, that's hard too because this is my job, and I'm getting paid to do it, therefore I should be doing it from 9 to 5 everyday. Sometimes it just doesn't work that way. When I force myself to come up with stuff it's never very good. You must give in to the demon that says, "I'm not going to play with you today."

Also (this may sound a little Shirley MacLaine-like) sometimes before I start to write

I'll meditate for awhile. I'll just let myself reach into that higher power, whatever that is, and ask any friendly little creative muse floating around the universe to come visit and sometimes it helps.

Jud: I tell people it's no big deal. If it's bad, I take the day off, relax, go fishing, play with my baby (Ariane Nicole—by the way, having a baby is a miraculous thing and she's inspired me a lot). Experience tells you that writer's block goes away eventually. I felt great when I read a book about Paul Simon. He said that there was a period of months when he felt like he wouldn't write anything good again. And I said to myself that if Paul Simon can feel that way, anyone can.

Catesby: I don't generally get creative block, it's more like there's nothing I want to say. Once I get an idea it's easy for me to get it out and into a song. When I get worn out or sick of my guitar or the sound of my voice I go sailing, work in the garden, play with my kids or take an afternoon nap. I love to work with wood and I have a couple of boxes full of all sorts of tools. I also get a kick out of playing the drums along with my favorite records. The music doesn't leave me for long. She comes back before I run out of distractions.

The Business of Songwriting

Those songwriters and performers who have been successful in their careers are those who have taken the time to learn as much as they can about the music business. Such an education can come by study or by experience or (more usually) by some combination of the two. It's best to learn all you can by study, because experience can often be a cruel teacher. As an example, would you rather take the time to learn what "work for hire" means before you sign a contract, or find out afterward that it effectively prohibits you from ever collecting royalties on that song? It is simply good sense to approach the business side of songwriting with as much seriousness and energy as you put into your musical creations.

The music business operates in accord with most of the economic principles of any industry. The law of supply and demand forms the heart of the business. Consumers want to hear music on the radio and buy it for their own use (in the form of records, tapes, CDs, etc.). Record companies attempt to meet that demand by offering a musical product that they hope will appeal to enough people to turn a profit. It is a fiercely competitive arena. Consumers don't have unlimited funds to spend on music, and the choices they make can spell success or failure for recording artists and record companies.

The same applies to songs. There is a finite number of artists releasing albums containing just nine or ten songs each, while there are thousands of songwriters trying to get their new songs recorded and their older songs re-recorded. So you can imagine how important it is for songwriters to understand how the business works. It's true that there would be no music industry without songs—the artists, producers, publishers and everyone involved need you. But because of the competition, you *must* understand the business of songwriting and function on a professional level as they do.

Getting started

First you need great songs. You have to write and polish and rewrite, and listen to the radio to learn what types of music are popular and judge how your songs stack up against the hits.

Some songwriters may think their efforts end with writing the song. Others know that it's necessary to go on to get their songs published and recorded, but they think once they sign a publishing contract or record deal, they're home free, waiting for the royalty checks to start rolling in. Unfortunately, that's not the case. Every step along the way to a successful record takes a team effort, and the songwriter needs to be a knowledgeable member of the team.

The structure of the music business

The music industry in the United States traditionally revolves around three hub cities: New York, Los Angeles and Nashville. Power is concentrated in those areas because that is where most of the record companies, publishers, songwriters and performers are. Many people who are trying to break into the music business—in whatever capacity—move to one of those three cities in order to be close to the people and companies they want to contact. From time to time a regional music scene will heat up in a non-hub city such as Austin, Seattle or Minneapolis. When this happens, songwriters and performers in that city experience a kind of musical renaissance complete with better paying gigs, a creatively charged atmosphere in which to work and active interest from the major labels. All this is not to say that a successful career cannot be nurtured from any city in the country. It can be, particularly if you are a songwriter. (Be sure to read Bloom Where You're Planted: Start Songwriting in Your Hometown, page 6.) The disadvantages one faces by not being in a major music center can be offset somewhat by phone and mail contact with industry people and, if possible, occasional trips to the music hub nearest you. For the serious songwriter, a well-planned, once-a-year trip to New York, Los Angeles or Nashville to attend a seminar or to call on record companies and music publishers can be of immense value in expanding music-industry contacts and learning how the business operates. There are, of course, many smaller, independent companies located in cities across the country. A career of international scope can be started on the local level, and some may find a local career more satisfying, in its own way, than the constant striving to gain the attention of a major label.

The perspective of any company, big or small, must begin with the buying public. Their support, in the form of money spent on records and other kinds of musical entertainment, keeps the record companies in business. Because of that, record companies are anxious to give the public what they want. In an attempt to stay one step ahead of public tastes, the record companies hire people who have a facility for spotting musical talent and anticipating trends and put them in charge of finding and developing new recording acts. These talent scouts are called "A&R representatives." "A&R" stands for artist and repertoire, which simply means they are responsible for finding new artists and matching songs to artists. The person responsible for the recording artist's finished product—the record—is called the producer. It is the producer's job to bring the recording artist out of the studio with a good-sounding, saleable product. His duties often involve choosing the songs to be included on the album, so record producers are great contacts for songwriters. Some A&R reps produce the bands they discover.

The A&R reps and the producers are helped in their search for songs (and sometimes artists) by the music publisher. A publisher is really a songwriter's representative who, for a percentage of the profits (typically 50% of all publisher/songwriter earnings), tries to find commercially profitable uses for the songs in his catalog. A good publisher stays in close contact with several A&R reps, trying to find out what kinds of projects are coming up at the record companies and whether any songs in his catalog might be of use.

When a song is recorded and commercially released, the record company, the recording artist, the producer, the publisher and the songwriter all stand to profit. Recording artists earn a negotiated royalty from their record company based on the number of records sold. Publishers and songwriters earn mechanical royalties (based on records sold) and performance royalties (based on radio air play). Producers are usually paid either a negotiated royalty based on sales or a flat fee. (For more information see Where the Money Goes, on page 29.)

Until you establish relationships with specific professionals in the industry who appreciate your music and are willing to work with you on a regular basis, you should submit your material to as many appropriate contacts as you can find. Based on what we've just discussed, you can see that appropriate contacts would include A&R reps, producers and publishers. You can add managers to that list. Depending on how "big" the artist is, he may have a personal and/or road manager. These people have direct access to the artists they manage, and they're always on the lookout for hit songs for them.

Any method of getting your song heard, published, recorded and released is the best way if it works for you. In this book music publishers, record companies, record producers and managers are listed with specifications on how to submit your material to each. If you can't find the person or company you're looking for, there are other sources of information you can try. Check trade publications such as *Billboard* or *Cash Box*, available at most local libraries. These periodicals list new companies as well as the artists, labels, producers and publishers for each song on the charts. There are several tipsheets available that name producers, managers and artists currently looking for new material. Album covers and cassette j-cards can be excellent sources of information. They give the name of the record company, producer, and usually the manager of the artist or group, and reveal who publishes the songs on the album. Liner notes can be revealing as well, telling how a song came to someone's attention, how a musical style evolved or what changes or new projects lie ahead for the artist. Be creative in your research—any clue you uncover may give you an edge over your competition.

Submitting your songs

When it comes to showing people what you have to offer, the tool of the music industry is a demonstration recording—a demo. Most people prefer cassettes because they're so convenient. Songwriters make demos showcasing their songs and musicians make demos of their performances. These demos are then submitted to various professionals in the industry. It's acceptable to submit your songs to more than one person at a time (this is called simultaneous submission). Most people try their best to return tapes if a self-addressed, stamped envelope is included in the submission, but even with the best intentions in the world sometimes it just doesn't happen. (A person screening tapes might open dozens of packages, take the tapes out and put them all in a bag or box, and listen to them in the car on his way to and from the office, thus separating the tapes from their SASEs. *Always* put your name, address and phone number on every item in your submission package, including the tape itself.)

The one exception to simultaneous submissions is when someone asks if he may put a song of yours on "hold." This means he intends to record it, and he doesn't want you to give the song to anyone else. Sometimes he'll give a song back to you without recording it, even if it's been on hold for months. Sometimes he'll record your song but decide that it's not as strong as his other material and so he won't include your song on his album. If either of these things happens, you're free to pitch that song to other people again. (You can protect yourself from having a song on hold indefinitely. Either establish a deadline for the person who asks for the hold, i.e., "You can put my song on hold for x number of months." Or modify the hold to specify that you will pitch the song to other people, but you will not sign a deal without allowing the person who has the song "on hold" to make you an offer.) When someone publishes your song, you grant that publisher exclusive rights to your song and you may not pitch it to other publishers (though you *may* pitch it to artists or producers who are interested in recording the song without publishing it themselves).

The production quality of demos can vary widely, but even simple demos with just piano/vocal or guitar/vocal need to sound clean, with the instrument in tune and the lyrics sung clearly with no background noise. Many songwriters are investing in equipment such as four- or eight-track recorders, keyboards and drum machines—for recording demos at home. Other writers like to book studio time, use live musicians, and get professional input from an engineer and/or producer. It's also possible to hire a demo service to do it all for you. Ultimately, you'll have to go with what you can afford and what you feel best represents your song. Once you have a master recording of your song, you're ready to make cassette copies and pitch your song to the contacts you've researched.

Some markets indicate that you may send for evaluation a video of your act in performance or a group doing your songs, in lieu of a standard cassette or reel-to-reel demo. Most of our listers have indicated that a videocassette is not required, but told us the format of their VCR should a songwriter or artist want to send one. It's always a good idea to check with the company first for appropriate video format and television system, especially if it's an international market. Be aware that the television systems vary from country to country. For example, a Beta or VHS format tape recorded using the U.S. system (called NTSC) will not play back on a standard English VCR (using the PAL system) even if the recorder formats are identical. It is possible to transfer a video demo from one system to another, but the expense in both time and money may outweigh its usefulness as opposed to a standard audio demo. Systems for some countries include: NTSC—U.S., Canada and Japan; PAL—United Kingdom, Australia and West Germany; and SECAM—France.

Submitting by mail

Here are guidelines to follow when submitting material to companies listed in this book:
• Read the listing and submit exactly what a company asks for and exactly how it asks that it be submitted.
• Listen to each demo before submitting to make sure the quality is satisfactory.
• Enclose a brief, neat cover letter of introduction. Indicate the types of songs you're submitting and recording artists you think they might suit. If you are a writer/artist looking for a record deal yourself, or pitching your demo for some reason other than for another artist to record your songs, you should say so in your letter. Have specific goals.
• Include typed or legibly printed lyric sheets. If requested, include a lead sheet. Place your name, address and phone number on each lead or lyric sheet.
• Neatly label each tape and tape box with your name, address, phone number and the names of the songs on the tape in the sequence in which they are recorded.
• Keep records of the dates, songs and companies you submit to.
• Include a SASE for the return of your material. Your return envelope to companies based in countries other than your own should contain a self-addressed envelope (SAE) and International Reply Coupons (IRC). Be certain the return envelope is large enough to accommodate your material, and include sufficient postage for the weight of the package.
• Wrap the package neatly and write (or type on a shipping label) the company's address and your return address so they are clearly visible. Your package is the first impression a company has of you and your songs, so neatness is very important.
• Mail first class. Stamp or write "First Class Mail" on the package and on the SASE you enclose. Don't send by registered mail unless the listing specifically requests it. The recipient must interrupt his day to sign for it and many companies refuse all registered mail.

If you are writing to inquire about a company's current needs or to request permission to submit, your query letter should be neat (preferably typed), brief and pleasant. Explain the type of material you have and ask for their needs and current submission policy.

To expedite a reply, you should enclose a self-addressed, stamped postcard asking the information you need to know. Your typed questions (see the Sample Reply Form) should be direct and easy to answer. Also remember to place the company's name and address in the upper lefthand space on the front of the postcard so you'll know which company you queried. Keep a record of queries, like tape submissions, for future reference.

Sample Reply Form

I would like to hear:
( ) "Name of Song" ( ) "Name of Song" ( ) "Name of Song"
I prefer:
( ) reel-to-reel ( ) cassette ( ) videocassette
( ) Beta ( ) VHS
With:
( ) lyric sheet ( ) lead sheet ( ) either ( ) both
( ) I am not looking for material at this time, try me later.
( ) I am not interested.

Name   Title

If a market doesn't respond within several weeks after sending your demo, don't despair. As long as your submission is in the possession of a market there is a chance someone is reviewing it. That opportunity ends when your demo is returned to you. If after a reasonable length of time you still haven't received word on your submission, follow up with a friendly letter giving detailed information about your demo package.

Submitting in person

A trip to Los Angeles, Nashville or New York will give you insight as to how the music industry functions. You should plan ahead and schedule appointments to make the most of your time while you're there. It will be difficult to get in to see some people, as many professionals are extremely busy and may not feel meeting out-of-town writers is their highest priority. Other people are more open to, and even encourage, face-to-face meetings. They may feel that if you take the time to travel to where they are, and you're organized and persistent enough to schedule meetings, you're more advanced and more professional than many aspiring songwriters who blindly submit inappropriate songs through the mail.

You should take several cassette copies and lyric sheets of each of your songs. More than one of the companies you visit may ask that you leave a copy. If the person who's reviewing material likes a song, he may want to play it for someone else. There's also a good chance the person you have the appointment with will have to cancel (expect that occasionally), but wants you to leave a copy of your songs so he can listen and contact you later. *Never* give someone the last or only copy of your material—if it is not returned to you, all the effort and money that went into your demo will be lost.

Many good songs have been rejected simply because they weren't deemed appropriate by one listener at one particular time, so don't take rejection personally. Realize that if one or two people didn't like your songs, they just could have been having a bad day. However, if there seems to be a consensus about your work, like the feel of the song isn't quite right or a lyric needs work, you should probably give the advice some serious thought. Listen attentively to what the reviewers say and summarize their comments when you return home. That information will be invaluable as you continue to submit material to those people who now know you personally.

Contracts

You may encounter several types of contracts as you deal with the business end of songwriting, beginning with a legal agreement between you and a co-writer as to what percentage of the writer's royalties each of you will receive, what you will do if a third party (e.g. a recording artist) wishes to change your song and receive credit as a co-writer, and other things. Usually as long as the issues at stake are simple, and co-writers respect each other and discuss their business philosophy in advance of writing a song, they can reach an agreement verbally. A written contract is not necessary. (A written contract is usually necessary only when one writer wishes to control the rights to the song or one of the writers wants to remove his contribution if no use is made of the song within a certain period of time, e.g., take his lyrics and have them set to different music or vice versa.) In other situations—if a publisher, producer or record company wants to do business with you— you need a contract. You should always have any contract offered to you reviewed by a knowledgeable entertainment attorney.

Single song contracts

Probably the most common type of contract you will encounter at first will be the single song contract. A music publisher offers this type of contract when he wants to sign one (or more) of your songs, but he doesn't want to hire you as a staff writer. This type of agreement rarely includes more than two or three songs. You assign your rights to a particular song to the publisher for an agreed-upon number of years (usually the life of the copyright).

Every contract should contain this basic information: the publisher's name, the writer's name, the song's title, the date, and the purpose of the agreement. The songwriter also declares that the song is an original work and he is the creator of the work. The contract must specify the royalties the songwriter will earn from various uses of the song. These include performance royalties, mechanical, print, synchronization, foreign subpublishing, and an agreement as to what will be paid for any uses not specifically set forth in the wording of the contract. The songwriter should receive no less than 50% of the income his song generates. That means, whatever the song earns in royalties, the publisher and songwriter should split 50/50. The songwriter's half is called the "writer's share" and the publisher's half is called the "publisher's share." If there is more than one songwriter, the songwriters split the "writer's share." Sometimes songwriters will negotiate for a percentage of the "publisher's share"; that is, a copublishing agreement. This is usually feasible only if the songwriter already has some hits and is unlikely for beginning songwriters.

Other issues a contract should address include whether or not an advance will be paid to the songwriter and how much it will be; when the royalties will be paid (quarterly or semi-annually); who will pay for the demos—the publisher, the songwriter or both; how lawsuits against copyright infringement will be handled, including the cost of such lawsuits; what will happen if a dispute over the contract needs arbitration; whether the publisher has the right to sell the song to another publisher without the songwriter's consent; and whether the publisher has the right to make changes in a song, or approve of changes written by someone else, without the songwriter's consent. In addition, the songwriter should have the right to audit the publisher's books if the songwriter deems it necessary and gives the publisher reasonable notice.

Songwriters should also negotiate for a reversion clause. This calls for the rights to the song to revert (return) to the songwriter if some provision of the contract is not met. The most common type of reversion clause is for the failure to secure a commercial recording or release of the song. Songwriters fear that a publisher will sign one of their songs and then forget about it while he actively pitches other songs in his catalog. Songwriters want a clause in the contract stating that if the publisher does not secure a commercial release of their song within a specified period of time (usually one or two years) the rights to the song revert back to the songwriter, who can then give the song to a more active publisher if he so chooses. Some publishers will agree to this, figuring that if they don't get some action on the song in the first year, they're not likely to ever get any action on it. Other publishers are reluctant to agree to this clause. They may invest a lot of time and money in a song, redemoing it and pitching it to a number of artists; they may be actively looking for ways to exploit the song. They may have even interested a few artists or producers in the song, but whether the song is recorded or not, and especially whether it's released or not after it's recorded, is usually beyond the publisher's control. If a producer puts a song on hold for a while and goes into a lengthy recording project, by the time the record company (or artist or producer) decides which songs to release as singles, a year can easily go by. That's why it's so important to have a good working relationship with your publisher. You need to trust that he has your best interests in mind. If a song really is on hold you can give him more time and/or know that if your song is recorded but ultimately not released by the artist, it's not your publisher's fault and he'll work just as hard to get another artist to record the song.

The Songwriter's Guild of America (SGA) has drawn up a Popular Songwriter's Contract which it believes to be the best minimum songwriter contract available. The Guild will send a copy of the contract at no charge to any interested songwriter upon request (they do ask that you include a self-addressed stamped envelope with your request). SGA will also review free of charge any contract offered to its members, checking it for fairness and completeness. (See the Guild's listings in the Organizations section.)

The following list, taken from a Songwriter's Guild of America publication entitled "10 Basic Points Your Contract Should Include" enumerates the basic features of an acceptable songwriting contract:

1. Work for Hire. When you receive a contract covering just one composition you should make sure that the phrases "employment for hire" and "exclusive writer agreement" are not included. Also, there should be no options for future songs.

2. Performing Rights Affiliation. If you previously signed publishing contracts, you should be affiliated with either ASCAP, BMI or SESAC. All performance royalties must be received directly by you from your performing rights organization and this should be written into your song contract. (The same goes for any third party licensing organization mutually agreed upon.)

3. Reversion Clause. The contract should include a provision that if the publisher does not secure a release of a commercial sound recording within a specified time (one year, two years, etc.) the contract can be terminated by you.

4. Changes in the Composition. If the contract includes a provision that the publisher can change the title, lyrics or music, this should be amended so that only with your previous consent can such changes be made.

5. Royalty Provisions. Basically, you should receive fifty percent (50%) of all publisher's income on all licenses issued. If the publisher prints and sells his own sheet music and folios, your royalty should be ten percent (10%) of the wholesale selling price. The royalty should not be stated in the contract as a flat rate ($.05, $.07, etc.).

6. Negotiable Deductions. Ideally, demos and all other expenses of publication should be paid 100% by the publisher. The only allowable fee is for the Harry Fox Agency collection fee, whereby the writer pays one half of the amount charged to the publisher. Today's rate charged by the Harry Fox Agency is 4.5%.

7. Royalty Statements and Audit Provision. Once the song is recorded and printed, you are entitled to receive royalty statements at least once every six months. In addition, an audit provision with no time restriction should be included in every contract.

8. Writer's Credit. The publisher should make sure that you receive proper credit on all uses of the composition.

9. Arbitration. In order to avoid large legal fees in case of a dispute with your publisher, the contract should include an arbitration clause.

10. Future Uses. Any use not specifically covered by the contract should be retained by the writer to be negotiated as it comes up.

For a more thorough discussion of the somewhat complicated subject of contracts, see these two books published by Writer's Digest Books: *The Craft and Business of Songwriting*, by John Braheny and *Protecting Your Songs and Yourself*, by Kent Klavens.

Copyright

When you create a song and put it down in some fixed or tangible form it is a property you own, and it is automatically protected by copyright. This protection lasts for your lifetime (or the lifetime of the last surviving author, if you co-wrote the song) plus 50 years. When you prepare demos, lyric sheets and lead sheets of your songs, you should put notification of copyright on all the copies of your song (on the lyric or lead sheet and on the label of a cassette). The notice is simply the word "copyright" or the symbol © followed by the year the song was created (or published) and your name: © 1992 by John L. Public.

For the best protection, you can register your copyright with the Library of Congress. Although a song is copyrighted whether or not it is registered, such registration establishes a public record of your claim to copyright that could prove useful in any future litigation involving the song. Registration also entitles you to a potentially greater settlement in a copyright infringement suit. To register your song, request a government form PA, available on request from the Copyright Office. Call (202)707-9100 to order forms. It is possible to register groups of songs for one fee, but you cannot add future songs to that particular collection.

Once you receive the PA form, you will be required to return it, along with a registration fee and a tape or lead sheet of your song, to the Register of Copyrights, Library of Congress, Washington DC 20559.

It may take as long as four months to receive your certificate of registration from the Copyright Office, but your songs are protected from the date of creation, and the date of registration will reflect the date you applied for registration.

If you ever feel that one of your songs has been stolen—that someone has unlawfully infringed on your copyright—you will need to have proof that you were the original creator of the work. Copyright registration is the best method of creating proof of a date of creation. You *must* have your copyright registered in order to file a copyright infringement lawsuit. One important way people prove a work is original is to keep their rough drafts and revisions of songs, either on paper or on tape, if they record different versions of the song as they go along.

True copyright infringement is rarer than many people think. For one thing, a title cannot be copyrighted, nor can an idea, nor can a chord progression. Only specific, fixed melodies and lyrics can be copyrighted. Second, a successful infringement suit would have to prove that another songwriter had access to your completed song and that he deliberately copied it, which is difficult to do and not really worthwhile unless the song is a smash hit. Song theft sometimes happens, but not often enough to allow yourself to become paranoid. Don't be afraid to play your songs for people or worry about creating a song that might sound similar to someone else's. Better to spend your time creating original songs, register the copyrights you intend to actively pitch to music professionals, and go ahead and make contacts to get your material heard.

The ripoffs

As in any other business, the music industry has its share of dishonest, greedy people who try to unfairly exploit the talents and aspirations of others. Most of them employ similar methods of attack which you can learn to recognize and avoid. These "song sharks" prey on beginners—those writers who are unfamiliar with ethical industry standards. Ethical companies hope to earn money with you as your quality songs earn royalties. Song sharks will take any song—quality doesn't count. They don't care about future royalties, because they get their money upfront from songwriters who don't know better.

Here are some guidelines to help you recognize such a person or company:

● Never pay to have your songs published. A reputable company interested in your songs assumes the responsibility and cost of promoting your material. That company invests in your song because it expects a profit once the song is recorded and released.

● Never pay to have your music "reviewed" by a company that may be interested in publishing, producing or recording it. Reviewing material—free of charge—is the practice of reputable companies looking for hits for their artists or recording projects. (Song critique and consultation by another songwriter or someone not in the market for original material is another matter.)

● Never pay to have your lyrics or poems set to music. "Music mills"—for a price—may use the same melody for hundreds of lyrics and poems, whether it sounds good or not. Publishers recognize one of these melodies as soon as they hear it.

● Read all contracts carefully before signing and don't sign any contract you're unsure about or that you don't understand. Don't assume any contract is better than no contract at all. Remember that it is well worth paying an attorney for the time it takes him to review a contract if you can avoid a bad situation that may cost you thousands of dollars in royalties if your song becomes a hit.

- Don't pay a company to pair you with a collaborator. Better ways include contacting organizations which offer collaboration services to their members. (See Co-writing.)
- Don't sell your songs outright. It's unethical for anyone to offer you such a proposition.
- If you are asked by a record company or some other type of company to pay expenses upfront, beware. Many expenses incurred by the record company on your behalf may be recoupable, but you should not be paying cash out of your pocket to a company that either employs you as an artist or owns your master recording. If someone offers you a "deal" that asks for cash upfront, it's a good idea to ask to speak with other artists who have signed similar contracts with them before signing one yourself. Weigh the expenses and what you have to gain by financing the project yourself, then make your decision. Read the stipulations of the contract carefully, however, and go over them with a music business attorney. Research the company and its track record, and beware of any company that won't answer your questions or let you know what it has done in the past. If it has had successes and good working relationships with other writers and artists, it should be happy to brag about them.
- Before participating in a songwriting contest, read all of the rules closely. Be sure that what you're giving up (in the way of entry fees, publishing rights, etc.) is not greater than what you stand to gain by winning the contest. See the introduction to our Contests and Awards section for more advice on this.
- There is a recent version of the age-old chain letter scheme with a special twist just for songwriters and musicians. The letter names five songwriters whose tapes you are supposed to order. You then add your name to the letter and mail it to five more songwriters who, in turn, send you $7 each for your tape. Besides the fact that such chain letter or "pyramid" schemes generally fail, the five "amateur" songwriters named in the letter are known song sharks. It's simply one more scheme to separate the unwise from their cash. Don't fall for it.
- Verify any situation about an individual or a company if you have doubts. Contact the performance rights organization with which it is affiliated. Check with the Better Business Bureau in the town where it is located or the state's attorney general's office. Contact professional organizations you're a member of (and the national ones listed in the Organization section of this book) and inquire about the reputation of the company.

Record keeping

It is a good idea to keep a ledger or notebook containing all financial transactions related to your songwriting. Your record keeping should include a list of income from royalty checks as well as expenses incurred as a result of your songwriting business: cost of tapes, demo sessions, office supplies, postage, traveling expenses, dues to songwriting organizations, class and workshop fees and publications of interest. It's also advisable to open a checking account exclusively for your songwriting activities, not only to make record keeping easier, but to establish your identity as a business for tax purposes.

Your royalties will not reflect tax or other mandatory deductions. It is the songwriter's responsibility to keep track of income and file appropriate tax forms. Contact the IRS or an accountant who serves music industry clients, for specific information.

International markets

Everyone talks about the world getting smaller, and it's true. Modern communication technology has brought us to the point at which media events and information can be transmitted around the globe instantly. No business has enjoyed the fruits of this progress more than the music industry. The music business of the 1990s is truly an international industry. American music is heard in virtually every country in the world, and music from all over the world has taken a firm hold on America's imagination over the past few years.

Those of you who have been buying *Songwriter's Market* over the years may have noticed a steady increase in the number of international companies listed. We believe these listings, though they may be a bit more challenging to deal with than domestic companies, provide additional opportunities for songwriters to achieve success with their music, and it is obvious from the response we get to our listing questionnaires that companies all over the world are very interested in music.

If you consider signing a contract with an enthusiastic publisher from a country outside the United States, use the same criteria that we referred to earlier when making a decision as to the acceptability of the contract.

Co-writing

Co-writing affects the creative side of your songwriting, and it also affects the business side. Many songwriters choose to collaborate because they like the instant feedback a writing partner can provide; they feel they are stronger in lyric or music writing skills and they seek someone whose talents will complement their own; they want to write in a style of music somewhat unfamiliar to them and so they seek someone more experienced in that genre. Or they feel the final outcome of two or more writers' experiences and creative input will be greater than the sum of its parts. While co-writing can be a boon to your creative output, you should think about how it will affect your business. You'll have to share the writer's royalties which means less money for you. On the other hand, your co-writer will be pitching your song to people you may not even know, thus expanding your network of contacts and increasing the possibilities for your song to get recorded.

Where do you find collaborators? Check the bulletin board at your local musician's union hall. If you don't see an advertisement that seems suitable for you, ask if you can post your own ad telling what type of writer you're looking for, what styles of music you're interested in, what experience you've had, what your goals are, etc. Other places to advertise are at music stores and college and university music departments, if they allow it.

Professional organizations like The National Academy of Songwriters, The Songwriters Guild of America, The Nashville Songwriters Association International and the Los Angeles Songwriters Showcase offer opportunities to meet collaborators or correspond with them through the mail. Check the Organizations section for addresses. Most local songwriters associations also provide names of potential co-writers. See if there's an organization in your area.

If there's not, why not start one? Having a local songwriting organization can be a great way to pool resources, critique each other's songs, help each other on demos and cooperate in many other ways. As you use *Songwriter's Market* and learn more about the music industry, you'll have much to share with the songwriters in your area.

Where the Money Goes

by Harvey Rachlin

Sure Thing Records recently released the first single of a hot new group, the Peptones, and their record, "Now I've Heard It All," quickly shot up to the top of the charts. Holy hit! Everybody's jubilant, excited. There's an international concert tour planned. There are invitations to appear on TV shows. Merchandising companies have approached the artists about licensing products based on the group's name and likeness. The possibilities seem endless!

Hit Heaven indeed seems paved with gold, but what can be earned from this record? After all, that's what started everything. Who earns what? That's a simple question with a complicated answer.

Let's start at the beginning—the song. Two writers, Bobby Righetti and Sue Thompson, wrote it. They took it to Miribank Publishing Company, whose professional manager, Arthur Camden, loved it and signed it up. Camden heard the Peptones had just been signed to Sure Thing and were looking for a single. He played "Now I've Heard It All" for their producer, who thought the group and tune would make a perfect marriage. The group agreed, as did the record company when it heard the master, and the record was released as the first single. The company's promotion staff went to work, getting the record played heavily on the air, and the distribution apparatus got the record into the stores. That in a nutshell is how the record became a hit.

So now it's payoff time and everybody wants to reap the rewards. Well, let's qualify that a little. It's a royalty period and the royalty participants are anxious to get paid. The record company pays the royalty participants from monies taken in from sales of the group's recording, manufactured in the form of CD's, cassettes and vinyl discs.

The label sells to rack jobbers and one-stops, which are wholesalers, and directly to retail chains and independent record stores. Product is sold to these entities at a discount, depending on quantity ordered and other factors.

As a hypothetical example, let's suppose the group's single sold 100,000 units in the first royalty period at a cost of $2.98 (remember that discount!). Again, the question: Who earns what? It's actually two questions in one: Who actually earns on the record? And what do these people earn? As to the first question, the royalty participants would be the artist, the songwriters and music publisher, and the producer.

The artist payment

The artist earns a percentage of the retail price of units sold. Typically, this percentage escalates as more units are sold, and there are certain conditions: Payment is made on 90 percent of units sold (a traditional record company clause to account for broken and defective records) and a reserve is held back for returns of records shipped. The Peptones' contract provides for a 10 percent royalty based on the retail price for the first 50,000 units

Harvey Rachlin is the author of The Songwriter's Handbook, The Encyclopedia of the Music Business, The Songwriter's and Musician's Guide to Making Great Demos and several other books. He is the winner of an ASCAP-Deems Taylor Award for excellence in music journalism and also runs a music management company.

sold and 12.5 percent for the next 50,000 units sold. Royalties are based on 100 percent of units sold and there is a 25 percent reserve for returns.

So, the group earns 10 percent of $2.98 for 50,000 units, and 12.5 percent for the second 50,000 units sold. That's $14,900 (from the first 50,000) plus $18,625 (for the second 50,000), for a total of $33,525. With 25 percent held back for reserves the group's earnings come to $25,143.75. Now that may not sound like a retirement fund, but remember that this is only for one royalty period (artists are typically paid on a semi-annual basis). But wait. The group, signed to a singles deal with the possibility of an album to follow, was given an advance of $10,000. That brings earnings down to $15,143.75. The group's personal manager takes his 20 percent cut from that, leaving the group $12,115. Finally, that sum is split among the group's four members, giving each $3,028.75.

Separate from the group, the producer negotiated a deal giving him two percent of the first 50,000 units sold and three percent of the next 50,000 sold. He received an advance of $1,000 and has the same 25 percent reserve clause. The producer's earnings may be computed by using the above example as a guideline.

The songwriter and music publisher

Now we switch our attention to the songwriter and the music publisher. For sales of units sold by the label, these participants collect recording (or mechanical) royalties. There are other sources for these guys, which we'll consider later. The federal copyright law provides a statutory recording royalty of 5.7 cents per composition or 1.1 cents per minute, or a fraction thereof, whichever is greater. (These rates are effective until December 31, 1991, after which they are scheduled to increase.) This is construed to be the maximum royalty and record companies are free to negotiate a lower royalty and often do. But in this case, Miribank Publishing Company, through its licensing agent, the Max Wolf Agency (most publishers have a representative for negotiating and licensing recording royalties), licensed "Now I've Heard It All" to Sure Thing for the full statutory royalty rate. That's 100,000 units times 5.7 cents per unit, or $5,700 (publishers and songwriters are typically paid semi-annually or quarterly). The Wolf Agency takes its fee of three percent off the top, leaving $5,529. This is split equally by the publisher and the writers. Thus, Miribank earns $2,764.50 and the two writers, Bobby Righetti and Sue Thompson, earn $2,764.50 (that's $1,382.25 each).

Tying up the loose ends

Is that it for the record company? Is that the end of its paying out money for the time being? Not exactly. There were background musicians and singers who performed on the record and although these people are not royalty participants per se, they are members of the American Federation of Musicians and the American Federation of Television and Radio Artists. These unions require labels to pay into special funds small percentages of earnings of records which in turn are paid out by the unions over time, according to complex formulas, to those who performed on the records.

We must remind ourselves that this is just the beginning. As mentioned, it's the first royalty period. The record will continue to sell over time. And for the artists there's the album that will follow. The success of the single prompted the group's label to sign them to an album deal, and there's a sizable advance. And there's also the benefits that may come from having a hit, including those mentioned before—concerts, television and merchandising.

It should also be remembered that we live in a hyphenated-talent era. Artists are not just artists, but songwriters, arrangers, producers, engineers, music publishers, film scorers and much more. In this article creative contributions have been kept separate for simplicity, but if the artist is also the writer, those separate revenues may simply be added together to get the hyphenated-talent's total earnings for a particular period.

Performance royalties and future earnings

Now we must return to the songwriter and the music publisher. A songwriter is what you are after all, and the above example does not account for all the earnings of a music copyright's earning universe. (Give me a hit recording or smash composition and I'll take the composition any day!)

The preceding example accounted for a song's recording royalties for one royalty period. Those are royalties for record sales. Didn't the song get played on the air? Didn't people hear the record played over and over on the radio before they bought it? Yes, let's not forget the very lucrative area of performance royalties, those paid for play of the song on the radio, as well as in other areas such as television, concert halls, theaters, hotels, amusement parks and much more. Music users pay fees to performing rights organizations in the U.S.—ASCAP, BMI and SESAC—and these groups in turn pay their member or affiliate songwriters and music publishers in a proportion that reflects the quantity and "quality" (for example, large radio station air play pays more than smaller stations') of the performance of their tunes.

If a song becomes popular there are no limits to its licensing potential. It may be licensed for a motion picture or a TV show or a commercial jingle. Print publishers may license it (on an advance-royalty basis) for sheet music and songbooks. Other companies may license it for a poster or music box or other product. And let's not forget that we're talking about a song made popular by one artist. There's a whole galaxy of other artists out there, artists who may want to adapt the song to their personal performance style, and the publisher works to obtain "cover" records. Even years down the line the song could become a hit again, in a new arrangement and with a new voice.

As I said before, given the record or the tune, I'll take the tune. The original artist's record will eventually fall off the charts, but a song may go on living forever! (Unfortunately, the royalties stop at the life plus 50, when the song enters the public domain.)

A chart which graphically depicts song revenue distribution is located on the back endleaves of this book.

Important information on market listings:

● *Although every listing in* Songwriter's Market *is updated, verified or researched prior to publication, some changes are bound to occur between publication and the time you contact any listing.*

● *Listings are based on interviews and questionnaires. They are not advertisements, nor are markets reported here necessarily endorsed by the editor.*

● *Looking for a particular market? Check the Index. If you don't find it there, it is because 1) It's not interested in receiving material at this time. 2) It's no longer in business or has merged with another company. 3) It charges (counter to our criteria for inclusion) for services a songwriter should receive free. 4) It has failed to verify or update its listing annually. 5) It has requested that it not be listed. 6) We have received reports from songwriters about unresolved problems they've had with the company. Check the '91-92 Changes list at the end of each section to find why markets appearing in the 1991 edition do not appear in this edition.*

● *A word of warning. Don't pay to have your song published and/or recorded or to have your lyrics — or a poem — set to music. Read "Rip offs" in the Business of Song-writing section to learn how to recognize and protect yourself from the "song shark."*

● Songwriter's Market *reserves the right to exclude any listing which does not meet its requirements.*

Key to Symbols and Abbreviations

* new listing
SASE self-addressed stamped envelope
SAE self-addressed envelope
IRC International Reply Coupon, for use on reply mail in countries other than your own

(for definitions of terms and abbreviations relating specifically to the music industry, see the Glossary in the back of the book)

The Markets

Music Publishers

The most versatile, grass roots cogs in the music industry machine are music publishers—those people who are the direct link between the song and the artist, the basic ingredient of the business. To say that a publisher is a song plugger would be accurate, but would far understate the broad range of duties the average music publisher maintains.

When a songwriter signs a binder (contract) with a music publisher, he's actually entering into a business—a partnership, if you will. The songwriter provides the creative work (the song) to the publisher. The publisher, in turn, uses his contacts in the field and business savvy to "exploit" the song to the fullest extent possible. That's the bottom line responsibility of the publisher: getting a song recorded by an artist and maximizing commercial success and monetary returns from the product. But, the publisher may also be responsible for copyrighting songs, collecting songwriter and publisher royalties, obtaining and managing foreign subpublishing rights for songs, and arranging appropriate demo production. Overall, the publisher must know all aspects of the music industry. He must be able to deal with and understand all the "specialists" in the field: producers, personal managers, A&R representatives, record distributors and entertainment lawyers.

When searching for a publisher for your songs, there are several important factors to consider before entering into any type of agreement. First, does the publisher deal with the type of music that you write? Obviously, a publisher who works mostly with country artists would be an unlikely candidate if you write rock 'n' roll. Find the publisher who specializes in your genre. Second, you must look at the publisher's track record. Find out what songwriters and artists he regularly works with. Talk with those people to get a good feel for his abilities. And ask a very important question: Has he been successful? Next, what is his personality like? If you're going to be in a working relationship with this person, you should probably get along smashingly with each other. Remember, he's representing your songs. If he doesn't come off as personable to you, he probably won't represent your songs the way you want.

If the publisher has a good track record and personality, and he works with your type of music, the next step is to consider the contract. Is it weighted heavily in his favor? Is he open to negotiations? If he isn't, and you think the contract is unfair, you may want to look elsewhere. If you think there is a problem with the contract, consult counsel. Many industry experts suggest hiring a lawyer before signing any contract. (For more information on contracts, refer to The Business of Songwriting, page 23.)

As in any business, the music industry has its share of unethical, greedy people. They're called "song sharks." No ethical publisher will ask you to sell your songs to him outright, nor will an ethical publisher ask you to pay to have your song published. A song shark will—that's how he makes his money. If you're asked to pay for publishing, don't do it. Although it's not illegal, it's unethical, and is not standard practice in the music industry.

To the best of our knowledge, the companies we have selected for inclusion in this year's *Songwriter's Market* are honest companies that are interested in hearing your music, not taking your money. (For more on "song sharks" see page 26.)

One more important point to keep in mind while looking for a publisher: bigger is not always better. There are small, independent publishers that may be able to cater to a new songwriter's needs more adeptly than a huge conglomerate publisher. And if you're just starting out in the business, a smaller publisher will usually offer more personal attention and will nurture a close-knit relationship. In most cases, this is more beneficial for a young, up-and-coming writer or artist, and ends up being better for the publisher as well. In larger corporations, songwriters may get "lost in the shuffle."

With each company you choose to submit to, remember that a professional, courteous approach goes a long way in making a good impression. When you submit through the mail, make sure your package is neat and that it meets the particular publisher's submission specifications. If it's not, it's likely that your package will end up at the bottom of the stack or in the trash. Also, never "shotgun" tapes to publishers. ("Shotgunning" refers to blind mailings to many listings in *Songwriter's Market*.) This approach rarely, if ever, works, and music publishers do not look favorably upon this type of approach. Instead of "shotgunning," submit only to the companies who are interested in the type of music that you write. This section is filled with helpful information and reflects the need for every conceivable style of music, from traditional country to rap to thrash metal to gospel. It's all here—but remember to be selective.

You may wish to try dealing with a foreign publisher—a healthy potential market for new material. Listings of companies in countries other than the U.S. will have the name of the country in bold type. You will also find an alphabetical list of these companies at the end of this section. At the end of this section is a geographic index of publishers in New York, Nashville and Los Angeles, which will be helpful in planning a trip to one of these major music centers.

A. M. PERCUSSION PUBLICATIONS, P.O. Box 436, Lancaster NY 14086. (716)937-3705. Administrative Assistant: Charlene C. Sparcino. Music publisher. Works with composers.
How to Contact: Submit a demo tape and sheet music (if possible) by mail—unsolicited submissions are OK. Prefers cassette. SASE.
Music: Only interested in percussion music pieces.

A STREET MUSIC, Suite 9W, 701 7th Ave., New York NY 10036. (212)764-3872. A&R Director: K. Hall. Music publisher, record company (A Street Records) and record producer (A Street Music). ASCAP. Estab. 1986. Publishes 25-30 songs/year; publishes 5 new songwriters/year. Receives 25-50 submissions/week. Works with composers. Pays standard royalty.
How to Contact: Write first to get permission to submit a tape. Prefers cassette with 3 songs. "No lyric sheets. SASE *only* will receive reply; for tape return include adequate postage."
Music: Mostly rock (heavy to pop/radio oriented); will listen to R&B (dance-oriented, radio/pop oriented). Published "I'll Be Alright" (by Mark Rohrbach), recorded by Without Warning; "I Won't Quit" (by Fred and Don Baker), recorded by Rockamatic; and "Stand and Deliver" (by Reggie Reese).
Tips: "Don't send sloppy, first-draft, off-the-cuff demos. Put your best foot forward. If you cannot sell it to us, then how can we hope to place it with an artist?"

ABIDING LOVE MUSIC PUBLISHING, P.O. Box 09045, Milwaukee WI 53209. President: L.L. Russell. Music publisher and record company (Creation Records and Kei Records). BMI. Estab. 1986. Publishes 1-7 songs/year; publishes 1-2 new songwriters/year. Receives 20-30 submissions/month. Works with composers and lyricists; teams collaborators. Pays standard royalty.
Affiliate(s): La-Net Music, Gospel Music Association, and American Music Network Inc.
How to Contact: Submit a demo tape by mail—unsolicited submissions are OK. Prefers cassette with 1-4 songs and lyric sheet. "Send a good tape, and make your first impression count." SASE or SAE and IRC. Reports in 1 month.
Music: Mostly gospel, MOR, R&B, pop and country/western. Published "There's Only One Way" written and recorded by Laf'eet' Russell on Creation Records (gospel).
Tips: "Send a good tape. We'll be more active in our quest for musical excellence. Make a good demo and believe in your ability as a writer."

ABINGDON PRESS, 201 8th Avenue, South, Nashville TN 37203. (615)749-6158. Music Editor: Gary Alan Smith. Music publisher. ASCAP. Publishes approximately 100 songs/year; publishes as many new songwriters as possible. Receives 20 submissions/month.
How to Contact: Submit a manuscript and/or a demo tape by mail—unsolicited submissions are OK. "Unsolicited material must be addressed with Gary Alan Smith's name on the first line." Prefers cassette with no more than 4 songs and lyric sheet. "Please assure name and address are on tapes and/ or manuscripts, lyric sheets, etc." SASE. Reports in 1 month.
Music: Mostly "sacred choral and instrumental; we do not publish separate octavos currently."
Tips: "Focus material on mid-size, volunteer church choirs and musicians."

*AEROSCORE MUSIC CO., P.O. Box 179, Westminster MA 01473. (508)852-8600. Publisher: John MacKay. Music publisher. BMI. Estab. 1989. Publishes 20 songs/year; publishes 4 new songwriters/ year. Works with composers and lyricists; teams collaborators. Pays standard royalty.
How to Contact: Submit a demo tape by mail—unsolicited submissions are OK. Prefers cassette or VHS videocassette. "Put name and how to contact on everything." Reports "only if interested."
Music: Mostly A/C, orchestrated rock; also "any potential standards regardless of musical lineage. We are not interested in rap unless it's interspersed with singing."
Tips: "Put best songs first. If you have good songs, then a simple but clean recording is fine."

*AIM HIGH MUSIC COMPANY (ASCAP), 1300 Division St., Nashville TN 37203. (615)242-4722. FAX: (615)242-1177. Producer: Robert Metzgar. Music publisher and record company (Stop Hunger Records International). Estab. 1971. Publishes 250 songs/year; publishes 5-6 new songwriters/year. Hires staff writers. Works with composers and lyricists; teams collaborators. "Our company pays 100% to all songwriters."
Affiliate(s): Aim High Music (ASCAP), Bobby & Billy Music (BMI).
How to Contact: Submit a demo tape by mail—unsolicited submissions are OK. Prefers cassette or VHS videocassette with 5-10 songs and lyric sheet. "I like to get to know songwriters personally prior to recording their songs." Does not return unsolicited material. Reports in 2 weeks.
Music: Mostly country, traditional country and pop country; also gospel, southern gospel and contemporary Christian. Publishes "Just the Two of Us" (by Metzgar/Patterson), recorded by Conway Twitty on MCA Records (country); "Stranger In My Arms" (by Curtis Wayne), recorded by George Strait on MCA Records (country); and "Standin' In the Shadows," written and recorded by Hank Williams, Jr. on Polygram International Records (country).
Tips: "Never write songs that have already been written a thousand times. Come to us with fresh, new and different material."

*AKRANA MUSIC, P.O. Box 535, College Place WA 99324. (509)529-4649. Vice President/Publishing: Benjamin Fenton. Music publisher and record company (Akrana Country, Akrana Visions, Tin Soldier Songs). ASCAP. Estab. 1989. Pays standard royalty.
How to Contact: Submit a demo tape by mail—unsolicited submissions are OK. Prefers cassette with 1-4 songs and lyric sheet. SASE. Reports in 2 weeks.
Music: Mostly contemporary Christian country, gospel and children's music.
Tips: "We want music with Christian values for today's country market. Write lyrics that paint graphic word pictures and tell a compelling story (i.e. Kathy Mattea's 'Where've You Been?'). The most successful songs seem to be those that reflect or address the needs of the heart."

ALA/BIANCA SRL, Mazzoni 34/36, Modena 41100 **Italy**. Phone: (059)223897. President: Toni Verona. Music publisher, record company (Bravo, Flea, River Nile), record producer (Idem) and video production (S.I.A.E.). Estab. 1978. Publishes 300 songs/year; publishes 10 new songwriters/year. Teams collaborators. Pays standard royalty.

The asterisk before a listing indicates that the listing is new in this edition. New markets are often the most receptive to unsolicited submissions.

How to Contact: Write first to get permission to submit a tape. Prefers cassette with 2-3 songs. Include biography. Does not return unsolicited material. "Be patient in receiving a response."
Music: Mostly pop, rock and dance; also instrumental. Published "No Sad Goodbyes" (by G. Romani), recorded by the Rocking Chairs on River Nile Records (rock); "Ala Li La (Sega')", written and recorded by D. Azor on Mighty Quinn Records (sega); and "Dedicated" (by various writers), recorded by R. Roberts on River Nile Records (rock/funky soul).

ALEXIS, P.O. Box 532, Malibu CA 90265. (213)463-5998. President: Lee Magid. Music publisher, record company, personal management firm, and record and video producer. ASCAP. Member AIMP. Estab. 1950. Publishes 50 songs/year; publishes 20-50 new songwriters/year. Receives 500 submissions/year. Works with composers. Pays standard royalty.
Affiliate(s): Marvelle (BMI), Lou-Lee (BMI) and D.R. Music (ASCAP).
How to Contact: Submit a demo tape—unsolicited submissions are OK. Prefers cassette (or VHS videocassette of writer/artist if available) with 1-3 songs and lyric sheet. "Try to make demo as clear as possible—guitar or piano should be sufficient. A full rhythm and vocal demo is always better." SASE. Reports in 1 month "if interested".
Music: Mostly R&B, jazz, MOR, pop and gospel; also blues, church/religious, country, dance-oriented, folk and Latin. Published "Jesus is Just Alright" (by Art Reynolds), recorded by Doobie Brothers on W/B Records (gospel rock); "What Shall I Do?" (by Quincy Fielding), recorded by Tramaine Hawkins on Sparrow Records (gospel); and "I Played the Fool" (by D. Alexis), recorded by The Clovers on Atlantic Records (R&B).
Tips: "Create a good melody-lyric and a good clean demo tape. A home recording will do."

ALL ROCK MUSIC, P.O. Box 2296, Rotterdam 3000 CG **Holland**. Phone: (1860)20180. President: Cees Klop. Music publisher, record company (Collector Records) and record producer. Estab. 1967. Publishes 50-60 songs/year; publishes several new songwriters/year. Pays standard royalty.
Affiliate(s): All Rock Music (England) and All Rock Music (Belgium).
How to Contact: Submit demo tape by mail. Prefers cassette. SAE and IRC. Reports in 4 weeks.
Music: Mostly 50s rock, rockabilly and country rock; also piano boogie woogie. Published "Loving Wanting You," by R. Scott (country rock) and "Ditch Digger" by D. Mote (rock), both recorded by Cees Klop on White Label Records; "Bumper Boogie" (by R. Hoeke), recorded by Cees Klop on Downsouth Records (boogie); and "Spring In April" by H. Pepping (rock).

*ALLEGED IGUANA MUSIC, 44 Archdekin Dr., Brampton ON L6V1Y4 **Canada**. President: Randall Cousins. Music publisher and record producer (Randall Cousins Productions). PROCAN, CAPAC, SOCAN. Estab. 1984. Publishes 80 songs/year. Works with composers and lyricists; teams collaborators.
Affiliate(s): Alleged Iguana (PROCAN), Secret Agency (CAPAC) and AAA Aardvark Music (SOCAN).
How to Contact: Write first and obtain permission to submit a tape. Prefers cassette or VHS videocassette with 3 songs and lyric sheet. SASE. Reports in 8 weeks.
Music: Mostly country, country-rock and A/C; also pop and rock. Published "Take Me in Your Arms" (by R. Cousins), recorded by Diane Raeside (country-rock); "Unfortunately" (by R. Materick), recorded by True Spirit (A/C); and "For Always" (by Hotchkiss-Terry), recorded by Lisa Logan (country); all on Roto Noto Records.

ALLISONGS INC., 1603 Horton Ave., Nashville TN 37212. (615)292-9899. President: Jim Allison. Music publisher, record company (ARIA Records), record producer (Jim Allison, AlliSongs Inc.) BMI, ASCAP. Estab. 1985. Publishes more than 50 songs/year. Receives 100 submissions/month. Works with composers and lyricists. 5 staff writers.
Affiliate(s): Jims' Allisongs (BMI), d.c. Radio-Active Music (ASCAP) and Annie Green Eyes Music (BMI).
How to Contact: Submit a demo tape by mail. Prefers cassette and lyric sheet. *Does not return material*. Will call or write if interested.
Music: Mostly country, pop and R&B. Published "What Am I Gonna Do About You" (by Allison/Simon/Gilmore), recorded by Reba McEntire on MCA Records (country); "Preservation of the Wild Life" (by Allison/Young), recorded by Earl Thomas Conley on RCA Records (country); and "Against My Will" (by Hogan), recorded by Brenda Lee on Warner Bros. Records (pop).

"How to Use Your Songwriter's Market" (at the front of this book) contains comments and suggestions to help you understand and use the information in these listings.

ALTERNATIVE DIRECTION MUSIC PUBLISHERS, Box 3278, Station D, Ottawa, Ontario K1P 6H8 **Canada.** (613)225-6100. President and Director of Publishing: David Stein. Music publisher, record company (Parade Records), record producer and management firm (Alternative Direction Management). PROCAN. Estab. 1980. Publishes 5-10 songs/year; publishes 2-3 new songwriters/year. Works with composers; teams collaborators. Pays standard royalty.
How to Contact: Prefers cassette (or Beta videocassette) with 2-4 songs. SASE if sent from within Canada; American songwriters send SAE and $2 for postage and handling. Reports in 6 weeks.
Music: Uptempo rock, uptempo R&B and uptempo pop. Published "Big Kiss" (by David Ray), recorded by Theresa Bazaar on MCA Records (pop/dance) and Cindy Valentine on CBS Records (rock), Kyana on Parade Records (R&B); The edge on Parade Records (rock) and "Paris in Red" on Parade Records.
Tips: "Make certain your vocals are up front in the mix in the demos you submit. I am looking only for uptempo R&B and pop songs with a strong chorus and killer hooks. Don't send me any MOR, country, blues or folk music. I don't publish that kind of material."

AMALGAMATED TULIP CORP., 117 W. Rockland Rd., Box 615, Libertyville IL 60048. (708)362-4060. President: Perry Johnson. Music publisher, record company and record producer. BMI. Estab. 1968. Publishes 12 songs/year; publishes 3-6 new songwriters/year. Pays standard royalty.
Affiliate(s): Mo Fo Music.
How to Contact: Submit a demo tape—unsolicited submissions are OK. Prefers cassette with 3-5 songs and lyric sheet. SASE. Prefers studio produced demos. Reports in 2 months.
Music: Mostly rock, top 40/pop, dance and R&B; also country, MOR, blues and easy listening progressive. Published "This Feels Like Love to Me" (by Charles Sermay), recorded by Sacha Distel (pop); "Stop Wastin' Time" (by Tom Gallagher), recorded by Orjan (country); and "In the Middle of the Night," recorded by Oh Boy (pop).
Tips: "Send commercial material."

AMBRA MUSIC, Liechtenstein Str.117/17, Vienna A-1090 **Austria**. Phone: (0222)310 9020. Contact: Blacky Schwarz. Music publisher, record company (Ambra) and record producer. AUME, AKM. Estab. 1988. Publishes 100 songs/year. Works with composers and lyricists. Pays 60% composer/lyricist, 40% publisher (payed by AKM directly) if original rights are by Ambra Music.
Affiliate(s): Cebra, Avox, Czech, Daniel, PZ, Timeless Music, Seagull, Giraffe and Wild Songs (all AKM, AUME).
How to Contact: Submit a demo tape by mail—unsolicited submissions are OK. Prefers cassette or 7.5 ips reel-to-reel with lyric sheets. "Folk music by singer/songwriters preferred. (Please include photo).
Music: Mostly pop, rock and new age; also dance/disco. Published "Sehr Aut" (by Scheutz/Scheutz/Spitzer), recorded by Wilfried on Bellaphon Records (pop/rock); "It's Not Easy" (by Fisher, Stocker Kochauf), recorded by El Fisher on CBS Records (mainstream power-rock); and "Die Leut san Alle Deppert!" (by Georg Danzer), recorded by Georg Danzer on Teldel (rock/pop).

AMERICAN SONGWRITER'S GROUP, (formerly Novelty Power Inc.), P.O. Box 409, East Meadow NY 11554-0409. (516)486-8699. President: Jay Gold. Music publisher. BMI. Estab. 1981. Publishes 25 songs/year; 1-2 new songwriters/year. Works with composers and lyricists; teams collaborators. Pays standard royalty.
How to Contact: Submit a demo tape by mail—unsolicited submissions are OK. Prefers cassette with 3 songs and lyric sheets. Reports in 6 weeks.
Music: Mostly pop, rock and country. Published "Tough Guy" (by Jay Gold), recorded by Jail Bait on *Star Search* TV show (pop); "All the Wrong Reasons," written and recorded by Jay Gold on Turbo Records (pop); and "Radio Riot" (by R. Freeman/J. Gold), recorded by Queen City Kids (rock).
Tips: "Make the best demo you can afford. It's better to have a small publisher pushing your songs than a large one keeping them on the shelf."

AMERICATONE MUSIC INTERNATIONAL, 1817 Loch Lomond Way, Las Vegas NV 89102-4437. (702)384-0030. FAX: (702) 382-1926. President Joe Jan Jaros. Estab. 1975. Publishes 5-10 songs/year. Receives 50 submissions/month. Pays standard royalty.
Affiliate(s): Americatone Records International, Christy Records International USA.
How to Contact: Prefers cassettes and "studio production with top sound recordings," a lyric sheets. SASE. Reports in 4 weeks.
Music: Mostly country, jazz, R&R, Spanish, classic ballads. Published "You're the Other Part of Me," by Owen, (ballad/western); "Edar Abbey," (by Patrick McElhoes) (western); and "I'm Leaving Alone," by Wally Jemmings (country), all recorded by Americatone International.

AMIRON MUSIC, 20531 Plummer St., Chatsworth CA 91311. (818)998-0443. Manager: A. Sullivan. Music publisher, record company, record producer and manager. ASCAP. Estab. 1970. Publishes 2-4 songs/year; publishes 1-2 new songwriters/year. Pays standard royalty.
Affiliate(s): Aztex Productions, and Copan Music (BMI).
How to Contact: Prefers cassette (or Beta or VHS videocassette) with any number songs and lyric sheet. SASE. Reports in 10 weeks.
Music: Easy listening, MOR, progressive, R&B, rock and top 40/pop. Published "Lies in Disguise," "Rapid," and "Let's Work It Out" (by F. Cruz), recorded by Gangs Back; and "Try Me," written and recorded by Sana Christian; all on AKO Records (all pop). Also "Boys Take Your Mind Off Things" (by G. Litvak), recorded by Staunton on Les Disques Records (pop).
Tips: Send songs with "good story-lyrics."

ANGELSONG PUBLISHING CO., 2714 Westwood Dr., Nashville TN 37204. (615)297-2246. President: Mabel Birdsong. BMI, ASCAP. Music publisher and record company (Birdsong Records). Publishes 2 albums/year; publishes 2 new songwriters/year.
How to Contact: Prefers cassette with maximum 4 songs and lyric sheet. Does not return unsolicited material. Reports in 2 weeks, "if requested."
Music: Mostly gospel, country and MOR; also pop. Published *Bless This House* by Junior Rutty; and *Go Where The Peace Is*, by the Songwriters.

ANOTHER AMETHYST SONG, 273 Chippewa Dr., Columbia SC 29210-6508. (803)750-5391. Contact: Manager. Music publisher, record company (Amethyst Group). BMI. Estab. 1985. Publishes 40 songs/year; publishes 20 new songwriters/year. Works with composers. Pays standard royalty.
How to Contact: Prefers cassette (or VHS videocassette) with 3-7 songs and lyric sheet; include any photos, biographical information. SASE. Reports in 5 weeks.
Music: Mostly metal, rock, pop, new wave and eclectic styles. Recently published "Complicated Love" and "Back in the Race" (by C. Sargent and C. Hamblin), recorded by True Identity; and "If You Had Your Mind Made Up" written and recorded by Kourtesy; and "Fugitive of Love," by Toni Land, all on Antithesis Records.
Tips: "Simplicity is the key. A hit is a hit regardless of the production. Don't 'overkill' the song! We mainly sign artist/writers."

ANOTHER EAR MUSIC, Box 110142 Nashville TN 37222-0142. General Manager: T.J. Kirby. BMI, ASCAP. Music publisher, record company (T.J. Records), record producer (T.J. Productions) and management firm (T.J. Productions). Publishes 2 songs/year; publishes 2 new songwriters/year. Works with composers and lyricists; teams collaborators. Pays standard royalty.
Affiliate(s): Peppermint Rainbow Music/ASCAP.
How to Contact: Submit a demo tape with 1-2 songs (or VHS videocassette) by mail. One song only on video with lyric sheets.
Music: Mostly country/pop and R&B: also gospel, rock and "concept songs." Published "Let it Be Me Tonight" (by Tom Douglas/Bob Lee/T.J. Kirby), recorded by Kathy Ford on Prerie Dust Records; and "Don't Take a Heart" (by Kirby/Lapp/Smith) and "Faster than a Speeding Bullet" (by Paul Hotchkiss), recorded by Deb Merrit on T.J. Records (all country/pop).
Tips: "Videos are great to help present a writer's concept but don't let the ideas of what you would put in a video stand in the way of writing a great song."

*ARS NOVA PUBLISHING, P.O. Box 191554, San Francisco CA 94119-1554. (415)554-8500. Professional Manager: Kent Phillips. Music publisher. ASCAP, BMI. Estab. 1984. Publishes 10 song/year. Receives 350 submissions/year. Works with composers and/or lyricists. Pays standard royalty.
How to Contact: Write first and obtain permission to submit a tape. Prefers cassette with 3 songs and lyric sheet. "Unsolicitied material will not be accepted." Reports in 1 month.
Music: Mostly R&B, jazz and pop. Published "People On A String" (by K.Wakefield), recorded by Roberta Flack on Atlantic Records (movie cut); "More Than Friends" (by J. Butler), recorded by Jonathan Butler on Zomba/Jive Records (R&B); and "Lovelines" (by R. Carpenter and J. Bettis), recorded by Karen Carpenter on A&M Records (pop).

ART AUDIO PUBLISHING COMPANY/TIGHT HI-FI SOUL MUSIC, 9706 Cameron Ave., Detroit MI 48211. (313)893-3406. President: Albert M. Leigh. Professional Manager: Dolores M. Leigh. Music publisher and record company. BMI, ASCAP. Pays standard royalty and publishers at equal rate.
How to Contact: Prefers cassette with 1-3 songs and lyric or lead sheets. "Keep lyrics up front on your demo." SASE. Reports in 2 weeks.
Music: Mostly MOR, R&B, soul and rock; also disco, easy listening, gospel and top 40/pop.
Tips: "Basically we are interested only in a new product with a strong sexual uptempo title with a (hook) story. Base it on the good part of your life—no sad songs; we want hot dance and rap. Arrange your songs to match the professional recording artist."

ASSOCIATED ARTISTS MUSIC INTERNATIONAL (AAMI), Maarschalklaan 47, 3417 SE Montfoort, The Netherlands. Phone: (0)3484-2860. FAX: 31-3484-2860. General Manager: Joop Gerrits. Music publisher, record company (Associated Artists Records), record producer (Associated Artists Productions) and radio and TV promotors. BUMA. Estab. 1975. Publishes 200 songs/year; publishes 50 new songwriters/year. Receives 100 submissions/month. "In 1987 subpublished more than 70 new songs, 27 local recordings by different record companies such as Phonogram, Polydor and EMI, released in The Netherlands, Belgium, Germany, Spain, Italy, Denmark and the United Kingdom." Works with composers; teams collaborators. Pays by agreement.
Affiliate(s): BMC Publishing Holland (BUMA); Hilversum Happy Music (BUMA); Intermelodie and Holland Glorie Productions.
How to Contact: Submit demo tape by mail. Prefers compact cassette (or VHS videocassette). SAE and IRC. Reports in 1 month.
Music: Mostly disco, pop and Italian disco; also rock, gospel (evangelic), musicals, MOR and country. Works with Electra Salsa, who "reached the top 40 in the Benelux countries, and the disco dance top 50." Older copyrights recorded by the Tremeloes, Whamm, Kayak and John Mackenzie. Published "Chains" (by Bortolotti), recorded by Mimmo Mix on Media Records (dance); "Words" (by Fitoussi), recorded by F.R. David on DDD Records (dance); and "Enter My Dreams" (by Garnett Embry), recorded by Garnett Embry on Images Records (ballad).
Tips: "Send good quality demos."

ASTRODISQUE PUBLISHING, Plum Sound and Video, 335 Merrimack St., Newburyport MA 01950. (617)465-5653. President: Richard Tiegen. Music publisher, record company (Plum Records) and record producer (Richard Tiegen/Magic Sound Productions). BMI. Estab. 1980. Publishes 15 songs/year; publishes 10 new songwriters/year. Works with composers and lyricists; teams collaborators. Pays standard royalty. "Charges recording and production fees."
How to Contact: Write or call first to obtain permission to submit. Prefers cassette (or VHS videocassette). Does not return unsolicited material. Reports in 3 weeks.
Music: Rock, R&B and country; also New Age and acoustic. Published "Star Train Express," "Too Hot to Handle" and "I Need Your Love," (all by Letourneau), recorded by Dixie Train on Plum Records (all country singles).

ATTID MUSIC CO., #1 Colony Rd., Gretna LA 70053. President: Carlo Ditta. Music publisher and record company (Orleans Records). ASCAP. Estab. 1986. Publishes 10 songs/year; publishes 5 new songwriters/year. Works with composers and lyricists. Pays standard royalty.
How to Contact: Write first and obtain permission to submit a tape. Prefers cassette with 5 songs and lyric sheets. Does not return unsolicited material. Reports in 6 weeks.
Music: Mostly soul, blues and folk; also gospel, country and R&B. Published "True Blue" (by C.P. Love), recorded by Carlo Ditta on Orleans (soul); "Pray" (by Carlo Ditta), recorded by Mighty Sam on Orleans (gospel); "Whatever It Takes" (by Jon Ayre and Carlo Ditta), recorded by Mighty Sam on Vivid Sound (inspirational).

AUDIO MUSIC PUBLISHERS, 449 N. Vista St., Los Angeles CA 90036. (213)653-0693. Contact: Ben Weisman. Music publisher, record company and record producer. ASCAP. Estab. 1962. Publishes 25 songs/year; publishes 10-15 new songwriters/year. Receives 100 submissions/month. Works with composers and lyricists; teams collaborators. Pays standard royalty.
How to Contact: Submit a demo tape—unsolicited submissions are OK. "No permission needed." Prefers cassette with 3-10 songs and lyric sheet. "We do not return unsolicited material without SASE. Don't query first; just send tape." Reports in 1 month.
Music: Mostly pop, R&B, rap, dance, funk, soul and country; also rock (all types).

*AUTHOR'S AGENCY LTD., ul. Hipoteczna 2, Warszawa 00-950 Poland. General Manager: Andrzej Januszewicz. Music publisher. Ziks/Poland. Estab. 1964. Publishes 60 songs/year; publishes 5 new songwriters/year. Works with composers. "We deal in promoting abroad mostly Polish composers, representing their rights, including contracts and mediating in the issue of options on translations abroad."
Affiliate(s): Ruch Muzyczny, Odra, Dialog, Tworczosc, Wydawnictwa, Muzyczne, Agencji Autorskiej, Literatura Na Świecie, Regiony.
How to Contact: Prefers cassette. "We are able to arrange the contracts for music which can be used mostly in Polish Radio." We do not return unsolicited material. Reports in 2-3 weeks.
Music: Mostly interested in rock, pop and New Age; also country and R&B.

*AVC MUSIC, #200, 6201 Sunset Blvd., Los Angeles CA 90028. (213)461-9001. President: James Warsinske. Music publisher. ASCAP. Estab. 1988. Publishes 30-60 songs/year; publishes 10-20 new songwriters/year. Works with composers and lyricists; teams collaborators. Pays standard royalty.

Affiliate(s): AVC Music (ASCAP) and Harmonious Music (BMI).
How to Contact: Call first and obtain permission to submit a tape. Prefers cassette or VHS videocassette with 2-5 songs and lyric sheet. "Clearly labelled tapes with phone numbers." SASE. Reports in 2 months.
Music: Mostly R&B/soul, pop and rock; also rap, metal and dance. Published "That's What Love Can Do" (by Curry/Nickerson), recorded by LeKlass (R&B); "In 2 The Night" (by Rocca/Taylor), recorded by Rocca (rap/pop); and "Checkmate" (by Madrok/Antron), Madrok (rap); all on Life Records.
Tips: "Be yourself, let your talents shine regardless of radio trends."

AVILO MUSIC, 8055 W. 21 Lane, Hialeah FL 33016. (305)822-9701 or (305)822-9708. President: Carlos Oliva. Music publisher, record company and record producer. Estab. 1979. BMI. Member NARM. Publishes 15 songs/year; publishes 2 new songwriters/year. Receives 50 submissions/year. Works with composers. Pays standard royalty.
Affiliate(s): Oliva Music (SESAC) and Santa Clara Music (ASCAP).
How to Contact: Submit a demo tape—unsolicited submissions are OK. Prefers cassette with any number of songs and lyric sheet. SASE. Reports in 2 weeks.
Music: Dance-oriented, Spanish and rock. Published "Iman" (merengue), "No Comprendo" (salsa) and "Pa Que Sufrir" (salsa) (all by Carlos Olivia), recorded by Los Sobrinos Del Juez on T-H-Rodven Records.
Tips: "Songs should have a strong hook, simple melody and sensible lyrics."

B. SHARP MUSIC, 24 rue Gachard, 1050 Brussels, **Belgium.** Phone: (02)241-41-86. Music publisher, record company (B. Sharp, Selection Records) and record producer (Pletinckx). Estab. 1950. Works with composers. Pays standard royalty.
Affiliate(s): Prestation Music and Multi Sound.
How to Contact: Write first and obtain permission to submit. Prefers cassette. Does not return unsolicited material. Reports in 1 month.
Music: Jazz, rock and instrumental music. Published "Speed Limit," written and recorded by M. Verderame (jazz fusion); "Modern Gardens," written and recorded by J.P. Catoul (jazz); and "Quadruplex," written and recorded by F. Degryse (jazz), all on B. Sharp Records (instrumentals).

*BABY RAQUEL MUSIC, #1235, 1204 Ave. U, Brooklyn NY 11239. (718)646-8969. President: Mark S. Berry. Music publisher. ASCAP, BMI. Estab. 1984. Publishes 5-10 songs/year; publishes 1-2 new songwriters/year. Teams collaborators. Pays standard royalty.
Affiliate(s): Raquels Songs (BMI), administered by All Nations Music.
How to Contact: Submit a demo tape by mail—unsolicited submissions are OK. Prefers cassette with 1-3 songs and lyric sheet. Does not return unsolicited material. Reports in 2-3 weeks.
Music: Mostly pop/dance and pop/rock. Published "Say Goodbye" (by M. Berry, M. Sukowski), recorded by Indecent Obsession on MCA Records (pop/rock); "I Feel Love" (by M. Smith, M. Berry), recorded by Fan Club on Epic Records (pop/dance); and "Crazy for You" (by M. Berry), recorded by White Heat on CBS/Canada Records (pop/rock).

BAD GRAMMAR MUSIC, Suite 306, 35918 Union-Lake Rd. Mt. Clemens MI 48043. Music Director: Joe Trupiano. Music publisher, record company (Rockit Records), record producer (Bad Grammar Enterprises) and management company. Estab. 1982. BMI. Publishes 10-20 songs/year; publishes 10-20 new songwriters/year. Receives 250 submissions/year. Works with composers and lyricists; teams collaborators. Pays standard royalty.
How to Contact: Submit a demo tape—unsolicited submissions are OK if submitting according to listing. Prefers cassette (or VHS videocassette) with 3-4 songs and lyric sheet. Reports in 6 weeks.
Music: Mostly dance-oriented, pop/rock and rock; also A/C, top 40/ballads and country. Published "Choose Life" (by Laya Phelps), recorded by Laya Phelps on Rockit Records (pop/rock); "Dances" (by James Elmore), recorded by J.D. Ruffcut on Rockit Records (pop/top 40); and "Sin Alley" (by Bob Josey), recorded by J.D. Ruffcut on Rockit Records (pop/top 40).
Tips: "We are presently screening material for our 'Power in Numbers' compilation CD, any material sent on 24-track format is given prompt attention and consideration. Be commercial and trendy and keep it hooky, but write from your soul. Listen to what's getting airplay, keep music and lyrics simple, and tell a definite story. We need songs that the public can walk away humming. The biggest sellers

Market conditions are constantly changing! If you're still using this book and it is 1993 or later, buy the newest edition of Songwriter's Market at your favorite bookstore or order directly from Writer's Digest Books.

in our industry today would have to be white pop/dance, pop/rock and love ballads."

BAGATELLE MUSIC PUBLISHING CO., 400 San Jacinto St., Houston TX 77002. (713)225-6654. President: Byron Benton. BMI. Music publisher, record company and record producer. Publishes 40 songs/year; publishes 2 new songwriters/year. Pays standard royalty.
Affiliate(s): Floyd Tillman Publishing Co.
How to Contact: Prefers cassette (or videocassette) with any number of songs and lyric sheet.
Music: Mostly country; also gospel and blues. Published "Everything You Touch," written and recorded by Johnny Nelms; "If I Could Do It All Over Again," written and recorded by Floyd Tillman; and "Mona from Daytona" (by Byron Benton), recorded by F. Tillman; all on Bagatelle Records (country).

BAL & BAL MUSIC PUBLISHING CO., P.O. Box 369, LaCanada CA 91012-0369. (818)548-1116. President: Adrian Bal. Music publisher, record company (Bal Records) and record producer. ASCAP. Member AGAC and AIMP. Estab. 1965. Publishes 2-6 songs/year; publishes 2-4 new songwriters/year. Receives 50 submissions/month. Works with composers; teams collaborators. Pays standard royalty.
Affiliate(s): Bal West Music Publishing Co. (BMI).
How to Contact: Submit a demo tape—unsolicited submissions are OK. Prefers cassette with 3 songs and lyric sheet. SASE. Reports in 1-3 months.
Music: Mostly MOR, country, rock and gospel; also blues, church/religious, easy listening, jazz, R&B, soul and top 40/pop. Published "Right To Know" and "Fragile" (by James Jackson), recorded by Kathy Simmons; "You're a Part of Me," "Can't We Have Some Time Together," "You and Me" and "Circles of Time," all written and recorded by Paul Richards (A/C); "Dance to the Beat of My Heart" (by Dan Gertz) recorded by Ace Baker (medium rock); all on Bal Records.

BANNERLEAGUE, LTD. T/A BOLTS MUSIC, 6/9 Salisbury Prom, Green Lanes, Harringay, London N8 ORX **England**. (01)809-1460. Contact: Nicky Price. Music publisher. Estab. 1987. Publishes 12 songs/year; publishes 2 new songwriters/year. Receives approximately 4 submissions/month. Hires staff songwriters. Works with composers and lyricists; teams collaborators. Pays 60% royalty to composer.
How to Contact: Submit a demo tape by mail—unsolicited submissions are OK. Prefers cassette with 3 songs and lyric or lead sheet. SAE. Reports in 3-5 weeks. "Does not return unsolicited material."
Music: Mostly dance. Published "Don't Stop" (by Wedge & Stickley), recorded by Dance Addiction on Bolts Records (house); "Trip on This" (by Asmo), recorded by Asmo on Bolts Records (techno); "Vindaloo Rap" (by Ferguson/Hopkins/Kalyan), recorded by Bhaji Jon on Bolts Records (rap comedy); "C'Mon & Dance" (by Wedge/Stickley/PRS), recorded by Partners Rime Syndicate on Hysteria Records (house dance rap); "Talk It Up" (by Nicky Price), recorded by Mirror Image on Bolts Records (house); and "I Can Dance All By Myself" (by Ewings/Townsend), recorded by Urbania on Hysteria Records (house).

BARTOW MUSIC, 68 Old Canton Rd N.E., Cartersville GA 30120. (404)382-1442. Publishing Administrator: Jack C. Hill; Producer: Tirus McClendon. Music publisher and record producer (HomeBoy, Ragtime Productions). BMI. Estab. 1988. Publishes 5 songs/year; 5 new songwriters/year. Works with composers and lyricists; teams collaborators. Pays royalty.
How to Contact: Submit a demo tape by mail—unsolicited submissions are O.K. Prefers cassette (or VHS videocassette) with 3 songs and lyric sheets. SASE. Reports in 1 month.
Music: R&B, pop, dance and house. Published"Oh Father" (by Maurice Carroll), recorded by Simply Suave (R&B); "I Need You Tonight" (by Maurice Carroll), recorded by Simply Suave (R&B) dance) and "New Day" (by Tirus McClendon), recorded by Celebrations (R&B dance) all on West View Records.

BEARSONGS, Box 944, Birmingham, B16 8UT **England**. Phone: 44-021-454-7020. Managing Director: Jim Simpson. Music publisher and record company (Big Bear Records). Member PRS, MCPS. Publishes 25 songs/year; publishes 15-20 new songwriters/year.
How to Contact: Prefers reel-to-reel or cassette. SAE and IRC. Reports in 2-3 weeks.
Music: Blues and jazz.

K. BEE PRODUCTIONS INC/BUZZ RECORDS, 8900 N. Central Penthouse 405, Phoenix AZ 85020. Mailing address: Box 399, Peoria AZ 85380-0399. (602)678-1444. President: Kenneth D. Belanger. Music publisher, record company (Buzz Records/Belhap Records), record producer (K. Bee Productions Inc.) ASCAP-BMI. Estab. 1989. Publishes 8-10 songs/year; 2 new songwriters/year. Hires staff songwriters. Works with composers and lyricists; teams collaborators. Pays varying royalty to artist on contract.

Affiliate(s): Belhap Music Publishers (ASCAP) and Pahleb Music Publishers (BMI).
How to Contact: Submit a demo tape by mail—unsolicited submissions OK. Prefers cassette (or ½" videocassette if available) with 1-3 songs and lyric sheet. "No phone calls. We will contact if intereted." Does not return unsolicited material. Reports in 1 month.
Music: Mostly rock, pop, country/R&B; also industrial A.V., novelty and heavy metal. Published "Secret Sea of Storm" recorded by Brats on Buzz Records (metal pop); "Lover Deceiver" (crossover/ pop) and "Kinda, Sorta, Maybe" (country) both recorded on Belhap Records all written by Rick Funk and Ken Belanger.
Tips: "Send a good clean, clear tape. We are looking for artists and writers with signature in their style."

EARL BEECHER PUBLISHING, P.O. Box 2111, Huntington Beach CA 92647. (714)842-8635. Owner: Earl Beecher. Music publisher, record company (Outstanding and Morrhythm Records) and record producer (Earl Beecher). BMI. Estab. 1968. Publishes varying number of songs/year. Works with composers. Pays standard royalty.
How to Contact: Submit a demo tape—unsolicited submissions are OK. Prefers cassette. SASE. Reports in 3 months.
Music: Mostly pop, ballads, rock and gospel; also country.
Tips: "I am interested mainly in people who want to perform their songs and release albums on one of my labels."

BEKOOL MUSIC, Box 31819, Dallas TX 75231-0819. (214)750-0720. A&R: Mike Anthony. Music publisher. ASCAP. Estab. 1987. Publishes 12-20 songs/year. Publishes 3 new songwriters/year. Pays standard royalty. Works with composers.
Affiliate(s): Forest Creek Music (BMI).
How to Contact: Write first and obtain permission to submit a tape. Prefers cassette with 1-2 songs and lyric sheet. "We do not return unsolicited material but will contact if interested."
Music: Mostly country and gospel. Published "You Hold My World Together" (by Mitchel, Penny, Grice), recorded by Charlie Pride on 16th Ave./Ritz Records (England) (country); "Lay it Down, Give it Up" (by T. Long, D. Liles and J. Chisum), recorded by Janet Paschal on Canaan Records/Word Records (gospel); and "High School Buddies" (by C. Jones, R. Muir), recorded by the Bama Band on Mercury/Polygram Records.

BENYARD MUSIC CO., P.O. Box 298, Queens NY 11415. (718)657-5363. President: Kevin Benyard. Music publisher and record producer (Stone Cold Productions). Member of Songwriter's Guild of America. BMI. Estab. 1987. Publishes 5 songs/year; publishes 3 new songwriters/year. Works with composers and lyricists. Pays standard royalty.
How to Contact: Write first and obtain permission to submit. Prefers cassette with 2-5 songs and lyric sheet. SASE (postcard). Reports in 4 weeks.
Music: Mostly R&B, jazz fusion, rock, rap, top 40; also pop. Published "Better Wait to Know Her" and "The Time is Right," both written and recorded by K. Benyard on Jeannae Records (dance). To be released: "Homeless Nation" (by K. Benyard) on A.A.I. Records (R&B single).
Tips: "I'm looking for music and songs that are totally new in approach. I'm interested in releasing the music of the 90's."

BERANDOL MUSIC LTD., Unit 220, 2600 John St., Marham ONT L3R 3W3 **Canada.** (416)475-1848. A&R Director: Tony Procewiat. Music publisher, record company (Berandol Records), record producer and distributor. BMI. Member CMPA, CIRPA, CRIA. Estab. 1969. Publishes 20-30 songs/year; publishes 5-10 new songwriters/year. Works with composers. Pays standard royalty.
How to Contact: Submit demo tape with 2-5 songs. Reports in 3 weeks.
Music: Mostly pop, serious, educational, top 40 and dance. Published "In Your Smile" written and recorded by Cyan on Berandol Records (dance); "Cosmic Love" (by Bruce Lord), recorded by Rob Liddell on Berandol (MOR); "Symphonie #3" (by Jacques Hetv), recorded on Centrediscs (serious).
Tips: "Strong melodic choruses and original sounding music receive top consideration."

HAL BERNARD ENTERPRISES, INC., P.O. Box 8385, 2612 Erie Ave., Cincinnati OH 45208. (513)871-1500. FAX: (513)871-1510. President: Stan Hertzman. Professional Manager: Chuck Fletcher. Music publisher, record company and management firm. Publishes 12-24 songs/year; 1-2 new songwriters/ year. Pays 25 submissions/month. Works with composers. Pays standard royalty.
Affiliate(s): Sunnyslope Music (ASCAP), Bumpershoot Music (BMI), Apple Butter Music (ASCAP), Carb Music (ASCAP), Saiko Music (ASCAP), TYI Music (ASCAP) and Smorgaschord Music (AS-CAP).

How to Contact: Submit a demo tape—unsolicited submissions are OK. Prefers cassette with 3 songs and lyric sheet. SASE. Reports in 6 weeks.

Music: Rock, R&B and top 40/pop. Published "Lone Rhino" and "Desire Caught By The Tail," written and recorded by Adrian Belew on Island Records (progressive); "Fear is Never Boring," "Trust" and "Aches and Pains," recorded by The Bears on PMRC/IRS Records (rock); "Young Lions," "Men in Helicopters" and Phone Call From the Moon," all written and recorded by Adrian Belew on Atlantic Records (progressive pop).

Tips: "Best material should appear first on demo. Cast your demos. If you as the songwriter can't sing it—don't. Get someone who can present your song properly, use a straight rhythm track and keep it as naked as possible. If you think it still needs something else, have a string arranger, etc. help you, but still keep the *voice up* and the *lyrics clear*."

M. BERNSTEIN MUSIC PUBLISHING CO., 2170 S. Parker Rd., Denver CO 80231. (303)755-2613. President: R.J. Bernstein. Music publisher, record company (Finer Arts Records) and record producer (Transworld Records). ASCAP, BMI. Estab. 1960. Publishes 15-25 songs/year; publishes 5-10 new songwriters/year.

How to Contact: Prefers cassette and lyric or lead sheet. Does not return unsolicited material. Reports in 1 month.

Music: Rock, country and jazz. Published "Over and Over" (R&B) and "Dance Baby Dance" (rap) (both by Pamela Dawn), recorded by Penda on Fine Arts Records.

Tips: "No *phone calls* please."

BEST BUDDIES, INC., , P.O. Box 121738, Nashville TN 37212-1738. (615)383-7664. Contact review committee. Music publisher, record company (X-cuse Me) and record producer (Best Buddies Productions). BMI. Estab. 1981. Publishes 18 songs/year. Publishes 1-2 new songwriters/year. Works with composers and lyricists. Pays standard royalty.

Affiliate(s): Swing Set Music (ASCAP), Best Buddies Music (BMI).

How to Contact: Write first and obtain permission to submit. Must include SASE with permission letter. Prefers cassette (or VHS videocassette) with maximum 3 songs. SASE. Reports in 8 weeks. Do not call to see if tape received.

Music: Mostly country, rock and roll and pop; also gospel and R&B. Published "Somebody Wrong is Looking Right" (by King/Burkholder), recorded by Bobby Helms; "Give Her Back Her Faith in Me" (by Ray Dean James), recorded by David Speegle on Bitter Creek Records (country); and "I Can't Get Over You Not Loving Me" (by Misty Efron and Bobbie Sallee), recorded by Sandy Garwood on Bitter Creek Records (country).

Tips: "Make a professional presentation. There are no second chances on first impressions."

*BETTER TIMES PUBLISHING/DORIS LINDSAY PUBLISHING, 1203 Biltmore Ave., Asheville NC 27260. (919)882-9990. President: Doris Lindsay. Music publisher, record company (Fountain Records) and record producer (Successful Productions). BMI, ASCAP. Estab. 1979. Publishes 40 songs/year; publishes 6 new songwriters/year. Works with composers and lyricists; teams collaborators. Pays standard royalty.

Affiliate(s): Doris Lindsay Publishing (ASCAP), Better Times Publishing (BMI).

How to Contact: Submit a demo tape by mail—unsolicited submissions are OK. Prefers cassette with 2 songs and lyric sheet. SASE. Reports in 2 months.

Music: Mostly country, pop, contemporary gospel. Also wedding songs, blues, southern gospel. Published "Share Your Love," written and recorded by Mitch Snow on Fountain Records (country); "What Did You Do With Your Old 45's" (by Hanna/Pickard), recorded by Bobby Vinton on Curb Records (country/pop); "Back In Time," written and recorded by Mitch Snow on Fountain Records (country); and "Another Notch on My Guitar," written and recorded by Larry Lovey on Fountain Records (blues).

Tips: "Have a professional demo made."

*BETTY JANE/JOSIE JANE MUSIC PUBLISHERS (C.E.R. RECORDS), 7400 N. Adams Rd., North Adams MI 49262. (517)287-4421. Professional Manager: Claude E. Reed. Music publisher and record company (C.E.R. Records). BMI, ASCAP. Estab. 1980. Publishes 5-10 songs/year; 10 new songwriters/year. Works with composers and lyricists; teams collaborators. Pays standard royalty.

How to Contact: Submit a demo tape by mail—unsolicited submissions are OK. Prefers cassette or 7½ ips reel-to-reel with up to 5 songs and lyric or lead sheets. "We prefer typewritten and numbered lyric sheets and good professional quality demo tapes." SASE. Reports in 3 weeks.

Music: Mostly gospel and country western; also R&B. Published "The Guiding Light" (by Rev. Charles E. Cravey), "Stand Up and Testify" (by Claude E. Reed) and "I'm Standing on the Promises" (by Rev. Cravey); all recorded by Rev. Cravey on C.E.R. Records (gospel).

Tips: "We are looking for professional, commercial song material presented on a good quality, well done demo tape. Keep in simple yet capture the listener's attention. A lot of artists are also writers, so your material has to be professional in order to compete."

BEVERLY HILLS MUSIC PUBLISHING, Division of Larrco Industries of Texas, Box 3842, Houston TX 77253-3842. President: Dr. Lawrence Herbst. Music publisher, record company (Best-Way, Beverly Hills, D.T.I., Larr, Lawrence Herbst and Total Sound Records) and record producer (Lawrence Herbst). BMI. Estab. 1966. Publishes 12 songs/year; publishes 3 new songwriters/year. Teams collaborators. Pays standard royalty.
Affiliate(s): K-Larrco Satellite Radio/TV and K-Larrco Music Publishing.
How to Contact: Prefers cassette (or VHS videocassette), lyric sheet and writer background information. Does not return unsolicited material. Reports in 6 weeks.
Music: Mostly rock; also country, top 40/pop, bluegrass, blues, easy listening, folk, jazz, progressive, R&B, gospel and soul.

*BIG CITY MUSIC, INC., 15 Gloria Lane, Fairfield NJ 07004. (201)808-8280. President: Gary Rottger. Music publisher. BMI. Estab. 1990. Publishes 10 songs/year; publishes 3 new songwriters/year. Teams collaborators. Pays standard royalty.
Affiliate(s): Doozen Music (BMI), Big City Music (BMI).
How to Contact: Submit a demo tape by mail—unsolicited submissions are OK. Prefers cassette and VHS videocassette with 3 songs and lyric sheet. Reports in 3 weeks.
Music: Mostly R&B, rap and rock. Published *I Still Dream About You* (by Byrd, Jett, Rottger), recorded by Joan Jett on CBS Records (rock); *Crushin'* (by Rottger and Fat Boys), recorded by Fat Boys on Polygram Records (rap); and *Rock Rulin'* (by Rottger and Fat Boys), Warner "Disorderlies" soundtrack on Polygram Records (rap).
Tips: "Good clean demo. Songs must compete with current radio."

BIG SNOW MUSIC, P.O. Box 279, Hopkins MN 55343. (612)942-6119. President: Mitch Viegut. Vice President and General Manager: Mark Alan. Music publisher. BMI. Estab. 1989. Publishes 20 new songs/year; publishes 8 new songwriters/year. Works with composers and lyricists; teams collaborators. Pays standard royalty.
How to Contact: Submit a demo tape by mail—unsolicited submissions are OK. Prefers cassette with 3 songs and lyric sheet. Does not return unsolicited material. Reports in 6 weeks.
Music: Mostly rock, pop and black. Published "Somewhere" (by Mitch Viegut), (pop); "Thief in the Night" (by Doug Dixon/Mitch Viegut) (rock); and "Rock City" (by Mitch Viegut) (rock), all recorded by Airkraft on Premiére Records.

BIG WEDGE MUSIC, P.O. Box 29-0186, Nashville TN 37229-0186. (615)754-2950. President: Ralph Johnson. BMI. Music publisher. Estab. 1960. Pays standard royalty. Publishes 1,000 songs and 200 new songwriters/year.
Affiliate(s): Wedge Entertainment Group, Wedge Records, Inc., Pro-Star Talent, Inc. and Pro Rite Music (ASCAP).
How to Contact: Prefers cassette (or videocassette) with maximum of 4 songs and lyric sheet or lead sheet. SASE. Reports in 2 weeks.
Music: Mostly country, pop and rock; also gospel and R&B. Published "Not Enough Country" (by Gary Newman); *That Little Green Worm*, (by Dave Martin); "Mr. Blue Eyes" (by Jackie Minarik/Chic Bixby/Billy Lee Napier), recorded by Will Beery (country/pop); and "My Dreams Came True" written and recorded by Stella Parton (country/pop), all on Wedge Records.

BLACK STALLION COUNTRY PUBLISHING, Box 368, Tujunga CA 91043. (818)352-8142. FAX: (718)507-5516. President: Kenn Kingsbury. Music publisher and book publisher (*Who's Who in Country & Western Music*). BMI. Member CMA, CMF. Publishes 2 songs/year; publishes 1 new songwriter/year. Pays standard royalty.
How to Contact: Prefers 7½ ips reel-to-reel or cassette with 2-4 songs and lyric sheet. SASE. Reports in 1 month.
Music: Bluegrass, country and R&B.
Tips: "Be professional in attitude and presentation. Submit only the material you think is better than anything being played on the radio."

BLADE TO THE RHYTHM MUSIC, 114-22 116th St., S. Ozone Pk. NY 11420. (718)672-8755 or (718)845-4417. FAX: (718)507-5516. President: Juan Kato Lemus. Music publisher and production company/Producers. ASCAP. Estab. 1990. Publishes 5-10 songs/year; publishes 2-4 new songwriters/year. Hires staff songwriters. "Depending on work." Pays "depending on work to be added or song to be changed."

Close-up

Mike Reid
Songwriter
Nashville, Tennessee

Back in the early '80s, songwriter Mike Reid drove down 16th Avenue, part of Nashville's Music Row, and pushed a button on his car radio. The song he heard playing was "Inside," which he had written for country singer Ronnie Milsap. That happy drive was the first time Reid heard one of his own songs on the air and the song soon became a hit.

"As I was pushing my buttons, I heard it, yeah," recalls Reid, who earned two Grammys in the '80s while he was a staff writer for Milsap's Lodge Hall Music publishing company. "When you get a song recorded, it's wonderful. You have the album and then, my God, you get the news that they're going to release it as a single. And from the release day on, you become the maddest radio button pusher that you've ever seen! You just scour the radio in search of that song."

While working for Milsap, Reid's songwriting flourished. In fact, he wrote or co-wrote such classic Milsap hits as "Stranger in My House" and "Lost in the Fifties" (his two Grammy winners) and "She Keeps the Home Fires Burning," "Prisoner of the Highway," "Show Her" and "Still Losing You." His duet single with Milsap, "Old Folks," went Top 5 on the country chart. Reid also has had substantial hits with "To Me" for Lee Greenwood and Barbara Mandrell, "Born to Be Blue" for The Judds, "There You Are" for Willie Nelson and "Forever Is as Far as I'll Go" for Alabama. ASCAP named Reid its 1985 Songwriter of the Year.

For most of his life, Reid has answered questions about why he would want to give up his brief career in pro football (he was a first-round draft pick for the Cincinnati Bengals) for a career in music, which he did in 1975. "My music started long before my sports did," he says. "I started piano lessons when I was six years old."

Reid was a star football player, honored as Rookie of the Year and All-Pro twice. But with the fame came numerous injuries, some of which still plague him. So this Penn State music graduate left the defensive line to write songs and play keyboard for a Cincinnati-based band. Then he toured the East Coast as a solo act, often billed as "The All-Pro Piano Player."

In 1980, Reid landed a job as a writer for a Nashville song publisher, then later worked for Milsap's company. Today, he writes for Almo-Irving Music. Looking back, he says it's taken him years and years to discover the most difficult task of learning to write songs: discovering what you intend to say. "I've had to write an enormous amount and make an awful lot of mistakes to teach myself what my intent as a writer is," he says. "But when I did begin to understand the intent of what I meant to say, it at least gave me something of a direction in which to work. And I found that when I latched onto an idea that I really loved and wanted to pursue and got the juices flowing, that then I could honestly say I enjoyed the hard work of writing as well."

Today Reid writes mostly at home. Instead of keeping a journal, he jots song ideas on large sheets of newsprint that he keeps on a drawing board. "I really believe in the notion of word relationships," he explains. "I think that's why I use the big page, because there's got to be some word, some sound, that you can relate to a given title. And even if it means filling up a page with nonsense that I'll never use, I do that."

Reid says one lesson he's learned is to make only demo tapes that have been written and recorded with commitment. In his words: "In most cases, when I hear demos from people, I get the feeling that they're saying, 'Well here, try this and see if you like it.' You cannot—you *must* not—possess the gall to ask people to believe in something you do not believe in. And if you're going to send material out to be judged and to be recorded, it has to be material that you would stake your whole songwriting life on; it has to be that good. And if it's not, people are going to start associating you with songs that they don't record."

Reid advises songwriters to be sure the person singing on their demo tape understands the emotional intent of the songs and sings them "with a sense of confidence and forceful-ness." He elaborates: "People really want to be convinced. Very often, a forceful, passion-ate performance of a song is what sells the singer on it. I happen to believe that people in this business . . . really *want* to find a good song. They really *want* to find a great singer. But they more than likely won't offer it to somebody who they feel has not sung or written a song that is committed, that says this is what it intends to be, this is what I mean to say. And you get that reflection in the way the demo is presented."

Reid's demo of possible songs for Willie Nelson impressed the staff at Columbia Re-cords enough to offer him a recording contract. The resulting debut album, *Turning for Home*, features 11 songs that Reid co-wrote. One of the cuts, "Walk on Faith," hit No. 1 on *Billboard*'s country charts in early 1991.

Some songwriters might look at Reid's many successes and think that he's never faced rejection or writer's block. Wrong. He's had his share.

"I deal with rejection every day," he says. "I would say that 80 percent of what I've written in my life has been rejected and will never be heard.

"I don't know how you deal with rejection. But I have found out over the years that the reasons people don't record songs are varied."

Songwriters, he says, should press on despite rejection. They should continue observing life, looking for song ideas. "But after that," he says, "it's rolling your sleeves up and working! And kind of arranging these symbols we call words in such a fashion that they say what you mean to say.

"You know, it's a distance of a couple of feet from your brain to your paper, but it takes years to learn how to make that trip clearly and in a concise way that the listener feels the same thing you do. And of course that's a crap shoot. You never know if they'll get it or not."

—Tyler Cox

Affiliate(s): Piedra Productions Music (ASCAP), Davidson Ospina Music (ASCAP), John Wilson Music (ASCAP) and Pavel De Jesus (ASCAP).
How to Contact: Submit a demo tape by mail—unsolicited submissions are OK. Prefers cassette with 2-4 songs and lyric sheet. "Send photo or bio." Does not return unsolicited material. Reports in 4 weeks.
Music: Mostly dance/pop, house and R&B; also freestyle, rap and ballads. Published "No Para" (by Bladerunners), recorded by Sound Factor on Warlock Records (house).

*BLENHEIM MUSIC, 14 Brickendon Green, Hertford S91 38PB **England.** (09)92-86404. Proprietor: John Dye. Music publisher. PRS, MCPS. Estab. 1982. Teams collaborators. Pays standard royalty.
How to Contact: Submit a demo tape by mail—unsolicited submissions are OK. Prefers cassette with any number of songs and lyric sheet. SASE. Reports in 6 weeks.
Music: Mostly pop, country and reggae; also comedy songs. Published *Ballad of Mr. Johnson*, written and recorded by Vivian Jones (reggae LP); "Losing Myself" (by Ariel), recorded by Delusions of Grandeur (pop single); and *Drake* (by Philip Evans), recorded by Tony Fayne (comedy LP); all on Rosie Records.

BLUE HILL MUSIC/TUTCH MUSIC, 308 Munger Lane, Bethlehem CT 06751. Contact: Paul Hotchkiss. Music publisher, record company (Target Records, Kastle Records) and record producer (Red Kastle Records). BMI. Estab. 1975. Published 20 songs/year; publishes 1-5 new songwriters/year. Receives 100 submissions/month. Pays standard royalty.

Affiliate(s): Blue Hill Music (BMI) and Tutch Music (BMI).

How to Contact: Write first and obtain permission to submit a tape. Prefers cassette with 2 songs and lyric sheet. "Demos should be clear with vocals out in front." SASE. Reports in 3 weeks.

Music: Mostly country and country/pop; also MOR and blues. Published "Everyday Man" (by M. Terry), recorded by M. Terry on Roto Noto Records (country/pop); "Thinking Bout You" (by P. Hotchkiss), recorded by Susan Manning on Target Records (country); and "Stop Look Listen" (by P. Hotchkiss), recorded by Beverly's Hillbilly Band on Trophy Records (country).

BLUE UMBRELLA MUSIC PUBLISHING CO./PARASOL MUSIC PUBLISHING CO., 3011 Beach 40th St., Brooklyn NY 11224. (718)372-6436. Contact: Mr. Kadish Millet. Music publisher. Publishes 15 songs/year; publishes 7 new songwriters/year. Pays standard royalty.

How to Contact: Submit a demo tape—unsolicited submissions are OK. Prefers cassette with 1-10 songs and lead sheet. Prefers studio produced demos. "Wrap cassette well; some cassette boxes have fairly sharp edges and break through envelope. I want a lead sheet and/or typed lyric sheet and accurate information on who owns the copyright and if it was registered in Washington at the time of submission. Affiliation of writers (ASCAP/BMI) needed to issue proper contract." SASE *"with proper amount of return postage."* Reports in 2 weeks.

Music: Country and/or anything "truly superior." Published "Through Love" (by Roy Ownbey), recorded by the Little Big Band on Track Records (sacred/country); "Boomerang" (by Ernie Scott), recorded by the Little Big Band on Track Records (country); and "What's More American Than Soccer?" (by Kadish Millet), recorded by Tony Ansems on Fox Records (novelty).

Tips: "Although there's no accounting for taste, you can't fool publishers and A&R personnel. Your song has to be memorable, unique, different in some way that makes the listener say 'Wow! That's incredible!' Otherwise, forget it. Come up with a great song lyrically and melodically. Songs are a dime a dozen. Great songs are few and far between."

JOHNNY BOND PUBLICATIONS, 1815 Division St., Nashville TN 37203. (615)327-8436. President: Sherry Bond. Music publisher. BMI/ASCAP. Estab. 1955. Publishes 100 songs/year; 1 new songwriter/ year. Works with composers. Pays standard royalty.

Affiliate(s): Red River Songs, Inc. (BMI), Crimson Creek Songs (ASCAP).

How to Contact: Write or call to arrange a personal interview. Prefers cassette with 1 song and lyric sheet. SASE. Reports in 1 month.

Music: Country only. Published "Blues Stay Away From Me" (by The Delmore Bros.), recorded by The Judds and Carl Perkins on Universal Records, K.D. Lang on Sire Records and Chris Austin on Warner Bros. Records (country).

Tips: "Because we receive so many requests to submit songs, we are very selective. Big corporations are buying up small publishing companies, making it more difficult to get songs recorded. Songwriters need to know as much as possible about the publishing companies they approach."

BONNFIRE PUBLISHING, P.O. Box 6429, Huntington Beach CA 92615-6429. (714)962-5618. Contact: Eva and Stan Bonn. Music publisher (Gather Round Music, BMI), record company (ESB Records) and record producer. ASCAP, BMI. Estab. 1987. Publishes 10-20 songs/year; publishes 2-10 new songwriters/year. Receives 20 submissions/month. Pays standard royalty.

How to Contact: Submit demo cassette with lyric sheet. Does not return unsolicited material.

Music: Country, country/crossover/pop and gospel. Published "Highway 44" (by Bobby Caldwell and Jim Weaver), "She's A Dance Hall Lady" (by Eva Bonn and Nancy Cyril), "She's a Lady By Day, Lover By Night" (by Bobby Caldwell); "Don't Watch Me Fall Apart" (by Bobby Lee Caldwell); "You're Workin' on Leavin Me" (by Eva Bonn, Nancy Cyril, Marda Philpott), recorded by Bobby Lee Caldwell (country); "There's a Memory in My Heart," written and recorded by Bobby Lee Caldwell (country), all on ESB Records; and "The Gold in This Ring" (by Tice Griffin and Todd Hartman), recorded by Pat Murphy on OL Records.

BOOGIETUNES MUSIKPRODUKTION GmbH, Seelingstrasse 33, 1000 Berlin 19, **West Germany.** Phone: 030/321 60 47. Managing Director: Timothy E. Green. Music publisher and record company. Estab. 1978. Publishes 100 songs/year; publishes 2 new songwriters/year. Teams collaborators. Pays standard GEMA rate.

How to Contact: Submit a demo tape—unsolicited submissions are OK. Prefers cassette. Does not return unsolicited material. "No cassette returns!"
Music: Mostly disco/dance, electronic, rap and house. Published "Silver Machine," recorded by Acieedo Domingo on TELDEC Records (house); "¾," recorded by Bass Mental on Dance Street Records (Rave Music); and "Radio Songs," recorded by Hold the Front Page on Up and Down Records (SKA Music)

BOOT SONGS, Box 1065, Stn. B., Mississauga, Ontario L4Y 3W4 **Canada**. (416)238-2783. President: Jury Krytiuk. Music publisher, record company (Boot, Cynda, Generation, Boot Leisure Corp.) and record producer (Jury Krytiuk). SOCAN. 1987. Publishes 100 songs/year. Pays standard royalty.
Affiliate(s): Boot Tunes (SOCAN), Boot House of Songs (ASCAP), Boot House of Tunes (BMI) and The Musical Boot (PRS).
How to Contact: Prefers cassette and lyric sheet. SAE and IRC. Reports in 2 weeks.
Music: Mostly country, folk and MOR. Published "For We Are the Irish" (by Ray Fynes), recorded by Mary Fynes on Boot Records (Irish); "Love is a Beautiful Song" (by Terry Dempsey), recorded by John McNally on Quality Records (MOR); and "Mama's Fiddle," written and recorded by Ray Keating on Boot Records (country).

*BRANCH GROUP MUSIC, #108-93 Lombard Ave., Winnipeg MB R3B 3B1 **Canada**. (204)957-0085. President: Gilles Paquin. Music publisher, record company (Oak Street Music) and record producer (Oak Street Music). SOCAN. Estab. 1987. Publishes 10 songs/year; publishes 2 new songwriters/year. Works with composers and lyricists; teams collaborators. Negotiable royalty.
Affiliate(s): Forest Group Music (SOCAN).
How to Contact: Submit a demo tape by mail—unsolicited submissions are OK. Prefers cassette or VHS videocassette with 2-3 songs and lyric and lead sheet. SASE. Reports in 1-2 months.
Music: Mostly children's and novelty. Published "Sandwiches" (by Bob King), "The Season" (by Fred Penner), and "Christmasy Kind of Day" (by Ken Whiteley); all recorded by Fred Penner on Oak Street Records.

*BROOZBEE MUSIC, INC., Suite 308, 37 East 28th St., New York NY 10016. (212)447-6000. President: Bruce B. Fisher. Music publisher. ASCAP. Estab. 1986. Publishes 8 songs/year; publishes 2 new songwriters/year. Works with composers; teams collaborators. Pays standard royalty.
How to Contact: Submit a demo tape by mail—unsolicited submissions are OK, or call to arrange a personal interview. Prefers cassette or VHS videocassette with 3 songs and lyric sheet. SASE. Reports in 2 months.
Music: Mostly house, dance, hip hop; also rap, R&B and pop. Published "Mission Accomplished," "Loose Flutes" and "Get Up" (by P. Punzone, G. Sicard and B.B. Fisher), all on Big Productions Records.
Tips: "The song has to fit in the musical styles we listed and be ready to be recorded for release."

*BUCKS MUSIC LTD., 1A Farm Pl., London W87SX **United Kingdom**. (071)221-4275. Director: Simon Platz. Music publisher and record company (Fly, Weekend, Sepia). PRS. Estab. 1979. Publishes 1000 songs/year; publishes 10-30 new songwriters/year. Hires staff writers. Works with composers and lyricists. Pays variable amount.
How to Contact: Submit a demo tape by mail—unsolicited submissions are OK. Prefers cassette with 3 songs and lyric sheets. SASE. Reports in 3 weeks.
Music: Mostly pop, jazz and dance; also rock and New Age.

BUG MUSIC, 6777 Hollywood, Los Angeles CA 90028. (213)466-4352. Contact: Fred Bourgoise. Music publisher. BMI, ASCAP. Estab. 1975. Hires staff songwriters. We handle administration.
Affiliate(s): Bughouse (ASCAP).
How to Contact: Prefers cassette. Does not return unsolicited material.
Music: All genres. Published "Joey," by Concrete Blonde; "Angel Eyes" (by John Hiatt), recorded by Jeff Healy on Artista Records; and "Full Moon Full of Love" (by Leroy Preston), recorded by K.D. Lang.

BURIED TREASURE MUSIC, 524 Doral Country Dr., Nashville TN 37221. Executive Producer: Scott Turner. Music publisher and record producer (Aberdeen Productions). ASCAP. Estab. 1972. Publishes 30-50 songs/year; publishes 3-10 new songwriters/year. Receives 1,500 submissions/year. Works with composers and lyricists. Pays standard royalty.
Affiliate(s): Captain Kidd Music (BMI).
How to Contact: Submit a demo tape—unsolicited submissions are OK. Prefers cassette (or VHS videocassette) with 1-4 songs and lead sheet. Reports in 3 weeks. "Always enclose SASE if answer is expected."

Music: Country and country/pop; also rock, MOR and contemporary. Published "I Still Can't Say Goodbye" (by J. Moore and B. Blinn), recorded by Chet Atkins; "You Did it All" (by D. Baumgartner and Scott Turner), recorded by Shelby Lynne on CBS Records (country); "All I Need Is You" (by P. Baer & G. Breen), recorded by Paulette Tyler (country); "The Lord of Birmingham" (by S. Rose), recorded by C. Kern on Badger Records (country); and "What If I Didn't Have You" (by Audie Murphy/S. Turner/D. Baumgartner), recorded by Roy Clark (country).
Tips: "*Don't* send songs in envelopes that are 15"x 20", or by registered mail. It doesn't help a bit. Say something that's been said a thousand times before . . . only say it differently. A great song doesn't care who sings it. Songs that paint pictures have a better chance of ending up as videos. With artists only recording 10 songs every 18-24 months, the advice is . . . Patience!"

*C.A.B. INDEPENDENT PUBLISHING CO., P.O. Box 26852, Oklahoma City OK 73126. Secretary: Christopher Stanley. Music publisher and record company (Ms'Que Records, Inc.). BMI. Estab. 1988. Publishes 10 songs/year; publishes 5 new songwriters/year. Works with composers. Pays standard royalty.
Affiliate(s): (C.A.B.) Creative Artistic Broadening Industries, Publishing (BMI).
How to Contact: Submit a demo tape by mail—unsolicited submissions are OK. Prefers cassette or VHS videocassette with 3 songs. SASe. Reports in 4 weeks-1 month.
Music: Mostly R&B, rock, pop; also jazz, New Age and gospel. Published "Attack" (R&B); "We Got Funky" (pop) and "Together" (pop), all written by C. Freeman and recorded by Cash & Co. on Ms'Que Records.
Tips: "Make sure you submit your best songs. It's best to get professional advice and demos."

C. P. I. MUSIC, %Franz B. Swegal, P.C., F. B. Swegal, Div. of Centaur®, P.O. Box 7320, Beverly Hills CA 90212. (818)762-7417. Principal: Franz B. Swegal Music publisher. ASCAP. Estab. 1984. Works with composers and lyricists; teams collaborators. Pays standard royalty.
How to Contact: Submit a demo tape by mail—unsolicited submissions are OK. "With simple release obviating C.P.I. Music from any liability with reference to copyright infringement." Prefers cassette with 3 songs. SASE. Reports in 3 weeks.
Music: Mostly AOR; also, pop, country, R&B, jazz and classical.

CALIFORNIA COUNTRY MUSIC, 112 Widmar Pl., Clayton CA 94517. (415)672-8201. Owner: Edgar. J. Brincat. Music Publisher, record company (Roll On Records). BMI. Estab. 1985. Publishes 30 songs/year; publishes 2-4 new songwriters/year. Receives 200 submissions/month. Works with composers and lyricists; teams collaborators. Pays standard royalty.
Affiliate(s): Sweet Inspirations Music (ASCAP).
How to Contact: Submit a demo tape by mail—unsolicited submissions are OK. Prefers cassette with 3 songs and lyric sheet. Any calls will be returned collect to caller. SASE. Reports in 6 weeks.
Music: Mostly MOR, contemporary country and pop; also R&B, gospel and light rock. Published "Jack Daniels" (by Barbara Finnicum, Edgar J. Brincat, Patti Leidecker), recorded by Carolyn Rae; "Southern Comfort" and "The Rain" (by Barbara Finnicum, Ed Davie) recorded by Ed Davie (country); all on Roll On Records.
Tips: "Listen to what we have to say about your product. Be as professional as possible."

CALVARY MUSIC GROUP, INC., 142 8th Ave. N., Nashville TN 37203. (615)244-8800. President: Dr. Nelson S. Parkerson. Music publisher and record company ASCAP, BMI, SESAC. Publishes 30-40 songs/year; publishes 2-3 new songwriters/year. Pays standard royalty.
Affiliate(s): Songs of Calvary, Music of Calvary and LifeStream Music, Soldier of the Light, Torchbearer Music.
How to Contact: Accepting material at this time.
Music: Church/religious, contemporary Christian, gospel and wedding music.

GLEN CAMPBELL MUSIC GROUP, Box 158717, Nashville TN 37215. (615)385-9875. Office Manager: Cherie Gamblin. Music publisher. BMI. Estab. 1970. Publishes 25 songs/year; publishes 1 new songwriter/year. Pays standard royalty.
Affiliate(s): Seventh Son (ASCAP), Keytee Kay (ASCAP), Latter End (BMI), Chapter IV (ASCAP), Allanwood (BMI).
How to Contact: Write or call first and obtain permission to submit a tape. Prefers cassette with 2 songs and lyric sheet. Does not return any material. Reports in 2 months. "We only call if we can use the material."
Music: Mostly country, contemporary or traditional; also female country/pop. Published "Breakin New Ground" (by Carl Jackson), recorded by Wild Rose on Universal Records (country); and "Blue Blooded Woman" and "Here In the Real World," written and recorded by Alan Jackson on Arista Records (country).

Tips: "Be ultra-selective; send only quality songs, as the business is more competitive than it's ever been."

*CANVIRG MUSIC, Ste. 101, 302 E. Pettigrew St., Durham NC 27701. (919)688-8563. President: Willie Hill. Music publisher and record company (Joy Records). BMI. Estab. 1987. Publishes 10 songs/year; publishes 3 new songwriters/year. Teams collaborators. Pays standard royalty.
Affiliate(s): Canvirg Music (BMI).
How to Contact: Submit a demo tape by mail—unsolicited submissions are OK. Prefers cassette with 4 songs and lyric sheet. Does not return unsolicited material. Reports in 2 weeks.
Music: Mostly R&B, pop and gospel. Published "Step by Step" (by Walter Hill), recorded by Inspire Productions Studio on Joy Records (R&B).

CAPAQUARIUS PUBLISHING & ARTIST MGT., INC., Suite 1106, 4525 Henry Hudson Parkway, Riverdale NY 10471. (212)549-6318 or 222-2933. Europe: Seeburgerstr 87, 1000 Berlin 20, West Berlin Germany. (030) 331-4568. President: P. Januari Watts. Music publisher, record producer and artist management firm. ASCAP. Publishes 3-4 songs/year; publishes 1 new songwriter/year. Works with composers and lyricists; teams collaborators. Pays standard royalty.
Affiliate(s): Yanita Music (BMI).
How to Contact: Prefers cassette (or NTSC/PAL/SECAM videocassette) with 2-3 songs and lead sheet. "Video should be 4-5 minutes in duration, black and white or color." SASE. Reports in 3-4 weeks. "We are also accepting material as listed above at our office in Germany, with return postage."
Music: Mostly rock and gospel rock; also top 40, contemporary gospel, R&B, soul and blues. Published "Being with You" and "Yahna's Blues" (blues), written and recorded by Queen Yahna and co-published with Marie-Marie Musikverlag; and "Doesn't Anybody (Wanna Fall in Love)" (by Q. Yahna/Danny Deutschmark), recorded by Q. Yahna for Another Record Company, GmbH.

CAPITOL STAR ARTIST ENTS., INC., 386 Clay Ave., Rochester NY 14613. (716)647-1617. Director: Don Redanz. Associate Director: Tony Powlowski. Music publisher, record company and record producer. BMI. Publishes 20 songs/year; publishes 5 new songwriters/year. Pays standard royalty.
Music: Country, gospel, and pop. Published "Dust on Mother's Bible," and "Away from Home," (by Anthony Powlowski), recorded by Tony Starr on Capitol Star (country); and "V-8 Detroit," by A. Powlowski.
Tips: "We like country songs with a heartwarming story."

CARAVELL MAIN SAIL MUSIC, P.O. Box 1646, Branson MO 65616. (417)334-7040. President: Keith O'Neil. Music publisher, record producer (Caravell Recording Studio). ASCAP. Estab. 1989. Publishes 5 new songwriters/year. Works with composers and lyricists; teams collaborators. Pays standard royalty of 50%.
How to Contact: Submit demo tape by mail—unsolicited submissions are OK. Prefers cassette with 3 songs and lyric sheet. SASE. Reports in 4 weeks.
Music: Mostly country, pop and gospel. Published "I've Been There Before" by Sue Ann Neal on Caravelle Records; "The Darlin' Boys" and "The Wizard of Song" by Rodney Dillard on Vanguard Records; and "In the Meadow" by Jackie Pope on Caravelle Records.

DON CASALE MUSIC, INC., 377 Plainfield St., Westbury NY 11590. (516)333-7898. President: Don Casale. Record producer, music publisher, artist management; affiliated recording studio. Estab. 1979. Deals with artists, songwriters, managers and agents. Fee derived from sales royalty.
Affiliate(s): Elasac Music (ASCAP), Don Casale Music (BMI).
How to Contact: "I will accept unsolicited cassettes (except during August and September) with 1-2 songs and a legible, typed lyric sheets (no registered mail). No lyrics-only submissions. Please include address and phone number and letter stating exact purpose (publishing deal? record deal? etc.). Anything else you'd like to say is welcome too (I frown on 'form' letters). Press kit, bio and photo(s) or VHS videocassette are helpful, if available. For return of your material, always include SASE (envelope *must* be large enough to handle contents). If you don't need your material returned, include a *signed* note stating so and only include SASE for my response letter. Sorry, but I will not listen or correspond without SASE. A call first is very welcome (between 12 noon and 12 midnight EST), but not necessary, or you may inquire first by mail (with SASE). I'll listen to every note of your music and respond to you as soon as possible, usually between two weeks and two months, depending on volume of submissions."
Music: Everything but jazz and classical.
Tips: "Submitted songs should have a 'special' nature about them; a different quality and lyric. Melodies should be particularly 'catchy' and memorable. Songs should be in tune with the current radio market. I want only 'career-starting,' top 10 singles; not B sides or album fillers. Please try to be selective and send me that one song you think is a killer; that one song that jumps off the tape! Don't

include a second song just because there's room on the cassette; if I hear something I like, I'll ask for more. Songwriters seeking a publishing contract need only a simple, in-tune, clear version of the song(s); a big production and recording, although welcome, is not necessary. Artists seeking a recording contract should submit a 'quality' performance (musically and vocally), incorporating their very best effort and their own, preferably unique, style. Your recording needn't be master quality, but your performance should be. I give extra points for following my instructions to the letter."

ERNIE CASH MUSIC, INC., 744 Joppa Farm Rd., Joppa MD 21085. (301)679-2262. President: Ernest W. Cash. Music publisher, record company (Continental Records, Inc.), record producer (Vision Music Group, Inc.) and Vision Video Production, Inc. BMI. Estab. 1987. Publishes 30-60 songs/year; publishes 10-15 new songwriters/year. Works with composers and lyricists; teams collaborators. Pays standard royalty.
Affiliate(s): Big K Music, Inc. (BMI), Guerriero Music (BMI) and Deb Music (BMI).
How to Contact: Submit a demo tape by mail—unsolicited submissions are OK. Write or call to arrange a personal interview. Prefers cassette (VHS videocassette if available) with 3 songs and lyric sheet. SASE. Reports in 2 weeks.
Music: Mostly country, gospel and pop; also R&B and rock. Published "A Man Called Jones" written and recorded by Jimmy Peppers; "If You're Not Here By Closing Time" (by Pam Hanna), recorded by Pam Bailey; and "Kansas Waltz" (by James Hession), recorded by Doug Lester, all on Go-Records, all country.
Tips: "Give me a call, I will review your material."

*CATHARINE COURAGE MUSIC LTD., 48 De Lisle Rd., Bournemouth Dorset BH3 7NG **England**. (202)529755. Director: Mike Shepstone. Music publisher. PRS/MCPS. Estab. 1981. Publishes 7 songs/year. Works with composers. Pays standard royalty of 50%.
How to Contact: Submit a demo tape by mail—unsolicited submissions OK. Prefers cassette with three songs and lyric sheet. SASE. Reports in 6 weeks.
Music: Mostly pop, rock/pop and R&B.
Tips: "We are urgently looking for Janis Joplin type songs (no sophistication) for new recording project."

*CENTER FOR THE QUEEN OF PEACE, P.O. Box 90035, Pasadena CA 91109. Music publisher and record company (Cosmotone Music, Cosmotone Records). ASCAP. Estab. 1984. Publishes 10-12 songs/year; publishes 10 new songwriters/year. Works with composers and lyricists; teams collaborators. Pays standard royalty "and by agreement."
Affiliate(s): Cosmotone Music (ASCAP) and Cosmotone Records.
How to Contact: Submit a demo tape by mail—unsolicited submissions are OK. "Will contact only if interested." Prefers cassette or VHS videocassette with lyric sheet.
Music: Mostly gospel and catholic marian music; also Christian new wave music and pop. Published "Peace of Heart," written and recorded by Rafael Brom (Christian New Wave); and "Padre Pio," written and recorded by Lord Hamilton (Christian pop/rock); both on Cosmotone Records.

*CENTURY CITY MUSIC PUBLISHING, 2207 Halifax Cres., Calgary T2M 4E2 **Canada**. (403)282-2555. Producer/Manager: Warren Anderson. Music publisher, record company (Century City Records) and record producer (Warren Anderson). SOCAN. Estab. 1983. Publishes 1-6 songs and 1-6 new songwriters/year. Works with composers and lyricists; teams collaborators. Pays standard royalty.
How to Contact: Write first and obtain permission to submit a tape. Prefers cassette or VHS videocassette with 4 songs and lyric and lead sheets. Reports in 1 month.
Music: Mostly country rock, rock and folk rock; also alternative. Published "Hand Me Down Clown" (by W.R. Hutchinson), recorded by W. Anderson (folk rock); "1000 Miles Away," written and recorded by Damian Follett (folk rock); and "Hot From The Streets," written and recorded by Warren Anderson (rock); all on Century City Records.
Tips: "Keep trying! To impress me you will have to send me more than one 4-song demo tape submission per year. I'm looking for consistency and quality. A small independent publisher can be much more effective in promoting a few good songwriters compared to a large multinational organization where the focus is diffused over a much broader market."

CHAPIE MUSIC (BMI), 228 West 5th, Kansas City MO 64105. (816)842-6854. Owner: Chuck Chapman. Music publisher, record company (Fifth Street Records), record producer (Chapman Recording Studios). BMI. Estab. 1977. Publishes 6 songs/year. Receives 4 submissions/month. Works with composers; teams collaborators. Pays standard 50% royalty.

How to Contact: Call to get permission to submit tape. Prefers cassette with 1-3 songs and lyric sheet. SASE. Reports in weeks.

Music: Mostly country, pop, gospel; also jazz, R&B and New Age. Published "Lonely Country Road" and "Talkin 'Bout," both written and recorded by Mike Eisel; and "Sometimes Takes A Woman" (by Greg Camp), recorded by Rick Loveall, all recorded on Fifth Street Records (country).

Tips: "Make it commercial—with a twist on the lyrics."

CHASANN MUSIC, P.O. Box 12151, Birmingham AL 35202. (205)786-6924. Owner: Charles Hall. Music publisher. BMI. Estab. 1975. Publishes 12 songs/year; publishes 4 new songwriters/year. Hires staff songwriters. Works with composers and lyricists; teams collaborators. Pays standard royalty.

Affiliate(s): Chasann Music (BMI).

How to Contact: Submit a demo tape by mail—unsolicited submissions are OK. Prefers cassette (videocassette if available) with 2 songs and lyric sheet. SASE. Reports in 3 weeks-1 month.

Music: Mostly pop, R&B and gospel.

CHIP 'N' DALE MUSIC PUBLISHERS, INC., 3950 N. Mt. Juliet Rd., Mt. Juliet TN 37122. (615)754-0417. Contact: Karen Jeglum Kennedy. Music publisher, record company (Door Knob Records, Society Records), record producer (Gene Kennedy Enterprises, Inc.). ASCAP. Estab. 1975. Publishes 20-25 songs/year; publishes 10-15 new songwriters/year. Works with composers and lyricists. Pays standard royalty.

Affiliate(s): Door Knob Music Publishing, Inc. (BMI), Lodestar Music, A Division of Gene Kennedy Enterprises, Inc. (SESAC).

How to Contact: Submit a demo tape by mail—unsolicited submissions are OK. Prefers cassette with 1-3 songs and lyric sheet. Include SASE for tape return and/or response. Send regular mail. SASE. Reports in 2 weeks.

Music: Mostly country, gospel. Published "I've Had Enough of You" (by Johnette Burton), recorded Debbie Rich; "She Was the Best Thing That Never Happened to Me" (by Charlie Pelligrini and Lou Fortunate), recorded by Ricky Lee Jackson; "What Kind of Girl Do You Think I Am" (by Sandy Ellwanger and Ralph Porter), recorded by Sandy Ellwanger; all country on Door Knob Records.

Tips: "Respect our submission policy and keep trying."

CHRIS MUSIC PUBLISHING, 133 Arbutus Ave., P.O. Box 396, Manistique MI 49854-0396. President: Reg B. Christensen. Chief Executive Officer: Ken Mathena. Music publisher and record company (Global Records/BMI and Bakersfield Records/BMI). Estab. 1956. Publishes 15-35 songs/year; publishes at least 20 new songwriters/year. Works with lyricists. Pays standard royalty with some exceptions.

Affiliate(s): Saralee Music Publishing (BMI).

How to Contact: Submit cassette *only* with 2-5 songs and lyric sheet. "No fancy, big band demo necessary; just one instrument with a clean, clear voice. Copyrighted material only. Send photocopy of copyright. If not registered with Copyright Office, let us know what you've done to protect your material." SASE. Reports in 1 month or ASAP.

Music: Mostly teen type novelty, gospel, MOR and novelty rock; also bluegrass, contemporary gospel and soul. Published "The Man Upstairs" and "Burning Flame," both written and recorded by Helen Debaker on Bakersfield Records (country/western); and "Don't You Cry" and "End of the Line," both written and recorded by Destiny Group on Global Records (rock).

Tips: "The writer should indicate if he has a certain singer in mind. Keep songs to 2-2½ minutes. Voice on demo should be clear—if one must strain to listen, interest is lost fast. Give us time—publishers put in a lot of time and money and we have to wait to hear back from managers and record companies, too. Songwriters are cautioned to be careful about writing flippant letters like 'answer or else,' which most publishers will ignore and deal no further with the writer."

CHRYSALIS MUSIC GROUP, 645 Madison Ave., New York NY 10022. (212)758-3555. Professional Manager: Michelle Mannies. Music publisher. ASCAP, BMI. Estab. 1972. Publishes 50-100 songs/year; publishes 1-2 new songwriters/year. Receives 40 submissions/month. Hires staff songwriters "in small quantities." Pays royalty—"standard in most cases, but negotiable."

Affiliate(s): Chrysalis Music (ASCAP) and Chrysalis Songs (BMI).

How to Contact: Call first and obtain permission to submit a tape. Prefers cassette with 3-5 songs and lyric sheet. "Quality is stressed instead of quantity." Returns unsolicited material with SASE. Reports in 3 weeks.

Music: Mostly pop/R&B and rock. Published "She Ain't Worth It" (by Armato/Prince), recorded by Glenn Mederios on MCA Records (single pop/R&B); "Sensible Shoes" (by Sturges/Morgan/Roth), recorded by David Lee Roth on WB Records (single-rock/pop); "Stick It to Ya," recorded by Slaughter on Chrysalis Records (album/rock); "Spend My Life" (by Mark Slaughter/Dana Strum), recorded by Slaughter on Chrysalis Records (rock); "I've Been Waiting For You" (by Antonina Armato/Scott

Cutler), recorded by Guys Next Door on SPK Records (pop/ballad); and "Pure" (by Dan Brodie), recorded by The Ligntning Seeds on MCA Records (pop/alternative).
Tips: "Really listen to the radio to hear what kind of songs are out there. Lyrics are very important. Don't just repeat one line several times—develop an idea and come up with a new way to say it."

CISUM, Box 192, Pittsburg KS 66762. (316)231-6443. Partner: Kevin Shawn. Music publisher, record company (Cisum), record producer (Cisum). BMI, SESAC and ASCAP. Estab. 1985. Publishes 100 songs/year. Works with composers and lyricists; teams collaborators. Pays standard royalty.
How to Contact: Write first and obtain permission to submit a tape. Prefers cassette (or VHS videocassette if available) and lyric sheet. "Unpublished, copyrighted, cassette with lyrics. Submit as many as you wish. We listen to everything, allow 3 months. When over 3 weeks please call."
Music: Mostly novelty, country and rock; also pop, gospel and R&B. Published "Angry Gun" (by R. Durst), recorded by Gene Straser on Antique Records (country); "Smooth Talk" (by Rhuems), recorded by Rich Rhuems on Antique Records (country); "Mailman Mailman" (by Strasser), recorded by Willie & Shawn on Cisum Records (novelty).
Tips: "Good demo, great song; always put your best effort on the tape first."

CITKO-SLOTT PUBLISHING CO., Suite 200, East 100 Merrick Rd., Rockville Centre NY 11570. (516)536-8341. President: James Citkovic. Music publisher and consultant. ASCAP. Estab. 1989. Works with composers and lyricists; teams collaborators.
Affiliate(s): Citko-Slott Publishing Co. (ASCAP).
How to Contact: Submit a demo tape by mail—unsolicited submissions are OK. Prefers cassette (VHS videocassette if available) with open number of songs and lyric sheet. "Send available information to help evaluate the songwriter/band, i.e., bio, press, pictures, etc." SASE. Reports in 5 weeks.
Music: Mostly pop, rock and dance/R&B; also nu-music, pop/rock and commercial hard rock. Published "Songs I Sing" (by Joe Costanzo, pop ballad).

R.D. CLEVÈRE MUSIKVERLAG, Postfach 2145, D-6078 Neu-Isenburg, **West Germany**. Phone: (6102)52696. Professional Manager: Tony Hermonez. GEMA. Music publisher. Estab. 1967. Publishes 700-900 songs/year; publishes 40 new songwriters/year. Works with composers, lyricists; teams collaborators. Pays standard royalty.
Affiliate(s): Big Sound Music, Hot Night Music, Lizzy's Blues Music, Max Banana Music, R.D. Clevère-Cocabana-Music, R.D. Clevère-Far East & Orient-Music, and R.D. Clevère-America-Today-Music.
How to Contact: "Do not send advanced letter(s) asking for permission to submit your song material, just send it." Prefers cassette with "no limit" on songs and lyric sheet. SAE and a minimum of two IRCs. Reports in 3 weeks.
Music: Mostly pop, disco, rock, R&B, country and folk; also musicals and classic/opera.
Tips: "If the song submitted is already produced/recorded professionally on 16/24-multitrack tape and available, we can use this for synchronization with artists of various record companies/record producers."

CLOTILLE PUBLISHING, 9 Hector Ave., Toronto, Ontario M6G3G2 **Canada**. (416)533-3707. Manager: Al Kussin. Music publisher, record company (Slak Record) and record producer (Slak Productions). PROCAN. Estab. 1988. Publishes 5 songs/year; publishes 1 new songwriter/year. Receives 10 submissions/month. Teams collaborators. Pays standard royalty of 50%.
How to Contact: Submit a demo tape by mail—unsolicited submissions are OK. Prefers cassette with 3 songs and lyric sheet. "Recording quality must be sufficient to convey the total impact of song." Reports in 4 weeks.
Music: Mostly pop, R&B and dance. Published "Go Baby" (by F. Fudge/A. Kussin), recorded by Frankie Fudge on Slak Records (rap); and "All Talk" and "Hold On Tight" (by L. Scott/A. Kussin), recorded by Lorraine Scott on Slak Records (R&B/pop).
Tips: "Submit good commercial material with strong hooks and interesting form. On most submissions, lyrics are usually cliched and substandard. Production quality must be adequate to get the song across."

COFFEE AND CREAM PUBLISHING COMPANY, 1138 E. Price St., Philadelphia PA 19138. (215)842-3450. President: Bolden Abrams, Jr. Music publisher and record producer (Bolden Productions). ASCAP. Publishes 20 songs/year; publishes 4 new songwriters/year. Works with composers and lyricists; teams collaborators. Pays standard royalty.
How to Contact: Prefers cassette (or VHS videocassette) with 1-4 songs and lyric or lead sheets. Reports in 2 weeks "if we're interested."
Music: Mostly dance, pop, R&B, gospel and country. Published "Beat Your Feet" (by Peter Crawford), recorded by Gabrielle on Saphire Rose Records (hip hop/dance/house); "No Time for Tears" (by Bolden Abrams/Keith Batts), recorded by Gabrielle (R&B ballad); "Sly Like a Fox," (by Regine

Urbach), recorded by Joy Duncan on Ultimate Records (pop/dance); "If I Let Myself Go" (by Jose Gomez/Sheree Sano), recorded by Evelyn "Champagne" King on RCA Records (pop/ballad); "My Rock" (by Sheree Sano & Peter Crawford), recorded by Ron Hevener (pop ballad); and "Lonely Man" (by Maurice Mertoli/Phil Nelson), recorded by Keith Bradford on MTT Records (pop/ballad).

CONTINENTAL COMMUNICATIONS CORP., 450 Livingston St., Norwood NJ 07648. (201)767-5551. President: Robert Schwartz. ASCAP, BMI. Estab. 1952. Music publisher and record company (Laurie Records and 3C Records). Publishes 50 songs/year; publishes 5-10 new songwriters/year. Works with composers and lyricists; teams collaborators. Pays standard royalty.
Affiliate(s): 3 Seas Music (ASCAP) and Northvale Music (BMI).
How to Contact: Prefers cassette. SASE. "Submit only a few of the most commercial songs with lead sheets and demo."
Music: Mostly rock. Published "Because of You," written and recorded by B. Sunkel on Laurie Records (pop); "Complicated," written and recorded by Allen Bros. on 3C Records (urban); and "Lament 62" (by D. Groom and P. Renari), recorded by D. Groom on Laurie Records (pop).

COPPELIA, 21, rue de Pondichéry, 75015 Paris France. Phone: 45 67 30 66. FAX: 43 06 30 26. Manager: Jean-Philippe Olivi. Music publisher, record company (Olivi Records), record producer (Coppelia) and music print publisher. SACEM. Publishes 150 songs/year; publishes 80 new songwriters/year. Works with composers and lyricists. Pays standard royalty.
How to Contact: Submit a demo tape—unsolicited submissions are OK. Prefers cassette (or VHS videocassette). SAE and IRC. Reports in 1 month.
Music: Mostly pop, rock and New Age; also background music and movies/series music. Published "A St. Germain de Prés," written and recorded by Bodin on Olivi Records (sax); "Sagapo," recorded by Ferchit on Olivi Records (accordion); and "Ambitions" (by Remy), recorded by Ferchit on Olivi Records (pop).

THE CORNELIUS COMPANIES, 803 18th Ave. South, Nashville TN 37203. (615)321-5333. Owner/Manager: Ron Cornelius. Music publisher and record producer (The Cornelius Companies, Ron Cornelius). BMI, ASCAP. Estab. 1987. Publishes 60-80 songs/year; publishes 2-3 new songwriters/year. Occasionally hires staff writers. Receives 250 submissions/month. Works with composers and lyricists; teams collaborators. Pays standard royalty.
Affiliate(s): RobinSparrow Music (BMI).
How to Contact: Write or call first and obtain permission to submit a tape. Prefers cassette with 2-3 songs. SASE. Reports in 2 months.
Music: Mostly country and pop. Published "Time Off for Bad Behavior" (by Larry Latimer), recorded by David Allen Coe; and "You're Slowly Going Out of My Mind" (by Gordon Dee), recorded by Southern Tracks; both on CBS Records; "These Colors Never Run" (by Gordon Dee).

COSMOTONE MUSIC, P.O. Box 71988, Los Angeles CA 90071-0988. Music publisher, record company (Cosmotone Records, Cosmotone Studios) and record producer. ASCAP. Estab. 1984. Publishes 10 songs/year; publishes 2 new songwriters/year. Works with lyricists; teams collaborators. Pays standard royalty.
How to Contact: Write first and obtain permission to submit a tape. Prefers cassette (VHS videocassette if available) with all songs and lyric sheet. "Will respond only if interested."
Music: All types. Published "Padre Pio," "Sonnet XVIII" and "O Let Me Be," all written and recorded by Lord Hamilton on Cosmotone Records (Christian/rock pop); and "Peace of Heart" by Rafael Brom (Christian new wave).

COTTAGE BLUE MUSIC, P.O. Box 121626, Nashville TN 37212. (615)726-3556. Contact: Neal James. Music publisher, record company (Kottage Records) and record producer (Neal James Productions). BMI. Estab. 1971. Publishes 30 songs/year; publishes 3 new songwriters/year. Receives 75 submissions/month. Works with composers and lyricists. Pays standard royalty of 50%.
Affiliate(s): James & Lee (BMI), Neal James Music (BMI) and Hidden Cove Music (ASCAP).
How to Contact: Write first and obtain permission to submit a tape. Prefers cassette with 2 songs and lyric sheet. SASE. Reports in 4 weeks.
Music: Mostly country, gospel and rock/pop; also R&B. Published "Shimmer" and "Share This Night" (by Neal James), recorded by Terry Barbay on Kottage Records (country/rock).
Tips: "Screen material carefully before submitting."

COUNTRY BREEZE MUSIC, 1715 Marty, Kansas City KS 66103. (913)384-4454 or 384-1020. President: Ed Morgan. Music publisher and record company (Country Breeze Records and Walkin' Hat Records). BMI, ASCAP. Estab. 1984. Publishes 100 songs/year; publishes 25-30 new songwriters/year. Receives 130 submissions/month. Teams collaborators. Pays standard royalty.

Affiliate(s): Walkin' Hat Music (ASCAP).

How to Contact: Submit a demo tape—unsolicited submissions are OK. Prefers cassette (or VHS videocassette) with 4-5 songs and lyric sheet. "The songwriter/artist should perform on the video as though on stage giving a sold-out performance. In other words put heart and soul into the project. Submit in strong mailing envelopes." Reports in 2 weeks.

Music: Mostly country (rock/pop/traditional), gospel (southern/bluegrass and black) and rock. Published "Guided by the Hand" (by Angela Daniels), recorded by Angela Daniels on Angel Star Records (gospel); "Ships that Pass in the Night" (by M. Spencer and R. Cowan), recorded by Mark Spencer and Nikiya on Midnight Shadow Records; "Let Freedom Ring" (by Greg Watson), recorded by Greg Watson on Villa Records; "Circle of Love" (by Lavonne English), recorded by Lavonne English and The Helping Hands on Country Breeze Records..

Tips: "Make sure your song is strong in both lyrics and melody and have vocal out front. Also if a writer believes they have a good song, put it on a good tape. A good tape makes a lot of difference in the sound. No SASE, no returns!"

COUNTRY CLASSICS MUSIC PUBLISHING CO., Box 15222, Oklahoma City OK 73115. (405)677-6448. General Manager: Sonny Lane. Music publisher and record company (Compo Records). BMI. Estab. 1972. Publishes 4-6 songs/year; publishes 2 new songwriters/year. Works with composers and lyricists; teams collaborators. Pays standard royalty.

How to Contact: Submit a demo tape—unsolicited submissions are OK. Prefers cassette with 2-4 songs and lyric sheet. SASE. Reports in 3 weeks.

Music: Mostly country western, gospel and MOR. Published "Ten Million and Two," "All's Right With the World" and "Sittin' in the Amen Seat," all written and recorded by Yvonne DeVaney on Compo Records (country).

Tips: "We like simple melodies with strong lyrics."

*COUNTRY SHOWCASE, America Productions, 385 Main St., Laurel MD 20707. President: Francis Gosman. Music publisher, record company (Country Showcase America Records) and record producer. BMI. Estab. 1971. Publishes 6 songs/year; publishes 1 new songwriter/year. Works with composers and lyricists; teams collaborators. Pays standard royalty.

Affiliate(s): Country Showcase Publishing.

How to Contact: Submit a demo tape by mail—unsolicited submissions are OK. Prefers cassette with 2 songs and lyric sheet. Does not return unsolicited material.

Music: Mostly country. Published "Tent Meeting Blues" (by L. Vague and F. Gosman), "Almost in Love" (by B. Fisher) and "More Than Once In a While" (by B. Fisher); all recorded by Johnny Anthony on CSA Records (country singles).

COUNTRY STAR MUSIC, 439 Wiley Ave., Franklin PA 16323. (814)432-4633. President: Norman Kelly. Music publisher, record company (Country Star, Process, Mersey and CSI) and record producer (Country Star Productions). ASCAP. Estab. 1970. Publishes 20-30 songs/year; publishes 2-3 new songwriters/year. Receives 400 submissions/year. Works with composers and lyricists; teams collaborators. Pays standard royalty.

Affiliate(s): Kelly Music Publications (BMI) and Process Music Publications (BMI).

How to Contact: Prefers cassette with 1-4 songs and lyric or lead sheet. SASE. Reports in 2 weeks.

Music: Mostly country (80%); also rock, gospel, MOR and R&B (5% each). Published "Pardon Me for Loving You" (by Robert Nailor), recorded by Tara Bailey on Country Star (country); "Time Between the Teardrops" (by Doog Davis), recorded by Junie Lou on Country Star Records (country); and "Every Bird's Gotta Fly" written and recorded by Ron Lauer on Country Star Records (country).

Tips: "Send only your best songs—ones you feel are equal to or better than current hits."

COWABONGA MUSIC, INC., P.O. Box 630755, Miami FL 33163. (305)935-4880. A&R Director: Jack Gale. Music Publisher, record company (Playback Records, Gallery 11 Records, Inc., Ridgewood Records and Caramba! Records) and record producer (Jack Gale). ASCAP. Estab. 1983. Publishes 70 songs/year; publishes 12 new songwriters/year. Receives 100 submissions/month. Pays standard royalty.

Affiliate(s): Lovey Music Inc. (BMI).

How to Contact: Submit a demo tape—unsolicited submissions are OK. Prefers cassette (or VHS vidoecassette) with maximum of 2 songs and lyric sheet. Does not return unsolicited material. Reports in 2 weeks.

Music: Mostly contemporary country and pop. Published "Everything's Mine" (by Margurita Bunch), recorded by Ginny Peters on Gallery II Records (country); "Just Pretend" (by Linsley/Spillton), recorded by Cheryl K. Warner on Playback Records (country); and "Southern Men" (by Curtiss/Byrum/Schapon), recorded by Cheryl K. Warner on Playback Records (country).

COWBOY JUNCTION FLEA MARKET AND PUBLISHING CO., Highway 44 West, Junction 490, Lecanto FL 32661. (904)746-4754. President: Elizabeth Thompson. Music publisher (Cowboy Junction Publishing Co.), record company (Cowboy Junction Records) and record producer. BMI. Estab. 1957. Receives 100 submissions/year. Publishes 5 songs/year. Pays standard royalty or other amount.
How to Contact: Submit demo tape (or VHS videocassette) by mail. SASE. Reports as soon as possible.
Music: Country, western, bluegrass and gospel. Published "Way Down in Alabama," "A Girl From the City" and "Way Up on the Mountain" (by Boris Max Pastuch), recorded by Buddy Max on Cowboy Junction Records (country).

CPA RECORDS & PUBLISHING CO., Suite 19, 135 Lassiter Dr., Hampton VA 23668. CEO: Christopher C. Carter. Music publisher and record company (CPA Records and Publishing Co.). BMI. Estab. 1989. Publishes 10 songs/year; publishes 5 new songwriters/year. Hires staff songwriters. Works with composers and lyricists; teams collaborators. Pays standard royalty.
How to Contact: Write first and obtain permission to submit a tape. Prefers cassette (VHS videocassette if available) with 3 or more songs. SASE. Reports in 1 month.
Music: Gospel only. Published "God Can Make a Way" and "Send Us a Blessing" on CPA Records (gospel).

*CREATIVE ENTERTAINMENT MUSIC, Suite 700, 6290 Sunset Blvd., Los Angeles CA 90028. Professional Manager: Mark Savage. Music publisher and management firm. BMI, ASCAP. Member NMPA. Estab. 1982. Publishes 35 songs/year; publishes 10 new songwriters/year. Receives 100 submissions/month. Teams collaborators.
Affiliate(s): Creative Entertainment Music (BMI), Weezy Music (ASCAP).
How to Contact: Submit a demo tape—unsolicited submissions are OK. Prefers cassette with 1-3 songs and lyric sheet. SASE. Reports in 1 month. "No telephone calls please!"
Music: R&B and dance. Published "Lead Me Into Love" (by Lane/Prentiss), recorded by Anita Baker on Elektra Records (R&B); "Ground Zero" (by Lauren Wood), recorded by Animotion on Polygram Records (rock); "So Happy" (by David Jones), recorded by Eddie Murphy on CBS Records (R&B); and "More Love" (by Steve Lane, Rodney Saulsberry, Peter Brown), recorded by Jasmine Guy on WB Records (R&B).
Tips: "Smart, crafty lyrics and the most up-to-date grooves and record quality demos aren't enough. You also need surprises."

CREEKSIDE MUSIC, 100 Labon St., Tabor City NC 28463. (919)653-2546. Owner: Elson H. Stevens. Music publisher, record company (Seaside Records) and record producer (Southern Sound Productions). BMI. Estab. 1978. Publishes 30 songs/year; publishes 5 new songwriters/year. Works with composers, lyricists; teams collaborators. Pays 25-50% royalty from record sales.
How to Contact: Write or call first and obtain permission to submit. Prefers cassette with 3 songs and lead sheets. SASE. Reports in 1 month.
Music: Mostly country, rock and gospel; also "beach music." Published "Here I Go Again" (by Elson Stevens), recorded by Angelia on SeaSide Records (country); "Little Bitty Country Boy," written and recorded by Lewie Allen on SeaSide Records (country); and "Loverboy" (by Jeff Knight), recorded by Kelly Devol on SeaSide Records (rock).
Tips: "Be original—search for 'the hook'."

*CREOLE MUSIC LTD., The Chilterns, France Hill Dr., Camberley, Surrey GU15 3QA **England**. Director: Bruce White. Music publisher. PRS/MCPS. Estab. 1966. Publishes 20-30 songs/year; publishes 2-3 new songwriters/year. Teams collaborators. Pays standard royalty of 50% ("sometimes higher, 60-40%").
How to Contact: Submit a demo tape by mail—unsolicited submissions OK. Prefers cassette with 3-4 songs. SASE. Reports in 6 weeks.
Music: Mostly pop, dance and rock. Published "Sweet Cherrie," recorded by UB40 on Dep/Virgin Records (reggae).

*CROWN MUSIC GROUP, 1015 16th Ave. S., Nashville TN 37212. (615)327-8100. Vice President of Creative Development: Eddie Burton. Music publisher and record producer (Crown Productions). BMI, ASCAP. Estab. 1989. Publishes 75 songs/year; publishes 5 or 6 new songwriters/year. Works with composers; teams collaborators. Pays standard royalty.

Affiliate(s): Southwing Publishing (ASCAP), Nashville Title Wave (BMI).
How to Contact: Write or call first and obtain permission to submit a tape. Prefers cassette with 4 songs and lyric sheet. Reports in 4 weeks.
Music: Mostly country, country rock and MOR. Published "Forever Yours" (by Burton/Westbun), recorded by Buck Owens on Capitol Records (country); "Talkin' To Your Picture" (by Lindsey/Bach), recorded by Jeff Chance on Mercury Records (country); and "Oceanfront Property" (by Dillon/Porter), recorded by George Strait on MCA Records (country).

*CRUSOE MUSIC LIMITED, 169-171 High Road, London NW10 2SE **England.** Phone: (01)451-3727. Professional Manager: Nigel Rush. Music publisher. PRS. Estab. 1987. Publishes 30 songs/year; publishes 2-3 new songwriters/year. Works with composers and lyricists; teams collaborators. Pays standard royalty.
How to Contact: Submit a demo tape by mail—unsolicited submissions are OK. Prefers cassette with 3 songs. SASE. Reports in 1 week.
Music: Mostly R&B/dance, pop/soul and rock. Published "Rich & Poor" (by Millar/C. Vearncombe), recorded by Randy Crawford on Warner Bros. (soul); "Hypnotised" (by S. Brown), recorded by Sam Brown on A & M Records (pop); and "Sunflower" (by Chap'pelle/Smith/Taylor), recorded by Vicki Brown on Ariola/BMG Records (MOR).

CSB KAMINSKY GMBH, Wilhelmstrasse 10, 2407 Bad Schwartau, **West Germany.** Phone: (0451)21530. General Manager: Pia Kaminsky. GEMA, PRS. Music publisher and collecting agency. Estab. 1978. Publishes 2-4 songs/year; 1 new songwriter/year. Teams collaborators. Pays 50% if releasing a record; 85% if only collecting royalties.
Affiliate(s): Leosong Copyright Management, Ltd. (London, United Kingdom and Sydney, Australia).
How to Contact: Write and submit material. Prefers cassette or VHS videocassette. Does not return unsolicited material. Reports in 4 weeks.
Music: Mostly pop; also rock, country and reggae.

CUDE & PICKENS PUBLISHING, 519 N. Halifax Ave., Daytona Beach FL 32118. (904)252-0381. A&R Director: Bobby Lee Cude. Music publisher, record company and record producer. BMI. Estab. 1978. Publishes 12 songs/year. Pays standard royalty.
How to Contact: "We are not accepting any new writers at this time."
Music: Mostly country; also easy listening, gospel, MOR, top 40/pop and Broadway show. Published "Tennessee's on My Mind" (country); "Texas Red, White and Blue Step" (country); "Who's Lovin You" (pop); and Shot in the Dark" (pop), all by Caz Allen.

CUMBERLAND MUSIC GROUP, INC., Suite 4, 30 Music Square West, Nashville TN 37203. (615)256-6822. CEO: Michael E. Lawson. Music publisher and record company (Psychotronic, Hitchcock-3). Works with musicians/artists and songwriters on contract. Royalty varies per contract; statutory rate to publishers per song on reocrds.
Affiliate(s): Obsidian Music (BMI), Obfuscated Music (ASCAP), Cucumberland Music (SESAC), Perspicacious Music (BMI), Psychotronic Publishing (BMI), S.U.Y.T. Publishing (BMI), zzi music (ASCAP).
How to Contact: Write first and obtain permission to submit. Prefers cassette, DAT or VHS videocassette (if available) with 3-5 songs and lyric sheet. SASE. Reports in 6-8 weeks.
Music: All types.

*CUNNINGHAM MUSIC, 23494 Lahser, Southfield MI 48034. (313)948-9787. President: Jerome Cunningham. Music publisher. BMI. Estab. 1988. Publishes 3-8 songs/year; publishes 2 new songwriters/year. Receives 4-6 submissions/month. Teams collaborators. Pays standard royalty.
How to Contact: Submit a demo tape by mail—unsolicited submissions are OK. Prefers cassette (or VHS videocassette if available) with 3 songs and lyric sheet. Does not return unsolicited material. Reports in 1 week.
Music: Mostly R&B, gospel and jazz; also pop and rock.
Tips: Main reason for rejection of submitted material includes: "Incomplete songs, no melody involved. Overall, just poorly prepared presentations."

*CUPIT MUSIC, P.O. Box 121904, Nashville TN 37212. (615)731-0100. President: Jerry Cupit. Music publisher and record producer (Jerry Cupit Productions). BMI and ASCAP. Publishes 30 songs/year; publishes 6 new songwriters/year. Receives 20-40 submissions/month. Hires staff songwriters. Works with composers and lyricists/ teams collaborators. Pays standard 50% royalty.

Affiliate(s): Cupit Music (BMI), Cupit Memories (ASCAP).
How to Contact: Submit a demo tape by mail—unsolicited submissions are OK. Prefers cassette with 5 songs and lyric sheet. "We do not return tapes." Reports in 8 weeks.
Music: Mostly country, southern rock and gospel; also R&B. Published "Thank God for America" recorded by Orion on Southern Tracks; and "The Greatest Gift," recorded by James Payne on Wind Chime (gospel).
Tips: "Keep vocals up front on demos."

CURRENT MUSICAL ENTERPRISES, INC., 418 Ontario Street, Toronto ON M5A 2W1 **Canada**. (416)921-6535. FAX: (416)921-7793. A&R, New Projects: Trevor G. Shelton. Music publisher, record company (Current Records, Rammit Records) and record producer (Trevor G. Shelton). SOCAN. Estab. 1983. Publishes 50 songs/year; publishes 2 new songwriters/year. Pays standard royalty.
Affiliate(s): Brand New Sounds Music (PROCAN), Current Sounds (CAPAC).
How to Contact: Submit a demo tape by mail—unsolicited submissions are OK. Prefers cassette with 4 songs and lyric sheet. "Please make sure that you include contact information (address and telephone number) and information on yourself." SASE. Reports in 2 weeks.
Music: Mostly rock, pop and dance; also acid, hip hop and rap. Published "Julian" (by Johnson/Orenstein), recorded by Alta Moda (dance/rock); "Love Becomes Electric" (by Kromm), recorded by strange advance (rock); and "So Far Away" (by Scullion), recorded by Mystery Romance (pop); all on Current Records.
Tips: "We understand that you, as a songwriter might not be able to present your material with pleasant vocals. We are interested in your ability to write good music. Please note: if you have material to be compared with the likes of The Jackson Five please by all means, send it in."

D.S.M. PRODUCERS INC., 161 W. 54th, New York NY 10019. (212)245-0006. Producer: Suzan Bader. Music publisher, record producer and management firm (Ameircan Steel Management Co.). ASCAP. Estab. 1979. Publishes 25 songs/year; publishes 10 new songwriters/year. Receives 1,000 submissions/year. Works with composers and lyricists. Pays standard royalty.
How to Contact: Write or call first and obtain permission to submit. Prefers cassette (or VHS videocassette) and lyric or lead sheet. SASE. "Include SASE or we do not review nor respond to material." Reports in 4 weeks.
Music: Mostly top 40, R&B/dance, CHR and rock; also jazz, country and instrumental tracks for background music. Published "On the Town," written and recorded by Frank Lakewood (jazz); "Welcome Home," written and recorded by Hal Gold/Mike Fink (pop); and "The Fields," written and recorded by Rick Resnick (AOR), all on AACL Records.
Tips: "Get your demo to sound like a master."

DAGENE MUSIC, P.O. Box 410851, San Francisco CA 94141. (415)822-1530. President: David Alston. Music publisher, record company (Cabletown Corp.) and record producer (Classic Disc Production). ASCAP. Estab. 1986. Hires staff songwriters. Works with composers; teams collaborators. Pays standard royalty.
Affiliate(s): Dagene Music, 1956 Music.
How to Contact: Write or call first and obtain permission to submit a tape. Prefers cassette with 2 songs and lyric sheet. "Be sure to obtain permission before sending any material." Does not return unsolicited material. Reports in 1 month.
Music: Mostly R&B/rap, dance and pop. Published "Visions" (by Marcus Justice), recorded by 2-Dominatorz on Dagene Records; "Serving 'Em" (by Rafael Bazile), recorded by Frisco Kid on Dagene Records; and "Started Life" (by David and M. Campbell), recorded by Primo on Cabletown Records (all rap).
Tips: "Keep an ear and eye to the street."

DAN THE MAN MUSIC, Suite 428, 16789 Brookpark Rd., Cleveland OH 44142. President: Daniel L. Bischoff. Music publisher, record company (Dan The Man Records) and management firm (Daniel Bischoff Management). ASCAP, BMI. "We have some major label connections. Always looking for top country hit material. Also interested in strong pop-rock material."
Affiliate(s): Bischoff Music Publishing Co. (BMI).
How to Contact: Please send cassette or VHS tape and lyrics. "When sending material to us please send a SASE with proper postage for return."
Music: Country, pop/rock. Published "Forget Him," written and recorded by Ted Makse (country); "Interview with Michael Jackson," written and recorded by Dan the Man (pop); and "The King Went on a Journey" (by Lambert Massey), recorded by Johnny Wright (country), all on the Dan the Man label.

DARBONNE PUBLISHING CO., Route 3, Box 172, Haynesville LA 71038. (318)927-5253. President: Edward N. Dettenheim. Music publisher and record company (Wings Record Co.). BMI. Estab. 1987. Publishes 50 songs/year; publishes 8-10 new songwriters/year. Works with composers and lyricists; teams collaborators. Pays standard royalty.
How to Contact: Submit a demo tape—unsolicited submissions are OK. Prefers cassette or 7½ ips reel-to-reel with up to 12 songs and lyric sheet. SASE. Reports in 6 weeks.
Music: Mostly country and gospel. Published "Bitter Taste of Leaving," written and recorded by T.J. Lynn on Wings Records (country); "Mama" (by E. Dettenheim), recorded by Donna Ray on Wings Records (country); and "Turner Hotel" (by E. Dettenheim), recorded by T.J. Lynn on Wings Records (country).
Tips: "The better the demo—the better your chances of interesting your listener."

DARK HEART MUSIC, 1236 S. Staples, Corpus Christi TX 78404. (512)882-7066. Music publisher, record company (Dark Heart Records) and record producer. Estab. 1984. BMI. Publishes 10-50 songs/year; publishes varying number of new songwriters/year. Pays standard royalty.
Affiliate(s): Roland Garcia Music, El Palacio Music, Dillettante Music and Alpen Glow Music.
How to Contact: Prefers cassette. Submissions must include complete name, address and phone number. Does not return unsolicited material. Reporting time varies.
Music: Mostly rock, Spanish and country; also gospel. Published "Ready as Hell," (by Jim Dandy), recorded by Black Oak Arkansas on Hacienda (rock); and "Time of Your Life" by Head East on Dark Heart Records (rock).

*JEFF DAYTON MUSIC, P.O. Box 9296, Scottsdale AZ 85252. (602)837-8650. President: Jeff Dayton. Music publisher and record company (Winners Circle). BMI. Estab. 1983. Publishes 10 songs/year; publishes 2 new songwriters/year. Pays standard royalty.
Affiliate(s): Not Yet Music (BMI).
How to Contact: Write first and obtain permission to submit a tape. Prefers cassette with 2 songs and lyric sheet. Does not return unsolicited material. Reports in 2-3 weeks.
Music: Mostly country; also bluegrass and pop. Published "So Blue" (by J. Dayton), recorded by J. Dayton Band (country); "It Ain't Over" (by J. Dayton), recorded by Blaine Brown (country); and "15 Minutes" (by Dayton/Rutowski), recorded by J. Dayton Band (swing), all on Winners Circle Records.

*DE DAN MUSIC, 200 Regent Dr., Winston-Salem NC 27103. (919)768-1298. Contact: Dave Passerallo. Music publisher, record company (Boom/Power Play Records) and record producer (Boom Productions Inc.). BMI. Estab. 1989. Publishes 24 songs/year; publishes 2 new songwriters/year. Teams collaborators. Pays standard royalty.
How to Contact: Write first and obtain permission to submit a tape. Prefers cassette or VHS videocassette with 2 songs and lead sheet. SASE. Reports in 3 weeks.
Music: Mostly pop and rock; also rap. Published "I Wanna Know," by Rodney Ballad and John Cody; "Ripped Jeans" and "The Good Ones," both written by John Cody; all produced by D. Passerallo for Boom Productions on Boom/Powerplay Records.
Tips: "Submissions must be worthy of national release and have mass appeal."

THE EDWARD DE MILES MUSIC COMPANY, 4475 Allisonville Rd., 8th Fl., Indianapolis IN 46205. (317)546-2912 or 549-9006. Attn: Professional Manager. Music publisher, record company (Sahara Records), management, bookings and promotions. BMI. Estab. 1984. Publishes 50-75 songs/year; publishes 5 new songwriters/year. Receives 250 submissions/year. Hires staff songwriters. Works with composers and lyricists; teams collaborators. Pays standard royalty of 50%.
How to Contact: Write or call first and obtain permission to submit a tape. Prefers cassette with 1-3 songs and a lyric sheet. SASE. Does not return unsolicited material. Reports in 1 month.
Music: Mostly top 40 pop/rock, R&B/dance and C&W; also musical scores for TV, radio, films and jingles. Published "No Mercy" (D. Evans/A. Mitchell), recorded by Multiple Choice (rap); "Don't Want Control" and "Mr. It," written and recorded by Steve Lynn (dance), all on Sahara Records.
Tips: "Copyright all songs before submitting to us."

Remember: Don't "shotgun" your demo tapes. Submit only to companies interested in the type of music you write. For more submission hints, refer to The Business of Songwriting on page 21.

*DEAN ENTERPRISES MUSIC PUBLISHING, P.O. Box 620, Redwood Estates CA 95044-0620. (408)353-1006. Attn: Executive Director. Music publisher (Whispering Echoes Music/ASCAP; Mikezel Music Co./ASCAP; and Teenie Deanie Music Co./BMI); Member: SGA, NAS, NCSA, TSA, CMRRA, Harry Fox Agency. Estab. 1989. Publishes 2-3 songs per year, publishes 2-3 new songwriters/ year. Receives 75 submissions/month. Pays standard royalty to writers and may split publishing with other publishers (25-50%).
How to Contact: Prefers chrome or metal cassette with 1-8 songs and typed lyric sheets and brief letter of introduction. Prefers to keep tapes on file, but will return if fully paid SASE is included. A free evaluation is given with SASE, even if tape not returned. Reports in 2-6 weeks. "*Please,* no phone calls. Show name, address, phone number on lyric sheets and cassette with © sign and year."
Music: Country, pop, MOR/easy listening, New Age, soft/easy rock, dance (high energy, house, pop), folk, top 40 and some instrumental music which could qualify as movie/TV themes or background music. No rap music, jazz, heavy metal, punk/acid rock. Published "Long Black Wall" (by Ron Tomich/ Geoff Stamm), recorded by Johnny Anthony on CSA Records (country single).
Tips: "Learn to handle rejection. Listen to the feedback you get. If you're not familiar with songwriting contracts, have an experienced music attorney review them for you. Join songwriting organizations, read songwriting books and network as much as possible. Opportunity, talent and connections are the name of the game in the music industry. Watch out for the sharks."

JASON DEE MUSIC, INC., 44 Music Sq. East, Nashville TN 37203. (615)255-2175. President: Charlie Fields. Music publisher, record company (Charta Records/Delux Records) and record producer (Charlie Fields). BMI. Estab. 1977. Publishes 15 or more songs and new songwriters/year. Receives 150-200 submissions/month. Works with composers. Pays standard royalty.
Affiliate(s): Jason Dee Music, Inc.(BMI), Mr. Mort Music, Inc. (ASCAP).
How to Contact: Submit a demo tape by mail—unsolicited submissions are OK. Prefers cassette with 3-4 songs. SASE. Reports in 4 weeks.
Music: Mostly country and country MOR. Published "Addicted to You" (J. Hitzler), recorded by Jeannie Marie; "I'm Layin' Down the Lovin' " (C.W. Fields), recorded by Lori Johnson; and "Multiple Choice" (J.J. Johnson), recorded by Jack Johnson, all country singles on Charta Records.
Tips: "Make sure you have a good clean demo and one of your best written songs. Also make sure you do the things that they tell you—follow submission instructions precisely. Don't send in 7-8 songs— they won't listen to them."

DELEV MUSIC COMPANY, 7231 Mansfield Ave., Philadelphia PA 19138-1620. (215)276-8861. President: W. Lloyd Lucas. Music publisher, record company (Surprize Records, Inc.), record producer and management. BMI, ASCAP, SESAC, SGA, NAS and CMRRA. Publishes 6-10 songs/year; publishes 6-10 new songwriters/year. Pays standard royalty.
Affiliate(s): Sign of the Ram Music (ASCAP) and Gemini Lady Music (SESAC).
How to Contact: Write first about your interest. Prefers cassette (or VHS videocassette) with 1-3 songs and lyric sheet. "Video must be in VHS format and as professionally done as possible. It does not necessarily have to be done at a professional video studio, but should be a very good quality production showcasing artist's performance." SASE. "We will not accept certified mail." Reports in 3 weeks.
Music: R&B ballad and dance-oriented, contemporary Christian/gospel, pop ballads, crossover and country/western. Published "Changes" (by Charles Green pka), recorded by Majesty The-All (rap); "Just Dance" (by Willie McClain/C. Hawthorne/W. McClain, Jr.), recorded by Lamar Lucas (dance/ rap); and "Money Won't Save You" (by D.L. Montague/W.L. Lucas), recorded by Two Hand Posse (rap). "All of the songs mentioned are very strong in message and melody and we are seeking to record them. We have very strong contemporary gospel material penned by Wayne Graber, a very prolific writer of religious music and are seeking artists for his material. We are seeking exceptional male vocalists, female vocalists and a male vocal group in the Philadelphia area who can both sing and dance."
Tips: "Songs submitted must be lyrically and melodically strong with good strong hook lines, and tell a story that will appeal to and be related to by the radio-listening and record-buying public. Most important is that the demo be a clear quality product with understandable vocal and lyrics out front."

DEMERIE MUSIC, 8667 Highway 101 North, Maple Grove MN 55369. (612)420-6300. Contact: Don Powell. Music publisher. ASCAP. Estab. 1984. Publishes 20 songs/year; publishes 2 new songwriters/ year. Pays 50% royalty.
How to Contact: Submit a demo tape by mail—unsolicited submissions are OK. Prefers cassette with 3 songs and lyric sheets. SASE. Reports in 6 weeks.
Music: Mostly R&B dance music, R&B ballads and pop. Published "Make It Real" (by D. Powell, R. Kelly and L. Mallan), recorded by The Jets on MCA Records (ballad); "You've Got Another Boyfriend" (by S. Lobelle and G. Felicetta), recorded by The Jets on MCA Records (R&B dance);

and "Do You Remember" (by L. Wolfgromm and G. Hunt), recorded by The Jets on MCA Records (R&B ballad).
Tips: "Send me a hit! Keep it simple."

DEMI MONDE RECORDS & PUBLISHING LTD., Foel Studio, Llanfair Caereinion, POWYS, **Wales**. Phone: (0938)810758 and (0952)883962. Managing Director: Dave Anderson. Music publisher, record company (Demi Monde Records & Publishing Ltd.), record producer (Dave Anderson). Member MCPS. Estab. 1983. Publishes 50-70 songs/year; publishes 10-15 new songwriters/year. Receives 20 submissions/month. Works with composers and lyricists; teams collaborators. Pays standard royalty.
How to Contact: Submit a demo tape—unsolicited submissions are OK. Prefers cassette (or VHS videocassette) with 3-4 songs. SAE and IRC. Reports in 1 month.
Music: Mostly rock, R&B and pop. Published "I Feel So Lazy" (by D. Allen), recorded by Gong on Demi Monde Records (rock); "Phalarn Dawn" (by E. Wynne), recorded by Ozric Tentacles on Demi Monde Records (rock); and "Pioneer" (by D. Anderson), recorded by Amon Dual on Demi Monde Records (rock).

DENNY MUSIC GROUP, 3325 Fairmont Dr., Nashville TN 37203-1004. (615)269-4847. Chief Executive Officer: John E. Denny. ASCAP, BMI, SESAC. Estab. 1983. Music publisher, record company (Dollie Record Co., Jed Record Production) and record producer. "Also owns Denny's Den, a 24-track recording studio designed for songwriters, which won a Grammy in 1990." Publishes 100 songs/year; 20 new songwriters/year. Works with composer and lyricists; teams collaborators. Pays standard royalty.
How to Contact: Write or call first and obtain permission to submit. Prefers cassette with 1 song and lyric sheet. Reports in 6 weeks.
Music: Mostly country, gospel and MOR. Published "Cashmere Cowboy" (by F. Hannaway, country); "Inside Information" (by J. Martin, R&B); and "Closer to You" (by T. Rooney, pop).

*DIAMOND STATE PUBLISHING CO., INC., P.O. Box 6239, Wilmington DE 19804. (302)836-3721. President: Ray Ballou Seemans. Music publisher. ASCAP. Estab. 1989. Publishes 10 songs/year; publishes 2 new songwriters/year. Receives 6 submissions/month. Works with composers and lyricists. Pays standard royalty.
How to Contact: Submit a demo tape by mail—unsolicited submissions are OK. Prefers cassette with 3 songs and lyric sheet. SASE. Reports in 3 weeks.
Music: Mostly country, rock/pop and R&B/blues; also spiritual. Published "Roses And Gold" (by R.B. Seemans), recorded by Ray Ballou on Fraternity Records; "Deep in Mary's Heart," written and recorded by John and Sue Sembiante; and "Special Lady," written and recorded by Brian Hildebrand.
Tips: "Be patient and keep writing. Nobody hits the first time. Have persistence and a good song."

DINGO MUSIC, 4, Galleria Del Corso, Milan **Italy** 20122. Phone: (02)76021141. FAX: 0039/2/76021141. Managing Director: Guido Palma. Music publisher and record company (Top Records). SIAE. Estab. 1977. Publishes 30-35 songs/year; publishes 5 new songwriters/year. Hires staff writers. Works with composers and lyricists. Pays standard royalty of 50% and 10% on printed copies.
Affiliate(s): U.C.P. (Ging).
How to Contact: Submit demo tape by mail-unsolicited submissions are OK. Prefers cassette with 2 songs. SAE and IRC. Reports in 2 weeks.
Music: Mostly interested in rock, pop and R&B (pop); also New Age and gospel. Published "Lambada" (by Do Berman) on Top Records; "Per Un Po" (by Palma) on Dingo Records (pop); and "La Vita di un Uomo" (by Caminiti) on Kiwi Records (pop).

*DIRECT MANAGEMENT GROUP, #G, 947 N. La Cienega Bl., Los Angeles CA 90069. (213)854-3535. Partners: Martin Kirkup and Steve Jensen. ASCAP, BMI. Estab. 1989. Publishes 10 songs/year; publishes 2-5 new songwriters/year. Works with composers and lyricists; teams collaborators. Pays variable royalty.
Affiliate(s): Direct World Music (ASCAP), Direct Planet Music (BMI).
How to Contact: Write first and obtain permission to submit a tape. Prefers cassette with 3 songs and lyric and lead sheet. SASE. Reports in 2 months.
Music: Mostly rock, pop and alternative. Published "Something New" and "So Much for Love" (by Hanes/Sheldon), recorded by S. Hoffs on Columbia (rock/pop).

DIRECTIONS, 6 Rue Laurencin, Lyon **France** 69002. (33)7240-9236. Managing Director: Andre. Music Publisher, record company (Lucky French Records). SACEM. Estab. 1988. Publishes 300 songs/year; 200 new songwriters/year. Receives 400 submissions/year. Works with composers; teams collaborators. Pays standard royalty.

Affiliate(s): Andre Records (SACEM), BPM (Salem).

How to Contact: Submit a demo tape—unsolicited submissions are OK. Prefers cassette with 3 songs and lyric sheets. SAE and IRC. Reports in 2 weeks.

Music: Interested in rock and pop; also classical. Published "To Be Free" (by Mel Muriell), recorded by BPM UK/London (house/dance); "Check the Beat" (by Mike/OXO), recorded by SGH/Brussells (house); and "Zen" (by Mamimo), recorded by Ligheira/Italy (house); all on BPM Records.

Tips: "The songs must interest us. If we don't reply in 2 weeks it's because the song is not for us."

*DOC PUBLISHING, #4 Lilac Court, Newport News VA 23601. (804)591-2717. A&R: Judith Guthro. Music publisher. SESAC, BMI, ASCAP, CAPAC. Estab. 1975. Publishes 30-40 songs/year; 20 new songwriters/year. Works with composers and lyricists; teams collaborators. Pays standard royalty.

Affiliate(s): Dream Machine (SESAC), Doc Holiday Music (ASCAP). Submit a demo tape by mail—unsolicited submissions are OK. Prefers cassette with 3 songs.

How to Contact: Submit a demo tape—unsolicited submissions are OK.

Music: Mostly country and cajun. Published "It's The Music" (by Tom Breeden and Doc Holiday), recorded by Ronn Craddock on Door Knob Records; "Juke Box King" (by Doc Holiday), recorded by Kevin Irwin on Door Knob Records; "Cajun Stripper" (by Doug Kershaw) on Tug Boat Records; "Mr. Jones The Final Chapter" (by Big Al Downing), on Tug Boat Records; and "Lady of the Evening" (by Jon Washington), recorded by Eagle Feather on Tug Boat Records.

DOOR KNOB MUSIC PUBLISHING, INC., 3950 N. Mt. Juliet Rd., Mt. Juliet TN 37122. (615)754-0417. Contact: Karen Jeglum Kennedy. Music publisher, record company (Door Knob Records, Society Records), record producer (Gene Kennedy Enterprises, Inc.). BMI. Estab. 1975. Publishes 20-25 songs/year; publishes 10-15 new songwriters/year. Works with composers and lyricists. Pays standard royalty.

Affiliate(s): Chip 'n' Dale Music Publishers, Inc. (ASCAP), Lodestar Music, A Division of Gene Kennedy Enterprises, Inc. (SESAC).

How to Contact: Submit a demo tape by mail—unsolicited submissions are OK. Prefers cassette with 1-3 songs and lyric sheet. Include SASE for tape return and/or response. Send regular mail. SASE. Reports in 2 weeks.

Music: Mostly country and gospel. Published "Forever" (by Tommye da Cerini), recorded by Brandy-Wine; "Can I Come Back To You" (by Larry Schmid), recorded by Perry La Pointe; and "Does It Matter That I Love You" (by Ed Dickey), recorded by Susan Thompson; (all country) on Door Knob Records.

Tips: "Respect our submission policy and keep trying."

BUSTER DOSS MUSIC, Box 13, Estill Springs TN 37330. (615)649-2577. President: Buster Doss. Music publisher and record company (Stardust). BMI. Estab. 1959. Publishes 500 songs/year; publishes 50 new songwriters/year. Teams collaborators. Pays standard royalty.

How to Contact: Write or call first and obtain permission to submit a tape. Prefers cassette with 2 songs and lyric sheets. SASE. Reports in 1 week.

Music: Mostly country; also rock. Published "What Th' Big Boys Do" (by Buster Doss), recorded by Cliff Archer on Wizard Records; "Small Town Country Girl" (by R.B. Stone), recorded by R.B. Stone on Stardust Records; and "A Little While," written and recorded by Rooster Quantrell on Stardust Records.

DUANE MUSIC, INC., 382 Clarence Ave., Sunnyvale CA 94086. (408)739-6133. President: Garrie Thompson. Music publisher. BMI. Publishes 10-20 songs/year; publishes 1 new songwriter/year. Pays standard royalty.

Affiliate(s): Morhits Publishing (BMI).

How to Contact: Prefers cassette with 1-2 songs. SASE. Reports in 1 month.

Music: Blues, country, disco, easy listening, rock, soul and top 40/pop. Published "Little Girl," recorded by The Syndicate of Sound & Ban (rock); "Warm Tender Love," recorded by Percy Sledge (soul); and "My Adorable One," recorded by Joe Simon (blues).

DUPUY RECORDS/PRODUCTIONS/PUBLISHING, INC., 2505 North Verdugo Rd., Glendale CA 91208. (818)241-6732. President: Pedro Dupuy. Music publisher, record company and record producer. ASCAP. Songwriters Guild. Estab. 1980. Publishes 50 songs/year; publishes 4 new songwriters/year. Works with composers and lyricists; teams collaborators. Hires staff writers. Pays standard royalty.

How to Contact: Write or call first about your interest or arrange a personal interview. Prefers cassette with 2-4 songs and lyric sheet. SASE. Reports in 1 month.

Music: Mostly R&B and pop; also easy listening, jazz, MOR, soul and top 40. Published "Find a Way," "I Don't Wanna Know," "Precious Love," "Livin for Your Love" and "Show Me The Way," all written and recorded by Gordon Gilman. Other artists include Robert Feeney, John Anthony, Joe Warner, Jon Rider and Kimo Kane.

Tips: "Songs should have very definitive lyrics with hook."

E. MINOR MUSIC, 310 B S. Gallatin Rd., Madison TN 37115. (615)860-2545. Owner: Carl Motsinger. Music publisher. BMI. Estab. 1987. Receives 15-20 submissions/month. Publishes 2 songs/year. Works with composers and lyricists; team collaborators. Pays standard royalty.

How to Contact: Submit a demo tape by mail—unsolicited submissions are OK. Prefers cassette with 1 song and lyric sheets. *Does not* return material.

Music: Mostly country and gospel.

Tips: "We need great songs. We have plenty of good ones. Send me your best song! Send me a different tune."

EARTH AND SKY MUSIC PUBLISHING INC., P.O. Box 4157, Winter Park FL 32793. (407)657-6016. President: Ernest Hatton. Music publisher, record company (Earth and Sky Records) and record producer (Hatton & Associates, Inc.). BMI. Estab. 1977. Publishes 25 songs/year; publishes 5-10 new songwriters/year. Receives 50 submissions/month. Works with composers and lyricists; teams collaborators. Pays standard royalty. "Evaluation services available. Write or call for details."

How to Contact: Submit a demo tape by mail—unsolicited submissions are OK. Prefers cassette (VHS videocassette if available) with 3 songs and lyric sheet. SASE. Reports in 2 months.

Music: Mostly pop/uptempo, pop ballads and rock (soft); also country. Published "All The Seasons" (by Hatton-Hurley), recorded by Sandy Contella (pop ballad); "With My Last Breath" (by Hatton-Contella), recorded by Sandy Contella (pop ballad); and "Catch a Snowflake" (by Hatton-Scott), recorded by Janet O. Neale (Christmas pop), all on E & S Records.

Tips: "We are looking *very hard* for uptempo songs—good lyrics for a young Debbie Gibson type. Have a great young gal but need material. Send demo with vocal *and also without (just tracks)* with lyric sheet."

EARTHSCREAM MUSIC PUBLISHING CO., Suite A, 2036 Pasket, Houston TX 77092. (713)688-8067. Contact: Jeff Johnson. Music publisher, record company and record producer. Estab. 1975. BMI. Publishes 12 songs/year; publishes 4 new songwriters/year. Pays standard royalty.

How to Contact: Prefers cassette (or videocassette) with 2-5 songs and lyric sheet. SASE. Reports in 1 month.

Music: New rock and top 40/pop. Published "Always Happens" (by Pennington/Smith), recorded by Barbara Pennington; "Show Me Reaction" (by Wells), recorded by Rick Bardon; and "New Guy" (by Wells), recorded by Valerie Starr (all pop/rock).

*ECCENTRAX MUSIC CO., Rt. 1 Box 1675-C, Grayling MI 49738. (517)348-1136. President: Debbie Bondar. Music publisher (Multi-Music Management). ASCAP. Estab. 1990. Publishes 3 songs/year; publishes 2 new songwriters/year. Works with composers and lyricists; teams collaborators. Pays standard royalty.

How to Contact: Submit a demo tape by mail—unsolicited submissions are OK. Prefers cassette with 3 songs and lyric sheet. "Please make sure lyrics are understandable." SASE. Reports in 1 month.

Music: Mostly pop, country and rock; also children's, R&B. Published "When I'm With You" (by A. Bondar and V. Ripp), recorded G. Worth (pop); and "Thank You" (by A. Bondar), recorded by L. Bondar.

EDICIONES MUSICALES PHONOGRAM S.A., Bartolome Mitre 1986, Buenos Aires 1093 **Argentina**. Phone: (541)953-2328. Publishing Manager: Olinda P. De Romera. Music publisher. SADAIC. Publishes 120 songs/year; publishes 10 new songwriters/year. Works with composers and lyricists.

Affiliate(s): "We belong to the PolyGram Music Group and our catalogues include: Island Music, Dick James Music, Welk Music Group, Sweden Music."

How to Contact: Write first and obtain permission to submit a tape. Prefers cassette with 2-3 songs and lyric or lead sheets. Always specify: "Sample Without Commercial Value." Does not return unsolicited material. Reports in 2 weeks.

Music: Mostly easy listening, pop and rock; also R&B, Latin and New Age. No country or gospel. Published "Coraje Y Amor" (by N. Gurvich and O. Valls), recorded by Paz Martinez; "Por Una Noche Contigo" (by Liliana Maturano), recorded by Tormenta; and "Que Quirre La Chola" (by R.

Diecas and O. Perez), recorded by Los Palmeras, all on CBS Records.

*EDUCATIONAL CIRCUS COMPANY, P.O. Box 3566, Kansas City KS 66103. President: Tony Osborne. ASCAP. 1989. Publishes 5 songs/year; publishes 2 new songwriters/year. Receives 50 submissions/year. Works with composers and lyricists; teams collaborators. Pays standard royalty of 50%. "Sometimes we will pay an advance to writer/artists."
How to Contact: Submit a demo tape by mail—unsolicited submissions are OK. Prefers cassette (Beta videocassette if available) with no more than 3 songs and lyric sheet. "Include SASE and photo, if possible." SASE. Reports in 2 weeks.
Music: Mostly rock, soul/R&B and children's; also gospel and Spanish. Published "Where Would I Be? (Anne's Song)," recorded by Lace (love song); "Heros," recorded by Langston (patriotic); and "Counting," recorded by Blood in the Saddle (metal); all written by Tony Osborne on ECC Records.

EKG MUSIC, P.O. Box 577, Waterloo Ontario N2J 4B8 **Canada.** (519)744-4350. President: Eric Gillespie. Music publisher, record producer. PROCAN. Estab. 1988. Publishes 20-30 songs/year; publishes 5 new songwriters/year. Works with composers and lyricists; teams collaborators. Pays standard royalty.
How to Contact: Submit a demo tape by mail—unsolicited submissions are OK. Prefers cassette (VHS videocassette if available) with 3 songs and lyric sheet. SASE. Reports in 4-6 weeks.
Music: Mostly rock and pop. Published "You Never Looked Back," "Say Hi" and "Flaunt It," all recorded by EKG on A&M Records (rock).
Tips: "Please make sure all submissions are commercially accessible rock or pop, suited for radio airplay."

*ELECT MUSIC PUBLISHING, P.O. Box 22, Underhill VT 05489. (802)899-3787. Founder: Bobby Hackney. Music publisher and record company (LBI Records). BMI. Estab. 1980. Publishes 24 songs/ year; publishes 3 new songwriters/year. Works with composers and/or lyricists; teams collaborators. Pays standard royalty.
Affiliate(s): Elect Music (BMI).
How to Contact: Submit a demo tape by mail—unsolicited submissions are OK. Prefers cassette and VHS videocassette with 3-4 songs and lyric sheet. SASE.
Music: Mostly reggae, R&B and rap; also New Age, rock and some country. Published "Samson & Delilah" (by Bobby Hackney), recorded by Lambsbread (reggae); "Sign of the Times" (by Rick Steffen), recorded by Lambsbread (reggae); and "This Love" (by Bobby Hackney), recorded by The Hackneys (R&B); all on LBI Records.
Tips: "Be patient. Our approach to the music business is ask not what the business can do for us, but what we can do for the business. We love to work with the underdogs of the industry."

ELEMENT MOVIE AND MUSIC, Box 30260, Bakersfield CA 93385. Producer: Jar the Superstar. Music publisher, record company and record producer. BMI. Publishes 2 songs/year; publishes 2 new songwriters/year. Hires staff writers. Pays standard royalty.
How to Contact: Write first about your interest or arrange personal interview. "Query with resume of credits. Do not mail songs without permission! We are taking interviews only." Prefers 15 ips reel-to-reel or cassette with 1-3 songs. Does not return unsolicited material. Reports in 3 months.
Music: Mostly R&B, rock, soul, gospel, jazz, progressive, easy listening and top 40/pop; also blues, children's, choral, church/religious, classical, country, dance-oriented, MOR, Spanish and music for feature films. Published "The Energy Conspiracy," from the soundtrack album on Element Records; "She's Sweet to Me" (by Jar the Superstar); "God Will Post Your Bail" (by Judge A. Robertson) (Christian pop); "What Could I'll Done Without Jesus Around" (by Jar the Superstar); and "Put Nothing Over God" (by Jar the Superstar) on Element Records (church rock).

EMANDELL TUNES, 10220 Glade Ave., Chatsworth CA 91311. (818)341-2264. President/Administrator: Leroy C. Lovett, Jr. Estab. 1979. Publishes 6-12 songs/year; 3-4 new songwriters/year. Receives 10-15 submissions/month. Pays standard royalty.
Affiliate(s): Ben-Lee Music (BMI), Birthright Music (ASCAP), Northworth Songs (SESAC), Chinwah Songs, Gertrude Music (SESAC), LMS Print/Publishing Co. and Nadine Music International in Zurich, Switzerland.
How to Contact: Write first to get permission to submit tape. Prefers cassette (or videocassette) with 4-5 songs and lead or lyric sheet. Include information about writer, singer or group. SASE. Reports in 5-6 weeks.

Listings of companies in countries other than the U.S. have the name of the country in boldface type.

Music: Inspirational, contemporary gospel and chorals. Published "High Places," (by Kevin Gaston); and "Surely Goodness and Mercy" (by Kevin Allen and Peppy Smith), both recorded by the Elect on WFL Records (urban contemporary); "Joy Great Joy" (by Dorinda Clark-Cole), recorded by UNAC 90-Mass Choir on WFL Records (gospel); "Renew Me" (by Eddie Howard), recorded by UNAC 90-Mass Choir on WFL Records (gospel); "The Center of Hope" (by Albert Hartdige), recorded by Voices of Rhoma on WFL Records (gospel). All above are SESAC selections.Licensed "How I Got Over" w/m Clara Ward Composition (Gertrude Music-SESAC) in the TV Mini Series "Call To Glory" and "Come On Children, Let's Sing," by Edwin Hawkins (Birthright Music-ASCAP) in a *LaVerne & Shirley* TV episode.
Tips: "Submit high quality demos but keep it simple—no production extras."

*EMPTY SKY MUSIC COMPANY, P.O. Box 626, 14th St., Verplanck NY 10596. Promotional Manager: Lisa Lancaster. Music publisher, record company (Empty Sky, Yankee, Verplanck) and record producer (Rick Carbone, for Empty Sky). ASCAP, BMI. Estab. 1982. Publishes 15-20 songs/year; publishes 10 new songwriters/year. Works with composer and lyricists; teams collaborators. Pays standard royalty.
Affiliate(s): Empty Sky Music (ASCAP) and Rick Carbone Music (BMI).
How to Contact: Submit a demo tape by mail—unsolicited submissions are OK. Prefers cassette with 3-5 songs and lyric sheet. SASE. Reports in 2-3 months.
Music: Mostly country, gospel and pop; also rap, rock and rap/gospel. Published "Letters (The Mailman Story)" (by B. Armocida, R. Sanders), recorded by Ray Sanders on Empty Sky Records (country); "Someday I'm Going to Heaven" (by Donald Mask), recorded by Wylie Justice on Empty Sky Records (gospel); "Giving Romance Another Try" (by Rick Carbone), recorded by The Sweetarts on Verplanck Records (country).

*ENTERTAINMENT SERVICES MUSIC GROUP, 27 Music Square East, Nashville TN 37203. (615)244-7171. Manager/Executive Administrator: Hannah Onassis. Music publisher. BMI. Estab. 1990. Publishes 10-15 songs/year; 2-4 new songwriters/year. Teams collaborators. Pays standard royalty.
How to Contact: Submit a demo tape by mail—unsolicited submissions are OK. Prefers cassette with 4 songs or less and lyric sheet. "Please submit quality demos. Full orchestration is not necessary. It's the tune and lyrics that will get our attention. Some killer demos have been achieved with 4-track recordings." SASE. Reports within 6 weeks.
Music: Mostly country (traditional), country rock and country pop; also country blues. Published "She Was Easy to Love" (by Michael Higgins), recorded by Mike Everett on Carrao Records (country traditional); "Hello Mexico" (by L.J. Hannah), recorded by Hannah Onassis on Trump Records (country); and "Stolen Moments," written and recorded by Nancy Lawson on Mega Cles Records (country blues).
Tips: "Keep the song commercial and under 3 minutes. Let your songs be one that the masses can relate to. When recording your demo, use a vocalist that can get your lyrics across."

*ERTIS MUSIC COMPANY, P.O. Box 80691, Baton Rouge LA 70898. (504)924-3327. Publisher: Johnny Palazzotto. ASCAP. Estab. 1977. Publishes 10-15 songs/year. Pays standard royalty.
Affiliate(s): Blue Rouge Music (ASCAP).
How to Contact: Submit a demo tape by mail—unsolicited submissions are OK. Prefers cassette with 3-5 songs. SASE. Reports in 2-4 weeks.
Music: Mostly country and zydeco. Published "Come on Home" (by Major Handy), recorded by Nathan & Cha-Chas on Rounder Records (zydeco); "Come on Home," written and recorded by Major Handy on Bedrock Records (zydeco); and "Laissez Les Bon" (by Kelly, J. Dideer), recorded by Queen Ida on Sonet Records (zydeco).

EURSONG, 6 Heath Close, London W5 **England.** Phone: 44-01-991-0993. Contact: Jan Olofsson. Music publisher and record company (Young Blood Records). Publishes 25-30 songs/year; publishes 12 new songwriters/year. Works with composers; teams collaborators. Pays standard royalty.
Affiliate(s): Birth Music Ltd./PRS, Olofsong/Basart (Holland), Blue Eyes/Careere (France), Olofsong Scandinavian Songs (Sweden), Olofsong Music, Inc. and Crazy Viking Music/BMI (USA).
How to Contact: Prefers cassette (or European VHS videocassette if possible for finished masters only) with 3-12 songs and lyric sheet. SAE and IRC. Reports in 3 weeks.
Music: Mostly dance music, rock bands, general pop, soul, rap, hip-hop and a little country; also R&B and rock. Published "Carefree Days," written and recorded by Time Gallery; "Let It Swing," written and recorded by Bobby Sock, and "Best Christmas," written and recorded by Shaky Stevens.
Tips: "Have a complete finished master recording that has hit appeal and can be released in Europe. We are an international music publisher."

EVER-OPEN-EYE MUSIC, Wern Fawr Farm, Pencoed, MID, Glam CF356NB **United Kingdom**. Phone: (0656)860041. Managing Director: M.R. Blanche. Music publisher and record company (Red-Eye Records). PRS. Member PPL and MCPS. Estab. 1980. Publishes 6 songs/year. Works with composers and lyricists; teams collaborators. Pays negotiable amount.
How to Contact: Submit a demo tape —unsolicited submissions are OK. Prefers cassette (or VHS videocassette). SAE and IRC.
Music: Mostly R&B, gospel and pop; also swing. Published "Rumba Time" (by G. Williams) on Red Eye Records (R&B); "For Ronnie" and "Night Stick" (by S. Campbell) on Red Eye Records (R&B); "Night Trains" (by I. Yandell) on Red Eye Records (ballad).

*EXCURSION MUSIC GROUP, P.O. Box 1170, Livermore CA 94551-1170. (415)373-6477. President: Frank T. Prins. Music publisher, record company (Excursion Records) and record producer. BMI, ASCAP. Estab. 1976. Publishes 25 songs/year; publishes 5 new songwriters/year. Hires staff writers. Works with composers and lyricists; teams collaborators. Pays standard royalty.
Affiliate(s): Echappee Music (BMI), Excursion Music (ASCAP).
How to Contact: Write or call first and obtain permission to submit a tape. Prefers cassette or VHS videocassette with 3 songs and lyric sheet. SASE. Reports in 2 weeks.
Music: Mostly pop, country and gospel; also rock & roll and R&B. Published "Mississippi Nights" (by Timothy Barnes), recorded by The Fabulous Flames (R&R); "Katrina" (by Robert Hepfner), recorded by Bobby C. (country); and "Fine, Fine, Fine" (by Marty Deradorian), recorded by The Fabulous Flames (R&B); all on Excursion Records.

*EYE KILL MUSIC, P.O. Box 242, Woodland PA 16881. A&R: John Wesley. Music publisher. ASCAP. Estab. 1987. Publishes 10 songs/year; publishes 6 new songwriters/year. Works with composers and lyricists. Pays standard royalty.
How to Contact: Submit a demo tape by mail—unsolicited submissions are OK. Prefers cassette with 3 songs and lyric sheet. SASE. Reports in 1 month.
Music: Mostly country and rock. Published "All Over For You" (by Cindy Stone) and "Here Again" (by Guy Stone), both recorded by Paul White; "Two Lonely Hearts," written and recorded by John Maine, Jr., all on Eye Kill Records (all country).

DOUG FAIELLA PUBLISHING, 16591 County Home Rd., Marysville OH 43040. (513)644-8295. President: Doug Faiella. Music publisher, record company (Studio 7 Records) and recording studio. BMI. Estab. 1984. Publishes 25 songs/year; publishes 5 new songwriters/year. Works with composers and teams collaborators. Pays standard royalty.
How to Contact: Write to obtain permission to submit a tape. SASE. Prefers cassette with 3 songs and lyric sheets. Does not return unsolicited material. Reports in 4 weeks.
Music: Mostly country, gospel and rock.

F&J MUSIC. 23, Thrayle House, Stockwell Road, London SW9 0XU **England**. (071)274-9533 and (818)962-6547. FAX: (071)737-7881 and FAX: (818)778-0225. Managing Director: Errol Jones. Music publisher and record company (Leopard Music/Jet Set International Records). PRS, BMI. Estab. 1978. Publishes 75 songs/year. Publishes 35 new songwriters/year. Works with composers and lyricists; teams collaborators. Pays standard royalty.
Affiliate(s): EURUSA Worldwide Publishing Affiliate (BMI).
How to Contact: Write first and obtain permission to submit. Prefers cassette (or VHS PAL videocassette) with 3 songs, lyric sheet and lead sheet. Include biography, resume and picture. SASE. Reports in 2 weeks.
Music: Mostly dance, soul and pop; also ballads, reggae and gospel. Published "Time After Time," (by Guy Spell), recorded by Rico J. on Leopard Music/Jet Set International Records (disco/soul); "I Need You," (by F. Campbell/E. North Jr.), recorded by Big Africa (soul/reggae); and "God is Beauty," written and recorded by Evelyn Ladimeji (gospel); both on Leopard Music.

*FAS-ENT MUSIC, 4060½ Laurel Canyon Bl., Studio City CA 91604. (818)753-1900. Vice President: Bob Bruning. Music publisher and record company (Fascination Entertainment). ASCAP. Estab. 1990. Publishes 40 songs/year; publishes 4 new songwriters/year. Works with composers and lyricists; teams collaborators. Pays standard royalty.
How to Contact: Submit a demo tape by mail—unsolicited submissions are OK. Prefers cassette with 3 songs and lyric sheet. Does not return unsolicited submissions. Reports in 1 month.
Music: Mostly children's and film and TV. Published "Land of Toys" (by Sam and Maria Libraty), recorded by Christina Veronica on Fascination Records (children's); "Wonderful You" (by Bob Bruning), recorded by Christina Veronica on Entertainment Records (children's); and "Jammy Jammin' Time" (by Pat Flanakin), recorded by Suzanne McSwanson on Entertainment Records (children's).
Tips: "Respect your audience, while giving them something to relate to."

FEZSONGS, 429 S. Lewis Rd., Royersford PA 19468. (215)948-8228. FAX: (215)948-4175. President: Jim Femino. Music publisher, record company (Road Records) and record producer (independent). ASCAP. Estab. 1970. Publishes 12-15 songs/year; publishes 1-2 new songwriters/year. Receives 12-20 submissions/month. Works with composers and lyricists; teams collaborators. Pays standard royalty. "Charges in advance for demo recording services, only if needed."
Affiliate(s): Fezsongs (ASCAP).
How to Contact: Submit a demo tape by mail—unsolicited submissions are OK. Prefers cassette (or VHS videocassette) with 3-4 songs and lyric sheet. Does not return unsolicited material. Reports in 6 weeks.
Music: Mostly rock, country and cross-over. Published "Dogs of War," "America" and "L.A.'s Callin'," all rock singles written and recorded by Jim Femino on Road Records.

FIRST MILLION MUSIC, INC., 50 Music Square West, #207, Nashville TN 37203. (615)329-2591. Vice President: Peggy Bradley. Music publisher. ASCAP. Estab. 1983. Publishes 4 songs/year; 2 new songwriters/year. Pays standard royalty.
Affiliate(s): Old Guide Music (BMI).
How to Contact: Submit a demo tape by mail—unsolicited submissions are OK. Prefers cassette with 3 songs and lyric sheet. SASE. Reports in 2 weeks.
Music: Mostly country, pop and R&B. Published "Love (by Ruddy), recorded by Jill Jordan on Maxx Records (country/uptempo); and "Jewel of the Mississippi" (by Lips Prat), recorded by Don Juan on Maxx Records (country/ballad).

*FIRST RELEASE MUSIC PUBLISHING, 6124 Selma Ave., Hollywood CA 90028. (213)469-2296. Creative Director: Danny Howell. Music publisher. BMI, ASCAP, SACEM, GEMA, PRS, MCPS. Publishes 30-50 songs/year. Hires staff songwriters. Pays standard royalty; co-publishing negotiable.
Affiliate(s): Fully Conscious Music, Criterion Music, Cadillac Pink, Atlantic Music, Illegeal Songs, I.R.S. Songs, Reggatta Music, Magnetic Publishing Ltd. and Animal Logic Publishing.
How to Contact: "We *never* accept unsolicited tapes or phone calls—you must have referral or be requested." Returns all unsolicited material. Reports only if interested, but "retain personally written critique for every song I agree to accept."
Music: "We are interested in great songs and great writers. We are currently successful in all areas." Published "One Touch" (by M. Anderson), recorded by Juice Newton on Capitol Records (country/rock); "Private Party" (by Pam Reswick/Allan Rich/Steve Werfel), recorded by Rege Burrell on Epic Records (R&B); "No Love In You" (by M. Anderson), recorded by John Fogerty on HBO/Warner Bros. Records (rock) and "Brother to Brother" (by E. Vidal/T. Kimmel), recorded by The Spinners and featured in the motion picture *Twins*.
Tips: "Don't always send what you think publishers want to hear—include a song that has personal meaning to you. If you feel very strongly about a song, don't wait. Send a demo of a single instrument and vocals if money or equipment is a problem. Always have vocals on demos at an audible level."

FIRST TIME MUSIC (PUBLISHING) U.K. LTD., Sovereign House, 12 Trewartha Road, Praa Sands, Penzance, Cornwall TR20 9ST **England.** Phone: (0736)762826. FAX: (0736)763328. Managing Director: Roderick G. Jones. Music publisher, record company (First Time Records, licensed and subsidiary labels), record producer and management firm (First Time Management and Production Co.). PRS. Member of MCPS. Estab. 1986. Publishes 500-750 songs/year; 20-50 new songwriters/year. Hires staff writers. Works with composers and lyricists; teams collaborators. Pays standard royalty; "50-60% to established and up-and-coming writers with the right attitude."
Affiliate(s): Subsidiary and administered music catalogues. Sub-publishing worldwide (new associations welcome).
How to Contact: Submit a demo tape—unsolicited submissions are OK. Prefers cassette, 1⅞ ips cassette (or VHS videocassette "of professional quality") with unlimited number of songs and lyric or lead sheets, but not necessary. Reports in 4-10 weeks. SASE in U.K.—SAE and IRC if outside U.K. "Postal costs in the U.K. are much higher than the U.S.—one IRC doesn't even cover the cost of a letter to the U.S., let alone the return of cassettes. Enclose the correct amount for return and contact as stated."
Music: Mostly country and folk, pop/soul/top 20/rock, country with an Irish/Scottish crossover; also gospel/Christian. Published "The Robinsons Back" (by Pete Arnold), recorded by Brendan Shine on Play Records (MOR/country); "Thanks" (by Rod Jones/Mike Cook), recorded by PJ Proby on J'ace Records (pop); "How Do You Do Those Things?" (by Charlie Landsborough), recorded by Charlie Landsborough on Roy Records (country/MOR).
Tips: "Have a professional approach—present well produced demo's. First impressions are important and may be the only chance you get. Remember that you as a writer/artiste are in a competitive market. As an active independent -international publisher we require good writers/artistes and product. As a company we seek to work with writers. If the product is good then we generally come up with something

in the way of covers. Writers are advised to join the Guild of International Songwriters and Composers in the United Kingdom."

FIVE ROSES MUSIC COMPANY, Twin Bridge Rd., Liberty NY 12754. (914)292-4042. President: Sammie Lee Marler. Music publisher. Consultant, management. BMI. Estab. 1989. Publishes 50-75 songs/year. Works with composers and lyricists; teams collaborators. Pays standard royalty.
How to Contact: Submit a demo tape by mail—unsolicited submissions are OK. Prefers cassette with 5 songs. SASE. Reports in 2 weeks.
Music: Mostly C&W, bluegrass, country rock, country gospel, light. Published "Who's Changin' the Rules" (by S. Marler), recorded by J. Oldania and Bobby Royce (C&W); "I'm Doing You A Favor," by D. Combs and S. Marler (country pop); and "Good Lord Willin," by Bobby Royce and Sammie Lee Marler (country gospel).
Tips: "We care about the songwriter and keep in personal contact with them. We are one happy family at Five Roses. Always include a SASE for material return."

FLAMING STAR WEST, P.O. Box 2400, Gardnerville NV 89410. (702)265-6825. Owner: Ted Snyder. Music publisher, record company (Fleming Star Records) and record producer (Flaming Star Records). BMI. Estab. 1988. Works with composers and lyricists; teams collaborators. Pays standard royalty.
How to Contact: Submit a demo tape by mail—unsolicited submissions are OK. Prefers cassette or VHS videocassette with up to 5 songs and lyric sheets. "If you are sure of your music, you may send more than 5 songs. No heavy metal. All other types." SASE. Reports in 3 weeks.
Music: Mostly country, pop and rock and country rock; also gospel, R&B, New Age and calypso. Published "Jezabel" (country rock) and "For the Sake of My Children" (ballad), both written and recorded by Ted Snyder on Flaming Star Records.
Tips: "Listen to what is on the radio, but be original. Put feeling into your songs. We're looking for songs and artists to promote overseas. Flaming Star Records is a launching pad for the new recording artist. We try to help where we can."

FLANARY PUBLISHING CO., P.O. Box 2220, Whittier CA 90610. (213)696-4941. Director of Submissions: Alicia Flanary. Music publisher. Estab. 1988. Hires staff writers for TV and film. Receives 12 submissions/month. Works with composers and lyricists. Pays standard royalty or open to negotiation.
How to Contact: Submit a demo tape by mail—unsolicited submissions are OK. Prefers cassette with 3 songs and lyric or lead sheets. SASE, otherwise does not return unsolicited material.
Music: Mostly pop/rock and country.
Tips: "When we send a songwriter's tape back to them, we stress submitting more material to us. Keep trying."

FOCAL POINT MUSIC PUBLISHERS (BMI), 920 McArthur Blvd., Warner Robins GA 31093. (912)923-6533. Manager: Ray Melton. Music publisher and record company. BMI. Estab. 1964. Publishes 4 songs/year; publishes 1 new songwriter/year. Receives 50 submissions/year. Works with composers. Pays standard royalty. "Songwriters must have BMI affiliation."
How to Contact: Write first to get permission to send a tape. Prefers cassette with 2-4 songs and lead sheet. Prefers studio produced demos. SASE.
Music: Mostly country and gospel; also "old-style pop and humor." Published "Walk Away," written and recorded by Bill Arwood on Bob Grady Records (country); "Troubles," written and recorded by Kenny Arledge on Club 45 (country); and "Band of Gold," written and recorded by Bill Arwood on Bob Grady Records (country). "We are getting overseas radio play on a lot of our material."

FOUR NEWTON PUBLISHING, Rt. 1, Box 187-A, Whitney TX 76692. (817)694-4047. President: Allen Newton. Music publisher, record company (Pristine Records, Pleasure Records, Cactus Flats, MFN). BMI. Estab. 1980. Publishes 14 songs/year; publishes about 10 new songwriters/year. Receives 120 submissions/year. Works with composers and lyricists; teams collaborators. Pays standard royalty.
How to Contact: Submit a demo tape by mail—unsolicited submissions are OK. Prefers cassette with 3 songs and lyric sheets. SASE. Reports in 3 weeks.
Music: Mostly country, rock and R&B; also pop, gospel and New Age. Published "I'm a Changed Man" (by Joel Nava), recorded by Nightrider on Pleasure Records (C&W); "Loud" (by Joseph Green), recorded by Diver on Pristine records (rock); and "On Your Wings" (by Richard Hankey), recorded by Fire on MFN Records (rock).

FOX FARM RECORDING, 2731 Saundersville Ferry Rd., Mt. Juliet TN 37122. (615)754-2444. President: Kent Fox. Music publisher and record producer and Demo Production Recording Studio. BMI, ASCAP. Publishes 20 songs/year; publishes 5 new songwriters/year. Works with composers and lyricists; teams collaborators. Pays standard royalty.

Affiliate(s): Blueford Music (ASCAP) and Mercantile Music (BMI).
How to Contact: SASE. Prefers cassette with 4 songs and lyric sheet. Reports in 1 month.
Music: Country, bluegrass and gospel.
Tips: "If your song is good enough to become a hit, its worth investing money for a good demo: drums, bass, guitar, keyboard, fiddle, sax, vocals."

FOXWORTHY MUSIC, 4002 Liggatt Dr., San Diego CA 92106. (619)226-4152. Vice President: Dottye Foxworthy. Music publisher, record company (Foxworthy Records) and record producer (Foxworthy Productions). BMI. Estab. 1982. Publishes 20 songs/year; publishes 1 new songwriter/year. Teams collaborators. Pays standard royalty.
Affiliate(s): Foxworthy Music (BMI), Expanding Universe Music (BMI).
How to Contact: Submit a demo tape by mail—unsolicited submissions are OK. Prefers cassette with 3 songs and lyric or lead sheets. Does not return unsolicited material. Reports in 4 weeks.
Music: Mostly pop, rock and R&B; also rap and New Age. Published "Black and White," "Mixed Emotions" and "CA" (by Mike Redmond), recorded by Street Poet Ray on Foxworthy Records (rap).

FRADALE SONGS, P.O. Box 121015, Nashville TN 37212. President: David Leone. BMI. Estab. 1981. Publishes 50 songs/year; publishes 1 new songwriter/year. Receives 10 submissions/month. Works with composers and lyricists; teams collaborators. Pays standard royalty.
Affilate: Reesha Music (BMI).
How to Contact: Unsolicited submissions are OK. Does not return unsolicited material. "We strongly suggest that developing writers contact us about critiquing their material—much of successful writing can be learned and Fradale offers workshops and correspondence courses for talented writers."
Music: Country and gospel. Published "My Heartache is Here To Stay" (by R. Alscomb), recorded by Pending (country); "Open to Your Love" (by R. Field), recorded by Cheri Lynn on Classic Records (country/pop); and "Red Beans and Rice," written and recorded by B. Slater on Classic Records (country).

*FREKO RECORDS, 417 E. Cross Timbers, Houston TX 77022. (713)694-2971. Engineers: Warren Jackson III and Freddie Kober. Music publisher, record company (Freko Records, Honeybee Records) and record producer (Freddie Kober Productions). BMI. Estab. 1976. Publishes 11 songs/year; publishes 3 new songwriters/year. Works with composers and lyricists. Pays standard royalty.
Affiliate(s): Anode Music (BMI).
How to Contact: Submit a demo tape by mail—unsolicited submissions are OK. Prefers cassette with 4-8 songs and lyric sheet. Does not return unsolicited material.
Music: Mostly R&B, rap and gospel; also country, rock and pop. Published "Aggravated Assult" (by Otis Berry), recorded by Aggravated Assult (rap single); *Mahogany's First* (by Warren Jackson), recorded by Mahogany (rap LP); and "It's Time to Chil" (by Tron Washington), recorded by Tron (rap single); all on Freko Records.

FRETBOARD PUBLISHING, Box 40013, Nashville TN 37204. (615)292-2047. Contact: A&R Department. Music publisher, record company (Mosrite Records), record producer (Mark Moseley). BMI. Estab. 1963. Publishes 25 songs/year; publishes 3 new songwriters/year. Works with composers and lyricists. Pays standard royalty.
Affiliate(s): Woodgrain Publishing Co. (ASCAP).
How to Contact: Submit a demo tape by mail. Prefers cassette with 2 songs and lyric sheets. Does not return unsolicited material. Reports in 6 weeks "only if we want to hear more."
Music: Mostly country, rock (not heavy), southern gospel. Published "Even Now" (by Mark Moseley), recorded by Marie Lester (country); "Mommy's Playing Santa Claus" (by Maurice Brandon), recorded by Marie Lester (Christmas); and "Queen For a Day" (by Billy Mize), recorded by Barbara Mandrell (country); all on Mosrite Records.
Tips: "Give us time to get to your songs before you make another contact."

FRICK MUSIC PUBLISHING CO., 404 Bluegrass Ave., Madison TN 37115. (615)865-6380. Contact: Bob Frick. Music publisher, record company and record producer. BMI. Publishes 50 songs/year; publishes 2 new songwriters/year. Works with lyricists. Pays standard royalty.
How to Contact: Call first to get permission to submit. Prefers 7½ ips reel-to-reel or cassette (or videocassette) with 2-10 songs and lyric sheet. SASE. Reports in 1 month.
Music: Mostly gospel; also country, rock and top 40/pop. Published "Follow Where He Leads" by Christine Starling; "I Found Jesus in Nashville" by Lin Butler; and "I Held Up My Hands" by Frank Conrad; all recorded by Bob Scott Frick on R.E.F. Records (gospel); also "My Little Girl" by Scott Frick, and "Time, Tricks and Politics" by Eddie Isaacs.

*THE FRICON ENTERTAINMENT CO., INC., 1048 S. Ogden Dr., Los Angeles CA 90019. (213)931-7323. Attn: Publishing Department. Music publisher. Music supervision (Fricon Music/BMI; Fricout Music/ASCAP). Pays standard royalty.
How to Contact: Write first and obtain permission to submit. Prefers cassette with 1 song and lyric sheet. Does not return unsolicited material without SASE. Reports in 6 weeks.
Music: Mostly TV and film. Also gospel, R&B, rock, pop, dance and country.

*FULLTILT MUSIC, 300 Linfield Dr., Vallejo CA 94590. (707)645-1615. President: Jack Walker. Music publisher. BMI. Estab. 1982. Publishes 1 song/year. Receives 3 submissions/year. Works with composers and lyricists; teams collaborators. Pays standard royalty
How to Contact: Submit demo tape, unsolicited submissions are OK. Prefers cassette (or VHS videocassette if available) with 3 songs and lyric sheet. SASE. Reports in 1 month.
Music: We are interested in all types of music. Published "Making Up Lies" (by Wally Jennings) on Americana Records (country single).

*FUTURE STEP SIRKLE, Box 2095, Philadelphia PA 19103. (215)848-7475. President: Krun Vallatine. Vice President: S. Deane Henderson. Music publisher, record company, record producer and management firm. ASCAP. Publishes 10-15 songs/year; 6 new songwriters/year. Pays standard royalty.
How to Contact: Prefers cassette (or VHS videocassette) with 4-8 songs and lyric sheets. Does not return unsolicited material. Reports in 2 weeks.
Music: Dance-oriented, easy listening, gospel, MOR, R&B, rock, soul, top 40/pop, funk and heavy metal. Published "Why Me" and "Love On the Left Hand Side," recorded by FSS; "Hot Number" (by John Fitch), recorded by The Racers (heavy rock); "Delirious," recorded by Molecules of Force (new wave); "Save and Cleanse Me Jesus" and "In God's Hand" (by Verdelle C. Bryant), recorded by Verdelle & Off Spring Gospel Singers (gospel); "Free the Godfather" and "Illusion of Love" (by Hall Sound Lab in collaborations with Future Step Sirkle); "He's Blessing You" by Jackie PaeyLord and *Sister Mary Deloatch & Her Guitar* (a new sound in gospel); all of Future Step Records.

*BOB GAFFNEY MUSIC, Suite A, 9375 SW 61 Way, Boca Raton FL 33428. President: Bob Gaffney. Music publisher and record producer (Bob Gaffney Productions). BMI. Estab. 1987. Publishes 20 songs/year; publishes 4-6 new songwriters/year. Works with composers and lyricists.
How to Contact: Submit a demo tape by mail—unsolicited submissions are OK. Prefers cassette with 1-4 songs and lyric sheet. SASE. Reports in 3 weeks.
Editor's Note: At press time, Bob Gaffney Music is no longer in operation. Refrain from submitting any material to this company.

GALAXIA MUSICAL S.A. De C.V., Leibnitz 130, D.F. 11590 **Mexico**. (905)511-6684. Managing Director: Arq. Jose G. Cruz. Music publisher. SACM. Publishes 50 songs/year. Receives 150-200 submissions/year. Works with composers and lyricists; teams collaborators. Pays standard royalty.
How to Contact: Write first and obtain permission to submit. "Will only accept submissions from writers who are very familiar with type of music currently being produced in Mexico and Spanish speaking territories." Prefers cassette (or VHS videocassette) with 1-5 songs. SAE and IRC. Reports in 2 weeks.
Music: Pop ballads and rock.
Tips: "A well-prepared demo signals good craftmanship."

LARRY GENE MUSIC, 435 Main St., Johnson City NY 13790. (607)729-2291. Owner: Larry Lupole. Music publisher, record company (Ice Records, Inc.) and record producer (Larry Lupole, Ice Records, Inc.). BMI. Estab. 1980. Publishes 2-3 songs/year; publishes 1-2 new songwriters/year. Hires staff writers. Teams collaborators. Pays standard royalty.
How to Contact: Write first and obtain permission to submit. Prefers cassette with 5 songs and lead sheet. SASE. Reports in 2 months.
Music: Mostly pop, rock and country; also R&B, gospel and new age. Published "Classic Fantasy" and "My Love," written and recorded by Larry Lupole; and "Zero Gravity," "Gardens in Orbit," and "Deep Space," written and recorded by David Sweet, all on Ice Records (all rock).

GENETIC MUSIC PUBLISHING, 10 Church Rd., Merchantville NJ 08109. (609)662-4428. Contact: Whey Cooler or Jade Starling. Music publisher, record company (Svengali) and record producer (Whey Cooler Production). ASCAP. Estab. 1982. Publishes 1-5 songs/year. Works with composers, lyricists; teams collaborators. Pays standard royalty.
How to Contact: Write or call first and obtain permission to submit a tape. Prefers cassette or VHS videocassette with songs. SASE. Reports in 2 weeks.
Music: Mostly dance, R&B and pop; also rock and jazz. Published "Catch Me I'm Falling," "Nightime" and "When I Look Into U'r Eyes" (by Starling/Cooler), recorded by Pretty Poison on Virgin (dance pop).

Tips: "Just submit it. If we think we can place it we'll hold it on file and submit it to projects as they arise. Should a song be chosen for a given project, we'll then publish the song."

GIFTNESS ENTERPRISE, Suite #5, 1315 Simpson Rd. NW, Atlanta GA 30314. (404)642-2645. Contact: New Song Department. Music publisher. BMI. Publishes 30 songs/year; publishes 15 new songwriters/ year. Employs songwriters on a salary basis. Works with composers and lyricsts; teams collaborators. Pays standard royalty.
Affiliate(s): Hserf Music (ASCAP).
How to Contact: Prefers cassette with 4 songs and lyric or lead sheet. SASE. Reports in 3 weeks.
Music: Mostly R&B, pop and rock; also country, gospel and jazz. Published "Vicious Rap," written and recorded by Eze T on Northwest Records (dance); "Only in America" (by E. Lyons), recorded by Mojo on Gold Key Records (dance); and "You're So Fine," written and recorded by Cirocco on Geffen Records (R&B).

GIL-GAD MUSIC, 6015 Troost, Kansas City MO 64110. (816)361-8455. General Manager/Publisher: Eugene Gold. ASCAP, BMI. Estab. 1969. Music publisher and record producer. Publishes 30 or more songs/year; publishes 10 or more new songwriters/year. Teams collaborators. Pays standard royalty.
Affiliate(s): 3G's Music Co., Eugene Gold Music.
How to Contact: Prefers cassette (or videocassette) with 4-6 songs and lyric sheet. SASE. Reports in 2 months.
Music: Mostly R&B, rock and top 40/pop; also disco/dance, gospel and jazz. Published "Magic" (by Cal-Green, Ronnie & Vicky), recorded by Suspension on 3G's (R&B/top pop); "Bootie Cutie," written and recorded by Robert Newsome on 3G's (R&B); and "Diamond Feather," (by M. Murf), recorded by Bad News Band on NMI (R&B).

GLOBEART PUBLISHING, A Division of GlobeArt Inc., Suite 21F, 1755 York Ave., New York NY 10128. (212)860-3023. President: Jane Peterer. Music publisher. BMI, ASCAP. Estab. 1989. Publishes 20 songs/year; publishes 2 new songwriters/year. Works with composers and lyricists. Pays standard royalty.
Affiliate(s): GlobeSound Publishing (ASCAP).
How to Contact: Submit a demo tape by mail—unsolicited submissions are OK. Prefers cassette (or videocassette) with 3-5 songs and lyric or lead sheet. SASE. Reports in 6 weeks.
Music: Mostly pop/R&B, jazz and gospel; also New Age and country. Published "Jamaica" (by Muralidhar), recorded by Muralidhar on AJ Records (pop); "Beautiful Morning," by Herbert Rehbein and his Orchestra on Pick Records (MOR); and "I Don't Want to Loose" (by M.L. Bryant), recorded by Muralidhar on AJ Records (pop).

*GMG MUSIC, 1226 17th Ave. South, Nashville TN 37212. (615)327-1632. Vice President: Maurice Godwin. Music publisher, management firm. BMI, ASCAP, SESAC. Estab. 1986. Publishes 15-20 songs/year; publishes 5 new songwriters/year. Receives 400 submissions/month. Works with composers; teams collaborators. Pays standard 50% royalty.
Affiliate(s): Old Empress Music (BMI), Un-Der 16 Songs (SESAC) and Paw Print Music (ASCAP). Write or call first and obtain permission to submit a tape. Prefers cassette with 4 songs. Chrome tape (high bias). Include SASE. Reports in 1 month.
Music: Mostly rock-a-billy, pop and R&B; also reggae and country. Published "So Far I," written and recorded by Greg Hansen on Rooney Record (reggae); "The Last Refrain," written and recorded by Bruce McMaster on Bullet Records (rock); "Real" (by Roy Cathey, Jr.), recorded by Mickey Dee on Rock City Record (rock).
Tips: "Know a little about the music business. Listen to commercial music."

GO STAR MUSIC, Suite #20, 4700 Belle Grove Rd., Baltimore MD 21225. (301)789-1005. FAX: (301)789-1006. Owner: William E. Baker. Music publisher, record company (Go Records) and record producer (International Music). Estab. 1988. Publishes 50-100 songs/year; 50 new songwriters/year. Receives 1,200 submissions/year. Pays standard royalty.
Affiliate(s): Billy Baker and Associates, Go Records, Infinity Productions and Independent International Music Associates.
How to Contact: Submit a demo tape. Unsolicited submissions are OK. "Limit 4 songs with lyric sheets, bio and photo. SASE with phone number. List what you would like to achieve." Prefers cassette and lyric or lead sheet. SASE. Reports in 3 weeks.
Music: Mostly rock, pop, country, R&B, New Age and gospel. Published "If You're Not Here" (by Paula Anderson/Pam Bailey), recorded by Closin' Time On Go Records (country); "Numbered Door" (by Roger Ware), recorded by Doug Beacham on Go Records (country); and "Carolina Blue (by Jim Hession), recorded by John Anthony on Go/Silver Dollar Records (country).

S.M. GOLD MUSIC, INC., % Compositions, Suite 6E, 295 Park Ave. S, New York NY 10010. President: Steven M. Gold. Music publisher and jingle/TV score producer. ASCAP. Publishes 5 songs/year. Receives 15 submissions/month. Works with composers. Hires staff writers. "We employ freelance and staff songwriters who are well-versed in all styles of popular music." Pays standard royalty or cash advance (buy-out).
How to Contact: Submit a demo tape—unsolicited submissions are OK. Prefers cassette with 1 song. Does not return unsolicited material. No calls please.
Music: Mainstream pop, R&B and dance/pop.
Tips: "We're not looking for 'album tracks' or 'B sides.' Hits only!"

*GOLD SOUND MUSIC INC., 3826 Commanche Ave., Las Vegas NV 89121. (702)458-3957. Producer and Publisher: Tom Devito. Music publisher, record company (Moontide Records) and record producer. BMI, ASCAP, SESAC. Estab. 1978. Publishes 30 songs/year; publishes 3 new songwriters/year. Pay standard royalty.
Affiliate(s): Moondance Music (SESAC), MoonDown Music (BMI) and Moontide Music (ASCAP).
How to Contact: Write or call to arrange a personal interview. Prefers cassette or VHS videocassette with 3 songs and lyric and lead sheets. SASE. Reports in 2 weeks.
Music: Mostly easy rock, country and R&B; also pop and MOR.
Tips: "We are looking for strong lyrics and a good melody."

*GOLDEN APPLE PRODUCTIONS, Hinton, Christchurch, Dorset BH23 7EA **England**. Phone: (0425)274993. Product Developer: Mrs. Alison Hedger. Music publisher. PRS. Estab. 1986. Member MPA (London). Publishes 4 albums (approximately 35 songs)/year; publishes 2 new songwriters/year. Receives 10 submissions/month. Works with composers and lyricists. Pays standard royalty, "contracts all at recognized current British rates."
How to Contact: Submit a demo tape—unsolicited submissions are OK. Prefers cassette and lyric or lead sheets. SAE and IRC. Reports in 1 month.
Music: Mostly children's educational and other children's material. Published *Tiny Bird* (Easter album), recorded by Caroline Hoile (children's educational); *Fife Connection* (recorded album), recorded by Bill McIntyre (educational); and *Wonderful Wish* (winter musical), recorded by Debbie Rigby (educational).
Tips: "We want attractive educational music (around a theme or story)."

GORDON MUSIC CO., INC., P.O. Box 2250, Canoga Park CA 91306. (818)883-8224. Owner: Jeff Gordon. Music publisher, record company (Paris Records). ASCAP/BMI. Estab. 1950. Publishes 10-20 songs/year. Works with composers and lyricists; teams collaborators. Pays standard royalty or arrangements of many kinds can be made between author and publisher.
Affiliate(s): Marlen Music (ASCAP), Sunshine Music (BMI).
How to Contact: Call first and obtain permission to submit a tape or to arrange a personal interview. Prefers cassette or VHS videocassette with 3-4 songs and lyric or lead sheets. Does not return unsolicited material.
Music: Mostly pop, children's and rock; also jazz. Published "New Leave It to Beaver Theme" (by D. Kahn, M. Lenard and M. Greene), recorded by Cabo Frio on MCA Records (jazz); "Jump Bop" and "Big Town" (by T. Lloyd and T. Mockler), recorded by Failsafe on Paris Records (pop-children's).

RICHARD E. GOWELL MUSIC, 45 7th St., Auburn ME 04210. (207)784-7975. Professional Manager: Rich Gowell. Music publisher and record company (Allagash Country Records, Allagash R&B Records, Gowell Records). BMI. Estab. 1978. Publishes 10-30 songs/year; 5-10 new songwriters/year. Works with composers and lyricists. Pays standard royalty.
How to Contact: Submit a demo tape by mail—unsolicited submissions are OK. Prefers cassette with 2-4 songs and lyric sheets. SASE. Reports in 2 months.
Music: Mostly country, pop and R&B. Published "It'll Be a Cold Day" (by L. Pritchett, R. Sanders), recorded by Ray Sanders on Allagash Country (country); "Workin' Overtime" (by R.E. Gowell), recorded by Phil Coley on Allagash Country Records (country); and "You Know I Have to Have Your Love" (by W. Stevenson), recorded by Tina Meeks on Allagash R&B Records (R&B).
Tips: "Have a great song with a professional demo and keep plugging to the right people."

GRADUATE MUSIC LTD., St. Swithun's Institute, The Trinity, Worcester WR1 2PN **United Kingdom**. Phone: (0905)20882. FAX: (0905)726677. Managing Director: David Virr. Music publisher and record company (Graduate Records Ltd.). PRS and MCPS. Estab. 1980. Publishes 25 songs/year; 2 new songwriters/year. Works with composers and lyricists. Pays standard royalty.

How to Contact: Submit a demo tape by mail. Prefers cassette (or VHS videocassette) with 3 songs. SASE. Reports in 2 weeks.
Music: Mostly rock, pop and anything original. Published "Heartache Avenue" (by Tibenham/Mason), recorded by The Maisonettes on Ready, Steady, Go! Records (60's pop); "Who Is Innocent" (by George Borowski), recorded by Guitar George on Graduate Records (rock); and "The Earth Dies Screaming," by UB40 on Graduate Records (reggae).

*GREAT PYRAMID MUSIC, P.O. Box 347008, San Francisco CA 94134. Administrator: Joe Buchwald. Music publisher. BMI. Estab. 1972. Pays standard royalty.
Affiliate(s): GPL Music (ASCAP), Diamondback Music Co.
How to Contact: Submit a demo tape by mail—unsolicited submissions are OK. Prefers cassette or VHS videocassette with 3-4 songs and lyric or lead sheet. "We do not return unsolicited material unless requested." Reports in 2 weeks.
Music: Mostly ballads, light rock and country. Published "Summer of Love" (by Marty Balin), recorded by Airplane on Epic Records (ballad).

*GREEN DOLPHIN MUSIC, Suite 2, 27 Fermanagh Ave., Toronto ON M6R1M1 **Canada**. Creative Director: Don Breithaupt. Music publisher. SOCAN. Estab. 1987. Publishes 20-30 songs/year; publishes 2 new songwriters/year. Works with composers and lyricists. Pays standard royalty.
How to Contact: Write first and obtain permission to submit a tape. No calls. Prefers cassette with 3 songs and lyric sheet. Does not return unsolicited material. Reports in 2 months.
Music: Mostly pop and A/C; also dance and R&B. Published "I Can Read Your Mind" (by Don Breithaupt), recorded by Joe Coughlin on RDR Records (A/C); "It's a Wonderful Life" (by Don Breithaupt), recorded by Rikki Rumball on Green Dolphin Records (A/C); and "Once More with Feeling" (by Don Breithaupt and James Collins), recorded by Carol Medina on Marigold Records (A/C).
Tips: "We're looking for hits, not album cuts!"

*MITCH GREENE MUSIC, 1126 S. Federal Hwy., Ft. Lauderdale FL 33316. (305)764-6921. Owner: Mitch Greene. Music publisher. BMI. Estab. 1990. Publishes 10 songs/year; publishes 4 new songwriters/year. Works with composers and lyricists; teams collaborators. Pays standard royalty.
Affiliate(s): Mitch Green Music (BMI).
How to Contact: Submit a demo tape by mail—unsolicited submissions are OK. Prefers cassette with 5 songs and lyric sheet. Submit typed cover letter with brief bio. SASE. Reports in 1 month.
Music: Mostly R&B, rock and pop; also country, blues and jazz. Published "Twice the Love" (by Greene-Cavalancia), recorded by Being Shopped By Angel Eyes (dance); "Make the Time" (by Greene-Scavone), recorded by Banyan Braves on Lo Conto Records (ballad); and "Here In the Arms of Love" (by Cavalancia-Greene), recorded by MC Nick on Lo Conto Records (R&B).

CHRIS GULIAN MUSIC, 424 West 33rd St., New York NY 10018. (212)704-9626 or 9627. Publishing Director: Margaret Liffey. Music publisher, record producer (Calliope Productions). ASCAP. Estab. 1985. Pubilshes 100 songs/year; publishes 10 new songwriters/year. Hires staff songwriters. Works with composers and lyricists; teams collaborators. Fee derived from percentage of publishing.
Affiliate(s): Calliope Productions.
How to Contact: Write or call first and obtain permission to submit a tape. Prefers cassette (or ½" VHS or ¾" videocassette if available) with up to 4 songs and lyric sheet. SASE. Reports in 6 weeks.
Music: Mostly rock, pop and R&B; also hip-hop, New Jack swing and house.
Tips: "Quality of demos getting better—needs to sound like a complete production."

HAMMER MUSIK GMBH, Christophstr. 38, 7000 Stuttgart 1, **West Germany**. Phone: (0711)6487620-27; FAX: (0711)6487629. Manager: Ingo Kleinhammer. GEMA. Estab. 1982. Music publisher and record company (Avenue and Boulevard). Publishes 100 songs/year; publishes 5 new songwriters/year. Works with composers and lyricists; teams collaborators. Pays standard royalty.
Affiliate(s): Belmont, Sound of the Future and Music Avenue, Westside.
How to Contact: Submit a demo tape—unsolicited submissions are OK. Prefers cassette or VHS videocassette. SAE and IRC.
Music: Mostly dance and disco; also jazz, rock and pop. Published "Perfect," written and recorded by Boys from Brazil on Ariola Records (disco); and "Passion and Pain" (by A. Henningo), recorded by Deborah Sasson on Eighty Eight Records (pop).

*HAMSTEIN PUBLISHING COMPANY, INC., P.O. Box 19647, Houston TX 77224. Contact: Director, Creative Services. Music publisher and record producer (Lone Wolf Productions). ASCAP, BMI, SESAC. Estab. 1968. Publishes 600 songs/year. Works with composers and lyricists; teams collaborators. Pays standard royalty.

Affiliate(s): Hamstein Music Company (ASCAP), Howlin' Hits Music, Inc. (ASCAP), Red Brazos Music, Inc. (BMI), Great Cumberland Music (BMI), Edge O'Woods Music (ASCAP), Risin' River Music (SESAC), Upala Music, Inc. (BMI).
How to Contact: Write first and obtain permission to submit a tape. Prefers cassette or VHS videocassette with 3 songs and lyric sheet. SASE. Reports in 1 month.
Music: Mostly pop/dance, rock and country; also R&B, gospel and instrumental. Published *Recycler* (by Gibbons, Hill, Beard), recorded by ZZ Top on Warner Bros. Records (rock); and *Killin' Time*, written and recorded by Clint Black on RCA/BMG Records (country).

MARK HANNAH MUSIC GROUP, Suite 250, 1075 NW Murray Road, Portland OR 97229. (503)642-4201. Owner: Mark Hannah. Music publisher, record company (Radioactive Records), record producer (Mark Hannah Productions) and Mark Hannah Management/Personal Management. BMI. Estab. 1988. Publishes 5-10 songs/year; publishes 1-3 new songwriters/year. Receives 30 submissions/month. Works with composers and lyricists; teams collaborators. Pays standard royalty.
How to Contact: Write first and obtain permission to submit a tape. Prefers cassette or 15 ips reel-to-reel (or VHS videocassette) with 1-3 songs and lyric or lead sheets. "The more professional the package and presentation, the better." SASE. Reports in 1 month.
Music: Mostly rock, pop and country; also fusion, New Age and jazz. Published *Modern Day Man*, written and recorded by M. Hannah (hard rock LP); "Crazy Fool," written and recorded by M. Harrop (pop ballad single); and "Billy," written and recorded by Syndi Helms (country single); all on Radioactive Records.
Tips: "Listen to the radio and try to emulate the styles and productions of hit records without infringing on copyrights. First impressions are very important. Be as professional as possible."

HAPPY DAY MUSIC CO., Box 602, Kennett MO 63857. President: Joe Keene. BMI. Publishes 12-20 songs/year; publishes 3-4 new songwriters/year. Pays standard royalty.
Affiliate(s): Lincoln Road Music (BMI).
How to Contact: Prefers reel-to-reel or cassette and lead sheet. SASE. Reports in 2 weeks.
Music: Gospel and religious. Published "I'm Going Up," recorded by the Inspirations (gospel); "Glory Bound," recorded by the Lewis Family (gospel); and "Keep Holding On" (by Jans Johnson/Joe Keene) on Cone Records.

HAPPY HOUR MUSIC, 5206 Benito St., Montclair CA 91763. (714)621-9903. FAX: (714)621-2412. President: Judith M. Wahnon. Music publisher and record company (Happy Hour Music). BMI. Estab. 1985. Publishes 5 songs/year; publishes 3 new songwriters/year. Works with composers.
How to Contact: Write first and obtain permission to submit a tape. Prefers cassette. SASE. Reports in 3 weeks.
Music: Mostly jazz and Brazilian contemporary. Published "The New Lambadas" (by Loão Parahyba); "Alemão Bem Brasileiro" (by Olmir Stocker); "Hermeto Pascoal Egrupo" (by Hermeto Pascoal); all on Happy Hour Records (Brazilian).

HAPPY NOTE MUSIC, Box 370, Round Rock TX. (512)448-6362. Owners: Robby Roberson and Karla Farrar. Music publisher. BMI. Publishes 60 songs/year; publishes 20 new songwriters/year. Hires staff songwriters. Works with composers. Pays standard royalty.
How to Contact: Prefers cassette with 3 songs and lyric sheet. "Vocals must be clear." SASE. Reports in 6 weeks.
Music: Mostly country, pop and gospel. Published *There* (by A. Sanifar), recorded by Oh Lamour on Top Secret Records (dance LP); *Angel's Face* (by N. Holley/R. Roberson) and *Walkin* (by Richard Laws/Steve Frye), both recorded by Nick Holley on Lana Records (pop LPs).

*HARMONY STREET MUSIC, Box 4107, Kansas City KS 66104. (913)299-2881. President: Charlie Beth. ASCAP. Estab. 1985. Music publisher, record company (Harmony Street Records), and record producer (Harmony Street Productions). Publishes 30-50 songs/year; publishes 15 new songwriters/year. Receives 50-70 submissions/month. Pays standard royalty.
Affiliate(s): Harmony Lane Music (BMI).
How to Contact: Prefers cassette (or VHS videocassette) with 1-3 songs and lyric sheet or lead sheet. SASE. "Due to the large amount of submissions that we receive we are no longer able to return unsolicited material. We will report within 3 weeks if we are interested."
Music: Country (all types) and gospel (all types). Published "I Came So Close To Lovin You" (by Paulette Howard and Don Bryant), recorded by Anna Jane and Cliff Dawne on Track Records of Canada (country); "Written In His Eyes" (by Paulette Howard and Bob Warren), recorded by J. Ferren on Harmony Street Records (country); and "An Old Fashioned Christmas" (by Charlie Beth), recorded by The Greenes on American Christian Artists Records (Christmas gospel).

Tips: "Start with a good strong hook and build your song around it. A song is only as good as the hook or idea. Make each line and verse say something. Keep your lyrics and melody fairly simple but interesting. Your chorus should stand out musically (usually up-lifting). Demos should be clear and clean with voice out front. Try to keep your songs three minutes or less. Songs must be original both musically and lyrically. Send only your best."

JOHANN HARTEL MUSIKVERLAG, Breitenseerstrasse 82a/4, Vienna, **Austria** 1140. (202)92-47-073. Contact: Hans Hartel. Music Publisher. AKM. Estab. 1985. Publishes 100 songs/year. Publishes 5 new songwriters/year. Hires staff writers. Works with composers and lyricists; teams collaborators. Pays "usual standard royalties per AKM/Austro Mechana."
Affiliate(s): Elisabeth Lindl, Edition Dum Dum, Edition Magnum.
How to Contact: Submit a demo tape by mail—unsolicited submissions OK. Prefers cassette with 3 songs and lyric sheet. SASE. Reports in 1 month.
Music: Mostly pop, German pop and instrumental; also ethno and New Age. Published "Ciao Amore" (by Jonny Blue), recorded by Hans Hartel (German pop single); and "Open Hearts" (by Gunter Rath), recorded by Gunter Rath (pop single), both on Cactus Records.

HEAVEN SONGS, C-300, 16776 Lakeshore Dr., Lake Elsinore CA 92330. Contact: Dave Paton. Music publisher, record company and record producer. BMI. Publishes 30-50 songs/year; publishes 10 new songwriters/year. Pays standard royalty.
How to Contact: Prefers 7½ ips reel-to-reel or cassette with 3-6 songs and lyric sheet. SASE. Reports in 2 weeks.
Music: Country, dance-oriented, easy listening, folk, jazz, MOR, progressive, R&B, rock, soul and top 40/pop. Published "Daddy's Blue Eyes" and "Hurry Home Soldier," both by Linda Rae and Breakheart Pass.
Tips: Looking for "better quality demos."

HEAVY JAMIN' MUSIC, Box 4740, Nashville TN 37216. (615)865-4740. Manager: S.D. Neal. Music publisher. BMI, ASCAP. Estab. 1970. Publishes 10 songs/year; publishes 4-10 new songwriters/year. Works with composers. Pays standard royalty.
Affiliate(s): Sus-Den (ASCAP), Valynn (BMI) and D. Canada (ASCAP).
How to Contact: Submit a demo tape—unsolicited submissions are OK. Prefers 7½ ips reel-to-reel or cassette (or VHS videocassette) with 2-6 songs and lyric sheet. SASE. Reports in 3 weeks.
Music: Mostly rock and country; also bluegrass, blues, easy listening, folk, gospel, jazz, MOR, progressive, Spanish, R&B, soul, top 40/pop and rock-a-billy. Published "Bright Lights" (by D. Derwald), recorded by Dixie Dee on Terock Records (rock-a-billy); "Home Again" (by L. Lynde), recorded by Linda Lynn on Terock Records (country); and "Lonesome and Blue" (by W. Curtiss), recorded by Wade Curtiss on Lee Records (R&B).

*HELLO TOMORROW MUSIC GROUP, Suite 31, 2201 Sycamore Dr., Antioch CA 94509. (415)757-3653. CEO: Don F. Scalercio. ASCAP, BMI, SESAC. Publishes 20-30 songs/year; 2-4 new songwriters/year. Collaborates with composers, A&R and producers. Pays standard royalty.
Affiliate(s): Person to Person Music Publishers (BMI) and Music is Life Publishing (BMI, ASCAP).
How to Contact: Send 3 songs per cassette with lyric sheet attached. All selected tapes will be submitted to major record companies. If tapes are to be returned, mail SASE. Reports in 6 weeks.
Music: Pop rock, R&B, MOR, C&W (all types), gospel. Published "Hal Blaine, world-renown percussionist with 8 grammys, over 200 gold and platinum records"—"Strangers in the Night," recorded by Frank Sinatra; "California Dreamin," recorded by The Mamas and the Papas; "Up Up and Away" (written by Jimmy Webb), recorded by The Fifth Dimension.
Tips: "Submit only top quality material. Be aware of artists' current style and direction."

*HENLY MUSIC ASSOCIATES, 45 Perham St., W. Roxbury MA 02132. (617)325-4594. President: Bill Nelson. Music publisher, record company (Woodpecker Records) and record producer. ASCAP. Estab. 1987. Publishes 5 songs/year; publishes 5 new songwriters/year. Works with composers and lyricists; teams collaborators. Pays standard royalty.
How to Contact: Submit a demo tape by mail—unsolicited submissions are OK. Prefers cassette with 4 songs and lyric sheet. Does not return unsolicited material. Reports in 4 weeks.
Music: Mostly country, pop and gospel. Published "Big Bad Bruce" (by J. Dean), recorded by B.N.O. (pop); "Do You Believe in Miracles" (by B. Nelson), recorded by Parttime Singers (country); and "Don't Hurry with Love" (by B. Nelson and B. Bergeron), recorded by Bill Nelson (country); all on Woodpecker Records.

HEUPFERD MUSIK VERLAG GmbH, Box 30 11 28, Ringwaldstr. 18, Dreieich D-6072 **West Germany**. Phone: (06103)86970. General Manager: Christian Winkelmann. Music publisher. GEMA. Publishes 60-100 songs/year; publishes 2-3 new songwriters/year. Works with composers and lyricists. Pays "royalties after GEMA distribution plan."
Affiliate(s): Edition Payador (GEMA) and Song Bücherei (book series).
How to Contact: Write first and obtain permission to submit. Prefers cassette and lead sheet. SAE and IRC. Reports in 1 month.
Music: Mostly folk, jazz, fusion; also New Age, rock and ethnic music. Published "Valse Mélancolique," written and recorded by Rüdiger Oppermann on Wuntertüte Records (new age); and "A Different Kind of Lovesong" (by Dick Gaughan), recorded by Dick Gaughan and others on Folk Freak Records (folk song).

HICKORY VALLEY MUSIC, 10303 Hickory Valley, Ft. Wayne IN 46835. President: Allan Straten. Music publisher, record company (Yellow-Jacket Records) and record producer (Al Straten Productions). ASCAP. Estab. 1988. Publishes 10 songs/year; publishes 5 new songwriters/year. Receives 20-25 submissions/month. Works with composers and lyricists; teams collaborators. Pays standard royalty.
How to Contact: Submit a demo tape by mail—unsolicited submissions are OK. Prefers cassette with 3-4 songs and lyric sheets. SASE. Reports in 4 weeks.
Music: Mostly country and MOR. "Love Is," written and recorded by April on Yellow-Jacket Records (country); and "A Rose and A Kiss" (by Grogg Straten), recorded by April on Yellow-Jacket Records (country).
Tips: "Accept suggestions and be prepared to rewrite."

HICKY'S MUSIC BMI, 2540 Woodburn Ave., Cincinnati OH 45206. (513)681-5436 or 559-3999. A&R Director: Smiley Hicks. Music publisher. BMI. Estab. 1985. Publishes 8 songs/year; publishes 4 new songwriters/year. Works with composers and lyricists; teams collaborators. Pays royalty.
How to Contact: Write first to get permission to submit a tape. Prefers cassette with 4 songs and lyric sheets. No porno or dirty lyrics, please. SASE. Reports in 4 weeks.
Music: Mostly R&B, gospel and danceable pop; also rap. Published "Stingy" (by Wavier, Hickland), recorded on Vibe Records (dance); and "Heartbeat" (by Barber, Hickland), recorded on Vibe Records (dance).
Tips: "Keep it clean."

HIGH DESERT MUSIC CO., 29512 Peoria Rd., Halsey OR 97348-9742. (503)491-3524. A/R: Karl V. Black. Music publisher, record company (Awsom Record). BMI. Estab. 1976. Publishes 30 songs/year. Receives 50 submissions/month. Works with composers and lyricists; teams collaborators. Pays standard royalty.
Affiliate(s): High Desert Music Co. (BMI), Lovin' Time Music (ASCAP).
How to Contact: Submit a demo tape by mail—unsolicited submissions are OK. Prefers cassette with 1 song and lyric sheet. "Be sure name is on everything submitted." Does not return material. No SASE required.
Music: Holiday music; also gospel. Published "Xmas in Heaven" (by T.D. Bayless), "High Desert Lullaby" (by Don McHan) and "We Know How Love Should Be" (by Higginbotham), all recorded by Higginbotham on Awsom Records (MOR).
Tips: Main problems with submissions include: "Verses don't time in with chorus or each other. A short story should have a beginning, middle and end. The chorus should blend them together. Somewhere out there there are other words besides I love you/blue/true."

HIGH POCKETS PUBLISHING, 527 Meadow Dr., West Seneca NY 14224. (716)675-3974. President: Nicholas Gugliuzza. Music publisher and record company. BMI and ASCAP. Estab. 1979. Publishes 3 songs/year; publishes 2 new songwriters/year. Receives 44 submissions/month. Works with composers. Pays standard royalty.
How to Contact: Submit a demo tape—unsolicited submissions are OK. Prefers cassette (or VHS videocassette) with 1-3 songs and lyric sheet. SASE. Reports in 1 month.
Music: Mostly rock; also bluegrass and blues. Published "Undeniable," "Don't Shoot My Dog" and "Down in the Valley," written and recorded by Paul Benhatzel on High Pockets Records (rock); "Dreamer," written and recorded by Don Trouble on High Pockets Records (rock); and "Empire," written and recorded by Dale Seawel on High Pockets Records (rock).

HIGH-MINDED MOMA PUBLISHING & PRODUCTIONS, Empire Ranch, 2329 Empire Grade, Santa Cruz CA 95060. (408)427-1248. Contact: Kai Moore Snyder. Music publisher and production company. BMI. Pays standard royalty.

How to Contact: Prefers 7½ ips reel-to-reel or cassette with 4-8 songs and lyric sheet. SASE. Reports in 1 month.
Music: Country, MOR, rock (country) and top 40/pop.
Tips: "We have just started to accept outside material."

HISTORY PUBLISHING CO., Box 7-11, Macks Creek MO 65786. (314)363-5432. President: B.J. Carnahan. Music publisher, record company (BOC, History) and record producer (AudioLoft Recording Studios). BMI. Estab. 1977. Publishes 10-15 songs/year; 2 new songwriters/year. Works with composer and lyricists. Pays standard royalty.
How to Contact: Write first and obtain permission to submit a tape. Prefers cassette with 2 songs and lyric sheets. "We prefer not to keep songs on file. Send a good, clean demo with vocal up front." SASE. Reports in 1 month.
Music: Mostly country and gospel. Published "Big Texas Waltz" (by G. Terry), recorded by Merle Haggard on Curb Records (country); "Remember the Alimony" (by J.B. Haynes), recorded by Bill and Roy on Gallery II Records (country); and "Grovespring Swing" (by F. Stowe), recorded by F. Stowe on History Records (country).

HIT & RUN MUSIC PUBLISHING INC., 1841 Broadway, Suite 411, New York NY 10023. Professional Manager: Joey Gmerek. Assistant: Jennifer Chin. Music publisher. ASCAP. Publishes 20-30 songs/year; publishes 2-4 new songwriters/year. Hires staff writers. Works with composers and lyricists; teams collaborators. Pays standard royalty.
Affiliate(s): Charisma Music Publishing USA Inc. (ASCAP), Hidden Pun Music Publishing Inc. (BMI).
How to Contact: Write or call first and obtain permission to submit a tape. Prefers cassette (or VHS videocassette) with lyric sheet. Does not return unsolicited material.
Music: Mostly pop, rock and R&B; also dance. Published "Bad of the Heart," recorded by George LeMond (Columbia); "Up All Night," recorded by Taylor Dayne (Arista Records); "The Flame" (by Nick Graham & Bob Mitchell), recorded by Cheap Trick on Epic (power ballad pop); "The Living Years" (by Mike Rutherford & B.A. Robertson), recorded by Mike & The Mechanics on Atlantic (pop); and "Two Hearts" (by Phil Collins & Lamont Dozier), recorded by Phil Collins on Atlantic (pop).

HITSBURGH MUSIC CO., P.O. Box 1431, 233 N. Electra, Gallatin TN 37066. (615)452-0324. President/General Manager: Harold Gilbert. Music publisher. BMI. Estab. 1964. Publishes 12 songs/year. Receives 30 submissions/month. Pays standard royalty.
Affiliate(s): 7th Day Music (BMI).
How to Contact: Prefers cassette (or quality videocassette) with 2-4 songs and lead sheet. Prefers studio produced demos. Does not return unsolicited material. Reports in 3 weeks.
Music: Country and MOR. Published "Make Me Yours" (by K'leetha Megal), recorded by Kim Gilbert (pop); "I'll Be Hurting" (by Hal Gilbert), recorded by Damon King (pop); and "One Step Away," recorded by Keith Walls (country) all on Southern City Records.

HITSOURCE PUBLISHING, INC., 606 Mulford, Evanston IL 60202. (708)328-4203. President: Alan J. Goldberg. Music publisher. BMI. Estab. 1986. Publishes 12 songs/year; publishes 3-6 new songwriters/year. Receives 150 submissions/year. Works with composers. Pays standard royalty.
Affiliate(s): Grooveland Music (ASCAP): 606 Milford, Evanston IL 60202. (708)328-4203.
How to Contact: Write or call first and obtain permission to submit. Prefers cassette with 2 songs and lyric sheet. SASE. Reports in 10 weeks.
Music: Country, pop, R&B and dance. Published "Right Lane Man" (by Tom Dundee), recorded by Tom Dundee on Flight Records (country); "Daddy Smoked His Life Away" (by Brian Gill), recorded by Brian Gill (country). "Evolution" (by Howard Berkman), recorded by Howard Berkman on Man-Hole Records (rock).
Also publishes material by T.S. Henry Webb, Maurice Irby, Rokko Jans, June Shellene, Dallas Wayne, Charles Stewart and John Sink.
Tips: "Use vocalists and musicians that can sing and play, not only well, but on key, so that the idea of the song is expressed as it should be."

HOLY GRAIL PUBLISHING, Ste. A222, 12609 Dessau Rd., Austin TX 78753. (512)251-0375. Vice President/A&R: Gary A. Coll. Music publisher and record company (Pendragon Records). BMI. Estab. 1987. Publishes 50 songs/year; 5-10 new songwriters/year. Works with composers. Pays standard royalty.
How to Contact: Write or call first and obtain permission to submit a tape. Prefers cassette with 3 songs and lyric sheet. "Include a self-addressed stamped envelope." Does not return unsolicited material. Reports in 2 weeks. "We now (freelance) produce for artists in the Texas area. Please write for terms and prices."

Music: Mostly jazz, rock and pop; also gospel. Published "Leather Lord" (by Tom Kross), recorded by Young Thunder on Pendragon Records (metal); "Wish A Day" (by J. Cook), recorded by Go Dog Go on Pendragon (pop-rock); and "Lion's Creed" (by Tom Kross and S. Wilcox), recorded by Young Thunder on Pendragon Records (metal).

*HOLYROOD PRODUCTIONS, 40 Sciennes, Edinburgh EK9 1NH **Scotland.** Contact: Gordon Campbell. PRS. Estab. 1973. Publishes 30-40 songs/year; publishes 10-15 new songwriters/year. Works with composers.
Affiliate(s): Ad-Chorel Music (PRS), Streamline (PRD).
How to Contact: Submit a demo tape by mail—unsolicited submissions are OK. Prefers cassette with 2-3 songs. SASE. Reports in 1 month.
Music: Mostly pop, dance, MOR; also traditional. Published "Your Wish," written and recorded by Santos on Holyrood Records (dance); "Come Together," written and recorded by Howie J & Co. on REL Records (pop).

HOPSACK AND SILK PRODUCTIONS INC., Suite 1A, 254 W. 72nd St., New York NY 10023. (212)873-2272. Associate Director: Ms. Tee Alston. Music publisher (Nick-O-Val Music). Estab. 1976. Deals with artists and songwriters.
How to Contact: Call first to get permission to submit a tape.
Music: R&B. Published "Hungry for Me Again" written and recorded by Ashford & Simpson on the Orpheus label (ballad).

*HOUSE OF REEDS PUBLISHING CO., #204, 11 Music Square East, Nashville TN 37203. (615)742-8845. Music publisher. Publishes 20 songs/year. Receives 300 submissions/year. BMI. Estab. 1988. Pays standard royalty.
How to Contact: Submit a demo tape, unsolicited submissions are OK. Prefers cassette with 2 songs and lyric sheets. "Send only completed songs—no more than 2—with lyrics and SASE."
Music: Mostly country, MOR and western. Published "Tell Me What You're Gonna Do" written and recorded by Melissa Kay on Reed Records (country).
Tips: "Remember, few hits are found from unsolicited writers. The charts seem to have a significant amount of all kinds of music called country. The 'anything goes' trend may be good news for writers and publishers."

HUMANFORM PUBLISHING COMPANY, Box 158486, Nashville TN 37215. (615)373-9312. Publisher: Kevin Nairon. BMI. Music publisher. Pays standard royalty.
How to Contact: Prefers cassette with 4 songs and lyric and lead sheets. SASE. Reports in 4 weeks.
Music: Mostly pop-oriented country.
Tips: "Please strive for maximum quality when making your demo."

*HYBNER MUSIC, P.O. Box 184, Sutherland Springs TX 78161. (512)947-3176. President: Mark Hybner. Music publisher. BMI. Estab. 1981. Publishes 30 songs/year; publishes 5 new songwriters/year. Hires staff writers. Works with composers and lyricists; teams collaborators. Pays standard royalty.
How to Contact: Submit a demo tape by mail—unsolicited submissions are OK. Prefers cassette with 3 songs and lyric sheet. SASE. Reports in 4 weeks.
Music: Mostly pop, rock and R&B; also country. Published "I'm Coming Home" (by Steve Carson); "Love Hurts" and "Breaking The Ice" (by Rob Wright), all recorded by PM Heat on Emotion Records (rock).

IMAGINARY MUSIC, 332 N. Dean Rd., Auburn AL 36830. (205)821-JASS. Publisher: Lloyd Townsend, Jr. Music publisher, record company (Imaginary Records) and record producer (Mood Swing Productions). Estab. 1982. Publishes 3-5 songs/year; publishes 1-2 new songwriters/year. Receives 10-15 submissions/month. Works principally with composers/performers recording for Imaginary Records. Pays standard royalty.
How to Contact: Submit a demo tape—unsolicited submissions are OK. Prefers cassette or 7½ ips reel-to-reel with 4 songs and lyric and lead sheets. "We do not return submissions unless accompanied by proper return envelope and postage." Reports in 3 months.
Music: Classical, jazz and blues. Published "Hexaphony" (by Somtow Sucharitkul), recorded by Bruce Gaston and Somtow Sucharitkul (improvisational world fusion); and "The Wanderer" (by Les and Mark Lyden), recorded by Nothing Personal (rock); both on Imaginary Records.
Tips: "Know music! How to write it, and how to present it (whether you play it yourself or have another band record it for you)."

Close-up

Matraca Berg
Singer/Songwriter
Nashville, Tennessee

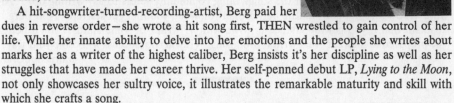

"If there's anything this town would teach you," RCA recording artist Matraca Berg says with a slow smile, "it's (that) you're not going to get around the struggle of learning your craft, of pulling your hair for years and years—just getting beat up all over the place. Eventually, it will come around; it came around to me."

A hit-songwriter-turned-recording-artist, Berg paid her dues in reverse order—she wrote a hit song first, THEN wrestled to gain control of her life. While her innate ability to delve into her emotions and the people she writes about marks her as a writer of the highest caliber, Berg insists it's her discipline as well as her struggles that have made her career thrive. Her self-penned debut LP, *Lying to the Moon*, not only showcases her sultry voice, it illustrates the remarkable maturity and skill with which she crafts a song.

Success came early and easily for Berg, the daughter of a well-known Nashville session singer and songwriter. At 18, her song, "Faking Love," co-written with songwriting legend Bobby Braddock, became a No. 1 duet for T. G. Sheppard and Karen Brooks. Adjusting to the "scrutiny of success" wasn't effortless, however. "It was paralyzing," she remembers. "I didn't write another song for months and months after that. I'd sit down, I'd try and it would just be a total blank. People were coming left and right wanting more songs and I didn't have any—at 18, you don't have a catalog. I wasn't ready, I didn't have enough time to get out there and work with other professionals—it was a fluke."

To gain her equilibrium, Berg left Nashville, joined a rock band in Louisiana and "didn't have another cut for three years." When she decided to return to her hometown, she was ready to work. She landed a writer's contract with Warner Music and managed to get a respectable number of cuts. "The songs I write aren't necessarily good singles," she shrugs. "They're always critically reviewed in the albums, but every now and then I'll get a single." And when she does, it's unforgettable—like Reba McEntire's No. 1 single, "The Last One to Know," which earned Berg a Grammy nomination, or Patty Loveless' hit "I'm That Kind of Girl."

Berg found acclaim easier to handle the second time around. "When 'The Last One To Know' went No. 1, it didn't bother me as much," she admits, "but I'd already had a lot of work under my belt."

The secret behind her successful tunesmithing? "When I started," she smiles, "I decided I was just going to do what I do and do it the best way I could. You can't be a mind reader in this business—you never know what they're going to like. If you go for what the last single was like, if you're shooting for a particular artist or style, you're usually way off because they're going to want to change, to stretch a little further. Your best bet is to do what comes to you and eventually, even if it's not right for this year, it'll come back around. "The Last One to Know" didn't get cut for almost four years; it just sat there waiting. As long as you've got good people working with your catalog, you're pretty safe in doing what feels right."

Despite the touring, the interviews, the photo shoots and TV appearances that are part of a recording career, Berg has managed to keep up her songwriting, something she credits to the discipline she learned during her years as a staff writer. "I've been a slave to a publishing house now for eight years," she explains. "You go in there and you write every day—it's almost a 9 to 5 existence for serious writers. You're trained to crank and tap into that loveable area we call creativity.

"Discipline is important if you want to make a living at songwriting. A lot of people don't make it. It depends on how committed you really are—the success rate is very, very low but it does happen.

"The best thing to do is get to know the songwriting community. Get your tunes together, go to the Bluebird (Cafe in Nashville) or any other place that has open mic writers' nights and get an audition. Go to the songwriters' clubs and listen. The songs that get on the radio aren't half as amazing as the songs you hear from new songwriters. Songwriters in this town never stop going to those clubs because it's just mind-blowing the stuff that comes out of some of these people—it's inspiring. The older writers go check them out because a lot of them are looking for a fresh perspective, a little new blood."

She also recommends what the songwriting community refers to as "writing up." "Always write with somebody a little better than you when you first get started." And Berg is adamant that if you get the chance to write with a "writer of some status," you'd better "be prepared to impress" that writer, promising, "(If you) do, success will come your way."

—Marjie McGraw

IN THE STUDIO PUBLISHING, 5209 Indian Head Hwy., Oxon Hill MD 20745. (301)839-6567. President: Steven Franco. Music publisher. BMI, ASCAP. Estab. 1983. Publishes 12 songs/year; 4-10 new songwriters/year. Hires staff writers. Works with composers and lyricists; teams collaborators.
How to Contact: Submit a demo tape by mail—unsolicited submissions are OK. Prefers cassette with 3 songs. Does not return unsolicited material. Reports in 2 weeks.
Music: Mostly dance, pop, R&B. Published "Girl You Know It's True," recorded by Milli Vinilli on Arista Records (pop); "Work It" (by Lisa Bellamy), on Sire Records.

INSURANCE MUSIC PUBLISHING, P.O. Box 288571, Chicago IL 60628. (312)326-5270. President: Bill Tyson. Music publisher. BMI. Publishes 12 songs/year. Receives 30 submissions/year. Pays standard royalty.
How to Contact: Submit a demo tape—unsolicited submissions are OK. Prefers cassette with 2-4 songs and lyric sheet. Does not return unsolicited material. Reports in 1 month.
Music: Blues, black church/religious/gospel and R&B.

*INTER-AMERICAN MUSICAL EDITIONS, 1889 F St. NW, Washington DC 20006. (202)458-3072. Director: Efrain Paesky. Record producer. Estab. 1978. Works with composers.
How to Contact: Prefers cassette with 3 or so songs. "Include bio (current one) and cassette."
Music: Mostly classical, folkloric and traditional.

INTERPLANETARY MUSIC, 7901 S. La Salle St., Chicago IL 60620; and 584 Roosevelt, Gary IN 46404. (219)886-2003. President: James R. Hall III. Music publisher, record company (Interplanetary Records), record producer and booking agency. Estab. 1972. BMI. Publishes 10 songs/year; publishes 4 new songwriters/year. Works with composers and teams collaborators. Pays standard royalty.
How to Contact: Call or write to arrange personal interview. Prefers cassette. SASE. Reports in 3 weeks.
Music: R&B, top 40/urban contemporary. Published "Make It Last" (by James R. Hall/Lamont Robin) and "No Love" (by James R. Hall/K. Henry), both recorded by Carolyn Hall on Interplanetary Records (pop/R&B).

ISBA MUSIC PUBLISHING, INC., 1327 Boul, St. Joseph Est, Montreal, Quebec H2J 1M1 **Canada**. (514)522-4722. FAX: (514)525-7550. General Manager: Maurice Velenosi. Music publisher, record company (ISBA) and record producer. SOCAN. Estab. 1983. Publishes 50 songs/year; publishes 10 new songwriters/year. Receives 25 submissions/year. Works with composers and lyricists. Pays standard royalty.

How to Contact: Write first and obtain permission to submit a tape. Prefers cassette with 3 songs. Does not return unsolicited material. Reports in 3 weeks.
Music: Mostly pop, rock and dance; also New Age, R&B. Published "Do You Really Love Me" (by Diodati), recorded by Diodation ISBA Records (dance); "Secrets," (by S. Merrick), recorded by HDV on ISBA Records (rap); and "Mlle Anne" (by A. Simard), recorded by Mitson on ISBA Records (pop/dance). Also represents Laymen Twaist, Paris Black, Les B.B. and Revolver,Robert Sart, Robert Leroux, Patsy, Claude De Chevieny.
Tips: "Prepare a good quality demo and work with a singer."

*IT'S REALLY ROB MUSIC, 14016 Evers Ave., Compton CA 90222. (213)438-5656 and (213)635-8522. Publisher: Robert E. Miles. Music publisher. BMI. Estab. 1988. Publishes 8 songs/year; publishes 8 new songwriters/year. Hires staff writers. Works with composers and lyricists; teams collaborators. Pays standard royalty.
Affiliate(s): Janet Marie Recording.
How to Contact: Submit a demo tape by mail—unsolicited submissions are OK. Prefers cassette (or VHS videocassette if available) with lyric sheet. SASE. Reports in 1 month.

*IVORY PALACES MUSIC, 3141 Spottswood Ave., Memphis TN 38111. (901)323-3509. President: Jack Abell. Music publisher, record producer and sheet music publisher. ASCAP. Estab. 1978. Publishes 5 songs/year; publishes 1 new songwriter/year. Works with composers and lyricists; teams collaborators. Pays standard royalty; sheet music: 10% of retail. "Computerized music typesetting services require a 50% deposit."
How to Contact: Write first and obtain permission to submit. Prefers cassette with 2-5 songs and lyric sheet. "Submit simple demo with clear vocal." SASE. Reports in 2 months.
Music: Mostly religious, educational and classical; also children's and folk. Published "Little One," written and recorded by T. Starr on Ivory Palaces (Christian); "Larkin's Dulcimer Book," written and recorded by Larkin Bryant on Ivory Palaces (folk); and "Sonatina Concertata" (by J.M. Spadden), recorded by L. Jackson on Ivory Palaces (classical).

JACLYN MUSIC, 306 Millwood Dr., Nashville TN 37217-1609. (615)366-9999. President: Jack Lynch. Music publisher, producer, recording company (Jaclyn, Nashville Bluegrass and Nashville Country, Recording Companies) and distributor (Nashville Music Sales). BMI. Estab. 1967. Publishes 50-100 songs/year; 25-50 new songwriters/year. Works with composers and lyricists. Pays standard royalties.
Affiliate(s): Jack Lynch Music Group (parent company) and Nashville Country Productions.
How to Contact: Submit a demo tape—unsolicited submissions are OK. Send good quality cassette recording, neat lyric sheets and SASE. Prefers 1-4 selections per tape. Reports in 2 weeks.
Music: Country, bluegrass, gospel and MOR. Published "Adieu False Heart" (by Ray Cline), recorded by Ralph Stanley (bluegrass); "Now She's Gone" (by Richard), recorded by Lynch (country); and "Goldmine of Love" (by J. Lynch and M. Adkins), recorded by Jack Lynch (bluegrass); all on Nashville Country Records.

JANA JAE MUSIC, P.O. Box 35726, Tulsa OK 74153. (918)749-1647. Secretary: Sue Teaff. Music publisher, record company (Lark Records) and record producer. BMI. Estab. 1977. Publishes 5-10 songs/year; publishes 1-2 new songwriters/year. Pays standard royalty.
How to Contact : Submit demo tape by mail—unsolicited submissions OK. Prefers cassette (or VHS videocassette) with 4-5 songs and lyric and lead sheet if possible. Does not return unsolicited material.
Music: Country, pop and instrumentals (classical or country). Published "Fiddlesticks," "Mayonnaise," "Bus 'n'Ditty" (by Steven Upfold), and "Let the Bible be Your Roadmap" (by Irene Elliot), all recorded by Jana Jae on Lark Records.

*JAMBOX MUSIC, 1241 Bay Ave., Ocean City NJ 08226. (609)398-3161. President: Doug Mann. Music publisher. ASCAP. Estab. 1987. Publishes 120 songs/year; publishes 2 new songwriters/year. Works with composers and lyricists; teams collaborators. Pays standard royalty.
How to Contact: Submit a demo tape by mail—unsolicited submissions are OK. Prefers cassette with 2-4 songs and lyric sheet. Does not return unsolicited material. Reports in 4 weeks.
Music: Interested in all types of gospel (pop, R&B, and ballad styles). Published "Sanity Obscure" (by D. Bachman, metal); "Tell" (by R. Campbell, post modern); and "Below the Grave" (by K. Ayers, metal); all recorded by Rex on Rex Records.

JAMMY MUSIC PUBLISHERS LTD., The Beeches, 244 Anniesland Rd., Glasgow G13 1XA, **Scotland.** Phone: (041)954-1873. Managing Director: John D. R. MacCalman. Music publisher and record company. PRS. Estab. 1977. Publishes 45 songs/year; publishes 2 new songwriters/year. Works with composers and lyricists. Receives 70 submissions/year. Pays royalty "in excess of 50%."

How to Contact: "We are not currently auditioning."
Music: Mostly rock, pop, country and instrumental; also Scottish. Published "The Wedding Song," (by Bill Padley/Grant Mitchell), recorded by True Love Orchestra on BBC Records (pop); "The Sheep Song" (by Craig Ferguson), recorded on Polydor Records; and "Glasgow" (by Forbes Masson & Alan Cumming), recorded on Jammy Records. "We also specialize in comedy material with artists Bing Hitler, Craig Ferguson, and Victor and Barry."
Tips: "We are now working with a small writers' roster and it's unlikely we would be able to take new writers in the future. We are now specialising in needledrop music."

JA/NEIN MUSIKVERLAG GMBH, Hallerstr. 72, D-2000 Hamburg 13, **West Germany.** Phone: (40)4102161. General Manager: Mary Dostal. Music publisher, record company and record producer. GEMA. Publishes 50 songs/year; publishes 50 new songwriters/year. Receives 30 submissions/month. Works with composers and lyricists; teams collaborators. Pays 50-60% royalty.
Affiliate(s): Pinorrekk Mv., Star-Club Mv., and Wunderbar Mv. (GEMA).
How to Contact: Submit a demo tape—unsolicited submissions are OK. Prefers cassette (or VHS videocassette) and lyric sheet. SAE and IRC. Reports in 6 weeks.
Music: Mostly rock, pop, MOR and blues. Published "Blue Pianos," written and recorded by J. McShann and A. Zwingenberger on Vagabond Records (boogie woogie); "When I'm Drinkin'," written and recorded by Champion Jack Dupree on Rounder Records (blues); and "Ballade Hour Adrenalin," written and recorded by Axel Zwingenberger on Vagabond Records (blues).
Tips: "Send single-A-side material only, plus photos (if artist). Leave 2-3 seconds space between the songs. Enclose lyrics. We only give negative reply if SAE and IRC is enclosed. Don't be polite!"

JANELL MUSIC, 195 S. 26th St., San Jose CA 95116. (408)286-9840. Owner: Gradie O'Neal. Music publisher. BMI. Estab 1960. Publishes 30-50 songs/year; 20-40 new songwriters/year. Works with composers; teams collaborators. Pays standard royalty.
Affiliate(s): O'Neal and Friend (ASCAP), Tooter Scooter (BMI).
How to Contact: Submit a demo tape by mail—unsolicited submissions are OK. Prefers cassette with 4 songs and lyric sheets. SASE. Reports in 2 weeks.
Music: Mostly top 40 pop, country and rock; also R&B, gospel and New Age. Published "Before and After" (by J. O'Neal), recorded by Sister Suffragette on Rowena (rap); "Texas in Your Eyes" (by S. Ellwanger), recorded by Johnny Gitar on Rowena Records (country); and "Where Are You Now That I Need You" (by C. Friend), recorded by Mel Tillis on Mercury Records (country).

JASPER STONE MUSIC (ASCAP)/JSM SONGS (BMI), P.O. Box 24, Armonk NY 10504. President: Chris Jasper. Vice President/General Counsel: Margie Jasper. Music publisher. ASCAP, BMI. Estab. 1986. Publishes 20-25 songs/year. Works with composers; teams collaborators. "Each contract is worked out individually and negotiated depending on terms."
How to Contact: Submit a demo tape by mail—unsolicited submissions are OK. Prefers cassette with maximum of 3 songs and lyric sheets. SASE. Reports in 6 weeks.
Music: Mostly R&B/pop, rap and rock. Published "Make It Last," recorded by Chaka Khan on Warner Bros. Records; "The First Time," recorded by Chris Jasper on Gold City/CBS Records; and "Dream Lover," recorded by Liz Hogue on Gold City/CBS Records; all written by C. and M. Jasper (R&B).
Tips: "Keep writing. Keep submitting tapes. Be persistent. Don't give it up."

JAY JAY PUBLISHING, 35 NE 62nd St., Miami FL 33138. (305)758-0000. Contact: Walter Jagiello. Music publisher, record company (Jay Jay Publishing) and record producer. BMI. Estab. 1958. One of the founders of NARAS. Publishes 30 songs/year. Pays standard royalty.
How to Contact: Submit a demo tape—unsolicited submissions are OK. Prefers 15 ips reel-to-reel (or VHS videocassette) with 2-6 songs and lyric sheet. SASE. Reports in 2 months.
Music: Mostly popular, country, polkas, waltzes and comedy. "The type of songs that were made in the 50's and 60's. No rock and roll." Published "Sexy Annie" (by W. Jagiello), recorded by Li'l Wally (polka); "Rainbow Polka," written and recorded by C. Siewierski (polka); "How I Love You Darlin'" (by W. Jagiello), recorded by Li'l Wally on Jay Jay Records (waltz); "I'd Love To Call You My Sweetheart" (by W. Jagiello), recorded by Li'L Wally on Jay Jay Records (polka) and "Thrill On The Hill" (by W. Jagiello), recorded by Li'l Wally on Jay Jay Records (polka).
Tips: "Make songs simple lyrics, simple melody, true to life! Send audio demo, sheet music with lyrics."

JELLEE WORKS MUSIC, P.O. Box 16572, Kansas City MO 64133. Phone: 1(800)283-SONG. President: Jimmy Lee. Music publisher, record company (Heart Land Records), record producer (Jellee Works Productions) and songwriter recording services. ASCAP, BMI. Estab. 1983. Publishes 24-36 songs/year; publishes 12-15 new songwriters/year. "Will work one on one with select songwriters to help them get started." Works with composers and lyricists; teams collaborators. Pays standard royalty.

Affiliate(s): Jellee Works Music (BMI) and Jellee Music Works (ASCAP).
How to Contact: Write first to get permission to submit a tape. Prefers cassette with no more than 2 songs per tape (or VHS videocassette) and lyric sheet. SASE. Reports in 6 weeks.
Music: Mostly country, gospel and MOR; also country crossover, rock-a-billy and pop. Published "Attic Full of Love" (by Priscilla McCann), recorded by Jackie Cotter (country); "It's Almost Christmas" (by Ethel Bankston), recorded by Max Berry (pop); and "Footprints" (by Richard Geddes), recorded by Geoff Clark, Max Berry, Jimmy Lee (gospel album); all on Heart Land Records.
Tips: "Learn to be professional. We put out a monthly newsletter dedicated to teaching the grassroots songwriter how to achieve success in this business by not only learning the craft but by opening the right doors."

*JENNACO-ALEXAS PUBLISHING CO. (BMI), 26111 Ynez Rd. B-30, Temecula CA 92390. (714)676-0006. A&R: Patrick Carrington. Music publisher and record company (Alexas Records). BMI. Estab. 1976. Publishes 6-10 songs/year; publishes 2-3 new songwriters/year. Hires staff writers. Works with composers and lyricists. Pays standard royalty.
Affiliate(s): Alexas Music Group (ASCAP).
How to Contact: Submit a demo tape by mail—unsolicited submissions are OK. Prefers cassette or VHS videocassette with 1-3 songs and lyric sheet. SASE. Reports in 2 months.
Music: Mostly country and pop; also New Age and gospel. Published "Daddy's Blue Eyes" (by Linda Noble), recorded by Linda Rae on Bermuda Dunes Records (country); "West Texas Woman," written and recorded by Fats Johnson on Wildomar Records (country); and "Mama You're an Angel in Disguise," written and recorded by Jeff Elder on Alexas Records (country).
Tips: "Be specific about your goals, and present material professionally. We are impressed with good marketing."

JERJOY MUSIC, P.O. Box 1264, Peoria IL 61654-1264. (309)673-5755. Professional Manager: Jerry Hanlon. Music publisher. BMI. Estab. 1978. Publishes 4 songs/year; publishes 2 new songwriters/year. Receives 15 submissions/month. Pays standard royalty.
How to Contact: Submit a demo tape—unsolicited submissions are OK. Prefers cassette with 4-8 songs and lyric sheet. SASE. Reports in 2 weeks.
Music: Country (modern or traditional). Published "E.T. We're Missing You," and "Scarlet Woman" (by Jerry Hanlon), recorded by Jerry Hanlon; "Rainy Nights and Honky Tonks," written and recorded by Jerry Hanlon; and "Fast Women and Expensive Toupes" (by Rodger and Jerry Hanlon), recorded by Jerry Hanlon; all on UAR Records (all country singles).
Tips: "Be 'real' in what you write. Don't submit any song that you don't honestly feel is strong in commercial value."

*JOEYBOY PUBLISHING CO., 3081 NW 24th St., Miami FL 33142. (305)633-7469. Director: Allen Johnston. Music publisher. BMI. Estab. 1985. Publishes 100-150 songs/year; publishes 12-15 new songwriters/year. Receives 50 submissions/month. Works with composers and lyricists; teams collaborators. Pays standard royalty.
Affiliate(s): Joeyboy Publishing Co. (BMI) and Rice & Beans Publishing (ASCAP).
How to Contact: Submit a demo tape by mail—unsolicited submissions are OK. Prefers cassette with no more than 3 songs and lyric sheets. "Type or print lyric sheet legibly please!" SASE. Reports in 6 weeks.
Music: Mostly R&B, rap; also dance, jazz and comedy. Published "One by One" (by Bettina), recorded by Joey Boy (dance); "Take It Off" (by Disco Rick), recorded by The Dogs on J.R. Records (rap); and "I'm the Gangster" (by Patrick Hall), recorded by Gangster Pat on Atlantic Records (rap).
Tips: "Write simple tunes about everyday occurrences."

LITTLE RICHIE JOHNSON MUSIC, 1700 Plunket, Belen NM 87002. (505)864-7441. Manager: Tony Palmer. Music publisher, record company (LRJ Records) and record producer. BMI. Estab. 1959. Publishes 50 songs/year; publishes 10 new songwriters/year. Works with composers. Pays standard royalty.

Market conditions are constantly changing! If you're still using this book and it is 1993 or later, buy the newest edition of Songwriter's Market at your favorite bookstore or order directly from Writer's Digest Books.

Affiliate(s): Little Cowboy Music (ASCAP)and Litlle Richie Johnson Music (BMI).
How to Contact: Submit a demo tape—unsolicited submissions are OK. SASE. Reports in 1 month.
Music: Country, gospel and Spanish. Published "Lisa," "Mona," and "June's Back in Town," written and recorded by Jerry Jaramillo on LRJ Records (C&W).

JOSENA MUSIC, P.O. Box 566, Los Altos CA 94022. President: Joe Nardone. Music publisher. SESAC. Estab. 1983. Publishes 30-40 songs/year; publishes 1-2 new songwriters/year. Hires staff songwriters. Works with composers and lyricists. Pays standard royalty.
Affiliate(s): Reigninme Music (SESAC).
How to Contact: Write first and obtain permission to submit a tape. Prefers cassette with 3 songs and lyric sheet. Does not return unsolicited material. Reports in 1 month if interested.
Music: Mostly Christian rock/pop, pop and gospel; also modern rock. Published "Coming Home," (by Dino Veloz/Joe Nardone), recorded by Joe Nardone (modern Christian rock); "Make Us One" (by Lee Kalem/Joe Nardone); recorded by Lillie Knauls (gospel); and "Go God's Way" (by Mike Palos/Joe Nardone); recorded by Joe Nardone (jazz).
Tips: "Be persistent and send commercial material only."

JUMP MUSIC, Langemunt 71, 9420 AAIGEM, **Belgium.** Phone: (053)62-73-77. General Manager: Eddy Van Mouffaert. Music publisher, record company (Jump Records) and record producer. Member of SABAM S.V., Brussels. Publishes 100 songs/year; publishes 8 new songwriters/year. Works with composers and lyricists. Pays royalty via SABAM S.V.
How to Contact: Submit demo tape by mail. Prefers cassette. Does not return unsolicited material. Reports in 2 weeks.
Music: Mostly easy listening, disco and light pop; also instrumentals. Published "Liefdeverdriet" (by Andy Free), recorded by Jo Vally (ballad); "Zonder Jon Ben Ik Verloren" (by Eddy Govert), recorded by Eddy Govert (ballad); and "Ach Eddy" (by Eddy Govert), recorded by Samantha and Eddy Govert (light pop); all on Scorpion Records.
Tips: "Music wanted with easy, catchy melodies (very commercial songs)."

JUST A NOTE, 1058 E. Saint Catherine, Louisville KY 40204. (503)637-2877. General Partner: John V. Heath. Music publisher (Two John's Music), record companies (Hillview, Estate) and record producer (MVT Productions). ASCAP and BMI. Estab. 1979. Publishes 35 songs/year; publishes 10-15 new songwriters/year. Works with composers and lyricists. Pays standard royalty.
Affiliate(s): Just a Note (BMI) and Two John's Music (ASCAP).
How to Contact: Submit a demo tape by mail—unsolicited submissions are O.K. Prefers cassette, 7½ ips reel-to-reel or VHS videocassette with 3 song and lead sheet. SASE. Reports in 2 weeks.
Music: Mostly pop, country, R&B and MOR; also gospel. Published "The Train," written and recorded by Whiskers on Estate Records (country); "Heartbreak," written and recorded by Johnny Vee on Estate Records (country); and "Sunshine," written and recorded by Adonis on Hillview Records (rock).

JOE KEENE MUSIC CO., P.O. Box 602, Kennett MO 63857. (314)888-2995. President: Joe Keene. Music publisher. BMI. Estab. 1968. Publishes 15-20 songs/year; 3-4 new songwriters/year. Pays standard royalty.
Affiliate(s): Lincoln Road Music Co. (BMI), Happy Day Music Co. (BMI); Cone Music Co. (BMI), Smooth Flight Music Co. (BMI).
How to Contact: Write first and obtain permission to submit a tape. Prefers cassette with 3-4 songs and lyric sheets. SASE. Reports in 2 weeks.
Music: Mostly country, gospel and rock. Published "One Old Guitar Man" (by Gill Blankenship) On KSS Records; "Scars On My Heart" (by Joe Jeene), on Texas Gold Records; and "Goodbyes Are All The Same" (by Gill Blankenship), on KSS Records.
Tips: "Pay attention to the market: write for it."

***KEEP CALM MUSIC LIMITED,** Falcon Mews, London SW12 9SJ **England.** Phone: FAX: (081)675-6313. Professional Manager: Zareena Hussain. Music publisher, record company and record producer (Don't Panic Productions Ltd.). PRS. Member MCPS. Publishes approximately 50-75 songs/year. Works with composers. Pays varying royalty.
Affiliate(s): Yo Bro, Low Spirit (UK office).
How to Contact: Prefers cassette with maximum 5 songs and lyric sheet. Does not return unsolicited material.
Music: Mostly R&B, also black/dance and pop; also high energy and rock. Sub-published "Pump Up the Jam," by Technotronic. Published "Hey You!" (by Titchener/Johnson), recorded by Divine (Hi/NRG), and "House of the Mountain King (by Tichener/Peter), recorded by Klassical Krew (house),

both on Dancetrax Records; and "Jazz House" (by Titchenor), recorded by C.D. Jay on Yo Bro! Records (house).

KEL-CRES PUBLISHING (ASCAP), 2525 East 12th St., Cheyenne WY 82001. (307)638-9894. A&R Manager: Gary J. Kelley. Music publisher, record company (Rough Cut Records) and record producer (Rough Cut Records). ASCAP. Estab. 1989. Publishes 2 songs/year. Receives 100 submissions/year. Works with team collaborators. Pays standard royalty.
Affiliate(s): Kelley-Kool Music (BMI).
How to Contact: Submit a demo tape by mail — unsolicited submissions are OK. Prefers cassette (or VHS videocassette) with 3 songs and lyric sheets. Guitar/piano demo with "words up front" is sufficient. SASE. Reports in 2 months.
Music: Mostly pop, soul and light-rock; also country, R&B and jazz-rock. Published "Just Say No" and "We Got Soul" (by G.J. Kelley & R.P. Creswell), on Rough Cut Records (rock).
Tips: "Be original. Don't copy someone else. We are a brand new company looking for new style songs. It's time record companies quit putting out albums and tapes with B songs (fill songs, junk songs) and only one or two hits. We want to help pave the way for the cassingle (cassette tape with only two hit songs). Don't be afraid to rewrite your songs."

BUTCH KELLY PRODUCTIONS AND PUBLISHING, 11 Shady Oak Trail, Charlotte NC 28210. (704) 554-1162. Manager: Butch Kelly. Music publisher, record company (KAM Executive Records, Fresh Avenue Records and Executive Records), record producer (Butch Kelly Productions), and songwriter. ASCAP, BMI. Estab. 1982. Publishes 10 songs/year; publishes 3 new songwriters/year. Receives 100 submissions/year. Teams collaborators. Pays standard royalty.
Affiliate(s): Music by Butch Kelly.
How to Contact: Write first and obtain permission to submit. Prefers cassette (or VHS videocassette) with 1-6 songs and lyric or lead sheet."Include bio and photo if possible." SASE. Reports in 4 months.
Music: Mostly R&B, pop, rap, gospel and rock; also dance oriented, easy listening, jazz, soul and top 40. Published "Power" (by Butch Kelly), recorded by Sunshine on KAM Records (R&B); "Money," written and recorded by Greg B. on KAM Records (R&B); and "War" (by McCrush), recorded by T.K. on KAM Records (pop).
Tips: "Send songs on Maxell UDS II tapes only."

GENE KENNEDY ENTERPRISES, INC., 3950 N. Mt. Juliet Rd., Mt. Juliet TN 37122. (615)754-0417. President: Gene Kennedy. Vice President: Karen Jeglum Kennedy. Music publisher, record company (Door Knob Records), record producer, distributor and promoter. ASCAP, BMI, SESAC. Estab. 1975. Publishes 30-40 songs/year; publishes 15-20 new songwriters/year. Works with composers and lyricists. Pays standard royalty.
Affiliate(s): Chip 'n Dale Music Publishers (ASCAP), Door Knob Music Publishing (BMI) and Lodestar Music (SESAC).
How to Contact: Prefers cassette or 7½ ips reel-to-reel with 1-3 songs and lyric sheet. "We will not accept anything we have to sign for." SASE. Reports in 3 weeks.
Music: Country and gospel. Published "Praise Ye The Lord" (by Linda Almond), recorded by Dave Jeglum (gospel); "Open For Suggestions" (by Wyndi Harp), recorded by Perry La Pointe (country); and "I've Had Enough of You" (by Johnette Burton), recorded by Debbie Rich (country); all on Door Knob Records.

KENNING PRODUCTIONS, Box 1084, Newark DE 19715. (302)737-4278. President: Kenneth Mullins. Music publisher and record company (Kenning Records). BMI. Publishes 30-40 songs/year.
How to Contact: Prefers cassette. Does not return unsolicited material.
Music: Mostly rock, new wave and country; also blues, jazz and bluegrass. Published "Crazy Mama," written and recorded by K. Mullins; "Work Me Over," (by J. Lehane/K. Mullins), recorded by K. Mullins, both on Kenning Records (both rock); and "This Time," (by K. Mullins).

*KENO PUBLISHING, P.O. Box 4429, Austin TX 78765-4429. (512)441-2422. Owner: Keith A. Ayres. Music publisher and record company (Glitch Records). BMI. Estab. 1984. Publishes 12 songs/year; publishes 10 new songwriters/year. Works with composers and lyricists; teams collaborators. Pays standard royalty.
How to Contact: Write first and obtain permission to submit a tape. Prefers cassette (and/or VHS videocassette if available) with 2-3 songs and lyric or lead sheets. Does not return unsolicited material.
Music: Rock, rap, reggae and pop; also metal, R&B alternative (all types). Published "I Wrote the Note," written and recorded by European Sex Machine (computerized); "Heav It Is," written and recorded by Cooly Girls (rap); and "Kick'em in the Ass" (by Los Deflectors), recorded by Ron Rogers (rock); all on Glitch Records.

*KERISTENE MUSIC, LTD., P.O. Box 390503, Denver CO 80239-1503. (303)399-8403. President: Kenneth H. Smith. Music publisher. BMI. Estab. 1972. Publishes 6-10 songs/year; publishes 6-10 new songwriters/year. Works with composers and lyricists; teams collaborators. Pays standard royalty.
Affiliate(s): Kenneth H. Smith Music (ASCAP).
How to Contact: Submit a demo tape by mail—unsolicited submissions are OK. Prefers cassette (or ½" VHS ¾" videocassette if available) with 3-6 songs and lyric or lead sheets. SASE. Reports in 2 months. "We report only if we're interested."
Music: Mostly C&W, pop and rock; also New Age, R&B and gospel. Published "Love Thang," written and recorded by Armel Jaccaro on D-Town Records (R&B/soul); "American Boy," written and recorded by Scott Mastro on Platinum Sound Records (rock); "Bad" (by K.H. Smith), recorded by Tammy Atwood on D-Town Records (dance); and "Back Streets" (by Ken Finton), recorded by The Fintons on HT Records.

KICKING MULE PUBLISHING/DESK DRAWER PUBLISHING, Box 158, Alderpoint CA 95411. (707)926-5312. Manager: Ed Denson. Music publisher and record company. BMI and ASCAP. Member NAIRD. Publishes 120 songs/year; publishes 7 new songwriters/year. Pays standard royalties.
How to Contact: Write first. Prefers cassette with 1-3 songs. Does not return unsolicited material. Reports "as soon as possible."
Music: Blues (fingerpicking); and folk (guitar/banjo only). Published "The Sweeper," written and recorded by George Gritzbach on KM Records (folk); "Thunder On The Run," written and recorded Stefan Grossman on KM Records (guitar instrumental); and "Pokerface Smile" (by Robert Force), recorded by Force & D'Ossche (country).
Tips: "We publish only material released on our albums. Since we record virtuoso guitar and banjo players, virtually the only way to get a tune published with us is to be such a player, or to have such a player record your song. We don't publish many 'songs' per se, our entire catalog is devoted 95% to instrumentals and 5% to songs with lyrics. As publishers we are not in the market for new songs. This listing is more of a hope that people will not waste their time and ours sending us blue-sky demos of material that does not relate to our very specialized business."

KING CREOLE, INC., Box 92763, Lafayette LA 70509. (318)268-2451. President: Ronald Bob. Music publisher and record company (King Creole and Bahama Records). BMI. Estab. 1987. Publishes 10 songs/year. Publishes 2 new songwriters/year. Works with composers and teams collaborators. Pays standard royalty.
Affiliate(s): Bob Fam Music (BMI).
How to Contact: Submit a demo tape by mail—unsolicited submissions are OK. Prefers cassette with 2 or more songs. "Include a picture." Does not return unsolicited submissions. Reports in 4 weeks.
Music: Mostly R&B, blues and zydeco; also rock and country. Published "Who's to Blame," written and recorded by Jude Taylor on King Creole Records (zydeco); "The Girl is Hot" (by Kip Guilbeaux), recorded by Gratitude Band on Roze Records (R&B); and "Why Baby" (by Jude Taylor), recorded by Burning Flames on King Creole Records (zydeco).

KINGSPORT CREEK MUSIC PUBLISHING, P.O. Box 6085, Burbank CA 91510. Contact: Vice President. BMI. Music publisher and record company (Cowgirl Records). Estab. 1980. Works with composers, lyricists; teams collaborators. Pays standard royalty.
How to Contact: Submit a demo tape—unsolicited submissions are OK. Prefers cassette (or VHS videocassette) with any number of songs and lyric sheet. Does not return unsolicited material. "Include photos and bio if possible."
Music: Mostly country and gospel; also R&B and MOR. Published "Heaven Bound" (gospel), "Only Life" (country) and "Tennessee Cowgirl" (country), all written and recorded by Melvena Kaye on Cowgirl Records.
Tips: "Videocassettes are advantageous."

KITTY GROUP INC., 1-8-4 Ohashi, Meguro-ku, Tokyo 153 **Japan.** Phone: (03)3780-8661. International Division: Hideki Ninomiya. Music publisher and record company (Kitty Records, Inc.). JASRAC. Estab. 1972. Publishes 400 songs/year; publishes 20 new songwriters/year. Employs songwriters on a salary basis. Works with composers and lyricists; teams collaborators. Pays standard royalty.
How to Contact: Prefers cassette with 5 songs and lyric sheet. "Include pictures and a personal history if you can." SAE and IRC. Reports in 1 month.
Music: Mostly rock and pop; also New Age (instrumental). Published "Mama Udongo" (by Kubota), recorded by Toshinobu Kubota (R&B); and "Forever Yours" (by T. Kubota & Oran J. Jones); recorded by Toshinobu Kubota and Alyson Williams (ballad/R&B) both on CBS/Sony Records.
Tips: "Please give a listen to Japanese pop music, if you have an opportunity. Our domestic songwriters are always listening to western pop and dance music."

KOKE, MOKE & NOKE MUSIC, P.O. Box 724677, Atlanta GA 30339. (404)355-0909. General Manager: Bryan Cole. Music publisher, record company (Ichiban). BMI. Estab. 1986. Publishes 30-40 songs/year. Receives 20 submissions/month. Works with composers and lyricists; teams collaborators. Pays standard royalty.
How to Contact: Submit a demo tape by mail—unsolicited submissions are OK. Prefers cassette with 4-5 songs and lyric sheets. "Put contact name and number on the tape." Does not return unsolicited material. Reports back in 2 weeks.
Music: Mostly blues, old R&B style, urban contemporary (dance, rap) and pop. Published "I'd Rather Be Alone" (by Buzz Amato), recorded by Billy Paul on Ichiban Records (R&B); "Straight From Heaven" (by Mark Ford, Joey Johnson), recorded by Rev. Charles McLean on Miracle Records (gospel); "What's the Name of That Thing?" (by Gary "B.B." Coleman), recorded on Ichiban Records (blues).
Tips: "Write from the heart and soul, not the head. Listen to some of our records for direction."

KOZKEEOZKO MUSIC, Suite 602, 928 Broadway, New York NY 10010. (212)505-7332. Professional Managers: Ted Lehrman and Libby Bush. Music publisher, record producer and management firm (Landslide Management). ASCAP. Estab. 1978. Publishes 5 songs/year; publishes 3 new songwriters/year. Receives 50 submissions/month. Pays standard royalty.
How to Contact: Write first and obtain permission to submit. Cassettes (or VHS ½″ videocassettes) with 2 songs maximum and typwritten lyric sheet for each song. SASE. Reports in 2 months.
Music: Mostly soul/pop, dance, pop/rock (no heavy metal), A/C and country. Published "Love Put Some Danger In Me," (Muzak, heavy rotation); "Video! TV-oh!," recorded by Scarlett on Coast-to-Coast Records; "Radio Free Nashville" and "Fool's Mountain," recorded by Jackie Cook on Silverado Records; and "This Heart's Gonna Heal," recorded by Deborah Dotson Livering on Triple R Records.

*KRUDE TOONZ MUSIC, P.O. Box 308, Lansdale PA 19446. (215)855-8628. President: G. Malack. Music publisher. ASCAP. Estab. 1988.
Affiliate(s): Teeze Me Pleeze Me Music (ASCAP).
How to Contact: Write first and obtain permission to submit a tape. Prefers cassette (or VHS videocassette if available) with 3 songs. SASE.
Music: Mostly rock and pop. Published "Tonight," "Fantasy" and "Love Or Lust" (by G. Malack), recorded by Roughhouse on CBS Records (rock).

RALF KRUEGER MUSIKVERLAG, Leopold St. 11-13, 4000 Dusseldorf NRW **Germany** 0211 364545. Director: Ralf Krueger. Music publisher and record company (AIA, BS Modern Music). GEMA. Estab. 1984. Publishes 10 songs/year; publishes 2 new songwriters/year. Works with composers and lyricists; teams collaborators.
How to Contact: Submit a demo tape by mail—unsolicited submissions are OK. Prefers cassette with lyric sheets. SASE. Reports in 1 month.
Music: Mostly new pop, funk/soul and dance, new house; also stylistic fusion. Published "Milky Way Kiss" (by Bop Whopper/Sira Ain), recorded by Frank Ananda on AIA (soul-pop-rap); and "Violins" (by George Rockwood, Victor Lovera, Sira Ain, Ama Donya), recorded by Frank Ananda on AIA (new pop).

L TRAIN PUBLISHERS, 3951 W. 178th Pl., Country Club Hills IL 60477. (312)939-5581. President: Frederick S. Koger. Music publisher and record company. ASCAP. Estab. 1987. Publishes 5 songs/year; publishes 2 new songwriters/year. Hires staff writers. Pays standard royalty.
How to Contact: Write or call to arrange a personal interview. Prefers cassette, 7½ ips reel-to-reel with 3-5 songs and lyric or lead sheets. SASE. Reports in 3 weeks.
Music: Mostly R&B, rap and pop; also rock and gospel. Published "Love Quarrel" (by Frederick S. Koger), recorded by Virgik/Rozlyn on Nickle Plate Records (single); and "Stop Watch," written and recorded by Jam 2000 on Nickle Plate Records (house dance).

THE LANGFORD COVE MUSIC GROUP, 2804 Columbine Place, Nashville TN 37204. (615)383-7209. Creative Director: Ted Barton. Office Manager: Charlie Gore. Music publisher. BMI, ASCAP. Estab. 1986. Publishes 200 songs/year; publishes 3 new songwriters/year. Hires staff writers. Works with composers and lyricists; teams collaborators. Pays standard royalty.
Affiliate(s): Ted Barton Music (BMI), Langford Cove Music (ASCAP).
How to Contact: Submit a demo tape by mail—unsolicited submissions are OK. Prefers cassette with 3 songs and lyric sheet. SASE.
Music: Mostly country, R&B and pop; also gospel. Published "Gonna Be A Long Time" (by Duncan Wayne/Jimmy Tittle), recorded by Jimmy Tittle on Dixie Frog France Records; "Jimmy 55," written and recorded by Joe Sun on Dixie Frog France Records; "Heart Trouble," written and recorded by Ottar Johansen on Sonet Norway Records; "Hank and Bogart Still Live" (by Ted Barton and Joe

Sun), recorded by Joe Sun on Dixie Frog France Records; "You Can't Stop These Trains" (by Ted Barton), recorded by Jimmy Tittle on CBS Records.
Tips: "You're competing with the world. You have to make your songs strong enough to be competitive."

LANSDOWNE AND WINSTON MUSIC PUBLISHERS, #318, 1680 Vine St., Hollywood CA 90028. (213)462-2848. Vice President/President: Lynne Robin Green. Music publisher. ASCAP, BMI. Estab. 1958. Publishes 20 songs/year; publishes 10 new songwriters/year. Receives 75 submissions/month. Works with composers and lyricists. Pays standard royalty.
Affiliate(s): Bloor Music Publishers (BMI); Ben Ross Music (ASCAP); Hoffman House Music Publisher (BMI); For Love Forever Music (ASCAP).
How to Contact: Submit a demo tape by mail—unsolicited submissions are OK. Prefers cassette with 1-3 songs and lyric sheets. SASE. Reports back in 3 weeks. "No calls."
Music: Mostly R&B (ballads), hip-hop, pop-rock; also alternative. Published "Global Music" (by King Errisson), recorded by Ichibar International on Swampdog Productions (fusion/funk worldbeat); "Best of the Dillards," written and recorded by The Dillards on Vanguard Records (classic bluegrass).
Tips: "Write from real life, touch the 'head', 'heart' or 'erogenous zone' with a solid story, and a melody that everyone can recall after a few plays. Be selective. A great, memorable melody and lyric will always be the vehicle into tomorrow's music, no matter what genre."

LANTANA, #308, 9430 Live Oak Pl., Ft. Lauderdale FL 33324. (305)472-7757. President: Jack Bluestein. Music publisher, record company (Twister Records, Quadraphonic Records) and record producer (Quadraphonic Talent/Records). BMI. Estab. 1974. Publishes 50-100 songs/year. Publishes 25-30 new songwriters/year. Works with composers and lyricists; teams collaborators. Pays standard royalty.
Affiliate(s): Pine Island Music (BMI) and Twister Music (ASCAP).
How to Contact: Write first and obtain permission to submit. Prefers cassette or 7½ ips. reel to reel with 3-6 songs and lyric sheet and/or lead sheet. SASE. Reports in 4 weeks.
Music: Country, country pop, R&B and gospel.

LARI-JON PUBLISHING, 325 West Walnut, Rising City NE 68658. (402)542-2336. Owner: Larry Good. Music publisher, record company (Lari-Jon Records) and record producer (Lari Jon Productions). BMI. Estab. 1967. Publishes 20 songs/year; publishes 2-3 new songwriters/year. Receives 100-150 submissions/year. Teams collaborators. Pays standard royalty.
How to Contact: Submit a demo tape by mail—unsolicited submissions are O.K. Prefers cassette with 5 songs and lyric sheet. "Be professional." SASE. Reports in 2 months.
Music: Mostly country, gospel—Southern and '50's rock. Published "Her Favorite Song" and "What Difference Would It Make," written and recorded by Johnny Nace on Lari-Jon Records (country); and "Between the Lies (by Mick Kovar), recorded by Johnny Nace on Lari-Jon Records (country).

LARRIKIN MUSIC, P.O. Box 78, Queen Victoria Building, Sydney NSW 2000 **Australia.** Phone: (02)267-7433. Professional Manager: John Boughtwood. Music publisher. APRA. Works with composers and lyricists.
Affiliate(s): Happy Valley Music (USA), Sleeping Giant (UK), Campbell Connelly (UK) and G. Schirmer (USA).
How to Contact: Write or call to arrange a personal interview. Prefers cassette with 3-4 songs and lyric sheet. SASE. Reports in 3 weeks.
Music: All types.

LAYMOND PUBLISHING CO., INC., Box 25371, Charlotte NC 28229. (704)537-0133. A&R Director: Dwight Moody. Music publisher, record company (Panhandle Records, Lamon Records) and record producer (David and Carlton Moody). BMI, ASCAP. Publishes 60-70 songs/year; publishes 20 new songwriters/year. Receives 1200 submissions/year. Works with composers. Pays standard royalty.
Affiliate(s): CDT Productions and Laymond Publishing Co.
How to Contact: Write first and obtain permission to submit. Prefers cassette. Does not return unsolicited material. Reports in 10 weeks.
Music: Mostly country, R&B and rock; also gospel. Published "Too Good To Turn Back Now" (by Rick Bowles), recorded by Vannesa Parker (pop); "If It Ain't Love," recorded by Moody Bros. (pop); "Listen Up Saddam," (by Desert Storm) (pop); and "I'm Through" (by Mildred Beard), recorded by Showdenes (R&B); all on Lamon Records.

LCS MUSIC GROUP, INC., P.O. Box 7409, Dallas TX 75209. (214)353-0472. Contact: Publishing Assistant. Music publisher. BMI, ASCAP, SESAC. Works with composers. Pays standard royalty.
Affiliate(s): Bug and Bear Music (ASCAP), Chris Christian Music (BMI), Court and Case Music (ASCAP), Home Sweet Home Music (ASCAP) and Monk and Tid Music (SESAC).
How to Contact: Submit a demo tape by mail—unsolicited submissions are OK. Prefers cassette with lyric sheet (only necessary if the words are difficult to understand). "Put all pertinent information on the tape itself. Such as how to contact the writer." Does not return unsolicited material.
Music: Mostly contemporary Christian and inspirational. Published "Thy Word" and "Find A Way" (by Amy Grant/M.W. Smith), recorded by Amy Grant on Myrrh Records (contemporary Christian); and "Hosanna" (by Gersmehl/Smiley), recorded by Sandi Patti on Word Records (inspirational).

LE MATT MUSIC, LTD., %Stewart House, Hillbottom Rd., Highwycombe, Buckinghamshire HP124HJ **England.** Phone: 063081374. FAX: 063081612. Art Director: Xavier Lee. Music publisher, record company and record producer. MCPS, PRS. Member MPA, PPL. Estab. 1971. Publishes 30 songs/year; publishes 10 new songwriters/year. Receives 60 submissions/month. Works with composers, lyricists; teams collaborators. Pays standard royalty.
Affiliate(s): Lee Music, Ltd., Swoop Records, Grenoville Records, Check Records, Zarg Records, Pogo Records, Ltd., R.T.F.M., R.T.L. Music.
How to Contact: Prefers 7½ or 15 ips reel-to-reel or cassette (or VHS/Beta 625/PAL system videocassette) with 1-3 songs and lyric and lead sheets. "Make sure name and address are on reel or cassette." SAE and IRC. Reports in 6 weeks.
Music: All types. Published "Not This Time" (by Daniel Boone), recorded by Lelly Boone (pop/jazz); "Together Again" (by Daniel Boone), recorded by Lelly and Daniel Boone (pop); and "Street Fighters" (by Daniel Boone), recorded by Daniel Boone (rock); all on Swoop Records.

LEMON SQUARE MUSIC, Box 671008, Dallas TX 75367-8008. (214)750-0720. A&R: Mike Anthony. Music publisher. ASCAP. Estab. 1979. Publishes 10 songs/year. Teams collaborators. Pays standard royalty.
Affiliate(s): Friends of the General Music (BMI).
How to Contact: Write first and obtain permission to submit a tape. Prefers cassette with 1-2 songs and lyric sheets. "We do not return unsolicited material. Will contact only if interested." Reports in 6 weeks.
Music: Mostly country and gospel. Published "He's My Gentleman" (by Stan Ratlift), recorded by Audie Henry on RCA Records (country); "Like Goin' Home" (by Allison Gilliam), recorded by Susie Calvin on Canyon Creek Records (pop-country).

*LEO-VINCENT MUSIC/OMINI-PRAISE MUSIC, 5934 Blairstone Dr., Culver City CA 90230. (213)558-8168. Owner: Leonardo Wilborn. Music publisher and record producer (LVW Entertainment). ASCAP, BMI. Estab. 1987. Publishes 9-12 songs/year; publishes 2 new songwriters/year. Works with composers and lyricists; teams collaborators. Pays standard royalty.
Affiliate(s): Leo-Vincent Music (ASCAP), Omni-Praise Music (BMI).
How to Contact: Write first and obtain permission to submit a tape, or to arrange a personal interview. Prefers cassette or VHS videocassette with 3 songs and lyric or lead sheet. "Doesn't need to be overproduced. Just a good clean demo. We'll let you know if more is needed." SASE. Reports in 6-8 weeks.
Music: Mostly nu-inspirational, R&B/dance, gospel; also concert pieces (for large ensembles), choral music and pop/country. Published "Lift Every Voice & Sing" (by J. Weldon Johnson, Arr: L. Wilborn), recorded by Federation of Love (gospel); "Free Again" (by Terence Thomas, Tameron Walker), recorded by Federation of Love (inspirational); and "Victory Is Won" (by Esau Joyner, Jr.), recorded by Daily Bread (Christian); all on IHS Records.
Tips: "Write strong material. Keep in touch every 6 months or so. Be patient, production schedules vary. Write lyrics that inspire with good story lines."

LEXINGTON ALABAMA MUSIC PUBLISHING CO., Rt. 1, Box 40, Lexington AL 35648. President: Darrell Glover. Music publisher, record company (Lamp Records), and record producer (Lamp Production Co.). BMI. Estab. 1981. Publishes 30 songs/year; publishes 3-5 new songwriters/year. Receives 20 submissions/month. Works with composers and lyricists; team collaborators. Pays standard royalty.
How to Contact: Prefers cassette with 3 songs and lyric sheet. Does not return unsolicited material. Reports in 1 month "only if material can be used by company."
Music: Mostly country, pop and R&B; also rock and gospel. Published "Off The Wall" (by Curtis Hall), recorded by Apul on Lamp Records (southern rock); "Whoa" (by Jeff Quillen, C. Hall), recorded by Apul on Lamp Records (rock); and "You Are To Me" (by Curtis Hall), recorded by Apul on Lamp Records (pop).
Tips: "We want strong hooks, unusual ideas, and a new way of expressing old ideas."

LIGHT FORCE MUSIC, P.O. Box 858, Sonoma CA 95476. (707)762-4858. Director of A&R: Shelly Trumbo. Music publisher (Victory, Bay City) and record producer (Victory Media Group). ASCAP. Estab. 1987. Publishes 5 songs/year. Receives 2 submissions/month. Works with composers; teams collaborators. Pays standard royalty.
Affiliate(s): Bay City Music (ASCAP).
How to Contact: Write first and obtain permission to submit a tape. Prefers cassette with 3 songs. Does not return unsolicited material. Reports in 3 months.
Music: Mostly rock, pop and Christian rock; also dance and folk/rock. Published "2 Empty Hearts" (by S. Trumbo), recorded by Shelly T. on Victory Records (rock); "New One" (by R. Prifer), recorded by Justin Sayne on Bay City Records (rock); and "Edge of the Storm" (by M. Allan/S. Trumbo), recorded by Shelly T. on Victory Records (rock).

LINEAGE PUBLISHING CO., Box 211, East Prairie MO 63845. (314)649-2211. (Nashville branch: 38 Music Sq. E., Nashville TN 37203. (615)255-8005.) Professional Manager: Tommy Loomas. Staff: Alan Carter and Joe Silver. Music publisher, record producer and record company. BMI. Pays standard royalty.
How to Contact: Query first. Prefers cassette with 2-4 songs and lyric sheet; include bio and photo if possible. SASE. Reports in 1 month.
Music: Country, easy listening, MOR, country rock, and top 40/pop. Published "Yesterdays Teardrops," and "Round & Round," (by Phil and Larry Burchett), recorded by the Burchetts on Capstan Records (country).

*LIN'S LINES, #434, 156 Fifth Ave., New York NY 10010. (212)691-5631. President: Linda K. Jacobson. Music publisher. ASCAP. Estab. 1978. Publishes 4 songs/year; publishes 4 new songwriters/year. Works with composers and lyricists; teams collaborators. Pays standard royalty.
How to Contact: Submit a demo tape by mail—unsolicited submissions are OK. Prefers cassette or VHS or ¾" videocassette with 3-5 songs and lyric or lead sheet.; SASE. Reports in 6 weeks.
Music: Mostly rock, pop and rap; also world music, R&B and gospel.

*LINWOOD MAXWELL MUSIC, P.O. Box 374, Fairview NJ 07022. (201)941-3987. Vice President Song Review: Irma Proctor. Music publisher (G.G. Music/ASCAP and Wazuri Music/BMI) and record producer (Cliffside Music, Inc.). Publishes 2-4 new songwriters/year. Teams collaborators. Pays standard royalty.
Affiliate(s): Linwood Maxwell Music (BMI), G.G. Music (ASCAP), Wazuri Music (BMI).
How to Contact: Submit a demo tape by mail—unsolicited submissions are OK. Prefers cassette with 2 songs. SASE.
Music: Mostly pop, R&B pop and gospel; also jazz and dance. Published "Maria Song" (by Linwood Simon), recorded by Gloria Gaynor on New Music (reggae); "Reason for the Season," written and recorded by Gloria Gaynor on Welcome Records (pop); and "Together We Can" (by L. Simon and Gloria Gaynor), recorded by Gloria Gaynor on New Music Records (pop).

LION HILL MUSIC PUBLISHING CO. (BMI), P.O. Box 110983, Nashville TN 37222-0983. (615)731-6640. Publisher: Wayne G. Leinsz. Music publisher. BMI. Estab. 1988. Publishes 40-50 songs/year; publishes a few new songwriters/year. Receives 100 submissions/year. Works with composers and lyricists; teams collaborators. Pays standard royalty.
How to Contact: Submit a demo tape by mail—unsolicited submissions are OK. Prefers cassette with 3 songs and lead sheets. SASE. Reports back in 4 weeks.
Music: Mostly country, pop, humorous; also easy rock, gospel and bluegrass. Published "Seems Like It Was Only Yesterday" (by Rudy Holiday), recorded by Hank Suzuki on Laurie Records (country); "Jesus Paid For It All" (by Bonnie Kirschner) and "The Devil Ain't Got Me Yet" (by Irene Elliott), both recorded by In One Accord on Psalms Records (both gospel).

*LION PUBLISHING, P.O. Box 71231, Milwaukee WI 53211-7331. (414)332-7474. President: Dr. Martin Jack Rosenblum. Music publisher and record company (Roar Records). Estab. 1969. Receives 20 submissions/month. Works with composers.
Affiliate(s): Roar Recording and American Ranger Incorporated.
How to Contact: Write or call first and obtain permission to submit a tape. Prefers cassette with an unspecified number of songs and lyric sheet. "No unsolicited submissions with inquiry."
Music: Mostly country, blues and country rock.
Tips: "Call first or write."

LITA MUSIC, 3609 Donna Kay Dr., Nashville TN 37211. (615)331-6056. Owner and President: Justin Peters. Music publisher. ASCAP. Estab. 1986.
How to Contact: Submit a demo tape by mail—unsolicited submissions are OK. Prefers cassette with 10 or less songs and lyric or lead sheets. Does not return unsolicited material. "Place code 525 on the left hand corner of any package submitted."
Music: Mostly pop, gospel and country; also reggae music. Published "Lost In The Shadow," recorded by Steven Curtis Chapman on Sparrow Records; "Tested By Fire," recorded by Al Denson on Benson Records; and "Somebody Prayed" (co-written by Mark Comden), recorded by Larry Howard on Forefront Records.

LIVE NOTE PUBLISHING (BMI), P.O. Box 16, Hampton Va 23669. (804)838-6930. A&R: Tom or Fonda Breeden. Music publisher. BMI. Estab. 1981. Publishes 20 songs/year; publishes 10 new song-writers/year. Works with composers and lyricists; teams collaborators. Pays standard royalty of 50%.
How to Contact: Submit a demo tape by mail—unsolicited submissions are OK. Prefers cassette with 2-3 songs and lyric sheets. SASE. Reports back in 4 weeks.
Music: Mostly country, rock and pop; also reviewing all types. Published "You Never Told Me" (by Doc Holiday and Tom Breeden), recorded by Savannah Ashley on Tug Boat Records (country); "It's The Music" (by Judith Guthro and Tom Breeden), recorded by Ronn Craddock on Door Knob Records (country); "Juke Box King" (by E. Wohanka, J. Guthro and T. Breeden), recorded by Kevin Irwin on Door Knob Records (country); and "But I Lie," written and recorded by Richie Balin on Door Knob Records (country).
Tips: "Send good quality tapes and typed lyric sheets, and always be sure to include address and phone numbers to contact."

LODESTAR MUSIC, A DIVISION OF GENE KENNEDY ENTERPRISES, INC., 3950 N. Mt. Juliet Rd., Mt. Juliet TN 37122. (615)754-0417. Contact: Karen Jeglum Kennedy. Music publisher, record company (Door Knob Records, Society Records), record producer (Gene Kennedy Enterprises, Inc.). SESAC. Estab. 1978. Publishes 5-10 songs/year; publishes 1-3 new songwriters/year. Works with composers and lyricists. Pays standard royalty.
Affiliate(s): Chip 'n' Dale Music Publishers, Inc. (ASCAP), Door Knob Music Publishing, Inc. (BMI).
How to Contact: Submit a demo tape by mail—unsolicited submissions are OK. Prefers cassette with 1-3 songs and lyric sheet. Include SASE for tape return and/or response. Send regular mail. SASE. Reports in 2 weeks.
Music: Mostly country and gospel. Published "Me Without You" (by Lance Middlebrook), recorded by Debbie Rich; "How I Love You In The Morning" (by Ed Jones and Elaine Jones), recorded by Joann Wintermute; both country, recorded on Door Knob Records.
Tips: "Respect our submission policy and keep trying."

LOMAN CRAIG MUSIC, P.O. Box 2955, Nashville TN 37219. (615)331-1219 or (615)331-3703. President: Loman Craig. Vice President: Nancy Craig. Engineer/Producer: Tommy Hendrick. Music publisher, record company (Bandit Records), record producer (Loman Craig Productions). BMI, ASCAP, SESAC. Estab. 1979. Publishes 15 songs/year; publishes 5 new songwriters/year. Works with composers and lyricists. Pays standard royalty.
Affiliate(s): Outlaw Music of Memphis (BMI), Doulikit Music (SESAC), and HIS Records.
How to Contact: Submit a demo tape by mail—unsolicited submissions are OK. Prefers cassette with 2-3 songs and lyric sheet. "Does not have to be a full production demo. Can be guitar/piano vocal demo." SASE. Reports in 3 weeks.
Music: Mostly country and pop; also bluegrass and gospel. Published "Love Me As Long" (by Craig-Craig), recorded by The Arbuckles on Bandit Records (bluegrass); "Mansion-Mind," written and recorded by Pat Riley on Bandit Records (pop); and "High on Music," written and recorded by Allen Gray on Bandit Records (country rock).

LONNY TUNES (BMI), P.O. Box 460086, Garland TX 75046. President: Lonny Schonfeld. Music publisher. BMI. Estab. 1988. Publishes 6-8 songs/year; publishes 2-3 new songwriters/year. Works with composers. Pays standard royalty.
How to Contact: Submit a demo tape by mail—unsolicited submissions are OK. Prefers cassette with 3-5 songs and lyric sheets. Make sure lyric and melody stand out. SASE. Reports in 6-8 weeks.
Music: Mostly pop, rock, children's and country. Published "Burning Bright" written and recorded by John Megert (pop) and "Living For Love" (by John Megert), recorded by Paul McCarthy (pop), both on Puzzle Records; and "The Little Bitty Chicken," by Charles Goodman (children's).
Tips: "Don't worry about market trends—a good song is a good song. Finding a market for a song is our job. Many artists are looking for outside material again. The songwriter is again becoming the backbone of the music industry. Send us your best. If you don't think it's great no one else will either."

THE LORENZ CORPORATION, 501 E. Third St., Dayton OH 45401-0802. (513)228-6118. Corp. Vice President: Larry F. Pugh. Music Publisher. ASCAP, BMI. Estab. 1890. Publishes 500 songs/year; 10 new songwriters/year. Hires staff writers. Works with composers and lyricists; teams collaborators. Pays standard royalty.
How to Contact: Submit manuscript (completely arranged); tape not necessary. SASE. Reports in 4 months.
Music: Interested in religious/Christian, high school choral and organ/piano music; also band music.

*LOUD & PROUD MUSIC, 6224 15th Ave., Brooklyn NY 11219. (718)234-0922. Contact: Ken Kriete. Music publisher. ASCAP. Estab. 1990. Publishes 12-24 songs/year; publishes 1-2 new songwriters/year. Works with composers; teams collaborators. Pays standard royalty.
How to Contact: Submit a demo tape by mail—unsolicited submissions are OK. Prefers cassette with 3 songs and lyric sheet. SASE. Reports in 2 weeks.
Music: Mostly rock, pop and country; also rap and dance. Published "Forever," "Still in Love" and "Shadow in the Dark," all written and recorded by Mitch Malloy on RCA/BMG Records (rock).

LOUX MUSIC PUBLISHING CO., 2 Hawley Lane, Hannacroix NY 12087-0034. (518)756-2273. Contact: Editorial Review Committee. Music publisher. ASCAP. Estab. 1976. Publishes 40 songs/year; publishes varying number of new songwriters/year. Receives 15 submissions/month. Works with composers. Pays 5-10%.
How to Contact: Write first and obtain permission to submit a tape. Prefers cassette. SASE. Reports in 4 months.
Music: Mostly classical, Medieval and Renaissance. Published "Dorian Weave" (by Catherine Blyther) for S.A.T. Records; "Jasmina" (by Thomas Sears) for AAA Records; and "Sonatina in C Major" (by Richard Eastman) for S.A.T. Records.
Tips: "We are publishers of music for early instruments, recorder and/or voice."

LOVEFORCE INTERNATIONAL, P.O. Box 241648, Los Angeles CA 90024. Submissions Manager: T. Wilkins. Music publishers, record company and international record promotion company. BMI. Estab. 1979. Publishes 5-10 songs/year; publishes 2 new songwriters/year. Receives 60 submissions/month. Pays standard royalty.
How to Contact: Write first and obtain permission to submit. Prefers cassette (or VHS videocassette) with 2 songs maximum and lyric sheet. "SASE a must." Reports in 6 weeks.
Music: Mostly pop, rock and R&B; also ballads, country and gospel. Published "One World One People," (reggae); "The Skids," "Blues Rock" and "Godfather of Love," recorded by Bandit on Loveforce International Records (soul/rap).
Tips: "We prefer Master quality demos and working with writer/artists who put their own records out. If you want a response, enclose an SASE."

LOVEY MUSIC, INC., P.O. Box 630755, Miami FL 33163. (305)935-4880. President: Jack Gale. Music publisher. BMI. Estab. 1981. Publishes 25 songs/year; publishes 10 new songwriters/year. Receives 200 submissions/year. Pays standard royalty.
Affiliate(s): Cowabonga Music, Inc. (ASCAP) and Lovey Music, Inc. (BMI).
How to Contact: Submit a demo tape by mail—unsolicited submissions are OK. Prefers cassette or VHS videocassette with 1-2 songs and lyric sheets. Does not return unsolicited material. "We report only if we can use a song."
Music: Mostly country crossover and country. Published "Southern Belle" (by Helms and Hall), recorded by Bobby Helms on Playback Records (country); "One Night A Week" (by Paul Hotchkiss), recorded by Robin Right on Roto Noto Records (country); and "Here We Lie" (by Gary Adams), recorded by Bonnie Guitar on Playback Records (country).

THE LOWERY GROUP of Music Publishing Companies, 3051 Clairmont Rd. NE, Atlanta GA 30329. (404)325-0832. General Professional Manager: Cotton Carrier. Music publisher. ASCAP, BMI. Estab. 1953. Publishes 100 songs/year; publishes varying number of new songwriters/year. Works with composers and lyricists. Pays standard royalty.
Affiliate(s): Lowery Music Co., Inc. (BMI); Low-Sal, Inc. (BMI); Low-Twi, Inc. (BMI); Low-Ab Music (BMI); Low-Bam Music (BMI); Low-Ja Music (BMI); Low-Rico Music (BMI); Low-Thom Music (BMI); Eufaula Music (BMI); Steel City Music (BMI); Wonder Music (BMI); Eternal Gold Music (BMI); New Testament Music (BMI); Songs of Faith (BMI); Brother Bill's Music (ASCAP); Miss Delta Music (ASCAP); Terri Music (ASCAP); and Holy Ground Music (ASCAP).
How to Contact: Prefers cassette with 3 songs and lyric sheet. Does not return unsolicited material. "No response unless we wish to publish the song."
Music: Mostly country, MOR and pop; also gospel, rock and New Age. Published "Every Time You Go Outside I Hope It Rains," by The Burch Sisters on Mercury Records; "Old Bridges Burn Slow" (by Joe South/Jerry Meaders/Sanford Brown), recorded by Billy Joe Royal on Atlantic American

Records; "Don't It Make You Wanta Go Home" (by Joe South), recorded by Butch Baker on Mercury Records (all country). Co-published "I Still Believe," recorded by Lee Greenwood, "Desperado Love" (by Conway Twitty), "The Flag's on Fire" (by Bertie Higgins), and 2 successful recordings by Waylon Jennings and Sammy Johns.

LUCKY'S KUM-BA-YA PUBLISHING CO., Box 6-9283 Evergreen, Brohman MI 49312. (616)745-2270. President: Ross "Lucky" Fulton. Music publisher and record company. ASCAP. Estab. 1976. Publishes 10-30 songs/year. Works with composers.
How to Contact: Write first and obtain permission to submit.
Music: Country, gospel and pop/light rock. Published "My First Truck (Kenworth 53)" (country); "The Junkyard Blues Band" (R&B); and "Princess Among Angels" (country), all written by R. Fulton.

HAROLD LUICK & ASSOCIATES MUSIC PUBLISHER (BMI), P.O. Box B, Carlisle IA 50047. (515)989-3676. President: Harold L. Luick. Music publisher, record company, record producer and music industry consultant. BMI. Publishes 25-30 songs/year; publishes 5-10 new songwriters/year. Receives 800 submissions/year. Pays standard royalty or will negotiate with established writer.
How to Contact: Write or call first about your interest or arrange a personal interview. Prefers cassette with 3-5 songs and lyric sheet. SASE. Reports in 3 weeks.
Music: Traditional country and hard core country. Published "Mrs. Used To Be" (by Joe E. Harris), recorded by River City Music, Inc. on River City Music Records (country); "Ballad of Deadwood S.P.," written and recorded by Don Laughlin on Kajac Records (historical country).
Tips: "Ask yourself these questions: Does my song have simplicity of lyric and melody? Good flow and feeling? A strong story line? Natural dialogue? Hook chorus, lyric hooks, melody hooks? If it doesn't, then why should a publisher or A&R person take the time to listen to it? Most material that is sent to us is also sent simultaneously to several other publishers. If we are going to publish a song, the writer must assure us that the same music submission isn't floating around out there somewhere."

*LYNCLAY PUBLICATIONS INC., 19938 Patton, Detroit MI 48219. (313)533-4506. Music publisher. ASCAP. Estab. 1989. Publishes 15 songs/year; publishes 1 new songwriter/year. Hires staff writers. Works with composers and lyricists; teams collaborators. Pays standard royalty.
How to Contact: Submit a demo tape by mail—unsolicited submissions are OK. Prefers cassette or VHS videocassette with minimum 3 songs and lyric and lead sheet. SASE. Reports in 1-2 weeks.
Music: All types. Published "Loose Lips" (by A. Taylor), recorded by Twan (pop); "Sally" (by A. Taylor), recorded by Twan (pop); and "Saucy Tip" (by L. Clay), recorded by Mr. Mill (rap); all on Torrid Records.

MAC-ATTACK PUBLISHING, Suite 6J, 14699 NE 18th Ave., N. Miami FL 33181. (305)947-8315. President: Michael J. McNamee. Music publisher and record producer (Mac-Attack Prod., Inc.). ASCAP. Estab. 1988. Publishes 3-10 songs/year; publishes 1-5 new songwriters/year. Receives 20-30 submissions/month. Works with composers and lyricists. Pays standard royalty.
How to Contact: Write or call first to get permission to submit a tape. Prefers cassette and VHS videocassete with a maximum of 3 songs and lyric sheet. SASE. Reports in 1-2 months.
Music: Mostly pop, rock, alternative; also R&B, New Age and new contemporary. Published "Give Me A Sign" and "The Face of Fear," written and recorded by Razor on Kinetic Records; and "What Time Is It" (by R. Rodrigeuz), recorded by D.K.Y. on Epic Records (dance/alternative).
Tips: "Less is more and simple is better. Great songs can usually be accompanied by just a guitar or a piano—think about it."

JIM McCOY MUSIC, Rt. 2, Box 114 H, Berkeley Springs WV 25411. Owners: Bertha and Jim McCoy. Music publisher, record company (Winchester Records) and record producer (Jim McCoy Productions). BMI. Estab. 1973. Publishes 20 songs/year; publishes 3-5 new songwriters/year. Receives 400 submissions/year. Pays standard royalty.
Affiliate(s): Alear Music and New Edition Music (BMI).
How to Contact: Submit a demo tape—unsolicited submissions are OK. Prefers cassette, 7½ or 15 ips reel-to-reel (or VHS or Beta videocassette) with 6 songs. Does not return unsolicited material. Reports in 1 month.
Music: Mostly country, country/rock and rock; also bluegrass and gospel. Published "This Woman" (by J. McCoy), recorded by Ronnie Flook; "She Loved Me Out of My Mind," written and recorded by D.Campbell; both on Winchester Records (country); "Leavin" (by Red Steed); "Same Ole Town" and "If I Threw Away My Pride" (by R. Lee Gray); and "One Time" and The Takin' Kind" (by J.B. Miller).

*DANNY MACK MUSIC, 3484 Nicolette Dr., Crete IL 60417. (708)672-6457. General Manager: Daniel H. Mackiewicz. Music Publisher and independent record producer. Estab. 1984. Publishes 1-8 songs/year. Pays standard royalty.

Affiliate(s): Syntony Publishers (BMI).
How to Contact: Submit a demo tape. Unsolicited submissions will not be returned. Prefers cassette, acetate or phono records with no more than 4 songs and typed lyric sheets. SASE. Reports in 2 weeks.
Music: Mostly country, gospel, (southern/country) polka. Published "He'll Lift You Up" (by Danny Mack), recorded by The Journeymen on Discovery Records (gospel); "No More Rocky Roads" (by Danny Mack), recorded by The Journeymen on Discovery Records (gospel); "Everything's Coming Up Roses" (by Danny Mack), recorded by Eddie Blazonczyk and Lenny Gomulka on Briar Hill Records (polka duet); and "Thank You Polka" (by Lenny Gomulka).

*MACMAN MUSIC, INC./FRESH FORCE MUSIC, INC., Suite 200, 3903 SW Kelly, Portland OR 97201. (503)224-7511. Secretary: David Leiken. Music publisher, record company (NuVisions/Lucky) and record producer (Macman Music, Inc., Dark Horse Entertainment). ASCAP, BMI. Estab. 1980. Publishes 20-30 songs/year; publishes 8-10 new songwriters/year. Works with compsers and lyricists; teams collaborators. Pays "deal by deal."
How to Contact: Submit a demo tape by mail—unsolicited submissions are OK. Prefers cassette with lyric sheet.
Music: Mostly R&B/pop, rock and rap; also jazz. Published "If You Were Mine" (by Larry Bell, Hakins, J-Mac), recorded by U-Krew on Enigma/Capitol Records (rap/funk); "Talk About Love" (by Roger Sause), recorded by Shock on Atlantic Records (dance/R&B); and "Be My Girl" (by Marlon McClain), recorded by Dennis Springer on Nasty Mix Jazz Records (jazz).

MAGIC MESSAGE MUSIC, P.O. Box 1345, Kings Beach CA 95719. (916)546-5381. Owner: Alan Redstone. Music publisher and record company (Sureshot Records). ASCAP. Estab. 1979. Publishes 6 songs/year; publishes 1 new songwriter/year. Receives 50-75 submissions/year. Pays standard royalty.
How to Contact: Currently not accepting new material.
Music: Mostly country, ballads and rock. Published "This Time Around," "Salomé" and "Cars Girls Dreams," all written and recorded by Alan Redstone on Sureshot Records (country rock).

*MAGNEMAR, #C-8, 900 Westgate Ln., Bossier City LA 71112. (318)742-5777. President: Lillian Mills. Music publisher, record company (Bunjak Records) and record producer (Bunjar Records). BMI, ASCAP, SESAC. Estab. 1980. Works with composers and lyricists; teams collaborators. pays standard royalty. "We pay acording to market."
How to Contact: Submit a demo tape by mail—unsolicited submissions are OK. Prefers cassette with unlimited songs. SASE. Reports in 4 weeks.
Music: Mostly country and gospel; also country ballads. Published "If This Ain't Love," "Crazy in Love" and "Country From the Heart" (all by Myrna Freeman and Bunnie Mills), recorded by Bunnie Mills on Bunjak Records (country).
Tips: "Make demo clear. Voice clear. Does not have to be any more than guitar or piano. Send lyric if you want to—lead sheet is not necessary."

*MAJESTIC CONTROL MUSIC, P.O. Box 330-568, Brooklyn NY 11233. (718)919-2013 and (718)486-6419. A&R Department: Alemo and Hank Love. Music publisher, record company (Majestic Control Records) and record producer (Alemo and Hank Love). BMI. Estab. 1983. Hires staff writers. Works with lyricists. Pays standard royalty.
How to Contact: Submit a demo tape by mail—unsolicited submissions are OK. Prefers cassette with 3 songs. SASE. Reports in 4 weeks.
Music: Mostly rap, R&B and reggae; also house. Published "Cold Sweat" (by Curtis, Moye, David), recorded by Majestic Productions (rap 12"); *Lovely, Lovely* (by M. Lowe), recorded by M.C. Lovely (rap LP); and "Front Line" (by Curtis, Moye, Davis), recorded by Majestic Productions (rap 12"); all on Majestic Control Records.

*MAJOR BOB/RIO BRAVO MUSIC, 1109 17th Ave. S., Nashville TN 37212. (615)329-4150. Professional Manager: Dan Ekback. Music publisher. ASCAP, BMI. Estab. 1986. Works with composers; teams collaborators.
Affiliate(s): Major Bob Music Co., Inc. (ASCAP) and Rio Bravo Music Co., Inc. (BMI).
How to Contact: Call first and obtain permission to submit a tape. SASE.
Music: Mostly country. Published "If Tomorrow Never Comes," "Unanswered Prayers" and "Not Counting You" recorded by G. Brooks; all on Capitol Records.

MAKIN TRACKS MUSIC, 17 Water St., Dracut MA 01826. (508)957-5781. Publisher: Henry Rowe. Music publisher, record company (Hazardous Records) and record producer (Henry Rowe). ASCAP. Estab. 1986. Publishes 4 songs/year; publishes 2 new songwriters/year. Works with composers and lyricists; teams collaborators. Pays standard royalty.

How to Contact: Submit a demo tape by mail—unsolicited submissions are OK. Prefers cassette (VHS videocassette if available) with 4-6 songs and lyric sheet. Does not return unsolicited material. Reports in 2 months.
Music: Mostly metal, rock and pop; also fusion, fazz and New Age. Published "Half Life" and "Danger Zone," by Hazardous Waste (metal); and "Candle to the Magic," by Johann Smith (rock), all recorded by Makin Tracks on Hazardous Records.
Tips: "Have a solid sound and good production."

THE MARCO MUSIC GROUP INC., P.O. Box 24454, Nashville TN 37202. (615)269-7074; FAX: (615)269-0131. General Manager: Terri Walker. Music publisher. Estab. 1988. Publishes approximately 50-75 songs/year; 14-15 new songwriters/year. Receives 1,000 submissions/year. Pays standard royalty.
Affiliate(s): Goodland Publishing Company (ASCAP), Marc Isle Music (BMI) and Gulf Bay Publishing (SESAC).
How to Contact: Call first to get permission to send a tape. Prefers cassette (or VHS videocassette) with 1-2 songs and lyric sheet. SASE.
Music: Country, MOR and contemporary. Published "My Way or The Highway" (by E. Reynolds/T. Fritz), recorded by Deborah Dubley on Concorde Records (country); "Mama's Rockin' Chair," (by Susan Clark), recorded by Deborah Dubley on Concorde Records (country); and "Let Your Music Do the Talking," (by B. Green, D&C Secreit), recorded by Tom Harrison on Buck Creek Records (country).
Tips: "Only send your best 2 or 3 songs with lyrics accompanying. Expect a reply within 4 weeks."

*MARIELLE MUSIC PUBLISHING CORP., P.O. Box 14324, Clearwater FL 34629. (813)862-9377. Vice President: Amy Polan. Music publisher, record company (Maximus Records) and record producer (Arnold Maxin). BMI. Estab. 1952. Publishes 2 new songwriters/year. Works with composers and lyricists; teams collaborators. Pays standard royalty.
Affiliate(s): Moorpark Music Corp. (ASCAP); Moo Moo Music Corp. (BMI).
How to Contact: Submit a demo tape by mail—unsolicited submissions are OK. Prefers cassette with several songs and lyric and lead sheets. SASE. Reports in 6 months.
Music: Mostly instrumentals, rock and soft rock; also country.

MARULLO MUSIC PUBLISHERS, 1121 Market St., Galveston TX 77550. (409)762-4590. President: A.W. Marullo Sr. Music publisher, record company (Red Dot) and record producer (A.W. Marullo Productions). BMI, SESAC. Estab. 1952. Publishes 27-37 songs/year; publishes 7-14 songwriters/year. Sometimes hires staff writers. Pays standard royalty.
Affiliate(s): Marullo Music (BMI), Don & Willie Music (SESAC).
How to Contact: Submit a demo tape by mail—unsolicited submissions are O.K. Cassette with only 4 songs. SASE. Reports in 7 weeks.
Music: Mostly country, pop and R&B; also rock, top 40 rock, country and dance songs. Published "Do You Feel Sexy" (by T. Pindrock), recorded by Flach Point on Puzzle Red Dot Records (top 40 rock); "Love Machine" (by T. Pindrock), recorded by Susan Moninger on Puzzle Red Dot Records (top 40 rock); and "You Put the Merry in My Christmas" (by E. Dunn), recorded by Mary Craig on Puzzle Red Dot Records (country and top 40 rock).
Tips: "Send only your best songs. The songwriter with a *new* idea is a crank, until the idea succeeds."

ANDY MARVEL MUSIC, P.O. Box 133, Farmingville NY 11738. President: Andy Marvel. Music publisher, record company (Alyssa Records) and record producer (Marvel Productions and Ricochet Records). ASCAP. Estab. 1981. Publishes 30 songs/year; publishes 10 new songwriters/year. Works with composers and lyricists; teams collaborators. Pays standard royalty.
Affiliate(s): Andysongs (BMI) and Bing, Bing, Bing Music (ASCAP).
How to Contact: Prefers cassette (or VHS videocassette) with 3 songs and lyric sheet. Returns only with SASE. "Do not call."
Music: Mostly pop, R&B and top 40; also country. Published "Learning to Live with a Heartache" (by Andy Marvel/Sheree Sano), recorded by Andy Marvel on Alyssa Records (pop); and "Love Will Never Be the Same Without You" (by Andy Marvel/Don Levy), recorded by John Wesley Shipp on Jamie Records (pop).
Tips: "Be patient. Your tape will be listened to. It helps if your song is produced, but it's not necessary."

*MASSMEDIA, 7105 Reynolds St., Pittsburgh PA 15208. (412)247-1301. President: Jon Gorr. Music publisher (MassMedia Records), record producer (Jon Gorr) and advertising/jingle agency. BMI. Estab. 1983. Publishes 10 songs/year; publishes 1-2 new songwriters/year. Hires staff writers. Works with composers and lyricists. Pays standard royalty.

How to Contact: Submit a demo tape by mail—unsolicited submissions are OK. Prefers cassette with 3 songs. Does not return unsolicited material. Reports in 1 month.
Music: Mostly rock, New Age and reggae. Published "It's No Life" (by Jon Gorr), recorded by Jon Gorr/Ram on MassMedia Records (pop); and "On the Right Track," written and recorded by Albert Griffiths on Heartbeat Records (reggae).

MASTER AUDIO, INC./MASTER SOUND, INC./LYRESONG, INC., 1227 Spring St. NW, Atlanta GA 30309. (404)873-6425. Contact: Babs Richardson. Music publisher and recording studio. BMI, ASCAP. Estab. 1960. Publishes 3-4 songs/year. Receives 10-12 submissions/month. Pays standard royalty.
Affiliate(s): Paydirt Music (ASCAP), Legal Tender (ASCAP) and Seyah Music (BMI).
How to Contact: Write or call first to get permission to send a tape. Prefers cassette with 2-3 songs. SASE. Reports in 1 month.
Music: Country, disco, gospel, R&B, soul and top 40/pop. Published *Great News*, (by Troy Ramey), recorded by T. Ramey and the Soul Searchers on Nashboro Records (black gospel); "Try Jesus, " recorded by T. Ramey (gospel); "Double Shot (of My Baby's Love)," recorded by Joe Stampley (country); "Forget The Man" (by Celia Lipton) on IRC Label; and several new groups in 1991.
Tips: "After submitting a requested tape, please allow us time to listen and allow us to contact the writer."

*MEDIA PRODUCTIONS/RESISTOR MUSIC, 1001½ Elizabeth St., Oak Hill WV 25901. (304)465-1298. Producer: Doug Gent. Music publisher, record company (Resistor Records) and record producer (Media Productions). ASCAP. Estab. 1985. Publishes 20 songs/year; publishes 3 new songwriters/year. Receives 100-120 submissions/year. Works with composers and lyricists; teams collaborators. Pays standard royalty.
Affiliate(s): Resistor Music (ASCAP).
How to Contact: Submit a demo tape by mail—unsolicited submissions are OK. Prefers cassette with 3 songs and lyric sheet. Does not return unsolicited material. Reports in 1 month.
Music: Mostly country, gospel and R&B; also top 40 and rock. Published "Mountain Man" (by Hiser/Rollins/Willis) and "Price Of Fame" (by Rollins/Dent), both recorded by Bitter Creek; "Free Love," "Still" and "Just Holdin' On," written and recorded by Cheryl Ormsbee (country); and "Veins of Coal" (by S. Bibb), recorded by Zephyr, all on Resistor Records (all country).
Tips: "I see an increasing role for the independent publisher/record label/studio in the music business. It is my sincere hope that the opportunities are not taken advantage of."

MEGA-STAR MUSIC, 248 W. 5th St., Deer Park NY 11729. (212)713-5229. General Manager: Barry Yearwood. Music publisher, record producer (Barry Yearwood) and management firm (Power Brokerage Management). Estab. 1984. Publishes 4 songs/year; publishes 4 new songwriters/year. Pays standard royalty.
How to Contact: Prefers cassette with 4 songs. Does not return unsolicited material. Reports in 1 month.
Music: Mostly dance and R&B; also pop. Published "Dancing to the Beat," written and recorded by Henderson and Whitfield on Park Place Records; "Solar Flight," written and recorded by Richard Bush on Island Records; and "Mind Your Own Business," written and recorded by R. Bush on Laser-7 Records.

*MERRY MARILYN MUSIC PUBLISHING, 33717 View Crest Dr., Lake Elsinore CA 92330. (714)245-2763. General Manager: Marilyn Hendricks. Music publisher. BMI. Estab. 1980. Publishes 10-15 songs/year; publishes 3-4 new songwriters/year. Receives 25 submissions/month. Pays standard royalty.
How to Contact: Submit a demo tape—unsolicited submissions are OK. No more than 3 songs per submission, one song per cassette. "No SASE. If we like the song, we'll contact you. Submit complete songs only. No lyrics without music."
Music: Mostly country; also MOR and pop. Published "Tears in Daddy's Eyes," by David Horn (country); "Set Me Free," written and recorded by J. Hendricks on Ribbit Records (country/MOR); and "Looking for a Woman" (by B. Schnieber), recorded by J. Hendricks on Ribbit Records (country/MOR).
Tips: "Be professional in your presentation. Make sure the tape is cued correctly. Make sure the lyric can be heard over the music. If possible, invest two dollars on a good quality tape. It really makes a difference to the listener."

*MIA MIND MUSIC, #4B, 500 ½ East 84th St., New York NY 10028. (212)861-8745. Professional Manager: Guy Torio. Music publisher, record company (Mindfield Records) and record producer (I.Y.F. Productions). ASCAP. Estab. 1986. Publishes 100 songs/year; publishes 3-4 new songwriters/year. Works with composers and lyricists; teams collaborators. Pays standard royalty.

How to Contact: Submit a demo tape by mail—unsolicited submissions are OK. Prefers cassette or VHS videocassette with 3 songs. SASE. Reports in 6 weeks.
Music: Mostly rap, house and hip-hop; also dance, top 40 and AOR. Published "Boyfriend," written and recorded by Baby Oil on Profile Records (rap); "Let's Go Dancing" (Bentzel/Torio), recorded by Madonna on Replay Records (house); and "Get Down" (by Bentzel/Torio), recorded by Madonna/Oho Von Warelerr on Replay Records (hip hop).
Tips: "Submit demos on DAT cassettes for best quality sound."

MICAH MUSIC, P.O. Box 348 Agin Court, Ontario M1S 3B9 **Canada**. (416)298-3108. President: Oswald L. Burke. Music publisher and record company (Micah Records). SOCAN. Estab. 1985. Publishes 15 songs/year; 3 new songwriters/year. Teams collaborators. Pays standard royalty.
Affiliate(s): Job Music (SOCAN).
How to Contact: Submit a demo tape by mail. Prefers cassette with 2-3 songs and lyric sheets. SASE.
Music: Gospel. Published "Make Us Better" (by E. Haughton); "I Wanna Be More" (by Elvis Boddie); and "One Day" (by K. Burke), all recorded by Sweet Sound on Micah Records (gospel).

*MICROSTAR MUSIC, #113, 5241 Cleveland St., Virginia Beach VA 23462. (804)499-4434. President: Mark Spencer. Music publisher, record company (MicroStar, MSM) and record producer (MicroStar Music). ASCAP. Estab. 1990. Publishes 60 songs/year; publishes 10 new songwriters/year. Hires staff writers. Works with composers and lyricists; teams collaborators. Pays standard royalty.
How to Contact: Write first and obtain permission to submit a tape. Prefers cassette with 4 songs and lyric sheets. Does not return unsolicited material. Reports in 4 weeks.
Music: Mostly pop, gospel and country; also R&B. Published "Heart's Desire" (by T. Beiderman), recorded by TK LLegs (pop); "Workin' Man's Dream," written and recorded by Buck Fisher (country); and "Little Miracle," written and recorded by Paul Van Valin (gospel); all on MicroStar Records.
Tips: "Don't send a poor quality demo. If you or someone you know doesn't believe in your material enough to invest your time and money than why should we?"

*MIGHTY SOUL-SONIC RECORDS, Suite 12G, 70 West 95th, New York NY 10025. (212)666-6454. President/Owner: Mark Carvel. Music publisher, record company (Mighty Soul-Sonic Records) and record producer (Mark Carvel). BMI, ASCAP. Estab. 1987. Publishes 10-17 songs/year; publishes 15-20 new songwriters/year. Hires staff writers. Works with composers and lyricists; teams collaborators. Pays 60%-40%.
Affiliate(s): Short & Sweet Publishing Company.
How to Contact: Write or call first and obtain permission to submit a tape. Prefers artist performance videocassette with 12 songs and lyric or lead sheets. SASE. Reports in 2 months.
Music: Mostly rap, rock and R&B; also jazz and gospel.

MIGHTY TWINNS MUSIC, 9134 S. Indiana Ave., Chicago IL 60619. (312)737-4348. General Manager: Ron Scott. Music publisher and record producer. BMI. Member NMPA, Midwest Inspirational Writers Association. Estab. 1977. Publishes 4-10 songs/year; publishes 5 new songwriters/year. Receives 20 submissions/month. Works with composers and lyricists; teams collaborators. Pays standard royalty.
How to Contact: Submit a demo tape—unsolicited submissions are OK. Prefers cassette with 2-4 songs and lyric sheet. SASE "only if you want material returned." Reports in 2 months.
Music: Mostly top 40, R&B, "hot" inspirational and gospel; also children's. Published "Dreams" and "Get Your Money On," recorded by Salaam on MTM Records (R&B).
Tips: Looking for "good hot songs with hot hooks. Please have tapes cued up. *Do not write for permission!* Submit a cued up cassette and wait for our response. No materials returned without proper postage. Take the time to write and re-write to get the song in its best form; then make a good clear/audible demo."

MILLHOUSE MUSIC, 1710 Roy Acuff Pl., Nashville TN 37203. (615)255-0428. Professional Manager: Russ Zavitson. Music publisher. BMI. Estab. 1978. Publishes 150 songs/year; publishes 10 new songwriters/year. Hires staff writers. Works with composers and lyricists; teams collaborators. Pays standard royalty.
Affiliate(s): Sheddhouse Music (ASCAP), Wooden Wonder Music (SESAC).
How to Contact: Write or call first and obtain permission to submit a tape. Prefers cassette with 3-5 songs and lyric sheet. Does not return unsolicited material. Reports in 3 weeks.
Music: Mostly country, pop and rock. Published "It Ain't Nothin" (by Tony Haselden), recorded by Keith Whitley on RCA Records (country); "80s Ladies," written and recorded by K.T. Oslin on RCA Records (country); and "Checkmate" (by Keith Hinton), recorded by Paul Rodgers on Atlantic Records (rock).

*MIMIC MUSIC, Box 201, Smyrna GA 30081. (404)432-2454. Manager: Tom Hodges. Music publisher, record producer, record company (Trend Records, Stepping Stones, BOAM, Trend/Side Records, Trendsetter Records and Atlanta Records) and management company. BMI, ASCAP. Estab. 1965. Publishes 25 songs/year; publishes 7 new songwriters/year. Works with composers and lyricists; teams collaborators. Pays standard royalty.
Affiliate(s): Skipjack Music (BMI), Stepping Stone (BMI) and British Overseas Airways Music/BOAM (ASCAP).
How to Contact: Submit a demo tape—unsolicited submissions are OK. Prefers cassette (or VHS videocassette) with 3-10 songs and lyric sheet. "Open to VHS and also for distribution on accepted videos." SASE. Reports in 2 weeks.
Music: Mostly country; also bluegrass, blues, church/religious, easy listening, gospel, MOR, R&B, rock, soul and top 40/pop. Published "Ivory Horse," written and recorded by Sue Sparth; "Take it or Leave It," written and recorded by Karen Dawson; and "Sad Song River," written and recorded by Dave Cole; all on Trend Records (country). "I also have Keith Bradford, Bill Price, Dell Wood, Lin Butler, Tara Bailey, Deb Watson and Frank Brannon on a mixed artists cassette album."

*MINI MAX PUBLISHING, 932 Nord Ave., Chico CA 95926. (916)345-3027. Publisher: Rich Carper. Music publisher and record company (Casaro Records). BMI. Estab. 1987. Publishes 50-60 songs/year; publishes 10-12 new songwriters/year. Works with composers and lyricists; teams collaborators. Pays standard royalties.
Affiliate(s): Starshine Audio Ent., RSA Productions.
How to Contact: Write first and obtain permission to submit a tape. Prefers cassette with 3 songs and lyric sheet. Does not return unsolicited material. SASE. Reports in 4 weeks.
Music: Mostly country, jazz and R&B; also gospel. Published "Back to Zero," written and recorded by John Peters (jazz/rock); "Sound of Christmas" (by Charlie Robinson), recorded by Lory Dobbs (big band); and "Another Side," written and recorded by Pam Dacus (new age); all on Casaro Records.

*MOFO MUSIC, 117 W. Rockland, Libertyville IL 60048. (708)362-4060. President: Perry Johnson. Music publisher and record company (Dharma, Future). ASCAP. Estab. 1980. Publishes 3 songs/year. Works with composers. Pays standard royalty.
How to Contact: Submit a demo tape by mail—unsolicited submissions are OK. Prefers cassette with 6 songs and lyric sheets. SASE. Reports in 3 months.
Music: Mostly top 40, pop and R&B; also blues, house and contemporary.

*MONEYTIME PUBLISHING CO. (BMI), 742 Rowley St., Owosso MI 48867. (517)723-1796. Director: Jon Harris. Music publisher and record company (Moneytime Records). BMI. Estab. 1990. Publishes 15 songs/year; publishes 3-5 new songwriters/year. Works with lyricists. Pays standard royalty.
Affiliate(s): Moneytime Publishing Co. (BMI).
How to Contact: Submit a demo tape by mail—unsolicited submissions are OK. Prefers cassette with 4-6 songs. Does not return unsolicited material. Reports in 4 weeks.
Music: Mostly rap, R&B and dance; also house, funk and soul. Published "Decibel Level," "Young Girls" and "My Jam Is King" (by Jon Harris), recorded by The Mad Rapper on Moneytime Records (rap).

*MONTINA MUSIC, P.O. Box 702, Snowdon Station, Montreal, Quebec H3X 3X8 **Canada**. Professional Manager: David P. Leonard. Music publisher. SOCAN. Estab. 1963. Pays standard royalty. Works with composers, lyricists; teams collaborators.
Affiliate(s): Sabre Music (SOCAN).
How to Contact: Submit a demo tape—unsolicited submissions are OK. Prefers cassette, phonograph record (or VHS videocasette) and lyric sheet. Does not return unsolicited material.
Music: Mostly top 40; also bluegrass, blues, country, dance-oriented, easy listening, folk, gospel, jazz, MOR, progressive, R&B, rock and soul.
Tips: "Maintain awareness of styles and trends of your peers who have succeeded professionally. Understand the markets to which you are pitching your material. Persevere at marketing your talents. Develop a network of industry contacts, first locally, then regionally and nationally."

 The asterisk before a listing indicates that the listing is new in this edition. New markets are often the most receptive to unsolicited submissions.

*MOON JUNE MUSIC, 4233 SW. Marigold, Portland OR 97219. President: Bob Stoutenburg. Music publisher. Estab. 1971. Pays standard royalty.
How to Contact: Prefers cassette (or VHS videocassette) with 2-10 songs. SASE.
Music: Country.

THE FRED MORRIS MUSIC GROUP, Suite 207, 50 Music Sq. West, Nashville TN 37203. (615)329-2591. Publishing Manager: Karen Morris. Music publisher and record company (Maxx Records). Publishes 10-15 songs/year; publishes 2-3 new songwriters/year. Receives 200 submissions/month. Pays standard royalty.
Affiliate(s): Karefree Music (BMI), Karlamor Music (ASCAP), Old Guide Music (BMI), First Million Music (ASCAP).
How to Contact: Submit a demo tape—unsolicited submissions are OK. Prefers cassette (or VHS videocassette) with 3 songs and lyric sheet. SASE. Reports in 1 month.
Music: Country, country/rock. No gospel. Published "Rocks, Rivers & Trees" (by Rod Wimmer), recorded by James Tiller on Maxx Records (country); "Feet of Clay" (by Mark Parsons), recorded by Jeff Davis on Maxx REcords (coungry); and "Strings of My Heart" (by Kevin Tuck Field), recorded by Don Stacy (country/crossover).

MOTHER BERTHA MUSIC PUBLISHING CO., INC., Penthouse Suite, 686 S. Arroyo Pkwy., Pasadena CA 91105. Administrative Director: Harold Esposito. Music publisher, record company (Phil Spector International) and record producer (Phil Spector Productions). BMI.
How to Contact: "We are not accepting or reviewing any new material or artists. Any unsolicited correspondence or material will not be returned."

MOUNT SCOTT MUSIC, 1119 Main St., Garland TX 75040. Professional Manager: Jim Brewer. Music publisher, record company (MSM Records, Hālo Records, Bronco Records), record producer; artists signed to labels only. BMI. Estab. 1979. Publishes 1-4 songs/year. Receives up to 200 submissions/year. Works with composers and lyricists; teams collaborators. Pays standard royalty.
Affiliate(s): Pick the Hits Music.
How to Contact: Write first and obtain permission to submit a tape. Prefers cassette with 2 songs and lyric sheets. SASE. Reports in 4 weeks.
Music: Mostly contemporary country, traditional country and pop-rock. Published "Here Comes the Rain Again" (by M. Lewis/M. Brush), recorded by Gwen Newton on Halo Records (country).
Tips: "Submit only material that you truly believe is worth an artist/label spending several thousand dollars on, otherwise, it's probably not good enough. While the market for writers/publishers getting a song recorded by a major artist/label is still tight and very hard to break into, more and more independents are getting records on the chart."

MOUNTAIN HERITAGE MUSIC CO., Rt. 3, Box 290, Galax VA 24333. (703)236-9249. Owner: Bobby Patterson. Music publisher and record company (Heritage Records, Frontier Productions and Mountain Records). BMI. Publishes 14 songs/year; publishes 2 new songwriters/year. Works with composers and lyricists. Pays standard royalty.
How to Contact: Prefers cassette with 3 songs and lyric sheet. SASE. Reports in 6 months.
Music: Mostly bluegrass, gospel and Christmas. Published "Back on the Front Line," "Till I'm Home Again" and "Almost a Romance," all recorded by Scott Freeman on Heritage Records (country).
Tips: "Words must tell a complete story within 2½-3 minutes."

MR. MORT MUSIC, 44 Music Square E., Nashville TN 37203. (615)255-2175. President: Charles Fields. Music publisher, record company (Charta Records and Delux Records) and record producer (Charlie Fields). ASCAP. Estab. 1977. Publishes 50 songs/year; publishes 8 new songwriters/year. Pays standard royalty.
Affiliate(s): Jason Dee Music (BMI).
How to Contact: Prefers cassette with 1-4 songs and lead sheet. SASE. Reports in 2 weeks.
Music: Mostly MOR, easy listening and country; also blues and top 40/pop. Published "Addicted to You" (by J. Hitzler), recorded by Jeannie Marie; "I'm Layin' Down the Lovin' " (by C.W. Fields), recorded by Lori Johnson; and "Multiple Choice" (by J.J. Johnson), recorded by Jack Johnson; all country singles on Charta Records.

*MUSIC FACTORY ENTERPRISES, INC., Suite 300, Ford & Washington, Norristown PA 19401. (215)277-9550. President: Jeffrey Calhoon. Music publisher, record company (MFE Records). BMI. Estab. 1984. Publishes 8 songs/year. Receives 4 submissions/month. Works with composers and lyricists; teams collaborators. Pays "royalty based on length of contract/quantity of records produced, and production expenses."

Affiliate(s): Robin Nicole Music (BMI).
How to Contact: Write or call first and obtain permission to submit a tape. Prefers cassette with 3-4 songs, lyric sheet and lead sheet. "Make sure notations are clear and legible." Does not return unsolicited material. Reports in 2 weeks.
Music: Mostly 20th Century Minimalism, world beat, alternative rock/pop and New Age. Published "Stillwater," "River Run" and "Shamont," all written and recorded by Gregory Darvis on MFE Records (New Age).
Tips: "Develop every song fully, be different, submit best quality product you can."

*MUSIC IN THE RIGHT KEYS PUBLISHING COMPANY, 3716 West 87th St., Chicago IL 60652. (312)735-3297. President: Bert Swanson. Music publisher. Estab. 1985. Publishes 150 songs/year; publishes 5 new songwriters/year. Works with composers; teams collaborators. Pays standard royalty.
Affiliate(s): Music In The Right Keys (BMI), High 'n Low Notes (ASCAP).
How to Contact: Submit a demo tape by mail—unsolicited submissions are OK. Prefers cassette with 3-5 songs and lyric and lead sheets. "Good demos only." SASE. Reports in 4 weeks.
Music: Mostly country, gospel and pop; also children's songs. Published "Drinking Got Out of Hand," written and recorded by Bert Swanson and C.R. Fisher on Write Keys Records (country); "Loving the Night Away," written and recorded by Bert Swanson and C.R. Fisher on Write Keys Records (country); and "She Sure Is Something Good," written and recorded by Bert Swanson and R. Spinnato on High n' Low Notes Records (rock).

*MUSICA ARROZ PUBLISHING, 5626 Brock St., Houston TX 77023. (713)926-4432. Administrator of Publishing: Barry E. Leavitt. Music publisher. ASCAP, BMI. Estab. 1986. Publishes 50 songs/year; publishes 10 new songwriters/year. Works with composers; teams collaborators. Pays standard 50% royalty.
Affiliate(s): Musica Arroz (ASCAP), Defiance Music (ASCAP), Tessitura Music Trust (BMI).
How to Contact: Write or call first and obtain permission to submit a tape. Prefers cassette with 5-6 songs and lyric sheet. SASE. Reports in 12 weeks.
Music: Mostly Latin (in Spanish), rap (in Spanish), jazz; also country and rock (in Spanish). Published "Rebelde" (by Alex Gallimore), recorded by Mercedez on Polygram Records (Latin); "Nose" (by Emily Cranz), recorded by Elsa Garcia on Polygram Records (Latin); "Dime Si Tu Me Quieres" (by Mary G. Henson), recorded by Laura Canales on Capitol/EMI Records (Latin).
Tips: "Do *not* send music other than that in which we are most interested."

MYKO MUSIC, #D203, 1324 S. Avenida, Tucson AZ 85710. (602)885-5931. President: James M. Gasper. Music publisher, record company (Ariana Records) and record producer (Future 1 Productions). BMI. Estab. 1980. Publishes 4 songs/year; publishes 2 new songwriters/year. Receives 5 submissions/month. Works with composers. Pays standard royalty.
How to Contact: Submit a demo tape—unsolicited submissions are OK. Prefers cassette (or ½″ VHS videocassette) with 3 songs and lyric sheet. SASE Reports in 5 weeks.
Music: Top 40, dance rock, AOR, R&B, ballads and pop/rock. Published "Longer Look" (by Jim Gasper, Tom Priuett, Mike Adair), recorded by Sketches; "Rip It Up" (by R. Ruiz), recorded by The Molecules on Ariand Records (AOR); "Her Love's Wrong" (J. Gasper), recorded by G.S.P. (Guys Seeking Paul) on Ariand Records (ballad).
Tips: "If the song's not there, no amount of production is going to make it work. Start with the words and music, worry about production later."

*CHUCK MYMIT MUSIC PRODUCTIONS, 9840 64th Ave., Flushing NY 11324. A&R: Chuck Mymit. Music publisher and record producer (Chuck Mymit Music Productions). BMI. Estab. 1978. Publishes 3-5 songs/year; publishes 2-4 new songwriters/year. Works with composers and lyricists; teams collaborators. Pays standard royalty.
Affiliate(s): Viz Music (BMI) and Tore Music (BMI).
How to Contact: Submit a demo tape by mail—unsolicited submissions are OK. Prefers cassette or VHS videocassette with 3-5 songs and lyric and lead sheets. "Bio and picture would be helpful." SASE. Reports in 1 month.
Music: Mostly pop, rock and R&B. Published "Giving You My Love" (by Nata and Schal), recorded by Laura Dees on VIN Records (pop/ballad); "To Love's a Mortal Sin" (by Chuck Mymit), recorded by The Dellmonts on Poly Records (pop/ballad); and "Juice" (by Favarelli), recorded by The Xogs on Rinidel Records (rock).
Tips: "Have strong confideence in your work but please follow our policy."

*MYSTIKOS MUSIC, P.O. Box 90936, Austin TX 78709-0936. (512)288-1044. FAX: (512)288-4748. Director: Chris or Martin Theophilus. Music publisher and record company (Phantom Records). BMI. Estab. 1987. Publishes 4-6 new songwriters/year. Pays standard royalty.

How to Contact: Submit a demo tape by mail—unsolicited submissions are OK. Prefers cassette or VHS videocassette with 4-5 songs and lyric sheet. SASE. Reports in 4 weeks.
Music: Mostly blues, rock and country; also dance and pop.

NADINE MUSIC, P.O. Box 2, Fronhof 100, CH-8260 Stein am Rhein **Switzerland**. Phone: (054)415415. FAX: (054)415420. Professional Manager: Freddy J. Angstmann. Music publisher, record producer, management firm and booking agency. SUISA, SESAC, BMI, ASCAP. Publishes 50-100 songs/year. Works with composers. Pays standard royalty.
Affiliate(s): Nadine Music (SESAC), Joecliff Music (BMI) and Lauren Music (ASCAP).
How to Contact: Submit a demo tape—unsolicited submissions are OK. Prefers cassette (or VHS videocassette [PAL]) with lyric and lead sheets. "Clearly label each item you send; include photo and bio if possible." Include SAE and IRC, or does not return unsolicited material. Reports in 6 weeks.
Music: Gospel, blues and jazz; also R&B and classical. Published "How Long Will My Journey Be," written and recorded by Rev. Thompson on Koch Records (gospel); "Goin' Home," written and recorded by Jerry Ricks on Bayer Records (blues); and "Medley" (by Gershwin/Baker), recorded by Baker on K Records (jazz).

*NAMAX MUSIC PUBLISHING, P.O. Box 24162, Richmond VA 23224. President: Nanette Brown. Music publisher. BMI. Estab. 1989. Publishes 2-4 songs/year; publishes 2 new songwriters/year. Works with composers; teams collaborators. Pays standard royalty.
How to Contact: Submit a demo tape by mail—unsolicited submissions are OK. Prefers cassette with 2 songs and lyric sheet. "No phone calls please." SASE. Reports in 6 weeks.
Music: Mostly R&B, urban contemporary and pop/top 40; also contemporary gospel. Published "Cynthia" (by Richard Williams), recorded by SoRich on Peak Records (R&B dance).
Tips: "Namax is looking for well constructed songs that deliver a positive message. Material should be as polished as possible."

NASHVILLE SOUND MUSIC PUBLISHING CO., P.O. Box 728, Peterborough, Ontario K9J 6Z8 **Canada**. (705)742-2381. President: Andrew Wilson Jr. Music publisher. PRO Canada, CAPAC. Estab. 1985. Publishes 10 songs/year; publishes 5 new songwriters/year. Receives 50 submissions/month. Pays standard royalty.
Affiliate(s): Northern Sound Music Publishing Co. (CAPAC).
How to Contact: Submit a demo tape—unsolicited submissions are OK. Prefers cassette or 7½ ips reel-to-reel with 2-4 songs and lyric sheet. "Please send only material you do not want returned. We have an open door policy. We will contact a writer if we hear something of interest."
Music: Mostly country, country/pop and crossover country; also MOR, top 40, pop/rock and gospel. Published "Leave Me the Memory," by I.M. South/A. Wilson Jr./L. Payne; "I'm Not a Fool" (by L. Payne), recorded by Wendy Tibbits; "Twin Fiddles Turn Me On" (by Mel Holt), recorded by Faron Young on Payne Records (country); and "A Hard Bridge to Cross" (by Frank H. Stanton, Ginni D. Johnson, Curtis Young and Andrew Wilson Jr.), recorded by Faron Young on Step One Records.

*NATIONAL TALENT, P.O. Box 14, Whitehall MI 49461. (616)894-9208. President: Sharon Leigh. Vice President: Jay Ronn. Music publisher and record company (United Country). BMI. Estab. 1985. Publishes 7-8 songs/year. Teams collaborators. Pays standard royalty.
Affiliate(s): House of Shar (BMI).
How to Contact: Submit a demo tape by mail—unsolicited submissions are OK. Prefers cassette with 1-10 songs and lyric sheet. SASE. Reports in 2 weeks.
Music: Country and gospel.

NAUTICAL MUSIC CO., Box 120675, Nashville TN 37212. (615)255-1068. Owner: Ray McGinnis. Music publisher and record company (Orbit Records, Ray McGinnis). BMI. Estab. 1965. Publishes 25 songs/year; 10 new songwriters/year. Receives 10-15 submissions/month. Works with composers. Pays standard royalty.
How to Contact: Submit a demo tape by mail—unsolicited submissions are OK. Prefers cassette with 4 songs and lyric sheets. SASE. Reports in 6-8 weeks.
Music: Mostly country ballads and country rock. Published "I Need The Real Thing" (by D. Acuff), recorded by Kim Tsoy (country); "Blame It On the Moonlight" (by T. Harrison), recorded by DaKota; and "I'm In the Yellow Pages Under Blue," recorded by Kim Tsoy (country); all on Orbit Records.

"How to Use Your Songwriter's Market" (at the front of this book) contains comments and suggestions to help you understand and use the information in these listings.

Tips: "The trend is back to traditional country music with songs that tell a story."

NEBO RIDGE PUBLISHING COMPANY, P.O. Box 194 or 457, New Hope AL 35760. President: Walker Ikard. Manager: Jim Lewis. Music publisher, promotions firm, record producer, record company (Nebo Record Company), management firm (Nebo Management) and booking agency (Nebo Booking Agency). ASCAP. Estab. 1985. Works with composers and lyricists; teams collaborators. Pays standard royalty.
How to Contact: Submit a demo tape—unsolicited submissions are OK. Prefers cassette demo tape (or VHS videocassette) with 1 song and lyric sheet. "A VHS video of a song would be helpful but not absolutely necessary." SASE always. Reports as soon as possible.
Music: Mostly modern and traditional country, modern and traditional gospel, country/rock, rock and roll, pop, MOR and bluegrass. Published "Nothin' Without You" (by Walker Ikard), recorded by Walker Ikard and Anita Biss (modern country); "Friend, About Jesus," written and recorded by Charles W. Cooper (gospel-modern); and "Blessin' Money Can't Buy," written and recorded by Osie W. Ikard (traditional gospel); all on Nebo Records.
Tips: "Submit in neat form with clear lyrics. Be original; send songs that produce a feeling or effect."

NEON NOTES, 2729 Westwood Dr., Nashville TN 37204. (615)297-2329. President: Roy Yeager. Music publisher and record producer (Rumble Productions). ASCAP, BMI. Estab. 1987. Works with composers; teams collaborators. Pays standard royalty.
Affiliate(s): Yeager Master (BMI).
How to Contact: Submit a demo tape by mail—unsolicited submissions are OK. Prefers cassette with 3-4 songs and lyric sheets. SASE. Reports in 1 month.
Music: Mostly rock, pop and country; also New Age.

*NERVOUS PUBLISHING, 4/36 Dabbs Hill Lane, Northolt, Middlesex, London **England**. Phone: (4481)963-0352. Managing Director: Roy Williams. Music publisher, record company and record producer. MCPS, PRS and Phonographic Performance Ltd. Estab. 1979. Publishes 100 songs/year; publishes 25 new songwriters/year. Receives 100 submissions/month. Works with composers and lyricists. Pays standard royalty; royalties paid directly to US songwriters.
How to Contact: Submit a demo tape—unsolicited submissions are OK. Prefers cassette with 3-10 songs and lyric sheet. "Include letter giving your age and mentioning any previously published material." SAE and IRC. Reports in 2 weeks.
Music: Mostly psychabilly, rockabilly and rock (impossibly fast music—ex.: Stray Cats but twice as fast); also blues, country, R&B and rock (50s style). Published "Who's He?" (by Clarke), recorded by Coffin-Nails on Nervous Records (Psychabilly); "Orgasmic Nightmare" (by Thomas), recorded by Demented Arego on Fury Records (psychabilly); and "Crazy Song" (by Verheij), recorded by Catmen on Nervous Records (rockabilly).
Tips: "Ignore the usual 'formula-rock.' Remember the UK is a different format to the U.S. Only send the kind of music we request. Don't waste our time or yours with other types."

NETWORK SOUND MUSIC PUBLISHING INC., 119 Peachwood Dr., Swedesboro NJ 08085. (609)467-1682. President, A&R: Vito Fera. Music publisher, record company (S.P.I.N. Records), record producer (Network Sound Productions) and songwriting organization. ASCAP. Estab. 1980. Publishes 10 songs/year. Receives 15 submissions/month. Hires staff writers "on agreement terms." Pays standard royalty. Publishes 6 new songwriters/year.
Affiliate(s): Fera Music Publishing (BMI).
How to Contact: Submit a demo tape by mail or UPS with 3 songs maximum and lyric sheet. "Package song material carefully. Always label (name, address and phone) both cassette and lyric sheet. Copyright songs." SASE. Reports in 4 weeks. Unsolicited submissions are OK. Prefers cassette (or VHS videocassette).
Music: Mostly dance/pop/disco, R&B/funk, rock/medium and adult contemporary. Published "Different Kinda Luv" and "Do You Mind" (by Steve Clarke), recorded by CHILL; "Moments" (by Fera/Burnett/Buchanan), recorded by Bobby Burnett; "Reindeer Rock" (children's Christmas album with associates RPL, KK&A and NSP), (by Fera/Lamborn/Clarke) recorded by Heather and Nicole Wilson, Kathy Lamborn, Steve Clarke and Vito Fera; and "Friends Across America," recorded by The Network Chorus. All selections recorded on S.P.I.N. Records.
Tips: "The 1990s are on their way to exhibiting the highest standards in music technology ever. Consequently, submitting music, especially in dance/pop, in 'raw or unpolished' form makes it somewhat more difficult to recognize the song's potential. The competition is stiff in the music industry and it's time to listen to the songs getting airplay, sharpen your writing skills, feel the 'hook line' and pay more attention to production. Record the best commercial demo you can afford with the lyrics clear and upfront. Best of luck!"

NEWCREATURE MUSIC, Box 148296, Nashville TN 37214-8296. President: Bill Anderson, Jr. Music publisher, record company, record producer and radio and TV syndicator. BMI. Publishes 5 songs/year; publishes 2 new songwriters/year. Pays standard royalty.
How to Contact: Prefers 7½ ips reel-to-reel or cassette (or videocassette) with 4-10 songs and lyric sheet. SASE. Reports in 1 month.
Music: Country, gospel, jazz, R&B, rock and top 40/pop. Published "Cotton, Popcorn, Peanuts and Jesus" (by H. Yates), recorded by Jeanne Cash on Jana Records (gospel); "His Love Is the Reason," written and recorded by Danny Vance on Livingsong Records (gospel); and "Ragged Ole Memory" (by J. Jerigan), recorded by Jim Chute on Cootico Records (country).

*NORTHWEST INTERNATIONAL ENTERTAINMENT, 5503 Roosevelt Way NE, Seattle WA 98105. (206)524-1020. FAX: (206)524-1102. Director of Publishing: Wendy Cook. Music publisher, record company (Etiquette Records, Suspicious Records) and record producer (Etiquette Productions/NIE). BMI. Estab. 1986. Publishes 5 songs/year; publishes 3-4 new songwriters/year. Receives 300 submissions/year. Works with teams collaborators. Pays standard royalty.
Affiliate(s): Valet Publishing Company (BMI).
How to Contact: Submit a demo tape by mail—unsolicited submissions are OK. Prefers cassette with 2-3 songs and lyric sheet. SASE. Reports in 2 months.
Music: Mostly dance, R&B and pop; also country and rock.
Tips: "Have professional looking lyric sheets and good quality tapes."

*NOW & THEN MUSIC, #2A, 412 E. 78 St., New York NY 10021. (212)879-4667. Owner: Shane Faber. Music publisher, record company (Now & Then Records) and record producer. BMI. Estab. 1980. Pays standard royalty.
How to Contact: Submit a demo tape by mail—unsolicited submissions are OK. Prefers cassette with 4 songs and lyric sheet. SASE. Reports in 2 months.
Music: Mostly pop, dance and R&B; also rap and New Age.

NRP MUSIC GROUP, 10 Pebblewood, Irvine CA 92714. (714)552-5231. Vice-President: Fred Bailin. Music publisher. BMI, ASCAP. Estab. 1975. Publishes 10-20 songs/year; 2 new songwriters/year. Receives 80-100 submissions/year. Works with composers; teams collaborators. Pays standard royalty.
Affiliate(s): New Ideas Music Co. (BMI), Simma Music Co. Division (ASCAP), Perspective Music Co. (BMI).
How to Contact: Submit a demo tape by mail—unsolicited submissions are OK. Prefers cassette with lead sheets. SASE. Reports in 2 weeks.
Music: Mostly R&B, pop and rock; also rap.

OBH MUSIKVERLAG OTTO B. HARTMANN, Box 2691, Ch-6901 Lugano **Switzerland.** FAX and Phone: 0041(91)685586. President: Otto B. Hartmann. Music publisher, record company (Kick/OBH) and record producer. Estab. 1968. Publishes 100 songs/year; publishes 2 new songwriters/year. Hires staff writers. Works with composers and lyricists. Pays standard royalty.
Affiliate(s): Edition Plural (classical).
Music: Mostly rock, jazz, folk, pop and R&B; also classical.

OCEAN WALK MUSIC, 13159 Glenoaks Blvd., Sylmar CA 91342. (818)364-2464. Owner: Mark Thornton. Music Publisher, record company and record producer (Tommark Records). BMI. Estab. 1989. Publishes 2-4 songs/year. Works with composers and lyricists. Pays standard royalty.
How to Contact: Submit a demo tape by mail—unsolicited submissions are OK. Prefers cassette (or VHS videocassette if available) with 4 songs and lyric and lead sheet. SASE. Reports in 2-3 months.
Music: Mostly country, western and instrumental; also novelty, R&B, gospel and bluegrass. Published "California Swing" (by Nat Wyner, David Zeigler, Sharon Lynne), recorded by American Made Band on Tommark Records; "Independence Day" (by Wylie Gustafson), recorded by Wylie Gustafson on Tommark Records (country); and "Those Famous Turkeys" (by Mark Thornton and Tom Willett), recorded by Tommark Records (rockabilly/country)..

*OH MY GOSH MUSIC, 5146 Hill Dr., Memphis TN 38109. (901)789-5296. Owner: Gerald McDade. Music publisher and record producer (Home Town Productions). BMI. Estab. 1985. Publishes 1-6 songs/year; publishes 1-6 new songwriters/year. Receives 10-20 submissions/year. Works with composers and lyricists; teams collaborators. Pays standard royalty.
How to Contact: Submit a demo tape by mail—unsolicited submissions are OK. Prefers cassette (or VHS videocassette if available) with 2-4 songs and lyric sheet. SASE. Reports in 6 weeks.
Music: Mostly traditional country, country rock and rock-a-billy; also gospel. Published "I Guess I Don't Have Sence Enough" (by Ken Prentiss), recorded by Eddie Ruth on Spinnin Wheel Records (country); "Flashback/AKA The Batman Song" (by Gerald McDade), recorded by Wierd Humour on

Hometown Records (country rock); and "Heartbreak" (by McDade Johnson and Rogers Grorren), recorded by Kannon on Hometown Records (rock).
Tips: "Be positive, be current, be different, be committed."

*OKISHER MUSIC, P.O. Box 20814, Oklahoma City OK 73156. (405)755-0315. President: Mickey Sherman. Music publisher, record company (Seeds Records, Okart Records, Homa Records and Okie Dokie Records), record producer and management firm (Mickey Sherman's Talent Management). BMI. Estab. 1973. Member OCMA. Publishes 10-15 songs/year; publishes 2-3 new songwriters/year. Receives 100 submissions/year. Works with composers and lyricists. Pays standard royalty.
How to Contact: Submit a demo tape—unsolicited submissions OK. Prefers 7½ ips reel-to-reel or cassette (or VHS videocassette) with 1-3 songs and lyric sheet. "Don't let the song get buried in the videocassette productions; a bio in front of performance helps. Enclose press kit or other background information." Does not return unsolicited material. Reports in 1 month.
Music: Mostly blues, country and ballads; also easy listening, jazz, MOR, R&B and soul. Published "Blues Monday Video," with Charlie "B" and Barbara Burton; "French Quarter Blues," written and recorded by JanJo on Seeds Records (blues); "Sincerely Yours" (by Charles Burton), recorded by Barabara Burton on Seeds Records (easy listening); and "Bluebird Fly Away," written and recorded by Benny Kubiak on Homa Records (country instrumental).
Tips: "Send 3 songs *only* on good tape with lyric sheet."

OLD EMPRESS MUSIC/DOGHOUSE PRODUCTIONS, Suite 3, 1226 17th Ave. S., Nashville TN 37212. Professional Manager: Maurice Godwin/Hal Godwin. Music publisher. BMI, ASCAP. Estab. 1987. Publishes 25-30 songs/year; publishes 5 new songwriters/year. Works with composers and lyricists; teams collaborators. Pays standard royalty.
Affiliate(s): Dish Bowl Music (ASCAP), UN-DER 16 Songs (SESAC).
How to Contact: Submit a demo tape by mail—unsolicited submissions are OK. Prefers cassette with 4 songs and lyric sheets. "Use chrome tape only." SASE. Reports in 3 weeks.
Music: Mostly dance, rock and pop; also country and R&B. Published "Real" (by Roy Cathey Jr.), recorded by Mickey Dee on Rock City Records (rock); "Sheila Likes Hollywood," written and recorded by Bruce McMaster on Black Gold Records (rock).
Tips: "Looking for completed masters for overseas releases. Know about publishing contracts."

O'LYRIC MUSIC, Suite 1, 1837 Eleventh St., Santa Monica CA 90404. (213)452-0815. President: J. O'Loughlin. Creative Director: Kathryn Haddock. Music publisher, manager (O'Lyric Music Management) and production company. BMI, ASCAP. Member California Copyright Conference. Estab. 1980. Publishes 50-75 songs/year; publishes 10-15 new songwriters/year. Hires staff writers; pays $20,000/year—"only duty expected is songwriting. Writers paid by royalties earned and by advances." Pays standard royalty to outside writers.
Affiliate(s): O'Lyrical Music (ASCAP).
How to Contact: Prefers cassette with 1-3 songs and lyric sheet. Does not return materials. Reports as soon as possible. SASE for reply. Please no phone calls.
Music: Mostly R&B, rock, top 40, dance and country; also contemporary jazz and soul. Published "I Live for Your Love" (by P. Reswick/S. Werfil/A. Rich), recorded by Natalie Cole on Manhattan Records (R&B/crossover); "Mr. Right" (by T. Shapiro/M. Garvin), recorded by Smokey Robinson on Motown Records (R&B/crossover); and "I've Still Got the Love We Made" (by Shapiro/Garvin/Waters), recorded by Reba McEntire (country/crossover). Production company works with Double T (Next Plateau Records), Cactus Choir (Atlantic Records), and The Biggs.
Tips: "Please follow our policy without exception."

OMNI RECORDS, INC., P.O. Box 917, Bala Cynwyd PA 19004. (215)828-7030. President: Steven Bernstein. Music publisher and record company. Estab. 1973. BMI. Publishes 50 songs/year; publishes 3-4 new songwriters/year. Employs songwriters on a salary basis. Teams collaborators.
How to Contact: Prefers cassette. Does not return unsolicited material.
Music: R&B and dance ONLY. Published "Closer than Close" (by Terri Price), recorded by Jean Carne; and "Lonely Road" (by Bryan Williams), recorded by Rose Royce, both on Omni Records (both R&B); and "Love Won't Let Me Wait" by Luther Vandross.

*ONE FOR THE MONEY MUSIC PUBLISHING CO. (BMI), P.O. Box 18751, Milwaukee WI 53218. (414)774-7489. President: Michael W. White. Music publisher, record company (World Class Record Co.) and record producer (MW Communications). BMI. Estab. 1989. Publishes 4-6 songs/year. Works with composers and lyricists; teams collaborators. Pays standard royalty.

How to Contact: Submit a demo tape by mail—unsolicited submissions are OK. Prefers cassette or VHS videocassette with 6-8 songs and lyric sheet (if possible). SASE. Reports in 1 month.
Music: Mostly country-rock, country-pop and country; also rock and R&B. Published "Whoops I'm in Love Again" (by White, Kowalski, Barker, Goetzke); "Twenty Three Days" (by M.W. White); and "Just Remember I'm Still Lovin' You" (by Kowalski, White, Barker); all recorded by Sky Harbor Band on World Class Records (country rock).

OPERATION PERFECTION, Suite 206, 6245 Bristol Pkwy., Culver City CA 90230. Contact: Larry McGee. Vice-President: Darryl McCorkle. Music publisher. BMI. Estab. 1976. Publishes 15 songs/year; publishes 1-2 new songwriters/year. Receives 200 submissions/year. Works with composers and lyricists. Pays standard royalty.
How to Contact: Submit a demo tape—unsolicited submissions OK. Prefers cassette (or VHS videocassette) with 1-4 songs and lyric sheet. "Please only send professional quality material!" Does not return unsolicited material. Reports in 8 weeks.
Music: Rock, rap, pop, MOR/adult contemporary and R&B. Published "We're Number One" (by Liz Davis), recorded by The Saxon Sisters on Boogie Band (rock); "Captain Freedom" and "Voices" (by Kenny Sims), recorded by Sheena Kriss on Mega Star Records (R&B).
Tips: "Study past, present and future trends in the music industry."

ORCHID PUBLISHING, Bouquet-Orchid Enterprises, Box 11686, Atlanta GA 30355. (404)355-7635. President: Bill Bohannon. Music publisher, record company, record producer (Bouquet-orchid Enterprises) and artist management. BMI. Member CMA, AFM. Publishes 10-12 songs/year; publishes 3 new songwriters/year. Works with composers and lyricists; teams collaborators. Pays standard royalty.
How to Contact: Prefers cassette with 3-5 songs and lyric sheet. "Send biographical information if possible—even a photo helps." SASE. Reports in 1 month.
Music: Religious ("Amy Grant, etc., contemporary gospel"); country ("George Strait, The Judds type material"); and top 100/pop ("Peter Cetera, Whitney Houston type material"). Published "Good Loving" (by Ralph Cherry), recorded by the Bandoleers; and "Let Me Be Your Lover" (by Clayton Russ), recorded by Susan Spencer.

ORDER PUBLISHING, 6503 York Rd., Baltimore MD 21212. (301)377-2270. President: Jeff Order. Music publisher and record producer (Jeff Order/Order Productions). ASCAP. Estab. 1986. Publishes 20 songs/year; publishes 3-4 new songwriters/year. Receives 20 submissions/month. Works with composers and lyricists. Pays standard royalty.
How to Contact: Write or call first to submit a tape. Prefers cassette with 4 songs. Does not return unsolicited material. Reports in 1 month.
Music: All types. Published "OH!," recorded by J. Order & Hiram Bullock (rock); "Won't You Dance With Me," recorded by Tiny Tim (dance); and "Sea of Tranquility" and "Isis Unveiled," written and recorded by Jeff Order and recorded on Order Productions Records (new A/C).
Tips: "Submit high-quality, well-recorded and produced material. Original styles and sounds. Don't waste our time or yours on copying the music of mainstream artists."

OTTO PUBLISHING CO., P.O. Box 16540, Plantation FL 33318. (305)741-7766. President: Frank X. Loconto. Music publisher, record company (FXL Records) and record producer (Loconto Productions). ASCAP. Estab. 1978. Publishes 25 songs/year; publishes 1-5 new songwriters/year. Pays standard royalty.
Affiliate(s): Betty Brown Music Co. (BMI), and Clara Church Music Co. (SESAC), True Friends Music (BMI).
How to Contact: Prefers cassette with 1-4 songs and lyric sheet. SASE. Reports in 1 month.
Music: Mostly country, MOR, religious and gospel. Published "Sewing Without Pins" (TV theme) and "Safety Sam" (novelty), both by Frank X. Loconto, recorded by Loconto Productions. Theme Song for "Nightly Business Reports," nationally syndicated TV show, written and recorded by Frank X. Loconto. Also published "Seminole Man" (by Loconto), recorded by James Billie on FXL Records (country).

*PADY MUSIC PUBLISHING CO., P.O. Box 3500, Pawtucket RI 02861. (401)728-1689. President: Karen Pady. Music publisher, record company (Pady Music Publishing Co.; Big K Records) and record producer (KA Productions, Karen Pady). ASCAP. Estab. 1986. Publishes 6 songs/year; publishes 1 new songwriter/year. Works with composers and lyricists; teams collaborators.
How to Contact: Write first and obtain permission to submit a tape. Prefers cassette or VHS videocassette with any number of songs and lyric sheet. SASE. Reports in 3 weeks.
Music: Mostly pop, rock and light rock; also country rock. Published "(You Were) My Best Friend," recorded by Karyn Krystal (country rock); "I Don't Need You," recorded by Karyn Krystal (rock); and "That's What I'm Living For," recorded by Midnight Fantasy (A/C); all by Karen Padykula on Big K Records.

*R.A. PAINTER MUSIC PUBLISHING, P.O. Box 111717, Nashville TN 37222-1717. (615)776-5188. President: Richard Allan Painter. Music publisher. BMI, ASCAP. Publishes 5-20 songs/year. Publishes 2-5 new songwriters/year. Pays standard royalty.
How to Contact: Send SASE for free information.
Music: Suited for audiences that appreciate pop, rock, and R&B; such that translates into broad commercial appeal and staying power in the target market.
Tips: "Pursue excellence and tell the truth as your only artistic moral imperative."

PALMETTO PRODUCTIONS, P.O. Box 1376, Pickens SC 29671. (803)859-9624. FAX: (803)859-3814. President: Brian E. Raines. Music publisher, record company (Palmetto Records), record producer and artist management/booking (Palmetto Productions). ASCAP. Publishes 10 songs/year; publishes 5 new songwriters/year. Receives 300 submissions/year. Works with composers and lyricists; teams collaborators. Pays standard royalty.
Affiliate(s): Brian Raines Music Co. (ASCAP) and Brian Song Music Co. (BMI).
How to Contact: Submit a demo tape, unsolicited submissions are OK. Prefers cassette (or VHS videocassette) with 2-3 songs and lyric sheet. "All demos are listened to whether professionally recorded or done at home." SASE. Reports "at earliest convenience."
Music: Country, gospel and Top 40. Published "Since I Met You," written and recorded by Brian Raines on Palmetto Records (country); "It Makes Me Glad" (by Jim Hubbard), recorded by Joe Russell on White Line Records (gospel); "Take It To Jesus" (by Dale Cassell), recorded by Trinity on Mark Five Records (gospel).
Tips: "Send good chart material. We also like a biography of the writer with a photo if possible. Try to send material that has been recorded by 'local' artists, or that is currently being performed on a local level. SASE required!"

J.S. PALUCH COMPANY, INC./WORLD LIBRARY PUBLICATIONS, INC., 3825 N. Willow Rd., P.O. Box 2703, Schiller Park IL 60176-0703. Music Editors: Mark G. Rachelski/Nicholas T. Freund, Betty Z. Reiber. Music publisher. SESAC. Estab. 1913. Publishes 50 or more songs/year; publishes varying number of new songwriters/year; recordings. Receives more than 300 submissions/year. Works with composers and lyricists; teams collaborators.
How to Contact: Submit demo tape by mail—unsolicited submissions are OK. Prefers cassette with any number of songs, lyric sheet and lead sheet. SASE. Reports in 3 months.
Music: Sacred music, songs, hymns, choral settings, descants, psalm settings, masses; also children's sacred music. Published "Sing Praise and Thanksgiving," by Michael Joncas (mass setting); "Come Christians, Join to Sing" by Mark Rachelski (congregations and choral setting); "Prayer of St. Francis," by James V. Marchionda, O.P. (song for choir).
Tips: "Make your manuscript as legible as possible, with clear ideas regarding tempo, etc. Base the text upon scripture."

PAMSCO INTERNATIONAL INC., 10022 NW 80th Ave., Hialeah Gardens FL 33016. (305)823-8147. Manager: Norbert L. Selasco. Music publisher, record company (Music Hall/Can Records/Sazam Records) and record producer (Sicamericana S.A.C.I.F.I.). SADAIC. Estab. 1950. Publishes 200 songs/year; 10 new songwriters/year. Works with composers and lyricists. Pays standard royalty.
How to Contact: Submit a demo tape, unsolicited submissions are OK. Prefers cassette with 8 songs and lead sheets. Does not return unsolicited material. Reports in 1½ months.
Music: Mostly New Age, ballads and tango. Published "Cuando Yo Amo," written and recorded by A. Vezzani; "Enterate Ya," written and recorded by Ian Simmons; and "Que Puedo Hacer Por Ti" (by Valeria Lynch), recorded by Marcelo Alejandro; all on Music Hall Records (ballad).

PANDISC RECORDS, 38 NE 167 St., Miami FL 33162. (305)948-6466. President: Bo Crane. Music publisher and record company (Pandisc, Jamarc). ASCAP, BMI. Estab. 1979. Publishes 50 songs/year; publishes 3-6 new songwriters/year. Receives 200 submissions/month. Works with composers and lyricists; teams collaborators. Pays standard royalty.
Affiliate(s): Whooping Crane Music (BMI) and Hombre Del Mundo (ASCAP).
How to Contact: Submit a demo tape by mail—unsolicited submissions are OK. Prefers cassette with 3 songs and lyric sheet. Does not return unsolicited material.
Music: Mostly rap and R&B. Published "B Girls" (by C. Trahan/L. Johnson), recorded by Young & Restless (rap); and "I Can't Let Go" (by Y. Israel), recorded by Joey Gilmore (blues), both on Pandisc Records; and "I Seen Your Boyfriend," (by Baily/Daniels), recorded by Get Fresh Girls on Breakaway Records (rap).

PAPE PUBLISHING, 7 Tansley Ave., Scarborough ON M1J 1P2 **Canada**. Phone: (416)267-7482. President: Peter Panayotu. Music publisher. CAPAC. Estab. 1980. Publishes 2 songs/year; 1 new songwriter/year. Receives 30 submissions/year. Works with composers; teams collaborators. Pays standard royalty.

How to Contact: Write first and obtain permission to submit a tape. Prefers cassette with 1-2 songs and lyric sheets. Does not return unsolicited material. Reports in 2 months.
Music: Mostly pop, country and R&B; also New Age, rock and ethnic. Published "Don't Stop This Feeling" (by Morrison/Panayotu), recorded by Pape Gang on Ravin' Records (pop); "What About Me?" (by Bleakley/Panayotu), recorded by Bobby Blake on Pape Records; and "Cool in Grade 10," written and recorded by Sean Lynch on Pape Records (country).

*PARCHMENT HARBOR MUSIC, 6920-214 Koll Center Pkwy., Pleasanton CA 94566. (415)846-6194.
CEO: Pam Hanna. Music publisher, record company (Wingate Records), record producer (Wingate) and artist management and talent agency (Wingate). BMI. Estab. 1989. Publishes 24 songs/year; publishes 6 new songwriters/year. Receives 50 submissions/month. Works with composers and lyricists; team collaborators. Pays standard royalty.
Affiliate(s): Hugo First Publishing (ASCAP).
How to Contact: Write or call first and obtain permission to submit a tape. Prefers cassette with 2 songs and lyric sheet. "Include SASE and brief writer bio/discography." SASE. Reports in 2 weeks.
Music: Mostly pop, country and R&B; also rock, contemporary Christian and A/C. Published "Last American Hero" (by Dave May and Rusty Colt), recorded by Robyn Banx (country); "Locomotive #3" (Bob Eggert/Joe Ryan), recorded by Bob Eggert (country); and "Sack the Quarterback" (Pam Hanna/Patty Markoch), recorded by Kathy Kennedy (rock); all on Wingate Records.

PDS MUSIC PUBLISHING, P.O. Box 412477, Kansas City MO 64141-2477. Contact: Submissions Department. Music publisher and record company (PDS Records, Universal Jazz, PDS Associated labels). ASCAP, BMI. Estab. 1988. Publishes 30 songs/year; publishes 3-4 new songwriters/year. Receives 4 submissions/month. Works with composers and lyricists. Pays standard royalty.
Affiliate(s): PDS Universal (ASCAP), PDS Worldwide (BMI).
How to Contact: Write first and obtain permission to submit a tape. Prefers cassette with 5-10 songs and lyric sheet. Does not return unsolicited material. Reports in 2 months.
Music: Mostly rap and R&B. Published "I Like the Things You Do," (by Derrick Peters/Kevin Griffin), recorded by Kevin Griffin on PDS Records (R&B); "The Way You Make Me Feel" (by D. Peters), recorded by Legacy on PDS Records (R&B).
Tips: "Follow directions and be patient."

PECOS VALLEY MUSIC, 2709 West Pine Lodge, Roswell NM 88201. (505)622-0244. President: Ray Willmon. Music publisher. BMI. Estab. 1989. Publishes 15-20 songs/year; publishes 3-4 new songwriters/year. Receives 20-30 submissions/month. Works with composers and lyricists; teams collaborators. Pays standard royalty.
How to Contact: Submit a demo tape by mail—unsolicited submissions are OK. Prefers cassette (or VHS cassette if available) with 2-4 songs and lyric sheet. SASE. Reports in 2 weeks.
Music: Mostly country, pop and rock. Published "Lifetime Guarantee" (by Ray Willmon), "And Took Your Love Away" (by Ron Ritzwater) and "You Don't Owe Me a Thing" by (Ray Willmon) (country).
Tips: "Good clear recorded lyrics with typed lyric sheet. Record companies seem to listen more these days to traditional country music."

PEERMUSIC, 8159 Hollywood Blvd., Los Angeles CA 90069. (213)656-0364. Contact: Director of A&R. Music publisher and artist development promotional label. ASCAP, BMI. Estab. 1928. Publishes 40 songs/year; publishes 2-5 new songwriters/year. Hires staff songwriters. Works with self-contained artists.
Affiliate(s): P.S.O. LTD (ASCAP), Peermusic (BMI).
How to Contact: Write first and obtain permission to submit a tape. Prefers cassette (VHS videocassette if available) with 2 songs and lyric sheet. Does not return unsolicited material. Reports in 1 month.
Music: Mostly R&B, pop and rock; also all types. Published "I Can't Cry Hard Enough" (by Williams/Etzioni), recorded by Williams Bros. (pop) on Warner Bros. Records; "Slow Burn" (by Bliss/Pisken), recorded by Louise Hoffsten on BMG Records (pop/rock); "I Don't Have the Heart" (by Jud Friedman/Allan Rich), recorded by James Ingram on Warner Bros. Records (#1 pop/R&B ballad); "Child Bride" (by Marvin Etzioni), recorded by Katy Moffatt on Philo/Rounder Records (blues rock); and "Metropolis" (by The Church), recorded by The Church on Arista Records (rock).

PEGASUS MUSIC, 27 Bayside Ave., Te Atatu, Auckland 8, **New Zealand**. Professional Manager: Errol Peters. Music publisher and record company. APRA. Estab. 1981. Publishes 20-30 songs/year; publishes 5 new songwriters/year. Receives 20-30 submissions/year. Works with composers and lyricists; teams collaborators. Pays 3-5% to artists on contract and standard royalty to songwriters; royalties paid directly to US songwriters.

How to Contact: Submit a demo tape—unsolicited submissions are OK. Prefers cassette with 3-5 songs and lyric sheet. SAE and IRC. Reports in 1 month.
Music: Mostly country; also bluegrass, easy listening and top 40/pop. Published "The Mirror" (by Ginny Peters), recorded by Dennis Marsh on Ode Records (country); "Ladybird," written and recorded by Tina Whall on Ode Records (folk/country); and "Any Old Time," written and recorded by Ginny Peters on Kiwi Pacific Records (country).
Tips: "Be fresh and original. We prefer direct lyrics."

PENNY THOUGHTS MUSIC, 484 Lexington St., Waltham MA 02154. (617)891-7800. President: John Penny. Music publisher, record company (Belmont Records and Waverly Records) and record producer. BMI. Publishes 12-15 songs/year. Receives 10-12 submissions/months. Pays standard royalty.
How to Contact: Write first to get permission to submit a tape. SASE. Reports in 2 weeks. Not accepting material at this time.
Music: Mostly country; also contemporary and rock (country). Published "Give It Away," written and recorded by Stan Anderson Jr. on Belmont Records (country); and "The Hurt That Hurts Me" and "You're the Right Love," by Mike Cummings (country).

*PERFECTION MUSIC PUBLICATION (BMI), P.O. Box 4094, Pittsburgh PA 15201. (412)782-4477. President: Edward J. Moschetti. Music publisher and record company (Century Records). Estab. 1953. Works with composers.
Affiliate(s): Regal Music Publications (ASCAP).
How to Contact: Write first and obtain permission to submit a tape. Prefers cassette. SASE. Reports in 1 month.
Music: Ballads, country and pop.

PHILIPPOPOLIS MUSIC, 12027 Califa St., North Hollywood CA 91607. President: Milcho Leviev. Music publisher. BMI. Member GEMA, NARAS. Estab. 1975. Publishes 3-5 songs/year; publishes 1-2 new songwriters/year. Works with lyricists. Pays standard royalty.
How to Contact: Submit a demo tape, unsolicited submissions are OK. Prefers cassette with 1-3 songs. Prefers studio produced demos. SASE. Reports in 1 month.
Music: Jazz and classical fusion. Published "Raga Todor" (by Spassov/Leviev); "Jim Gem Jay" and "Just Another Blues" (by Leviev), all recorded by L.S. Duo on Balkanton Records (jazz).

PIN PUBLISHING, 11 Shady Oak Trail, Charlotte NC 28210. (704)554-1162. Director: Butch Kelly. Music publisher, record company (Kam Executive, Fresh Aire, New Town Records) and record producer (Butch Kelly Productions). ASCAP, BMI. Estab. 1981. Publishes 10 songs/year; publishes 3 new songwriters/year. Teams collaborators. Pays standard royalty.
Affiliate(s): Pin Publishing (ASCAP), Music by Butch Kelly (BMI).
How to Contact: Write first and obtain permission to submit a tape. Prefers cassette (VHS videocassette) with 3 songs and lyric sheets. SASE. Reports in 2 months.
Music: Mostly pop, R&B and rock; also rap. Published "Power" (by Butch Kelly), recorded by Sunshine on KAM Records (R&B); "Money" (by Greg B.), recorded by Greg B. on KAM Records (R&B); and "War" (by McCrush), recorded by T.K. on KAM Records (pop).

PINE ISLAND MUSIC, #308, 9430 Live Oak Place, Ft. Lauderdale FL 33324. (305)472-7757. President: Jack P. Bluestein. Music publisher, record company and record producer. BMI, ASCAP. Estab. 1973-1974. Publishes 50-100 songs/year; publishes 25-30 new songwriters/year. Receives 100 submissions/month. Works with composers, lyricists; teams collaborators. Pays standard royalty.
Affiliate(s): Lantana Music (BMI) and Twister Music (ASCAP).
How to Contact: Submit a demo tape—unsolicited submissions OK. Prefers cassette or 7½ ips reel-to-reel (or VHS videocassette) with 3 songs and lyric sheet. SASE. Reports in 2-4 months.
Music: Mostly country and pop; also gospel, soft rock and contemporary. Published "Golden Penny" written and recorded by Walt Sambor on Quadrant Records (children's country); "Lucky Is A Man" (by Larry Coen), recorded by Al Williams on Quadrant Records (country/pop); "Kathy, Dear" (by Al Williams), recorded by Kathy Ratzburg on Quadrant Records (pop/C&W).

PLACER PUBLISHING, Box 11301, Kansas City KS 66111. (913)287-3495 (night). Owner: Steve Vail. Music publisher, record company (System Records) and record producer. ASCAP. Estab. 1980. Publishes 2 songs/year; publishes 1 new songwriter/year. Receives 10 submissions/months. Works with composers and lyricists. Pays standard royalty.
How to Contact: Submit a demo tape—unsolicited submissions are OK. Prefers cassette (or VHS or Beta ½″ videocassette) with 10-12 songs. Does not return unsolicited material. Reports in 6 weeks.
Music: Mostly classic rock, New Age and jazz. Published "Echo Lake," "Mother Earth, Father Sky" and "The Path" (all by Vail), recorded by Realm on System Records (progressive rock).

PLANET DALLAS, P.O. Box 191447, Dallas TX 75219. (214)521-2216. Producer, Music publisher, record producer (Rick Rooney) and recording studio (Planet Dallas). BMI, ASCAP. Estab. 1985. Publishes 50 songs/year; 2-3 new songwriters/year. Receives 20 submissions/month. Works with composers and lyricists; teams collaborators. Pays standard royalty; also depends on deal/studio work.
Affiliate(s): Stoli Music (ASCAP).
How to Contact: Write or call first and obtain permission to submit. Prefers cassette with 1-3 songs and lyric sheet. SASE for reply. Reports in 4-6 weeks.
Music: Mostly modern rock and top 40. Published "This Property is Condemned" (by P. Sugg), recorded by Maria McKee on Geffen Records (pop); "Tickle" (by U Know Who), recorded by U Know Who on WE–Mix Records (rap); and "Hydrogen City" (by Hydrogen City), recorded by Hydrogen City on H1 Records (rock).

PLATINUM BOULEVARD PUBLISHING, 523 East Prater Ave., Reno NV 89431. (702)358-7484. President: Lawrence Davis. Music publisher. BMI. Estab. 1984. Publishes 12 songs/year; 1 new songwriter/year. Receives 30 submissions/month. Works with composers and lyricists. Pays standard royalty, but will negotiate.
How to Contact: Submit a demo tape by mail–unsolicited submissions are OK. Prefers cassette (or VHS videocassette), with unlimited songs and lyric or lead sheets. "Songs must be in English." Does not return unsolicited material. "We report only if interested."
Music: Mostly rock, country and R&B; also country, jazz and New Age. Published "Long Haul," "Crazy Thing" and "Don't Shut Me Out," all written and recorded by Lawrence Davis on Platinum Boulevard Records (AOR).
Tips: "We own a 24-track studio and are willing to provide inexpensive recording time to qualified artists wishing to improve their demo sound."

*POLLYBYRD PUBLICATIONS LIMITED, P.O. Box 8442, Universal CA 91608. (818)506-8533. Professional Manager: Maxx Diamond. Music publisher (Kelli Jai, Pollyann, Ja Nikki, Lonnvaness Branmar and PPL Music). ASCAP, BMI, SESAC. Estab. 1979. Publishes 100 songs/year; publishes 25-40 new songwriters/year. Hires staff writers. Works with composers and lyricists; teams collaborators. Pays standard royalty.
Affiliate(s): Kellijai Music (ASCAP), Pollyann Music (ASCAP), Ja'Nikki Songs (BMI), Branmar (BMI), Lonnvanness (SESAC) and PPL Music (ASCAP).
How to Contact: Write first and obtain permission to submit a tape. Prefers cassette or VHS videocassette with 4 songs and lyric and lead sheet. SASE. Reports in 4-6 weeks.
Music: Published "This Time" (by Jae Jarrett), recorded by B. Fynne on Credence Records (dance); "Shakedown" (by Jae Jarrett), recorded by Band AKA on Bouvier/CBS Records (R&B, dance); and "Love Song" (by Dale Mitchell), recorded by D.M. Groove on Bouvier Records (R&B).

PPI/PETER PAN INDUSTRIES, 88 St. Francis St., Newark NJ 07105. (201)344-4214. Product Manager: Marianne Eggleston. Music publisher, record company (Compose Records, Current Records, Parade Video, Ironbound Publishing, Compose), record producer (Dunn Pearson, Jr.); also outside producers. ASCAP, BMI. Estab. 1928. Publishes over 100 songs/year. Hires staff songwriters. Works with composers and lyricists; teams collaborators. Pays standard royalty "based on agreements."
Affiliate(s): Ironbound Publishing (ASCAP), Triloka Records, DA Music.
How to Contact: Submit a demo tape by mail–unsolicited submissions are OK. Prefers cassette (or VHS videocassette if available) with 3-5 songs. "Please include name, address and phone numbers on all materials, along with picture, bio and contact information. SASE. Reports in 3-4 months.
Music: Mostly children's–audio, R&B and jazzy; also exercise–video, rock and classical. Published "Ring My Bell" (by Fredrick Knight), recorded by Karen King on Power Records (Dance/12'); "Beautiful Lullabyes" (by Dunn Pearson, Jr.), recorded by Tawatha Agee and Bill Rippone on Compose Records (children's CD/cass.); and "Sing A Long," on Peter Pan Records (children's CD/cassette).

PRATT AND MCCLAIN MUSIC (ASCAP), Box 852, Beverly Hills CA 90213. (818)769-2842. President: Jeremy McClain. Music Publisher (Happy Days Music) and record producer. Deals with artists and songwriters. Voting member of NARAS. Gold record and Grammy winner on "Happy Days" (theme from TV show).
How to Contact: Prefers cassettes, video or audio.
Music Mostly pop, rock and some progressive gospel.
Tips: "Direct access to Donna Summer, Christopher Cross, Debbie Boone and Michael Omartian."

*PREJIPPIE MUSIC GROUP, Box 2849, Trolley Station, Detroit MI 48231. (313)581-1267. Partner: Bruce Henderson. Music publisher, record company (PMG Records) and record producer (PMG Productions). BMI. Estab. 1990. Publishes 50-75 songs/year; publishes 2-3 new songwriters/year. Hires staff writers. Teams collaborators. Pays standard royalty.

How to Contact: Submit a demo tape by mail—unsolicited submissions are OK. Prefers cassette with 3-4 songs and lyric sheet. SASE. Reports in 1 month.
Music: Mostly rap, funk rock and dance; also alternative, rock and experimental music. Published "Ego-Trip," "Feel That Groove" and "Redd Hott (Breathless)" (by Bruce & Victoria Henderson), recorded by The Prejippes on PMG Records (hip house).

PRESCRIPTION COMPANY, 70 Murray Ave., Port Washington NY 11050. (516)767-1929. President: David F. Gasman. Music publisher and record producer. BMI. Pays standard royalty.
How to Contact: Call or write first about your interest. Prefers cassette with any number of songs and lyric sheet. "Send all submissions with SASE (or no returns)." Reports in 1 month.
Music: Bluegrass, blues, children's, country, dance-oriented, easy listening, folk, jazz, MOR, progressive, R&B, rock, soul and top 40/pop. Published "You Came In," "Rock 'n' Roll Blues" and "Seasons" (by D.F. Gasman), all recorded by Medicine Mike on Prescription Records.
Tips: "Songs should be good and written to last. Forget fads—we want songs that'll sound as good in 10 years as they do today. Organization, communication and exploration of form are as essential as message (and sincerity matters, too)."

PRESTATION MUSIC, 24 Gachard St., Brussels **Belgium** 1050. (02)6492847. General Manager: Pierre Pletinckx. Music publisher, record company (B. Sharp Selection Multi Sound Music). SABAM. Works with composers; teams collaborators. Pays standard royalty 50%.
How to Contact: Submit a demo tape by mail—unsolicited submissions are OK. Prefers cassette. SASE. Reports in 1 month.
Music: Mostly instrumental, jazz and New Age.

JIMMY PRICE MUSIC PUBLISHER, Sun-Ray Production Company, 1662 Wyatt Parkway, Lexington KY 40505. (606)254-7474. Owner: Jimmy Price. Music publisher, record company (Sun-Ray, Sky-Vue) and record producer (Jimmy Price Music Publisher). BMI. Estab. 1950. Works with composers and lyricists. Pays standard royalty.
Affiliate(s): Jimmy Price Productions (BMI).
How to Contact: Submit a demo tape by mail—unsolicited submissions are OK. Prefers cassette or track ½ or Full 7½ ips reel-to-reel with 3-7 songs and lyric sheet. SASE. Reports in 1½ months.
Music: Mostly country, gospel and bluegrass. Published "My High Country," written and recorded by Charles Stephens (country); "Walk with Jesus" (by Jimmy Price), recorded by Charles Stephens (gospel), all on Sun-Ray.
Tips: "I must have the lyrics to meter. If a person does not know what I mean about bringing lyrics to meter, please check a gospel hymn song book. You will see in each and every staff there is a music note for each and every word or syllable. This way, should I want to add a composition in print I can do so."

PRIMAL VISIONS MUSIC, Suite 133, 3701 Inglewood Ave., Redondo Beach CA 90278. (213)214-0370. Creative Director: Jeffrey Howard. Music publisher, record company (Primal Records) and record producer (Primal Productions, Inc.). BMI. Estab. 1989. Publishes 10-15 songs/year. Works with composers and lyricists; teams collaborators. Pays standard royalty or other amount "depending on the deal per artist or writer."
How to Contact: Write or call to arrange a personal interview. Prefers cassette (or VHS videocassette if available) with 1-5 songs and lyric sheet. SASE. Reports in 6 weeks.
Music: Mostly pop/rock, hard rock and dance/R&B; also rap, rock and country. "Mirror, Mirror," "Piece of the Action" and "Locked In a Box," (all written and recorded by Jeffrey Howard) all on Primal Records (rock).

PRIMAVERA SOUND PRODUCTIONS, 6283-3410 Shelbourne St., Victoria, British Columbia V8P 5L5 **Canada.** Professional Manager/Producer: Eduardo Pereira. Music publishers and record company (PSP Records). SOCAN. Estab. 1986. Publishes 5-10 songs/year; publishes 1-2 new songwriters/year. Works with composers. Pays standard royalty.
How to Contact: Prefers cassette (or Beta videocassette) with 3 songs. Unsolicited material OK. Does not return material but we keep it on file. Reports in 6 weeks.
Music: Mostly pop, rock; also Latin jazz, salsa, merengue, cumbia. Published "Papa Nicolas" (by Hugo Beltran), recorded by Hugo Beltran (merengue); "Let Me Know" (by DeGrassi/Walker), recorded by Julie Coy (top 40/rock); and "Pienso Tanto En Ti" (by Ruben Zunica), recorded by Yizeth.

***PRINCE/SF PUBLICATIONS,** 1135 Francisco St., San Francisco CA 94109. (415)775-9627. Artists Representative: Ken Malucelli. Music publisher (Auriga, Christmas) and record producer (Prince/SF Productions). ASCAP. Estab. 1975. Publishes 2 songs/year; publishes 2 new songwriters/year. Works with composers and lyricists "under personal management"; teams collaborators. Pays statutory rate.

How to Contact: Write first and obtain permission to submit a tape. Prefers cassette with VHS videocassette with 3 songs and lyric or lead sheet. "Primarily interested in a cappella, novelty, theatrical material." SASE. Reports ASAP.

Music: Mostly original pop, Christmas and satire; also unusual, humorous. Published "Oh What a Heavenly Morn!" (by Ken Malucelli), recorded by Merrie Olde Christmas Carolers on Christmas Records (holiday); "Freedomsong" (by Eric Morris), recorded by The Edlos on Auriga Records (pop); and "Package" (by Eric Morris), recorded by The Edlos on Auriga Records (pop).

Tips: "Work should be unique, high quality, not derivative."

PRITCHETT PUBLICATION (Branch), P.O. Box 725, Daytona Beach FL 32114-0725. (904)252-4848. Vice President: Charles Vickers. Music publisher and record company. (Main office in California.) BMI. Estab. 1975. Publishes 21 songs/year; publishes 12 new songwriters/year. Works with composers and lyricists. Pays standard royalty.

Affiliate(s): Alison Music (ASCAP).

How to Contact: Write first and obtain permission to submit. Prefers cassette with 6 songs and lyric or lead sheet. SASE.

Music: Gospel, rock-disco and country. Published *Walkin On The Water* (by Charles Vickers), recorded by Charles Vickers on King of Kings Records (gospel); and "It'll Be A Cold Day" (by Leroy Pritchett), recorded by Ray Sanders on Alagash Country Records (country).

PROPHECY PUBLISHING, INC., P.O. Box 4945, Austin TX 78765. (512)452-9412. President: T. White. Music publisher. ASCAP. Pays standard royalty, less expenses; "expenses such as tape duplicating, photocopying and long distance phone calls are recouped from the writer's earnings."

Affiliate(s): Black Coffee Music (BMI).

How to Contact: "We now only accept songs which are currently on the charts or have a very good chance of entering them next week."

Music: Published "The Sun and Moon and Stars" and "Woman of the Phoenix," (by Vince Bell), performed by Lyle Lovett (country/jazz).

Tips: "Only songs with immediate projected income would entice us to add to our roster."

PUBLISHING CENTRAL, (formerly Alltold Music Publishing), 7251 Lowell Dr., Overland Park KS 66204. (913)384-6688. Director of Publishing: Mark David Pine. Music publisher. "We are also a theatrical agency." SAG, ITAA. Estab. 1961. Publishes 5 songs/year; publishes 3 new songwriter/year. Teams collaborators. Pays standard royalty.

Affiliate(s): Jac-Zang (ASCAP), Bunion (BMI).

How to Contact: Submit a demo tape by mail—unsolicited submissions are O.K. Prefers cassette with 1-3 songs and lead sheets. Does not return unsolicited material. Reports in 2 months.

Music: Mostly country rock, pop and rock; also gospel reggae, alternative, cutting edge and soul (southern). Published "It Did Me In" (by Mark Baysinger), recorded by Brewer/Shipley on Capitol (country/rock).

Tips: "There is a trend toward more professionalism. More songwriters can actually write music. They provide lead sheets and not just lyrics and tapes. Take advantage of the advances in music technology and put a part of your soul in your composition."

PURPLE HAZE MUSIC, P.O. Box 1243, Beckley WV 25802. President: Richard L. Petry. (304)252-4836. A & R: Carol Lee. Music publisher. BMI. Estab. 1968. Publishes 3-5 songs/year; publishes 3-4 new songwriters/year. Receives 150 submissions/year. Works with composers and lyricists; teams collaborators. Pays standard royalty.

How to Contact: Prefers cassette with 3-5 songs and lyric sheet. SASE. Reports in 4 weeks.

Music: Country, pop/top 40 and R&B/crossover. Published "Keep Movin' " (by Chuck Paul), recorded by Chuck Paul on Rising Sun Records; "A Little Night Lovin' " (by Carol Lee), recorded by Victor Jackson on Rising Sun Records (R&B); and "Blue Kentucky Boy" (by Ron Miller/Don MacClean), recorded by Cypress Creek on Country Road Records (country).

Tips: "Songs should be well thought out with clever hooks and lines. We now only accept a professional demo. All songs should be typed up neatly! We have a Nashville songwriters program for those who qualify."

PUSTAKA MUZIK EMI (Malaysia) SDN. BHD., Suite 10.01, 10th Floor, Exchange Square, off Jalan Semantan, Damansara Heights, 50490 Kuala Lumpur, Malaysia. Phone: 03-6277511. Contact: Publishing Manager. Music publisher and record company. Publishes 50 songs/year; publishes 15 new songwriters/year. Receives 200-300 submissions/month. Works with composers and lyricists; teams collaborators. Pays standard royalty

How to Contact: Prefers cassette and lyric or lead sheet. Does not return unsolicited material.
Music: Mostly MOR, country and commercial jazz; also blues and rock. Published "Sepi Sekuntum Mawar Merah" (by Fauzi Marzuki), recorded by Ella on WEA Records (pop rock); "Boom Boom Boom" (by A. Ali), recorded by Krystal on EMI Records (pop); and "Bunga Larangan" (by Wom), recorded by UG14 on Polygram Records (pop).
Tips: "Please send us properly recorded demo tape with commercial pop, rock musical material."

*QMARK MUSIC, 1201 Carlisle Ave., York PA 17404. (717)843-4228. President: Lewis Quintin. Music publisher. BMI. Estab. 1985. Publishes 12 songs/year; publishes 3 new songwriters/year. Pays standard royalty.
Affiliate(s): Barquin Music (ASCAP).
How to Contact: Write first and obtain permission to submit a tape. Prefers cassette with 2 songs and lyric sheet. Does not return unsolicited material. Reports in 6 weeks.
Music: Mostly country and R&B. Published "José" (by B. Belton), "Subway Casanova" (by Barken) and "Walking Down the Avenue" (by Belton), all recorded by Spyke on Qmark Records (pop/rock).

QUARK, INC., #1212, 1650 Broadway, New York NY 10019. (212)489-7260. Manager: Curtis Urbina. Music publisher, record company (Quark Records and Q-Rap Records), record producer (Curtis Urbina). Estab. 1986. Publishes 12 songs/year; 2 new songwriters/year. Receives 50 submissions/month. Teams collaborators. Pays standard royalty of 50%.
Affiliate(s): Quarkette Music (BMI) and Freedurb Music (ASCAP).
How to Contact: Write first and obtain permission to submit a tape. Prefers cassette with 2 songs and lyric sheet. Does not return unsolicited material. Reports in 2 weeks.
Music: Mostly pop, R&B and New Age. Published "Come To Me" (by Laluna), recorded by Laluna (dance); "What Am I Gonna Do" (by Larry Tee), recorded by Larry Tee (pop); and "Dreams" (by Ray Rusarco/Jimmy Sands), recorded by Quiet Storm (dance), all on Quark Records.

R. J. MUSIC, 10A Margaret Rd., Barnet, Herts. EN4 9NP **England**. Phone: (01)440-9788. Managing Directors: Roger James and Laura Skuce. Music publisher and management firm (Roger James Management). PRS. Pays negotiable royalty (up to 75%).
How to Contact: Prefers cassette with 1 song and lyric or lead sheet. Does not return material.
Music: Mostly MOR, blues, country and rock; also chart material. "No disco or rap!"

R.T.L. MUSIC, LEE MUSIC, LE MATTE MUSIC, POSO RECORDS, Stewart House, Hill Bottom Road, Sands-Ind. Est., Highwycome, Buckinghamshire HP12 4HJ **England**. Telephone 063081374. FAX: 063081612. A&R: Xavier Lee. Music publisher. PRS (UK). Estab. 1971. Works with composers and lyricists; teams collaborators. Pays standard royalty. Publishes 120 songs/year; publishes 50 new songwriters/year. Receives 10-15 submissions/month.
How to Contact: Submit a demo tape by mail—unsolicited submissions are OK. Prefers cassette, VHS videocassette with 3 songs and lyric or lead sheets. SASE. Reports in 6 weeks.
Music: Mostly all types. Published "Better Believe It" (pop rock); "Beautiful Sunday '91" (disco); and "Missing You" (ballad), all written and recorded by Daniel Boone on Swoop Records.

*RADIO TELE MUSIC S.A., Ch. de Waterloo Stwg. 868/870(B. 7) B-1180 Brussels **Belgium**. Phone: (02)375.65.60. Managing Director: Ray Van Cant. Music publisher and record company. SABAM. Estab. 1965. Publishes 150 songs/year; publishes 20 new songwriters/year. Works with composers and lyricists. "Writers get their writer's shares through collection societies."
How to Contact: Write or call and request submission policy.
Music: Mostly pop/easy listening. Published "She's In Love With Her Teacher" (by McKenny, Roefs), recorded by Ruth McKenny on Sonybel Records (rock); "1, 2, 3 Ole" (by Caerts), recorded by Nicole Mery on Nirola Records (pop); and "Mi Vida Tu" (by Jonet, Michael and Angel), recorded by Frank Michael on Carrere Records (Spanish).

RAINBARREL MUSIC COMPANY, P.O. Box 292101, Nashville TN 37229-2101. Director: Teresa Parks Bernard. BMI. Estab. 1972. Music publisher, record company (Paragold Records) and record producer. Publishes 10 songs/year; publishes 5 new songwriter/year. Receives 25 submissions/month. Teams collaborators. Pays standard royalty.

Listings of companies in countries other than the U.S. have the name of the country in boldface type.

How to Contact: Write first to get permission to submit. Prefers cassette with 2 songs and lyric and lead sheets. SASE. "No SASE, no answer."Reports in 6 weeks.
Music: Mostly country; also top 40. Published "Devil's Guitar" (by J. Bernard), recorded by Johnny Bernard on Paragold Records; "Muddy Mississippi" (by J. Bernard/Julie Jones), recorded by Reba McEntire on Mercury Records; and "Love" (by J. Bernard/J. Jones), recorded by Johnny Bernard/Julie Jones on Paragold Records (all country).
Tips: "Send only the most outstanding material you have."

*THE RAINBOW COLLECTION LTD., P.O. Box 300, Solebury PA 18963. (215)838-2295. President: Herb Gart. BMI, ASCAP. Music publisher, record company and record producer. Publishes 125 songs/year; publishes 10 new songwriters/year. Receives 50 submissions/month.Occasionally hires staff songwriters. Pays standard royalty.
How to Contact: Prefers cassette (or VHS videocassette) with 1-6 songs. Does not return unsolicited material. Reports in 2 months.
Music: Mostly rock, rap, pop, R&B and country; also blues, reggae, TV and movie scores and jazz. Published "Twisted Heart" (by Arens/Sundet), recorded by Minneapolis Funhouse on The Rainbow Collection Label (rock); "Pretty in Pink," by Mike Hughes (rock/film score); "Grizzly Bear," (by Jerry Corbitt, top 10 hit); and "A Mother Knows" (by Moser/Viereck), recorded by Mikki on Rainbow Collection (AC/c&s).
Tips: "Send me your finest work. If you are original and great and know it—if you believe in yourself and your artistry and are looking for a believer, contact me."

*RECORD COMPANY OF THE SOUTH (RCS) & VETTER MUSIC PUB., P.O. Box 14685, Baton Rouge LA 70898. (504)766-2996. General Manager: Johnny Palazzotto. Music publisher. ASCAP, BMI. Estab. 1978. Pays standard royalty.
How to Contact: Submit a demo tape by mail—unsolicited submissions are OK. Prefers cassette with 3-5 songs. SASE. Reports in 2-4 weeks.
Music: Mostly rock, R&B and country. Published "Knockin' Around" (by B. Hornsby), recorded by Joe Doe on Geffen Records (rock); and "Grovin' Out" (by C. Vetter), recorded by Joe Stampley on Paula Records (rock).

REN MAUR MUSIC CORP., 521 5th Ave., New York NY 10175. (212)757-3638. President: Rena L. Feeney. Music publisher and record company. BMI. Member AGAC and NARAS. Publishes 6-8 songs/year. Pays 4-8% royalty.
Affiliate(s): R.R. Music (ASCAP).
How to Contact: Prefers cassette with 2-4 songs and lead sheet. SASE. Reports in 1 month.
Music: R&B, rock, soul and top 40/pop. Published "Same Language," "Do It to Me and I'll Do It to You," and "Once You Fall in Love" (by Billy Nichols), recorded by Rena; and "Lead Me to Love" (by Brad Smiley), recorded by Carmen John (ballad/dance), all on Factory Beat Records.
Tips: "Send lead sheets and a good, almost finished cassette ready for producing or remixing."

RHYTHMS PRODUCTIONS, Whitney Bldg., P.O. Box 34485, Los Angeles CA 90034. President: Ruth White. Music publisher and record company (Tom Thumb Records). ASCAP. Member NARAS. Publishes 6 cassettes/year. Receives 10-12 submissions/month. Pays negotiable royalty.
Affiliate(s): Tom Thumb Music.
How to Contact: Submit tape with letter outlining background in educational children's music. SASE. Reports in 1 month.
Music: "We're only interested in children's songs that have educational value. Our materials are sold in schools and homes, so artists/writers with a teaching background would be most likely to understand our requirements." Published "Professor Whatzit®," series including "Adventures of Professor Whatzit & Carmine Cat,"(cassette series for children). "We buy completed master tapes."

RIC RAC MUSIC, Ric Rac Inc., Box 712, Nashville IN 47448. (812)837-9569. Professional Manager: Sue Hanson. Music publisher, record company (Ric Rac Records and Country Bump Records), record producer (Rich Hanson Productions) and Ric Rac Inc. (marketing and promotion). ASCAP. Publishes 10-15 songs/year; publishes 5-10 new songwriters/year. Works with composers and lyricists; teams collaborators. Pays standard royalty.
Affiliate(s): Rick Hanson Music (BMI).
How to Contact: Write first and obtain permission to submit. Phone calls accepted during office hours only, 9 a.m. to 4 p.m. weekdays except Wednesday. Prefers cassette (or VHS videocassette) with 1-4 songs and lyric sheet. SASE. Reports in 8 weeks.
Music: Mostly country; also pop/rock, rock, gospel, folk, pop, jazz, R&B, easy listening instrumental. Published "Same Old Barroom Melody," written and recorded by Rick Hanson; and "My Love is Safe With You" (by Hanson/Harland), recorded by Rick Hanson; both on Ric Rac Records (country).

Tips: "Be as professional as possible. Get involved with local and regional songwriting workshops and/or music associations in your area."

*G. RICORDI & C. SPA, Via Berchet 2, Milano 20121 **Italy**. Phone (02)8881234. Publishing Manager: Federico Monti Arduini. Music publisher and record producer (Ricordi). S.I.A.E. Estab. 1808. Publishes 100 songs/year; publishes 4-5 new songwriters/year. Hires staff writers. Works with composers and lyricists; teams collaborators.
Affiliate(s): Radio Record RRR, Fama, Ritmi e Canzoni, Pegaso, Fono Film, Iller, Jubal, Edir, Mondia Music, Metron, Editori Associati, Fado, SO.E.DI. Musica, Settebello, Life.
How to Contact: Submit a demo tape by mail—unsolicited submissions are O.K. Prefers cassette (or videocassette if available) with 3/5 songs and lyric or lead sheets. Does not return unsolicited material. Reports in 1 month.
Music: Mostly pop and rock; also New Age.

RIDGE MUSIC CORP., 38 Laurel Ledge Ct., Stamford CT 06903. President/General Manager: Paul Tannen. Music publisher and manager. Estab. 1961. BMI, ASCAP. Member CMA. Publishes 12 songs/year. Pays standard royalty.
Affiliate(s): Tannen Music Inc. and Deshufflin, Inc.
How to Contact: Write first to get permission to submit a tape. Prefers cassette with 3 songs and lyric sheet. SASE. Reports in 1 month.
Music: Country, rock, top 40/pop and jazz.

RISSON MUSIC (PUBLISHING) UK, 127 Aldersgate St., London EC1A 4JQ **United Kingdom**. Phone: (44)71-2501910. Contact: A&R Department. Music publisher, record company (Presidential; XXI St. Century, record producer. PRS. Estab. 1987. Publishes 20-30 songs/year; 4-5 new songwriters/year. Receives 8 submissions/month. Works with composers and lyricists; team collaborators. Pays 60% to writers and 40% to publisher.
How to Contact: Write or call first and obtain permission to submit a tape. Prefers cassette with 2-5 songs and lyric sheet. Does not return unsolicited material. Reports in 2 weeks.
Music: Mostly house and hip-hop. Published "Reason," written and recorded by Chris Payne (pop/dance); "As One" (by Vargus), recorded by Qwerty (house), both on XXIst Century records; and "Hungry for Your Love" (by Vargus), recorded by Seerot Wisugs (house/pop) on Disco Club records.
Tips: "Don't overproduce. Send simple instrumental backing with strong vocal performance."

FREDDIE ROBERTS MUSIC, P.O. Box 203, Rougemont NC 27572. (919)477-4077. Manager: Freddie Roberts. Music publisher, record company, record producer (Carolina Pride Productions), and management firm and booking agency. Estab. 1967. BMI. Publishes 45 songs/year; publishes 15 new songwriters/year. Works with composers, lyricists; teams collaborators. Pays standard royalty.
How to Contact: Write first about your interest or arrange personal interview. Prefers 7½ ips reel-to-reel or cassette with 1-5 songs and lyric sheet. SASE.
Music: Mostly country, MOR and top 40/pop; also bluegrass, church/religious, gospel and southern rock (country). Published "Any Way You Want It" (by B. Fann), recorded by Sleepy Creek (southern rock) on Bull City Records; "Just A Little" (by C. Justis), recorded by Dean Phillips (country) on Ardon Records; and "He Knows What I Need" (by J. Dobbs), recorded by the Roberts Family (gospel) on Bull City Records.
Tips: "Write songs, whatever type, to fit today's market. Send good, clear demos, no matter how simple."

*ROB-LEE MUSIC, P.O. Box 37612, Sarasota FL 34237. Vice Presidents: Rodney Russen, Eric Russen, Bob Francis. Music publisher, record company (Castle Records, Rock Island Records and Jade Records), record producer, and manager. ASCAP. Estab. 1965. Publishes 18-36 songs/year; publishes 6 new songwriters/year. Teams collaborators. Pays standard royalty.
Affiliate(s): Heavy Weather Music (ASCAP).
How to Contact: Submit a demo tape—unsolicited submissions OK. Prefers cassette (or VHS videocassette) with 4-8 songs and lyric sheet. Does not return unsolicited material. Reports in 2 weeks.
Music: Dance-oriented, easy listening, MOR, R&B, rock, soul, top 40/pop and funk. Published "Paradise" (MOR) and "Wide Open" (funk), (both by David Lawrence), recorded by Phoenix on Jade Records; and "Calm After the Storm" (by Rob Russen), recorded by Snow on Castle Records (rock).

ROCKER MUSIC/HAPPY MAN MUSIC, P.O. Box 73, 4501 Spring Creek Rd., Bonita Springs, FL 33923-6637. (813)947-6978. Executive Producer: Dick O'Bitts. BMI, ASCAP. Estab. 1960. Music publisher, record company (Happy Man Records, Condor Records and Air Corp Records), record producer (Rainbow Collections Ltd.) and management firm (Gemini Complex). Publishes 25-30 songs/

Close-up

Randy Poe
Executive Vice-President/
General Manager
Leiber & Stoller
Los Angeles, California

Randy Poe's formula for success in the music business is simple: "It's based on attitude," he says. "Whether you're a songwriter, a music publisher, a record company executive or whatever, you have to have the right attitude. It's a matter of being very headstrong without being insulting."

This is especially applicable when a songwriter is negotiating a contract with a music publisher, says Poe. "On the business side, a songwriter must have a general lack of fear in order to get a good deal. If an aggressive publisher can see fear or uncertainty in your eyes, he will take advantage of that."

The attitude Poe speaks of has nothing to do with being ruthless, rude or unkind. It has to do with not settling for less than what you think a particular song is worth. Of course, there are many considerations, he says, and one of the most important factors early in a writer's career is "songwriter status." As a new songwriter, one must realize that a publisher is dealing with untested talent, and there is a risk factor involved. "It's logical that you don't just start at the top in any field. You can't make unreasonable demands if you don't have success. You shouldn't expect the 'best Songwriter's Guild contract ever' the first time out. But at the same time, you don't want to be taken advantage of. Know what you're doing; then, once you get a little bit of success, bargaining power will accompany it."

After years of working in several different capacities in the industry, Poe is now the Executive V.P. of Leiber & Stoller, a company whose publishing catalog includes such classics as "Stand By Me," "Under the Boardwalk" and "Jailhouse Rock," among many. He's also written a book entitled *Music Publishing: A Songwriter's Guide*, in which he explains all the intricacies of music publishing.

In the book, as in person, he stresses to the songwriter the importance of knowing and considering all the options for your songs. And that means considering the specific markets applicable, the publisher (size and influence) and the amount of control over the song in the future. Also, learn as much as possible about contracts, negotiations and the music industry in general before getting intensely involved.

"I'm a big believer in learning how to do things by reading books. That's what I did when I first got into this business, and I still do it," Poe says. He continues, mentioning that the sources for information are readily available, but it's a situation that a songwriter must confront—research is necessary in all cases, even if it's not enjoyable for the individual. Poe relays the example of his educational career: "I didn't enjoy school at all, period. When my high school teacher said 'You'd better learn this algebra, because you'll need it someday,' I thought it was the biggest crock I'd ever heard. But in the end, he was right. I use algebra in my job today. It's the same thing with songwriters—they need to know music theory and music business history, even if they don't 'like it' . . . and then they'll be able to better understand the way things work in this business. Eventually that research pays off."

With mergers of large music companies, the Sonys and Warners of the industry buying and consuming smaller publishers, Poe suggests to new songwriters the small to medium-size companies. "In some situations, there are huge conglomerates with staff members who have no idea who their songwriters are. Those writers are getting lost in the shuffle. It's not that these companies mean to do it, but there are so many people and so many things going on that it sometimes can work against the songwriter." He says that with a smaller publisher a more nurturing relationship is developed, thus being more beneficial to the personal and professional development of the tunesmith. Also with a smaller company it is usually easier to keep accurate track of financial concerns.

As far as how much of an advance a songwriter should get for a published song, it varies so that a concrete figure is impossible. But, he says the songwriter should ask the simplest economic question: "What will the market bear?" And that should be the goal. "Why settle for something less than the going rate?" Poe asks. "If the songwriter gives in and doesn't negotiate for a larger advance or more of the publishing, then if the song becomes a hit, he could lose thousands of dollars. Hindsight doesn't work here. It's a question of knowing what you're doing before you do it. Once the deal is signed, that's it, you must live with it."

Poe mentions that it's conceivable that a single song can earn millions of dollars over the course of time. He stresses that "In the same sense, a successful song can earn you next to nothing if you don't know what you're supposed to do with it . . . or if you don't have the right people working deals for you."

—Brian C. Rushing

---

year; publishes 8-10 new songwriters/year. Works with composers; teams collaborators. Pays standard royalty.
Affiliate(s): Happy Man Music.
How to Contact: Submit a demo tape—unsolicited submissions are OK. Prefers cassette (or VHS videocassette if possible) with 4 songs and lyric sheet or lead sheet. SASE. Do not call. "You don't need consent to send material."
Music: Country, rock, pop and off-the-wall. Published "Anyone Like Me in Tennessee," (by Kevin Thomas), recorded by Holly Ronick on Happy Man Records (country); "Between A Rock & A Heartache," (by Cow Estes), recorded by Holly Ronick on Happy Man Records (country); "Can We Talk" (by Chris and Bob Thompson), recorded by Chris and Lenny; and "When Daddy Did the Driving" (by Chris Thompson), recorded by Chris and Lenny; all on Happy Man Records (country).
Tips: "For speedier response send material to be reviewed to Bonita Springs address."

ROCKFORD MUSIC CO., Suite 6-D, 150 West End Ave., New York NY 10023. Manager: Danny Darrow. Music publisher, record company (Mighty Records), record and video tape producer. BMI, ASCAP. Publishes 1-3 songs/year; publishes 1-3 new songwriters/year. Teams collaborators. Pays standard royalty.
Affiliate(s): Corporate Music Publishing Company (ASCAP) and Stateside Music Company (BMI).
How to Contact: Submit a demo tape—unsolicited submissions are OK. Prefers cassette with 3 songs and lyric sheet. "SASE a must!" Reports in 2 weeks. *"Positively no phone calls."*
Music: Mostly MOR and top 40/pop; also adult pop, country, adult rock, dance-oriented, easy listening, folk and jazz. Published "Falling in Love" (by Brian Downen) and "A Part of You" (by B. Downen/ Randy Lakeman), both recorded by D. Darrow on Mighty Records (rock ballad and blues); *Doomsday* (by various songwriters), recorded by Danny Darrow on Colley Records (Euro disco LP); and *Great Folk Songs* (by various songwriters), recorded by Danny Darrow on Mighty Records (folk LP).
Tips: "Listen to top 40 and write current lyrics and music."

ROCKLAND MUSIC, INC., 117 W. Rockland, Libertyville IL 60048. (708)362-4060. Contact: Perry or Rick Johnson. Music publisher, record company and record producer. BMI. Estab. 1980. Publishes 5 songs/year. Publishes 2 new songwriters/year. Pays standard royalty.
How to Contact: Submit a demo tape—unsolicited submissions are OK. Prefers cassette with 5 songs and lyric sheet. SASE. Reports in 3 months.
Music: Mostly rock/pop, dance/R&B and country; also blues. Published "This Feels Like Love to Me" (by C. Sermay), recorded by S. Distel (pop).

ROOTS MUSIC, Box 111, Sea Bright NJ 07760. President: Robert Bowden. Music publisher, record company (Nucleus Records) and record producer (Robert Bowden). BMI. Estab. 1979. Publishes 2 songs/year; publishes 1 new songwriter/year. Receives 10 submissions/year. Works with composers and lyricists; teams collaborators. Pays standard royalty.
How to Contact: Submit a demo tape. Prefers cassette (or VHS videocassette) with 3 songs and lyric sheet; include photo and bio. "I only want inspired songs written by talented writers." SASE. Reports in 1 month.
Music: Mostly country and pop; also church/religious, classical, folk, MOR, progressive, rock (soft, mellow) and top 40. Published "Henrey C," "Oh How Miss You Tonight" and "Hurting," all written and recorded by Robert Bowden (country); all recorded on Nucleus Records.

STEVE ROSE MUSIC, 790 Boylston St., Boston MA 02199. (617)267-0886. Manager: Steve Rose. "Uses two Nashville songpluggers and other contacts to pitch to majors and maintains active relationships with charting indie record labels. Uses Songwriter's Guild contract with two year reversion when a song is held by a producer or label."
Affiliate(s): Has ASCAP, SESAC and BMI companies.
How to Contact: "Unfortunately we can now accept new submissions ONLY from serious Nashville-oriented writers who have had at least one independent cut. Call first, but only if this is the case. Send up to three of your best with a 29¢ SASE for return of lyrics and comments only. Publishing must be open. Put your phone number on everything."
Music: "Country exclusively. And then only well-demoed competitive, pitchable songs. They must be positive and mid- to uptempo. We had three charted singles by press time in 1991."
Tips: "We'll help you revise a good song and we'll team complimentary talents. We are building a national network to show that Music Row is wherever country hits are written. Our best advice is to pitch songs direct to indie labels 'til you get a country cut, then contact us. And don't ever pay upfront for anything except demos when you're starting. Half the demos we take, we redemo at our expense or via a co-writer. Don't send a title that's listed in Phono-Log."

*ROSEMARK PUBLISHING, 12 Lorkim Lane, Atco NJ 08004. (609)767-8037. Manager: Robert Fitzpatrick. Music publisher, record producer (Studio B) and copyright consultant for artists. BMI. Estab. 1988. Publishes 12 songs/year; publishes 3 new songwriters/year. Receives 400 submissions/year. Hires new staff writers. Works with composers and lyricists. Pays standard royalty.
How to Contact: Submit a demo tape, unsolicited submissions are OK. Prefers cassette with 3 songs and lyric or lead sheets. "Demo can be 2 or more tracks. But it must be clean." Does not return unsolicited material. Reports in 4 weeks.
Music: Mostly top 40/pop, easy listening and country; also MOR, gospel and R&B. Published "Daddy I Love You" (by Bob Thomas), recorded by Katie Rose on SBR Records (novelty); "I'll Always Love You" (by Bob Thomas), recorded by Mark Daniel on SBR Records (MOR); and "I Don't Need A Man" (by Nancy Lee), recorded by Nancy Lee on SBR Records (country).
Tips: "Be professional and have patience. Music has become too "programmed" and over-produced. We need to get back to honest simplicity."

*ROUGH TRADE MUSIC LIMITED, 61 Collier St., London N19BE UK. (44)71-837-6747. General Manager: Cathi Gibson. Music publisher. Estab. 1979. Publishes 75 songs/year; 12 new songwriters/year. Receives 15 submissions/month. Works with composers. Pays "per contract."
How to Contact: Submit a demo tape by mail—unsolicited submissions are OK. Prefers cassette with up to 10 songs and lyric sheet. SASE.
Music: Mostly rock, pop and dance. Published "Admiral of the Sea" (by Grant Hart), recorded by Nova Mob on Rough Trade Records (rock); "Black and White" (by Henry Rollins), recorded by Rollins Band on Texas Hotel Records (rock); and "Moyo Wansu," written and recorded by Thomas Mapfumo on Island Records (World).
Tips: "We want original, well-written, coverable material."

ROWILCO, Box 8135, Chicago IL 60680. (312)224-5612. Professional Manager: R.C. Hillsman. Music publisher. BMI. Publishes 8-20 songs/year.
How to Contact: Arrange personal interview. Prefers cassettes or 7½ or 15 ips ¼" reel-to-reel with 4-6 songs (on VHS or Beta Videocassette) and lyric sheet. Submissions should be sent via registered mail. SASE. Reports in 3 weeks.
Music: Blues, church/religious, country, disco, easy listening, gospel, jazz, MOR, rock and top 40/pop.

ROYAL FLAIR PUBLISHING, Box 438, Walnut IA 51577. (712)366-1136. President: Bob Everhart. Music publisher and record producer. BMI. Estab. 1967. Publishes 5-10 songs/year; publishes 1-2 new songwriters/year. Works with composers and lyricists. Pays standard royalty.

How to Contact: Submit a demo tape—unsolicited submissions are OK with SASE. Prefers cassette with 2-6 songs. SASE. Reports in 9 weeks.
Music: Traditional country, bluegrass and folk. Published "Hero of Gringo Trail," "Time After Time," and "None Come Near," written and recorded by R. Everhart on Folkways Records; and "Smoky Mountain Heartbreak," written and recorded by Bonnie Sanford (all country).
Tips: "Song definitely has to have old-time country flavor with all the traditional values of country music. No sex, outlandish swearing, or drugs-booze type songs accepted. We have an annual Hank Williams Songwriting Contest over Labor Day weekend and winners are granted publishing."

RUSHWIN PUBLISHING, Box 1150-SM92, Buna TX 77612. (409)423-2521.Owner/General Manager: James L. Gibson. Music publisher and record producer (James L. Gibson/Rushwin Productions). BMI. Member GMA. Estab. 1985. Receives over 500 submissions/year. Works with composers and lyricists. Pays standard royalty.
Affiliate(s): Rushwin Productions.
How to Contact: Write first to get permission to submit a tape. Prefers cassette with 1-4 songs and typed lyric sheet. Clearly label each item sent. SASE (6x9 or larger).
Music: Southern/Country Gospel. Published "Holy Rolling" (by Ronald T. Sparks), recorded by the Helmsmen (southern gospel) on Morning Star Records; "You're a Saint or You Ain't" (by Randy Lawrence/Bill Fisher), recorded by the Harbingers (southern gospel) on Gold Street Records; and "The Third Day" (by Stephen Mattox), recorded by The Third Day (contemporary southern gospel) on New Breeze Records.
Tips: "We are interested in the type material suited for the recording artist that appear in the music charts published by *The Gospel Voice* and *The Singing News*."

RUSTRON MUSIC PUBLISHERS, 1156 Park Lane, West Palm Beach FL 33417. (407)-686-1354. Professional Managers: Rusty Gordon, Ron Caruso and Davilyn Whims. Music publisher and record producer (Rustron Music Productions). ASCAP, BMI. Estab. 1974. Publishes 100-150 songs/year; publishes 10-20 new songwriters/year. Works with composers and lyricists; teams collaborators. Pays standard royalty.
How to Contact: Submit a demo tape (cassette)—unsolicited submissions are OK, or write or call first to get permission to submit a tape. Prefers cassette with 1-3 songs and lyric or lead sheet. "Clearly label your tape and container. Include cover letter." Must include SASE. Reports in 2 months.
Music: Mostly pop (ballads, blues, theatrical, cabaret), progressive country, folk/rock; also R&B and New Age. Published "Lily May" and "No Place In Kansas Is Home Anymore" (by Sue Massek), recorded by Reel World String Band on Flying Fish Records (country/bluegrass); "I'm A Reptile" (by Jill Jarboe), recorded by The Singing Rainbows Youth Ensemble on Sister's Choice Records (children's music); "Heartbeat" and "Turning," written and recorded by Deb Criss on Catalyst Records (New Age folk fusion).
Tips: "Write strong hooks. Keep song length 3½ minutes or less. Avoid predictability—create original lyric themes. Tell a story."

*S & R MUSIC PUBLISHING CO., 71906 Highway III, Rancho Mirage CA 92270. (619)346-0075. Contact: Dolores Gulden. Music publisher. ASCAP. Member AIMP and NMPA. Publishes 100 songs/year; publishes 50 new songwriters/year. Receives 10 submissions/month. Pays standard royalty.
Affiliate(s): Meteor Music (BMI) and Boomerang Music (BMI).
How to Contact: Prefers cassette with 1-4 songs and lyric sheet. SASE.
Music: "We are mostly interested in lyrics or melodies for instrumentals." Published "Bluescape," written and recorded by Jay Thomas (pop/instrumental); "Misty Morning," written and recorded by Louis Cope (pop/instrumental); and "Flaus A Banana" (by Johan van Heerden, Jeri Sullivan), recorded by Jeri Sullivan (novelty); all on Accent Records.

S.M.C.L. PRODUCTIONS, INC., P.O. Box 84, Boucherville, Quebec J4B 5E6 **Canada.** (514)641-2266. President: Christian Lefort. Music publisher and record company. BMI, SOCAN. Estab. 1968. Publishes 25 songs/year.
Affiliate(s): A.Q.E.M. Ltee (SOCAN), Bag Enrg. (SOCAN), C.F. Music (SOCAN), Big Bazaar Music (SOCAN), Sunrise Music (SOCAN), Stage One Music (SOCAN), L.M.S. Ltee (SOCAN), ITT Music (SOCAN), Machine Music (SOCAN), Dynamite Music (SOCAN), Danava Music (SOCAN), Coincidence Music (SOCAN), Music and Music (SOCAN), Cinemusic Inc. (SOCAN), Cinafilm (SOCAN), Editions La Fete Inc. (SOCAN), Groupe Concept Musique (SOCAN), Editions Dorimen (SOCAN), C.C.H. Music (SOCAN) and Lauagot Music (SOCAN).
How to Contact: Write first to get permission to submit a tape. Prefers cassette with 4-12 songs and lead sheet. SAE and IRC. Reports in 1 month.
Music: Dance, easy listening, MOR, top 40/pop and TV and movie soundtracks. Published "Where Is My Man," recorded by the Eartha Kitt on Able Records (dance); and "Sex Over the Phone," recorded by Village People on Celsius Records (dance). Also publishes the songs of Kaschtin and

Nathalie Carsen; and many soundtracks of French-Canadian TV series.

SABRE MUSIC, P.O. Box 702, Snowdon Station, Montreal, Quebec H3X 3X8 **Canada**. Professional General Manager: D. Leonard. Music publisher. SOCAN. Estab. 1963. Works with composers and lyricists; teams collaborators. Pays standard royalty.
Affiliate(s): Montina Music (SOCAN).
How to Contact: Submit a demo tape—unsolicited submissions are OK. Prefers cassette or record (or VHS videocassette) and lyric sheet. Does not return unsolicited material.
Music: Mostly top 40; also blues, country, dance-oriented, easy listening, folk, gospel, jazz, MOR, progressive, R&B, rock, soul and pop.

SABTECA MUSIC CO., Box 10286, Oakland CA 94610. (415)465-2805. President: Duane Herring. Music publisher and record company (Sabteca Record Co.). ASCAP, BMI. Estab. 1980. Publishes 8-10 songs/year; 1-2 new songwriters/year. Works with composers and lyricists; teams collaborators. Pays standard royalty.
How to Contact: Write or call first and obtain permission to submit a tape. Prefers cassette with 2 songs and lyric sheet. SASE. Reports in 4 weeks.
Music: Mostly R&B, pop and country. Published "Come Into My Arms" and "I Dare You" (by Duane Herring), recorded by Johnny B and the Rhythm Method (rock) on Sabteca Records; and "Make Love Stay" (by Walter Coleman), recorded by Lois Shayne (R&B) on Sabteca Records.
Tips: "Improve your writing skills. Keep up with music trends."

*SADDLESTONE PUBLISHING, 264 "H" St., Box 8110-21, Blaine WA 98230. Canada Address: 2954 O'Hara Lane, Surrey, B.C., V4A 3E5 **Canada**. (604)535-3129. President: Rex Howard. Music publisher, record company (Saddlestone) and record producer (Silver Bow Productions). PROCAN, BMI. Estab. 1988. Publishes 100 songs/year; publishes 12-30 new songwriters/year. Receives 70 submissions/month. Hires staff writers. Works with composers and lyricists; teams collaborators. Pays standard royalty.
Affiliate(s): Silver Bow Publishing (SOCAN, ASCAP).
How to Contact: Submit a demo tape by mail—unsolicited submissions are OK. Prefers cassette with 5-7 songs and lyric sheet. "Make sure vocal is clear." SASE. Reports in 3 months.
Music: Mostly country, rock and pop; also gospel and R&B. Published "Stand There" (by Champion/Wilson), recorded by Elmer Fudpucker on Vista Records (country); "Never Be Mine" (by E. Johnson), recorded by Michael Austin Nelson on Saddlestone Records (country); and "Every Mornin' Blues" (by Moberg), recorded by Alan Moberg on Saddlestone Records (easy listening).
Tips: "Submit clear demos, good hooks and avoid long intros or instrumentals."

TRACY SANDS MUSIC, Suite 119, 2166 W. Broadway, Anaheim CA 92804-2446. (714)525-5223. Vice President, A&R: Harold Shmoduquet. Music publisher, record company (Orange Records, Beet Records), record producer (Orange Productions). BMI. Estab. 1977. Publishes 12 songs/year; publishes 4 new songwriters/year. Receives 600 submissions/year. Pays standard royalty of 50%.
Affiliate(s): Fat Cat Music (BMI), Lipstick Traces Music (BMI) and Bastion Music (BMI).
How to Contact: Submit a demo tape by mail—unsolicited submissions are OK. Prefers cassette with 2-3 songs and lyric sheet. SASE. Reports in 2 months.
Music: All types. Published "Hot Summer Days" (by Daniel Dailey and Ted Greenberg), recorded by Wilson Dailey on Orange Records; "Dinah Wants Religion" (by Ellis, Clark, Cammack), recorded by The Fabs on Swak Records and "We're Not What We Are" (by Robert Wahlsteen), recorded by Jubal's Children on Swak Records (all rock).

SARISER MUSIC, Box 211, Westfield MA 01086. (413)783-8386. Operations Manager: Alexis Steele. Music publisher and record company (Sweet Talk Records). BMI. Publishes 6-12 songs/year; publishes 1-2 new songwriters/year. Works with composers and lyricists; teams collaborators. Pays standard royalty.
How to Contact: Write first and obtain permission to submit. No calls. Prefers cassette or 7½ IPS reel-to-reel with 3-4 songs and lyric or lead sheet. "Lyrics should be typed; clear vocal on demo." SASE. Reports in 6 weeks.
Music: Mostly country/pop, country/rock and educational material; also soft rock and rockabilly. "We're interested in 50s/60s style 4-part harmony." Published "One Last Kiss" (by Sparkie Allison), recorded by Moore Twinz on MMT Records (country); "Sweet Talk" and "Ride a Rainbow," written and recorded by Sparkie Allison and Ginny Cooper on Sweet Talk Records (country/pop).
Tips: "Lyrics must have positive message. No cheatin' songs. Be unique. Try something different."

*E.C. SCHIRMER MUSIC COMPANY INC., 138 Ipswich St., Boston MA 02215. (617)236-1935. President: Robert Schuneman. Music publisher. ASCAP, BMI. Estab. 1931. Publishes 200 songs/year; publishes 3 new songwriters/year. Hires staff writers. Works with composers. Print sales: pays 10% list price. Performance & license: pays 50%.
Affiliate(s): Galaxy Music Corporation (ASCAP), Highgate Press (BMI), Ione Press (BMI).
How to Contact: Submit a demo tape and score by mail—unsolicited submissions are OK. Prefers cassette. SASE. Reports in 3-12 months.
Music: Mostly serious, concert, educational, piano/organ, choral, orchestral/opera; also vocals and instrumental.
Tips: "Have clean, readable score, good demo tape."

SCHMERDLEY MUSIC, #G3, 7560 Woodman Pl., Van Nuys CA 91405. (818)994-4862. Owner: Tom Willett. Music publisher, record company (Tomark Records) and record producer (Tomark Records). BMI. Estab. 1969. Publishes 10 songs/year; 2-4 new songwriters/year. Receives 125 submissions/year. Pays standard royalty.
How to Contact: Submit a demo tape by mail—unsolicited submissions are OK. Prefers cassette (or VHS videocassette). SASE. Reports in 4 weeks.
Music: Mostly country and novelty; also rock. Published "So Many Men, So Little Time" (by Lynne), recorded by Wynen on American Made Band Records (country); "Sacker Bill" (by William Farley), recorded by Tom Willett on Tomark Records (country); and "Christopher Columbus" (by Thornton/ Willett), recorded by Tom Willett on Tomark Record (country.

SCOTTI BROTHERS MUSIC PUBLISHING, 2114 Pico Blvd., Santa Monica CA 90405. (213)450-4143. Professional Manager: Richie Wise. Music publisher and record company. BMI, ASCAP. Member NMPA, AIMP, RIAA and CMA. Publishes 40 songs/year; publishes 2 new songwriters/year. Pays standard royalty.
Affiliate(s): Flowering Stone and Holy Moley.
How to Contact: Prefers cassette with 1-2 songs and lyric sheet. Does not accept unsolicited material; "we report only if we're interested."
Music: Mostly top 40/pop and country; also easy listening, MOR and rock. Published "Eye of the Tiger" (by J. Peterick/F. Sullivan), recorded by Survivor on Scotti Bros.-CBS Records (rock); "How Do You Fall Out of Love," recorded by Janie Fricke on CBS Records (country-pop); and "Them Good Ol' Boys Are Bad" (J. Harrington/J. Pennig), recorded by John Schneider on Scotti Bros.-CBS Records (country).

SCRAMROCK MUSIC CO., 139 E. Harding Rd., Springfield OH 45504. (513)399-6708. Professional Manager: Robert T. "Dusty" Jones. Music publisher, record company (War Minister Records, Spike Opera, Paragon, and Scram Records) and management firm ("Dusty" Jones Management Co.). BMI. Estab. 1980. Publishes 15-20 songs/year; publishes 14-15 new songwriters/year. Receives 100 submissions/year. Works with composers "having full bands only." Pays standard royalty.
How to Contact: Submit a demo tape—unsolicited submissions are OK. Prefers cassette (or VHS videocassette—high energy showmanship-stage clothes). "Include photo of artist or group." SASE. Reports in 2 days.
Music: Heavy metal, thrash metal, hard rock and speed metal. Published "Change of Seasons," "Land of Dreams" and "Stand Alone" (all by S. Smith, K. Wood and J. Faber), recorded by Paragon on Paragon Records (Progressive Metal).
Tips: Submit "hard driving, high energy tunes with good catchy hooks and melodies. Have a full band whose music is hard driving with high energy with good catchy hooks and melodies and whose band has super high energy showmanship with a killer look, stage clothes, etc."

SCRUTCHINGS MUSIC, 429 Homestead St., Akron OH 44306. (216)773-8529. Owner/President: Walter E.L. Scrutchings. Music publisher. BMI. Estab. 1980. Publishes 35 songs/year; publishes 10-20 new songwriters/year. Receives 125 submissions/year. Hires staff songwriters. Works with composers and lyricists; teams collaborators. Pays standard royalty of 50%. "Songwriters pay production costs of songs."
How to Contact: Submit a demo tape by mail—unsolicited submissions are OK. Prefers cassette (or videocassette if available) with 2 songs, lyric and lead sheet. Does not return unsolicited material. Reports in 4-6 weeks.
Music: Mostly gospel, contemporary and traditional. Published "The Joy He Brings" (by R. Hinton), recorded by Akron City Mass; "Come by Hear" (by J. Mingo), recorded by The Refuge Family; and "He Keeps Blessing Me" (by Scrutchings), recorded by Arch Angels; all on Scrutchings Music Records (gospel).

SEA DREAM MUSIC, 236 Sebert Rd., Forest Gate, London E7 0NP **England**. Phone: (081)534-8500. Senior Partner: Simon Law. PRS. Music publisher and record company (Plankton Records, Embryo Arts (Belgium) and Radio Records). Estab. 1976. Publishes 50 songs/year; publishes 2 new songwriters/year. Works with composers and lyricists; teams collaborators. Pays 66⅔% royalty.
Affiliate(s): Scarf Music Publishing, Really Free Music, Ernvik Musik (Sweden).
How to Contact: Submit a demo tape—unsolicited submissions are OK. Prefers cassette with 3 songs and lyric sheet. "Technical information about the recording is useful, as are the songwriter's expectations of the company—i.e., what they want us to do for them." SAE and IRC. Reports in 6 weeks.
Music: Mostly funk/rock, rock and blues; also gospel. Published "Kid In a Hostile World" (by Paul Crick/Greg Nash/Keith Dixon), recorded by Medals (jazz/rock); "Pictures of You" (by Rue Randall), recorded by Solid Air (rock); and "A Choice of Shadows" (by Simon Law), recorded by Fresh Claim (blues/rock), all on Plankton Records.
Tips: "We are specifically interested in material with a Christian bias to the lyrics."

SEGAL'S PUBLICATIONS, Box 507, Newton MA 02159. (617)969-6196. Contact: Charles Segal. Music publisher and record producer (Segal's Productions). BMI, SAMRO. Estab. 1963. Publishes 80 songs/year; publishes 6 new songwriters/year. Works with composers and lyricists. Pays standard royalty.
Affiliate(s): Charles Segals Publications (BMI).
How to Contact: Call first and obtain permission to submit or to arrange a personal interview. Prefers cassette (or VHS videocassette) with 3 songs and lyric or lead sheet. Does not return unsolicited material.
Music: Mostly rock, pop and country; also R&B, MOR and children's songs. Musicals published include "Everyday Things" and "Magical Mystery Man" as well as traditional children's stories on EMI records (children's); "Forste Saga" (by Segal), recorded by the SABC Orchestra on Decca (ballad); "You're Not Alone" (by Brilliant), recorded by Bibby Stewart on Spin Records (rock).
Tips: "Listen to what is going on in the music business via TV and radio. Write for a specific artist. Do a simple demo cassette, voice/keyboard; write a clean lead sheet."

SELLWOOD PUBLISHING, 170 N. Maple, Fresno CA 93702. (209)255-1717. Owner: Stan Anderson. Music publisher, record company (Trac Record Co.) and record producer. BMI. Estab. 1972. Publishes 10 songs/year; publishes 3 new songwriters/year. Receives 30-35 submissions/month. Pays standard royalty.
How to Contact: Submit a demo tape. Unsolicited submissions are OK. Prefers cassette (or VHS videocassette) with 2 songs and lyric sheet. SASE. Reports in 2 weeks.
Music: Mostly country, gospel, pop and rock. Published "Don't Walk Away," by B.G. White (country); "Bare Your Soul," by Denise Benson (country); "Overnight Sensation," by Ric Blake (top 40); and Nevada State Of Mind," by Barry Best (country); all on Trac Records.

SHAOLIN MUSIC, P.O. Box 387, Hollywood CA 90078. (818)506-8660. President: Richard O'Connor. Vice President, A&R: Michelle McCarty. Music publisher, record company (Shaolin Film and Records) and record producer (The Coyote). ASCAP. Estab. 1984. Works with groups that have own material. Royalties negotiated.
How to Contact: Prefers cassette with 3-4 songs and lyric sheet. Include bio and press kit. Does not return unsolicited material. Reports in 3 months.
Music: Mostly rock, hard rock and pop; also soundtracks. Published "Show Girls," recorded by The Rich; releasing soundtrack album "Coyote In a Graveyard" (by Coyote), on Shaolin Film and Records (rock).

***SHO-DOE MUSIC**, #252, 1840 South Gaffey St., San Pedro Peninsula CA 90731. (213)514-0920. Independent Music Publisher/President: C. Kunde. Music publisher, record company (domestic and international indy labels) and record producer (Galaxy Music Productions). ASCAP. Estab. 1991. Publishes 12-36 songs/year. Works with composers and studio musicians; teams collaborators.
Affiliate(s): Sho-Doe Music.
How to Contact: Write first and obtain permission to submit a tape. Prefers cassette and any number of lyric and lead sheets. SASE. Reports in 2 weeks.
Music: Mostly easy listening/AOR, New Age (international) and R&B; also A/C, soft rock/pop and cross-over/fusion.

***SHU'BABY MONTEZ MUSIC**, 1447 North 55th St., Philadelphia PA 19131. (215)473-5527. President: Leroy Schuler. Music publisher. BMI. Estab. 1986. Publishes 25 songs/year; publishes 15 new songwriters/year. Pays standard royalty.

How to Contact: Submit a demo tape by mail—unsolicited submissions are OK. Prefers cassette with 4 songs and lyric sheet. SASE. Reports in 3 weeks.
Music: Mostly R&B, pop and jazz; also rock. Published "I'd Rather Be By Myself" (by L. Schuler/J. Freeman/A. Felder), recorded by EBO on Domino Records (R&B); "I'll Do Better" and "Here We Go Again" (written and recorded by Mack Atkinson), both on Bang-Bang Records (pop).

*SIEBENPUNKT VERLAGS GMBH, Habsburgerplatz 1 Rückgebäude, D-8000 München 40 **West Germany.** Phone: 089-331808. General Manager: Mr. Schmidt. Music publisher. GEMA. Estab. 1978. Publishes 250 songs/year; publishes 7 new songwriters/year. Works with composers and lyricists; and teams collaborators. Pays standard royalty or by contract.
How to Contact: Submit a demo tape—unsolicited submissions OK with SAEs and IRCs. Prefers cassette (or VHS videocassette) with 2-3 songs. Reports in 3 weeks.
Music: Rock, dance and pop; also fusion-jazz and New Age. Published *Seen One Earth*, written and recorded by Pete Bardens (LP); "On the Air Tonight" (by Pete Bardens), recorded by Southside Johnny on RCA Records (rock); "Listen," written and recorded by Stephen Petit on Blackbird Records (dance/rock); and "Solo," by Leo Sayer on Chrysalis Records.

SIEGEL MUSIC COMPANIES, 2 Hochlstr, 80 Munich 8000 **West Germany.** Phone: 089-984926. Managing Director: Joachim Neubauer. Music publisher, record company, (Jupiter Records and Zip Records) and record producer. Estab. 1948. GEMA. Publishes 2,000-3,000 songs/year; publishes 50 new songwriters/year. Hires staff songwriters. Works with composers and lyricists. Pays standard royalty according to individual society.
Affiliate(s): Ed. Meridian, Old Friends/Golden Bridge (Nashville), Sound of Jupiter Ltd. (England), Sounds of Jupiter, Inc. (USA), Step Two (Austria), Step One (Holland), Step Two (Austria), Step Four (France), Step Five (Brazil), Step Six (Scandinavia), Step Seven (Australia), Step Eight (Belgium) and Yellowbird (Switzerland).
How to Contact: Prefers cassette (or VHS videocassette, but not necessary). Reports in 8 weeks.
Music: Mostly pop, disco and MOR; also country and soul. Published "So Many People," written and recorded by Hirschburger Hubert on Kah Curb Records (pop); "Let There Be House" (by West Bam), recorded by Deskee on RCA Records (dancehouse); and "Still Beatin' " (by Schudde), recorded by World on Edge on Virgin Records (pop rock).

SILICON MUSIC PUBLISHING CO., Ridgewood Park Estates, 222 Tulane St., Garland TX 75043. President: Gene Summers. Vice President: Deanna L. Summers. Public Relations: Steve Summers. Music publisher and record company (Domino Records, Ltd. and Front Row Records). BMI. Estab. 1965. Publishes 10-20 songs/year; publishes 2-3 new songwriters/year. Pays standard royalty.
How to Contact: Prefers cassette with 1-2 songs. Does not return unsolicited material. "We are usually slow in answering due to overseas tours."
Music: Mostly rockabilly and 50s material; also old-time blues country and MOR. Published "Ready to Ride/Ode to a Stuntman" (from the HBO presentation "Backlot"), written and recorded by Pat Minter on Domino Records; "Loco Cat" (by Eddie Hill/Tom Toms), recorded by Gene Summers on White Label; "Love Me Til I Do," written and recorded by Joe Hardin Brown on Domino Records; "Rockaboogie Shake" (by James McClung), recorded by Gene Summers on Jan Records (Sweden); and "Stevie Ray Vaughn" (by Joe Hardin Brown) and "My Yearbook" (by Deanna Summers), both recorded by Gene Summers on Teardrop Records.
Tips: "We are very interested in 50s rock and rockabilly *original masters* for release through overseas affiliates. If you are the owner of any 50s masters, contact us first! We have releases in Holland, Switzerland, England, Belgium, France, Sweden, Norway and Australia. We have the market if you have the tapes! Sample recordings available! Send SASE for catalogue."

SILVERFOOT PUBLISHING, 4225 Palm St., Baton Rouge LA 70808. (504)383-7885. President: Barrie Edgar. BMI. Music publisher, record company (Gulfstream Records) and record producer (Hogar Musical Productions). Estab. 1977. Publishes 20-30 songs/year; publishes 8-20 new songwriters/year. Receives 200 submissions/year. Pays standard royalty.
How to Contact: Submit a demo tape—unsolicited submissions are OK. Prefers cassette with maximum 4 songs and lyric sheet. "Patience required on reporting time." SASE.
Music: Mostly rock, pop, blues ("not soul") and country. Published "Just Getting By," written and recorded by Beckie Joe Benson (country); "Sound of A Heartbreak," written and recorded by John Clark (country); and "Stuck Up Girls," written and recorded by Jack Denton (rock).

SIMPLY GRAND MUSIC, (formerly Beckie Publishing Group), P.O. Box 41981, Memphis TN 38174-1981. (901)272-7039. President: Linda Lucchesi. Music publisher. ASCAP, BMI. Estab. 1965. Publishes 1-5 songs and new songwriters/year. Works with composers and lyricists; teams collaborators. Pays standard royalty.

Affiliate(s): Memphis Town Music, Inc. and Simply Grand Music, Inc.
How to Contact: Write or call first to get permission to submit a tape. Prefers cassette with 1-3 songs and lyric sheet. SASE. Reports in 3 months.
Music: Mostly pop and soul; also R&B, country and soft rock.
Tips: "We're the publishing home of 'Wooly Bully'!"

SINGING ROADIE MUSIC, 342 Ogle St., Costa Mesa CA 92627. (714)548-1908. General Manager: Garth Shaw. Music publisher, member of ACM and CMA. ASCAP. Estab. 1984. Publishes 3-10 songs/year; publishes 1-3 new songwriters/year. Pays standard royalty.
Affiliate(s): Singing Roadie Music (ASCAP), Helioplane Music (BMI).
How to Contact: Submit a demo tape by mail—unsolicited submissions are OK. Prefers cassette with 1-3 songs and lyric sheets. SASE. Reports in 3 months.
Music: Country, all styles, from traditional to contemporary. Co-published "Follow the Path" (by Garth Shaw, Jim Turner), recorded by Jim Turner on Earthtone Records (gospel); "Rescue Me" (by Paul Hotchkiss), recorded by Pam Rogers on Trophy Records (country); "Bed of Roses" (by Rex Benson, Steve Gillette), recorded by The Oak Ridge Boys on MCA Records (country).
Tips: "If you're a great writer and a terrible singer, find a great demo singer!"

SINGLE PHASE MUSIC, Box 67, Covina CA 91723. (714)592-3098. President: Steve Mortensen. Music publisher, record company (Blue Sun), record producer (Blue Sun Productions). BMI. Estab. 1986. Publishes 15-20 songs/year; publishes 1-5 new songwriters/year. Works with composers and lyricists; teams collaborators. Pays standard royalty.
Affiliate(s): Single Phase Music (BMI).
How to Contact: Submit a demo tape by mail—unsolicited submissions are OK. Prefers cassette wityh 2-3 songs and lyric sheet. Does not return unsolicited material. Reports in 1-2 months.
Music: Mostly pop-European, rock and R&B. Published "Off and On" (by Basque), recorded by single phase; "Private Masquerade" and "One World" (by Basque), recorded by Single Phase; and "She's a Beauty" (by Mortensen/Amato), recorded by Emotion (pop); all on Blue Sun Records.

*SISAPA MUSIC, 6200 Eiterman Rd., Amlin OH 43002. (614)764-4777. Director of Publishing: Rick Cooper. Music publisher. BMI. Estab. 1990. Publishes 55 songs/year; publishes 16 new songwriters/year. Hires staff writers. Works with composers and lyricists; teams collaborators. Pays standard royalty of 50%.
Affiliate(s): Sisapa Music (BMI), twentytwo music, inc. (ASCAP).
How to Contact: Write or call first and obtain permission to submit a tape. Prefers cassette with 3 songs and lyric sheet. "Put identification on all materials submitted." SASE. Reports in 2 months.
Music: Mostly R&B, rock and country; also pop and alternative. Publishes "Rock of Ages" (by John Schwab and Rick Cooper), recorded by John Schwab (rock); "Can I Play My Horn for You?" written and recorded by Vince Andrews (R&B); and "Her Heart is Mine," written and recorded by Bob Sauls (blues); all on Sisapa Records.
Tips: "Don't overproduce your demo—a good song should stand on its own. Send us your strongest material first."

*SNEAK TIP MUSIC, 2R, 102-40 62nd Ave., Forest Hills NY 11375. (718)271-5149. President: Gerald Famolari. Music publisher, record company (Sneak Tip Records, Sneak Tip Music) and artist. BMI. Estab. 1990. Publishes 10 songs/year. Works with composers and lyricists.
Affiliate(s): Sneak Tip Music (BMI).
How to Contact: Write to arrange a personal interview. Prefers cassette. Reports in 1-4 weeks.
Music: Mostly house, club and freestyle; also rap and R&B. Published "Treat Me Right," by J. Suriff (hip-house); "Without Your Love," by Rhingo (freestyle-house); and "Emotional Pain," by Xavier (Euro-Freestyle); all recorded by DieHard Productions on Sneak Tip Records.

*SOCIETE D'EDITIONS MUSICALES ET ARTISTIQUES "ESPERANCE", 85 Rue Fondary, Paris 75015 France. Phone: (1) 45 77 30 34. Manager: Michel David. Music publisher and record company (Societe Sonodisc). SACEM/SDRM. Estab. 1972. Publishes 50 songs/year; 20 new songwriters/year. Receives 30 submissions/month. Pays negotiable rates.
How to Contact: Submit a demo tape, unsolicited submissions are OK. Prefers cassette (or VHS videocassette). SAE and IRC. Reports in 1 month.
Music: African, West Indian, Arabian and salsa music. Published "Exile" (by Ina Cesaire), recorded by Ralph Tamar on GD Production (West India); "Les Années Folles" (by Roland Brival), recorded by Ralph Tamar on GD Production (West India); "Wakaele" (by Sekou Diabate), recorded by Bambeya Jazz Esperance (African); and "Diniya," written and recorded by Kante Manfila on Esperance (African).
Tips: "See that the style of your songs fits in with the music we distribute."

SONG FARM MUSIC, P.O. Box 24561, Nashville TN 37202. (615)321-4875. President: Tom Pallardy. Music publisher and record producer (T.P. Productions). BMI. Member NSAI. Estab. 1980. Publishes 2-5 songs/year; publishes 1-2 new songwriters/year. Works with team collaborators. Receives 2000 songs/year. Pays standard royalty.
How to Contact: Submit a demo tape—unsolicited submissions are OK. Prefers cassette with maximum 2 songs and lyric or lead sheet. SASE required. Reports in 1 month.
Music: Mostly country, R&B and pop; also crossover and top 40. Published "Mississippi River Rat" (by J. Hall, R. Hall, E. Dickey), recorded by Tom Powers on Fountain Records (Cajun country); "Today's Just Not the Day" (by J. Bell, E. Bobbitt), recorded by Liz Draper (country); and "I Know I've Got Her Leanin'," (by B. Dellaposta, S. Stephens), recorded by Rick Thompson on Radioactive Records (country).
Tips: "Material should be submitted neatly and professionally with as good quality demo as possible. Songs need not be elaborately produced (voice and guitar/piano are fine) but they should be clear. Songs must be well constructed, lyrically tight, good strong hook, interesting melody, easily remembered; i.e., commercial!"

SONGFINDER MUSIC, 4 Reina Lane, Valley Cottage NY 10989. (914)268-7711. Owner: Frank Longo. Music publisher. ASCAP. Estab. 1987. Publishes 20 songs/year; publishes 5-10 new songwriters/year. Receives 200 submissions/month. Works with composers; teams collaborators. Pays standard royalty.
Affiliate(s): Spring Rose Music (BMI).
How to Contact: Submit a demo tape by mail—unsolicited submissions are O.K. Prefers cassette with 2 songs and lyric sheets. SASE. "No SASE—no returns." Reports in 4 weeks.
Music: Mostly MOR, top 40, soft rock, country/pop and uptempo country. Published "You Make It Magic," written and recorded by John Capplan on Caprice Records (MOR); "Nobody Cheated, Nobody Lied" (by John Capplan and Frank Longo), recorded by John Capplan on Caprice Records (MOR); and *Clocks and Calendars* (by Frank Longo), recorded by Lydia Tarketon on Lost Gold Records (country pop); and "There's No Easy Way to Forget You" (by Jimmy Crane), recorded by Kimberly Carter on KRC Records.
Tips: "Listen to what's being played on the radio. Be professional. Good demos get good results. Up tempo positive lyrics are always wanted. Success needs no apology—failure provides no alibi."

SONGWRITERS' NETWORK MUSIC PUBLISHING, P.O. Box 190446, Dallas TX 75219. (214)824-2739. President: Phil Ayliffe. Music publisher and record company (Songwriters' Network Records). ASCAP. Estab. 1983. Publishes 3 songs/year. Receives 5-8 submissions/year. Works with composers and lyricists; teams collaborators. Pays standard royalty.
How to Contact: Write first to get permission to submit a tape. Prefers cassette with 3 songs and lyric sheets. SASE. Reports in 6 weeks.
Music: Mostly pop, MOR and adult contemporary country. Published "Crazy About You," written and recorded by Phil Ayliffe on Songwriters' Network Records (jazz/pop).

SOTEX MUSIC, P.O. Box 27, Converse TX 78109-0027. (512)658-6748; 653-3898. Partners: Delbert Richerson and Frank Willson. Music publisher (BSW Records). BMI. Estab. 1989. Publishes 30 songs/year; publishes 5-10 new songwriters/year. Receives 10-15 submissions/month. Works with composers and lyricists; team collaborators. Pays standard royalty.
Affiliate(s): Sotex Music (BMI), Cinder Music Publishing (BMI), Delleon Records, Delrich Productions and Buffalo Valley Productions.
How to Contact: Submit a demo tape by mail—unsolicited submissions are OK. Prefers cassette or ½" VHS videocassette with 3 songs and lyric sheets. Include name, address, phone number and social security number with submissions.
Music: Mostly country, country/rock, country/gospel and rock. Published "Guessin' Game," written and recorded by Candace Howard; "Tried For Love," written and recorded by Eric Scott; "Alone With You," written and recorded by Eric Scott; and "I'll Be Home When I Get There," (by Barry Roberts), recorded by Lost Prairie; all on BSW Records.

*SOUL STREET MUSIC PUBLISHING INC., 265 Main St., East Rutherford NJ 07073. (201)933-2297. President: Glenn La Russo. Music publisher. ASCAP. Estab. 1988. Publishes 20 songs/year; publishes 5 new songwriters/year. Works with composers. Pays standard royalty.
How to Contact: Submit a demo tape by mail—unsolicited submissions are OK. Prefers cassette with 3 songs and lyric sheet. SASE. Reports in 1 month.
Music: Mostly R&B, dance and rap. Published "Touch Me" (by Carmichael), recorded by Cathy Dennis on Polydor Records (dance); "Symptoms of True Love" (by Harman/Weber), recorded by Tracey Spencer on Capitol Records (R&B); and "Thinking About Your Love," written and recorded by Skipworth and Turner on Island Records (R&B).

SOUND ACHIEVEMENT GROUP, P.O. Box 24625, Nashville TN 37202. (615)883-2600. President: Royce B. Gray. Music publisher. Estab. 1985. Publishes 120 songs/year; publishes 4 new songwriters/year. Works with composers and lyricists; teams collaborators. Pays standard royalty.
Affiliate(s): Song Palace Music (ASCAP) and Emerald Stream Music (BMI).
How to Contact: Submit a demo tape by mail—unsolicited submissions are OK. Prefers cassette (or VHS videocassette if available) with 3 songs and lyric sheet. SASE. Reports in 2 months.
Music: Gospel. Published "You Are," (by Penny Strandberg Miller), recorded by Revelations on Newind Records (gospel); "I Want My Life To Count" (by Sammy Lee Johnson), recorded by Sammy Lee Johnson on Image Records (gospel); and "The Wonder of Christmas" (by Giorgio Longno/John Ganes), reocrded by Giorgio Longno on Candle Records (gospel).

*SOUND ADVISORS LTD., 400 West Lancaster Ave., Devon PA 19333. (215)975-9212. President: Greg Mizii. Vice Presidents: Steven Bernstein and Howard Scott III. "Negotiated recording and publishing contracts with major companies that resulted in the worldwide sale of over 35 million records, tapes and CDs." ASCAP, BMI. Publishes 20-30 songs/year; 5-7 new songwriters/year. Negotiates royalties with companies and songwriters. Recording producers on staff.
How to Contact: Write first with SASE to obtain permission to submit. Prefers cassette tapes, CDs or records. Reports ASAP. Does not accept or return unsolicited material. Prefers correspondence by mail.
Music: Rock, R&B, rap, metal, pop, folk rock, country, contemporary Christian, Christian rock, gospel, jazz, blues, New Age, punk, new wave and reggae. Negotiated "*Sideshow*" (platinum record), by Blue Magic, "*Double Dutch Bus*," by Frankie Smith (a gold 7″ and 12″ single), "*Love Won't Let Me Wait*," by Major Harris (gold record). Also handled deals with Jean Carne, Luther Vandross, Cool C, Sweet Sensations, Fat Larry's Band and Bobby Rydell. Covers all aspects of the business—from law and management to production and promotion.
Tips: "Present yourself as professionally as possible. If you are great we can sign you or get you signed."

*SOUND CEREMONY RECORDS, 23 Selby Rd., London NW1 E11 **United Kingdom**. Phone: (01)081-503-1687 or 081503-1689. Director: R.W. Ganderton. Music publisher and record producer (Celestial Sound Productions). PRS. Publishes various number of songs and new songwriters/year. Works with composers and lyricists; teams collaborators. Pays standard or negotiable royalty.
Affiliate(s): Centridge Publishing.
How to Contact: Prefers cassette (or videocassette) and lyric sheet. SAE and IRC. Reports in 3 weeks.
Music: Mostly rock, pop and country; also jazz and soul. Published "giggle Amidst the Tears" on Centridge Records (rock); "You're Breaking My Heart" on Celestial Sound Records (rock); and "Dream Girl" and "Good News for Lovers" on Sound Ceremony Records (pop), all by R.W. Ganderton and recorded by Sound Ceremony.

*SOUND COLUMN COMPANIES, P.O. Box 70784, Salt Lake City UT 84170. (801)355-5327. President/General Manager: Ron Simpson. Music publisher, record company (SCP Records) and record producer (Sound Column Productions). BMI, ASCAP, SESAC. Member CMA, AFM. Estab. 1968. Publishes 50 songs/year; publishes 2 new songwriters/year. Receives 30 submissions/month. Hires staff writers. Works with composers and lyricists. Pays standard royalty.
Affiliate(s): Ronarte Publications (ASCAP), Mountain Green Music (BMI), Macanudo Music (SESAC).
How to Contact: Query first. Prefers cassette with 1-3 songs and lyric sheet. "We can't listen to outside submissions unless they are complete songs." SASE. Reports as time permits.
Music: Mostly pop, country and A/C; "lean toward power ballads." Published "Norma Jean Riley" (by Honey, Powell, Truman), recorded by Diamond Rio on Arista Records (contemporary country); "In Your Loving Hands" (by Romney), recorded by Kevin & Lita on Deseret Records (A/C); and "Personal Attention" (by Romney-Simpson-Trumen), recorded by The Jensens on SCP Records (country).
Tips: "We very rarely accept outside submissions so be careful about song form and quality of demo. No correspondence or return of materials without SASE. We would like to hear from more SESAC writers."

SOUND IMAGE PUBLISHING, 6556 Wilkinson, North Hollywood CA 91606. (818)762-8881. President: Marty Eberhardt. Vice President and General Manager: David Chatfield. Music publisher, record company, record producer and video company. BMI. Member NARAS. Publishes 160 songs/year; publishes 10 new songwriters/year. Pays standard royalty.

How to Contact: Prefers cassette (or VHS videocassette) with 3 songs and lyric sheet. Does not return unsolicited material. Reports in 2 months.
Music: Mostly rock; also dance, R&B.
Tips: "Demos should be professionally recorded. We suggest 16-24 track recording on cassette submissions."

SOUND SPECTRA MUSIC, P.O. Box 2474, Auburn AL 36831-2474. (205)821-4876. President: Larry L. Barker. Music publisher, record company (Rainbow River Records) and record producer (Spectra Productions). BMI. Estab. 1978. Publishes 20 songs/year; 3-5 new songwriters/year. Receives 20 submissions/month. Works with composers and lyricists. Pays standard royalty.
How to Contact: Write first and obtain permission to submit a tape. Prefers cassette with 3-4 songs and lyric sheets. Include SASE for reply. Does not return unsolicited submissions. Reports in 6 weeks.
Music: Mostly rock, R&B and New Age; also jazz, gospel and country. Published "Don't Hold Back" (by Ronald La Pread and Larry Barker), recorded by Ronald La Pread on Little Records (R&B); "It's Not Easy" (by Larry Barker), recorded by Lennie Hartzog on Rainbow River Records (pop); and "The Trash Bag's Been Ripped" (by Bruce Yandle), recorded by Mr. Resistor on Rainbow River Records (rock).
Tips: "Write first to determine current needs—then send only your tightest material."

SPEEDSTER MUSIC, P.O. Box 96, Glendale AZ 85311. (602)435-0314. Owner: Frank E. Koehl. Music publisher, record company (Auburn Records and Tapes). BMI. Estab. 1988. Publishes 2-8 songs/year; 2 new songwriters/year. Receives 25 submissions/month. Works with composers. Pays standard royalty.
How to Contact: Submit a demo tape by mail—unsolicited submissions are OK. Prefers cassette with 2-4 songs and lyric sheets. "Send only traditional, acoustic country music." SASE. Reports 3 weeks.
Music: Mostly country, traditional and bluegrass. Published "Shade Tree" and "Lottery Fever," written and recorded by Troy McCourt on Auburn (traditional country); and "Gonna Go To Houston" written and recorded by Frank Koehl on Auburn Records (country).
Tips: "Keep it country and acoustic. Tell a story simply."

SPHEMUSATIONS, 12 Northfield Rd., Onehouse, Stowmarket Suffolk 1P14 3HR **England**. Phone: 0449-613388. General Manager: James Butt. Music publisher. Estab. 1963. Publishes 200 songs/year; publishes 6 new songwriters/year. Receives 500 submissions/year. Works with lyricists; teams collaborators. Pays standard royalty.
How to Contact: Submit demo tape—unsolicited submissions are OK. Prefers cassette (or VHS or Beta videocassette). SAE and IRC. Reports in 3 months.
Music: Mostly country, blues and jazz, also "serious modern music." Published "Satyr's Song" (by J. Playford, J. Butt), "The Weeper" (by J. Playford, J. Butt); and "O. Moon" (by J. Keats, J. Butt), all on Sphemusations Records (light).

SPRADLIN/GLEICH PUBLISHING, P.O. Box 80083, Phoenix AZ 85060. (602)840-8466. Manager: Lee Gleich. Music publisher. BMI. Estab. 1988. Publishes 4-10 songs/year; 2-4 new songwriters. Works with composers and lyricists; teams collatorators. Pays standard 50% royalty.
Affiliate(s): "We work very closely with Country City Record Co., Port Pirie, **Australia**."
How to Contact: Submit a demo tape by mail—unsolicited submissions are OK. Prefers cassette with 3 songs and lyric sheet or lead sheet. "It must be very good material, as I only have time for promoting songwriters who really care."
SASE. Reports in 4 weeks.
Music: Mostly country geared to the US and Australian country markets; also pop, gospel (all types; also rock, theme music and piano jazz). Published "Tommy's Song" and "Friends Like These," both written and recorded by Lorri Rizzo on RTF Records.
Tips: "Don't use me for a sounding board only. I will comment on every tape submitted, if you send postage. I want good, clean lyrics, with something to say. Statement songs are coming in again. (Country music leaning to its roots but lyrics are better than ever!)"

SRSF RECORDINGS/ENTERTAINMENTS ENTERPRISES PUBLISHING®, A Division of SORIA Engerprizes®, P.O. Box 14131, Denver CO 80214. Publisher/Producer: Sharon Smith Fliesher Soria. Music publisher, record company (SRSF Recordings/Entertainments Enterprises®) and record producer (SRSF Recordings/Entertainments Enterprises®). ASCAP. Estab. 1980. Publishes 2 or more songs/year. Receives 4 submissions/month. Works with composers and lyricists; teams collaborators. Pays royalty of 95%. "A 10% markup is charged over clients cost of manufacturing pressings/videos, etc."
How to Contact: Submit a demo tape—unsolicited submissions are OK. Prefers cassette with 3 songs and lyric or lead sheet. "For our protection please enclose a signed and dated statement with your submissions stating you are enclosing 'title of song #1, #2, #3, no others follow.' Submissions without this statement will be disposed. Professional multitrack demo, with media kit a must." Reports in 6

weeks. "Send SASE postcard for our number disclosing publishing information."
Music: Mostly folk and country. "Our Time Has Come" (by Luanna Soria), recorded by Sharon Soria on Lambda Records®, Soria Enterprizes® (lesbian folk).
Tips: "We have changed our policy to cater only to the lesbian community working in conjunction with the Lambda Performing Arts Guild of America®. We encourage all interested to contact us. Our purpose is to legitimize and recognize lesbian artists. Please send only professionally mixed demos. Send for the 1-900-Nationwide phone number explaining our producing/publishing information."

*TERRY STAFFORD MUSIC, Box 6546, Burbank CA 91510. Music publisher. BMI. Estab. 1966. Publishes 25 songs/year. Publishes varying number of new songwriters/year. Pays standard royalties.
How to Contact: Prefers cassette with 3-5 songs and lyric sheet. "We will listen to all songs."
Music: Country, rockabilly and western. Published "Bear Country," by T. Stafford/J. Fortune (theme song for cable TV series); "Paradise," by T. Stafford/S. Howell/P. Fraser; and "Amarillo By Morning," by T. Stafford/P. Fraser.

STANG MUSIC INC., 753 Capitol Ave., Hartford CT 06106. (203)951-8175. Producer: Jack Stang. Music publisher, record company (Nickel Records) and record producer (Jack Stang). BMI. Estab. 1970. Publishes 20 songs/year; publishes 2 new songwriters/year. Receives 100 submissions/month. Hires staff writers. Works with composers; teams collaborators. Pays standard royalty.
How to Contact: Submit a demo tape by mail—unsolicited submissions are OK. Prefers cassette with 3 songs and lyric sheets. SASE. Reports in 3 weeks.
Music: Mostly rock, pop, top 40 and R&B; also country. Published "We Have It All" and "Free That Girl," both written and recorded by Ray Alaire on Stang Music (top 40).

STAR INTERNATIONAL, INC., P.O. Box 470346, Tulsa OK 74147. (918)663-7700. President: MaryNell Jetton. Senior Vice President: Michael Brown. Music publisher. ASCAP. Estab. 1989. Publishes 1-20 songs/year. Works with composers and lyricists; teams collaborators. Pays standard 50% royalty.
How to Contact: Submit a demo tape by mail—unsolicited submissions are OK. Prefers cassette (or VHS videocassette if available) with 1-2 songs and lyric sheet. "If we are interested in your first two songs, we will request more of your material. We respond only if we're interested."
Music: "We accept any type of music material, if it's professional."
Tips: "We are looking for new talent and are interested in songwriters who have material suitable for today's top recording artists in all music categories. We are also interested in new singer/songwriters."

*STARQUEST MUSIC, #295, 24318 Hemlock G2, Moreno Valley CA 92387. (714)485-0740. Manager: Cynthia Jule. Music publisher, record company (Starquest Records). BMI, ASCAP. Estab. 1985. Publishes 30 songs/year; publishes 5 new songwriters/year. Works with composers or lyricists; teams collaborators. Pays standard royalty of 50%.
Affiliate(s): Starquest Music (BMI), Moonmaid Music (ASCAP).
How to Contact: Submit a demo tape by mail—unsolicited submissions are OK. Prefers cassette (or VHS videocassette if available) with 4 songs and lyric sheet. SASE. Reports in 1 month.
Music: Mostly country and pop. Published "Lucky Guy" and "Don Do," both written and recorded by Don Malena on Starquest Records (country)

STONEHAND PUBLISHING, P.O. Box 895, Station E, Victoria BC V8W 2R9 **Canada.** (604)386-0507. Project Director: Linda Ehlers. Music publisher, record companies (Stonehand Records). SOCAN, CMRRA. Estab. 1984. Publishes 6 songs/year; publishes 2-3 new songwriters/year. Receives 20 submissions/month. Pays standard royalty.
How to Contact: Submit a demo tape by mail—unsolicited submissions are OK. Prefers cassette or VHS videocassette with 3 songs and lyric sheets. SAE with IRC. Reports in 6 weeks.
Music: Mostly pop/rock, AOR/MOR and country; also folk. Released the album *Leave Me Standing,* by Kin Cain (independent). Published "I'm Not Normal," written and recorded by Lord Horizontal on Indie Records (pop); and "Love Never Stops At the Heart," written and recorded by Kin Cain on Indie Records (rock).
Tips: "Develop strong, visual lyrics, imaginative musical ideas and a persistent belief in yourself."

STRAWBERRY SODA PUBLISHING, 15 Exeter Rd., Kingston NH 03848. (603)642-8493. Coordinator: Harry Mann. Music publisher. ASCAP. Estab. 1988. Publishes 15 songs/year. Publishes 2-4 new songwriters/year. Works with composers and lyricists. Pays standard royalty.
How to Contact: Submit a demo tape by mail—unsolicited submissions are OK. Prefers cassette, 15 IPS reel-to-reel, or VCR videocassette with 3 songs and lyric sheets. SASE. Reports in 6-8 weeks.
Music: Mostly rock, country and pop; "no heavy metal." Published "2 Lane Highway," and "Flight 17" (by Doug Mitchell), both recorded by Doug Mitchell Band (A/C singles); on Kingston Records.
Tips: "Simple, understandable lyrics with a flow. Sequenced, electronic music is going too far. I think the acoustic sound might be ready for a comeback."

STREET SINGER MUSIC, 117 W. 8th, Hays KS 67601. (913)625-9634. President: Mark Meckel. BMI. Music publisher, record company (MDM Records) and record producer (Sunset Productions). Estab. 1980. Publishes 60 songs/year; publishes 4 new songwriters/year. Receives 600 submissions/year. Works with composers and lyricists. Pays standard royalty.
How to Contact: Submit a demo tape—unsolicited submissions are OK. Prefers cassette with 2-4 songs and lyric sheet.
Music: Mostly pop/rock; also country swing, country rock, 50s rock, Christmas, R&B, country, gospel and country R&B. Published "Bandito," written and recorded by C. Conley; "Full Moon Crazy" (by Val Stecklein), recorded by Brent Ronen; and "Showdown" (by M. Benish, Jack Routh, Brent Ronen), recorded by Brent Ronen; all on MDM Records (country).
Tips: "Be willing to make changes and work with a producer."

JEB STUART MUSIC CO., Box 6032, Station B, Miami FL 33123. (305)547-1424. President: Jeb Stuart. Music publisher, record producer and management firm. BMI. Estab. 1975. Publishes 4-6 songs/year. Teams collaborators. Pays standard royalty.
How to Contact: Submit a demo tape—unsolicited submissions are OK. Prefers cassette or disc with 2-4 songs and lead sheet. SASE. Reports in 1 month.
Music: Mostly gospel, jazz/rock, pop, R&B and rap; also blues, church/religious, country, disco and soul. Published "Saucy Music," written and recorded by Jeboria Stuart on Esquire Records (jazz/pop/ R&B); "Maxie-D" (by Stuart, Shapiro), recorded by J. Stuart on Esquire Records (rap); and "Have a Party Tonight" (by Stuart, Shapiro), recorded by J. Stuart on Esquire Records (R&B).

STYLECRAFT MUSIC CO. INC., P.O. Box 802, 953 Highway 51, Madison MS 39110. (601)856-7468. Professional Manager: Style Wooten. Music publisher, record company (Style Records, Styleway Records and Good News Records), record producer and booking agency (Style Wooten Inc.). BMI. Estab. 1964. Publishes 20-35 songs/year; publishes 10 new songwriters/year. Receives 100 submissions/ month. Pays standard royalty.
How to Contact: Write or call first. Prefers cassette with 2-4 songs and "typewritten lyric sheet." SASE. Reports in 1 month.
Music: Country, R&B and black gospel. Published "Bitter and the Sweet," "I'll Fight Goliath" and "Hard Love Affair" (all by Rev. Douglas Bell), all recorded by the Rev. Douglas Bell and The Stage Cruisers on Four Winds Records (black gospel).

SUBAR MUSIC PUBLISHING CO. LTD., 21, Any Ma'amin St., Ramat-Hasharon 47212 **Israel.** Phone: (03)5491323. FAX: (3) 5403490. TELEX: (3)32353. Manager: Dr. Ophira Bar-Elan. Music publisher. ACUM Ltd. Estab. 1961. Publishes 20-25 songs/year; publishes 2-3 new songwriters/year. Works with composers and lyricists. Pays standard royalty.
Affiliate(s): Sharon Music Publishing (ACUM Ltd.), Pa'amonim Music Publishers (ACUM Ltd.).
How to Contact: Write first to get permission to submit a tape. Prefers cassette and lyric or lead sheet. Does not return unsolicited material. Reports in 1 month.
Music: Mostly pop, rock and country.

SUGAR MAMA MUSIC, #805, 4545 Connecticut Ave. NW, Washington DC 20008. (202)362-2286. President: Jonathan Strong. Music publisher, record company (Ripsaw Records) and record producer (Ripsaw Productions). BMI. Estab. 1983. Publishes 3-5 songs/year; publishes 2 new songwriters/year. Works with composers and lyricists. Pays standard royalty.
Affiliate(s): Neck Bone Music (BMI) and Southern Crescent Publishing (BMI).
How to Contact: Prefers cassette and lyric sheet. SASE. Reports in 1 month.
Music: Mostly rockabilly and traditional rock. Published "No Use Knockin'," "Let Me Give You Lovin' " and "I'm Gonna Have to Send You Back," all written by Arthur Gerstein and recorded by the Uptown Rhythm Kings (jump blues).

SUGARBAKERS MUSIC, 404 Bluegrass Ave., Madison TN 37115. (615)865-6380. President: Bob Frick. Music publisher. ASCAP. Estab. 1988. Publishes 20 songs/year; publishes 5 new songwriters/year. Works with composers and lyricists. Pays standard royalty.
How to Contact: Submit a demo tape by mail—unsolicited submissions are OK. Prefers cassette with 2 songs and lyric sheets. Does not return unsolicited material. Reports in 2 weeks.
Music: Mostly gospel, country and pop. Published "Follow Where He Leads" (by Christine Starling); "Jesus is the Answer" (by Esther Stewart); and "Peace Within My Heart" (by Katz/Hopwood); all recorded by Bob Scott Frick on R.E.F. (gospel).

SULTAN MUSIC PUBLISHING, P.O. Box 461892, Garland TX 75046. (214)271-8098. President: Don Ferguson. Music publisher, record company (Puzzle Records), record producer and booking agency (Don Ferguson Agency). BMI. Publishes 15 songs/year, including some new songwriters. Receives 50

submissions/month. Works with composers and lyricists; teams collaborators. Pays standard royalty.
Affiliate(s): Illustrions Sultan (ASCAP).
How to Contact: Prefers cassette with 3 songs and lyric sheet. SASE. Reports in 3 weeks.
Music: Mostly country; also MOR. Published "What Does It Take," written and recorded by Derek Hartis on Puzzle Records (C&W); "After Burn," written and recorded by Phil Rodgers (jazz); and "Ain't No Way" (by G. Duke), recorded by Flash Point (rock), all on Puzzle Records.
Tips: "The best quality demo makes the listener more receptive."

*SULTRY LADY MUSIC, Suite 205, 380 Lafayette Rd., St. Paul MN 55107. (612)228-0719. Professional Manager: Thomas A. Del Vecchio. Music publisher. Publishes 1-2 songs/year; publishes 1 new songwriter/year. Pays standard royalty.
How to Contact: Prefers cassette with 3-5 songs "and a lyric sheet for each song. No submissions will be returned without SASE." Reports in 8 weeks.
Music: Mostly rock, MOR and jazz; also pop, top 40 and blues.

SULZER MUSIC (BMI), P.O. Box 142, Madisonville TX 77864. (409)348-6978. President: Claire Wilson. BMI. Estab. 1965. Publishes 30 songs/year; publishes 20 new songwriters/year. Receives 120 submissions/year. Works with composers and lyricists; teams collaborators. Pays standard royalty.
How to Contact: Submit a demo tape by mail—unsolicited submissions are OK. Prefers cassette (or VHS videocassette if available) with lyric sheet and lead sheet. SASE. Reports in 1 month.
Music: Mostly country, country rock and soft rock; also big band, gospel and R&B. Published "Something Special" (by Mike Dineen), recorded by John Mendell (country); "I Loved You The First time I Saw You," written and recorded by John Mendell (country); and "The Lottery Song" (by Eugene Schrader), recorded by Schrader; all on Regime Records (MOR/country).

SUNSET PRODUCTIONS, 117 W. 8th, Hays KS 67601. (913)625-9634. President: Mark Meckel. Music publisher, record company (M.D.M. Records), record producer (Sunset Productions), and management firm. BMI. Member CASK and SRS. Estab. 1978. Publishes 20 songs/year; publishes 3-4 new songwriters/year. Works with composers and lyricists; teams collaborators. Pays standard royalty. Sales royalty when song or artist is recorded, outright fee from recording artist, outright fee from record company.
Affiliate(s): Street Singer Music (BMI).
How to Contact: Prefers cassette with minimum 3 songs and lyric sheet.
Music: Mostly pop, country rock, 50s rock, Christian rock, R&B and Christmas; also MOR, gospel, blues and dance-oriented. Published "Just Like the Rain" (by Corey Gonzales), recorded by Dave Pfeiffer (pop rock); "Showdown" (by J. Routh, B. Ronen, M. Benish), recorded by Brent Ronen (country); and "Nobody Left to Save" (by M. Benish), recorded by Bren Ronen (country); all on M.D.M. Records.
Tips: "Be willing to change and work with a producer."

SUNSONGS MUSIC/MARS TALENT, (formerly Rigo Music Enterprises), 57 N. Perkins Ave., Elmsford NY 10523. (914)620-0944; and (914)592-2563. Professional Manager: Michael Berman. Music publisher, record producer and talent agency. Estab. 1981. BMI, ASCAP. Publishes 20 songs/year; publishes 10 new songwriters/year. Pays standard royalty; co-publishing deals available for established writers.
Affiliate(s): Media Concepts Music and Venus Music Inc. (BMI).
How to Contact: Prefers cassette with 3-4 songs and lyric sheet. SASE. Reports in 5 weeks.
Music: Dance-oriented, techno-pop, R&B, rock (all styles) and top 40/pop. Published "Big Girl" (by Michael Christian), "What You Get Is What You See" (Etoll/Kalem), and "Nothing But Trouble" (by Robbie Rigo), all recorded by Jailbait and performed on *Star Search* (pop/rock; Jailbait was a finalist and was signed to Atlantic Records). Published *Sunrise* (early 80s LP) on Buddah/Arista Records. Also handles nostalgia material.

SUPER RAPP PUBLISHING, 9305 Dogwood Place, Gainesville GA 30506. (404)889-8624. President: Ron Dennis Wheeler. Music publisher. BMI. Estab. 1964. Publishes 100 songs/year; 20-25 new songwriters/year. "Sometimes hires staff writers for special projects." Pays standard royalty.
How to Contact: "Send a demo tape/professionally recorded—if not, response time may be delayed. If you need a tape produced or song developed, contact Rapp Productions Inc. first before submitting a badly produced tape. Unsolicited submissions are OK. Send music trax with and without lead vocals. Lyric sheet and chords. Also send music score if possible. Prefers 15 ips and a cassette copy. Video is also better than cheap cassette. Clarity is most important. SASE is a must if you want submission returned. Will try to respond within 3 months."

Music: Mostly gospel, rock and pop; also country and R&B. "No new age." Published "No Exception To The Rule" (pop), "Ordinary Hero" (country pop), and "Echoes" (ballad/pop), all written and recorded by T. Prichard on Rapp/RRR Records.

SYNCHRO SOUND MUSIC AB, P.O. Box 1049, Sundbyberg 172 21 **Sweden.** Phone: (46)8-28 13 46. Publishing Manager: Douglas E. Lawton. Music publisher, record company (Synchro Sound Records) and record producer (Synchro Sound Records). STIM (Sweden). Estab. 1986. Publishes 50-75 songs/year; publishes 10-15 new songwriters/year. Hires staff writers. Works with composers and lyricists; teams collaborators. Pays standard royalty.
Affiliate(s): Desert Music AB, Midnight Sun Music AB, and Coste Apetrea Music AB.
How to Contact: Submit a demo tape—unsolicited submissions are OK. Prefers cassette or 15" ips reel to reel (or videocassette) with 4 songs and lyric sheet. Does not return unsolicited material. Reports in 6 weeks.
Music: Mostly pop, rock, classical and New Age; also R&B, country and gospel. Published "Angels," written and recorded by M. Siverling on Airplay Records (MOR); "Aliens," written and recorded by D. Saxon on Elektra Records (soul); and "The Way That I Did" (by Bacal), recorded by Sulphuric Sister on Vinyl Mania Records (soul).

*TABITHA MUSIC, LTD., 39 Cordery Rd., St. Thomas, Exeter, Devon EX2 9DJ, **England.** Phone: 44-0392-79914. Managing Director: Graham Sclater. Music publisher, record company (Tabitha and Willow Records) and record producer. MCPS, PRS. Member MPA. Estab. 1975. Publishes 25 songs/year; publishes 6 new songwriters/year. Works with composers. Pays standard royalty; royalties paid directly to US songwriters.
Affiliate(s): Domino Music and Dice Music.
How to Contact: Submit a demo tape—unsolicited submissions are OK. Prefers cassette with 1-4 songs and lyric sheet. SAE and IRC. Reports in 2 weeks.
Music: Mostly MOR and pop; also country, dance-oriented, Spanish, rock, soul and top 40. Published "Aliens" (by Mark Fojo), recorded by Sovereign on Tabitha Records; "Not A Chance," written and recorded by Simon Galt on Tabitha Records; "Video Boys" (by Goode/Partimeton), recorded by Circuit on Micro Records (electro pop); and "Teenage Love," written and recorded by A. Ford on Tabitha Records (pop).

TANGER-MUSIC PUBLISHING CO., INC., % British Record Corp., 1015 Gayley Ave,. Los Angeles CA 90024. Contact: A&R Department. Music publisher. ASCAP, BMI. Estab. 1981. Publishes 20 songs/year. Receives 150 submissions/month. Works with composers and lyricists; teams collaborators. Pays standard royalty 50%.
Affiliate(s): AKA Music (ASCAP) and Michelina's High Notes.
How to Contact: Submit a demo tape by mail—unsolicited submissions are OK. Prefers cassette with 3-4 songs and lyric and lead sheet. Does not return unsolicited material.
Music: Mostly rock, heavy metal and pop; also blues, folk and R&B. Published "Rock Me" (by Geoff Gibbs), recorded by Janet Lee on British Records (rock); "Never End This Love," by Ryan White (rock ballad); and "When I'm Alone," by Geoff Gibbs (rock ballad).

*TAS ENTERPRISES, P.O. Box 6096, Wausau WI 54402. (715)842-8176. Editor: Theodore A. Salvi. Music publisher. Estab. 1988. Publishes 2 songs/year. Receives 10 submissions/year. Works with composers. Pays standard royalty.
How to Contact: Submit a demo tape by mail—unsolicited submissions are OK. Prefers cassette with 4 songs and lyric and lead sheets. SASE. Reports in 4 weeks.
Music: Mostly sacred, gospel and educational; also church organ, piano and harp. Published "Two Christmas Pastorales," by R.R. McMahon (sacred organ); "Minuet," by R.R. McMahon (orchestra music); and "Two Hymn Accompaniments," R.R. McMahon (sacred).

DALE TEDESCO MUSIC CO., 16020 Lahey St., Granada Hills CA 91344. (818)360-7329. President: Dale T. Tedesco. General Manager: Betty Lou Tedesco. Music publisher. BMI, ASCAP. Estab. 1981. Publishes 20-40 songs/year; publishes 20-30 new songwriters/year. Receives 80-100 submissions/month. Works with composers and lyricists; teams collaborators. Pays standard royalty.
Affiliate(s): Dale Tedesco Music (BMI) and Tedesco Tunes (ASCAP).
How to Contact: Submit a demo tape—unsolicited submissions are OK. Prefers cassette with 1-2 songs and lyric sheet. SASE or postcard for critique. "Dale Tedesco Music hand-critiques all material submitted. Free evaluation." Reports in 2 weeks.

Music: Mostly pop, R&B and A/C; also dance-oriented, R&B, instrumentals (for television & film), jazz, MOR, rock and soul.
Tips: "Listen to current trends and touch base with the publisher."

*TEK PUBLISHING, P.O. Box 1485, Lake Charles LA 70602. (318)439-8839. Administrator: Eddie Shuler. Music publisher, freelance producer. ASCAP, BMI. Estab. 1956. Publishes 50 songs/year; publishes 35 new songwriters/year. Teams collaborators. Pays standard royalty of 50%.
Affiliate(s): TEK Publishing (BMI), Nassetan (BMI) and EMFS Music (ASCAP).
How to Contact: Submit a demo tape by mail—unsolicited submissions are OK. Prefers cassette with 3 songs and lyric sheet. "Return postage is required for return of material." SASE. Reports in 2 months.
Music: Mostly country and R&B; also cajun, humorist and zydeco. Published "Sands of Arabia" (by Ray Prince) and "So Many Things Make a Memory" (by Inez Polazzi & Ray Sanders), both recorded by Skip Dowers on Goldband Records (country); and "Whiskey, My Zydeco Horse," written and recorded by Herman Guiee on Jador Records (zydeco).

*TEN OF DIAMONDS MUSIC PUBLISHING (BMI), 880 Front St., Suite 661, Lahaina, Maui HI 96761. (808)661-5151 and (808)244-1100. A&R Director: Jack Carrington. Music publisher, record company (Survivor Records/Dream Makers Records/H.I.T. Records) and record producer (Maui). BMI, AS-CAP. Estab. 1974. Publishes 1-3 songs/year; publishes 1-3 new songwriters/year. Works with composers and lyricists; teams collaborators. Pays standard royalty.
Affiliate(s): Maui No Ka Oi Publishing (ASCAP), Ten of Diamonds Music (BMI).
How to Contact: Submit a demo tape by mail—unsolicited submissions are OK. Prefers cassette and VHS videocassette with 3-4 songs and lyric or lead sheet. SASE. Reports in 1 month.
Music: Mostly pop, country and R&B; also classical, Hawaiian and jazz/fusion. Published "Dreamer," written and recorded by Michael Condon (pop ballad); "Sunny Side of Reality" (by Walt Rosansky an Jason Schwartz), recorded by Jason (pop); and "Tangueray," written and recorded by Mark Cohen (jazz/fusion); all on Survivor Records.

*TERRA LITHIC MUSIC, P.O. Box 272, Garden City AL 35070. (205)352-4873. President: Dennis N. Kahler. "Growing publisher, always on the lookout for new material. Presently expanding contacts within the Nashville area, pitching to various artists. Critique/work with new writers whose material appeals to us." Publishes 12 songs/year. ASCAP affiliated. Affiliations with BMI pending. Pays standard royalty.
How to Contact: Unsolicited submissions welcomed. "Send cassette tape with no more than 4 songs, including lyric sheets, along with SASE mailer if you wish your tape returned (or $1.25 money order to cover cost of mailer and postage) to our letterhead address. We will reply as soon as possible, with comments on your material."
Music: "Primarily Terra Lithic is interested in country/western and gospel music. We look for songs emotionally charged, unique and with good word pictures." Recently published "Silent Night, Lonely Night" and "It Sure Feels Like Christmas to Me," by John Foster and James Cameron, respectively.
Tips: "We will be frank in our comments, as we believe no one ever learns if not told of his/her weaknesses as well as strong points. We are a new company, established in 1990. Presently we have close working relationship with 6 writers, having signed songs from 4."

*THEMA-VERLAG, Lacknergasse 6-8/3, Vienna 1170 **Austria**. Phone: (0222)454746. FAX: (0222)459503. Contact: Dr. Georg Strzyzowski. Music publisher, record company (Thema Records) and record producer. AKM, AUME, IFPI, LSG. Estab. 1985. Publishes approximately 100 songs/year; 5 new songwriters/year. Works with composers and lyricists; teams collaborators. Pays standard royalty.
Affiliate(s): Merco, Bronco, Airlift, Firebird, Recon, Novale, Jump, Enterprises, Continent.
How to Contact: Submit a demo tape by mail—unsolicited submissions are OK. Prefers cassette or 38 ips reel-to-reel (or VHS videocassette) with lyric or lead sheets. SASE. Reports in 1 month.
Music: Mostly MOR, pop and jazz; also classic, rock and folk. Published "Video" (by P. Meissner); "The Way Home" (by Rooner Meye, folk); and "Disco Nt" (by Voyage, MOR); all recorded by Strzyzowski on Thema Records.

"How to Use Your Songwriter's Market" (at the front of this book) contains comments and suggestions to help you understand and use the information in these listings.

MIKE THEODORE MUSIC, P.O. Box 841, Montclair NJ 07042. Contact: Mike Theodore. Music publisher and record producer. BMI and ASCAP. Estab. 1970. Publishes 20 songs/year; publishes 10 new songwriters/year. Works with composers and lyricists; teams collaborators. Pays standard royalty.
How to Contact: Submit a demo tape by mail—unsolicited submissions are O.K. Prefers cassette. SASE. Reports in 2 weeks.
Music: Mostly R&B and pop.

THIRD MILLENNIUM MUSIC, 301 Exhibition, Guelph, Ontario N1H-4R8 **Canada.** (519)821-3701. President: John Gandor. Music publisher. ASCAP. Estab. 1988. Publishes 15 songs/year; publishes 2-5 new songwriters/year. Pays standard royalty.
How to Contact: Submit a demo tape by mail—unsolicited submissions are OK. Prefers cassette (or VHS videocassette) with 1-3 songs and lyric sheets. "Only send material that you feel can compete with the best!" SASE. Reports in 4 weeks.
Music: Mostly pop, rock and country.
Tips: "We are looking for 'radio-oriented' hit singles."

TIKI ENTERPRISES, INC., 195 S. 26th St., San Jose CA 95116. (408)286-9840. President: Gradie O'Neal. Music publisher, record company (Rowena Records) and record producer (Jeannine O'Neal and Gradie O'Neal). BMI, ASCAP. Estab. 1967. Publishes 40 songs/year; publishes 12 new songwriters/year. Receives 1,200 submissions/year. Works with composers; teams collaborators. Pays standard royalty.
Affiliate(s): Tooter Scooter Music (BMI), Rememberance Music (ASCAP), and Janell Music (BMI).
How to Contact: Submit a demo tape—unsolicited submissions are OK. Prefers cassette with 3 songs and lyric or lead sheets. SASE. Reports in 3 weeks.
Music: Mostly rock/pop, country and gospel; also international, jazz/fusion, rock, R&B and New Age. Published "Don't Make Me Hurt Before My Time," by Leon Coleman; "By Another Man," by Cleveland Anderson; "Can You Feel It," by J. O'Neal (crossover); "Without Me," by B. Bingham and T. Eller (country); and "Out of the Blue," by J. O'Neal (country); all recorded by Charlie on Rowena Records.

***TIME MINSTREL MUSIC,** Box 241, Cameron MO 64429. (816)632-6039. Director: E.K. Bruhn. BMI. Music publisher, record company (Crusader and Songwriter Showcase), record producer (Crusader Records & Tapes). Estab. 1979. Publishes 10-15 songs/year; publishes 2-5 new songwriters/year. Works with composers and lyricists; teams collaborators. Pays standard royalty.
How to Contact: Write for immediate styles needed. Prefers cassette or 7½ ips reel-to-reel with 1-3 songs and "optional" lyric sheet or lead sheet. "Include short write-up about your interests." SASE. Reports in 10 weeks.
Music: Novelty/show songs, pop, country, soft rock and some gospel; also "clean" comedy show material.
Tips: "We like upbeat songs that are unique in subject matter."

TOMPAUL MUSIC CO., 628 South St., Mount Airy NC 27030. (919)786-2865. Owner: Paul E. Johnson. Music publisher, record company, record producer and record and tape distributor. BMI. Estab. 1960. Publishes 25 songs/year. Receives 250 submissions/year. Works with composers. Pays standard royalty.
How to Contact: Submit a demo tape—unsolicited submissions are OK. Prefers cassette tapes with 4-6 songs and lyric or lead sheet. SASE. Reports in 2 months.
Music: Mostly country, bluegrass and gospel; also church/religious, easy listening, folk, MOR, rock, soul and top 40. Published "Love Valley," written and recorded by Bobby Atkins on Stark Records (country); "My Favorite Way To Cry," written and recorded by Don Sawyers on Stark Records (country); and "I Had to Step Aside," written and recorded by Eddy Johnson on Triad Records (country).
Tips: "Try to write good, commercial songs. The lyrics should match the music. Use new ideas; don't try to make alterations in a song that is already established."

***TONE RECORDS,** 4057 McClung Dr., Los Angeles CA 90008. (213)294-3359. Operations Manager: Chris Roe. Music publisher, record company (Tone Records) and record producer (Total Trak Productions). ASCAP. Estab. 1988. Hires staff writers. Works with composers and lyricists; teams collaborators. Pays standard royalty.
How to Contact: Submit a demo tape by mail—unsolicited submissions are OK. Prefers cassette (or VHS videocassette if available) with 3 or more songs and lyric sheet. SASE. Reports in 2 weeks.
Music: Mostly R&B, dance and rap; also pop, funk/soul and rock. Published "Woman Intuition," "I Love Music" and "You're On The Ball," written and recorded by Margaret Coleman and Courtney Branch on Tone Records (R&B).

TOOTER SCOOTER MUSIC (BMI), 195 S. 26th St., San Jose CA 95116. (408)286-9840. Owner: Gradie J. O'Neal. Music publisher. BMI. Estab. 1985. Publishes 15 songs/year; 6 new songwriters/year. Works with composers and lyricists. Pays standard 50% royalty.
Affiliate(s): Janell Music (BMI), O'Neal & Friend (ASCAP) and Remembrance Music (ASCAP).
How to Contact: Submit a demo tape by mail—unsolicited submissions are OK. Prefers cassette with 2-4 songs and lyric sheet. SASE. Reports in 3 weeks.
Music: Country, gospel, pop/rock, Mexican. Published "Sweet Street Cowboy" (by D. Henry); "Lift Me Up, Lay Me Down" (by M. Eagen); and "Could Have Heard a Heart Beat" (by C.W. Childers), all recorded by Charlie.

TOPOMIC MUSIC, 105 Rue de Normandie, Courbevoie 92400 **France**. (1)4333 6515. President: Pierre Jaubert. Music publisher and record producer. SACEM, ASCAP. Estab. 1974. Publishes 60 songs/year; publishes 10 new songwriters/year. works with composers and lyricists; teams collaborators. Pays SACEM royalty which is usually 50/50.
How to Contact: Submit demo tape by mail.
Music: "Looks for new songs for movie soundtracks. Also needs top 40 style singers for movie soundtracks and dance records productions. Topomic Music is looking for new lyricists in English, to write words on compositions already published by Topomic. Writer will receive writer shares only, no publisher share, and lyrics will be published by Topomic for the world." Published "You Call It Love" movie soundtrack), performed by Norwegian singer Karoline Kruger. Also publishes composer Jean Coignoux.

TOULOUSE MUSIC PUBLISHING CO., INC., Box 96, El Cerrito CA 94530. Executive Vice President: James Bronson, Jr. Music publisher, record company and record producer. BMI. Member AIMP. Publishes 1 new songwriter/year. Hires staff writers. Pays standard royalty.
How to Contact: Prefers cassette with 2-4 songs and lyric sheet. SASE. Reports in 1 month.
Music: Bluegrass, gospel, jazz, R&B and soul.

*TRANSCONTINENTAL MUSIC PUBLICATIONS, 838 Fifth Ave., New York NY 10021. (212)249-0100. Senior Editor: Dr. Judith B. Tischler. Music publisher. ASCAP. Estab. 1941/1977. Publishes 2 new songwriters/year. Works with composers. Pays 10% royalty. "We publish serious solo and choral music. The standard royalty is 10% except for rentals—there is no cost to the songwriter."
How to Contact: Call first and obtain permission to submit a tape. Prefers cassette. "We usually do not accept lead sheets. Most all of our music is accompanied. Full and complete arrangements should accompany the melody." Reports in 10-12 months.
Music: Mostly Jewish vocal and Jewish choral.

TREASURE TROVE MUSIC, P.O. Box 48864, Los Angeles CA 90048. (213)739-4824. Contact: Professional Manager. Music publisher and record company (L.S. Disc). BMI. Estab. 1987. Publishes 3-15 songs/year; publishes 1-5 new songwriters/year. Receives 10-30 submissions/month. Works with composers and lyricists; teams collaborators. Pays standard royalty.
Affiliate(s): Treasure Trove Music (BMI).
How to Contact: Submit a demo tape by mail—unsolicited submissions are OK. Prefers cassette (or VHS videocassette) with 1-10 songs and lyric sheet. SASE. Reports in 3 months.
Music: Mostly rock, pop and folk rock; also unique crossover, novelty and New Age. Published "Kathleen" (rock), "More Than Friends" (pop), and "Never Gonna Work" (novelty punk), all written and recorded by Larry Rosenblum on L.S. Disc Records.
Tips: "Nobody really knows where music will be 2 years down the road. Anything can be a hit in the 1990's. So if you believe in your songs, keep on plugging. I can see folk music making a major comeback, especially on environmental issues. I also think people are getting a little bored with the current marketing and labeling. Music should be more than 'just entertainment.' "

TRI-SHE KIETA PUBLISHERS, INC., #825, 122 W. Monroe, Chicago IL 60603. President: John Bellamy. Music publisher, record company (Source Records), record producer (Anthony Stephens). BMI. Estab. 1974. Publishes 12 new songs/year; 1-2 new songwriters/year. Works with composers and lyricists; teams collaborators. Pays standard royalty of 50%.
Affiliate(s): Light & Sound Music, Inc. (ASCAP).
How to Contact: Submit demo tape by mail—unsolicited submissions are OK. Prefers cassette (or VHS videocassette if available) with 3 songs and lyric sheet. Does not return unsolicited material. Reports in 3 weeks.
Music: Mostly R&B, pop and gospel. Published "You Got The Love" (by A. Stephens), recorded by Candi Staton (inspiration); "Everybody Dance," written and recorded by Darnell Owens (R&B); and "Keeper of the Dream" (by M. Hughes), recorded by Clear Vision (rap), all on Source Records.

TRUSTY PUBLICATIONS, 8771 Rose Creek Rd., Nebo KY 42441. (502)249-3194. President: Elsie Childers. Music publisher, record company (Trusty Records) and record producer. BMI. Member CMA, NAS. Estab. 1960. Publishes 2-3 songs/year; publishes 2 new songwriters/year. Receives 8-10 submissions/month. Works with composers. Pays standard royalty.
Affiliate(s): Sub-publishers: Sunset Music (Italy) and White Label (Holland).
How to Contact: Submit a demo tape—unsolicited submissions are OK. Prefers cassette (or VHS videocassette) with 2-4 songs and lead sheet. SASE. Reports in 1 month.
Music: Mostly country/blues, contemporary Christian, Southern gospel and dance tunes; some rap. Published "Get Up," by Joey Benjamin (rap).
Tips: "We consider songwriters who are also on the road with a band, or as a single act, before we consider just songwriters."

21st CENTURY SPIRITUALS, Box 48661, St. Petersburg FL 33743. Coordinator: Pamela Krizmanich. Music publisher. ASCAP. Estab. 1989. Publishes 12 songs/year. Receives 80 submissions/year. Works with composers. Pays standard royalty.
How to Contact: Submit a demo tape by mail—unsolicited submissions are OK. Prefers cassette with 1-3 songs and lyric sheets. "Be professional. We prefer typed lyric sheet and studio production." SASE. Reports in 4 weeks.
Music: Mostly New Age, pop and modern jazz; also folk-rock. Published "States of Grace," "Between Life & Living," and "Lost in the Hurrah," all written and recorded by Michael Kris on Dustco Records (New Age).
Tips: "Sometimes success is only three minutes away. We prefer the music to speak through the person, not the person to speak through the music. There are enough people trying to be somebody else."

*TWIN TOWERS PUBLISHING CO., 8833 Sunset Blvd., Penthouse, Los Angeles CA 90069. (213)659-9644. President: Michael Dixon. Director of Publishing: Dave Powell. Music publisher and booking agency (Harmony Artists, Inc.). Works with composers and lyricists. Publishes 24 songs/year. Receives 200 submissions/month. Works with composers and lyricists. Pays standard royalty.
How to Contact: Call first to get permission to submit a tape. Prefers cassette with 3 songs and lyric sheet. SASE. Will respond only if interested.
Music: Mostly pop, rock and R&B. Published "Magic," from *Ghostbusters* soundtrack on Arista Records; and "Kiss Me Deadly" (by Lita Ford), on RCA Records.

TWL PUBLISHING GROUP, P.O. Box 11227, Detroit MI 48211-0227. Attention: A&R Department. ASCAP, BMI, SESAC. Music publisher and management firm (L2 Management). Estab. 1982. Publishes 10-15 songs/year; publishes 1-2 new songwriters/year. Works with composers; teams collaborators. Pays standard royalty; negotiates foreign subpublishing.
Affiliate(s): Lady Marion, Isle Cay Music, Sunscape Publishing and The Clearwind Publishing Group.
How to Contact: "Solicited submissions only." Write and obtain permission to submit. SASE. Prefers cassette with 2 songs and typed lyric sheet. Reports in 12 weeks.
Music: "Highly commercial" pop/dance, pop/rock and R&B. Published "Don't Stop" (by M. Grabowski), recorded by Cerberus on Starstream (rock); *Champion*, and "What a Friend," written and recorded by Ron Moore on Morada (pop); and "Crazy in Your Ways," written and recorded by R.R. Jackson on Windguest Records (pop).
Tips: "The writer must be flexible and have the (obvious) potential to write not just one commercial success but many. The writer must also have a great amount of persistence, patience and perseverance. The goal of the writer should be close to that of his or her publisher."

TWO & TWO PUBLISHING, 2305 Dickey Ave., N. Chicago IL 60064. (312)689-2726. Vice President: Walter T. Barnett. Music publisher, record company (WMB Records, Two & Two Publishing) and record producer (Barnett Productions). BMI. Estab. 1980. Publishes 50 songs/year; 4 new songwriters/year. Hires staff writers occasionally. Receives 1,000 submissions/year. Works with composers and lyricists; teams collaborators. Pays standard royalty.
How to Contact: Submit a demo tape by mail—unsolicited submissions are OK. Prefers cassette with 4 songs and lyric sheets. SASE. Reports in 1 month.
Music: Mostly R&B, rock and rap; also house, reggae and soul. Published "Heavy On My Mind" (by Jackie Bell), recorded by Jackie Bell on WMBN Records (rap); "Get Next To You" (by W. Barnett), recorded by Shibeli on WMB Records (R&B); and "So Much Pain" (by R. Coleman), recorded by Fulldeck on WMB Records (rap).
Tips: "Make sure you have your song put together as close as you would want it to be heard. If you don't sing, have a singer do it."

*TWO FOLD MUSIC, P.O. Box 388, Goodlettsville TN 37072. (615)831-6242. Manager: Roland Pope. Music publisher. BMI. Estab. 1978. Publishes 50 songs/year. Teams collaborators. Pays standard royalty of 50%.
Affiliate(s): Two Fold Music (BMI).
How to Contact: Submit a demo tape by mail—unsolicited submissions are OK. Prefers cassette with 4 songs and lyric sheet. "Include return address and phone number." SASE. Reports in 3 weeks.
Music: Mostly country, gospel and rock.

*UDDER PUBLISHING/GOLDEN GELT PUBLISHING, P.O. Box 93457, Hollywood CA 90093. (213)960-9447. President: Adam Rodell. Music publisher, record company (Rodell Records) and record producer (Rodell Records). BMI, ASCAP. Estab. 1984. Publishes 200-300 songs/year; publishes 25-50 new songwriters/year. Works with composers and lyricists; teams collaborators. Pays negotiable royalty.
How to Contact: Submit a demo tape by mail—unsolicited submissions are OK. Prefers cassette (or VHS videocassette if available) with 3 songs and lyric sheet. Does not return unsolicited material. "We will report back only if we are interested."
Music: Mostly rock, country and pop; also fusion-progressive, R&B and rap. Published "Birdie Dance" (by Clyde Brewer), recorded by River Road Boys (country); "Pine Tar Bat" (by Dave McEmery), recorded by Red Rover Dave (novelty); and "Rodell Rhapsody," written and recorded by Andrew Rodell (rock); all on Longhorn Records.
Tips: "Send studio or studio quality cassettes only with bio. We openly welcome all types of music. We run periodic nationwide talent searches. Aggressively seeking new material."

*UNITED ENTERTAINMENT MUSIC, 4024 State Line, Kansas City KS 66103. (913)262-3555. Director of Publishing: Dave Maygers. Music publisher, record company (United Entertainment Productions) and record producer. BMI. Estab. 1972. Publishes 30-40 songs/year; publishes 30-40 new songwriters/year. Pays negotiable royalty.
How to Contact: Prefers cassette or 15 or 30 ips reel-to-reel and lyric sheet. Does not return unsolicited material.
Music: Mostly rock, R&B/blues and jazz; also country and pop. Published "Steal Away" and "So Lucky" (by R. Lucente), recorded by Bon Ton Band on Stress Records; "Mr. Misery" (by D. Blake), recorded by Tic Toc Boom; and "Weak Heart, Strong Memory," written and recorded by Spike Blake on Stress Records.
Tips: "We are looking for music that suits our artists and has a message that is positive and current. Music should have commercial value."

UNIVERSAL STARS MUSIC, INC., HC-80, Box 5B, Leesville LA 71446. National Representative: Sherree Stephens. Music publisher and record company (Robbins Records). BMI. Publishes 12-24 songs/year; publishes 1 new songwriter/year. Pays standard royalty.
Affiliate(s): Headliner Stars Music Inc.
How to Contact: Prefers cassette with 1-6 songs and lyric or lead sheets. Does not return unsolicited material. Reports in 1 month, if interested.
Music: Mostly religious; also bluegrass, church, country, folk, gospel and top 40/pop. Published "Jesus, You're Everywhere," "I Can Depend On You," and "I Just Came to Thank You Lord," (all by Sherree Stephens), all recorded by J.J. and S. Stephens on Robbins Records (religious).

UTTER NONSENSE PUBLISHERS, Box 1583, Brantford Ontario N3T 5V6 **Canada**. Phone: (519)753-2081. President: John Mars. Music publisher, record company (Ugly Dog Records) and record producer. CAPAC. Estab. 1979. Publishes 2-5 songs/year; publishes 1 new songwriter/year. Receives 10 submissions/month. Works with composers and lyricists; teams collaborators. Pays standard royalty.
How to Contact: Submit a demo tape by mail—unsolicited submissions are OK. Prefers cassette (or videocassette if available) with lyric or lead sheet. "Send picture of artist(s). We regret that (due to the large number of submissions we receive) we now can only reply to those artists that we wish to express interest in."
Music: Mostly rock & roll; also new jazz and R&B. Published "Love Ya Babe" (by Mars, Guest, Todd), recorded by The Red Shrimps; and "Dance Hall Girl" (by Mars, Guest), recorded by The Popp Tarts; both on Ugly Dog Records (rock & roll).
Tips: "We are mainly interested in basic, rootsy R&R, and very little of that is sent to us. Also, 9 out of 10 demos are of quality that is virtually undecipherable. Do not waste time with poor quality demos."

VAAM MUSIC GROUP, P.O. Box 29688, Hollywood CA 90029-0688. (213)664-7765. President: Pete Martin. Music publisher and record producer. ASCAP, BMI. Estab. 1967. Publishes 9-24 new songs/year; varying number of new songwriters per year. Receives 50-200 submissions/month. Pays standard royalty.

Affiliate(s): Pete Martin Music.
How to Contact: Prefers cassette with 2 songs maximum and lyric sheet. SASE. Reports in 1 month. "Small packages only."
Music: Top 40/pop, country and R&B. "Submitted material must have potential of reaching top 5 on charts." Published "Good Girls" (by Kevin Bird), recorded by Valerie Canon on Carrere/CBS Records (R&B dance); "The Greener Years," recorded by Frank Loren on Blue Gem Records (country/MOR); "Bar Stool Rider" (by Peggy Hackworth); and "I Love a Cowboy," written and performed by Sherry Weston in the feature film "Far Out Man," with Tommy Chong (of Cheech & Chong comedy team) and also co-starring Martin Mull.
Tips: "Study the top 10 in charts in the style that you write. Stay current and up to date to today's market."

TOMMY VALANDO PUBLISHING GROUP, Suite 2110, 1270 Avenue of the Americas, New York NY 10020. (212)489-9696. President: Tommy Valando. General Manager: Arthur Valando. Director of Publications: Paul McKibbins. Music publisher. BMI, ASCAP. Member NMPA. Publishes varying number of songs/year. Pays standard royalty. Printed material percentage—rate varies.
Affiliate(s): Revelation Music Publishing Corp. (ASCAP) and Fiddleback Music Publishing Co., Inc. (BMI).
How to Contact: Call first. Prefers cassette with 1-3 "clear" songs. SASE. Reports "as quickly as possible."
Music: Musical theater scores primarily; occasionally pop and country.
Tips: "We prefer writer to perform own songs to give a true idea of what he or she is trying to convey. Demo does not have to be elaborate."

VALENTINE MUSIKVERLAG, Box 203312, D-2000 Hamburg 20 **West Germany.** Phone: (040) 4300339. FAX: (040)439 65 87.General Manager: Arno H. van Vught. GEMA. Music publisher, record company (Bandleader Records, Range Records) and record producer. Estab. 1973. Publishes 350 songs/year; publishes 50 new songwriters/year. Pays standard royalty.
Affiliate(s): Mento Music Group KG, Edition RCP Music and Auteursunie.
How to Contact: Submit a demo tape—unsolicited submissions are OK. Prefers cassette and lyric sheet and lead sheet. SAE and IRC. Reports in 2 weeks.
Music: Mostly country, jazz, big band, background music and MOR; also film music. Published "Ach Lass Es" (by Martin), recorded by A. Körber on TeBiTo Records (pop); "Weites Land," written and recorded by P. Reifegerste on DA Records (soft pop); and "Bulles De Savon," written and recorded by D. Brun on Playbones Records (pop).
Tips: "Send full lead sheet and information about the writer(s)."

VALET PUBLISHING CO., #273, 2442 N.W. Market, Seattle WA 98107. (206)524-1020; FAX: (206)524-1102. Publishing Director: Buck Ormsby. Music publisher and record company (Etiquette/Suspicious Records). BMI. Estab. 1961. Publishes 5-10 songs/year. Receives 300-350 submissions/year. Hires staff songwriters. Pays standard royalty.
How to Contact: Submit a demo tape—unsolicited submissions OK. Prefers cassette or VHS videocassette with 3-4 songs and lyric sheets. SASE. Reports in 1 month.
Music: Mostly R&B, rock, pop; also dance and country. Published "Black Lace" (by Roger Rogers), recorded by Kinetics on Etiquette Records (rock); "Hunger and Emotion" (by Rogers/Caldwell), recorded by Kinetics on Etiquette Records (pop); and "One More Time" (by Morrill/French), recorded by Kent Morrill on Suspicious Records (R&B).
Tips: "Production of tape must be top quality; or lyric sheets professional."

VIN-JOY MUSIC, 872 Morris Park Ave., Bronx NY 10462. (212)792-2198. Contact: Vice President. Music publisher, record company (Dragon Records) and record producer. BMI, ASCAP. Estab. 1960. Publishes 14-16 new songs/year; publishes 3-4 new songwriters/year. Works with composers, lyricists; teams collaborators. Pays negotiable amount.
How to Contact: "We accept material by recommendation only." Write or call first to get permission to submit a tape.
Music: Easy listening, MOR, top 40/pop and country. Published "Promise Me" (by Heath), recorded by Smokey on Agon Records (country); "Cousins," written and recorded by Badale (mood-background); and "Letters" (by Gagliano), recorded by Smokey Heath on Dragon Records (country).
Tips: "Material has to be exceptional—not amateurish."

*VIRGIN BOY PUBLISHING, 2613 Castle, Irving TX 75038. (214)255-8015. President: James Yarborough. Music publisher, record company (Virgin Boy Records) and record producer. ASCAP. Estab. 1988. Publishes 25 songs/year; publishes 10 new songwriters/year. Works with composers and lyricists; teams collaborators. Pays standard royalty.

Affiliate(s): Virgin Boy Publishing (ASCAP).
How to Contact: Submit a demo tape by mail—unsolicited submissions are OK. Prefers cassette with 3 songs and lyric sheet. Does not return unsolicited material. Reports in 2 months.
Music: Mostly pop, rock and country. Published "A Woman Of Mystery," "Angel In White Satin" and "Looking All Over," (all written and recorded by James Yarborough) on Virgin Boy Records (pop singles).

VOKES MUSIC PUBLISHING, Box 12, New Kensington PA 15068-0012. (412)335-2775. President: Howard Vokes. Music publisher, record company, booking agency and promotion company. BMI.
How to Contact: Submit cassette (3 songs only), lyric or lead sheet. SASE. Reports within a week.
Music: Traditional country-bluegrass and gospel. Published "The Howard Vokes Yodel," "When You Meet Your Lord," "Judge of Hearts," "Your Kisses and Lies" and "If This World Wants Peace."

*VOLITION MUSIC, 38 Thomson St., East Sydney NSW 2010 **Australia**. Phone: (02)3322270. General Manager: C. Ready. Music publisher. APRA (Austalian). Estab. 1984. Publishes 30 songs/year; publishes 5 new songwriters/year. Works with composers and lyricists; teams collaborators.
How to Contact: Call first and obtain permission to submit a tape. Prefers cassette. Does not return unsolicited material.
Music: Mostly pop/dance, R&B/dance and rock/dance; also electronic/dance and rock. Published "Insect" and "Free Mason," written and recorded by Boxcar, on Arista Records (pop/dance); and "All Saint's Day," written and recorded by Severed Heads on Network Records (electronic/dance).

*WALK ON WATER MUSIC, Rt. 2, Box 566-H, New Braunfels TX 78130. (512)625-2768. Producer/Manager: Kenneth D. Brazle. ASCAP, BMI. Estab. 1984. Music publisher, record company, record producer and recording studio. Publishes 3-6 songs/year; publishes 1 new songwriter/year. Receives 10-15 submissions/month. Works with composers and lyricists; teams collaborators. Pays negotiated royalty.
How to Contact: Write first and obtain permission to submit. Prefers cassette or 7½ ips reel-to-reel (or VHS videocassette if available, though not necessary) with 2-3 songs and lyric sheet. SASE. Does not return unsolicited material. Reports in 6 weeks.
Music: Mostly rock; also AOR-pop/rock, new music and country. Published "Longbone," "No Time," and "Stand By Me," (by Innerview), on Walk on Water Records (rock).

WARNER/CHAPPELL MUSIKVERLAG GESELLSCHAFT m.b.H., Diefenbachgasse 35, Vienna A 1150 **Austria**. Phone: (0222) 894 19 20; FAX: (0222) 894 16 15. Contact: Franz Handler. Music publisher. AKM. Works with composers and lyricists; teams collaborators.
Affiliate(s): Schneider Musikverlag, Gloria Musikverlag, and Aberbach Musikverlag.
How to Contact: Prefers cassette (or VHS videocassette). SAE and IRC. Reports in 3 months.
Music: Mostly pop, rock and country; also musicals.

WARNER/CHAPPELL MUSIC, INC., 1290 6th Ave., New York NY 10019. (212)399-6910. Creative Manager: Kenny McPhearson. Music publisher. ASCAP, BMI. Estab. 1811. Publishes hundreds of songs/year; publishes hundreds of new songwriters/year. Hires staff songwriters. Works with composers and lyricists; teams collaborators.
Affiliate(s): WB Music Corp. (ASCAP), Warner Tamerlane Publishing Corp. (BMI), W.B.M. Music Corp. (SESAC), Warner/Elektra/Asylum Music Inc. (BMI), Warner/Refuge Music Inc. (ASCAP), Warner/Noreale Music Inc. (SESAC), Chappell & Co. (ASCAP), Intersong U.S.A. Inc. (ASCAP), Rightsong Music Inc. (BMI), Unichappell Music Inc. (BMI), Tri-Chappell Music, Inc. (SESAC), Lorimar Music A Corp (ASCAP), Lorimar Music B Corp (BMI), Roliram Lorimar Music (BMI), Marilor Music (ASCAP), Goldline Music (ASCAP) Silverline Music (BMI) and Oakline Music (SESAC).
How to Contact: "Must be solicited by an attorney or management firm." Company policy prohibits unsolicited submissions.
Music: Mostly pop, rock, R&B and country; also rap, jazz and new music.
Tips: "Submit your best song because sometimes you only get to make a first impression. Submit a song you feel most comfortable writing regardless of style."

WATCHESGRO MUSIC, P.O. Box 1794, Big Bear City CA 92314. (714)585-4645. President: Eddie Carr. Music publisher. BMI. Estab. 1987. Publishes 100 songs/year; publishes 5 new songwriters/year. Receives 200 submissions/year. Teams collaborators. Pays standard royalty.
How to Contact: Submit a demo tape by mail—unsolicited submissions are OK. Prefers cassette. Does not return unsolicited material. Reports in 1 week.
Music Published "7th & Sundance" (by Aileen/Dempsey), recorded by Rita Aileen (country); "Eatin' My Words" (by M. Jones), recorded by Michael Jones; and "Precious Memories" (by D. Horn), recorded by Cindy Jane, all on Interstate 40 Records (country singles).

WAVEWORKS, 2000 P. St. NW, Washington DC 20036. (202)861-0560. Contact: Patrick Smith. Music publisher. BMI. Estab. 1987. Produces and publishes 20 songs/year; publishes 1 new songwriter/year. Hires staff writers. Works with composers and lyricists; teams collaborators.
How to Contact: Submit a demo tape by mail—unsolicited submissions are O.K. Prefers cassette (or ¾" videocassette if available). Does not return unsolicited material.
Music: Primarily music for television, film and video.

WAYNE AND LACEY, 4305 So. 70th St., Tampa FL 33619. (813)621-7055. Publisher: Wayne Lacey. Music publisher, record company (Music City Records) and record producer (Music City Records). BMI. Estab. 1982. Publishes 50 songs/year; publishes 10-15 new songwriters/year. year. Works with composers. Pays standard royalty.
How to Contact: Prefers cassette with 4 songs. Does not return unsolicited material. Reports in 1 month.
Music: Mostly gospel. Published "Only the Blood," "What A Wonderful Day," and "Land Of Promise," (all written by Wayne Lacey), recorded by The Laceys on Music City Records.
Tips: "Submit gospel, southern, bluegrass and traditional."

WEEDHOPPER MUSIC, 1916 28th Ave. S., Birmingham AL 35209-2605. (205)942-3222. President: Michael Panepento. BMI. Estab. 1985. Music publisher and record company (Pandem Records, Inc.). Publishes 4-6 songs/year; publishes 3 new songwriters/year. Receives 10 submissions/month. Works with composers and lyricists. Pays standard royalty.
Affiliate(s): Panepentunes (ASCAP).
How to Contact: Write first and get permission to submit. Prefers cassette or 15 ips reel-to-reel with 3 songs. SASE. Reports in 3 weeks.
Music: Mostly pop/rock, AOR, R&B/jazz and rock; also all others. Published "Money Talks" (by A.J. Vallejo), recorded by Vallejo Bros.; "Elvis' Grave" and "I'm the One" (by Phillips/Panepento) recorded by Soundtrack; all on Pandem Records (rock). Also "Paris" on Pandem Records Inc. (rock), and "I am the One," by Phillips/Panepento on Pandem Records (soundtrack).
Tips: "Send us the best possible demo/example of your work."

BERTHOLD WENGERT (MUSIKVERLAG), Hauptstrasse 100, D-7507 Pfinztal-Soellingen, **West Germany.** Contact: Berthold Wengert. Music publisher. Pays standard GEMA royalty.
How to Contact: Prefers cassette and complete score for piano. SAE and IRC. Reports in 4 weeks.
Music: Mostly light music and pop.

*BOBE WES MUSIC, P.O. Box 28609, Dallas TX 75228. (214)681-0345. President: Bobe Wes. Music publisher. BMI. Publishes 20 songs/year. Receives 4 submissions/month. Pays standard royalty.
How to Contact: Submit a demo tape—unsolicited submissions are OK. Prefers cassette. "State if songs have been copyrighted and if you have previously assigned songs to someone else. Include titles, readable lyrics and your full name and address. Give the same information for your co-writer(s) if you have one. State if you are a member of BMI, ASCAP or SESAC. Lead sheets are not required. Comments will follow only if interested." SASE. No certified mail accepted.
Music: Blues, country, disco, gospel, MOR, progressive, rock (hard or soft), soul, top 40/pop, polka, Latin dance and instrumentals. "Special interest in Christmas songs."

*WEST BROADWAY MUSIC, 201-1505 W. 2nd Ave., Vancouver, BC V6H 3Y4 **Canada.** (604)731-3535. Professional Manager: Carey Fok. Music publisher and management company. SOCAN. Estab. 1989. Publishes 12-15 songs/year; publishes 1-3 new songwriters/year. Works with composers; teams collaborators. Pays standard royalty.
How to Contact: Write or call first and obtain permission to submit a tape. Prefers cassette with 3-5 songs and lyric sheet. SASE. Reports in 4-6 weeks.
Music: Mostly pop, dance and rock; also R&B. Published "Might as Well Party," written and recorded by Al Rodger on Criminal Records (pop); and "Your Place or Mine" (by Al Rodger), recorded by Sharon Lee Williams on Virgin Records (R&B/dance).

WESTUNES MUSIC PUBLISHING CO., Suite 330, 1115 Inman Ave., Edison NJ 08820-1132. (908)548-6700. FAX: (908)548—6748. A&R Director: Kevin McCabe. Music publisher and management firm (Westwood Entertainment Group). ASCAP. Publishes 15 songs/year; publishes 2 new songwriters/year. Receives 300-400 submissions/year. Works with composers and lyricists. Pays standard royalty.
How to Contact: Write first and obtain permission to submit. Prefers cassette with 3 songs and lyric sheet. SASE. Reports in 6 weeks.
Music: Mostly rock; also pop. Published *Greetings From New Jersey* (various artists) on Westwood Records; released *Breakout USA* (various artists) on Westwood Records (CD), "Inside Out," "We Love the Radio" and "Heaven on Earth," all rock singles written by K. McCabe and recorded by The Numbers on Westwood Records.

Tips: Submit a "neat promotional package; attach biography of the songwriter."

*WHIMSONG PUBLISHING ASCAP, 1156 Park Lane, West Palm Beach FL 33417. (407)686-1354. Professional Managers: Rusty Gordon, Ron Caruso and Davilyn Whims. Music publisher and record producer (Rustron Music Productions). Estab. 1991. Works with composers and lyricists; teams collaborators. Pays standard royalty.
How to Contact: Submit a demo tape—unsolicited submissions are OK. Prefers cassette with 1-3 songs and lyric or lead sheet. "Clearly label your tape and container. Include cover letter." SASE required for all correspondence. Reports in 1-2 months.
Music: Mostly pop (ballads, blues, theatrical, cabaret), progressive country, folk/rock; also New Age and R&B. Published "What Will We Leave the Children?" (by Gary Gonzalez and Patricia White Gonzalez); "Remember," written and recorded by Gary Gonzalez; and "Lottery Game" (by Gary Gonzalez), all recorded by Relative Viewpoint (on RV Records & Tapes).
Tips: "Write for the market as it really exists, create songs for the recording artists who accept original material, read label credits. Stay tuned to the trends and fusions indicative of the '90s."

WHITE CAR MUSIC (BMI), 11724 Industriplex, Baton Rouge LA 70809. (504)755-1400. Contact: Nelson Blanchard. Music publisher, record company (White Car Records/Techno Sound Records), record producer. BMI, ASCAP. Estab. 1988. Publishes 15 songs/year; publishes 2 new songwriters/year. Receives 6 submissions/month. Works with composers and lyricists; teams collaborators. Pays standard royalty.
Affiliate(s): Char Blanche Music (ASCAP).
How to Contact: Submit a demo tape by mail—unsolicited submissions are OK. Prefers cassette with 4 songs. Does not return unsolicited material. Reports in 2 weeks.
Music: Mostly country, rock and pop; also R&B. Published "Leading Man" (by Butch Reine), recorded by Atchafalaya on White Car Records (country); "Sail On" (by Blanchard, Watts, Bullion), recorded by Johnsteve on Stebu Records (rock); and "Crazy Bound" (by Blanchard), recorded by Tareva on White Car Records (country).

WHITE CAT MUSIC, Suite 114, 10603 N. Hayden Rd., Scottsdale AZ 85260. (602)951-3115. Professional Manager: Frank Fara. Producer: Patty Parker. Music publisher. Member CMA, CARAS, CCMA, BCCMA and BBB. Estab. 1978. Publishes 30 songs/year; publishes 20 new songwriters/year. Receives 60 submissions/month. "50% of our published songs are from non-charted and developing writers." Pays standard royalty.
Affiliate(s): Rocky Bell Music (BMI).
How to Contact: Submit a demo tape—unsolicited submissions are OK. Cassettes only with 2 songs and lyric or lead sheet. SASE. Reports in 2 weeks.
Music: Mostly A/C, traditional country and contemporary country. Published "By Your Side (by Richard Schrum), recorded by Jess Owen (contemporary country); "Paint Me Blue" (by Jesse Dyas), recorded by Monte Causey on Comstock Records (C&W); "In Need Of A Miracle" (by Richie Milton), recorded by Rick Page on Comstock Records (contemporary country); and "Your Daddy Would Be Proud," written and recorded by Paul Gibson (modern C&W).
Tips: "Send only 2 songs—they will be heard faster and listened to more intently! Send up-tempo songs—this will increase your chances."

WHITEWING MUSIC, 413 N Parkerson Ave., Crowley LA 70526. (318)783-1601. Owner: Jay Miller. Music publisher, record company (Master-Trak, Showtime, Par T, MTE, Blues Unlimited, Kajun, Cajun Classics) and record producer (Master-Trak Productions). BMI. Estab. 1969. Publishes 25 songs/year. Works with composers and lyricists. Pays standard royalty.
Affiliate(s): Jamil Music (BMI), Whitewing Music (BMI).
How to Contact: Submit a demo tape by mail—unsolicited submissions are OK. Prefers cassette with 3-4 songs and lyric sheets. Does not return unsolicited material.
Music: Mostly country, rock & roll and novelty; also blues, party and cajun. Published "Johnny Can't Dance" (by Mike Doucet, Wayne Toups), recorded by Wayne Toups on Master-Trak (rock) and "Fish Out of Water" (by Wayne Toups) recorded by Zydecajun.

*WILCOM PUBLISHING, Box 4456, West Hills CA 91308. (818)348-0940. Owner: William Clark. Music publisher. ASCAP. Estab. 1989. Publishes 10-15 songs/year; publishes 1-2 new songwriters/year. Works with composers and lyricists. Pays standard royalty.
How to Contact: Write first and obtain permission to submit a tape. Prefers cassette with 1-2 songs and lyric sheet. SASE. Reports in 3 weeks.
Music: Mostly R&B, pop and rock; also country. Published "Girl Can't Help It" (by W. Clark, D. Walsh and P. Oland), recorded by Stage 1 on Rockit Records (top 40).

WILCOX MUSIC ORGANIZATION, 1099A Finchley Rd., London NW11 **England**. Phone: (01)455-6620. Managing Director: Herb W. Wilcox. PRS, MCPS, SGGB. Music publisher, record company (Zodiac Records) and record producer (Zodiac-Wilcox). Publishes 10 songs/year; publishes 6 new songwriters/year. Pays negotiable royalty.
How to Contact: Prefers cassette and lyric sheet. Reports in 1 month.
Music: Mostly jazz, rock and blues; also ballads, instrumentals and gospel.

*WILD ANGEL, 3500 Llan Beris Ave., Bristol PA 19007. (215)788-2723. President: Johnny Kline. Music publisher, record company (Silver Jet) and record producer (Silver Jet Production). BMI. Estab. 1989. Pays standard royalty.
How to Contact: Submit a demo tape by mail—unsolicited submissions are OK. Prefers cassette with 3 songs and lyric sheet. "No phone calls please." SASE. Reports in 2 weeks.
Music: Mostly rockabilly, country and rock; also gospel. Published "Rockabilly Baby" and "Dean of Rock n Roll," written and recorded by Johnny Kline, on Silver Jet Records (rockabilly).

SHANE WILDER MUSIC, P.O. Box 3503, Hollywood CA 90078. (818)508-1433. President: Shane Wilder. Music publisher (BMI), record producer (Shane Wilder Productions) and management firm (Shane Wilder Artists Management). Estab. 1960. Publishes 25-50 songs/year; publishes 15-20 new songwriters/year. Receives 400 submissions/month. Works with composers. Pays standard royalty.
How to Contact: Prefers cassette (or VHS videocassette) with 3 songs and lyric sheet. "Include SASE if you wish tape returned. Photo and resume should be sent if you're looking for a producer." Reports in 1 month.
Music: Mostly traditional country and crossover. Published "Are There Any Angels in Nashville," "I'm Not Cookin' Your Eggs No More" and "I Just Love A Good Story," by Jane Tyler; "Here Comes Another Lonely Week," by Allan Karl on Century 2 Records; "Love Em' & Leave Em'," and "If You Touch Me," by Wynn Hammons on Eagle International Records.
Tips: "We no longer accept songs with a reversion clause."

MAURICE WILSON'S MUSIC CO., 1771 Clearwater Drive, Cumarillo CA 93012. (805)484-4303. President: Morris Lee Wilson. Music publisher, record company (Wilson Records) and record producer (Wilson Music Co.). BMI. Estab. 1978. Publishes 20 new songs/year; publishes 1-20 new songwriters/year. Hires staff writers. Works with composers and lyricists; teams collaborators. Pays standard royalty of 50%.
Affiliate(s): Wilson's Music Co., Kat and Morris Wilson Publications, Jack of Diamond Publishing, Country Creations.
How to Contact: Submit a demo tape by mail—unsolicited submissions are OK. Prefers cassette (or VHS videocassette) with any number of songs and lyric and lead sheet. SASE, "but we prefer to keep it on file." Reports in 2 weeks.
Music: Mostly easy listening, country and MOR; also R&B, jazz and children's. Published "Special Lady" (by Alex Zaneztis and Morris Wilson), recorded by Matt Vincent on Jack of Diamonds (country); "Freedom Man" (by Bonnie Lee Young and Morris Wilson), recorded by Matt Vincent on Jack of Diamonds (country); and "Burning Bridges" (by Maurine Moore and Morris Wilson), recorded by Morris Wilson on Wilson's Records (MOR).
Tips: "We look for songs that have a good hook line, have something to say and are different from the norm. Publishers are looking for songs that will sound as good in 20 years as they do today."

WONDERWAX PUBLISHING, P.O. Box 4641, Estes Park CO 80517. (303)586-9005. President: James Haber. Music publisher, record company (DG Records; ? Records). BMI. Estab. 1983. Publishes 5 songs/year; publishes 5 new songwriters/year. Works with composer and lyricists; teams collaborators. Pays standard royalty.
How to Contact: Submit a demo tape by mail—unsolicited submissions are OK. Prefers cassette with 4 songs and lyric sheets. "Listen to your submitted cassette beforehand—check for clarity." SASE. Reports in 4-6 weeks.
Music: Mostly rock, pop and R&B; also British 60s rock, novelty and folk. Published "Exploding Myths" recorded by Byla gois on Wonder Wax Records.
Tips: "Looking for 60s guitar rock like the Birds and the Beatles—strong hooks and please, no garage band recordings."

WOODEN IRON MUSIC, 601 NW 80th St., Seattle WA 98117. (206)789-7569. President: Paul Scoles. Music publisher, record company (Ironwood Records) and record producer (Ironwood Productions). BMI. Estab. 1978. Publishes 25 songs/year; publishes 1-2 new songwriters/year. Works with composers and lyricists and teams collaborators. Pays standard royalty.

Close-up

Eric Lowen & Dan Navarro
Songwriters/Artists
Los Angeles, California

The music of Lowen & Navarro is "sincere," says Eric Lowen. "People sense the honesty in our music and they feel
good about it. And they really enjoy listening to it as a result.

"We don't put on a mask," says Dan Navarro. "If we're
on stage and someone makes a mistake, we laugh—we don't
pretend to be too serious about it, because we're not. We
like to be upfront and loose."

Performing is the first love of the singer/songwriter duo of Lowen & Navarro, a Los
Angeles-based tandem with an acoustic rock sound (with "a hint of the blues and a bit of
country," says Dan) and an honest, real-life lyrical disposition. But the two didn't reach a
point of being able to perform until they scored a Top 5 hit for Pat Benatar in 1985, "We
Belong."

After that smash, the two were thrust into professional songwriting, which gave them
insight into the business and the experience they wouldn't have gotten otherwise. What
emerged was the development of one-off songwriting projects for several artists, including
The Bangles, Nile Rodgers, Dave Edmunds and David Lee Roth. Most recently, the two
broke the Billboard Top 20 with a song called "You Don't Have to Go Home Tonight,"
recorded by the Triplets. They also secured a record deal with the fledgling record company
Chameleon Records, on whose label they released their first album, *Walking on a Wire*.

For a time, the two were "chasing down styles," which, explains Lowen, is hard not to
do when you're beginning. "Now, we don't find ourselves trying to *be* anything but ourselves. Instead of worrying about what type of music we're writing, we're concentrating on
the content of the music. It comes much easier for us that way, and we've gotten a good
response. People are feeling what we're feeling when we compose a song—the personal
aspect, the heartfeltness."

"Yeah," adds Navarro, "and we write about things we care about, so that other people
might care about them too."

Both Eric and Dan have written individually and with other people, but their collaboration efforts have yielded the best results. Although the two are self-proclaimed "opposites,"
their competitive natures work in a positive manner. "It's more motivating to write together," says Eric. "We really trust each other's opinions. The collaborative process involves editing each other, and since Dan and I are naturally competitive, it pushes us and
makes us do our best work." Navarro mentions that a third person is occasionally brought
into the L&N songwriting arena, and this sometimes improves their songwriting even more.
"The reason we write with a third person from time to time is that he will further moderate
us. The third writer acts as a referee between us, in a way, and he'll direct us in the right
path. That way, our egos don't get the best of the project."

At some point, no matter how hard they try, there reaches a point at which writing
becomes fruitless. Creative block, says Navarro, is not necessarily bad. "It's a sign that
you're changing levels. Your old material suddenly seems perfunctory . . . you don't think
it's cutting the edge it used to. It means it's time to change. Your expansion as a writer

needs something else." Not to worry, he says. There is a solution: "Write a bad song. *Try* to write anything at all, even if it's terrible. Just fill the space."

And if the block is unpenetrable, to the extent of not even being able to write a bad song, Navarro advises to "go do something else productive. Go demo a song that you've already written, or try to add a chorus to an existing song. Anything to get your mind off of it."

Eric mentions that in essence, a songwriter goes through creative block every time he or she writes a song, until it is finished. "You just have to plug through it. Keep trying crummy phrases and chords and progressions. Keep pulling the thread, and most of the time it will break off. But you'll eventually find the thread that will pull everything together, usually when you least expect it."

Although Lowen & Navarro are a songwriting team, they also have had individual projects outside of their work together. Since the business aspect of songwriting could "eventually become confusing," each has kept separate deals in the past. They had a mutual deal with Chameleon at one time, but only as performers. Currently Dan's songwriting royalties are administered by Sony, Eric's by BMG. "It just makes good sense to split up the business part of it because there are so many incidentals that could get in the way when you're tied together," advises Eric. "And when the business side of songwriting turns into a hassle, it gives you less time to work on the important things . . . like songwriting or developing as an artist."

— Brian C. Rushing

How to Contact: Write or call first and obtain permission to submit a tape. Prefers cassette (or VHS videocassette if available) with 3 songs and lyric sheet. "Good quality demos are a must." Reoprts in 1 month.
Music: Mostly rock, pop and country; also New Age and jazz. Published "In Your Face" written and recorded by Steve Adamek on North Coast Productions Records (film theme song, rock), "Poco Loco" (by Paul Scoles), recorded by The IRS on North Coast Productions Records (film score, rock) and "Neptune's Garden" written and recorded by Michael Lynch on MNTEX (New Age).

WOODRICH PUBLISHING CO., P.O. Box 38, Lexington AL 35648. (205)247-3983. President: Woody Richardson. Music publisher and record company (Woodrich Records) and record producer. BMI. Estab. 1959. Publishes 25 songs/year; publishes 12 new songwriters/year. Receives 3,000 submissions/year. Works with composers; teams collaborators. Pays 50% royalty less expenses.
Affiliate(s): Mernee Music (ASCAP) and Tennesse Valley Music (SESAC).
How to Contact: Submit a demo tape—unsolicited submissions are OK. Prefers cassette with 2-4 songs. Prefers studio produced demos. SASE. Reports in 1 month.
Music: Mostly country and gospel; also bluegrass, blues, choral, church/religious, easy listening, folk, jazz, MOR, progressive, rock, soul and top 40/pop. Published "Welcome Back to Me," written and recorded by S.J. Celia on Woodrich Records (modern country); "First Step" (by James Robinson), recorded by Beverly Robinson on Petra Records (black gospel); and "Androids in Love," written and recorded by Thom Rathburn on Woodrich Records (jazz).
Tips: "Use a studio demo if possible. If not, be sure the lyrics are extremely clear. Be sure to include a SASE with *sufficient* return postage."

WORD MUSIC, Division of Word, Inc., Suite 1000, 5221 N.O'Connor Blvd., Irving TX 75039. (214)556-1900. Creative Director: Debbie Atkins, Word Records: Suite 110, 33 Music Square W., Nashville TN 37203. Music publisher and record company. ASCAP. Member GMA. Publishes 200 songs/year; publishes 1-2 new songwriters/year. Teams collaborators. Pays standard royalty.
Affiliate(s): Rodeheaver (ASCAP), Dayspring (BMI), The Norman Clayton Publishing Co. (SESAC), Word Music (ASCAP), and 1st Monday (ASCAP).
How to Contact: Write or call first to get permission to submit a tape. Prefers cassette (or VHS videocassette) with 1-3 songs and lead sheet. SASE. "Please send a demonstration tape of a choir singing your anthem to Ken Barker, Print Director." Reports in 10 weeks.
Music: Mostly contemporary Christian, Southern gospel, Black gospel, inspiration. Published "Make His Praise Glorious," recorded by Sandi Patti on Word Records (inspirational) and "Watercoloured Ponies," written and recorded by Wayne Watson on Dayspring Records.

Tips: "Lead sheets, or final form—anything submitted—should be legible and understandable. The care that a writer extends in the works he submits reflects the work he'll submit if a working relationship is started. First impressions are important."

*WORLD ARTIST, (formerly Geoffrey Hansen Ents., Ltd.), Box 405, Alamo CA 94507. A&R Representative: Randal Larsen. BMI. Music publisher, record company (World Artist), record producer and personal management-production of TV, concerts and sporting events (Geoffrey Hansen Ents. Ltd.). Publishes 20 songs/year; publishes varying number of new songwriters/year. Pays standard or negotiable royalty.
How to Contact: Prefers cassette (or ¾ U-matic or ½" VHS videocassette) with lyric and lead sheets. SASE. Reports in 6 weeks.
Music: Mostly top 40, MOR, jazz and country-rock; also TV, motion picture and theatrical music, blues (French and Spanish).
Tips: "Send a neat and clear package. We are not interested in form letters or material that is sent to other companies."

WORLD FAMOUS MUSIC CO., 1830 Spruce Ave., Highland Park IL 60035. (708)831-4162. President: Chip Altholz. Music publisher, record producer. ASCAP. Estab. 1986. Publishes 25 songs/year; 3-4 new songwriters/year. Works with composers and lyricists. Pays standard royalty of 50%.
How to Contact: Submit a demo tape by mail-unsolicited submissions are OK. Prefers cassette with 3 songs and lyric sheet. Does not return unsolicited material. Reports in 1 month.
Music: Mostly pop, R&B and rock. Published "Let Me Show You Love" and "Oo La La," recorded by Ten-28 on Pink Street Records (pop/dance).

WW MUSIC, Box 201, Wageningen NL, 6700 AE **Holland**. Music publisher, record company (Timeless, Timeless Traditional Records) and record producer (Timeless Records BV). STEMRA. Publishes 10 songs/year. Works with composers.
How to Contact: Write first and obtain permission to submit. Does not return unsolicited material.
Music: Mostly jazz and blues.

YOUNG GRAHAM MUSIC (BMI), 19 Music Square W., Nashville TN 27203. (615)255-5740. Vice President: Valerie Graham. Music publisher, record company (Bear Records) and record producer (Bear Records). BMI. Estab. 1989. Publishes 10 songs/year; publishes 4-5 new songwriters/year. Works with composers and lyricists; teams collaborators. Pays standard royalty.
How to Contact: Submit a demo tape by mail—unsolicited submissions are OK. Prefers cassette with 3 songs and lyric sheet. SASE. Reports in 2 weeks.
Music: Mostly country and traditional. "Red Neck" (by Sanger Shafer), recorded by J. Wright; "Eyes As Big As Dallas" (by Gary McCray), recorded by Autumn Day; and "Girls Like Her" (by Wimberly-Hart), recorded by J. Wright; on Bear Records (all country).

Geographic Index
Music Publishers

The U.S. section of this handy geographic index will quickly give you the names of music publishers located in the music centers of Los Angeles, New York and Nashville. Of course, there are many valuable contacts to be made in other cities, but you will probably want to plan a trip to one of these established music centers at some point in your career and try to visit as many of these companies as you think appropriate. The International section lists, geographically, markets for your songs in countries other than the U.S.

Find the names of companies in this index, and then check listings within the Music Publishers section for addresses, phone numbers and submission details.

Los Angeles
Audio Music Publishers
AVC Music
Bug Music
Cosmotone Creative Entertainment Music
Direct Management Group
Fas-Ent Music
First Release Music Publishing
The Fricon Entertainment Co., Inc.
Loveforce International
PeerMusic
Pollybyrd Publications Limited
Rhythms Production
Terry Stafford Music
Tanger Music Publishing Co.
Tone Records
Treasure Trove Music
Twin Towers Publishing Co.
Udder Publishing/Golden Gelt Publishing
Shane Wilder Music

Nashville
Abingdon Press
Aim High Music Co. (ASCAP)
Angelsong Publishing Co.
Another Ear Music
Best Buddies, Inc.
Big Wedge Music
Johnny Bond Publications
Buried Treasure Music
Calvary Music Group, Inc.
Glen Campbell Music Group
The Cornelius Companies
Cottage Blue Music
Crown Music Group
Cumberland Music Group
Cupit Music
Jason Dee Music, Inc.
Denny Music Group
Entertainment Services Music Group
First Million Music, Inc.
Fradale Songs
Fretboard Publishing
GMG Music

Heavy Jammin' Music
House of Reeds Publishing Co.
Humanform Publishing Co.
Jaclyn Music
Lion Hill Music Publishing Co.
Lita Music
Loman Craig Music
Major Bob/Rio Bravo Music
The Marco Music Group, Inc.
Millhouse Music
The Fred Morris Music Group
Mr. Mort Music
Nautical Music Co.
Neon Notes
Newcreature Music
Old Empress Music/Doghouse Productions
R.A. Painter Music Publishing
Rainbarrel Music Company
Songfarm Music
Sound Achievement Group
Young Graham Music (BMI)

New York
A Street Music
Baby Raquel Music
Broozbee Music, Inc.
Chrysalis Music Group
D.S.M. Producers Ent. Publishing Co.
Globeart Publishing
Chris Gulian Music
S.M. Gold Music, Inc.
Hit & Run Music Publishing Inc.
Hopsack and Silk Productions, Inc.
Kozkeeozko Music
Lift Him Up Music
Lin's Lines
Loud & Proud Music
Majestic Control
Mia Mind Music
Mighty Soul—Sonic Records
Now & Then Music
Quark, Inc.
Ren Maur Music Corp.
Rockford Music Co.

Transcontinental Music Publications
Tommy Valando Publishing Group
Warner/Chappell Music, Inc.

International

Argentina
Ediciones Musicales Phonogram S.A.

Australia
Larrikin Music
Volition Music

Austria
Ambra Music
Warner/Chappell Musikverlag Gesellschaft m.b.H.
Thema—Verlag

Belgium
B. Sharp Music
Jump Music
Prestation Music
Radio Tele Music S.A.

Canada
Alternative Direction Music Publishers
Berandol Music Ltd.
Boot Songs
Branch Group
Century City Music Publishing
Clotille Publishing
Current Musical Enterprises, Inc.
EKG Music
ISBA Music Publishing, Inc.
Micah Music
Montina Music
Nashville Sound Music Publishing Co.
Pape Publishing
Primavera Sound Productions
S.M.C.L. Productions, Inc.
Sabre Music

Saddlestone Music
Stonehand Publishing
Third Millennium Music
Utter Nonsense Music
West Broadway Music

England
Bannerleague, Ltd. T/A Bolts
Music
Bearsongs
Blenheim Music
Bucks Music, Ltd.
Catharine Courage Music Ltd.
Creole Music
Crusoe Music Limited
Eursong
Ever-Open-Eye Music
F&J Music
First Time Music (Publishing)
U.K. Ltd.
Golden Apple Productions
Keep Calm Music Ltd.
Lematt Music, Ltd.
Nervous Publishing
Sound Ceremony Records
R.J. Music
R.T.L. Music, Lee Music, Le
Matte Music, Poso Records
Risson Music Publishing U.K.
Rough Trade Music Limited
Sea Dream Music
Sphemusations
Tabitha Music, Ltd.

France
Coppelia

Directions
Societe D'Editions Musicals Et
Artistiques "Esperance"

Germany
Boogietunes Musikproduktion
Gmbh
R.D. Clevere Musikverlag
CSB Kaminsky Gmbh
Hammer Musik Gmbh
Heupferd Musik Verlag Gmbh
Ja/Nein
Ralf Krueger Musikverlag
Siebenpunkt Verlags Gmbh
Siegel Music Companies
Valentine Musikverlag
Berthold Wengert Musikverlag

Holland
All Rock Music
WW Music

Hong Kong
BMG Pacific Music Publishing
Ltd.

Israel
Subar Music Publishing Co.
Ltd.

Italy
Ala/Bianca SRL
Dingo Music
G. Ricordi & C. Spa

Japan
Kitty Group

Malaysia
Pustaka Muzik EMI

Mexico
Galaxia Musical S.A. De C.V.

The Netherlands
Associated Artists International (Holland)

New Zealand
Pegasus Music

Poland
Author's Agency, Ltd.

Scotland
Holyrood Productions
Jammy Music Publishers Ltd.

Sweden
Synchro Sound Music AB

Switzerland
Capricorn Ltd. Publishing
OBH Musikverlag, Otto B.
Hartmann

Wales
Demi Monde Records & Pub-
lishing Ltd.

Music Publishers/'91-'92 Changes

The following markets appeared in the 1991 edition of *Songwriter's Market* but are absent
from the 1992 edition. Most of these companies failed to respond to our request for an
update of their listing. Others are not listed for a variety of reasons, which is indicated in
parentheses following the company name. For example, they may have gone out of business,
or they may have requested deletion from the 1992 edition because they are backlogged
with material.

After You Publishing Co.
Alhart Music Publishing Co.
Allora Music Publishing
Antioch Ministries Interna-
tional, Inc. (out of business)
Apon Publishing Co.
Apple-Glass Music
Arcade Music
Nicholas Astor Grouf Enter-
prises
Auntie Argon Music
Avatar Productions (asked to
be deleted)
Axbar Productions
B.A.M. Music
Bay Tone Music Publishing
Big Ears Music Ltd.
Big Ron Production and Pub-
lishing Inc.
Bluefield Music

BMG Music Publishing
BMG Pacific Music Publishing
Ltd.
Branch International Music
Brentwood Music, Inc.
Broad River Pubishing
Satchel Brown Music
Button Music
Cactus Music and Gidget Pub-
lishing
Ca-Song Music Publisher
Charis Music
Cherie Music Co.(asked to be
deleted)
Chestler Publishing Co. (asked
to be deleted)
Cindy Jane Music Publishing
(BMI) (out of business)
City Publishing Co.
Continental Sound Music

Cornish Legend Music
Cousins Music (asked to be de-
leted)
Data Processing Music (out of
business)
Different Stokes Publishing
(asked to be deleted)
Dileo Music Group (asked to
be deleted)
Discapon Publishing Co.
Discovering Music Ltd.
Tomy Don Publishing
Don't Call Me (D.M.C.) Music
Edition Musica
Ellymax Music Co. (asked to be
deleted)
Emmell Music Inc.
Eschenback Editions
Essex Music of Australia Pty.
Ltd.

Express Music (London) Ltd.
Gallo Music Publishers, A Division of Gallo Africa (Pty.) Ltd.
Geimsteinn HF
Get A Hit Publishing
Gil Con Music
Gracenote Music Publishing Company, Inc.
Graduate Music Ltd.
Jody Grenier Words & Music Ltd. (asked to be deleted)
Frank Gubala Music
Harris-Richardson Music Group (asked to be deleted)
Hobo Railways (Music Publishing) Ltd.
Holy Spirit Music
Home Key Music
The Image Music Group Pty., Ltd. (asked to be deleted)
Irish Indian Music (BMI)
Iza Music Corp.
Jay-Tam Publishing Company
Jimco Records
Jimerlean Music
Jodunn Music
Al Jolson's Black & White Music
Jongleur Music
Kamishi Publishing/A Division of Arway Records
Karlamor Music Publishing
Keeny-York Publishing
Kimtra Music
Koch Music Publishing
L.S. Records
Ty Lemly Music (Tymena Music) (asked to be deleted)
Lemmel Music Ltd.
Listen Again Music
Little, Bitty, Midi City Music Committy
Lo Pine Music
Looking Good Music

Louie B. Publishing
Love Dove Productions
Maine-ly Country Music
Marks Central Publishing Unit
Master's Collection Publishing & T.M.C. Publishing
The Mathes Company
Mayhem Music/Bugtussle Recording Co.
MCR Records
More of the Same (BMI)
MSM Musikverlag Wien
Music City Music (Australia)
New Music Enterprises
Next to Impossible Music
Nightflite Music Publishing (moved; left no forwarding address)
Northcott Music/Tancot Music
Nu-Trayl Publishing Co.
One Hundred Grand Music
Pancho's Music Co.
Park J. Tunes
Pathetic Music
Pentachord/Pentarch Music
Pluto Music
Portage Music
Ragland Publications
Random Image Music (moved; left no forwarding address)
Reata Music
Red River Songs/Crimson Creek Songs
Jack Redick Music
Reid Publishing International
Righteous Records (out of business)
Rocksong Music Publishing Ltd.
Rollin' in the Dough, Bro Music (BMI)
S.U.Y.T. Publishing
Sci-Fi Music
William Seip Music Incorporated

Seychelles Music
Shan-Darlyn Publishing Co.
Singnorbert Musichouse
Seizemore Music
Sleeping Giant Music International Ltd.
Sometimes Y Publishing (moved; left no forwarding address)
Sound Spectra Music
Soundtrax Recording
Southern Most Publishing Co. (moved; left no forwarding address)
The Sparta Florida Music Group, Ltd. (asked to be deleted)
James Lee Stanley Music
Storz Group of Companies
Sugarfoot Productions
Sundance Music
Sweet Singer Music
Tenalina Music (asked to be deleted)
Tone Science Music
Toro'na Music
Uncle Rikki's Music Project
Undercover Music
Unimusica Inc.
Valance Enterprises
Voice Notes Publishing
W/A Music Corporation
Weaver Words of Music
Don White Publishing/Dew Music
Wilcox Music Organization
Wild West Music of Canada Ltd.
Wood Monkey Music (out of business)
Wyoming Brand Music
Young Bob Publishing Co.
Zip Kid Publishing

Music Print Publishers

The sheet music publisher's function is much more specific than that of the music publisher. Music publishers try to exploit a song in many different ways: on records, videos, movies and radio/TV commercials, to name a few. But, as the name implies, sheet music publishers deal in only one publishing medium: print.

Although the role of the music print publisher has virtually stayed the same over the years, his demand has declined substantially. Today there are only a few major sheet music publishers in operation, along with many minor ones.

Most songs and compositions fall into one of two general categories: popular or educational music. Popular songs are pop, rock, adult contemporary, country and other hits heard on the radio. They are printed as sheet music (for single songs) and folios (collections of songs). Educational material includes pieces for chorus, band, orchestra, instrumental solos and instructional books. In addition to publishing original compositions, print publishers will sometimes print arrangements of popular songs.

Many major publishers of pop music won't print sheet music for a song until a popular recording of the song has become a hit single, or at least is on *Billboard*'s Hot 100 chart. Some companies listed here indicate the lowest chart position held by a song they've published, to give you a better idea of the market for your songs.

Chart action is obviously not a factor for original educational material. What the print publishers look for is quality work that fits into their publishing program and is appropriate for the people who use their music, such as school and church choirs, junior high school bands or high school orchestras.

When dealing with sheet music publishers, it is generally unacceptable to send out simultaneous submissions. That is, sending identical material to different publishers at the same time. Since most of the submissions they receive involve written music, whether single lead sheets or entire orchestrations, the time they invest in evaluating each submission is considerable—much greater than the few minutes it takes to listen to a tape. It would be discourteous and unprofessional to ask a music print publisher to invest a lot of time in evaluating your work and then possibly pull the deal out from under him.

Writers' royalties for music in print range from 10-15% of the retail selling price. For educational material that would be a percentage of the price of the whole set (score and parts). For a book (folio), the 10-15% would be pro-rated to the number of songs in the book. Royalties for sheet music are paid on a flat rate per sheet, which is usually about one-fifth of the retail price. If a music publisher licenses print publishing to a different music print publisher, print royalties are usually split between the music publisher and songwriter 50-50, but it may vary. You should read any publishing contract carefully to see how print deals fit in, and consult your attorney if you have any questions.

A & C BLACK (PUBLISHERS) LTD., 35 Bedford Row, London WC1R 4JH **England**. Phone: (071)242-0946. Commissioning Editor: Sheena Roberts. Publishes educational material. Prints 6 items/year. Pays a fee per 1,000 copies printed. Query with complete score and tape of piece. Prefers cassette. SASE. Reports in 4-8 weeks.
How to Contact: Query or write first and obtain permission to submit.
Music: Methods books and children's songs/musicals. Published "Phantasmagoria," by Kaye Umansky (children's songbook); "Abracadabra Clarinet," (graded pieces for clarinet); and "Okki-Tokki-Unga," (children's song compilation).

Tips: "We keep a list of good children's songwriters whom we commission to write songs that fit the needs of our compilations. A compilation may consist of around 30-50% commissioned songs. Look at our children's catalogue (available on request) to see what sort of books we publish."

BOSTON MUSIC CO., 172 Tremont St., Boston MA 02111. (617)426-5100. Contact: Editorial Department. Prints 100 pieces/year, both individual pieces and music books. Pays standard royalty.
How to Contact: Submit "legible manuscript." Do not send tapes. Reports in 6 months.
Music: Choral pieces, educational material, instrumental solo pieces, methods book and "piano instructional materials that piano teachers would be interested in."

BOURNE COMPANY, 5 W. 37th St., New York NY 10018. (212)391-4300. Contact: Editorial Department. Estab. 1917. Publishes education material and popular music. Prints 50 pieces/year, mostly individual pieces.
How to Contact: Submit unsolicited demo tape, lead sheet and complete score.
Music: Band pieces, choral pieces and handbell pieces.

DAVIKE MUSIC CO., P.O. Box 8842, Los Angeles CA 90008. (213)296-2302. Owner: Isaiah Jones, Jr. Estab. 1965. Prints 4 songs/year, mostly individual songs. Publishes 3 new songwriters/year. Pays 50% royalty. Works with composers and lyricists; team collaborators.
How to Contact: Prefers cassette and lead and lyric sheets or complete score. SASE.
Music: Mostly gospel, pop, R&B and inspirational; also folk and country. Published "The Miracle God" by I. Jones and G. Cowart (contemporary gospel).

EMANDELL TUNES, 10220 Glade Ave., Chatsworth CA 91311. (818)341-2264. SESAC affiliate. Administrator: Leroy C. Lovett Jr. Prints 15-20 songs/year, both individual songs and folios. Lowest chart position held by song published in sheet form is 36. Pays statutory royalty or 15¢/song to songwriter for each sheet sold or parts thereof for folios.
Affiliates: Birthright Music (ASCAP), Northworth Songs (SESAC), Ben-Lee Music (BMI) and Adarom Music (ASCAP).
How to Contact: Write and obtain permission to submit. Prefers cassette (or videocassette showing performance—will return) and lyric and lead sheets. SASE. Reports in 6 weeks.
Music: Inspirational, contemporary and traditional gospel, and chorals. Published "The Center of Hope" (by Al Hartidge), recorded by Voices of Rhema; "Re-new Me" (by Eddie Howard), recorded by Mattie Moss Clark; "No Greater Love" (by Robert Montgomery), recorded by The Montgomereys, all on WFL Records.

HAMMER MUSIK GMBH, Christophstr. 38, 7000 Stuttgart 1, **West Germany.** Phone: (0711)648-7620-7. FAX: (0711)648-7625. Contact: Ingo Kleinhammer. Prints mostly individual songs. Interested in receiving band pieces, choral pieces and orchestral pieces. Pays 10% royalty/song to songwriter for each sheet sold. Publishes 100 original songs/year.
How to Contact: Prefers cassette. SAE and IRC. Reports in 2 weeks.
Music: Mostly dance, disco and pop; also rock and jazz. Published "Hit You" (by Volker Barber), "Stop The World" (by Jerome Des Arts and Deborah Sasson), and "I'll Be Forever Your Man" (by Jerome Des Arts and Maria Monrose), all recorded by Oh Well (all dance/just released).

IVORY PALACES MUSIC, 3141 Spottswood Ave., Memphis TN 38111. (901)323-3509. Estab. 1978. President: Jack Abell. Publishes educational material. Prints 5 songs/year, mostly book/tape combinations. Pays 10% retail price or 50% license income.
How to Contact: Write first and obtain permission to submit. Prefers cassette and lyric sheet. SASE. Reports in 2 months.
Music: Orchestral pieces, instrumental solo pieces, instrumental ensemble pieces, methods books and religious songs. Published "Sonatina Concertata" (by Joe McSpadden), recorded by Linda Jackson and Strings by Archive (classical); "Chamber Music Primer" (by Taylor), recorded by Abell/Jackson/Long (classical); and "Sonatina Concertata 2" (by McSpadden), recorded by Jackson (classical).

JUMP MUSIC, Langemunt 71, 9420 Aaigem, **Belgium.** Phone: (053)62-73-77. Estab. 1976. General Manager: Eddy Van Mouffaert. Publishes educational material and popular music. Prints 150 songs/year, mostly individual songs. Pays 5% royalty.
How to Contact: Prefers cassette and lead sheet or complete score. Does not return unsolicited material. Reports in 2 weeks.
Music: Pop, ballads, band pieces and instrumentals. Published "In Jouw Armen," written and recorded by Eddy Govert (ballad); "Niet Met Jij" (by Henry Spider), recorded by Samantha (Flemish); and "Do the Twist" (by Eddy Govert), recorded by Rudy Silvester (Flemish popular).

LANTANA MUSIC, #308, 9430 Live Oak Place, Ft. Lauderdale FL 33324. (305)472-7757. President: Jack P. Bluestein.
How to Contact: Query with complete score and tape of piece or submit demo tape (unsolicited submissions are OK). Prefers cassette or 7½ ips reel-to-reel. SASE. Reports in 4 weeks.
Music: Pop, country, musical comedy and gospel.

THE LORENZ CORPORATION, P.O. Box 802, Dayton OH 45401. ASCAP and BMI affiliates. Member NMPA and CMPA. Publishes approximately 350 songs/year; publishes 10 new songwriters/year. Pays standard royalty or outright purchase.
Affiliates: Lorenz Publishing Company (publishes easy sacred music for youth and adult choirs as well as for hand bells, piano and organ); Sacred Music Press (publishes "traditional sacred choral and keyboard music for church"); Heritage Music Press (school music); Roger Dean Publishing Co. ("sophisticated sacred and secular music"); Triune Music, Inc. (traditional to contemporary Christian); Kirkland House (Childrens sacred music); Sunshine Productions (Evangelica Music); and Laurel Press (contemporary Christian).
How to Contact: Send manuscripts only—"no demo tapes." SASE. Reports in 1 month.
Music: Church music publisher. Also interested in band pieces, choral pieces and method books.
Tips: "Send to an appropriate publisher for the style in readable format and persevere."

HAROLD LUICK & ASSOCIATES, Box B, Carlisle IA 50047. (515)989-3748 and 989-3676. BMI affiliate. President: Harold Luick. Prints 4-5 songs/year, mostly individual songs. Lowest chart position held by a song published in sheet form is 98. Pays 4% royalty.
How to Contact: Write and obtain permission to submit or submit through publisher or attorney. Prefers cassette or reel-to-reel and lyric sheet. SASE. Reports in 3 weeks.
Music: Mostly traditional country; also novelty songs. Published "Waylon Sing to Mama," written and recorded by Darrell C. Thomas (country, #78 on charts when music was printed).

*PHOEBUS APOLLO MUSIC PUBLISHERS, 1126 Huston Dr., Pittsburgh PA 15122-3104. (412)469-1713. FAX: (412)469-3579. Member MPA. Estab. 1989. President: Keith V.A. Bajura. Prints 30-50 works/year. Pays 10% royalty.
Affiliates: KVAB Music Publishers (BMI).
How to Contact: Submit a maximum of 2-3 unsolicited clear and legible manuscripts. Cassette tapes may be sent in addition to the written scores. Lyrics and/or tapes alone are not acceptable. Enclose SASE for the return of your works. Unsolicited works without return postage cannot be returned. Reports sent in 2-4 months.
Music: Sacred and secular choral music. Serious and educational works. The majority of our music is sacred church music. "We do not publish pop, country, R&B or rap music. Solo piano, piano/vocal, and other small ensemble works are occasionally considered."
Tips: "We are mostly interested in well written and easily accessible sacred and secular choral music. Traditional or moderately contemporary works for SATB choir with or without accompaniment stand the best chance for serious consideration."

PLYMOUTH MUSIC CO., INC., 170 NE 33rd St., Ft. Lauderdale FL 33334. (305)563-1844. General Manager: Bernard Fisher. Prints 50-60 pieces/year: individual pieces, individual songs, music books and folios. Pays 10% of list price to composer per sheet or book sold.
How to Contact: Prefers cassette and lead sheet or complete score. SASE. Reports in 1 month.
Music: Choral pieces and methods books.

THEODORE PRESSER CO., Presser Place, Bryn Mawr PA 19010. (215)525-3636. ASCAP, BMI and SESAC affiliate. Contact: Editorial Committee. Member MPA. Publishes 90 works/year. Works with composers. Pays varying royalty.
Affiliates: Merion Music (BMI); Elkan Vogel, Inc. (ASCAP); and Mercury Music Corp. (SESAC).
How to Contact: Prefers cassette with 1-2 works and score. "Include return label and postage." Reports in 1 month.
Music: Serious, educational and choral music. "We primarily publish serious music by emerging and established composers, and vocal/choral music which is likely to be accepted in the church and educational markets, as well as gospel chorals of high musical quality. We are *not* primarily a publisher of song sheets or pop songs."

R.T.F.M., % Stewart House, Hillbottom Rd., Highwycombe Buckinghamshire, HP124HJ **England**. Phone: 063081374. FAX: 063081612. A&R: Xavier Lee. Publishes educational material and popular music. Prints 40 songs/year, mostly individual songs. Lowest chart position held by a song published in sheet form is 140. Royalty varies.

Affiliates: Lee Music Ltd., Pogo Records Ltd. and R.T.L. Music.
How to Contact: Prefers cassette or 7½ or 15 ips reel-to-reel and lyric and lead sheets or complete score. SAE and IRC. Reports in 6 weeks.
Music: All types: band, orchestral, instrumental solo and instrumental ensemble pieces; also radio, TV and film music (specializes in jingles/background music). Published "Groovin" (15), "Wish You Well" (90) and "Alligator Man" (27), all by M.I. Lawson, recorded by "Emmit Till Band."

*E.C. SCHIRMER MUSIC COMPANY INC., 138 Ipswich St., Boston MA 02215. (617)236-1935. President: Robert Schuneman. Prints 200 pices/year, mostly individual pieces and music books. Pays 10% royalty on sales and 50% on performance/license.
How to Contact: Query with complete score and tape of piece. Prefers cassette. "Submit a clean, readable score." SASE. Reports in 3-12 months.
Music: Choral pieces, orchestral pieces, instrumental solo pieces, instrumental ensemble pieces, methods books, books on music, keyboard pieces.

SEA DREAM MUSIC, 236 Sebert Rd., London E7 ONP **England**. Phone: (081)534-8500. Senior Partner: Simon Law. Publishes educational material and popular music. Estab. 1976. Prints 20 songs/year, mostly individual songs. Has printed sheet music for uncharted songs. Pays 10% royalty per sheet sold.
How to Contact: Prefers cassette and lyric sheet. SAE and IRC. Reports in 6 weeks.
Music: Band and choral pieces. Mostly funk/rock, rock, blues and gospel; also "music with a Christian bias to the lyrics." Published "Shipshapes Song" (pop) and "Everyone Matters to Jesus" (rock 'n' roll), both by Derek & Jackie Llewellyn; and "God Loves You So Much" (rock), by Derek Llewellyn; all recorded by Fresh Claim and all uncharted.

WILLIAM GRANT STILL MUSIC, Suite 422, 22 S. San Francisco St., Flagstaff AZ 86001-5737. (602)526-9355. ASCAP affiliate. Estab. 1983. Manager: Judith Anne Still. Publishes educational material and popular music. Prints 2-3 arrangements/year; 2-3 new arrangers/year. Works with arrangers only. Pays 10% royalty for arrangements sold. "We publish arrangements of works by William Grant Still. This year we are especially interested in developing a catalog of guitar arrangements, though other sorts of arrangements may be considered."
How to Contact: Query. Does not return unsolicited material. Reports in 1 month.
Music: Mostly instrumental solo pieces. Published "Mother and Child" by Timothy Holley; "Memphis Man" by Bert Coleman, for organ (classical); and "Coquette," by Anthony Griggs (classical).
Tips: "We suggest that the prospective arranger familiarize himself with the music of William Grant Still, prepare a sample arrangement and submit it after having been given permission to do so."

3 SEAS MUSIC/NORTHVALE MUSIC, 450 Livingston St., Norwood NJ 07648. (201)767-5551. Vice President: Gene Schwartz. Prints mostly individual songs. Lowest chart position held by a song published in sheet form is 20. Pays 14¢/song to songwriter for each sheet sold.
How to Contact: Prefers cassette and lead sheet or complete score. SASE. Reports in 1 month.
Music: Rock.

THE WILLIS MUSIC COMPANY, 7380 Industrial Rd., Florence KY 41042. (606)283-2050. SESAC affiliate. Estab. 1899. Editor: David B. Engle. Publishes educational material. Prints 100 publications/year; "no charted songs in our catalog." Pays 5-10% of retail price or outright purchase.
How to Contact: Prefers fully notated score. SASE. Reports in 3 months.
Music: Mostly early level piano teaching material; also instrumental solo pieces, methods books and "supplementary materials-educational material only."

Music Print Publishers/'91-'92 Changes

The following markets appeared in the 1991 edition of *Songwriter's Market* but are absent from the 1992 edition. These companies failed to respond to our request for an update of their listing.

Blue Umbrella Music Publishing Company (ASCAP)
C. Chase Music Productions

Genevox Music Group
Hinshaw Music Inc.

Music Sales Corp.
Brian Raines Music Co.

Record Companies

Record companies are responsible for recording and releasing records, cassettes and CDs – the mechanical products of the music industry. They sign artists to recording contracts, decide what songs those artists will record, and finally determine which songs to release. They are also responsible for providing recording facilities, securing producers and musicians, and overseeing the manufacture, distribution and promotion of new releases.

Unlike music publishers, record companies have a lot to lose monetarily if a product doesn't sell. Music publishers may only spend a limited amount of money on songs – usually just for a good demo and the salary of those pushing the songs. Record companies always take a gamble with an untested product, and thousands of dollars are usually budgeted for a single project.

Because such a great financial investment is required of the record companies, they are extremely selective in choosing songs for their artists, and even more particular about the acts they sign. It's the people in the record company's A&R (Artists and Repertoire) department who decide which songs and artists to take a chance on. They find, sign and develop talent, help artists polish their material or help choose outside material for them. All of this is done with one goal in mind: to sell records. They want their songs and artists to be hits. And what A&R departments are looking for from outside writers are hits – the rest of the "album cuts" (songs not released as singles) are usually written by the producer or artist.

Unfortunately, getting that hit song to an A&R representative is a difficult task for most beginning songwriters, especially with a decrease in record sales in the past year. Most major record labels, on the advice of their attorneys, do not accept unsolicited material. They accept tapes only from industry people, such as publishers, producers and managers, whom they know and whose judgment they respect. If you happen to have contacts, you're halfway there. If not, you may have trouble getting any of your material heard by a major label.

So how do you gain these valuable contacts? It's logical that a good way to gain notice from industry people is by networking. Songwriters must take into consideration that talent alone does not guarantee success in the music industry. You must be recognized through contacts (networking). Networking is the process of building an interconnecting web of acquaintances within the music business. The more industry people you meet, the broader your contact base becomes, and your chances of befriending someone who has the clout to get your demo heard increase. Some people may call it brown-nosing; others call it schmoozing. But, if you want to get ahead, and you want to get your music on the desk of an important A&R representative, networking is imperative.

There are also networking opportunities at regional and national music conferences and workshops. If you can afford to attend one or two of these events each year, you will benefit from an immediate increase in the number and quality of your music industry contacts.

Major labels needn't be, or shouldn't be, a songwriter's only outlet and/or goal. Good contacts and good companies also exist on the grass roots level of the music industry. There are many independent record labels out there anxious to hear songs by undiscovered talent. Many successful acts began their careers at smaller record companies, only to be picked up later by a major label. Other acts that found success at a small company have stayed right there.

Many of the following listings are independent labels. They are the most receptive to new material. Just because the companies are small doesn't mean you should forget professionalism. When submitting material to a record company, be very specific about what you are submitting and what your goals are. If you are strictly a songwriter and the label carries a band who you believe would properly present your song, state that in your cover letter. If you are an artist looking for a contract, make sure you showcase your strong points as a performer in the demo package. Whatever your goals are, follow submission guidelines closely, be as neat as possible and include a top-notch demo. If you need more information concerning a company's requirements, write or call for more details.

At the end of this section, you will find a Geographic Index listing alphabetically the record companies in the major music centers—New York, Los Angeles and Nashville—in order to help you plan a trip in the future to one or more of these cities. There is also an alphabetical list of international listings appearing in this section.

AARSON RECORDS %Entertainment Management Enterprises, 454 Alps Rd., Wayne NJ 07470. (201)694-3333. President: Richard Zielinski. Labels include Aarson Records and Unicorn Records. Record company and manager. Estab. 1983. Works with musicians/artists on contract.
How to Contact: Submit demo tape by mail. Unsolicited submissions are OK. Prefers cassette (or VHS videocassette) with 4 songs and lyric sheet. SASE. Reports in 1 month.
Music: Mostly rock, metal and urban. Artists include Mirror's Image and Sinful.

ABACUS, Box 111, Newburg WI 53060. (414)675-2839. Producer: Bob Wiegert. Record company, record producer and music publisher (RobJen Music). Works with musicians/artists on contract and musicians on salary for in-house studio work. Pays negotiable royalty to artists on contract; statutory rate to publishers for each record sold.
How to Contact: Write first about your interest. Submit cassette only with 1-3 songs and lyric sheet. Does not return unsolicited material. Reports in 1 month.
Music: New Age, soundtrack productions and fine arts.
Tips: "We are always on the lookout for a talented composer, but write first. Unsolicited material will not be sent back."

*ADOBE RECORDS, P.O. Box W, Shallowater TX 79363. (806)873-3537. President: Tom Woodruff. Record company. Estab. 1989. Releases 5 LPs/year. Works with musicians/artists, storytellers and poets on contract. Pays statutory rate.
How to Contact: Write or call first and obtain permission to submit. Prefers cassette or VHS videocassette with 3 songs and lyric or lead sheet. Does not return unsolicited material. Reports in 3 months.
Music: Mostly interested in western, bluegrass and cowboy. Released *Texas When Texas Was Free*, written and recorded by A. Wilkinson; and *Moon Light on the Colorado* (by A. Wilkinson), recorded by J. Stephenson; both on Adobe Records (LPs).

AIA RECORDS, Leopold Str. 11-13, 4000 Dusseldorf NRW **Germany**. Phone: (0211)364545. Director: Ralf Krueger. Labels include AIA and BS Modern Music. Record company, music publisher (Ralf Krueger Musikverlag) and record producer (Sira Ain/Trance Palace Productions). Estab. 1984. Releases 2 12″ singles, 2 LPs and 1 CD/year. Works with musicians/artists and songwriters on contract and hires musicians for in-house studio work.
How to Contact: Submit demo tape by mail. Unsolicited submissions are okay. Prefers cassette with lyric sheet. SASE. Reports in 2 months.
Music: Mostly new pop, funk/soul and dance/new house; also stylistic fusion. Released "Milky Way Kiss" (by Bop Whopper/Sira Ain), recorded by Frank Ananda on AIA (soul-pop-rap); and "Violins" (by Georgie Rockwood, Victor Lovera, Sira Ain, Ama Donya), recorded by Frank Ananda on AIA (new pop). Other artists include S.A., FreeDome, The Soul and Female Invasion.

AKO RECORDS, 20531 Plummer, Chatsworth CA 91311. (818)998-0443. President: A.E. Sullivan. Labels include Dorn Records and Aztec Records. Record company, music publisher (Amiron Music) and record producer (AKO Productions). Estab. 1980. Releases 2 singles/year. Works with musicians/artists and songwriters on contract. Pays negotiable royalty to artists on contract. Pays statutory rate.

How to Contact: Write first and obtain permission to submit. Prefers cassette (or Beta or VHS videocassette) and lyric sheet. SASE. Reports in 2 months.
Music: Top 40/pop, rock and pop/country. Released *Touch of Fire*, by Touch of Fire; *Gang Back*, by F. Cruz; "Sana Christian," by Sana Christian, and "Helpless" (by R. Black), recorded by Les Staunton, all on AKO Records. Other artists include Rozzi and Cemas.

*AKRANA COUNTRY, P.O. Box 535, College Place WA 99324. (509)529-4649. Founder/CEO: Loren Fenton. Labels include Akrana Visions. Record company and music publisher (Akrana Music/AS-CAP). Estab. 1990. Releases 1-2 singles and 1 LP/year. Works with musicians/artists and songwriters on contract. Pays statutory rate.
How to Contact: Submit demo tape by mail. Unsolicited submissions are OK. Prefers cassette or VHS videocassette with 1-4 songs and lyric sheet. SASE. Reports in 2-3 weeks.
Music: Mostly contemporary Christian country, gospel and children's music. Released "Throw Wide the Windows," by Benjamin Fenton/Kelly Santee (single); and *Forever Free!*, (LP); both recorded by Loren Fenton on Akrana Music Records.
Tips: "We are looking for contemporary Christian country. Listen for recent songs by Paul Overstreet, Garth Brooks, etc. We want music that can be played on today's country radio stations. Songs must have lyrics with Christian values but not be preachy."

ALCAZAR RECORDS, P.O. Box 429, Waterbury VT 05676. (802)244-7845. Manager: Murray Crugman. Labels include Alcazar, Cole Harbor, Fogarty's Cove, Fretless, Alacazam!, Record Rak Records and TOAD. Estab. 1977. Releases 12 LPs and 12 CDs/year. Works with musicians/artists on record contract, songwriters on royalty contract and musicians on salary for in-house studio work. Pays 5-15% royalty to artists on contract. Pays statutory rate to publishers per song on records.
How to Contact: Write or call first and obtain permission to submit. Prefers cassette or VHS videocassette if available with 3 songs and lyric sheet. Does not return unsolicited materials. Reports in 4 weeks.
Music: Children's, folk and blues: also pop/soft rock and avant-garde. Released *Where . . . Fast Lane*, written and recorded by Fred Koller on Alcazar Records (folk LP); Amy and Leslie, written and recorded by *Amy and Leslie* on Alcazar Records (folk LP); and *Peter and the Wolf*, written and recorded by Dave Van Ronk on Alcazam! Records (children's LP). Other artists include Doc Watson, Odetta, George Gritzbach, Priscilla Herdman and Rory Block.
Tips: "Study our releases; are you/your songs appropriate for us? If someone knows everything we've put out and insists they're right for the label, that person/artist will get a serious listen."

ALEAR RECORDS, % McCoy, Route 2, Box 114, Berkeley Springs WV 25411. (304)258-2175. Labels include Master Records, Winchester Records and Real McCoy Records. Record company, music publisher (Jim McCoy Music, Clear Music, New Edition Music/BMI), record producer and recording studio. Releases 20 singles and 10 LPs/year. Works with artists and songwriters on contract; musicians on salary. Pays 2% minimum royalty to artists; statutory rate to publishers for each record sold.
How to Contact: Prefers 7½ ips reel-to-reel or cassette with 5-10 songs and lead sheet. SASE. Reports in 1 month.
Music: Bluegrass, church/religious, country, folk, gospel, progressive and rock. Released "Like Always," by Al Hogan (country single); *Mr. Bluegrass Here's to You*, by Carroll County Ramblers (bluegrass LP); "One Time" and "The Takin' Kind" (by J.B. Miller), "Leavin" and "Tulsa" (by Red Steed), and "Same Ole Town" and "If I Throw Away My Pride" (by R. Lee Gray). Other artists include Alvin Kesner, Jubilee Travelers, Jim McCoy, and Middleburg Harmonizers.

ALHART MUSIC PUBLISHING, P.O. Box 1593, Lakeside CA 92040. (619)443-2170. President: Richard Phipps. Labels include Alhart Music. Record company and music publisher (Alhart Music Publishing/BMI). Estab. 1981. Releases 4 singles/year. Receives 35-60 submissions/month. Works with songwriters on contract. Pays statutory rate.

 The asterisk before a listing indicates that the listing is new in this edition. New markets are often the most receptive to unsolicited submissions.

How to Contact: Write or call first and obtain permission to submit. Prefers cassette with 2 songs and lyric or lead sheets. Does not return unsolicited material. Reports in 4 weeks.
Music: Mostly country; also R&B. Released "Party For One," "Don't Turn My Gold To Blue," and "Blue Lady" (by Dan Michaels), on Alhart Records (country). Other artists include Leo Boek, Michel Sealy, Dan Michaels and T.E. Powell (The American Empire) Group.

ALLAGASH COUNTRY RECORDS, 45 7th St., Auburn ME 04210. (207)784-7975. President/A&R Director: Richard E. Gowell. Labels include Allagash Country Records, Gowell Records and Allagash R&B Records. Record company, music publisher (Richard E. Gowell Music/BMI) and record producer. Estab. 1986. Releases 3-5 singles and 1-3 LPs/year. Receives 50 submissions/month. Works with musicians/artists and songwriters on contract. Pays 3-50% royalty to artists on contract; statutory rate to publisher per song on record.
How to Contact: Prefers cassette with 2-10 songs and lyric or lead sheet. Returns unsolicited material, with SASE, 1-2 months.
Music: Mostly country, pop/country and country rock; also R&B/pop. Released "It'll be a Cold Day," (by L. Pritchett and R. Sanders), recorded by Ray Sanders on Allagash Country Records (country); "Savannah's Song" (by E. Seville), recorded by Eddie Seville on Allagash Country Records (progressive country/rock); "Long Way Home" (by E. Seville), recorded by Eddie Seville on Allagash Country Records (country/rock) and "Bump Goes Baby" (by Rick Johnson), recorded by Rick Johnson on Allagash Country Records (western swing C/W).
Tips: "Our label is currently seeking high quality finished masters with publishing open. Submit chrome cassette, copyrighted and ready for record pressing. Never send original master – copies only."

ALPHABEAT, Box 12 01, D-6980 Wertheim/Main, **West Germany**. Phone: (09342)841 55. Owner/ A&R Manager: Stephan Dehn. A&R National Manager: Marga Zimmermann. Press & Promotion: Alexander Burger. Disco Promotion: Matthias Marth. Music Service: Wolfgang Weinmann. Creative Services: Heiko Köferl. Labels include Alphabeat. Record company and record producer. Releases vary "depending on material available." Works with musicians/artists on contract; hires musicians for in-house studio work. Also works through "license contract with foreign labels." Payment to artists on contract "depends on product." Payment: conditional on German market.
How to Contact: Prefers cassette (or PAL videocassette) with maximum of 3 songs and lyric sheet. "When sending us your demo tapes, please advise us of your ideas and conditions." SAE and IRC. Reports in 1 month.
Music: Mostly dance/disco/pop, synth/pop and electronic; also R&B, hip hop/rap and ballads. Artists include Martin King, Red Sky, Fabian Harloff, Silent Degree, Mode Control, Mike M.C. & Master J., Skyline, Lost in the Dessert, Oriental Bazar, Voice In Your Head, Love Game, Alpha W. Synthoxx and Interface (ZYX Records).
Tips: "We are a distributor of foreign labels. If foreign labels have interest in distribution of their productions in West Germany (also Switzerland and Austria) they can contact us. We distribute all styles of music of foreign labels. Please contact our department (Distribution Service)."

ALTERNATIVE RECORD CO. LTD., 140 Prospect St., S.I. NY 10305. (718)447-3986. President/Chief Executive: Vinny DeGeorge. Record company and producer. Estab. 1976. Releases 5 singles/year, 2 12″ singles, 3 LPs and 1 EP/year. Works with musicians/artists and songwriters on contract and hires musicians for in-house studio work and promotion for live acts. Royalty is negotiable; statutory rate to publishers per song on records.
How to Contact: Write first to arrange personal interview. Prefers cassette (or videocassette if available) with 3 songs. Does not return unsolicited material. Reports in 10 weeks.
Music: Interested in all types of music. Released *Rule of Thumb* (by Rule of Thumb), recorded by F.V. Sound on Alternative Records (pop LP); "Hot Strokes" (by Vinny DeGeorge), recorded by F.V. Sound on Alternative Records (reggae/rock song). Other artists include Social Numbers and Kenny and The Hearthrobs.

*ALTERNATIVE RECORDS, 1610 Riverview St., Eugene OR 97403. (503)344-5716. A&R: KC Layton. Labels include Alternative Records, Alternative Archive. Record company. Estab. 1979. Releases 3-4 singles, 5 LPs, 1 EP and 5 CDs/year. Works with musicians/artists on record contract. Pays 17% royalty to artists on contract; statutory rate to publisher per song on record.
How to Contact: Write first and obtain permission to submit. Prefers cassette (or VHS videocassette if available) with 5 songs and lyric sheet. SASE. Reports in 4 weeks.
Music: Mostly rock (alternative), pop (again, alternative in nature), country/rock; also experimental and industrial. Released *Songs from the Riverhouse*, written and recorded by Robert Vaughn; *Lost Horizon*, written and recorded by Steve Scott; and *More Miserable Than You'll Ever Be*, written and recorded by 77; all CD/cassettes on Alternative Records.

Tips: "Our label appeals to the thoughtful/creative type of consumers. Artists that approach their work like a Bruce Cockburn or Mark Knopfler are most likely to be signed by us."

ALYSSA RECORDS, Box 133, Farmingville NY 11738. President: Andy Marvel. Labels include Ricochet Records and Alyssa Records. Record company, music publisher (Andy Marvel Music/ASCAP, Bing Bing Bing Music/ASCAP, and Andysongs/BMI), and record producer (Marvel Productions). Estab. 1981. Releases 12-15 singles, 1 12" single and 4 LPs/year. Works with musicians/artists and songwriters.
How to Contact: Prefers cassette (or VHS videocassette) with 3 songs and lyric sheet. Return only with SASE. "Do not call."
Music: Mostly pop, R&B, and Top 40; also country. Released "You Can't Hide Your Fantasies," by Andy Marvel, Steve Perri and Tom Siegel; "Express (10 Items Or Less)," by Andy Marvel; and "Meant To Be," by Andy Marvel and Don Levy, all recorded by Andy Marvel on Alyssa Records.

AMALGAMATED TULIP CORP., 117 W. Rockland Rd., Libertyville IL 60048. (708)362-4060. Director of Publishing and Administration: P. Johnson. Labels include Dharma Records. Record company and music publisher. Works with musicians on salary; artists and songwriters on contract. Pays royalty to artists and songwriters on contract.
How to Contact: Prefers cassette with 2-5 songs. SASE. Reports in 1-3 months.
Music: Rock (progressive and easy listening), dance/R&B and top 40/pop. Released *Songs by the Group Milwaukee*, by Milwaukee; "Sunday Meetin' In the Morning," by Ken Little and the Band; and "This Feels Like Love to Me," by Mirrors.

AMAZING RECORDS, P.O. Box 2164, Austin TX 78768. (512)477-7055. Owner: Cass Hook. Record company, music publisher (Munificent Music/BMI) and record producer (Branch Productions). Estab. 1985. Releases 2-4 LPs and 2-4 CDs/year. Works with musicians/artists on record contract. Pays 7-10% royalty to artists on contract; statutory rate to publisher per song on record. Charges artists upfront for production.
How to Contact: Write or call first to arrange personal interview. Prefers cassette (or VHS videocassette) with 3 songs and lyric sheet. Does not return unsolicited material.
Music: Mostly rock & roll-all types, country rock and rhythm n' blues; also jazz, folk and reggae. No rap. Released *Texana Dames* (by Conni Hancock), recorded by Lloyd Maines (country rock LP); *Ty Gavin* (by Ty Gavin), recorded by Hunt Sales (hard rock LP); and *Juke Jumpers* (by Jim Colegrove), recorded by Jive (rock LP), all on Amazing Records. Other artists include B.W. Stevenson, Freddie Steady's Wild Country, Teddy and the Tall Tops, Rosie Flores, Junior Brown and Eric Hokannen.
Tips: "Get in touch, submit materials, play Austin, keep in touch."

AMERICAN MUSIC COMPANY/CUCA RECORD AND CASSETTE MANUFACTURING COMPANY, Box 8604, Madison WI 53708. Vice-President: Daniel W. Miller. Labels include American, Cuca, Jolly Dutchman, Age of Aquarius, Top Gun, Sound Power and Night Owl Records. Record company and music publisher (American Legend Music/ASCAP and Apple-Glass Music/BMI). Works with artists and songwriters on contract. Pays 10% royalty to artists on contract; 50% royalty to songwriters on contract.
How to Contact: Prefers reel-to-reel tape (but will accept cassettes) with 2-20 songs; include photo and complete information. SASE. "No calls, please." Reports within 6 months.
Music: "Old time" (polkas, waltzes), bluegrass, folk and ethnic. Released "Hupsadyna," by Styczynski (ethnic single); *Polka 76*, by Meisner (ethnic LP); and "Muleskinner Blues," by the Fendermen.
Tips: "Cuca has an extensive catalog and is known as 'America's leading line of ethnic and old-time music.' Artists may have a superior chance of having their material released on Cuca, American or affiliated labels, if they present *studio-quality* tapes of *all original* material."

*AMERICANA RECORDS, INC., 300 Linfield Dr., Vallejo CA 94590. (707)645-1615. President: Jack Walker. Labels include SUS Americana. Record company, music publisher (Americana/BMI) and record producer (Fulltilt Music). Estab. 1982. Releases 2 singles/year. Receives 40-50 submissions/month. Works with musicians/artists on contract. Pays 1-5% royalty to artists on contract; statutory rate to publisher per song on record.
How to Contact: Submit demo tape by mail. Unsolicited submissions are OK. Prefers cassette (or VHS videocassette if available) with 3 songs and lyric sheet. SASE. Reports in 1 month.
Music: Mostly country and bluegrass. Released "Minimum Wage" and "Goodbye Heartache" (by Tommy Johnson), recorded by Wally Jammings on SUS Americana Records (country single).
Tips: "Have a complete package and identify your wants. Our company helps get artists started in the business. The artist should also be aware that our company as well as other small companies don't have big budgets like the majors, so be prepared to spend money on production."

*AMERICATONE RECORDS INTERNATIONAL USA, 1817 Loch Lomond Way, Las Vegas NV 89102-4437. (702)384-0030. FAX: (702)382-1926. Estab. 1975. Record company, producer and music publisher. Publishes 50 songs/year. Releases 5 12″ singles, 5 EPs and 5 CDs/year. Receives 50 submissions/month. Pays standard royalty.
Affiliates: Americatone Music International (BMI), The Rambolt Music International (ASCAP).
How to Contact: Prefers cassettes and studio production with top sound recordings and lyric sheets. SASE. Reports in 4 weeks.
Music: Mostly country, jazz, R&R, Spanish, classic ballads. Published "You're The Other Part Of Me" (by Anita Johnson), "Memories Search For You" (by Patrick McElhoes); "Good Time Charlies" (by Patrick McElhoes); "Willie" (by Patrick McElhoes) and "I Love Your Waltz" (by Patrick McElhoes), all recorded on Americatone International Records.

THE AMETHYST GROUP LTD./ANTITHESIS RECORDS, 273 Chippewa Dr., Columbia SC 29210-6508. No phone calls please. Contact: A&R. Labels include Amethyst Records and Antithesis Records. Record company, music publisher (Another Amethyst Song/BMI) and management firm. Estab. 1979. Releases 10 singles and 3 LPs/year. Works with musicians/artists on contract. Pays 5-15% royalty to artists on contract. Pays statutory rate to publishers per song on record. International distribution, management, marketing firm. "Our forte is management, with overseas marketing."
How to Contact: Prefers cassette (or VHS videocassette) with 3-7 songs and lyric sheet. SASE. Reports within 5 weeks only if interested. "Always include return postage for any reply."
Music: Mostly mainstream, pop and R&B; also rock, new music, jazz/rap and heavy metal. Released "Long Distance Lovers" recorded by Ted Neiland on Amethyst Records (pop); and "Age of Modern Man" recorded by Synthetic Meat on Antithesis Records (new music). Other artists include J. Blues, Knightmare, Jeromeo, Carnage, True Identity, Toniland, Danny D/X and I-Rock.
Tips: "We develop and market recording artists, models, actresses and songwriters for international promotion. We promote to radio stations, promoters, distributors, and most major manufacturers of products. Also to booking agents, TV and movie production companies."

AMIRON MUSIC/AZTEC PRODUCTIONS, 20531 Plummer St., Chatsworth CA 91311. (213)998-0443. General Manager: A. Sullivan. Labels include Dorn Records and Aztec Records. Record company, booking agency and music publisher (Amiron Music). Releases 2 singles/year. Works with artists and songwriters on contract. Pays 10% maximum royalty to artists on contract; standard royalty to songwriters on contract. Pays statutory rate to publishers.
How to Contact: Prefers 7½ ips reel-to-reel or cassette and lead sheet. SASE. Reports in 3 weeks.
Music: Dance, easy listening, folk, jazz, MOR, rock ("no heavy metal") and top 40/pop. Released "Look In Your Eyes," by Newstreet; and "Midnight Flight," recorded by Papillon.
Tips: "Be sure the material has a hook; it should make people want to make love or fight. Write something that will give a talented new artist that edge on current competition."

ANGEL STAR RECORDS, 1715 Marty, Kansas City KS 66103. (913)384-4454. President: Ed Morgan. Record company, music publisher (Country Breeze Music/BMI, and Walkin' Hat Music/ASCAP). Releases 15 singles, 12 EPs and 15 cassette albums/year. Receives 130 submissions/month. Works with musicians/artists and songwriters on contract. Pays 18% royalty to artists on contract, statutory rate to publisher per song on record.
How to Contact: Prefers cassette with 3 songs and lyric sheet. SASE. Reports as time allows.
Music: Gospel, southern, country and bluegrass. Released "Streets of Glory" (by Wilma Bell), recorded by Wilma Bell on Angel Star Records; "Guided By The Hand" (by Angela Daniels), recorded by Angela Daniels on Angel Star Records; "That Great Day" (by Stanley Johnston) on Angel Star Records; "God's Not Finished With Me" (by Jim Watters), recorded by Rev. Jim Watters on Angel Star Records; "Let Him Carry You" (by Jim & Stephanie Watters), recorded by Joanne Hite & Covenant on Angel Star Records.
Tips: "When submitting a song make sure the song is strong in lyrics and melody. We are looking for single material, not album fillers."

ARIANA RECORDS, 1324 S. Avenida Polae, #0203, Tucson, AZ 85710. (602)577-8669. President: James M. Gasper. Vice President: Thomas M. Dukes. Record company, record producer (Future 1 Productions) and music publisher (Myko Music). Estab. 1980. Releases 1 single and 2 LPs/year. Works with musicians/artists on contract; hires musicians for in-house studio work.

"How to Use Your Songwriter's Market" (at the front of this book) contains comments and suggestions to help you understand and use the information in these listings.

How to Contact: Prefers cassette with 3-5 songs and lyric sheet. Does not return unsolicited material. Reports in 1 month.
Music: Mostly top 40; also R&B, rock, dance rock, pop and AOR. Released "Longer Look" (by J. Gasper, T. Privett), recorded by Sketches on Ariana Records; "Love Gun" (by Scott Smith), on Ariana Records (pop rock); "Rip It Up" (by Ruben Ruiz), recorded by Biff Turbo on Ariana Records (country rock). Other artists include 4 Walls, The El Caminos, Guys Seeking Paul (G.S.P.), Ronnie G, Scott Smith and Damn Shame.
Tips: "Be professional; first impressions are very important."

ASSOCIATED ARTISTS RECORDS INTERNATIONAL, Maarschalklaan 47, 3417 SE Montfoort, The Netherlands. Phone: (0)3484-2860. FAX: 31-3484-2860. Release Manager: Joop Gerrits. Labels include Associated Artists, Disco-Dance Records and Italo. Record company, music publisher (Associated Artists International/BUMA-STEMRA, Hilversum Happy Music/BUMA-STEMRA, Intermedlodie/BUMA-STEMRA and Hollands Glorie Productions), record producer (Associated Artists Productions) and TV promotions. Estab. 1975. Releases 10 singles, 25 12″ singles, 6 LPs and 6 CDs/year. Works with musicians/artists and songwriters on contract. Pays 10-16% royalty per record sold.
How to Contact: Prefers compact cassette or 19 cm/sec reel-to-reel (or VHS videocassette) with any number of songs and lyric or lead sheets. Records also accepted. SAE and IRC. Reports in 5 weeks.
Music: Mostly dance, pop, house, hip hop, and rock. Released: "Life is Life" (by Bortolotti), recorded by Sharada House Gang on Media Records; "MacArthur Park" (by J. Webb), recorded by D.F. Girls and Kim Taylor on DDD Records; and "The Rhythm, The Rebel" (by Leoni), recorded by RAF on Media Records, all dance singles.
Tips: "We invite producers and independent record labels to send us their material for their entry on the European market. Mark all parcels as 'no commercial value—for demonstration only.' We license productions to record companies in all countries of Europe and South Africa."

ATLANTIC RECORDING CORP., 9229 Sunset Blvd., Los Angeles CA 90069. (213)205-7460. A&R Director: Kevin Williamson, Contact: Paul Cooper. Labels include Atco, Cotillion, East-West and Atlantic. "We distribute Island and Virgin." Record company, music publisher. Estab. 1948. Works with artists on contract, songwriters on royalty contract and musicians on salary for in-house studio work.
How to Contact: Prefers cassette with 3 songs (or VHS videocassette). SASE. Reports in 2 weeks. Does not return unsolicited material.
Music: Blues, disco, easy listening, folk, jazz, MOR, progressive, R&B, rock, soul and top 40/pop. Artists included Debbie Gibson, Mike & the Mechanics, INXS, Yes, AC/DC, Pete Townsend, Bette Midler, Ratt, Skid Row, Crosby, Stills, Nash & Young.

AUBURN RECORDS AND TAPES, P.O. Box 96, Glendale AZ 85311. (602)435-0314. Owner: Frank E. Koehl. Record company and music publisher (Speedster Music/BMI). Estab. 1962. Releases 1-4 singles/year. Receives 15 submissions/month. Works with musicians/artists and songwriters on contract. Pays statutory rate.
How to Contact: Submit a demo tape by mail. Unsolicited submissions are OK. SASE. Reports in 3 weeks.
Music: Mostly country, folk and bluegrass. Released "Shade Tree" (by Troy McCort), recorded by Troy McCort on Auburn Records (acoustic country); "Lottery Fever" (by Troy McCourt), recorded by Troy McCourt on Auburn (acoustic country); and "Burglar Man" (by Al Ferguson), on Auburn Records (acoustic folk comical).
Tips: "Keep it simple; I want to hear the words. We are recording traditional music and we want mostly songs featuring acoustic music."

AUDEM RECORDS, Box 32A, Albany Post Road, Wallkill NY 12589. (914)895-8397. President: Tom Destry. Record company and record producer (Destry Music). Estab. 1986. Releases 2 singles, 2 LPs/year. Works with musicians/artists and songwriters on contract. Pays 4-9% royalty to artists on contract; statutory rate to publisher per song on record.
How to Contact: Submit demo tape by mail. Unsolicited submissions are okay. Prefers cassette, 7½ ips reel-to-reel (or VHS videocassette) with 3 songs and lyric sheet. SASE. Reports in 6 weeks.
Music: Mostly pop, rock and country; also contemporary gospel, R&B and dance. Released "I Hear You Knocking" (by Barthomomeu, King & Domino), recorded by Dave Kennedy and the U.S.A. Band (rock); "I'm Looking for a Miracle" and "Light of My Life" written and recorded by Tom Destry (pop), all on Audem Records (all singles). Other artists include Susan Stanley (country), Helen Angelo (gospel) and Michele Lee (pop).
Tips: "The radio will give you your best key to creativity. Listen to the hits of today, then mold your talents around them. In turn, the combination makes you new."

AUTOGRAM RECORDS, Burgstr. 9, 4405 Nottula 1, **West Germany**. (02502) 6151. FAX: 1825. Contact: A&R Department. Labels include Autonom, Folk-Record, Autophon and Roots. Record company. Releases 20-25 CDs and 10 LPs/year. Works with musicians/artists and songwriters on contract. Pays "above average" royalty to artists on contract.
How to Contact: Prefers cassette with minimum 3 songs and lyric sheet. SAE and IRC. Reports in 1-10 weeks. "No stylistic imitations, (no cover versions)."
Music: Mostly ethnic folk music, blues and contemporary guitar music; also classical, contemporary, bluegrass and historical (reissues).

*AVALANTIC RECORDS, P.O. Box HP2, Leeds Yorkshire LS6 1LN **United Kingdom** Phone: (0532)310145. Label Manager: Tony Doyle. Labels include Rebel Records (Germany) and New Rose (France). Record company and artist or tour management specialists. Estab. 1988. Releases 14 12" singles, 12 LPs, 12 EPs and 12 CDs/year. Works with musicians/artists on record contract. Pays negotiable rate to artists on contract; statutory rate to publisher per song on record.
How to Contact: Write first and obtain permission to submit. Prefers cassette or VHS videocassette with "at least 4" songs. Does not return unsolicited material. Reports in 2 months.
Music: Mostly pop, rock and Indie dance. Released *I Believe* on Rebel Records (EP); *A Peace Inside* on Avalantic Records (EP/3" CD); and *String'a'Beads* on Avalantic/Rebel/New Rose Records; all by Phil Morris, recorded by The Rose of Avalanche. Other artists include Thing Fish, Window Panes, Inert and Samsong.

AVANT-GARDE RECORDS CORP., 12224 Avila Dr., Kansas City MO 64145. (816)942-8861. Director A&R/President: Scott Smith. Record company, music publisher and record producer. Estab. 1983. Releases 3 LPs and 3 CDs/year. Receives 10 submissions/month. Pays statutory rate.
How to Contact: Write or call first and obtain permission to submit. Prefers cassette (or VHS videocassette if available) with 4 songs. SASE. Reports in 2 weeks.
Music: Mostly themes, new standards and pop classical, on piano only. Released *30th Anniversary on Stage*, *Dos Amigos*, *American Fantasy*, and *Favorites-On Stage* recorded by Ferrante & Teicher on Avant-Garde Records (LPs).
Tips: "Dedicated solo/duo-pianist—no vocals. Variety of pianistic styles—no lightweights. We request piano recordings, not electric keyboards."

*AVC ENTERTAINMENT INC., Suite 200, 6201 Sunset Blvd., Hollywood CA 90028. (213)461-9001. President: James Warsinske. Labels include AVC Records. Record company and music publisher (AVC Music/ASCAP, Harmonious Music/BMI). Estab. 1988. Releases 6-12 singles, 6-12 12" singles, 3-6 LPs and 3-6 CDs/year. Works with musicians/artists and songwriters on contract. Pays rate of 75% to publishers.
How to Contact: Call first and obtain permission to submit. Prefers cassette and VHS videocassette with 2-4 songs and lyric sheet. SASE. Reports in 3-5 weeks.
Music: Mostly R&B/rap, pop and rock; also funk/soul, dance and metal. Released *That's What Love Can Do* (by Curry/Nickerson), recorded by LeKlass (R&B LP); *In 2 the Night* (by Taylor/Rocca), recorded by Rocca (rap/dance LP); and *Skin Tight* (by Ohio Players/Madrok), recorded by Madrok (rap LP); all on Life Records. Other artists include N-Demand, James Richard, 7th Stranger and Duncan Faure.
Tips: "Perfect your individuality, don't sound like everyone else or who's hot now, take time for us to get to know you and your talents. We don't make rash decisions. It has to feel right to commit."

AZRA INTERNATIONAL, P.O. Box 459, Maywood CA 90270. (213)560-4223. A&R: Jeff Simins. Labels include Azra, Iron Works, Not So Famous David's Records and Masque Records. Record company. Estab. 1978. Releases 10 singles, 5 LPs, 5 EPs and 5 CDs/year. Receives 20 submissions/month. Works with artists on contract. "Artists usually carry their own publishing." Pays 10% royalty to artists on contract; statutory rate to publishers for each record sold.
How to Contact: Prefers cassette (or VHS videocassette) with 3-5 songs and lyric sheet. Include bio and photo. SASE. Reports in 1 month.
Music: Mostly rock, heavy metal, Christian and New Age; also novelty. Released *Guitar and Lute*, written and recorded by Allan Alexander on Condor Classix Records (CD); *Raving Mad*, written and recorded by Raving Mad on World Metal Records (EP); and *Industrial Strength*, written and recorded by Industrial Strength on World Metal Records (CD).
Tips: "We prefer groups that have been together a minimum of 6 months and solo artists who can write for specific projects."

BAGATELLE RECORD COMPANY, 400 San Jacinto St., Houston TX 77002. (713)225-6654. President: Byron Benton. Record company, record producer and music publisher (Floyd Tillman Music Co.). Releases 20 singles and 10 LPs/year. Works with songwriters on contract; musicians on salary for in-house studio work. Pays negotiable royalty to artists on contract.

How to Contact: Prefers cassette and lyric sheet. SASE. Reports in 2 weeks.
Music: Mostly country; also gospel. Released "This is Real," by Floyd Tillman (country single); "Lucille," by Sherri Jerrico (country single); and "Everything You Touch," by Johnny Nelms (country single). Other artists include Jerry Irby, Bobby Beason, Bobby Burton, Donna Hazard, Danny Brown, Sonny Hall, Ben Gabus, Jimmy Copeland and Johnny B. Goode.

BAL RECORDS, P.O. Box 369, La Canada CA 91012-0369. (818)548-1116. President: Adrian Bal. Record company, record producer and music publisher (Bal & Bal Music Publishing Co./ASCAP, Bal West Music Publishing Company/BMI). Estab. 1965. Releases 2-6 singles/year. Receives 50 submissions/month. Works with artists and songwriters on contract; musicians on salary for in-house studio work. Works with composers and lyricists; teams collaborators. Pays standard royalty to artists on contract; statutory rate to publishers for each record sold.
How to Contact: Prefers cassette (or videocassette) with 1-3 songs and lyric or lead sheet. SASE. Reports in 15-20 weeks.
Music: Rock, MOR, country/western, gospel and jazz. Released "Fragile" (by James Jackson), recorded by Kathy Simmons (med. rock); "Right to Know" (by James Jackson), recorded by Kathy Simmons (med. rock); "Dance to the Beat of My Heart" (by Dan Gertz), recorded by Ace Baker (med. rock) and "You're A Part of Me," "Can't We Have Some Time Together," "You and Me" and "Circles of Time" by Paul Richards (adult contemporary).
Tips: "Consider: Will young people who receive an allowance go out and purchase the record?"

BARNETT PRODUCTIONS INC., 2305 Dickey Ave., No. Chicago IL 60064. (312)689-2726. Vice President: Walter T. Barnett. Labels include W.M.B. Records. Record company and music publisher (BMI, Barnett). Estab. 1980. Releases 2 singles and 3 12″ singles/year. Works with songwriters on contract and hires musicians for in-house studio work. Pays 6-12% royalty to artists on contract; pays statutory rate to publishers.
How to Contact: Submit demo tape by mail. Unsolicited submissions are OK. Prefers cassette with 4 songs and lyric sheets. SASE. Reports in 1 month.
Music: Mostly R&B, rock and rap; also reggae, house music, soul, country, dance music, and ballads. Released "Emotional Man" (by W. Barnett), recorded by Shibeli on WMB Records (R&B/ballad); "Get Next To You" (by W. Barnett), recorded by Shibeli on WMB Records (R&B/dance) and "Do You Wanna Party" (by Fulldeck) on WMB Records (rap/dance).
Tips: "Never say never, believe in your music and never stop trying to reach and expand, first impression could be the last, so make it good."

BASSMENT RECORDS, 234 Columbus Drive, Jersey City NJ 07302. (201)963-1560. A&R Department: Craig Bevan or Barry Zeger. Record company. Estab. 1986. Releases 20 12″ singles and 3 LPs/year. Works with musicians/artists on contract and hires musicians on salary for in-house studio work. Royalties vary.
How To Contact: Submit demo tape by mail. Unsolicited submissions are OK. Prefers cassette (or VHS videocassette if available) with 1-3 songs and lyric sheet. SASE. Reports in 2 weeks.
Music: Released "Counting The Days" (by C. Bevan), recorded by Joey Kid (dance 12″); "Feelin' Moody" (by Loose Bruce), recorded by Loose Bruce (rap 12″); and "Lose Control" (by C. Bevan, B. Zeger and C. Pridgen), recorded by Like This (rap 12″), all on Bassment Records.
Tips: "We are interested in artist/songwriters with an awareness of the sounds/styles demanded by the marketplace, and a desire to work with a label whose production/songwriting expertise can guide and nurture their careers effectively and profitably."

BEAU-JIM RECORDS INC., Box 2401, Sarasota FL 34230-2401. President: Buddy Hooper. Record company, music publisher (Beau-Jim Music, Inc./ASCAP and Beau-Di Music, Inc./BMI), record producer and management firm. Estab. 1972. Member CMA, NSAI, NMA, AGAC. Releases 4 singles and 2 LPs/year. Receives 20 submissions/month. Works with artists and songwriters on contract.
How to Contact: Prefers cassette with lyrics (or videocassette) with 3-5 songs on demo. SASE. Reports in 3 weeks.
Music: Country. Artists include Debbie Kay and Joe Neddo.

*BELMONT RECORDS, 484 Lexington St., Waltham MA 02154. (617)891-7800. President: John Penny. Labels include Belmont Records and Waverly Records. Record company and record producer. Works with musicians on salary for in-house studio work. Pays standard royalty to artists on contract; statutory rate to publisher per song on record.
How to Contact: Write first and obtain permission to submit. Prefers cassette with 3 songs and lyric sheet. SASE. Reports in 2-3 weeks.
Music: Mostly country. Released *One Step At a Time*, recorded by Cheri Ann on Belmont Records (C&W LP); and *Tudo Bens Sabe*, recorded by Familia Penha (gospel LP). Other artists include Stan Jr., Tim Barrett, Jackie Lee Williams, Robin Right, Mike Walker and Dwain Hathaway.

BGM RECORDS, 4265 Gate Crest, San Antonio TX 78217-3824. (512)654-8773. Contact: Bill Green. Labels include Zone 7, BGM and Rainforest Records. Record company, music publisher (Bill Green Music) and record producer. Estab. 1979. Releases 10 singles and 2-3 LPs/year. Works with songwriters on contract.
How to Contact: Prefers cassette. SASE. Reports in 2 months.
Music: Mostly contemporary country and traditional country. Released "Cajun Baby" (by H. Williams, H. Williams Jr.), recorded by Doug Kershaw (country cajun); "Photographic Memory" (by B. Boyd), recorded by Billy Mata (country); and "Boogie Queen" (by Jenkins, Green), recorded by Doug Karrhau (country cajun); all on BGM Records. Other artists include David Price.

BGS PRODUCTIONS LTD., Newtown St., Kilsyth, Glasgow G65 0JX, **Scotland**. Phone: 44-0236-821-81. Contact: Dougie Stevenson or Bill Garden. Labels include Scotdisc and Country House Records. Record company, record producer (Bill Garden) and music publisher (Garron Music). Estab. 1978. Member ARRS, PPL, MCPS. Releases 5 singles, 15 LPs and 10 CDs/year. Receives 100 submissions/year. Works with artists and songwriters on contract. Statutory rate paid to publishers for each record sold. Royalties paid to US songwriters and artists through US publishing or recording affiliate.
How to Contact: Prefers cassette (or videocassette) with 2-3 songs and lyric sheet. SAE and IRC. "Unable to report on submissions. When submitting please mention *Songwriters Market*."
Music: Mostly country and folk; also easy listening and gospel. Released "Wee Laddie" (by MacLeod/Kerr), recorded by Jim MacLeod; *Play the Game*, (by Tommy Scott), recorded by Tommy Scott's Pipes and Dixie Banjo Band; and *The Ghostie* (by Garden), recorded by Stuart Anderson, Jr., all on Scotdisc Records.

BIG BEAR RECORDS, Box 944, Birmingham, B16 8UT, **England**. Phone: 44-021-454-7020. FAX: 44-021-454-9996. A&R Director: Jim Simpson. Labels include Big Bear, Truckers Delight and Grandstand Records. Record company, record producer and music publisher (Bearsongs). Releases 6 LPs/year. Works with artists and songwriters on contract; teams collaborators. Pays 8-10% royalty to artists on contract; 8¼% to publishers for each record sold. Royalties paid directly to the songwriters and artists or through US publishing or recording affiliate.
How to Contact: Prefers 7½ or 15 ips reel-to-reel, DAT, or cassette (or videocassette) and lyric sheet. SAE and IRC. Reports in 2 weeks.
Music: Blues, jazz. Artists include King Pleasure & the Biscuit Boys, Lady Sings the Blues, Bill Allred, Poorboys and jazz and blues artists. Released *This Is It* recorded by King Pleasure on Big Bear Records (R&B LP/CD/MC).

***BIG K RECORDS**, P.O. Box 3500, Pawtucket RI 02861. (401)728-1689. President: Karen Pady. Record company, music publisher (Big K Records, Pady Music Publishing Co./ASCAP) and record producer (KA Productions, Karen Pady). Estab. 1980. Releases 2 LPs/year. Works with musicians/artists and songwriters on contract and hires musicians.
How to Contact: Write first and obtain permission to submit. Prefers cassette or VHS videocassette with any number of songs and lyric sheet. SASE. Reports in 3 weeks.
Music: Mostly pop, rock and light rock; also A/C, country rock. Released "Cause I Love You" (adult contemporary); "My Friend" (adult contemporary); and "Will I Ever Make It Thru" (rock); all by Karen Pady Kula, recorded by Karyn and Steph on Big K Records. Other artists include Image w/ Camy and Gina, Midnight Fantasy, Pauline Silvia, Ronnie Woods, Together Again and Karyn Krystal.
Tips: "Work to please yourself. Write, sing, or play the type of music that you enjoy. I enjoy many types of music. If I like your demo material or ideas, I will work with you."

***BIG L PRODUCTIONS LTD., INC.**, Box 37490, Denver CO 80237. President: Mr. Lonnie Salazar. Labels include I.C.A. Records. Record company, music publisher (Hungry Bear Publishing, Happy Bear Publishing, Scuffy Bear Publishing) and record producer. Estab. 1971. Releases 10 singles, 10 12" singles, and 5 LPs/year. Works with musicians/artists and songwriters on contract and hires musicians for in-house studio work. Pays 6½% royalty to artists on contract; statutory rate to publisher per song on record.
How to Contact: Write first and obtain permission to submit. Submit cassette, picture if available and brief history. SASE.
Music: Mostly country and MOR/light rock (50s style). Released "Promise Her Anything" (by Joe Bob Barnhill), recorded by Tom Shoemaker on ICA Records (country); "Old Sam" (by Jimmy Platts), recorded by Tom Shoemaker on ICA Records (country) and "Sorry Isn't Always Easy to Say" (by Blake Emmons), recorded by Tom Shoemaker on ICA Records (country). Other artists include Butch Onstott and Yellowstone.

***BIG PRODUCTIONS RECORDS**, Suite 308, 37 East 28th St., New York NY 10016. (212)447-6000. President: Paul Punzone. Record company, music publisher (Humongous Music/ASCAP) and record producer (Big Productions and Publishing Co., Inc.). Estab. 1989. Releases 10 12" singles/year. Works

with musicians/artists and songwriters on contract and hires musicians for in-house studio work. Pays 40% royalty to artists on contract; statutory rate to publisher per song on record.
How to Contact: Submit demo tape by mail. Unsolicited submissions are OK. Prefers cassette or VHS videocassette with 3 songs and lyric sheet. SASE. Reports in 2 months.
Music: Mostly 12″ house tracks, vocal house and hip hop; also rap, R&B and pop. Released "Mission Accomplished," recorded by Big Baby; "Loose Flutes," recorded by Picture Perfect; and "Get Up," recorded by Big Baby; all written by P. Punzone, G. Sicard and B.B. Fisher on Big Productions Records (house track 12″). Other artists include Sheron Neverson and Cheryl Alter.
Tips: "We are seeking completed house/sample mixer for immediate release. Send best representation of your work for song or artist submissions."

BLACK DOG RECORDS, Rt. 2 Box 38, Summerland Key FL 33042. (305)745-3164. Executive Director: Marian Joy Ring. A&R Contact: Rusty Gordon, (Rustron Music Productions), 1156 Park Lane, West Palm Beach, FL 33417. (407)686-1354. Record company. Estab. 1989. Releases 2-6 singles and 3 LPs/ year. Pays standard royalty to artists on contract; statutory rate to publishers per song on record.
How to Contact: Submit demo tape by mail to W. Palm Beach address. Write or call first and obtain permission to submit. Prefers cassette with 3-6 songs and lyric or lead sheet. SASE required for all correspondence. Reports in 4-6 weeks.
Music: Mostly pop, R&B and folk-rock; also New Age and cabaret. Released *Rising Cost of Love*, "Song for Pedro," "Reflections" and "Same Moon," all written and recorded by Marian Joy Ring on Black Dog Records.

BLACK MOON RECORDS, INC. % **Chris Owens**, 328 Flatbush Ave., #271, Brooklyn NY 11238. (718)297-4907. President: Spencer McAdams. Record company. Estab. 1989. Works with musicians/ artists and producers on record contract. Pays 4-10% royalty to artists on contract for each record sold; statutory rate to publishers per song on record.
How to Contact: Submit demo tape by mail—unsolicited submissions are OK. Prefers cassette (or VHS videocassette) with 4 songs and lyric sheet. Material wil not be returned.
Music: Mostly rap and R&B.
Tips: "Submit clean demos. Vocals must be clear! Be original and to the point. We don't need 'bad attitudes'—just a willingness to work, patience and creativity!"

*BLUE GEM RECORDS, P.O. Box 29688, Hollywood CA 90029. (213)664-7765. Contact: Pete Martin. Record company and record producer (Pete Martin Productions). Estab. 1981. Receives 50-200 submissions/month. Works with musicians/artists on contract. Pays 6-15% royalty to artists on contract; statutory rate to publisher per song on record.
How to Contact: Submit demo tape by mail. Prefers cassette with 2 songs. SASE. Reports in 3 weeks.
Music: Mostly country and R&B; also pop/top 40 and rock. Released "The Greener Years," written and recorded by Frank Loren (country); "It's a Matter of Loving You" (by Brian Smith), recorded by Brian Smith and Renegades (country); and "Two Different Women" (by Frank Loren and Greg Connor), recorded by Frank Loren (country); all on Blue Gem Records. Other artists include Sherry Weston and Brian Smith & The Renegades (all country).
Tips: "Study top 10 on charts in your style of writing and be current!"

BLUE WAVE, 3221 Perryville Rd., Baldwinsville NY 13027. (315)638-4286. President/Producer: Greg Spencer. Labels include Blue Wave and Blue Wave/Horizon. Record company, music publisher (G.W. Spencer Music/ASCAP) and record producer (Blue Wave Productions). Estab. 1985. Releases 3 LPs and 3 CDs/year. Receives 300 submissions/year. Works with musicians/artists on contract. Royalty varies; statutory rate to publishers per song on records.
How to Contact: Submit demo tape by mail. Unsolicited submissions are OK. Prefers cassette (or VHS or Beta videocassette—live performance only) if available and as many songs as you like. Does not return unsolicited material. "We contact only if we are interested. Allow 6 weeks.
Music: Mostly blues, roots rock & roll and roots R&B; also cutting edge rock & roll, garage/60's rock & roll and roots country and rockabilly. Released *Jungle Fever* (by Mark Doyle and Joe Whiting), recorded by Backbone Slip (blues/rock); *What Will It Take* (by Joe Whiting and Dan Eaton), recorded by Jumpin' Joe Whiting (R&B); and *Motherless World* (by Pete McMahon), recorded by Kingsnakes (blues); all on Blue Wave Records.
Tips: "Don't send it unless it is great. I have enough good songs and I don't have the time or money to invest in good artists, only those who are great or unique. Please do not call; if it knocks me out I'll call you for sure! Don't send lyric sheets or photo."

BOLTS RECORDS, Arena Hse 6/9 Salisbury Prom, Green Lanes, Harringay, London N8 ORX **England**. (01)809-1460. Chairman: J.S. Batten. Labels include Bolts Records, Boy Records, Soultown Records, Hysteria Records. Record company. Estab. 1986. Releases 12 singles, 2-3 LPs and 2 CDs/

year. Receives 4 submissions/month. Works with musicians/artists and songwriters on contract and hires musicians for in-house studio work. Pays 3-15% royalty to artists on contract; statutory rate to publisher per song.

How to Contact: Submit demo tape by mail. Unsolicited submissions are OK. Prefers cassette with 3 songs and lyric or lead sheets. Does not return unsolicited material. Reports in 5 weeks.

Music: Mostly house/high NRG and dance music. Released "Don't Stop" (by Wedge and Stickley), recorded by Dance Addiction (house 12"); "Trip On This," written and recorded by Asmo (techno 12"); "Vindiloo Rap" (by Ferguson/Hopkins/Kalyan), recorded by Bhaji Jon (comedy rap 7"); "C'mon and Dance" (by Wedge/Stickley/PRS), recorded by Partners Rime Syndicate on Hysteria Records (house dance rap); "Jack It Up" (by Nicky Price), recorded by Mirror Image on Bolts Records (house); and "I Can Dance All By Myself" (by Ewings Townsend), recorded by Urbania on Hysteria Records (house). Other artists include Lisa Lee and Mirror Image.

BOOGIE BAND RECORDS, Suite 206, 6245 Bristol Pkwy., Culver City CA 90230. Contact: Larry McGee. Labels include Dollar Bill Records and Mega Star Records. Record company, music publisher (Operation Pefection Publishing), record producer (Intrigue Productions) and management firm (LMP Management). Estab. 1976. Releases 6 singles, 3 12" singles, 1 LP, 4 EPs and 2 CDs/year. Receives 200-300 submissions/year. Works with musicians/artists and songwriters on contract; musicians on salary for in-house studio work. Pays 10% royalty to artists on contract; statutory rate to publishers per song on record.

How to Contact: Prefers cassette with 1-4 songs and lyric sheet. Does not return unsolicited material. Reports in 2 months. "Please only send professional quality material."

Music: Urban contemporary, dance, rock, MOR/A/C, pop, rap and R&B. Released "Captain Freedom," "Voices" and "Snake," all written and recorded by Captain Freedom on Boogie Band Records. Other artists include the S-Quires, Jim Sapienza, The Allen Brothers, Terri Parondi, Roz Smith, Gary Walker, and Cindi Tulk.

*BOOM/POWER PLAY RECORDS, 200 Regent Dr., Winston-Salem NC 27103. (919)768-1298. President: David D. Passerallo. Record company, music publisher (DeDan Music/BMI) and record producer (Boom Productions Inc.). Estab. 1989. Releases 2 singles, 2 LPs and 2 CDs/year. Works with musicians/artists and songwriters on contract and "musicians and artists on production contracts." Pays 8-10% royalty to artists on contract; statutory rate to publisher per song on record.

How to Contact: Write first and obtain permission to submit. Prefers cassette or VHS videocassette with 2 songs and lead sheet. SASE. Reports in 2-3 weeks.

Music: Mostly pop and rock; also rap. Released "Ripped Jeans" (pop/rock); "I Wanna Know" (ballad) and "Lay It Back" (rock/rap); all written and recorded by John Cody on Boom Records. Other artists include China Blue.

Tips: "Have a good positive attitude and be very flexible."

BOUQUET RECORDS, Bouquet-Orchid Enterprises, Box 11686, Atlanta GA 30355. (404)355-7635. President: Bill Bohannon. Record company, music publisher (Orchid Publishing/BMI), record producer (Bouquet-Orchid Enterprises) and management firm. Releases 3-4 singles and 2 LPs/year. Works with artists and songwriters on contract. Pays 5% maximum royalty to artists on contract; pays statutory rate to publishers for each record sold.

How to Contact: Prefers cassette with 3-5 songs and lyric sheet. SASE. Reports in 1 month.

Music: Mostly religious (contemporary or country-gospel, Amy Grant, etc.), country ("the type suitable for Clint Black, George Strait, Patty Loveless, etc.") and top 100 ("the type suitable for Billy Joel, Whitney Houston, R.E.M., etc."); also rock and MOR. Released "Good Loving" by the Bandoleers, "Starting All Over" by Adam Day and "Let Me Be Your Lover" by Susan Spencer.

Tips: "Submit material that relates to what is currently being charted. A strong story line will help."

*BOVINE INTERNATIONAL RECORD COMPANY, 593 Kildare Rd., London, Ontario N6H 3H8 **Canada**. A&R Director: J.A. Moorhouse. Labels include Bovine and Solid Ivory Records. Record company. Estab. 1977. Releases 1-10 singles and 1-5 LPs/year. Receives 60 submissions/month. Works with musicians/artists on contract and musicians on salary for in-house studio work. Pays 30-40% royalty to artists on contract; statutory rate to publisher per song on record.

How to Contact: Cassette only with 2-3 songs and lyric and lead sheets. SAE and IRC. Reports in 1 month.

Music: Mostly country, pop and R&B; also children's records, blues and jazz. Released "San Antonio Truckers' Christmas" and "Keep It In Mind," written and recorded by J. Moorhave; and "Reconsider Me" (by J. Moorhave), recorded by Keynotes, all country singles on Bovine International Records. Other artists include Merle Morgan and The Rockin Renegades.

*BRIER PATCH MUSIC, 3825 Meadowood, Grandville MI 49418. (616)534-6571. Promotion Associate: Sharon Knol. Record company. Estab. 1985. Releases 1 or 2 LPs and 1 CD/year. Works with "our own artists." Pays negotiable royalty to artists on contract.

How to Contact: Write or call first and obtain permission to submit. Prefers VHS videocassette with 3 songs and lyric or lead sheet. SASE. Reports in 6 weeks.

Music: Mostly light rock, pop and gospel; also New Age instrumental, children's and peace/justice/folk. Released "Flying Upside Down" (light rock); "November Tomatoes" (New Age); and "How Do You Build a Love House" (children's); all written and recorded by Ken Medema on Brier Patch Records.

Tips: "Original music, with proficient musical background."

BRITISH RECORDS, 1015 Gayley Ave., Los Angeles CA 90024. A&R Representative: Geoff Gibbs. Labels include Songster Records. Record company. Estab. 1978. Works with musicians/artists and songwriters on contract. Releases 2-4 LPs/CDs per year.

How to Contact: Submit demo tape by mail. Unsolicited submissions are OK. Prefers cassette (or VHS videocassette) with 3-4 songs and lyric and/or lead sheet. SASE. Reports in 6 weeks.

Music: Mostly rock, heavy metal and pop; also blues, folk and R&B. Released "Rock Me" and "The Need In Love" (by Geoff Gibbs), recorded by Janet Lee (pop/single); *Face of a Stranger*, written and recorded by Janet Lee (pop/rock LP); and "Dress to Kill," written and recorded by Rick Montgomery (rock), all on British Records. Other artists include Montgomery/Silk, Chambermaid and Chris Ford/U.K.

*BROKEN RECORDS INTERNATIONAL, 305 S. Westmore Ave., Lombard IL 60148. (708)916-6874. International A&R: Roy Bocchieri. Labels include Broken Records International. Record company. Estab. 1984. Works with musicians/artists on contract. Payment negotiable.

How to Contact: Submit demo tape by mail. Unsolicited submissions are OK. Prefers cassette or VHS videocassette with at least 2 songs and lyric sheet. Does not return unsolicited material. Reports in 8 weeks.

Music: Mostly rock, pop and dance; also acoustic and industrial. Released *Electric*, written and recorded by LeRoy on Broken Records (pop LP-CD-MC).

BULL CITY RECORDS, Box 6, Rougemont NC 27572. (919)477-4077. Manager: Freddie Roberts. Record company, record producer and music publisher (Freddie Roberts Music). Releases 20 singles and 6 LPs/year. Works with songwriters on contract. Pays standard royalty to artists on contract; statutory rate to publishers for each record sold.

How to Contact: Write or call first about your interest or to arrange personal interview. Prefers 7½ ips reel-to-reel or cassette (or videocassette) with 1-5 songs and lyric sheet. "Submit a clear, up-to-date demo." SASE. Reports in 3 weeks.

Music: Mostly country, MOR, southern rock and top 40/pop; also bluegrass, church/religious, gospel and rock/country. Released "Redeemed" (by Jane Durham), recorded by Roberts Family on Bull City Records (southern gospel); "Almost" (by Rodney Hutchins), recorded by Billy McKellar on Bull City Records (country) and "Not This Time" (by D. Tyler), recorded by Sleepy Creek on Bull City Records (southern rock).

C.P.I. RECORDS, %F.B. Swegal, division of Centaur®, P.O. Box 7320, Beverly Hills CA 90212. (818)762-7417. Contact: Franz B. Swegal, P.C. Record company and record producer. Estab. 1984. Royalties vary.

How to Contact: Submit demo tape by mail. Unsolicited submissions are OK. "Simple release must absolve C.P.I. Records and/or affiliated Companies from infringement." Prefers cassette (or ½" VHS videocassette if available) with best songs. SASE.

Music: Mostly AOR; also pop, country, R&B.

CACTUS RECORDS, Breitenstrasse 82a/4, Vienna **Austria** 1140. (222)92-47-073. Contact: Hans Hartel. Labels include Cactus Records and Ha Ha Soundwave. Record company, music publisher and record producer (Hans Hartel). Estab. 1985. Releases 10 singles, 2 12" singles, 4 LPs and 2 CDs/year. Works with musicians/artists on contract, songwriters on contract and musicians on salary for in-house work.

How to Contact: Submit demo tape by mail. Prefers cassette with 3 songs and lyric sheet. SASE. Reports in 1 month "only if interested."

Music: Mostly pop, German pop and instrumentals; also ethno and New Age. Released "S.O.S," recorded by Chris White and "Kids Can't Wait (Children of the World)" recorded by Kids Can't Wait, both Johnny Blue Productions, and "Foxey" (instrumental images series). Other artists include Charly Hloch, Duncan Mlango, Christoph Hornstein, Chris White and Jonny Blue.

Tips: "You should have enough material for at least one LP."

THE CALVARY MUSIC GROUP, 142 8th Ave. N., Nashville TN 37203. (615)244-8800. Contact: Artist Development Department. Labels include Calvary, Lifestream, Heart Song and Wedding Song. Record company, record producer, music publisher and distribution company. Member GMA. Releases 8 singles and 8 LPs/year. Works with artists and songwriters on contract. Pays statutory rate or negotiates rate to publishers for each record sold.

How to Contact: Not accepting unsolicited material at this time.

Music: Mostly gospel; also wedding music. Released "Going Back" (by Shifflet), recorded by the Freemans on Calvary Records (southern gospel); "I Prayed Through Today," written and recorded by Ronny Hinson on Calvary Records (southern-inspirational); and "Lonely Tonight" (by Wilson), recorded by Karen Wheaton on Life Stream Records (inspirational).

CAMBRIA RECORDS & PUBLISHING, Box 374, Lomita CA 90717. (213)831-1322. Director of Recording Operations: Lance Bowling. Labels include Charade Records. Record company and music publisher. Estab. 1979. Releases 5 cassettes and 6 CDs/year. Works with artists on contract; musicians on salary for in-house studio work. Pays 5-8% royalty to artists on contract; statutory rate to publisher for each record sold.

How to Contact: Write first. Prefers cassette. SASE. Reports in 1 month.

Music: Mostly classical. Released *Songs of Elinor Remick Warren* on Cambria Records (CD). Other artists include Marie Gibson (soprano), Mischa Leftkowitz (violin), Leigh Kaplan (piano), North Wind Quintet, Sierra Wind Quintet and many others.

CANYON CREEK RECORDS, Box 31351, Dallas TX 75231. (214)750-0720. Chief Executive Officer: Bart Barton. A&R: Mike Anthony. Record company, record producer. Estab. 1983. Works with musicians/artists and songwriters on contract. Pays 25% royalty to writers on contract. Releases 12 singles/year, 4 LP/year.

How to Contact: Write first and obtain permission to submit. Prefers cassette (or VHS videocassette) with 2 songs and lyric sheet. Reports in 10 weeks.

Music: Country and gospel. Artists include Audie Henry, Dana Presley, Billy Parker and Susie Calvin. Released "She's Sittin' Pretty" (by Bart Barton), recorded by Billy Parker on CCR/RCA Records (country); "I Didn't Know You" (by D. Kirkpatrick/M. McClain), recorded by Audie Henry on CCR/RCA Records (country) and "Alive and Lovin' It" (by D.Kirkpatrick/M. McClain) recorded by Geo Marie on Canyon Creek Records (country).

CAPSTAN RECORD PRODUCTION, Box 211, East Prairie MO 63845. (314)649-2211. Nashville Branch: 38 Music Sq. E., Nashville TN 37203. (615)255-8005. Contact: Joe Silver or Tommy Loomas. Labels include Octagon and Capstan Records. Record company, music publisher (Lineage Publishing Co.) and record producer (Silver-Loomas Productions). Works with artists on contract. Pays 3-5% royalty to artists on contract.

How to Contact: Write first about your interest. Prefers cassette (or VHS videocassette) with 2-4 songs and lyric sheet. "Send photo and bio." SASE. Reports in 1 month.

Music: Country, easy listening, MOR, country rock and top 40/pop. Released "Dry Away the Pain," by Julia Brown (easy listening single); "Country Boy," by Alden Lambert (country single); "Yesterday's Teardrops," by The Burchetts (country single); and "Round & Round," by The Burchetts. Other artists include Bobby Lee Morgan, Skidrow Joe and Fleming.

CAROLINE RECORDS, INC., 114 W. 26th St., 11th Fl., New York NY 10001. (212)989-2929. Director Creative Operations: Janet Billig. Labels include Caroline Records, exclusive manufacturing and distribution of Plan 9 Records, exclusive distribution in the U.S. of EG, Editions EG and Sub-Pop. Record company, music publisher (26th St. Songs, 26th St. Music) and independent record distributor (Caroline Records Inc.). Estab. 1985. Releases 3-4 12" singles, 10 LPs, 1-2 EPs and 10 CDs/year. Works with musicians/artists on record contract. Pays varying royalty to artists on contract; statutory rate to publisher per song.

How to Contact: Submit demo tape by mail. Unsolicited submissions are OK. Prefers cassette with lead sheets and press clippings. SASE. Reports in 3 weeks.

Music: Mostly metal, "hardcore," and alternative/indie rock. Released *Quickness*, written and recorded by Bad Brains on Caroline Records (rock LP); *Bridge* (by Neil Young), recorded by V/A on NO.6 Records/Caroline Records (rock LP): and *God of Thunder* (by Kiss), recorded by White Zombie on Caroline Records (metal EP). Other artists include Naked Raygun, War Zone, Excel, Snake Nation, Unrest, Reverend, Mind Over 4, Pussy Galore, Primus.

Tips: "When submitting a demo keep in mind that we have never signed an artist who does not have a strong underground buzz and live track record. We listen to all types of 'alternative' rock, metal, funk and rap but do not sign mainstream hard rock or dance. We send out rejection letters so do not call to find out what's happening with your demo."

*CASARO RECORDS, 932 Nord Ave., Chico CA 95926. (916)345-3027. Partner: Hugh Santos. Record company, music publisher (Mini Max Publishing/BMI), record producer (RSA Productions). Estab. 1988. Releases 5-8 LPs/year. Works with musicians/artists and songwriters on contract; session players. Pays 7% royalty to artists on contract; statutory rate to publisher per song on record.
How to Contact: Write first and obtain permission to submit. Prefers cassette with full project demo and lyric sheet. Does not return unsolicited material. Reports in 4 weeks.
Music: Mostly jazz and country; also R&B and pop. Released *Trad Jazz* (by various), recorded by Charlie Robinson (jazz LP); *Off to Paradise* (by Harvey Borthwick), recorded by Harvey (country folk/LP); and *Sound of Christmas* (by various), recorded by Lory Dobbs on Casaro Records (big band/LP), all on Casaro Records. Other artists include Marcia Dekorte, Pam Dacus, John Peters and Charlie Robinson.
Tips: "We only contract with owners of ready-to-release masters that fit our catalog style. The bulk of our releases are from RSA Productions which is an inhouse production company that is supervised by Casaro Records."

CDE RECORDS AND TAPES, P.O. Box 310551, Atlanta GA 30331. (404)344-7621. President: Charles Edwards. Labels include TBS Records, Tapes Inc. and Nationwide Black Radio. Record Company. Estab. 1978. Releases 4-8 singles, 2-3 12″ singles, 2-5 LPs and 2-5 CDs/year. Receives 3-5 submissions/month. Works with musicians/artists on contract. Pays negotiable royalty to artists on contract.
How To Contact: Submit demo tape by mail. Prefers cassette (or VHS videocassette) with "several" songs. Does not return unsolicited material. Reports ASAP.
Music: Mostly interested in urban and rap; also gospel, R&B, jazz and pop. Released "Come Inside the Radio" (written and recorded by Chago) on CDE (urban single).
Tips: "Be strong; keep the faith and don't give up. The music business needs new and creative people."

*CENTURY CITY RECORDS AND TAPES OF CANADA, 2207 Halifax Cres. N.W., Calgary Alberta T2M 4E1 **Canada**. (403)282-2555. Vice President: Deborah Anderson. Labels include Century City Records. Record company, music publisher (SOCAN) and record producer (Century City). Estab. 1983. Releases 1-2 singles, 1-2 12″ singles, 1-2 LPs, 1-2 EPs and 1-2 CDs/year. Works with musicians/artists and songwriters on contract and hires musicians for in-house studio work. Pays 5-10% royalty to artists on contract; statutory rate to publishers per song on record.
How to Contact: Write or call first and obtain permission to submit. Prefers cassette or VHS videocassette with 4 songs, lyric sheets and lead sheets ("if available"). SASE. Reports in 1-4 weeks.
Music: Mostly country rock, rock and folk rock; also alternative, New Age and blues. Released "Hand Me Down Clown" (by W. R. Hutchinson), recorded by Warren Anderson (folk rock single); "1,000 Miles Away," written and recorded by Damian Follett (folk rock single); and *Hot From the Streets*, written and recorded by Warren Anderson (rock LP); all on Century City Records. Other artists include Thieves of Silence, Johnny 7, and Rattle Snake Kane.
Tips: "We are very interested in working with artists who have a proven background demonstrated by previous record sales statistics, cult following, media attention, etc. We are also interested in Alberta bands with a western flavour such as K.D. Lang, George Fox, Steve Earle-type music."

CENTURY RECORDS, INC., P.O. Box 4094, Pittsburgh PA 15201. (412)781-4557. President: Edward J. Moschetti. Labels include Star Records. Record company. Works with songwriters on contract.
How to Contact: Prefers cassette. SASE.
Music: Country; all types of music.

CHA-CHA RECORDS, 902 North Webster St., Port Washington WI 53074. (414)284-3279. President: Joseph C. De Lucia. Labels include Cha-Cha, Cap and Debby. Record company, record producer, and music publisher (Don-Del Music/BMI and Don-De Music/ASCAP). Estab. 1955. Releases 1 single and 1 LP/year. Receives 3 submissions/month. Works with artists/musicians and songwriters on contract.
How to Contact: Prefers cassette with 4-6 songs and lyric sheet. SASE. Reports in 2 months.
Music: Country, folk, acoustic jazz, rock, and religious. Released *99 Chicks*, by Ron Haydock and the Boppers (rock LP); and "The Jogging Song" by J. DeLucia. Other artists include Don Glasser and Lois Castello.

*CHALLEDON RECORDS, 5th Floor, Pembroke One Bldg., Virginia Beach VA 23462. General Counsel: Richard N. Shapiro. Record company, music publisher (Challedon Publishing Co./BMI) and record producer (Challedon Productions). Member NAIRD. Estab. 1990. Releases 1-2 singles and 1-2 LPs/year. Works with musicians/artists and songwriters on contract.

How to Contact: Write first and obtain permission to submit. Prefers cassette with 3 songs and lyric sheet. Reports in 4 weeks.

Music: Mostly rock/pop, college radio rock and some R&B. Released *Hired Gun* (by J. Sullivan), recorded by Hired Gun at Master Sound for Challedon Records (LP).

Tips: "Want acts with existing live show, prefer acts proximate to Virginia area, but not mandatory. Looking for rock acts with very unique sound. Want players, not poseurs."

CHARTA RECORDS, 44 Music Sq. E., Nashville TN 37203. (615)255-2175. President: Charlie Fields. Labels include Delux Records. Record company, music publisher (Jason Dee Music, Inc./BMI and Mr. Mort Music/ASCAP), and record producer (Charlie Fields Productions). Estab. 1977. Releases 15 singles and 6-8 LPs/year. Works with musicians/artists on contract. Pays standard royalty to artists on contract; pays statutory rate to publisher per song on record.

How to Contact: Call first to arrange personal interview. Prefers cassette or reel-to-reel (or VHS videocassette) with 2-3 songs and lyric or lead sheets. Does not return unsolicited material. Reports in 3 weeks.

Music: Mostly uptempo MOR, blues and country; also light rock, pop and bluegrass. Released "Somewhere In Canada" (by D. Walsh, J. Louiselle and P. Monet), recorded by David Walsh on Charta Records (country); "You Won the Battle" (by D. Erickson and J. Walker), recorded by Eddie Rivers on Charta Records (country); and "She's Layin' Down the Lovin" (by C.W. Fields), recorded by Ronny C. Collins on Delux Records (country). Other artists include Donna Darlene and Nina Wyatt.

Tips: "Have good clean quality tape and production with typewritten lyrics."

*CHERRY RECORDS, 9717 Jensen Dr., Houston TX 77093. (713)695-3648. Vice President: A.V. Mittelstedt. Labels include AV Records, Music Creek. Record company, music publisher (Pen House Music/BMI) and record producer (AV Mittelstedt Productions). Estab. 1970. Releases 10 singles and 5 LPs/year. Works with musicians/artists and songwriters on contract and hires musicians for in-house studio work. Pays varying royalty to artists on contract; statutory rate to publishers per song on record.

How to Contact: Submit demo tape by mail. Unsolicited submissions are OK. Prefers cassette with 2 songs. SASE. Reports in 3 weeks.

Music: Mostly country and pop. Released "Too Cold at Home" (by B. Hardin), recorded by Mark Chestnutt on Cherry Records (country); "Girls Like Her" (by Wimberly-Hart), recorded by Mark Chesnutt on Cherry Records (country); and "Half of Me" (by Wimberly/Trevino), recorded by Geronimo Trevino on AV Records (country crossover). Other artists include Randy Cornor, Roy Hilad, Georgie Dearborne, Kenny Dale, Karla Taylor and Borderline.

CHRYSALIS RECORDS, 645 Madison Ave., New York NY 10022. (212)758-3555. Senior Director of A&R: Paul Burton. Labels include Ensign, Cool Tempo. Record company. Works with musicians/artists and songwriters on contract and hires musicians for in-house studio work. Pays 12-14% royalty to artists on contract.

How to Contact: Call first and obtain permission to submit. Prefers cassette with 2-3 songs and lyric sheets. SASE. Reports in 2 months.

Music: Mostly pop, rock and rap; R&B, cross-over and modern/alternative. Recent releases include albums by Paul Carrack, Kevin Paige and The Angels. Other artists include Trouble Tribe, Ray Conteras, T.P.O.H., Child's Play, The Next School and Billy Idol.

THE CHU YEKO MUSICAL FOUNDATION, Box 10051, Beverly Hills CA 90213. (818)761-2646. Branch: Box 1314, Englewood Cliffs NJ 07632. Messages: (201)567-5524. Producer: Doris Chu. Labels include The Chu Yeko Musical Foundation, Take Home Tunes! Record Co., Original Cast Records and Broadway Baby Records. Record company and music publisher (Broadway/Hollywood International Music Publishers/ASCAP). Releases 5-10 LPs/year. Works with songwriters on contract. Teams collaborators. Pays 1-10% royalty to artists on contract; statutory rate or less to publishers for each record sold.

How to Contact: Prefers cassette (or VHS videocassette) with any number of songs and lyric sheet. "Final mix, top professional quality only." SASE. Reports in 1 month.

Music: Pop, rock, R&B and musicals in entirety.

Tips: "Need female singer or rock/pop/group touring L.A./CA area. Also need final mix songs for film scores and compilation albums: rock and pop, R&B, New Age. Only highly professional tapes are accepted. Include phone, address, SASE and cassette tape. We're seeking a "name" male rock, pop or R&B singer who can act for a major motion picture. Send tape, photo, resume, and VHS if available with SASE."

CIMIRRON/RAINBIRD RECORDS, 607 Piney Point Rd., Yorktown VA 23692. (804)898-8155. President: Lana Puckett. Vice President: Kim Person. Record company. Releases 2-3 singles, 3 LPs, 1 EP and 1 CD/year. Works with musicians/artists on contract. Pays variable royalty to artists on contract. Pays statutory rate.

Close-up

Michel Camilo
Jazz Composer/Performer
New York, New York

Jazz is once again in the spotlight. After a decline in the early to mid-eighties, there's a re-emergence of classic jazz in pop markets—jazz oriented radio is cropping up and record sales in the genre are at a high point. Much of jazz's recent climb is due to the success of several young jazz musicians. Harry Connick, Jr., the Marsalis brothers, Marcus Roberts and Michel Camilo have brought jazz newfound prominence in the mainstream.

According to Camilo, there's been a change in the way jazz artists approach the music. "It's less self-indulgent," he says. "People in the past thought of jazz as too complicated. But now we have to compress and compact the music for the sake of making radio. And I think in that regard it's good that we're trimming and shaping up. There's a bright future for jazz because people are really beginning to understand it—it has more continuity now and people can relate to it better."

And thousands of new jazz fans have definitely been relating. Each of Camilo's last three albums has hit No. 1 on the jazz charts. But, even though he wants his music to continue to be commercially acceptable, Camilo assures that he writes from within and he writes for himself. Along with his desire to create wonderful music comes the need to be heard. He doesn't completely discount commercialism, as long as it doesn't negatively affect his writing. "Radio won't play anything that's over five or six minutes; they insist on variety. And it has actually been good for me as a composer. I've become more focused."

A native of the Dominican Republic, the fiery Camilo recognizes the importance of a broad base of musical exposure, as well as a high curiosity level, in order to improve one's creative edge. "Don't think that everything creative is going to come from music and music only, because it doesn't," he says. "Read a lot—including the newspaper, books on a variety of topics—as well as listen to many types of music."

Along the same lines, he advises songwriters and composers to never close out new ideas. Once you block out other styles and different opinions and stop experiencing new things, your music may suffer. A creative person should tap into his or her surroundings, he says. "Music is a reflection of life. You really have to have life experiences in order to make inspired music. Songwriters and composers are basically telling a story . . . and what better place to get an intriguing story than from your own life and our world?" He offers the examples of the music of Tracy Chapman, Phil Collins and Sting (in the pop vein) as "inspired by the world."

Camilo has already made his mark in the jazz world, but he first gained professional success as a composer for Score Productions in New York. He wrote the theme songs for CNN Headline News, the reorchestration of the theme for Peter Jennings' World News Tonight, and themes for the New York Marathon and the Winter Olympics in Sarajevo. His composition for the Goodwill Games earned an Emmy, as did his breakthrough hit "Why Not?", recorded by the Manhattan Transfer.

His work with Score supplied "the discipline to be able to write every day," another component of success for any songwriter, he says. "I learned that when you write constantly, you open internal channels that stay open more often."

In addition to continuing to hone the songwriting craft, an objective look at oneself and one's music is imperative, says Camilo. "A very old musician once told me: 'Don't ever stop looking at yourself in the mirror.' And what he meant was that you must always question yourself—What can I improve? How far have I come? Where am I going? It's a constant evaluation of your music. If people don't like your music, find out why, but don't let the ego get in the way. You must be able to take criticism (by yourself and others), analyze it and take it as constructive. That's the only way you'll get better."

—Brian C. Rushing

How to Contact: Write to obtain permission to submit. Prefers cassette with 1-3 songs and lyric sheet. SASE. Reports in 3 months.
Music: Mostly country-bluegrass, New Age and pop. Released "Nutcracker Suite," written and recorded by Steve Bennett (guitar) and "Forever and Always" (by Lana Puckett and Kim Person), recorded by Lana & Kim (country LP); all on Cimirron/Rainbow Records.

CITA COMMUNICATIONS INC., 676 Pittsburgh Rd., Butler PA 16001. (412)586-6552. A&R/Producer: Mickii Taimuty. Labels include Phunn! Records and Tropē Records. Record company. Estab. 1989. Releases 6 singles, 3 12″ singles, 3 LPs, 2 EPs and 5 CDs/year. Works with musicians/artists on record contract. Pays artists 10% royalty on contract. Pays statutory rate to publishers per song on records.
How to Contact: Call first and obtain permission to submit. Prefers cassette (or VHS, Beta or ¾″ videocassette if available) with a maximum of 6 songs and lyric sheets. SASE. Reports in 8 weeks.
Music: Interested in rock/dance music and contemporary gospel; also rap, jazz and progressive country. Released "Forged by Fire", written and recorded by Sanxtion on Tropē Records; "I Cross My Heart" (by Taimuty/Nelson), recorded by Melissa Anne on Phunn! Records; and "Fight the Fight," written and recorded by M.J. Nelson on Tropē Records. Other artists include Most High, Sister Golden Hair and Countdown.

CITY PIGEON RECORDS, P.O. Box 43135, Upper Montclair NJ 07043. (201)857-2935. President: Richard Reiter. Record company. Estab. 1983. Releases 3 LPs and 3 CDs/year. Receives 25-30 submissions/year. Works with musicians/artists on contract. Pays 10-13% royalty to artists on contract; statutory rate to publishers per song on record.
How to Contact: Write first and obtain permission to submit. Prefers cassette with 3 songs and lyric or lead sheet. SASE.
Music: Mostly jazz; also pop. Released "Wishful Thinking," "Song for Martha," and "Mel's Barbecue," written by Richard Reiter, recorded by Crossing Point on City Pigeon/Optimism Records (contemporary jazz singles). Other artists include Lou Caimano.

*CLAY & CLAY, INC., 19938 Patton, Detroit MI 48219. (313)533-4506. Labels include Torrid, Scorcher, Claycastle, 2 Hot. Record company, Music publisher (Lynclay Publications/ASCAP) and record producer. Estab. 1988. Releases 12 singles and 4 LPs/year. Works with musicians/artists and songwriters on contract and hires musicians for in-house studio work. Payment negotiable.
How to Contact: Submit demo tape by mail. Unsolicited submissions are OK. Prefers cassette or VHS videocassette with minimum of 3 songs and lyric or lead sheets. SASE. Reports in 1 month "if interested."
Music: Released "I Want to Be Ready" (by D. Arnold), recorded by Mighty Wings on Claycastle Records (gospel single); "Gettin' 'Em On" (by L. Clay), recorded by Mr. Mill on Torrid Records (rap 12″); and "I Ain't Buyin' It" (by D. Davis/D. Fielderl, M. Field), recorded by D.O.P. on Scorcher Records (rap 12″). Other artists include Jesse Douglas, Relana Harris, Total Darkness, Jamal Morson, Brenda Wilson-Johnson, TCs Tempo, Twan.
Tips: "Submit your best work and understand it doesn't happen overnight."

CLOUDBURST RECORDS, Box 31, Edmonton KY 42129. (502)432-3183. President: Rev. Junior Lawson. Record company and music publisher (Holy Spirit Music). Releases 3 singles and 4 LPs/year. Works with songwriters on contract. Pays 4% royalty to artists on contract.
How to Contact: Call first. Prefers 7½ ips reel-to-reel or cassette and lyric sheet. SASE. Reports in 3 weeks.
Music: Mostly southern gospel; also country, gospel, MOR and progressive. Released *Introducing the Cornerstones* and *Extra! Extra!,* by The Cornerstones (southern gospel LPs); and *Old-Fashioned Ways,* by the Sounds of Joy (southern gospel LP). Other artists include The Southern-Aires.

*CLOWN RECORDS, P.O. Box 357, Ridgefield NJ 07660. (201)641-5749. President: C.A. Pruitt. Record company (BMI). Estab. 1987. Works with musicians/artists and songwriters on contract and hires musicians for in-house studio work. Pays negotiable royalty to artists on contract; statutory rate to publisher per song on record. Charges for services in advance "depending on the contract."
How to Contact: Submit demo tape by mail. Unsolicited submissions are OK. Prefers cassette or videocassette with two or more songs and lyric or lead sheet. SASE.

COLLECTOR RECORDS, Box 2296, Rotterdam 3000 CG **Holland**. Phone: (1860)20180. Research: Cees Klop. Labels include All Rock, Downsouth, Unknown, Pro Forma and White Label Records. Record company, music publisher (All Rock Music Pub.) and record producer (Cees Klop). Estab. 1967. Releases 10 singles and 30 LPs/year. Works with musicians/artists and songwriters on contract. Pays standard royalty to artist on contract.
How to Contact: Prefers cassette. SAE and IRC. Reports in 1 month.
Music: Mostly 50's rock, rockabilly, hillbilly boogie and country/rock; also piano boogie woogie. Released "Spring in April" (by Pepping/Jellema), recorded by Henk Pepping on Down South Records (50's rock); "Go Cat Go" (by Myers), recorded by Jimmy Myers on White Label Records (50's rock) and "Knocking On the Backside" (by T. Redell), recorded by T. Redell on White Label Records (50's rock).

COMMA RECORDS & TAPES, Postbox 2148, 6078 Neu-Isenburg, **West Germany**. Phone: (6102)52696. General Manager: Roland Bauer. Labels include Big Sound, Comma International and Max-Banana-Tunes. Record company. Estab. 1969. Releases 50-70 singles and 20 LPs/year. Works with musicians/artists and songwriters on contract. Pays 7-10% royalty to artists on contract.
How to Contact: Prefers cassette and lyric sheet. Reports in 3 weeks. "Do not send advanced letter asking permission to submit, just send your material, SAE and minimum two IRCs."
Music: Mostly pop, disco, rock, R&B and country; also musicals.

COMPO RECORD AND PUBLISHING CO., Box 15222, Oklahoma City OK 73115. (405)677-6448. President: Yvonne DeVaney. General Manager: Sonny Lane. Record company and music publisher (Country Classics Music/BMI). Estab. 1972. Releases 4-6 singles and 1-2 LPs/year. Works with musicians/artists and songwriters on contract. Pays negotiable royalty to artists and songwriters on contract; statutory rate to publishers for each record sold.
How to Contact: Prefers cassette with 2-4 songs and lead sheet. SASE, with correct postage. Reports in 3 weeks. "If not contacted in that time, material is unsuited for our use."
Music: Mostly country/western, gospel and MOR. Released "Lovers Waltz"; "Yodel Love" and "Yodel Waltz" (all by Yvonne DeVaney), recorded by Wes Onley and Yvonne DeVaney on Compo Records (country duet).
Tips: "Songwriter: We like a simple song with a simple melody—a song you can whistle and hum. Artists: Develop a style."

COMSTOCK RECORDS LTD., Suite 114, 10603 N. Hayden Rd., Scottsdale AZ 85260. (602)951-3115. Canadian, United States and European distribution on Paylode & Comstock Records. Production Manager/Producer: Patty Parker. President: Frank Fara. Record company, music publisher (White Cat Music/ASCAP, Rocky Bell Music/BMI), Nashville Record Production, and International Record Promotions. Member CMA, BBB, CCMA, MACE, BCCMA, British & French C&W Associations, and CARAS. "Comstock Records, Ltd. has three primary divisions: Production, Promotion and Publishing. We distribute and promote both our self-produced recordings and outside master product." Releases 24-30 singles, 2 LPs and 2-4 CDs/year. Receives 30-40 submissions/month. Works with artists and songwriters on contract; musicians on salary. Pays 10% royalty to artists on contract; statutory rate to publishers for each record sold. "Artists pay distribution and promotion fee to press and release their masters."
How to Contact: Prefers cassette (or VHS videocassette) with 1-4 songs "plus word sheet. Enclose stamped return envelope if cassette is to be returned." Reports in 2 weeks.
Music: Western music, A/C and country. Released "Cherokee" recorded by Anne Lord; "Half A Fighting Chance" by Singer Steve Heske; "We Rise Again" by Priscilla Wright and "You're the Reason I Live" by Cheryl Maxim. Other artists include Anne Lord, Jess Owen, Randy Owen Bishop, Brent McAthey, Ogden Harless, Gwen Bishop, Johnny Ramone, Ray Dean James, Richard and Mary and The Roberts Sisters.
Tips: "We have an immediate need for country material for our European division. Our international division consists of master distribution and promotion to the following nations: England, France, Germany, Belgium, Ireland, Luxembourg, The Netherlands, Scotland, Switzerland, Norway and Canada. Also Denmark and Austria. We do video promotion with air play promotions to C&W networks across North America."

*CONCORDE INTERNATIONAL RECORDS, P.O. Box 24454, Nashville TN 37202. (615)269-7074. FAX: (615)269-0131. Publishing Director: Terri Walker. Record company. Estab. 1990. Releases 3-4 singles and 1-2 LPS/year. Pays statutory rate.

How to Contact: Submit demo tape by mail. Unsolicited submissions are OK. "No more than 2 at a time." Prefers cassette. SASE. Reports in 4-6 weeks.

Music: Mostly country, A/C and Christian; also MOR and Christmas. Released "Mamas Rockin' Chair" (by S. Clarke) and "My Way or the Highway" (by E. Reynolds and T. Fritz); both recorded by D. Dudley on Concorde Records (country single).

COSMOTONE RECORDS, P.O. Box 71988. Los Angeles CA 90071-0988. Labels include Cosmotone Music and Center for the Queen of Peace. Record company and music publisher. Estab. 1984. Releases 1 single, 1 12″ single and 1 LP/year. Works with songwriters on contract and hires musicians on salary for in-house studio work. Pays statutory rate to publishers per song on record.

How to Contact: Write first and obtain permission to submit. Prefers cassette (or VHS videocassette). "Will contact only if interested."

Music: All types. Released "Padre Pio", written and recorded by Lord Hamilton on Cosmotone Records (Christian/pop/rock); and "Peace of Heart," by Rafael Brom (Christian New Wave).

COUNTRY BREEZE RECORDS, 1715 Marty, Kansas City KS 66103. (913)384-4454. President: Ed Morgan. Labels include Country Breeze Records, Angel Star Records and Midnight Shadow Records. Record company, music publisher (Country Breeze Music/BMI and Walkin' Hat Music/ASCAP). Releases 15 7″ singles and 20 cassettes/year. Receives 130 submissions/month. Works with musicians/artists and songwriters on contract. Pays 18% royalty to artists on contract; statutory rate to publisher per song on record.

How to Contact: Prefers studio-produced demo with 3 songs and lyric sheet. SASE. Reports "as time allows."

Music: All types country, top 40, rock/pop. Released "Love on the Borderline" (by John Maines, Jr.), recorded by John Maines, Jr. on Country Breeze Records; "Once More" (by Dusty Owens), recorded by Carolina Country on Country Breeze Records; "Ships that Pass in the Night" (by Mark Spencer & Richard Cowan), recorded by Mark Spencer & Nikiya on Midnight Shadow Records; "Only in September" (by J. Schwitzerlette and K. Janny), recorded by Jonathan Keith on Country Breeze Records; "Saudi Sand" (by J. Grimes, T. Toler, J. Evans, G. Mitchell), recorded by Southern Strings on Country Breeze Records. Other artists include Chill Factor, Edging West.

Tips: "When submitting an artist package we require 3 of your best songs, a short bio and recent photo. Make sure your voice is out front and the songs are strong, both in lyrics and melody."

COUNTRY SHOWCASE AMERICA, 14134 Brighton Dam Rd., Clarksville MD 21029-1327. (301)854-2917. President: Francis Gosman. Record company. Estab. 1971. Releases 5 singles/year. Receives 6 submissions/month. Works with musicians/artists and songwriters on contract. Pays 3% royalty to artists on contract; statutory rate to publishers for each record sold.

How to Contact: Prefers cassette and lyric sheet. SASE.

Music: Country. Released "The Iowa, Remember Terret #2" (by Gosman); "The Long Black Wall" (by Lomich/Stamm); "More Than Once In A While" (by Blake/Fisher); "Wave The Flag" (by Gosman/Vagus); "Blue Gray" (by Gosman/Vague); "I Just Built a Wall" (by Gosman/Vague); "Starting Over" (by Vagus); "Almost in Love" (by Fisher and Weller); "Tent Meeting Blues" (by Gosman/Vague); all recorded by Johnny Anthony on CSA (all country).

COUNTRY STAR INTERNATIONAL, 439 Wiley Ave., Franklin PA 16323. (814)432-4633. President: Norman Kelly. Labels include CSI, Country Star, Process and Mersey Records. Record company, music publisher (Country Star/ASCAP, Process and Kelly/BMI) and record producer (Country Star Productions). Member AFM and AFTRA. Estab. 1970. Releases 10-15 singles and 8-10 LPs/year. Receives 400 submissions/year. Works with musician/artists and songwriters on contract. Works with lyricists and composers. Pays 8% royalty to artists on contract; statutory rate to publishers for each record sold. "Charges artists in advance only when they buy records to sell on personal appearances and show dates."

How to Contact: Prefers cassette with 2-4 songs and lyric or lead sheet. SASE. Reports in 2 weeks.

Music: Mostly country western, bluegrass, pop, easy listening; also rock, gospel, MOR and R&B. Released "A Part Of Me" (by Lisa Hadley Patton), on Country Star Records (country); "Your Place Or Mine" (by Tommy Davidson), on Country Star Records (country) and "Spinning In My Heart" (by Junie Lou) on Country Star Records (country). Other artists include Don Earl Mabury, Tara Bailey and Shelley Harris.

Tips: "Send only your best efforts."

COWBOY JUNCTION FLEA MARKET AND PUBLISHING CO., Highway 44 W., Lecanto FL 32661. (904)746-4754. Contact: Elizabeth Thompson. Record company, record producer (Cowboy Junction Publishing Co.)and music publisher (Cowboy Junction Flea Market and Publishing Co.). Estab. 1957. Releases 3 or more singles, 1-2 12″ singles and 1-2 LPs/year. Receives 100 submissions/year. Works with musicians/artists and songwriters on contract. Pays 50% royalty.
How to Contact: Prefers cassette with 1-4 songs and lyric sheet. SASE. Reports ASAP.
Music: Country, gospel, bluegrass and country western. Released "Way Down In Alabama," "Mr. and Mrs. Dixie," and "Way Up on the Mountain" (by Boris Max Pastuch), recorded by Buddy Max on Cowboy Junction Records (country & western). Other artists include Izzy Miller, Wally Jones, Leo Vargason, Johnny Pastuck, Troy Holliday and Pappy Dunham.
Tips: "Come to one of our shows and present your song (Flea Market on Tuesdays and Fridays, country/bluegrass show every Saturday) or send a tape in."

COWGIRL RECORDS, P.O. Box 6085, Burbank CA 91510. Contact: Vice President. Record company and music publisher (Kingsport Creek). Estab. 1980. Works with musicians/artists and songwriters on contract. Pays statutory rate to publishers for each record sold.
How to Contact: Prefers cassette (or VHS videocassette) with any number of songs and lyric sheet or lead sheet. Does not return unsolicited material. "Include a photo and bio if possible."
Music: Mostly country, R&B, MOR and gospel. Released "Heaven Bound," "Only Life," and Tennessee Cowgirl" written and recorded by Melvena Kaye on Cowgirl Records.

*CREOLE RECORDS, LTD., The Chilterns, France Hill Dr., Camberley Surrey GU153QA **England**. 0276-686077. Managing Director: Bruce White. Labels include Creole, Dynamic, Revue, Cactus, Big, Past Replay. Record company and music publisher (PRS/MCPS—Creole Music Ltd.). Estab. 1966. Releases 15 singles, 15 12″ singles; 20-30 LPs and 20-30 CDs/year. Receives 30-40 submissions/month. Works with musicians/artists and songwriters. Pays artists 8-16% royalty; publishers standard MCPS.
How to Contact: Submit demo tape by mail. Unsolicited submissions are OK. Prefers cassette with 3 songs. SASE. Reports in 8 weeks.
Music: Mostly dance, pop and reggae; also oldies. Released *Worst of* (by various artists), recorded by Judge Dread (pop); *Reggae Hits* written and recorded by various artists (reggae); and *English Language* written and recorded by David Donaldson (spoken), all on Creole Records. Artists include Boris Gardiner, Peter Green, In Crowd, Desmond Dekker, Byron Lee, and 2 Dragonaires.

CRYSTAL RAM/APRIL RECORDS, 827 Brazil Pl., El Paso TX 79903. (915)772-7858. Owner: Harvey Marcus. Labels include Crystal Ram, April, T.S.B., and M.C.R. Records. Record company, music publisher and record producer (April Productions). Releases 1-3 singles, 1-3 12" singles, 1-5 LPs, 1-5 EPs, and 1-3 CDs/year. Works with musicians/artists and songwriters on contract; hires musicians for in-house studio work. Pays 25% royalty to artists on contract; statutory rate to publisher per song on record.
How to Contact: Prefers cassette or 7½ ips reel-to-reel (or VHS videocssette) with one song and lyric or lead sheet. SASE. Reports in 6 weeks.
Music: Mostly jazz/pop, top 40 (ballads) and tex-mex; also country, New Age and Christian/rock. Released *Are We In This for Love* (EP) and "Baby Blue Baby" (single), written and recorded by The Street Boys on T.S.B. Records; and *Endless Dreams*, written and recorded by Ruben Castillo on Crystal Ram Records (LP). Other artists include Ray Justin Vega.

CURTISS RECORDS, Box 4740, Nashville TN 37216. (615)865-4740. President: Wade Curtiss. Record company and producer. Works with artists and songwriters on contract. Pays 8¢/record royalty to artists on contract; 2½¢/record royalty to songwriters on contract.
How to Contact: Prefers cassette with 2-8 songs and lead sheet. SASE. Reports in 3 weeks.
Music: Bluegrass, blues, country, disco, folk, gospel, jazz, rock, soul and top 40/pop. Released "Book of Matches," by Gary White; and "Rompin' " and "Punsky," by the Rhythm Rockers.

*D.J. INTERNATIONAL, INC., 727 W. Randolph St., Chicago IL 60661. (312)559-1845. A&R: Martin Luna. Labels include Underground, Fierce, Gangster, Rythm, Mutant. Record company and record producer. Estab. 1985. Releases 75 12″ singles and 35 LPs/year. Works with musicians/artists and songwriters on contract and hires musicians for in-house studio work. Payment varies.
How to Contact: Submit demo tape by mail. Unsolicited submissions are OK. Prefers cassette with 3 songs and lyric sheets. Does not return unsolicited material.
Music: Mostly dance, house, alternative; also tracks.

DAGENE RECORDS, P.O. Box 410851, San Francisco CA 94141. (415)822-1530. President: David Alston. Labels include Dagene Records and Cabletown Corp. Record company, music publisher (Dagene Music) and record producer (David-Classic Disc Productions). Estab. 1987. Works with musicians/artists and songwriters on contract and hires musicians on salary for in-house studio work. Pays statutory rate to publishers per song on record.

How to Contact: Write or call first and obtain permission to submit. Prefers cassette (or VHS videocassette) with 2 songs and lyric sheet. Does not return unsolicited material.

Music: Mostly R&B/rap, dance and pop; also gospel. Released "Serving 'Em" (written and recorded by Frisco Kid) on Dagene Records; "Visions" (by Marcus Justice), recorded by 2-Dominatozs on Dagene Records; and "Started Life" (by David/M. Campbell), recorded by Primo on Cabletown Records, (all rap 12"). Other artists include "The D."

DA-MON RECORDS, Orisa Productions Inc., 646 East Madison St., Lancaster PA 17602. (717)393-9115. President: Daoud A. Balewa. Labels include The Creative InterFace/TCI and Da-Mon Records/TCI. Record company and music publisher (DABA Music Publishers/BMI). Estab. 1979. Releases 3 LPs and 3 CDs/year. Works with songwriters on contract and musicians on salary for in-house studio work. Pays statutory rate to publishers per song on records. Charges prospective artists for promotion.

How To Contact: Submit demo tape by mail. Unsolicited submissions are OK. Prefers cassette (or Beta/VHS videocassette if available) with 3 songs, lyric sheet, artist bio, PR photos and contact information. SASE. Reports in 3-6 weeks.

Music: Mostly jazz/fusion, New Age and black urban contemporary; also pop, crossover. Released "Raw Savage," written and recorded by Lady E on DaMon Records (pop/rap single); "I'll Make It Up," written and recorded by E. Laws on DaMon Records (pop single); and *Colours In Spaces*, written and recorded by Ambiance on DaMon/TCI (LP). Other artists include Matt Nathan, Jim Lum, Carol Merriwether and M.C. Penetrator.

DARK HORSE PRODUCTIONS, 1729 N. Third Ave., Upland CA 91786. (714)946-1398. A&R Director: Bill Huff. Record company, music publisher (see Lizard Licks Music, BMI), record producer (Dark Horse Productions). Estab. 1988. Releases 2 LPs and 2 CDs/year. Works with musicians/artists on contract. Pays 6-9% royalty on retail price; statutory rate to publishers per song on records.

How to Contact: Submit demo tape by mail. Prefers cassette with 3-5 songs. SASE. Reports in 4 weeks.

Music: Mostly contemporary jazz, New Age, and traditional jazz. Released *Iridescence* (by Brad Kaenel), recorded by Polyhedra on Dark Horse Records (contemporary jazz) and *Simply Simon* (by D.J. Alverson), recorded by Polyhedra on Dark Horse (contemporary jazz).

DEMI MONDE RECORDS AND PUBLISHING, LTD., Foel Studio, Llanfair Caereinion, Powys, Wales, United Kingdom. Phone: (0938)810758. Managing Director: Dave Anderson. Record company and music publisher (Demi Monde Records & Publishing, Lts.) and record producer (Dave Anderson). Estab. 1983. Releases 5 12" singles, 10 LPs and 6 CDs/year. Works with musicians/artists and songwriters on contract; hires musicians for in-house studio work. Pays 10-12% royalty to artists on contract; statutory rate to publisher per song on record.

How to Contact: Prefers cassette with 3-4 songs. SAE and IRC. Reports in 1 month.

Music: Rock, R&B and pop. Released *Hawkwind* and *Amon Doul II & Gong* (by Band), and *Groundhogs* (by T.S. McPhee), all on Demi Monde Records (LPs).

DHARMA RECORDS, 117 W. Rockland Rd., Box 615, Libertyville IL 60048. (708)362-4060. Vice President: Rick Johnson. Labels include Future and Homexercise. Record company, record producer and music publisher (Amalgamated Tulip Corp.). Releases 3 singles and 2 LPs/year. Works with artists and songwriters on contract. Pays negotiable royalty to artists on contract; negotiable rate to publishers for each record sold.

How to Contact: Prefers cassette with 3-5 songs and lyric sheet. Prefers studio produced demos. SASE. Reports in 3 months.

Music: Rock, top 40/pop, country, dance/R&B, MOR and progressive rock. Released *Active Music for Children*, by Bill Hooper (education LP); "Oh Boy," by Oh Boy (pop rock single); and *Not Marmosets Yet*, by Conrad Black (rock LP).

DIGITAL MUSIC PRODUCTS, INC., 94-1301 Southfield Ave., Stamford CT 06902. (203)327-3800. Marketing: Paul Jung. Record company. Estab. 1983. Releases 6-8 CDs/year. Pays ¾ rate to publishers per song on record.

How to Contact: Write or call first and obtain permission to submit. Prefers cassette. SASE. Reports in 2 months.

Music: Mostly jazz. Released *Home Again* (written and recorded by Thom Rotella); *Magic Fingers* (by Chuck Loeb), recorded by Chuck Loeb/Andy Laverne; and *Bob's Diner* (by Bob Smith), recorded by Bob's Diner, all on DMP Records (jazz CD). Other artists include Bob Mintzer, The Dolphins, Joe Beck, Warden Bernhardt, Manfredo Fest and Bill Mays.

Tips: "Can you record direct to two-track? We are *not* a multi-track label."

DIRECTIONS, 6 Rue Laurenlin, Lyon **France** 69002. (33)7240-9236. Managing Director: Andre. Labels include Lucky French, Scycla and Elsa. Record company and music publisher (Directions, SACEM). Estab. 1988. Releases 124 singles, 50 12″ singles, 90 LPs and 20 CDs/year. Receives 200 submissions/year. Works with musicians/artists on record contract, songwriters on royalty contract. Pays artists 6-12% royalty; statutory rate to publishers per song on record.
How to Contact: Write first to arrange interview. Prefers cassette with 3 songs and lyric sheet. SASE. Reports in 2 weeks.
Music: Interested in rock and house; also classical. Released "Zen" (by Massimo), recorded by Deux (house/maxi); *To Be Free* (by d), recorded by Mel Muriell (dance/LP); and "Check the Beat" (by Mike), recorded by Oxo (house/maxi), all on BPM Records. Other artists include The Suns, Lanterne Rouge, Deux and Philippe Richard.

*DISCOS CBS SAICF, Bartolome Mitre 1986, Buenos Aires 1039 **Argentina**. Phone: (541)953-2328. A&R Manager: Raul Tortora. Record company. Releases 5 12″ singles and 140 LPs/year. Works with musicians/artists on contract. Royalty depends on each contract, between 5 or 17%, over 90%. Pays statutory rate to publishers per song on records.
How to Contact: Submit demo tape by mail. Unsolicited submissions are okay. Prefers cassette (or Pal U-Matic videocassette). Does not return unsolicited submissions. Only reports back if interested.
Music: Mostly easy listening, pop or rock; also R&B, Latin and New Age. Released *Bad English* (by John Waite/ETC), recorded by Bad English on Epic Records (rock LP); *Como Una Luz* (written and recorded by Jose Manuel Soto), on Epic Records (melodic LP); and *Sonrie* (by R. Carlos/Others), recorded by Roberto Carlos on CBS Records (Latin LP). Other artists include Paz Martinez, Maria Martha Serra Lima, Soda Stereo, Tormenta, Los Fabulosos Cadillacs and Los Perros Calientes.
Tips: "Our policy is to work with artists on a long-term basis, avoiding short deals except for those world hits such as Lambada. We prefer artists with catalogue which we can develop."

DISQUES NOSFERATU RECORDS, C.P. 304 Succ. S, Montreal Quebec H4E 4J8 **Canada**. (514)769-9096. Promotion Director: Ginette Provost. Record company. Estab. 1986. Releases 1 12″ single and 1 cassette/year. Receives 100 submissions per year. Works with musicians/artists on contract and hires musicians for in-house studio work. Pays statutory rate to publishers per song on records.
How to Contact: Write. Prefers cassette or VHS videocassette with 3 songs and lyric sheet. SASE. Reports in 1 month.
Music: Mostly rock and blues; also instrumental and heavy metal. Released "Brulee Parle Blues" (by Fee Ross), recorded by Nosferatu (blues/rock); "Hollywood" (by Fee Ross), recorded by Nosferatu (rock); and "Barracuda Blues" (by J.J. LaBlonde), recorded by Nosferatu (blues/rock).
Tips: "Any artist who signs with us must have stage experience."

DOMINO RECORDS, LTD., Ridgewood Park Estates, 222 Tulane St., Garland TX 75043. Contact: Gene or Dea Summers. Public Relations/Artist and Fan Club Coordinator: Steve Summers. Labels include Front Row Records. Record company and music publisher (Silicon Music/BMI). Estab. 1968. Releases 5-6 singles and 2-3 LPs/year. Works with artists and songwriters on contract. Pays negotiable royalties to artists on contract; standard royalty to songwriters on contract.
How to Contact: Prefers cassette (or VHS videocassette) with 1-3 songs. Does not return unsolicited material. SASE. Reports ASAP.
Music: Mostly 50's rock/rockabilly; also country, bluegrass, old-time blues and R&B. Released "The Music of Jerry Lee," by Joe Hardin Brown (country single); "Ready to Ride," (from the HBO Presentation *Backlot*), by Pat Minter (country single); and *Texas Rock and Roll* and *Gene Summers Live In Scandinavia*, by Gene Summers (50's LPs). Also *Gene Summers In Nashville* and *Early Rockin' Recordings* by Gene Summers (both are 50s LPs).
Tips: "If you own masters of 1950s rock and rock-a-billy, contact us first! We will work with you on a percentage basis for overseas release. We have active releases in Holland, Switzerland, Belgium, Australia, England, France, Sweden, Norway and the US at the present. We need original masters. You must be able to prove ownership of tapes before we can accept a deal. We're looking for little-known, obscure recordings. We have the market if you have the tapes! Sample records available. Send SASE for catalogue."

DUPUY RECORDS/PRODUCTIONS/PUBLISHING, INC., 2505 North Verdugo Rd., Glendale CA 91208. (818)241-6732. President: Pedro Dupuy. Record company, record producer and music publisher (Dupuy Publishing, Inc./ASCAP). Releases 5 singles and 3 LPs/year. Works with artists and songwriters on contract; musicians on salary for in-house studio work. Pays negotiable rate to publishers for each record sold.

How to Contact: Write or call first or arrange personal interview. Prefers cassette with 2-4 songs and lyric sheet. SASE. Reports in 1 month.
Music: Easy listening, jazz, MOR, R&B, soul and top 40/pop. Artists include Joe Warner, John Anthony, Robert Feeney, Jon Rider and Kimo Kane.
Tips: Needs "very definite lyrics with hook."

*E.S.R. RECORDS, 61 Burnthouse Lane, Exeter Devon EX2 6AZ U.K.. Phone: (0392)57880. M.D: John Greenslade. Labels include E.S.R. Label. Record company (P.R.S.) and record producer (E.S.R. Productions). Estab. 1965. Releases 4 singles and 10 LPs/year. Works with musicians on salary for in-house studio work. Pays standard royalty; statutory rate to publisher per song on records.
How to Contact: Submit demo tape by mail. Unsolicited submissions are OK. Prefers cassette with 4 songs and lyric sheet. SASE. Reports in 1 month.
Music: Mostly country and MOR. Released "The Best Is Yet To Come" (by John Greenslade), recorded by Marty Henry (country single); "Tomorrow" (by John Greenslade), recorded by Mascarade (MOR); and "A Kind Of Loving" (by T. Jennings), recorded by Mike Scott (MOR), all on E.S.R. Records.

*EAST COAST RECORDS INC., 604 Glover Dr., Runnemede NJ 08078. (609)931-8389. President: Anthony J. Messina. Record company and music publisher. Releases 10 singles and 3 LPs/year. Works with artists and songwriters on contract. Pays 4-7% royalty to artists on contract; standard royalty to songwriters on contract.
How to Contact: Prefers 7½ ips reel-to-reel or cassette with 3-12 songs and lyric sheet. SASE. Reports in 3 weeks.
Music: Classical, MOR, rock, and top 40/pop. Released "Remembering," by Lana Cantrell (MOR single); "Drifting Away," by Uproar (rock single); and *England Made Me* (soundtrack from the motion picture), by London Philharmonic (classical LP). Other artists include Lynn Redgrave, Harold Melvin & The Bluenotes, Dakota and Aviator.

ELEMENT RECORD(S), Box 30260, Bakersfield CA 93385-1260. President: Judge A. Robertson. Record company. Estab. 1978. Releases 5 singles and 5 EPs/year. Works with musicians/artists on contract. Pays standard royalty.
How to Contact: Write first to arrange personal interview. Prefers cassette with 1 or more songs and lyric sheet.
Music: All types. Released "I'll Like You The Way You Are" written and recorded by Jar The Superstar (funk); "God They May Not Love You," by Judge A. Robertson (gospel); and "Spirits of Truth," by Jar The Superstar (Christian pop).

*EMOTIVE RECORDS, Ste. 615, 160 5th Ave., New York NY 10010. (212)645-7330. Vice President: Josh DeRienzis. Record company. Estab. 1989. Releases 4 12″ singles/year. Works with musicians/artists on record contract. Pays 7-12% royalty to artists on contract; statutory rate to publisher per song on record.
How to Contact: Submit demo tape by mail. Unsolicited submissions are OK. Prefers cassette. Does not return unsolicited material.
Music: Mostly dance, club and house; also industrial. Released "Feel the Vibe" (by L. Gomez), recorded by Louie Lou; "Get On the Move" (by Maude), recorded by Maude; and "Work It Out" (by T. Bey), recorded by Together Bros., all on Emotive Records (12″ singles). Other artists include Joe Smooth, On Point.
Tips: "Looking for club music similar to what's on *Billboard's* dance charts."

*EMPTY SKY RECORDS, P.O. Box 626, Verplanck NY 10596. Producer/Manager: Rick Carbone. Labels include Empty Sky, Verplanck, Yankee Records. Record company, music publisher (ASCAP and BMI) and record producer (Rick Carbone-Empty Sky). Estab. 1982. Releases 15-20 singles, 2 12″ singles, 2 LPs, 1 EP and 1 CD/year. Works with musicians/artists and songwriters on contract. Pays 8-10% royalty to artists on contract; statutory rate to publisher per song on record.
How to Contact: Submit demo tape by mail. Unsolicited submissions are OK. Prefers cassette with 3-5 songs and lyric sheet. SASE. Reports in 2-3 months.
Music: Mostly country, gospel and pop; also rap, rock and rap/gospel. Released "The Bowling Ball" (by Carl Becker), recorded by GutterBall Band on Empty Sky Records (pop single); "I Wanna Be In NY City" (by M. LaJiness, R. Sanders), recorded by Ray Sanders on Yankee Records (rock single); and "White Water" (by Eleanor Aldridge), recorded by Phil Coley on Verplanck Records (country single). Other artists include The Dependents, The Sweetarts, Bosco, The Sack Dance Band, True Blue, Wylie Justice, Leo Stephens and Denny and Ray.

ESB RECORDS, P.O. Box 6429, Huntington Beach CA 92615-6429. (714)962-5618. Executive Producers: Eva and Stan Bonn. Record company, music publisher (Bonnfire Publishing/ASCAP, Gather' Round/BMI), record producer (ESB Records). Estab. 1987. Releases one 1 single, 1 LP and 1 CD/ year. Receives 20 submissions/month. Works with musicians/artists and songwriters on contract. Pays negotiable royalty to artists; pays statutory rate to publisher per song on record.
How to Contact: Call first. Does not return unsolicited material. Reports in one month.
Music: Mostly country, country/pop, MOR/country; also gospel. Released "It's So Nice To See You Again" (by Bobby Lee Caldwell), "Don't Watch Me Fall Apart" (by Bobby Lee Caldwell) and "She's a Dance Hall Lady" (by Nancy Cyril/Eva Bonn); all recorded by Bobby Lee Caldwell on ESB Records (country).
Tips: "Studio demos preferred."

ETIQUETTE/SUSPICIOUS RECORDS, 2442 N.W. Market #273, Seattle WA 98107. (206)524-1020; FAX: (206)524-1102. President: Buck Ormsby. Labels include Etiquette Records and Suspicious Records. Record company and music publisher (see Valet Publishing). Estab. 1962. Releases 2-3 LPs and 2-3 CDs/year. Receives 300-900 submissions/year. Works with musicians/artists and songwriters on contract. Pays varying royalty to artists on contract. Pays statutory or negotiated rate to publisher per song on record.
How to Contact: Prefers cassette or VHS videocassette with 3-4 songs and lyric sheets. SASE. Reports in 1 month.
Music: Mostly R&B, rock and pop; also country. Released *Crazy 'Bout You* (by Roger Rogers), recorded by Kinetics on Etiquette Records (rock cassette). Other artists include Kent Morrill and Jerry Roslie.
Tips: "Tapes submitted should be top quality—lyric sheets professional."

*EXCURSION RECORDS, P.O. Box 1170, Livermore CA 94551-1170. (415)373-6477. President: Frank T. Prins. Labels include Echappee Records. Record company, music publisher. ASCAP, BMI. Record producer (Frank T. Prins). Estab. 1982. Releases 2-5 singles, 1 LP and 1 EP/year. Works with musicians/artists and songwriters on contract. Pays 5-6% royalty to artists on contract; statutory rate to publisher per song on record.
How to Contact: Write or call first and obtain permission to submit. Prefers cassette (or VHS videocassette if available) with 3 songs and lyric sheet and lead sheet. SASE. Reports in 2 weeks.
Music: Mostly pop, rock and country; also gospel and R&B. Released "Fine, Fine, Fine" (by M. Deradoorian), recorded by The Fabulous Flames (R&B single); "Mississippi Nights" (by Tim Barnes), recorded by The Fabulous Flames (rock single); and "Katrina" (by Robert Hepfner), recorded by Bobby C (country single), all on Excursion Records. Other artists include Bobby C, Tim Patrick and Destiny.

EXECUTIVE RECORDS, 18 Harvest Lane, Charlotte NC 28210. (704)554-1162. Executive Producer: Butch Kelly Montgomery. Labels include KAM, Executive and Fresh Avenue Records. Record company, record producer (Butch Kelly Productions), music publisher (Butch Kelly Publishing/BMI and Music by Butch Kelly/BMI) and songwriter. Member AGAC. Estab. 1982. Releases 10 singles, 7 12″ singles, 3 LPs and 1 CD/year. Receives 100 submissions/year. Works with musicians/artists songwriters on contract; hires musicians for in-house studio work. Pays 50% to artists on contract; statutory rate to publishers for each record sold. "$10 consulting fee."
How to Contact: Prefers cassette "on Maxell UDS-II tapes only" (or videocassette) with 3 songs and lyric sheet, pictures and bio. SASE. Submit pictures with demo. Reports in 2 months.
Music: Mostly R&B, pop dance, rock, top 40, rap and country. Released "War" (by TK), recorded by McCrush (pop); "Power" (by Butch Kelly), recorded by Sunshine (R&B); and "Money," written and recorded by Greg B. (R&B); all on KAM Records.

*EYE KILL RECORDS, Box 242, Woodland PA 16881. A&R: John Wesley. Record company and music publisher (Eye Kill/ASCAP). Estab. 1987. Releases 4 singles, 6 12″ singles, 10 LPs, 10 EPs and 10 CDs/year. Works with songwriters on contract. Pays statutory rate to publisher per song on record.
How to Contact: Submit demo tape by mail. Unsolicited submissions are OK. Prefers cassette with 3 songs and lyric sheets. SASE. Reports in 3 weeks.
Music: Mostly country and rock; also southern rock. Released "JC Carr," written and recorded by Lori Gator (country); "So Far Away," written and recorded by Lori Gator (country); and "Helpless," written and recorded by RJ Walli (country); all on Eyekill Records.
Tips: "Send good clean cassettes of your best three songs."

FACTORY BEAT RECORDS, INC., 521 5th Ave., New York NY 10175. (212)757-3638. A&R Director: Rena L. Romano. Labels include R&R, Ren Rom and Can Scor Productions, Inc. Record company, record producer and music publisher (Ren-Maur Music Corp.). Member NARAS, BMI and Songwriters Guild. Releases 4 12" singles and 2 LPs/year. Works with musicians/artists and songwriters on contract; hires musicians for in-house studio work. Pays 4-12% royalty to artists on contract; statutory rate to publishers for each record sold.

How to Contact: Submit cassette with 4 songs and lead sheet. SASE. Reports in 1 month. "Do not phone—we will return material."

Music: Mostly R&B, pop rock and country; also gospel. Released "That's Hot" (by B. Nichols) and "Rise Up" (by B. Nichols/R. Feeney), both recorded by Rena on Factory Beat Records (12" singles).

FAME AND FORTUNE ENTERPRISES, P.O. Box 121679, Nashville TN 37212. (615)244-4898. Producer: Jim Cartwright or Scott Turner. Labels include National Foundation Records and Fame and Fortune Records. Record company, music publisher (Boff Board Music/BMI) and record producer. Estab. 1976. Releases 6 singles, 6 LPs and 6 CDs/year. Receives 200-400 submissions/month. Works with musicians/artists and songwriters on contract. Pays statutory rate to publishers per song on records. Charges for "production services on recordings sessions."

How to Contact: Submit demo tape by mail. Unsolicited submissions are OK. Prefers cassette or VHS videocassette with 4 songs and lyric sheet. SASE. Reports in 3 weeks.

Music: Mostly country, MOR, med. rock, and pop. Released "I Can Be Tempted" (by George Wurzbach/Hank Bones) recorded by Teresa Dalton (country blues R&B); "When Blondes Go Bad" (by Don Kennedy) recorded by Johnny Hernandez (pop/dance); and "Love Enough" (by Anthony Cirillo) (pop), all on Fame & Fortune Records. Other artists include Angel Connell, Teresa Dalton, Paulette Tyler, Robert Wood and Mary James.

FAMOUS DOOR RECORDS, 1A-1 Estate St. Peter, St. Thomas USVI 00802. (809)775-7428. Contact: Harry Lim. Record company. Member NARAS. Releases 6 LPs/year. Works with artists on contract. Pays 5% in royalty to artists on contract; statutory rate to publishers for each record sold.

How to Contact: Write first. Prefers cassette with minimum 3 songs. Prefers studio produced demos. SASE. Reports in 1 month.

Music: Jazz. Released *L.A. After Dark*, by Ross Tomkins Quartet; *More Miles and More Standards*, by the Butch Miles Sextet; and *Buenos Aires New York Swing Connections*, by George Anders Sextet.

Tips: Looking for "good instrumentals."

*FASCINATION ENTERTAINMENT, Ste. #205, 17939 Chatsworth, Granada Hills CA 91344. (818)360-7111. President: Rick Greenhead. Vice President: Bob Bruning. Record company and music publisher (Fas-Ent Music/ASCAP). Estab. 1987. Releases 3 LPS/year. Works with musicians/artists and songwriters on contract and hires musicians for in-house studio work. Pays 5-50% royalty to artists on contract; statutory rate to publisher per song on record.

How to Contact: Submit demo tape by mail. Unsolicited submissions are OK. Prefers cassette with 3 songs and lyric sheet. SASE. Reports in 1 month.

Music: Mostly children's, film and TV. Released *Unicorn Dreams* (by various artists), recorded by Christina Veronica; *Suzanne McSwanson* (by various artists), recorded by Suzanne McSwanson; and *Pat Flanakin*, written and recorded by Pat Flanakin; all on Fascination Entertainment Records (children's LPs). Other artists include Mark Moulin, Paul Hobbs, Bob Bruning, John Hoke, Sam Libraty, and Debbie Clemmer.

Tips: "Optimism, enthusiasm, determination, tempered with a grasp of reality are qualities shared by all our artists."

FINER ARTS RECORDS/TRANSWORLD RECORDS, 2170 S. Parker Rd., Denver CO 80231. President: R.J. Bernstein. Record company, music publisher (M. Bernstein Music Publishing Co.) and record producer. Estab. 1960. Releases 6 singles, 3 LPs and 2 CDs/year. Receives 100 submissions/month. Works with musicians/artists and songwriters on contract; musicians on salary for in-house studio work. Pays artists on contract 5-7% per record sold.

How to Contact: Write first and obtain permission to submit. Prefers cassette (or VHS videocassette) and lyric sheet or lead sheet. Reports in 3 weeks. "Please no telephone calls."

Music: Mostly interested in R&B, pop and rap. Also interested in jazz and country.

FIRST TIME RECORDS, Sovereign House, 12 Trewartha Rd., Praa Sands, Penzance, Cornwall TR20 9ST **England.** Phone (0736)762826. FAX: (0736)763328. Managing Director A&R: Roderick G. Jones. Labels include Pure Gold Records, Rainy Day Records, Mohock Records and First Time Records. Record company and music publisher (First Time Music Publishing U.K. Ltd./MCPS/PRS), and record producer (First Time Management & Production Co.). Estab. 1986. Works with musicians/artists and songwriters on contract; hires musicians for in-house studio work and as commissioned. Royalty to artists on contract varies; pays statutory rate to publishers per song on record subject to deal.

How to Contact: Prefers cassette with unlimited number of songs and lyric or lead sheets, but not necessary. SAE and IRC. Reports in 1-3 months.
Music: Mostly country/folk, pop/soul/top 20, country with an Irish/Scottish crossover; also gospel/Christian and HI NRG/dance. Released "Songwriters and Artistes Compilation Volume III," on Rainy Day Records; "The Drums of Childhood Dreams," (by Pete Arnold), recorded by Pete Arnold on Mohock Records (folk) and *The Light and Shade of Eddie Blackstone* (by Eddie Blackstone), recorded by Eddie Blackstone on Digimix International Records (country).
Tips: "Writers should learn patience, tolerance and understanding of how the music industry works, and should present themselves and their product in a professional manner and always be polite. Listen always to constructive criticism and learn from the advice of people who have a track record in the music business. Your first impression may be the only chance you get, so it is advisable to get it right from the start."

JOHN FISHER & ASSOCIATES, Suite 201, 1300 Division St., Nashville TN 37203. (615)256-3616. President: John Fisher. Labels include Player International, Crusader, Gold Country and Pulsation. Record company, music publisher and record producer. Releases 2 singles and 1 LP/year. Works with musicians/artists on contract.
How to Contact: Prefers cassette with up to 6 songs and lyric or lead sheets. SASE. Reports in 2 weeks.
Music: Mostly country, 50s rock and blues; also rock-a-billy. Artists include Terry Stafford, Steve Ricks, Henson Cargill, Ray Peterson and Webb Pierce.

*FLAMING STAR WEST, P.O. Box 2400, Gardnerville NV 89410. (702)265-6825. Owner: Ted Snyder. Record company (Flaming Star Records) and record producer. BMI. Estab. 1988. Works with composers and lyricists; teams collaborators. Pays standard royalty.
How to Contact: Submit a demo tape by mail—unsolicited submissions are O.K. Prefers cassette or VHS videocassette with up to 5 songs and lyric sheets. "If you are sure of your music, you may send more than 5 songs. No heavy metal. All other types." SASE. Reports in 3 weeks.
Music: Mostly country, pop and rock and country rock; also gospel, R&B, and calypso. Published "Jezabel" (country rock) and "For the Sake of My Children" (ballad) both written and recorded by Ted Snyder on Flaming Star Records.
Tips: "Listen to what is on the radio, but be original. Put feeling into your songs. We're looking for songs and artists to promote overseas. If you have 45 records or masters we may be interested. We have a juke box program where we can sell your 45s. If you need your record produced we may be able to help. Flaming Star Records is a launching pad for the new recording artist. We try to help where we can."

*FLYING FISH RECORDS, INC., 1304 W. Schubert, Chicago IL 60614. (312)528-5455. A&R Assistant: J. Seymour Guenther. Record company and music publisher (Flying Fish Music/BMI, Swimming Bird Music/ASCAP). Estab. 1974. Releases 35-40 LPs and 35-40 CDs/year. Works with musicians/artists on contract. Pays "up to statutory" rate to artists on contract and to publisher per song on record.
How to Contact: Write first and obtain permission to submit. Prefers cassette with 3-5 songs. Reports in 6 months.
Music: Mostly folk, bluegrass and country; also blues, gospel and Latin.

FLYING HEART RECORDS, 4026 NE 12th Ave., Portland OR 97212. (503)287-8045. Owner: Jan Celt. Labels include Flying Heart Records. Record company. Estab. 1982. Releases 2 LPs and 1 EP/year. Works with musicians/artists and songwriters on contract and hires musicians for in-house studio work. Pays 2-10% royalty to artists on contract; negotiable rate to publisher per song on record.
How to Contact: Submit a demo tape by mail. Unsolicited submissions are okay. Prefers cassette with 1-10 songs and lyric sheets. Does not return unsolicited material. Reports in 3 months.
Music; Mostly R&B, blues and jazz; also rock. Released "Get Movin" (by Chris Newman), recorded by Napalm Beach (rock); "Down Mexico Way" (by Chris Newman), recorded by Napalm Beach (rock); and "Which One Of You People" (by Jan Celt), recorded by The Esquires (R&B); all on Flying Heart Records. Other artists include Janice Scroggins, Tom McFarland and Obo Addy.
Tips: "Express your true feelings with creative originality and show some imagination."

FM-REVOLVER RECORDS LTD., 152 Goldthorn Hill, Wolverhampton WV23JA **England.** (902)345345. A&R Director: David Roberts. Labels include Heavy Metal Records, Heavy Metal America, Heavy Metal Worldwide, Revolver Records, Black, and FM Dance. Record company, music publisher (Rocksong Music Publishing Ltd./PRS). Estab. 1980. Releases 5 singles, 5 12″ singles, 20 LPs, 5 EPs and 20 CDs. Works with musicians/artists and songwriters on contract; also licenses masters. Pays 8-16% royalty to artists on contract; statutory rate to publisher per song on record.

How to Contact: Submit demo tape by mail. Prefers cassette with 4 songs. SASE. Reports in 4 weeks.
Music: Mostly AOR, alternative rock, hard rock, heavy metal, and rock. Released *Sally Cinamon* (by Squire/Brown), recorded by The Stone Roses on Black Records (indie pop); *Pure Sex* (by Bomb), recorded by Adam Bomb on FM Records (hard rock) and *Radar Love* (by Band), recorded by Golden Earring on FM Records (rock). Other artists include Vibrators, Torino, Lisa Dominique, MaccLads, Cloven Hoof and White Sister.

FOUNTAIN RECORDS, 1203 Biltmore Ave., High Point NC 27260. (919)882-9990. President: Doris W. Lindsay. Record company, music publisher (Better Times Publishing-BMI, Doris Lindsay Pub.-ASCAP) and record producer. Estab. 1979. Releases 3 singles and 1 LP/year. Works with musicians/artists and songwriters on contract. Pays 5% royalty to artists on contract; statutory rate to publishers per song on record.
How to Contact: Write first and obtain permission to submit. Prefers cassette with 2 songs and lyric sheets. SASE. Reports in 2 months.
Music: Mostly country, pop and gospel. Released "Right Smack Dab in the Middle of Love" (by P.A. Hanna), recorded by Pat Repose; "Sweet Baby" (by P.A. Hanna), recorded by Tim Sloan; and "Two Lane Life" (by D. Lindsay), recorded by Mitch Snow; all on Fountain Records (country). Other artists include Tom Powers, J.R. Bevers, George Pickard and Lisa De Lucca.
Tips: "Send a well recorded demo. Do not send more than 2 songs per submission. I prefer up tempo and positive, clean lyrics."

FRANNE RECORDS, Box 8135, Chicago IL 60680. (312)224-5612. A&R Director/Executive Producer: R.C. Hillsman. Labels include Superbe Records. Record company, music publisher and producer. Pays 3½% royalty to artists and songwriters on contract.
How to Contact: Write or call to arrange personal interview. Prefers 7½ or 15 ips ¼" reel-to-reel or cassette with 4-6 songs (or videocassette) and lyric sheet. Send material "by registered mail only." SASE. Reports in 3 weeks.
Music: Church/religious, country, disco, gospel, jazz, MOR, rock and top 40/pop. Released "He's Love" and "You Better Get Right," by Allen Duo (gospel singles).

*FREKO RECORDS, 417 E. Cross Timbers, Houston TX 77022. (713)694-2971. Engineer/Producer: Freddie Kober. Labels include HoneyBee Records and Freko Records. Record company, music publisher (Anode Music/BMI) and record producer (Freddie Kober Productions). Estab. 1976. Releases 6 singles, 2 12" singles and 3 LPs/year. Works with musicians/artists and songwriters on contract.
How to Contact: Submit demo tape by mail. Unsolicited submissions are OK. Prefers cassette with 4-8 songs and lyric sheet. Does not return unsolicited material.
Music: Mostly R&B, rap and gospel; also country, rock and pop. Released "Aggravated Assult" (by Otis Berry), recorded by Aggravated Assult; *Mohagany's First* (by Warren Jackson), recorded by Mahongany; "It's Time to Chill" (by Tron Washington), recorded by Tron; all on Freko Records (rap). Other artists include Chateau Lynch and Boss Man.

FRESH ENTERTAINMENT, Ste. 5, 1315 Simpson Rd. NW, Atlanta GA 30351. (404)642-2645. Vice President, Marketing/A&R: Willie Hunter. Record company and music publisher (Hserf Music/ASCAP). Releases 5 singles and 2 LPs/year. Works with musicians/artists and songwriters on contract. Pays standard royalty to artists on contract.
How to Contact: Prefers cassette (or VHS videocassette) with at least 3 songs and lyric sheet. SASE. Reports in 2 weeks.
Music: Mostly R&B, rock and pop; also jazz, gospel and rap. Released "Girls with Me," written and recorded by Ede' (pop single); "Tell the Story" (by W. Gates), recorded by J. Gates (dance 12" single); and "Love to Live" (by F. McKinney/B. James), recorded by Heart to Heart (R&B 12" single), all on Fresh Records. Other artists include Sir Anthony with Rare Quality, and Larion.
Tips: "We're a new label looking for new ideas and acts."

FUTURE STEP SIRKLE RECORDS, P.O. Box 2095, Philadelphia PA 19103. (215)848-7475. Vice President: S. Deane Henderson. A&R: Sonny Knight. Labels include FSS Records. Record company, record producer, music publisher (Communciation Concept) and management firm. Releases 6-10 singles and 3-6 LPs/year. Works with artists and songwriters on contract. Pays 4-10% royalty to artists on contract; statutory rate to publishers for each record sold.
How to Contact: Prefers cassette (or VHS videocassette) with 4-8 songs and lyric sheet. "Lyrics only are returned." Reports in 2 weeks. "No phone calls are necessary."
Music: Mostly R&B, funk, rock and heavy metal; also dance-oriented, easy listening, gospel, MOR, soul and top 40/pop. Released *In God's Hands*, by Verdell; *Save Me Jesus*, by Offspring Gospel (gospel LP); and "Exercise," by M.O.F. (dance single). Other artists include Dean Morrow and William K. Hall, Jr. (Natural Vibes).

*G FINE RECORDS, P.O. Box 180 Cooper Station, New York NY 10276. (212)995-1608. President: P. Fine. Record company, music publisher (Rap Alliance) and record producer (Lyvio G.). Estab. 1986. Works with musicians/artists on contract. Pays 7-12% royalty to artists on contract; statutory rate to publisher per song on record. ·

How to Contact: Submit demo tape by mail. Unsolicited submissions are OK. Prefers cassette. Include SASE for return of tape.

Music: Mostly rap, R&B, progressive rock and dance.

GALLERY II RECORDS, INC., P.O. Box 630755, Miami FL 33163. (305)935-4880. President: Jack Gale. Labels include Playback, Ridgewood and Caramba Records. Record company, music publisher (Lovey Music/BMI, Cowabonga Music/ASCAP). and record producer. Estab. 1983. Releases 25 singles, 6 LPs and 12 CDs/year. Receives 200 submissions/year. Works with musicians/artists and songwriters on contract and hires musicians for in-house studio work. Pays statutory rate to publishers per song on record.

How to Contact: Submit demo tape by mail. Unsolicited submissions are OK. Prefers cassette (or VHS videocassette) with 2 songs and lyric sheet. Reports in 1 week "if interested."

Music: Mostly contemporary country and traditional country. Released "Hundred Proof Woman" (by Lynne Thomas), recorded by Whiskey Creek on Gallery II Records; "Free" written and recorded by Jeannie C. Riley on Playback Records; and "Thoughts on the Flag" (by Tom T. Hall), recorded by Tommy Cash on Playback Records (all country). Other artists include Jim Newberry, Sammi Smith, Del Reeves, Eddie Carpenter, Margo Smith, Kitty Wells, Mickey Rooney, Lynn Thomas, Dennis Yost and the Classics IV and Bobby Bare.

Tips: "Have determination, be realistic; have a clear demo."

GATEWAY, 4960 Timbercrest, Canfield OH 44406. (216)533-9024. President: A. Conti. Labels include Endive. Record company, music publisher (Ashleycon, BMI), and record producer. Estab. 1987. Releases 6 singles and 3 cassettes/year. Receives 6-8 submissions/month. Works with musicians/artists and songwriters on contract. Pays 1-7% royalty to artists on contract; statutory and negotiable rate to publisher per song on record.

How to Contact: Submit demo tape by mail. Prefers cassette with 3 songs and lyric sheets. Reports in 6 weeks.

Music: Mostly new algorithmic, computer generated, organized sound. Released "Communications I," (by A. Conti), on Endive Records (algorithmic); "Can-Can-Canfield" (by A. Conti), on Endive Records (amerothrust); "Thank You Cows" (by M. Eckert), recorded by Artboyz on Endive Records (amerothrust); and "Busy Business" (by A. Conti) on Endive Records (Incan). Other artists include Compose, Ada Vice, and Tootsweet.

GENLYD GRAMMOFON ApS, Haraldsgade 23, 8260 Viby J **Denmark**. Contact: A&R Director. Record company, music publisher (Genlyd Publishing, NCB/Denmark) and record producer (Genlyd Grammofon ApS.) Estab. 1975. Works with musicians/artists on contract and also licenses foreign companies.

How to Contact: Submit demo tape by mail. Unsolicited submissions are OK. Prefers cassette with 1-3 songs and lyric sheets. SAE and IRC. Reports in 4 weeks.

Music: Mostly R&B, rock, pop and country. Artists include Gnags, Sos Fenger, Arvid, Thomas Helmig, and Henning Staerk. Released *Even Cowgirls*, by SOS Fenger (C&W); *Cheque Book*, by Henning Staerk (rock) and *I Don't Mind* by Henning Staerk.

Tips: "Being a Danish/Scandinavian label we are from time to time in need of experienced lyricists capable of working with highly successful local acts on English versions of local hits. That should, however, not prevent songwriters from getting in touch, since we are always interested in good songs for those of our acts who don't write their own material."

GET WIT IT PRODUCTION RECORDS, Mott Haven Station, Box 986, Bronx NY 10454. (212)292-8104. Executive Producer: Eddie Rivera. Labels include Get Wit It Production Records. Record company (G.W.I.P Records/ASCAP) and record producer (G.W.I.P Records). Estab. 1988. Releases 3 12" singles, 2 LPs, 3 EPs, and 2 CDs/year. Receives 400-500 submissions/year. Works with musicians/artists on contract. Pays 7% royalty to artists on contract; statutory rate to publisher per song on record.

How to Contact: Submit demo tape by mail. Unsolicited submissions are OK. Prefers cassette, 30 ips reel-to-reel or VHS videocassette with song and lyric sheets. Does not return unsolicited material. Reports in 3 weeks.

Music: Mostly R&B, rap and ballads. Released "Let It Rock," "Peace" and "Zion" (by Dwayne/Eddie), recorded by Emperial Brothers on G.W.I.P. Records (rap). "Also released on G.W.I.P. Records in 1991 include an explosive educational rap album by "The Emperial Brothers" titled *Coming Out Strong*."

Tips: "The quickest way to get our A&R director's attention is to prepare your demo the way you think the public would most accept your production. We focus and work on the artist's interest if we feel your style has potential."

*THE GHETTO RECORDING COMPANY, 1, Star St., Paddington, London W2 1QD **England.** (071)258-0093. A&R Department: Paul Kinder. Record company. Estab. 1987. Releases 10 singles, 10 12" singles, 4 LPs and 4 CDs/year. Works with musicians/artists on record contract. Pays statutory rate.
How to Contact: Submit demo tape by mail. Unsolicited submissions are OK. Prefers cassette with 3 songs. SASE. Reports in 4 weeks.
Music: Mostly pop/rock. Released "Pure" (by Ian Broudie), recorded by Lightening Seeds; "I Know You Well" (by Michael Head), recorded by Shack; and "You Used To" (by Edwards/Fitzpatrick), recorded by Distant Cousins; all on Ghetto Records (pop singles). Other artists include The Dave Howard Singers and Kev Hopper.

GLOBAL RECORD CO., P.O. Box 396, 133 Arbutus Ave., Manistique MI 49854-0396. President: Reg B. Christansen. Labels include Bakersfield Record Company. Record company and music publisher (Chris Music/BMI and Sara Lee Music/BMI). Estab. 1956. Releases 20-40 singles and 5 CDs/year. Works with artists and songwriters on contract. Pays 10-20% royalty to artists on contract; statutory rate to publishers for each record sold.
How to Contact: Prefers cassette with 3 songs and lyric sheet. SASE. Reports in 1 month.
Music: Mostly top 40, R&B, country, MOR, rock, and novelty types. Released "Burning Flame" and "The Man Upstairs," both written and recorded by Helen Debaker on Bakersfield Records (country/western); and "End of the Line" and "Don't You Cry," both written and recorded by Destiny Group on Global Records (rock).
Tips: "Send us clean, technically correct tapes—a single guitar, a single piano accompaniment is very fine."

GOLD CASTLE RECORDS, Ste. 470, 3575 Cahuenga Blvd., West, Los Angeles CA 90068. (213)850-3321. President: Paula Jeffries. Record company. Estab. 1986. Releases 10 singles, 12 LPs and 12 CDs/year. Works with musicians/artists and songwriters on contract.
How to Contact: Write first and obtain permission to submit. Prefers cassette. SASE. Reports in 3 months.
Music: Mostly folk, new age/acoustic jazz. Released *Speaking of Dreams*, recorded by Joan Baez (folk LP); *Vanilla*, recorded by Cybill Shepherd (jazz vocal); and *Cardboard Confessional*, recorded by Darius (folk); all on Gold Castle Records. Other artists include Don McLean, Eliza Gilkyson, Eric Andersen, Peter, Paul and Mary, David Hayes, Bruce Cockburn and The Washington Squares.
Tips: "Don't just blindly send a tape. Find out our needs first. The best possible thing would be to submit through a manager, publisher or personal contact with the company. We return all unsolicited tapes!"

GOLD CITY RECORDS, INC., Box 24, Armonk NY 10504. (914)273-6457. President: Chris Jasper. Vice President/General Counsel: Margie Jasper. Labels include Gold City Label (independent distribution and distribution through majors, including CBS). Record company. Estab. 1986. Releases 5-10 singles, 5-10 12" singles, 3-5 LPs and 3-5 CDs/year. Works with musicians/artists and songwriters on contract and hires musicians for in-house studio work. Pays negotiable rate to publisher per song on record.
How to Contact: Submit demo tape by mail. Unsolicited submissions are okay. Prefers cassette with 3 songs and lyric sheets. SASE. Reports in 6 weeks.
Music: Mostly R&B/rap, pop and rock. Released *TimeBomb* and "The First Time," written and recorded by Chris Jasper; and *Vicious & Fresh*, recorded by Liz Hogue; all on Gold City/CBS Records (all R&B/pop).

GOLDBAND RECORDS, Box 1485, Lake Charles LA 70602. (318)439-8839. President: Eddie Shuler. Labels include Folk-Star, Tek, Tic-Toc, Anla, Jador and Luffcin Records. Record company and record producer. Works with artists and songwriters on contract; musicians on salary for in-house studio work. Pays 3-5% royalty to artists on contract; standard royalty to songwriters on contract.
How to Contact: Prefers cassette with 2-6 songs and lyric sheet. SASE. Reports in 2 months.
Music: Blues, country, easy listening, folk, R&B, rock and top 40/pop. Released *Katie Webster Has the Blues* (blues LP) and "Things I Used to Do" (blues single), by Katie Webster; "Waiting For My Child," by Milford Scott (spiritual single); "Gabriel and Madaline," by Johnny Jano (cajun country single); and "Cajun Disco," by the La Salle Sisters (disco single). Other artists incude Jimmy House,

Listings of companies in countries other than the U.S. have the name of the country in boldface type.

John Henry III, Gary Paul Jackson, Junior Booth, Rockin Sidney, Ralph Young, Tedd Dupin, R. Sims, Mike Young and Everett Brady.

GOLDEN BOY RECORDS, 16311 Askin Dr., Pine Mountain Club CA 93222. (805)242-0125. A&R Director: Eddie Gurren. Labels include Golden Boy and Alva. Record company. Releases 6 singles and 2 LPs/year. Works with artists on contract.
How to Contact: Prefers cassette (or videocassette) with maximum 3 songs and lyric sheet. Reports in 3 weeks.
Music: Mostly R&B, urban, dance and soul; also jazz.

GOLDEN TRIANGLE RECORDS, 1051 Saxonburg Blvd., Glenshaw PA 15116. Producer: Sunny James. Labels include Rocken Robin. Record company (Golden Triangle/BMI) and record producer (Sunny James). Estab. 1987. Releases 8 singles, 6 12″ singles, 10 LPs and 19 CDs/year. Receives 5 submissions/ year. Works with musicians/artists and songwriters on contract and hires musicians for in-house studio work. Pays 10% royalty to artists on contract; statutory rate to publishers per song on record.
How to Contact: Submit demo tape by mail. Unsolicited submissions are OK. Prefers cassette, 15 IPS reel-to-reel (or ½″ VHS videocassette) with 3 songs and lyric or lead sheets. Does not return unsolicited material.
Music: Mostly progressive R&B, rock and adult contemporary; also jazz and country. Released "Baby Blue," written and recorded by Fred Johnson; "After You," written and recorded by Fred Johnson; and "Don't Wait for Me" (by Fred Johnson), recorded by The Marcels; all on Golden Triangle Records (7″). Other artists include The original Mr. Bassman Fred Johnson of the Marcels (Blue Moon), Arnel (Elvis) Pomp and Steve Grice (The Boxtops).

GO-ROC-CO-POP RECORDS, 1611 Hickory Valley Rd., Chattanooga TN 37421. (615)899-9685. President: B.J. Keener. Labels include WAR Records. Record company. Estab. 1984. Releases 4-5 singles and 2-5 LPs/year. Works with musicians/artists and songwriters on contract and hires musicians for in-house studio work. Pays standard royalty to artists on contract.
How to Contact: Write first and obtain permission to submit. Prefers cassette with 1-2 songs and lyric and lead sheets. SASE. Reports in 3 months.
Music: Mostly country, gospel and MOR; also jazz, R&B and pop. Released *I Wonder* (by Stan Ramey), recorded by Tim Whalen (pop/cassette); *Tennessee Hills*, written and recorded by Tim Whalen (country/cassette); and *The Child* (by Dick Bell), recorded by Rapture (MOR/cassette); all on Go-Roc-Co-Pop Records. Other artists include LaWanda, Topaz, Joe Cleve, Johnny Sue, Scotty Duran and Billy Joe.
Tips: "Be sincere, hard working and flexible, with a desire to succeed."

GRASS ROOTS RECORD & TAPE/LMI RECORDS, P.O. Box 532, Malibu CA 90265. (213)463-5998. President: Lee Magid. Labels include Grass Roots and LMI Records. Record company, record producer, music publisher (Alexis/ASCAP, Marvelle/BMI, Lou-Lee/BMI) and management firm (Lee Magid Management Co.). Also SESAC. Member AIMP, NARAC. Estab. 1967. Releases 4 LPs and 4 CDs/year. Works with musicians/artists and songwriters on contract. Pays 2-5% royalty to artists on contract; pays statutory rate to publishers per song record.
How to Contact: Prefers cassette with 3 songs and lyric sheet. "Please, no 45s." SASE. Reports in 1 month minimum.
Music: Mostly pop/rock, R&B, country, gospel, jazz/rock and blues; also bluegrass, children's and Latin. Released "What Shall I Do?" (by Quincy Fielding Jr.), "Whenever You Call" (by Calvin Rhone), and "I Got Joy" (by Quincy Fielding Jr.) all recorded by Tremaine Hawkins on Sparrow Records (gospel/R&B).Other artists include Gloria Lynne, L.A. Jazz Choir, Papa John Creach and Kim and Sam.

*GREEN LINNET RECORDS, 43 Beaver Brook Rd., Danbury CT 06810. (203)730-0333. Managing Director: Steve Katz. Record company. Estab. 1978. Releases 16 CDs/year. Works with musicians/ artists on contract. Payment negotiable.
How to Contact: Submit demo tape by mail. Unsolicited submissions are OK. Prefers cassette or VHS videocassette with 3 songs and lyric or lead sheet. Does not return unsolicited material. Reports in 1 month.
Music: Mostly folk. Released *Jane Gillman*, recorded by Jane Gillman; *Red Crow*, recorded by Altan; and *Best of The Tannahill Weavers*, recorded by Tannahill Weavers; all CDs on Green Linnet Records.
Tips: "You must have a very special talent as a musician or writer (or preferably, both)."

GULFSTREAM RECORDS, 4225 Palm St., Baton Rouge LA 70808. (504)383-7885. President: Barrie Edgar. Record company, music publisher (Silverfoot) and record producer (Hogar). Estab. 1980.Works with musicians/artists and songwriters on contract; musicians on salary for in-house studio

work. Pays 3-6% royalty to artists on contract. Pays statutory rate to publishers per song on records.
How to Contact: Prefers cassette with 4 songs and lyric sheet. SASE. "Patience required on reports."
Music: Mostly rock and country. Released "Louisiana's Basin Child," by Top Secret on Gulfstream Records (rock single). Other artists include Joe Costa.

HACIENDA RECORDS, 1236 S. Staples, Corpus Christi TX 78404. (512)882-7066. Owner: Roland Garcia. Producer: Rick Garcia. Labels include Las Brisas. Record company, music publisher (Alpenglow Music, Dark Heart Music, El Palacio Music, Roland Garcia Music) and record producer. Releases 20-100 singles and 5-20 LPs/year. Works with artists and songwriters on contract; musicians on salary for in-house studio work. Pays royalties or per LP to artists on contract.
How to Contact: Prefers cassette. Does not return unsolicited material. Reporting time varies.
Music: Rock, Spanish and country, pop, MOR, international and gospel. Released "Ready as Hell," (by Jim D./Ricky R./Johnny C.), recorded by Jim Dandy's Black Oak Arkansas (rock single & LP), "It's Majic," (by Pio Trevino), recorded by Majic (English single from Spanish LP); and "Ran Kan Kan," (by Tito Puente), recorded by Steve Jordan (Spanish single), all on Hacienda Records. Other artists include Freddy Fender, Romance, Gary Hobbs, Fuego, Janie C., Steve Borth and Rowdy Friends.

*HAPPY MAN RECORDS, 4501 Spring Creek Dr., Box 73, Bonita Springs FL 33923. (813)947-6978. Executive Producer: Dick O'Bitts. Labels include Happy Man, Condor, Con Air. Record company, music publisher (Rocker Music/BMI, Happy Man Music/ASCAP) and record producer (Rainbow Collection Ltd.). Estab. 1972. Releases 4-6 singles, 4-6 12″ singles, 4-6 LPs and 4 EPs/year. Works with musicians/artists and songwriters on contract. Pays statutory rate to publishers per song on records.
How to Contact: Submit demo tape by mail. Unsolicited submissions are OK. Prefers cassette (or VHS videocassette if available) with 3-4 songs and lyric sheet. SASE.
Music: Mostly country. Released "Diamonds and Chills" (by D.N Goodwin/Mary Ann Kennedy); and "Ain't No One Like Me" (by Kevin Thomas), both recorded by Holly Ronick on Happy Man Records (all singles). Other artists include Colt Gipson, Ray Pack and Chris and Lenny.

HARD HAT RECORDS AND CASSETTES, 519 N. Halifax Ave., Daytona Beach FL 32118. (904)252-0381. President: Bobby Lee Cude. Labels include Hard Hat, Maricao, Blue Bandana and Indian Head. Record company, record producer and music publisher (Cude & Pickens Publishing/BMI). Estab. 1978. Releases 12 singles and 12 LPs/year.
How to Contact: Write first. Does not use outside material.
Music: Mostly country; also easy listening, gospel, MOR, top 40/pop and Broadway show. Released "V-A-C-A-T-I-O-N," (by Cude & Pickens) recorded by the Hard Hatters; "Just a Piece of Paper," and "Worried Worried Man," (both by Cude & Pickens) recorded by Blue Bandana Country Band; "Who's Lovin' You" and "Shot In the Dark" by Caz Allen (pop); "Tennessee's On My Mind" and "Texas Red, White and Blue Step" by Caz Allen (country); all are singles on Hard Hat Label. Other artists include "Pic" Pickens, Hula Kings, Caribbean Knights and Cityfolks Country Band.

HARMONY STREET RECORDS, Box 4107, Kansas City, KS 66104. (913)299-2881. President: Charlie Beth. Record company, music publisher (Harmony Street Music/ASCAP and Harmony Lane Music/BMI), and record producer (Harmony Street Productions). Estab. 1985. Releases 15-30 singles and 4-6 LPs/year. Works with musicians/artists and songwriters on contract; musicians on salary for in-house studio work. Pays 10% royalty (retail) to artists on contract; pays statutory rate to publishers per song on record.
How to Contact: Prefers cassette (or VHS videocassette) with no more than 3 songs and lyric or lead sheet. OK for artists to submit album projects, etc., on cassette. Also photo and bio if possible. "Due to the large amount of submissions that we receive we are no longer able to return unsolicited material. We will report within 3 weeks if interested. Please include a full address and telephone number in all submitted packages."
Music: Mostly country (all types) and gospel (all types). Released "The One You've Left Behind" (by John Sullivan, William M. Watson and Sylvia Winters), recorded by Sylvia Winters (country); "Cheatin List" (by John Coburn and Dawn Anita), recorded by Dawn Anita (country); "Rainbows and Roses" (by A. Glenn Duke), recorded by Jeanette Dorel (country); all on Harmony Street Records. Other artists include Terry Allen, J. Ferren, Scott Hansgen, The Harmonettes, Tony Mantor and Dusty Martin.
Tips: "Songs submitted to us must be original, commercial and have a good strong hook. Submit only your best songs. Demos should be clear and clean with voice out front. We are interested in working with commercial artists with a commercial style and sound, professional attitude and career goals. In 1990 Harmony Street Records was nominated in the top five of all Independent record labels in the U.S. and also received a nomination for record single of the year. Our records are released world wide and also available for sales world wide. Our standards are high and so are our goals."

HEART LAND RECORDS, P.O. Box 16572, Kansas City MO 64133. (816)358-2542. Executive Producer: Jimmy Lee. Record company, music publisher (Jellee Works Music/BMI, Jellee Music Works/ASCAP), record producer (Jimmy Lee/Heart Land Records) and Jellee Works Productions—"We do own and operate our own recording studios. We produce demos for songwriters that ask for and need our help." Estab. 1982. Releases 6-8 singles and 4-6 LPs/year. Works with musicians/artists and songwriters on contract and hires musicians for in-house studio work. Pays 10-14% royalty to artists on contract; statutory rate to publisher per song on record.

How to Contact: Write first and obtain permission to submit. Prefers cassette (or VHS videocassette) with no more than 2 songs and lyric sheets. SASE. Reports in 5 weeks.

Music: Mostly country, gospel & pop; some R&B and light rock. Released "Dustin' Off My Dreams" (by Priscilla McCann), recorded by Jackie Cotter (country blues); "It's Almost Christmas (by Ethel Kean Bankston), recorded by Karen Williams (country); and *Footprints* (by Richard Geddes), recorded by Geoff Clark, Max Berry and Jimmy Lee (gospel album), all on Heart Land Records. Other artists include Joe Donovan, Kevin Eason, Geoff Clark and Stephanie Sieggen.

Tips: "Be professional and follow guidelines for submitting material. We put out a newsletter dedicated to teaching and helping songwriters."

HEATH & ASSOCIATES, #1058, E. Saint Catherine, Louisville KY 40204. (502)637-2877. General Partner: John V. Heath. Labels include Hillview Records and Estate Records. Record company, music publisher (Two John's Music/ASCAP), record producer (MTV Productions and Just a Note/BMI). Estab. 1979. Releases 8-10 singles, 3 12″ singles, 4-5 LPs, 3 EPs and 3 CDs/year. Receives 8-12 submissions/month. Works with musicians/artists and songwriters on contract. Pays 5-10% royalty to artists on contract; statutory rate to publisher per song on record.

How to Contact: Submit demo tape by mail. Unsolicited submissions are OK. Prefers cassette, 7½ ips reel-to-reel or VHS videocassette with 3 songs and lead sheets. SASE. Reports in 2 weeks.

Music: Mostly pop, country, R&B and MOR; also gospel. Released "Heartbreak," written and recorded by Johnny Vee on Estate Records (country); "The Train," written and recorded by Whiskers on Estate Records (country); and "Sunshine," written and recorded by Adonis on Hillview Records (rock). Other artists include Artis Steel.

HELION RECORDS, Suite 216, 8306 Wilshire Blvd., Beverly Hills CA 90211. (818)845-2849. Vice President, Record Division: Nick Schepperle. Record company and record producer (Greg Knowles). Estab. 1984. Releases 4 LPs and 4 CDs/year. Works with musicians/artists on contract; hires musicians for in-house studio work. Pays 3-6% royalty to artists on contract; statutory rate to publisher for each record sold.

How to Contact: Prefers cassette with 3-4 songs and lyric or lead sheet. Does not return unsolicited material. Reports in 3 weeks.

Music: Mostly R&B and pop; also country and comedy. Released *Angel* and "Telephone Blues," by Diana Blair; *A Family of Friends* by Country West; a jazz album by Miriam Cutler and Swingstreet and *Groove With Me* by Jan Marie (R&B).

Tips: "Treat your work as a business first and an art form second. You need the business head to get you into the door—then we can see how good your music is."

HOLLYROCK RECORDS, Suite C-300, 16776 Lakeshore Dr., Lake Elisnore CA 92330. A&R Director: Dave Paton. Record company, record producer and music publisher (Heaven Songs/BMI). Releases 4 singles and 6 LPs/year. Works with artists and songwriters on contract; musicians on salary for in-house studio work. Pays negotiable royalty to artists on contract; statutory rate to publishers for each record sold.

How to Contact: Prefers 7½ ips reel-to-reel or cassette with 3-6 songs and lyric sheet. SASE. Reports in 2 weeks.

Music: Progressive, top 40/pop, country, easy listening, folk, jazz, MOR and rock. Released *Everything* (movie soundtrack). Presently working on Linda Rae and Breakheart Pass Album (country), and Gene Mitchener comedy album (sit down comic).

HOTTRAX RECORDS, 1957 Kilburn Dr., Atlanta GA 30324. (404)662-6661. Vice President, A&R: Oliver Cooper. Labels include: Dance-A-Thon, Hardkor. Record company and music publisher (Starfox Publishing). Releases 12 singles and 3-4 LPs/year. Receives 3000-4000 submissions/year. Works with musicians/artists and songwriters on contract. Pays 5-7% royalty to artists on contract.

How to Contact: Prefers cassette with 3 songs and lyric sheet. SASE. "We will not return tapes without adequate postage." Reports in 3 months. "When submissions get extremely heavy, we do not have the time to respond/return material we pass on. We do notify those sending the most promising work we review, however."

Music: Mostly top 40/pop, rock and country; also hard core punk and jazz-fusion. Released *P Is For Pig*, written and recorded by The Pigs (top 40/pop LP); "The World May Not Like Me" (by Mike Fitzgerald), recorded by Mike Angelo (rock single); and *Introducing The Feel*, written and recorded by The Feel (new rock LP) all on Hottrax Records; also "The Condom Man," recorded by Big Al Jano, and "Ms. Perfection," by Larry Yates (urban contemporary). Other artists include Burl Compton (country), Michael Rozakis & Yorgos (pop), Starfoxx (rock), The Night Shadows (rock), The Bop (new wave), and Secret Lover.

*HYSTERIA RECORDS, Arena House 6/9 Salisbury Prom, Green Lanes, London N8 0RX **England**. (081)809-1460. A&R Manager: Nicky Price. Record company. Estab. 1988. Releases 12 singles, 12 12″ singles, 2 LPs and 2 CDs/year. Works with musicians/artists and songwriters on contract and hires musicians for in-house studio work. Pays 1-12% royalty to artists on contract.
How to Contact: Write or call first and obtain permission to submit. Prefers cassette or videocassette with 3 songs and 3 lyric sheets. SASE. Reports in 1 month.
Music: Mostly house/rap, dance house, and funk-soul dance; also New Age and pop. Released "C'Mon and Dance," recorded by Partners Rime Syndicate (house/rap single); "Don't Stop Believing," recorded by Richard Davis (soul single); and "Party On," recorded by System X (dance/house); all on Hysteria Records. Other artists include Enrapture (Feul Jessica George), Urbania and Omaze Isiatic.
Tips: "Try to be as individual as possible but in keeping with today's music."

*IHS RECORDS, 5934 Blairstone Dr., Culver City CA 90230. (213)558-8168. Vice President, General Manager: Leonardo V. Wilborn. Record company. ASCAP/BMI. Estab. 1990. Releases 2 12″ singles and 2 LPs/year. Works with musicians/artists and songwriters on contract. Pays statutory rate to publisher per song on record.
How to Contact: Write first and obtain permission to submit. Prefers cassette or VHS videocassette with 3 songs and lyric sheet. SASE. Reports in 6-8 weeks.
Music: Mostly nu-inspirational, dance/rap and concert; also R&B, gospel and pop. Released "Second Coming" on IHS Records (nu-inspirational); "Righteous" on IHS Records (dance/inspirational); and "Positive Force" on LVW Records (nu-inspirational); all recorded by Federation of Love. Other artists include Daily Bread, Nasa and M.C. Smiley.
Tips: "Be sincere. Stay on top of industry trends. Monitor production schedules."

*I'LL CALL YOU (I.C.Y.) RECORDS, P.O. Box 94, London SWIR 4PH **England**. Phone: (071)834-8337. Managing Director: E. Richard Bickersteth. Labels include I.C.Y. Records and G.N.M.C. Records. Record company. Estab. 1986. Releases 4 LPS and 4 CDs/year. Works with musicians/artists on contract. Pays negotiable royalty to artists on contract; statutory rate to publisher per song on record.
How to Contact: Submit demo tape by mail. Unsolicited submissions are OK. Prefers cassette (or VHS videocassette) with 3 songs and lyric or lead sheets. SAE and IRC. Reports in 2 weeks.
Music: Mostly rock and pop; also blends of music. Released *Aggressive Sunbathing* written and recorded by Fat and Frantic (rock skiffle LP); *The Mystery of The Universe*, written and recorded by The Clarinet Connection (classical rock LP); and *Mind the Gap*, written and recorded by Mind the Gap (pop/gospel LP); all on I.C.Y. Records. Other artists include John Peters and Andy McCullough.
Tips: "A commitment to live performance is vital as well as an interesting fusion of musical styles."

IMAGINARY RECORDS, 332 N. Dean Rd., Auburn AL 36830. (205)821-JASS. Proprietor: Lloyd Townsend, Jr. Record company, music publisher (Imaginary Music), record producer (Mood Swing Productions) and distribution firm (Imaginary Distribution). Estab. 1982. Releases 1-2 singles, 1-2 12″ singles, 1 LP, 1-2 EPs and 2-3 CDs/year. Receives 15-20 submissions/month. Works with musicians/artists and songwriters on contract; "will manufacture custom cassettes for a set price." Pays 10-12% royalty to artists on contract; statutory rate to publisher per song on record.
How to Contact: Prefers cassette or 7½ ips reel-to-reel with 4 songs and lyric or lead sheet. Submissions not returned unless accompanied by SASE. Tapes may be retained for future reference unless return is specifically requested. Reports in 3 months.
Music: Mostly jazz, blues and rock; also classical, folk and spoken word. Released "Violent Romance" (by Bruce Yandle), recorded by Mr. Resistor (rock); "Surfin' Aliens" (Tommy Smeltzer and Tom Royston), recorded by Friction Pigs (60s rock); and "Don't Mess with My Shades" (by Robert Orr and Tim Chambliss), recorded by Kidd Blue and The Blues Kings (R&B); all on Imaginary Records. Other artists include Slow Natives, Kidd Blue, The Moderns, Paul and The Quest, Bone Dali, Nothing Personal, Bob Richardson, Patrick Mahoney, Auburn Knights Orchestra and Yardbird Orchestra.

*INTERSTATE 40 RECORDS, Box 1794, Big Bear City CA 92314. (714)585-4645. President: Eddie Lee Carr. Labels include Tracker Records. Record company and music publisher (Watchesgro Music/BMI and Watch Us Climb/ASCAP). Estab. 1979. Releases 12 singles, 1 LP and 2 CDs/year. Works with musicians/artists on contract. Pays 20% royalty to artists on contract; statutory rate to publisher per song on record.

How to Contact: Submit demo tape by mail. Unsolicited submissions are OK. Prefers cassette with 3 songs. SASE. Reports in 2 weeks.

Music: Mostly country.

INTREPID RECORD, Ste. 1409, 808 Travis, Houston TX 77002. Director of Operations: Rick Eyk. Record company and record producer (Rick Eyk). Recently produced Mary Mazza, The Ink Spots, The Jaguars, Elice Ditmar, Walter Stewart, Little Edward and the G Men.

How to Contact: Prefers cassette (or VHS videocassette) or 7½ ips reel-to-reel with maximum of 7 songs, lyric sheet and bio. SASE. Reports in 1 month.

Music: Mostly rock, new music, country and jazz; also classical and blues. Recently produced Mary Mazza, The Ink Spots, The Jaguars, Elice Ditmar, Walter Stewart, Little Edward and The G Men.

Tips: "Along with your demo, it's nice to have a personal bio which includes some insight into the artist beyond the usual hype."

*IRS RECORDS LTD., Bugle House, 21A Noel St, London W1V 3PD **England**. Phone (671)439-2282. Managing Director: Steven Tannett. Labels include I.R.S. Record Company and Tribe Records. Estab. 1979. Works with musicians/artists on contract.

How to Contact: Submit demo tape by mail. Unsolicited submissions are OK. Prefers cassette (or VHS videocassette if available) with several songs. SASE. Reports in 2 weeks.

Music: Mostly rock/folk, pop and R&B; also dance, rap and house.

ISBA RECORDS, INC., Ste. 607, 18 The Donway East, Don Mills Ontario M3C 1X9 **Canada**. (416)443-8756. A&R: Maurice Velenosi. Record company and record producer. Estab. 1984. Releases 20 singles, 5 12" singles, 10 LPs and 10 CDs/year. Works with musicians/artists on contract. Pays 5-7% royalty to artists on contract; statutory rate to publisher per song on record.

How to Contact: Write first and obtain permission to submit. Prefers cassette (or VHS videocassette) with 3 songs. Does not return unsolicited material. Reports in 4 weeks.

Music: Mostly rock, pop and dance. Released "Conspiracy" (M. Bolton/Halligan), recorded by Paris Black (pop dance); "Secrets" (by Merrick), recorded by HDV (rap); and "Do You Really Love Me," written and recorded by Diodati (dance); all on ISBA Records. Other artists include Robert Sart, Robert Stefan, Robert Leroux, Laymen Twaist, The Bryan Hughes Group, Patsy, Nancy Martinez, Claude de Chevigny, Sylvie Boucher, Mitsou, Les B.B., Collage and Revolver.

J.L.I. RECORDS, Box 74-R, Romeoville IL 60441. (815)886-3929. President: Julian Leal. Record company, music publisher (J.L.I. Music/BMI) and record producer (J.L.I. Productions). Estab. 1984. Releases 1-2 singles, 1 12" single, 2 LPs, 1-2 EPs and 1-2 CDs/year. Works with musicians/artists and songwriters on contract. Pays "standard" royalty to artists on contract. Pays statutory rate to publisher per song on record.

How to Contact: Write first and obtain permission to submit. Prefers cassette (or VHS videocassette) with 3-6 songs. SASE. Reports in 6 weeks.

Music: Mostly rock and pop; also metal. Released "Just a Dream," written and recorded by Julian Leal (pop-rock single); "Little Darling" (by Julian Leal), recorded by The Villains (rock single); and *Forever*, written and recorded by The Villains (rock LP); all on J.L.I. Records. Other artists include The Villains, Fuller Forces, Comfort South, Beatwalker, and Duke Rocky.

Tips: "When writing for permission to submit, please enclose a press-sheet or bio information."

JALYN RECORDING CO., 306 Millwood Dr., Nashville TN 37217. (615)366-9999. President: Jack Lynch. Labels include Nashville Bluegrass and Nashville Country Recording Company. Record company, music publisher (Jaclyn Music/BMI), record producer, film company (Nashville Country Productions) and distributor (Nashville Music Sales). Estab. 1963. Releases 1-12 LPs/year. Works with musicians/artists and songwriters on contract; hires musicians for in-house studio work; also produces custom sessions. Pays 5-10% royalty to artists on contract; statutory rate to publisher per song on record.

How to Contact: Write or call first. Prefers cassette with 1 song and lyric sheet. SASE. Reports in 1 week.

Music: Country, bluegrass, gospel and MOR. Released "I Wonder Why" (by Ray Cline), recorded by Ralph Stanley on Nashville Country Records (bluegrass); "In My Mind" (by Richard Lynch), recorded by Richard Lynch on Nashville Country Records (country) and "Goldmine of Love" (by Lynch & Adkins), recorded by Jack Lynch on Nashville Country Records (bluegrass).Other artists include Ralph Stanley, Dave Evans, Country Gentlemen, Larry Sparks and Benny Williams.

Tips: "We prefer songs with good lyrics that tell a story with a certain amount of rhyming, a good melody sung by a good singer, and as good a production as is feasible. Our biggest need is good, commercial country songs. Send a good quality cassette recording and a neat lyrics sheet, picture and resume, if available."

JAMAKA RECORD CO., 3621 Heath Ln., Mesquite TX 75150. (214)279-5858. Contact: Jimmy Fields. Labels include Felco, and Kick Records. Record producer and music publisher (Cherie Music/BMI). Estab. 1955. Releases 2 singles/year. Works with artists and songwriters on contract; hires musicians for in-house studio work. Works with in-house studio musicians on salary. Pays 5% royalty to artists on contract; statutory rate to publishers for each record sold.
How to Contact: Prefers cassette with songs and lyric sheet. "A new singer should send a good tape with at least 4 strong songs, presumably recorded in a professional studio." Does not return without return postage and proper mailing package. "The post office has written me about returning cassettes in envelopes; they crush, and damage their equipment. I am holding over 5,000 tapes that came without return postage." Reports ASAP.
Music: Country and progressive country. Released "Stand Up For Your Country (And the Color of Your Flag)" (by J. Fields/D. Fields/Kern/Ray), recorded by Ronnie Ray; "Jessie James" and "Let's Save the Memories" (by Curk Ryles), recorded by Ronnie Ray; "Big Iron House" (by George McCoy), recorded by Cliff Price; all on Jamaka Records (modern country). Other artists include Bobby Belev, The Blue Lady, Jim Kern, George McCoy, Lucky LaRue, Bobby Crown, Billy Taylor and Susan Stutts.
Tips: "Songs should have strong lyrics with a good story, whether country or pop."

*JANET MARIE RECORDING, 14016 Evers Ave., Compton CA 90272. President: Robert E. Miles. Labels include Milon Entertainment. Record company, music publisher (BMI) and record producer. Estab. 1988. Works with musicians/artists and songwriters on contract. Pays statutory rate to publishers per song on records.
How to Contact: Submit demo tape by mail. Unsolicited submissions are OK. Prefers cassette (or VHS videocassette if available) with lyric sheet. SASE. Reports in 1 month.

J/L ENTERTAINMENT GROUP, 8730 Sunset Blvd., Los Angeles CA 90069. (213)657-1836. President: Jack Heller. Labels include Crown Records. Produces Japanese songs in English and vice-versa. Estab. 1985. Releases 100 CDs/year. Works with musicians/artists on record contract. Pays 25% royalty to artists on contract. Pays statutory rate to publishers per song on records. Charges for distribution.
How to Contact: Write or call first and obtain permission to submit. SASE. Reports in 1 month.
Music: Rock, R&B and pop.

JOEY BOY RECORDS INC., 3081 N.W. 24th St., Miami FL 33142. (305)635-5588. Contact: Cheryl Randol. Labels include J.R. Records, On Top Records. Record company. Estab. 1985. Releases 50 singles, 50 12″ singles, 15-20 EPs and 15-20 CDs/year. Receives 50-75 submissions/month. Works with musicians/artists on contract. Pays 6% royalty to artists on contract; statutory rate to publisher per song on record.
How to Contact: Write or call first and obtain permission to submit. Prefers cassette with 3 songs and lyric sheets. SASE. Reports in 6 weeks.
Music: Mostly rap and dance; also jazz and comedy. Released "The Dogs," "Disco Rick," and "Success-N-Effect," by A.N.M. Other artists include Eric G. and Bettina.
Tips: "Be creative in your writing and exercise patience in your business dealings."

*JOYFUL SOUND RECORDS, 130 87th Ave. N., St. Petersburg FL 33702. A&R: Mike Douglas. Record company and music publisher (Nite Lite Music/BMI). Releases various number of singles and LPs/year. Receives 6-8 submissions/month.
How to Contact: "When submitting, send a cassette with 3 songs and lyric or lead sheets. Clearly label each item you send with your name and address." SASE. Reports in 21 days.
Music: Children's music and gospel music (no heavy metal gospel).

JUMP RECORDS & MUSIC, Langemunt 71, 9420 Aaigem **Belgium**. Phone: (053)62-73-77. General Manager: Eddy Van Mouffaert. Labels include Jump, Yeah Songs and Flower. Record company, music publisher (Jump Music) and record producer. Estab. 1976. Releases 40 singles, 3 LPs and 1 CD/year. Works with musicians/artists and songwriters on contract. Pays 5% royalty to artists on contract; statutory rate to publisher per song on record.
How to Contact: Prefers cassette. Does not return unsolicited material. Reports in 2 weeks.
Music: Mostly easy listening, disco and light pop; also instrumentals. Released "Laat Je Hart Toch Even Spreken," and "Summer Holiday," written and recorded by Eddy Govert; "First Day of Spring" (by Eddy Govert), recorded by Franky Francis, all on Scorpion Records (all singles). Other artists include Rocky, Le Grand Julot, Eigentijdse Jeugd, Marijn Van Duin, Connie-Linda, Guy Lovely, Tom

Davys, Laurie, Cindy, Patrik, Allan David, Peggy Christy, Aswin, Little Cindy, Sandra More, Dolly, Danny Brendo, Christle Love, Sandra Tempsy, Dick Benson, Angie Halloway and Ricky Morgan.

*JUSTIN TIME RECORDS INC., Suite 101, 5455 Pare, Montreal Quebec H4P 1P7 **Canada**. (514)738-9533. A&R Director: Jean-Pierre Leduc. Labels include Justin Time Records and Just a Memory Records. Record company, music publisher (Justin Time Publishing and Janijam Music/SOCAN) and record producer (Jim West). Estab. 1982. Releases 12 LPs and 12 CDs/year. Works with musicians/artists and songwriters on contract. Pays statutory rate to publisher per song on record.
How to Contact: Submit demo tape by mail. Unsolicited submissions are OK. Prefers cassette (or VHS videocassette if available) with at least 5 songs and lyric sheet. Does not return unsolicited material. Reports in 3 months.
Music: Mostly jazz, blues and gospel; also French pop, comedy and cajun. Released *Northern Summit*, written and recorded by Oliver Jones (jazz CD/MC); *Blues Under A Full Moon* (by Stephen Barry), recorded by Stephen Barry Band (blues CD/MC); and *Montreal Jubilation Gospel Choir* (by various), recorded by M.J.G.C. (gospel CD/MC), all on Justin Time Records.
Tips: "Include a good representation of your work, for example several different styles if applicable. Also, be prepared to *tour* and *promote*."

KAM EXECUTIVE RECORDS, 11 Shady Oak Trail, Charlotte NC 28910. (704)554-1162. Director: Butch Kelly. Labels include Fresh Ave Records, KAM Records, Newtown. Record company (KAM/BMI) and record producer (Butch Kelly Production). Estab. 1981. Releases 5 singles, 5 12″ singles and 10 CDs/year. Works with musicians/artists on contract. Pays 6% royalty to artists on contract. Pays statutory rate.
How to Contact: Write or call first and obtain permission to submit. Prefers cassette (or VHS videocassette) with 3-6 songs and lyric or lead sheets. SASE. Reports in 2 months.
Music: Mostly R&B, pop and rock; also rap and gospel. Released "Waiting" (by Butch Kelly), recorded by A. Brown on KAM Records (R&B); "Miss You" (by Greg Johnston), recorded by Fresh Air on KAM Records (R&B); and "Stumping Blues" (by Kelly Montgomery), on KAM Records (pop). Other artists include The Prep of Rap, Sharon Jordan (R&B), Richard Kirkpatrick (R&B) and Caro (R&B).

KICKING MULE RECORDS, INC., Box 158, Alderpoint CA 95411. (707)926-5312. Head of A&R: Ed Denson. Record company and music publisher (Kicking Mule Publishing/BMI and Desk Drawer Publishing/ASCAP). Member NAIRD. Releases 12 LPs/year. Works with artists on contract. Pays 10-16% royalty to artists on contract; standard royalty to songwriters on contract.
How to Contact: Prefers reel-to-reel or cassette with 3-5 songs. SASE. Reports in 1 month.
Music: Bluegrass, blues and folk. Released *Solo Guitar* by Tom Ball (folk); *Christmas Come Anew* by Maddie MacNeil (folk); and *Cats Like Angels* by Bob Griffin (piano folk). Other artists include Michael Rugg, Neal Hellman, Bert Jansch, John Renbourn, Stefan Grossman, John James, Happy Traum, Fred Sokolow, Bob Stanton, Bob Hadley, Leo Wijnkamp, Jr., Mark Nelson, Lea Nicholson and Hank Sapoznik.
Tips: "We are a label mostly for instrumentalists. The songs are brought to us by the artists but we contract the artists because of their playing, not their songs. First, listen to what we have released and don't send material that is outside our interests. Secondly, learn to play your instrument well. We have little interest in songs or songwriters, but we are quite interested in people who play guitar, banjo, or dulcimer well."

KILGORE RECORDS, INC., 706 West Mechanic St., Leesville LA 71446-3446. (318)239-2850. President: Mr. John E. Kilgore. Labels include Gotown Records and Kilgore Records. Record company, record producer and music publisher (Gotown Publishing Company/BMI). Releases 6 singles/year. Works with artists and songwriters on contract. Pays statutory rate to publishers for each record sold.
How to Contact: Prefers cassette with 2 songs and lead sheets. SASE. Include 5×7 photo. Reports in 3 months.
Music: Mostly gospel; also urban, contemporary gospel. Released "Rescue Me" (by Pearl Warren) on Kilgore Records; and "The Uneducated Grandmother" (by Evangelists).
Tips: "I don't listen to poor quality demos that I can't understand. Submit good material with potential in today's market. Use good quality cassettes."

KIMBO EDUCATIONAL, 10 N. Third Ave., Box 477, Long Branch NJ 07740. (201)229-4949. Production: James Kimble/Amy Laufer. Labels include Kimbo, KBH Productions Inc., S&R Records. Estab. 1962. Releases 8 LPs/year. Works with musicians/artists and songwriters on contract. Pays approximately 7% royalty to artists on contract; statutory rate to publisher per song on record.

How to Contact: Submit demo tape by mail. Unsolicited submissions are OK. Prefers cassette with 8-10 songs and lyric sheets. SASE. Reports in 2 months.
Music: Mostly children's music (ages 1-10) and simple rock or pop (easy for child to relate to). Released *Journey Into Space* (by Jane Murphy), recorded by Kimbo; *A Rainbow of Songs*, written and recorded by Bing Bingham; and *Me and My Bean Bag*, recorded by The Learning Station; all on Kimbo Records (all kids LPs). Other artists include Slim Goodbody, Carol Hammett, Dennis Buck, Georgiana Stewart, Priscilla Hegner and Laura Johnson.
Tips: "Kimbo seeks contemporary sounds with limited instrumentation so as not to appear too sophisticated or distracting for young children. Song lyrics should present topics that are of interest to today's children."

*KING KLASSIC RECORDS, P.O. Box 8532, Waukegan IL 60079. (708)336-5619. Executive Producer: Dennis Bergeron. Labels include King Klassic Records and Zoinks! Label. Record company. Estab. 1985. Releases 2 EPs and 2 CDs/year. Receives more than 100 submissions/year. Works with musicians/artists on contract. Pays 9% royalty to artists on contract.
How to Contact: Submit demo tape by mail. Unsolicited submissions are OK. Prefers cassette. SASE. Reports in 2 weeks.
Music: Mostly heavy metal, new rock and industrial dance; also HIP/House and soft rock. Released *Hellcats* (by Hellcats), recorded by Record Plant (hard rock LP); *Genocide* (written and recorded by Genocide, heavy metal LP) and *Solitude* (written and recorded by Solitude, doom metal LP), all on King Klassic Records. Other artists include Johnny Chainsaw, Winterhawk, Slauter Xstroyes, Jordan D. Macarus and Masada.
Tips: "Be creative. Write well, play well, send us a tape and we'll talk."

KING OF KINGS RECORD CO., 38603 Sage Tree St., Palmdale CA 93551-4311. (Branch office: P.O. Box 725, Daytona Beach FL 32015-0725. (904)252-4849.) President: Leroy Pritchett. A&R Director: Charles Vickers. Labels include King of Kings, L.A. International. Record company and music publisher (Pritchett Publications/BMI). Estab. 1978. Releases 1 single and 1 LP/year. Receives 5 submissions/month. Works with musicians/artists and songwriters on contract. Pays 10% royalty to artists on contract; statutory rate to publishers per song on record.
How to Contact: Write first for permission to submit. Prefers cassette and lyric or lead sheet. SASE. Reports in 1 month.
Music: Mostly gospel; also country. Released "Let Your Light Shine," "Heaven Is Just Over the Hill," and "Glory To Jesus Name," all written and recorded by Charles Vickers on King of Kings Records (gospel).

KINGSTON RECORDS, 15 Exeter Rd., Kingston NH 03848. (603)642-8493. Coordinator: Harry Mann. Labels include Kingston Records. Record company, music publisher (Strawberry Soda Publishing/ASCAP). Estab. 1988. Releases 3-4 singles, 2-3 12″ singles, 3 LPs and 2 CDs/year. Receives 50 submissions/year. Works with musicians/artists and songwriters on contract. Pays 3-5% royalty to artists on contract; statutory rate to publisher per song.
How to Contact: Submit demo tape by mail. Unsolicited submissions are OK. Prefers cassette, 15 ips reel-to-reel, VCR videocassette with 3 songs and lyric sheet. SASE. Reports in 6-8 weeks.
Music: Mostly rock, country and pop; "no heavy metal." Released "Sunshine Where She Goes," "Angeline" and "Hard to Find" (by D. Mitchell), recorded by Doug Mitchell Band on Kingston Records (all A/C singles).

KITTY RECORDS, INC., 1-8-4 Ohashi, Megro-Ku, Tokyo 153 **Japan**. Phone: (03)3780-8661. International Division: Hideki Ninomiya. Record company and music publisher (Kitty Music Corporation). Estab. 1982. Releases 30 LP/cassettes and 30 CDs/year. Receives 5 submissions/month ("excluding domestic artists"). Works with musicians/artists and songwriters on contract. Pays 1% royalty to artists on contract.
How to Contact: Prefers cassette with 5 songs and lyric sheet. Does not return unsolicited material. Reports in 1 month.
Music: Mostly rock, pop and dance; also New Age (instrumental), jazz (with classical music flavor) and soul (pop-soul). Released "Ikanaide" (by K. Tamaki and D. Matsui), recorded by Kohgi Tamaki; "Johnetsu" (by K. Tamaki and J. Matsui), recorded by Auzenchitai; and "Yumeyori Tohkue" (by T. Kisugi and E. Kisugi); recorded by Takao Kisugi; all pop singles on Kitty Records.

SID KLEINER MUSIC ENTERPRISES INC., 10188 Winter View Dr., Naples FL 33942. (813)566-7701 and (813)566-7702. Contact: Sid Kleiner. Labels include Musi-Poe, Top-Star, This Is It, Token and Country-King Records. Record company and consulting firm to music industry. Releases 10 LPs/year. Works with musicians and songwriters on contract. Charges for some services: "We may, at our option, charge *actual* production expense. We are not get-rich-quickers or rip-off artists. But we are too small to pay all of these bills!"

How to Contact: Prefers cassette (or VHS videocassette) and lead sheet. SASE, "otherwise materials aren't returned." Reports in 3 weeks.

Music: Bluegrass, country, easy listening, folk, jazz, and "banjo and guitar soloists and features." Released *Burd Boys on Stage* and *Chartbusters and Other Hits* (country LPs), by the Burd Boys; and *Find a Simple Life*, by Dave Kleiner (folk/rock LP). Other artists include Sid Kleiner.

KOTTAGE RECORDS, P.O. Box 121626, Nashville TN 37212. (615)726-3556. President: Neal James. Record company, music publisher (Cottage Blue Music, BMI) and record producer (Neal James). Estab. 1979. Releases 4 singles, 2 LPs and 3 CDs/year. Receives 75 submissions/month. Works with musicians/artists on contract. Pays 5% royalty to artists on contract; statutory rate to publisher per song on record.

How to Contact: Write or call first and obtain permission to submit. Prefers cassette with 2 songs and lyric sheet. SASE. Reports in 4 weeks.

Music: Mostly country, rock/pop and gospel; also R&B. Released "Shimmer" (by Neal James), recorded by Terry BarBay; and "Lookin 4 A Boyfriend" (by Neal James), recorded by Ted Yost; both on Kottage Records (contemporary-country).

KRYSDAHLARK MUSIC, P.O. Box 26160, Cincinnati OH 45226. President: Jeff Krys. Works with musicians and artist on contract. Production company and publisher designed to produce and shop music to record labels and producers. Estab 1986.

How to Contact: Not accepting unsolicited submissions at this time.

Music: Billy Larkin and Chris Dahlgren of EKIMI; Terri Cantz of Blanche and Deux Boys; Sylvain Acher; Chris Philpotts; Modern Rock group, and Sleep Theatre (Robert Hamrick, Chris Sherman, Johnny Miracle).

L.S. RECORDS, 120 Hickory St., Madison TN 37115. (615)868-7171. Publisher: Kevin L. Stoller. Labels include L.S. Records. Record company, music publisher (ASCAP, BMI, SESAC) and record producer (Lee Stoller—L.S. Records). Estab. 1972. Releases 2 singles and 3-4 12" singles/year. Works with songwriters on contract. Pays 50% royalty to artists on contract; statutory rate to publisher per song on record.

How to Contact: Call first and obtain permission to submit. Prefers cassette with 1 song and lyric or lead sheet. SASE. Reports in weeks.

Music: Mostly gospel, country and pop; also rock, rap and AC. Released *All in His Hands* and *He Sees My Heart* (both by Jimmie Young), and *How Great Thou Art*; all recorded by Cristy Lane on L.S. Records (LPs).

LA LOUISIANNE RECORDS, 711 Stevenson St., Lafayette LA 70501. (318)234-5577. Labels include Tamm and Belle. President: (Mr.) Carol J. Rachou, Sr. Record company, record producer, recording studio and music publisher (La Lou Music/BMI). Releases 10-20 singles and 4-6 LPs/year. Works with artists and songwriters on contract. "We also deal with promoters, managers, agents, etc." Pays statutory rate to publishers for each record sold.

How to Contact: Prefers 7½ ips reel-to-reel or cassette with 1-6 songs and lyric sheet. "If possible, submit different musical variations of songs (tempos, styles, keys, etc.)." SASE.

Music: Mostly Cajun/French; also blues, church/religious, classical, country, folk, gospel, jazz, MOR, progressive, R&B, rock, top 40/pop, comedy, French comedy and instrumental. Released *Lache Pas La Patate*, by Jimmy C. Newman (French Cajun LP—Gold record in Canada); *A Cajun Tradition Vol. 2*, by Nathan Abshire (French Cajun LP); *Cajun Fiddle*, by Rufus Thibodeaux (Cajun/country LP); *That Cajun Country Sound*, by Eddy Raven (French and English Cajun/country LP); and *Authentic French Music*, by Ambrose Thibodeaux (traditional Cajun LP). Other artists include Vin Bruce, Aldus Roger, Merlin Fontenot, L.J. Foret, Blackie Forestier, The Dusenbery Family, Alex Broussard and Bud Fletcher.

LAMAR MUSIC GROUP, (formerly PULSE Music Group), Box 412, New York NY 10462. (914)668-3119. Associate Director: Darlene Barkley. Labels include Lamar, MelVern, Wilson, We-Us and Co. Pub. Record company, music publisher (BMI), and workshop organization. Estab. 1984. Releases 10-12 12" singles and 2-4 LPs/year. Works with musicians/artists and songwriters on contract and hires musicians for in-house studio work. Pays standard royalty to artists on contract; statutory rate to publisher per song. "We charge only if we are hired to do 'work-for-hire' projects.

How to Contact: Write first and obtain permission to submit. Prefers cassette with 2 songs. Does not return unsolicited material. Reports in 1 month.

Music: Mostly R&B, rap and pop. Released "So In Love" (by R. Robinson), recorded by L. Williams on Macola Records (R&B/dance); "Lose You Love" (by R. Robinson), recorded by Vern Wilson on Lamar Records (R&B/dance); and "Feel Like a Woman" (by Wilson/Johnson), recorded by S. Taylor on MelVern Records (R&B/ballad). Other artists include Barry Manderson and Co/Vern.

Tips: "Members of our company function as singers, songwriters, musicians, producers, executive producers. We basically have all graduated from college in areas related to music or the music business. We either teach about music and the music business or we perform in the business. If you sincerely want to be in this industry this is the type of work you will need to do in order to succeed. It is not as easy as you think."

LAMBDA RECORDS®, A Division of Soria Enterprizes®, P.O. Box 14131, Denver CO 80214. Executive Producer: Sharon Soria. Partner: Luanna Soria. Record labels include SRSF Records®, SRSF Recordings/entertainments enterprises®, SRS Records®. Record Company, music publisher (Lambda Guild®/ASCAP) and record producer (Lambda Performing Arts Guild of America®). Estab. 1987. "We are a non-profit organization." Releases 2 or more 12" singles/year. Receives 4 submissions/month. Pays 95% royalty to artists on contract. "A 10% markup above costs for manufacturing pressings etc."

How to Contact: Submit demo tape by mail. Unsolicited submissions are okay. Prefers cassette (or VHS videocassette) with 1 song and lyric or lead sheets. Reports in 3 months. Send SASE postcard for our number disclosing Lambda Records® Publishing/Producing Information.

Music: Mostly pop, country and MOR; also easy listening, bluegrass and folk. Released "Our Time Has Come" (by Luanna Soria), recorded by Sharon Soria on Lambda Records® and Soria Enterprizes® (lesbian folk).

Tips: "We currently only work with Lesbian artists. Our mission is to recognize and legitimize lesbian performers. As a Lesbian operated organization working with artists, managers, producers, etc., we have noticed a change in attitudes towards Lesbian artists. Please send only professionally mixed demos. Send for the 1-900-nationwide telecommunications number explaining our producing/publishing information."

LANA RECORDS, Box 370, Round Rock TX 78680. (512)448-6362. Executive Producer: Robby Roberson. Labels include Lana Records, Country Roots Records, GGT Records and El Country Records. Record company, music publisher (Happy Note Music), and record producer. Releases 3 singles and 2 LPs/year. Works with musicians/artists and songwriters on contract; musicians on salary for in-house studio work. Pays 7-10% royalty to artists on contract; statutory rate to publisher per song on record.

How to Contact: Prefers cassette with 3 songs and lyric sheet. SASE. Reports in 1 month.

Music: Mostly country, gospel, pop, Tex-Mex and soft rock. Released "The Master's Touch," "Mountain House Rendezvous," "Save the Train" and "The Western Iron Rail." Artists include Robby Roberson, Mikal Masters, Rosemarie Reedy and Jimmy Walker.

LANDMARK COMMUNICATIONS GROUP, P.O. Box 148296, Nashville TN 37214. Producer: Bill Anderson, Jr. Labels include Jana, and Landmark Records. Record company, record producer and music publisher (Newcreature Music/BMI and Mary Megan Music/ASCAP) and management firm (Landmark Entertainment). Releases 10 singles, 8 LPs, and 8 CDs/year. Receives 40 submissions/month. Works with musicians/artists and songwriters on contract; hires musicians for in-house studio work. Teams collaborators. Pays 5-7% royalty to artists on contract; statutory rate to publishers for each record sold.

How to Contact: Prefers 7½ ips reel-to-reel or cassette with 4-10 songs and lyric sheet. SASE. Reports in 1 month.

Music: Country/crossover, gospel, jazz, R&B, rock and top 40/pop. Released *Joanne Cash Yates Live . . . w/Johnny Cash,* on Jana Records (gospel LP); *Play It Again Sam,* recorded by Michael L. Pickern on Landmark Records (country LP); *Millions of Miles,* recorded by Teddy Nelson/Skeeter Davis (Norway release) (country LP); *Always,* recorded by Debi Chasteen on Landmark Records (country LP); "You Were Made For Me" by Skeeter Davis and Teddy Nelson on Elli Records/Norway; and *Someday Soon,* recorded by Pam Fenelon on Bil-Mar Records (country LP).

LANOR RECORDS, 329 N. Main St., Box 233, Church Point LA 70525. (318)684-2176. Contact: Lee Lavergne. Labels include Lanor and Joker Records. Record company and music publisher (Country Classics Music/BMI). Releases 12-18 singles and 1-3 LPs/year. Works with artists and songwriters on contract. Pays 3-5% royalty to artists on contract; statutory rate to writers for each record sold.

Remember: Don't "shotgun" your demo tapes. Submit only to companies interested in the type of music you write. For more submission hints, refer to The Business of Songwriting on page 21.

How to Contact: Prefers cassette with 2-6 songs. SASE. Reports in 2 weeks.
Music: Mostly country; also rock, and soul. Released "Good Hearted Man" and "Rockin' Zydeco," by Rockin' Sidney and Jim Olivier.
Tips: Submit "good material with potential in today's market. Use good quality cassettes—I don't listen to poor quality demos that I can't understand."

LARI-JON RECORDS, 325 West Walnut, Rising City NE 68658. (402)542-2336. Owner: Larry Good. Record company, music publisher (LariJon Publishing/BMI) and record producer (Lari-Jon Productions). Estab. 1967. Releases 15 singles and 5 LPs/year. Receives 100-150 submissions/year. Works with songwriters on royalty contract.
How to Contact: Submit demo tape by mail. Unsolicited submissions are OK. Prefers cassette with 5 songs and lyric sheet. SASE. Reports in 2 months.
Music: Mostly country, gospel-Southern and '50s rock. Released "Between the Lies," recorded by Johnny Nace (country); "The Time is Spent with You," recorded by Johnny Nace (country); and "Her Favorite Song," recorded by Johnny Nace (country LP), both on Lari-Jon Records.

*LARK RECORD PRODUCTIONS, INC., Suite 520, 4815 S. Harvard, Tulsa OK 74135. (918)749-1648. Vice-President: Sue Teaff. Record company, music publisher (Jana Jae Music/BMI) and record producer (Lark Talent and Advertising). Estab. 1980. Works with musicians/artists on contract. Payment to artists on contract negotiable; statutory rate to publishers per song on record.
How to Contact: Submit demo tape by mail. Unsolicited submissions are OK. Prefers cassette or VHS videocassette with 3 songs and lead sheets. Does not return unsolicited material.
Music: Mostly country, bluegrass and classical; also instrumentals. Released "Fiddlestix" (by Jana Jae); "Mayonnaise" (by Steve Upfold); and "Flyin' South" (by Cindy Walker); all country singles recorded by Jana Jae on Lark Records. Other artists include Syndi, Hotwire and Matt Greif.

*LE DISQUE HOLLAND B.V./B&B RECORDS, Huizerweg 13, 1261 AS Blaricum, **The Netherlands**. Phone: (2153)87574 or (2153)83323. FAX: (2153)12523. General Manager: Michael C. Lambrechtsen. Production company (Le Disque Holland B.V.), record label (B&B Records), studio (Bolland Studios B.V.) and music publishers (Le Disque Music Publishing, Bolland Music and B&B Music Publishing). Estab. 1981. "All companies owned by producers and composers Robert Bolland and Ferdi Bolland. The company produces for record companies and for own record label." Releases 10 singles, 10 12″ singles, 10 LPs and 10 CDs/year. Works with musicians/artists on contract. Payment to be negotiated. Pays statutory rate to publishers per song on record.
How to Contact: Prefers cassette (or VHS videocassette if available) with 3-5 songs and lyric or lead sheet. SAE and IRC. Reports in 6 weeks.
Music: Mostly rock, pop and dance. Released "Love House," recorded by Samantha Fox on Jive Records; "Baby You're a Star," recorded by Suzi Quatro on Teldec/WEA Records; multi-million selling hits for Falco ("Rock me Amadeus"); all by Bolland and Bolland (all 7″ and 12″ singles). Other artists include Academy of Modern Dance, Cosmic Company, Bolland & Bolland, 1st Avenue, Shaun Cassidy, Ethnic Dance Project and many others.

LE MATT MUSIC LTD., % Stewart House, Hill Bottom Rd., Highwycombe, Buckinghamshire, HP12 4HJ **England**. Phone: 063081374. FAX: 063081612. Contact: Ron or Cathrine Lee. Labels include Swoop, Zarg Records, Genouille, Pogo and Check Records. Record company, record producer and music publisher (Le Matt Music, Ltd., Lee Music, Ltd., R.T.F.M. and Pogo Records, Ltd.). Member MPA, PPL, PRS, MCPS. Estab. 1972. Releases 30 12″ singles, 20 LPs and 20 CDs/year. Receives 10-15 submissions/month. Pays negotiable royalty to artists on contract; statutory rate to publishers for each record sold. Royalties paid to US songwriters and artists through US publishing or recording affiliate.
How to Contact: Prefers 7½ or 15 ips reel-to-reel or cassette (or VHS videocassette) with 1-3 songs and lyric sheet. Include bio and photo. SAE and IRC. Reports in 3 weeks.
Music: Mostly interested in pop/Top 40; also interested in bluegrass, blues, country, dance-oriented, easy listening, MOR, progressive, R&B, 50s rock, disco, new wave, rock and soul. Released "Annabel" (pop); and "Skydiver" (pop), both written and recorded by D. Boone; and "Gotta Do It All Again" by (D. Boone) recorded by D. Boone and Lolly Boone (pop/rock), all on Swoop Records. Other artists include Emmitt Till, Touche, Orphan, Jonny Moon, Ian "Sludge" Lees and Kyro Groucho.

LEOPARD MUSIC, 23 Thrayle House, Stockwell Rd., London, SW9 0XU **England**. Phone: (071)274-9533. FAX: (071)737-7881. Executive Producer: Errol Jones. Vice President: Terry Schiavo. Phone: (818)962-6547. FAX: (818)960-8737. Labels include Jet Set Records International (USA). Record company (PRS, BMI) and record producer. Releases 15 singles and 2 LPs/year. Works with musicians/artists and songwriters on contract and hires musicians for in-house studio work. Pays 4-12% royalty to artist on contract and hires musicians for in-house studio work. Pays 4-12% royalty to artist on contract. Pays statutory rate to publishers per song on record.

How to Contact: Write first and obtain permission to submit. Prefers cassette (or VHS/PAL videocassette) with 3 songs. SASE. Reports in 2 weeks.

Music: Mostly dance music, soul and pop; also ballad, reggae and gospel. Released "Time After Time" (by Guy Spell), recorded by Rico J (single); "I Need You" (by E. Campbell and E. North Jr.), recorded by Big Africa (single); and "God is Beauty," written and recorded by Evelyn Ladimeji (LP); all on Leopard Music Records. Other artists include Zoil Foundations, Michael Eytle.

Tips: "Create strong original songs, and artists must have good image."

*LION HUNTER MUSIC, Box 110678, Anchorage AK 99511. Vice President: Clive Lock. Record company (BMI). Estab. 1989. Releases 1 single and 1 CD/year. Works with musicians/artists on contract. Pays negotiable royalty to artists on contract; statutory rate to publisher per song on record.

How to Contact: Write first and obtain permission to submit. Prefers cassette with 3 songs and lyric sheet. Does not return unsolicited material.

Music: Mostly rock, pop and R&B. Released *Wild Horse Road* (CD); and "The Lion Hunters" (single); both recorded by Abandon on Lion Hunter Music. Other artists include The Undertakers (rock).

*LIPHONE RECORDS, Box 51, S-451 15 Uddevalla **Sweden.** Phone: 4652262081. FAX Int.: +4652262222. Owner: Borge Lindquist. Record company and music publisher (LiTUNE Music). Estab. 1970. Releases 3-5 singles and 15-20 LPs and 2-3 CDs/year. Works with musicians/artists and songwriters on contract. Pays 3-8% royalty to artists on contract; pays statutory rate to publisher per song on record.

How to Contact: Prefers cassette and lyric sheet; disc to ATARI ST is also OK. Does not return unsolicited material. Reports in 5 weeks.

Music: Mostly country, pop and rock; also folk, R&B, jazz, fusion and gospel. Released "Soft Landing" (by Rolf Jardemark), recorded by Michael Ruff (LA) (CD and LP); "Jon Nagourney," recorded by Jon Nagourney (LA) (CD); and "It's Still Time," written and recorded by Bjorn Vickhoff (LP); all on Liphone Records. Other artists include "about 40 artists from the Scandinavian countries."

*LOADING BAY RECORDS, 586, Bristol Road, Selly Oak, Birmingham B29 6BQ **England.** Phone (21)472-2463. FAX: (21)414-1540. M.D.: Duncan Finlayson. Labels include Loading Bay Records, Two Bears Music and Made Up Records. Record company and record producer (Loading Bay Productions). Estab. 1988. Releases 20 12″ singles, 3 LPs and 3 CDs/year. Works with musicians/artists on contract and "negotiates one-off licensing deals." Pays 10% royalty; statutory rate to publishers per son on record.

How to Contact: Submit demo tape by mail. Unsolicited submissions are OK. Prefers cassette (or D.A.T.) with several songs. Does not return unsolicited material. Reports in 1 month.

Music: Mostly Hi-NRG-dance and disco dance. Released "Somewhere" (by Bernstein and Sondheim), recorded by Vicki Shepard; "Over the Rainbow" (by Arlen and Marburg), recorded by Paradise; and "We Stand Together" (written and recorded by Nick John), all on Loading Bay Records (Hi-NRG 12″). Other artists include Rofo, Samantha Gilles, Sheila Steward, Claudia T., Ross Alexander and Kelly Marie.

LRJ, Box 3, Belen NM 87002. (505)864-7441. Manager: Tony Palmer. Labels include LRJ, Little Richie, Chuckie. Record company. Estab. 1959. Releases 5 singles and 2 LPs/year. Works with musicians/artists on contract.

How to Contact: Submit demo tape by mail. Unsolicited submissions are OK. Prefers cassette. SASE. Reports in 1 month.

Music: Mostly country. Released "Step Aside" and "Yellow Bandana," recorded by Jerry Jaramillo on LRJ Records (singles).

LUCIFER RECORDS, INC., Box 263, Brigantine NJ 08203-0263. (609)266-2623. President: Ron Luciano. Labels include TVA Records. Record company, music publishers (Ciano Publishing and Legz Music), record producers (Pete Fragale and Tony Vallo) and management firm and booking agency (Ron Luciano Music Co. and TVA Productions).Works with artists and songwriters on salary and contract. "Lucifer Records has offices in South Jersey, Palm Beach, Florida, Sherman Oaks, California and Las Vegas, Nevada."

How to Contact: Arrange personal interview. Prefers cassette with 4-8 songs. SASE. Reports in 3 weeks.

Music: Dance, easy listening, MOR, rock, soul and top 40/pop. Released "I Who Have Nothing," by Spit-N-Image (rock single); "Lucky," and "Smoke Ya," by Legz (rock singles); and "Loves a Crazy Game," by Voyage (disco/ballad single).

MAIN TRIPP RECORDS INC., 2804 Beechtree Dr., Sanford NC 27330. (919)774-8926. President: Bill Tripp. Record company and music publisher (BMI). Estab. 1982. Releases 12 singles, and 12 LPs/ year. Works with musicians/artists and songwriters on contract. Pays statutory rate to publisher per song on record. Write first and obtain permission to submit or to arrange personal interview. Prefers cassette with 3 songs and lyric sheet. Does not return unsolicited material. Reports in 3 months.
Music: Mostly country, gospel and bluegrass. Released *Forever*, written and recorded by Raymond Barns (R&B); *Empty Places*, written and recorded by Don Keatley/Jim Watters (country gospel) both on MTR Records; and *Empty Places*, (by Jim Watters), recorded by The Helmsmen (gospel) on Morning Star Records. Other artists include Pioneers (gospel), Don Keatley, Shine On, Clyde Frazier, Raymond Barnes, Jim Watters.

*MAJESTIC CONTROL RECORDS, P.O. Box 330-568, Brooklyn NY 11233. (718)919-2013. A&R Department: Alemo. Record company, music publisher (Majestic Control Music/BMI) and record producer (Alemo and Hank Love). Estab. 1983. Works with musicians/artists on contract.
How to Contact: Submit demo tape by mail. Unsolicited submissions are OK. Prefers cassette with 3 songs. SASE. Reports in 4 weeks.
Music: Mostly rap, dance and reggae; also house. Released "Cold Sweat" (by Curtis, Moye, Davis), recorded by Majestic Productions (rap, single); *Lovely, Lovely* (by M. Lowe), recorded by M.C. Lovely (rap LP); and "Front Line" (by Curtis, Moye, Davis), recorded by Majestic Productions (rap single); all on Majestic Control Records. Other artists include M.C. Cuba.

MARIAH RECORDS, P.O. Box 310, Carmichael CA 95609-310. President: Mari Minice. Record company (Mariah Records). Estab. 1986. Releases 1 single/year. Receives 50 submissions/year. Works with musicians/artists on contract. Pays varying royalty to artists on contract; statutory rate to publishers per song on records.
How to Contact: Submit demo tape by mail. Unsolicited submissions are OK. Prefers cassette with any number of songs and lyric sheets. Does not return unsolicited material. Reports in 2 months.
Music: Mostly country/contemporary, pop and rock. Released "Closer to Heaven" (by Jill Wood), recorded by Rachel Minke on Mariah Records (country single).
Tips: "Submit songs with wide vocal ranges, with a country feel."

*MARZ RECORDS, 2602 NW 5th Ave., Miami FL 33127. (305)573-5400. Label Manager: Joe Alonso. Labels include Marz Records, Kinetic Records (manufacture and distribute only). Record company and music publisher (Marz Need Music/BMI). Estab. 1990. Releases 6-8 12″ singles, 3-5 LPS and 3-5 CDs/year. Works with musicians/artists on record contract. Pays statutory rate to publisher per song on record.
How to Contact: Submit demo tape by mail. Unsolicited submissions are OK. Prefers cassette with 3-5 songs and lyric sheet. SASE. Reports in 1 month.
Music: Mostly industrial/progressive and dance; also progressive rock. Released "Algorythm," written and recorded by Force Dimension on Marz Records (industrial, 12″); "Move Out," written and recorded by Another Nation on Kinetic Records (industrial 12″); and "Give Me a Sign," written and recorded by Razor on Kinetic Records (industrial 12″).

*MASSMEDIA, 7105 Reynolds St., Pittsburgh PA 15208. (412)247-1301. President: Jon Gorr. Record company, music publisher (BMI) and record producer (Jon Gorr). Estab. 1983. Releases 5 singles and 2 LPs/year. Works with musicians/artists and songwriters on contract. Pays statutory rate to publisher per song on record.
How to Contact: Submit demo tape by mail. Unsolicited submissions are OK. Prefers cassette with 3 songs. Reports in 1 month.
Music: Mostly rock, New Age and reggae. Released "It's No Lie" (by Jon Gorr), recorded by J. Gorr/ Ram on Massmedia Records (pop); and *On the Right Track* (by Albert Griffith), recorded by J. Gorr/ Ram on Heartbeat Records (reggae LP). Other artists include Albert Griffiths and The Gladiators, The I-Tones, Steve Recker Band and Bo Diddley.

MASTER-TRAK ENTERPRISES, 413 N. Parkerson, Crowley LA 70526. (318)788-0773. General Manager and Chief Engineer: Bobby Terry. Labels include Master-Trak, Showtime, Kajun, Blues Unlimited, Par T and MTE Records. Recording studio and record companies. Releases 20 singles and 6-8 LPs/year. Works with musicians/artists on contract. Pays 6% artist royalty. (No studio charges to contract artists.) Studio available on an hourly basis to the public. Charges for some services: "We charge for making audition tapes of any material that we do not publish."
How to Contact: Prefers cassette and lead sheet. SASE. Reports in 1 month.
Music: Mostly country, rock, R&B, cajun, blues and Zydeco. Released "Johnny Can't Dance" by Wayne Toups (Zydeco), "Tell Me What I Want to Hear Tonight" by Tammy Lynn, and "Only Passing Through" by Freddie Pate on MTE Records (country). Other artists include Al Ferrier, and Fernest & The Thunders.

Tips: "The song is the key. If we judge it to be a good song, we record it and it sells, we are happy. If we misjudge the song and/or the artist and it does not sell, we must go back to the drawing board."

MAXIMA RECORDS, Suite 234, 24285 Sunnymead Blvd., Moreno Valley, CA 92388-9971. (714)653-1556. Professional Manager: LaDonna Kay. Record company, music publisher (KayDay Music) and record producer (Country Charts and OurWay Music). Releases 4-5 singles and 1-2 LPs/year. Works with musicians/artists and songwriters on contract. Pays standard royalty to artists on contract; compulsory rate to publisher per song on record.
How to Contact: Prefers cassette (or VHS videocassette) with 1-10 songs and lyric sheet. Reports in 1 month. "Please include a stamped and addressed postcard if you wish to know the date your material is received. We do not return any cassettes."
Music: Mostly contemporary country; also MOR and pop. Released "She Looks Like a Heartache" and "Small Town Dreams," recorded by Don Malena on Maxima Records (both singles).

*MAXIMUS RECORDS, P.O. Box 14324, Clearwater FL 34629. (813)862-9377. President: Don Seat. Record company and music publisher (Marielle Music/BMI). Estab. 1955. Works with musicians/artists and songwriters on contract. Pays statutory rate to publisher per song on contract.
How to Contact: Submit demo tape by mail. Unsolicited submissions are OK. Prefers cassette with several songs and lead sheet. SASE.
Music: Mostly rock, country and rap; also classical, pop and piano works.

MAXX RECORDS, Suite 207, 50 Music Square W., Nashville TN 37203. (615)329-2592. Publishing Manager: Karen Morris. Record company, music publisher (Maxx) and record producer (Fred Morris Music Group). Estab. 1987. Releases varying number of singles/year. Works with musicians/artists and songwriters on contract. Pays varying royalty to artists on contract; pays statutory rate to publisher per song on record.
How to Contact: Prefers cassette (or VHS videocassette, if artists) with 3-5 songs and lyric sheet. SASE. Reports in 1 month.
Music: Mostly country, pop and rock; "no gospel." Released *Calendar Blues* (by Karren Pell/Dan E. James), recorded by Jill Jordan; and *We're Gonna Love Tonight* (by Eddy Rager/Vernis Pratt), recorded by Don Juan (both singles, LPs and CDs); *Panic* (by Fran Weber), recorded by Don Juan (country rock LP); and "Ease My Mind" (by Sing Me Publishing), recorded by Jill Jordan (country LP); all on Maxx Records.
Tips: "Remember that the music business is that, a business. Talent is not enough anymore. You need an awareness of marketing and what is involved in making commercial decisions of where you are headed."

MCA RECORDS, 1755 Broadway, 8th Fl., New York NY 10019. (212)841-8000. East Coast A&R Director: Susan Dodes. East Coast Vice President: Bruce Dickinson. Labels include Costellation, Cranberry, Curb, IRS, Motown, London, Zebra and Philly World. Record company and music publisher (MCA Music). Works with musicians/artists on contract.
How to Contact: Call first and obtain permission to submit. Prefers cassette (or VHS videocassette) and lyric or lead sheet. SASE.

*MCI ENTERTAINMENT GROUP, Suite 830, Universal City Plaza, Universal City CA 91608. (818)506-8533. Vice President A&R: Jaeson Effantic. Labels include Bouvier, Credence, PPL. Record company. Estab. 1979. Releases 50-60 singles, 12 12" singles, 6 LPs and 6 CDs/year. Works with musicians/artists and songwriters on contract and hires musicians for in-house studio work. Pays 8-15% royalty to artists on contract; statutory rate to publisher per song on record.
How to Contact: Write first and obtain permission to submit. Prefers cassette or videocassette with 2 songs. SASE. Reports in 4-6 weeks.
Music: Released *Night Song* (by Gip Noble), recorded by Phuntaine on Bouvier Records (jazz LP); *Fynne as I can B* (by Santiono), recorded by I.B. Fynne on Credence Records (pop LP); and *Love Song* (by DM Groove), recorded by Dale Mitchell on Bouvier Records (R&B LP). Other artists include Big Daddy and Blazers, Lejenz and Condottiere.
Tips: "Don't limit yourself to just one style of music. Diversify and write other styles of songs."

MEDA RECORDS INC., 19457 Shrewsbury, Detroit MI 45221. (313)862-5139. West Coast: 1621 Virginia Rd., Los Angeles CA 90019. (213)732-7009. A&R Director: Joe Hunter. Vice President/Marketing & Promotion: Mable John. Record company, record producer and music publisher (Mertis Music Company). Releases 4 singles and 4 LPs/year. Works with artists and songwriters on contract. Pays 4-12% royalty to artists on contract; statutory rate to publishers for each record sold.

How to Contact: Prefers cassette with 4-8 songs and lead sheet. SASE. Reports in 1 month or ASAP.
Music: Mostly R&B and pop; also gospel, jazz and top 40. Released "Christmas Comes Once a Year," by The Lamp Sisters (pop single); *A New Day*, by Mertis John (pop LP); *Heaven Bound*, by Mable John (gospel LP); *Where Can I Find Jesus?*, by Mable John (contemporary gospel) and *For Thee Lord I Sing*, by Lorine Thompson (gospel LP).

MEGA RECORDS APS., Frederiksborggade 31, 1360 Copenhagen K **Denmark**. Phone: (4533)11 77 11. FAX: (4533)13 40 10. A&R Director: Martin Dodd. Labels include Mega Records, Mega Rock and Doctor Tilt. Record company and music publisher. Estab. 1982. Releases 150-200 singles, 75-100 12" singles, 50-75 LPs and 50-75 CDs/year. Works with musicians/artists and songwriters on contract; hires musicians for in-house studio work.
How to Contact: Write or call first and obtain permission to submit. Prefers cassette with 1 song and lyric sheet. Does not return unsolicited material. Reports in 3 weeks.
Music: Mostly crossover dance, pop/rock and hard rock; also strong ballads. Released "Mel & Kim," written and recorded by S.A.W. on Mega Records. Other artists include Disneyland After Dark, The Overlords, The Colours Turn Red, Laban, Seventy'Leven, Sky High, Technotronic, Jive Bunny, Sybil, Eric & The Good Good Feeling, De La Soul, Information Society, Digital Underground, Fancy, Camouflage and many more.

METAL BLADE RECORDS, #311, 18653 Ventura, Tarzana CA 91356. (818)981-9050. A&R: Chris Leibendgud. Labels include Death Records and No Wonder. Record company. Estab. 1982. Releases 4 singles, 2 12" singles, 30 LPs, 3 EPs and 33 CDs/year. Works with musicians/artists.
How to Contact: Write or call first and obtain permission to submit. Prefers cassette, (or ½" videocassette if available) with 3 songs and lyric and lead sheet. Does not return unsolicited submissions. Reports in 6 weeks.
Music: Mostly metal, rock and alternative; also rap and commercial. Released *Thrashzone* (by DRI), recorded by Bill Metoyes on Metal Blade Records (metal LP); *Perfect Symmetry* (by Fates Warning), recorded by Roger Probert on Metal Blade Records (progressive LP); and *Princess Pang*, (by Princes Pang) recorded Ron St. Germain on MB/Capitol Records (rock LP). Other artists include Artch, Bitter End, Goo Goo Dolls and Masi.
Tips: "Be organized, send complete promo pack, be familiar with Metal Blade and all that is involved in acquiring a record deal. Have a representative for the band."

*MICROSTAR MUSIC, #113, 5241 Cleveland St., Virginia Beach VA 23462. (804)499-4434. President: Mark Spencer. Labels include MicroStar, MSM. Record company, music publisher (ASCAP) and record producer (MicroStar). Estab. 1990. Releases 6 LPs and 6 CDs/year. Works with musicians/artists and songwriters on contract; and musicians on salary for in-house studio work. Pays for in-house studio work 15-20% wholesale. Pays statutory rate to publisher per song on record.
How to Contact: Write first and obtain permission to submit. Prefers cassette with 4 songs and lyric sheet. Does not return unsolicited material. Reports in 4 weeks.
Music: Mostly pop, gospel and country; also R&B. Released *Do You Think We Have a Chance* (by K. Cleveland), recorded by TK Lleggs; *Wearing White With No Shame* (by P. Van Valin), recorded by P. Van Valin; and *Workin' Man's Dream*, written and recorded by B. Fisher; all on MicroStar Records (LPs). Other artists include Don Burford, Tony Hawkins, Charity Jackson, David Givens, Matt Vollmer, and Pam Osborn.
Tips: "Work hard and don't cut corners on your demo. However, don't overproduce it either. If you can't raise enough support on your own to pay for a well-produced demo, then we don't have confidence in your ability to be successful."

MIGHTY RECORDS, Suite 6-D, 150 West End, New York NY 10023. (212)873-5968. Manager: Danny Darrow. Labels include Mighty Sounds & Filmworks. Record company, music publisher, record producer (Danny Darrow). Estab. 1958. Releases 1-2 singles, 1-2 12" singles and 1-2 LPs/year. Works with songwriters on royalty contract and hires musicians for in-house studio work. Pays standard royalty to artists on contract; statutory rate to publishers per song on records.
How to Contact: Submit demo tape by mail. Unsolicited submissions are OK. "No phone calls." Prefers cassette with 3 songs and lyric sheet. SASE. Reports in 1 week.
Music: Mostly pop, country and dance; also jazz. Released *Carnival Nights* (by Vincent C. DeLucia and Raymond Squillacote), recorded by Danny Darrow (country LP); *Impulse* written and recorded by Danny Darrow (dance LP); and *Corporate Lady* (by Michael Greer), recorded by Danny Darrow (pop) all on Mighty Records.
Tips: "Listen to the hits of Richie, Manilow, Houston and Rogers and write better songs."

*MIGHTY SOUL-SONIC RECORDS, Suite 12G, 70 West 95th, New York NY 10025. (212)666-6454 and (212)541-7600. President/Owner: Mark Carvel. Labels include Rocket in Space Record Company and Lift Off Record Company. Record company, music publisher (Mighty Soul-Sonic Records/Short

& Sweet Publishing Co./BMI) and record producer (Mark Carvel). Estab. 1987. Releases 12 singles, 2 12″ singles, 7 LPs, 4 EPs and 7 CDs/year. Works with musicians/artists and songwriters and hires musicians for in-house studio work. Pays statutory rate to publishers per song on records. Write or call first and obtain permission to submit. Prefers cassette (or VHS videocassette if available) with 12 songs and lyric or lead sheets. SASE. Reports in 2 months.
Music: Mostly rap, rock and R&B; also jazz and gospel.

*MINDFIELD RECORDS, 4B, 500 ½ E. 84th St., New York NY 10028. (212)861-8745. A&R: Guy Torio. Record company, music publisher (Mia Mind Music/ASCAP) and record producer (I.Y.F. Productions). Estab. 1985. Releases 10 singles, 6 12″ singles, 4 LPs and 4 CDs/year. Works with musicians/artists and songwriters on contract. Payment to artists on contract varies; statutory rate to publisher per song on record.
How to Contact: Submit demo tape by mail. Unsolicited submissions are OK. Prefers cassette or VHS videocassette with 3 songs. SASE. Reports in 6 weeks.
Music: Mostly rap, house and hip hop; also dance, top 40 and AOR. Released "Cosmic Climb" (by Werner/Sargent), recorded by Madonna (dance); "Gods" (by Werner/Sargent), recorded by Madonna (dance); and "I've Fallen," written and recorded by Baby Oil (house); all on Mindfield Records. Other artists include P.O.A., Electric Sun, Clark After Dark and Papa HaHa.
Tips: "Submit demos on DAT cassettes for best sound quality."

MISSILE RECORDS, Box 5330 Kreole Station, Moss Point MS 39563. (601)475-2098. "No collect calls." President/Owner: Joe F. Mitchell. Record company, music publisher (Bay Ridge Publishing/BMI) and record producer (Missile Records; have also produced for Happy Holllow Records, Myra Records, JB Records, RCI and Wake Up Records). Estab. 1974. Releases 20 singles and 6 LPs/year. Works with artists on contract. Pays 8-10¢ royalty to artists on contract.
How to Contact: Write first and obtain permission to submit. Include #10 SASE. "All songs sent for review must include sufficient return postage." Prefers cassette with 3-6 songs and lyric sheets. Does not return unsolicited material. Reports in 6 weeks.
Music: Mostly country, gospel, rap and R&B; also soul, MOR, blues, rock, pop, and bluegrass. Released "Standing In Your Way," "Baby," "In the Hollow of His Hand" and "He Will Not Come From Texas," recorded by T.C. Bullock; "No One Loves Me at Home" and "The Mountains and Eagles," recorded by Jimmy Dale Bullock; and "Grandmama Can I Read to You" and "Crying Melody," recorded by Big Sam Frazier, Jr. (all country singles). Other artists include Herbert Lacey, Ann Black, Lori Mark, Jerry Wright, Danny Keebler and Jerry Ann. "Also considering songs on master tape for release in the US and abroad."
Tips: "If a recording artist has exceptional talent and some backing then Missile Records will give you our immediate attention. A bio and cassette tape and picture of the artist should be submitted along with sufficient return postage."

*MODERN MUSIC VENTURES, INC., 5626 Brock St., Houston TX 77023. (713)926-4436. Chief Operations Officer: Art Gottschalk. Labels include Discos MM, Double M Records and Foundation. Record company. Estab. 1986. Releases 12 singles, 2 12″ singles, 6 LPs, 2 EPs and 6 CDs/year. Works with musicians/artists on record contract. Pays statutory rate to publisher per song on record.
How to Contact: Write first and obtain permission to submit. Prefers cassette with 5 songs and lyric sheets. SASE. Reports in 12 weeks.
Music: Mostly Latin (in Spanish), country and jazz; also rap and rap (in Spanish). Released *Simplemente,* recorded by Elsa Garcia; *Rebelde,* recorded by Mercedez; and *La Primera Vez,* recorded by The Choice; all on PolyGram Records (LPs). Other artists include Mary Maria, Dallazz, and Michael Flores.

*MONEYTIME RECORDS, 742 Rowley St., Owosso MI 48867. (517)723-1796. Director: Jon Harris. Record company and music publisher (Moneytime Publishing Co./BMI). Estab. 1990. Releases 6 singles, 2 12″ singles, 3 LPs, 2 EPs and 3 CDs/year. Works with musicians/artists on record contract. Pays 10% royalty to artists on contract; statutory rate to publisher per song on record.
How to Contact: Submit demo tape by mail. Unsolicited submissions are OK. Prefers cassette with 4-6 songs and lyric sheets (picture and bio if possible). Does not return unsolicited material. Reports in 4 weeks.

Market conditions are constantly changing! If you're still using this book and it is 1993 or later, buy the newest edition of Songwriter's Market at your favorite bookstore or order directly from Writer's Digest Books.

Music: Mostly rap, R&B, dance; also house, funk and soul. Released *Corporate MC* and "Censored for Suckers" (by Jon Harris), recorded by The Mad Rapper; and *P.O.D.* (by Brian Hammock), recorded by Mass Hysteria; all on Moneytime Records (rap). Other artists include King RV and MC Tay.
Tips: "Be persistent, be professional, be yourself, but don't be annoying."

MONTICANA RECORDS, P.O. Box 702, Snowdon Station, Montreal, Quebec H3X 3X8 **Canada**. General Manager: David P. Leonard. Labels include Dynacom and Monticana Records. Record company, record producer, and music publisher (Montina Music/SOCAN). Estab. 1963. Works with artists and songwriters on contract. Pays negotiable royalty to artists on contract; statutory rate to publishers for each record sold.
How to Contact: Prefers phonograph record (or VHS videocassette) and lyric sheet. Does not return unsolicited material.
Music: Mostly top 40, blues, country, dance-oriented, easy listening, folk, gospel, jazz, MOR, progressive, R&B, rock and soul.

MOR RECORDS, 17596 Corbel Court, San Diego CA 92128. (619)485-1550. President: Stuart L. Glassman. Record company and record producer. Estab. 1980. Releases 3 singles/year. Receives 250 submissions/year. Works with musicians on salary for in-house studio work. Pays 4% royalty to artists on contract.
How to Contact: Prefers cassette (or VHS videocassette). Does not return unsolicited material. Reports in 2 months.
Music: Mostly pop instrumental/vocal MOR; also novelty songs. Released "As Time Goes By" (by Herman Hupfeld) recorded by Al Rosa on MOR Records (pop); and "What a Difference a Day Makes" (by S. Adams and Maria Grever) recorded by Al Rosa and Danny Winchell on MOR Records (Spanish/English pop).
Tips: "Send original work. Do not send 'copy' work."

*MSB, LTD., #1235, 1204 Ave. V, Brooklyn NY 11229. (718)646-8969. President: Mark S. Berry. Record company, music publisher (Baby Raquel Music/ASCAP) and record producer (Mark S. Berry, Ltd.). Estab. 1984. Releases 1-2 12″ singles and 1-2 LPs/year. Works with musicians/artists on contract.
How to Contact: Submit demo tape by mail. Unsolicited submissions are OK. Prefers cassette or VHS videocassette with 3 songs and lyric sheet. Does not return unsolicited material. Reports in 2-3 weeks.
Music: Mostly pop/dance and pop/rock.

*MS'QUE RECORDS INC., P.O. Box 26852, Oklahoma OK 73126. A&R Representative: Christopher Stanley. Record company and music publisher (CAB Industries, Inc./BMI). Estab. 1988. Releases 20 singles, 20 12″ singles, 6 LPs and 2 CDs/year. Works with musicians/artists and songwriters on contract and hires musicians for in-house studio work. Pays statutory rate to publisher per song on record.
How to Contact: Submit demo tape by mail. Unsolicited submissions are OK. Prefers cassette or VHS videocassette with 3 songs and lead sheet. SASE. Reports in 1 month.
Music: Mostly R&B, pop and rock; also gospel and jazz. Released "Together" (by C. Freeman), recorded by Cash & Co.; "We've Just Begun" (by C. Freeman), recorded by Cash & Co.; and "Everybody Sing" (by S. DeBrown), recorded by Emotions; all on Ms'Que Records.

*MULE KICK RECORDS, 5341 Silvewode Dr., Placerville CA 95667. (916)626-4536. Owner: Doug McGinnis, Sr. Record company and music publisher (Freewheeler Publishing/BMI). Estab. 1949. Works with musicians/artists and songwriters on contract and hires musicians for in-house studio work.
How to Contact: Submit demo tape by mail. Unsolicited submissions are OK. Prefers cassette with 6-10 songs and lyric and lead sheet. Reports in 1 month.
Music: Mostly C&W, jazz-AB, and c-rock; also pop. Released "Paying My Dues" (by Alona Knight), recorded by Kim Moore; "Without Me," written and recorded by Kelly Marie; and "You're Not There" (by Alona Knight), recorded by CJ Bowlin; all singles on Mule Kick Records. Other artists include Don McGinnis, Tiny Moore, Dub Taylor, Rome Johnson and Roy Lanham.

MUSCLE SHOALS SOUND GOSPEL, P.O. Box 915, Sheffield AL 35660. (205)381-2060. Executive Director: Butch McGhee. Record company and record producer (Butch McGhee). Estab. 1986. Releases 6 LPs/year. Receives 50-60 submissions/year. Works with musicians/artists and songwriters on contract and hires musicians for in-house studio work. Pays 8% royalty to artists on contract; statutory rate to publisher per song.
How to Contact: Write first and obtain permission to submit. Prefers cassette or VHS videocassette with 4 songs. Does not return unsolicited material. Reports in 8 weeks.
Music: Mostly gospel, inspirational. Released "Bow Down and Praise Him" (by Butch McGhee, Shawn Lee Sr. and Harvey Thompson Jr.), recorded by Loretta Handy (gospel); "Caught in Your Own Mess" (by Butch McGhee, Shawn Lee Sr. and Harvey Thompson Jr.), recorded by Denise

LaSalle (blues); and "Stop That Zero" (by Butch McGhee and Harvey Thompson Jr.) recorded by Denise LaSalle (blues); all on Maleco Records.

MUSIC FOR LITTLE PEOPLE, P.O. Box 1460, Redway CA 95560. (707)723-3991. Director: Jim Deerhawk. Labels include Music For Little People and Earth Beat! Record company, music pubilsher (Music For Little People/BMI), record and video producer (Music For Little People). Estab. 1985. Releases 6-12 cassettes and 6-12 CDs/year. Receives 200 submissions/year. Works with musicians/ artists on contract and hires musicians for in-house studio work. Pays 2-12% royalty to artists on contract; negotiable rate to publisher per song on record.
How to Contact: Write or call first and obtain permission to submit. Prefers cassette with 3 songs and lyric sheet. SASE. Reports in 3 months.
Music: Mostly children's music, world music and children's stories. Released *All For Freedom* (by various), recorded by Sweet Honey in the Rock; *Dirt Made My Lunch* (by S. Van Zandt), recorded by Banana Slug String Band; *Percival The Froggy* (by D. Connolly), recorded by David Connolly; *On the Sunny Side* (by various), recorded by Maria Muldaur; and *Family Folk Festival* (by various), all on MLP Records (kids cassette).
Tips: "We're interested in music that empowers children with creativity, self-respect, interactive choices and that promotes peace and environmental consciousness and celebrates cultural diversity."

*MUSIC OF THE WORLD, P.O. Box 3620, Chapel Hill NC 27515-3620. President: Bob Haddad. Record company and music publisher (Owl's Head Music/BMI). Estab. 1982. Releases 10 LPs and 10 CDs/ year. Works with musicians/artists on contract and hires musicians for in-house studio work. Royalty paid to artists on contract varies; statutory rate to publisher per song on record.
How to Contact: Write first and obtain permission to submit. Prefers cassette. SASE. Reports in 2 weeks.
Music: Only world music. Released *Brazil Encanto* (by Tico da Costa); *Laya Vinyas* (by Tricky Sankoran); and *Ramana* (by Glen Velez); all on M.O.W. (cassettes/CDs).
Tips: "Submit only traditional world music, or ethnic-influenced modern music."

MÚSICA ARROZ (ASCAP), 5626 Brock St., Houston TX 77023. (713)926-4436. Publications Manager: Barry Leavitt. Labels include Discos MM. Record company and publishing company. Estab. 1986. Releases 10 singles, 5 12″ singles, 10 LPs, 5 EPs and 10 CDs/year. Works with musicians/artists and songwriters on contract and hires musicians for in-house studio work. Pays 10-11% royalty to artists on contract; statutory rate to publisher per song on record.
How to Contact: Submit demo tape by mail. Unsolicited submissions are okay or write to arrange personal interview. Prefers cassette with less than 10 songs and lyric sheets. SASE. Reports in 6 months.
Music: Mostly Spanish pop, Spanish rock and Spanish regional and Tejano. Released "Todos Me Dicen" (by Albert Gonzales) recorded by Rick Gonzales & The Choice, on Mercury Latino Records (discos MM); "Otro Día" (by Gerardo Rodriguez) recorded by Jerry Rodriguez & Mercedez; and "Dime Si Tú Quieres" (by Maria G. Henson), recorded Laura Canales on Capitol/EMI (Latin Tejano).
Tips: "We're interested in anything with a Latin feel, of any type, English or Spanish. We translate if necessary."

*MUSICLAND PRODUCTIONS, Suite C, 1627 E. Silver Springs, Ocala FL 32670. (904)622-5599 and 1-800-330-1627 (Florida residents). Contact: Bobby Land. Music publisher, recording studio and printing shop. BMI. Estab. 1987. Releases 12 songs/year; 4 new songwriters/year. Works with composers. Pays 6% royalty.
Affiliate: Big Sun Music (BMI).
How to Contact: Submit a demo tape—unsolicited submissions are OK. Prefers cassette with 4 songs and lyric sheet. If possible come in person. "We do not return tapes."
Music: Mostly rock, pop and gospel; also country. Produced "Sold Out Of Love" (by B.L. & D.B.), recorded by David Mathis on Musicland Records (country); "20 to Life" (by R.S. BL. J.W.), recorded by Ron Stephens on Musicland Records (country) and "Standing In My Shoes" (by R.S. B.L. J.W.), recorded by Ron Stephens on Musicland Records (country).
Tips: "Stick with one type of music and do it well."

NADINE MUSIC, P.O. Box 2, Fronhof 100, CH-8260 Stein am Rhein **Switzerland.** Phone: 054-415-415. FAX: 054-415-420. President: Freddy J. Angstmann. Music publisher and record producer. Releases 12 LPs/year. Works with musicians/artists and songwriters on contract.
How to Contact: Prefers cassette (or VHS/PAL videocassette). SAE and IRC.
Music: Mostly gospel, blues and jazz; also classical. Released *Christmas Album*; and *Who Shall Abide* (by Johnny Thompson), and *Gospel at the Opera* (by Radio Zürich) both on Capricorn Records (all LPs). Other artists include Mickey Baker, Erich Lauer, Errol Dixon, Anne Morrëe, Philadelphia Terry Ricks and Champion Jack Dupra.

NARADA PRODUCTIONS, 1845 North Farwell Ave., Milwaukee WI 53202. (414)272-6700. Contact: Dan Chase. Labels include Narada Equinox, Narada Lotus, Narada Mystique, Sona Gaia. Record company. Estab. 1979. Releases 25 LPs/year. Works with musicians/artists on contract.
How to Contact: Submit demo tape by mail. Unsolicited submissions are OK. Prefers cassette (or VHS videocassette if available). Does not return unsolicited material. Reports in 2 months.
Music: Mostly instrumental. Released *Mil Amones* written and recorded by Doug Cameron, on Euinox Records; *Dr. D* written and recorded by Spencer Brewer, on Equinox Records; and *Citizen of Time* written and recorded by David Arkenstone, on Mystique Records (instrumental).

NEON RECORDS, 88 Lenox Ave., Paterson NJ 07502. (201)790-7668. A&R Department: Scott Lea. Record company, music publisher (BMI, ASCAP), record producer (Scott Lea Productions) and Scott Lea Publishing. Estab. 1988. Releases 3-6 singles, 2-4 12″ singles, 1-2 LPs, 1-2 EPs and 1-2 CDs/year. Works with musicians/artists and songwriters on contract and hires musicians for in-house studio work. Pays varying royalty to artists on contract; negotiated rate to publisher per song on record.
How to Contact: Call first and obtain permission to submit. Prefers cassette with 3-5 songs and lyric sheet. SASE. Reports in 6 weeks.
Music: Mostly R&B, club, dance, A/C and rock; also pop and jazz. Released "World Without Love" (by Claude S.), recorded by Anything Box on Neon Records (club/ballad); "Stop" (by R. Bonagura and D. Cintron), recorded by Myth on Neon Records (rock) and "How Does Your Heart Feel?" (by P. Castgilin and S. Lea), recorded by Paul Cast on Neon Records (adult contemporary/rock ballad).

NERVOUS RECORDS, Unit 6, 7-11 Minerva Rd., London NW10 6HJ, **England**. Phone: 4481-963-0352. Managing Director: R. Williams. Record company, record producer and music publisher (Nervous Publishing and Zorch Music). Member MCPS, PRS, PPL. Releases 10 LPs and 4 CDs/year. Receives 100 submissions/year. Works with songwriters on royalty contract. Pays 5-12% royalty to artists on contract; statutory rate to publishers per song on records. Royalties paid directly to US songwriters and artists or through US publishing or recording affiliate.
How to Contact: Submit demo tape with 4-15 songs and lyric sheet. SAE and IRC. Reports in 2 weeks.
Music: Psychobilly and rockabilly. "No heavy rock, AOR, stadium rock, disco, soul, pop—only wild rockabilly and psychobilly." Released "Who's He?" (by Clarke), recorded by Coffin-Nails (psychobilly); "Help Me" (by Peisey), recorded by Scamps (psychobilly); and "Alien Nation" (by Brand), recorded by Torment (psychobilly), all on Nervous Records. Other artists include The Griswalds, Rusti Steel, The Tintax Torment and The Nitros.
Tips: "Want wild and fast music—really demented rockabilly, not punk."

***NEXT STEP RECORDS**, Studio 104, 912 E. Third St., Los Angeles CA 90013. (213)617-3362. President: Barbara Wright. Record company. Estab. 1990. Releases 3-4 cassettes and 3-4 CDs/year. Works with musicians/artists and songwriters on contract. Pays 1-10% royalty to artists on contract; statutory rate to publisher per song on record.
How to Contact: Write or call first and obtain permission to submit. Prefers cassette. SASE. Reports in 2-3 weeks.
Music: Mostly A/C, pop/jazz, Latin and R&B. Released *Neon Ballroom* (by Rick Rhodes), recorded by Marc Green on Next Step Records (A/C LP). Other artists include David Perry and Nobody's Baby.
Tips: "Our label specializes in original contemporary music for ballroom dancing. We do mostly instrumental music and look for strong melodies which can be adapted for ballroom dancing: i.e., Foxtrot, Waltz, Tango, Swing, Rumba, Cha cha, Samba."

***NFS RECORDS, INC.**, 502 Park Avenue, New York NY 10022. (212)644-2290. National Director: Cathy Bergman. Record company. Estab. 1986. Releases 6-8 12″ singles, 6-8 LPs and 4 CDs/year. Works with musicians/artists, songwriters and producers on contract; hires musicians on salary for in-house studio work. Pays statutory rate to artists and publishers per song on records.
How to Contact: Submit demo tape by mail. Unsolicited submissions are OK. Prefers cassette or VHS videocassette with 2-3 songs and lyric sheet. SASE. Reports in 3-4 weeks.
Music: Mostly pop/dance, pop/rock and rock. Released "Doctor's Orders" (by Stephen Greenway Cook), recorded by Andree Maranda (pop/dance); "45 Reasons'" (by Arnie Roman and Hard Times Productions), recorded by Andree Maranda (pop); and "Stagger Lee '89," written and recorded by Lloyd Price, all on NFS Records.

NICKLE PLATE RECORDS, 3951 W. 178th Pl., Country Club Hills IL 60477. President: Frederick S. Koger. Record company and music publisher ("L" Train Publishers/ASCAP). Estab. 1987. Releases 3 singles and 3 12″ singles/year. Works with musicians/artists and songwriters on contract. Pays 10% royalty to artist on contract.

How to Contact: Write or call first to arrange personal interview. Prefers cassette or 7½ ips reel-to-reel with 3-5 songs and lyric or lead sheets. Reports in 3 weeks.

Music: Mostly R&B, rap and pop; also rock and gospel. Released "Love Quarrel" (by Frederick S. Koger), recorded by Virgil/Rozlyn on Nickle Plate Records (single) and "Stop Watch" written and recorded by Jam 2000 and Derick on Nickel Plate Records (dance house). Other artists include Steven Lee and Orlando Sifney.

NORTH STAR RECORDS, 95 Hathaway St., Providence RI 02907. (401)785-8400. Executive Vice President: Bruce R. Foulke. Record company and music publisher (Blue Gate Music/ASCAP). Estab. 1985. Releases 4-5 LPs/year. Works with musicians/artists and songwriters on contract. Pays statutory royalty to artists on contract; statutory rate to publisher per song on record.

How to Contact: Write first and obtain permission to submit. Prefers cassette with 4-5 songs and lyric sheets. Does not return unsolicited material. Reports in 1 month.

Music: Mostly country, R&B and rock/folk; also acoustic traditional, classical and children's music. Released *Cheryl Wheeler* on North Star Records and *Half-A-Book* on Cypress Records, written and recorded by Cheryl Wheeler (rock/country LPs); and *Time Can Be So Magic*, written and recorded by Bill Thomas on North Star Records (children's LP). Other artists include Chili Brothers, Arturo Delmoni, New England Music Collection, Mair-Davis Duo and Hubbards.

Tips: "A professional, well thought-out presentation of your best material is necessary to attract the attention of record label personnel."

NORTHEASTERN RECORDS, P.O. Box 3589, Saxonville MA 01701-0605. (508)820-4440. General Manager: L.E. Joiner. Record company. Estab. 1980. Releases 10 CDs/year. Pays statutory rate to publishers per song on records.

How to Contact: "We are interested in performers only, not individual songs." Submit demo tape by mail. Unsolicited submissions are OK. "Include SASE if you want anything back." Prefers cassette, "preferably a copy of final studio cut." Reports in 3 months.

Music: Interested in country/bluegrass, folk/international and jazz; also rock 'n roll. Released *That Old Mill*, written and recorded by John Lincoln Wright (country/folk CD/cassette); and *Manic Traditions*, written and recorded by Les Miserables Brass Band (worldbeat/folk CD/cassette), both on Northeastern Records. Other artists include Didi Stewart (pop), The Fringe (jazz), Barry and Holly Tashian (country), Shirim Klezmer Orchestra and Andanzas (folk/Latin).

Tips: "We are presently licensing finished masters for CD and cassette release, and are mainly interested in artists with a developed, original sound, who are also touring. We are not looking for songs."

*NOW & THEN RECORDS, #2A, 412 E. 78 St., New York NY 10021. (212)879-4667. Contact: Shane Faber. Record company, music publisher (Now & Then Music/BMI) and record producer (Shane "the Dr." Faber). Estab. 1980. Works with musicians/artists and songwriters on contract. Pays 10% royalty to artists on contract; statutory rate to publisher per song on record.

How to Contact: Submit demo tape by mail. Unsolicited submissions are OK. Prefers cassette with 4 songs and lyric sheet. SASE.

Music: Mostly pop, dance and R&B; also rap and New Age. Released *Sneak Attack*, *Beat the Meter* and *Big Ducks*, all LPs recorded by Bad Sneakers. Other artists include Tenita Jordon (R&B), T.T. (dance), Blackhearts (rap), Shane Faber (pop) and Audrey Smith-Bey (pop).

NUCLEUS RECORDS, P.O. Box 111, Sea Bright NJ 07760. President: Robert Bowden. Record company and music publisher (Roots Music/BMI). Member AFM (US and Canada). Estab. 1979. Releases 2 singles and 1 LP/year. Works with musicians/artists on contract and hires musicians for in-house studio work. Pays up to 10% royalty for each record sold; 50% rate to publisher per song on record. Charges artists/songwriters up-front for demo work.

How to Contact: Prefers cassette (or videocassette) with any number songs and lyric sheet. Prefers studio produced demos. SASE. Reports in 1 month.

Music: Mostly country and pop; also church/religious, classical, folk, MOR, progressive, rock (soft, mellow) and top 40. Released "Always," written and recorded by Marco Sison (pop singles); "Selfish Heart," written and recorded by Robert Bowden; and "Henrey C.," written and recorded by Robert Dowden (country); all on Nucleus Records.

*NUDE RECORDS, P.O. Box 460, Kings Cross NSW 2011 **Australia**. Phone: (02)3572350. Managing Director: C. Read. Record Company. Estab. 1986. Releases 3 12″ singles, 3 LPs and 4 CDs/year. Works with musicians/artists on contract. Payment varies.

How to Contact: Call first and obtain permission to submit. Prefers cassette with 1-4 songs. Does not return unsolicited material. "If we like it, you will hear from us."
Music: Mostly pop/R&B/dance and electronic/dance; also rock, country and avant-guard. Released *Flesh D-Vice*, written and recorded by Flesh D-Vice (LP); *Crush The Lily* (by M. Snarski), recorded by Chad's Tree (LP); and "Sweet Jesus" (by M. Snarski), recorded by Chad's Tree (12″ single), all on Nude Records.

*ONE-EYED DUCK RECORDING AND PUBLISHING, 22 Rainsford Rd., Toronto, ON M4L3N4 Canada. (416)694-6900. General Manager: Patricia Erlendson. Record company, music publisher (PROCAN) and record producer. Estab. 1983. Releases 1 LP/year. Works with musicians/artists and songwriters on contract. Pays negotiable rate to artists on contract; statutory rate to publisher per song on record. Charges up-front for production.
How to Contact: Write first and obtain permission to submit. Prefers cassette.
Music: Mostly children's. Released "I Can Do Anything," "Sharing" and "Kickoff," recorded by Sphere Clown Band on One-Eyed Duck Records (children's).

THE ORANGE RECORD COMPANY, Suite 119, 2166 W. Broadway, Anaheim CA 92804-2446. (714)525-5223. Vice President A&R: Harold Shmoduquet. Labels include Orange Records and Beet Records. Record company, music publisher (Tracy Sands Music/BMI) and record producer (Orange Productions). Estab. 1989. Releases 1-2 singles, 6-12 12″ singles, 4 LPs, 2 EPs and 4 CDs/year. Receives 600 submissions/year. Works with musicians/artists and songwriters on contract. Pays 1-9% royalty to artists on contract; statutory rate or negotiable rate to publishers per song on record. "Artists may, depending on negotiation, be responsible for a percentage of production costs in relation to the finished master tape. Songwriters are never charged for any reason."
How to Contact: Submit demo tape by mail. Unsolicited submissions are OK. Prefers cassette (or VHS videocassette) with 2-3 songs and lyric sheet. SASE. Reports in 2 months.
Music: Mostly melodic metal, progressive rock and sixties-sound; also ethnic, R&B and gospel. Released "The Hunter," written and recorded by J.C. Hope on Orange Records (pop); "My Pants Are Way Too Tight" (by Bo Antin), recorded by Benny Grunch on Beat Records (R&B); and "Woman's World" (by Robert and Herb Wahlsteen), recorded by Jubal's Children on Swak Records (rock). Other artists include Mary Hart, Bastille, No Sweat and Manhunter.
Tips: "If you sound like the Beatles, we'll talk."

ORBIT RECORDS, P.O. Box 120675, Nashville TN 37212. (615)255-1068. Owner: Ray McGinnis. Record company, music publisher (Nautical Music Co.) and record producer (Ray Mack Productions). Estab. 1965. Releases 6-10 singles, 6 12″ singles and 4 LPs/year. Receives 15-20 submissions/month. Works with musicians/artists on contract. Pays 8-12% royalty to artists on contract; statutory rate to publisher per song on record.
How to Contact: Prefers cassette with 4 songs and lead sheet. Does not return unsolicited material. Reports in 6-8 weeks.
Music: Country (ballads), country rock and R&B. Released "Burning Love," written and recorded by Alan Warren (hard rock); "I Need the Real Thing," written and recorded by Don Acuff (country); and "She's a Heartbreaker" (by L. Oldham), recorded by LeRoy Steele (country rock); all on Orbit Records. Other artists include LeRoy Steele, and Da-Kota, "a supercharged country rock group."
Tips: "We like artists with individual styles, not 'copy cats'; be original and unique."

ORINDA RECORDS, Suite 200, 111 Deerwood Place, San Ramon CA 94583. (415)831-4890. A&R Director: Harry Balk. Record company. Releases 30 LPs/year. Works with musicians/artists and songwriters on contract. Pays varying royalty to artists on contract; statutory rate to publishers.
How to Contact: Prefers cassette with lyric and lead sheet. SASE. Does not return unsolicited material. Reports in 2 months.
Music: Rock, pop, and jazz; also classical.

*ORLEANS RECORDS, 828 Royal St., #536, New Orleans LA 70016. President: Carlo Ditta. Labels include Tomohawk Discs. Record company and music publisher (Attid Music/ASCAP). Estab. 1984. Releases 2 singles, 3 LPs, 2 EPs and 2 CDs/year. Works with musicians/artists and songwriters on contract and master lease agreements. Pays 5-6% royalty to artists on contract; statutory rate to publisher per song on record. Unsolicited submissions are OK. Prefers cassette (or VHS videocassette) with 5 songs and lyric sheets. SASE. Reports in 6 weeks.
How to Contact: Submit demo tape by mail. Unsolicited submissions are OK. Prefers cassette (or VHS videocassette) with 5 songs and lyric sheets. SASE. Reports in 6 weeks.
Music: Mostly blues, soul, gospel and folk; also R&B, pop and traditional jazz. Released *Victory Mixture*, by Willy DeVille; *Your Perfect Companion* (by K. Bertucci/Loria/Mclain), recorded by Mighty Sam; *New Orleans, New Orleans*, written and recorded by A.J.Loria; and *The Story of My Life* (by Eddie Jones), recorded by Guitar Slim Jr. (1988 Traditional Blues Grammy nominee); all on Orleans Records

(all LPs). Other artists include Mighty Sam, A.J. Loria, Guitar Slim Jr., Robert Lowery, and The New Indians.

*PACIFIC & PLANET PACIFIC RECORDS, Pacific House, Vale Rd., London N4 **U.K.**. Phone (81)800-3288. A&R: B. Dollman. Record company. Estab. 1990. Releases 8 singles, 8 12″ singles, 1 LP and 1 CD/year. Works with musicians/artists on contract. Pays 10-12% royalty; statutory rate to publisher per song on records.
How to Contact: Submit demo tape by mail. Unsolicited submissions are OK. Prefers cassette (or VHS PAL videocassette if available) with 3-6 songs. SASE. Reports in 2 weeks.
Music: Mostly dance music and psychedelic dance.
Tips: "Interested in groups with interesting grooves, style, hybriding of music."

PALMETTO PRODUCTIONS, P.O. Box 1376, Pickens SC 29671. (803)859-9614. FAX: (803)859-3814. President: Brian E. Raines. Labels include Palmetto Records (country) and Rosada Records (gospel). Record company, music publisher (Brian Raines Music Co./ASCAP and Brian Song Music Co./BMI) and record producer (Brian E. Raines/Palmetto Productions). Estab. 1985. Releases 1-3 singles and 2 LPs/year. Works with musicians/artists and songwriters on contract and hires musicians as independent contractors. Pays 20% royalty to artists on contract; statutory rate to publishers per song on record.
How to Contact: Submit demo tape by mail. Unsolicited submissions are okay. Prefers cassette (or VHS videocassette) with 2 songs and lyric sheet. SASE. Reports in 3 weeks.
Music: Mostly country, gospel and top 40; also contemporary Christian. Released "Since I Met You" (written and recorded by Brian Raines), on Palmetto Records (country, single); *Take It To Jesus* (by Dale Cassell), recorded by Trinity on Mark Five Records (gospel LP); and *From the Heart* (written and recorded by Jim Hubbard), on Hubbit Records (country LP).

PANDEM RECORDS INC., 1916 28th Ave. South, Birmingham AL 35209. (205)870-3239. President: Michael Panapento. Labels include Polymusic Records. Record company. Estab. 1985. Releases 4 LPs, 2 EPs and 1 CD/year. Works with musicians/artists on contract and hires musicians for in-house studio work; artist development. Pays 50% royalty to artists on contract; varying rate to publishers per song on record.
How to Contact: Write first and obtain permission to submit. Prefers cassette with 3 song and lyric sheets. Reports in 6 weeks.
Music: Mostly pop/top 40, rock and R&B; also country and jazz. Released *Pass the Buck*, written and recorded by F. Fatts on Pandem Records (jazz LP), *The RAW Sessions*, by the Vallejo Bros. on Pandem Records (rock); "This Time" (by J. Bradley), recorded by Dee Bradley on Smoke Stack Records (R&B 45); "Money Talks" (by A.J. Vallejo), recorded by Vallejo Brothers on Pandem Records (rock); "Elvis' Grave" (by Phillips/Panepento) (soundtrack); and "I Wish" (by S. Morris), recorded by The Diptones on Pandem Records (vocal/AC).

PARADE, 88 St. Francis St., Newark NJ 07105. (201)344-4214. Senior Vice President, Product Development/A&R Director: Joey Porello. Labels include Peter Pan, Power, Compose Records, Tronbound, Third Ear, Connection and Jammo. Record company. Estab. 1928. Releases 10-20 singles and 5-10 12″ singles, 10-20 LPs, and 10-20 CDs/year. Works with artists and songwriters on contract. Pays varying royalty to artists on contract; statutory rate to publishers for each record sold.
How to Contact: Prefers cassette with 1-3 songs and lyric sheet. SASE. Reports in 2 months.
Music: Mostly dance, children's and MOR; also country, R&B, New Age rock, novelty and classical. Released *Aerobics*, by Joanie Greggains (exercise LP). Other artists include Morton Downey, Jr. (country) and Gilead Limor (New Age).

PARAGOLD RECORDS & TAPES, P.O. Box 292101, Nashville TN 37216. (615)391-5955. Director: Teresa Bernard. Record company, music publisher (Rainbarrel Music Co./BMI) and record producer. Estab. 1972. Releases 5 singles, 5 LPs and 1 EP/year. Works with musicians/artists and songwriters on contract. Pays statutory rate to publishers.
How to Contact: Write first and obtain permission to submit. Prefers cassette (or VHS videocassette) with 2 songs and lyric or lead sheets. SASE. "Unpublished songs are welcome. Send only outstanding material." Reports in 6 weeks.
Music: Country and top 40. Released "Devil's Guitar," "Rock'n Roll Revival," and "I Worked with O'l Lefty," both written and recorded by Johnny Bernard on Paragold Records (country). Other artists include Sunset Cowboys.

PARC RECORDS INC., Suite 205, 5104 N. Orange Blossom Trail, Orlando FL 32810. (407)292-0021. Executive Assistant: Leslie A. Schipper. Record company (Mister Sunshine Music/BMI). Estab. 1985. Releases 4+ singles, 2 12″ singles, 2 LPs and 2 CDs/year. Works with musicians/artists and songwriters on contract.

How to Contact: Prefers cassette (or VHS videocassette) with 3-5 songs and lyric sheet. SASE. Reports in 6-8 weeks.
Music: Mostly rock/metal, dance and jazz/new wave; also A/C and R&B. Released *Lighting Strikes* recorded by Molly Hatchet on Parc/Capitol Records (rock LP); *China Sky* recorded by China Sky on Parc/CBS Records (rock LP); and *Ana* recorded by Ana on Parc/CBS Records (dance LP) (all by various). Other artists include Glen Kelly and Deryle Hughes.
Tips: "Quality songs with good hooks are more important than great production. If it's good, we can hear it."

PARHAM SOUND STUDIO, Rt. 3, Box 243-B, Stephenville TX 76401. (817)965-4132. Contact: Carroll Parham. Label: Scotty Records of Texas. Record company, music publisher and record producer. Releases 4 LPs/year. Works with musicians/artists and songwriters on contract. Pays standard royalty to artists on contract; pays statutory rate to publishers.
How to Contact: Prefers cassette. Does not return unsolicited material. "Please make sure demo is clean and presentable."
Music: Mostly country, gospel and swing. Released *Do You Ever Think of Me* (by Joan Hathcox), recorded by Joanie on Scotty Records; *What's Left of A Man*, (by J. Green), recorded by Curtis Lovejoy on Scotty Records; and *Texas Ranger Swing*, (by D. Rowell/J. Hathcox/ C. Parham), recorded by Country Express on GBC Records, (all LPs). Other artists include Tommy Horton, Derwood Rowell, and Ray Jones.

PAULA RECORDS/JEWEL RECORDS/RONN RECORDS, P.O. Box 1125, Shreveport LA 71163-1125. (318)227-2228. Owner: Stanley J. Lewis. Labels include Jewel Records and Ronn Records. Record company and music publisher. Works with musicians/artists and songwriters on contract.
How to Contact: Submit demo tape by mail. Unsolicited submissions are OK. Prefers cassette with 3 songs and lyric sheet. SASE.
Music: Mostly R&B, gospel and country.

PDS RECORDS, P.O. Box 412477, Kansas City MO 64141. (816)921-7621. Contact: A&R, Dept. 100. Labels include Universal Jazz, PDS Associated labels. Record company, music publisher (PDS Music Publishing/ASCAP/BMI) and record producer (PDS Productions). Estab. 1988. Releases 8-10 singles, 8-10 12" singles, 3-5 LPs, 8-10 EPs and 3-5 CDs/year. Works with musicians/artists on contract.
How to Contact: Write first and obtain permission to submit. Prefers cassette (or VHS videocassette) with 4-5 songs and lyric sheet. Does not return unsolicited material. Reports in 2 months.

*PENDRAGON RECORDS, Suite A222, 12609 Dessau Rd., Austin TX 78753. (512)251-0375. Vice President/A&R: Gary A. Coll. Music publisher (Holy Grail Publishing/BMI) and record producer (Freelance). Estab. 1987. Releases 5 singles, 5 LPs and 3 EPs/year. Works with musicians/artists on contract and hires musicians for in-house studio work. Pays 30-50% royalty to artists on contract; statutory rate to publisher per song on record. Charges prospective artists for production, promotion and distribution.
How to Contact: Write first and obtain permission to submit. Prefers cassette or VHS videocassette with 3 songs with lyric or lead sheet. Reports in 2 months.
Music: Mostly rock, pop and jazz; also R&B, gospel and country. Released *Charlie Chaplin's Factory* (by J. Cook), recorded by Wallflowers (LP); *Young Thunder* (by T. Kross-S. Wilcox), recorded by Young Thunder (EP); and *Goat Suite #2, 3* (by R. Cooper), recorded by Richard Cooper (EP); all on Pendragon Records. Other artists include Olin Murrell.
Tips: "If you need advice – don't submit!"

PENGUIN RECORDS, INC., P.O. Box 1274, Miami FL 33261. Product Manager: Michael J. McNamee. Operation Manager: Gregory J. Winters. Labels include Straitgate Records, Penguin Records and Kinetic Records, distributed by Marz Records. Record company, music publisher. Estab. 1990. Releases 6 singles, 6 12" singles, 3 LPs and 3 CDs/year. Works with musicians/artists and songwriters/year. Pays varying royalty.

 The asterisk before a listing indicates that the listing is new in this edition. New markets are often the most receptive to unsolicited submissions.

How to Contact: Obtain permission to submit before sending submissions. Prefers cassette (or VHS videocassette if available) with 3 songs and lyric sheets. Does not return unsolicited material. Reports in 2 months.

Music: Mostly dance, pop, rock R&B/rap and alternative/dance; also industrial and Christian. Released "What Time Is It?" (by R. Rodriguez), recorded by Don't Know Yet on Penguin Records (distributed by Epic), and "Move Out" (by Another Nation), recorded by Another Nation on Kinetic Records.

Tips: "Be patient! There's a lot of music out there. Everyone will get a chance."

PENTHOUSE MUSIC, 6728 Eton Ave., Canoga Park CA 91303. (818)992-4777. Director: Toni Biggs-Andrews. Record company, music publisher (Tonina Music Publishing) and record producer.
How to Contact: "We are not looking for outside material at the present time."
Music: Mostly pop, New Age and rock; also R&B, dance, easy listening, progressive, soul, top 40/pop and "space wave/mod hot." Released "Bad to The Bone" (by George Thorogood) and "Summertime" (by George Gershwin), both recorded by Threshold on Penthouse Records (12″ singles).

PHOENIX RECORDS, INC., Box 121076, Nashville TN 27212-1076. (615)244-5357. President: Reggie M. Churchwell. Labels include Nashville International Records. Record company and music publisher (affiliated with both BMI and ASCAP). Estab. 1971. Releases 5-6 singles, 2-3 12″ singles, 2-3 LPs and 1-2 CDs/year. Works with musicians/artists and songwriters on contract. Pays standard royalty to artists on contract; statutory rate to publisher per song on record.
How to Contact: Write first and obtain permission to submit. "You must have permission before submitting any material." Prefers cassette with lyric sheets. Does not return unsolicited material. Reports in 2-3 weeks.
Music: Mostly country, rock and pop; also gospel. Released "Left of Center Line" (by Howard Lips), recorded by Catfish on Phoenix Records (country/rock); and "Littlest Cowboy" written and recorded by Sonny Shroyer on Hazzard Records (children's). Other artists include Conrad Pierce and Clay Jerrolds.
Tips: "We are looking for songs with strong hooks and strong words. We are not simply looking for songs, we are looking for hits."

PILOT RECORDS AND TAPE COMPANY, 628 S. South St., Mount Airy NC 27030. (919)786-2865. President and Owner: Paul E. Johnson. Labels include Stork, Stark, Pilot, Hello, Kay, Sugarbear, Southcoast, Songcraft and Blue Jay. Record company, music publisher (Tompaul Music Company/BMI) and record producer. Estab. 1960. Releases 12 singles and 75 LPs/year. Works with songwriters on contract; musicians on salary for in-house studio work. Pays 30% royalty to artists on contract; statutory rate to publishers per song on record.
How to Contact: Prefers cassette or 7 ½ ips reel-to-reel with 6 songs and lyric sheet. SASE. Reports in 1 month. "The songwriters should give their date of birth with submissions. This information will be used when copyrighting a songwriter's song."
Music: Mostly country, gospel and bluegrass; also rock, folk and blues. Released "Devil's Sweetheart," written and recorded by Clyde Johnson (country); "Heartache Street," written and recorded by Clyde Johnson (country); and "Jesus Is Waiting (Just Over the Way)," written and recorded by Cleo Taylor (gospel); all on Pilot Records. Other artists include Bobby Atkins, Carl Tolbert, Sam Bray, Ralph Hill, Early Upchurch, Sanford Teague and Don Sawyers.

PLANKTON RECORDS, 236 Sebert Rd., Forest Gate, London E7 0NP **England**. Phone: (081)534-8500. Senior Partner: Simon Law. Labels include Plankton, Sea Dream, Embryo Arts (licensed, Belgium), Gutta (licensed, Sweden), and Radio (licensed, United Kingdom). Record company and music publisher (Sea Dream Music, Scarf Music Publishing and Really Free Music). Estab. 1977. Releases 1 single, 4 LPs, and 1 EP/year. Works with musicians/artists and songwriters on contract. Pays 10% royalty to artists on contract; statutory rate to publishers per song on record.
How to Contact: Prefers cassette with 3 songs and lyric sheet. SAE and IRC. Reports in 6 weeks.
Music: Mostly funk/rock, R&B and gospel; also blues. Released *Gotta Keep Moving*, (by Paul Crick/Greg Nash/Keith Dixon), recorded by Medals (jazz/rock); *Surrender*, (by Rue Randall), recorded by Solid Air (rock); and *Paris Airshow*, (by Simon Law), recorded by Fresh Claim (rock); (all LP/cassette) all on Plankton Records. Other artists include Pete Ward, Catch 22, Really Free, Ruth Turner and Cheryl Mead.

"How to Use Your Songwriter's Market" (at the front of this book) contains comments and suggestions to help you understand and use the information in these listings.

Tips: "We specialize in bands with a Christian bias, regardless of their musical style."

*PLATINUM BOULEVARD RECORDS, 523 East Prater Way, Reno NV 89431. (702)358-7484. President: Lawrence Davis. Record company. Estab. 1986. Releases 2 singles and 1 LP/year. Works with musicians/artists on contract. Pays negotiable royalty to artists on contract; negotiable rate to publisher per song on record.
How to Contact: Submit demo tape by mail. Unsolicited submissions are OK. Prefers cassette (or VHS videocassette) with songs and lyric or lead sheets. Does not return unsolicited material. "We report back only if interested."
Music: Mostly rock, pop and R&B; also country, jazz and New Age. Released *Davis*, written and recorded by L.R. Davis on Platinum Blvd. Records (rock LP).
Tips: "Be willing to learn."

PLAY RECORDS, Box 6541, Cleveland OH 44101. (216)467-0300. President: John Latimer. Record company. Estab. 1985. Releases 3 LPs/year. Works with musicians/artists and songwriters on contract.
How to Contact: Submit demo tape by mail. Unsolicited submissions are OK. Prefers cassette (or VHS or ¾″ videocassettes) with 5 songs and lyric or lead sheets. SASE. Reports in 6 weeks.
Music: Mostly rock, pop and alternative; also blues, jazz and R&B. Released "There Was a Time," written and recorded by The Bellows; "Bombs Away," written and recorded by Serious Nature; and "Mr. Sensible," written and recorded by Mr. Sensible; all on Play Records (rock). Other artists include The French Lenards, 15 60 75, The Adults, Cool Down Daddy, The Bomb, Earl Rays, Zero One, Holy Cows and Ronald Koal.
Tips: "Be patient but persistent. Please correspond by mail only."

PLAYBONES RECORDS, Box 203312, D-2000 Hamburg 20, **West Germany**. Phone: (040) 4300339. FAX: (040)439.65.87. Producer: Arno v. Vught. Labels include Rondo Records. Record company, music publisher (Mento Music Group KG.) and record producer (Arteg Productions). Estab. 1975. Releases 30 CDs/year. Works with musicians/artists and songwriters on contract. Pays 8-16% royalty to artists on contract.
How to Contact: Prefers cassette and lyric or lead sheet. SAE and IRC. Reports in 2 weeks.
Music: Mostly instrumentals, country and jazz; also background music, rock and gospel. Released "I Need to Hold" (by Eggert), recorded by O. Bendt on VS-Verlag Records (CD); "Weites Land" written and recorded by P. Reifegerste on DA-Music Records (CD); and "Ach Lass Es" (by Martin), recorded by Achim Körber on TeBiTo Records (CD). Other artists include H.J. Knipphals, Gaby Knies, Jack Hals, H. Hausmann, Crabmeat and M. Frommhold.

PLEASURE RECORDS, Rt. 1, Box 187-A, Whitney TX 76692. (817)694-4047. President: Allen Newton. Labels include Cactus Flats, Pristine, MFN. Record company and music publisher (Four Newton Publishing/BMI). Estab. 1986. Releases 12 singles, 1 12″ single and 1 LP/year. Works with musicians/artists and songwriters on contract. Pays statutory rate to publisher per song on record.
How to Contact: Submit demo tape by mail. Unsolicited submissions are OK. Prefers cassette with 3 songs and lyric or lead sheets. SASE. Reports in 4 weeks.
Music: Mostly country, gospel and rock; also rock-a-billy, R&B and Spanish. Released "I'll Hear Your Call" (by V. Smeaton), recorded by Victoria on Pristine Records (R&B single); "Dim Lit Bars," written and recorded by Charlie Locke on Pleasure Records (C&W single); "Carry Me Back,' written and recorded by Mickey Drum on Pleasure Records (C&W single); and "Starin-A-Haze," written and recorded by Thin Ice on Pristine Records (rock single). Other artists include Denny Glenn, Arch Brown, Sherry Fontaine, Blessed Carrion, Felix Van Slyke, Stylle and J. Sam.

*PMG RECORDS, Box 2849, Trolley Station, Detroit MI 48231. (313)581-1267. Partner: Bruce Henderson. Record company, music publisher (Prejippie Music Group/BMI) and record producer (PMG Productions). Estab. 1990. Releases 2-4 12″ singles, 1 LP and 1 EP/year. Works with musicians/artists on contract. Pays statutory rate.
How to Contact: Submit demo tape by mail. Unsolicited submissions are OK. Prefers cassette or VHS videocassette with 3-4 songs and lyric sheet. Include photo if possible. SASE. Reports in 1 month.
Music: Mostly funk rock, rap, dance; also alternative, rock and new age. Released "Shake Your Body" and "Redd Hott," recorded by The VIC and The CUT; and "Good Times," recorded by DOS (featuring Coco); all on PMG Records (hip house). Other artists include The Prejippies, Sacred Places, and Vicky and The Poetics.
Tips: "We're looking for creativity/originality. The songs that are most imaginative get our attention first. Also have your own look/style."

POLYGRAM RECORDS, 810 7th Ave., New York NY 10019. (212)333-8000. Contact: A&R Assistant. Record company. Works with artists on contract.

How to Contact: "We review songs submitted by established publishers. Not accepting unsolicited material, but welcome queries when accompanied by press and/or chart clippings and SASE. Do *not* send recordings or lyrics until requested." Recommends referral from a reputable industry source.

Music: Rock, top 40/pop, R&B and dance/urban. Current roster includes Bon Jovi, John Mellencamp, Cinderella, Robert Cray, The Rainmakers, Tom Kimmel, Billy Branigan, Kiss, The Everly Brothers, Kool and the Gang, Cameo, Commodores, Fat Boys, Gwenn Guthrie, Rush, Moody Blues, ELP and Scorpions.

Tips: "Be patient—you will be contacted if there's interest. Keep in mind that most of the artists write their own material. We're most open to female-oriented and pop acts to balance out heavy-hitting hard rock and R&B roster."

POP RECORD RESEARCH, 17 Piping Rock Dr., Ossining NY 10502. (914)762-8499. Director: Gary Theroux. Labels include Surf City, GTP and Rock's Greatest Hits. Record company, music publisher (Surf City Music/ASCAP), record producer and archive of entertainment-related research materials (files on hits and hitmakers since 1877). Estab. 1962. Works with musicians/artists and songwriters on contract and writers/historians/biographers/radio, TV and film producers requiring research help or materials. Pays statutory rate to publisher per song on record.

How to Contact: Submit demo tape, press kits or review material by mail. Unsolicited submissions are OK. Prefers cassette (or VHS videocassette). Does not return unsolicited material.

Music: Mostly pop, country and R&B. Released "The Declaration" (by Theroux-Gilbert), recorded by An American on Bob Records; "Thoughts From a Summer Rain," written and recorded by Bob Gilbert on Bob Records; and "Tiger Paws," written and recorded by Bob Gilbert on BAL Records; all pop singles. Other artists include Gary and Joan, The Nightflight Singers and Ruth Zimmerman.

Tips: "Help us keep our biographical file on you and your career current by sending us updated bios/press kits, etc. They are most helpful to writers/researchers in search of accurate information on your success."

POSITIVE FEEDBACK STUDIOS, (formerly Counterpart Creative Studios), 4010 North Bend Rd., P.O. Box 11333, Cincinnati OH 45211. (513)661-8810. President: Shad O'Shea. Record company, music publisher (Hurdy Gurdy Music Co., Counterpart Music/BMI) and jingle company. Member RIAA. Releases 24 singles and 6 LPs/year. Works with musicians on salary.

How to Contact: Write first. Prefers 7½ ips reel-to-reel with 1-2 songs. Does not return unsolicited material. Reports in 1 week.

Music: Bluegrass, blues, children's, choral, church/religious, classical, country, dance, easy listening, folk, gospel, jazz, MOR, progressive, rock, funk, soul and top 40/pop. Released "McLove Story," by Shad O'Shea on Plantation Records; "Hot Fun in the Summertime," by Dayton on Capitol Records; "Freakazoid" and "Wet My Whistle," by Midnight Star on Warner Bros. Records.

PPI/PETER PAN INDUSTRIES, 88 St. Francis St., Newark NJ 07105. (201)344-4214. Product Manager: Marianne Eggleston. Labels include Compose Records, Current Records, Parade Video, Iron Bound Publishing/Guess Star Records. Record company, music publisher, record producer (Dunn Pearson, Jr.) and outside producers are used also. Estab. 1928. Releases 12 singles, 6 12″ singles, over 28 LPs and 28 CDs/year. Works with musicians/artist and songwriters on contract. Pays royalty per contract; statutory rater per contract to publisher per song on records. "All services are negotiable!"

How to Contact: Write or call first to obtain permission to submit. Prefers cassette (or VHS videocassette if available) with 3-5 songs and lyric sheet. SASE. Reports in 3 months. Does not return unsolicited submissions.

Music: Pop, R&B; also jazz and New Age. Released "Go For The Gusto" (R&B); "Programmed For Love" (jazz); and "Color Tapestry" (jazz) all written and recorded by Dunn Pearson, Jr. on Compose Records.

PRAIRIE MUSIC RECORDS LTD., Box 438, Walnut IA 51577. (712)366-1136. President: Robert Everhart. Record company (BMI) and record producer (Prairie Music Ltd.). Estab. 1964. Releases 2 singles and 2 LPs/year. Works with musicians/artists and songwriters on contract. Pays 5% royalty to artists on contract; statutory rate to publisher per song on record.

How to Contact: Submit demo tape by mail. Unsolicited submissions are OK. Prefers cassette. SASE. Reports in 4 months.

Music: Mostly traditional country, bluegrass and folk. Released "Time After Time," "Street Sleepers" and "Rock of Hollywood," all written and recorded by Bob Everhart on Folkways Records (traditional country). Other artists include Gospel Pilgrims.

Close-up

Harold Shedd
Creative Vice President
PolyGram
Nashville, Tennessee

Harold Shedd has never been afraid to take chances. He's also never been shy about sticking his neck out if he believes in something. But Shedd is also used to winning and by trusting his gut instinct—in this case, his ears—he has produced some of country music's biggest superstars: Alabama, K.T. Oslin, The Kentucky Headhunters, Reba McEntire and Glen Campbell. Each act has a unique sound, look and feel, which is exactly what attracts and delights Shedd.

His search for the unusual is part of what helps keep country music fresh. He's quick to give credit to the songwriters "who write these great songs" and the musicians who play them, but disagrees with those tunesmiths who complain of the difficulty in getting their songs cut. "If they come here and do unique things, not rewrites and rehashes of old things that have been done over and over, and are totally dedicated to their craft, it's unbelievable what can happen for aspiring songwriters. (Nashville is) a great town to be in and it's not as closed as it gets the reputation of being. It is in an expansion stage that demands better and more creative types of projects, and that includes creative songs and writers."

How does Shedd define a hit song? He laughs, points at eye-level stacks of tapes covering his desk and says, "A lot of people have different definitions. It's pretty hard to describe a hit before it is cut; it becomes so personal and individual for that artist. You just look for a certain type of song that you feel is the vehicle for where you want to go. Different artists and different projects call for particular types of songs. The flow of the album, the flow of the music is important—when you hear a song you know if it's in the ballpark or not."

Shedd doesn't believe a songwriter needs to live in Nashville or in any other music center to be successful. "Some of the greatest songs were written before the writers came to town," he says. He cites Bob Corbin and Dave Hanner (two PolyGram songwriters who live in Pittsburgh), K.T. Oslin and the group Alabama as good examples. Sometimes, he says, moving to Nashville may disrupt a songwriter's development. "Sometimes moving to Nashville can be detrimental because you can get into that sameness or co-writing routine of music that sounds like everything else that's been written."

At the same time, Shedd loves what Nashville has to offer tunesmiths, and says that if the timing is right, it's the place to be. "What you really have to be is dedicated and willing to learn. Try to find your niche with people who write good music, that's a given. And you can do that from anywhere. But, if you're going to write country music . . . there's not a better place to be than here. Nashville seems to be the place where the attitude is toward the music and the product."

—Marjie McGraw

PREMIÉRE RECORDS, P.O. Box 279, Hopkins MN 55343. (612)942-6119. President: Mitch Viegut. V/P and General Manager: Mark Alan. Record company. Estab. 1988. Releases 6 singles, 3-5 LPs, 3-5 cassettes and 3-5 CDs/year. Receives 150 submissions/year. Works with musicians/artists and songwriters on contract. Pays 7-10% royalty to artists on contract.
How to Contact: Submit demo tape by mail. Submissions must be solicited. Prefers cassette (or VHS videocassette) with 3-4 songs. Does not return unsolicited material. Reports in 1 month.
Music: Mostly rock, pop and black contemporary. Released "Footsteps" (by Azhaar/Cavanagh), (pop single); "Midnight Confessions" (by Lou Josie), (pop single); and *Airkraft* (rock LP), all recorded by Airkraft on Premiére Records. Other artists include Airkraft and Zwarté.

PRESIDENTIAL ENTERPRISES LTD., 127 Aldergate St., London **England** EC1A 6JQ. (44)71-2501910. Contact: Roland A. Radelli. Labels include Presidential; XXIst Century. Record company, music publisher (Risson Music (UR PRS) and record producer (The Club Studios). Estab. 1986. Releases 12-15 12" singles and 3-5 LPs/year. Receives 8-10 submissions/month. Works with musicians/artists and songwriters on contract; also Disc-jockeys and remixers. Pays 6-15% royalty to artists on contract; statutory rate to publisher per song on record.
How to Contact: Write or call first. Prefers cassette with 2-5 songs and lyric sheet. Does not return unsolicited material. Reports in 2 weeks.
Music: Mostly house, pop/dance and hardcore rap; also hip-hop, soul, rock and reggae. Released "If I Can't Have You" (by R. & B. Gibbs), recorded by Project Joy (pop/dance 12"); "As One" (by various), recorded by Qwerty (house 12"); and "Reason" written and recorded by Chris Payne (pop/dance 12"), all on XXIst Century Records.
Tips: "Will accept finished masters for licensing in UK and Europe."

PRESTO RECORDS, P.O. Box 1081, Lowell MA 01853. (617)893-2144. President: Christopher Porter. Record company. Affiliated with Chris Porter Productions Inc. (a booking and management company). Estab. 1989. Releases 3-4 LPs and 2-4 CDs/year. Receives 60 submissions/year. Work with musicians/artists on contract. Pays statutory rate to publisher per song on record.
How to Contact: Submit demo tape by mail. Unsolicited submissions OK. Prefers cassette with 3-4 songs. SASE or SAE and IRC. Reports in 1-2 months.
Music: Mostly guitar-oriented alternative rock. Released *Ruins Cafe* (by Frank Rowe), recorded by Classic Ruins; *Girsl Like the Criminal Types* (by Adam Boc), recorded by Miranda Warning; *When I'm Waiting* (by Alan Grandy), recorded by The Terrible Parade; and *Laughing at Me* (by Buck Cherry), recorded by The Visigoths; all recorded on Presto Records (all rock LPs). Other artists include Miles Dethmuffen.
Tips: "We mainly deal with guitar-oriented rock—accessible but not overly commercial. If a songwriter has a band together and they are playing out live regularly, we would be happy to hear their material if it fits in our guidelines."

*PRINCE/SF PRODUCTIONS, 1135 Francisco St., San Francisco CA 94109. (415)775-9627. Artists Representative: Ken Malucelli. Labels include Auriga and Christmas. Music publisher (Prince/SF Publications/ASCAP) and record producer (Prince/SF Productions). Estab. 1975. Releases 1 LP and 1 CD/year. Works with artists under personal management. Pays standard royalty to artists on contract; statutory rate to publishers per song on record.
How to Contact: Write first and obtain permission to submit. Prefers cassette or VHS videocassette with 3 songs and lyric and lead sheet. SASE. Reports "ASAP."
Music: Mostly pop and Christmas; also satirical and humorous. Released *The Merrie Olde Christmas Carolers* (by Ken Malucelli, arranger), recorded by MOC Carolers on Christmas Records (holiday cassette); *Loud is Good*, written and recorded by The EDLOS on Auriga Records (pop, cassette); and "Freedomsong" (by Eric Morris, composer), recorded by The EDLOS on Auriga Records (pop single).
Tips: "Work should be unique, high quality, not derivative."

PRISTINE RECORDS, Route 1, Box 187-A, Whitney TX 76692. (817)694-4047. President: Allen Newton. Labels include Cactus Flats, MFN, Pleasure Records. Record company and mailing/distributor/promotion. Estab. 1981. Releases 10-12 singles; 1-2 12" singles and 10-12 LPs/year. Works with musicians/artists on contract. Pays negotiable royalty to artists on contract.
How to Contact: Submit demo tape by mail. Unsolicited submissions are OK. Prefers cassette or 7½ ips reel-to-reel (or VHS videocassette) with 2 songs and lyric or lead sheets. SASE. Reports in 4 weeks.
Music: Mostly country, R&B and rock; also gospel. Released "Starin-A-Haze" and "All I Ever Wanted," (by J.Sylvis/F. Redder), recorded by Thin Ice on Pristine Records (rock); and "Styllin," (by Andre), recorded by Stylle on Pristine Records (R&B). Other artists include Linda Roper, Samuel Green, Mickey Drum, Thin Ice, Sherry Fontaine, Stylle.
Tips: "Read, study, listen, and prepare."

PSP RECORDS, 6283-3410 Shelbourne St., Victoria, British Columbia V8P 5L5 **Canada**. (604)598-3651. Producer: Eduardo Pereira. Music publishers (Primavera Sound/SOCAN). Releases 3-5 singles and 1-2 LPs/year. Works with musicians/artists on contract and hires musicians for in-house studio work. Pays 6-8% royalty to artists on contract; statutory rate to publishers per song on record.
How to Contact: Prefers cassette (or BETA videocassette) with 3 songs. Does not return material but we keep it on file. Reports in 6 weeks.
Music: Mostly pop, rock; also Latin/jazz, salsa, merengue and cumbia. Released "Papa Nicolas" (merengue), written and recorded by Hugo Belran; "Let Me Know" (by DeGrassi/Walter), recorded by Julie Coy (rock); and "Pienso Tanto en Ti" (by Ruben Zunica), recorded by Yizeth.

PUZZLE RECORDS, P.O. Box 461892, Garland TX 75046. (214)271-8098. A&R Director: Don Ferguson. Record company, music publisher (Sultan Music Publishing/BMI and Illustrious Sultan/ASCAP), record producer and booking agency (Don Ferguson Agency). Estab. 1972. Releases 7-8 singles and 1-2 LPs/year. Works with artists and songwriters on contract.
How to Contact: Accepts unsolicited material.
Music: Mostly country; also MOR, jazz and light rock. Released "Leave Me Right Now," written and recorded by Bobby Teesdale (MOR); "Ain't No Way," (by Duke/Osborn/Fox), recorded by Flash Point (rock); and "I'm Hurtin" (by Roy Orbison/Joe Melson), recorded by Mary Craig (country); all on Puzzle Records.

R.E.F. RECORDS, 404 Bluegrass Ave., Madison TN 37115. (615)865-6380. Contact: Bob Frick. Record company, record producer and music publisher (Frick Music Publishing Co./BMI). Releases 10 LPs/year. Works with artists and songwriters on contract. Pays 3-5¢ royalty to artists on contract; statutory rate to publishers for each record sold.
How to Contact: Call first. Prefers 7½ ips reel-to-reel or cassette with 2-10 songs and lyric sheet. SASE. Reports in 1 month.
Music: Country, gospel, rock and top 40/pop. Released "I Love You In Jesus," "Warm Family Feeling," and "Our Favorites," all by Bob Scott Frick. Other artists include Larry Ahlborn, Francisco Morales, Candy Coleman, Peggy Beard, Bob Myers, The Backwoods Quartet, Jim Mattingly, David Barton, Jim Pommert, The Vision Heirs, Eddie Issacs and Craig Steele.

*RABADASH RECORDS INC., 4805 Baudin St., New Orleans LA 70119. (704)486-7646. President: John G. Autin. Record company, music publisher (Rabadash Music/ASCAP) and record producer. Estab. 1982. Releases 1 LP and 1 CD/year. Works with musicians/artists and songwriters on contract.
How to Contact: Submit demo tape by mail. Unsolicited submissions are OK. Prefers cassette or VHS videocassette and lyric sheet. SASE. Reports in 3 months.
Music: Mostly R&B, pop and country; also jazz, gospel and rock. Other artists include Anders Osbourne, Lori Frazier.

RADIOACTIVE RECORDS, 1075 N.W. Murray Rd., Suite 250, Portland OR 97229. (503)642-4201. Contact: A&R Dept. Record company, music publisher (Mark Hannah Music Group/BMI), record producer (Mark Hannah Productions) and Mark Hannah Management/Personal Management. Estab. 1985. Releases 5-10 singles, 3-5 12″ singles, 1-3 LPs, 1-3 EPs and 1-3 CDs/year. Receives 30 submissions/month. Works with musicians/artists and songwriters on record contract. Pays 5-10% royalty to artists on contract; statutory rate to publisher per song on record.
How to Contact: Write first and obtain permission to submit. Prefers cassette or 15 ips reel-to-reel with 1-3 songs and lyric or lead sheets. SASE. Reports in 1 month.
Music: Mostly rock, pop and country; also fusion, New Age and jazz. "Forced to Have Sex With An Alien," written and recorded by M. Harrop (comedy single); "You Stole My Heart Away," written and recorded P. Witt (pop/rock single); *Desert Moon*, written and recorded by M. Hannah (New Age LP); *Modern Day Man* written and recorded by M. Hannah (hard rock LP); "Crazy Fool" written and recorded by M. Herrop (pop/ballad single); and "Billy," written and recorded by Syndi Helms (country single), all on Radioactive Records. Other artists include Rex E. Plew and Messenger (rock band).
Tips: "Learn as much as you can about the music business."

RAILROAD RECORDS, 300 Bedford St., Manchester NH 03101. (603)669-6353. President: Michael Skinner. Labels include Railroad Records. Record company and record producer (Skinner Productions) and talent manager. Estab. 1985. Releases 3 LPs and 3 EPs/year. Works with musicians/artists on contract. Pays negotiable royalty to artist on contract; statutory rate to publisher per song on record.
How to Contact: Submit demo tape by mail. Unsolicited submissions are OK. Prefers cassette with 3-4 songs and lyric sheets. SASE. Reports in 3 weeks.
Music: Mostly rock/hard rock and pop. Released "Blondes Have More Fun," recorded by T.T. Strip (hard rock EP); "Gypsy," written and recorded by First Strike (hard rock EP); and "Dreams," written and recorded by Marathon; all on Railroad Records. Other artists include Roxx, T.T. Strip, Marathon, Uncontrollable Urge and Photograph.

*RAMBO STAR RECORDS, 129 N. Cortez St., Prescott AZ 86301. (602)778-1776. Owner: Frank Harris. Record company (BMI). Estab. 1987. Releases 2 singles and 3 LPs/year. Works with musicians/artists and songwriters on contract; hires musicians for in-house studio work. Pays statutory rate to publishers per song on records.
How to Contact: Write or call first to arrange personal interview. Prefers cassette with 1 song and lyric sheet. "Include permission to record at the statutory royalty rate." Does not return unsolicited material. "Reports immediately if interested."
Music: Mostly pop, country and R&B; also gospel and Christmas. Released *Cry* (pop LP); *Cry* (country LP); and *To Worship You* (gospel LP) by various, all recorded by Adriann E. Harris on Rambo Star Records.

*RAZOR & TIE MUSIC, 60 Third Ave., New York NY 10003. (212)473-9173. President: Cliff Chenfeld. Labels include Razor Edge Records. Record company. Estab. 1990. Releases 15-20 CDs/year. Works with musicians/artists on contract.
How to Contact: Write first and obtain permission to submit. Prefers cassette with 3 songs and lyric sheet. SASE. Reports in 2 weeks.
Music: Mostly rock, pop/R&B and country. Released *The Up Escalator*, written and recorded by Graham Parker on Razor Edge Records (rock CD); *Men Without Women*, written and recorded by Little Steven on Razor Edge Records (rock CD); and *Those Funky '70s*, written and recorded by various artists on Razor & Tie Records (oldies/CD/cassette).
Tips: "We have only released reissues. We only began signing new artists and songwriters in late 1991."

RAZOR RECORDS, 2623 Bosworth, Chicago IL 60614. (312)549-3227. Owner: Mark Lefens. Record company. Estab. 1979. Releases 1 single and 1 LP/year. Works with musicians/artists on contract. Pays statutory rate to publisher per song on record.
How to Contact: Submit demo tape by mail. Unsolicited submissions are OK. Prefers cassette. SASE. "Will report only if interested."
Music: Mostly blues and R&B. Released *After Work* (by various writers), recorded by John Embry; *Set Me Free* (by various writers), recorded by Gloria Hardiman; and *Housefire* (written and recorded by Byther Smith), all on Razor Records (blues LPs) reissued on Rounder's "Bullseye" label.
Tips: "Come up with some good new blues."

REALITY RECORDS PRODUCTIONS, 19 Roxborough Place, Willingboro NJ 08046. (609)877-7653. Producer: "Hank" Strasser. Record company and record producer (Reality Productions). Estab. 1972.
How to Contact: Prefers cassette; bios appreciated. Does not return unsolicited material. Reports "to selected artists only."
Music: Jazz and electronic music. Released "Mirage," "Warm Wind," and "Idaho Snow," all written and recorded by Christopher Adrian on Reality Records (jazz).
Tips: "We're looking for commercially viable jazz. Product choices probably won't stray too far from mainstream jazz. New Age, fusion and electronic music welcome, but no vocals please."

RECA MUSIC PRODUCTION, Nykobingvej 18, 4571 Grevinge DK 4571 **Denmark.** Phone: (45)345-9389. Director: Finn Reiner. Labels include Reca and Favorit. Record company and music publisher (Top Music). Releases 10 singles, 10 LPs and 5 CDs/year. Works with musicians/artists and songwriters on contract; hires musicians for in-house studio work. Pays 5% royalty to artists on contract; statutory rate to publishers per song on record.
How to Contact: Write or call first and obtain permission to submit. Prefers cassette (or VHS videocassette) with 2 songs. SAE and IRC. Reports in 2 weeks.
Music: Mostly pop, country and folk; also classical. Released *Skyrider with Tomboola Band*, by various writers (country LP); *Fast Train With Van Dang*, by Svend Petersen (shuffle LP); and *Classic*, by Peter Vesth (folk LP), all on RECA Records. Other artists include Bent Larsen, Peter Langberg, Jodle Johnny and The Kuhlau Quartet.

*RECORD COMPANY OF THE SOUTH, P.O. Box 14685, Baton Rouge LA 70809. (504)766-3233. General Manager: Johnny Palazzotto. Record company. Estab. 1978. Works with musicians/artists on contract. Pays 8% royalty to artists on contract; statutory rate to publisher per song on record.
How to Contact: Submit demo tape by mail. Unsolicited submissions are OK. Prefers cassette with 3-5 songs. SASE. Reports in 2-4 weeks.
Music: Mostly rock, R&B and country. *Safe With Me*, recorded by Irma Thomas on RCS Records (R&B LP, CD). Other artists include Luther Kent.

RED DOT/PUZZLE RECORDS, 1121 Market, Galveston TX 77550. (409)762-4590. President: A.W. Marullo Sr. Record company, record producer and music publisher (A.W. Marullo Music/BMI). Estab. 1952. "We also lease masters from artists." Releases 14 12" singles/year. Works with artists and songwriters on contract; musicians on salary for in-house studio work. Pays 8-10% royalty to artists on contract; statutory rate to publishers for each record sold.
How to Contact: Prefers cassette with 4-7 songs and lyric sheet. SASE. Reports in 2 months.
Music: Rock/top 40 dance songs. Released "Do You Feel Sexy," (by T. Pindrock), recorded by Flash Point (Top 40/rock); "You Put the Merry in My Christmas," (by E.Dunn), recorded by Mary Craig (rock/pop country) and "Love Machine," (by T. Pindrock), recorded by Susan Moninger; all on Puzzle/Red Dot Records.

*RED SKY RECORDS, P.O. Box 7, Stonehouse, Glos. GL10 3PQ **United Kingdom**. 0453-826200. Producer: Johnny Coppin. Record company (PRS) and record producer (Red Sky Records). Estab. 1985. Releases 2 singles, 3 LPs and 3 CDs/year. Works with musicians/artists and songwriters on contract and hires musicians for in-house studio work. Pays 8-10% to artists on contract. Pays statutory rate to publisher per song on record.
How to Contact: Submit demo tape by mail. Unsolicited submissions are OK. Prefers cassette with 3 songs and lyric sheet. SASE. Reports in 3 months.
Music: Mostly rock/singer-songwriters, modern folk and roots music. Released *Edge of Day*, written and recorded by Laurie Lee & Johnny Coppin; *Songs on Lonely Roads (The Story of Ivor Gurney)*, recorded by David Goodland; and *West Country Christmas*, written and recorded by Johnny Coppin; all on Red Sky Records (LPs). Other artists include Desperate Men and White Leaved Oak.

RED-EYE RECORDS, Wern Fawr Farm, Pencoed, Mid-Glam CF35 6NB **United Kingdom**. Phone: (0656)86 00 41. Managing Director: M.R. Blanche. Record company, music publisher (Ever-Open-Eye Music/PRS). Estab. 1979. Releases 4 singles and 2-3 LPs/year. Works with musicians/artists on contract.
How to Contact: Prefers cassette (or VHS videocassette) or 7½ or 15 ips reel-to-reel with 4 songs. SAE and IRC.
Music: Mostly R&B, rock and gospel; also swing. Released "River River" (by D. John), recorded by The Boys; "Billy" (by G. Williams), recorded by The Cadillacs; and "Cadillac Walk" (by Moon Martin), recorded by the Cadillacs, all on Red-Eye Records. Other artists include Cartoon and Tiger Bay.

RELATIVITY RECORDS INC., 18707 Henderson Ave., Hollis NY 11423. (718)740-5700. National Labels Director: Anne Adams. Labels include Relativity, Combat, Ineffect. Record company. Estab. 1979. Releases 35 LPs and 10 EPs/year. Works with musicians/artists on contract.
How to Contact: Submit demo tape by mail. Unsolicited submissions are OK. Prefers cassette or ½" videocassette. SASE. Reports in 8 weeks.
Music: Mostly metal and hard rock.

*REX MUSIC INC., 1241 Bay Ave., Ocean City NJ 08226. (609)398-3161. President: Doug Mann. Labels include Rex Music and Rex Rap. Record company (ASCAP). Estab. 1987. Releases 12 LPs and 12 CDs/year. Works with musicians/artists and songwriters on contract. Pays 6-10% royalty to artists on contract; statutory rate to publisher per song on record.
How to Contact: Submit demo tape by mail. Unsolicited submissions are OK. Prefers cassette with 4 songs and lyric sheet. Does not return unsolicited material. Reports in 4 weeks.
Music: Mostly gospel-rock/metal, gospel rap, and gospel R&B. Artists include Sacrament, The Lead, The Throes, Living Sacrafice, Pure Heart and NLM.

*RHINO RECORDS LTD., The Chilterns, France Hill Dr., Chamberley Surrey GU153QA **England**. 0276-686077. Director: Bruce White. Record company. Estab. 1970. Releases 12 singles, 12 12" singles, 10-15 LPs and 10-15 CDs/year. Receives 20 submissions/month. Works with musicians/artists on record contract. Pays 8-16% royalty to artists on contract. Pays statutory rate to publisher per song on record.
How to Contact: Submit demo tape by mail. Unsolicited submissions are OK. Prefers cassette with 3-4 songs. SASE. Reports in 6 weeks.
Music: Interested in "most types of music." Released "Take Care," written and recorded by Boris Gardiner (reggae); and "This Is" (by D. Dacres), recorded by Desmond Dekker (reggae), both on Rhino Records; and "Carnival 90," written and recorded by Byron Lee on Dynamic Records (reggae).

RIC RAC RECORDS, % Ric Rac, Inc., Box 712, Nashville IN 47448. (812)837-9569. President: R.L. Hanson. Labels include Country Bump. Record company, music publisher (Ric Rac Music/ASCAP and Rick Hansen Music/BMI), record production and promotion firm, and management firm (Ric Rac, Inc.). Estab. 1985. Releases 4-6 singles/year. Works with musicians/artists and songwriters on contract. Pays 3-6% royalty to artists on contract; statutory rate to publishers for each record sold.

How to Contact: Write first and obtain permission to submit. Prefers cassette with 1-4 songs and lyric or lead sheet. SASE. Reports in 2 months. "Do not make phone inquiries as to status of material submitted. Material submitted to A&R must be represented by publisher. We are only interested in videos of live performances."

Music: Mostly country; also rock, gospel, folk and easy listening (MOR). Released "Same Old Barroom Melody," written and recorded by Rick Hanson; "Little Girl Blue" and "Down For More," recorded by Glori McFall; all on Ric Rac Records (country).

Tips: "Be as professional as possible and become active in songwriters workshops in your area."

RICOCHET RECORDS, P.O. Box 133, Farmingville NY 11738. President: Andy Marvel. Labels include Alyssa Records. Record company, music publisher (Andy Marvel Music), and record producer (Marvel Productions). Releases 9 singles, 18 CDs and 6 LPs/year. Receives 4000 submissions/month. Works with musicians/artists and songwriters on contract.

How to Contact: Submit a demo tape—unsolicited submissions are OK. Prefers cassette (or VHS videocassette) with 3 songs and lyric sheet. Returns only with SASE. "Do not call."

Music: Mostly pop, R&B and top 40; also country pop.

RIDGEWOOD RECORDS, Box 630755, Miami FL 33163. (305)935-4880. President: Jack Gale. Labels include Playback, Gallery II, Caramba! Record company, music publisher (Lovey Music/BMI, Cowabonga Music/ASCAP) and record producer (Jack Gale). Estab. 1983. Releases 48 singles, and 8 CDs/year. Works with musicians/artists and songwriters on contract. Pays statutory rate to publisher per song on record. "Ridgewood Records is primarily for 'new' artists."

How to Contact: Submit demo tape by mail. Unsolicited submissions are okay. Prefers cassette (or VHS videocassette) with 2 songs and lyric sheet. Reports in 2 weeks.

Music: Mostly country and contemporary country. Released "Cry Cry Darling" (written and recorded by J.C. Newman); "Have it Your Way" (by J. Fuller), recorded by Brittany; and "Tossin' & Turnin'", recorded by Stacy, all on Ridgewood Records (country). Other artists include Donnie Bowser, Lynne Thomas, Cailyn Tanner, Amy Jo Larson, Kathy Reed and Eleanor Paris.

Tips: "Don't be afraid to keep submitting. We listen to everything."

RIPSAW RECORD CO., Suite 805, 4545 Connecticut Ave. NW, Washington DC 20008. (202)362-2286. President: Jonathan Strong. Record company, record producer and music publisher (Southern Crescent Publishing/BMI and Sugar Mama Music/BMI). Estab. 1976. Releases 1-2 LPs/year. Works with musicians/artists and songwriters on contract. Payment negotiable with artists on contract. Pays standard royalty to songwriters on contract; statutory rate to publishers for each record sold.

How to Contact: Prefers cassette and lyric sheet. SASE. "Invite us to a club date to listen." Reports as soon as possible.

Music: Blues, rockabilly and "traditional" rock 'n' roll. Released *Oooh-Wow!*, by the Uptown Rhythm Kings (jump blues). Other artists include Bobby Smith, Billy Hancock, Kid Tater and Cheaters.

Tips: "Keep it true roots rock 'n' roll."

ROAD RECORDS, 429 S. Lewis Rd., Royersford PA 19468. (215)948-8228. Fax: (215)948-4175. President: Jim Femino. Labels include Road Records. Record company and music publisher (Fezsongs/ASCAP). Estab. 1980. Releases 2-5 singles, 1 LP and 1 CD/year. Receives 20 submissions/month. Works with musicians/artists and songwriters on contract. Pays varying royalty to artists on contract; statutory rate to publisher per song on record.

How to Contact: Write first and obtain permission to submit. Prefers cassette (or VHS videocassette) with 1-3 songs and lyric sheets. SASE. Reports in 8 weeks.

Music: Mostly rock, country and crossover. Released *All Night Party* (by Jim Femino), "Party Tonight" (by Jim Femino), *Just The Good Stuff* (album/CD) and "Nancy's Song" (by Jim Femino); all recorded by Jim Femino on Road Records (rock). Other artists include Paul Waltz Band.

ROBBINS RECORDS, INC., HC80, Box 5B, Leesville LA 71446. National Representative: Sherree Scott. Labels include Headliner Stars Records. Record company and music publisher (Headliner Stars Music and Universal Stars Music/BMI). Estab. 1973. Releases 12-14 singles and 1-3 LPs/year. Works with artists and songwriters on contract. Pays standard royalty to artists on contract; statutory rate to publishers for each record sold.

How to Contact: Prefers cassette with 1-6 songs and lyric sheet. Does not return unsolicited material. Reports only if interested.

Music: Mostly church/religious; also bluegrass, country, folk, gospel, and top 40/pop. Released "Jesus, You're Everywhere," "I Can Depend on You," and "I Just Came to Thank You Lord," by J.J. and Sherree Stephens (religious singles). Other artists include Renee Wills and Melodee McCanless.

ROCK CITY RECORDS, (A Division of Rock City Entertainment Co.) P.O. Box 6553, Malibu CA 90264. (813)287-5057 (FLA), (813)225-3847 (FLA). CEO: Mike Danna. Rock City Entertainment Co. (Rock City Records) and record producer (Mike Danna). Estab. 1984. Releases 3 singles, 3 cassette singles and 1 CD/year. Works with musicians/artists on contract. Pays negotiable royalty to artists on contract. Pays statutory rate to publishers per song on records.
How to Contact: Prefers cassette (or VHS videocassette) with 2-3 songs and lyric sheet. Does not return unsolicited material. Reports in 2 weeks. Send SASE for return of tapes.
Music: Mostly pop and rock; also soundtracks. Released "Words of Love" (by Mickey Dee), recorded by Mickey Dee/Bobbi Heart (pop single); and *Now Or Never* (pop/rock LP) and "Lovelights" (pop single), both written and recorded by M. Dee, all on Rock City Records.
Tips: "Sacrifice, patience, persistence, and knowing your abilities will ultimately get you where you're looking to go."

ROCK IN RECORDS, Haven Commercial Bldg. 24/F, Room A Tsing Fung Street, **Hong Kong.** General Manager: Keith Yip. Record company. Estab. 1981. Releases 6 LPs and 6 CDs/year. Receives 20-30 submissions/year. Works with musicians/artists on contract and hires musicians for in-house studio work. Pays 5-7% royalty to artists on contract; statutory rate to publishers per song on record.
How to Contact: Submit demo tape by mail. Unsolicited submissions are OK. Prefers cassette (or VHS videocassette if available) with 2 or more songs. SASE.
Music: Mostly new age, rock and R&B, pop. Released "Tonight" (by Yvonne Lau), recorded by Paradox; "Feeling" (by Keith Yip and Yvonne Lau), recorded by Paradox; and "Winter Love" (by Keith Yip and Max Wong), recorded by Cass Phang, all pop singles on Rock In Records.

ROCKIT RECORDS, INC., Suite 306 35918 Union Lake Rd., Mt. Clemens MI 48043. (313)792-8452. Music Director: Joseph Trupiano. Receives 30 submissions/month. Record company and music publisher (Bad Grammar Music, Inc. BMI). Estab. 1985. Releases 360 cassette LPs/year. Works with musicians/artists and songwriters on contract. Pays statutory rate to publisher per song on records.
How to Contact: Submit demo by mail. Unsolicited submissions are OK. Prefers cassette (or VHS videocassette if available) with 3 songs and lyric sheet. SASE. Reports in 3 months.
Music: Mostly pop/dance, pop rock and rock; also alternative rock, new age and urban and R&B. Released "Runaround Sue" (by D. Dimucci), recorded by The Joey Harlow Project (CD and cassette single); "Choose Life," written and recorded by Laya Phelps (CD); and "Busy," written and recorded by Kurt Deitz (CD); all on Rockit Records. Other artists include, The Mix, Bob's Night Off, David Hansen, Atlas, Michael Duhnzigger and Oscar Charles.
Tips: "Presently we are most responsive to reviewing material for our compilation CD project. Our artists receive national exposure to major labels (USA), college radio nationally, trade publications, commercial European radio, and European independent labels. Through this project we have generated much exposure for artists and have gotten several acts signed to major labels."

*RODELL RECORDS, P.O. Box 93457, Hollywood CA 90093. (213)960-9447. President: Adam Rodell. Record company, music publisher (Udder Publishing/BMI) and record producer (Golden Gelt/AS-CAP). Recently established company. Works with musicians/artists and songwriters on contract and hires musicians for in-house studio work. Pays statutory rate to publisher per song on record.
How to Contact: Submit demo tape by mail. Unsolicited submissions are OK. Prefers cassette or VHS videocassette with 3 songs and lyric sheet. Does not return unsolicited material. "We will report back only if we are interested."
Music: Mostly rock, country and pop; also R&B, progressive fusion and rap.
Tips: "Send studio or studio quality cassettes only. Actively seeking new acts and material."

ROLL ON RECORDS®, 112 Widmar Pl., Clayton CA 94517. (415)672-8201. Owner: Edgar J. Brincat. Record company. Estab. 1985. Releases 2-3 LPs/cassettes/year. Receives 200+ submissions/month. Works with musicians/artists and songwriters on contract and hires musicians for in-house studio work. Pays 10% royalty to artists on contract; statutory rate to publisher per song on record.
How to Contact: Submit demo tape by mail. Unsolicited submissions are OK. Prefers cassette with 3 songs and lyric sheet. SASE. Reports in 2-4 weeks.
Music: Mostly contemporary/country, MOR and R&B; also pop, light rock and modern gospel. Released "Jack Daniels" (by Barbara Finnicum/Edgar J. Brincat/Pattie Leidecker) and "Southern Comfort" (by Barbara Finnicum), both recorded by Carolyn Rae; "The Rain" (by Barbara Finnicum/Ed Davie) and "I Only Put it On" (by Barbara Finnicum/Ed Davie), both recorded by Ed Davie; and "The Saddest Goodbye" (by Barbara Finnicum/Ed Davie) and "Back In Time" (by Barbara Finnicum/Ed Davie), both recorded by Ed Davie.
Tips: "Be professional, write clearly and always enclose an SASE (many people don't)."

ROSEWOOD RECORDS, P.O. Box 364, New Castle PA 16103. (412)654-3023. Owner: Wes Homner. Production Manager: Jay Ed Moore. Record company, music publisher (Mountain Therapy Music/ BMI) and record producer (Rosewood Productions). Estab. 1975. Releases 2 singles, 5 cassettes, 2 LPs and 2 CDs/year. Works with musicians/artists and songwriters on contract. Pays according to contract signed with artist; statutory rate to publisher per song on record.
How to Contact: Submit demo tape by mail. Unsolicited submissions are OK. Prefers cassette with 3 songs and lyric sheets. Does not return unsolicited material. Reports in 3 weeks.
Music: Mostly southern gospel and bluegrass; also country. Produced "Grave Digger," written and recorded by Ron Mesing for Heritage Records (bluegrass); "Just Like You" (by Pete Wernick), recorded by Full House; and "Sing A Song of Seasons" (by Judy Minouge), recorded by Millcreek Ramblers; "Rock Me Gently" (by Wes Homner), recorded by Jay Moore on Rosewood Records (bluegrass gospel); "Rainbow's End" (by Jim Fiest), recorded by Full House on Rosewood Records (bluegrass); and "Just Can't Win" (by Jim Metz), recorded by Tim Berline on Rosewood Records (bluegrass). Other artists include Rainbow Valley Boys, Mac Martin, Bill Wright, Buzz Matheson, Wildwood Express, Judy Minouge, Timberline, The Ascensions and The Meadors Family.
Tips: "Please submit only, clean positive love songs and bluegrass/gospel."

*ROSIE RECORDS, 14 Brickendon Green, Hertford Herts SG138PB **England**. Phone: 0992-86404. Proprietor: John Dye. Labels include Rosie Records and Musical Time Box. Record company (Performing Rights Society, MCPS and PPL). Estab. 1982. Releases 2 singles, 2 12" singles, 2 LPs and 1 CD/year. Works with musicians/artists on contract. Pays 8-12% royalty to artists on contract; statutory rate to publisher per song on record.
How to Contact: Submit demo tape by mail. Unsolicited submissions are OK. Prefers cassette with any song and lyric sheet. SASE. Reports in 1 month.
Music: Mostly country, pop and reggae; also comedy songs. Released *Vivian Jones I.*, written and recorded by Vivian Jones (reggae LP); "Donegan's Dancing Band," written and recorded by Lonnie Donegan (country single); and *Tony Fayne's Back*, recorded by Tony Fayne (comedy LP); all on Rosie Records. Other artists include Delusion of Grandeur, Joe Turone and Lucy Stan.
Tips: "Please submit good quality demos and your own material only."

ROTO-NOTO MUSIC, 148 Erin Ave., Hamilton Ontario L8K 4W3 **Canada**. (416)796-8236. President: R. Cousins. Labels include Roto-Noto, Marmot, Chandler. Record company, music publisher and record producer. Estab. 1979. Releases 20 singles, 2 12" singles, 5 LPs and 6 CDs/year. Works with musicians/artists and songwriters on contract and hires musicians for in-house studio work.
How to Contact: Write first and obtain permission to submit. Prefers cassette with 2 songs and lyric sheets. SASE. Reports in 4 weeks.
Music: Mostly country, pop and rock; also R&B and jazz. Released *Here Comes Trouble*, written and recorded by Mark La Forme (LP); "Hangin' By A Thread" (by S. Younger), recorded by Jenny Lee West (single); and *Rapid Transit* (by K. King), recorded by Rapid Transit (CD); all on Roto-Noto Records. Other artists include Bobby McGee, Jack Diamond Band, Eleven Degrees, Harrison Kennedy and Frequency.

ROUND SOUND MUSIC, RR 2, Box 111-C, Cresco PA 18326. (717)595-3149. Owner: Tommy Lewis, Jr.. Labels include Round Sound Music, Geodesic Records; Positive Alternative. Record company and record producer. Estab. 1983. Releases 3-5 singles, 5 LPs and 5 CDs/year. Receives 5-10 submissions/month. Works with musicians/artists and songwriters on contract and hires musicians on salary for in-house studio work. Pays statutory rate to publishers per song on record.
How to Contact: Write or call first and obtain permission to submit. Prefers cassette, 15 ips reel-to-reel or VHS videocassette with 3 songs and lyric and lead sheet. SASE. Reports in 3 months.
Music: Mostly pop, jazz, also New Age, country, R&B, and gospel. Released *You're the Only One* (by T. Lewis), recorded by Joey Price on Geodesic Records (pop); *Some Jazz*, written and recorded by T. Lewis on Positive Alternative Records (jazz); and *Still Thinking of You* (by T.Lewis), recorded by Charade on Geodesic Records (pop).
Tips: "Be honest with yourself, and professional with your presentation."

ROWENA RECORDS, 195 S. 26th St., San Jose CA 95116. (408)286-9840. A&R Director: G.J. O'Neal. Labels include Rowena Records, Chance Records and Jan-Ell Records. Record company. Releases 4 singles, 4 12" singles and 4 LPs/year. Works with musicians/artists and songwriters on contract; hires musicians for in-house studio work. Pays 10% royalty to artists on contract; pays statutory rate to publishers per song on record.

Listings of companies in countries other than the U.S. have the name of the country in boldface type.

How to Contact: Prefers cassette with 4 or more songs and lyric sheet. SASE. Reports in 1 month.
Music: Mostly gospel, country and R&B; also pop, rock and new age. Released "Dear Hearts" by Eddie Lee; "Lady's Choice" by Jeannie O'Neal; "Can You Feel It" by Charlie; "Kacey Ann" by Larry Martinez; and "Me & Grandpa," "Papa Runs a Gold Mine," "First Grade Dream" and "Why Not Wynette" all by Jacque Lynn.

ROXTOWN RECORDS, 2124 Darby Dr., Massilon OH 44646. (216)833-2061. President: Nick Boldi. Labels include Roxtown Records and Bold One Records. Record company, music publisher (Bolnik Music/BMI) and record producer (NRB Productions). Estab. 1986. Releases 6 singles and 2 LPs/year. Works with musicians/artists and songwriters on contract. Pays 4-5% royalty to artists on contract; pays statutory rate to publishers per song on record.
How to Contact: Prefers cassette with 6 songs maximum and lyric sheet (1 per song). SASE. Reports in 6 weeks.
Music: Mostly country, rock and pop; also R&B. Released "Lover's Dreamland" (by N. Boldi/D. Glasser), recorded by Danny Pellegrine (country rock); "The Thief" (by Lewis Mischeff), recorded by Big Lou (contemporary rock); and "Stay" (by Werner/Mischeff), recorded by Big Lou (ballad); all on Roxtown Records.

ROYAL RECORDS, 41-1100 Watkupanaha St., Watmanalo HI 96795. (808)259-8570. President: Fred Jones. Record company and music publisher (Fred Jones/ASCAP). Estab. 1984. Releases 6 singles, 6 12″ singles and 6 LPs/year. Receives 200 submissions/year. Works with musicians/artists and songwriters on contract and hires musicians for in-house studio work. Pays 15% royalty to artists on contract.
How to Contact: Write and obtain permission to submit. Prefers cassette with 3 songs and lead sheet. SASE. Reports in 2 weeks.
Music: Mostly country, gospel and pop. Released "By My Side," written and recorded by Ed Riley; "Stay With Me," by Warren Johnson; and "Silver Seas" (by Fred Jones), recorded by Roland Atone; recorded on Royal Records (single). Other artists include Leroy Daves, Lou Canady, Al Romero, Taran Ericson, Jean Howard.
Tips: "Don't give up, keep writing and be dedicated to your work."

RR&R RECORDS, 9305 Dogwood Place, Gainsville, GA 30506. (404)889-8624. Contact: Ron Dennis. Labels include Rapture Records, Ready Records, Rapp Records, Y'Shua Records and RR&R Records. Record company, music publisher (Super Rapp Publishing/BMI and Do It Now Publishing/ASCAP), record producer (Ron Dennis Wheeler). Estab. 1966. Releases 5 singles, 5 12″ singles, 5 LPs, 5 EPs and 5 CDs/year. Works with musicians/artists and songwriters on contract; hires musicians for in-house studio work. Pays statutory rate to publishers per song on record.
How to Contact: Prefers cassette (or VHS videocassette) or 15 ips reel-to-reel with lyric or lead sheet. SASE. Reports in 3 months. "Master track demos."
Music: Mostly gospel, rock, pop, country and R&B. Released "If Were Not In Love," recorded by Patty Weaver; "She Knows About Me" and "Your Music Make Me Cry," recorded by Jez Davidson; all performed on the Young and Restless Show. "K-Mart Christmas" and "Tribute to a King," by Chuck Carter. Other artists include Rita Van and Rob McInnis, Dan Carroll, Taylor Prichard and Peter Burwin.
Tips: "Send songs that are positive with good moral overtones in the message—melodic tunes with less electric synthesizer sound. Also if these tapes are of music previously published they must be mastered and ready for release—otherwise you are only auditioning the artist not the music."

S.O.C., P.O. Box 897, Hartford CT 06101. (203)548-0212. A&R: Linda "Bottles" Polite. Labels include S.O.C., Light Source and Silsar Records. Record company, music publisher and record producer (Silver Sargent Silsar). Estab. 1986. Releases 4-12 singles, 4-12 12″ singles 13 LPs, 13 EPs and 13 CDs/year. Works with musicians/artists and songwriters on contract. Pays 5-12% royalty to artists on contract; negotiable rate to publishers per song on record.
How to Contact: Submit demo tape by mail. Unsolicited submissions are OK. Prefers cassette (or VHS videocassette) with 4-5 songs and lyric sheet. SASE. Reports in 6 weeks.
Music: Mostly funk, R&B and soul and gospel; also rap. Released "Handwriting on the Wall," written and recorded by Silver Sargent (R&B single); *Meet Muffin* (by Herb Superb), recorded by Sarge "Muffin" (rap LP); and *Jesus is Real*, written and recorded by Silver Sargent (gospel LP), all on S.O.C. Records. Other artists include Drum Possie, Native American, The Uniques and Officer Muffin.
Tips: "Have a good hook, and a great look. A photo may help."

SABTECA RECORD CO., P.O. Box 10286, Oakland CA 94610. (415)465-2805. President: Duane Herring. Creative Manager: Sean Herring. Record company and music publisher (Sabteca Music Co./ASCAP, Toyiabe Music Co./BMI). Estab. 1980. Releases 3 singles and 1 12″ single/year. Works with songwriters on contract and hires musicians for in-house studio work. Pays statutory rate to publisher per song on record.

How to Contact: Write first and obtain permission to submit. Prefers cassette with lyric sheet. Reports in 3 weeks.

Music: Mostly R&B, pop and country. Released "Come Into My Arms" and "I Dare You," (by Duane Herring), recorded by Johnny B and The Rhythm Method; both on Sabteca Records.

Tips: "Improve your writing skills. Keep up with music trends."

*SADDLESTONE RECORDS, 264 "H" Street Box 8110-21, Blaine WA 98230. Canada address: 2954 O'Hara Ln., Surrcy BC **Canada** V4A 3E5. (604)535-3129. President: Candice James. Labels include Silver Bow Records. Record company, music publisher (SOCAN, Saddlestone/BMI) and record producer (Silver Bow Productions). Estab. 1988. Releases 15 singles, 4-6 LPs and 6 CDs/year. Works with musicians/artists on contract. Pays 10-20% royalty to artists on contract; statutory rate to publishers per song on record.

How to Contact: Submit demo tape by mail. Unsolicited submissions are OK. Prefers cassette with 3-5 songs and lyric sheet. SASE. Reports in 3 months.

Music: Mostly country, pop and rock; also R&B and gospel. Released "Whiskey" (written and recorded by Joe Lonsdale) and "You Gotta Love" (by Arledge/McBee), recorded by Barbra Farrell (singles); and *Wild One* (by Friskie/Hillis), recorded by Randy Friskie (CD and single); "The Face Behind Those Bottles" (by Joe Lonsdale) (country); "Wild One" (by Friskie/Hillis), recorded by Randy Friskie (rock); and "Close to You," written and recorded by Chris Brighton (pop/contemporary), all on Saddlestone Records. Other artists include Elmer Fudpucker, Gerry King, Hank Sasaki, Razzy Bailey, Matt Audette, Ray St Gerhain, Rex Howard, Dorrie Alexander, Patty Mayo and Hulio Heart.

Tips: "Send original material, studio produced, with great hooks."

SAHARA RECORDS AND FILMWORKS ENTERTAINMENT, Suite 829, 4475 Allisonville Rd., Indianapolis IN 46205. (317)549-9006. President: Edward De Miles. Record company, music publisher (EDM Music/BMI) and record producer. Estab. 1981. Releases 15-20 12″ singles and 5-10 LPs/year. Works with musicians/artists and songwriters on contract and hires musicians for in-house studio work. "Pays varying royalty to artists on contract." Pays statutory rate to publishers per song on record.

How to Contact: Write or call first and obtain permission to submit. Prefers cassette with 3-5 songs and lyric sheet. Does not return unsolicited material. Reports in 1 month.

Music: Mostly R&B/dance, top 40 pop/rock and contemporary jazz; also TV-film themes, musical scores and jingles. Released "Need A Lover" (by S. Lynn), recorded by Steve Lynn (R&B single); "High Off Rhymes" (by D. Evans/A. Mitchell), recorded by Multiple Choice (rap single); and "Break Your Promise" recorded by Klas (R&B single), all on Sahara Records.

Other artists include "Lost in Wonder" and "Dvon Edwards".

Tips: "We're looking for strong mainstream material. Lyrics and melodies with good hooks that grab people's attention."

SAM RECORDS INC., 76-05 51st Ave., Elmhurst NY 11373. Vice President: Michael Weiss. Record company. Estab. 1976. Releases 12 singles, 6 12″ singles, 2 LPs and 2 CDs/year. Receives 2 submissions/month. Works with musicians/artists on contract. Pays 10-12% royalty to artists on contract; statutory rate to publishers per song on record.

How to Contact: Sumit demo tape by mail. Unsolicited submissions are OK. Prefers cassette with 2 songs. Does not return unsolicited material.

Music: Mostly R&B, rap and dance. Released "This Dub Is Mine" (by D. Nabritt and L. Vega) (rap); "Spread A Little Love" (by S. Burks and C.Alexander) (R&B); and "Feel The Love Magic" written and recorded by John Davis (dance), all on Sam Records. Other artists include Brothers From Another Planet, Gee Wise and Charm One.

Tips: "Be sure to include artist's name on tape so we can direct the material to the right person."

SAN-SUE RECORDING STUDIO, P.O. Box 773, Mt. Juliet TN 37122-3336. (615)754-5412. Labels include Basic Records. Owner: Buddy Powell. Record company, music publisher (Hoosier Hills/BMI) and recording studio (16-track). Estab. 1975. Works with artists and songwriters on contract. Releases 7 singles and 3 LPs/year. Pays 8% royalty to artists on contract; statutory rate to publishers for each record sold.

How to Contact: Prefers 7½ ips reel-to-reel or cassette with 2-4 songs. "Strong vocal with piano or guitar is suitable for demo, along with lyrics." SASE. Reports in 2 weeks.

Music: Church/religious, country, and MOR. Released "You'd Think I'd Learn," by Stacy Armstrong; "Slow Walk Out of Town," by Donny Abney; and "When I Woke Up You Were Gone," by Donny Abney; all country pop singles on Basic Records. Other artists include Camillo Phelps.

SCENE PRODUCTIONS, Box 1243, Beckley WV 25802. (304)252-4836. President/Producer: Richard L. Petry. A&R: Carol Lee. Labels include Rising Sun and Country Road Records. Record company, record producer and music publisher (Purple Haze Music/BMI). Member of AFM. Releases 1-2 singles and 1-2 LPs/year. Receives 150-200 submissions/year. Works with musicians/artists and songwriters on contract. Pays 4-5% minimum royalty to artists on contract; standard royalty to songwriters on contract; statutory rate to publishers for each record sold. Charges "initial costs, which are conditionally paid back to artist."
How to Contact: Write first about your interest (recording only). Prefers cassette with 2-5 songs and lyric sheet. Prefers studio produced demos. SASE. Reports in 1 month.
Music: Mostly country, top 40, R&B/crossover and pop/rock; also MOR, light and commercial rock. Released "No Time for Play" and "I'm In Deep" (written and recorded by Chuck Paul) (pop). Other artists includes Dave Runion.
Tips: "Songs should be well thought-out and well constructed with good demo."

SCORE PRODUCTIONS, 3414 Peachtree Rd. NE 640, Atlanta GA 30326-1113. (404)266-8990. A&R Director: Amy Davis. Record company, music publisher and record producer (Score Productions, Inc.). Releases 10 singles, 1000 LPs and 5 CDs/year. Works with musicians/artists and songwriters on contract. Pays negotiable royalty to artists on contract.
How to Contact: Call first and obtain permission to submit. Prefers cassette with 1 song and lyric sheet. SASE. Reports in 1 month.
Music: Rock, country, MOR and pop. Released "Tone Up," "In Concert," and "Silver Anniversary Tribute to the Beatles," all on Perfect Pitch Records.

SCP RECORDS, Division of the Sound Column Companies, P.O. Box 70784, Salt Lake City UT 84170. (801)355-5327. A&R Professional Manager: Ron Simpson. Record company with affiliated record producer and music publisher (Ronarte Publications/ASCAP, Mountain Green Music/BMI and Macanudo Music/SESAC). Member CMA, AFM. Estab. 1970. Releases 3 singles and 4 cass/CDs/year. Works with artists and songwriters on contract; hires musicians for in-house studio work. Pays negotiable royalty to artists on contract; statutory rate to publishers for each record sold.
How to Contact: "Unsolicited submissions OK this year (pop ballads, pop uptempo, dance, country, R&B ballad and uptempo). Three songs max on demo tape, please include lyric sheets. No return or correspondence without SASE and sufficient postage. We'll eventually listen to everything. No calls, please."
Music: Pop (dance and A/C), country and contemporary religious. Released *His Love* (by various), recorded by Janine Lindsay (contemporary religious); "So Excited" (by Grant), recorded by Shawn K. (pop dance); and "Goodbye I Love You" (by K. Simpson and E. Pearson), recorded by Emily Pearson (contemporary folk), all on SCP Records.

*SCRAPBOOK RECORDS, 1840 South Gaffey St., #252, San Pedro Peninsula CA 90731. (213)514-0920. President: R. Perez. Record company, music publisher (Scrapbook Records/ASCAP) and record producer (Galaxy Music Productions). Estab. 1980. Releases 24 singles, 12 12″ singles, 6 LPs and 4 EPs/year. Works with musicians/artists and songwriters on contract, and L.A. Session Men (musicians union local #47). Pays royalty percentage to publisher per song on record.
How to Contact: Prefers cassette with any number of songs and lyric and lead sheet. SASE. Reports in 2 weeks.
Music: Mostly easy listening/AOR, New Age (international), R&B/blues, and 1950s oldies (doo-wop, rock-a-billy, California surf sounds); also A/C, soft rock/pop and instrumentals. Released "Samurai Warrior," recorded by King Neptune and The Sea Serpents; "From the '50s Big Beat to the '60s Surf Beat," recorded by King Neptune and The Sea Serpents; and "Instrumental Rock-A-Billys," recorded by The Galaxies; all written by various artists, recorded on Scrapbook Records (LPs/EPs). Other artists include The Ventures, Johnny and The Hurricanes, Dick Dale and The Del-Tones, Duane Eddy and The Rebels, Link Wray and The Raymen and The Virtues.

SEALED WITH A KISS, INC., Suite 119, 2166 W. Broadway, Anaheim CA 92804-2446. (714)992-2677. Vice President A&R: Tracy Sands. Labels include Swak Records. Record company and music publisher (Lipstick Traces Music Publishing/BMI). Estab. 1989. Releases 6-12 singles, 4 LPs, 2 EPs and 4 CDs/year. Receives 600 submissions/year. Works with musicians/artists and songwriters on contract. Pays 1-9% royalty to artists on contract; statutory rate or negotiable rate to publisher per song.
How to Contact: Submit demo tape by mail. Unsolicited submissions are OK. Prefers cassette. SASE. Reports in 2 months.
Music: Mostly rock and psychedelic. Released "The Bomb" (by Robert Wahlsteen), recorded by Jubal's Children (psychedelic); "Dance Time" (by Jeff Schreibman), recorded by The Royalites (rock); "My Silver Lining" (by David Rangel and Harry Watkins), recorded by The Yorkshires (rock), all on SWAK Records. Other artists include Tracy Sands.

Tips: "If you own unsigned masters, demos, live recordings, garage rehearsal tapes of 1960's rock and psychedelic, contact us first! We're looking for obscure, little known groups from any region. Must prove ownership and authenticity. Then we talk."

SEASIDE RECORDS, 100 Labon St., Tabor City NC 28463. (919)653-2546. Owner: Elson H. Stevens. Labels include SeaSide and JCB. Record company, music publisher and record producer. Estab. 1978. Releases 10 singles and 15 LPs/year. Works with musicians/artists and songwriters on contract; musicians on salary for in-house studio work, and producers. Receives 15 submissions/month. Pays 3-10% royalty to artists on contract; statutory rate to publisher per song on record.
How to Contact: Write or call first to obtain permission to submit. Prefers cassette with 3 songs and lyric or lead sheet. SASE. Reports in 1 month.
Music: Mostly country, gospel and rock; also "beach music." Released "Here I Go Again" (by E. Stevens), recorded by Angelia; "Little Bitty Country Boy" (by Lewis Allen), recorded by Lewie Allen Jr; "Lover Boy" (by Jeff Knight), recorded by Kelly Devol; "Miracles Happen" (by G. Jones, M. Jones and R. Jones), recorded by Rhonda Jones; and "I Found Jesus in Nashville" (by Len Butler), recorded by The Watson Family.

SEPHORA DIFFUSION, B. P. 30, 51170 Fismes **France.** Phone: (26) 48-8348. FAX: (26)48-8730. Director/Manager: Marc Brunet. Labels include MAYIM. Record company and record producer. Estab. 1984. Releases 10 LPs and 6 CDs/year. Works with musicians/artists on contract. Pays 7% royalty to artists on contract.
How to Contact: Submit demo tape by mail. Unsolicited submissions are OK. Prefers cassette with 3-4 songs and lyric sheets. SASE. Reports in 2 months.
Music: Mostly gospel, rock and MOR; all in French. Released "Der Jours Faus Toi" (by Jean-luc Gadreau), recorded by Label 7 on Mayim Records (gospel rock); "Councun Rayen" (by Christian Bertrand), recorded by C. Berhand on Mayim Records (MOR); "Ezets Sarat" (by Eliahu Gaulick), recorded by Mynam Klein on EVI Records (traditional). Other artists include David Durham and Jude 25.

SHAOLIN FILM & RECORDS, P.O. Box 387, Hollywood CA 90078. (818)506-8660. President: Richard O'Connor. A&R: Michelle McCarty. Record company, music publisher (Shaolin Music/ASCAP) and record producer (The Coyote). Estab. 1984. Releases 2 singles, 1 LP, 1CD and 1EP/year. Receives 30 submissions/month. Works with musicians/artists on record contract.
How to Contact: Prefers cassette with 3-4 songs and lyric sheet. Include bio and press kit. Does not return unsolicited material. Reports in 3 months.
Music: Mostly rock, hard rock and pop; also soundtracks. Released ""It's Your Shadow" (single), and soundtrack album *Coyote In A Graveyard*, written and recorded by Coyote on Shaolin Film and Records (rock).

SILENT RECORDS, Suite 315, 540 Alabama, San Francisco CA 94110. (415)864-7815. President: Kim Cascone. Record company and record producer (Kim Cascone). Estab. 1986. Releases 5 CDs/year. Works with musicians/artists on contract. Accepts LPs and CDs for consideration and distribution.
How to Contact: Write first and obtain permission to submit. Prefers cassette (or VHS videocassette) with press kit (press clips, bio, etc.). Does not return unsolicited material. Reports in 6 months.
Music: Mostly experimental and industrial. Released "Kill The King" (by A. McKenzie), recorded by The Hafler Trio; and "Fetish" (by D. Myers and K. Casone), recorded by Arcane Device/PGR; both on Silent Records (experimental). Other artists include Organum, The Haters, Pelican Daughters.

*SILVER JET PRODUCTIONS, 3500 Llanberis Ave., Bristol PA 19007. (215)788-2723. President: Johnny Kline. Record company, music publisher (BMI) and record producer (Silver Jet). Estab. 1984. Releases 1-2 singles/year. Receives 1-2 submissions/month. Works with musicians on salary for in-house studio work. Pays 10% royalty to artists on contract; statutory rate to publishers per song on record.
How to Contact: Submit demo tape by mail. Unsolicited submissions are OK. "No phone calls please." Prefers cassette with 3 songs and lyric sheet. "Submit professional quality tapes." SASE. Reports in 2 weeks.
Music: Mostly rockabilly and rock 'n roll; also gospel and country. Released "Poor Little Fool" (rockabilly single by Shari Sheely); "I'm Walkin" (by Fats Domino) and "Memphis" (by Chuck Berry) (R&B singles), all Recorded by Johnny Kline on Silver Jet Records.

*SIREN RECORDS, 807 E. Fayle, Baytown TX 77520. (713)420-3189. Executive Producer: Richard E. Cagle. Labels include Saturn Records. Record company (Siren Records). Estab. 1989. Releases 3 LPs and 1 EP/year. Works with musicians/artists and songwriters on contract; hires musicians on salary for in-house studio work. Pays 7-10% royalty to artists on contract; statutory rate to publishers per song on records.

How to Contact: Submit demo tape by mail. Unsolicited submissions are OK. Prefers cassette with 4-6 songs and lyric sheet. SASE. Reports in 6 weeks.

Music: Mostly rock, metal and pop; also blues, reggae and country. Released *Dream Come True* (by Kevin Blessington), recorded by Elevator Up (LP); *Premonition* (by Todd Good), recorded Premonition (LP); and *Experiment* (by Spike Jacobs), recorded by Earth Army (EP), all on Siren Records. Other artists include MXD Emotions, Third Person, Joe "King" Carrasco, Reality, Mickey Jones Project and Academy Black.

Tips: "Send good demo without too many effects. Just keep it simple!"

SIRR RODD RECORD & PUBLISHING CO., Box 58116, Philadelphia PA 19102-8116. President: Rodney J. Keitt. Record company, music publisher, record producer and management and booking firm. Releases 5 singles, 5 12″ singles and 2 LPs/year. Works with musicians/artists and songwriters on contract. Pays 5-10% royalty to artist on contract; statutory rate to publishers for each record sold.

How to Contact: Prefers cassette (or videocassette) with 3-5 songs and lyric sheet. SASE. Reports in 1 month.

Music: Top 40, pop, gospel, jazz, dance and rap. Released "Ghetto Jazz" and "Listen To Me" (by R.J. Keitt), "Fashion," "West Oak Lane Jam" and "I'm Serious" (by Klassy K/rap); "U-Crazy" and Strangelove" (by Ernie Kool); and *Monét The First Album* by Monét.

*SISAPA RECORD CO., INC., 6200 Eiterman Rd., Amlin OH 43002. (614)764-4777. National Coordinator: Stephanie Timberlake. Record company. Estab. 1988. Releases 9 singles, 2 12″ singles, 12 LPs and 12 CDs/year. Works with musicians/artists and songwriters on contract. Pays variable rate to artists on contract; statutory rate to publisher per song on record.

How to Contact: Write first and obtain permission to submit. Prefers cassette or VHS videocassette with 3 songs and lyric sheet. SASE. Reports in 2 months.

Music: Mostly R&B, rock and country. Released *Darwin's Finch vs. The Flying Saucers*, recorded by Zero One (pop/alternative LP); *Frontline*, recorded by The Marshall Tucker Band (souther rock LP): and *Crack of Dawn*, recorded by John Schwab (rock LP); all on Sisapa Records. Other artists include: Crazy Horse, Vince Andrews, Network 23, Paul Cotton, Karla and Bob Sauls.

Tips: "The songwriter should listen to our current releases to learn the types of songs our artists are recording. The songwriter/artist should submit a complete package—demo tape, photos, biography and video (if available)."

SLAK RECORDS, 9 Hector Ave., Toronto, ON M6G3G2 **Canada**. (416)533-3707. President: Al Kussin. Record company, music publisher (Clotille Publishing/SOCAN) and record producer (Slak Productions). Estab. 1986. Releases 2 singles, 2 12″ singles and 1 LP/year. Receives 10 submissions/month. Works with musicians/artists on contract. Pays 8-12% per record sold. Pays statutory rate to publisher per song on record.

How to Contact: Submit demo tape by mail. Unsolicited submissions are OK. Prefers cassette with 3 songs and lyric sheets. SASE.

Music: Mostly pop, R&B and dance. Released "Go Baby" (by F. Fudge and A. Kussin), recorded by Frankie Fudge; "All Talk" and "In Love" (by Lorraine Scott and A. Kussin), recorded by Lorrain Scott; all on Slak Records (R&B).

Tips: "Most of the material on Slak has been written by me. However, I wish to expand. A small label needs commercial, solid songwriting with good hooks and interesting lyrics."

*SNEAK TIP RECORDS, INC., 102-40 62nd Ave., 2R, Forest Hills NY 11375. (718)271-5149. President: Gerald Famolari. Record company and music publisher (Sneak Tip/BMI). Estab. 1990. Works with musicians/artists and songwriters on contract. Pays 10% to artists on contract; statutory rate to publisher per song on record.

How to Contact: Submit demo tape by mail. Unsolicited submissions are OK. Prefers cassette. Reports in 1-4 weeks.

Music: Mostly house, club and freestyle; also rap and R&B. Released "Treat Me Right" (by J. Swift) (hip-house); "Without Your Love" (by Rhingo) (freestyle-house); and "Emotional Pain" (by Xavier) (euro-freestyle); all recorded by Die Hard Productions on Sneak Tip Records.

SONY MUSIC, 34 Music Square E., Nashville TN 37203. (615)742-4321. Labels include Columbia and Epic. Record Company.

How to Contact: Write and ask for submission policy.

SOUND DEVELOPMENT RELEASING GROUP LTD., 1320 Sherman, Evanston IL 60201. (708)328-0400. Contact: A&R Department. Record company. Estab. 1988. Works with musicians/artists and songwriters on contract. Releases 40 CDs/year. Pays 6-10% royalty to artists on contract; ¾ rate to publishers per song on record.
How to Contact: Submit demo tape by mail. Unsolicited submissions are OK. Prefers cassette with 3 songs. SASE.
Music: Released "Ego" and "Kill That Sucka" written and recorded by Bad Boys (rap); and "High Style" (by M. Davis) recorded by Michael Davis (jazz), all on Sound Development Records.

SOUND IMAGE RECORDS, 6556 Wilkinson, North Hollywood CA 91606. (818)762-8881. President: Marty Eberhardt. Vice President Sales and Studio Manager: Chuck Kopp. Vice President and General Manager: David Chatfield. Vice President Business Affairs: John Bishop. Vice President A&R: Cathy Gibson. Labels include Sound Image and Harmony. Record company, record producer, music publisher (Sound Image Publishing), management firm (Sound Image Management), 24 track recording studio and video company. Member NARAS. Releases 8 singles and 4 LPs/year. Works with artists and songwriters on contract; hires musicians for in-house studio work. Pays 5-12% royalty to artists; statutory rate to publishers for each record sold.
How to Contact: Prefers cassette with 3 songs and lyric sheet. Include photo and bio. SASE. Prefers studio produced demos. Reports in 2 months.
Music: Mostly rock, AOR and R&B; also dance oriented. Currently working with *Brickyard* (songs include "Break the Ice" "Piece of Action") and *Joey McCall* (songs include "Arizona" and "The Wave").

SOUNDS OF WINCHESTER, Rt. 2, Box 116-H, Berkeley Springs, WV 25411. Contact: Jim or Bertha McCoy. Labels include Alear, Winchester and Real McCoy Records. Record company, music publisher (Jim McCoy Music, Alear Music and New Edition Music/BMI) and recording studio. Estab. 1973. Releases 20 singles and 20 LPs/year. Works with artists and songwriters on contract; musicians on salary for in-house studio work. Pays 2% royalty to artists and songwriters on contract; statutory rate to publishers for each record sold.
How to Contact: Arrange personal interview. Prefers 7½ ips reel-to-reel with 4-12 songs. Does not return unsolicited material. Reports in 1 month.
Music: Bluegrass, country, country rock, gospel and top 40/pop. Released "If I Throw Away My Pride" (by R. Lee Gray); "The Taking Kind" (by J.B. Miller); and "I've Got a Hold On You," written and recorded by Ronnie Flook; all on Winchester Records (country). Other artists include Carroll County Ramblers, Alvin Kesner, Bob Myers, George Dove, Bud Armel and Terry McCumbee.

SOURCE RECORDS, INC., #825, 39 S. LaSalle St., Chicago IL. (312)287-2227. President: John Bellamy. Record company. Estab. 1974. Releases 2 singles, 3 12″ singles and 2 LPs/year. Works with musicians/artists and songwriters on contract. Pays statutory rate to publisher per song on record.
How to Contact: Submit demo tape by mail. Unsolicited submissions are OK. Prefers cassette (or VHS or ¾″ videocassette if available) with 2 songs and lyric sheet. Does not return unsolicited material. Reports in 3 weeks.
Music: Mostly R&B, pop and gospel. Released "You Got The Love" (by A. Stephens), recorded by Candi Staton; "Everybody Dance" (by D. Owens), recorded by Darnell Owens; and "Keepers of the Dream" (by N. Hughes), recorded by Clear Vision all on Source Records.

SOURCE UNLIMITED RECORDS, 331 E. 9th St., New York NY 10003. (312)473-7833. Contact: Santo. Record company. Estab. 1982. Releases 4 CDs/year. Receives 30 submissions/month. Works with songwriters on contract. Pays 20% royalty to artists on contract; statutory rate to publisher per song on record.
How to Contact: Write first and obtain permission to submit. Prefers cassette and lyric sheet. SASE. Reports in 2 months.
Music: Mostly modern folk and gospel. Released *Trick or Treat, Games For Fools* and *Sex on the Mind* all written and recorded by Santo on Source Records (acoustic blues).
Tips: "Write about what you know! Be original."

SOUTHERN TRACKS RECORDS, 3051 Clairmont Rd. NE, Atlanta GA 30329. (404)325-0832. Contact: Mr. Carrier. Record company and record producer. Releases 15 singles and 2 LPs/year. Works with musicians/artists and songwriters on contract. Pays average of 5% royalty to artists on contract.
How to Contact: Prefers cassette with 3 unpublished songs and lyric sheet. Does not return unsolicited material.
Music: Interested in all types of music. Released "Burns Like a Rocket," recorded by Billy Joe Royal; and "We Always Agree on Love," recorded by Atlanta on Southern Tracks Records. Other artists include Bertie Higgins, Sammy Johns and Scooter Lee.

SPHEMUSATIONS, 12 Northfield Rd., Onehouse, Stowmarket Suffolk 1P14 3HF **England**. Contact: General Manager. Record company and music publisher. Estab. 1963. Releases 8 singles, 8 LPs, 8 EPs, 8 CDs/year. Receives 500 submissions/year. Works with musicians/artists and songwriters on contract and hires musicians for in-house studio work. Pays 6% royalty to artists on contract; statutory rate to publisher per song on record.
How to Contact: Write first and obtain permission to submit; write to arrange personal interview. Prefers cassette. SAE and IRC. Reports in 3 months.
Music: Mostly country, blues and jazz; also "serious modern." Released "The Weeper" (by J. Playford and J. Butt), recorded by K. Van Kampen; "The Lark" (by J. Playford and J. Butt), recorded by Simon Dresorgmer and "O Moon" (by J. Kears and J. Butt), recorded by Lorraine Anderson, all on Sphemusations Records (light music).

STARCREST PRODUCTIONS, INC., 209 Circle Hills Dr., Grand Forks ND 58201. (701)772-6831. President: George J. Hastings. Labels include Meadowlark and Minn-Dak Records. Record company, management firm and booking agency. Estab. 1970. Releases 2-6 singles and 1-2 LPs/year. Works with artists and songwriters on contract. Payment negotiable to artists on contract; statutory rate to publishers for each record sold.
How to Contact: Write first. Prefers cassette with 1-6 songs and lead sheet. SASE. Reports in 1 month.
Music: Country and top 40/pop. Released "Mr. Youcon Man" (by John Bass), recorded by Mary Joyce on Meadowlark (country) and "Ballad of Teddy Roosevelt" (by Bob Angle and George Hastings), recorded by Mary Joyce on Meadowlark (country).

STARDUST, Box 13, Estill Springs TN 37330. (615)649-2577. President: Buster Doss. Labels include Stardust, Wizard, Doss, Kimbolon, Flaming Star. Record company, music publisher (Buster Doss Music/BMI) and record producer (Colonel Buster Doss). Estab. 1959. Releases 50 singles and 25 LPs/year. Works with musicians/artists and songwriters on contract and hires musicians for in-house studio work. Pays 8% royalty to artists on contract; statutory rate to publisher per song on record.
How to Contact: Write or call first and obtain permission to submit. Prefers cassette with 2 songs and lyric sheets. SASE. Reports in 1 week.
Music: Mostly country; also rock. Released "Red Hot Fire," written and recorded by Benny Ray; "Where Were You" (by Buster Doss), recorded on Rooster Q.; and "Sad Memories," written and recorded by R.B. Stone; all on Stardust Records (all country singles). Other artists include Johnny Buck, Hobson Smith, Cliff Archer, Linda Wunder, Buck Cody and Tony Andrews.

STARGARD RECORDS, P.O. Box 138, Boston MA 02101. (617)296-3327. Artist Relations: Anthony Greenaway. Labels include Oak Groove Records. Record company, music publisher (Zatco Music/ASCAP and Stargard Publishing/BMI) and record producer. Estab. 1985. Releases 9 singles and 1 LP/year. Receives 25-30 submissions/month. Works with musicians/artists on contract; hires musicians for in-house studio work. Pays 5-6% royalty to artists on contract; statutory rate to publisher per song on record.
How to Contact: Write first to arrange personal interview. Prefers cassette and lyric and lead sheet. SASE. Reports in 2 months. "Sending bio along with picture or glossies is appreciated but not necessary."
Music: Mostly R&B, dance/hip hop. Released "Pipe Dreaming" (by Troy DeVoe), recorded by Tow Zone on Stargard Records (12″ single); and "Playing With Time" (by Joseph Williams), recorded by Tiger Brown on Oak Groove Records (12″ single). Other artists include Down Time and En-Control.

STARK RECORDS AND TAPE COMPANY, 628 S. South St., Mount Airy NC 27030. (919)786-2865. President and Owner: Paul E. Johnson. Labels include Stark, Pilot, Hello, Sugarbear, Kay and Red Bird. Record company, music publisher (Tompaul Music Company/BMI) and record producer (Stark Records and Tape Company). Estab. 1960. Releases 8 singles and 3 LPs/year. Works with songwriters on contract. Pays statutory rate to publisher per song on record.
How to Contact: Submit demo tape by mail. Unsolicited submissions are OK. Prefers cassette with 3-5 songs and lyric or lead sheets. SASE. Reports in 2 months.
Music: Mostly pop, country and country gospel; also bluegrass, bluegrass gospel and C&W. Released "Blue Eyes Crying in the Rain" (by Paul E. Johnson), recorded by Bobby Atkins (country); "Love Valley," written and recorded by Bobby Atkins; all on Stark Records (C&W). Other artists include Carl Tolbert, Sam Bray, Ralph Hill, Early Upchurch, Sanford Teague and Don Sawyers.

*STARMAN RECORDS, P.O. Box 245569, Sacramento CA 95824. (916)441-1080. A&R: Virgal Covington. Record company, record producer (Starman Records), (SAA, independent label) and in-house studio. Estab. 1976. Deals with artists and songwriters. Produces 3-4 singles and 2-3 LPs/year. Fee derived from outright fee from recording artist or record company. Sometimes charges artists in

advance for services; "depends on their input and willingness to be produced on a professional level."
How to Contact: Call first and obtain permission to submit. Prefers cassette or VHS videocassette with 6 songs and lyric and lead sheet. SASE.
Music: Mostly popular MOR, AOR and R&B, New Age and soundtrack; also spoken word, sound effects and novelty or specialties. Produced *Starbreak Vol.1* (compilation), recorded by A.V. Covington (country LP); *Starbreak Vol.2* (by Gospel Choirs), recorded by John Irving (rock Gospel); and "The War Song" (by A.V. Covington), recorded by The Virg (AOR/pop); all on Starman Records. Other artists include Mary Murphy, Duane Kennedy, Devotion, Kevin Archie, Vincente Michael, and Jimmy Malone and Gerry Brennan.

*STATUE RECORDS, 2810 McBain St., Redondo Beach CA 90278. President: Jim Monroe. A&R Director: Brian Gunther. Record company. Releases 5-10 singles and 10-20 LPs/year. Works with musicians/artists and songwriters on contract. Pays 5-10% or negotiable royalty to artists on contract.
How to Contact: Prefers "high quality" cassette with 3-5 songs and lyric sheet. Accepts unsolicited material. Reports in 1 month. "Please include glossy photo(s) if you are a group looking for a recording deal."
Music: Mostly "up-tempo rock, with *strong* hooks and new wave." Released *Ring Leader* (rock LP), *Chosin Few* (rock LP), *England 402* (rock LP), *Voyager* (rock LP), *Bob Dato* (rock LP), *Hollywood Bears* (rock LP) and *New Dynasty* (rock LP).

*STOP HUNGER RECORDS INTERNATIONAL, 1300 Division St., Nashville TN 37203. (615)242-4722. FAX: (615)242-1177. Producer: Robert Metzgar. Record company and music publisher (Aim High Music/ASCAP, Bobby and Billy Music/BMI). Estab. 1971. Releases 16-17 singles, 25 LPs and 25 CDs/year. Works with musicians/artists and songwriters on contract and hires musicians for in-house studio work. Pays statutory rate to publisher per song on record.
How to Contact: Submit demo tape by mail. Unsolicited submissions are OK. Prefers cassette or VHS videocassette with 5-10 songs and lyric sheet. Does not return unsolicited material. Reports in 2 weeks.
Music: Mostly country, traditional country and pop country; also gospel, southern gospel and contemporary Christian. Released *George and Merle* (by H. Cornelius), recorded by Alan Jackson on Arista Records (CD/cassette); *Return of the Ghost Riders* (by Jack Patton), recorded by J. Cash on Polygram Records (CD/cassette); and *Just the Two Of Us* (by Metzgar/Patterson), recorded by C. Twitty on MCA Records (CD/cassette). Other artists include Tommy Cash/Mark Allen Cash (CBS-Sony), Carl Butler (CBS-Sony), Tommy Overstreet (CBS-Sony), Mickey Jones (Capitol), Glen Campbell Band and others.

*STREET MUSIC RECORDS, #17, 61 Canal St., San Rafael CA 94901. (415)454-0906. A&R Director: Steven Britto. Record company. Estab. 1987. Releases 9 singles and 9 12" singles/year. Works with musicians/artists and songwriters on contract and producers on royalty and points.
How to Contact: Prefers cassette or VHS videocassette with 2 songs and lyric sheet. SASE. Reports in 2 weeks.
Music: Mostly rap, R&B and dance; also house and pop. Released "Talking That Bad Talk," recorded by CIA (rap); "Pop Music IZ" (by Corey A. Powell and Mike Pantaleone), recorded by Corey Andre (dance); and "Just Another Sucka" (by Russell L. Montiero and Suzanne Amadeo), recorded by Niten-Day (rap); all on Street Music Records. Other artists include: City Street Council, Dávida, Joe Barros III, and Rudy C.

*STRESS RECORDS, 4024 State Line, Kansas City KS 66103. (913)262-3555. Director of A&R: Dave Maygers. Labels include Graphic Records. Record company and music publisher (United Entertainment Music/BMI). Estab. 1982. Releases 1-2 12" singles, 2-4 LPs, 1-2 EPs and 2-4 CDs/year. Receives 4-6 submissions/month. Works with musicians/artists and songwriters on contract. Pays 10% royalty to artists on contract; negotiable rate to publisher per song on record.
How to Contact: Write first and obtain permission to submit. Prefers cassette (or VHS videocassette) or 15 or 30 ips reel-to-reel with 3-5 songs and lyric sheet. SASE.
Music: Mostly rock and country; also jazz, R&B and pop. Released *We Only In It For the Monkey* (by R. Lucente), recorded by the Bon Ton Band on Stress Records (LP zydeco); *American Tradition*, written and recorded by The Verandas on Stress Records (LP rock); *The Clique*, written and recorded by The Clique on Graphic Records (LP rock); *Rodeo Rocks Vol 1* (heavy metal LP compilation) on Stress Records and *Weak Heart, Strong Memory* by Spike Blake on Stress Records (country LP). Other artists include The Hollowmen and That Statue Moved.

STUDIO RECORDS INC., 5209 Indian Head Hwy., Oxon Hill MD 20745. (301)839-6567. President: Steven Franco. Vice President: Michael Pipitone. Record company (BMI). Estab. 1983. Releases 4-10 12" singles, 4 CDs, 4 EPs and 4 LPs/year. Works with musicians/artists and songwriters on contract and hires musicians for in-house studio work and commercial production. Pays 6-10% royalty to artists on contract; statutory rate to publisher per song on record.

How to Contact: Submit demo tape by mail. Unsolicited submissions are OK. Prefers cassette with 3 songs. Does not return unsolicited material. Reports in 2 weeks.

Music: Mostly pop, dance and R&B. Released "Girl You Know Its True" (by Anedo, Lyles, Dehewy, Spencer, Hollang), recorded by Numarx on Studio Records (pop). Other artists include Tommi Gee, Patrick Adams and Lisa Bellamy.

STUDIOEAST RECORDING, INC., 5457 Monroe Rd., Charlotte NC 28212. (704)536-0424. Owner: Tim Eaton. Labels include Pyramid Records, Metro Records, Sandblast Records, Sandman, East Coast Records and Peach. Record company, music publisher (Eastwood Publishing) and record producer. Releases 50 singles and 20 LPs/year. Works with musicians/artists and songwriters on contract; hires musicians for in-house studio work. Pays standard royalty to artists on contract.

How to Contact: Prefers cassette or 15 ips reel-to-reel (or VHS videocassette) with any number of songs. Does not return unsolicited material. Reports in 2 months. "If we feel material is unusable we will not contact artist. We will, however, keep material on file for possible future use."

Music: Mostly R&B, country and jazz; also rhythm and black gospel. Released "One More Step" by the Band of Oz on Metro Records; "Lovers' Holiday," by Dink Perry and the Breeze Band on Metro Records; "They Call Me Mr. Bassman"; "Whadja Do That Fo' " by the Catalinas on Metro Records (single). Presently recording: General Johnson & The Chairman Of The Board for Surfside Records, The Fantastic Shakers for Metro Records, The Catalinas for Metro Records and Part Time Party Time Band for Metro Records.

SUNDOWN RECORDS, P.O. Box 241, Newbury Park CA 91320. (805)499-9912. Owners: Gilbert Yslas and Richard Searles. Record company, distributor. Estab. 1985. Releases 2 CDs/year. Works with musicians/artists on contract.

How to Contact: Submit demo tape/CD by mail. Prefers cassette. SASE. Reports in weeks.

Music: Contemporary classical/New Age. Released "A Christmas Gift" written and recorded by Yslas/Searles on Sundown Records (New Age); "Dance of the Renaissance" (acoustic); and "Dream of the Troubadour" (acoustic).

SURESHOT RECORDS, Box 1345, Kings Beach CA 95719. (916)546-5381. Contact: Alan Redstone. Record company and music publisher (Magic Message Music/ASCAP). Estab. 1979. Releases 1 single and 1 LP/year. Works with songwriters on contract.

How to Contact: Currently not accepting new material.

Music: Mostly country, A/C and rock; also ballads. Released "This Time Around," written and recorded by Alan Redstone on Sureshot Records (country/rock).

*SURPRIZE RECORDS, INC., 7231 Mansfield Ave., Philadelphia PA 19138-1620. (215)276-8861. President: W. Lloyd Lucas. Executive Director A&R: Brian L. Lucas. Labels include Surprize and SRI. Record company and record producer (Surprize Records, Inc.). Estab. 1981. Releases 4-6 singles, 1-3 12″ singles and 2 LPs/year. Works with musicians/artists and songwriters on contract. Pays 6-10% royalty to artists on contract; statutory rate to publisher per song on record.

How to Contact: Write or call first and obtain permission to submit. Prefers cassette or VHS videocassette with 4 songs and lyric or lead sheet. SASE. Reports in 3 weeks.

Music: Mostly R&B ballads, R&B dance oriented and positive rap (no profanity); also crossover country, gospel and contemporary Christian. Released "Pledging My Love" (by Cobb/McCoy), recorded by Bill Lucas on Surprize Records (R&B single); "Shadow People" (by August/Trantham), recorded by Trilogy on Surprize Records (R&B single); and "Changes" (by Charles Green) and "The Nightstalker" (by Lucas/Hernandez/Alleca), recorded by C.G. Majesty The-All (rap single). Other artits include Lamar Lucas, Tasha Fulmore, and Two Hand Posse (rap group).

Tips: "Be dedicated and steadfast in your chosen field whether it be songwriting and/or performing. Be aware of the changing trends. Watch other great performers and try to be as good, if not better. 'Be the best that you can be.' And as Quincy Jones says, 'Leave your egos at the door" and take all criticisms as being positive, not negative. There is always something to learn."

*SURVIVOR RECORDS/H.I.T. RECORDS, Suite 661, 880 Front St., Lahaina HI 96761. (808)244-1100. A&R Director: Jack Carrington. Labels include Survivor and H.I.T. Record Company (Suvivor and H.I.T.), music publisher (Ten of Diamonds/BMI, Main No KaOi/ASCAP) and record producer (Jason Schwartz). Estab. 1974. Releases 1-3 singles, 1-3 LPs and 1-3 CDs/year. Works with musicians/artists and songwriters on contract. Pays 3-15% royalty to artists on contract; statutory rate to publisher per song on record.

How to Contact: Submit demo tape by mail. Unsolicited submissions are OK. Prefers cassette or CD, VHS videocassette with 3-4 songs. SASE. Reports in 1 month.

Music: Mostly pop, country and R&B; also classical, Hawaiian and jazz/fusion. Released "Dreamer" (by Michael Condon), recorded by Doc Michaels (pop single); *Sunnyside of Reality* (by Walt Rosansky and Jason Schwartz), recorded by Jason (pop album); and "Tanqueray," written and recorded by Mark Cohen (jazz/fusion single); all on Survivor Records. Other artists include Greta Warren, Amber, Michael Thompson and Rambona.

Tips: "The song is the basis of our interest. Only the best artists will be considered for their own recording, but songs—aah! That's our goal."

SUSAN RECORDS, Box 4740, Nashville TN 37216. (615)865-4740. A&R Director: D. Daniels. Labels include Denco Records. Record company and music publisher. Releases 2-20 singles and 1-5 LPs/year. Works with artists and songwriters on contract. Pays 15¢/record to artists on contract. Buys some material outright; payment varies.

How to Contact: Prefers cassette with 1-6 songs and lead sheet. SASE. Reports in 2 weeks.

Music: Blues, country, dance, easy listening, folk, gospel, jazz, MOR, rock, soul and top 40/pop.

SWEET TALK RECORDS, P.O. Box 211, Westfield MA 01086. (413)783-8386. Operations Manager: Alexis Steele. Labels include Sweet Talk Records. Record company and music publisher (Sariser Music/BMI). Estab. 1987. Releases 2 LPs/year. Receives 10-15 submissions/year. Works with musicians/artists and songwriters on contract. Pays statutory rate to publisher per song on record.

How to Contact: Write first and obtain permission to submit. No phone calls. Prefers cassette or 7½ ips reel-to-reel (or VHS ¼" videocassette) with 3-4 songs and lyric or lead sheet. SASE. Reports in 6 weeks.

Music: Mostly country/pop, country/rock and educational material; also soft rock and rockabilly. Released "Magic & Music" written and recorded by Sparkie Allison on Sweet Talk Records (jazz) and "One Last Kiss" (by Sparkie Allison) recorded by The Moore Twins on MMT Records (country).

Tips: "Be unique. Try something different. Avoid the typical love songs. We look for material with a universal positive message. No cheatin' songs, no drinkin' songs."

SWOOP RECORDS, Stewart House, Hillbottom Rd., Highwycombe, Bucks, HP124HJ **England**. Phone: (063)081374. FAX: (063)081612. A&R Director: Xavier Lee. Labels include Grenoullie, Zarg, Pogo and Check. Record company, music publisher (R.T.L. Music) and record producer (Ron Lee). Estab. 1976. Releases 50 singles, 50 12" singles, 60 LPs and 60 CDs/year. Receives 10-15 submissions/month. Works with musicians/artists and songwriters on contract. Royalty paid to artists varies; statutory rate to publishers per song on record.

How to Contact: Prefers cassette, (or VHS videocassette) with 3 songs and lyric or lead sheet. SAE and IRC. Reports in 3 weeks.

Music: Interested in all types. Released "99" (by R.C. Bowman), recorded by The Chromatics on Swoop Records (hillbilly rock & roll); "Asylum" (by M.J. Lawson), recorded by Emmitt Till on Swoop Records (rock) and "Not Me" (by D. Boone) recorded by Daniel Boone on Swoop Records (rock). Other artists include Orphan, Groucho, Sight-n-Sound, Mike Sheridan, The Night Riders and Studs.

Tips: "Be original."

TABITHA RECORDS, Sandpiper Court, Harrington Lane, Exeter HX6 8N5 **England**. Phone: (0392)79914. Managing Director: Graham Sclater. Labels include Willow and Domino. Record company (PRS/MCPC/PPL) and record producer (Graham Sclater). Estab. 1975. Releases 6 singles, 2 12" singles, 4 LPs and 2 CDs/year. Works with musicians/artists on contract. Pays 4-8% royalty to artists on contract; statutory rate to publisher per song on record.

How to Contact: Submit demo tape by mail. Unsolicited submissions are OK. Prefers cassette (or VHS videocassette if available) with 4 songs. SASE. Reports in 1 month.

Music: Mostly pop, rock and country; also R&B and folk. Released "Aliens," written and recorded by Mark Fojo; "Fuzzin' The Tracks" (by Sting), recorded by Flic; and "Not A Chance," written and recorded by Simon Galt; all on Tabitha Records (all pop singles). Other artists include Andy Ford, Deparate Measures and 'Ot Nuts.

Tips: "Send good quality demos."

"How to Use Your Songwriter's Market" (at the front of this book) contains comments and suggestions to help you understand and use the information in these listings.

TARGET RECORDS, Box 163, West Redding CT 06896. President: Paul Hotchkiss. Labels include Kastle Records. Record company, music publisher (Tutch Music/Blue Hill Music) and record producer (Red Kastle Prod.). Estab. 1975. Releases 6 singles and 2 LPs/year. Works with songwriters on contract. Pays statutory rate to publisher per song on record.
How to Contact: Write first and obtain permission to submit. Prefers cassette with 2 songs and lyric sheet. SASE. Reports in 3 weeks.
Music: Country and crossover. Released "Luv Radio" (by P. Hotchkiss/M. Terry), recorded by M. Terry (country pop); "Honky Tonk Darling" (by Paul Hotchkiss), recorded by Tony Worsley (country); and "Standing on Mountain" (by Cal Stewart), recorded by Lynn and Rebels (country rockabilly); all on Target/Roto Noto Records. Other artists include Fran Taylor, Malone & Hutch, Jimmy Hartley, Beverly's Hillbilly Band, Randy Burns, Susan Rose Manning and Donna Maine and Rodeo.

TEROCK RECORDS, P.O. Box 4740, Nashville TN 37216. (615)865-4740. Manager: S.D. Neal. Labels include Terock, Susan, Denco, Rock-A-Nash-A-Billy. Record company, record producer, and music publisher (Heavy Jamin' Music/ASCAP). Estab. 1959. "We also lease masters." Member ASCAP, BMI. Releases 8-12 singles and 3-6 12″ singles/year. Receives 300 submissions/month. Works with musicians/artists and songwriters on contract and hires musicians for in-house studio work. Pays artists on contract 15-25¢ per record sold; standard royalty to songwriters on contract.
How to Contact: Prefers cassette with 3-6 songs and lyric sheet. SASE. Reports in 3 weeks.
Music: Mostly rock'n'roll, country and rockabilly; also bluegrass, blues, easy listening, folk, gospel, jazz, MOR, progressive, Spanish, R&B, soul and top 40/pop. Released "That's Why I Love You," by Dixie Dee (country); "Born to Bum Around," by Curt Flemons (country); and "Big Heavy," by the Rhythm Rockers (rock).
Tips: "Send your best."

*TEXAS CRUDE, 5224 N. Lamar, Austin TX 78751. (512)440-1976. Managers: Lance Keltner/Bobby Lockhart. Labels include Harvest and Texas Crude. Record company (Texas Crude Publishing Inc.). Works with musicians on salary for in-house studio work. Pays varying royalty to artists on contract.
How to Contact: Submit demo tape by mail. Write or call first to arrange a personal interview. Prefers cassette with 1-3 songs and lyric sheet. SASE. Reports in 1 month.
Music: Mostly country, rock and gospel; also jazz, swing and pop/dance. Released *Living For a Song*, recorded by Roy Head on Texas Crude Records (LP). Other artists include Jimmy Mac, Lance Kelter, and Tom Holden (in 1989, had #22 country single with "That Old Wheel," by Johnny Cash on Polygram Records).

*LEE THORP ENTERTAINMENT, Box 70, Observatory, Capetown 7935 **South Africa**. Phone: (21)471358. Managing Director: Lee Thorp. Labels include Sea Records and Mountain Records. Record company, music publisher and record producer. Estab. 1974. Releases 4 12″ singles, 6-8 LPs and 6-8 CDs/year. Works with musicians/artists and songwriters on contract; hires musicians on salary for in-house studio work. Pays statutory rate to publishers per song on records.
How to Contact: Submit demo tape by mail. Unsolicited submissions are OK. Prefers cassette. SASE. Reports in 3 months.
Music: Mostly pop, rock and jazz; also ethnic, folk and blues. Released "Vastrap," recorded by R. Jansen on Sea Records (rock/jazz); "LDV," recorded by A. DeVilliams on Mountain Records (pop/rock); and "The Voice," recorded by A. deWilliams/Zayn Adam on Mountin Records (pop/MOR). Other artists include Basil Coetzee and Tracey Butler.

3 G'S INDUSTRIES, 6015 Troost, Kansas City MO 64110. (816)361-8455. General Manager: Eugene Gold. Labels include NMI, Cory, 3 G's and Chris C's Records. Record company, record producer and music publisher (Eugene Gold Music and Gid-Gad Music). Releases 8 singles and 6 LPs/year. Works with musicians/artists and songwriters on contract; hires musicians for in-house studio work. Pays 4-6% royalty to artists on contract; statutory rate to publishers for each record sold.
How to Contact: Prefers cassette (or videocassette) with 4-8 songs and lyric sheet. SASE. Reports in 1 month.
Music: Mostly R&B and jazz; also church/religious, gospel and soul. Released "Solitude," written and recorded by Jeff Lucas; "Young Tender" (by M. Gilmore/J. Spradlin), recorded by Mark Gilmore; and "Remember" recorded by Wings of Graces, all on 3G's Records (singles). Other artists include Suspension, L. Washington, Thrust's, James "Fuzzy" West, Cal Green and L.S. Movement Band.

TIMELESS ENTERTAINMENT CORP., 10 Pebblewood, Irvine CA 92714-4530. (714)552-5231. Vice President: Fred Bailin. Labels include Perfect, Goldisc. Record company. Estab. 1978. Releases 3 singles, 3 12″ singles, 4 LPs and 4 CDs/year. Receives 100-150 submissions/year. Works with musicians/artists and songwriters on contract. Pays 9% royalty to artists on contract; statutory or negotiated rate to publisher per song on record.

How to Contact: Submit demo tape by mail. Unsolicited submissions are OK. Prefers cassette with 3 songs and lead sheets. SASE. Reports in 2 weeks.
Music: Mostly R&B, pop and rock; also rap. Artists include Ecstacy, Passion and Pain.

*TIMELESS PRODUCTIONS, 5050 Traverse Creek Rd., Garden Vally CA 95633. (916)333-1335. Owner: David A. Blonski. Labels include Timeless Productions; Natures Symphonies. Record company (Timeless Productions) and record producer (Timeless Productions/David Blonski). Estab. 1986. Releases 4 LPs and 2-4 CDs/year. Works with musicians/artists and songwriters on contract and hires musicians for in-house studio work; also collaborators. Pays 5-10% royalty to artists on contract.
How to Contact: Submit demo tape by mail. Unsolicited submissions are OK. Prefers cassette with 4 songs. SASE. Reports in 3 weeks.
Music: Mostly New Age, instrumental folk, light jazz; also self-help/health, children's, relaxation and motivation. Released *Land of the Midnight Sun,* written and recorded by David Blonski and Jon Allasia on Timeless Records (New Age LP); *Sierra Passage* (by David Blonski and Ken Craig), recorded by David Blonski on Timeless Records (new folk LP); and "Thundering Skies," written and recorded by David Blonski on Nature's Symphonies Records (environmental). Other artists include Ken Craig, Dan Bowman and The Singing Nuns.
Tips: "I am extremely busy working on my own projects in our in-house recording studio. But it is available for other projects especially when collaborations are involved."

TOM THUMB MUSIC (Division of Rhythms Productions), Box 34485, Los Angeles CA 90034. President: R.S. White. Labels include Rhythms Productions and Tom Thumb. Record company. Estab. 1955. Works with songwriters on contract. Pays negotiable royalty to artists on contract. Requires completed tape masters.
How to Contact: Submit demo tape by mail. Unsolicited submissions are OK. Prefers cassette. SASE. Reports in 1 month.
Music: Mostly "children's concept albums with educational content. Can be songs or musical stories."
Tips: "Experience with children and educational content is desirable."

TOMARK RECORDS, 7560 Woodman Pl., #G3, Van Nuys CA 91405. (818)994-4862. Owners: Tom Willett and Mark Thornton. Labels include Tomark Records. Record company, music publisher (Schmerdley Music and Ocean Walk Music/BMI) and record producer. Estab. 1988. Releases 1 single and 1 LP/year. Receives 125 submissions/year. Works with artists and songwriters on contract.
How to Contact: Submit demo tape by mail. Unsolicited submissions are OK. Prefers cassette or 7½ ips reel-to-reel (or VHS videocassette) with songs. SASE. Reports in 4 weeks.
Music: Mostly country and novelty; also rock. Released "My Ex-Ex Wife" (by Tom Willett), recorded by Tomark (country novelty); "Christmas Will Be Blue in California," by Mark Thornton (Christmas country); and "Christopher Columbus," by Mark Thornton and Tom Willett (country).

TOMMY BOY MUSIC, INC., 1747 First Ave., New York NY 10128. (212)722-2211. A&R Director/ R&B, Dance/Rap: Kevin Maxwell. Record company, music publisher (T-Boy/T-Girl). Releases 15-20 singles and 5-10 LPs/year. Works with musicians/artists on contract; pays varying royalty to artists on contract.
How to Contact: Call first and obtain permission to submit. Prefers cassette with 1-3 songs and lyric sheet, clearly marked with submitter name and phone number. Materials not returnable. "When submitting a demo, please do not call to see if we are going to use it. If we are, you will be the first to know."
Music: Mostly rap, R&B and dance/pop. No rock or New Age. 1989 releases included "Me Myself and I", "Say No Go" and "Buddy" by De La Soul; "Doowutchyalike" and "The Humpty Dance" by Digital Underground; "You Are the One" by TKA; "Dance for Me" and "Ladies First" by Queen Latifah.

TOP RECORDS, Gall. del Corso, 4 Milano 20122 **Italy.** Phone: (02)76021141. FAX: (0039)276021141. Manager/Director: Guido Palma. Labels include United Colors Productions, Dingo Music, Telex Music and Records, KIWI Record, Smoking Records and Tapes. Estab. 1979. Record company and music publisher. Releases 20 singles, 20 12″ singles, 30 LPs, 15 EPs and 40 CDs/year. Receives 200 submissions/year. Works with musicians/artists and songwriters on contract and hires in-house studio musicians. Pays 10% royalty to artists on contract.
How to Contact: Prefers cassette (or videocassette) with 5 songs and lyric sheet. Does not return unsolicited material.
Music: Mostly pop and dance; also soundtracks. Released "Manbo Jumbo" (by Prado), recorded by Mirella Banti (dance); "Unastoria" (by Politano), recorded by Giannini (pop); and "Capricci di Donna" written and recorded by Daiano (Italian style), all on Top Records. Other artists include Tina Charles, Gisa, Marisa Sacchetto, Gil Ventura, Antonio Gallo, Santarosa and Petula Clark.

*TOP TRAX, P.O. Box 111717, Nashville TN 37222-1717. (615)776-5188. President: Richard Allan Painter. Record company, music publisher (R.A. Painter Music/ASCAP, Richard Painter Music/ BMI), Painter Music TelePro-Motions. Member NARAS, GMA, NAPE. Top Trax has three primary divisions: Song Production, Promotion and Publishing. Manufactures and markets self-produced recordings and outside master product. Releases quarterly compilation CD sampler with up to 40 singles/ year. Works with artists and songwriters on contract; musicians on salary. Pays 7% royalty to artists on contract; statutory rate to publishers for each record sold. Artists pay manufacturing and marketing fee to press and release their masters.
How to Contact: Send SASE for free information.
Music: Suited for radio formats CHR, AOR, A/C, and UC; such that translates into broad commercial appeal and staying power in the target market.
Tips: "Be yourself. Offer a unique style, versatility and musical diversity to your audience. Pursue excellence and tell the truth as your only artistic moral imperative. Replicate your studio sound on stage. Be prepared to embark on an ambitious promotional appearance schedule in support of your released recording(s)."

TOUCHE RECORDS, Box 96, El Cerrito CA 94530. Executive Vice President: James Bronson, Jr. Record company, record producer (Mom and Pop Productions, Inc.) and music publisher (Toulouse Music Co./BMI). Member AIMP. Releases 2 LPs/year. Works with artists and songwriters on contract; musicians on salary for in-house studio work. Pays statutory rate to publishers per song on record.
How to Contact: Prefers cassette with 2-4 songs and lyric sheet. SASE. Reports in 1 month.
Music: Mostly jazz; also bluegrass, gospel, jazz, R&B and soul. Released *Bronson Blues* (by James Bronson), *Nigger Music* and *Touché Smiles* (by Smiley Winters), all recorded by Les Oublies du Jazz Ensemble on Touché Records (all LPs). Other artists include Hi Tide Harris.

TRAC RECORD CO., 170 N. Maple, Fresno CA 93702. (209)255-1717. Owner: Stan Anderson. Record company and music publisher (Sellwood Publishing/BMI). Estab. 1972. Releases 10-20 singles and 5 LPs and 2 CDs/year. Receives 30-35 submissions/month. Works with musicians/artists on contract, songwriters on royalty contract and in-house musicians on contract. Pays 13% royalty to artists on contract. Pays statutory rate to publisher per song on record.
How to Contact: Prefers cassette (or VHS videocassette) with 2-4 songs and lyric sheet. SASE. Reports in 2 months.
Music: Country, top 40 gospel and rock. Released "Nevada State of Mind" and "West Coast Girl" written and recorded by Barry Best (country); "Don't Walk Away" written and recorded by B.G. White (country); and *Bare Your Soul*, written by Denise Benson, recorded by Jessica James (country), all on Trac Records. Other artists include Gil Thomas, Ron Arlen and Ric Blake, in one accord.

*TREND RECORDS, P.O. Box 201, Smyrna GA 30081. (404)432-2454. President: Tom Hodges. Labels include Trendsetter, Trend/Side Atlanta, British Overseas Airways Music and Stepping Stone Records. Record company, music publisher (Mimic Music/BMI, Skipjack Music/BMI and British Overseas Airways Music/ASCAP), record producer and management firm. Estab. 1965. Releases 12 singles, 3 12″ singles, 15 LPs and 5 CDs/year. Works with musicians/artists and songwriters on contract. Pays 15% royalty to artists on contract; standard royalty to songwriters on contract; statutory rate to publisher per song on records.
How to Contact: Prefers cassette with 3-6 songs and lead sheet. SASE. Reports in 3 weeks.
Music: Country, bluegrass, gospel, MOR, rock and soul. Released "Don't Mess With the IRS" (by Rita/Rita), recorded by Marlon Frizzell (country); "Papa Says" (by B. Buic and J. Cobb), recorded by Jim Single; "Put it Where," written and recorded by Dave Sanborn; and "My Life's Book," written and recorded by Frank Brannon; all on Trend Records (country). Other artists include Jimmy Moore, Ray Macdonald, Jimmy Williams, Bobby Martin, Soul-jers and Dennis & The Times, Ginny Peters, Deb Watson, Charlotte Bradford and Fred Eubanks.

TRUSTY RECORDS, 8771 Rose Creek Rd., Nebo KY 42441. (502)249-3194. President: Elsie Childers. Record company and music publisher (Trusty Publications/BMI). Member NSAI, CMA. Estab. 1950. Releases 2 singles and 2 LPs/year. Receives 8-10 submissions/month. Works with musicians/artists and songwriters on contract. Pays 3% royalty to artists on contract; statutory rate to publishers for each record sold.
How to Contact: Prefers cassette with 2-4 songs and lead sheet. SASE. Reports in 1 month.
Music: Mostly country; also blues, church/religious, dance, easy listening, folk, gospel, MOR, soul and top 40/pop. Released "Mystical Magic" "Rainy Nights Are Made for Love" and "I Did Something Wrong Just Right" all written by Elsie Childers and recorded by Noah Williams on Trusty Records (hard country).
Tips: "Writers with road tours are given top consideration."

TUG BOAT RECORDS, #4 Lilac Court, Newport News VA 23601. (804)591-2717. A&R: Judith Guthro. Record company, music publisher (Doc Publishing/BMI, Dream Machine/SESAC) and record producer (Doc Holiday Productions). Estab. 1967. Releases 12 singles, 15 12″ singles, 15 LPs, 15 EPs, and 4 CDs/year. Works with musicians/artists and songwriters on contract and hires musicians for in-house studio work. Pays varying royalty to artists on contract; statutory rate to publisher per song on record.
How to Contact: Submit demo tape by mail. Unsolicited submissions are OK. Prefers cassette with 1 song and lyric sheets.
Music: Mostly country, top 40 and rock. Released "Here Comes That Rainy Day Feeling" recorded by Jon Washington (top 40); "Cajun Stripper" written and recorded by Doug "The Ragin' Cajun" Kershaw (country); and "My Guy" recorded by Diane Darrah (top 40), all on Tug Boat Records. Other artists include Ronn Craddock, Tracy Wilson, Doc Holiday, Big Al Downing Jolene, Eagle Feather, John Lockhart M.D.

UGLY DOG RECORDS, Box 1583, Brantford ON N3T 5V6 **Canada.** (519)753-2081. President: John Mars or A&R: Marilyn Guest. Labels include Ugly Dog Records. Record company, music publisher (Utter Nonsense Publishing/SOCAN) and record producer (John Mars). Estab. 1979. Releases 1 single and 1 LP/year. Works with musicians/artists and songwriters on contract. Pays 5-10% royalty to artists on contract; negotiated or 50% rate to publisher per song on record.
How to Contact: Submit demo tape by mail. Unsolicited submissions are OK. Prefers cassette (or videocassette if available). "We regret that (due to the large number of submissions we receive) we now can only reply to those artists that we wish to express interest in."
Music: Mostly rock and roll, new jazz and R&B. Released "Oh Yeah" (by Mars/Templeton), recorded by Children and Daniel Lanois (single); *Annihilated Surprise* (by Broomer/Mars), recorded by J. Mars and Mark Wright (LP); and *Electric Playground* (by Mars/Lanzalone/Sinkowski/Tremblay), recorded by J. Mars and Bob Doidge (LP); all on Ugly Dog Records. Other artists include The Recognitions, The Martians and The Popp Tarts.
Tips: "Send high quality demo with lots of songs. Send pictures or video."

UNIVERSAL-ATHENA RECORDS, P.O. Box 1264, Peoria IL 61654-1264. (309)673-5755. A&R Director: Jerry Hanlon. Record company and music publisher (Jerjoy Music/BMI). Estab. 1978. Releases 1-2 singles and 1 LP/year. Receives 15 submissions/month. Works with musicians/artists on contract; hires musicians on salary for in-house studio work. Pays statutory rate to publishers for each record sold.
How to Contact: Prefers cassette with 4-8 songs and lyric sheet. SASE. Reports in 2 weeks.
Music: Country. Released "Look At Me" (by Robby Hill and Jerry Hanlon), recorded by Jerry Hanlon (country ballad); and "Leavin for Illinois" and "Rainy Nights & Honky Tonks," both written and recorded by Jerry Hanlon, all on Universal Athena Records.

VELVET PRODUCTIONS, 517 W. 57th St., Los Angeles CA 90037. (213)753-7893. Manager: Aaron Johnson. Labels include Velvet, Kenya, Normar and Stoop Down Records. Record company, booking agency and promoter. BMI. Estab. 1965. Releases 5 singles, 2 12″ singles and 3 EPs/year. Works with artists and songwriters on contract. Pays 5% royalty to artists on contract.
How to Contact: Submit demo and/or lead sheet by mail. Arrange personal interview. Prefers cassette with 3-5 songs and lead sheet. SASE. Reports in 2 months.
Music: Blues, gospel, rock, soul and top 40/pop. Released "How I Wish You" (by Arlene Bell/Delais Ene), recorded by Arlene Bell on Velvet Records (single).

VIBE RECORDS, 2540 Woodburn Ave., Cincinnati OH 45206. (513)961-0602. A&R Director: Smiley Hicks. Record company. Estab. 1985. Releases 2 singles and 3 12″ singles/year. Works with musicians/artists on contract. Pays varying royalty to artists on contract; statutory rate to publisher per song.
How to Contact: Write first and obtain permission to submit. Prefers cassette with 4 songs and lyric sheet. SASE. Reports in 4 weeks.
Music: Mostly R&B, gospel and pop; also rap and dance. Released "Heartbeat" (by Hicks) (R&B dance); "All About Town" (by Barber) (pop); and "Stingy" (by Waiver) (R&B dance); all on Vibe Records. Other artists include Kenny Hill, Greg Jackson, Trina Best, Sandy Childress, Tim Napier and Kim Seay.

VICOR MUSIC CORP., 782 Aurora Blvd., Cubao, Quezon City, **Philippines.** Phone: 721-3331 to 34. President: Florendo Garcia, Jr. Labels include Blackgold Records, Sunshine Records and Vicor International. Record company, music publisher (Bayanihan Music Phils., Inc.), record producer (Vicor Music and Blackgold Records), and booking firm (Vicor Entertainment Corporation). Releases 60 singles, 10 CDs and 50 LPs/year. Receives 12 submissions/month. Works with musicians/artists and songwriters on contract; musicians on salary for in-house studio work. Pays 4-10% royalty to artists on contract.

How to Contact: Write or call first and obtain permission to submit. Prefers cassette or reel-to-reel with 2 songs and lyric or lead sheet. SAE and IRC. Reports in 3 weeks.

Music: Mostly ballads, country, rock and disco. Released "Narito Ako" (by Nonong Pedero), recorded by Tadao Hayashi and Regine Velasquez on Sunshine Records (ballad); "Ipagpatawad" (by Marvic Sotto and Joey de Leon), recorded by Janno Gibbs on Sunshine Records (ballad); and "Maybe" (by Jimmy Antiporda), recorded by Neocolours on Blackgold Records (pop). Other artists include Randy Santiago, Basil Valdez, Louie Heredia and Joanne Lorenzana.

*VIRGIN BOY RECORDS, 2613 Castle, Irving TX 75038. (214)255-8015. President: James Yarbrough. Labels include Virgin Boy Records. Record company, music publisher (Virgin Boy Records & Publishing/ASCAP) and record producer (James Yarbrough). Estab. 1988. Releases 4 singles and 2 LPs/year. Receives 15 submissions/year. Works with songwriters on contract; hires musicians on salary for in-house studio work. Pays statutory rate to publishers per song on records.

How to Contact: Submit demo tape by mail. Unsolicited submissions are OK. Prefers cassette with 3 songs and lyric sheet. Does not return unsolicited material. Reports in 2 months.

Music: Mostly pop, rock and country. Released "Something's Got Me," "Don't Wanna Run" and "In the Moonlight" all written and recorded by James Yarbrough on Virgin Boy Records (pop singles).

VOKES MUSIC PUBLISHING & RECORD CO., Box 12, New Kensington PA 15068. (412)335-2775. President: Howard Vokes. Labels include Vokes and Country Boy Records. Record company, booking agency and music publisher. Releases 8 singles and 5 LPs/year. Works with artists and songwriters on contract. Pays 2½-4½¢/song royalty to artists and songwriters on contract.

How to Contact: Submit cassette only and lead sheet. SASE. Reports in 2 weeks.

Music: Country, bluegrass, gospel-old time. Released "From Dusk Til Dawn" by Lenny Gee and "For The Sake of The Children" by Laura Lee Reddig, both on Vokes Records; and "Tribute To Riley Puckett" by Uncle Rufus Brewster on Country Boy Records.

*VOLITION RECORDS, 38 Thomson St., East Sydney NSW 2010 **Australia**. Phone: (02)3322270. Labels include Volition Acquisitions. Record company. Estab. 1984. Releases 6 12″ singles, 5 LPs and 10 CDs/year. Works with musicians/artists on contract. Payment varies for artists on contract and publishers.

How to Contact: Call first and obtain permission to submit. Prefers cassette with 1-4 songs and lyric sheet. Does not return unsolicited material. "If we like it, we call you, if we don't, we won't."

Music: Mostly pop, R&B, dance, rock/dance and electronic/dance; also rock. Released *Insect*, written and recorded by Boxcar on Arista Records (12″ single, CD); *All Saints Day* and *Rotund for Success*, written and recorded by Severed Heads on Nettwerk Records. Other artists include Falling Joys and JB Love.

WALK ON WATER RECORDS, Rt. 2 Box 566-H, New Braunfels TX 78130. (512)625-2768. Producer/Manager: Kenneth D. Brazle. Record company, music publisher, record producer and recording studio. Estab. 1984. Releases 1-2 singles and 1 CD/year. Receives 10-15 submissions/month. Works with musicians/artists and songwriters on contract. Pays royalty to artists on contract. "Each deal is negotiated separately." Pays statutory rate to publisher per song on record.

How to Contact: Write first and obtain permission to submit. "Include SASE for reply." Prefers cassette, 7½ ips reel-to-reel (or VHS videocassette) with 2-3 songs and lyric sheet. Does not return unsolicited material. Reports in 6 weeks.

Music: Mostly AOR-pop/rock, blues, jazz, new music and country. Released "Long Gone" "No Time" and "Stand By Me" written and recorded by Innerview on Walk on Water Records (rock). Other artists include Fax and Secrets.

Tips: "Give me something original with a good melody that people can sing to themselves."

WATCHESGRO MUSIC, Box 1794, Big Bear City CA 92314. (714)585-4645. Watch Us Climb Music President: Eddie Carr. Interstate 40 Records and videos by Watchesgro Productions. Estab. 1987. Releases 12 singles/year. Works with songwriters on contract. Pays 100% royalty to artists on contract; statutory rate to publisher per song on record.

How to Contact: Submit demo tape by mail. Unsolicited submissions are okay. Prefers cassette with minimum of 2 songs. Does not return unsolicited material. Reports in 1 week.

Music: Mostly country and country rock.

WEDGE RECORDS, P.O. Box 290186, Nashville TN 37229-0186. (615)754-2950. President: Ralph D. Johnson. Labels include Wedge Records, Dome Records and Fleet Records. Record company, music publisher (Big Wedge Music/BMI and Pro-Rite Music/ASCAP), record producer (Ralph D. Johnson) and Pro-Star Talent Agency. Estab. 1960. Releases 10 singles, 2 LPs and 2 CDs/year. Works with musicians/artists and songwriters on contract. Pays 10% royalty to artists on contract; statutory rate to publisher per song on record.

How to Contact: Write or call first to arrange personal interview. Prefers cassette and lyric or lead sheet. SASE.

Music: Mostly country and country crossover; also rock, gospel, pop and R&B. Released "They Final Got Around to You" (by L. Joe Christine); "Closest Thing to Love" (by Dean Mitchell); and "In the Middle of the Night Time" (by Joey Weltz), all on Wedge Records (all singles).

WESTPARK MUSIC - RECORDS, PRODUCTION & PUBLISHING, Box 260227, Rathenauplatz 4 D-5000 Cologne 1 **West Germany.** Phone: (49)221 247644. FAX: (49)221 231819. Contact: Ulli Hetscher. Labels distributed by BMG Ariola. Estab. 1986. Releases 3-4 singles, 10-12 LPs and 10-12 CDs/year. Receives 50-60 submissions/month. Works with musicians/artists on contract; tape lease. Pays 8-14% royalty to artists on contract.

How to Contact: Submit demo tape by mail. Unsolicited submissions are OK. Prefers cassette with 5-6 songs and lyric sheets.

Music: Everything apart from mainstream-pop, jazz, classical. "The only other criterion is: we simply should love it." Released "New Coat of Paint" (by T. Waits), recorded by Soul Cats (blues/soul); "Mad" written and recorded by A. Brown (punk-blues/gringo-rock); and "Besame Mucho" recorded by Salsa Picante (Latin American), all on Westpark Records.

Tips: "Mark cassette clearly. No high quality cassettes expected. We only send letters back!!"

WHITE CAR RECORDS, 10611 Cal Rd., Baton Rouge LA 70809. (504)755-1400. Owner: Nelson Blanchard. Labels include Techno Sound Records. Record company, music publisher (White Car Music/BMI, Char Blanche/ASCAP) and independent record producer. Estab. 1980. Releases 6 singles, 4 12″ singles, 6 LPs, 1 EP and 2 CDs/year. Receives 4 submissions/month. Works with musicians/artists and songwriters on contract. Pays 7½-20% royalty to artists on contract; statutory rate to publisher per song.

How to Contact: Submit demo tape by mail. Unsolicited submissions are OK. Prefers cassette with 4 songs. Does not return unsolicited material. Reports in 2 weeks.

Music: Mostly country, rock and pop; also R&B. Released "Time, You're No Friend of Mine" written and recorded by Howard Austin on Techno Sound Records; "Closer to Heaven" written and recorded by Joey Dupuy on Techno Sound Records; and "I Read Between the Lines (by Stan Willis) recorded by Nelson Blanchard on White Car Records; all country singles. Other artists include John Steve, B.J. Morgan and Bayon Country Band.

*WHITESTOCKING RECORDS, P.O. Box 250013, Atlanta GA 30325. (404)352-2263. A&R Department: Steve Hill. Labels include Tigersteeth and Nancy Belle. Estab. 1990. Releases 4 12″ singles, 4 LPs and 4 CDs/year. Works with musicians/artists and songwriters on contract. Pays 5-7% royalty to artists on contract; statutory rate to publisher per song on record.

How to Contact: Submit demo tape by mail. Unsolicited submissions are OK. Prefers cassette with 3 songs and lyric sheets. SASE. Reports in 1 month.

Music: Mostly dance, pop and R&B or Latin; also metal, alternative and industrial. Released "Black Limosine" (by S. Ball), recorded by T. Brock on Whitestocking Records (single). Other artists include: Jennifer Ferren, Phil Thompson and Lillian Garcia.

Tips: "We listen for danceability, musicality and lyrical content."

WILD PITCH RECORDS LTD., 231 West 29th St., New York NY 10001. (212)594-5050. President: Stu Fine. Record company and music publisher (Frozen Soap Songs/ASCAP). Estab. 1989. Releases 1 single, 8-10 12″ singles and 5 LPs/year. Works with musicians/artists and songwriters on contract. Pays ¾ rate to publishers per song on records.

How To Contact: Submit demo tape by mail. Unsolicited submissions are OK. Prefers cassette (or ½″ videocassette if available) with 1-3 songs and lyric sheet. Does not return unsolicited material. Reports in 2 weeks.

Music: Mostly rap, dance and R&B. Released *Manifest* (by Elam Martin), recorded by Gary Starr and *Let Me Show You* (by R. Frazier), recorded by Chill Rob G all on Wild Pitch Records (LP; 12″). Other artists include Gary Starr, Lord Finesse and Chill Rob G.

Tips: "Work hard; write about something real!"

WILSON'S MUSIC CO.; MAURICE/NE PRODUCTIONS, 1771 Clearwater Dr., Camarille CA 93012. (805)484-4303. President: Morris Lee Wilson. Labels include Wilson Records, Time West Records and Imma Banks Records. Record company, music publisher (BMI) and record producer (Wilson Music Co.). Estab. 1978. Releases 10 singles, 5 LPs and 2 CDs/year. Receives 12 submissions/month. Works with musicians/artists and songwriters on contract and hires musicians on salary for in-house studio work. Pays statutory rate.

How to Contact: Submit demo tape by mail. Unsolicited submissions are OK. Prefers cassette (VHS videocassette) with any number of songs and lyric and lead sheet. SASE for return "but we prefer to keep it on file." Reports in 2 weeks.

Music: Mostly easy listening, country and MOR; also R&B, jazz and children's. Released "Special Lady" (by Alex Zanetis and Morris Wilson), on Jack O'Diamonds Records (country); "Freedom Man" (by Morris Wilson and Bennie Lee Young), on Jack O'Diamonds (country); and "Burning Bridges" (by Morris Wilson and Maurine Moore), on Wilson's Records (MOR), all recorded by Morris Wilson. Other artists include Bonnie Lou Young, Linda Moore, Duane Crone, Bonnie Skinner, Greg Coleman and Wayne St. John.

Tips: "Songs must have a good hook line, have something to say, and be different from the norm."

WINCHESTER RECORDS, Rt. 2, Box 114H, Berkeley Springs WV 25411. Owners: Bertha or Jim McCoy. Labels include Master, Mountain Top and Winchester. Record company, music publisher and record producer (Jim McCoy Productions). Estab. 1973. Releases 12 singles, 6 CDs and 6 LPs/year. Works with musicians/artists and songwriters on contract; musicians on salary for in-house studio work. Pays standard royalty to artists on contract.

How to Contact: Write or call first and obtain permission to submit. Prefers cassette, or 7½ or 15 ips reel-to-reel (or VHS or Beta videocassette) with 6 songs and lyric or lead sheet. SASE. Reports in 1 month.

Music: Mostly country, rock and gospel; also country/rock and bluegrass. Released "They Call the Wind Mariah" and *A Tribute to Patsy Cline* (by Mariah); "She Must Have Loved You Out of My Mind" (written and recorded by Don Campbell); and "She's Different" (written and recorded by E. Howard), all on Winchester Records (country). Other artists include Bud Armel, Terry McCumbee, George Dove, J.B. Mitler and R. Lee Gray.

WINDHAM HILL PRODUCTIONS, Box 9388, Palo Alto CA 94305. Contact: A&R Department. Labels include Windham Hill and Windham Hill Jazz. Record company. Estab. 1976. Works with musicians/artists on contract.

How to Contact: Write first and obtain permission to submit. "We are not accepting unsolicited material. Detailed queries are welcome. Do not send recordings until requested. We prefer a referral from a reputable industry person." Prefers cassette with 3 songs. SASE. Reports in 2 months.

Music: Mostly pop, jazz and original instrumental. Released *Metropolis*, recorded by Turtle Island String Quartet (new acoustic jazz LP); *Sampler '89*, written and recorded by various artists on Windham Hill Records (instrumental LP); and *Switchback* (by S. Cossu, Van Manakas), recorded by Scott Cossu on Windham Hill Records (jazz, ensemble LP). Other artists include William Ackerman, George Winston, Philip Aaberg, Michael Hedges, The Nylons and Montreux.

*WINGATE RECORDS, 6920-214 Koll Center Parkway, Pleasanton CA 94566. (415)846-6194. CEO: P. Hanna. Record company, music publisher (Parchment Harbor Music/BMI and Hugo First Publishing/ASCAP), record producer (Wingate Productions) and Artist Management and Talent Agency. Estab. 1989. Releases 12 singles, 2 LPs and 2 EPs/year. Works with musicians/artists and songwriters on contract. Pays statutory rate to publishers per song on record.

How to Contact: Write or call first and obtain permission to submit. Prefers cassette (or VHS videocassette if available) with 2 songs and lyric sheet. SASE. Reports in 2 weeks.

Music: Mostly pop, country and rock; also contemporary Christian and A/C. Released "Lovin' You Forever Blues" (by Bill Johnson), recorded by Ron Kimball (country/blues); "I Can't Play In Tennessee Tonight" (by Pam Hanna), recorded by Kayla Moore (contemporary country); and "Old Weepin Willow" written and recorded by Bob Eggert (country), all on Wingate Records. Other artists include Debbie Eden, Marty Ross, Robyn Banx, Kelli Crofton and Julissa Lynn.

WINGS RECORD COMPANY, Route 3, Box 172, Haynesville LA 71038. (318)927-5253. President: E. Dettenheim. Record company and music publisher (Darbonne Publishing Co./BMI). Estab. 1987. Releases 4 singles and 4-8 LPs/year. Works with musicians/artists on record contract. Pays 5-10% royalty to artists on contract; statutory rate to publishers per song on record.

How to Contact: Prefers cassette, 7½ ips reel-to-reel with at least 3 songs and lyric sheeet. Does not return unsolicited material. Reports in 3 months.

Music: Mostly country, rock and gospel; also pop and R&B. Released "Man in the Mirror" written and recorded by Leon Martin on Wings Records (country); "Still Haven't Let You Go" written and recorded by Kate Chandler on Wings Records (contemporary country); and "Turner Hotel" written by E. Dettenheim performed by Skidrow Joe on Wings Records (country).

WOODRICH RECORDS, P.O. Box 38, Lexington AL 35648. (205)247-3983. President: Woody Richardson. Record company and music publisher (Woodrich Publishing Co./BMI, Mernee Music/ASCAP and Tennessee Valley Music/SESAC) and record producer (Woody Richardson). Estab. 1959. Releases 12 singles and 12 LPs/year. Works with songwriters on contract. Pays 10% royalty to writers on contract; statutory rate to publisher per song on records.

How to Contact: Prefers cassette with 4 songs and lyric sheet. "Be sure to send a SASE (not a card) with sufficient return postage." Reports in 2 weeks. "We prefer a good studio demo."

Music: Mostly country; also gospel, comedy, bluegrass, rock and jazz. Released "I'm Headin Out" (by Benny Ray), recorded by Jerry Wright "Welcome Back to Me," written and recorded by Sandra Celia; and "Androids in Love," written and recorded by Thom Rathburn; all on Woodrich Records.

WORLD ARTIST, Box 405, Alamo CA 94507. A&R Representative: Randal Larsen. Record company, music publisher (Hansen Music Company), record producer (Geoffrey Hansen Enterprises) and personal management firm. Releases varying number of singles and LPs/year. Works with musicians/artists and songwriters on contract; musicians on salary for in-house studio work. Pays negotiable royalty to artists on contract.

How to Contact: Prefers cassette (or videocassette) and lyric sheet or lead sheet. SASE. Reports in 6 weeks. "We do not want the same material that you are sending to other companies. We are looking for the 50s and 60s style rock and doo-wop vocal harmony plus new artists with star quality. Do not send a form letter."

Music: Mostly top 40/MOR, rock-a-billy and country-rock; also blues, French and Spanish. Artists include various Hawaiian artists, and artists in Japan, Philippines, Korea and Latin America.

*WORLD WIDE ENTERTAINMENT, INC., #602, 134 W. 32nd St., New York NY 10001-3201. (212)265-5458. President: Darrin McGillis. Labels include Baila Records and Hurricane Records. Record company and record producer (World Wide Entertainment). Estab. 1987. Releases 5 singles, 5 12″ singles, 2 LPs and 2 CDs/year. Works with musicians/artists and songwriters on contract. Pays 3-4% royalty to artists on contract; statutory rate to publisher per song on record. Charges prospective artists for production and promotion.

How to Contact: Submit demo tape by mail. Unsolicited submissions are OK. Prefers cassette or VHS videocassette with 2 songs and lyric or lead sheet. SASE. Reports in 3 weeks.

Music: Mostly dance, pop and house; also country, acid house and rap. Released "Don't Keep Me Holding On" (by Lewis A. Martinez), recorded by Angelo on W.W.E. Records (dance 12″); "Move" (by Papo Gely), recorded by Ruber Goner on W.W.E. Records (dance 12″); and "Anything for Love" (by Phil Castellano), recorded by Kiko on Baila Records (dance 12″).

YELLOW JACKET RECORDS, 10303 Hickory Valley, Ft. Wayne IN 46835. President: Allan Straten. Record company. Estab. 1985. Releases 8-10 singles, 1 LP and 1 CD/year. Receives 20-25 submissions/year. Works with musicians/artists and songwriters on contract; hires musicians for in-house studio work. Pays 10-20% royalty to artists on contract; statutory rate to publisher per song on records.

How to Contact: Prefers cassette with 3-4 songs and typed lyric sheet. SASE. Reports in 1 month.

Music: Country and MOR. Released singles "A Rose and a Kiss" (by April) and "Love Is" (by S. Grogg and A. Straten); and *April In Love* (LP), all on Yellow Jacket Records.

*YOUNGHEART MUSIC, P.O. Box 6017, Cypress CA 90630. (714)995-7888. President: James Connelly. Record company. Estab. 1975. Releases 1-2 LPs/year. Works with musicians/artists and songwriters on contract. Pays statutory rate.

How to Contact: Write first and obtain permission to submit. SASE. Reports in 1-2 months.

Music: Mostly children's and educational. Released *Holidays & Special Times*, written and recorded by Greg Scelsa (LP); "Kids in Motion," written and recorded by Steve (children's); and "We All Live Together," written and recorded by Millang; all on Youngheart Records.

Tips: "We are looking for original, contemporary, motivating music for kids. Songs should be fun, educational, build self-esteem and/or multicultural awareness. New original arrangements of classic songs or nursery rhymes will be considered."

*ZANZIBAR RECORDS, 2019 Noble St., Pittsburgh PA 15218. (412)351-6672. A&R Manager: John C. Antimary. Labels include A.W.O.L. Records. Record company and music publisher (RTD Music/BMI). Estab. 1980. Releases 6-12 singles, 4-8 12″ singles and 6 LPs/year. Receives 22 submissions/month.Works with musicians/artists and songwriters on contract and hires musicians for in-house studio work. Pays 8-10% royalty to artists on contract; statutory rate to publisher per song on record.

How to Contact: Submit demo tape by mail. Unsolicited submissions are OK. Or call first to arrange personal interview. Prefers cassette (or VHS videocassette) with 4 songs and lyric sheet. SASE. Reports in 1 month.

Music: Mostly rock, progressive and R&B; also pop, rap and metal. Released "We Are Boomerang" by Affordable Floors (progressive rock); "This Old Town" by Lenny Collini (rock) and "Monster Zero" by Monster Zero (rock); all on Zanzibar Records. Other artists include Bunky Gooch, Necropolis, Post Mortem, Good Earth and Corky Zapple.
Tips: "When sending demos of your songs, please make sure that they are recorded on good cassette tapes."

Geographic Index
Record Companies

The U.S. section of this handy geographic index will quickly give you the names of record companies located in the music centers of Los Angeles, New York and Nashville. Of course, there are many valuable contacts to be made in other cities, but you will probably want to plan a trip to one of these established music centers at some point in your career and try to visit as many of these companies as you think appropriate. The International section lists, geographically, markets for your songs in countries other than the U.S.

Find the names of companies in this index, and then check listings within the Record Companies section for addresses, phone numbers and submission details.

Los Angeles
Atlantic Recording Co.
AVC Entertainment
Blue Gem Records
British Records
C.P.I. Records
Cosmotone Records
Gold Castle Records
Golden Boy Records
Helion Records
J/L Entertainment Group
Next Step Records
Rodell Records
Sound Image Records
Tom Thumb Music
Velvet Productions

Nashville
The Calvary Music Group
Concorde International Records
Curtiss Records
Fame and Fortune Enterprises
John Fisher & Associates
Jalyn Recording Co.
Kottage Records
Landmark Communications Group
Maxx Records
Orbit Records
Paragold Records & Tapes
Phoenix Records, Inc.
Sony Music
Stop Hunger Records International
Susan Records
Terock Records
Top Trax
Wedge Records

New York
Alternative Record Co. Ltd.
Big Productions Records
Black Moon Records, Inc.
Caroline Records
Chrysalis Records
Emotive Records
G Fine Records
Get Wit It Production Records
Jump Street Records
Lamar Music Group
Majestic Control Records
MCA Records
Mighty Records
Mighty Soul/Sonic Records
Mindfield Records
MSB, Ltd.
NFS Records, Inc.
Now & Then Records
PolyGram Records
Razor & Tie Music
Source Unlimited Records
Tommy Boy Music, Inc.
Wild Pitch Records, Inc.
World Wide Entertainment

International

Argentina
Discos CBS Saief

Austria
Cactus Records

Australia
Nude Records
Volition Records

Belgium
Jump Records & Music

Canada
Bovine International Record Co.
Century City Records & Tapes of Canada
Disques Nosferatu Records
ISBA Records, Inc.
Justin Time Records, Inc.
Montican Records
One-Eyed Duck Records and Publishing
PSP Records
Roto-Noto Music
Saddlestone Records
Slak Records
Ugly Dog Records

Denmark
Genlyd Grammafon APS
Mega Records APS
Reca Music Production

England
Avalantic Records
Big Bear Records
Bolts Records
Creole Records
Demi Monde Records and Publishing, Ltd.
E.S.R. Records
First Time Records
FM-Revolver Records, Inc.
The Ghetto Recording Co.
Hysteria Records
IRS Records
Le Matt Music, Ltd.
Leopard Music
Loading Bay Records

Nervous Records
Pacific & Planet Pacific Records
Plankton Records
Presidential Enterprises Ltd.
Red-Eye Records
Red Sky Records
Rhino Records
Rosie Records
Sphemusations
Swoop Records
Tabitha Records

France
Directions
Sephora Diffusion

Germany
AIA Records
Alphabeat Autogram & Folk Records
Comma Records
Playbones Records
Westpark Music Productions

Hong Kong
Rock in Records

Italy
Top Records

The Netherlands
Associated Artists

Collector Records (Holland)
Le Disque Holland B.V./B&B Records

Phillipines
Vicor Music Corp.

Scotland
BGS Productions Ltd.

South Africa
Lee Thorp Entertainment

Sweden
Liphone Records

Switzerland
Nadine Music

Record Companies/'91-'92 Changes

The following markets appeared in the 1991 edition of *Songwriter's Market* but are absent from the 1992 edition. Most of these companies failed to respond to our request for an update of their listing. Others are not listed for a variety of reasons, which is indicated in parentheses following the company name. For example, they may have gone out of business, or they may have requested deletion from the 1992 edition because they are backlogged with material.

A&M Records, Inc.
Allegiance Records
Apon Record Company (asked to be deleted)
Arway Records & Enterprises, Inc.
Arzee Record Company
AVM Records/Star Maker Int'l
Billy Baker & Associates — Go-Records
Beachwood Records (asked to be deleted)
Berandol Records
Best West Productions
Beverly Hills Music Publishing
Blind Pig Records (asked to be deleted)
Bolivia Records
Bright & Morningstar Records
Caritas Records
Carlyle Records, Inc.
Carousel Records, Inc.
The CCC Group
Charge-Coupled Device Records (CCD Records) (asked to be deleted)
Charta Records
Chattahoochee Records
Chiltown Records
Codiscos
Colt Records
Continental Records (moved; left no forwarding address)
Cosmopolitan Country Records (CCR Records)
Cue Management Pty Ltd.
Current Records
Downtown Record Company
Dupuy Records/Productions/Publishing, Inc.

Dynamic Recording Co. (asked to be deleted)
Dynamite
EMI
Factory Beat Records, Inc.
Four Winds Record Productions Inc.
Frontline Music Group
Futura International Records Inc.
Geimsteinn HF
Genesee Records, Inc.
Global Pacific Records
Groove and Move Records
H&S Records
Happy Beat Records
Hazardous Records
Heavy Metal Records
Highland Records
Hix Studios
Ice Records Inc.
J&J Musical Enterprises Ltd.
Jewish Family Productions
Jimco Records
JRM Records
JTM Records
Jump Street Records, Inc.
Justice Records
Kansa Records Corp.
Katron Record
Kilgore Records, Inc.
Lemon Records
John Lennon Records
Love Dove Productions
Lunar Records
Lee Mace's Ozark Opry Records, Inc.
Mad Rover Records (asked to be deleted)
Madlyn Records

Mainroads Music Inc. (moved; left no forwarding address)
Majega Records
The Master's Collection Limited
Mel Vern Records (out of business)
Micah Records
Mirror Records
Monotone Records
Music City Records
Musica Schallplatten Vertrieb GES.M.B.H.
Nephelim Record (Studio Works)
Neptune Records
Nettwerk Productions
New Music Enterprises
Newstar International Records
Nickel Records
Nise Productions Inc.
O.L. Records, Inc.
Opus — Records and Publishing House
Paris Records
Parsifal PVBA
Pegasus Records
Pholk Records
PMA Records
Post-Ambient Motion (asked to be deleted)
Prestation Music
Prodisc (Prodisc Limitada)
Productions Diadem
Psychotronic Records
Rainbow River Records
Random Records (moved; left no forwarding address)
Red Bus Records (Int.) Ltd.
Revonah Records

Righteous Records
Rogue Records
Rohit International Records
ROM Records (asked to be deleted)
RTP International
San Francisco Sound
Seeds Records
Shanachie Records
Sheperd Records
Signature Records
Slamdek/Scramdown

Sound Masters
Soundshine Productions, Inc.
Phil Spector International and Warner/Spector Records Inc.
Sun Dance Records
Sundance Music
Swen-Daug Record Inc.
Tawas Records (asked to be deleted)
Time Capsule Records (asked to be deleted)

Titan International Productions, Ltd.
Top's Records
True North Records
Turf Handler Records
Underground Release Records
Walden Records
Webco Records
Thomas Wiggins Associates
Z-Gweet Records (moved; left no forwarding address)
Zone Record Co.

Demo Materials Checklist

When submitting a demonstration tape to a record company, music publisher or producer, be sure to include the following:
- *a quality cassette with a clean recording of your best songs*
- *a sturdy but easy-to-open mailer that will get your demo to its destination securely*
- *a brief, neat cover letter of introduction*
- *typed or clearly printed lyric sheets*
- *labels on each tape, tape box and lyric sheet giving your name, address and phone number*
- *a stout self-addressed stamped envelope (SASE) with enough postage to cover the cost of returning your demo to you.*

Remember: first impressions are critical. A professionally presented demo package will give you an immediate advantage over most of the competition.

Record Producers

The independent producer can best be described as a creative coordinator. He's usually the one with the most creative control over the recording project and is ultimately responsible for the finished product. Although some larger record companies have their own in-house producers, it's more common for a record company today to contract out-of-house, independent producers for recording projects.

Producers can be valuable contacts for songwriters because they work so closely with the artists whose records they produce. They are usually creative and artistic people, typically with a lot more freedom than others in executive positions, and they are known for having a good ear for hit song potential. Many producers are songwriters, musicians and artists themselves. Since they have the most influence on a particular project, a good song in the hands of the producer at the right time stands a good chance of being cut. And even if the producer is not working on a specific project, they are well-acquainted with record company executives and artists, and they can often get material through doors not open to you.

Even so, it can be difficult to get your tapes to the right producer at the right time. Many producers write their own songs and even if they don't write, they might be involved in their own publishing companies so they have instant access to all the songs in their catalogs. It's important to understand the intricacies of the producer/publisher situation. If you pitch your song directly to a producer first, before another publishing company publishes the song, the producer may ask you for the publishing rights (or a percentage thereof) to your song. You must decide whether the producer is really an active publisher who will try to get the song recorded again and again, or whether he merely wants the publishing because it means extra income for him from the current recording project. You may be able to work out a co-publishing deal, where you and the producer split the publishing of the song. That means that he will still receive his percentage of the publishing income, even if you secure a cover recording of the song by other artists in the future. But, even though you would be giving up a little bit initially, you may benefit in the future.

The listings that follow outline which aspects of the music industry each producer is involved in, what type of music he is looking for, what records and artists he's recently produced and what artists he produces on a regular basis. Study the listings carefully, noting the artists he works with, and consider if any of your songs might fit a particular artist's or producer's style.

*A & R RECORDING SERVICES, 71906 Highway 111, Rancho Mirage CA 92270. (619)346-0075. Producer-Engineer: Wade Perluss. Record producer. Estab. 1978. Deals with artists. Fee derived from sales royalty when song or artist is recorded, outright fee from recording artist and outright fee from record company.
How to Contact: Submit demo tape by mail. Unsolicited submissions are OK. Prefers cassette (or VHS videocassette if available) with 4 songs and lyric or lead sheets. SASE. Reports in 2 months.
Music: Mostly pop, country and gospel; also rock. Produced "What Will You Say" (by Richard Carl), recorded by Positive Influence (single); *By Request*, written and recorded by Brent Streeper (LP); and *One Fine Touch*, recorded by Scott Beaty (LP), all on Accent Records. Other artists include Paul Gerkin, Mike Babbitt, David Powell and Diann Torrey.

ABERDEEN PRODUCTIONS, (A.K.A. Scott Turner Productions), 524 Doral Country Dr., Nashville TN 37221. (615)646-9750. President: Scott Turner. Record producer and music publisher (Buried Treasure/ASCAP, Captain Kidd/BMI). Estab. 1971. Deals with artists and songwriters. Works with

30 new songwriters/year. Produces 10 singles, 15-20 12″ singles, 8 LPs and 8 CDs/year. Fee derived from sales royalty and production fee.

How to Contact: Prefers cassette with maximum 4 songs and lead sheet. SASE. Reports in 3 weeks.

Music: Mostly country, MOR and rock; also top 40/pop. Produced "We Are All Americans" (by S.C. Rose), recorded by Roy Clark (country); "Appalachian Blue" (by S.C. Rose), recorded by Roy Clark (country); and "Coming to My Senses" (by Audie Murphy, S. Turner, M. Jaden), recorded by Jim Cartwright (country). Other artists include Slim Whitman, Jonathan Edwards, Don Malena, Hal Goodson, Jimmy Clanton, Bobby Lewis and Del Reeves.

Tips: "Be unique. A great song doesn't care who sings it . . . but there is a vast difference between a good song and a great song."

*ACRAM PRODUCTIONS, #10 Gonzales Terrace, Gonzales P.O.S., **Trinidad W.I.** Managing Director: Andy R. Salandy. Record producer, music publisher (Acram Music/ASCAP), record company (Acram Records) and artist management and consultations. Estab. 1988. Deals with artists, songwriters and record labels. Produces 3 singles and 3 12″ singles/year. "An advance payment is needed only if the artist/songwriter is funding the production."

How to Contact: Submit demo tape by mail. Unsolicited submissions are OK. Prefers cassette with 4 songs and lyric sheet. "We listen and answer all material submitted, we welcome piano/guitar and vocal demos also." SASE. Reports in 5 weeks.

Music: Mostly urban dance, soca/calypso and reggae; also R&B ballads, pop ballads and jazz. Produced "Take Me Home With You" (by Andy and Pierre Salandy/Heather Charles-Salandy), recorded by New Generation on CVC Records (soca 12″ single); "Sandy" (by Tex Smith), recorded by TH2 on Bupbap Records (reggae 12″ single); and "Party Mash Up" (by George Kirton/Anslem Serrette/Russel Cadogan), recorded by Russell Cadogan on Bupbap Records (soca 12″ single).

Tips: "Be patient, and try to learn as much as you can about the entertainment industry."

*ACTIVE SOUND PRODUCTIONS, 314 C St., So. Boston MA 02127. (617)269-0104. Owner: Larry Lessard. Record producer and recording studio. Estab. 1981. Deals with artists and songwriters. Produces 5 singles, 2 12″ singles, 3 LPs, 2 EPs and 2 CDs/year. Fee derived from sales royalty when song or artist is recorded. Charges for studio time.

How to Contact: Submit demo tape by mail. Unsolicited submissions are OK. Prefers cassette (or 15 IPS reel-to-reel or DAT videocassette if available) with 3-5 songs and lyric sheet. SASE. Reports in 3 weeks.

Music: Mostly pop (A/C), dance and rock; also R&B. Produced *Accused*, written and recorded by Blind Rhino on Fast Track Records (rock CD-LP); *Down Avenue*, written and recorded by D.A. on 6L6 Records (pop LP); and *Mary*, written and recorded by Vasco Da Gama on Major Label Records (alternative LP). Other artists include The Reprieve, Mike Freestone, Adrianne, Dave Doms and Candy Machine.

Tips: "Concentrate on melody. Make the song honest. Know what market you're trying to go for. But most of all have fun and do music that satisfies you."

MICHAEL AHARON MUSIC, 1439 S. 2nd St., Philadelphia PA 19147. (215)336-6339. Owner: Michael Aharon. Record producer. Estab. 1984. Deals with artists and songwriters. Produces 3 LPs, 4 EPs and 3 CDs/year. Receives 20 submissions/month. Fee derived from outright fee from recording artist or record company. "Fee covers arrangement, production, pre-production and programming. For demos, fee also covers all recording costs. Fully arranged song demos are available for $700 per song. For album tracks, additional studio costs apply."

How to Contact: Submit demo tape by mail. Unsolicited submissions are OK. Prefers cassette with 3-6 songs. SASE. Reports in 3 weeks.

Music: Mostly folk-rock and pop/urban contemporary; also New Age, world-beat and experimental. Produced *I Will Stand Fast*, written and recorded by Fred Small on Flying Fish Records (folk/rock LP); *Out of the Darkness*, written and recorded by Tom Juravitch on Flying Fish Records (folk/rock LP); and *Vaguar*, written and recorded by Fred Small on Flying Fish Records (folk rock LP). Other artists include Heather Mullen, Charlie Cooper Project and Julia Haines.

The asterisk before a listing indicates that the listing is new in this edition. New markets are often the most receptive to unsolicited submissions.

Tips: "Send material which exhibits your personal style and creativity, even if it is not 'commercial' material. Individuality is starting to matter again. Lyrics are starting to matter again. Singer-songwriters are on the radio again."

AKO PRODUCTION, 20531 Plummer, Chatsworth CA 91311. (818)998-0443. President: A. Sullivan. Record producer and music publisher (Amiron). Deals with artists and songwriters. Produces 2-6 singles and 2-3 LPs/year. Fee derived from sales royalty.
How to Contact: Write first and obtain permission to submit. Prefers cassette (or Beta or VHS videocassette if available) and lyric sheet. SASE.
Music: Pop/rock and modern country. Produced *Lies in Disguise,* by Gang Back (pop LP); and *Touch of Fire* (LP) and "Try Me" (pop single) by Sana Christian; all on AKO Records.

***ALA BIANCA PUBLISHING GROUP**, V Mazzoni 34136, Modena 41100 **Italy**. Phone: (59)223897. President: Toni Verona. Managing Director: Mr. Maurizio Bettelli. International Manager: Mr. David J. Smith. A&R Dance Manager: Mr. Guido Felicani. Record producer, music publisher (S.I.A.E.-Italy), record company (Flea/River Nile/Bravo) and video production company. Estab. 1978. Deals with artists and songwriters. Produces 10 singles, 120 12" singles, 10 LPs and 10 CDs/year. Fee derived from sales royalty.
How to Contact: Write or call first and obtain permission to submit or to arrange personal interview. Prefers cassette with 3 songs and lyric or lead sheets. Include biography. SASE. Reports in 3 weeks.
Music: Mostly pop, rock and dance; also R&B. Produced *New Egypt,* written and recorded by Rocking Chairs on River Nile Records (rock LP); *H. Gualdi,* written and recorded by H. Gualdi on Bravo Records (pop LP).

***ALL STAR PRODUCTIONS**, P.O. Box 49524, Gold Tree Station, Sarasota FL 34278. (813)953-4447. President: Rob Russen. Record producer, music publisher (Rob-Lee Music) and record company (Castle Records). Estab. 1966. Deals with artists and songwriters. Produces 12 singles, 6 12" singles, 6-10 LPs, 3 EPs and 6-10 CDs/year. Fee derived from sales royalty.
How to Contact: Submit demo tape by mail. Unsolicited submissions are OK. Prefers cassette (or VHS videocassette if available) with 3-6 songs. "We do not return tapes." Does not return unsolicited material. Reports in 2 weeks.
Music: Mostly R&B/funk, rock and pop. Produced "Who's to Blame," written and recorded by Gigolo on Castle Records (R&B 12"); "Gotcha," written and recorded by Sheldon Price on TCB Records (R&B single); and *Wide Open* (by D. Lawrence), recorded by Phoenix on Castle Records (R&B LP). Other artists include Westside, TCB Band, Rob Russen, Jammer and Dream Warriors.
Tips: "Supply master quality demos."

***ALLEN-MARTIN PRODUCTIONS INC.**, 9701 Taylorville Rd., Louisville KY 40299. (502)267-9658. Audio Engineer: Nick Stevens. Record producer and music publisher (Always Alive Music, Bridges Music/ASCAP, BMI). Estab. 1965. Deals with artists. Produces 10 singles, 5 12" singles, 20 LPs, 5 EPs and 20 CDs/year. Fee derived from sales royalty when song or artist is recorded, outright fee from recording artist or outright fee from record company.
How to Contact: Submit demo tape by mail. Unsolicited submissions are OK. Prefers cassette (or ¾" or ½" videocassette if available) with several songs and lyric sheet. Artist photo is desirable. Does not return unsolicited material. Reports in 2 months.
Music: Mostly country, gospel and pop; also rock, R&B and rap. Produced *Delta,* written and recorded by Duke Robillaro on Rovrene Records (R&B LP); *Exquisite Fashion,* written and recorded by Duke Robillaro on X Mode Records (rock LP); and *More Praise* (by Harold Moore), recorded by Duke Robillaro on X Mode Records (gospel LP). Other artists include J.P. Pennington, Larnelle Harris, Turley Richards, Shaking Family and Michael Jonathon.

JIM ALLISON/ALLISONGS INC., 1603 Horton Avenue, Nashville TN 37212. (615)292-9899. A&R: Anne Reeves. Record producer, music publisher (Jim's AlliSongs/BMI; Annie Green Eyes Music/BMI) and record company (ARIA Records). Estab. 1985. Deals with artists and songwriters. Produces 8-12 singles and 3-5 LPs/year. Receives 100 submissions/year. Fee derived from sales royalty.
How To Contact: Submit demo tape by mail. Unsolicited submissions are OK. Prefers cassette with 3 songs and lyric sheet. "Prefer chrome tape; clear and clean sound." Does not return unsolicited material. Reports in 6 weeks.

"How to Use Your Songwriter's Market" (at the front of this book) contains comments and suggestions to help you understand and use the information in these listings.

Music: Mostly country and pop. Produced "Hard Headed Heart" (by Allison), recorded by Bruce VanDyke (country single); "Stop Pickin' on Willie" (by Allison), recorded by Del Reeves on Aria Records (country/novelty); and "The Line In the Sand" (by Lee), recorded by Sandy Lee on Aria Records (A/C). Regularly produces Brent Burns, Kari Reeves and Billy Montana.
Tips: "Submit top-of-the-line material; be organized."

*BUZZ AMATO, A-15, 1150 Collier Rd., Atlanta GA 30318. (404)352-3509. Producer: Buzz Amato. Record producer and record company (Ichiban, Gold Key, Curton, J&S). Estab. 1987. Deals with artists. Produces 8 singles, 4 12″ singles, 10 LPs and 10 CDs/year. Fee derived from sales royalty when song or artist is recorded.
How to Contact: Submit demo tape by mail. Unsolicited submissions are OK. Prefers cassette with 3 songs and lyric or lead sheets. "List how material was cut—instruments, outboard, tape format, etc." SASE. Reports in 1 month.
Music: Mostly R&B (urban), blues and pop; also jazz. Produced "Chi-Lites" (R&B), "Synethia Foster" (R&B-blues), and "Trudy Lynn," all recorded by James O'Neill on Ichiban Records. Other artists include Three Degree, Jerry McCairi, Slave and Louise Freeman.
Tips: Trends in the music industry include: "The marriage of rap with other styles of music."

AMETHYST RECORDS, INC., P.O. Box 82158, Oklahoma City OK 73148. (405)632-2000. General Manager: Russell Canaday. Record company (Amethyst Records, Inc.). Estab. 1988. Deals with artists and songwriters. Produces 10 singles, 25 LPs, 3 EPs and 3 CDs/year. Recording cost derived from recording artist or Amethyst record company. "If artist is unknown, we sometimes charge an outright fee. It depends on exposure and work."
How to Contact: Submit demo tape by mail. Unsolicited submissions are OK. Prefers cassette with 3 songs and lyric or lead sheets. SASE. Reports in 2 months.
Music: Mostly country, gospel, easy listening; also R&B. Produced *Jehovah God* (by Danny Chambers), recorded by Sherman Andrus (gospel LP); *Blues Man* (by Hank Williams, Jr.), recorded by Henson Cargi (country); and *Just Us Two* (by Mark Bryant), recorded by Sherman Andrus (R&B); all on Amethyst Records. Other artists include Cissie Lynn, Wanda Jackson, Branson Brothers and several Oklahoma Opry artists.
Tips: "Don't get on the record company's bad side by encouraging us to use your material. Don't call us, we will contact you if you have the right stuff. Don't send your only copy of the songs you want us to consider."

BILL ANDERSON JR., Box 148296, Nashville TN 37214. (615)889-4977. Record producer. Estab. 1976. Deals with artists only. Produces 4 singles and 5 LPs/year. Fee derived from outright fee from recording artist and record company.
How to Contact: Submit demo tape by mail. Unsolicited submissions are OK. Prefers cassette with 4 songs and lyric sheets. SASE.
Music: Mostly country, gospel and pop/crossover. Produced "Jesus Is Lord" (by Randy Weiss), recorded by Joanne Cash Yates with Johnny Cash on Crosstalkin' Records (gospel); and *Debi Chasteen*, recorded by Debi Chasteen on Lan Records (country LP). Other artists include Vernon Oxford (country), Skeeter Davis and Teddy Nelson (country).

*WARREN ANDERSON, 2207 Halifax Cres NW, Calgary Alta. T2M 4E1 **Canada**. (403)282-2555. Producer/Manager: Warren Anderson. Record producer (Century City Music-SOCAN) and record company (Century City Records). Estab. 1983. Deals with artists and songwriters. Produces 1-6 singles, 1-2 LPs, 1-2 EPs and 1-2 CDs/year. Fee derived from sales royalty (typically 2%) and/or outright fee from record company.
How to Contact: Write first and obtain permission to submit. Prefers cassette or VHS videocassette with 4 songs and lyric or lead sheet. SASE. Reports in 4 weeks.
Music: Mostly country rock, rock and folk rock; also alternative, jazz and C&W. Produced "Angel" (by Warren Anderson), recorded by Fran Thieven on Bros. Records; "Hot from the Streets" (by Warren Anderson) recorded by Robert Bartlett on Century City Records; "1000 Miles Away" (by Damian Follett), recorded by Warren Anderson on Century City Records; all rock singles.
Tips: "Rockers moved over to C&W and took it places that the cowboy wouldn't recognize. I'm into Chris Isaak, Steve Earl, Blue Rodeo, K.D. Lang, Roger McGuinn, John Couger Mellencamp. I'm into pushing the envelope of country rock into the 21st century."

*ANDREW & FRANCIS, Box 64-1008, Chicago IL 60664-1008. (708)755-2928. Talent Representative: Katie Major. Record producer and management agency. Estab. 1984. Deals with artists and songwriters. Produces 4 LPs, 5 EPs and 1 CD/year. Fee derived from sales royalty when song or artist is recorded.

How to Contact: Submit demo tape by mail. Unsolicited submissions are OK. Prefers cassette (or VHS videocassette if available) with 1-7 songs and lyric sheet. "Don't be afraid to submit! We are here to help you by reviewing your material for possible representation or production." Does not return unsolicited material. Reports in 5 weeks.

Music: Mostly rock (commercial), hard rock and dance rock; also classical guitar, instrumental rock and solo guitar. Produced *Paul Henry* (classical LP by Manuel deFalla); *Blake Clifford* (rock LP by Blake Clifford); and *Mike Martis* (rock LP by Mike Martis), all produced by Pacific Talent on Demo Records. Other artists include Brian Kalan, Descendent, Mail Order, Joe Johnson, Project Z and Sampled Heroes.

Tips: "If you're not sure of yourself, send it anyway. You don't have anything to lose. We aren't a huge corporation and we aren't trying to be, but we are professionals who may be able to help you and you may be able to help us."

APON RECORD COMPANY, INC., P.O. Box 3082, Steinway Station, Long Island City NY 11103. (718)721-5599. Manager: Don Zemann. Record producer and music publisher (Apon Publishing). Estab. 1957. Deals with artists and songwriters. Produces 100 singles, 50 LPs and 50 CDs/year. Fee derived from sales royalty and outright fee from recording artist or record company.

How to Contact: Prefers cassette with 2-6 songs and lyric sheet. SASE. Reports in 1 month.

Music: Classical, folk, Spanish, Slavic, polka and Hungarian gypsy (international folk music). Produced *Czech Polkas* (by Slavko Kunst), recorded by Prague Singers on Apon Records; "Hungarian Gypsy" (by Deki Lakatos), recorded by Budapest on Apon Records; and "Polka - Dance With Me" (by Slavko Kunst), recorded by Prague on Apon Records.

APRIL RECORDING STUDIOS/PRODUCTIONS, 827 Brazil Pl., El Paso TX 79903. (915)772-7858. Owner: Harvey Marcus. Record producer, music publisher (Crystal Ram Records Publishing/BMI), record company (April and Crystal Ram Records) and recording studio. Deals with artists and songwriters. Produces 1-3 singles, 1-3 12" singles, 1-5 LPs, 1-5 EPs and 1-3 CDs/year. Receives 35 submissions/month. Fee derived from sales royalty and/or outright fee from record company.

How to Contact: Prefers cassette or 7½ ips reel-to-reel (or VHS videocassette) with 1-3 songs and lyric or lead sheets. "Include current updated listing of all available past recordings, publishing and performances of your material." SASE. Reports in 2 months.

Music: Mostly jazz, R&B and new wave/rock; also "all ballads and material with crossover possibilities, such as Mex/Tex, country and instrumental." Produced *Topaz* (compilation), recorded by Topaz (Christian/pop); *Foot Prints*, written and recorded by Jaime Gallindo (Christian/easy listening); and *Sinai* (compilation), recorded by Sinai (Christian/Spanish pop); all on Xavier Records. Other artists include Patricia and Pamela Thoreson, Ruben Cruz and Robert Cast.

Tips: "Please be patient! We answer and listen to all material. Also, leave out all the flashy solos unless the song is an instrumental."

*ARCADIA PRODUCTIONS, INC., 425 Windsor Pkwy. NE, Atlanta GA 30342. (404)255-3284. FAX: (404)255-8723. Owner: Sammy Knox. Record producer, music publisher (Axl's Gruv Music-ASCAP) and record company (Arista). Estab. 1986. Deals with artists and songwriters. Produces 20 singles, 6 12" singles and 2 LPs/year. Fee derived from sales royalty or outright fee from record company.

How to Contact: Submit demo tape by mail. Unsolicited submissions are OK. Prefers cassette (or VHS videocassette if available) with 3 songs. SASE. Reports in 2 weeks.

Music: Mostly R&B, rock and pop; also gospel. Produced "Good Old Days" (by K. Kendrick/S. Knox); "Do You Still Remember Love" (by Tommy Dean, Marty Kearns, S. Knox); and "I Just Laugh" (by K. Kendrick, S. Knox, Ken Cummings); all recorded by Geoff McBride on Arista Records. Other artists include Shiela Jackson and Michael Meredith.

aUDIOFILE TAPES, 209-25 18th Ave., Bayside NY 11360. Sherriff, aT County: Carl Howard. Cassette-only label of alternative music. Estab. 1984. Deals with artists and songwriters. Produces about 25 cassettes/year. Receives 15-20 submissions/year. "Money is solely from sales. Some artists ask $1 per tape sold."

How to Contact: Submit demo tape by mail. Unsolicited submissions are OK. Prefers cassette. "Relevant artist information is nice. Master copies accepted on metal cassette. We trade submissions for cassettes on the label." Reports in 1-2 weeks.

Music: Mostly psych/electronic rock, non-rock electronic music, progressive rock; also free jazz and world music. Produced "News You Can Choose," recorded by Nomuzic (electronic rock); "The Inner Chamber," recorded by LG Mair, Jr. (electronic jazz-funk); and "Space Trip," recorded by Through Black Holes Band (space rock); all on audiofile Tapes. Other artists include Alien Planetscapes, Doug Michael and The Outer Darkness, and Paradox.

Tips: "Please, no industrial music, no deliberately shocking images of racism and sexual brutality. And no New Age sleeping pills. Outside of that, go go go."

BAL RECORDS, P.O. Box 369, LaCanada CA 91012-0369. (818)548-1116. President: Adrian Bal. Record producer and music publisher (Bal & Bal Music). Estab. 1965. Bal West estab. 1988. Deals with artists and songwriters. Produces 3-6 singles/year. Fee derived from sales royalty.
How to Contact: Prefers cassette with 3 songs and lyric sheet. SASE.
Music: Mostly MOR, country, jazz, R&B, rock and top 40/pop; also blues, church/religious, easy listening and soul. Produced "Right To Know" and "Fragile" (by James Jackson), recorded by Kathy Simmons on BAL Records (rock); "Dance To The Beat of My Heart" (by Dan Gertz), recorded by Ace Baker on BAL Records (rock); and "You're A Part of Me," "Can't We Have Some Time Together," "You and Me" and "Circles of Time," written and recorded by Paul Richards on BAL Records (A/C).
Tips: "Write and compose what you believe to be commercial."

BARNETT PRODUCTIONS INC., 2305 Dickey Ave., No. Chicago IL 60064. (312)689-2726. Vice President: Walter T. Barnett. Record producer, music publisher (BMI) and record company (WMB Records). Estab. 1980. Deals with artists and songwriters. Produces 2 LPs and 10 singles/year. Fee derived from sales royalty or outright fee from record company.
How to Contact: Submit demo tape by mail. Unsolicited submissions are OK. Prefers cassette with 4 songs and lyric sheets. SASE. Reports in 1 month.
Music: Mostly R&B, rock, ballads, blues, pop and rap; also reggae, house and soul. Produced "Takin' Applications," written and recorded by Jackie "B" (dance/R&B); *Shibeli* (by W. Barnett), recorded by Shibeli (dance/R&B LP); and *Full Deck* (by M. Sanders/T. Pierson/R. Coleman/B. Jackson), recorded by Full Deck; all on WMB Records.
Tips: "Be persistent and patient; send only your best material."

*TED BARTON, 2804 Columbine Place, Nashville TN 37204. (615)383-7209. Producer: Ted Barton. Record producer and music publisher (Ted Barton Music/BMI, Langford Cove Music/ASCAP). Estab. 1986. Deals with artists and songwriters. Produces 3-4 singles, 2-3 LPs and 2-3 CDs/year. Fee derived from sales royalty when song or artist is recorded and outright fee from record company.
How to Contact: Submit demo tape by mail. Unsolicited submissions are OK. Prefers cassette with maximum of 3 songs and lyric sheet. "Send only your best material." Does not return unsolicited material.
Music: Mostly country, R&B and pop; also gospel. Produced "Hank & Bogart Still Live" (by Joe Sun/Ted Barton), recorded by Joe Sun on Dixie Frog France Records (country single); "Blue Norweigian Moon" (by Don Goodman/Richie Rector), recorded by Ottar Johanson on Sonet Norway (country single); and "Have Heartache Will Travel" (by M & J. Harrison/Ted Barton), recorded by Julie Harrison on S&H UKA (country single). Other artists include Smith/Harrison, Jimmy Tittle and Steve Crunk.

*BAY FARM PRODUCTIONS, P.O. Box 2821, Duxbury MA 02364. (617)585-9470. Producer: Paul Caruso. Record producer and in-house 24-track recording facility. Estab. 1985. Deals with artists and songwriters. Produces 6 singles, 4 LPs, 2 EPs and 6 CDs/year. Fee derived from sales royalty when song or artist is recorded, outright fee from recording artist, or outright fee from record company.
How to Contact: Submit demo tape by mail. Unsolicited submissions are OK. Prefers cassette or VHS videocassette with 3 songs and lyric and lead sheet (if available). "Please use a high quality cassette." SASE. Reports in 1 month.
Music: Mostly A/C, pop and rock. Produced *Dawna Hammers*, written and recorded by Dawna Hammers on New Dawn Records (A/C LP); "West" (by V. and D. West), recorded by West (rock single); and *Caruso*, written and recorded by Caruso on Bay Farm Records (rock LP).
Tips: "We are happy to see more acoustic instruments being integrated into modern productions. We believe this is the direction for the music of the 90s."

*THE BEAU-JIM AGENCY, INC., Box 2401, Sarasota FL 34230. President: Buddy Hooper. Record producer and music publisher (Beau-Jim Music, Inc.—ASCAP; Beau-Di Music, Inc.—BMI). Deals with artists and songwriters. Produces 4 singles and 1 LP/year.
How to Contact: Prefers cassette (or videocassette) with 3-5 songs and lyric sheet. SASE. Reports in 3 weeks.
Music: Mostly country.

*BELL RECORDS INTERNATIONAL, P.O. Box 725, Daytona Beach FL 32115-0725. (904)252-4849. President: Leroy Pritchett. Record producer, music publisher and record company (Bell Records International). Estab. 1985. Deals with artists and songwriters. Produces 12 singles, 12 LPs and 12 CDs/year. Fee derived from sales royalty when song or artist is recorded.

How to Contact: Write first and obtain permission to submit. Prefers cassette.
Music: Mostly R&B, gospel and rock; also country and pop. Produced *Hot In The Gulf* (R&B LP by Billy Brown) and *Hold To God's Hand* (gospel LP by James Martin), both recorded by Charles Vickers on Bell Records. Other artists include Bobby Blue Blane and Little Anthony.

HAL BERNARD ENTERPRISES, INC., P.O. Box 8385, Cincinnati OH 45208. (513)871-1500. President: Stan Hertzmann. Record producer and music publisher (Sunnyslope Music Inc. and Bumpershoot Music Inc.). Deals with artists and songwriters. Produces 5 singles and 3-4 LPs/year. Fee derived from sales royalty.
How to Contact: Prefers cassette with 1-3 songs and lyric sheet. SASE. Reports in 1 month.
Music: Produced *Lone Rhino* and *Desire Caught By The Tail*, by Adrian Belew on Island Records (rock LPs); *The Bears* and *Rise and Shine*, by The Bears on PMRC/MCA records (rock LPs); and *Mr. Music Head* and "Young Lions," by Adrian Belew on Atlantic Records.

RICHARD BERNSTEIN, 2170 S. Parker Rd., Denver CO 80231. (303)755-2613. Contact: Richard Bernstein. Record producer, music publisher (M. Bernstein Music Publishing Co.) and record label. Deals with artists and songwriters. Produces 6 singles, 2 12″ singles, 6 LPs and 6 CDs/year. Receives 200 submissions/month. Fee derived from sales royalty, outright fee from songwriter/artist and/or outright fee from record company.
How to Contact: Prefers cassette and lyric or lead sheets. Does not return unsolicited material. Reports in 6-8 weeks.
Music: Rock, jazz and country.
Tips: "No telephone calls *please*."

BEST BUDDIES PRODUCTIONS, Box 121738, Nashville TN 37212-1738. (615)320-7664. President: Phil Efron. Record producer, music publisher (Best Buddies Music—BMI, Swing Set Music—ASCAP) and record company (X-cuse Me Records). Estab. 1981. Deals with artists and songwriters. Produces 5-8 singles and 2-3 LPs/year. Fee derived from outright fee from recording artist or record company.
How to Contact: Write first and obtain permission to submit. Prefers cassette or VHS videocassette with 4-6 songs and lyric sheets. "Include bio and promo package, details on management, etc." SASE. Reports in 3 months.
Music: Mostly country, rock, R&B; also gospel. Produced *Tie Me Up* (by Jamie O'Hara), recorded by David Speegle on Bitter Creek Records; "I Want to Be the Cowgirl in the Drifting Cowboy Band" (by Efron), recorded by Misty on Universal Records (Holland); and "If I Were You," written and recorded by Sandy Garwood on Bitter Creek Records; all country.
Tips: "Send professional package. Be well organized and businesslike."

BIG BEAR, Box 944, Birmingham, B16 8UT, **England.** 44-21-454-7020. Managing Director: Jim Simpson. Record producer, music publisher (Bearsongs) and record company (Big Bear Records). Works with lyricists and composers and teams collaborators. Produces 10 LPs/year. Fee derived from sales royalty.
How to Contact: Write first about your interest, then submit demo tape and lyric sheet. Reports in 2 weeks.
Music: Blues and jazz.

*BIG CITY MUSIC, INC., 15 Gloria Lane, Fairfield NJ 07004. (201)808-8280. President: Gary Rottger. Estab. 1990. Deals with artists and songwriters. Produces 6 singles, 6 12″ singles and 2 LPs/year. Fee derived from sales royalty or outright fee from record company.
How to Contact: Submit demo tape by mail. Unsolicited submissions are OK. Prefers cassette (or VHS videocassette if available) with 3 songs and lyric sheet. Does not return unsolicited material. Reports in 3 weeks.
Music: Mostly dance, rap and rock. Produced "Ring My Bell" (by Knight), recorded by Karen King on Power Records (dance single); *Crushin* and *Comin' Back Hard Again* (by Rottger and Fat Boys), recorded by Fat Boys on Polygram Records.
Tips: "Have a good clean demo which competes with current radio."

*BIG PICTURE RECORD CO., #7A, 101 E. 9th Ave., Anchorage AK 99501. (907)279-6900. Producer/ Owner: Patric D'Eimon. Record producer and record company (Big Picture Records). Estab. 1983. Deals with artists and songwriters. Produces 5 LPs/year. Fee derived from outright fee from recording artist.
How to Contact: Submit demo tape by mail. Unsolicited submissions are OK. Prefers cassette or VHS videocassette with 4 songs and lyric sheet. SASE. Reports in 6 weeks.
Music: Mostly country, pop/rock, R&B; also folk, New Age, "in between styles." Produced *Back Streets*, written and recorded by Patric D'Eimon on Big Picture Records (pop LP); *Chris Watkins* (by Alone/In Style), recorded by Patric D'Eimon on Home Town Records (rock LP); and *Shirley English*

(by Shirley English), recorded by Patric D'Eimon on Comai Music Records (folk LP). Other artists include Susan Grace, PBL, Marge Ford, Button Box Gang, Jim Shepard.

Tips: "We are a small company looking to help artists get to a better level in the industry. Be willing to share responsibility for the project and work hard."

*BIG PRODUCTIONS AND PUBLISHING CO. INC., Suite 308, 37 E. 28th St., New York NY 10016. (212)447-6000. FAX: (212)447-6003. President: "Big" Paul Punzone. Record producer, music publisher (Humongous Music Publishing/ASCAP) and record company (Big Productions). Estab. 1989. Deals with artists and songwriters. Produces 12 12″ singles/year. Fee derived from sales royalty when song or artist is recorded, and outright fee from recording artist or record company. Charges upfront "only when hired for independent projects."

How to Contact: Write or call first to arrange personal interview. Prefers cassette with 3 songs and lyric sheet. "We are looking for artists and independent productions for release on Big Productions Records. Artists will be signed as a production deal to shop to other labels. We mainly release 12″ house tracks on Big Productions Records." SASE. Reports in 6 weeks.

Music: Mostly house, hip-hop and pop dance. Produced "Big House" (by P. Punzone/H. Romero) and "Mission Accomplished" (by P. Punzone/B. Fisher/G. Sicard), both recorded by Big Baby; and "Loose Flutes" (by P.Punzone/B. Fisher/G. Sicard), recorded by Picture Perfect, all on Big Productions Records (all house 12″ singles).

Tips: "Please submit only musical styles listed. We want finished masters of 12″ house material."

BLADE TO THE RHYTHM MUSIC PRODUCTIONS, 114-22 116th St., Ozone Park NY 11420. (718)672-8755 or 845-4417. President: Juan-Kato Lemus. Record producer, music publisher (Blade to the Rhythm/ASCAP) and production company. Estab. 1987. Deals with artists and songwriters. Produces 4 12″ singles, 2 LPs and 6 EPs/year. Fee derived from sales royalty or outright fee from record company. "May charge in advance for services, depending on deal made with artist or songwriter."

How to Contact: Submit demo tape by mail. Unsolicited submissions are OK. Prefers cassette with 2-4 songs and lyric sheet. "Send photograph and brief bio and tell us what type of music you do." Does not return unsolicited material. Reports in 1 month.

Music: Mostly dance/pop, house and R&B; also rap, freestyle and ballads. Produced "What Was I Thinking Of" (by Vince DeMar and Rob Caputo), on 2nd Self Records (freestyle); "The Afterworld" (by J. Lemus and R. Checo), recorded by Orchestra Three on Blade to the Rhythm Records (house); and "Leave Me This Way" (by D. Ospina), recorded by Margie Martineé on Metropolitan Records (freestyle). Other artists include Aviance, Mari, Max, Hugo Fernandez, Magic Juan and Davidson.

Tips: "Be patient and the time and effort will pay off. The good songs sell because of the proper steps taken at the appropriate time."

*BLAZE PRODUCTIONS, Box 1002, Maywood NJ 07607. (201)845-9175. Record producer. Estab. 1978. Deals with artists and songwriters. Fee derived from sales royalty, outright fee from recording artist or record company.

How to Contact: Prefers cassette (or VHS videocassette) with 1 or more songs and lyric sheet. Does not return unsolicited material.

Music: Pop, rock and dance.

BLUE SUN PRODUCTIONS, P.O. Box 67, Covina CA 91723. (714)592-3098. President: Steve Mortensen. Record producer, music publisher (Single Phase Music/BMI) and record company (Blue Sun Records). Estab. 1986. Deals with artists and songwriters. Produces 12-15 singles, 2 LPs and 3 EPs/year. Receives 100 submissions/year. Fee derived from sales royalty or outright fee from recording artist or record company.

How to Contact: Submit demo tape by mail. Unsolicited submissions are OK. Prefers cassette with 2-3 songs and lyric sheet. Submit demo tape by mail. Unsolicited submissions are OK. Prefers cassette with 2-3 songs and lyric sheet. Does not return unsolicited material. Reports in 1-2 months.

Music: Mostly pop-European, rock and reggae. Produced "Rough Around the Edges," recorded by Emotion (European pop); "The Single Phase Collection," recorded by Single Phase (pop); and "Emotion," recorded by Emotion (European pop); all on Blue Sun Records. Other artists include Sean Amato, Leslie Harder and Stacey Venne.

JACK P. BLUESTEIN, P.O. Box 630175, Miami FL 33163. (305)472-7757. President: Jack Bluestein. Record producer and music publisher (Twister Music, Lantana Music and Pine Island Music). Estab. 1973. Deals with artists and songwriters. Produces 50 singles and 1-2 LPs/year. Works with 10-15 new songwriters/year. Fee derived from sales royalty.

How to Contact: Prefers reel-to-reel or cassette with 2-6 songs and lyric sheet. SASE. Reports in 1 month.
Music: Blues, country, gospel, MOR, R&B, rock and top 40/pop. Produced "It's Over" and "Dreaming For Two," recorded by Beth Thliveris on Twister Records (pop); "Kathy, Dear" (by Al Williams); "Lucky is a Man" (by Larrry Coen); "Say, Don't Go" (by Winthrop Marcinak); and "Mardi Gras" (by Nan Beeson), all new releases.

PETER L. BONTA, 1518 Pr. Anne St., Fredericksburg VA 22401. (703)373-6511. Studio Manager: Chris Ippolito. Record producer. Estab. 1980. Deals with artists and songwriters. Produces 8-12 singles, 5-8 LPs and 4-6 CDs/year. Fee derived from sales royalty, outright fee from recording artist or record company.
How to Contact: Write or call first and obtain permission to submit. Prefers cassette with 3-4 songs and lyric sheet. SASE. Reports in 6 weeks.
Music: Mostly roots rock, country rock and blues; also country and Bluegrass. Other artists include Gary Herrewig (Artful Dodger).

*BOOM PRODUCTIONS, INC., 200 Regent Dr., Winston-Salem NC 27102. (919)768-1881. President: Dave Passerallo. Record producer, music publisher (DeDan Music/BMI) and record company (Boom/Power Play Records). Estab. 1989. Deals with artists and songwriters. Produces 2 singles, 2 LPs and 2 CDs/year. Fee derived from sales royalty.
How to Contact: Write first and obtain permission to submit. Prefers cassette (or VHS videocassette if available) with 2 songs and lead sheet. SASE. Reports in 2-3 weeks.
Music: Mostly pop, rap and rock. Produced "Ripped Jeans," by John Cody (pop); and "Guilty," by Paul Krege (rock/pop); both produced by Dave Passerallo for Boom Productions on Boom Powerplay Records.
Tips: "Artist must be able to sign a production agreement."

*BRIEFCASE OF TALENT PRODUCTIONS, 1612 Marlbrook Dr., Atlanta GA 30307. (401)371-8583. Owner: Kevin Howell. Record producer and live recording engineer. "Offers sound reinforcement services." Deals with artists. Produces 3 singles, 1 LP, 2 EPs and 1 CD/year. Fee derived from outright fee from recording artist or outright fee from record company.
How to Contact: Write first and obtain permission to submit. Prefers cassette (or VHS videocassette if available) with 4 songs and lyric sheet. Does not return unsolicited material. Reports in 2 weeks.
Music: Mostly alternative, rock (classic) and heavy metal; also R&B. Produced *Chunks This Big* (by Stan Hodgin), recorded by Living Industry on Briefcase Records (thrash LP); and *Ready To Rock*, written and recorded by Scott Fairchild on Childman Records (rock LP). Other artists include Problem Child, Seventh Heaven and Piece Dogs.
Tips: "Make it sound finished and professional. Nothing catches an engineer/producer's ear better than a quality, pro demo."

RAFAEL BROM, P.O. Box 71988, Los Angeles CA 90071-0988. Producer: Rafael Brom. Record producer, music publisher (ASCAP), record company (Cosmotone Records). Estab. 1984. Deals with artists and songwriters. Produces 1 LP/year.
How to Contact: Write first to obtain permission to submit. Prefers cassette (or VHS videocassette if available) with several songs and lyric sheet. Does not return unsolicited material. "Will contact only if interested."
Music: All types. Produced "Padre Pio," Sonnet XVIII," and "Peace of Heart," all written and recorded by Lord Hamilton on Cosmotone Records (Christian/rock pop). Other artists include Adrian Romero and Thomas Emmett Dufficy.

*BROOZBEE MUSIC, INC., Suite 308, 37 East 28th St., New York NY 10016. (212)447-6000. President: Bruce B. Fisher. Record producer and music publisher (Broozbee Music, Inc./ASCAP). Estab. 1986. Deals with artists and songwriters. Produces 8 12″ singles/year. Fee derived from sales royalty or outright fee from recording artist (if hired for independent project) or record company.
How to Contact: Submit demo tape by mail. Unsolicited submissions are OK. Prefers cassette (or VHS videocassette if available) with 3 songs and lyric sheet. "Send what you consider to be the best representation of your talent." SASE. Reports in 2 months.
Music: Mostly house, hip hop and dance; also rap, R&B and pop. Produced "Mission Accomplished," recorded by Big Baby; "Loose Flutes," recorded by Picture Perfect; and "I'm the Other Lover," recorded by Picture Perfection; all written by P. Puzone/B.B. Fisher/G. Sicard on Big Productions Records (all house). Other artists include Sheron Neverson.
Tips: "Quality, not quantity, is the most important."

Close-up

Jessica Baron
Children's Music Consultant
Topanga, California

Jessica Baron is not your average, everyday music publisher. She isn't looking for a big hit that instantly makes thousands of dollars. She's not searching for a "new sound" that will revolutionize the music industry. And she's not working for a publisher whose interests lie strictly in acquiring the rights to popular music and creating a publishing empire. Not at all.

Baron looks for children's music—a limited, yet ever-growing market for songwriters. As a children's music consultant and former Founder/Director of Gibson Kids (a multi-arts and music educational program), Baron has been building a repertoire of children's music which correlates to visual art, movement and drama as the main vehicles of pre-school and elementary education. And she uses a special formula for the selection of guitar/vocal music for youngsters in a classroom environment.

This formula involves a lengthy process in which Baron custom-fits children's songs into programs to create a learning experience for young students. She receives many submissions, but only the songs that interest her the most are input into a computer database, where they are then broken down by category. For example, she documents the signature, tempo, the primary and secondary music style the song can be used in, whether the song is multicultural or internationally based, the theme and the chord structure (among other specifics).

With the song, a certain issue or topic will be studied, either of social or academic value. For instance, dealing with and recognizing racism is a topic for the kids. "What we're trying to do is give the children a forum in which they can explore their feelings and express themselves in a creative way, and you can use music to do it. To learn about racism, we might have a song about all the colors in the rainbow, and we'll talk about how the skin colors differ. I might ask them to put the color of their skin (or the color of others in the class) into the song. So, they're singing about what they know. We aren't forcing anything on them." Then, an art project or related movement or drama exercise may accompany the song.

Baron, who has a degree in child development and has experience in music education and therapy, says that writing for children is much more difficult for songwriters not intensely involved with children. "The best writers are around children a lot. They may have kids of their own, or they're teachers and happen to have an affinity for music and songwriting as well." And many of the submissions she receives reflect the songwriters' inexperience with children.

Although it seems that writing children's music would be easier than typical pop or other "adult" genres, Baron is the first to disagree. Writing for adults is much different, she says, because children's perceptions and feelings are changing constantly, and it's hard to pinpoint their needs sometimes, especially with music. The development of adults slows tremendously, and their feelings do not vary as radically as a youngsters. Often times the songwriters themselves do not approach the child's needs appropriately. "I think a lot of people attempting songwriting for children are writing from the wrong perspective. They're writing as a parent, or they're using their memories of childhood to create a storyline. A good song for children isn't written this way—it's written completely from a child's view, so nothing in the 'adult world' interferes.

"Many people who send in submissions are writing from the perspective of their own inner-child, but sometimes they don't realize that. The difference between their inner-child and real children is that an adult's inner-child has acquired all of the intellectual and communications skills of an adult—and the adult may need to release an old feeling not necessarily relevant to children today." A successful children's songwriter is able to make the distinction.

The process of listening for good songs begins with Baron listening to a tape from beginning to end, usually in her car. "I listen to it with the ears of a child, or at least as much as a child as I can. And I imagine what they might like about it, whether it's the lyric or melody or production or whatever." After that, if there is potential, she lets the tape sit for a few days, and then goes back to review it again. "I'll evaluate the songs further to see if they're really appropriate for children to sing from beginning to end."

Baron advises children's songwriters to "go hang out with children. Take your guitar (or voice or your marimba or whatever) and go to a pre-school or an after school program and play your songs for them." This will indicate whether or not the kids can relate to the music. Also, "read about child development," she urges, "specifically Erik Eriksen and Abraham Maslow," two accomplished developmental psychologists. This will help the songwriter better understand the needs of children, and the way kids think and react.

The children's songwriter must remember that the entire song is important too. Lyrically, one catchy hook is not enough. "A lot of good songs are wonderful for children to listen to, but they aren't the type that kids can memorize entirely. You must consider whether the lyrics can be sung, understood and memorized by 6 and 7-year olds. It's very important to use appropriate language. If you want children to sing along with you, use words that they would use themselves. And use a lot of repetition. They follow that the best."

—Brian C. Rushing

BURNING TYGER MUSIC, 684 Indiana, San Francisco CA 94107. (415)821-2321. President/Producer: Michael Molenda. Staff Producers: Neal Brighton, Frank Macchia, Buddy Saleman and Jerry Stucker. Record producers and music publisher (Burning Tyger Music/BMI). Deals with artists and songwriters. Produces 1 12″ single, 3 CDs and 3 LPs/year. Fee derived from sales royalty (songwriters), or outright fee from recording artist or record company (artists). "Contract production services for demos or records are on a fee basis. Percentage contracts or conventional songwriter-royalty contracts are, of course, offered at no advance fee."
How to Contact: Write first and obtain permission to submit. Prefers cassette with 3 songs, lyric sheet, and photo. "A few concise lines detailing your artistic concepts or goals are helpful." SASE. Reports in 1 month.
Music: Mostly modern rock, dance, and pop; also gospel, R&B and jazz. Produced LP master by *The Sextants* for Barebones Productions; "Symphony of Life," by Slaves of Orpheus on Sound & Vision Records (modern rock CD); *St. Christopher's Sin* on Sound & Vision Records (modern rock EP); "Hold Back the Night," by *Boom Box Orchestra*; "Movietron" by Neal Brighton (rock-u-drama video of WWII); *Danse Orkestra* (dance EP) on Sound & Vision Records; and "Way-er Out West," by Frankie Maximum on Sound & Vision Records (jazz CD).
Tips: "We develop 'visionary' artists who approach the 'song' like a film director stages a movie scene. Lyrics should be meaningful and alive with images—the music should evoke a mood consistent with the message inherent in the work."

CALLIOPE PRODUCTIONS, 265 W. 37th St., New York NY 10018. (212)704-9626. Attn: Andy Lasseter. Record producer, music publisher (Gizzard/ASCAP) and record company (Calliope Records). Estab. 1985. Deals with artists and songwriters. Produces 2 singles, 2 12″ singles, 2 LPs, 2 EPs and 2 CDs/year. Receives 20 submissions/month. Fee derived from combination of sales royalty when song or artist is recorded, outright fee from recording artist, outright fee from record company and percentage of publishing.

How to Contact: Write first and obtain permission to submit. Prefers cassette (or ½" or ¾" videocassette if available) with 3 songs and lyric sheet. Does not return unsolicited material. Reports in 1 month.

Music: Mostly R&B, pop and rock; also rap, gospel and jazz. Produced "Baby Baby" (by Christian Julian), on RKO Records (pop); "Why," written and recorded by Roland Clark on Atlantic Records (dance single); and "Save Yourself," "Where Were You," "Good Enough" and "Life A.D.," for Alta Dustin on Atlantic Records. Other artists include Kinky Pink and Justin Time.

PETER CARDINALI, 12 Ecclesfield Dr., Scarborough ON M1W 3J6 **Canada**. (416)494-2000. Record producer/Arranger (Peter Cardinali Productions Inc./CAPAC) and Cardstar Music (publishing), CAPAC, BMI, PROCAN. Estab. 1975. Deals with artists and songwriters. Produces 6-8 singles, 4-5 12" singles, 8-10 LPs and 8-10 CDs/year.

How to Contact: Write or call first and obtain permission to submit. Prefers cassette with 4-6 songs and lyric sheets. SASE. Reports within weeks.

Music: Mostly pop, R&B, dance and funk/jazz. Produced *Big Fat Soul*, written and recorded by John James on Attic/A&M Records (dance LP); "The Bear Walks" (by P. Cardinali/H. Marsh), recorded by Hugh Marsh on Duke St./WEA Records (R&B/jazz LP); and "Moments" (by J. Nessle), recorded by See on A&M Records (pop single). Other artists include Rick James and Teena Marie.

*CARLYLE PRODUCTIONS, 1217 16th Ave. South, Nashville TN 37212. (615)327-8129. President: Laura Fraser. Record producer, record company (Carlyle Records) and production company. Estab. 1986. Deals with artists and songwriters. Produces 6 singles and 6 LPs/CDs per year.

How to Contact: Submit demo tape by mail. Unsolicited submissions are OK. Prefers cassette with 3 songs and lyric sheet. Does not return unsolicited material. Reports in 1 month.

Music: Mostly rock, pop and country. Produced *Exercise in Tension*, written and recorded by Dessau (dance LP); *Songs From Beneath the Lake*, written and recorded by The Shakers (acoustic LP); and *I Play Jupiter*, written and recorded by The Grinning Plowman (rock LP), all on Carlyle Records, Inc.

CAROLINA PRIDE PRODUCTIONS, Box 6, Rougemont NC 27572. (919)477-4077. Manager: Freddie Roberts. Record producer, music publisher (Freddie Roberts Music/BMI), record company, management firm and booking agency. Estab. 1967. Deals with artists, songwriters and session musicians. Produces 12 singles, 7 LPs, 2 EPs and 3 CDs/year. Fee derived from sales royalty.

How to Contact: Call or write first. Prefers 7½ ips reel-to-reel or cassette with 1-5 songs and lyric sheet. SASE. Reports in 3 weeks.

Music: Mostly country, MOR and top 40/pop; also bluegrass, church/religious, gospel and country rock. Produced "Restless Feeling," written and recorded by Rodney Hutchins (country/rock) on Catalina Records; "Empty" (by David Laws), recorded by Jerry Harrison (country) on Celebrity Circle Records; and "Redeemed" (by Jane Durham), recorded by The Roberts Family (Southern gospel) on Bull City Records. Other artists include Sleepy Creek, Lady Luck, Billy McKellar and C.J. Jackson.

STEVE CARR, % Hit & Run Studios, 18704 Muncaster Rd., Rockville MD 20855. (301)948-6715. Owner/Producer: Steve Carr. Record producer (Hit & Run Studios). Estab. 1979. Deals with artists and songwriters. Produces 10 singles, 2 12" singles, 8 LPs, 4 EPs and 10 CDs/year. Fee derived from outright fee from recording artist.

How to Contact: Write or call first and obtain permission to submit. Prefers cassette with 3 songs. "Do NOT send unsolicited material! Write name and phone number on cassette shell. Will call back if I can do anything with your material."

Music: Mostly pop, rock and R&B; also country. Produced/recorded *Billy Kemp* (by Billy Kemp), on Essential Records (LP); *Classic Rock*, written and recorded by various artists (oldies digital remaster) on Warner Bros. Records; "Frontier" (by R. Kelley), recorded by Frontier Theory on TOP Records (rock CD); *The Wolves* (by Band), on Top Records (LP); and "Bomb Squad" (by Lorenzo), on Their Own Records (single); all recorded by Hit & Run. Other artists include Beyond Words, Steve Nally/ Deep End, Oho, Voodoo, Love Gods, Necrosis, Debra Brown and Universe. Produces and digitally remasters Time-Life Music's Rock n' Roll, Country Classics and R&B Series.

*MARK CARVEL, Suite 12G, 70 West 95th St., New York NY 10025. (212)666-6454. Producer/Owner: Mark Carvel. Record producer, music publisher (BMI, ASCAP affiliate) and record company (Mighty Soul-Sonic Records). Estab. 1987. Deals with artists and songwriters. Produces 12 singles, 2 12" singles, 7 LPs, 4 EPs and 7 CDs/year. Fee derived from sales royalty when song or artist is recorded, outright fee from recording artist or outright fee from record company.

How to Contact: Write or call first and obtain permission to submit. Prefers cassette (or artist performance videocassette if available) with 12 songs and lyric or lead sheets. SASE. Reports in 2 months.
Music: Mostly rap, rock and R&B; also jazz and gospel.

JAN CELT, 4026 NE 12th Ave., Portland OR 97212. (503)287-8045. Owner: Jan Celt. Record producer, music publisher (Wiosna Nasza Music/BMI) and record company (Flying Heart Records). Estab. 1982. Deals with artists and songwriters. Produces 2 LPs, 1 EP and 2 CDs/year. Receives 300 submissions/month.
How to Contact: Submit demo tape by mail. Unsolicited submissions are OK. Prefers cassette with 1-10 songs and lyric sheets. Does not return unsolicited material. Reports in 3 months.
Music: Mostly R&B, rock and blues; also jazz. Produced "Voodoo Garden," written and recorded by Tom McFarland (blues); "Bong Hit" (by Chris Newman), recorded by Snow Bud & the Flower People (rock); and "She Moved Away" (by Chris Newman), recorded by Napalm Beach, all on Flying Heart Records. Other artists include The Esquires and Janice Scroggins.
Tips: "Be sure your lyrics are heartfelt; they are what makes a song your own. Abandon rigid stylistic concepts and go for total honesty of expression."

*CHALLEDON PRODUCTIONS, 5th Floor, Pembroke One Bldg., Virginia Beach VA 23462. General Counsel: Richard Shapiro. Record producer and record company (Challedon Records). Estab. 1990. Deals with artists and songwriters. Produces 1-2 singles, 1-2 LPs and 1-2 CDs/year. Fee derived from sales royalty.
How to Contact: Write first and obtain permission to submit. Prefers cassette (or VHS videocasette if available) with up to 3 songs and lyric sheet. Reports in 4 weeks.
Music: Mostly rock, pop and alternative/college rock; also some R&B. Produced *Hired Gun* (by J. Sullivan), recorded by Challedon Productions at Master Sound on Challedon Records (LP). Other artists include High Energy.

*CHUCK CHAPMAN, 228 W. 5th St., Kansas City MO 64105. (816)842-6854. Office Manager: Gary Sutton. Record producer and music publisher (Fifth Street Records/BMI). Estab. 1973. Deals with artists and songwriters. Fee derived from sales royalty when song or artist is recorded, outright fee from recording artist or outright fee from record company. "Charges upfront for recording only."
How to Contact: Write or call first and obtain permission to submit. Prefers cassette (or ½" or ¾" videocassette if available) with 3 songs and lyric sheet. Include SASE. Does not return unsolicited material. Reports back in 1 month.
Music: Mostly country, gospel and rock; also rap, jazz and spoken word. Produced "Rumor Has It" (by Sheli), recorded by Freddie Hunt on Fifth Street Records (country single); and "Cold As Ashes" (by Lee Bruce), recorded by Montgomery Lee on Opal Records (country single). Other artists include Conrad Morris and Eisel & The Haymakers.

CHROME DREAMS PRODUCTIONS, 5852 Sentinel St., San Jose CA 95120. (408)268-6066. Owner: Leonard Giacinto. Record producer. Estab. 1982. Deals with artists and songwriters. Produces 15 singles and 8 12" singles/year. Fee derived from outright fee from recording artist.
How to Contact: Submit demo tape by mail. Unsolicited submissions are OK. Write or call first to arrange personal interview. Prefers cassette (or ½" VHS videocassette if available). SASE. Reports in 1 month.
Music: Mostly rock, New Age, avant-garde and college radio. Produced "Seal Your Love" (by F. Barbaccia), recorded by Vidiots (rock); "Get It Now," written and recorded by B. Linden (rock); and "Why Get Up?," recorded by Hurrican's; all on independent record labels. Other artists include Waxed Dolphin (cover band), Love Stooges (European electronic), The Krells, Certain Words and The John Amato Blues Band. Also produced soundtrack for V. Volkoff's film *The Garage Door*.
Tips: "Try to get emotion across in your work."

*CLAY/TWAN, 19938 Patton, Detroit MI 48219. (313)533-4506. Record producer. Deals with artists and songwriters. Produces 25 singles and 6 LPs/year. Fee derived from sales royalty or outright fee from recording artist. Charges artists in advance for services "only if artist or songwriter contracts our services."
How to Contact: Submit demo tape by mail. Unsolicited submissions are OK. Prefers cassette (or VHS videocassette if available) with 3 songs and lyric sheet. "We will make contact if we plan to use your material." SASE. Reports in 1 month.
Music: Produced "Shadows" (by Grady Quiett), recorded by Brenda Wilson-Johnson on Scorcher Records (pop single); *Doing It to the Maximum* (by A. Taylor), recorded by Twan on Torrid Records (R&B LP); and *I Ain't Buyin It* (by D. Fielder/D. Davis/M. Fields), recorded by D.O.P. on Scorcher Records (rap EP). "All artists signed to Clay & Twan, Inc."

THE CLUB STUDIOS, 127 Aldersgate St., London EC1A 4JQ **England**. (66)71-2501910. Contact: Roland A. Radaelli. Record producer, music publisher (Risson Music UK-PRS) and record company (Presidential Enterprises, Ltd.). Estab. 1986. Deals with artists and songwriters. Produces 20-30 12″ singles and 3-5 LPs/year. Receives 8 submissions/month. Fee derived from sales royalty or outright fee from recording artist or record company. Charges for services in advance "only when productions are for other labels or publishers."
How to Contact: Prefers cassette with 2-5 songs and lyric sheet. Does not return unsolicited material. Reports in 2 weeks.
Music: Mostly house and hip-hop. Produced "Yo!" (by J.S.Gray), recorded by Fly Girls on Happy Music Records (pop-rap); "Low Frequency Overload" (by various writers), recorded by 100HZ on Optimism Records (house); and "If I Can't Have You" (by Gibbs), recorded by Project Joy on XXIst Century Records (pop-dance). Other artists include Tube Generation and Alberto.

COLLECTOR RECORDS, Box 2296, Rotterdam Holland 3000 CG **The Netherlands**. Phone: (1860)20180. Research: Cees Klop. Record producer and music publisher (All Rock Music). Deals with artists and songwriters. Produces 8-10 singles and up to 30 LPs/year. Fee derived from sales royalty.
How to Contact: Prefers cassette. SAE and IRC. Reports in 1 month.
Music: Mostly 50s rock, rockabilly and country rock; also piano boogie woogie. Produced *Eddie Bond* (by Bond), recorded by Bond/Klop on White Label Records (rock LP); *Louis Gittens*, written and recorded by Gittens on White Label Records (rock LP); and *Rob Hoeke* (by Hoeke), recorded by Cees Klop on Downsouth Records (boogie LP). Other artists include Teddy Redell, Gene Summers and Benny Joy.

MICHAEL COLLINS/REFINED RECORDS, 2105 Maryland Ave., Baltimore MD 21218. (301)685-8500. Deals with artists only. Produces 3 LPs/year. Receives 50 submissions/month. Fee derived from outright fee from recording artist.
How to Contact: Prefers cassette with at least 4 songs. Does not return unsolicited material.
Music: Mostly rock. Produced *Two Thirds*, by Bazooka Joe; *Funk Wagon McGuillicuddy*, by Krack; "Pride and Passion" (by When Thunder Comes), recorded on Frantic Records (rock); and "Black Friday" (by Black Friday), on Refined Records (rock).

*COM'TECH PRODUCTIONS, INC., P.O. Box 28816, Philadelpha PA 19151. (215)473-5527. General Manager: Leroy Schuler. Record producer. Estab. 1990. Deals with artists and songwriters. Fee derived from outright fee from record company. Produces 6 singles, 25 12″ singles and 3 LPs/year.
How to Contact: Submit demo tape by mail. Unsolicited submissions are OK. Prefers cassette with 4 songs and lyric sheet. SASE. Reports in 3 weeks.
Music: Mostly R&B, pop and jazz. Artists include Lavelle, Clint Washington and Felice. Produced "Here We Go Again," "I'll Do Better" (by SBmm), recorded by Mack Atkinson on Bend-Bang Records (single 7″); and "Do Me Right" (by SBmm), recorded by Debra Scott on Big Bang Records (LTD cassette).

*CONTINENTAL COMMUNICATIONS CORP., Suite 212, 450 Livingston St., Norwood NJ 07648. (201)767-5551. Vice President: Gene Schwartz. Record producer and music publisher (3 Seas Music/ASCAP and Northvale Music/BMI) and record company (3C Records and Laurie Records). Estab. 1985. Deals with artists and songwriters. Produces 25 singles, 12 12″ singles, 20 LPs and 10 CDs/year. Fee derived from sales royalty.
How to Contact: Prefers cassette and lyric sheet. "Send only a few of your most commercial songs." SASE. Reports in 2 weeks.
Music: Mostly rock and pop, urban; also dance-oriented and top 40/pop. Artists include Human Beings, Barbara M and Bill Sunkel.

COPPELIA, 21 rue de Pondichery, Paris 75015 **France**. Phone: (1)45673066. FAX: (1)43063026. Manager: Jean-Philippe Olivi. Record producer, music publisher (Coppelia/SACEM), record company (Olivi Records) and music print publisher. Deals with artists and songwriters. Produces 8 singles and 4 LPs/year. Fee derived from sales royalty or outright fee from recording artist or record company.
How to Contact: Prefers cassette. SAE and IRC. Reports in 1 month.
Music: Mostly pop, rock and New Age; also background music and film/series music. Produced "No'mad" written and recorded by Alain Mion (jazz); "Fille Facile," written and recorded by Henry Stoltz (pop); and "Carte Postale" (by Remy-Ferchit), recorded by Dominique Bodin (French folk), all on Olivi Records. Other artists include Pino Lattuca, Christian Chevallier and Robert Quibel.

*JOHNNY COPPIN/RED SKY RECORDS, P.O. Box 7, Stonehouse, Glos. GL10 3PQ U.K. 0453-826200. Record producer, music publisher (PRS) and record company (Red Sky Records). Estab. 1985. Deals with artists and songwriters. Produces 2 singles, 3 LPs and 3 CDs/year. Fee derived from sales royalty when song or artist is recorded.

How to Contact: Submit demo tape by mail. Unsolicited submissions are OK. Prefers cassette with 3 songs and lyric sheet. SASE. Reports in 3 months.

Music: Mostly rock, modern folk and roots music. Produced *Edge of Day*, written and recorded by Laurie Lee and Johnny Coppin (LP); *Songs on Lonely Roads*, recorded by Johnny Coppin and David Goodland (musical drama LP); and *West Country Christmas*, written and recorded by Johnny Coppin (LP); all on Red Sky Records. Other artists include Desperate Men, White Leaved Oak.

RON CORNELIUS, 803 18th Ave. South, Nashville TN 37203. (615)321-5333. Owner/Manager: Ron Cornelius. Record producer and music publisher (The Cornelius Companies). Estab. 1987. Deals with artists and songwriters. Produces 3-4 singles and 1-2 LPs/year. Receives 200-300 submissions/month. Fee derived from sales royalty or outright fee from record company.

How to Contact: Call first and obtain permission to submit. Prefers cassette with 2-3 songs. SASE. Reports in 2 months.

Music: Mostly country and pop. Published "These Colors Never Run," written and recorded by Gordon Dee; and "The 'F' Word," written and recorded by Bertie Higgins; both country singles on Southern Tracks Records.

DANO CORWIN, 5839 Silver Creek, Azle Rd., Azle TX 76020. (817)281-7988. Record producer, music video and sound production company. Estab. 1986. Works with artists and songwriters. Produces 6 singles, 3 12″ singles, 5 EPs and 2 CDs/year. Receives 200 submissions/year. Fee usually derived from sales royalty, but negotiated on case-by-case basis.

How to Contact: Prefers cassette (or VHS videocassette if available) with 3 songs and lyric sheet. "Keep songs under 4 minutes. Only copyrighted material will be reviewed. Please do not send material without copyright notices." SASE, "but prefers to keep material on file." Reports in 6 weeks.

Music: Mostly rock; also pop, New Age and dance. Produced "Say Goodbye to Love" (by Craig Cole/Keny McClurg), recorded by Sound Dog (rock/single) on MLM records; "In the Meantime" (by Craig Cole/Keny McClurg), recorded by Sound Dog (rock EP/CD) on MLM Records; and "Intense" (by P. Aziz), recorded by Nuclear Power (rock/single) on Big M Records. Other artists include Demur Cull, The Kindreds and The W-4's.

Tips: "Keep songs simple and melodic. Write as many songs as possible. Out of a large quantity, a few quality songs may emerge."

*DAVE COTTRELL, 1602 8th Ave. South, Fort Dodge IA 50501. Producer: Dave Cottrell. Record producer. Estab. 1969. Deals with artists and songwriters. Producers 25 singles, 10 LPs, 10 EPs and 25 CDs/year. Receives 15 submissions/month. Fee derived from outright fee from recording artist or outright fee from record company.

How to Contact: Write or call first to arrange personal interview. Prefers cassette with 4 songs and lyric sheet. Reports in 1 month.

Music: Mostly rock, pop and gospel; also country, R&B and disco. Produced "Change Of Address," written and recorded by Donna Rogers (country single); *Verne Fibiker* (by various songwriters), recorded by Verne Fibiker (accordian LP); and *Battalian*, written and recorded by Battalian (metal LP), all on Independent Records. Credits include work with Ray Manzerak of The Doors, Jan & Dean, Bobby Vee, The Beach Boys and more.

Tips: "Avoid clutter and multi-track overkill. Too many sounds and tracks ruin the sound. Write music that you enjoy. Be honest and creative. There is no room for the weak and insane in the music business."

*COUNTERPOINT PRODUCTIONS, 6903-A E. Harris Blvd., Charlotte NC 28215. (704)532-2277. Manager/Owner: Greg Auch. Estab. 1990. Deals with artists and songwriters. Produces 4-5 singles, 3-4 12″ singles and 5-7 LPs/year. Deposit usually required for studio. Payment depends upon the particular situation and the artist.

How to Contact: Submit demo tape by mail. Unsolicited submissions are OK. Prefers cassette with 2 songs and lyric sheet. "Would also like a SASE for response return." SASE. Reports in 1 month.

Music: Mostly gospel (southern and contemporary), country and R&B; also jazz and rock. Produced *Time*, written and recorded by The Difference, on Lamon Records (gospel LP); *The Lambert Family*, written and recorded by Lambert Family (gospel LP); and *Tight Dress* (by M. Giggy), recorded by Gypsie (rock). Other artists include Phill Ruff, Will Hoguild, Steve Newell, Sudden Impulse, The Kinney Family and Keith Gardner.

*COUNTRY REEL ENTERPRISES, P.O. Box 99307, Stockton CA 95209. (209)473-8050. President: Mr. Dana C. Copenhaver. Record producer, music publisher (BMI) and record company (Country Reel Records). Estab. 1981. Deals with artists and songwriters. Fee derived from sales royalty.
How to Contact: Write first and obtain permission to submit. Prefers cassette or VHS videocassette with lyric and lead sheets. "Send promo package (include copyrights)." SASE.
Music: Traditional country and country gospel. Artists include Dana Clark, Jennifer Celeste and D.J. Birmingham.
Tips: "Write traditional type songs—country music is going back to traditional country sounds."

COUNTRY STAR PRODUCTIONS, P.O. Box 569, Franklin PA 16323. (814)432-4633. President: Norman Kelly. Record producer, music publisher (Country Star Music/ASCAP, Kelly Music/BMI and Process Music/BMI) and record company (Country Star, Process, Mersey and CSI Records). Estab. 1970. Deals with artists and songwriters. Produces 5-8 singles and 5-8 LPs/year. Receives 100 submissions/year. Works with 3-4 new songwriters/year. Works with composers and lyricists; teams collaborators. Fee derived from sales royalty or outright fee from recording artist or record company.
How to Contact: Prefers cassette with 2-4 songs and lyric or lead sheet. SASE. Reports in 2 weeks.
Music: Mostly country (80%); also rock (5%), MOR (5%), gospel (5%) and R&B (5%). Produced "America I Love You" (by A. Barri), recorded by Bob Stamper; "The Holiday Waltz" (by Wrightman-Stelezer), recorded by Debbie Sue; and "Rose of Cherokee" (by K. Casteel), recorded by Virge Brown; all country singles on Country Star Records. Other artists include Bob Stamper, Elmer Blanchard, John York, Vince Smith, Virge Brown, Bonnie Baldwin, Junie Lou, Lisa Hadley Patton, Debbie Sue, Tommy Davidson, Ron Lauer, J.C. Young and Silver Dollar Country Band.
Tips: "Submit only your best efforts."

THE COYOTE, P.O. Box 387, Hollywood CA 90078. (818)506-8660. Producer: The Coyote. Record producer, music publisher (Shaolin Music/ASCAP) and record company (Shaolin Film & Records). Estab. 1984. Deals with artists and songwriters. Produces 3 singles, 2 LPs and 2 CDs/year. Receives 25-30 submissions/month. Fee derived from sales royalty or outright fee from record company.
How to Contact: Write first and obtain permission to submit. Does not return unsolicited material.
Music: Mostly rock, hard rock and pop; also soundtracks. Produced "Temptation," "Coyote In A Graveyard" and "Love, Always & Forever," written and recorded by Coyote (rock) on Shaolin Records. Other artists include Soho, The Rich and The Streethearts.
Tips: "Perform your songs."

*CREATIVE ARTWORKS INC./B&W Productions, 705 Taywood Rd., Englewood OH 45322. (513)832-1785. President: Mark Herres. Record producer, music publisher and record company (Creative Artworks Records). Estab. 1985. Deals with artists and songwriters. Produces 40 singles, 40 12″ singles and 10 CDs/year. Fee derived from sales royalty when song or artist is recorded.
How to Contact: Submit demo tape by mail. Unsolicited submissions are OK. Prefers cassette (or VHS videocassette if available) with 3 songs and lyric sheet. Does not return unsolicited material. Reports in 6 weeks.
Music: Mostly danceable pop/R&B; also country, house and jazz. Produced *Nothing Qwest* (by Johnny Qwest, alternative pop); *Nothing Definite* (by Mark Herres, rock-pop LP); and *Dave Simon Quartet* (by Dave Simon, jazz LP), all recorded by Mark Herres on Creative Artworks Records. Other artists include Dave Deal (pop), Daryl Thomas (R&B) and Cliche (R&B).
Tips: "Be honest with yourself. Listen to what you send with big ears, not a big head. Put your ideas on tape, don't expect us to imagine what it should sound like."

*CRUSADER RECORDS AND TAPES, Box 241, Cameron MO 64429. (816)632-6039. Manager: E.K. Bruhn. Record producer, music publisher (Time Minstrel Music) and record company (Crusader Records). Estab. 1984. Deals with artists, songwriters and other producers. Produces 3-6 singles and 2-5 LPs/year. Fee is derived from sales royalty or outright fee from artist/songwriter or record company.
How to Contact: "Write about your interest." Submit cassette, reel-to-reel or record with 2 songs." SASE. Reports in 10 weeks.
Music: Country/rock and top 40/pop. Artists include Terry Alden and Hope Jackson.

*JERRY CUPIT PRODUCTIONS, PO Box 121904, Nashville TN 37212. (615)731-0100. Producer: Jerry Cupit. Record producer and music publisher. Estab. 1984. Deals with artists and songwriters. Releases 10 singles, 6 LPs and 6 CDs/year. Fee derived from sales royalty or outright fee from record company. "I produce artists and I charge a fee; sometimes budget comes from record company, sometimes from the artist. I never charge songwriters to demo songs I publish."
How to Contact: Write or call first to arrange interview. Does not return unsolicited material.
Music: Mostly country, rock and gospel; also R&B. Produced *Guilty*, written and recorded by David and Faye Brewer on Mercury/Polygram Records (country LP); *Thank God for America* (by Randy Roberts), recorded by Orion on Southern Tracks Records (country LP); and "Tennessee Plea," writ-

ten and recorded by Johnny Die on Premier One Records (country single). Other artists include Freddie Hart, Judy Bailey, San Antonio Rose, James Payne (gospel), Gere Simmons (Haunted House), Rhet Bradey, Ken Mellons, Liz Lyndell and John Wesley Ryles.

WADE CURTISS, P.O. Box 4740, Nashville, TN 37216. A&R Director: Wade Curtiss. Record producer and record company (Terock Records). Estab. 1959. Deals with artists and songwriters. Produces 12-20 singles, 6 12″ singles, 12-20 LPs, 4 EPs and 6 CDs/year. Fee derived from outright fee from recording artist. Charges "artists for sessions."
How to Contact: Submit demo tape by mail. Unsolicited submissions are OK. Prefers IPS reel-to-reel or "all kinds" of videocassettes (if available) with 4-10 songs and lyric sheets. SASE.
Music: Interested in "all kinds." Produced "Changes," written and recorded by R. Derwald; and *Rock*, written and recorded by Mickey Finn (rock LP), both on Terock Records. Other artists include Dixie Dee, Greg Paul and Rhythm Rockers.

S. KWAKU DADDY, P.O. Box 4794, San Francisco CA 94101. (415)239-3640. President: S. Kwaku Daddy. Record producer and record company (African Heritage Records Co.). Deals with artists and songwriters. Produces 6 LPs/year.
How to Contact: Prefers cassette. Sometimes returns unsolicited material. Reports in 3 weeks.
Music: Mostly African pop, R&B and gospel. Produced *Times of Change, Life's Rhythms* and *Heritage IV*, all by S. Kwaku Daddy, all on African Heritage Records (LPs).

DANNY DARROW, Suite 6-D, 150 West End Ave., New York NY 10023. (212)873-5968. Manager: Danny Darrow. Record producer, music publisher (BMI, ASCAP), record company (Mighty Records) and Colley Phonographics—Europe. Estab. 1958. Deals with songwriters only. Produces 1-2 singles, 1-2 12″ singles and 1-2 LPs/year. Fee derived from royalty.
How to Contact: Submit demo tape by mail. Unsolicited submissions are OK. "No phone calls." Prefers cassette with 3 songs and lyric sheet. SASE. Reports in 1 week.
Music: Mostly pop, country and dance; also jazz. Produced *Carnival Nights*, by Vincent C. Delucia and Raymond Squillacote (country LP); *Impulse*, by Danny Darrow (dance LP); and *Corporate Lady*, by Michael Greer (pop), all recorded by Danny Darrow on Mighty Records.
Tips: "Listen to the hits of Richie, Manilow, Houston and Rogers and write better songs."

*REMY DAVID'S AUDIO OASIS, 4526 Orr Dr., Chantilly VA 22021. (800)YO-OASIS. Independent Producer: Remy David. Estab. 1981. Deals with artists and songwriters. Fee derived from sales royalty when song or artist is recorded, outright fee from recording artist, or outright fee from record company.
How to Contact: Submit demo tape by mail. Unsolicited submissions are OK. Prefers cassette.
Music: Mostly jazz, rock and pop/blues; also opera.
Tips: "I produce live recordings."

*MAL DAVIS, 730 S. Harvey, Oak Park IL 60304. (708)386-7355 or (708)653-1919. Producer: Mal Davis. Record producer and engineer. Deals with artists and songwriters. Produces 4 singles and 4 LPs/year. Fee derived from sales royalty or outright fee from songwriter/artist or record company.
How to Contact: Prefers cassette, 7½ or 15 ips reel-to-reel (or VHS videocassette or DAT) with 2-6 songs and lyric or lead sheet. Does not return unsolicited material; SASE for reply. Reports in 8 weeks.
Music: Mostly contemporary gospel, MOR rock, progressive rock and jazz; also country. Co-produced and engineered "Time To Fly," written and recorded by Chris Christensen (contemporary Christian); "Random Factor" (instrumental); engineered "Master and Musician," by Phil Keaggy; and engineered "Over All the World," by James Ward.

*MIKE DE LEON PRODUCTIONS, 14146 Woodstream, San Antonio TX 78231. (512)492-0613. Owner: Mike De Leon. Record producer, music publisher (BMI) and record company (Antonio Records). Estab. 1983. Deals with artists and songwriters. Produces 15 singles and 5 LPs/year. Receives 10 submissions/month. Fee derived from sales royalty when song or artist is recorded and outright fee from record company.
How to Contact: Submit demo tape by mail. Unsolicited submissions are OK. Prefers cassette (or VHS videocassette if available) with any number of songs and lyric or lead sheets. "Include contact number and any promo materials." SASE. Reports in 2 months.
Music: Mostly pop/rock, R&B and Latin. Produced *Marina's Momento*, recorded by Marina Chapa; *Elegante*, written and recorded by DeLeon Bros.; and *Debut*, written and recorded by Claudia (all LPs).
Tips: "Feel free to submit material, but be patient. New material is constantly being sought by everyone. All *good* material consistently succeeds."

EDWARD DE MILES, 8th Floor, 4475 Allisonville Rd., Indianapolis IN 46205. (317)549-9006. President: Edward De Miles. Record producer, music publisher (Edward De Miles Music Co./BMI), record company (Sahara Records). Estab. 1981. Deals with artists and songwriters. Produces 15-20 singles, 15-20 12″ singles, 5-10 LPs and 5-10 CDs. Receives 100 submissions/year. Fee derived from sales royalty.
How to Contact: Write or call first and obtain permission to submit. Prefers cassette (or VHS or Beta ½″ videocassette if available) with 1-3 songs and lyric sheet. Does not return unsolicited material. Reports in 1 week.
Music: Mostly R&B/dance, top 40 pop/rock and contemporary jazz; also country, TV and film themes—songs and jingles. Produced "Mr It," written and recorded by Steve Lynn (R&B); "No Mercy" (by D. Evans, A. Mitchel), recorded by Multiple Choice (rap); and "Forever," written and recorded by Steve Lynn (ballad); all on Sahara Records. Other artists include Lost in Wonder, D'von Edwards and Ultimate Force.
Tips: "Copyright all material before submitting. Equipment and showmanship a must."

DEMI MONDE RECORDS & PUBLISHING LTD., Foel Studio, Llanfair Caereinion, Powys, SY21 0RZ Wales. 0938-810758. Managing Director: Dave Anderson. Record producer, music publisher (PRS & MCPS) and record company (Demi Monde Records). Estab. 1982. Deals with artists and songwriters. Produces 5 singles, 15 12″ singles, 15 LPs and 10 CDs/year. Fee derived from combination of sales royalty, outright fee from recording artist, outright fee from record company and studio production time.
How to Contact: Submit demo tape by mail. Unsolicited submissions are okay. Prefers cassette with 3 or 4 songs and lyric sheet. SASE. Reports in 2 months.
Music: Mostly rock, pop and blues. Produces *Hawkwind* (by D. Brock); *Atomic Rooster* (by J. Ducann); and *Ozril Tentacles* (by E. Wynn), all on Demi Monde Records (LP).

***DETROIT PRODUCTIONS,** Box 265, N. Hollywood CA 91603-0265. (818)569-5653. President/Executive Producer: Randy De Troit. Vice President: Ciara Dortch. Co-Producer: Porter Stewart. Independent Television Producer of network TV shows, cable-TV series. Works with freelance producers/promoters for local and national broadcast on assignment basis only; gives unlimited assignments per year. Buys all rights outright or pays percentage if applicable.
How to Contact: "Send edited version of work on VHS or broadcast quality tape. All categories above plus surrealism, new concept, idealistic or abstract material by mail for consideration; provide resume/bio with photos (if available) for filing for possible future assignments." SASE. Reports within one month.
Music: Produces weekly Cable-TV series—"Inner-Tube Presents." Features actors, actresses, singers, bands, models, dancers, rappers and whole independent production companies for Chicago Access Network channels 19 and 21. Produces documentaries, industrials, commercials, musicals, talent showcases (new performers), news, plays, lectures, concerts, talk-show format with host, music-videos, contests. Uses all types of programming; formats are color Super-VHS, broadcast quality ¾″ and 1″ Videotape, or film to video.
Tips: "An imaginative freelance producer is an invaluable asset to any production house, not only as a constant source of new and fresh ideas, but also for pre- and post-production supportive elements, contributing just as much as any staffer. Because of the nature of the business, we tend to be more open to outside sources, especially when it is to our benefit to keep new blood flowing. Indies tend to lean towards seeking unknowns, because their styles are usually, in our opinion, more unique."

CARLO DITTA, #563, 828 Royal St., New Orleans LA 70116. Contact: Carlo Ditta. Record producer, music publisher (Attid Music Co./ASCAP) and record company (Orleans Records). Estab. 1986. Deals with artists and songwriters. Produces 3 LPs and 2 CDs/year. Fee derived from sales royalty when song or artists is recorded or outright fee from record company. Charges artists for production services.
How to Contact: Submit demo tape by mail. Unsolicited submissions are OK. Prefers cassette (or VHS videocassette) with 5 songs and lyric sheets. SASE.
Music: Mostly soul, folk and country; also pop, gospel, blues and R&B. Produced *Why* (by Carlo Ditta), recorded by Mighty Sam; *Miss Bea* (by Sam McClain), recorded by Mighty Sam; and *The Story of My Life* (by Eddie Jones), recorded by Guitar Slim Jr.; all on Orleans Records (all LPs). Other artists include The New Indians, Willy Deville and Robert Lowery.

DRAGON RECORDS, INC., 872 Morris Park Ave., Bronx NY 10462. (212)792-2198. Vice President: Mr. "G". Record producer and music publisher (Vin-Joy Publishing). Estab. 1954. Deals with artists and songwriters. Produces 16 singles, 20 LPs and 10 CDs/year. Receives 100 submissions/month. Fee derived from sales royalty.

How to Contact: "We accept material by recommendation only."
Music: Easy listening, country, MOR and top 40/pop. Produced "Promise Me" (by J. Heath), recorded by Smokey Heath; "A Letter to D.J." (by V. Gagliano) and "One Prayer" (by Gagliano and Heath), both recorded by Joyce Heath (both singles). Other artists include Dickie Do and The Don'ts, The Go-Go's and Prometheus.

*DUANE MUSIC, INC., 382 Clarence Ave., Sunnyvale CA 94086. (408)739-6133. President: Garrie Thompson. Record producer and music publisher. Deals with artists and songwriters. Fee derived from sales royalty.
How to Contact: Prefers cassette with 1-2 songs. SASE. Reports in 1 month.
Music: Blues, country, rock, soul and top 40/pop. Produced "Wichita," on Hush Records (country single); and "Syndicate of Sound," on Buddah Records (rock single).

*JAMIE DYCE/RADIO ACTIVE RECORDS, 210 Academy Dr., Thunder Bay ON P7B 5N6 **Canada**. Phone: (807)344-0357. Producer: Jamie Dyce. Record producer, music publisher (Cybernetic Music/CAPAC), record company (Radio Active Records) and mail order demo service, Amazon Advertizing. Estab. 1987. Deals with artists and songwriters. Produces 10 singles and 3 LP/year. Receives 20 submissions/month. Charges outright fee for mail order demo service.
How to Contact: Submit demo tape by mail. Unsolicited submissions are OK. Prefers cassette with 3 songs and lyric sheets. "We are accepting submissions by lyricists to combine with songwriters who are weak lyrically. The theme of the lyric should be intense or moving. Lyrics should bring images to mind. Have a sense of humor." SASE. Reports if interested.
Music: Mostly rock, pop and country; also heavy metal. Produced "Daystar Shine Down on Me," written and recorded by Agnes Seargeant on Radioactive Records (gospel); "Fallen Angel," written and recorded by Fallen Angel on Radioactive Records (metal/rock); and "Criwolf" (Gleeson/Isherwood/Dyce), recorded by Criwolf on Wave/Radioactive Records (rock/pop). Other artists include Jamie Dyce, Lori L, Elaine Lai, Rick Hautala and Baby Huey.
Tips: "Learn to be objective about your material as well as other people's material. Try to identify the factors that make a great song and apply these principles to your music."

*E P PRODUCTIONS, 7455 Lorge Cr., Huntington Beach CA 92647. (714)842-5524. Business Manager: Billy Purnell. Record producer and record company (Venue Records, Branden Records). Estab. 1987. Deals with artists and songwriters. Produces 5-10 singles, 1-2 12″ singles, 2-5 LPs, 1-5 EPs and 1 CD/year. Receives 15-20 submissions/year. Fee derived from sales royalty when song or artist is recorded, outright fee from recording artist and outright fee from record company. (All terms are negotiable.) "Some artists come to us for production work only—not on our label. For this we charge a flat fee. We *never* charge songwriters unless for demos only."
How to Contact: Submit demo tape by mail. Unsolicited submissions are OK. Prefers cassette with 1-3 songs and lyric sheet. Does not return unsolicited material. Reports in 2 weeks.
Music: Mostly pop, R&B and contemporary Christian; also country and rock. Produced *Blushed*, written and recorded by London Issue on Venue Records (techno dance EP); "Cactus Walk," written and recorded by Debbie Kay on Branden Records (country/pop); and "Brand New Morning," written and recorded by Christopher Schadt on Branden Records (new folk). Other artists include Jeremy Davis, Howard Cowles, Billie Courtright, Joanna Duffin, Patty Booker, Reiko Takahashi and Bob Curran.
Tips: "Be professional—typed lyric sheets and cover letter are so much easier to work with along with a well-produced demo. Don't compromise on the quality of your songs or your package."

*E.S.R. PRODUCTIONS, 61 Burnthouse Lane, Exeter Devon EX2 6AZ **U.K.**. Phone: (0392)57880. Contact: John Greenslade. Record producer and record company (E.S.R.). Estab. 1965. Deals with artists and songwriters. Produces 4 singles and 10 LPs/year. Receives 10 submissions/year. Fee derived from outright fee from recording artist.
How to Contact: Submit demo tape by mail. Unsolicited submissions are OK. Prefers cassette with 4 songs and lyric sheet. SASE. Reports in 1 month.
Music: Mostly country, pop and R&B. Produced "I Will Ask Again" (by Mike Scott), recorded by J. Greenslade (pop single); *Mascarade* (by J. Greenslade), recorded by Mascaradde (MOR LP); and *Can't Imagine* (by J. Greenslade), recorded by Mike Scott (pop album); all on E.S.R. Records. Other artists include Johnny Ramone, Barracuda, Johnny Solo, Karen and Marty O'Henry.

Listings of companies in countries other than the U.S. have the name of the country in boldface type.

LEO J. EIFFERT, P.O. Box 5412, Buena Park CA 90620. (213)721-7260. Owner: Leo J. Eiffert, Jr. Record producer, music publisher (Eb-Tide Music/BMI, Young Country Music/BMI) and record company (Plain Country). Estab. 1967. Deals with artists and songwriters. Produces 15-20 singles and 5 LPs/year. Fee derived from sales royalty.
How to Contact: Submit demo tape by mail. Unsolicited submissions are OK. Prefers cassette with 2-3 songs, lyric and lead sheet. SASE. Reports in 3 weeks.
Music: Mostly country and gospel. Produced "Summer School" (by Mario Burnes and Leo J. Eiffert), recorded by Leo J. Eiffert, Jr.; "Tears Will Never Fall," written and recorded by Joe Eiffert; and "Single Life" (by Leo J. Eiffert, Jr.), recorded by Donna Jean; all on Plain Country Records (single). Other artists include Duane Austin, Crawfish Band, Wayne Meadows, Teeci Clarke, Debbie Collins and David Busson.
Tips: "Just keep it real country."

GEOFFREY ENGLAND, 2810 McBain, Redondo Beach CA 90278. (213)371-5793. Contact: Geoffrey England. Record producer. Deals with artists and songwriters. Produces 10 singles/year. Fee derived from sales royalty and/or outright fee from record company.
How to Contact: Prefers cassette and lyric sheet. SASE. Reports in 2 weeks.
Music: Mainstream melodic rock. Produced "Steppenwolf Live," on Dunhill Records; and "If Licks Could Kill," by Virgin on Statue Records.

*ENGLISH VALLEY MUSIC, 383 Forest Retreat Rd., Hendersonville TN 37075. (615)822-6341. Owner/ Producer: Jan Pulsford. Record producer (ASCAP) and record company (English Valley Music). Estab. 1988. Deals with artists' and songwriters. Produces 6 LPs and 2 CDs/year. Fee derived from sales royalty when song or artist is recorded; outright fee from recording artist; or outright fee from record company.
How to Contact: Submit demo tape by mail. Unsolicited submissions are OK. Prefers cassette with 3 songs. "Emphasize good quality songs, not good quality demos." SASE. Reports in 4 weeks.
Music: Mostly pop, dance and R&B; also rock, alternative and underground. Produced *Better Than Nothing* (by Craig Wiseman/J. Pulpeto), recorded by Tentu on EVM Records (LP); *Waiting for the Right Time*, written and recorded by Gilly Elkin on Mantabridge Records (LP); and *Identity*, written and recorded by Jan Pulsford on Atmosphere Records (CD). Other artists include The Few, Felicia Collins and Garth Hewitt.
Tips: "Work hard and leave your ego at the door. Be professional . . . our aim is to record music for music's sake but we all have to make a living. Drugs and booze went out in the 60s."

ESQUIRE INTERNATIONAL, Box 6032, Station B, Miami FL 33123. (305)547-1424. President: Jeb Stuart. Record producer, music publisher and management firm. Deals with artists and songwriters. Produces 6 singles and 2 LPs/year. Fee derived from sales royalty or independent leasing of masters and placing songs.
How to Contact: Write or call first. Prefers cassette or disc with 2-4 songs and lead sheet. SASE. Reports in 1 month.
Music: Blues, church/religious, country, dance, gospel, jazz, rock, soul and top 40/pop. Produced "Can't Count the Days," (R&B single, Kent Records); "Sitba," (R&B single, King Records); and "You're So Right For Me," (disco single, Esquire Records), all by Jeb Stuart. Other artists include Valerie and Stone Foxx.
Tips: "When sending out material make sure it is well organized, put together as neatly as possible and it is of good sound quality."

*SHANE FABER, #2A, 412 E. 78 St., New York NY 10021. (212)879-4667. Contact: Shane Faber. Record producer, music publisher (Now & Then Music/BMI) and record company (Now & Then Records). Estab. 1980. Deals with artists and songwriters. Produced 6 singles and 2 LPs/year. Fee derived from sales royalty or outright fee from recording artist or record company.
How to Contact: Submit demo tape by mail. Unsolicited submissions are OK. Prefers cassette with 4 songs and lyric sheet. SASE. Reports in 2 months.
Music: Mostly pop, dance and R&B; also rap and New Age. Produced "Partyline," recorded by 5th Platoon on SBK Records; "Turtle Power," recorded by Partners In Krime on SBK Records; and "U Shouldn't Wonder" (by Audrey Smith Bly). Other artists include Tenita Jordon (R&B), Blackhearts (rap) and T.T. (dance).

DOUG FAIELLA PRODUCTIONS, 16591 County Home Rd., Marysville OH 43040. (513)644-8295. President: Doug Faiella. Record producer, music publisher (Doug Faiella Pubishing/BMI), record company (Studio 7 Records) and recording studio. Estab. 1984. Deals with artists and songwriters. Produces 10 singles and 5 LPs/year. Fee derived from outright fee from recording artist. "Charges a flat rate per song."

How to Contact: Write first and obtain permission to submit. Include SASE. Prefers cassette with 3 songs and lyric sheets. Does not return unsolicited material. Reports in 4 weeks.
Music: Mostly country, gospel and rock. Produced *Yesterday Country*, recorded by Dago Red on Studio 7 Records (country LP).
How to Contact: Submit demo tape by mail; call first and obtain permission to submit. Prefers cassette with 3-4 songs and lyric sheets. SASE. Reports in 4 weeks.

FARALLONE PRODUCTIONS, P.O. Box 156, Saratoga CA 95071. Producer: B.H. Yoshida. Record producer, music publisher (Farallones/BMI) and record company (Farallones Productions). Estab. 1982. Deals with artists and songwriters. Produces 25 LPs and 25 CDs/year. Fee derived from sales royalty, outright fee from songwriter/artist and/or outright fee from record company.
How to Contact: Write first and obtain permission to submit. Prefers cassette. Does not return unsolicited material. Reports ASAP if interested.
Music: Mostly light rock, jazz fusion, New Age and country; also radio/TV commercials.

*R. L. FEENEY, 17th Fl., 521 5th Ave., New York NY 10175. (212)757-3638. Producer: R.L. Feeney. Record producer and record company (Factory Beat Records, Inc.). Estab. 1979. Deals with artists and songwriters. Produces 1-2 LPs/year. Fee derived from sales royalty when song or artist is recorded.
How to Contact: Submit demo tape by mail. Unsolicited submissions are OK. Prefers cassette with 4 songs. SASE. Reports in 1 month.
Music: Mostly R&B, pop and contemporary. Produced "Once You Fall In Love" (R&B ballad single) and "Same Language" (R&B single by Billy Nichols), recorded by Rena on FBR, Inc. Records.

DON FERGUSON PRODUCTIONS, P.O. Box 461892, Garland TX 75046. (214)271-8098. Producer: Don Ferguson. Record producer (Sultan Music/BMI and Illustrious Sultan/ASCAP), record company (Puzzle Records). Estab. 1972. Deals with artists and songwriters. Produces 10-15 singles, 4-5 cassettes and 2-3 CDs/year. Receives 15-75 submissions/year. "Fees are negotiated."
How to Contact: Submit demo tape by mail. Unsolicited submissions are OK. Prefers cassette with 3 songs and lyric sheet. "Include bio." SASE. Reports in 2 weeks.
Music: C&W, pop and MOR. Produced "Knock on Wood" (by S. Cropper, E. Floyd), recorded by Diane Elliott (C&W); "The Woman on Your Mind" (by L. Schonfeld), recorded by Lonny Jay (pop); and "Eight Days a Week" (by Lennon, McCartney), recorded by Mary Craig (C&W); all on Puzzle Records. Other artists include Heartland (band), Flashpoint (band), Charlie Shearer, Derek Hartis, Phil Rodgers and Jimmy Massey.

*FESTIVAL STUDIOS, 2112 17th St., Kenner LA 70062. (504)469-4403. Engineer/Producer: Rick Naiser/Michael Borrello. Record producer, music publisher (Homefront Music/BMI), record company (Homefront Records) and recording studio (Festival Studios). Estab. 1988. Deals with artists and songwriters. Produces 12 singles, 6 12″ singles, 15 LPs, 10 EPs and 5 CDs/year. Fee derived from sales royalty or outright fee from reocrding artist or record company.
How to Contact: Submit demo tape by mail. Unsolicited submissions are OK. Prefers cassette, DAT or ½″ VHS or Beta videocassette with 4 songs. "Send any pictures, press clips, reviews and any promo material available." Reports in 1 month.
Music: Mostly rock, pop and New Age; also rap, R&B and other. Produced *In It To Win It* (by Def Boyz), on Big T Records (rap LP); *EHG* (by EHG), on Intellectual Convulsion Records (sludge metal LP); and *Red Headed Step Children of Rock* (by Force of Habit), on Riffish Records (pop LP); all recorded by Festival. Other artists include Ice Mike, Ice Nine, RSBR, Common Knowledge and Mooncrikits.
Tips: "Concentrate on songwriting as a craft—don't spend time or money on embellishing demos. Raw demos leave room for the producer's creative input. Record demos quickly and move on to the next project."

CHARLIE FIELDS, 44 Music Sq. E., Nashville TN 37203. (615)255-2175. President: Charlie Fields. Record producer, music publisher (Jason Dee Music/BMI and Mr. Mort Music/ASCAP) and record company (Charta Records and Delux Records). Deals with artists and songwriters. Produces 10 singles/year, 6-8 12″ singles, 8 LPs and 8 CDs/year. Receives 150-200 submissions/month. Fee derived from sales.
How to Contact: Prefers cassette or reel-to-reel with 3-4 songs and lyric sheet. SASE. Reports in 3 weeks.
Music: Mostly rock, pop and country; also bluegrass. Produced "Addicted to You" (by J. Hitzler), recorded by Jeannie Marie; "I'm Layin' Down the Law" (by C.W. Fields), recorded by Lori Johnson; and "Multiple Choice," written and recorded by Jack Johnson; all country singles on Charta Records. Other artists include Lori and Jack Johnson, Donna Darlene, Fran Nickens and Jeannie Marie.

FIRST TIME MANAGEMENT & PRODUCTION CO., Sovereign House, 12 Trewartha Rd., Praa Sands, Penzance, Cornwall TR20 9ST **England.** Phone (0736)762826. FAX: (0736)763328. Managing Director: Roderick G. Jones. Record producer, music publisher (First Time Music Publishing U.K. Ltd. MCPS/PRS), record company (First Time, Mohock Records, Rainy Day Records and Pure Gold Records), licensed and subsidiary labels and management firm (First Time Management & Production Co.). Estab. 1986. Deals with artists and songwriters. Produces 5-10 singles and 5 LPs/year. EPs and CDs subject to requirements. Fee derived from sales royalty.
How to Contact: Prefers cassette with unlimited number of songs and lyric or lead sheets. SAE and IRC. Reports in 10 weeks.
Music: Mostly country/folk, pop/top 40, country with an Irish/Scottish crossover, rock, soul, jazz funk, fusion, dance and reggae. Produced "Jazz" (by Lockwood/Pusey), recorded by Fadermaster and the Beat (dance) on Digimix International Records; "Here I Stand" (by Jones/Cook), recorded by Colin Eade on First Time Records (instrumental library music); and "When Tomorrow Never Comes" (by C. Eade/Q. Hafeez), recorded by Kenny McKie on Rainy Day Records (pop ballad). Other artists include Willow (pop-folk), Nick White (country) and compilation of artists on LPs (pop-soul).

FM-REVOLVER RECORDS LTD., 152 Goldthorn Hill, Penn, Wolverhampton, WV2 3JA, **England**. Also, 28 Talbot Rd., London W2 JLJ **England**. Tel. 071-243-0992, 44-(0)902-345345. A&R: Carl Slater. Record producer, music publisher (Rocksong Music Publishing Co.) and record company (Heavy Metal America, Heavy Metal Records, Heavy Metal Worldwide, FM Records and Black, Revolver Records). Works with artists, songwriters and label producers. Produces 35 LPs/year.
How to Contact: Prefers cassette (or VHS/PAL or NTJC videocassette if available) with 1-3 songs. Does not return unsolicited material. Reports in 1 month.
Music: Pop, rock, AOR, dance and alternative. Artists include White Sister, Jack Green and King Kobra.
Tips: "Send good photographs, short bio (50-100 words maximum); and *relevant* press clippings, i.e., charts, etc."

FOLSOM PRODUCTIONS, 43 McKee Dr., Mahwah NJ 07430. (201)529-3550. President: Edward Feldsott. Vice President: Robert Feldsott. Record producer and artist management company. Estab. 1988. Deals with artists and songwriters. Produces 2 singles, 1 LP and 4 EPs/year. Receives 5-10 submissions/month. Fee derived from sales royalty.
How to Contact: Submit demo tape by mail. Unsolicited submissions are OK. Prefers cassette with 1-3 songs. SASE. Reports in 2 months.
Music: Mostly rock, pop and blues. Produced "Stranger in Town," written and recorded by Mick Taylor on Mate Records (blues/rock). Artists include Paul Dianno, Stone Poets and Dash Rip Rock.
Tips: "Keep in mind the artist you are writing for and his/her limits."

FOX FARM RECORDING, 2731 Saundersville Ferry Rd., Mt. Juliet TN 37122. (615)754-2444. President: Kent Fox. Record producer (Mercantile Productions) and music publisher (Mercantile Music/BMI and Blueford Music/ASCAP). Estab. 1970. Deals with artists and songwriters. Produces 20 singles/year. Fee derived from outright fee from recording artists. Charges in advance for studio time.
How to Contact: Submit demo tape by mail. Unsolicited submissions are OK. Prefers cassette (or VHS videocassette if available). SASE. Reports in 3 months.
Music: Country, bluegrass and gospel.

BOB SCOTT FRICK, 404 Bluegrass Ave., Madison TN 37115. (615)865-6380. Contact: Bob Scott Frick. Record producer and music publisher (R.E.F.). Estab. 1958. Deals with artists and songwriters only. Produces 12 singles, 30 12″ singles and 30 LPs.
How to Contact: Submit demo tape by mail. Unsolicited submissions are OK. Write first and obtain permission to submit.
Music: Produced "I Found Jesus in Nashville," recorded by Bob Scott Frick; "Love Divine," recorded by Backwoods; and "A Tribute," recorded by Visionheirs on R.E.F. (gospel). Other artists include Larry Ahlborn, Bob Myers Family, David Barton, The Mattingleys and Jim Pommert.

*THE FRICON ENTERTAINMENT CO., INC., 1048 S. Ogden Dr., Los Angeles CA 90019. (213)931-7323. Attention: Publishing Department. Music publisher (Fricon Music Co./BMI, Fricon Music Co./ASCAP) and library material. Estab. 1981. Deals with songwriters only. Fee derived from sales royalty.
How to Contact: Write first and obtain permission to submit. Prefers cassette with 1 song and lyric and lead sheet. SASE. Reports in 6 weeks.
Music: Mostly TV/film, R&B and rock; also pop, country and gospel.

*G FINE, Box 180, Cooper Station, New York NY 10276. (212)995-1608. Vice President: Lyvio G. Record producer, music publisher (Rap Alliance, Inc.) and record company (G Fine). Estab. 1986. Fee derived from sales royalty or outright fee from recording artist or record company.

How to Contact: Submit demo tape by mail. Unsolicited submissions are OK. Prefers cassette with 3 or more songs. "Send photo, if possible." SASE. Reports in 1 month.
Music: R&B, rap and progressive rock; also dance.

*BOB GAFFNEY PRODUCTIONS, Suite A, 9375 SW 61 Way, Boca Raton FL 33428. President: Bob Gaffney. Record producer and music publisher (Bob Gaffney Music/BMI). Estab. 1987. Deals with artists and songwriters. Produces 6 singles, 6 12" singles, 6 LPs and 6 CDs/year. Fee derived from sales royalty or outright fee from recording artist or record company.
How to Contact: Submit demo tape by mail. Unsolicited submissions are OK. Prefers cassette with 1-4 songs and lyric sheet. "Please, no phone calls." SASE. Reports in 3 weeks.
Music: Pop, R&B and rock; also dance, rap and country. Produced "Rumor Has It" (by Gaffney/Walker), recorded by Phil Walker (country/single); "Hear My Hands," written and recorded by Suzie Vigon (ballad/single); and "Broken Hearted" (by Robert and Sue Oveits), recorded by Eyes of Pandora (rock/single).
Editor's Note: As of press time, Bob Gaffney Productions is no longer in operation. Refrain from submitting any material to this company.

JACK GALE, P.O. Box 630755, Miami FL 33163. (305)935-4880. Contact: Jack Gale. Record producer, music publisher (Cowabonga Music/ASCAP) and record company (Playback Records). Estab. 1983. Deals with artists and songwriters. Produces 48 singles, 10 LPs and 10 CDs/year. Fee derived from sales royalty.
How to Contact: Submit demo tape by mail. Unsolicited submissions are OK. Prefers cassette (or VHS videocassette if available) with 2 songs and lyric sheets. Does not return unsolicited material. "We report back immediately if we are interested."
Music: Mostly contemporary country and country crossover. Produced "Shame on the Moon" (by Rodney Crowell), recorded by Bonnie Guitar; "Another One of My Near Mrs. (Misses)" (by Gillon/Hammond), recorded by Bobby Bare and Donnie Bowser; and "Blue Christmas," by David Frizzell; all on Playback Records (country). Other artists include PJ Allman, Del Reeves, Dennis Yost & Classics Four, Juanita Rose, Sammi Smith, Darnell Miller, Sylvie & Her Silver Dollar Band, Mac Bailey and David Heavener.
Tips: "Our doors are always open to new artists and writers, just keep at it. If you have talent and are persistent, it will happen. Just learn to overcome the magic word in the music business . . . rejection."

*GEORGE D. PRODUCTIONS, INC., #3, 19300 SW 106 Ave., Miami FL 33157. (305)573-5767. Director/Producer: George D. Record producer, music publisher (BMI) and a newly developed demo label (Custom Sounds). Estab. 1990. Deals with artists and songwriters. Fee derived from sales royalty when song or artist is recorded, outright fee from recording artist or outright fee from record company.
How to Contact: Submit demo tape by mail. Unsolicited submissions are OK. Prefers cassette with 2 songs and lyric sheet. SASE. Reports in 3 weeks.
Music: Mostly R&B, rap and dance; also jazz, reggae and pop. Produced "Mary Goes Round" (by L. Harrington), recorded by A.M.N. (12" record); "Break It On Down" (by T. Higgins), recorded by Mellow J. (12" record); and "Stranger," written and recorded by C. Robeldo (12" record); all on Amran Records.
Tips: "We are a new registered label looking for all new and dedicated talent. We do not want hype, we want substance. We're starting out as a demo label for the first 6 months until our success grows. We invite all to grow with us."

THE GLAND PUPPIES, INC., 203 Westmoreland, Naperville IL 60540. (708)357-3353. President: John Klopp. Record producer. Estab. 1989. Deals with artists and songwriters. Produces 7-10 singles, 3 LPs and 3 EPs/year. Fee derived from sales royalty.
How to Contact: Submit demo tape by mail. Unsolicited submissions are OK. Prefers cassette with 4-8 songs and lyric sheet. "Send *your* favorite songs, not the songs your friends like, just because they sound like what's being played on the radio." SASE. Reports in 3 weeks.
Music: Mostly New Age, pop/dance and folk songs; also comedy, gypsy/dance and thrash metal. Produced *Secret Love*, written and recorded by The Gland Puppies on Sick Dog Records (rock LP); "Mr. Hamburger" (by Exotic Food), recorded by Edy Heady on Bland Yuppy Records (single); *Two Late Four Love* (by Exotic Food), recorded by Edy Heady on Bland Puppy Records (cassette LP).
Tips: "Don't try to be a Bon Jovi sound alike. Go for something new! It's the only way to make it to the top. Playing covers may make you money to get by, but doing something new is the best way to actually start the new trend."

*JON GORR/MASSMEDIA, 7105 Reynolds St., Pittsburgh PA 15208. (412)247-1301. President: Jon Gorr. Record producer, music publisher (BMI) and record company (Massmedia). Estab. 1983. Deals with artists and songwriters. Produces 5 singles and 2 LPs/year. Fee derived from sales royalty or outright fee from recording artist.

How to Contact: Submit demo tape by mail. Unsolicited submissions are OK. Prefers cassette with 3 songs. Does not return unsolicited material. Reports in 1 month.
Music: Mostly rock, New Age and reggae. Artists include Albert Griffiths and The Gladiators, Steve Recker Band, The I-Tones and Bo Diddley.

*GRAPEVINE STUDIOS, P.O. Box 8374, Gadsden AL 35902. (205)442-3330. Owner: Chris Mahy. Recording studio. Estab. 1988. Deals with artists and songwriters. Produces 20 LPs and 10 CDs/year. Fee derived from outright fee from recording artists or outright fee from record company. "Charges artists 10% in advance to book studio time."
How to Contact: Write or call first and obtain permission to submit. Prefers cassette with several songs and lead sheet. SASE. Reports in 2 months.
Music: Mostly gospel, pop and jazz; also country and rock. Produced *Get Ready* (by Penny Halloway) and *Welcome To The Human Race* (by Bob McLeod), recorded by Glory Bound Trio on Independent Records (LP).

*GRASS RECORDING AND SOUND, 800 Arbor Place, Del Rey Oaks CA 93940. (408)394-1065. Owner: Michael Grass. Record producer, record company (Blackend Earth, Rabid Records) and recording studio (Live Sound Service). Estab. 1989. Deals with artists and songwriters. Produces 2 singles, 1 LP and 4 EPs/year. Fee derived from sales royalty when song or artists is recorded and outright fee from recording artist. "We sometimes require 50% cash deposit for recording only."
How to Contact: Submit demo tape by mail. Unsolicited submissions are OK. Prefers cassette (or VHS videocassette if available) with 1-5 songs and lyric sheet. "Don't be overly persistent. I will listen to *all* tapes, and if I like you, I'll call you." Does not return unsolicited submissions. Reports in 2 months.
Music: Mostly thrash metal, mainstream metal and hard rock; also punk, rap and fusion. Produced *3 Faces* (by Bilac), recorded by Cremation on Blackend Earth Records (thrash EP); *Endless* (by Lopez), recorded by Labyrinth on Rabid Records (metal EP); and *R.P.M* (by Goyat), recorded by Speed Demon on Rabid Records (thrash EP). Other artists include Gary Souza, The Broadway Band and Bradley Burchell.
Tips: "Too many posers! No Milli Vanilli! I like the funk/thrash fusion bands that are literally exploding on the West Coast."

*RL HAMMEL ASSOCIATES,INC., P.O. Box 531, Alexandria IN 46001-0531. Contact: Randal L. Hammel. Record producer, music publisher (Ladnar Music/ASCAP) and consultants. Estab. 1973. Deals with artists and songwriters. Produces 4 singles, 4 LPs, 2 EPs and 4 CDs/year. Receives 50-75 submissions/month. Fee derived from sales royalty, outright fee from artist/songwriter or record company, or negotiable fee per project.
How to Contact: Write first and obtain permission to submit, include brief resume (including experience, age, goal). Prefers cassette with 3 songs maximum. "Lyrics (preferably typed) *must* accompany tapes." SASE. Reports as soon as possible.
Music: Blues, church/religious, country, easy listening, gospel, MOR, progressive, R&B, rock (usually country), soul and top 40/pop. Produced *E-Z KE1* on Imday Records; *At The Table*, recorded by Casey Lardry on Epoch Records (Catholic); and *Dare To Believe*, on Word Records (contemporary Christian). Other artists include Overeasy, Heigh-Liters, Morris Chapman, Jeff Steinberg, Carlton-Taylor Band, Carey Landry and Shannon.
Tips: "Only those who have a full knowledge of the sacrifice involved with this industry (or those willing to hear it) should consider contacting this office. We shoot straight, and it is *always* explained our observations are just that—'ours', and another company/production team will present a different opinion. Always get a second opinion (or more)."

MARK HANNAH PRODUCTIONS, Suite 250, 1075 N.W. Murray Rd., Portland OR 97229. (503)642-4201. Owner: Mark Hannah. Record producer, music publisher (Mark Hannah Music Group/BMI), record company (Radioactive Records) and Mark Hannah Management/personal manager. Estab. 1985. Deals with artists and songwriters. Produces 5-10 singles, 1-3 LPs and 1-3 EPs/year. Fee derived from sales royalty.
How to Contact: Write first and obtain permission to submit. Prefers cassette or 15 ips reel-to-reel with 1-3 songs and lyric or lead sheets. SASE. Reports in 1 month.
Music: Mostly rock, pop and country; also fusion, New Age and jazz. Produced *Modern Day Man*, written and recorded by M. Hannah (hard rock LP); "Crazy Fool," written and recorded by M. Harrop (pop ballad single); "Billy," written and recorded by Syndi Helms (country single); "You Stole My Heart Away," written and recorded by P. Witt (pop-rock single); "Forced to Have Sex with an Alien," written and recorded by M. Harrop (comedy single); and *Desert Moon*, written and recorded by M. Hannah (New Age LP); all on Radioactive Records. Other artists include Ray Overton, Rex E. Plew and Messenger (rock band).

HARD HAT PRODUCTIONS, 519 N. Halifax Ave., Daytona Beach FL 32118-4017. (904)252-0381. President/Producer: Bobby Lee Cude. Record producer, music publisher (Cude & Pickens Publishing) and record company (Hard Hat). Estab. 1978. Works with artists only. Fee derived from contract. Produces 12 singles and 4 LPs/year.
How to Contact: Produces "only in-house material." Write first and obtain permission to submit. Prefers cassette with 4 songs and lyric sheet "from performing artists only."
Music: Mostly pop, country and easy listening; also MOR, top 40/pop and Broadway show music. Produced "V-A-C-A-T-I-O-N" (by Cude/Pickens), recorded by The Hard Hatters (pop single); "Just a Piece of Paper" and "Worried Worried Men" (by Cude/Pickens), recorded by the Blue Bandana Country Band (country singles); all on Hard Hat Records. Also, "Blow Blow Stereo," "Don't Stop," "Hootchie Cootch Girl" and "There Ain't No Beer in Heaven That's Why I Drink It Here," all by Caz Allen on Hard Hat Records.

STEPHEN A. HART/HART PRODUCTIONS, 1690 Creekview Cir., Petaluma CA 94954. (707)762-2521. Executive Producer: Stephen A. Hart. Record producer. Estab. 1975. Deals with artists and songwriters. Produces 8 LPs and 8 CDs/year. Fee derived from outright fee from recording artist or record company.
How to Contact: Submit demo by mail. Prefers cassette with 3 songs and lyric sheet. Does not return unsolicited material. Reports in 6 weeks.
Music: Mostly pop, rock and instrumental. Produced *Liberi-Liberi* (by Vasco Rossi), on EMI Records; *Stien/Walder* (by Stien/Walder) on Narada/MCA Records; and *Uzeb Club* (by Carron/Brouchu/Cusson) on Select Records (CD/LP); all recorded by Stephen Hart.

ERNIE HATTON/BILL WINBORNE/SANDY CONTELLA, P.O. Box 4157, Winter Park FL 32793. (407)657-6016. Contact: Producer. Record producer, music publisher (BMI) and record company (Earth & Sky Records). Estab. 1977. Deals with artists and songwriters. Fee derived from royalty.
How to Contact: Submit demo tape by mail. Unsolicited submissions are OK. Prefers cassette (or VHS videocassette if available) with 3 songs and lyric sheet. "Send tape with vocal and without vocal (background tracks)." SASE. Reports in 2 months.
Music: Mostly up-tempo pop, pop ballad and soft rock; also country. Produced "Catch a Snowflake" (by Hatton-Scott), recorded by Janet O. Neale (pop Christmas); "Plant a Tree" (by Hatton-Baumer), recorded by Beach Girls (pop); and "Seasons" (by Hatton-Hurley), recorded by Sandy Contella (pop ballad), all on E&S Records.
Tips: "Send good demo—strong lyrics and very good hook; up-tempo material (pop) needed now for young teenage female (Gibson—Tiffany type material). Also ballads for strong Englebert type and pop jazz for female."

*HEARING EAR, 730 S. Harvey, Oak Park IL 60304. (708)386-7355. Owner: Mal Davis. Record producer. Estab. 1985. Deals with artists and songwriters. Produces and/or engineers 6 LPs and 4 CDs/month. Receives 6 submissions/month. Fee derived from sales royalty when song or artist is recorded, outright fee from recording artist or outright fee from record company.
How to Contact: Write first and obtain permission to submit. Prefers cassette (or VHS videocassette if available) with up to 6 songs and lyric or lead sheets. Does not return unsolicited material.
Music: Mostly pop, gospel and rock; also R&B, rap and metal. Engineered *Over All The World* (by James Ward), on MTD Records (contemporary gospel LP); "40 Seconds" (by Ken Medema), on Briar Patch Records (contemporary gospel single); and *Time To Fly*, by Chris Christensen (contemporary gospel LP).

LAWRENCE HERBST, P.O. Box 3842, Houston TX 77253. President: Lawrence Herbst. Record producer, music publisher (Beverly Hills Music Publishing/BMI, Klarr Music Publishing) and record company (Beverly Hills, Lawrence Herbst, Best-Way, Total Sound, D.T.I. and Larr Records) and Klarrco Satellite Radio and TV. Estab. 1966. Deals with songwriters and artists. Produces 1 single and 1 LP/year. Fee derived from sales royalty or outright fee from record company.
How to Contact: Prefers 7½ ips reel-to-reel (or VHS videocassette if available) with 1 song and lead sheet. "Do a professional recording tape in a studio if you want to work with us." SASE. Reports in 6 weeks.
Music: Mostly rock, country and gospel.

*HERITAGE MUSIC, #311, 41 Antrim Cr., Scarborough ON M1P4T1 **Canada.** (416)292-4724. President: Jack Boswell. Record producer and record company (Condor-Oak). Estab. 1967. Deals with artists and songwriters. Produces 10-15 LPs/year. Fee derived from sales royalty.
How to Contact: Submit demo tape by mail. Unsolicited submissions are OK. Prefers cassette with 3-4 songs and lyric sheet. Reports in 4-5 weeks.
Music: Mostly country, country gospel and instrumental.

HIGHLAND RECORDS, P.O. Box 554, Los Gatos CA 95031. (408)353-3952. Producer: Joe Weed. Record producer, music publisher (Highland Records/BMI) and record company (Highland Records). Estab. 1986. Deals with artists and songwriters. Produces 3-4 LPs and 3-4 CDs/year. Fee derived from sales royalty or outright fee from recording artist.
How to Contact: Write to obtain permission to submit. Prefers cassette with 3 songs; no vocals. Instrumental music only. Does not return unsolicited material. Reports in 4-6 weeks.
Music: Mostly acoustic New Age, new acoustic, folk; also country. Produced *Dream of the Manatee*, written and recorded by Weed/Hellman on Gouro Music (New Age/folk CD); *Indiana Moon*, written and recorded by Scott Freed on LKA Records (country LP cassette); *Waltz of the Whippoorwill*, written and recorded by Joe Weed on Highland Records (new acoustic LP). Other artists include Steve Kritzer.
Tips: "Submit only well-composed, all-instrumental music in new acoustic, New Age or folk styles."

HOBAR PRODUCTION, 27 Newton Pl., Irvinston NJ 07111. (201)375-6633. President: Randall Burney. Record producer, record company (Independent). Estab. 1987. Deals with artists and songwriters. Produces 4 singles, 6 12″ singles and 2 LPs/year. Fee derived from outright fee from record company.
How to Contact: Submit demo tape by mail. Unsolicited submissions are OK. Prefers cassette (or VHS videocassette if available) with 4 songs and lyric or lead sheets. SASE. Reports in 3 weeks.
Music: Mostly R&B, pop and gospel; also country and rap.

HOGAR MUSICAL PRODUCTIONS, 4225 Palm St., Baton Rouge LA 70808. (504)383-7885. President: Barrie Edgar. Record producer and music publisher (Silverfoot). Deals with artists and songwriters. Produces 0-5 singles and 0-2 LPs/year. Receives 75 submissions/year. Fee derived from outright fee from record company.
How to Contact: Prefers cassette with maximum 4 songs and lyric sheet. SASE.
Music: Mostly rock, blues ("not soul"), country and pop. Produced "Louisiana's Basin Child," by Top Secret (rock single, Gulfstream Records).
Tips: "Send me a happy story song (light hearted beat)."

*HORIZON RECORDING STUDIO, Rte. 1, Box 306, Seguin TX 78155. (512)372-2923. Owner/Producer: H.M. Byron. Record producer, music publisher (Route One Music/BMI) and record company (Route One Records, Starmaker Records). Estab. 1988. Deals with artists and songwriters. Produces 25-30 singles and 5-7 LPs/year. Fee derived from sales royalty when song or artist is recorded or outright fee from recording artist.
How to Contact: Prefers cassette (or VHS videocassette if available) with a maximum of 5 songs and lyric sheet. Reports in 3 weeks.
Music: Mostly country, gospel and pop. Produced "The Last Song" (by B. Dees, R. Orbison), recorded by Mike Lord on BSW Records (country); and "Mother's Lullabye," written and recorded by Dee Spillman on Route One Records (gospel). Other artists include Stan Crawford and Bobby O'Neal.
Tips: "Before spending megabucks to demo a song, submit it for appraisal. Piano or guitar and voice are all that is necessary."

HORRIGAN PRODUCTIONS, P.O. Box 41243, Los Angeles CA 90041. (213)256-0215. President/Owner: Tim Horrigan. Record producer and music publisher (Buck Young Music—BMI). Estab. 1982. Deals with artists and songwriters. Produces 5-10 singles, 3-5 LPs, 3-5 EPs and 3-5 CDs/year. Receives 100 submissions/year. Fee derived from sales royalty or outright fee from recording artist or record company. "We do some work on spec but the majority of the time we work on a work-for-hire basis."
How to Contact: Submit demo tape by mail. Unsolicited submissions are OK. Prefers cassette (or VHS videocassette if available) with 1-5 songs and lyric sheets. "Please do not call first; just let your music do the talking." SASE. Reports in 2 weeks.
Music: Mostly R&B, pop and rock; also country. Produced "Rubber Room" (by Porter Wagner), recorded by Johnny Legend on Dionysus Records (rock); "Just For Awhile," recorded by Jimmy Roland on SGP Records (R&B); and "Golden Lady" (by Stevie Wonder), recorded by Mike Quick on SGP Records (R&B). Other artists include Keo.
Tips: "Write from the heart with eyes on the charts."

*I.Y.F. PRODUCTIONS, 4B, 500 ½ E. 84th St., New York NY 10028. (212)861-8745. A&R: Steven Bentzel. Record producer, music publisher (Mia Mind Music/ASCAP) and record company (Mixedfield Records). Estab. 1990. Deals with artists and songwriters. Produced 30 singles, 8 12″ singles, 6 LPs and 8 CDs/year. Fee derived from sales royalty.

How to Contact: Submit demo tape by mail. Unsolicited submissions are OK. Prefers cassette (or VHS videocassette if available) with 3 songs. SASE. Reports in 6 weeks.
Music: Mostly rap, house, hip hop; also dance, top 40 and AOR. Produced "Boyfriend," written and recorded by Baby Oil on Profile/CBS Records (rap, single); "I've Fallen," written and recorded by Baby Oil on Profile/CBS Records (house); and "Get Down" (by Bentzel/Torio), recorded by Madonna on Replay Records (hip house). Other artists include P.O.A., Electric Sun, Clark After Dark, Papa Haha, Q.O.S. and Datman.
Tips: "Submit demos on DAT cassettes for best sound quality."

*INSPIRE PRODUCTIONS, INC., Ste. 101, 302 E. Pettigrew St., Durham NC 27701. (919)688-8563. President: Willie Hill; Vice President: Sylvestor Howell. Record producer (BMI) and record company (Joy Records). Estab. 1988. Deals with artists and songwriters. Produces 10 singles, 1 12″ single, 1 LP and 1 CD/year. Fee derived from sales royalty when song or artist is recorded.
How to Contact: Submit demo tape by mail—unsolicited submissions are OK. Prefers cassette with 4 songs and lyric sheet. Include bio and picture. Reports in 2 weeks.
Music: R&B, gospel and pop. Produced "Step By Step" (by Walter Hill), recorded by Inspire on Joy Records (R&B LP/CD).
Tips: "Do your homework."

INTRIGUE PRODUCTION, Suite 206, 6245 Bristol Parkway, Culver CA 90230. (213)417-3084, ext. 206. Producer: Larry McGee. Record producer and record company (Intrigue Productions). Estab. 1986. Deals with artists and songwriters. Produces 6 singles, 3 12″ singles, 1 LP, 4 EPs and 2 CDs/year. Fee derived from sales royalty.
How to Contact: Submit demo tape by mail. Unsolicited submissions are OK. Prefers cassette or reel-to-reel (or VHS videocassette if available) with 1-4 songs and lyric sheets. "Please put your strongest performance upfront. Select material based on other person's opinions." Does not return unsolicited material. Reports in 8 weeks.
Music: Mostly R&B, pop, rap and rock; also dance and A/C. Produced "We're No. 1" (by Liz Davis), recorded by Saxon Sisters on Boogie Band Records (pop 12″); "Captain Freedom" and "Voices" (by Kenny Simms), recorded by Shena Kriss on Mega Star Records (R&B single and EP); and *Feels So Good*, written and recorded by Bill Sawyer on Dollar Bill Records (R&B LP). Other artists include S-Quires, Jim Sapienza, Terri Parondi, Roz Smith, Allen Brothers and Gary Walker.
Tips: "Decide which marketplace you would be most competitive in. Then create a commercial concept for you or your group."

*J.L. PRODUCTIONS, 4303 Teesdale Ave., Studio City CA 91604. (818)760-7651. Owner: Jeff Lorensen. Record producer and engineer. Estab. 1988. Deals with artists only. Produces 10 singles, 15 12″ singles, 4 LPs and 4 CDs/year.
How to Contact: Submit demo tape by mail. Unsolicited submissions are OK. Prefers cassette (or VHS videocassette if available) with 3 songs and lyric sheet. SASE. Reports in 1 month.
Music: Mostly pop, rock and R&B; also alternative and New Age. Produced "Too Young to Love You," written and recorded by Timmy T. on Quality Records (pop). Mixed "Fallen Angel" (by Sami McKinney), recorded by Lisa Taylor on Giant Records (pop/R&B); and "I Want To Fall In Love" (by K.C. Porter), recorded by Lisa Taylor on Giant Records (pop/R&B). Other artists include Paul Young, Fine Young Cannibals, Kim Bassinger, Isley Bros., Troy Johnson and Earth Wind and Fire.
Tips: "Make it simple, meaningful. Write from your soul, not your mind."

*JAG STUDIO, LTD., 3801-C Western Blvd., Raleigh NC 27606. (919)821-2059. Record producer, music publisher (Electric Juice Tunes/BMI), record company (Jab Records) and recording studio. Estab. 1981. Deals with artists and songwriters. Produces 10 singles, 12 LPs and 4 CDs/year. Receives 6 submissions/month. Fee derived from outright fee from recording artist or record company.
How to Contact: Write or call first and obtain permission to submit. Does not return unsolicited material.
Music: Mostly pop/dance, rap and rock; also country and gospel. Produced *Jamie Pauhl* (by Jamie Pauhl), recorded by Byron McCay and John Custer on Mission Entertainment (LP); *Insurgence* (by Insurgence), recorded by Byron McCay on Crisis Record (LP); and *Me & the Boyz* (by Poetic Justice), recorded by Jag on Triamid Records (LP). Other artists include Johnny Quest, The Accelerators, Bad Checks, Hootie & the Blowfish, Annabel Lee, Doctor Die and Ellen Harlow.
Tips: "Be prepared. Learn something about the *BUSINESS* end of music first."

*NEAL JAMES PRODUCTIONS, P.O. Box 121626, Nashville TN 37212. (615)726-3556. President: Neal James. Record producer, music publisher (Cottage Blue Music/CBMI, Neal James Music/BMI) and record company (Hidden Cove Music/ASCAP), Estab. 1971. Produces 16 singles and 4 CDs and LPs/year. Receives 75-100 submissions/year. Deals with artists and songwriters. Fee derived from sales royalty when song or artist is recorded, outright fee from recording artist and outright fee from record company.

How to Contact: Write first and obtain permission to submit. Prefers cassette (or VHS videocassette if available) with 2 songs and lyric sheet. SASE. Reports in 1 month.

Music: Mostly country, pop/rock and R&B; also gospel. Produced *Tell Me* (by Neal James), recorded by Ted Yost on Kottage Records (country/rock); *Some Ole Dude* (by Neal James), recorded by Kenny Carr on Kottage Records (country); and *Quite Like You* (by Neal James), recorded by Phil Schmidt (country). Other artists include Reed Wilcox, Reggie Whitaker, Paula Andrea, Willie T. Buerkett and Terry Barbay. "We also produce television specials and music videos. Currently we are producing projects featuring Merle Haggard, Johnny Paycheck, Hank Cochran, George Jones, Willie Nelson and Dottie West."

SUNNY JAMES, 1051 Saxonburg Blvd., Glenshaw PA 15116. Producer: Sunny James. Record producer, music publisher, record company (Golden Triangle). Estab. 1987. Deals with artists only. Produces 2 singles, 8 12″ singles, 18 LPs and 9 CDs/year. Receives 100 submissions/month. Fee derived from sales royalty or outright fee from record company.

How to Contact: Submit demo tape by mail. Unsolicited submissions are OK. Prefers cassette, 15 ips reel-to-reel (or ½″ VHS videocassette if available) with 3 songs and lyric or lead sheet. SASE. Reports in 1 month.

Music: Mostly R&B, country, rock; also A/C and jazz. Produced "Baby Blue," written and recorded by F. Johnson (12″); "Dean Don't Wait For Me" (by F. Johnson), recorded by The Marcels (7″); and "After You," written and recorded by F. Johnson (singles); all on Golden Triangle Records. Other artists include Loney Smith, Joe DeSimone, Arnel (Elvis) Pomp., Steve Grice (The Boxtops), The Original Marcels, Bingo Mundy, Cornelius Harp, Fred Johnson, Richard Harris, Brian (Badfinger) McClain and City Heat.

ALEXANDER JANOULIS PRODUCTIONS, 1957 Kilburn Dr., Atlanta GA 30324. (404)662-6661. President: Alex Janoulis. Record producer. Deals with artists and songwriters. Produces 6 singles and 2 LPs/year. Fee derived from sales royalty or outright fee from recording artist or record company.

How to Contact: Write first and obtain permission to submit. "Letters should be short, requesting submission permission." Prefers cassette with 1-3 songs. "Tapes will not be returned without SASE." Reports in 2 months.

Music: Mostly top 40, rock, pop; also black and disco. Produced "He's A Rebel," (by Gene Pitney), recorded by Secret Lover on HotTrax Records (pop single); *Stop!*, written and recorded by the Chesterfield Kings on Mirror Records (rock LP); and *P is For Pig*, written and recorded by The Pigs on HotTrax Records (pop LP). Other artists include Night Shadows, Starfoxx, Splatter and Big Al Jano. "Album produced for Chesterfield Kings was reviewed in *Rolling Stone*."

PIERRE JAUBERT, 105 Rue De Normandie, Courbevoie 92 400 **France**. Phone: (1)4333-6515. Contact: President. Casting agent for singers to perform songs in movie soundtracks. Estab. 1959. Deals with singers and songwriters. Produces 3 singles, 2 12″ singles and 5 LPs/year. Fee derived from sales royalty.

How to Contact: Submit demo tape by mail. Prefers cassette with one song only.

Music: Dance and pop/top 40. Produced "You Call It Love" (by Karoline Kruger), by Virugen on Carrere Records (pop); "Si Je Te Mens" (by Xenia), recorded by Cariaire on Carrere Records (disco/pop); "Mirabelle" (by E. Dooh), recorded by Farid Feajer on Marshall Records (ballad) and "I Know It's a Lie" by Karoline Kruger on Carrere Records. Other artists include Richard Sanderson, Cook da Books and Katla Blas.

JAY JAY PUBLISHING & RECORD CO., 35 NE 62nd St., Miami FL 33138. (305)758-0000. Owner: Walter Jagiello. Record producer, music publisher (BMI) and record company (Jay Jay Record, Tape and Video Co.). Estab. 1951. Deals with artists and songwriters. Produces 12 singles, 12 LPs and 12 CDs/year. Fee derived from sales royalty.

How to Contact: Submit demo tape by mail. Prefers cassette (or VHS videocassette if available) with 6 songs and lyric and lead sheet. "Quality cassette or reel-to-reel, sheet music and lyrics." SASE. Reports in 2 months.

Music: Mostly ballads, love songs, country music and comedy; also polkas and waltzes. Produced *If I Was the President We'd Have Polkas in Washington* (LP), "Lover Come Back To Me" and "All Night with Lil' Wally" (all by Walter Jagiello), all recorded by Lil' Wally on Jay Jay Records. Other artists include Casey Siewierski.

JAZZANO, 12 Micieli Pl., Brooklyn NY 11218. (718)972-1220. President: Rick Stone. Record producer, music publisher (BMI) and record company. Estab. 1984. Deals with artists only. Produces 1 LP/year. Fee derived from outright fee from recording artist or record company.

How to Contact: Write or call first and obtain permission to submit. Prefers cassette. Does not return unsolicited material. Reports in 2 weeks.

Music: Mostly jazz (straight ahead), bebop and hard bop. Produced *Blues for Nobody* and *Far East* (CDs), both written and recorded by Rick Stone on Jazzano Records (jazz).

Tips: "We are a small artist-owned label. We may in the future consider doing collaborative projects with other artists and labels. Our main concern is good music; we don't expect to get rich doing this."

JAZZMARK SOUND, Suite 513, 146 E. 49th St., New York NY 10017. (718)706-7071. Owner, Engineer/Producer: Mark J. Romero. Estab. 1984. Deals with artists only. Fee derived from any combination of sales royalty when song or artist is recorded, outright fee from recording artist and outright fee from record company. Receives up to 6 submissions/month. Charges depending upon contract status of the artist.

How to Contact: Submit demo tape by mail. Unsolicited submissions are OK. Prefers cassette with 4 songs. "If artist wants the material returned, he/she should provide mailing materials and postage." SASE. Reports in 4 weeks.

Music: Mostly jazz, R&B and funk; also New Age and pop. Artists include Jorge Nila and the Jazz Ninjas and The Scott Napoli Band.

Tips: "I'm glad to see musicians playing with each other in the studio again. I'm all for live tracking sessions with everyone playing together, sometimes even directly to 2-track."

*JERICHO SOUND LAB, P.O. Box 407, Jericho VT 05465. (802)899-3787. Owner: Bobby Hackney. Record producer, music publisher (Elect Music/BMI) and record company (LBI Records). Estab. 1988. Deals with artists and songwriters. Produces 5 singles, 2 12" singles and 3 LPs/year. Fee derived from sales royalty.

How to Contact: Submit demo tape by mail. Unsolicited submissions are OK. Prefers cassette or VHS videocassette with 3-4 songs and lyric sheet. SASE.

Music: Mostly reggae, R&B and pop; also New Age and rock. Produced *Officer Can I Plead?* (by B. Hackney), recorded by Lambsbread (reggae LP); *Sign of the Times* (by R. Steffen), recorded by Lambsbread (reggae); and "The Mighty Train" (by B. Hackney), recorded by The Hackneys (reggae single); all on LBI Records.

Tips: "Be patient, send your best works. Our approach to the music business is ask not what the music business can do for us, but what we can do for the music business—we love to work with and encourage the underdogs of the business."

JOHNNY JET RECORDS, 101-1431 Howe St., Vancouver B.C. V6Z 1R9 **Canada.** (604)685-2002. A&R: Dale Penner or John Livingston. Record producer, music publisher (Johnny Jet Music/BMI, PRO-CAN) and record company (Johnny Jet Records). Estab. 1990. Deals with artists and songwriters. Produces 12 singles and 6 LPs/year. Receives 45 submissions/month. Fee derived from sales royalty. Distribution in Canada by A&M Records.

How to Contact: Submit demo tape by mail. Unsolicited submissions are OK. Prefers cassette with a maximum of 3 songs and lyric sheet. "Artists should include photo." Reports in 2 months.

Music: Mostly pop, dance and R&B. Produced *Dream A Little Dream* and *Tima B!* (by John Dexter & others), recorded by various artists on A&M Records (pop LP).

RALPH D. JOHNSON, 114 Catalpa Dr., Mt. Juliet TN 37122. (615)754-2950. President: Ralph D. Johnson. Record producer, music publisher (Big Wedge Music) and record company. Estab. 1960. Deals with artists and songwriters. Produces 10 singles/year. Fee derived from sales royalty and outright fee from record company.

How to Contact: Write or call first to arrange personal interview. Prefers cassette with maximum of 4 songs.

Music: Mostly country and novelty. Recorded "Little Green Worm" (by Cal Veale), recorded by Dave Martin (novelty); "In the Middle of the Nighttime" (by Ralph D. Johnson), recorded by Joey Weltz (country); and "They Finally Got Around to You" (by T. J. Christian), recorded by T. J. Christian (country), all on Wedge Records.

Remember: Don't "shotgun" your demo tapes. Submit only to companies interested in the type of music you write. For more submission hints, refer to The Business of Songwriting on page 21.

JUMP PRODUCTIONS, 71 Langemunt, 9420 Aaigem **Belgium.** (053)62-73-77. General Manager: Eddy Van Mouffaert. Record producer and music publisher (Jump Music). Estab. 1976. Deals with artists and songwriters. Produces 25 singles, 2 LPs/year. Fee derived from sales royalty.
How to Contact: Prefers cassette. Does not return unsolicited material. Reports in 2 weeks.
Music: Mostly ballads, up-tempo, easy listening, disco and light pop; also instrumentals. Produced "Ach Eddy" (by Eddy Govert), recorded by Samantha and Eddy Govert on Carrere Records (light pop); "Al Wat Je Wilt" (by Eddy Viaene) recorded by Fransis on Scorpion Records (light pop); and "International" (by Eddy Govert), recorded by Le Grand Julot on Dureco Records (ambiance).Other artists include Angie Halloway, Debby Jackson, Ricky Morgan and Sandra Tempsy.

JUNE PRODUCTIONS LTD., "Toftrees," Church Rd., Woldingham, Surrey CR3 7JH **England.** Managing Director: David Mackay. Record producer, music producer (Sabre Music) and record company (Tamarin, PRT Records). Estab. 1970. Produces 6 singles, 3 LPs and 3 CDs/year. Deals with artists and songwriters. Fee derived from sales royalty.
How to Contact: Prefers cassette with 1-2 songs and lyric sheet. SAE and IRC. Reports in 2 weeks.
Music: MOR, rock and top 40/pop. Produced "Paris," the rock opera, soon to be released. Currently producing: Up With People, Jon English, Peter Hewitt and Smith-Wade Band. Past hits include "It's a Heartache" (by Bonnie Tyler); "I'd Like to Teach the World to Sing," and "Look What They've Done To My Song," by the New Seven; and hits for Cliff Richard, Cilla Black, Frankie Miller, Blue Mink, Gene Pitney and Joe Fagin.

*WARREN DENNIS KAHN, 540 B. E. Todd Rd., Santa Rosa CA 95407. (707)585-1325. President/Owner: Warren Dennis Kahn. Record producer and independent producer. Estab. 1976. Deals with artists and songwriters. Produces 10 LPs and 10 CDs/year. Fee derived from sales royalty when song or artist is recorded, outright fee from recording artist, or outright fee from record company. Does not return unsolicited submissions.
How to Contact: Write or call first and obtain permission to submit. Prefers cassette with 2-3 songs and lyric sheet. Reports in 1 month. Does not return unsolicited submissions.
Music: Mostly New Age, pop and gospel; also country, rock and R&B. Produced *Music to Disappear in 2* (by Rafael), recorded by WDK on Hearts of Space Records (New Age LP); *Tokewki* (by Tokewki) on TKM Records (world LP); and *Stone by Stone* (by M. Pomer) on Peartree Records (Christian LP); all recorded by WDK. Other artists include Michael Pomer, Buddy Comfort and Constance Demby.
Tips: "Have a clear understanding of who you wish to reach and what you're trying to accomplish."

*JOHANN KAPLAN MUSIC GROUP, Bürgergasse 17-19/2/12, 1100 Vienna **Austria** (office address). Ö.G.F.K.T. Box 233, 1014 Vienna **Austria** (mailing address). (1)602-22-18. President: Johann Kaplan, Jr. Record producer, music publisher and artist management firm. Estab. 1976. Deals with artists and songwriters. Produces 80 singles, 110 LPs and 30 CDs/year. Fee derived from sales royalty, outright fee from songwriter/artist or record company.
How to Contact: Write first and obtain permission to submit or to arrange personal interview. Prefers cassette or reel-to-reel (or VHS videocassette) with 2 songs and lyric or lead sheet. SAE and IRC. Reports in 2 months.
Music: All kinds of music. Produced "Tell Me More, Tell Me Sweet" (by J. Kaplan), recorded by Anna Long on Sunshine Records (pop); "I Need You" (by A. Flickentanz), recorded by Theresa on Caplan Music Records (disco); and "I Love You" (by J. Kaplan/A. Flickentanz), recorded by Kathy Piao on Tou Fu Music Records (soft rock). Other artists include The Revolution, A. Flickentanz and Group, and The Commercials.

BUTCH KELLY PRODUCTION, 11 Shady Oak Trail, Charlotte NC 28210. (704)554-1162. Executive Director: Butch Kelly. Record producer, music publisher (Butch Kelly Publishing/ASCAP and Music by Butch Kelly/BMI) and record company (KAM Executive and Fresh Avenue Records). Estab. 1985. Deals with artists and songwriters. Produces 4 singles, 4 12″ singles 4 EPs/year. Receives 500 submissions/month. Fee derived from sales royalty or outright fee from recording artist or record company.
How to Contact: Write first and obtain permission to submit. Prefers cassette (or VHS videocassette if available) with 1-6 songs and lyric or lead sheet. "Send your best song on Maxell UDS II tape, along with picture and bio." SASE. Reports in 4 months.
Music: Mostly pop and R&B; also rock and jazz. Produced "Waiting" (by B. Kelly), recorded by Caro; "Love You" (by B. Kelly), recorded by Sunshine; and "Where Have You Been" (by A. Brown); all R&B singles on KAM Records. Other artists include Melissa Kelly.

GENE KENNEDY ENTERPRISES, INC., 3950 N. Mt. Juliet Rd., Mt. Juliet TN 37122. (615)754-0417. President: Gene Kennedy. Vice President: Karen Jeglum Kennedy. Record producer, independent distribution and promotion firm and music publisher (Chip 'N' Dale Music Publishers, Inc./ASCAP,

Door Knob Music Publishing, Inc./BMI and Lodestar Music/SESAC). Estab. 1975. Deals with artists and songwriters. Produces 40-50 singles and 3-5 LPs/year. Fee derived from sales royalty or outright fee from recording artist or record company.
How to Contact: Prefers 7½ ips reel-to-reel or cassette with up to 3 songs and lyric sheet. "Do not send in a way that has to be signed for." SASE. Reports in 3 weeks.
Music: Country and gospel. Produced "I've Had Enough of You" (by Johnette Burton), recorded by Debbie Rich (country); "Praise Ye the Lord" (by Linda Almond), recorded by Dave Jeglum (gospel); "Change of Heart" (by Lanier O. Smith), recorded by Sandy Ellwanger (country); "For Cryin' Out Loud" (by Hugh Cunningham), recorded by Bobby G. Rice; all on Door Knob Records.

KINGSPORT CREEK MUSIC, P.O. Box 6085, Burbank CA 91510. Contact: Vice President. Record producer and music publisher. Deals with artists and songwriters.
How to Contact: Prefers cassette (or VHS videocassette). Does not return unsolicited material. "Include photo and bio if possible."
Music: Mostly country, MOR, R&B, pop and gospel. Produced "Tennessee Cowgirl" (country); "Heaven Bound" (gospel); and "Only Life" (country), written and recorded by Melvena Kaye on Cowgirl Records.

*JOHNNY KLINE, 3500 Llanberis Ave., Bristol PA 19007. (215)788-2723. President: Johnny Kline. Record producer, music publisher (BMI) and record company (Silver Jet Records). Estab. 1984. Deals with artists and songwriters. Produces 2-3 singles/year. Fee derived from outright fee from recording artist.
How to Contact: Submit demo tape by mail. Unsolicited submissions are OK. Prefers cassette with 3 songs and lyric sheet. "No phone calls please." SASE. Reports in 2 weeks.
Music: Mostly rockabilly, country and rock; also gospel. Produced "Poor Little Fool" (rockabilly single by Shari Sheely); "I'm Walkin" (rock and roll single by Fats Domino) and "Memphis" (rock and roll single by Chuck Berry), all recorded by Johnny Kline on Silver Jet Records.

FRANK E. KOEHL, P.O. Box 96, Glendale AZ 85311. (602)435-0314. Owner: Frank E. Koehl. Record producer and music publisher (Auburn Records & Tapes, estab. 1962. Speedstar Music/BMI, estab. 1989). Deals with artists and songwriters. Produces 3-5 singles and 7 LPs/year. Receives 25 submissions/month. Fee derived from sales royalty.
How to Contact: Submit demo tape by mail. Unsolicited submissions are OK. Prefers cassette with 2-4 songs and lyric sheet. SASE. Reports in 3 weeks.
Music: Mostly country, bluegrass and traditional music. Produced "Shade Tree" and "Lottery Fever," recorded by Troy McCourt on Auburn Records (acoustic country); also "Buglarman," "I Wish I Was Single," "I Know An Old Lady" and "It Ain't Gonna Rain No More," recorded by Al Ferguson on Auburn Records. Other artists include Cherry River Boys.
Tips: "Keep it country. No rock. Looking for traditional country and bluegrass, mostly acoustic. Country is going back to the older traditional songs."

ROBERT R. KOVACH, P.O. Box 7018, Warner Robins GA 31095-7018. (912)953-2800. Producer: Robert R. Kovach. Record producer. Estab. 1976. Deals with artists and songwriters. Produces 6 singles, 2 cassettes and 1 CD/year. Receives 200 submissions/year. Works with composers. Fee derived from sales royalty.
How to Contact: Prefers cassette with 4 songs and lyric sheet. SASE. Reports in 3 months.
Music: Mostly country and pop; also easy listening, R&B, rock and gospel..

*JURY KRYTIUK PRODUCTIONS, P.O. Box 1065, Station B, Mississauga, Ontario L4X 2P1 Canada. (416)238-2783. Contact: Jury Krytiuk. Record producer, Music publisher (Boot Songs/CAPAC) and record company (Boot Leisure Corp.). Deals with artists and songwriters. Produces 24 singles, 15 LPs and 15 CDs/year. Receives 50 submissions/year. Fee derived from sales royalty or outright fee from recording artist. Charges production fee for all projects undertaken.
How to Contact: Prefers cassette (or VHS videocassette optional). Submissions should include artist bio and photo. SAE and IRC. Reports in 2 weeks.
Music: Mostly country, folk, old time; also ethnic and MOR. Produced "Mr. Big Stuff" (by Joe Broussard, Ralph Williams and Carol Washington), recorded by Precious Metal on A&M Records (rock).

LAMON RECORDS/PANHANDEL RECORDS, P.O. Box 25371, Charlotte NC 28229. (704)537-0133. President: Dwight Moody. A&R: Carlton Moody. Record producer and music publisher (Laymond Publishing Co. and CDT Productions). Estab. 1962. Deals with artists, songwriters and publishers. Produces 35 singles, 4 12″ singles, 20 LPs and 5 CDs/year. Receives 300-750 submissions/year. Fee derived from outright fee from recording artist.

How to Contact: Write first and obtain permission to submit. Prefers cassette (or VHS videocassette if available) with minimum 2 songs. Does not return unsolicited material. Reports in 1 month.

Music: Mostly country, beach, gospel, rock & roll and R&B. Produced "You Are the One" (by J. Lone, W. Smothers), recorded by The Lyke Bros. (rock); "Land of Plenty" (by W. Carson, D. Stanton), recorded by Dusty Stanton (county); and "On My Way" (by Sony Tunner), recorded by The Luaner Family (gospel); all on Lamon Records. Other artists include Allen Ray, Hutchins Brothers, Routabouts, Nelson Young, George Hamilton, IV Dale Upton, Hege V, Marshall and Vaughan, The Diffence Jeffrey Newberry, Province, Bubba and Angle, The Briarhopper and Dusty Stanton.

*LARK TALENT & ADVERTISING, P.O. Box 35726, Tulsa OK 74153. (918)749-1648. Owner: Jana Jae. Record producer, music publisher (Jana Jae Music/BMI) and record company (Lark Record Productions, Inc.). Estab. 1980. Deals with artists and songwriters. Fee derived from sales royalty when song or artist is recorded.

How to Contact: Submit demo tape by mail. Unsolicited submissions are OK. Prefers cassette or VHS videocassette with 3 songs and lead sheet. Does not return unsolicited material.

Music: Mostly country, bluegrass and classical; also intstrumentals. Produced "Fiddlestix" (by Jana Jae); "Mayonnaise" (by Steve Upfold); and "Flyin' South" (by Cindy Walker); all country singles recorded by Jana Jae on Lark Records. Other artists include Sydni, Hotwire and Matt Greif.

*JOHN LATIMER, Box 6541, Cleveland OH 44101. (216)467-0300. Producer: John Latimer. Record producer, record company (Play Records) and independent. Estab. 1985. Deals with artists and songwriters. Produces 1-2 LPs/year. Fee derived from sales royalty or outright fee from recording artist or record company.

How to Contact: Submit demo tape by mail. Unsolicited submissions are okay. Prefers cassette (or ¾" or VHS videocassette if available) with 5 songs and lyric or lead sheets. SASE. Reports in 6 weeks.

Music: Mostly rock and alternative. Produced *Exhibit A*, *Exhibit B* and *Exhibit C* (compilations) on Play Records. Other artists include The Bellows, I-TAL U.S.A., Serious Nature, Hipshot and Mike O'Brien.

*SCOTT LEA PRODUCTIONS, 88 Lenox Ave., Paterson NJ 07502. (201)790-7668. President: Scott Lea. Record producer, music publisher (Scott Lea Publishing/BMI) and record company (Neon Records). Estab. 1988. Deals with artists and songwriters. Produces 5 singles, 20 12" singles, 2 LPs, 1 EP and 2 CDs/year. Fee derived from outright fee from recording artist or record company.

How to Contact: Submit demo tape by mail. Unsolicited submissions are OK. Prefers cassette or VHS videocassette with 2-4 songs. SASE. Reports in 2-4 weeks.

Music: Mostly club, R&B and rap; also house, jazz and rock. Produced *What Exit?*, written and recorded by various artists on Neon Records (various rock LP); *Pursuit of Peace*, written and recorded by Scott Lea on Neon Records (contemporary jazz LP); and *Ebony* (by various artists), recorded by Ebony on World One Records (club/dance LP). Other artists include Bugle Boyz, Dana Way, Latin Lover, Maja Hall, Ari Goodman and The Fiendz.

*JOHN LEAVELL, 2045 Anderson Snow, Spring Hill FL 34609. (904)799-6102. Producer: John Leavell. Record producer and recording studio. Estab. 1980. Deals with artists and songwriters. Produces 10-12 singles/year. Fee derived from outright fee from recording artist. Charges artist upfront for demo production.

How to Contact: Write or call first to arrange personal interview. Prefers cassette (or VHS videocassette if available) with 4-5 songs and lyric sheet. Does not return unsolicited material. Reports in 2-3 weeks.

Music: Mostly Christian rock, Christian contemporary and gospel; also rock and country. Produced *Patricia Plays Christmas* (by Patricia Tassie) on Patricia Records (classical CD); *Tom Martin #1* (by Tom Martin), on Leavell Records (rock LP); and *Tom Butler* (by John Leavell/Tom Butler), on Leavell Records (Christian rock LP), all recorded by Leavell Sound Studio. Other artists include Johnny Grubbs, Greg Eadler, East From West and Tye Dowdy.

LEE SOUND PRODUCTIONS, RON LEE, VALUE FOR MONEY, HOPPY PRODUCTIONS, Stewart House, Hill Bottom Road, Sands-Ind. Est., Highwycombe, Buckinghamshire HP12-4HJ **England.** 063081374. FAX: 063081612. Contact: Catherine Lee. Record producer. Affiliates are: Value For Money and Hoppy Productions. Estab. 1971. Deals with artists and songwriters. Fee derived from sales royalty or outright fee from recording artist and record company.

How to Contact: Submit demo tape by mail. Unsolicited submissions are OK. Prefers cassette (or VHS/PAL videocassette if available) with 3 songs and lyric sheet or lead sheets. SASE. Reports in 6 weeks.

Music: All types. Produced *Not This Time* (by D. Boone), recorded by Lelly Boone (pop/jazz); *Together Again* (by D. Boone), recorded by Daniel and Lelly Boone (pop); and *Don't Test My Love*, written and recorded by Daniel Boone (disco); all on Swoop Records. Other artists include Nightmare, The Chromatics, Sight-N-Sound, Suburban Studs and Groucho.

LEMON SQUARE PRODUCTIONS, P.O. Box 31819, Dallas TX 75231. (214)750-0720. A&R: Mike Anthony. Producer: Bart Barton. Record producer, music publisher and record label. Deals with artists and songwriters. Produces 2 singles and 3 LPs/year. Fee derived from sales royalty.
How to Contact: Write first and obtain permission to submit. Prefers cassette and lyric sheet or lead sheet. Does not return unsolicited material. Reports in 2 months.
Music: Mostly country and gospel. Produced "Like Goin' Home" (by Allison Gilliam), recorded by Susie Calvin on Canyon Creek Records (country); "Still Fallin' " (by Dave Garner), recorded by Audie Henry on RCA/Canada Records (country); and "Lord If I Make It To Heaven" (by Dale Vest/T. Overstreet), recorded by Billy Parker on RCA/Canada Records (country). Other artists include Glen Baily, Susie Calvin and Bev Marie.

TOMMY LEWIS, JR., RR 2, Box 111-C, Cresco PA 18326. (717)595-3149. Owner/Producer: Tommy Lewis, Jr. Record producer and record company (Round Sound Music). Estab. 1983. Deals with artists and songwriters. Produces 3-5 singles, 2-3 LPs and 2-3 CDs/year. Receives 100 submissions/month. Fee derived from sales royalty. "Generally doesn't charge up-front, but if co-production is desired, advance payment is negotiated."
How to Contact: Write or call first and obtain permission to submit. Prefers cassette (or VHS videocassette if available) with 3 songs and lyric and lead sheet. "Be professional in your presentation." SASE. Reports in 6-8 weeks.
Music: Mostly pop and jazz; also New Age, country, R&B and gospel. Produced "I'm All Alone," written and recorded by J. Schick (pop/single); *He Died For You*, recorded by Ransomed on W.C. Productions Records (Christian rock/album); "No Easy Way" (by T. Lewis, Jr.), recorded by Gloria Kay (country/single); and "On the Other Side" (by Adam Lenox). Other artists include Charade and J. Hendershedt.
Tips: "Be honest with yourself, do what you believe in, and always give your absolute very best!"

LINEAR CYCLE PRODUCTIONS, P.O. Box 2827, Carbondale IL 62902. (618)687-3515. Producer: R. Borowy. Record producer. Estab. 1980. Deals with artists and songwriters. Produces 15-25 singles, 6-10 12″ singles, 15-20 LPs and 10 CDs/year. Fee derived from sales royalty or outright fee from recording artist.
How to Contact: Prefers cassette or 7⅞ ips reel-to-reel (or ½″ VHS or ¾″ videocassette if available). Does not return unsolicited material. Reports in 1 month.
Music: Mostly rock/pop, R&B/blues and country; also gospel and comedy. Produced "Workin' The Grind" (by B. Roit), recorded by The Bag Boys on Rix Records (rock); "I Love to Love Your Lovin' " (by H. Tank), recorded by Wide Ranch on Caktis Records (country); and "Missil Kikin," written and recorded by M.C. Pee on G.E.T.A. Records (rap). Other artists include Eugene Cornblatt, Off The Bus and No Soap Boys.

LISTEN PRODUCTIONS, P.O. Box 1155, Hollywood CA 90078. (213)473-7480. President: Daniel Keller. Record producer. Estab. 1986. Deals with artists and songwriters. Fee derived from sales royalty or outright fee from recording artist or record company.
How to Contact: Call or write first to get permission to submit. Prefers cassette (or VHS videocassette if available) with 4 songs and lyric sheet. "If artist, submit photos if available." SASE. Reports in 6 weeks.
Music: Mostly R&B (uptempo and ballads), pop and rock/alternative; also New Age and acoustic.

*LIVE PRODUCTIONS INC., P.O. Box 448, Hanover VA 23069. (804)730-1765. President: Patrick D. Kelley. Record producer, music publisher (Studley Publishing), record company (Live Productions) and recording studio (The Fishing Hole). Estab. 1988. Deals with artists and songwriters. Produces 6 LPs/year. Fee derived from sales royalty. "We charge clients on not our label for studio time."
How to Contact: Submit demo tape by mail. Unsolicited submissions are OK. Prefers cassette (or VHS videocassette if available) with any number of songs and lyric sheet. "Be specific on what you are seeking (publishing, recording contract, etc.)." SASE. Reports in 1 month.
Music: Mostly country, gospel and pop; also rock, folk and children's. Produced "The Magical Toy" (by Cover Tunes), recorded by Andy and Cindy (children's); "Allen Watkins," written and recorded by Allen Watkins (folk); and "Highway and Heartaches," written and recorded by Highway and Heartache (country); all on Live Productions.

LOCONTO PRODUCTIONS, P.O. Box 16540, Plantation FL 33318. (305)741-7766. President: Frank X. Loconto. Record producer and music publisher. Estab. 1978. Deals with artists and songwriters. Produces 20 singles and 20 LPs/year. Fee derived from sales royalty, outright fee from songwriter/artist and/or outright fee from record company.
How to Contact: Write first and obtain permission to submit. Prefers cassette. SASE.
Music: Produced "Calypso Alive and Well," written and recorded by Obediah Colebrock (island music); "Standing on the Top" (by various artists), recorded by Mark Rone (C&W); and "Walking On Air" (by Ken Hatch), recorded by Frank Loconto (motivational); all on FXL Records. Other artists include Bruce Mullin, Bill Dillon and James Billie (folk music).

HAROLD LUICK & ASSOCIATES, P.O. Box B, Carlisle IA 50047. (515)989-3676. Record producer, music industry consultant and music publisher. Deals with artists and songwriters. Produces 20 singles and 6 LPs/year. Fee derived from sales royalty, outright fee from artist/songwriter or record company, and from consulting fees for information or services.
How to Contact: Call or write first. Prefers cassette with 3-5 songs and lyric sheet. SASE. Reports in 3 weeks.
Music: Traditional country, gospel, contemporary country and MOR. Produced Bob Everhart's LP *Everhart*; Don Laughlin's *Ballads of Deadwood S.D.* LP; Lee Mace's Ozark Opry albums; and Darrell Thomas' singles and LPs. "Over a 12-year period, Harold Luick has produced and recorded 412 singles and 478 albums, 7 of which charted and some of which have enjoyed independent sales in excess of 30,000 units."
Tips: "We are interested in helping the new artist/songwriter make it 'the independent way.' This is the wave of the future. As music industry consultants, our company sells ideas, information and results. Songwriters can increase their chances by understanding that recording and songwriting is a business. 80% of the people who travel to large recording/publishing areas of our nation arrive there totally unprepared as to what the industry wants or needs from them. Do yourself a favor. Prepare, investigate and only listen to people who are qualified to give you advice. Do not implement anything until you understand the rules and pitfalls."

*LVW ENTERTAINMENT, 5934 Blairstone Dr., Culver City CA 90230. (213)558-8168. Owner: Leonardo V. Wilborn. Record producer and music publisher (Leo-Vincent Music/ASCAP, Omini-Praise/BMI). Estab. 1987. Deals with artists and songwriters. Produces 2 12″ singles and 2 LPs/year. Fee derived from sales royalty.
How to Contact: Write first and obtain permission to submit. Prefers cassette (or VHS videocassette if available) with 3 songs and lyric sheet. SASE. Reports in 8 weeks.
Music: Mostly R&B, gospel and pop/country; also musicals, concert pieces and choral music. Produced "Victory is Won" (by Eau Joyner, Jr.), recorded by Daily Bread on IHS Records (gospel); "Temptation" (by T. Walker), recorded by Federation of Love on IHS Records (nu-inspirational); and "Heartache & Pain" (by L. Wilborn), recorded by Marsha Stewart on Gallery Records II (R&B). Other artists include M.C. Smiley and Nasa.
Tips: "Have patience, versatility, strong general office skills, self-motivation and an original concept."

*JACK LYNCH/NASHVILLE COUNTRY PRODUCTIONS, 306 Millwood Dr., Nashville TN 37217. (615)366-9999. Producer: Col. Jack Lynch. Record producer, music publisher (BMI), record company and distributor (Nashville Music Sales). Estab. 1963. Deals with artists and songwriters. Produces 12 LPs/year. Fee derived from sales royalty or outright fee form recording artist.
How to Contact: Submit demo tape by mail. Unsolicited submissions are OK. Prefers cassette with 1-4 songs and lyric sheet. "Send picture and resume, if available. Send good quality demo cassette recording, neat lyric sheets." SASE. Reports in 2 weeks.
Music: Mostly country, bluegrass and religious; also MOR, folk and comedy/novelty. Produced *Did You Lose My Number* (by Vicki Watts), recorded by Glenda Rider on NCP #301 Records (country); *She Took Me For a Fool* (by Art Scharinger), recorded by Paul Woods on NCP #302 (country); and *Bedroom Bar Room Blues* (by Otis Johnson), recorded by Paul Woods on NCP #302 (country). Other artists include Jack Lynch, Larry Sparks, Ralph Stanley, Richard Lynch, Ricky Skaggs and Keith Whitley.

*LYX MUSIC PRODUCTION & RECORDING STUDIOS, 25 Foster St., Worcester MA 01608. (508)752-6010. Producer: Andy Celley. Record producer, music publisher (LYX Music Publishing/ASCAP) and record company. Estab. 1987. Deals with artists and songwriters. Produces 40 singles, 10 12″ singles, 4 LPs and 10 EPs/year. Fee derived from sales royalty when song or artist is recorded, outright fee from recording artist and outright fee from record company.

How to Contact: Write or call first and obtain permission to submit. Prefers cassette (or VHS videocassette if available) with unlimited number of songs and lyric sheet. SASE. Reports in 1 month.
Music: Mostly rock (all types), pop and dance; also rap, easy listening and folk. Produced *Hot Lyx 1*, a compilation of music by several artists, on LYX Records (LP); LYX Records (LP); *Drive It To Ya Hard*, written and recorded by Roxxi, on Rock Hard Records (LP/CD); and *Arlindo*, written and recorded by Arlindo, on Alemar Records (LP/CD). Other artists include Transit, Scared of Horses, Ephesus, Bad Rationale, Big Red Bus, Jim Perry, Mad House, Heartbeats, Danimal's Animals, Brother Blue, Angry Salad, Angel of Monz, Bottom Line, Scuff and Sassa.
Tips: "Individualism has always been and will always be the biggest money maker for any artist/band/act. As many modern writers and producers copy and emulate the sounds, melodies, lyrics and styles, it's the individual(s) unique interpretation that makes it special."

MAC-ATTACK PRODUCTIONS, INC., Ste. #6J, 14699 N.E. 18th Ave., N. Miami FL 33181. (305)947-8315. President: Michael J. McNamee. Record producer and music publisher (see Mac-Attack Publishing/ASCAP). Estab. 1987. Deals with artists and songwriters. Produces 10-12 singles, 3-10 LPs and 3-10 CDs/year. Fee derived from sales royalty or outright fee from recording artist or record company. "Depending upon the contract, a percentage to cover expenses that *will* be made."
How to Contact: Write or call first and obtain permission to submit. Prefers cassette (or VHS videocassette if available) with a maximum of 3 songs and lyric sheet. "I can't stand formalities. Be yourself when writing your letter. Communication is the key to a great relationship." SASE. Reports in 1-2 months.
Music: Mostly Progressive rock and alternative; also progressive dance, R&B and "anything different." Produced "The Face of Fear" and "Give Me a Sign," written and recorded by Razor on Kinetic Records (cutting single); *No Shadow of Turning*, written and recorded by Nina Llopis on R.E.X. Records (Progressive LP); *Water and Walls*, written and recorded by Forget the Name on Unforgettable Records (Progressive Blues LP). Regularly produces Blowfly, Don't Know Yet, The Maxxturs.
Tips: "There's no need to rush anything. Let it come naturally—don't try to force it. Remember, you and I will be gone one day, but our songs will never die."

*JIM McCOY PRODUCTIONS, Rt. 2, Box 114, Berkeley Springs WV 25411. President: Jim McCoy. Record producer and music publisher (Jim McCoy Music/BMI). Estab. 1964. Deals with artists and songwriters. Produces 12-15 singles and 6 LPs/year. Fee derived from sales royalty.
How to Contact: Write or call first and obtain permission to submit. Prefers cassette or 7½ or 15 ips reel-to-reel (or Beta or VHS videocassette if available) with 6 songs and lyric or lead sheets. Does not return unsolicited material. Reports in 1 month.
Music: Mostly country, rock and gospel; also country/rock and bluegrass. Produced "Same Ole Town" and "If I Throw Away My Pride" by R. Lee Gray; and "Leavin' " and "Tulsa" by Red Steed. Other artists include Mel McQuain and Terry McCawhee.

RANDY B. MCCOY, P.O. Box 678, Baird TX 79504. (915)893-2616. Producer: Randy B. McCoy. Record producer. Estab. 1985. Deals with artists and songwriters. Produces 10 singles and 4 LPs/year. Receives 150-200 submissions/year. Fee derived from outright fee from artist. Charges artist up front for "all phases of project from start to finish, including production, arrangements, presentation, etc."
How to Contact: Prefers cassette with 3-4 songs and lyric sheet. "Make sure vocals can be clearly heard, and keep the arrangments simple and basic." SASE. Reports in 3 weeks.
Music: Produced "It's Christmas Time in Texas" (by various artists), recorded by John Secord on Code of the West Records (country); "Reflections" (by various artists), recorded by Reflections on ACU Records (contemporary Christian); and "My Daddy" (by Mike Schuler), recorded by Children of America on Duke Records (pop novelty). Other artists include Dan Griffing, Willy Ray Band and Abilene Christian University.
Tips: "Submit material that is upbeat and pertains to the events and feelings of today. Be basic—originality presents itself in simple form."

BUTCH MCGHEE, TYRA MANAGEMENT GROUP, P.O. Box 915, Sheffield AL 35660. (205)381-2060. President: Butch McGhee. Record producer and record company (Muscle Shoals Sound Gospel Records, Ameika Records). Estab. 1985. Deals with artists and songwriters. Produces 4 12″ singles, 10 LPs and 10 CDs/year. Fee derived from sales royalty. "Before project a production fee is charged."
How to Contact: Write first and obtain permission to submit. Prefers cassette (or VHS videocassette if available) with 3 songs and lyric sheets. "Send biography and photo if possible." Does not return unsolicited material. Reports in 8 weeks.
Music: Mostly gospel, R&B and country. Produced *2nd Chance*, recorded by Loretta Handy on Ameika Records (LP); *Anybody Can, God Can*, recorded by Voices of Cosmo on MSSG Records (LP); and *Pamela Davies and True Spirit*, recorded on MSSG Records (LP). Other artists include Keith Pringle, Stefania Stone Fierson, Vanessa Bell Armstrong, Charles Fold and Fold Singers.

Tips: "Supply gospel and inspirational material with a strong message. Clean demos and lyric sheets."

DAVID MACKAY, "Toftrees," Church Rd., Woldingham, Surrey CR3 7JH **England**. Managing Director: David Mackay. Record producer (June Productions) and music publisher. Works with artists and songwriters. Produces 10 singles, 10 12″ singles, 4 LPs and varying number of CDs/year. Fee derived from sales royalty.
How to Contact: Prefers cassette with 2 songs. SAE and IRC. Reports in 1 month.
Music: Mostly contemporary and rock. Produced "It Should've Been Me," recorded by David Ride on Phonorac Records; and "Younger Days,'" recorded by John English on Mushroom Records (both rock singles). Other artists include Joe Fagin, Ornella Mutti, Marica Hines, Upwith People and Barry Humphries.

*MADISON STATION PRODUCTIONS, 217 Highway 51, Box 98, Madison MS 39110. Producer: Jason S. Wooten. Record producer and record company (Madison Station Records). Estab. 1988. Works with artists and songwriters. Produces 5 singles and 5 LPs/year. Fee derived from sales royalty or outright fee from record company.
How to Contact: Write first and obtain permission to submit. Prefers cassette with 1-3 songs and lyric sheet. SASE.
Music: Mostly rock, R&B and country.

*LITO MANLUCU (Magic Music Production), 4121 N. Laramie, Chicago IL 60641. (312)545-7388. Producer: Lito Manlucu. Record producer. Estab. 1991. Deals with artists and songwriters. Produces 1 single, 1 LP and 1 CD/year. Fee derived from outright fee from recording artist.
How to Contact: Write first and obtain permission to submit. Prefers cassette with 3 songs and lyric sheet. Does not return unsolicited material. Reports in 2 weeks.
Music: Mostly pop, R&B and rock; also foreign music.

*HARVEY MARCUS, 827 Brazil, El Paso TX 79903. Owner: Harvey Marcus. Record producer, music publisher and record company (Crystal Ram, April Records). Works with artists and songwriters. Produces 1-3 singles, 1-3 12″ singles, 1-5 LPs, 1-5 EPs and 1-3 CDs/year. Fee derived from sales royalty or outright fee from record company.
How to Contact: Prefers cassette or 7½ ips reel-to-reel (or VHS videocassette if available) with 1 song and lyric or lead sheet. SASE. "No SASE, no answer." Reports in 6 weeks.
Music: Mostly jazz/pop, top 40 (ballads) and Tex-Mex; also country, New Age and Christian rock. Produced *Are We In This For Love* (EP) and "Baby Blue Baby" (single), written and recorded by The Street Boys on T.S.B. Records; and *Endless Dreams*, written and recorded by Ruben Castillo on Crystal Ram Records (LP). Other artists include Bob Cast (M.C.R. Records recording artist).

*MARKETUNES INC., 106 Lynbrook Rd., Mastic Beach NY 11951. (516)399-5479. President: Joe Costanzo. Record producer, music publisher (Marketunes/ASCAP) and producer for solo artists and songwriters. Estab. 1979. Deals with artists and songwriters. Produces 50 singles and 4 LPs/year. Fee derived from sales royalty when song or artist is recorded or outright fee from recording artist.
How to Contact: Write or call first and obtain permission to submit. Prefers cassette with 3 songs and lyric sheet. Does not return unsolicited material.
Music: Interested in all styles.

*PATRICK MELFI, B-30, 26111 Ynez Rd., Temecula CA 92390. (714)676-0006. Contact: Patrick Melfi. Record producer, music publisher (BMI) and record company (Alexas Records). Estab. 1984. Deals with artists and songwriters. Produces 6 singles, 2 LPs, 1 EP and 2 CDs/year. Fee derived from outright fee from recording artist or record company.
How to Contact: Submit demo tape by mail. Unsolicited submissions are OK. Prefers cassette (or VHS videocassette if available) with 1-6 songs and lyric or lead sheet. Does not return unsolicited submissions. Reports in 2 months.
Music: Mostly country and pop; also New Age and gospel. Produced "Mama, You're an Angel," written and recorded by Jeff Elder; "She's On Her Own" (by P. Melfi/AJ Masters), recorded by AJ Masters; and "West Texas Woman," written and recorded by Fats Johnson; all on Alexas Records (all C&W singles). Other artists include Linda Rae, Jenny Lynn and Joe Neddo.

*METROMEDIA PRODUCTIONS, Suite 306, 822 11th Ave. SW, Calgary AB T2R 0E5 **Canada**. President: Lanny Williamson. Record producer, music publisher (Zimmy Music/SOCAN) and recording studio. Estab. 1988. Deals with artists and songwriters. Produces 20 singles, 3 LPs and 3 CDs/year. Fee derived from outright fee from recording artist.

How to Contact: Submit demo tape by mail. Unsolicited submissions are OK. Prefers cassette with 4 songs and lyric sheet. "Please enclose picture and bio." SASE. Reports in 2 weeks.
Music: Mostly pop, R&B and rock; also funk, country and alternative. Produced "Say It" (by Ray MacDonald), recorded by IN on Indie Records (single); *Boys Say Go* (by Ray MacDonald), recorded by IN on Indie Records (LP); and *Between Friends* (by Rio/Leitl), recorded by Leitl on Freedom Records (LP). Other artists include Bob Erlundson, Tera Lynn, Ballooner Landing, Richard Samuels and Kathy Shane.

*MICROSTAR MUSIC, #113, 5241 Cleveland St., Virginia Beach VA 23462. (804)499-4434. President: Mark Spencer. Record producer, music publisher and record company (MircoStar, MSM). Estab. 1990. Deals with artists and songwriters. Produces 6 LPs and 6 CDs/year. Fee derived from sales royalty.
How to Contact: Write first and obtain permission to submit. Prefers cassette with 4 songs and lyric sheet. Does not return unsolicited material. Reports in 4 weeks.
Music: Mostly pop, gospel and country; also R&B. Produced *Do You Think We Have a Chance?* (by K. Cleveland), recorded by TK Llegs; *Wearing White With No Shame*, written and recorded by P. VanValin; and *Workin' Man's Dream*, written and recorded by B. Fisher; all on MicroStar Records (LP). Other artists include Don Burford, Tony Hawkins, Charity Jackson, David Givens, Matt Vollmer and Pam Osborn.
Tips: "Work hard and don't cut corners on your demo. If you won't spend your time and money on it than why should we?"

*MIDWEST RECORDS, 2748 Apple, Lincoln NE 68503. (402)476-0986. Producer: Harold Dennis. Record producer, record company (Midwest Records) and Country Music Promotions. Estab. 1983. Deals with artists and songwriters. Produces 2 singles, 2 12″ singles and 2-3 LPs/year. Fee derived from outright fee from recording artist. "We do not charge songwriters; but we do charge artists."
How to Contact: Submit demo tape by mail. Unsolicited submissions are OK. Prefers cassette with 2 songs and lyric sheets. Does not return unsolicited material. Reports in 6 weeks.
Music: Mostly country and crossover country. Produced "Shutters and Boards" (by C. Turner/A. Murphy), recorded by Ron Royer on Midwest Records (country). Other artists include Barbara Ramos, Angel Miller, Tracy Hartsharn and Jack Elliott.

MIGHTY SOUNDS AND FILMWORKS, Suite 6-D, 150 West End Ave., New York NY 10023. (212)873-5968. Manager: Danny Darrow. Record producer, music publisher (Rockford Music Co./BMI) and record company (Mighty Sounds and Filmworks). Works with artists and songwriters. Produces 1-2 singles, 1-2 12″ singles, 1-2 LPs and 1-2 EPs/year. Receives 200 submissions/month. Fee derived from sales royalty.
How to Contact: Prefers cassette with 2-3 songs. SASE. No phone calls. Reports in 1 week.
Music: Mostly A/C, country and adult rock. Produced "Let There Be Real," by P. Zinn (rock gospel); "Wonderland of Dreams," by Danny Darrow (lullaby); and "Power of Love," by Herb Miller (rock ballad); all recorded by Danny Darron on Mighty Records.

*ROBERT E. MILES/King Eugene Productions, 14016 Evers Ave., Compton CA 90222. (213)438-5656 or (213)639-8522. A&R: Robert E. Miles. Record producer, music publisher (King Eugene Productions/BMI). Estab. 1988. Deals with artists and songwriters. Fee derived from sales royalty when song or artist is recorded or outright fee from record company.
How to Contact: Submit demo by mail. Unsolicited submissions are OK. Prefers cassette (or VHS videocassette if available) with several songs and lyric sheet. SASE. Reports in 1 month.
Music: Mostly rap, R&B and pop/dance. Produced "Kickin' It," written and recorded by King Eugene Revue on Janet Marie Records (R&B single); "Home Girl," written and recorded by Cassie 'D' on Janet Marie Records (rap single); and "Blow My Thang," written and recorded by Mig-X on Micon Records (rap single).

JAY MILLER PRODUCTIONS, 413 N. Parkerson Ave., Crowley LA 70526. (318)783-1601 or 788-0773. Contact: Jay Miller. Record producer and music publisher. Deals with artists and songwriters. Produces 50 singles and 15 LPs/year. Fee derived from sales royalty.

Market conditions are constantly changing! If you're still using this book and it is 1993 or later, buy the newest edition of Songwriter's Market at your favorite bookstore or order directly from Writer's Digest Books.

How to Contact: Arrange personal interview. Inquiries are invited. Prefers cassette for audition.
Music: Mostly country; also blues, Cajun, disco, folk, gospel, MOR, rock, top 40/pop and comedy. Working on video productions. Produced *Zydecajun*, by Wayne Toups on Mercury Records (LP); "I Wish I Had A Job," by Paul Marx (single); and "The Likes Of Texas," by Sammy Kershaw (single). Other artists inlcude Wayne Toups, Tammy Lynn, John Fred and Camey Doucet.

*MĪMÁC PRODUCTIONS, 1433 Cole Pl., Hollywood CA 90028. (213)856-8729. Artist Services: Robyn Whitney. Record producer and studio-TRAX recording. Estab. 1979. Deals with artists and songwriters. Fee derived from sales royalty or outright fee from recording artist or record company. "If not a spec deal, we are for hire for production services."
How to Contact: Submit demo tape by mail. Unsolicited submissions are OK. Prefers cassette (or VHS videocassette if available) with 4 songs and lyric sheets. "Not interested in rap, pop/dance or country. We specialize in hard rock, heavy metal, unique R&B and some mature pop." SASE. Reports in 5 weeks.
Music: Mostly hard rock, heavy metal and funk/rock; also unique R&B, mature pop and mature Latin pop. Produced *Music Speaks Louder Than Words* (by American and USSR writers), recorded by various artists on Epic Records (pop/R&B LP); "One Heart, One Mind" (by Gregory Abbott), recorded by Emmanual on Epic Records (single); and *Jerry Riopelle*, written and recorded by Jerry Riopelle on Warner (LP). Other artists include Total Eclipse and Charlie Mitchell.
Tips: "We do not believe that image alone can sustain a market for an artist. You must train, practice, constantly update your image and stretch your abilities."

MR. MORT ENTERPRISES, 44 Music Sq. E, Nashville TN 37203. (615)255-2175. Vice President: Bernice Fields. Music publisher (BMI, ASCAP) and record company (Charta Records, Deluxe Records). Estab. 1977. Deals with artists and songwriters. Produces 20 singles and 8 LPs/year. Fee derived from sales royalty.
How to Contact: Submit demo tape by mail. Unsolicited submissions are OK. Prefers cassette (or VHS videocassette if available) with 3-4 songs and lyric sheets. SASE. Reports in 4 weeks.
Music: Mostly country and MOR. Produced "Home Is Where The Love Is" (by C. Fields), recorded by Eddie Rivers; "Jealous Hearts and Suspicious Minds" (by C. Fields), recorded by Ronnie Klein; and "All The Things We Are Not" (by M. Taylor), recorded by David Walsh; all on Charta Records (all country singles). Other artists include Fran Nickens, Donna Darlene and Nina Wyatt.
Tips: "Call or write for an appointment. Have a good quality cassette of 3-4 songs and a video cassette or pictures with bio. A super talented artist or group has a chance to make it in the business today."

MR. WONDERFUL PRODUCTIONS, INC., 1730 Kennedy Rd., Lousiville KY 40216. (502)774-1066. President: Ronald C. Lewis. Record producer, music publisher (Ron "Mister Wonderful" Music/BMI and 1730 Music/ASCAP) and record company (Wonderful Records and Ham Sem Records). Estab. 1984. Deals with artists and songwriters. Produces 2 singles and 3 12″ singles/year. Fee is derived from outright fee from recording artist or record company. "We also promote records of clients nationwide to radio stations for airplay."
How to Contact: Prefers cassette with 4 songs and lyric sheet. SASE. Reports in 3 weeks.
Music: Mostly R&B, black gospel and rap. Produced "Wanted" (by Ricky Henderson), recorded by Foul Play on Wonderful Records (rap); "Connect" (by Harold Johnson), recorded by Jerry Green on BroFeel Records; "First on the Dance Floor," written and recorded by Jerry Green on Wonderful Records; and "I'm the One for You" (by Jerry Green) on HamSem Records (all singles). Other artists include Tabitha Brown, Margaret Beaumont, Maxx Franklin, Nocomo and Golden Crowns (gospel).

*A.V. MITTELSTEDT, 9717 Jensen Dr., Houston TX 77093. (713)695-3648. Producer: A.V. Mittelstedt. Record producer and music publisher (Sound Masters). Works with artists and songwriters. Produces 100 singles and 10 LPs and 20 CDs/year. Receives 500 submissions/year. Fee derived from sales royalty and outright fee from recording artist.
How to Contact: Prefers cassette. SASE. Reports in 3 weeks.
Music: Mostly country, gospel, crossover; also MOR and rock. Produced "Too Cold at Home" (by Bobby Harding), recorded by Mark Chestnutt on Cherry Records (country); "Two Will Be One," written and recorded by Kenny Dale on Axbar Records (country); and "Shake Your Hiney" (by Gradual Taylor), recorded by Roy Head on Cherry Records (cross over country). Other artists include Randy Corner, Bill Nash, Ron Shaw, Borderline, George Dearborne and Good, Bad and Ugly.

*MJM PRODUCTIONS, P.O. Box 654, Southbury CT 06488. Owner: Michael McCartney. Record producer and music publisher (On The Button/BMI). Estab. 1988. Deals with artists and songwriters. Produces 5 singles. Fee derived from sales royalty or outright fee from recording artist.

How to Contact: Submit demo tape by mail. Unsolicited submissions are OK. Prefers cassette with 3-5 songs and lyric sheet. "Give details as to what your goals are: artist in search of deal or writer wishing to place songs." SASE. Reports in 3-4 weeks.
Music: Mostly country/rock, pop rock and R&B.

*MODERN MUSIC VENTURES, INC., 5626 Brock St., Houston TX 77023. (713)926-4431. President: David R. Lummis. Record producer and music publisher. Estab. 1986. Deals with artists and songwriters. Produces 12 singles, 2 12″ singles, 12 LPs, 2 EPs and 12 CDs/year. Fee derived from sales royalty and outright fee from record company.
How to Contact: Write first and obtain permission to submit. Prefers cassette (or VHS videocassette if available) with 5 songs and lyric sheet. "Include press kit with bio, picture, news clippings, etc." SASE. Reports in 12 weeks.
Music: Mostly Tejano, Conjunto (Norteño) and jazz; also classical (contemporary), rap (in Spanish), and rock (in Spanish). Produced *Abre El Corazón*, recorded by Mary Maria; *Simplemente*, recorded by Elsa Garcia; *Rebelde*, recorded by Mercedez; and *La Primera Yez*, recorded by Rick Gonzales and The Choice, all on Polygram Records (LPs). "Recently signed a distribution deal with Capitol/EMI Latin."
Tips: "Establish a successful live performance career before contacting the record company."

MOM AND POP PRODUCTIONS, INC., P.O. Box 96, El Cerrito CA 94530. Executive Vice President: James Bronson, Jr. Record producer, record company and music publisher (Toulouse Music/BMI). Deals with artists, songwriters and music publishers. Fee derived from sales royalty.
How to Contact: Prefers cassette with 2-4 songs and lyric sheet. SASE. Reports in 1 month.
Music: Bluegrass, gospel, jazz, R&B and soul. Artists include Les Oublies du Jazz Ensemble.

*MONKEY'S UNCLE PRODUCTIONS, 434 W. Harrison Rd., Lombard IL 60148. (708)620-5338. Producer/Engineer: Jeff Perry. Record producer. Estab. 1933. Deals with artists and songwriters. Fee derived from sales royalty when song or artist is recorded and outright fee from recording artist or record company.
How to Contact: Submit demo tape by mail. Unsolicited submissions are OK. Prefers cassette (or VHS videocassette if available) with 4 songs. Does not return unsolicited material. Reports in 2 months.
Music: Mostly rock, pop and R&B; also country and comedy.

MOOD SWING PRODUCTIONS, 332 N. Dean Rd., Auburn AL 36830. (205)821-JASS. Contact: Lloyd Townsend, Jr. Record producer, music publisher (Imaginary Music), record company (Imaginary Records) and distribution (Imaginary Distribution). Estab. 1982. Deals with artists. Produces 1-2 singles, 1-2 LPs, 1-2 EPs and 1-2 CDs/year. Receives 10-15 submissions/month. Fee derived from sales royalty.
How to Contact: Prefers cassette or 7½ ips reel-to-reel with 4 songs and lyric sheet or lead sheet. "Submissions not returned unless accompanied by SASE; may be retained for future reference unless return specifically requested." Reports in 3 months.
Music: Mostly jazz; also classical, blues and rock. Produced "Electronic Syncopations" (by Scott Joplin), recorded by Patrick Mahoney on Imaginary Records (ragtime); "Sonic Defense Initiatives Vol. 2," written and recorded by various artists (rock); and "Auburn Knights Orchestra 60th Anniversary" (by various artists), recorded by Auburn Knights Orchestra on Custome Records (rag band). Other artists include The Yardbird Orchestra.

MORE COFFEE PRODUCTIONS/WESLEY BULLA, Suite B, 2113 Elliott Ave., Nashville TN 37204. (615)297-6939. A&R Director: Wesley Bulla. Record producer, music publisher (Sadhana Music Publishing/ASCAP). Estab. 1981. "We mostly work with major labels: EMI, Curb, Warner-Chappel, RCA." Fee derived from sales royalty or outright fee from recording artist or record company.
How to Contact: Submit demo tape by mail. Unsolicited submissions are OK. Prefers cassette (or VHS videocassette if available) with 3 songs and lyric sheet. SASE.
Music: Mostly pop/rock, country, R&B; also gospel and New Age/jazz.
Tips: "Know your market, find a producer with music industry contacts. Produce quality demos. Publishers and record companies are expecting record quality demos."

ERIC MORGESON, 5619 N. Beech Daly, Dearborn Heights MI 48127. President: Eric Morgeson. Record producer. Estab. 1980. Deals with artists and songwriters. Produces more than 15 singles and 5 albums/year. Fee derived from sales royalty or outright fee from recording artist or record company.
How to Contact: Submit demo tape by mail. Unsolicited submissions are OK. Prefers cassette with 3 songs and lyric sheet. Include SASE. Reports in 6 weeks.
Music: Mostly R&B, pop and rock. Produced "Don't Call My House," recorded by Ada Dyer on Motown Records (R&B); "Something 'Bout Your Touch," recorded by Sharon Bryant on Wing Records (R&B) and "Stay With Me," recorded by Gerry Woo on Polygram Records (R&B). Other artists

include Tamika Patton, Billy Always, Fred Hammond, Krystol and Chris Bender.
Tips: "Be willing to rewrite. We just need A-sides."

GARY JOHN MRAZ, 1324 Cambridge Dr., Glendale CA 91205. (818)246-PLAY. Producer: Gary Mraz. Record producer. Estab. 1984. Deals with artists and songwriters. Produces 6-12 12″ singles and 2-6 LPs/year. Fee derived from sales royalty or outright fee from record company.
How to Contact: Submit demo tape by mail. Unsolicited submissions are OK. Prefers cassette (or VHS videocassette if available) with 3 songs and lyric sheets. "Does not return unsolicited material." Reports in 6 weeks.
Music: Mostly dance, pop and R&B. Produced "Flip" (by Ray/Sooen), recorded by Mraz/Ray on Draw Records (dance) and "Fontana/Game of Love" (by Jinni Fontana), recorded by Mraz on Banana Records (dance). Other artists include Jon Holland, Stacy O, Bunji Jumpers and The Moosters.
Tips: "Give me grooves that make you move. Just do what you do best."

MUNICH PRODUCTIONS/RECORDS, B.V., Edeseweg 33, P.O. Box 81, Bennekom 6720 AB **Holland**. (31)8389-16777 and 19377. FAX: (31)16588. Producer/President: Job Zomer. Record producer, music publisher (Munich Music) and record company (Munich Records B.V.). Deals with artists and song-writers. 24-track studio. Produces 20 CD singles, 20 7″ singles and 20 CDs/year. Fee derived from "percentage of net income."
How to Contact: Prefers cassette (or Beta or VHS PAL videocassette if available). Does not return unsolicited material.
Music: Mostly jazz, reggae and blues; also new classical. Produced *Turning Point*, written and recorded by Rory Block; *Jack of Hearts*, written and recorded by Jack of Hearts; *16 Titles* (by Mr. & Mrs. Bergman), recorded by Greed & Kauffeld; all on Munich Records (all LP/CD/cassettes).

*ROSS MUNRO/RANDOM ENTERTAINMENT INC., #104, 185 Frederick St., Toronto Ontario M5A 4L4 **Canada**. (416)863-6994. FAX: (416)868-0100. Producer: Ross Munro. Record producer, music publisher (Toon Town Music/CAPAC, ASCAP). Estab. 1980. Deals with artists and songwriters. Produces 4-6 singles and 3-4 albums/year. Fee derived from fees and/or sales royalty.
How to Contact: Write or call first to obtain permission to submit. Prefers cassette (or VHS videocassette if available) with 2-4 songs and lyric sheets. "Does not return unsolicited material." Reports in 1 month.
Music: Mostly rock, pop and country. Produced *Thrill of the Chase*, written and recorded by Simon Chase on Axe Records (rock LP); *Breathless*, written and recorded by Jannetta on Trilogy Records (rock LP); *After The Storm*, written and recorded by Danny Brooks on Trilogy Records (rock LP) and "Mark On My Heart," by Janetta on Trilogy Record (rock/pop album).

*MUSIC HOUSE PRODUCTIONS, 23 Maureen Dr., Mt. Sinai NY 11766. (516)928-2425. President: Michael Dominici. Record producer. Estab. 1986. Deals with artists and songwriters. Produces 3 singles, 2 LPs and 2 EPs/year. Fee derived from sales royalty or outright fee from recording artist.
How to Contact: Submit demo tape by mail. Unsolicited submissions are OK. Prefers cassette with 3 songs and lyric sheet. "Send bio if you have one." SASE. Reports in 3 weeks.
Music: Mostly rock, pop and R&B. Produced "A Cut Above" (by Michael Dominici), recorded by Off the Edge on M.H. Records (alternative EP); and "Without You," written and recorded by Tony Clay on M.H. Records (pop single).
Tips: "Let us hear your best songs, but you must be open for changes or different feels within the song."

*CHUCK MYMIT MUSIC PRODUCTIONS, 9840 64th Ave., Flushing NY 11374. Contacts: Chuck and Monte Mymit. Record producer and music publisher (Chuck Mymit Music Productions/BMI). Estab. 1978. Deals with artists and songwriters. Produces 8-10 singles, 2-4 12″ singles, 3-5 LPs and 3-5 CDs/year. Fee derived from sales royalty or outright fee from recording artist or record company.
How to Contact: Submit demo tape by mail. Unsolicited submissions are OK. Prefers cassette (or VHS videocassette if available) with 3-5 songs and lyric or lead sheet. SASE. Reports in 1 month.
Music: Mostly pop, rock and R&B. Produced "Easy Lovin' " (by Donnell and Cody), recorded by Linda Li on RCA Records (pop single); *For Your Love* (by Tonsend), recorded by Tony Spataro on Candi Records (pop LP); and "Juice" (by Favarelli), recorded by The Xogs on Rinidel Records (rock single). Other artists include Chuck Mymit, Rita Rose, Eddie Tyrell, and The Dellmonts.

*NARADA PRODUCTIONS, 1845 North Farwell, Milwaukee WI 53202. (414)272-6700. A&R Coordinator: Richard Morton. Record producer, music publisher and record company (Narada Records). Estab. 1980. Deals with artists only. Produces 30 LPs and 30 CDs/year. Fee derived from sales royalty when song or artist is recorded.

How to contact: Submit demo tape by mail. Unsolicited submissions are OK. Prefers cassette (or VHS videocassette if available) with 5 songs. Does not return unsolicited material. Reports in 1 month.
Music: New Age, instrumental and world beat.
Tips: "We want instrumental music."

NASHVILLE COUNTRY PRODUCTIONS, 351 Millwood Dr., Nashville TN 37217. (615)366-9999. President/Producer: Colonel Jack Lynch. Record producer, music publisher (Jaclyn Music/BMI), record company (Jaclyn and Nashville Country Productions) and distributor (Nashville Music Sales). Estab. 1987. Works with artists and songwriters. Produces 1-12 LPs/year. Fee derived from sales royalty or outright fee from artist or record company; "We do both contract and custom producing."
How to Contact: Submit demo tape, or write or call first and obtain permission to submit or arrange personal interview. Prefers cassette with 1-4 songs and lyric or lead sheet. SASE. Reports in 10 days.
Music: Mostly country, bluegrass, MOR and gospel; also comedy. "We produced Keith Whitley and Ricky Skaggs' first album." Produced *Please Don't Let the Fire Go Out,* a 9 song cassette album by Glenda Rider; and *Easy This Time,* a 10 song cassette album by Paul Woods. Other artists include Jack Lynch and The Nashville Travelers and Ralph Stanley and The Clinch Mountain Boys.
Tips: "Prepare a good quality cassette demo, send to us along with a neat lyrics sheet for each song and a resume and picture."

*BILL NELSON, 45 Perham St., W. Roxbury MA 02132. Contact: Bill Nelson. Record producer and music publisher (Henly Music/ASCAP). Estab. 1987. Deals with artists and songwriters. Produces 6 singles and 6 LPs/year. Fee derived from outright fee from recording artist.
How to Contact: Submit demo tape by mail. Unsolicited submissions are OK. Prefers cassette with 3-4 songs and lyric sheet. SASE. Reports in 3-4 weeks.
Music: Mostly country, pop and gospel. Produced "Big Bad Bruce" (by J. Dean), recorded by B.N.O.; "Do You Believe in Miracles" (by B. Nelson), recorded by Part-Time Singers; and "Don't Hurry With Love" (by B. Bergeron), recorded by B.N.O.; all on Woodpecker Records (all singles).

NEON JUKEBOX PRODUCTION, P.O. Box 16, Hampton VA 23669. (804)838-6930. Producer: Doc Holiday; Producer & Engineer: Tom Breeden. Record producer and music publisher (Live Note Publishing/BMI, Doc Publishing/BMI). Estab. 1985. Deals with artists and songwriters. Produces 15-20 singles, 3-5 LPs and 5-10 EPs/year. Fee derived from sales royalty or outright fee from recording artist or record company.
How to Contact: Submit demo tape by mail. Unsolicited submissions are OK. Prefers cassette with 2-3 songs and lyric sheets. "Artist: bios and photos helpful but not a must." SASE. Reports in 4 weeks. "Send good quality demos with lyric sheets and be sure to include SASE and phone number for reply."
Music: All types. Produced "If You Could Only See" (by Judith Guthro/Richie Balin), recorded by Richie Balin (country/single); "Seven Wonders of the World", written and recorded by Richie Balin (country/single); and "Canadian State of Mind" (by Tom Breeden/Judith Guthro), recorded by Doc Holiday (country folk EP); all recorded on Tugboat Records. Other artists include Kevin Irwin and Jon Washington. "Although to date a majority of product has been focused on a country market, we are expanding to also include A&R departments for rock and top-40 projects."
Tips: "Produced 16 records charting in the top 100's on Cashbox and Billboard charts in the last 20 months. 'If You Could Only See' went #1 on Cashbox Country Indies Charts and to #44 on Cashbox 100's Country Singles Chart. 'Seven Wonder's of the World' is presently at #49 on Cashbox Top 100's Country Charts and at #5 on Cashbox Country Indies Charts and still climbing!"

*NEW DAWN PRODUCTIONS/SOUTH BOUND PRODUCTIONS, Box 111, Newbury WI 53060. (414)675-2839. Producer: Robert Wiegert. Record producer and music publisher (RobJen Music, Trinity Music and Great Northern Lights Music). Works with artists and songwriters. Fee derived from sales royalty.
How to Contact: Prefers 7½ ips reel-to-reel or cassette with 3 songs and lyric sheet. Does not return unsolicited material. Reports in 1 month.
Music: New Age and fine arts music.
Tips: "If we feel a song is a hit, we do everything possible to get it cut. But writers must be self critical and write, write, write."

*NEW EXPERIENCE RECORDS, P.O. Box 683, Lima OH 45802 (419)226-3509. Music Publisher: James L. Milligan Jr. Vice President: Tonya Milligan. Record producer, music publisher (BMI/CMA, a Division of Party House Publishing) and record company (New Experience Records, Grand-Slam Records, Rap Label). Estab. 1989. Deals with artists and songwriters. Produces 5 12″ singles, 2 LPs, 1 EP and 2 CDs/year. Fee derived from sales royalty when song or artist is recorded, outright fee from recording artist or outright fee from record company, "depending on services required."

How to Contact: Call first to arrange personal interview, if in the area. If not write or call first and obtain permission to submit. Contact is Tonya Milligan, VP of A&R. Prefers cassette with a minimum of 3 songs and lyric or lead sheets (if available). "If tapes are to be returned, proper postage should be enclosed and all tapes and letters should have SASE for faster reply." Reports in 1 month.

Music: Mostly pop, R&B and rap; also gospel, contemporary gospel and rock. Produced "Lawman" (by Ray Smith), recorded by M.C.Y.T. on N.E.R. (rap, single); "Blue Haze" and "Young and Freaky" (by J. Milligan), recorded by James Junior on N.E.R. (singles). Other artists include Melie-D-DJ-Deff, Melvin Milligan and Robert Perry.

Tips: "I'm seeing a big change in the music industry. The major labels are open to more independent products, songwriters, singers and artists. Find a good indie label for your material and work your way to the top."

NEW HORIZON RECORDS, 3398 Nahatan Way, Las Vegas NV 89109. (702)732-2576. President: Mike Corda. Record producer. Deals with singers preferably. Fee derived by sales royalty.

How to Contact: Prefers cassette with 1-3 songs and lyric sheet. SASE.

Music: Blues, easy listening, jazz and MOR. Artists include Mickey Rooney, Bob Anderson, Jan Rooney, Joe Williams and Robert Goulet.

NIGHTWORK RECORDS, 355 W. Potter Dr., Anchorage AK 99502. (907)562-3754. Contact: Kurt Riemann. Record producer and music licensor (electronic). Deals with artists and songwriters. Produces 2 singles, 8 LPs and 2 CDs/year. Fees derived from sales royalty or outright fee from recording artist.

How to Contact: Prefers cassette or 15 ips reel-to-reel with 2-3 songs "produced as fully as possible. Send jingles and songs on separate reels." Does not return unsolicited material. Reports in 1 month.

Music: Mostly electronic and electronic jingles. Produced *Aurora*, by Kurt Riemann on Nightworks Records (electronic); *T/B/A*, by Jeanene Walker on Windsong Records (country); and *Midnight Run*, by Robby Dennis (pop).

*DAVID NORMAN PRODUCTIONS, #1632, 639 Garden Walk Blvd., College Park GA 30349. (404)994-1770. Producer/Engineer: David Norman. Record producer. Estab. 1986. Deals with artists and songwriters. Produces 6 singles, 8 12″ singles, 5 LPs, 5 EPs and 4 CDs/year. Receives 200 submissions/year. Fee derived from outright fee from recording artist or outright fee from record company.

How to Contact: Submit demo tape by mail. Unsolicited submissions are OK. Prefers cassette with 5 songs. "Please send photo." Does not return unsolicited material. Reports in 2 weeks.

Music: Mostly funk and R&B; also techno-music. Produced "The Mack" (by Ervin Hunter), recorded by DJ Noah on Trianta Records (rap single); "Living Voice" (by Billy Kaplin), recorded by Living Voice on Kudzu Records (techno); and "The Power" (by Derek Coile), recorded by The Power on Ichiban Records (dance). Otherartists include Kid Gloves, Rane, So Inclined, H^2O, Tony St. Anthony.

Tips: "I see the music industry being overkilled by musical programming on computers. Hopefully, in the coming years, music will once again resort to real drummers and musicians actually playing the music themselves."

*NOW+THEN MUSIC, #2A, 412 E. 78 St., New York NY 10021. (212)879-4667. President: Shane Faber. Record producer, music publisher (Now+Then Music/BMI) and record company (Now+Then Records). Estab. 1980. Deals with artists and songwriters. Produces 10 singles and 2 LPs/year. Fee derived from sales royalty when song or artist is recorded, outright fee from recording artist and outright fee from record company. "I'm usually hired to produce and record masters for artists by their management or labels—or to mix their material."

How to Contact: Submit demo tape by mail. Unsolicited submissions are OK. Prefers cassete (or DAT or VHS videocassette if available) with 4 songs and lyric sheet. SASE. Reports in 2 months.

Music: Mostly rap, R&B and rock; also quiet storm, New Age and world beat. Produced "Turtle Power" (written and recorded by Partners In Kryme), on SBK Records (rap single); "Work" (by Faber/King Davis), recorded by BTXpress (R&B single); and "Partyline," recorded by 5th Platoon on SBK Records (rap single).

*NRB PRODUCTIONS, 2124 Darby Dr. NW, Massillon OH 44646. (216)833-2061. A&R Director: Nick Boldi. Record production, music publisher (Bolnik Music) and record company (RoxTown Records). Works with artists and songwriters. Produces 4-6 singles and 4 LPs/year. Receives 60 submissions/year. Fee derived by sales royalty.

How to Contact: Prefers cassette with 1-6 songs and lyric sheet. SASE. Reports in 6 weeks.

Music: Mostly country, rock and pop; also New Age and R&B. Produced "Aerobic Rock & Roll" (by Misheff/Boldi), recorded by Big Lou; "He'll Always Be My Daddy To Me" (by Pellegrini) and "Lover's Dreamland" (by Boldi), both recorded by Danny Pellegrini; all on Roxtown Records (45s). Other artists include Charles Davenport, Dew Watson and Kody Storma.

Tips: "We like an unusual, interesting, good story with hook line and mostly country songs."

*OGDENHOUSE MUSIC PRODUCTIONS, Los Angeles CA 90046. (213)851-0458. President: Byron De Lear. Record producer and songwriter (De Lear Music/ASCAP). Estab. 1987. Deals with artists and songwriters. Produces 3-5 singles, and 3-4 LPs/year.
How to Contact: Call first and obtain permission to submit. Prefers cassette with 3 songs and lyric sheets. Reports in 6 weeks.
Music: Mostly pop, rock and R&B; also MOR and country. Produced *Warren Hill,* recorded by Warren Hill on BMG/Novus Records (R&B/jazz LP); "Ready," recorded by Joey Diggs on Capitol Records (pop single); and "Cold Shoulder," written and recorded by Taz on Monster Records (rock EP).

JEANNINE O'NEAL PRODUCTIONS, 195 S. 26th St., San Jose CA 95116. (408)286-9840. Producer: Jeannine O'Neal. Record producer and arranger. Deals with artists and songwriters. Produces 10 singles, 5 12″ singles, 6 LPs and 2 CDs/year. Fee derived from sales royalty, outright fee from songwriter/artist and/or outright fee from record company.
How to Contact: Submit demo tape or write or call first to arrange personal interview. Prefers cassette with 3 songs and lyric or lead sheets. SASE.
Music: Mostly rock/pop, country and gospel; also jazz and international. Produced "Before, After" and "Oh Why," recorded by Sister Suffragette (pop/rap); *Up On the Edge,* by Jaque Lynn (country LP); "Lady's Choice"/"Catfish on a Stick," by Jeannine O'Neal (instrumental country); *Can You Feel It* by Charlie (country LP); "Get Me to the Country," by Larry Martinez (country); and "One From the Heart," by Practical Jokes (New Age/alternative rock).

*KEITH O'NEIL/Caravell Records, HCR 9 Box 2400, Branson MO 65616. (417)334-7040. Owner: Keith O'Neil. Record producer, music publisher (Caravell Main Sail/ASCAP, White River Music/BMI) and record company (Caravell Records). Estab. 1988. Deals with artists and songwriters. Produces 10 singles, 20 LPs and 4 CDs/year. Fee derived from sales royalty when song or artist is recorded and outright fee from recording artist.
How to Contact: Submit demo tape by mail. Unsolicited submissions are OK. Prefers cassette with 3 songs and lyric sheet. Include SASE. Reports in 1 month.
Music: Mostly interested in country, gospel and pop; also rock. Produced "I've Been There Before" (country single by Sue Ann O'Neal); *It Hurts To Be Alone* (country LP by Karen Rhodes); and "Somethin' Tells Me This Must Be The Blues" (single by Marla Cagle), all recorded by Caravell Studio on Caravell Records. Other artists include Doug Gabriel, Larry Whaley and Moore Brothers.
Tips: "Early submissions, vocal guitar or piano, but don't be afraid to take it to a full-blown demo stage."

ORANGE PRODUCTIONS, Suite 119, 2166 W. Broadway, Anaheim CA 92804-2446. (714)992-2677. CEO: Maxwell Edison. Record producer, music publisher (Tracy Sands Music/BMI) and record company (Orange, Beat, Swak Records). Estab. 1989. Deals with artists and songwriters. Produces 12 singles, 12 12″ singles, 8 LPs, 2-3 EPs and 8 CDs/year. Receives 600 submissions/year. Fee derived from sales royalty or outright fee from recording artist or record company.
How to Contact: Submit demo tape by mail. Unsolicited submissions are OK. Prefers cassette with 2-3 songs and lyric sheet. SASE. Reports in 2 months.
Music: All types. Produced "She's My Girl" (by Dave Kern/Doug Brown), recorded by Jonah (rock); "My Dreams Come True" (by Robert Wahlsteen/Brad Stanfield), recorded by Bob Chance (country); and "Thoughts Of A Wooden Soldier" (by Robet Wahlsteen/Herb Wahlsteen), recorded by Paul and Jeri (country); all on Orange Records. Other artists include Tracy Sands, Marcae Taurus and Manhunter.
Tips: "Looking for high skill level; craftsmen—artisans."

ORDER PRODUCTIONS, 6503 York Rd., Baltimore MD 21212. (301)377-2270. President: Jeff Order. Record producer and music publisher (Order Publishing/ASCAP). Estab. 1986. Deals with artists and songwriters. Produces 3 singles, 3 LPs, 3 EPs and 2 CDs/year. Fee derived from sales royalty and outright fee from recording artist and record company.

 The asterisk before a listing indicates that the listing is new in this edition. New markets are often the most receptive to unsolicited submissions.

How to Contact: "Lyric sheets without recorded music are unacceptable." Submit demo tape by mail. Unsolicited submissions are OK. Prefers cassette with 4 songs and lyric sheet. Does not return unsolicited material. Reports in 1 month.
Music: Works with all types of music. Produced "Won't You Dance With Me" (by Jeff Order), recorded by Tiny Tim (dance/single); *Sea of Tranquility* and *Isis Unveiled*, written and recorded by Jeff Order (New Age LPs). Other artists include R&B artist Tracy Hamlin and rock group Lost Angels.
Tips: "We only work with songwriters and artists who are seriously committed to a career in music. Submissions should be professionally recorded."

JOHN "BUCK" ORMSBY/ETIQUETTE PRODUCTIONS, Suite 273, 2442 N.W. Market, Seattle WA 98107. (206)524-1020. FAX: (206)524-1102. Publishing Director: John Ormsby. Record producer (Etiquette/Suspicious Records) and music publisher (Valet Publishing). Estab. 1980. Deals with artists and songwriters. Produces 1-2 singles, 3-5 LPs, and 3-5 CDs/year. Fee derived from sales royalty.
How to Contact: Prefers cassette (or VHS videocassette if available) with lyric or lead sheet. SASE.
Music: R&B, rock, pop and country. Produced *Snake Dance* (by Rogers), recorded by Kinetics on Etiquette Records (LP); and *Hard to Rock Alone*, written and recorded by K. Morrill on Suspicious Records (LP); and *Crazy 'Bout You*, (by R. Rogers), recorded by Kinetics on Etiquette Records. Other artists include Jerry Roslie.
Tips: "Tape production must be top quality; lead or lyric sheet professional."

OUTLOOK PRODUCTIONS, Box 180, Star Route, Bethel ME 04217. (207)824-3246. Record producer. Deals with artists and songwriters. Produces 12 singles and 6 LPs/year. Fee derived from sales royalty and/or outright fee from record company.
How to Contact: Prefers cassette or 15 ips reel-to-reel (or VHS videocassette if available) with 1 song and lyric sheet. "Please include your name and phone number on the tape." Does not return unsolicited material.
Music: Mostly rock, pop and country; also new wave, heavy metal and avant-garde. Produced *Private WA I&II*, by Willie Alexander (rock/avant garde EPs, Tourmaline Records); "Orgone Box," by The Twitch on Tourmaline Records (rock cassette album); *Sky Frontier* and *Innocent Condemned* by Sky Frontier on Tourmaline Records (rock albums); "Facets," by Jewel Clark on Tourmaline Records (country EP).

*KAREN PADY-KA PRODUCTIONS, P.O. Box 3500, Pawtucket RI 02861. (401)728-1689. President: Karen Pady. Record producer, music publisher (KA Productions, Pady Music Publishing Co./ASCAP) and record company (Big K Records). Estab. 1980. Deals with artists and songwriters. Produces 2 LPs/year. Fee derived from outright fee from recording artist.
How to Contact: Write first and obtain permission to submit. Prefers cassette (or VHS videocassette if available) with any number of songs and lyric sheet. Include SASE. Does not return unsolicited material. Reports in 3 weeks.
Music: Mostly pop, rock and light rock; also A/C and country rock. Produced "Will I Ever Make It Thru," recorded by Karyn and Steph (rock); "You Were My Best Friend," recorded by Karyn Krystal (country rock); and "That's What I'm Living For," recorded by Midnight Fantasy (A/C); all written by Karen Padykula on Big K Records. Other artists include Together Again, Image with Camy and Gina, Pauline Silvia and Ronnie Woods.
Tips: "We produce all types of music. If we like it, we'll go for it."

*JOHNNY PALAZZOTTO/PAL PRODUCTIONS, P.O. Box 80691, Baton Rouge LA 70898. (504)924-3327. Owner: Johnny Palazzotto. Record producer and music publisher (Ertis Music Co./ASCAP). Estab. 1980. Deals with artists and songwriters. Produces 1 single, 1 LP and 1 CD/year.
How to Contact: Submit demo tape by mail. Unsolicited submissions are OK. Prefers cassette with 3-5 songs. "Please try to be objective regarding your own material, maybe let someone whose opinion you respect choose your submissions." Reports in 2-4 weeks.
Music: Mostly rock n' roll, R&B and country; also zydeco, cajun and gospel. Produced "TeNiNeNi Nu" (by Slim Harpo) and *Keep on Walkin'* (by Major Handy); both recorded by Major Handy on Maison de Soul (zydeco). Other artists include Raful Neal, Rudy Richard and Henry Gray.

MICHAEL PANEPENTO/AIRWAVE PRODUCTION GROUP INC., 1916 28th Ave. South, Birmingham AL 35209. (205)870-3239. Producer: Michael Panepento. Record producer, music publisher (Panelips Music/BMI) and record company (Pendem Records Inc.). Estab. 1985. Deals with artists and songwriters. Produces 5 singles, 2 12" singles, 4 LPs, 5 EPs and 3 CDs/year. Fee derived from sales royalty.
How to Contact: Write first and obtain permission to submit. Prefers cassette with 3 songs and lyric sheet. SASE. Reports in 2 months.
Music: Mostly rock, R&B and pop; also jazz and country. Produced *Raw Sessions* (by A.J. Vallejo), recorded by The Vallejo Bros. on Pandem Records (rock LP); "Kickin Up a Fuss" (by Steven Hanks), recorded by Slick Lilly on Slick Lilly Records (rock EP); and *The Diptones* (by various songwriters),

recorded by Diptones on Pandem Records (MOR CD). Other artists include Syntwister, Kelly O'Neal, Baghdad and Elvis' Grave.

PANIO BROTHERS LABEL, P.O. Box 99, Montmartre, Saskatchewan S0G 3M0 **Canada**. Executive Director: John Panio, Jr. Record producer. Estab. 1977. Deals with artists and songwriters. Produces 1 single and 1 LP/year. Receives 6 submissions/month. Works with lyricists and composers and teams collaborators. Fee derived from sales royalty or outright fee from artist/songwriter or record company.
How to Contact: Prefers cassette with any number of songs and lyric sheet. Does not return unsolicited material. Reports in 1 month.
Music: Country, dance, easy listening and Ukrainian. Produced "Christmas Is Near," by the Panio Brothers Band (Christmas single); "Celebrate Saskatchewan," by the Panio Brothers (Ukrainian); and *Best of the Panio Brothers*, by the Panio Brothers on PB Records (cassette).

*GEORGE PAPPAS/CHESHIRE SOUND STUDIOS, 2093 Faulkner Road, N.E., Atlanta GA 30324. (404)321-3886. Producer/Engineer: George Pappas. Record producer, engineer. Estab. 1967. Deals with artists and songwriters. Produces 5 singles, 5 12″ singles, 3 LPs, 4 EPs and 5 CDs/year. Fee derived from outright fee from recording artist or record company.
How to Contact: Call first to arrange personal interview. Prefers cassette with 3-5 songs and lyric or lead sheets. "In order for any material to be returned a SASE must accompany any and all material submitted." Reports in 2 months.
Music: Alternative rock, rap and R&B; also gospel, rock and pop. Produced *Scarred But Smarter* recorded by Drivin'n'Crying on Island Records; and *Stiff Kitty* on Drastic Measures Records and *Nihilist*, written and recorded by Nihilist on Metal Blade Records. Recently credited work: Bobby Brown/Big Daddy Kane; Lateasha (Motown); Kinetic Dissent (Road Racer); Michelle Shocked (Polygram); Georgia Satellites (Elektra).

MICK PARKER, Gateway Studio, Kingston Hill Centre, Surrey KT2 7LB **England**. Managing Director: Mick Parker. Record producer. Also produces and writes TV commercials and film soundtracks. Estab. 1985. Works with artists and songwriters. Produces 4-6 singles, 2-3 LPs and 2-3 CDs/year. Fee derived from sales royalty or outright fee from record company.
How to Contact: Prefers cassette with up to 5 songs and lyric or lead sheet. SAE and IRC. Reports in 3 weeks.
Music: Mostly rock, jazz/rock, dance; also pop, soul and funk. Produced "From Be-Bop to Hip-Hop" (by R. Marcangelo), recorded by Streetbeat U.K. on Polydor Records (rap); "Christmas Wrapping" (by Mick Parker), recorded by Tony Robinson on Marco Polo Records (comedy); "Central Lobby," written and recorded by Mick Parker (TV theme, instrumental). Other artists include Kit Rolfe and Reuben Richards.
Tips: "Don't worry about the production too much. I want to hear good songs, well sung and with the minimum of fussy arrangement."

PATTY PARKER, Suite 114, 10603 N. Hayden Rd., Scottsdale AZ 85260. (602)951-3115. Producer: Patty Parker. Record producer, record company (Comstock, Paylode), miscellaneous independent releases. Estab. 1978. Deals with artists and songwriters. Produces 18 singles, 3 LPs and 3-4 CDs/year. Receives 60 submissions/month. Fee derived from outright fee from recording artist or recording company. "We *never* charge to songwriters!! Artist's fee for studio production/session costs."
How to Contact: Submit demo tape by mail. Unsolicited submissions are OK. Prefers cassette, (or VHS videocassette if available) with 4 songs and lyric sheet. Voice up front on demos. SASE. Reports in 2 weeks.
Music: Mostly country—traditional to crossover, western and some A/C. Published "Lonesome Road," written and recorded by Jess Owen on Comstock Records (country); "Granddaddy Was a Lawman" (by Sharon Chadwick), recorded by The Roberts Sisters on Comstock Records (country); and "Never A Night Like That Before" (by Sharon Johnson, Bill Yeats and Kelley Pettigrew), recorded by Bill Yeats on Paylode (A/C). Also produces Paul Gibson, Jodie Sinclair, Colin Clark, Jacquelyn Moore and Rodney Young.
Tips: "Writers should strive to write medium to uptempo songs—there's an abundance of ballads. New artists should record medium to uptempo material as that can sometimes better catch the ear of radio programmers."

*CHRIS PATI PRODUCTIONS, INC., 289 Littleneck Rd., Centerport NY 11721. (516)754-6800. Vice President: John Tabacco. Record producer, music publisher (Patitude Publishing), record company (Backdoor Records Inc.) and recording studio (Modern Voices). Estab. 1984. Deals with artists and songwriters. Produces 2 singles, 2 12″ singles and 1 CD/year. Receives 1 submission/month. Fee derivation varies per situation. "Charges a studio fee (only)."

How to Contact: Submit demo tape by mail. Unsolicited submissions are OK. Prefers cassette (or VHS ½" videocassette if available) with 4 songs and lyric sheet. Does not return unsolicited material. Reports in 1 month.
Music: Mostly pop, dance/house and rock (metal, etc.); also alternative, jazz and classical. Produced *Spontaneous Repetition*, written and recorded by Mike Crum on NAB Publishing (alternative) and *Go House Yourself* (by Pati/DiMauro/Tabacco), recorded by Soled Out on Backdoor Records (house). Other artists include Jim Dexter, Jenean Claps, Fuzzy Gray Matter, Mike Crum, Mathews & Bach and John Tabacco.

DAVE PATON, The Idea Bank, 16776 Lakeshore Dr., C-300, Lake Elsinore CA 92330. Contact: Dave Paton. Record producer and music publisher (Heaven Songs/BMI). Deals with artists and songwriters. Produces 20 singles and 3-5 LPs/year. Fee negotiable.
How to Contact: Write first to obtain permission to submit. Prefers 7½ ips reel-to-reel or cassette with 3-6 songs and lyric sheet. SASE. Reports in 2 weeks.
Music: Country, dance, easy listening, jazz, MOR, progressive, R&B, rock, top 40/pop and comedy. Produces Linda Rae and Breakheart Pass and Gene Mitchener (world's only sit down, stand up comic).

*DAVE PELL PRODUCTIONS/Digital, 5635 Corteen Pl., No. Hollywood CA 91607. (818)980-1021. Owner: Dave Pell. Record producer, music publisher (Dave Pell Enterprises, Inc./ASCAP, BMI) and record company (Headfirst Records). Estab. 1982. Deals with artists and songwriters. Produces 10 LPs and 10 CDs/year. Fee derived outright from record company.
How to Contact: Submit demo tape by mail. Unsolicited submissions are OK. Prefers cassette with 4 songs and lyric sheet. Does not return unsolicited material. Reports in 1 month.
Music: Mostly jazz, fusion and New Age. "We produced 17 CDs in first 2 years."

JOHN PENNY, 484 Lexington St., Waltham MA 02154. (617)891-7800. President: John Penny. Record producer, music publisher (Penny Thoughts Music/BMI) and record company (Belmont Records, Waverly Records). Produces 15 singles and 6 LPs/year. Deals with songwriters and artists. Fee derived from fee from recording artist.
How to Contact: Write first and obtain permission to submit. Prefers cassette with 3-4 songs. SASE. Reports in 2 weeks.
Music: Mostly C&W, rock. Produced *Hands of a Dreamer*, written and recorded by Larry Flint (LP and single); "Good Timer," written and recorded by Stan Jr. Anderson (single); and "Nights Out at the Days Inn" (by J. Fox/L. Wilson/R. Ball), recorded by Jimmy Allen; all country/western on Belmont Records. Other artists include Jackie Lee Williams, Tim Barrett, John Hicks, Paul Metcalf, Rick Robinson and The Bayou Boys and Mike Cummings.

*PHANTOM PRODUCTIONS, INC., P.O. Box 90936, Austin TX 78709-0936. (512)288-1044. FAX: (512)288-4748. Director: Chris or Martin Theophilus. Record producer, music publisher (Mystikos Music/BMI) and record company (Phantom Records, US and UK). Estab. 1964. Deals with artists and songwriters. Produces 20 singles, 10 LPs and 5 CDs/year. Fee derived from sales royalty when song or artist is recorded.
How to Contact: Submit demo tape by mail. Unsolicited submissions are OK. Prefers cassette (or VHS videocassette if available) with 4-6 songs and lyric sheet. SASE. Reports in 1 month.
Music: Mostly pop, New Age, alternative rock and country; also R&B, gospel, jazz and Latin. Produced *Shadow Of A Doubt* (country CD/LP written and recorded by Mark Luke Daniels); *Chambridge Circus* (rock LP written and recorded by John Cambridge); and *Bare Bones and Railroad Tones* (country LP/cassette written and recorded by Mark Luke Daniels), all on Phantom Records. Other artists include Tracy Lyn, The Twins, James Hinkle and Lucian Turk.
Tips: "Most of the artists we work with are singer/songwriters. We find we react best to artists who know what they want, have spent some amount of time developing their skill and following . . . and who have a well produced demo with professional packaging. We look for artists with international potential."

*PHILLY BREAKDOWN, 216 W. Hortter St., Philadelphia PA 19119. (215)848-6725. President: Matthew Childs. Record producer, music publisher (Philly Breakdown/BMI) and record company (Philly Breakdown). Estab. 1974. Deals with artists and songwriters. Produces 3 singles and 2 LPs/year. Fee derived from sales royalty when song or artist is recorded.
How to Contact: Submit demo tape by mail. Unsolicited submissions are OK. Prefers cassette with 4 songs and lead sheet. SASE. Reports in 6 weeks.
Music: Mostly R&B, hip hop and pop; also jazz, gospel and ballads. Produced *Taste Of The Blues* (by Jimmy Thompson/Matt Childs), recorded by Leroy Christy (blues LP); "Say No To Drugs" (by Matt Childs/Jim Thompson), recorded by Mark Adam (single); and "U Changed Me" (by Clarence Patter-

son), recorded by Gloria Clark (single), all on Philly Breakdown Records.
Tips: "Be original and creative and stay current. Be exposed to all types of music."

PLANET DALLAS, P.O. Box 191447, Dallas TX 75219. (214)521-2216. Manager: Marian Ross. Record producer, music publisher (Planet Mothership/BMI, Stoli Music/ASCAP) and recording studio (Hot Dog Productions Co.). Estab. 1985. Deals with artists and songwriters. Produces 30 singles, 30 12″ singles, 20 LPs, 30 EPs and 20 CDs/year. Fee derived from sales royalty or outright fee from recording artist or record company.
How to Contact: Submit demo tape by mail or write first and obtain permission to submit. Prefers cassette (or VHS videocassette if available) with 4 songs and lyric sheet. Reports in 4-6 weeks. Send SASE for reply.
Music: Mostly modern rock and top 40. Produced *Princess Tex*, (by Hal West) recorded by Princess Tex (pop/LP) on Horsehead Records; *King*, written and recorded by The Daylights (punk/funk EP) on 109 Records; and *To Hell and Back*, written and recorded by Nemesis (rap LP) on Profile Records. Other artists include Shock Tu, The Trees and The Mystics.

*PLAYTOWN SOUND PRODUCTIONS, 625 Connable Ave., Petoskey MI 49770. (616)347-0063. Owner: Bob Bollinger. Record producer and engineer/producer. Estab. 1987. Deals with artists and songwriters. Produces 50 singles and 10 LPs/year. Fee derived from outright fee from recording artist. Charges upfront: "We receive a deposit for orchestrating services."
How to Contact: Submit demo tape by mail.Unsolicited submissions are OK. Prefers cassette with 4 songs and lyric or lead sheets. "Telephone us after mailing cassette." SASE.
Music: Mostly pop, rock and folk/rock; also country, folk and metal. Produced *Deep Into the Windy Night* (folk rock LP by Terry Becks); *Puff And The Urge* (rock LP by Kurt Puffpaff); and *Infinity*, all recorded by Playtown Sound. Other artists include Sean Ryan, Kirby Snively, Christopher James, Kerry West, Randy Newsted and Bryan Connolly.
Tips: "Learn patience. Steady hard work always yields good results."

POPS NEON ENTERPRISES, P.O. Box 4125, West Hills CA 91308. Director: Steve Hobson. Record producer and music publisher (Auntie Argon Music/BMI). Estab. 1988. Deals with artists and songwriters. Produces 2 singles/year. Fee derived from sales royalty or outright fee from recording artist. Retainer required for production services.
How to Contact: Write first and obtain permission to submit. Prefers cassette with 1-3 songs and lyric sheets. "Type lyric sheets. Don't overproduce demos. Piano/vocal or guitar/vocal are OK. Unsolicited tapes go straight in the trash, unopened and unheard."
Music: Mostly mainstream pop/top 40. Produced "City Boy Gone Country" and "Go Mountaineers," recorded by Daddy Hoedown on Pops Neon Records (country singles).
Tips: "Submit songs that best represent your direction and best showcases your talents as an artist."

PRAIRIE MUSIC LTD., P.O. Box 438, Walnut IA 51577. (712)366-1136. President: Robert Everhart. Record producer, music publisher (BMI) and record company (Prairie Music). Estab. 1964. Deals with artists and songwriters. Produces 2 singles and 2 LPs/year. Fee derived from outright fee from recording artist or record company.
How to Contact: Submit demo tape by mail. Unsolicited submissions are OK. Prefers cassette. SASE. Reports in 4 months.
Music: Traditional country, bluegrass and folk. Produced "Time After Time," "Street Sleepers" and "Rock of Hollywood," all written and recorded by Bob Everhart on Folkways Records (traditional country). Other artists include Bonnie Sanford and Fiddlin' Grandad Kephart.

*PREJIPPIE MUSIC GROUP, Box 2849, Trolley Station, Detroit MI 48231. (313)581-1267. Partner: Bruce Henderson. Record producer, music publisher (Prejippie Music Group/BMI) and record company (PMG Records). Estab. 1990. Deals with artists and songwriters. Produces 2-4 12″ singles, 1 LP and 1 EP/year. Negotiates between sales royalty and outright fee from artist or record company.
How to Contact: Submit demo tape by mail. Unsolicited submissions are OK. Prefers cassette with 3-4 songs and lyric sheets. SASE. Reports in 1 month.
Music: Mostly rap, funk/rock and R&B; also alternative, rock and experimental music. Produced "Shake Your Body," recorded by The VIC and The CUT (hip house); "Redd Hott (Breathless)," recorded by The VIC and the CUT; and "Good Times," recorded by DOS (featuring Coco); all by PMG Productions on PMG Records. Other artists include The Prejippies, Sacred Places and Vicky and the Poetics.
Tips: "We're looking for songwriters who have a good sense of arrangement, a fresh approach to a certain sound and a great hook for each song."

THE PRESCRIPTION CO., 70 Murray Ave., Port Washington NY 10050. (516)767-1929. President: David F. Gasman. Vice President A&R: Kirk Nordstrom. Tour Coordinator/Shipping: Bill Fearn. Secretary: Debbie Fearn. Record producer and music publisher (Prescription Co./BMI). Deals with artists and songwriters. Fee derived from sales royalty or outright fee from record company.
How to Contact: Write or call first about your interest then submit demo. Prefers cassette with any number of songs and lyric sheet. Does not return unsolicited material. Reports in 1 month. "Send all submissions with SASE or no returns."
Music: Bluegrass, blues, children's, country, dance, easy listening, jazz, MOR, progressive, R&B, rock, soul and top 40/pop. Produced "You Came In" and "Rock 'n' Roll Blues," by Medicine Mike (pop singles, Prescription Records); and *Just What the Doctor Ordered*, by Medicine Mike (LP).
Tips: "We want quality—fads mean nothing to us. Familiarity with the artist's material helps too."

PRIMAL PRODUCTIONS, INC., Suite 133, 3701 Inglewood Ave., Redondo Beach CA 90278. (213)214-0370. Vice President/Producer: Jeffrey Howard. Record producer, music publisher (Primal Visions Music/BMI) and record company (Primal Records). Estab. 1985. Deals with artists and songwriters. Produces 6 singles, 3 LPs and 3 CDs/year. Production charges vary from artist to writer. Charges in advance for services. "This doesn't always apply, but generally we get 50% production fees in advance on projects we produce, 50% on delivery of finished masters."
How to Contact: Write or call first and obtain permission to submit or to arrange personal interview. Prefers (DAT) cassette (or VHS videocassette if available) with 1-5 songs and lyric sheet. "Send only your best and strongest material. Demos are OK but use of high quality cassettes and packaging does reflect on your level of professionalism." SASE. Reports in 6 weeks.
Music: Mostly rock and hard rock, pop and R&B/dance/rap; also country, New Age and heavy metal. Produced *The Passion*, written and recorded by Jeffrey Howard for Primal Records (rock/hard-rock); and *Keeper of the Flame*, written and recorded by Jeff Laine. Other artists include Christopher Fedrov and Cynne Eslin.
Tips: "Always believe in yourself and your material. Don't write what you think *we* want to hear. We're interested in strong material performed by people with a passion for what they do. I have recently seen a trend toward rap music on the West Coast, and there seems to be no end in sight to that. Commercial hard rock has literally turned radio into the 'Rock 40' and that also will continue to be a strong contender in the commercial music market."

*PRINCE/SF PRODUCTIONS, 1135 Francisco St., San Francisco CA 94109. (415)775-9627. Artists Representative: Ken Malucelli. Record producer, music publisher (Prince/SF Publications/ASCAP) record company (Auriga, Christmas). Estab. 1975. Deals with artists only. Produces 1 LP and 1 CD/ year. Fee derived from sales royalty when song or artist is recorded.
How to Contact: Write first and obtain permission to submit. Prefers cassette (or VHS videocassette if available) with 3 songs and lyric and lead sheet. "Primarily interested in a cappella, novelty, theatrical material." SASE. Reports ASAP.
Music: Mostly original pop, Christmas and satire; also unusual and humorous. Produced *The Merrie Olde Christmas Carolers*, by Ken Malucelli), recorded by MOCCarolers on Christmas Records (Holiday, cassette); *Loud is Good* (by The Edlos), recorded by The Edlos on Auriga Records (pop, cassette); and "Freedomsong" (by Eric Morris), recorded by The Edlos on Auriga Records (pop single).
Tips: "Work should be unique, high quality, not derivative."

QUADRAPHONIC TALENT, INC., P.O. Box 630175, Miami FL 33163. (305)472-7757. President: Jack P. Bluestein. Record producer and music publisher. Estab. 1973. Deals with artists and songwriters. Produces 5-10 singles/year. Fee derived from sales royalty.
How to Contact: Artist: query, submit demo tape. Songwriter: submit demo tape and lead sheet. Prefers cassette or 7½ ips reel-to-reel with 1-4 songs. SASE. Reports in 1 month.
Music: Blues, country, easy listening, folk, gospel, jazz, MOR, rock, soul and top 40/pop. Produced "Three Things" and "A Miracle in You," by Ray Marquis on Twister Records (country singles); "Red Velvet Clown" and "Love Day," by Dottie Leonard on AMG Records (pop singles); "Terrorism" and "Ginger," by Winn Thumpkins; "It's Over" and "Dreaming For Two" by Beth Thliveris, "Kathy, Dear" by Al Williams, "Lucky Is A Man" by Larry Coen, "Say, Don't Go" by Winthrop Marcinak and "Masquerade" by Nan Beeson.

R.E.F. RECORDS, 404 Bluegrass Ave., Madison TN 37115. (615)865-6380. President: Bob Frick. Manager: Shawn Frick. A&R Director: Scott Frick. Record producer and music publisher (Frick Music Publishing Co./BMI). Deals with artists, songwriters and producers. Produces 2 singles and 10 LPs/ year. Fee derived from sales royalty.

How to Contact: Write or call first and obtain permission to submit, then submit 7½ ips reel-to-reel or cassette with 2-10 songs and lyric sheet. SASE. Reports in 1 month.
Music: Mostly gospel; also country, rock and top 40/pop. Produced "Unworthy," recorded by Bob Myers; "One Day Closer to Jesus" and "Heading for Heaven," recorded by Bob Scott Frick; "My Little Girl" by Scott Frick; "She's Gone Forever," by Craig Steele; "Time Tricks and Politics," by Eddie Isaacs; and "I Found Jesus in Nashville," by Bob Scott Frick (all gospel singles on R.E.F. Records). Other artists include Larry Ahlborn.

*RANDALL PRODUCTIONS, Box 265, N. Hollywood CA 91603-0265. (708)450-8283 and (818)569-5653. President: Monique O'Neal. Record producer, video producer and musical services to artists/songwriters. Produces 5 singles, 2 LPs and 2 music videos/year. Fee derived from sales royalty.
How to Contact: Prefers cassette (or VHS videocassette if available) with 3-5 songs and lyric sheet. "Clearly label each item you send. Include photo/bio if available." SASE. Does not return material with no return postage. Reports in 1 month, "but be patient."
Music: Mostly R&B, soul, funk, pop, blues, gospel; also accepting finished masters of these and rock (heavy, hard, metal, some acid) for Grandville Rock Sampler album. Produced *Mama Was Right*, recorded by Mack Simmons on Grandville Records (blues/R&B LP); and *Mr. Joy*, recorded by The Jade (LP), with newest singles "Mr Joy/Sweet Love," "Thunderkeeper/The Poetry of You" released overseas and distributed by Timeless Records/London (R&B/pop).

RAPP PRODUCTIONS, INC., 9305 Dogwood Place, Gainesville GA 30506. (404)889-8624. Owner/President: Ron Dennis. Record producer, music publisher (Super Rapp Publishing/BMI and Do It Now Publishing/ASCAP) and record company (RR&R, Rapp Records, Rapture, Ready Records and Yshua Records). Estab. 1964. Works with artists and songwriters. Produces 10-20 singles, 10-20 LPs, 10-20 EPs and 10-20 CDs/year.
How to Contact: Prefers cassette (Type II) or 15 or 30 ips reel-to-reel (or VHS videocassette if available) with lyric chords and lead sheet. "Demo should have lead vocal and music and also a recording of music tracks without vocals." SASE. Reports in 3 months.
Music: Mostly gospel and pop rock. Produced *Free At Last*, written and recorded by Mike Bell on Rapture Records (gospel); *Tommow Looks Like Yesterday* (by Louis Brown), recorded by Ron Dennis on (Sony) CBS/Epic Records (country crossover); and "Tribute to a King," by Chuck Carter on RR&R Records (pop). Other artists include Lisa Westmoreland and Mike Bell, Dan Carroll, Sydney Australia's Stephen Concon, Chuck Carter, Peter Bunwen, Taylor Prichard, Wesley Furumoto, Jan Nielson and Otis Reding; also Patty Weaver on Warner Brothers and approximately 50 others in the past to reach the charts.

*RAY MACK PRODUCTIONS, Box 120675, Nashville TN 37212. (615)255-1068. Owner: Ray McGinnis. Record producer, music publisher (Nautical Music Co./BMI), (Orbit Records). Estab. 1965. Deals with artists and songwriters. Produces 8 singles, 2 12″ singles and 4 CDs/year. Fee derived from sales royalty.
How to Contact: Submit demo tape by mail. Unsolicited submissions are OK. Prefers cassette with 4 songs and lyric sheet. SASE. Reports in 6 weeks.
Music: Mostly country, rock and country rock. Produced *Super Country*, recorded by Da-Kota (country rock); *Pure Country*, recorded by Kim Tsoy; and *I've Always Been Country*, recorded by Sonny Martin (LP); all on Orbit Records. Other artists include LeRoy Steele and Traci Trudeau.
Tips: "Have a good demo tape available with top-notch songs. You will have a better chance of being heard."

RED KASTLE PRODUCTIONS, P.O. Box 163, West Redding CT 06896. (203)438-5366. President: Paul Hotchkiss. Record producer and music publisher. Deals with artists and songwriters. Produces 10 singles, 2 EPs, 2 LPs and 2 CDs/year. Fee derived from sales royalty.
How to Contact: Prefers cassette with 2 songs and lyric sheet. Include bio. SASE. Reports in 3 weeks.
Music: Mostly country and country/pop. Produced "Honky Tonk" (by P.Hotchkiss), recorded by Susan Rose on Direct Records (country); "Darlin' Not Enough Time," written and recorded by Michael Berry on Roto Noto Noto Records (country); and "Thinking About You" (by P. Hotchkiss), recorded by Susan Rose on Target Records (country). Other artists include Big John Hartman, Beverly's Hill-Billy Band, Susan Rose and Leigh Henry.

GARY REVEL, #106, 9015 Owensmouth Ave., Canoga Park CA 91304. (818)341-7125. Record producer and record company (produces for Top's Records). Estab. 1973. Deals with artists and songwriters. Produces 4 singles, 2 LPs and 6 CDs/year. Fee derived from sales royalty.

How to Contact: Write first and obtain permission to submit. "Referrals from agent, manager or lawyer are preferred." Does not return unsolicited material.
Music: Mostly rock, pop and country; also gospel and R&B. Produced "Maria" (by G. Revel, D. Tuttle, A. Meza), recorded by Dale Tuttle (country single); "I Know (We're Gonna Make It Love)" (by Gary Revel), recorded by Dale Tuttle (country); and "Hollywood Star," written and recorded by Gary Revel (rock); all on Top's Records. Other artists include Czar Tuck and Todd Taylor.

*RIDGE RECORDING STUDIOS, 399 Cahaba Road, Greenville AL 36037. (205)382-7800. Record producer and recording studio. Deals with artists and songwriters. Produces 3-5 singles and 3 LPs/year. Receives 3 submissions/year.
How to Contact: Submit demo tape by mail. Unsolicited submissions are OK. Prefers cassette with 3 songs and lyric sheet. "Also will accept standard MIDI files for production purposes." SASE. Reports in 2 months.
Music: Mostly country/rock, country and pop; also rock and jazz. Produces Ralph Sutton (jazz) and Danny Black (country/pop).

ROBBY ROBERSON PRODUCTIONS, Box 370, Round Rock TX 78680. (512)448-6362. Owner: Robby Roberson, Executive Producer for Lana Records, Top Secret Records, Lair Music and GGT Music Group, Inc. Record producer, music publisher (Three Kings Music/BMI) and television and record production. Estab. 1964. Produces 10 singles, 4 12″ singles and 4 LPs/year. Fee derived from sales royalty or outright fee from record company.
How to Contact: Prefers cassette with 3 songs and lyric sheet. SASE.
Music: C&W, gospel, soft rock and crossover. Produced *Iron Butterfly*, written and recorded by Mikal Masters on Top Secret Records (rock LP); *Secret Place*, written and recorded by Robert Hooks on GGT Records (Christian LP); and "By Family Request," written and recorded by Robby Roberson on Lana Records (country). Other artists include Hud Rose, The Jacksons (Christian), Cottonmouth (country rock) and Alexandria (Spanish country).
Tips: "Get educated as to what is really happening in the business, before you make application."

*ROB ROBERTS/OCEAN HILLS MUSIC GROUP, 522 Jones Place, Walnut Creek CA 94596. Producer: Rob Roberts. Record producer (Ocean Hills Music Group). Estab. 1987. Works with artists and songwriters. Fee derived from sales royalty and outright fee from recording artist or record company.
How to Contact: Write first and obtain permission to submit. Prefers cassette with 1-4 songs and lyric sheet. SASE.
Music: Mostly contemporary rock, pop/AOR crossover and contemporary Christian; also jazz/rock with vocals and jazz/rock instrumental. Artists include Paulinho Da Costa, Paul Harris, Chuck Kirkpatrick and David Cochrane.

*ROCK & TROLL PRODUCTIONS, 19 Chase Park, Batavia NY 14020. (716)343-1722. Vice President: Guy E. Nichols. Record producer, music publisher and record company (Rock & Troll Records). Estab. 1981. Deals with artists and songwriters. Produces 25 singles and 2 LPs/year. Fee derived from sales royalty or outright fee from recording artist.
How to Contact: Submit demo tape by mail. Unsolicited submissions are OK. Prefers cassette with 4 songs and lyric sheet. SASE. Reports in 4 weeks.
Music: Mostly rock, pop and R&B. Produced *Heartbreaker*, written and recorded by Lost Angels; and *Little Trolls*, written and recorded by Little Trolls; both on R&T Records (rock LPs).

ROCKIT RECORDS, INC., Suite 107, 35918 Union Lake Rd., Mt. Clemens MI 48043. Production Director: Joe Trupiano. Record Producer: J. D. Dudick. Record producer, music publisher, in-house studio (Ruffcut Recording Studio, Bad Grammar Music/BMI and Broadcast Music, Inc./BMI), record company (Bad Grammar Records) and management company. Estab. 1982. Deals with artists and songwriters. Produces 10-20 singles and 4 CDs/year. Receives 20 submissions/month. Fee derived from outright fee from recording artist.
How to Contact: Prefers cassette (or videocassette if available) with 3-4 songs and lyric sheet. SASE. Reports in 6 weeks.
Music: Mostly pop/rock, R&B/pop, mainstream rock, New Age and heavy metal; also jingles, easy listening, ballads, dance-oriented and MOR. Produced "Choose Life," written and recorded by Laya Phelps (rock); "Main Emotion," written and recorded by Oscar Charles; and "Sin Alley" (by Bob Josey), recorded by Johnny Terry (pop); all on Rockit Records. Other artists include Tuff Kids, Thionne Carpenter, Bamboo Blonde, David Hensen and Jami Bauer.
Tips: "We are presently open for producing outside projects *with self-supporting budget*. This allows our clients the opportunity to shop their own master or sign it to Bad Grammar Records *if* our A&R approves and also considering whether we have an open door policy at the time. We are also accepting material for our upcoming compilation CD projects, which gain valuable exposure for artists seeking

national and European coverage. Through this project several acts have been signed to major labels in the U.S., as well as indie labels in Europe. We have charted many of our acts on commercial radio in Europe."

ROCKY MOUNTAIN HEARTLAND PRODUCTIONS, Box 6904, Denver CO 80206. (303)841-8208. Executive Producer: Steve Dyer. Record and video producer and advertising firm (full service – brochures, demo kits, promo packs, graphics, photography). Deals with artists and songwriters. Fee derived from sales royalty or outright fee from songwriter/artist or record company.
How to Contact: Submit demos. Prefers cassette (or videocassette if available) with 3-5 songs and lyric sheet or lead sheet. Does not return unsolicited material.
Music: Mostly gospel, top 40 and rock; also jazz and country. "Music open and not limited to these types." Produced *The Best Is Yet to Come,* by Kent Parry (big band and orchestra gospel LP); *From Here to Kingdom Come,* by Heart Song (mild gospel/top 40 LP); and *Going, Going, Gone,* by Heart Song (gospel rock LP); all on Record Harvest Records; and *From My Heart,* by Beth Chase.
Tips: "We are interested in new, up and coming artists."

*ADAM RODELL/RODELL RECORDS, P.O. Box 93457, Hollywood CA 90093. (213)960-9447. President: Adam Rodell. Record producer, music publisher (Udder Publishing/BMI, Golden Gelt/ASCAP) and record company (Rodell Records). Estab. 1989. Deals with artists and songwriters. Fee derived from sales royalty or outright fee from recording artist or record company.
How to Contact: Submit demo tape by mail. Unsolicited submissions are OK. Prefers cassette (or VHS videocassette if available) with 3 songs and lyric and lead sheet. Does not return unsolicited material. "We will report back only if we are interested."
Music: Mostly rock, country and pop; also R&B, progressive fusion and rap.
Tips: "We aggressively seek well-produced and professionally recorded demos."

*ROLLING ROAD PRODUCTIONS, INC., Suite 434, 3960 Laurel Cyn., Studio City CA 91614. (818)506-4606. President: Frosty Harton. Estab. 1985. Deals with artists and songwriters. Produces 10 singles, 5 LPs, 2 EPs and 4-5 CDs/year.
How to Contact: Submit demo tape by mail. Unsolicited submissions are OK. Prefers cassette with no more than 4 songs and lyric sheet (optional). Include bio and picture, along with press kit, if available. "Please submit only from categories listed, in which I specialize. I do not do rap, metal or gospel. We will reply only if interested."
Music: Mostly modern/alternative rock (i.e. Pixies, Smithereens), or contemporary jazz (i.e. Metheny). Also pop songwriters/vocalists (i.e. Tracy Chapman, Lyle Lovett). Produced *Blue Solitaire* (by Swanson), recorded by The Telling on Music West Records (alternative rock LP); *Perfectly Human* (by Sloniken), recorded by Mark Sloniken on Music West Records (contemporary jazz LP); and *Rage On River* (by Weathersby), recorded by Shad Weathersby on Dancing Cat/A&M Records (rock EP). Other artists include The Hooligans, George Winston, Bobby McFerren, Cher, Scott Fitzgerald and VINX.
Tips: "Write brilliant songs, perform them brilliantly, and don't use a blowdrier."

*ROOSTER PRODUCTIONS, 1234 W. 6th Ave., Vancouver, British Columbia V6H 1A5 **Canada.** (604)734-1217. Contact: Rolf Hennemann. Record producer. Estab. 1979. Deals with artists and songwriters. Produces 2-3 LPs and 2-3 CDs/year. Receives 20 submissions/month. Fee derived from sales royalty, outright fee from songwriter/artist and/or outright fee from record company.
How to Contact: Prefers cassette. Does not return unsolicited material.
Music: Rock, pop and country blues. Produced "Human Kind," written and recorded by Roy Forbes (country); "The Project," written and recorded by UHF on CBC Variety Records (folk/pop); and "Rocker," written and recorded by Mark Perry (country-rock).
Tips: "Be prepared for some constructive criticism and hard work."

MIKE ROSENMAN, 45-14 215 Pl., Bayside NY 11361. (718)224-7424. Producer: Mike Rosenman. Record producer and arranger. Estab. 1984. Deals with artists and songwriters. Produces 4-6 singles, 1-2 LPs and 1 EP/year. Fee derived from sales royalty or outright fee from recording artist.
How to Contact: Write before submitting. Prefers cassette (or VHS videocassette if available), with 2-4 songs and lyric sheet. Include address and phone number. Put phone number on cassette. Does not return unsolicited material. Will not return solicited tapes without SASE. Reports in 8 weeks.
Music: Mostly pop, R&B, dance/disco and rock; also hard rock, rap and foreign languages. Produced "Jamie Morad," written and recorded by Jamie Morad (foreign language dance cassette); "Lawn Chair Hero," written and recorded by The Upstartz on Tab Records (rock 7″ single); and "Here She Comes," written and recorded by The Upstartz on Tab Records (rock 7″ single). "We also produce jingles and 'sound-alike' song parodies."
Tips: "Send simple demos of good songs. Please write, don't phone to ask about sending tapes. Include SASE if you want your tape back."

HENRY ROWE, 17 Water St., Dracut MA 01826. (508)957-5781. Producer: Henry Rowe. Record producer, music publisher and record company (Hazardous Records). Estab. 1986. Deals with artists and songwriters. Produces 50 singles and 5 LPs/year. Fee derived from sales royalty or outright fee from recording artist or record company.

How to Contact: Write or call first to arrange personal interview. Prefers cassette with 4 songs and lyric sheet. Does not return unsolicited material. Reports in 6-8 weeks.

Music: Mostly metal, rock and pop; also fusion, jazz and New Age. Produced "Half Life" and "Danger Zone" (by Hazardous Waste) (metal); and "Candle to the Magic," by Johann Smith (rock), all recorded by Making Tracks on Hazardous Records.

RUSHWIN PRODUCTIONS, P.O. Box 1150-SM92, Buna TX 77612. (409)423-2521. Owner/Manager: James L. Gibson. Record producer, music publisher (Rushwin Publishing). Estab. 1985. Deals with artists and songwriters. Receives 500 submissions/year. Fee derived from sales royalty, outright fee from songwriter/artist and/or outright fee from record company, depending on the project.

How to Contact: Prefers cassette with 1-4 songs and "typed lyric sheet. Clearly label each item sent. Include photo and bio if available. SASE (6x9 or larger)." Reports ASAP.

Music: Southern/country only. Produced "Reachin' Thru The Thorns" (by James Gibson), recorded by the Gibsons (gospel single); *You're a Saint or You Ain't* (by Randy Lawrence and Bill Fisher), recorded by The Harbringers (gospel LP); and *Jesus I Love You* (by Paul A. Hammock), recorded by The Gibsons (gospel LP); all on Gold Street Records.

Tips: "We consider sincere, hard working artists who are willing to grow with us. We are a small independent operation on the grow. It would be most helpful if the artists would include a press package with their submissions. This would familiarize us with their ministry/music (past, present and future plans). We have an open door policy for songwriters. We utilize material similar to that which is on the charts published by *The Gospel Voice* and *The Singing News*."

RUSTRON MUSIC PRODUCTIONS, 1156 Park Lane, West Palm Beach FL 33417. (407)686-1354. A&R Directors: Rusty Gordon and Davilyn Whims. Record producer, manager and music publisher (Rustron Music Publishers/BMI, Whimsong Publishing/ASCAP). Estab. 1970. Works with artists and songwriters. Produces 2-4 singles and 6-10 LPs/cassette albums/year. Fee derived from sales royalty or outright fee from record company. "This branch office reviews all material submitted for the home office in Rustron NY."

How to Contact: Prefers cassette with 1-3 songs and lyric or lead sheet. "Songs should be 3½ minutes long or less and must be commercially viable for today's market. Singer/songwriters and collaborators are preferred." SASE required for all correspondence. Reports in 1-3 months.

Music: Mostly progressive country, pop (ballads, blues, theatrical, cabaret) and folk/rock; also R&B, New Age folk fusion and New Age. Produced "Seafood Mama," written and recorded by Marianne Flemming on Mermaid Records (blues/rock/R&B); "What Will We Leave the Children," written and recorded by Relative Viewpoint on RVP Records & Tapes; "Verse Ability," written and recorded by Helen Hooke on Montana Blake Records (rock fusion); "Jupiter Light," written and recorded by Robin Plitt on Florida Daze Records (historical folk). Other artists include Sue Massek and Reel World String Band, Deb Criss, Stephanie Shore, Circle & Star, Coconut Heads, Elaine Silver, Terry Andrews, Gordon Johnson and Florida Trails, Marian Joy Ring.

Tips: "Avoid redundant lyrics. Follow a theme, tell a story. Create innovative phrase hooks. Seek original ideas for songs."

JOJO ST. MITCHELL, 273 Chippewa Dr., Columbia SC 29210-6508. Executive Producer and Manager: Jojo St. Mitchell. Record producer. Deals with artists and songwriters. Produces 10 singles and 4 LPs/year. Fee derived from sales royalty, booking and licensing.

How to Contact: Prefers cassette (or VHS videocassette if available) with 3-7 songs; include any photos, biography. SASE. Reports in 3-6 weeks, if interested. Enclose return postage.

Music: Mostly mainstream, pop and R&B; also rock, new music and jazz/rap. Produced *Wheels of Steel* (by R. Clavon/J. Aiken), recorded by Unique Force (rap LP); *Can't Stop Thinking of You* (by L.S. Skinkle), recorded by Jr. Ellis (pop ballad, LP); "Complicated Love," recorded by True Identity; and *Miracle* (by K. Lyon/T. Lyon), recorded by Kat Lyon (pop LP). Other artists include Carnage, Synthetic Meat, Toni Land and Progress In April.

*SAND HAND RECORDS, INC., 3703 Edgewood Rd., Baltimore MD 21215. (301)466-0188. Owner/ Producer: Christopher David III. Record producer (BMI) and record company (Sand Hand, Inc.). Estab. 1988. Deals with artists and songwriters. Produces 1 single, 2 12″ singles, 2 LPs, 2 EPs and 4 CDs/year. Fee derived from outright fee from recording artist and "creation fee."

Close-up

Edward Bilous
Composer/Arranger/Producer
New York, New York

After earning a doctorate in composition from Julliard, Ed
Bilous had a few career options to consider. He could have
pursued classical composition, which despite eight years of
study didn't exactly interest him. But he still wanted music
as a major part of his life.

"I loved learning about the music and the craft of composition, but my heart and soul longed for other kinds of
sounds that existed outside the classical domain," says Bilous. "I was faced with a dilemma:
What is my own personal musical style, and how will I pay the rent?"

Bilous began to pound the pavement of New York, searching for freelance jobs as an
arranger and composer. Working mainly on music for small films, advertising jobs and TV
shows, Bilous continued to learn and develop his writing. "All the time I was freelancing
I wasn't as concerned about finding my own voice as I was about improving my craft. And
along the way I discovered a very new craft, which was using the recording studio as an
instrument and a creative resource."

Being in the "last generation of pre-MIDI composers," it was necessary for Bilous to
branch out to electronic music, or else pay the cost of having less work. His fascination
with the studio paid off. Bilous now owns his own production company, Edward Bilous
Productions, a relatively young company whose forte is music for film and TV.

Although the bread and butter job for Bilous' company is music for advertising (among
his clients are AT&T, Fisher-Price Toys and Norelco), he's also produced the soundtrack
for a film entitled "Le Bain," which premiered at the 1990 Paris Film Festival. He's produced a New Age record (called "Bridge to Infinity") using all African, Asian and Indian
instruments and is preparing to branch out into other projects to produce on his new record
label. Bilous' work on commercials for the African Wildlife Foundation won an award at
the Cannes Film Festival in 1988 for the best public service announcement.

Bilous mentions that although his classical training has helped him succeed in the music
production field, it's not absolutely necessary. What is necessary is to study music that is
novel, that has been influential in film and TV. For example, Bilous cites the movies *The
Witness* and *The Mission* as having important film scores. "Go and buy the CDs to a few
important films like that, and really sit down and pay attention to exactly how those scores
were done. Pluck the notes out on a piano and notice how the music blends with the scene.
Every parameter of sound should be analyzed."

As far as presentation goes, Bilous says that "production does mean something," even
in demo tapes. He recommends, to both the pop songwriter and commercial composer,
investing a little money to accurately depict one's music. If you don't have a good recording,
the message may get muddled. "Even if the writing is terrific," he says, "a lot of people
who listen to the tape (even at music companies) have trouble bridging the gap between
the demo stage and what you envision if it were fully produced. The instant you add real
instruments and real players, your music takes a major leap forward into listenability."
And if it's possible, get familiar with MIDI and electronic music along the way, without

basing all of your music on it. "As soon as you do a demo tape that's MIDI from beginning to end, it puts you in a category with about 99% of all the other inexperienced writers and arrangers that have a computer, synthesizer and tape recorder at home."

Making music for TV and movie scores and advertising is a tough business to break into, and to succeed one must not only have talent and perseverance, but a knack for knowing what to write. "There are so many gifted composers out there who haven't developed the skill to read between the lines or to listen to descriptions of what is needed. Unlike every other aspect of the creative process, music is one that has such a specific language and vocabulary that if you don't know it then you can never really speak specifically about it — even if you are a musician. You start talking about chord voicings and inversions and other technical terms and it becomes confusing. The more successful producers and writers are ones that can maintain their own personality while still identifying what it is the creatives are looking for."

Bilous mentions a book by George Martin (producer of The Beatles) called *All You Need Is Ears*, and offers that title as the basis for success. "That's what it boils down to. If you have the ability to close your eyes and envision sound in your head, then all the rest is just a matter of practice."

—Brian C. Rushing

How to Contact: Write or call first and obtain permission to submit. Prefers cassette (or VHS ½″ videocassette if available) with 2 songs and lyric sheet. SASE. Reports in 2 months.
Music: Mostly pop, rap and rock; also R&B and jazz. Produced *More* (by Christopher David), recorded by Brad Crew on Unisex Records (LP); and *Five Steps* (by David Jones), recorded by Brad Crew on Sand Hand Records (cassette LP).

*SILVER J. SARGENT, P.O. Box 897, Hartford CT 06120. (203)548-0212. Producer: Silver J. Sargent. Record producer, music publisher (LUV Sound/BMI and Silsar Music/BMI) and recording label (Sounds of Connecticut — S.O.C.). Estab. 1984. Deals with artists and songwriters. Produces 4 singles, 4 12″ singles, 2 LPs, 2 EPs, and 2 CDs/year. Receives 30 submissions/month. Fee derived from sales royalty or outright fee from record company.
How to Contact: Prefers cassette (or VHS videocassette) with 4-5 songs and lyric or lead sheet. SASE. Reports in 6 weeks.
Music: Mostly funk, soul and R&B; also gospel, light rock and jazz. Produced "Bite It," (by Herb Superb), recorded by Drum (rap); "Shoot Your Best Shot," (by Silver Sargent), recorded by Carol (dance); and "Merci-ba-coup," (by Silver Sargent), recorded by Scarph (ballad), all singles on S.O.C. Records. Other artists include X.Y. Eli, Kimberlee, Barbara Fowler, Native American and Angie Champaigne.
Tips: "Send only your best, make sure your vocals are understood."

*SATURN PRODUCTIONS, 807 E. Fayle, Baytown TX 77520 (713)420-3189. Executive Producer: Richard E. Cagle. Record producer (Saturn Productions) and record company (Siren Records). Estab. 1989. Deals with artists and songwriters. Produces 3 LPs and 1 EP/year. Fee derived from sales royalty when song or artist is recorded, outright fee from recording artist or outright fee from record company.
How to Contact: Submit demo tape by mail. Unsolicited submissions are OK. Prefers cassette with 4-6 songs and lyric sheet. "Send a complete promo pack (pictures, tapes, and bio). SASE. Reports in 6 weeks.
Music: Mostly funk, heavy rock and top 40; also thrash, reggae and blues. Produced *Royal & Loyal* (written and recorded by Joe "King" Carrasco), on Royal Rio Records; *Voices of Red God* (by compilation of various songwriters and recording artists), on Saturn Redords; and *MXD Emotions* (written and recorded by MXD) on Saturn Records (all LPs). Other artists include Dead Horse, Flesh Mop, Panjam Drum, Elevator Up, Social Deceit and Hunger.
Tips: "Funk will get much bigger in the 90s. New labeling laws are just the beginning, unfortunately."

*JASON SCHWARTZ-U.S.A. ENTERTAINMENT, Suite 661, 880 Front St., Lahaina HI 96761. (808)661-5151. FAX: (808)244-1100. Contact: A&R Director. Record producer, music publisher (Ten of Diamonds/BMI, Mavi No Ka Oi/ASCAP) and record company (Survivor and H.I.T. Records). Estab. 1974. Deals with artists and songwriters. Produces 1-3 singles/year. Fee derived from sales royalty or outright fee from record company.

How to Contact: Submit demo tape by mail. Unsolicited submissions are OK. Prefers cassette (or VHS videocassette if available). SASE. Reports in 1 month.

Music: Mostly pop, country and R&B; also classical, Hawaiian and jazz/fusion. Produced "Dreamer" (by Michael Condon), recorded by Doc Michaels (pop ballad single); *Sunny Side of Reality* (by Walt Rosansky and Jason), recorded by Jason (pop LP); and *Our Love Will Shine On Thru* (by Mark Cohen and Jason), recorded by Jason (rock LP); all on Survivor Records. Other artists include Greta Warren, Amber, Michael Thompson and Rambona.

Tips: "I'm real discriminating; send only your best."

*SCRAPBOOK MUSIC PRODUCTIONS, #252, 1840 South Gaffey St., San Pedro Peninsula CA 90731. (213)514-0920. President: R. Perez. Record producer, music publisher (ASCAP) and record company (Scrapbook Records). Estab. 1980. Deals with artists and songwriters. Produces 24 singles, 12 12" singles, 6 LPs and 4 EPs/year. Fee derived from sales royalty.

How to Contact: Submit demo tape by mail. Unsolicited submissions are OK. Prefers cassette with any number of songs and lyric and lead sheets. SASE. Reports in 2 weeks.

Music: Mostly easy/listening/AOR, New Age (international), R&B/blues, and 1950s oldies (doo-wop, rockabilly, California surf sounds); also A/C, soft rock/pop and instrumentals. Produced *Samurai Warrior*, recorded by King Neptune and The Sea Serpents; *From the 50s Big Beat to the 60s Surf Beat*, recorded by King Neptune and The Sea Serpents; *Instrumental Rock-A-Billy*, by The Galaxies; all written by various artists on Scrapbook Records (LPs/EPs). Other artists include Johnny and The Hurricanes, The Virtues, Duane Eddy and The Rebels, Lind Wray and The Raymen, Dick Dale and The Del-Tones and The Ventures.

*SEPTEMBER MUSIC PRODUCTIONS, P.O. Box 1181, St. Louis MO 63031. (314)837-4095. Producer/Director: Russ Kirkland. Record producer and music publisher (Solid Jammin' Music/ASCAP). Estab. 1979. Deals with artists and songwriters. Produces 3-4 12" singles, 7-10 LPs, 1-2 EPs and 3-4 CDs/year. Fee derived from sales royalty when song or artist is recorded, outright fee from recording artist or outright fee from record company. "Usually, we work with advances from record company, but sometimes 50% and shared profits with speculative artists."

How to Contact: Call first and obtain permission to submit. Prefers cassette (or VHS videocassette if available) with 3 songs and lyric sheet. "Don't send me rap!" Does not return unsolicited material. Reports in 1 month.

Music: Mostly rock, pop and gospel; also metal and country. Produced "Armored Choir" (by artists and producers), recorded by Arsenal on Regency Records (CD and cassette); *Xara* (written and recorded by Xara), on Sugar Records (cassette LP); and "Christmas In St. Louis" (written and recorded by various artists), on Fox Association Records (cassette and single). Other artists include September and Randy Mayfield.

*JON E. SHAKKA PRODUCTIONS, 176 B Woodridge Cres., Nepean ON K2B 7S9 **Canada**. (613)596-5638. President: Jon E. Shakka. Record producer (PROCAN/SOCAN). Estab. 1988. Deals with artists and songwriters. Produces 1 single and 1 12" single/year. Fee derived from sales royalty when song or artist is recorded, outright fee from recording artist or outright fee from record company.

How to Contact: Submit demo tape by mail. Unsolicited submissions are OK. Prefers cassette (or VHS videocassette if available) with 4 songs and lyric sheet. SASE. Reports in 3 months.

Music: Mostly funk, rap and house music; also pop, ballads and funk-rock. Produced "Shake Your Pants" (by J. Poku/E. Poku), recorded by Jon E. Shakka on Sizzle Records (rap 12" single).

Tips: "Believe in God; be positive; be patient; get to know the business; work hard; be trustful."

*SHARPE SOUND PRODUCTIONS, 3016 Delta Queen Dr., Nashville TN 37214. (615)391-0650. Producer/Engineer: Ed Sharpe. Record producer. Estab. 1990. Deals with artists and songwriters. Fee derived from sales royalty or outright fee from recording artist or record company.

How to Contact: Submit demo tape by mail. Unsolicited submissions are OK. Prefers cassette (or VHS videocassette if available) with 4 songs and lyric sheet. SASE. Reports in 2 months.

Music: Mostly pop, R&B and rock; also folk, country, contemporary Christian and storytelling. Produced *Cherokee Legends*, recorded by Kathi Smith on Cherokee Pub Records (spoken stories LP); "Higher Power" (by Betsy Koonce), recorded by B.K. Group on SSP Records (folk single); and "Pick It Up" (by John Weber), recorded by Heavy Boy J on SSP Records (rap single).

Tips: "Put best work first on demos with emphasis on vocal."

*SIERRA WEST MUSIC, 13 Winter Creek Ln., Canyon CA 94516. (415)376-6135. Producer: Neil J. Young. Record producer (8- and 24-track studios). Estab. 1969. Deals with artists and songwriters. Produces 15-40 LPs and 3 12" singles/year.

How to Contact: Call first and obtain permission to submit or to arrange a personal interview. Prefers cassette (or VHS videocassette if available) with 5 songs and lyric sheet. "Authors must have songs copywritten in their name." Does not return unsolicited material. Reports in 3 weeks.
Music: Mostly acoustic or vocal story songs, country rock or folk rock; also ballads. Produced "She Can" (by Steve Sesken), recorded by Alabama (country single); "Wrong" (by Steve Sesken), recorded by Waylon Jennings (country singles); *Feelin' Good*, written and recorded by David Rea on Canadian River (LP); and *One Voice*, by David Maloney (LP).

*SILICON CHIP RECORDING COMPANY, 1232 Cedar Rd., Ambler PA 19002. (215)542-0785. President: Christian Barth. Record producer and demo and jingle studio. Estab. 1986. Deals with artists and songwriters. Produces 35-40 singles, 5-6 LPs and 5-6 CDs/year. Fee derived from sales royalty or outright fee from recording artist and record company.
How to Contact: Submit demo tape by mail. Unsolicited submissions are OK. Prefers cassette with 3 songs and lyric sheet. "We will respond only if interested." SASE. Reports in 4 weeks.
Music: Mostly rock, dance and pop; also gospel, country and New Age. Produced *First Flower*, written and recorded by Patrick Robinson (New Age); *Before It's Too Late* (by Thomas Stokes), recorded by Robin Lynx (dance); and *Blue Heartache* (by Mike Mattera), recorded by Ichshe (pop). Other artists include The Cause, Lee Wright, Rudy Greaux, Judy Green, Ken Fox, Top Knowledge Gangsters.
Tips: "Write lots of songs; don't concentrate on only two or three. You may have to write 10 songs to discover one great one."

SILSAR PRODUCTIONS, P.O. Box 897, Hartford CT 06101. (203)548-0212. A&R: Linda "Bottles" Polite. Music publisher (BMI) and record company (S.O.C. Records and Silsar Music). Estab. 1986. Deals with artists and songwriters. Produces 4-12 singles, 4-12 12″ singles, 13 LPs, 13 EPs and 13 CDs/year. Fee derives from sales royalty.
How to Contact: Submit demo tape by mail. Unsolicited submissions are OK. Prefers cassette (or VHS videocassette if available) with 4-5 songs and lyric sheet. SASE. Returns in 6 weeks.
Music: Mostly funk, R&B/soul and gospel; also rap. Produced "Keepers of the Dream" (by Silsar), recorded by Silver Sargent (R&B single); "Co-Co," written and recorded by Muffin (rap single); and *Dreamin* (by The Uniques), recorded by Silsar (R&B LP), all on S.O.C. Records. Other artists include Drum and Red Rappin' Hood.

SILVER BLUE PRODUCTIONS, Penthouse, 220 Central Park S, New York NY 10019. (212)586-3535. Executive Vice President: Sarah Moon. Contact: Joel Diamond. Record producer and music publisher. Deals with artists and songwriters. Receives 40 submissions/month. Fee derived from sales royalty.
How to Contact: Prefers cassette with 1-3 songs and lyric sheet. SASE.
Music: Dance, easy listening, country, R&B, rock, soul and top 40/pop. Produced "Love is the Reason," by Engelbert Humperdinck on BMG Records; "Do You Love Me" by David Hasselhoff on BMG Records; "Heaven In The Afternoon," by Lew Kyrton on Timeless; "I Am What I Am," by Gloria Gaynor (single); "Where the Boys Are," by Lorna; "One Night In Bangkok," by Robey; and "Love is the Reason" (by Cline/Wilson), recorded by E. Humperdinck and G. Gaynor on Critique Records (A/C).

*SINGING CAT MUSIC, BMI, 910 Herbert St., Richmond VA 23225. (804)231-7235. A&R: Julie Fulcher. Record producer, music publisher (Singing Cat Music/BMI) and record company (Singing Cat Records). Estab. 1990. Deals with artists and songwriters. Produces 4 singles, 4 LPs and 2 CDs/year. Fee derived from sales royalty when song or artist is recorded.
How to Contact: Submit demo tape by mail. Unsolicited submissions are OK. Prefers cassette with 3-10 songs and lyric sheet. "Do not call. If interested we will call you." SASE. Reports in 1 month.
Music: Mostly pop, R&B and country; also gospel. Produced "One More Time For Love," written and recorded by Julie Fulcher on Singing Cat Records (R&B single).
Tips: "We are an infant record company looking to produce top-notch unknown artists. We have access to a 24-track digital studio for unbeatable production. If your demo lacks production quality but has heart, take a chance, send it to us."

SIR GARRETT PRODUCTIONS, 10346 NE Chowning, Kansas MO 64155. (816)734-2159. Contact: Auska Garrett. Record producer (Sir Garrett Productions) and record company. Estab. 1987. Deals with artists and songwriters. Produces 2 singles, 3 12″ singles and 2 LPs. Fee derived from sales royalty.
How to Contact: Submit demo tape by mail. Unsolicited submissions are OK. Prefers cassette (or VHS videocassette if available) with 3 songs and lyric sheets. "Include a short resume of music background along with cassette and picture." SASE. Reports in 1 month.
Music: Mostly R&B, rock, pop and gospel; also jazz, soul and blues. Produced "Point It Out" and "I'll Wait For You," written and recorded by Ricky Dotson (uptempo R&B); and "On Our Honeymoon," written and recorded by Auska Garrett. Other artists include Rap Inc., Ralf Dixon, Gavin Johnson, Cal Green, Unidos Band and Mac Lace Band.

Tips: "Keep your songs short and simple. Always have a good beat."

*MIKE SISKIND, 285 Chestnut St., W. Hempstead NY 11552. (516)489-0738. Staff Producer: Mike Siskind. Record producer and record company (Storehouse Records). Deals with artists only. Produces 1 singles, 1-3 LPs and 1-3 EPs/year. "Fee varies project to project."
How to Contact: Submit demo tape by mail. Unsolicited submissions are OK. Prefers cassette (or VHS videocassette if available) with 5-8 songs and lyric sheet. "If interested in pursuing project, I will contact you." Does not return unsolicited material. Reports in 6 weeks.
Music: Mostly rock, folk and soul; also pop. Produced "No Reason" (by Larry Andrews), recorded by Off the Wall (rock); "The Personals" (by L. Andrews/M. Ellis), recorded by Off the Wall (rock); and "New York City Night" (by M. Siskind), recorded by Michael Ellis (rock); all on Storehouse Records.
Tips: "Let the producer produce. He may hear a diamond in the rough that you don't even realize you have."

*GARY R. SMITH PRODUCTION, 2154 McKinley Ct., Grand Junction CO 81503 (303)243-7551. Owner: Gary Smith. Record producer (ASCAP). Estab. 1974. Deals with artists and songwriters. Produces 10-12 singles 5-8 LPs and 5-8 CDs/year. Fee derived from outright fee from recording artist or record company. "Charges based on estimate, 50% up front."
How to Contact: Write or call first and obtain permission to submit. Prefers cassette with 3 songs and lead sheet. Does not return unsolicited material. Reports in 1 month.
Music: Mostly country, pop and jazz. Produced *Turquoise* (by Mike Barone) on TBA Records (jazz LP); *Follow Your Heart* (gospel LP) and *Just Good Music* (country LP), both by Lloyd Mabry, on Slow Foot Records. Other artists include Ed Stabler, Walt Smith, Dave Gann, Jim Petty and Ed Carpenter.
Tips: "Be willing to accept constructive criticism. And willing to rewrite."

*SNEAK TIP RECORDS INC., 2R, 102-40 62nd Ave., Forest Hills NY 11375. (718)271-5149. Record producer, music publisher (Sneak Tip Music) and record company (Sneak Tip Records). Estab. 1990. Deals with artists and songwriters. Produces 5-10 singles/year. Fee derived from sales royalty.
How to Contact: Write or call first to arrange a personal interview. Prefers cassette. Reports in 4 weeks.
Music: Mostly house, club and rap; also pop, R&B and freestyle. Produced "Treat Me Right," by J. Swift (hip house); "Without Your Love," by Rhingo (freestyle-house); and "Emotional Pain," by Xavier (Euro-freestyle); all recorded by Die Hard Productions on Sneak Tips Records.

SONGWRITERS' NETWORK, P.O. Box 190446, Dallas TX 75219. (214)824-2739. President: Phil Ayliffe. Record producer, music publisher (Songwriters' Network Music Publishing/ASCAP), and record company (Songwriters' Network Records). Estab. 1983. Deals with artists and songwriters. Produces 1 LP/year. Receives 5-8 submissions/month. Fee derived from sales royalty.
How to Contact: Prefers cassette (or videocassette if available) with 5 songs and lyric sheet. "Five songs should include an uptempo opener; an uptempo, positive song; a ballad; a hand-clapping rouser; and a dramatic, personal philosophy song as a closer. Vocal must be mixed up-front. Any straining to hear the lyric and the tape is immediately rejected. Material is returned only if accompanied by an SASE." Reports in 6 weeks.
Music: A/C, pop and MOR. Produced "Flying Free," written and recorded by Phil Ayliffe on Songwriters Network Records (New Age/pop).
Tips: "We are most interested in working with the singer/songwriter/producer entrepreneur, so we would like the best produced material possible, though vocal and instrument demo is OK. Be patient with me and the process."

*SOUND ADVISORS LTD., 400 West Lancaster Ave., Devon PA 19333 (215)975-9212. President: eg Mizii Vice Presidents: Howard Scott II and Steven Bernstein. Secretary/Treasurer: Bernard M. Resnick, Esq. "Covers all aspects of the music business—from producing and promotion to law and management. Negotiated recording and publishing contracts with CBS, Atlantic, Capitol, Virgin, Vogue and Polygram, that resulted in the sale of over 35 million records, tapes and CDs." Recording producers on staff. Deals with artists and songwriters. 5-7 new songwriters/year. Publishes 20-30 songs/year.
How to Contact: Write first with SASE to obtain permission to submit. Prefers cassette tapes, CDs or records. Reports ASAP. Does not accept or return unsolicited material. Prefers correspondence by mail.
Music: R&B, rock, pop, metal, folk rock, country, gospel, jazz, New Age, contemporary Christian, Christian rock, blues, punk, new wave, hardcore and reggae. Negotiated *"Side Show"* (platinum record) by Blue Magic; *"Double Dutch Bus"* by Frankie Smith (a gold 7" and 12" single); *"Love Won't*

Let Me Wait" (gold record) by Major Harris. Also worked with Luther Vandross, Cool C., Jean Carne, Code Vogue and many others.
Tips: "Send all styles to show versatility. We are always searching for great songs and musical talent. We have what it takes to expose a great artist."

SOUND ARTS RECORDING STUDIO, 2036 Pasket, Houston TX 77092. (713)688-8067. President: Jeff Wells. Record producer and music publisher (Earthscream Music). Deals with artists and songwriters. Estab. 1974. Produces 12 singles and 3 LPs/year. Fee derived from outright fee from recording artist.
How to Contact: Prefers cassette with 2-5 songs and lyric sheet. SASE. Reports in 1 month.
Music: Mostly pop/rock and dance. Produced "Always Happens," written and recorded by Barbara Pennington; "Show Me Reaction" (by Wells), recorded by Rick Bardon; and "New Guy" (by Wells), recorded by Valerie Starr, all on Earth Records.

SOUND COLUMN PRODUCTIONS, Division of Sound Column Companies, 160 Westgate Fine Arts Center, 342 W. Second South, Salt Lake City UT 84101. (801)355-5327. President/General Manager: Ron Simpson. Record producer, media producer, music publisher (Ronarte Publications/ASCAP, Mountain Green Music/BMI and Macanudo Music/SESAC) and record company (SCP Records, Big Sky Records). Estab. 1970. Looking for songs our artists can record. Produces 3 singles and 5 LPs/year. Fee derived from sales royalty or outright fee on media productions, demos and albums produced for outside labels..
How to Contact: Unsolicited submissions of three songs maximum (with pop or R&B ballads and uptempo and contemporary Christian). No metal or rap. "We listen to everything, eventually. Remember, we can't return materials or correspond unless you include SASE. No phone calls please."
Music: Pop, R&B, country, contemporary Christian. "We produce albums under contract for various labels, and demo packages for client artists."
Tips: "We respond to clean production and must have current-style songs. We accepted several songs by outside writers this past year."

*SOUND CONTROL PRODUCTIONS, 2813 Azalea Pl., Nashville TN 37204. (615)269-5638. Producer: Mark. Record producer and record company (Mosrite Records). Estab. 1982. Deals with artists and songwriters. Produces 30 singles, 8 LPs and 2 CDs/year. Fee derived from sales royalty or outright fee from recording artist or record company—"sometimes all or a combination of these." Charges 50% in advance for services. "I don't want to pay studio time and musicians when the client doesn't show."
How to Contact: Submit demo tape by mail. Unsolicited submissions are OK. Prefers cassette with 3 songs and lyric sheet. "Don't submit anything in which you need to explain what the song or you are trying to say—let the performance do that." Does not return unsolicited material. Reports in 8 weeks.
Music: Mostly country, gospel and bluegrass; also Christmas. Produced *Paddy Kelly* (by various artists), recorded by Paddy Kelly (country LP); *The Thorntons* (by various), recorded by Thorntons on Bridge Records (gospel LP); and *The Lewis Family* (by various artists), recorded by The Lewistown on Benson Records (gospel bluegrass LP).

SOUNDS OF WINCHESTER, Rt. 2 Box 114 H, Berkley Springs WV 25411. Contact: Jim McCoy. Record producer, music publisher (New Edition Music, Jim McCoy Music and Sleepy Creek Music) and record company (Winchester, Faith and Master Records). Deals with artists and songwriters. Produces 20 singles and 10 LPs/year. Fee derived from sales royalty.
How to Contact: Prefers 7½ ips reel-to-reel or cassette with 4-10 songs and lead sheet. SASE. Reports in 1 month.
Music: Bluegrass, country, gospel and country/rock. Produced *Tribute to Patsy Cline*, by Mariah (LP); "Always," written and recorded by Alvin Kesner (single); "Run-away-Girl," written and recorded by Earl Howard (single); and *Tryin to Quit*, written and recorded by Jim McCoy (LP), all on Winchester Records. Other artists include Dave Elliott, R. Lee Gray, Red Steed, Kim Segler, Carroll County Ramblers and Troubadour Band.

*SOUNDSTAGE SOUTH, 5183 Darlington Dr., Memphis TN 38118. (901)363-3345. President: Fred B. Montgomery. Rock & "New" country production and artist development. Estab. 1990. Deals with artists and songwriters. Fee derived from sales royalty when song or artist is recorded.
How to Contact: Submit demo tape by mail. Unsolicited submissions are OK. Prefers cassette (or VHS videocassette if available) with 3 songs and lyric sheet. Does not return unsolicited material. Reports in 1 month.
Music: Mostly rock, blues rock and contemporary country; also country/rock.
Tips: "I represent selected songwriters/artists in the Memphis/Mid-South area in development, pre-production, demo production and general support in shopping original material to publishers and labels." Music trends: "I see young rock musicians moving away from metal and back to more melodic, less shock oriented presentation and performance, and I see an enormous crossover occurring in

contemporary country, i.e. Highway 101, Restless Heart, Desert Rose Band."

SOUTHERN SOUND PRODUCTIONS, 100 Labon St., Tabor City NC 28463. (919)653-2546. President: Elson H. Stevens. Record producer, music publisher (Creekside Publishing, SeaSide Records/BMI) and record company. Estab. 1978. Deals with artists, songwriters and radio stations. Produces 15 singles, 16 EPs and 16 LPs/year. Fee derived from sales royalty or outright fee from recording artist.
How to Contact: Write first about your interest. Prefers cassette or 8-track tape with 1-3 songs and lyric or lead sheets. SASE. Reports in 1 month.
Music: Mostly country; also bluegrass, gospel, rock (country and hard) and beach music. Produced "Being in Love" (by J. Knight), recorded by Angela (country); "Child of the King" (by W. Ormond), recorded by Twilights (black gospel); "Here I Go Again" (by E. Stevens), recorded by Angela (country); and "On the Downside" (by J. Gibson), recorded by T.J. Gibson, all recorded on Seaside Records (country singles). Other artists include Mitch Todd, T.J. Gibson, Crossroads, Coppper Creek, Gospel Entertainers, Glin Todd, Sheila Gore, Gayle Mathies, Gospel Echoes, Don Casper, Mary Jane Cooper and Buck Johnson.
Tips: "Please make sure that all songs submitted have a very strong hook. Limit of 3 songs per submission."

SPHERE PRODUCTIONS, P.O. Box 991, Far Hills NJ 07931-0991. (908)781-1650. FAX: (908)781-1693. President: Tony Zarrella. Record producer, artist development, management and placement of artists with major/independent labels. Produces 5-6 singles, 2 LPs and 1 CD/year. Receives 150-300 submissions/quarterly. Estab. 1988. Deals with artists and songwriters. Fee derived from percentage royalty of deal, outright fee from record company.
How to Contact: Submit demo tape by mail. Unsolicited submissions are OK. Prefers cassette (or VHS videocassette) with 3-5 songs and lyric sheets."Include as much information as possible: photos, press, resume, goals and specifics on character of project submitted, etc." SASE. Reports in 8 weeks.
Music: Specialize in pop (mainstream), progressive/rock, New Age and cross-over country/pop. Also film soundtracks. Produced "All Heart" (by T. Zarrella), recorded by 4 of Hearts (pop/rock); and Speed of Light" recorded by Traveller, both on Sphere Records. Also produces Oona Falcon and The Snowmen.
Tips: "Be able to take direction and have trust and faith in your producer or manager."

JACK STANG, 753 Capitol Ave., Hartford CT 06106. (203)524-5656. Producer: Jack Stang. Record producer, music publisher (Stang Music/BMI) and record company (Nickel Records). Estab. 1970. Deals with artists and songwriters. Produces 5 singles and 5 12″ singles/year. Fee derived from sales royalty.
How to Contact: Submit demo tape by mail. Unsolicited submissions are OK. Prefers cassette with 3 songs and lyric sheets. SASE. Reports in 3 weeks.
Music: Mostly pop, rock and dance; also country. Produced "For What We've Got," written and recorded by Ray Alaire (top 40); "Shortest Distance" (by Cléntel), recorded by Dagmar (top 40/dance); and "We Have It All," by Ray Alaire and Sky (A/C), all on Nickel Records (all singles).

*STAR SOUND AND RECORDING, 618 Georgia, Bethalto IL 62010. (618)377-5569. Executive Producer: Mark Church. Record producer and recording studio. Estab. 1984. Deals with artists and songwriters. Produces 12 singles, 12 12″ singles, 12 LPs and 6 EPs/year. Fee derived from outright fee from recording artist. "Payment usually 50% down, 50% at completion. Hourly rate $40/hour or project price."
How to Contact: Write or call first to arrange personal interview. Prefers cassette with 1-3 songs. Does not return unsolicited material. Reports in 3 weeks.
Music: Mostly gospel, R&B and pop; also rock, country and jazz. Produced *Shoe Bob*, written and recorded by Judge Nothing on Custom Records (alternative rock LP); and *Brad Horshberger*, written and recorded by Brad Horshberger on Custom Records (gospel LP). Other artists include Dead Planet, Power Source and The Undecided.

*STEPPIN OUT MUSIC, #5B, 31 E. 1st St., New York NY 10003. (212)460-9191. President: Richard Wilder. Estab. 1989. Deals with artists and songwriters. Produces 2 singles and 2 LPs/year. Receives 12 submissions/month. Fee derived from outright fee from recording artist or outright fee from record company.
How to Contact: Submit demo tape by mail. Unsolicited submissions are OK. Prefers cassette (or VHS videocassette if available) with 3-5 songs and lyric sheet. Does not return unsolicited material. Reports in 3 weeks.
Music: Mostly pop, rock and R&B. Produced "Refuse and Resist," written and recorded by Tom Steele on OS Records (single); "Electric President," written and recorded by Tony Matta on EP Records (EP); and "A Few Who Dared to Trust God" (by Ken Howard and Clifton Davis), recorded

by American Bible Society. Other artists include Georgina, Rob Stoner and Dan Cazio.

Tips: "Be original, define your style and be very aware of who your audience is and how to present music to them."

*A. STEWART PRODUCTIONS, 22146 Lanark St., Canoga Park CA 91304. (818)704-0629. President: Art Stewart. Record producer and music publisher (Famosonda Music/BMI and Sonada/ASCAP). Estab. 1975. Deals with artists and songwriters. Produces 1 single and 1 LP/year. Receives 8 submissions/year. Fee determined by sales royalty.

How to Contact: Prefers 7½ ips reel-to-reel or cassette with 1-4 songs and lyric sheet. SASE. Reports in 1 month.

Music: All types; mostly soul. Produced "Got To Give It Up" (by M. Gaye), recorded by Sterling (soul); "Come Into These Arms," written and recorded by Dion Pride (pop/rock); and *Second Son*, written and recorded by Dion Pride (pop/rock). Co-produced "You and I" (by R. James) and "Sucker For Your Love" (by Teena Marie).

*STONE COLD PRODUCTIONS, P.O. Box 298, Queens NY 11415. (718)657-5363. Producer: Kevin Benyard. Record producer and music publisher (K. Benyard Music Co./BMI). Estab. 1990. Deals with artists and songwriters. Produces 4 singles, 4 12″ singles and 5 LPs/year. Fee derived from outright fee from recording artist or record company.

How to Contact: Call first and obtain permission to submit. Prefers cassette (or VHS videocassette if available) with 5-9 songs and lyric or lead sheet. Reports in 4 weeks.

Music: Mostly R&B, rock and R&B/rap; also pop and dance. Produced "Homeless Nation" (by K. Benyard), recorded by Teshome on A.A.I. Records (R&B single); and "I'm All Yours" (by Glen Turner), recorded by T-Love on A.A.I. Records (R&B single).

*STREET MUSIC, Suite 17, 61 Canal St., San Rafael CA 94901. (415)453-6270. Managing Partner: Jeff Britto. Record producer, music publisher (ASCAP) and record company (Street Music Records). Estab. 1987. Deals with artists and songwriters. Produces 6 singles, 6 12″ singles and 6 LPs/year. Receives 10-20 submissions/month. Fee derived from sales royalty when song or artis is recorded.

How to Contact: Write first and obtain permission to submit. Prefers cassette (or VHS videocassette if available) with 4 songs and lyric sheet. Include 8 × 10 glossy photo if available. SASE. Reports in 2 weeks.

Music: Mostly rap, R&B and dance/house; also pop. Produced "Pop Music IZ" (by Corey André), recorded by Panta Productions (dance single); "Talking That Bad Talk" (by C.I.A.), recorded by Tony Star Prod. (rap single); and "Just Another Sucker" (written and recorded by Nite-N-Day, rap single), all on Street Music Records. Other artists include City Street Council, Rudy. C and Da'Vidá.

Tips: "Don't short change your lyrics or music production by taking short cuts to meet production schedules. An assembly-line approach to songwriting is not good. Never release substandard material for consideration unless you like rejection. I see a definite trend in CHR formats accepting more ethnically diverse music, thus showcasing artists who until recently were locked out of the top 40 market."

*STUDIO CITY PRODUCTIONS, 2810 McBain, Redondo Beach CA 90278. (213)371-5793. Staff Producer: Geoff England. Record producer. Estab. 1982. Deals with artists and songwriters. Produces 15 singles, 20 12″ singles, 10 LPs, 5 EPs and 35 CDs/year. Fee derived from sales royalty or outright fee from recording artist or record company.

How to Contact: Submit demo tape by mail. Unsolicited submissions are OK. Prefers cassette (or VHS videocassette if available) with 1-5 songs and lyric sheet. SASE. Reports in 2 weeks.

Music: Mostly rock and pop. Produced *Steppenwolf Live*, recorded by Steppenwolf on ABC Records (LP); *Ring Leader*, recorded by Ring Leader on Statue Records (LP); and *Rock City*, recorded by John Verla on Statue Records (LP).

*SUCCESSFUL PRODUCTIONS, 1203 Biltmore Ave., High Point NC 27260. (919)882-9990. President: Doris Lindsay. Record producer, music publisher (Better Times Publishing/BMI) and record company (Fountain Records). Estab. 1979. Deals with artists and songwriters. Produces 3 singles and 2 LPs/year. Fee derived from sales royalty.

How to Contact: Submit demo tape by mail. Unsolicited submissions are OK. Prefers cassette with 2 songs and lyric sheet. "Send a professional demo." SASE. Reports in 2 months.

Music: Mostly country, pop and contemporary gospel; also blues, children's and southern gospel. Produced *Another Notch on My Guitar*, written and recorded by Larry Lovey (blues LP); "Share Your Love," written and recorded by Mitch Snow (country); and "Right Smack Dab in the Middle of Love" (by P. Hanna), recorded by Pat Repose (country); all on Fountain Records.

SUNSET PRODUCTIONS, 117 W. 8th, Hays KS 67601. (913)625-9634. President: Mark Meckel. Record producer, music publisher (Street Singer Music/BMI) and record company. Estab. 1980. Deals with artists and songwriters. Produces 6 singles, 6 LPs and 2 CDs/year. Fee derived from sales royalty.
How to Contact: Prefers cassette with 3 songs and lyric or lead sheet. SASE.
Music: Mostly pop, country rock, gospel and 50s rock. Produced "I'm Gonna Win You Over," written and recorded by M. Selby (slow rock); "20," written and recorded by C. Connelly (rock); "Getting Nothen Done At All," written and recorded by M. Benish (country); *The Heat* (various songwriters), recorded by The Heat (rock); and *The Jimmy Dee Band 50's Rock 'n Roll*; all recorded on M.D.M. Records. Other artists include Mark Selby and C. Connelly.

SURPRIZE RECORDS, INC., P.O. Box 42707, Philadelphia PA 19101-2707. (215)276-8861. President: W. Lloyd Lucas. Record producer, music publisher (Delev Music Co./BMI, Sign of the Ram Music/ASCAP, Gemini Lady Music/SESAC) and management firm. Estab. 1981. Deals with artists, songwriters and publishers. Produces 3-6 singles, 2-3 12″ singles and 3-6 LPs/year. Fee derived from sales royalty.
How to Contact: Write or call first and obtain permission to submit. Prefers cassette with 1-3 songs and lyric or lead sheet. SASE. Reports in 1 month.
Music: R&B, soul, top 40/pop, dance-oriented and MOR. Produced a Charles Green composition titled "Changes." Also produced the four member rap group called Two Hand Posse. They recorded 3 songs, "Dreamseeds," "Child's Play" and "Money Won't Save You." Other artists that are scheduled to be produced are Lamar Lucas, who will be performing "Just Dance" (written by Willie McClain, C. Hawthrone and Willie McClain, Jr.), and female group, The Next Step, who are looking for material.
Tips: "We are impressed with very positive lyrics and great hooklines and near finished demo 'masters'. It does not matter if the artist has had extensive experience working in front of an audience, but it does matter if his or her attitude is in a positive posture. Determination and the ability to take constructive criticism is most important. We have no time for ego trippers."

SWEET INSPIRATION MUSIC, 112 Widmar Pl., Clayton CA 94517. (415)672-8201. Owner: Edgar J. Brincat. Record producer, music publisher (California Country Music/BMI, Sweet Inspirations Music/ASCAP) and record company (Roll On Records). Estab. 1986. Deals with artists and songwriters. Produces 2-4 singles/year. Pays standard royalty.
How to Contact: Submit demo tape by mail. Unsolicited submissions are OK. Prefers cassette with 3 songs and lyric sheets. SASE. Reports in 6 weeks.
Music: Mostly MOR, contemporary country or pop; also R&B, gospel and light rock. Published "I'll Take Country Music Anytime" (by John Covert, Ann Leisten, Phil Monton), recorded by John Covert on Roll On Records.

F.B. SWEGAL, division of Centaur®, P.O. Box 7320, Beverly Hills CA 90212-7320. (213)286-1448. Contact: Franz B. Swegal, P.C. Estab. 1979. Fee derived from sales royalty.
How to Contact: Submit demo tape by mail. Unsolicited submissions are OK. Prefers cassette (or ½″ videocassette if available) with best songs. "Unsolicited submissions should be released to simply 'absolve F.B. Swegal, division of Centaur® and affiliated and/or associated companies from infringement per each titled submission.' " SASE. Reports in 3 weeks.
Music: Mostly AOR, rock & roll, pop, country and R&B; also classical.

SYNDICATE SOUND, 311 Poland Ave., Struthers OH 44471. (216)755-1331. Owner: Jeff Wormley. Record producer and recording studio. Estab. 1987. Deals with artists and songwriters. Produces 1-2 singles, 1-2 12″ singles, 15-20 LPs, 10-15 EPs and 1-2 CDs/year. Receives 10 submissions/year. Fee derived from combination of sales royalty when song or artist is recorded, outright fee from recording artist or record company and third party financing.
How to Contact: Submit demo tape by mail. Unsolicited submissions are OK. "Please send a promo package or biography (with pictures) of band, stating past and present concerts and records." SASE. Reports in 1 month.
Music: Mostly rock, pop and Christian rock; also country, R&B and hardcore. Produced "Does Your Father Know" (by Brent Young), recorded by As Big As Love on Sad Face Records (cassette single); "Stone Cold Wall" (by Terry Barrett), recorded by Bangorilas on TNT Records (cassette single); "Saturday Night" (by Wayne Mackie), recorded by Count Down on Syndicate Sound Records (cassette single). Other artists include Blood Bath, John Horvath, Yellow #5, Picture Red and February's.

SYSTEM, P.O. Box 11301, Kansas City KS 66111. (913)287-3495. Executive Producer: Steve Vail. Record producer, management firm, booking agency and film company. Estab. 1978. Deals with artists and songwriters. Produces 1-3 LPs/year. Fee derived from outright fee from songwriter/artist or record company.

How to Contact: Prefers cassette or 7½ ips reel-to-reel (or ½″ or ¾″ VHS or ½″ Beta videocassette if available) with 1-10 songs and lyric sheet. Does not return unsolicited material. Reports in 6 weeks.
Music: "Classical rock, New Age, jazz fusion and art rock." Produced *The Path*, recorded by Realm (proressive rock LP/CD); *Outlines*, recorded by Navigator (dance rock LP); and *Rituals*, written and recorded by Vail, all on System Records.

TABITHA PRODUCTIONS, Sandpiper Court, Harrington Lane, Exeter EX4 8N5 **England**. Phone: 44-0392-79914. Producer: Graham Sclater. Record producer, music publisher (Tabitha Music, Ltd.) and record company (Tabitha/Willow Records). Works with artists and songwriters. Produces 6 singles and 2 LPs/year. Works with 6 new composers and songwriters/year. Fee derived from sales royalty.
How to Contact: Prefers cassette with 2-6 songs and lyric sheet. SAE and IRC. Reports in 3 weeks.
Music: Mostly AOR, MOR and pop; also country, dance, soul and rock. Produced "I'm Your Man," written and recorded by Tony Carey on Tabitha Records (pop); "Groovy Kind of Love" (by Bayer-Sager), recorded by Andy Ford (pop/reggae); and "Summer Love Affair" (by Bradbury/Artes), recorded by Beat the Heat (pop). Other artists include Shoot to Kill, Colin Wilson, FLIC, Simon Galt and Mark Fojo.

*__GARY TANIN__, 2139 N. 47th St., Milwaukee WI 53208. (414)444-2404. Producer: G. Tanin. Record producer. Estab. 1970. Deals with artists and songwriters. Produces 4 singles and 2 LPs/year. Fee derived from outright fee from recording artist or record company.
How to Contact: Submit demo tape by mail. Unsolicited submissions are OK. Prefers cassette with 3 songs and lyric sheet. "On demos, piano line and vocals are OK. Prefer as complete a submission as possible." SASE. Reports in 2 months.
Music: Mostly rock, pop and New Age. Produced *Otto and The Elevators*, written and recorded by G. Tanin on Vera Records (rock LP); *Coming Home*; (by Billy Wallace), recorded by Billy Wallace (jazz LP); and "Cheap Love, Easy Money," written and recorded by White Lie on White Lie Records (pop rock single). Other artists include Junior Brantley (formerly keyboardist with Fabulous Thunderbirds, now with Roomful of Blues on Black Top Records).

*__TCC PRODUCTIONS__, (Division of Tech-Coh Communications), 6331 Bahama Shores Drive S., St. Petersburg FL 33705-5437. (813)867-8546. FAX: (813)867-8330. President/Producer: Paul Hayes. Record producer, music publisher (Hayes Publishing Group/BMI) and record company (TCC Records, Seyah Records, Nivik Records). Estab. 1959. Deals with artists and songwriters. Fee derived from sales royalty when song or artist is recorded and outright fee from record company.
How to Contact: Submit demo tape by mail. Unsolicited submissions are OK. Prefers cassette with no more than 3 songs and lyric sheet. "If an artist, do not submit photos or video. Submit a *brief* bio if available, but it's not required." SASE. Reports in 2 weeks. "All unsolicited material must have a notification of copyright on the package in addition to a copyright notice on each enclosed submission. Material not bearing a copyright notice will be returned unopened."
Music: Mostly R&B, country and pop. Produced "I'm Serious," written and recorded by JJ Johnson on Capitol Records (R&B 12″ single); "Fantasy" (by Rufus Spencer), recorded by Alma Davis on Macola Records (R&B 12″ single); and "Taking Care Of Business" (by Randy Bachman), recorded by Alma Davis on TCC/Macola Records (R&B 12″ single). Other artists include Laurie Kittle, Hal O'Neil and Michael Battle.
Tips: "Songwriter: Write material that listeners can relate to with a strong hook. Artist: Believe in yourself and be willing to give 200% to a project. Be *unwilling* to do material that you don't believe in. Provide assigned producer with your input. You are the frosting on the cake so share your thoughts."

TEROCK RECORDS, Box 4740, Nashville TN 37216. President: Wade Curtiss. Record producer and music publisher. Deals with artists and songwriters. Fee derived from sales royalty.
How to Contact: Prefers cassette tape with 2-6 songs and lyric sheet. SASE. Reports in 3 weeks.
Music: Bluegrass, blues, country, dance, easy listening, folk, gospel, progressive, R&B, hard rock, soul, top 40/pop, rockabilly and rap.

*__THIRD FLOOR PRODUCTIONS__, P.O. Box 40784, Nashville TN 37204. (615)331-1469. Producer: Steven Ray Pinkston. Record producer. Estab. 1982. Deals with artists and songwriters. Produces 3 singles, 10 LPS and 10 CDs/year. Fee derived from outright fee from recording artist and/or record company.
How to Contact: Submit demo tape by mail. Unsolicited submissions are OK. Prefers cassette (or VHS videocassette if available) or DAT with 2 songs. SASE. Reports in 2 months.
Music: Mostly pop, rock and contemporary Christian. Produced *Face the Nation*, recorded by 4 Him on Benson Records (Christian LP); *What Are You Made Of* (by Koch), recorded by Brian Becker on Benson Records (Christian LP cut); and *Draw the Line*, recorded by Brian White on White Brook Records (rock-Christian LP).

Tips: "Great song, great demo, great voice. I'm looking for a female or band that has all the above."

THE THOMAS GROUP, 3649 Norwood Rd., Shaker Heights OH 44122. (216)991-9217. CEO: Tony Thomas. Record producer and advertising/music production company. Deals with artists and songwriters. Produces varying number of singles and LPs/year. Receives 1-3 submissions/month. Fee depends on project.

How to Contact: Submit demo tape by mail. Prefers cassette or 7½ ips reel-to-reel (or videocassette if available) and lyric sheet. "Please label submissions." Does not return unsolicited material. Reports in 6 weeks.

Music: Pop, jazz/fusion instrumentals and R&B; also jingles, "stingers/music beds and bumpers."

Tips: "Develop your own style and make sure that style shines through on your demo."

TOMSICK BROTHERS PRODUCTIONS, 21271 Chardon Rd.,Euclid OH 44117. (216)481-8380. President: Ken Tomsick. Record producer and record company (Recording Studio). Estab. 1982. Deals with artists and songwriters. Produces 2-5 LPs/year. Also produces original music for TV, radio, video and ad jingles. Fee derived from outright fee from recording artist. Charges in advance for studio time.

How to Contact: Write first and obtain permission to submit. Prefers cassette. "We have arrangers to help produce your sound." Does not return unsolicited material. Reports in 1 month.

Music: Mostly ethnic, polka and New Age/experimental. Produced *Joey T & Lynn Marie*, by Joey Tomsick (ethnic LP); *Proud of Cleveland*, by Joey Tomsick Orchestra (polka LP); "Encore" (by Joey Tomsick), recorded by Joey T and Lynn Marie on T.B.P. Records (buttonbox-polka); "Sweet 16," written and recorded by Nancy Hlad on F. Hlad Records (buttonbox-polka); and *Tag YR It*, by Dale Stevens (electronic LP), all recorded by Tomsick Brothers on TBP Records.

TORO'NA INT'L., P.O. Box 88022, Indianapolis IN 46208. Contact: Inga McDaniel. Professional record producer and musical arranger. A&R Director: Anthony Wiggins. Estab. 1987. Produces 3 singles and 1 12″ single/year. Fee derived from sales royalty.

How to Contact: Write first and obtain permission to submit. Prefers cassette with 3 songs. Does not return unsolicited material. Reports in 8 weeks.

Music: Mostly top 40, R&B and gospel; also rap. Produced "I'm Black and Proud" (by E. Walker/G. Brumfield), recorded by Second Power on Black Ivory Records (rap); and "Hooked On Your Love" (by I. McDaniel), recorded by Derryck Weeden on Toro'na Records (r&b). Other artists include Connee Draper, Leturah Jackson, Mazeo, D.J.Rock and M. Ware.

Tips: "Write first about your interests. No phone calls."

*TOTAL TRAK PRODUCTIONS, 4057 McClune Dr., Los Angeles CA 90008 (213)294-3359. Operations Manager: Chris Roe. Record producer and music publisher (ASCAP). Estab. 1989. Deals with artists and songwriters. Produces 5 singles, 5 12″ singles, 2 LPs, 3 EPs and 2 CDs/year.

How to Contact: Submit demo tape by mail. Unsolicited submissions are OK. Prefers cassette (or VHS videocassette if available) with 3 or more songs and lyric sheet. "Photo would be helpful." SASE. Reports in 2 weeks.

Music: Mostly R&B, dance and rap; also pop, funk/soul and rock.

*TOUGH GUYS PRODUCTIONS, INC., P.O. Box 381463, Miami FL 33238. (305)757-7038. Chairmen: David and Chancy. Estab. 1986. Deals with artists and songwriters. Fee derived from sales royalty when song or artist is recorded.

How to Contact: Write or call first and obtain permission to submit. Prefers cassette (or VHS videocassette if available) with 2-3 songs and lyric sheet. "Pictures and/or bios are recommended, but not necessary." SASE. Reports in 2 weeks.

Music: Mostly pop/dance, R&B/dance and rap; also pop/rock. Produced "I Got To Have You" (by Carolle/T.G.P.), recorded by Carolle on Champion Records (dance single); "Raw Deal" (by Latine Bros.), recorded by Hard Core on Magic Apple Records (rap single); and "Is It Him Or Is It Me," written and recorded by Latin Xtasy on Survivor Records (pop/dance single). Other artists include Plio and Cap, Nardy.

TRAC RECORD CO., 170 N. Maple, Fresno CA 93702. (209)255-1717. Owner: Stan Anderson. Record producer, music publisher (Sellwood Publishing/BMI) and record company (Trac Records). Estab. 1972. Works with artists and songwriters. Produces 10-20 12″ singles, 5 LPs and 1 CD/year. Fee derived from sales royalty or outside investors.

How to Contact: Prefers cassette with 3 songs and lyric sheet. "Studio quality." SASE. Reports in 2 weeks.
Music: Mostly country, gospel, pop and rock. Produced "Nevada State of Mind," written and recorded by Barry Best; "Don't Walk Away," written and recorded by B.G. White (country); and "Overnight Sensation," written and recorded by Rick Blake (top 40), all on Trac Records. Other artists include Jessica James, Robin Sharkey, Ron Arlen and The Deacon.

*ROBIN TRACY, 109 E. 73rd St., New York NY 10028 (212)734-1953. Executive Secretary: Cathy Bergman Record producer and record company (NFS Inc.). Estab. 1986. Deals with artists and songwriters. Produces 6-8 singles and 6-8 12″ singles/year. Fee derived from sales royalty when song or artist is recorded and outright fee from record company. "Charges 50% on start date and 50% on project completion."
How to Contact: Submit demo tape by mail. Unsolicited submissions are OK. Prefers cassette with 1-3 songs. Include one 8×10″ glossy photo and bio on goals and direction. SASE. Reports in 2-3 weeks.
Music: Mostly R&B/dance, pop/dance and R&B and pop ballads. Produced "Do You Really?" (by R. Tracy/A. Miranda), "As My Heart Breaks" and "Untangle Me" (by Robin Tracy), all recorded by A. Miranda on NFS Records (12″ singles).
Tips: "Establish a style, in voice and/or melody. Try to write a song or idea for a song every day. With 365 ideas, you're sure to have at least one hit song."

*TREND PRODUCTIONS, Box 201, Smyrna GA 30081. (404)432-2454. Manager: Tom Hodges. Record producer, music publisher (Mimic Music, Stepping Stone Music, Skip Jack Music/BOAM, ASCAP), record company (Trend, Atlanta, Stepping Stone and Trendsetter Records and British Overseas Airways Music) and artist management. Estab. 1965. Deals with artists, songwriters and musicians. Produces 7 singles, 3 12″ singles, 8 LPs and 3 CDs/year. Fee derived from sales royalty or outright fee from record company or music publisher.
How to Contact: Prefers cassette with 3-10 songs and lyric sheet. SASE. Reports in 3 weeks.
Music: Mostly country, gospel and MOR; also bluegrass, blues, R&B, rock, soul and top 40/pop. Produced "Jessica," written and recorded by G. Peters on BOAM #1 Records; "Don't Mess with the IRS" (by Dan/Rita/Al Rita), recorded by Marion Frizzell on Trend Records (country novelty); and "Another Footprint," recorded by Joann Johnson on Trend Records (country). Other artists include Rick Sumner, Terry Brand, Keith Bradford and Bobby Martin.

TURNER PRODUCTIONS, P.O. Box 64895, Baton Rouge LA 70896. (504)925-0988. Indie Producer: Henry Turner. Record producer (BMI) and record companies (Hit City Records and Genesis Gospel Records). Estab. 1984. Deals with artists and songwriters. Produces 2-5 singles and 2-5 LPs/year. Fee derived from sales royalty or outright fee from recording artist or record company. "We charge a production fee."
How to Contact: Write or call first and obtain permission to submit. Prefers cassette with 3 songs and lyric sheet. "Stay basic in your ideas." Does not return unsolicited material. Reports in 1 month.
Music: All types. Produced "What A Wonderful God We Serve," written and recorded by Marvin Griffin, formerly of the Five Blind Boys, on Genesis Records (gospel single); "Little Heart," written and recorded by Valaree Brock on Hit City Records (country single); and "The Fall of Englatine," written and recorded by Tim Grabus & Once Upon A Time, on Hit City Records (rock single). Other artists include Eldon Ray and Cross Kountry (country), Henry Turner Jr. and Flavor (R&B/reggae/soul/funk), Radical Rhadd Hunt (funk/reggae), Jerry Stanley (country), Jack Smith (country).
Tips: "Think reality and be prepared to work for the things you want."

*27TH DIMENSION INC., P.O. Box 1149, Okeechobee FL 34973-1149. (800)634-6091. President: John St. John. Record producer, music publisher (ASCAP, BMI) and music library. Estab. 1986. Deals with artists and songwriters. Produces 10 CDs/year. Fee derived from outright fee from record company and "performances."
How to Contact: Write or call first and obtain permission to submit. Prefers cassette with several songs. Does not return unsolicited submissions. Reports in 1 week.
Music: Mostly industrial, pop jazz and industrial fusion; also pop, impressionism and descriptive.

*UNITED RECORDING STUDIO, 4024 State Line Rd., Kansas City KS 66103. (913)262-3558. Producer/Engineer: Mike Frazier. Record producer, record company (Stress Records) and 24-track recording facility. Estab. 1980. Deals with artists and songwriters. Fee derived from sales royalty when song or artist is recorded, outright fee from recording artist or record company, "depending upon situation."

How to Contact: Submit demo tape by mail. Unsolicited submissions are OK. Prefers cassette (or VHS videocassette if available) with 4 songs. Does not return unsolicited material. Reports in 1 month.
Music: Mostly pop, country and rock; also jazz, heavy metal and industrial. Produced "Weak Heart, Strong Memory," written and recorded by Spike Blake (country); "Rodeo Rocks," written and recorded by various artists (rock), both on Stress Records; and "Rumor Has It," recorded by Freddie Hart on 5th Street Records (country). Other artists include Donnie Miller, Prism, Psychowelders, Foxy-Foxy, Prism Hollowpoint and Delissa Dawn.

*LUCIEN VECTOR, #3, 4747 N. Kenneth, Chicago IL 60630. (312)685-4815. Producer: Lucien Vector. Composer/arranger. Estab. 1985. Produces 5-10 singles, 0-3 12″ singles, 2-4 LPs and 2-4 CDs/year. Receives 5-10 submissions/month. Fee derived from sales royalty when song or artist is recorded, outright fee from recording artist or outright fee from record company.
How to Contact: Submit demo tape by mail. Unsolicited submissions are OK. Prefers cassette with 1-4 songs and lyric sheet. Does not return unsolicited material. Reports in 1 month.
Music: Mostly pop-rock, world beat, ethno-pop and dance/rap; also electronic, soundtracks and theatrical. Produced *Healthy System* (by Johny K), recorded by TIC Productions on TIC Productions Records (pop LP); *Recitations of Norwid* (by Stan Borys), recorded by Chicago Trax on Nike Records (ethno-pop LP); and *The Mark* (by Dr Pepper and the X Factor), recorded by Fast Forward Sound Design on St. Christopher Records (pop-rock LP). Other artists include Nancy Davis, Tony Brajer and Miroslaw Rogala. Also produced soundtracks for "Ditka On Motivation" with Mike Ditka; "Great Crimes of the Century," "Nature Is Leaving Us" and many others.
Tips: "Work on the details only after the foundation is sound."

CHARLES VICKERS MUSIC ASSOCIATION, Box 725, Daytona Beach FL 32015-0725. (904)252-4849. President/Producer: Dr. Charles H. Vickers D.M. Record producer, music publisher (Pritchett Publication/BMI, Alison Music/ASCAP) and record company (King of Kings Records and L.A. International Records). Deals with artists and songwriters. Produces 3 singles and 6 LPs/year. Works with 1 new songwriter/year. Teams collaborators. Fee derived from sales royalty.
How to Contact: Write first and obtain permission to submit. Prefers 7½ ips reel-to-reel or cassette with 1-6 songs. SASE. Reports in 1 week.
Music: Mostly church/religious, gospel and hymns; also bluegrass, blues, classical, country, easy listening, jazz, MOR, progressive, reggae (pop), R&B, rock, soul and top 40/pop. Produced "Walking on the Water," "Let Us Pray," "Always Depend on Jesus," "The Lord is My Proctor" and "Everyday is a Holy Day," all written and recorded by C. Vickers on King of King Records.

WILLIAM F. WAGNER, Suite 218, 14343 Addison St., Sherman Oaks CA 91423. (818)905-1033. Contact: Bill Wagner. Record producer. Estab. 1957. Deals with artists and songwriters. Produces 4-6 singles, 2-4 LPs and 2-4 CDs/year. Works with 25 new songwriters/year. Fee derived from sales royalty or outright fee from recording artist record company.
How to Contact: Prefers cassette with 1-5 songs and lead sheets. "No lyric sheets. Material should be copyrighted." SASE. Reports in 1 month.
Music: Mostly top 40, pop, country and jazz; also blues, choral, gospel, easy listening, MOR, progressive, rock, soul and pop. Produced "Sings Mercer," recorded by Dewey Erney on Legend Records (MOR jazz); "Digital Page," recorded by Page Cavanaugh on Legend Records (jazz); "Sandy Graham," recorded by Sandy Graham on Muse Records. Other artists include Frank Sinatra, Jr., Candace Bennett and Mike Randall.
Tips: "Tune up the band and/or piano. Let's hear the singer. Quit using 'friends'; use pro players and singers instead."

*WALK ON WATER PRODUCTIONS, 245 S. Seguin, New Braunfels TX 78130. (512)625-2768. Producer/Manager: Kenneth D. Brazle. Record producer, music publisher and recording studio. Deals with artists and songwriters. Produces 2 singles/year. Receives 15 submissions/year. Fee derived from sales royalty or specific contract negotiation.
How to Contact: Write first and obtain permission to submit. "Include SASE for reply." Prefers cassette or 7½ ips reel-to-reel (or VHS videocassette if available) with 2-3 songs and lyric sheet. Does not return unsolicited material. Reports in 6 weeks.

Remember: Don't "shotgun" your demo tapes. Submit only to companies interested in the type of music you write. For more submission hints, refer to The Business of Songwriting on page 21.

Music: Mostly AOR, pop/rock, new music and country.
Tips: "Don't trust everyone - but when you find someone/company you do trust, be prepared to go for it, both mentally and financially."

*JACK WALKER II, 300 Linfield Dr., Vallejo CA 94590. (707)645-1615. President: Jack Walker. Record producer. Estab. 1982. Deals with artists and songwriters. Produces 2 singles/year. Fee derived from outright fee from recording artist or record company.
How to Contact: Write or call first and obtain permission to submit. Prefers cassette (or VHS videocassette if available) with 3 songs and lyric sheet. SASE. Reports in 2-4 weeks.
Music: Mostly country, R&B and jazz; also New Age, pop and other.
Tips: "Be prepared to spend the money if you want to make it in the music business. My company can guide you in the right direction, and if you have a good attitude then you should have no problem making it in the business."

*WATERFALL PRODUCTIONS, P.O. Box 14461, Greenville SC 29610. (803)230-5391. Executive Producer: James L. King, III. Estab. 1990. Deals with artists and songwriters. Produces 2 singles, 1 LP, 1 EP and 1 CD/year. Receives 2-3 submissions/month. Fee derived from percentage of sales or outright fee from artist.
How to Contact: Prefers cassette (or VHS videocassette if available) with 2-6 songs and lyric sheets. SASE. Reports in 2-4 weeks. Does not return unsolicited material.
Music: Pop, rock, R&B, folk, New Age, Christian and alternative (college rock). Produced "Le-Grand," written and recorded by JLK III (New Age); "Don't Throw Us Away" (by JLK III/Wa7), recorded by Brotherhood (pop); and "Another Chance for Love" (by James Brazel), recorded by Brazel (R&B); all on Waterfall Records.
Tips: "Unless you've got a master tape ready to press, don't overproduce your songs—just make sure we can hear the words clearly."

THE WEISMAN PRODUCTION GROUP, 449 N. Vista St., Los Angeles CA 90036. (213)653-0693. Contact: Ben Weisman. Record producer and music publisher (Audio Music Publishers). Estab. 1965. Deals with artists and songwriters. Produces 10 singles/year. Receives 50-100 submissions/month. Fee derived from sales royalty.
How to Contact: Prefers cassette with 3-10 songs and lyric sheet. SASE. "Mention *Songwriter's Market*. Please make return envelope the same size as the envelopes you send material in, otherwise we cannot send everything back. Just send tape." Reports in 1 month.
Music: Mostly R&B, soul, dance, rap and top 40/pop; also all types of rock.
Tips: "Work on hooks and chorus, not just verses. Too many songs are only verses."

SHANE WILDER PRODUCTIONS, P.O. Box 3503, Hollywood CA 90078. President: Shane Wilder. Record producer and music publisher. Deals with artists and songwriters. Produces 10-15 singles and 5 LPs/year. Receives 100-150 submissions/month. Fee derived from sales royalty and production fees.
How to Contact: Prefers cassette with 6-8 songs and lyric sheet. SASE. Reports in 4 weeks.
Music: Country. Produced "Are There Any Angels in Nashville," "I'm Not Cookin' Your Eggs No More" and "I Just Love a Good Story," by Jane Tyler; "We Graduate This Summer," by Teresa O'Dell (country single); "Part Time Love," by Crystal Blue (disco single); and "Old Liars, Umpires and a Woman Who Knows," by Mike Franklin (country single, N.S.D. Records). Other artists include Priscilla Emerson, Laurie Loman (MCA recording artist) and Terry Brooks (rock artist, Jet Records).
Tips: "Looking for top country acts for record contract and management. Must be very commercial."

TOM WILLETT, TOMMARK RECORDS, #G3, 7560 Woodman Pl., Van Nuys CA 91405. (818)994-4862. Owners: Tom Willett and Mark Thornton. Record producer, music publisher (Schmerdley Music/BMI) and record company (Tomark Records). Estab. 1988. Deals with artists and songwriters. Produces 1 single and 1 CD/year. Receives 150 submissions/year.
How to Contact: Submit demo tape by mail. Unsolicited submissions are OK. Prefers cassette (or VHS videocassette if available) with any number of songs and lyric sheets. SASE. Reports in 4 weeks.
Music: Mostly country and novelty; also folk. Produced "Joe's Blues," written and recorded by Joe Wolverton (country instrumental); "Please Don't Play My Record On The Radio" (by Tom Willett), recorded by Herman Schmerdley (novelty country); and "So Many Men So Little Time" (by Nat Wyner/Sharon Lynne), recorded by American Made Band (C&W swing), all on Tommark Records.
Tips: "Submit bio, resume, cassette. Send a good quality recording. Music is becoming even more lucrative than before. A good song can generate a good album or even a TV program or movie."

FRANK WILLSON, P.O. Box 2297, Universal City TX 78148. (512)653-3989. Producer: Frank Willson. Record producer (BMI) and record company (BSW Records). Deals with artists and songwriters. Estab. 1987. Produces 4 singles, 12-15 12″ singles, 10-12 LPs, 3 EPs and 5 CDs/year. Receives 20 submissions/month. Fee derived from sales royalty.

How to Contact: Submit demo tape by mail. Unsolicited submissions are OK. Prefers cassette with 3-4 songs and lyric sheets. SASE. Reports in 4 weeks.
Music: Mostly country and rock. Produced "Someone Wrote A Love Song," recorded by Jess De-Maine; "High Cost of Lovin," written and recorded by Dale McBride; and "Guessin Game," written and recorded by Candace Howard, all country singles on BSW Records. Other artists include Larry Noland and Candee Land.

*WIR (WORLD INTERNATIONAL RECORDS), A-1090 Vienna, Servitengasse 24, **Austria**. Tel: 0043-222-7737-10. FAX: 0043-222-7784-22. Contact: Peter Jordan. Record producer, music publisher (Aquarius) and record company (WIR). Estab. 1986. Deals with artists and songwriters. Produces 5-10 singles and 5-8 LPs/year. Fee derived from outright fee from recording artist or record company.
How to Contact: Write or call first and obtain permission to submit or to arrange a personal interview. Prefers cassette.
Music: Produced "Talk To Me" (by Brenner), recorded by Tina K.; "Fire And Heat" (by Nicodemo), recorded by Fussy Cussy; and "Living On This Earth" (by Herzog), recorded by Without Words; all CDs on WIR Records.

*WIZARDS & CECIL B, 1111 Second St., San Rafael CA 94901. (415)459-6714. Producer: David Lew-ark. Record producer and music publisher. Estab. 1978. Deals with artists and songwriters. Produces 10 singles, 10 12″ singles, 15 LPs and 15 CDs/year. Fee derived from sales royalty when song or artist is recorded, outright fee from recording artist, outright fee from record company and/or 24-track studio income.
How to Contact: Submit demo tape by mail. Unsolicited submissions are OK. Prefers cassette with several songs. Reports in 2 months.
Music: All kinds of music. Produced "New Rider of Purple Sage," recorded by W&CB on MU Records; "Nick Gravenities," recorded by In Mix on MU Records; and "Sarah Campbell," recorded by W&CB on Kalidascope Records, all written by J. Dawson (C&W). Other artists include Caribbean All Stars and Richie Barron.

*RAY WOODBURY/OUTERSPACE COMMUNICATIONS MANAGEMENT, Suite 244, 112 N. Harvard Ave., Claremont CA 91711. (714)626-4245. Record producer and record company (OuterSpace Records). Estab. 1990. Deals with artists and songwriters. Produces 4 singles, 2 12″ singles, 3 LPs and 3 CDs/year.
How to Contact: Call first and obtain permission to submit. Prefers cassette (or VHS videocassette if available) with 5 songs and lyric sheet. SASE.
Music: Interested in all types of music. Produced "Pretty Wiped Out" (by Jerry Joseph), recorded by Little Women on OuterSpace Records (rock single); "Hot Diggitty Dogs" (by Mr. P), recorded by Desperation Sound on OuterSpace Records (alternative rock single); and "Alternate Roots," written and recorded by Cardiff Reefers on Grow Records (reggae single).

WORLD ARTIST, Box 405, Alamo CA 94507. A&R Representative: Randal Larsen. Record producer, music publisher (Hansen Music Company), record company (World Artist Records), personal man-agement and production firm. Produces varying number of singles and LPs/year. Fee derived from sales royalty, outright fee from songwriter/artist or record company or contract.
How to Contact: "Do not call in advance. It's a waste of time to call before we hear the material." Prefers cassette (¾″ or VHS videocassette if available) and lyric or lead sheet. "Send a neat and clean package. We are looking for new talent with star quality." SASE. Reports in 6 weeks.
Music: Mostly top 40/MOR, rockabilly, jazz (big-band) and country rock; also blues, French and Spanish. "We are looking for 50s and 60s style rock 'n' roll and do-wop vocal harmony tunes, plus TV, motion picture and theatrical music."
Tips: "We do not read form letters. Do not send the same thing to us that you send to others."

*WORLD RECORD COMPANY, P.O. Box 691161, Houston TX 77070-1161. (713)894-2840. A/R Direc-tors: Jackie Barton/Baxter Sexton. Record producer and record company (Sheldon, Southern Thun-der, Gulf Coast Gold Records). Estab. 1988. Deals with artists and songwriters. Produces 6 singles and 4 12″ singles/year. Fee derived from sales royalty when song or artist is recorded. Produces on contract.
How to Contact: Submit demo tape by mail. Unsolicited submissions are OK. Prefers cassette (or VHS videocassette if available) with 1-5 songs and lyric sheet. SASE. Reports in 1 month.
Music: Mostly dance, country and ballads; also calypso, gospel and rock. Produced "Suspicious Minds" (by Mark James), recorded by Stephanie Dawn on Sheldon Records (12″ dance single); "Baby, Baby, Don't Get Hooked On Me" (by Mac Davis), recorded by Stephanie Dawn on Southern Thunder Records (country single); and "Where's The Fire?" (by Stephanie Dawn) (12″ dance single).

Tips: "We see (or hope to see) everyone in the industry cleaning up their acts and we're doing our best to help the trend succeed."

CHRISTOFF WYBOUW, 21A Oude Dorpsweg, Varsenare 8690 **Belgium.** (050)387910. FAX: 050/382835. Producer: Christoff Wybouw. Record producer, music publisher (Onadisc) and recording studio. Estab. 1980. Deals with artists and songwriters. Produces 10 singles, 5 12″ singles, 2 LPs and 5 EPs/year. Fee derived from sales royalty.
How to Contact: Prefers cassette. SAE and IRC. Reports in 1 month.
Music: Mostly disco, rock and new wave; also "crooners." Produced "Azabeat" (by C. Wybouw), recorded by Bingo (disco/ambiance); "Eena Ena" (by C. Wybouw/S. Feys), recorded by Otto Rongo (disco); and "I Was Daring" (by C. Wybouw/S. Feys), recorded by T'Pah (disco), all on Holy Hole Records.

*JAMES YARBROUGH, 2613 Castle, Irving TX 75038. (214)255-8015. President: James Yarbrough. Record producer, music publisher (ASCAP) and record company (Virgin Boy Records). Estab. 1988. Deals with artists and songwriters. Produces 3 singles, 4 12″ singles and 2 LPs/year. Fee derived from sales royalty when song or artist is recorded.
How to Contact: Submit demo tape by mail. Unsolicited submissions are OK. Prefers cassette with 3 songs and lyric sheet. Does not return unsolicited material.
Music: Mostly pop, rock and country. Produced "Seems Too Late," "Something's Got Me" and "Looking All Over," all written and recorded by James Yarbrough, on Virgin Boy Records (all pop singles).

JOHN YOUNG, Suite 101, 19 Music Square W., Nashville TN 37203. (615)255-5740. Record producer, music pubilsher, record company (Bear Records) and Young Graham Music. Estab. 1989. Deals with artists and songwriters. Produces 10 singles/year. Fee derived from sales royalty and outright fee from recording artist. Charges artists in advance for services.
How to Contact: Write or call first and obtain permission to submit. Prefers cassette with 3 songs and lyric sheet. SASE.
Music: Mostly country and gospel. Produced "Girls Like Her" (by Gant), recorded by J. Wright; "Red Neck, Blue Monday" (by Shafer), recorded by J. Wright; and "Down Home" (by Shephard), recorded by T. Roberson, all on Bear Records (all country). Other artists include Patton Ray, Autumn Day and Jimmy Peacock.

*JOHN ZAPPLE, 2019 Noble St., Pittsburgh PA 15218. (412)351-6672. A&R Department: John Zapple. Record producer. Estab. 1980. Deals with artists and songwriters. Produces 5 LPs and 4 EPs/year. Receives 20 submissions/month. Fee derived from sales royalty.
How to Contact: Submit demo tape by mail. Unsolicited submissions are OK. Prefers cassette with 5 songs and lyric sheets. SASE. Reports in 2 weeks.
Music: Mostly rock, R&B/dance and new music; also gospel rock. Produced "Give Me Liberty Or Give Me Death," written and recorded by various artists (metal); and "Fire In Faith," written and recorded by Revelation's Fire (gospel rock). Other artists include Seance and Post Mortem.
Tips: "Send 5 to 8 of your best song's with photos and press kit."

ZAR MUSIK, Dreilindenstr. 42, Saint Gall, CH 9011 **Switzerland.** Phone: (071)255-666. A&R Director: Victor Waldburger. Record producer, music publisher and record company (Masters Records). Deals with artists and songwriters. Estab. 1980. Produces 5 singles, 5 LPs and 5 CDs/year. Fee derived from sales royalty, outright fee from recording artist or record company.
How to Contact: Send cassette (or VHS videocassette if available) and lyric or lead sheet. Reports only if interested.
Music: Mostly commercial pop, dance and rock/heavy metal. Produced "Miracles" (by Tony Sachary) on CBS Records (pop); "Gold for Iron" (by Ex-Yello Carlos Perou) on WEA Records (techno); and "Check and Mate" (by Sultan) on CTE/BNE Germany.

Record Producers/'91-'92 Changes

The following markets appeared in the 1991 edition of *Songwriter's Market* but are absent from the 1992 edition. Most of these companies failed to respond to our request for an update of their listing. Others are not listed for a variety of reasons, which is indicated in parentheses following the company name. For example, they may have gone out of business, or they may have requested deletion from the 1992 edition because they are backlogged with material.

A Street Music
Jerry Abbott
Accent Records
All Star Sound Studios
Stuart J. Allyn
American Communications
    Enterprises (moved; left no
    forwarding address)
Angela Productions
April Recording Studios/Pro-
    ductions
Art of Music Productions
Arzee, Arcade and Clymax Re-
    cords
Associated Music Producers
Suzan Bader/D.S.M. Producers
John Bauers Music Productions
Black Diamond Music Publish-
    ing & Production Group
Black Olive
Nelson Blanchard
Bolden Productions
Brooke Productions, Inc.
L. Marion Brown
Carrie/Tribal Records Co.
Don Casale Music, Inc.
Lou Cicchetti (asked to be de-
    leted)
Colossal Records
Creative Productions
Cummings Productions
Dark Horse Productions
Ed Dettenheim
DKP Productions, Inc.
Dodgy Productions
Downtown Record Productions
8th Street Music
Jesse Evatte
Factory Beat Records
Foxworthy Productions
Fun City Record Co. (moved;
    left no forwarding address)
Fydaq Productions
Geimsteinn, Thor Baldursson,
    Runar Juliusson
Golden Goose Productions
Go-Records
Bill Greeen
Tommy Greene
Charles Hall
Rick Hanson Productions
Happy Days Music/Jeremy Mc-
    Clain
Jay Henry/Visual Music

Gordon Hickland
Homeboy/Ragtime Produc-
    tions
John R. Hudson
Humanity Productions
Indie Music Productions, Inc.
Ironwood Productions
David Ivory Productions
JK's Underground Recording
    Service
Tolga Katas Productions
Matthew Katz Productions
Kingston Records and Talent
Howard Knight Enterprises
Greg Knowles
Known Artist Productions
Laurel Canyon Productions
Little Richie Johnson
Loman Craig Productions
    (moved; left no forwarding
    address)
Love Dove Productions
M.R. Productions
Lee Magid Productions
Cookie Marenco
John Mars
Pete Martin/Vaam Music Pro-
    ductions
Marvel Productions (moved;
    left no forwarding address)
David Mathes Productions
Meda Records
Micah Production
Midi City
MJD Productions, Inc.
Monticana Productions
Mark J. Morette/Mark Manton
Fred Morris Music Group
Mother's Productions
Gary John Mraz
Music for Little People
Musideo (asked to be deleted)
Tommy Musto/Northcott Pro-
    ductions, Ltd.
Nashville International Enter-
    tainment Group
Nebo Record Company
Nervous Music
Nick Nack Paddywack Records
    (moved; left no forwarding
    address)
Not-2-Perfect Productions
Michael Panepento (moved;
    left no forwarding address)

Paradise Records
Sandy Perlman, Inc.
Persia Studios
Paul Person Creative Manage-
    ment
Michael Robert Phillips
Jim Pierce
Nicky Price
Productions Diadem (asked to
    be deleted)
Radio Magic/BSO Records
Random Image Productions
    (moved; left no forwarding
    address)
Ravenshead Productions
Fritz Riha
Ripsaw Productions
Rockland Music, Inc.
Rockstar Productions
Mark J. Romero/Jazzmark
    Sound
Rose Hill Group
Ruf-Mix Productions Incorpo-
    rated
Sacco Productions
Saggitar Records
Sceptre Productions
SCI Productions
Segal's Productions
SGB Production
Mark S. Shearer
Silver Loomas Productions
Donovan "Sound" Smith
    Audio Achievements, Inc.
Sometimes Y Music
Sound Column Productions
Sound Image Productions
Sovereign Productions
Spectra Productions
Starmaker Int'l Inc.
Stephen Stewart-Short
Lee Stoller
Straight Arrow Recordings
Mike Theodore Productions
Timeless Records BV
Tony's Production
The Victory Label
Cornell Ward
WE-B Records and Promotions
Thomas Wiggins Associates
Albert Kennedy Williams
Winbern Coup Productions
Steve Wytas Productions
Zeke Productions

Managers and Booking Agents

Managers and booking agents work closely with artists, helping them gain needed exposure and, in general, guiding artists in the right direction. Although a personal manager's job description may vary from firm to firm, he is, like the music publisher, a versatile and vital part of an act's career.

The artist manager is a valuable contact, both for the songwriter trying to get songs to a particular artist and for the songwriter/performer. Often the manager is the person closest to the artist, and he may have heavy influence in what type of material the performer uses. Remember that managers of nationally-known acts are usually located in the major music hubs. Don't expect these "big time" managers to be the easiest people to approach, because they're not. Many songwriters are trying to get songs to these people, and in most cases they only accept material from music publishers or producers who they know personally or professionally.

You need not go further than your own hometown, however, to find artists hungry for good, fresh material. Managers of local acts often have more to say in the choice of material their clients perform and record than managers in major hubs, where the producer often makes the final decision on what songs are included. Locally, it could be the manager who not only chooses songs for a recording project, but also selects the producer, the studio and the musicians.

If you are a writer/performer seeking a manager, be selective. A manager should have an excellent grasp of the entire music business: copyright law, A&R, publicity and promotion and financial management. As one industry source says: "There are many more good artists out there than there are managers." Keep this in mind. A good, well-rounded manager who possesses the style you need may be hard to find.

Managers may also be booking agents, although some people specialize solely in booking acts. Agents tend to represent many more clients than managers, mainly because they have less personal and developmental contact with the act. They may review material for the artists they work with, but usually don't get to know them as well as personal managers. Each listing in this section will specify whether the company is a manager, booking agent or both. A manager usually charges anywhere from 15-20% of the act's gross earnings. A booking agent generally charges a bit less.

Talent, originality, credits, dedication, self-confidence and professionalism are qualities that will attract a manager to an artist—and a songwriter. Before submitting to a manager or booking agent, be sure he's searching for the type of music you offer. And, just as if you were contacting a music publisher or producer, always be as organized and professional as possible. *Billboard* also publishes a list of managers/booking agents in *Billboard's International Talent and Touring Directory*. Although listings do not include submission requirements or other relevant information, an address, phone number and contact name are provided.

*A•C•E TALENT MANAGEMENT, Unit 24, 4544 Dufferin St., Downsview Ont. M3H 5X2 **Canada.** President: Raymond A Sare. Management firm. Estab. 1984. Represents local, regional or international individual artists, groups, songwriters, models and actors; currently handles 15 acts. Receives 15% commission. Reviews materials for acts.

How to Contact: Call first to arrange personal interview. Prefers cassette (or VHS videocassette if available) with 5 songs and lyric sheets. Does not return unsolicited material. Reports in 1 week.
Music: Mostly rock, pop and dance; also country and R&B. Deals with groups, vocalists and songwriters. Current acts include Sweettalk, SRO and Joyride.
Tips: "Visualize your goal, stick to your product development and invest all your resources into your career."

ACADEMY AWARD ENTERTAINMENT, 11 Shady Oak Trail, Charlotte NC 28210. (704)554-1162. Agent: Butch Kelly. Management firm, music publisher (Butch Kelly Productions, Music By Butch Kelly/BMI), record company (KAM Executive and Fresh Avenue Records), record producer and promoter (Sunshine Record Promotions). Estab. 1987. Represents national acts and comedians. Currently handles 10 acts. Receives 20% commission. Reviews material for acts.
How to Contact: Prefers cassette or records (or VHS videocassette if available) with 5-10 songs. "Send bio information, 8x10 photo, press kit or news clips if possible." SASE. Reports in 2 months.
Music: Rock, pop, R&B, rap, beach, soul, gospel, country and comedy. Works primarily with show and dance groups, vocalists, bar bands and concerts. Current acts include Fresh Air (R&B), Lady Crush (rapper), Dean Mancuso (country), Melisa Kelly (R&B/pop), L.A. Star (R&B), Caro (R&B) and Platters (show).

AFTERSCHOOL PUBLISHING COMPANY, P.O. Box 14157, Detroit MI 48214. (313)873-5449. President: Herman Kelly. Management firm, booking agency, record company (Afterschool Co.) and music publisher (Afterschool Pub. Co.). Estab. 1978. Represents individual artists, songwriters, producers, arrangers and musicians. Currently handles 8 acts. Receives 20% commission. Reviews material for acts.
How to Contact: Prefers cassette with 3 songs and lyric or lead sheet. SASE. Reports in 1 month.
Music: Mostly pop, jazz, rap, country and folk. "What we are seeking now is comedy on the subjects of food, clothes, sports, cars and love." Works primarily with small bands and solo artists. Current acts include Herman Kelly, Rendell Star (singer/songwriter), Raymond Ellis (pop/jazz/folk), James Garland (pop/jazz,folk) and T. Stevenson.

AIM HIGH PRODUCTIONS/IMA, #210, 2022 Powers Ferry Rd., Atlanta GA 30339. (404)956-8742. Contact: Jim Stephens. Management firm, booking agency and record company (JDS Records). Estab. 1982. Represents local, Southeast and national individual artists and groups. Currently handles 10 acts. Receives 15-20% commission. Reviews material for acts.
How to Contact: Submit demo tape by mail. Unsolicited submissions are OK; or call first to arrange personal interview. Prefers cassette (or VHS videocassette if available) with 4 songs. SASE. Reports in 2 weeks.
Music: Mostly pop, metal, top 40 and R&B. Works primarily with top 40 dance bands, show bands, bar bands, soloists, duos and vocalists. Current acts include Desaint (rock/writers), Party Boys (top 40) and Ouija (heavy rock/writers).
Tips: "Have a complete kit on yourself pointing out your best talents and the type of material that you are best suited for. Your presentation should be brief but to the point. Your tapes should be labeled clearly and always have a phone number on them. As long as your tape is clear it doesn't have to be 24-track master quality. Send material that is current. Watch the charts in the trades to see what is up and coming."

AKO PRODUCTIONS, 20531 Plummer, Chatsworth CA 91311. (818)998-0443. President: A.E. Sullivan. Management firm, booking agency, music publisher and record company (AKO Records, Dorn Records, Aztec Records). Estab. 1980. Represents local and international artists, groups and songwriters; currently handles 3 acts. Receives 10-25% commission. Reviews material for acts.
How to Contact: Write first and obtain permission to submit. Prefers cassette with maximum of 5 songs and lyric sheet. Does not return unsolicited material. Reports in 1 month.
Music: Mostly pop, rock and top 40. Works primarily with vocalists, dance bands and original groups. No heavy metal. Current acts include Les Staunton's, Touch of Fire and The Stereo Band.

MARK ALAN AGENCY, P.O. Box 279, Hopkins MN 55343. (612)942-6119. President: Mark Alan. Management firm and booking agency. Represents individual artists, groups and songwriters; currently handles 8 acts. Receives 15% commission. Reviews material for acts.
How to Contact: Prefers cassette (or VHS videocassette if available). Does not return unsolicited material. Reports in 90 days.
Music: Rock, pop, R&B (black) and new wave. Works primarily with groups and solo artists. Current acts include Airkraft (contemporary rock band), Mercedez, Zwarté (rock band), Raggedy Ann, Montage, Constable Jones, Audra Shay and Bridges (pop dance band).

Tips: "We work with rock bands that tour nationally and regionally and record their original songs and release them on major or independent labels. We book clubs, colleges and concerts."

*ALEXAS MUSIC GROUP, B-30, 26111 Ynez Rd., Temecula CA 92390. (714)676-0006. President: Patrick Melfi. Management firm, booking agency (BMI) and record company (Alexas Records/AS-CAP). Estab. 1976. Represents local, regional or international individual artists, groups and songwriters; currently handles 10 acts. Receives 15% commission. Reviews material for acts.
How to Contact: Submit demo tape by mail. Unsolicited submissions are OK. Submit VHS videocassette only with 1-3 songs and lyric sheets. Does not return unsolicited material. Reports in 2 months.
Music: Mostly country and pop; also New Age and gospel. Represents well-established bands and vocalists. Current acts include A.J. Masters (singer/songwriter), Fats Johnson (entertainer/songwriter), Joe Neddo (entertainer/songwriter), Crossfire, Hardriders and Midnight Country.

*GREG ALIFERIS MANAGEMENT, 3406 N. Ocean Blvd., Ft. Lauderdale FL 33308. (305)561-4880. President: Greg Aliferis. Management firm, music publisher (Rumrunner Music/BMI) and record company (Rumrunner Records, Inc.). Estab. 1980. Represents local and southeast individual artists, groups and songwriters; currently handles 5 acts. Reviews material for acts.
How to Contact: Submit demo tape by mail. Unsolicited submissions are OK. Prefers cassette or VHS videocassette with 3 songs and lyric sheet. SASE. Reports in 1 month.
Music: Mostly dance, rap and pop. Works primarily with rap groups, dance groups and female vocalists. Current acts include Side F-X (rap), Mario (rap) and Don't Know Yet (dance).

*ALL STAR TALENT & PROMOTIONS, P.O. Box 37612, Sarasota FL 34237. (813)377-1877. Executive Vice President: Lynn Russen. Management firm, booking agency, music publisher (Rob Lee Music/BMI) and record company (Castle, TCB, Jade, Rock Island). Estab. 1965. Represents local, regional and international individual artists and groups; currently handles 32 acts. Receives 15-25% commission. Reviews material for acts.
How to Contact: Submit demo tape by mail. Unsolicited submissions are OK. Prefers cassette (or VHS videocassette if available). Reports in 2 weeks.
Music: Mostly rock, pop and dance. Current acts include Dreta Warriors, Fantastics and Derrek Dukes.

*ALLIGATOR RECORDS AND ARTIST MANAGEMENT, P.O. Box 60234, Chicago IL 60660. (312)973-7736. Vice President/Director of Artist Relations: Nora Kinnally. Management firm. Estab. 1971. Represents local, regional and international individual artists and groups; currently handles 20-25 recording artists. Reviews material for acts.
How to Contact: Submit demo tape by mail. Unsolicited submissions are OK. Prefers cassette with 3 songs and lyric sheet. Reports in 6 months.
Music: Mostly blues and roots rock. Current acts include Koko Taylor, Lonnie Brooks and Elvin Bishop.
Tips: "The majority of musicians are looking for a record contract. However we have limited room on our roster for singing acts. We do have 20 acts who will be recording in the next year—and they all need good songs."

*ALOHA ENTERTAINMENT, P.O. Box 2204, 14 Sherman St., Auburn NY 13021. (315)252-1863. Publicist/Manager: Art Wenzel. Management and public relations firm. Estab. 1982. Represents local, Central New York, international and national touring acts and groups. Unsolicited submissions are OK. Prefers cassette.
How to Contact: Submit demo tape by mail. Unsolicited submissions are OK. Prefers cassette.
Music: Mostly rock, metal and blues; also jazz and R&B. Current acts include Sacred Death (speed metal band), The Kingsnakes (real blues) and Ruff Haus (R&B).

AMERICAN ARTIST, INC., 604 Glover Dr., Runnemede NJ 08078-1225. (609)931-8389. President: Anthony Messina. Management firm. Represent local, regional or international individual artists, groups and songwriters; currently handles 4 acts. Receives 15% commission. Reviews material for acts.

 The asterisk before a listing indicates that the listing is new in this edition. New markets are often the most receptive to unsolicited submissions.

How to Contact: Submit demo tape by mail. Unsolicited submissions are OK. Prefers cassette or 7½ ips reel-to-reel (or VHS videocassette if available) with 3 songs and lyric sheets. Does not return unsolicited material. Reports in 6 weeks.

Music: Mostly MOR, rock and R&B. Works primarily with vocalists and dance bands. Current acts include Harold Melvin, Delfonics, Electric City and The Bluenotes.

ANJOLI PRODUCTIONS, 24 Center Square Rd., Leola PA 17540. (717)656-8215. President: Terry Gehman. Management firm, booking agency and music publisher (Younger Bros. Music). Estab. 1984. Represents individual artists, groups and songwriters; currently handles 20 acts. Receives 15% commission. Reviews material for acts.

How to Contact: Prefers cassette or VHS videocassette (preferably a live show video, good quality. Segments of a variety of material with 15-minute maximum length) with 5 songs and lyric sheet. Does not return unsolicited material.

Music: Country, pop and R&B. Works primarily with vocalists and show groups. Current acts include Shucks (country show), Crossover (country shows), Marsha Miller (country show) and Anita Stapleton (country vocalist).

ARISTO MUSIC GROUP, Box 22765, Nashville TN 37202. (615)269-7074. President: Jeff Walker. Publishing Manager: Terri Walker. Publicity/media management firm. Represents artists, groups and songwriters. "We deal with artists on a national and international level." Currently handles 8 clients. Receives negotiable commission for public relations services "based on estimated time and services involved." Reviews material for acts.

How to Contact: Query by mail. "At present we are only interested in artists with national distribution." Prefers cassette with 1-2 songs (or videocassette if available). Prefers a "low-key, patient approach." SASE. Reports in 1 month.

Music: Country, easy listening, MOR and top 40/pop. Works primarily with country groups and artists. Current acts include the Nashville roster of Atlantic Records including Billy Joe Royal, Martin Del Ray, Ray Kennedy, Robin Lee and Jeff Stevens and the Bullets; the Nashville roster of the Entertainment Artists Agency; and the Nashville Roster of DPI Records, which includes Hoyt Axton and Mel McDaniel.

Tips: Songwriters "need to be professional in their approach to the music business. Have established affiliated publishing companies. See the Marco Music Group Inc."

THE ARTIST GROUP, 13176 Royal Pines Dr., St. Louis MO 63146. (314)576-7625. Manager: Keith Davis. Management firm and booking agency. Estab. 1987. Represents individual artists and groups from anywhere; currently handles 3 acts. Receives 15-25% commission. Reviews material for acts.

How to Contact: Submit demo tape by mail. Unsolicited submission are OK. Prefers cassette (or VHS videocassette if available) with 4 songs and lyric sheet. Does not return unsolicited material. Reports in 1 month.

Music: Mostly rock, alternative (new music) and funk. Works primarily with rock bands—dance funk bands. Current acts include Aynthem (objectivist rock), Red Rover (rock show group) and Saturn Cats (pop metal show group).

Tips: "Submit quality demos, lyric sheets. Wait for a response. We will respond within 4 weeks of receipt."

*ARTISTIC DEVELOPMENTS INTERNATIONAL, INC. (A.D.I.), P.O. Box 6386, Glendale CA 91225. (818)501-2838. Management Director: Lisa Weinstein. Management firm. Estab. 1988. Represents local, regional and international individual artists, groups and songwriters. Reviews material for acts.

How to Contact: Call first and obtain permission to submit. Prefers cassette with unlimited number of songs and lyric sheet. Reports in 4-6 weeks.

Music: Mostly cross-over artists, AC/pop and alternative/rock; also world beat/pop and R&B/dance. Works primarily with singer/songwriters, bands and performance artists.

ARTISTS'/HELLER AGENCY, Ste. 100, 21860 Burbank Blvd., Woodland Hills CA 91367. (818)710-0060. President: Jerry Heller. Management firm. Represents artists, groups and songwriters; currently handles 15 acts. Reviews material for acts. Receives 15-25% commission.

"How to Use Your Songwriter's Market" (at the front of this book) contains comments and suggestions to help you understand and use the information in these listings.

How to Contact: Query by mail. Prefers cassette with 4-7 songs. SASE. Reports in 1 month.
Music: Mostly R&B, rap and jazz; also rock, soul and progressive. Works primarily with concert groups. Current acts include Rose Royce (R&B), Rodney Franklin (jazz/R&B), Bobby Jimmy & The Critters, Russ Parr, World Class Wreckin' Cru, C.I.A., Eazy E, N.W.A., J.J. Fad, The D.O.C. and Michélle.

*ASA PRODUCTIONS MANAGEMENT, P.O. Box 244, Yorba Linda CA 92686. (714)693-7629. President: Craig Seitz. Management firm. Estab. 1986. Represents local, regional or international individual artists and groups; currently handles 2 acts. Receives 20% commission. Reviews material for acts.
How to Contact: Submit demo tape by mail. Unsolicited submissions are OK. Prefers cassette (or VHS videocassette if available). SASE. Reports in 1 month.
Music: Mostly country and bluegrass. Works primarily with show/concert groups. Current acts include Barbara Morrison and Sierrah Band.

ATTRACTIONS, LTD., P.O. Box 10013, Dallas TX 75207. (214)941-6971. President: R. Edward Cobb. Management firm. Estab. 1977. Represents individual artists and groups from anywhere; currently handles 2 acts. Reviews material for acts.
How to Contact: Submit demo tape by mail. Unsolicited submissions are OK. Prefers cassette (or VHS videocassette if available). Does not return unsolicited material.
Music: Mostly pop, country and rock; also variety. Current acts include Chisholm and Vince Vance.
Tips: "Send your best and simplest."

BABY SUE, Box 1111, Decatur GA 30031-1111. (404)288-2073. President: Don W. Seven. Management firm, booking agency, record company (Baby Sue); "we also publish a magazine which reviews music." Estab. 1983. Represents local, regional or international individual artists, groups and songwriters; currently handles 3 acts. Receives 10% commission. Reviews material for acts.
How to Contact: Submit demo tape by mail. Unsolicited submissions are OK. Prefers cassette (or VHS videocassette if available) with 4 songs and lyric sheets. Does not return unsolicited material. Reports in 2 weeks.
Music: Mostly rock, pop and alternative; also country and religious. Works primarily with multi-talented artists (those who play more than 1 instrument). Current acts include LMNOP (rock), Stephen Fievet (pop) and Bringbring (poetic music).

*BACK DOOR MANAGEMENT, P.O. Box 1696, Batavia NY 14021-1696. (716)343-6502. President: Richard Anselmo. Management firm and booking agency. Estab. 1990. Represents local, regional and international individual artists, groups, songwriters and comedians; currently handles 6 acts. Receives 15-25% commission. Reviews material for acts.
How to Contact: Write or call first and obtain permission to submit. Prefers cassette or VHS videocassette with 3-6 songs and lyric and lead sheets. Reports in 3-5 weeks.
Music: Mostly rock, folk and pop; also R&B, heavy metal and industrial. Works primarily with individual artists, duos/groups and songwriters. Current acts include Dresden (rock-pop group), Dominic DeSantis (folk singer/songwriter) and Lorie McCloud (singer/songwriter).
Tips: "Hard work coupled with originality produces results."

GARY BAILEY ENTERTAINMENT AGENCY, 207 Queen St., Port Stanley, Ontario, **Canada.** (519)782-3570. President: Gary Bailey. Booking agency. Represents artists and groups in Ontario; currently handles 15 acts. Receives 15-20% commission. Reviews material for acts.
How to Contact: Query by mail. Prefers cassette or videocassette with 3-5 songs. Does not return unsolicited material. Reports in 2 weeks.
Music: Mostly MOR, 50s-60s and top 40; also dance, easy listening and rock. Works primarily with dance bands and bar bands. Current acts include Player (MOR), Wildcats, Dolly Hartt (country recording artist), Footloose (50s/60s) and Destiny (top 40).
Tips: "Be honest, hard working and have a clean appearance."

BARNARD MANAGEMENT SERVICES (BMS), 2219 Main St., Santa Monica CA 90405. (213)396-1440. Agent: Russell Barnard. Management firm. Estab. 1979. Represents artists, groups and songwriters; currently handles 3 acts. Receives 10-20% commission. Reviews material for acts.
How to Contact: Write first and obtain permission to submit. Prefers cassette with 3-10 songs and lead sheet. Artists may submit VHS videocassette (15-30 minutes) by permission only. SASE. Reports in 1 month.
Music: Mostly country crossover; also blues, country, R&B, rock and soul. Works primarily with country crossover singers/songwriters and show bands. Current acts include Helen Hudson (singer/songwriter), Mark Shipper (songwriter/author), Mel Trotter (singer/songwriter) and Sally Spurs (singer).

Tips: "Semi-produced demos are of little value. Either save the time and money by submitting material 'in the raw,' or do a finished production version."

BDO SEIDMAN, 1200 Statler Towers, Buffalo NY 14202. (716)853-9333. Partner: Richard A. Romer. Management firm. Estab. 1982. Represents individual artists and groups; currently handles 5 acts. Commission is "based on hourly rate of $175/hour." Reviews material for acts.
How to Contact: Prefers cassette. "Would like to see live performance videocassette." Does not return unsolicited material. Reports in 2 weeks.
Music: Mostly R&B and rap. Works primarily with R&B acts and vocalists. Current acts include Rick James (R&B), Erskine Williams (R&B) and Val Young (R&B).
Tips: "Have original material that has a different sound."

BE-ALL AND END-ALL, 34 Walton Ave., South Harrow, Middlesex HA2 8QX **England**. Phone: (081)864-7978. Personal Assistant: Louise Mobbs. Management firm and booking agency. Estab. 1980. Represents local, regional or international individual artists, groups and songwriters. Currently handles 4 acts. Receives 15% commission. Reviews material for acts.
How to Contact: Submit demo tape by mail. Unsolicited submissions are OK. Prefers cassette (or videocassette of live performance, if available) with 3 songs and lyric sheet. SASE. Reports in 2 weeks.
Music: Mostly rock, pop, R&B and soul. Represents rock, R&B and solo acts. Current acts include The Babysitters, Errol Shaker, Brian Knight and Martin Connelly.
Tips: "Try and be patient. Keep on knocking on the door."

BELKIN PERSONAL MANAGEMENT, 44 N. Main St., Chagrin Falls OH 44022. (216)247-2722. Assistant: Susan Haffey. Management firm. Represents local, regional or international individual artists, groups and songwriters; currently handles 4 acts. Receives 10-20% commission.
How to Contact: Submit demo tape by mail. Unsolicited submissions are OK. Prefers cassette with 3 songs. SASE. Reports in 3 weeks.
Music: Mostly rock, pop and R&B; also female vocalists. Works primarily with rock performance bands and female vocalists. Current acts include Mason Ruffner (blues rock singer/songwriter), Donnie Iris and The Cruisers (rock) and Cellarful of Noise (pop).

BEST BUDDIES, INC., Box 121738, Nashville TN 37212-1738. (615)383-7664. Professional Manager: Paul Sanders. Management firm and music publisher (Swing Set Music/ASCAP and Best Buddies Music/BMI). Estab. 1981. Represents individual artists, groups and songwriters from anywhere. Prefers "self-contained songwriter/artists." Currently handles 5 acts. Receives 10-20% commission. Reviews material for acts.
How to Contact: Write first and obtain permission to submit a demo. Prefers cassette (or VHS videocassette if available) with 4-5 songs and lyric sheet. Does not return unsolicited material. Reports in 6 weeks.
Music: Mostly country, rock and pop; also gospel and R&B. Works primarily with vocalists/musicians. Current acts include Ray Lynch (singer/writer), Sandy Garwood (singer/writer) and Jamie Bowles (singer/writer).
Tips: "Shoot your very best shot. This is a business and has to be treated as such."

J. BIRD BOOKING – THE ENTERTAINMENT AGENCY, 250 N. Kepler Rd., Deland FL 32724. (904)734-9446. Contact: John R. Bird II. Management firm and booking agency. Estab. 1963. Represents artists, groups and songwriters; currently handles 55 acts. Receives 15-25% commission. Reviews material for acts.
How to Contact: Prefers cassette with 3-4 songs (or VHS videocassette, 3-10 minutes, segments of performance. Preview a varity of material. Original songwriters should submit complete version of song). "Initial interview is usually by phone; after demo material is received we usually ask person to contact us again in 1 week-10 days." Does not return unsolicited material.
Music: Mostly folk, rock, dance and top 40/pop. Works primarily with dance bands, vocalists and recording acts. Current acts include The Drifters, Greg Allman, Molly Hatchet, Doobie Brothers, Tams, Swinging Medallions and Nantucket (original concert rock/RCA label).
Tips: "We solicit established professional acts interested in touring full time. The groups should have or be willing to prepare a promotional package containing audio and/or videotape, photos, and personnel and equipment lists."

WILLIS BLUME AGENCY, Box 509, Orangeburg SC 29116. (803)536-2951. President: Willis Blume. Management firm and booking agency. Estab. 1972. Represents artists and groups in the southeast; currently handles 30 acts. Receives minimum 15% commission. Reviews material for acts.

How to Contact: Query by mail. Prefers cassette with maximum of 4 songs. Artists may submit videocassette. SASE.
Music: "Only interested in A/C songs and artists." Motown type, R&B, dance and top 40. Works primarily with show and dance bands with horns. Current acts include Shagtime, The Swingin' Medalions and The Catalinas (all show and dance bands/recording acts), the Tams (beach/top 40/pop artists), Archie Bell, The Kicks, The Impressions, Bank of Oz, The Drifters, The Clovers and The Entertainers.

BOJO PRODUCTIONS INC., 3935 Cliftondale Pl., College Park GA 30349. (404)969-1913. Management firm and record company (Bojo Records). Estab. 1982. Represents local, regional or international individual artists, groups and songwriters; currently handles 5 acts. Receives 15% commission. Reviews material for acts.
How to Contact: Submit demo tape by mail. Unsolicited submissions are OK. Prefers cassette (or videocassette if available) with 3 songs and lyric or lead sheets. SASE. Reports in 2 weeks.
Music: Mostly R&B, gospel and country; also MOR. Works primarily with vocalists and dance bands. Current acts include Francell Burton (R&B), Flavor (R&B and MOR), Rose McCoy (songwriter), Cathie Knight (contemporary gospel) and George Smith (country and jazz and MOR).

BONNIE LOU ENTERPRISES, RD 3, Box 322-B, Seaford DE 19973. (302)629-0401. Manager: Bonnie L. Carver. Management firm and booking agency (April One Inc.). Estab. 1983. Represents individual artists and groups. Currently handles 1 act. Receives 10-20% commission. Reviews material for acts.
How to Contact: Prefers cassette (or VHS videocassette if available) with 3 songs and lyric sheet. SASE. Reports in 3 weeks.
Music: Country. Works primarily with dance and show bands and new artists.
Tips: "Make sure your songs have good hooks and are original and commercial. We are looking for hardworking and disciplined people who are honest and not into drugs. You must have the perseverance to hang in there over the long haul. Be professional at all times."

T.J. BOOKER LTD., Box 969, Rossland, B.C. V0G 1YO **Canada**. (604)362-7795. Contact: Tom Jones. Management firm, booking agency and music publisher. Estab. 1976. Represents local, regional or international individual artists, groups and songwriters; currently handles 25 acts. Receives 10-15% commission. Reviews material for acts.
How to Contact: Submit demo tape by mail. Unsolicited submissions are OK. Prefers cassette (or videocassette if available) with 3 songs. Does not return unsolicited material.
Music: Mostly MOR, crossover, rock, pop and country. Works primarily with vocalists, show bands, dance bands and bar bands. Current acts include Kirk Orr (Comedian), Tommy and T Birds (50s show band) and Lanzee (top 40/pop).
Tips: "There is always a market for excellence."

BOUQUET-ORCHID ENTERPRISES, Box 11686, Atlanta GA 30355. (404)355-7635. President: Bill Bohannon. Management firm, booking agency, music publisher (Orchid Publishing/BMI) and record company (Bouquet Records). Represents individuals and groups; currently handles 4 acts. Receives 10-15% commission. Reviews material for acts.
How to Contact: Prefers cassette (or videocassette if available) with 3-5 songs, song list and lyric sheet. Include brief resume. SASE. Reports in 1 month.
Music: Mostly country, rock and top 40/pop; also gospel and R&B. Works primarily with vocalists and groups. Current acts include Teresa Gilbert, Adam Day and the Bandoleers (top 40/pop group).

*BRIER PATCH MUSIC, 3825 Meadowood, Grandville MI 49418. (616)534-6571. Promotions Associate: Sharon Knol. Booking agency and record company (Brier Patch Records). Estab. 1987. Represents local, regional and international individual artists; currently handles 3 acts. Receives 20% commission.
How to Contact: Write or call first and obtain permission to submit. Prefers 3 songs and lyric and lead sheets. SASE. Reports in 6 weeks.
Music: Mostly light rock, pop and gospel; also New Age instrumental, children's and peace/justice/folk. Current acts include Ken Medema (light rock singer, keyboardist, composer), Garth Hewitt (folk singer, guitarist, activist, gospel) and Darrell Adams (folk singer, gospel).
Tips: "Have original music or unique presentation. Theme of peace and justice."

DAVID BRODY PRODUCTIONS, 4086 Royal Crest, Memphis TN 38115. (901)362-1719. President: David or Gina Brody. Management firm and music publisher (Brody-Segerson Publishing/BMI). Estab. 1986. Represents international individual artists, groups and songwriters; currently handles 5 acts. Reviews material for acts.

How to Contact: Call first and obtain permission to submit. Prefers cassette (or VHS videocassette if available) with 3 songs and lyric sheet.
Music: Interested in all music. Works primarily with comedians, announcers, singer and actors. Current acts include Cousin Bubba (comedian), Jonathan Michaels (actor), Billy Davis, Jr. (singer) and Frazer Smith (radio personality).

BROTHERS MANAGEMENT ASSOCIATES, 141 Dunbar Ave., Fords NJ 08863. (201)738-0880 or 738-0883. President: Allen A. Faucera. Management firm and booking agency. Estab. 1972. Represents artists, groups and songwriters; currently handles over 100 acts. Receives 15-20% commission. Reviews material for acts.
How to Contact: Query by mail. Prefers cassette (or VHS videocassette if available) with 3-6 songs and lyric sheets. Include photographs and resume. SASE. Reports in 2 months.
Music: Mostly pop, rock, MOR and R&B. Works primarily with vocalists and established groups. Current acts include Ben E. King, Makana (rock), Waterfront (top 40/show), Chelsea (top 40/rock), Benny Troy and Company (top 40/show), James Brown and other track artists.
Tips: "We need very commercial, chart-oriented material."

*BRUSCO/PACE MANAGEMENT CO., 1073 Green St., Roswell GA 30342. (404)642-9999. Vice President: David Prescher. Management firm. Estab. 1972. Represents local, southeast and international individual artists and groups; currently handles 4 acts. Receives 15-20% commission. Reviews material for acts.
How to Contact: Submit demo tape by mail. Unsolicited submissions are OK. Prefers cassette or VHS videocassette with 3-5 songs and lyric sheet. Does not return unsolicited material. Reports in 1 month.
Music: Mostly rock, pop and rap. Works most often with self-contained rock groups. Current acts include Flags on Fire (alternative rock), Hard Corps (rock n' rap) and Slaughter House (metal blade/heavy metal).

BSA INC., P.O. Box 1516, Champaign IL 61820. (217)352-8700. Management firm and booking agency. Estab. 1983. Represents local, regional or international individual artists, groups and songwriters; currently handles 6 acts. Receives 10-15% commission. Reviews material for acts.
How to Contact: Submit demo tape by mail. Prefers cassette (or Beta videocassette of live performance if available). Does not return unsolicited material.
Music: Mostly pop, country and rock; also jazz, blues and R&B. Works primarily with dance bands, concert acts and vocalists. Currently represents Pink Flamingoes and Ken Carlysle.

BSC PRODUCTIONS, INC., P.O. Box 368, Tujunga CA 91043. (818)352-8142. President/General Manager: Kenn E. Kingsbury, Jr. Management firm and music publisher (Black Stallion Country Publishing, BMI). Estab. 1979. Represents individual artists and songwriters. Deals with local, national and international artists. Currently handles 2 acts. Reviews material for acts. Producer of "Bear Show," TV show.
How to Contact: Submit demo tape by mail. Unsolicited submissions are OK. Prefers cassette (or 7½ IPS reel-to-reel if available) with 3 songs and lyric sheets. SASE. Reports back in 6 weeks.
Music: Country, blues and A/C. Works primarily with vocalists, comedians, magicians and film/TV actors and actresses. Current acts include Jenny James (singer/songwriter), Lane Brudy (performer/actress) and Gene Bear (performer/actor).

*JOE BUCHWALD, P.O. Box 347008, San Francisco CA 94134. Administrator: Joe Buchwald. Management firm (BMI). Estab. 1972. Represents local, regional and international individual artists and songwriters. Receives 10% (or more) commission. Reviews material for acts.
How to Contact: Submit demo tape by mail. Unsolicited submissions are OK. Prefers cassette (or VHS videocassette if available) with 3 or 4 songs and lyric and lead sheet. Reports in 2 weeks.
Music: Mostly ballads, light rock and country. Works primarily with vocalists and dance bands. Current acts include Marty Balin and Rock Justice.

*BUTTERFLY PROMOTIONS, 20 Princess Highway, Figtree NSW **Australia** 2525. Phone: (042)29-7293. Manager: Bob Ebsworth. Management firm, booking agency and record company (Butterfly Records). Estab. 1971. Represents local, regional or international individual artists and groups; currently handles 11 acts. Receives 10% commission. Reviews material for acts.
How to Contact: Write or call first and obtain permission to submit. Prefers cassette (or VHS videocassette if available) with an unlimited number of songs and lyric sheets (helpful). "Make them easy to watch and/or listen to. Don't misrepresent the songs." SASE. Reports in 1 month.

Music: Prefers rock, R&B and dance. Primarily works with dance bands, vocalists and show bands. Current acts include Sue Samson (female vocalist), The Great Bite (dance show band) and David Mason-Cox (singer/songwriter/arranger).
Tips: "Be frank—do not misrepresent yourself. Send only finished product."

C & M PRODUCTIONS INC., 6312 Landmark, Waco TX 76710. (817)772-6357. Manager: Ronald W. Cotton. Management firm, booking agency, music publisher (Triangle Songworks/ASCAP) and C.M.R. Music Group (BMI). Estab. 1980. Represents international individual artists; currently handles 2 acts on Polygram Records. Receives 15% commission.
How to Contact: Submit demo tape by mail—unsolicited submissions are OK. Prefers cassette (or VHS videocassette if available) with 3 songs and lead sheets. SASE. Reports in 2 weeks.
Music: Mostly country, gospel and pop. Current acts include Rowne Reeves and B.B. Watson.

*C.I.A., 3rd Floor, 114 Chambers St., New York NY 10007-1059. (212)732-8111. President: Tony Grifasi. Booking agency. Estab. 1989. Represents local, regional and international individual artists, groups and songwriters; currently handles 15 acts. Receives 15% commission. Reviews material for acts.
How to Contact: Call first and obtain permission to submit. Prefers cassette (or VHS videocassette if available) with 3 or 4 songs and lyric sheet. SASE. Reports in 1-3 weeks.
Music: Mostly R&B, blues and rock; also folk and ballads. Works primarily with R&B groups and blues artists. Current acts include Tino Gonzales (blues), Phenix Horns Revue (Phil Collins horn section) and The Blues Brotherhood.
Tips: "Be original, have a sense of humor and be real."

C.M. MANAGEMENT, 7957 Nita Ave., Canoga Park CA 91304-4706. (818)704-7800. President: Craig Miller. Management firm and music publisher. Estab. 1975. Represents individual artists; currently handles 5 acts. Receives 15-20% commission—"occasional flat fee."
How to Contact: Write or call first and obtain permission to submit. Prefers cassette with 3 songs and lyric sheet. Submit material "with the best package (representation) possible." Does not return unsolicited material. SASE. Reports in 1 month.
Music: Mostly instrumental and session artists; also jazz, new acoustic and fusion. Works primarily with highest caliber recording artists. Current acts include David Grisman (Acoustic Disc recording act), Mark O'Connor (WB Recording act), Strength In Numbers (MCA Records recording act) and Danny O'Keefe (singer/songwriter).
Tips: "Unless you feel that you are really *exceptional*, don't bother to contact us."

CAM MUSIC, LTD., 1423 Lee Blvd., Berkeley IL 60163. (708)544-4771. President: Chip Messineo. Management firm, booking agent, producer and publisher. Estab. 1983. Represents local and regional individual artists, groups and songwriters; currently handles 6 acts. Receives 15-25% commission. Reviews material for acts.
How to Contact: Write first and obtain permission to submit. Prefers cassette (or videocassette of performance, if available) with 3 songs, lyric sheets and SASE. "Do not send full songs. 60-90 seconds is enough." Does not return unsolicited material. Reports in 2 months.
Music: Mostly country, bluegrass and folk; also MOR, jazz and children's. Works primarily with concert tour bands, show bands and festival bands. Current acts include Wendy Como, Strait Southern (country) and Special Concensus (bluegrass).
Tips: "A career in music does not happen overnight. If it did you wouldn't know what to do with your overnight success. You have to work for it. Be professional. Don't send out sloppy promotional kits. Your demo is the first impression that we hear and see. Impress me. One of the things that will make me turn off the tape machine is a demo that does not have the vocal UP front and solos. I want to hear the song."

*CAPITAL ARTISTS LTD., No. 1, Leighton Rd., **Hong Kong**. Phone: (852)833-9192. General Manager: Tong Ching Chuen. Management firm, booking agency, music publisher (Capital Artists Ltd., Cash) and record company. Estab. 1971. Represents local, regional and international individual artists and songwriters; currently handles 10 acts. Receives 5-30% commission. Reviews material for acts.
How to Contact: Submit demo tape by mail. Unsolicited submissions are OK. Prefers cassette or PAL videocassette. Does not return unsolicited material. Reports in 4 weeks.
Music: Mostly pop and R&B. Works primarily with vocalists.

*CAPITAL PRODUCTIONS, Liebigstrasse 1-3, Kaiserslautern 6750 **Germany**. Phone: (011)49-631-50948. President: Ron Boswell. Management firm and booking agency. Estab. 1989. Represents local, regional or international individual artists and groups; currently handles 23 acts. Receives 15-25% commission. Reviews material for acts.

How to Contact: Submit demo tape by mail. Unsolicited submissions are OK. Prefers cassette (or NTSC videocassette if available) with 3 songs and lyric sheet. SASE. Reports in 6 weeks.
Music: Mostly gospel, R&B and pop; also full shows and jazz. Works primarily with young vocalists and bands looking to get started in the business. Current acts include Drema Leonard (singer), Samuel Boswell (singer/songwriter) and Technique (R&B band).
Tips: "Know your trade, be confident, prepare to work hard. Most of all, be patient and persistent."

*CAPITOL MANAGEMENT, 1300 Division St., Nashville TN 37203. (615)242-4722. Producer: Robert Metzgar. Management firm, booking agency, music publisher (Aim High Music Co.) and record company (Stop Hunger Records International, Bobby & Billy Music). Estab. 1971. Represents local, regional or international individual artists, groups and songwriters; currently handles 24 acts. Receives 15% commission. Reviews material for acts.
How to Contact: Submit demo tape by mail. Unsolicited submissions are OK. Prefers cassette (or videocassette of live performance, if available). SASE. Reports in 1 week.
Music: Mostly traditional country, contemporary country and southern gospel; also pop rock, rock-a-billy and R&B. Works primarily with major label acts and new acts shopping for major labels. Current acts include Carl Butler (CBS records), Tommy Cash (CBS Records), Tommy Overstreet (CBS Records), Mark Allen Cash, Mickey Jones and The Glen Campbell Band.
Tips: "Getting us on your team is the single best thing you could ever do for your career in the city of Nashville."

CARMAN PRODUCTIONS, INC., 15456 Cabrito Rd., Van Nuys CA 91406. (213)873-7370. A&R: Joey Vieira. Management firm, music publisher (Namrac/BMI, Souci/ASCAP) and record production company. Estab. 1969. Represents local, regional and international individual artists, groups, songwriters, producers and actors. Currently handles 6 acts. Receives 15% commission. Reviews material for acts.
How to Contact: Write first and obtain permission to submit. Prefers cassette with 5 songs and lyric sheets. Does not return unsolicited material. Reports in 2 months.
Music: Mostly rock, dance, R&B, pop and country; also dance and R&B. Current acts include Richard Carpenter, Tom Harriman, Michael Botts, Kuh Ledesma, the Dressler Sisters, J.J. White, James Intveld, Ron Keel & Fair Game, Timothy Pantea and Casanova.

CAT PRODUCTION AB, Rörstrandsgatan 21, Stockholm 11340 **Sweden**. Phone: (08)317-277. Managing Director: Christina Nilsson. Management firm and booking agency. Estab. 1972. Represents individual artists, groups and songwriters; currently handles 3 acts. Receives 15% commission. Reviews material for acts.
How to Contact: Prefers cassette (or VHS videocassette if available) with 4-6 songs and lyric or lead sheet. SAE and IRC. Reports in 2 months.
Music: Mostly R&B, rock and gospel; also "texts for stand-up comedians." Works primarily with "concert bands like Janne Schaffers' Earmeal. Rock-blues-imitation shows." Current acts include Jan Schaffer (lead guitar, songwriter), Tod Ashton (singer, blues/rock guitar and harmonica player, stand up comedian) and Malou Berg (gospel singer).

CHARTA RECORDS, 44 Music Sq. E., Nashville TN 37203. (615)255-2175. President: Charlie Fields. Record company (Charta Records/Delux Records) and public relations firm (Debbie Dean & Associates). Estab. 1972. Represents local, regional and international individual artists and groups. Currently handles 4-5 acts. Reviews material for acts.
How to Contact: Submit demo tape by mail. Unsolicited submissions are OK. Prefers cassette (or VHS videocassette if available) with 3 songs and lyric sheets. SASE. Reports in 1 week.
Music: Mostly country, pop and R&B. "So far we have worked with single vocalists, though we have had a duo." Current acts include David Walsh (country singer/songwriter), Nina Wyatt (country singer/songwriter) and Ronnie Klein (country).

*CHASIMONÉ ENTERPRISES, 24 Maple Dr., Roosevelt NY 11575. (516)378-7803. President: Mindy Carter; Vice President: James Citkovic. Management/consultant firm. Estab. 1990. Represents local, regional and international artists. Individual artists, groups and songwriters; currently handles 3 acts. Reviews material for acts.
How to Contact: Submit demo tape by mail. Unsolicited submissions are OK. Prefers cassette with 4 songs and lyric sheets. SASE. Reports in 3 weeks.
Music: Mostly R&B, rap and pop; also gospel and rock. Works primarily with vocalists, bands and producers. Current acts include G.M. Web D. (rap), EM-SEE Prime (rap) and M.C. Kev-Rock (rap).

*PAUL CHRISTIE MANAGEMENT, P.O. Box 96, Avalon NSW 2107 **Australia**. Phone: (02)918-2562. Managing Director: Paul Christie. Management firm (Paul Christie Management/APRA). Estab. 1982. Represents local, regional and international individual artists, groups and songwriters; currently handles 5 acts. Receives 20% commission. Reviews material for acts.
How to Contact: Submit demo tape by mail. Unsolicited submissions are OK. Prefers cassette or VHS videocassette with 4 songs and lyric or lead sheet. Reports in 1 week.
Music: Mostly rock, pop/rock and pop/R&B. Works primarily with rock acts, singer/writers, all composers. Current acts include Party Boys (2-guitar power rock), Dorian West (writer/performer) and Tim Gaze (singer/writer).
Tips: "Divorce yourself from all the rock music industry mythology and all the emotional issues, and assess yourself in terms of 'what really is'."

*CLIFFSIDE MUSIC INC., P.O. Box 374, Fairview NJ 07022. (201)941-3987. Song Review: Irma Proctor. Management firm and music publisher (Wazuri/BMI, G.G./ASCAP). Represents local, regional and international individual artists and songwriters; currently handles 3 acts. Receives 20-25% commission. Reviews material for acts.
How to Contact: Submit demo tape by mail. Unsolicited submissions are OK. Prefers cassette with 2 songs. Does not return unsolicited material.
Music: Mostly R&B crossover, pop/MOR and gospel; also jazz. Represents recording and touring singers, backup bands and songwriters (known and unknown). Current acts include Gloria Gaynor (R&B/pop/gospel), Linwood Simon (songwriter) and Cornell Johnson (singer/songwriter).
Tips: "Get real! Do not try to write every song overnight."

*CLOANA MUSIC GROUP, 4th Floor, 177 West 7th Ave., Vancouver BC V5Y 1K5 **Canada**. (604)876-3005. President: Diana J. Kelly. Management firm and music publisher (Diclo Publishing/BMI, Cloana Publishing/ASCAP, SOCAN). Estab. 1982. Represents local, regional and international individual artists, groups and songwriters; currently handles 2 acts. Reviews material for acts.
How to Contact: Call first and obtain permission to submit. Prefers cassette with 3 songs and lyric and lead sheets. Does not return unsolicited material. Reports in 1 month.
Music: Mostly country and pop; also gospel. Works primarily with country vocalists, vocal groups and songwriters. Current acts include Alibi (contemporary country group) and Colin Weinmaster (producer/songwriter).

CLOCKWORK ENTERTAINMENT MANAGEMENT AGENCY, P.O. Box 1600, Haverhill MA 01831. (508)373-6010. President: Bill Macek. Management firm and booking agency. Represents groups and songwriters throughout New England; currently handles 2 acts. Receives 15% commission. Reviews material for acts.
How to Contact: Query or submit demo tape. Prefers cassette with 3-12 songs. "Also submit promotion and cover letter with interesting facts about yourself." Does not return unsolicited material unless accompanied by SASE. Reports in 1 month.
Music: Rock (all types) and top 40/pop. Works primarily with bar bands and original acts. Current acts include Head First (4 piece cover/original rock) and Take One (5 piece cover/original rock).

*RAYMOND COFFER MANAGEMENT, S. The Lake, Bushey Herts WD2 1HS UK. Phone: (44)8195-05489. FAX: (44)8195-07617. Contact: Raymond Coffer. Management firm. Estab. 1984. Represents local, regional and international individual artists and groups; currently handles 5 acts. Receives 20% commission. Reviews material for acts.
How to Contact: Submit demo tape by mail. Unsolicited submissions are OK. Prefers cassette (or PAL or VHS videocassette if available) with 4 songs and lyric sheet. Does not return unsolicited material. Reports in 4 weeks.
Music: Mostly rock and pop. Works primarily with bands. Current acts include Love & Rockets, Cocteau Twins and Ian McCulloch.

COLE CLASSIC MANAGEMENT, Suite 207, 4150 Riverside Dr., Burbank CA 91505. (818)841-6365. A&R Manager: Earl Cole. Management firm. Represents local, regional, international individual artists, groups and producers. Currently handles 6 acts. Receives 10-15% commission. Reviews material for acts.
How to Contact: Submit demo tape by mail. Unsolicited submissions are OK. Prefers cassette with 2-3 songs and lyric sheets. Does not return solicited material. Reports in 3-4 weeks.
Music: Mostly R&B, pop and jazz; also gospel. Works primarily with vocalists and dance bands. Current acts include Atlantic Starr (R&B band/songwriters), Mac Band (R&B) and Surface (R&B group/songwriters/producers).

COMMUNITY MUSIC CENTER OF HOUSTON, 5613 Almeda, Houston TX 77004. (712)523-9710. Managing Director: Ron Scales. Management firm and booking agency. Estab. 1979. Represents international individual artists and groups; currently handles 6 acts. Receives 10-20% commission. Reviews material for acts.
How to Contact: Submit demo tape by mail. Unsolicited submissions are OK. Prefers cassette (VHS videocassette if available) with 4 songs and lyric or lead sheet. SASE. Reports in 2 months.
Music: Jazz, R&B and blues; also gospel and folk. Works primarily with solo vocalists, vocal groups and jazz bands. Current acts include Rhapsody (jazz vocal ensemble), Scott Joplin Chamber Orchestra (classical music by African-American composers) and Diedre Curnell (folk singer/songwriter).

BURT COMPTON AGENCY, P.O. Box 160373, Miami FL 33116. (305)271-6880. Contact: Burt Compton. Booking agency. Estab. 1978. Represents groups; currently handles 42 acts. Receives 10-20% commission. Reviews material for acts.
How to Contact: Query by mail, then submit demo tape. Prefers cassette (or videocassette) with 3-6 songs. "Include complete repertoire, 8x10 photo and resume." Does not return unsolicited material.
Music: Mostly top 40/nostalgia ('50, '60s). Works primarily with dance bands. Current acts include Heroes (dance band), Fantasy (recording/concert group) and Wildlife (recording/concert group).
Tips: "Have your promotional materials professionally packaged. We don't like having to decipher handwritten resumes with misspelled words and incomplete sentences."

MIKE CONSTANTIA ENTERTAINMENT, 41 Manchester Rd., Warrington, Cheshire WA1 4AE **England.** Phone: (0925)810979. Managing Director: M. Constantinou. Booking agency. Represents local individual artists and groups; currently handles 400 acts. Receives 15% commission. Reviews material for acts.
How to Contact: Prefers cassette (or VHS videocassette). SAE and IRC. Reports in 3 weeks.
Music: Mostly pop, country and R&B. Works primarily with vocalists and bands. Current acts include Billy Brown and Mark Williamson.

COUNTRY MUSIC SHOWCASE INTERNATIONAL, INC., P.O. Box 368, Carlisle IA 50047. (515)989-3676. President: Harold L. Luick. Vice President: Barbara A. Lancaster. Management firm and booking agency "for acts and entertainers that are members of our organization." Estab. 1984. Represents individual artists, groups and songwriters; currently handles 18-20 acts. Receives 5-20% commission.
How to Contact: Prefers cassette with 3 songs and lyric sheet (or VHS videocassette showing artist on the job, 3 different venues). SASE. Reports in 3 weeks. "Must be paid member of Country Music Showcase International, Inc., to receive review of work."
Music: Mostly contemporary, hard core country and traditional country; also bluegrass, western swing and comedy. Works primarily with "one person single acts, one person single tape background acts and show bands." Current acts include Mr. Elmer Bird (banjo virtuoso), Country Classics USA (12-piece stage show), The Dena Kaye Show, Britt Small and Allen Karl.
Tips: "We want artists who are willing to work hard to achieve success and songwriters who are skilled in their craft. Through educational and informative seminars and showcases we have helped many artist and songwriter members achieve a degree of success in a very tough business. For information on how to become a member of our organization, send SASE to the above address. Memberships cost $20.00 per year for artist or songwriter memberships."

COUNTRY STAR ATTRACTIONS, 439 Wiley Ave., Franklin PA 16323. (814)432-4633. Contact: Norman Kelly. Management firm, booking agency, music publisher (Country Star Music/ASCAP) and record company (Country Star, Process, Mersey and CSI Records). Estab. 1970. Represents artists and musical groups; currently handles 4-6 acts. Receives 10-15% commission. Reviews material for acts.
How to Contact: Prefers cassette with 2-4 songs and lyric or lead sheet; include photo. SASE. Reports in 2 weeks.
Music: Mostly country (80%); rock (5%) and gospel (5%). Works primarily with vocalists. Current acts include Junie Lou, Ron Lauer and Debbie Sue, all country singers.
Tips: "Send only your very best efforts."

COUNTRYWIDE PRODUCERS, 2466 Wildon Dr., York PA 17403. (717)741-2658. President: Bob Englar. Booking agency. Represents individuals and groups; currently handles 8 acts. Receives 10-15% commission. Reviews material for acts.
How to Contact: Query or submit demo with videocassette of performance, if available. Include photo. SASE. Reports in 3 weeks.
Music: Bluegrass, blues, classical, country, disco, folk, gospel, jazz, polka, rock (light), soul and top 40/pop. Works primarily with show bands. Current acts include Carroll County Ramblers (bluegrass), Ken Lightner (country), Rhythm Kings (country), Junction (variety), the Bruce Van Dyke Show (variety) and Big Wheeley & the White Walls (country rock).

*COURTRIGHT MANAGEMENT INC., 201 E. 87th St., New York NY 10128. (212)410-9055. Contacts: Hernando or Doreen Courtright. Management firm. Estab. 1984. Represents local, regional and international individual artists, groups, songwriters and producers. Receives 20% commission. Reviews material for acts.
How to Contact: Write or call first and obtain permission to submit. Prefers cassette (or VHS videocassette if available) with 4 songs and lyric sheet. Does not return unsolicited material. Reports in 3 weeks.
Music: Mostly rock and metal; also pop and blues. Current acts include Mass (group), Eddie Kramer (producer), Peter Wood (writer) and Rosetta Stone (writer).

COVER AGENCY, 300 North 240 West #103, Salt Lake City UT 84103. (801)364-9706. Booking Agent: William Larned. Management firm and booking agency. Estab. 1984. Represents local, regional and international individual artists and groups. Currently handles 180 acts. Receives 15% commission. Reviews material for acts.
How to Contact: Submit demo tape by mail. Unsolicited submissions are OK. Prefers cassette (or VHS videocassette if available) with 4 songs and lead sheets. Does not return unsolicited material.
Music: Mostly modern, funk, top 40, reggae and rock. Works primarily with dance bands, show bands, touring acts and bar bands. Current acts include Irie Heights (reggae), Tempo Timers (R&B/blues) and The Gamma Rays (modern).
Tips: "We are not really interested in original material, we are looking for cover bands that can play clubs in the intermountain area."

CRASH PRODUCTIONS, P.O. Box 40, Bangor ME 04402-0040. (207)794-6686. Manager: Jim Moreau. Booking agency. Estab. 1967. Represents individuals and groups; currently handles 9 acts. Receives 10-25% commission.
How to Contact: Query. Prefers cassette (or VHS videocassette if available) with 4-8 songs. "To all artists who submit a video: We will keep it on file for presentation to prospective buyers of talent in our area—no longer than 15 minutes please. The quality should be the kind you would want to show a prospective buyer of your act." Include resume and photos. "We prefer to hear groups at an actual performance." SASE. Reports in 3 weeks.
Music: Mostly 50s-60s and country rock, top 40; also rock and polish. Works primarily with groups who perform at night clubs (with an average of 150-200 patrons) and outdoor events (festivals and fairs). Current acts include Coyote (country rock), Bushwhack (50s and 60s), Air Fare (top 40), Boot Leg (country/rock) and Kaktus (country).
Tips: "We are a small company with no big promises that we cannot fulfill. Our main business is as a booking agency for acts. We do not reject material from songwriters, but very seldom do we get to use their services; we do keep them on file."

CRAWFISH PRODUCTIONS, P.O. Box 5412, Buena Park CA 90620. (213)721-7260. Producer: Leo J. Eiffert, Jr. Music publisher (Young Country/BMI) and record company (Plain Country Records). Estab. 1968. Represents local and international individual artists and songwriters; currently handles 4 acts. Commission received is open. Reviews material for acts.
How to Contact: Submit a demo tape by mail. Unsolicited submissions are OK. Prefers cassette with 2-3 songs and lyric sheet. SASE. Reports in 3 weeks.
Music: Mostly country and gospel. Works primarily with vocalists. Current acts include Brandi Holland, Duane Austin (country), Joe Eiffert (country/gospel) and Crawfish Band (country).

BOBBY LEE CUDE'S GOOD AMERICAN MUSIC/TALENT/CASTING AGENCY, 519 N. Halifax Ave., Daytona Beach FL 32118-4017. FAX: (904)252-0381. CEO: Bobby Lee Cude. Music publisher (BMI) and record company (Hard Hat). Estab. 1978. Represents international individual artists. Receives 15% commission. Reviews material for acts.
How to Contact: Write first and obtain permission to submit. Prefers cassette (or videocassette) with 2 songs, lyrics and lead sheets. "No unsolicited material reviewed."
Music: Mostly pop and country. Current acts include Caz Allen and "Pic" Pickens.
Tips: "Read music books for the trade."

D.A.G. PROMOTIONS LTD., 28 Bolton St., London WI **England**. Phone: (01)876-4433. Director: D. Gordon. Management firm. Estab. 1983. Represents individual artists and groups; currently handles 5 act. Receives 20% commission. Reviews material for acts.
How to Contact: Write or call first and obtain permission to submit. Prefers cassette with 4 songs and lyric sheet. Does not return unsolicited material.
Music: Mostly pop and rock. Works primarily with singer/songwriters, solo artists and rock bands. Current acts include Julian Lennon (singer/songwriter), Paul Jackson (singer/songwriter), Shannon Sweeney (singer/songwriter), Hold The Frame (rock) and Eddie Kidd (rock).

D MANAGEMENT COMPANY, Box 121682, Nashville TN 37212. President: Douglas Casmus. Management firm and music publisher (N2D/ASCAP and Breezeway/BMI). Estab. 1987. Represents individual artists and songwriters; currently handles 2 acts. Receives 15-25% commission. Reviews material for acts.
How to Contact: Write first and obtain permission to submit (include SASE for response). Prefers cassette with 2 songs and lyric sheets. Does not return unsolicited material. "Will contact only if interested."
Music: Mostly rock, pop and country. Current acts include Dobie Gray and David Murphy.

D&D TALENT ASSOCIATES, P.O. Box 308, Burkeville VA 23922. (804)767-4150. Owner: J.W. Dooley, Jr. Booking agency. Estab. 1976. Represents international individual artists and groups; currently handles 2 acts. Receives 10% commission. Reviews material for acts.
How to Contact: Write first and obtain permission to submit. Prefers cassette (or videocassette) with 1-6 songs and lead sheet. SASE. Reports in 1-2 weeks.
Music: Mostly jazz, 40's-50's music, and country. Works primarily with vocalists, comics. Current acts include Johnny Pursley (humorist) and David Allyn (vocalist).
Tips: "Just send the best songs possible—although I am doing no booking now, for practical reasons, I will try to give free advice if possible. Since I am not in a metro area, possible contacts are probably out at this time. Don't contact me to produce miracles. I can be a sounding board for the music only—someone to at least listen and hopefully, make suggestions."

D & R ENTERTAINMENT, 308 N. Park, Broken Bow OK 74728. (405)584-9429. President: Don Walton. Management firm. Estab. 1987. Represents international individual artists and groups; currently handles 4 acts. Receives 15-20% commission. Reviews material for acts.
How to Contact: Submit demo tape by mail. Unsolicited submissions are OK. Prefers cassette with any number of songs and lyric or lead sheet. SASE. Reports in 1 month.
Music: Mostly country, country metal rock or hard rock; also pop country. Current acts include Dixie Lee (metal), Nanette Garner (country), Rick Thompson (country) and Rachel Garrett (country).
Tips: "Make sure everything submitted is copyrighted! If it isn't I won't consider it."

DANGEROUS MANAGEMENT, (formerly Nicholas Rubenstein Organization), 438 Poole Rd., Branksome, Dorset BH12 1DG **England**. Phone: Bourngmouth 768766. Principal: Nick Rubenstein. Management firm. Estab. 1975. Represents individual artists, groups, songwriters; currently handles 5 acts. Receives 20% commission. Reviews material for acts.
How to Contact: Prefers cassette (or VHS videocassette if available) with lyric or lead sheet. "Basic live performance (even home video) tells a lot." SAE and IRC. Reports in 1 month.
Music: Mostly pop, rock, R&B; soul, also most music forms, if not *all*. Works primarily with vocalists (male and female) and rock bands. Current acts include Jon Jack Christie (solo rock/pop singer/songwriter), Law (solo rock/pop singer/songwriter), The 4 Waltons (rock), Astro Galaxy (dance), and Cartoon Boyfriend (soul).

*BRAD DAVIS INC., P.O. Box 158125, Nashville TN 37215. (615)298-2134. President: Brad Davis. Management firm, booking agency and music publisher (Green Chili Music/BMI). Represents local, regional and international individual artists and groups. Reviews material for acts.
How to Contact: Submit demo tape by mail. Unsolicited submissions are OK. Prefers cassette with 3 songs and lyric or lead sheets. Does not return unsolicited material. Reports in 1 month.
Music: Mostly rock, country and R&B. Current acts include Leon Russell (singer/songwriter).

THE EDWARD DE MILES COMPANY, Vantage Point Towers, 4475 N. Allisonville Rd., 8th Floor, Indianapolis, IN 46205. (317)549-9006. FAX: (317)549-9007. President & CEO: Edward De Miles. Management firm, booking agency, entertainment/sports promoter and TV/radio broadcast producer. Estab. 1984. Represents film, television, radio and musical artists; currently handles 15 acts. Receives 10-20% commission. Reviews material for acts. Regional operations in Chicago, Dallas, Houston and Nashville through marketing representatives. Licensed A.F. of M. booking agent.
How to Contact: Write first about your interest. Prefers cassette with 3-5 songs, 8x10 black and white photo and lyric sheet. "Copyright all material before submitting." SASE. Reports in 1 month.
Music: Mostly country, dance, R&B/soul, rock, top 40/pop and urban contemporary; also looking for material for television, radio and film productions. Works primarily with dance bands and vocalists. Current acts include Lost in Wonder (progressive rock/dance band), Steve Lynn (R&B/dance) and Multiple Choice (rap).
Tips: "Performers need to be well prepared with their presentations (equipment, showmanship a must)."

*DEBBIE DEAN AND ASSOC., P.O. Box 687, Ashland City TN 37015. (615)792-3223. FAX: (615)746-8608. Contact: Debbie Dean. Overseas booking agency and public relations firm. Estab. 1988. Represents local, regional and international individual artists; currently handles 6 acts. Receveives 15% commission. Reviews material for acts.
How to Contact: Submit demo tape by mail. Unsolicited submissions are OK. Prefers cassette with 3 songs and lyric sheet. SASE. Reports in 2 weeks.
Music: Mostly country traditional and MOR country. Works primarily with artists who can also play a guitar or some instrument. Current acts include Jack and Lori Johnson (duo group-singer/songwriter) and Bobby G. Rice (artist-songwriter).

*DE-EL MUSIC MANAGEMENT, INC., P.O. Box 6193, New York NY 10128. (212)587-1197. Vice President-A&R: Diane Gowman. Management firm. Estab. 1986. Represents local, regional or international individual artists, groups, songwriters and entertainers in general. Reviews material for acts.
How to Contact: Call first and obtain permission to submit. Prefers cassette with 3 songs and lyric sheet. Does not return unsolicited material. Reports in 1 month.
Music: Mostly rock, pop and R&B. Works primarily with vocalists and solo artists. Current acts include Gregg Allman.
Tips: "We only listen to material solicited prior to its arrival . . . "

*BILL DETKO MANAGEMENT, 127 Shamrock Dr., Ventura CA 93003. (805)644-0447. Owner: Bill Detko. Management firm. Estab. 1987. Represents local, regional and international individual artists, groups and songwriters; currently handles 4 acts. Receives 15% commission. Reviews material for acts.
How to Contact: Write first and obtain permission to submit. Prefers cassette (or VHS videocassette if available) with 3-4 songs and lyric sheet.
Music: Mostly rock, metal and jazz; also pop. Works with "recording of artists of all genres." Current acts include Stuart Hamm (bass player/writer/solo artist), Scott Henderson and Gary Willis (tribal tech fusion group/composers) and Watchtower (metal).
Tips: "The music must knock me out."

DMR AGENCY, Suite 250, Galleries of Syracuse, Syracuse NY 13202-2416. (315)475-2500. Contact: David M. Rezak. Booking agency. Represents individuals and groups; currently handles 50 acts. Receives 15% commission.
How to Contact: Write first and obtain permission to submit. Submit cassette (or videocassette) with 1-4 songs and press kit. SASE.
Music: Mostly rock (all styles), pop and blues. Works primarily with dance, bar and concert bands; all kinds of rock for schools, clubs, concerts, etc. Current acts include Tryx (rock) and Windsong (dance/pop).
Tips: "We strictly do booking and have no involvement in artist repetoire. We prefer regionally-based bands with a high percentage of cover material."

COL. BUSTER DOSS PRESENTS, Drawer 40, Estill Springs TN 37330. (615)649-2577. Producer: Col. Buster Doss. Management firm, booking agency, record company (Stardust Records) and music publisher (Buster Doss Music/BMI). Estab. 1959. Represents individual artists, groups, songwriters and shows; currently handles 15 acts. Receives 15% commission. Reviews material for acts.
How to Contact: Prefers cassette with 2-4 songs and lyric sheet. SASE. Reports in 2 weeks.
Music: Country, gospel and progressive. Works primarily with show and dance bands, single acts and package shows. Current acts include Rooster Quantrell, Sonny Carson, R. B. Stone, Hobson Smith, Tony Caldarona, Buck Cody, Cliff Archer, Linda Wunder, Benny Ray, Clayton Michaels, Honey James, Gilbert Gann, The Border Raiders, Tony Andrews and Jess Demaine.
Tips: "Tell the truth! No hype."

*DOUBLE TEE PROMOTIONS, INC., Suite 200, 3903 SW Kelly, Portland OR 97201. (503)221-0288. President: David Leiken. Management firm, music publisher (Macman Music, Inc./ASCAP, Fresh Force Music, Inc./BMI) and record company (Lucky/NuVisions). Estab. 1972. Represents local, regional and international individual artists, groups, songwriters and producers; currently handles 5 acts. Receives 15% commission. Reviews material for acts.
How to Contact: Submit demo tape by mail. Unsolicited submissions are OK. Prefers cassette with 3-5 songs and lyric sheet.
Music: Mostly R&B/pop, rock and blues/rock; also hit songs and some jazz. Current acts include Curtis Salgado (R&B singer on CBS Records), U-Krew (rap/dance/R&B on Capitol Records) and Dazz Band (funk/R&B on Impact/MCA Records).

*DOYLE-LEWIS MANAGEMENT, 1109-17th Ave. South, Nashville TN 37212. (615)329-9447. Management firm. Estab. 1988. Represents local, regional and international individual artists and groups; currently handles 5 acts. Reviews some material for acts.
How to Contact: Call first and obtain permission to submit. Prefers cassette (or VHS videocassette if available) with 3 songs. SASE.
Music: Mostly country; also pop. Current acts include Garth Brooks, Trisha Yearwood and Great Plains.

*DSI THEATRICAL PRODUCTIONS, 660 NE 139th Street, N. Miami FL 33161. (305)891-4449 or (305)891-0158. Artistic Director: Scott Evans. Management firm and booking agency. Estab. 1979. Represents local, regional or international individual artists, groups, songwriters, comedians, novelty acts, dancers and theaters; currently handles more than 200 acts. Receives 10-25% commission. Reviews material for acts.
How to Contact: Submit demo tape by mail. Unsolicited submissions are OK. Prefers cassette (or ½″ videocassette if available) with 3 songs. Does not return unsolicited material.
Music: Mostly pop, R&B and Broadway. Deals with "all types of entertainers; no limitations."
Tips: "Submit neat, well put together, organized press kit."

DUNCAN MANAGEMENT INC., Suite 401, 366 Fifth Ave., New York NY 10001. (212)564-2100. President: Ellis Duncan. Management firm. Estab. 1988. Represents local and regional (Central-East Coast) individual artists and groups; currently handles 2 acts. Receives 20% commission. Reviews material for acts.
How to Contact: Submit demo tape by mail. Unsolicited submissions are OK. Prefers cassette (or VHS videocassette if available) with 3-5 songs. Does not return unsolicited material. Reports in 2 months.
Music: Mostly R&B, pop, rock and country; also gospel and bluegrass. "All types are considered, but usually individual artist and showbands." Current acts include Danny Gatton (guitarist), David Quick (rock & roll singer/guitarist) and Blue Chieftains (country rock/swing).

JIM DUNLOP PRODUCTIONS, 1272 Pinehurst Place, London, Ontario **Canada** N5X 2K9. (519)663-9039. FAX: (519)679-1812. President: Jim Dunlop. Management firm and record company (Auto Records). Estab. 1985. Represents international individual artists, groups and songwriters; currently handles 5 acts. Receives 10-20% commission. Reviews material for acts.
How to Contact: Submit demo tape by mail. Unsolicited submissions are OK. Prefers cassette (or VHS videocassette if available) with 3-5 songs and lyric sheet. SASE. Reports in 3-4 weeks.
Music: Mostly country, pop and rock; also children's and classical. Works primarily with individuals and groups. Current acts include Michael Dee (country), Monkey See (rock) and Glenn Bennett (children's music).
Tips: "Send only your very best songs. You need to be totally committed if you want to make it in this business. If you're not, then save yourself the headaches and heartaches."

EARTH TRACKS ARTISTS AGENCY, (formerly David Aleksander Productions), Suite 286, 4712 Avenue N, Brooklyn NY 11234. Managing Director-Artist Relations: David Krinsky. Management firm. Estab. 1990. Represents individual artists, groups and songwriters from anywhere; currently handles 3 acts. Receives 10-25% (depends) commission. Reviews material for acts.
How to Contact: Submit demo tape by mail. Unsolicited submissions are OK, accompanied by release form and SASE. "Do not call to submit tapes. Mail in for review. No calls will be returned, unsolicited or accepted, under any conditions." Prefers cassette (or VHS and/or ¾″ videocassette) with 3-6 songs and lyric sheet. "We do not return unsolicited material if international." Reports in 2 months.
Music: Mostly commercial rock (all kinds), pop/dance/rap, post modern rock/folk rock; also novelty/comedy songs. Works primarily with commercial, original, solo artists and groups, songwriters in the rock, pop, dance areas (no country, thrash or punk). Current acts include Heavy Connection (rock), Bella (pop/dance artist) and Bi-Coastals (comedy/satire artist). "We're looking for original acts who wish to be signed to record labels in the rock, pop and rap categories. (No 'show bands' 'cover bands', etc.)."
Tips: "Submit a package of completed songs along with lyrics, photo of artist/group, or songwriter credits if any. A video on VHS accepted if available. If no package available send a cassette of what you as an artist consider best represents your style. Strong meaningful songs are preferred, as well as light pop rock for top 40 release. Will submit quality songwriter's material to name artists. All materials must be accompanied by a release form and all songs must be copyrighted."

*ECI, INC., 1646 Bonnie Dr., Memphis TN 38116. (901)346-1483. Vice President: Bernice Turner. Management firm, booking agency, music publisher and record company (Star Trek). Estab. 1989. Represents local, regional and international individual artists and groups; currently handles 3 acts. Receives 25% commission. Reviews material for acts.

How to Contact: Submit demo tape by mail. Unsolicited submissions are OK. Prefers cassette with 2 songs. Does not return unsolicited material. Reports in 2 weeks.
Music: Mostly R&B and country. Works primarily with show groups. Current acts include Kool and The Gang, Robby Turner and Something Special.

*TOM ELLIOTT PRODUCTIONS, 4002 Stearns Hill Rd., Waltham MA 02154. (617)647-2825. President: Tom Elliott. Booking agency. Estab. 1975. Represents New England individual artists and groups. "We specialize in musical novelty acts." Currently handles more than 100 acts. Receives 15% commission. Reviews material for acts.
How to Contact: Prefers cassette (or VHS videocassette if available) with several songs. Does not return unsolicited submissions.
Music: Mostly novelty acts, original folk and street acts; also ethnic groups. Works primarily with folksingers, streetsingers, one-man bands and ethnic bands. Current acts include Ruth Anna (streetsinger), Stephen Baird (street/folksinger) and the Gloucester Hornpipe and Clog Society (ethnic dance music).
Tips: "Be focused on your goals and remember that 'slow and steady wins the race.' Be flexible, accommodating; don't be a prima donna."

ELLIPSE PERSONAL MANAGMENT, % Boxholder 665, Manhattan Beach CA 90266. (310)546-2224. Contact: Mr. L. Elsman. Management firm. Represents local individual artists, vocalists and vocalist/songwriters. Receives 15% commission and up (P.M. contract). Reviews material for acts.
How to Contact: Write or call first and obtain permission to submit. Prefers cassette with 3 songs and lyric sheet. Does not return unsolicited material. Reports in 5 weeks.
Music: Mostly pop rock, mellow rock and soft rock; also MOR, easy listening and ballads. Works primarily with vocalists and vocalist/songwriters.
Tips: "We usually will listen to unsolicited material, however we do not return audio tapes and we may not even reply. Songwriters, do not neglect to put the copyright notice (©, your name, year) on all your original material. We have a self-imposed limitation of just 2 acts. Vocalists, if you are past your voice change, send your name, age, address, a snapshot and a brief outline of your ambitions."

EMARCO MANAGEMENT, P.O. Box 867, Woodland Hills CA 91365. President: Mark Robert. (818)712-9069. Management firm and record company (Burbank Records). Estab 1982. Represents local, regional or individual artists, groups and songwriters. Currently handles 6 acts. Receives 15% commission. Reviews material for acts.
How to Contact: Write first and obtain permission to submit. Prefers cassette with 3 songs or less and lyric sheets. Returns with SASE. Reports in 3 weeks.
Music: Mostly pop and rock. Current acts include Paul Pope, Gabriela Rozzi, and Wonderboy (rock).

ENTERTAINING VENTURES MANAGEMENT INC., 86 Bayview Road, Halifax NS **Canada** B3M 1N9. (902)443-7324. Artist Representative: Robert McLellan. Management firm. Estab. 1988. Represents international individual artists; currently handles 3 acts. Receives 15% commission. Reviews material for acts.
How to Contact: Call first and obtain permission to submit. Prefers cassette (or VHS videocassette of performance) with 3-4 songs and lyric sheet. SASE. Reports in 1-2 months.
Music: Mostly contemporary country, pop and traditional. Works primarily with show bands, and corporate and concert acts. Current acts include Jimmy Flynn—"Canada's top musical comedy act," the Steve Ambrose Band (R&B) and Jakki Rogue (contemporary country).
Tips: "Call first, but our doors are always open."

ENTERTAINMENT MANAGEMENT ENTERPRISES, 454 Alps Rd., Wayne NJ 07470. (201)694-3333. President: Richard Zielinski. Management firm. Estab. 1982. Represents artists and musical groups; currently handles 2 acts. Receives minimum of 20% commission. Reviews material for acts.
How to Contact: Prefers cassette (or VHS videocassette) with 4-6 songs and lyric sheet. Include 8×10 glossy and bio. "Let us know, by mail or phone, about any New York area performances so we can attend." SASE. Reports in 2 weeks.
Music: Mostly rock. Works primarily with rock groups with vocals, synthesized rock, contemporary singers and club bands. Current acts include Voyager (progressive rock) and Mirrors' Image (metal).
Tips: "A good press kit is important."

*ENTERTAINMENT UNLIMITED ARTIST INC., 64 Division Ave., Levittown NY 11956. (516)735-5550. Senior Agent: George I. Magdaleno. Management firm and booking agency. Estab. 1960. Represents local, regional and international individual artists, groups and songwriters; currently handles 30 acts. Receives 15% commission. Reviews material for acts.

How to Contact: Submit demo tape by mail. Unsolicited submissions are OK. Prefers cassette (or VHS videocassette if available) with 4 songs and lyric and lead sheet. SASE. Reports in 3-4 weeks.
Music: Mostly rock, pop and R&B; also country and jazz. Current acts include Orleans (rock group), Belmonts (oldies rock) and Ben E. King (rock-pop).

*ENTERTAINMENT WORKS, 22 Walden Cypress Court, Baltimore MD 21207. (301)788-5095. President: Nancy Lewis. Management firm, booking agency and public relations/publicity firm. Estab. 1989. Represents local, regional and international groups; currently handles 5 acts. Receives 10-15% commission. Reviews material for acts.
How to Contact: Submit demo tape by mail. Unsolicited submissions are OK. Prefers cassette with 3 songs "plus biography/publicity clips/photo." Reports in 1 month.
Music: Mostly reggae and African. Works primarily with vocalists/dance bands. Current acts include Uprising (reggae band), Cool Runnings (reggae band) and Awareness Art Ensemble (reggae band).
Tips: "Start with a phone call to introduce yourself, followed by a well-recorded 3-song demo, band member biographies, and all publicity clips."

*SCOTT EVANS PRODUCTIONS, 660 NE 139th St., N. Miami FL 33161. (305)891-4449. Artistic Director: Scott Evans. Management firm and booking agency. Estab. 1979. Represents local, regional and international individual artists, groups and songwriters; currently handles over 200 acts. Receives 15-25% commission. Reviews material for acts. Does not charge a fee for reviewing material "if reviewing of material was referred by associate."
How to Contact: Write or call first to arrange personal interview. Contact "initially by mailing promotional to Attention: Casting. Appointments are $50." Prefers cassette with ½ inch videocassette with 3 songs and lyric or lead sheet.
Music: Mostly Broadway, international and pop/top 40.
Tips: "Please present a complete, neat and self-explanatory promotional package for our perusal. Clever approaches do get more immediate responses. Cassette/video/resume etc. assist in quick responses."

JIM FEMINO PRODUCTIONS, (formerly Music Services of America), 429 South Lewis Rd., Royersford PA 19468. (215)948-8228. FAX: (215)948-4175. President: Jim Femino. (Fezsongs/ASCAP) publishing branch, record company (Road Records) and independent producer/engineer with own 24-track facility. Estab. 1970. Represents singer/songwriters; currently handles 2 acts.
How to Contact: Prefers cassette with two songs only. Replies in 2-4 weeks.
Music: Country and rock. Works primarily with vocalists and songwriters. Currently working with Jim Femino (writer/artist) and Ed Festor (writer).

FRED T. FENCHEL ENTERTAINMENT AGENCY, 2104 S. Jefferson Avenue, Mason City IA 50401. (515)423-4177. General Manager: Fred T. Fenchel. Booking agency. Estab. 1964. Represents local and international individual artists and groups. Receives 15% commission. Reviews material for acts.
How to Contact: Submit demo tape by mail (videocassette if available). Unsolicited submissions are OK. Does not return unsolicited material.
Music: Mostly country, pop and some gospel. Works primarily with dance bands, show groups; "artists we can use on club dates, fairs, etc." Current acts include The Memories, D.C. Drifters, Convertibles and Cadillac. "We deal primarily with established name acts with recording contracts, or those with a label and starting into popularity."
Tips: "Submit good material with universal appeal and be informative on artists background."

FESTIVAL FAMILY ENTERPRISES, LTD., P.O. Box 87, Skidmore MO 64487. (816)928-3631. Personal Manager: Jonnie Kay. Management firm (Max Stout Publishing/BMI) and record company (Max Stout Records). Estab. 1973. Currently handles 2 acts. Receives 10-15% commission. Reviews material for acts.
How to Contact: Submit demo tape by mail. Unsolicited submissions are OK. Prefers cassette (or videocassette of performance) with 2 songs with lyric and lead sheets. Reports in 1 year.
Music: Mostly ballads, pop and country; also patriotic. Works primarily with variety showbands and dance bands. Current acts include Britt Small and Festival (brass band/variety) and Matt and Robyn Rolf (country show band).

Remember: Don't "shotgun" your demo tapes. Submit only to companies interested in the type of music you write. For more submission hints, refer to The Business of Songwriting on page 21.

Tips: "We're looking for ballads written for a bass voice, mass vocals and brass; also looking for comedy tunes and patriotic songs."

FIRST TIME MANAGEMENT, Sovereign House, 12 Trewartha Rd., Praa Sands-Penzance, Cornwall TR20 9ST **England**. Phone: (0736)762826. FAX: (0736)763328. Managing Director: Roderick G. Jones. Management firm. Estab. 1986. Represents local, regional and international individual aritsts, groups and songwriters. Receives 20% commission. Reviews material for acts.
How to Contact: Submit demo tape by mail. Unsolicited submissions are OK. Prefers cassette or 15 ips reel-to-reel (or VHS videocassette) with 3 songs and lyric sheets. SASE. Reports in 4-8 weeks.
Music: Mostly dance, top 40, rap, country, gospel and pop; also all styles. Works primarily with songwriters, composers, vocalists, groups and choirs. Current acts include Pete Arnold (folk) and Willow.
Tips: "Become a member of the Guild of International Songwriters and Composers. Keep everything as professional as possible. Be patient and dedicated to your aims and objectives."

FIVE STAR ENTERTAINMENT, 10188 Winter View Dr., Naples FL 33942. (813)566-7701 and (813)566-7702. Assistant Manager: Sid Kleiner. Management firm, booking agency (Kleiner Entertainment Services), record company and audiovisual firm (Sid Kleiner Music Enterprises, Inc.) and record producer. Represents individual artists and groups; currently handles over 15 acts. Receives 15-25% commission. Reviews material for acts.
How to Contact: Prefers VHS (or super VHS) videocassette only with maximum of 6 songs. SASE. Reports in 1 month.
Music: Mostly swing, MOR and country; also ethnic, pop and rock. Works primarily with organized dance bands and self-contained singles. Current acts include Sid Kleiner (guitar/one-man band), Ron Hart (vocal/instrumental single), Ray King (vocal/piano/band) and Johnny Dee ("All Stars").
Tips: "Furnish as much information as possible: glossies, VHS video demo tapes (1½ choruses), song lists, equipment lists, availability, price per single engagement, price per on-going weekly engagement, costuming, etc."

*FLASH ATTRACTIONS AGENCY, 38 Prospect St., Warrensburg NY 12885. (518)623-9313. Agent: Wally Chester. Management firm and booking agency. Estab. 1952. Represents artists and groups; currently handles 106 acts. Receives 15-20% commission. Reviews material for acts. "We are celebrating 40 years in business, and are fully licensed by the American Federation of Musicians and the State of New York."
How to Contact: Query by mail. Prefers cassette for singers, VHS videocassette for acts, with 1-6 songs with lead and lyric sheets. Songwriters and artists may submit "professionally done" videocassettes. SASE. Reports in 1 month.
Music: Mostly country, calypso, Hawaiian and MOR; also blues, dance, easy listening, jazz, top 40, country rock and Latin, plus American Indian Shows. Works primarily with vocalists, dance bands, lounge acts, floor show groups and ethnic shows. Current acts include Prince Pablo's Caribbean Extravaganza (steel drum band and floor show), Mirinda James (Nashville recording artist and her country cross/over show band), Loi Afo and "Island Call," The Country Belles (all girl variety band), The Ronnie Prophet Country Music Show (Canada's #1 recording and TV star), N.C. Preservation Dixieland Jazz Band, The Robin Right Country Music Show (voted New England's #1 entertainer and band), Wally Chester's "Spark and a Flame Duo" (lounge act), Kit McClure and her all female 17 piece big band sound.
Tips: "Submit songs that have public appeal, good story line and simplicity. Good cassettes and band-show videos are mandatory for promotion."

*THE FLYING DUTCHMAN, P.O. Box 9027, Amsterdam HOL 1006AA **Netherlands**. Phone: (020)669-1981. Artist Manager: TJ Lammers. Management firm and music publisher (Rock Rose-BUMA/STEMRA). Estab. 1980. Represents local, regional and international individual artists, groups and songwriters; currently handles 7 acts. Receives 20% commission. Reviews material for acts.
How to Contact: Submit demo tape by mail. Unsolicited submissions are OK. Prefers cassette (or VHS videocassette if available) with 2-4 songs. Does not return unsolicited material. Reports in 1 month.
Music: Mostly rock, pop and alternative; also country, folk and blues. Works primarily with hard rock, rock, pop and folk rock bands and singers. Current acts include Gringos Locos (hard rock band), Personnel (roots rock band), A Girl Called Johnny (female rock/R&B singer/songwriter) and Powerplay (rock).
Tips: "Put name and number on the cassette."

*WILLIAM FORD PERSONAL MANAGEMENT INC., #5D, 17 E. 7th St., New York NY 10003. (212)477-5586. President: Bill Ford. Estab. 1983. Represents local individual artists and groups; currently handles 2 acts. Receives 20% commission. Reviews material for acts.

How to Contact: Submit demo tape by mail. Unsolicited submissions are OK. Prefers cassette (or VHS videocassette if available) with 3 or 4 songs and lyric sheet. SASE. Reports in 4 weeks.
Music: Mostly pop, rock and R&B. Works primarily with pop vocalists, performing rock bands and acts. Current acts include Rev. Conner Tribble (rock performer and band writer) and Loni Singer (vocalist, pop and dance).
Tips: "Have a considerable amount of patience and work very hard on the performance of the right song."

THE FRANKLYN AGENCY, #312, 1010 Hammond St., West Hollywood CA 90069. (213)272-6080. President: Audrey P. Franklyn. Management firm, public relations firm and cable production company plus part owner of A&E Productions. "Producing weekend singer showcases." Represents artists, musical groups and businesses; currently handles 3 acts. Receives 10-15% commission. Reviews material for acts.
How to Contact: Query by mail, arrange personal interview, or submit demo. Prefers cassette (or videocassette if available) with 4 songs and lead sheet. SASE. Reports in 1 month.
Music: Mosly rock, country and pop; also blues, easy listening, gospel, jazz, MOR, progressive and R&B. Works primarily with rock bands and single soloist singers. Current acts include Merrell Fank-hauser (writer of "Wipe Out"), Exetta Murphy (singer) and Carol Metcalf (comic).
Tips: "No amateurs—be funded for promotional efforts."

FREADE SOUNDS ENTERTAINMENT & RECORDING STUDIO, North 37311 Valley Rd., Chattaroy WA 99003. (509)292-2201. FAX: (509)292-2205. Agent/Engineer: Tom Lapsansky. Booking agency and recording studio. Estab. 1967. Represents groups; currently handles 10-13 acts. Receives 10% commission. Reviews material for acts.
How to Contact: Query by mail or submit demo. Prefers cassette (or videocassette, "please pick best vocal song, best instrumental and best song performer likes to perform") with 4-6 songs and pictures/song list. SASE. Reports in 2 weeks.
Music: Mostly top 40/rock; also R&B and production rock. Works primarily with dance/concert groups and bar bands. Current acts include Top Secret, Nasty Habit, Justin Sayne, Lynx, Defiant, Nobody Famous, City Boy, Criminal Minds, Rockaholics and Unchained.

BOB SCOTT FRICK ENTERPRISES, 404 Bluegrass Ave., Madison TN 37115. (615)865-6380. President: Bob Frick. Booking agency, music publisher (Frick Music Publishing Co./BMI and Sugarbaker Music Publishing/ASCAP) and record company (R.E.F. Recording Co). Represents individual artists and songwriters; currently handles 5 acts. Reviews material for acts.
How to Contact: Submit demo tape by mail, or write or call first to arrange personal interview. Prefers cassette with 3 songs and lyric sheet. SASE. Reports in 1 month.
Music: Mostly gospel, country and R&B. Works primarily with vocalists. Current acts include Bob Scott Frick (guitarist, singer), Larry Ahlborn (singer) and Bob Myers (singer).

*FULL CIRCLE TALENT AGENCY, P.O. Box 578190, Chicago IL 60657. (312)348-1234. President: John Boncimino. Management firm and booking agency. Estab. 1987. Represents individual artists and groups; currently handles 2 acts. Reviews material for acts.
How to Contact: Write or call first and obtain permission to submit. Prefers cassette with any number of songs and lyric sheet. Reports in 6-8 weeks.
Music: Mostly blues-rock and traditional blues. "We represent the blues acts Albert Collins and The Kinsey Report, as well as Big Daddy Kinsey."
Tips: "Submit songs with our artists in mind (be familiar with our artists)."

GANGLAND ARTISTS, 707-810 W. Broadway, Vancouver, British Columbia V5Z 1J8 **Canada.** (604)872-0052. Contact: Allen Moy. Management firm, production house and music publisher. Estab. 1985. Represents artists and songwriters; currently handles 5 acts. Reviews material for acts.
How to Contact: Prefers cassette (or VHS videocassette if available) and lyric sheet. "Videos are not entirely necessary for our company. It is certainly a nice touch. If you feel your audio cassette is strong—send the video upon later request. Something wildly creative and individual will grab our attention." SAE and IRC. Reports in 1 month.
Music: Rock, pop and R&B. Works primarily with "original rock/left of center" show bands. Current acts include 54-40 (rock/pop), Sons of Freedom (hard/rock), Mae Moore (pop) and Phaedra (dance).

*GLO GEM PRODUCTIONS, INC., P.O. Box 427, Port Huron MI 48061. (313)984-4471. Public Affairs Coordinator: James David. Management firm and booking agency. Estab. 1974. Represents local, Midwestern and international individual artists, groups and songwriters; currently handles 35 acts. Receives 15-20% commission. Reviews material for acts.

How to Contact: Write first and obtain permission to submit. Prefers cassette or 7½ ips reel-to-reel (or ½ VHS videocassette of live performance, if available) with 2 songs and lyric or lead sheets. Does not return unsolicited material. Reports in 3 weeks.
Music: Mostly country, MOR and blues; also folk, jazz and pop. Works primarily with vocalists, show groups and dance bands. Current acts include Cliff Erickson (songwriter/entertainer), Jimmy Cox (show person/songwriter) and Burnwood (showband/songwriters).

*MICHAEL GODIN MANAGEMENT, INC., #201-1505 West 2nd Ave., Vancouver BC V6H 3Y4 **Canada.** (604)731-3535. Professional Manager: Carey Fok. Management firm and music publisher (West Broadway Music/SOCAN). Estab. 1986. Represents local, regional and international individual, groups, songwriters and record producers/engineers; currently handles 4 acts. Receives 20% commission.
How to Contact: Write or call first and obtain permission to submit. Prefers cassette or VHS videocassette with 3-5 songs and lyric sheet. SASE. Reports in 4-6 weeks.
Music: Mostly pop, rock and dance. Work primarily with pop singers/songwriters. Current acts include Paul Janz (pop singer/songwriter), Carson Cole (heartland rock singer/songwriter) and Fear of Flying (rock/pop group).

*GOLDBERG TALENT MANAGEMENT, Penthouse A-21st Floor, 620 Peachtree St., Atlanta GA 30308. (404)874-5500. Contact: Director of A&R. Management firm. Estab. 1977. Represents local and Southeast individual artists, groups and songwriters; currently handles 12 acts. Receives 8-20% commission. Reviews material for acts.
How to Contact: Submit demo tape by mail. Unsolicited submissions are OK. Prefers cassette with several songs. SASE. Reports in 4 weeks.
Music: Mostly pop, rock and R&B. Works primarily with vocalists, songwriters and bands. Current acts include Actors on Call, Blu Maxx and The Dancing Spirits.

GOLDEN CITY INTERNATIONAL, P.O. Box 410851, San Francisco CA 94141. (415)822-1530. Manager: Mr. Alston. Management firm, booking agency and record company (Dagene Records, Cabletown). Estab. 1987. Represents regional (Bay area) individual artists, groups and songwriters; currently handles 3 acts. Receives 25% commission. Reviews material for acts.
How to Contact: Write or call first and obtain permission to submit. Prefers cassette with 2 songs and lyric sheet. Does not return unsolicited material. Reports in 3 weeks.
Music: Mostly R&B/dance, rap and pop; also gospel. Current clients include Marcus Justice (songwriter), Primo (artist) and David Alston (producer).

GRAVITY PIRATES MANAGEMENT, G.P.O. Box 697, Sydney NSW **Australia** 2001. Phone: (2)332-2929. Manager: Steven Hindes. Management firm. Estab. 1983. Represents local artists and groups; currently handles 1 act. Receives 10% commission. Reviews material for acts.
How to Contact: Submit demo tape by mail. Unsolicited submissions are OK. Prefers cassette with 2 songs and lyric or lead sheet. Does not return unsolicited material. Reports in 1 month.
Music: Mostly rock, pop and R&B. Works primarily with rock bands. Current acts include Gravity Pirates (rock band).
Tips: "We prefer songs that lend themselves to different arrangements and styles."

*CHRIS GREELEY ENTERTAINMENT, P.O. Box 593, Bangor ME 04402-0593. (207)827-4382. General Manager: Christian D. Greeley. Management firm and booking agency. Estab. 1986. Represents local, regional and international individual artists, groups, songwriters and disc-jockeys; currently handles 4 acts. Receives 10-15% commission. Reviews material for acts.
How to Contact: Submit demo tape by mail. Unsolicited submissions are OK. Prefers cassette (or VHS videocassette if available) with 1-4 songs. SASE. Reports in 1 month.
Music: Mostly rock, country and pop. "I'm open to anything marketable." Wide range of musical styles. Current acts include Rick Finzel (original artist/songwriter) and Soundtrac (regional top 40 dance band).
Tips: "Be positive! Work hard and smart. Treat your music interest as a business. Be open to other ideas. Be willing to spend money on your craft."

BILL HALL ENTERTAINMENT & EVENTS, 138 Frog Hollow Rd., Churchville PA 18966. (215)357-5189. Contact: William B. Hall III. Booking agency and production company. Represents individuals and groups; currently handles 30 acts. Receives 15% commission. Reviews material for acts, depending on engagement and type of attraction.
How to Contact: "Letter of inquiry preferred as initial contact." Prefers cassette (or videocassette of performance) with 2-3 songs "and photos, promo material and record or tape. We need quality material, preferably before a 'live' audience." Does not return unsolicited material. Reports in 1 month.

Music: Marching band, circus and novelty ethnic. Works primarily with "unusual or novelty attractions in musical line, preferably those that appeal to family groups." Current acts include Fralinger and Polish-American Philadelphia Championship Mummers String Bands (marching and concert group); Erwin Chandler Orchestra (show band); "Mr. Polynesian" Show Band and Hawaiian Revue (ethnic group); the "Phillies Whiz Kids Band" of Philadelphia Phillies Baseball team; Phillies organist-entertainer Paul Richardson; Wm. (Boom-Boom) Browning Circus Band (circus band); Philadelphia German Brass Band (marching band); and numerous solo pianists and vocalists.

*GEOFFREY HANSEN ENTERPRISES, LTD., Box 63, Orinda CA 94563. Agent: J. Malcom Baird. Management firm and booking agency. Represents artists, groups and songwriters. Receives 15-25% commission. Also paid on a contract basis. Reviews material for acts.
How to Contact: Submit demo tape, lead sheet, photograph, song list and cover letter. Prefers cassette. SASE.
Music: Top 40/country, R&B, MOR and jazz in English, Spanish, French and Japanese. Works with top 40 and standard jazz recording acts and overseas international stars.
Tips: "We are always looking for new talent. Anyone who has a demo and is interested in international bookings and career development, contact us. We are ready to listen. We are looking for female vocalists, girl groups, show bands, jazz, western swing, cajun and Tex-Mex musical acts to tour overseas in Europe, the Far East, Hawaii, Japan and various foreign markets as well as in the USA. Send photos, bio, song list, demo tape and SASE. All styles of music wanted."

GEORGE HARNESS ASSOCIATES, 1 Timberline Dr., Springfield IL 62707. (217)529-8550. President: George Harness. Management firm and booking agency. Estab. 1978. Represents artists and groups; currently handles 12 acts. Receives 15-20% commission. Reviews material for acts.
How to Contact: Query by mail. Prefers cassette (or videocassette of live perfomance, if available) with 6-8 songs and lyric sheet. SASE. Reports in 2 weeks.
Music: Mostly R&B, top 40 and ballads; also dance. Current acts include 7th Heaven, Earl Turner & Earl Turner Group, Todd Bradley and Next Level, Phlash, Alcazar, Crush and Moses & Highbrows (all show & dance acts).

HAWKEYE ATTRACTIONS, 102 Geiger St., Huntingburg IN 47542. (812)683-3657. President: David Mounts. Booking agency. Estab. 1982. Represents individual artists and groups. Currently handles 1 act. Receives 10% commission. Reviews material for acts.
How to Contact: Prefers cassette with 4 songs and lyric sheet. SASE. Reports in 6 weeks.
Music: Mostly country and western swing. Works primarily with show bands, Grand Ole Opry style form of artist and music. Current acts include Bill Mounts (singer/songwriter) and His Midwest Cowboys (country/western swing).
Tips: "Don't copy anybody, just be yourself. If you have talent it will show through."

HEAD OFFICE MANAGEMENT, Suite #305, 296 Richmond St., W., Toronto, Ontario M5V 1X2 Canada. (416)979-8455. FAX: (416)979-8766. Los Angeles office: Head Office Management, 523 23rd St., Manhattan Beach, CA 90266. (213)546-6670. FAX: (213)546-3454. President: Stephen Prendergast. Vice President: Pat Arnott. Management firm and music publisher (Auto-Tunes, Dee Songs and Steeler Music/Fraze-songs, Sonicsongs/Towntunes). Estab. 1982. Represents individual artists, groups and songwriters, producers and engineers; currently handles 3 acts. Receives 15-25% commission. Reviews material for acts. "They are mostly self-contained. We solicit music, and are willing to listen."
How to Contact: Prefers cassette (or VHS ½" videocassette if available) with 3 songs and lyric sheet. Does not return any material. Reports in 2 months.
Music: Mostly rock, pop, metal and dance. Works primarily with rock/pop recording artists and songwriters. Current acts include Big House (rock band), Nick Heyward (pop band/songwriter) and Michael Hanson (pop band/songwriter).
Tips: "Have a business attitude, style in presentation, sincerity, honesty, hunger. Include photo, lyrics, contact information (with phone number) and brief history of songwriters/band and members involved."

*HEADQUARTERS ENTERTAINMENT CORPORATION, 273 Richmond St. W, Toronto Ont M5V 1X1 Canada. (416)348-9811. President: Wayne G. Thompson. Management firm. Estab. 1973. Represents local, regional or international individual artists, groups, songwriters and record producers; currently handles 3 acts. Receives 20% commission. Reviews material for acts.
How to Contact: Write or call first and obtain permission to submit. Prefers cassette and bio if available. SASE. Reports in 2 months.
Music: Mostly pop, R&B and classical. "We are interested in any type of musical entertainer, as long as they are quality." Current acts include The Nylons (a capella), Billy Newton-Davis (R&B) and Molly Johnson.

Tips: "Patience, persistence (follow-up, but don't 'nag')."

*HEAVYWEIGHT PRODUCTIONS & UP FRONT MANAGEMENT, 2734 East 7th St., Oakland CA 94601. (415)436-5532. Vice President: Charles M. Coke. Management firm, music publisher and record company (Man Records). Estab. 1988. Represents local, regional and international individual artists, groups, songwriters and producers; currently handles 6 acts. Receives 20% commission. Reviews material for acts.
How to Contact: Submit demo tape by mail. Unsolicited submissions are OK. Prefers cassette with 4 songs and lyric or lead sheet (optional). Does not return unsolicited material. Reports within 2 weeks.
Music: Mostly R&B, rock and country; also pop, Latin and jazz. Works primarily with vocalists. Current acts include Derick Hughes, John Payne, Black Moriah and Ronnie Kimball.
Tips: "Listen to trends in today's market place. If you're writing with someone in mind, research their music. Write strong hooks, and don't forget people will always be dancing no matter the type of music. Don't write over the listeners' heads."

BOB HINKLE MANAGEMENT/THE CHILDREN'S GROUP, 17 Cadman Plaza West, Brooklyn NY 11201. (718)858-2544. President: Bob Hinkle. Management firm. Represents individual artists, groups and songwriters. Currently handles 5 artists. Receives 15-25% commission. Reviews material for acts.
How to Contact: Unsolicited submissions are OK. Prefers cassette (or ¾" or VHS videocassette if available) with 3-5 songs and lyric sheet. Artist should send a videocassette of his/her performance. Does not return unsolicited material. Report in 1 month.
Music: Mostly pop and rock; also R&B, gospel and children's. Works primarily with recording bands, soloists and children's performers. Current acts include Red Grammar, Wilton Banks and Peter Combe (all children's performers) and Mack/Shockley (a rock band recording for BMG International).
Tips: "Tailor writing to needs of artists without losing what makes your writing unique."

HITCH-A-RIDE MANAGEMENT, P.O. Box 1001, Florence KY 41022-1001. (606)371-5469. Manager: J.H. Reno. Management firm, booking agency and publishing company. Represents professional individuals, groups and songwriters; currently handles 4 acts. Receives 15% commission. Reviews material for acts.
How to Contact: Prefers cassette (or videocassette – "be natural") with 1-4 songs and lyric sheet. SASE. Reports in 1 month.
Music: Mostly modern country and light cross-over rock. Works primarily with vocalists. Current acts include Sheila Reno, Pam Hanna, Mike Tomlin and Jack Reno (country vocalists).

*HOLIDAY PRODUCTIONS, 1786 State Line Road, Lagrange GA 30240. (404)884-5369. President: Phyllis Imhoff. Management firm and music publisher (Silverstreak Music/ASCAP). Estab. 1983. Represents local, regional and international individual artists and songwriters; currently handles 2 acts. Receives 15-20% commission. Reviews material for acts.
How to Contact: Submit demo tape by mail. Unsolicited submissions are OK. Prefers cassette or VHS videocassette with an unspecified number of songs and lyric sheet. SASE. Reports in 2 weeks.
Music: Mostly country and pop. Works primarily with dance bands and show bands with strong lead vocalists. Current acts include Scooter Lee (country singer) and Dealer's Choice (country band).

DOC HOLIDAY PRODUCTIONS, 5405 Echo Pines Circle W., Fort Pierce FL 34951. (804)591-2717. Vice President: Judith Guthro. Management firm, booking agent, music publisher (BMI, ASCAP, SESAC) and record company (Tug Boat Records). Estab. 1985. Represents international individual artists, groups and songwriters; currently handles 47 acts. Receives 15-25% commission. Reviews material for acts.
How to Contact: Submit demo tape by mail. Unsolicited submissions are okay. Prefers cassette with 1 song and lyric sheet. Does not return unsolicited material. Reports in 2 weeks.
Music: Mostly country, pop and rock. Works primarily with vocalist dance bands. Current acts include Richie Balin (country singer/writer), Jon Washington (pop singer/writer), Ronn Craddock (country singer), Doug Kershaw (cajun), Eagle Feather (country rock), Galaxy of Stars (top 40) and others.

*HOLLANDER-LUSTIG ENTERTAINMENT, Suite 103, 321 Northlake Blvd., N. Palm Beach FL 33408. (407)863-5800. Vice President: Richard Lustig. Booking agency. Estab. 1990. Represents local, regional and international individual artists and groups. Receives 10-20% commission. Reviews material for acts.
How to Contact: Submit demo tape by mail. Unsolicited submissions are OK. Prefers cassette or VHS videocassette.
Music: All types. Works primarily with dance and show bands. Current acts include Bill Haley's Comets, Tiny Tim and Joey Dee & The Starlighters.
Tips: "Have good promo kit. Be easy to work with. Do a professional job for the client."

*HOT HITS, #326, 2505 Chamber-Tucker, Chamblee GA 30341. (404)452-0494. Vice President: Lesley K. Scott. Management firm, music publisher (Alan White Music/ASCAP) and record company (Hot Hits Records). Estab. 1988. Represents local, regional and international individual artists and groups; currently handles 4 acts. Receives 20% commission. Reviews material for acts.
How to Contact: Submit demo tape by mail. Unsolicited submissions are OK. Prefers cassette with any number of songs and lyric sheet. SASE. Reports in 2 weeks.
Music: Mostly dance, pop and country; also R&B and rock. Works primarily with dance bands. Current acts include Jane Doe (dance band), Sharrone (pop band) and Gayle Short (country vocalist).

*HOT ROCK ARTIST MANAGEMENT, 19673 W Cambridge, Mundelein IL 60060. (708)566-7417. FAX: (708)566-4046. President: John Hochrek. Management firm. Estab. 1985. Represents local, regional and international individual artists and groups; currently handles 2 acts. Reviews material for acts.
How to Contact: Submit demo tape by mail. Unsolicited submissions are OK. Prefers cassette with 2-3 songs and lyric or lead sheets. Does not return unsolicited material. Reports in 1 month.
Music: Mostly rock, pop and alternative; also blues. Current acts include The Luck of Eden Hall (alternative rock band) and Like This (pop/dance band).

*INERJÉ PRODUCTIONS, RECORDS, MANAGEMENT, 661 N. 13th St., Philadelphia PA 19123. (215)236-5358. President: Inerjé Barrett. Management firm, music publisher (Inerjé Publishing/ASCAP) and record company (Inerjé Records). Estab. 1990. Represents local, regional and international individual artists, groups, songwriters and producers; currently handles 5 acts. Receives 20% commission. Reviews material for acts.
How to Contact: Submit demo tape by mail. Unsolicited submissions are OK. Prefers cassette (or VHS videocassette if available) with 3-5 songs. Does not return unsolicited material. Reports in 4 weeks.
Music: Gospel. Works primarily with vocalists and choirs. Current acts include Tony Gilmore (vocalist), Bryant Pugh (producer, writer, musician) and Damien Cove (artist).
Tips: "Please be sure that you are interested in gospel music. Write clearly or type information. Please give ample time for the review of material. Be vocally strong."

INTERMOUNTAIN TALENT, P.O. Box 942, Rapid City SD 57709. (605)348-7777. Owner: Ron Kohn. Management firm, booking agency and music publisher (Big BL Music). Estab. 1978. Represents invididual artists, groups and songwriters; currently handles 30 acts. Receives 10-20% commission. Reviews material for acts.
How to Contact: Query. Prefers cassette with 3 songs and lyric sheet. Artist may submit videocassette. SASE. Reports in 3 weeks.
Music: Mostly rock; also top country/rock. Works with solo acts, show bands, dance bands and bar bands. Current acts include Dial 911 (hard rock), Road House Band (rock) and Missoura Brakes (country band).

*INTERNATIONAL TALENT NETWORK, 17580 Frazho, Roseville MI 48066. Executive Vice President of A&R: Ron Geddish. Booking agency. Estab. 1980. Represents Midwest groups; currently handles 3 acts. Receives 20% commission. Reviews material for acts.
How to Contact: Submit demo tape by mail. Unsolicited submissions are OK. Prefers cassette (or VHS videocassette of performance if available) with 3-5 songs and lyric sheet. Does not return unsolicited material. Reports in 1 month.
Music: Works primarily with rock, pop and alternative-college acts. Current acts include His Name Is Alive (group/alternative), Elvis Hitler (Hollywood rock group) and The Look (A&M/Canada rock group).
Tips: "If we hear a hit tune—rock, pop, alternative college—we are interested."

*INTERNATIONAL TALENT SERVICES, INC., Fourth Floor, 177 West 7th Ave., Vancouver BC V5Y 1K5 **Canada.** (604)872-2906. General Manager: Claude Lelievre. Management firm and music publisher (SOCAN). Estab. 1988. Represents local, regional and international individual artists, groups and songwriters; currently handles 5 acts. Reviews material for acts.
How to Contact: Call first and obtain permission to submit. Prefers cassette with 3 songs and lyric sheets. Does not return unsolicited material. Reports in 1 month.
Music: Mostly country, pop and gospel. Works primarily with vocalists, vocal groups and songwriters. Current acts include Ron Tarrant (singer/songwriter), Heidi Marlaine (singer/songwriter) and Step by Step (gospel group).

ISSACHAR MANAGEMENT, (formerly Murphy's Law Entertainment Group Ltd.), Suite 10F, 111 Third Ave., New York NY 10003. (212)477-7063. FAX: (212)477-1469. President: Jack Flanagan. Management firm and booking agency. Estab. 1990. Represents international individual artists and groups; currently handles 4 acts.
How to Contact: "Submit all tapes by mail. Non-returnable—no guarantee of reply."
Music: Mostly rock, R&B and reggae; also pop. Current acts include The Mighty Mighty Bosstones (rock), Mikey Dread (reggae), David Simeon (reggae) and Technikill (thrash metal).

J. BIRD ENTERTAINMENT AGENCY, 250 North Kepler Ave., Deland FL 32724. (904)734-9446. President: John R. Bird II. Management firm and booking agency. Estab. 1963. Represents local, regional and international individual artists, groups, songwriters and recording acts; currently handles 55 acts. Receives 15-20% commission. Reviews material for acts.
How to Contact: Submit demo tape by mail. Unsolicited submissions are OK. Prefers cassette (or VHS videocassette of live performance, if available) with 2-3 songs and lyric or lead sheets. "Videos should be 3-15 minutes in length." Does not return unsolicited material. Reports in 2 weeks.
Music: Mostly top 40, rock, pop and country; also R&B. Works primarily with dance bands and recording acts in concert format. Current acts include Greg Allman (recording act), The Drifters (nostalgia) and Molly Hatchet (concert act).
Tips: "J. Bird agency represents established, concert and copy bands and solo and duo acts to national club circuit and national college concert circuit. Bands should have adequate equipment and transportation and perform either original concert material, period-nostalgia material, or current top 40. We stress professional promotional packages including: $8 \times 10''$ photo, audio and videocassette tape."

JACKSON ARTISTS CORP., (Publishing Central), Suite 200, 7251 Lowell Dr., Shawnee Mission KS 66204. (913)384-6688. President: Dave Jackson. Management firm, booking agency (Drake/Jackson Productions), music publisher, (All Told Music/BMI, Zang/Jac Publishing/ASCAP and Very Cherry/ASCAP), record company and record producer. Represents artists, groups and songwriters; currently handles 12 acts. Receives 15-20% commission from individual artists and groups; 10% from songwriters. Reviews material for acts.
How to Contact: Query, arrange personal interview or submit demo. Prefers cassette (or VHS videocassette of performance if available) with 2-4 songs and lead sheet. "List names of tunes on cassettes. May send up to 4 tapes. Although it's not necessary, we prefer lead sheets with the tapes—send 2 or 3 that you are proud of. Also note what 'name' artist you'd like to see do the song. We do most of our business by phone. We prefer good enough quality to judge a performance, however, we do not require that the video or cassettes be of professional nature." Will return material if requested with SASE. Reporting time varies.
Music: Mostly gospel, country and rock; also bluegrass, blues, easy listening, disco, MOR, progressive, soul and top 40/pop. Works with acts that work grandstand shows for fairs as well as bar bands that want to record original material. Current acts include "Ragtime Bob" Darch (songwriter/entertainer), Dixie Cadillacs (country/rock), Impressions (50's and 60's), Gary Adams Players (pop), Tracie Spencer, Paul & Paula, Bill Haley's Comets, Max Groove (jazz) and The Dutton Family (classical to pop).
Tips: "Be able to work on the road, either as a player or have a group. Invest your earnings from these efforts in demos of your originals that have been tried out on an audience. And keep submitting to the industry."

*JACKSON/JONES MANAGEMENT, 5917 West Blvd., Los Angeles CA 90043. (213)296-8742. Manager: E.J. Jackson. Management firm. Estab. 1984. Represents local, regional and international individual artists and groups; currently handles 4 acts. Receives 25% commission. Reviews material for acts.
How to Contact: Write or call first and obtain permission to submit. Prefers cassette (or VHS videocassette if available) with 3 songs and lyric sheet. SASE. Reports in 3 weeks.
Music: Mostly R&B, pop and top 40. Works primarily with vocalists, producers and dance bands. Current acts include Vesta (R&B/pop singer), Ken Williams (producer), Rio Lawrence (songwriter, producer) and Andre C. (R&B).

JAM MANAGEMENT, P.O. Box 6588, San Antonio TX 78209. (512)828-1319. Production: Scudder Miller. Management firm and booking agency. Estab. 1970. Represents local, regional and international individual artists, groups and songwriters. Currently handles 3 acts. Receives 20% commission. Reviews material for acts.
How to Contact: Submit demo tape by mail. Unsolicited submissions are OK. Prefers cassette with 3 songs and lyric sheets. Does not return unsolicited material. Reports in 2 weeks.
Music: Rock, country and pop. Works primarily with show and bar bands. Current acts include Scudder Moon (rock), Flash Cadillac (50's rock) and Rio Trouble (rock).
Tips: "Have good material, good attitude and be persistent."

ROGER JAMES MANAGEMENT, 10A Margaret Rd., Barnet, Herts EN4 9NP **England**. Phone: (01)440-9788. Professional Manager: Laura Skuce. Management firm and music publisher (R.J. Music/PRS). Estab. 1977. Represents songwriters. Receives 50% commission; reviews material for acts.
How to Contact: Prefers cassette with 3 songs and lyric sheet. Does not return unsolicited material.
Music: Mostly pop, country and "any good song."

*****JAMPOP LTD.**, 41 Trevennion Pk. Rd., Kingston 5 J.A. W.I. **Jamaica**. Phone: (809)92-21236-7. President: Michael Lihyte. Management firm and booking agency. Estab. 1990. Represents local, regional and international individual artists, groups and songwriters; currently handles 30 acts. Receives 10% commission. Reviews material for acts.
How to Contact: Submit demo tape by mail. Unsolicited submissions are OK. Prefers cassette with lyric sheets. SASE. Reports in 4 weeks.
Music: Mostly R&B and pop; also gospel. Works primarily with vocalists. Current artists include Chalice, Sophia George and Calypso Rose.

JANA JAE ENTERPRISES, #520, 4815 S. Harvard, Tulsa OK 74135. (918)749-1647. Vice President: Diana Robey. Booking agency, music publisher (Jana Jae Publishing/BMI) and record company (Lark Record Productions, Inc.). Estab. 1979. Represents individual artists and songwriters; currently handles 12 acts. Receives 15% commission. Reviews material for acts.
How to Contact: Prefers cassette (or videocassette of performance if available). SASE. Reports in 1 month.
Music: Mostly interested in country, classical and jazz instrumentals; also pop. Works with vocalists, show and concert bands, solo instrumentalists. Represents Jana Jae (country singer/fiddle player), Matt Greif (classical guitarist), Sydni (solo singer) and Hotwire (country show band).

JANC MANAGEMENT, Box 5563, Rockford IL 61125. (815)398-6895. President: Nancy Lee. Management firm, booking agency and record company. Represents individual artists, groups and songwriters; currently handles 2 acts. Reviews material for acts.
How to Contact: Prefers cassette (or VHS videocassette if available) with 4 songs and lyric sheet. SASE. Reports in 2 weeks.
Music: Mostly country (contemporary) and pop; also up-tempo songs, ballads and novelty. Works primarily with vocalists, dance bands and show bands. Current acts include George James and the Mood Express.
Tips: "Be very neat and professional with your submissions."

*****JBK PRODUCTIONS, LTD.**, 12045 Lincolnshire Drive, Austin TX 78758. (512)834-0765. General Partner: Scott Hoyt. Management firm, booking agency, music publisher (Scott Hoyt Music/BMI) and record company (Twitchy Records). Estab. 1989. Represents local, regional and international individual artists; currently handles 1 act. Receives 15-20% commission. Reviews material for acts.
How to Contact: Call first and obtain permission to submit. Prefers cassette with 3 songs and lyric sheet. Does not return unsolicited material. Reports in 3 weeks.
Music: Country.

JMAR PRODUCTIONS, P.O. Box 2393, Beverly Hills CA 90213-2393. President: Jeff Rizzotti. Management firm and booking agency. Estab. 1969. Currently handles 3 acts. Reviews material for acts.
How to Contact: Query by mail. Prefers cassette with 3-6 songs. SASE. Reports in 2 weeks.
Music: Mostly 60s renditions; also top 40, country, jazz and soul. Works primarily with vocalists and bar bands.
Tips: "Friedrich Nietzsche once said 'Without music, life would be a mistake.' "

JOHNS & ASSOCIATES, % Ward Johns and Sabian Simpson, Suite 101, 550 E. Plumb Lane, Reno NV 89502. (702)827-3648. Management firm and booking agency. Estab. 1981. Represents artists, groups and songwriters; currently handles 6-12 acts. "We represent all types of music to record labels and booking/management firms throughout the world." Currently handles 12 acts. Receives 10-15% commission. Reviews material for acts.
How to Contact: Query by mail, arrange personal interview or submit demo tape. Prefers cassette (or VHS or Beta videocassette of live performance, if available) with 4-10 songs and lyric sheet. "It's important to have VHS or Beta tape and a professional 16-24 track demo. Also send pictures and printed resume."

Listings of companies in countries other than the U.S. have the name of the country in boldface type.

Music: Mostly commercial: top 40 original music; up to date rock'n'roll; cross-over pop and country western. Works primarily with show and dance bands: rock groups, original jazz artists and original rock/pop/soul/R&B artists. Current acts include Geary Hanley (country), Ron Shirrel (country), Robin Baxter (rock), Jessica Hart (rock), Larry Elliot (MOR/rock), Michael Stosic (pop), Michael Shiflett (pop) and Rich Chaney (pop/C&W).
Tips: "Send new material with strong hooks. Although it is not mandatory, a videocassette is a big help for an artist's marketing potential. We have music mortgage brokers helping to find financial opportunities for booking agencies, management firms and record labels as our secondary income resource."

*C. JUNQUERA PRODUCTIONS, P.O. Box 393, Lomita CA 90717. (213)325-2881. Co-owner: C. Junquera. Management firm and record company (NH Records). Estab. 1987. Represents local, regional and international individual artists and songwriters; currently handles 1 act. Receives a flat fee, depending on project costs. Reviews material for acts.
How to Contact: Write first and obtain permission to submit. Prefers cassette with 1-3 songs and lyric sheet. SASE.
Music: Mostly traditional country and country pop; also easy listening. Works primarily with vocalists. Current acts include Nikki Hornsby (singer/songwriter).

*KA PRODUCTIONS, P.O. Box 3500, Pawtucket RI 02861. (401)728-1689. President/General Manager: Karen A. Pady. Management firm, booking agency, music publisher (Pady Music Publishing Co/ ASCAP) and record company (Big K Records). Estab. 1980. Represents local, regional and international individual artists, groups and songwriters "if I believe I can assist." Currently handles 5 acts. Receives 10-30% commission. Reviews material for acts.
How to Contact: Submit demo tape by mail. Unsolicited submissions are OK. Prefers cassette with an unlimited number of songs and lyric and lead sheets. SASE. Reports in 2 weeks.
Music: Mostly pop, rock and A/C; also light rock and country. Works primarily with duos, trios and quartets (musicians/vocalists). Current acts include Karyn Krystal (contemporary singer/songwriter), Karyn and Steph (light rock/top 40 duo, songwriters), Lee Carol and The Burgandies (female top 40/ rock quartet, musicians/vocalists) and Pauline Silvia (contemporary singer/songwriter).
Tips: "Satisfy yourselves with your work, in case it is turned down; and you will have at least accomplished something for yourself that you believe in."

*KALIMBA PRODUCTIONS, INC., #210, 1990 Westwood Blvd., Los Angeles CA 90025. (213)475- 3203. Contact: Jack Stein or Art Macnow. Management firm, music publisher (ASCAP, BMI), music production company and personal management firm. Estab. 1972. Represents local, regional and international individual artists, groups and songwriters; currently handles 7 acts. Receives 15% commission. Reviews material for acts.
How to Contact: Write or call first and obtain permission to submit. Prefers cassette or VHS videocassette with 3 songs and lyric sheet. SASE. Reports within 4 weeks.
Music: R&B, rock and A/C. Current acts include Earth, Wind and Fire, Susan Anton and Maurice White.

*R.J. KALTENBACH PERSONAL MANAGEMENT, P.O. Box 510, Dundee IL 60118-0510. (708)428- 4777. President: R.J. Kaltenbach. Management firm. Estab. 1980. Represents national touring acts only (individual artists and groups); currently handles 3 acts. Receives 15-20% commission. Reviews material for acts.
How to Contact: Submit demo tape by mail. Unsolicited submissions are OK. Prefers cassette or VHS ½" videocassette with 3 songs and lyric sheet. Reports in 1 month "if we are interested in material."
Music: Country, rock/pop and contemporary Christian. Works primarily with "national acts with recording contracts or deals pending." Current acts include T.G. Sheppard (national recording artist), Ron David Moore (new Christian artist) and Mike Redmond and Magazine (Chicago-based rock act).
Tips: "We deal only with professionals who are dedicated to their craft and show lots of promise."

KAUFMAN HILL MANAGEMENT, Suite 613, 410 S. Michigan Ave., Chicago IL 60605. (312)477-6644. Contact: Don Kaufman or Shawn Hill. Management firm (also Mozart Midnight Productions, Inc.) and record company (Vamp Records). Estab. 1982. Represents individual artists, groups and songwriters; currently handles 8 acts. Receives 20-25% commission. Reviews material for acts.
How to Contact: Prefers cassette (or VHS videocassette if available) with 2-6 songs and lyric sheet. Does not return any material. Reports in 1 month.
Music: Mostly R&B, pop, rock and rap. Works primarily with singer/songwriters, bands, groups and vocalists. Current acts include Kevin Irving (lead singer of Club Nouveau, R&B), Jeannie Withrow, Darksyde (rap) and Tribal Opera (progressive band).

Tips: "Submit by mail. If you have what we need, we will be in touch."

HOWARD KING AGENCY, INC., 7050 Babcock Ave., North Hollywood CA 91605. President: Howard King. Management firm and booking agency. Estab. 1962. Represents artists, groups and songwriters. Receives 10-20% commission. Reviews material for acts.
How to Contact: Write or call first and obtain permission to submit. Prefers cassette or VHS videocassette with maximum 3 songs, photo, publicity material and lyric sheet. SASE.
Music: Mostly top 40; also country, dance-oriented, easy listening, jazz, MOR, rock and pop. Works primarily with top 40 artist singles, duos and groups.

JEFF KIRK, 515 Inwood Dr., Nashville TN 37211. (615)331-0131. Owner/President: Jeff Kirk. Management firm and booking agency. Estab. 1981. Represents regional (mid-South) individual artists; currently handles 1 act. Commission varies. Reviews material for acts.
How to Contact: Submit demo tape by mail. Unsolicited submissions are OK. Prefers cassette (or VHS videocassette if available) with 1-3 songs and lyric or lead sheet. SASE. Reports in 6 weeks.
Music: Mostly jazz, pop and rock. Works primarily with jazz groups (4-6 members), instrumental and vocal. Current acts include Jeff Kirk Quartet (mainstream jazz) and New Vintage (jazz fusion).
Tips: "Please submit brief demos with as high audio quality as possible."

L.D.F. PRODUCTIONS, P.O. Box 406, Old Chelsea Station, New York NY 10011. (212)925-8925. President: Mr. Dowell. Management firm and booking agency. Estab. 1982. Represents artists and choirs in the New York area. Currently handles 2 acts. Receives 20-30% commission.
How to Contact: Write first and obtain permission to submit. Prefers cassette (or videocassette of performance—well-lighted, maximum 10 minutes) with 2-8 songs and lyric sheet. SASE. Reports in 1 month. "Do not phone expecting a return call unless requested by L.D.F. Productions. Videos should be imaginatively presented with clear sound and bright colors."
Music: Mostly black gospel; also choral and church/religious. Works primarily with inspirational soloists and church groups. Current acts include L.D. Frazier (gospel artist/lecturer).
Tips: "Those interested in working with us must be original, enthusiastic, persistent and sincere."

LANDMARK DIRECTION COMPANY, INC., P.O. 132, Amelia OH 45102. (513)752-0611. President: James B. Williams. Management firm, booking agency, music publisher (Landmark Publishing/BMI) and record company (JAB Production Co., Inc.). Estab. 1987. Represents regional (Midwest) individual artists, groups and songwriters; currently handles 6 acts. Receives 10-35% commission. Reviews material for acts.
How to Contact: Submit demo tape by mail. Unsolicited submissions are OK. Prefers cassette (or VHS videocassette of performance if available) with best 3 songs and lyric or lead sheets. SASE. Reports in 6 weeks.
Music: Country, pop and R&B. Works primarily with individual and group recording artists/road acts. Current acts include Just Another Band (country group), Bobby Joe Mueller (traditional country solo) and Michael Denton (country crossover solo).
Tips: "Only send your best material, and send it only to *one* company at a time. Make your presentations brief and as described above. Have all your material copyrighted before submitting."

LANDSLIDE MANAGEMENT, 928 Broadway, New York NY 10010. (212)505-7300. Principals: Ted Lehrman and Libby Bush. Management firm and music publisher (KozKeeOzko Music). Estab. 1978. Represents singers, singer/songwriters and actor/singers; currently handles 2 singing acts. Reviews material for acts.
How to Contact: Submit demo tape and lyric sheet "of potential hit singles only—not interested in album cuts." SASE. "Include picture, resume and (if available) ½" videocassette if you're submitting yourself as an act." Reports in 6 weeks.
Music: Dance-oriented, MOR, rock (soft pop), soul, top 40/pop and country/pop. Current acts include Deborah Dotson (soul/pop/jazz) and Loretta Valdespino (pop).

LARI—JON PROMOTIONS, P.O. Box 216, 325 W. Walnut, Rising City NE 68658. (402)542-2336. Owner: Larry Good. Music publisher (Lari-Jon Publishing Co./BMI) and record company (Lari-Jon Records). "We also promote package shows." Represents individual artists, groups and songwriters; currently handles 5 acts. Receives 15% commission. Reviews material for acts.
How to Contact: Prefers cassette with 5 songs and lyric sheet. SASE. Reports in 1 month.
Music: Mostly country, gospel and 50s rock. Works primarily with dance bands and show bands. Represents Larry Good (singer/writer), Tommy Campbell (singer/songwriter), Kent Thompson (singer), Nebraskaland 'Opry (family type country show) and Brenda Allen (singer/comedienne).

Close-up

Steve Tracy
Blues Singer/Songwriter
Cincinnati, Ohio

On paper, it's an odd combination. A man with a doctorate in English who is a high school English teacher, a historian and writer, a harmonica player and (here's the odd one) a blues singer/songwriter.

For Steve Tracy, it's not unorthodox; he's been writing and playing the blues since his high school days. Even though it's only a part-time endeavor, Tracy and his band, The Crawling Kingsnakes, got a record deal with a label in Holland called Blue Shadow. "This is relatively late for a band to get a recording," says Tracy, who fronts the band composed of men in their late 30s and early 40s. "But music means a lot to us. I think it's a big part of our lives."

Since Tracy and his band didn't want to tour, but still wanted to get a record out to the public, they finally decided to pool their money, produce a solid master demo and attempt to locate a suitable record company to press and distribute their album. Unfortunately, the plan didn't go as scheduled. "We submitted our CD to a number of record companies in the U.S., none of whom answered us. We had kind of given up, but I saw an advertisement in the back of *Living Blues* magazines by Blue Shadow. I sent it to them and they responded immediately."

Shortly after, Blue Shadow released the album under the title *Going to Cincinnati* by Steve Tracy and the Crawling Kingsnakes. The band was given a chance to travel to Holland and play clubs for 10 days—a dream of Tracy's and his band.

Although the band hails from Cincinnati, Tracy claims to have more of a following in Holland. "We're better known there because of the CD and our brief tour. And it was a real thrill going to Amsterdam, coming out on stage and having people on the front row requesting our songs . . . and then singing along. It was a very special thing, yet very strange."

Judging from reviews of their performances, they were quite a hit. One said: "It really became a party when the highly energetic Steve Tracy started his performance . . . the harp-player from Cincinnati and his real tight band . . . blew the festival tent almost to pieces." Another said: "Singer and harp-player Steve Tracy . . . is capable of putting on a perfect, unbelievably energetic blues show in front of any audience in the world."

Tracy believes that European acceptance of music from the United States will continue to expand. "There is such a big market in Europe for this kind of music—and other alternative types of music too. Many labels there are really hot to get people to submit tapes."

As far as a lack of acceptance in the U.S., Tracy responds with indifference. "I don't think that the reason we didn't hear from domestic labels was because we aren't any good. What people want to hear in the U.S. or what the record labels value here is not what the people or record labels value somewhere else. Europeans want to hear American blues and rock. They are really interested in diversity."

—Brian C. Rushing

DAVID LEFKOWITZ MANAGEMENT, 3470 Nineteenth St., San Francisco CA 94110. (415)777-1715. Contact: David Lefkowitz. Management firm. Represents individual artists, groups and songwriters from northern California; currently handles 4 acts. Receives 15-20% commission. Reviews material for acts.
How to Contact: Prefers cassette with 3-5 songs and lyric sheet. Does not return unsolicited material. Reports in 3 weeks.
Music: Mostly alternative music, rock, pop and R&B. Works with modern rock bands. Represents Capture the Flag (modern rock band), Limbomaniacs (funk/rock band), Primus (funk/thrash band) and Smoking Section (R&B, pop group).

LEMON SQUARE MUSIC, Box 671008, Dallas TX 75367-8008. (214)750-0720. Contact: Bart Barton. Production company. Represents artists, groups and songwriters; currently handles 7 acts. Reviews material for acts.
How to Contact: Query by mail, then submit demo tape. Prefers cassette with 2-4 songs. SASE. Reports in 1 month.
Music: Country and gospel. Works primarily with show bands. Current acts include Dania Presley (country), Freed (progressive country artist), Craig Solieau (comedy act), Audie Henry (progressive country singer), Susie Calvin (country), Billy Parker (traditional country) and Bev Marie (traditional country).

LEROI AND ASSOCIATES, 104 Chapin Pkwy., Buffalo NY 14209. (716)855-2644. Secretary: Camille Hudson. Management firm. Estab. 1985. Represents individual artists and groups. Deals with artists from anywhere. Currently handles 3 acts. Receives 10-20% commission.
How To Contact: Submit demo tape by mail. Unsolicited submissions are OK. Prefers cassette (or videocassette of performance if available) with 4 songs. Does not return unsolicited material. Reports in 1 month.
Music: R&B and gospel; also pop. Works mainly with concert and show bands. Current acts include Rick James, Val Young and Mary Jane Girls.

THE LET US ENTERTAIN YOU CO., Suite 204, 900 19th Ave. S., Nashville TN 37212-2125. (615)321-3100. Administrative Assistant: Corrine. Management firm, booking agency and music publisher (ASCAP/SESAC/BMI). Estab. 1968. Represents groups and songwriters; currently handles 50-60 acts. Receives 15% commission. Reviews material for acts.
How to Contact: Prefers cassette (or videocassette if available) and lyric sheet. Does not return unsolicited material.
Music: Mostly country, pop, R&B; also rock and new music. Works with all types of artists/groups/songwriters. Current acts include C.N. Double (showband), Wizzards (dance/show band), Colours (dance/showband), Broadway (showband) and Max (dance/showband).

***PAUL LEVESQUE MANAGEMENT INC.**, 154 Grande Cote, Rosemere QC J7A 1H3 **Canada**. A&R Director: Jean Lemieux. Management firm, music publisher and record company (Artiste Records). Estab. 1987. Represents local, regional and international individual artists, groups and songwriters; currently handles 6 acts. Reviews material for acts.
How to Contact: Submit demo tape by mail. Unsolicited submissions are OK. Prefers cassette (or VHS/Beta videocassette if available) with 3-6 songs and lyric sheet. "Send photos and bio if possible." SASE. Reports in 1 month.
Music: Mostly rock and pop. Current acts include Paradox (rock band), The Tribes of March (rock band) and Sonya Papp (pop singer/songwriter).

LEVINSON ENTERTAINMENT VENTURES INTERNATIONAL, INC., Suite 650, 1440 Veteran Avenue, Los Angeles CA 90024. (213)460-4545. President: Bob Levinson. Management firm. Estab. 1978. Represents national individual artists, groups and songwriters; currently handles 4 acts. Receives 15-20% commission.
How to Contact: Write first and obtain permission to submit or to arrange personal interview. Prefers cassette (or VHS videocassette) with 6 songs and lead sheet. "Inquire first. Don't expect video to be returned unless SASE included with submission and specific request is made." Does not return unsolicited material. Reports in 1 month.
Music: Rock, MOR, R&B and country. Works primarily with rock bands and vocalists.
Tips: "Should be a working band, self-contained and, preferably, performing original material."

LINE-UP PROMOTIONS, INC., 9A, Tankerville Place, Newcastle-Upon-Tyne NE2 3AT **United Kingdom**. Phone: (091)2816449. FAX: (091)212-0913. Director: C.A. Murtagh. Management firm, booking agency, record company (On-Line Records), music publisher (On Line Records & Publishing) and record producer. Represents individual artists, groups and songwriters; currently handles 6-8 acts. Receives 15% commission. Reviews material for acts.

How to Contact: Prefers cassette (or videocassette if available) and lyric sheet. "Send full press kit, commitments and objective." Does not return unsolicited material. Reports in 1 month. "We're looking for professional acts who can entertain in city centers and unusual situations; e.g., tea dances, supermarkets, metro stations and traditional venues."

Music: Mostly acoustic pop, rock, new world, Afro and reggae. Works primarily with original groups (not MOR). Current acts include Moonlight Drive (rock), Fan Heater (post punk/new wave/psychedelic), Swimming Pool (fine art rock), Royal Family (post punk exploitative), Leg Theory (rock/pop), APU (Andean music), The Light Programme (swing jazz) and Big Life (C&W/folk/pop).

LMP MANAGEMENT FIRM, Suite 206, 6245 Bristol Pkwy., Culver City CA 90230. Contact: Larry McGee. Management firm, music publisher (Operation Perfection, Inc.) and record company (Boogie Band Records Corp.). Represents individual artists, groups and songwriters; currently handles 40 acts. Receives 15% commission. Reviews material for acts.

How to Contact: Prefers cassette (or videocassette of performance) with 1-4 songs and lead sheet. "Try to perform one or more of your songs on a local TV show. Then obtain a copy of your performance. Please only send professional quality material. Keep it simple and basic." Does not return unsolicited material. Reports in 2 months.

Music: Mostly pop-oriented R&B; also rock and MOR/adult contemporary. Works primarily with professionally choreographed show bands. Current acts include Sheena-Kriss (self-contained band) and Bill Sawyer (showband).

Tips: "Do research on current commercial marketplace. Take the necessary steps, time, talent and money to present a professional product."

LOCONTO PRODUCTIONS, 10244 NW 47 St., Sunrise FL 33351. (305)741-7766. Contact: Phyllis Finney Loconto. Management firm. Estab. 1978. Represents 3 clients. Receives 5% commission. Reviews material for acts.

How to Contact: "Not presently soliciting material."

Music: All types, including dance music, Latin and country; also bluegrass, children's, church/religious, country, easy listening, folk, gospel, MOR and top 40/pop. Works primarily with country vocalists, country bands, MOR vocalists and bluegrass artists. Current acts include Bill Dillon, Rob Mellor, Jennifer Geiget, The Lane Brothers and Frank X. Loconto.

Tips: "Material must be 'top shelf.' "

*LONG DISTANCE ENTERTAINMENT PRODUCTIONS INC., 6801 Hamilton Ave., Cincinnati OH 45224. (513)522-9999. Vice President: Gary R. Kirves. Booking agency. Estab. 1985. Represents groups; currently handles 25 acts. Receives 15-20% commission. Reviews material for acts.

How to Contact: Submit demo tape by mail. Unsolicited submissions are OK. Prefers cassette or videocassette with 2 songs and lyric sheet. SASE. Reports in 1 month.

Music: Mostly rock and pop. Deals with metal to mainstream rock bands. Some top 40. Current acts include Cub-Koda, The Take and Za-Za.

Tips: "Send photos with tape so we can get visual about project. Also information about any current G.G.'s."

JEFFREY LOSEFF MANAGEMENT, Suite 205, 4521 Colfax Ave., N. Hollywood CA 91602. (818)505-9468. President: Jeffrey C. Loseff. Management firm. Represents local individual artists; currently handles 5 acts. Receives 15% commission. Reviews material for acts.

How to Contact: Write or call first and obtain permission to submit. Prefers cassette (or VHS videocassette if available) with 3 or more songs and lead sheet. SASE. Reports in 6 weeks.

Music: Mostly pop, jazz, cabaret, light rock; also blues. Works primarily with film and TV composers. Current acts include Sarah Coley (jazz vocalist), Bill Payne Duo (jazz instrumental) and Hayden Wayne (film, stage TV scoring).

Tips: "Have an ear for the public and present unique material."

*LOTUS PRODUCTIONS, 1724 NW 9th St., Oklahoma City OK 73106. (405)239-6460. President/CEO: Terry "Big Daddy" McCann. Management firm and booking agency. Estab. 1975. Represents local, Midwestern U.S. and international individual artists and groups; currently handles 8 acts. Receives 10% commission. Reviews material for acts.

How to Contact: Write first to arrange personal interview. Prefers cassette (or VHS or ¾" videocassette if available) with 3-6 songs. Reports in 6 weeks.
Music: Mostly blues, R&B and AOR; also jazz, some New Age and funk. Current acts include Lindsey/Reeder (AOR), Brownston Blues Band (blues) and Jay Minor (jazz).
Tips: "Take your project one step at a time. Do the best you can do, then move on to the next part of your project. Set goals that are realistic. If you're serious, never settle for second best, and above all never quit or give up your dreams."

*LOUD & PROUD MANAGEMENT, 6224 15th Ave., Brooklyn NY 11219. (918)234-0922. Manager: Ken Kriete. Management firm and music publisher (Loud and Proud Music/ASCAP). Estab. 1983. Represents national recording individual artists, groups and songwriters; currently handles 5 acts. Reviews material for acts.
How to Contact: Submit demo tape by mail. Unsolicited submissions are OK. Prefers cassette with 3 songs and lyric sheet. SASE. Reports in 2 weeks.
Music: Mostly rock, pop and country; also rap and dance. Works primarily with rock groups. Current acts include White Lion (Atlantic recording artist), Tyketto (Geffen/DGC recording artist) and Eric Gaies Band (Elektra recording artist).

LOWELL AGENCY, 4043 Brookside Ct., Norton OH 44203. (216)825-7813. Contact: Leon Seiter. Booking agency. Estab. 1985. Represents regional (Midwest and Southeast) individual artists; currently handles 3 acts. Receives 10% commission. Reviews material for acts.
How to Contact: Submit demo tape by mail. Unsolicited submissions are OK. Prefers cassette with 4 songs and lyric sheet. SASE. Reports in 1 month.
Music: Mostly country. Works primarily with country vocalists. Current acts include Leon Seiter (country singer/entertainer/songwriter), Ford Nix (bluegrass singer and 5 string banjo picker) and Tom Durden (country singer, co-writer of "Heartbreak Hotel").

*RON LUCIANO MUSIC CO., P.O. Box 263, Brigantine NJ 08203. (609)266-2623. President: Ron Luciano. Management firm, booking agency and record company (Lucifer Records Inc.). Represents local, regional and international individual artists and groups; currently handles 4 acts. Receives 10-20% commission. Reviews material for acts. "There is a $25 fee for reviewing, due to the heavy amount of mail we receive each week. The fee is good for 1 year on all submissions."
Affiliates: Ciano Publishing and Legz Music.
How to Contact: Submit demo tape by mail. Unsolicited submissions are OK. Prefers cassette with 4-8 songs. SASE. Reports in 4 weeks to 3 months.
Music: Mostly oldies, rock and top 40; anything commercial. Current acts include Bobby Fisher (singer/songwriter), Tony Vallo (comedian/songwriter) and Jay and The Techniques (oldies group).

*M.S. ASSOCIATES, 29 Almroth Dr., Wayne NJ 07470. (201)595-0050. New Artists Development Group. Management firm. Estab. 1984. Represents local, regional and international individual artists, groups and songwriters; currently handles 15 acts. Receives 10-33% commission. Reviews material for acts.
How to Contact: Submit demo tape by mail. Unsolicited submissions are OK. Prefers cassette (or VHS videocassette if available) with up to 6 songs and lyric or lead sheet. SASE. Reports in 3 months.
Music: Mostly soft rock, top 40 and pop; also country. "We work with a wide variety of artists/groups, from the individual songwriter/singer to a polished act."

KEVIN MABRY ENTERPRIZES, 8 E. State, Milford Center OH 43045. (513)349-2971. Owner/Artist: Kevin Mabry. Management firm and booking agency. Represents local and regional artists and groups. Receives 10-15% commission.
How to Contact: Prefers cassette or 7½ ips reel-to-reel with 4 songs and lyric sheet. Does not return unsolicited material.
Music: "Positive" country, contemporary Christian and MOR/gospel. Works primarily with show bands, vocalists, country groups and contemporary Christian acts. Current acts include Kevin Mabry and Jubilation
Tips: "I'm looking for MOR Christian songs. Also great positive country songs. Positive material is in demand."

*MĆ LAVENE & ASSOCIATES, P.O. Box 26852, Oklahoma OK 73126. Vice President: S. McCurtis. Management firm, booking agency, music publisher (C.A.B. Independent Publishing Company/BMI) and record company (MśQue Records). Estab. 1988. Represents local, regional and international individual artists, groups and songwriters; currently handles 3 acts. Receives 15-20% commission. Reviews material for acts.

How to Contact: Submit demo tape by mail. Unsolicited submissions are OK. Prefers cassette (or VHS videocassette if available) with 3 songs and lead sheet. SASE. Reports in 1 month.
Music: Mostly pop, R&B and rock; also jazz and gospel. Works primarily with dance bands and vocalists. Current acts include C. Freeman (songwriter), Cash & Co. (rap group) and MśQue (R&B singer).
Tips: "We are looking for new artists and songwriters, and we are looking forward to being a stepping stone to the majors."

*ANDREW MCMANUS MANAGEMENT, 1017173 Victoria St., Sydney NSW 2011 **Australia.** Phone: (02)358-4377. Manager: Andrew McManus. Management firm. Estab. 1986. Represents local, regional and international individual artists, groups, songwriters and producers; currently handles 4 acts. Receives 15-20% commission. Reviews material for acts.
How to Contact: Write first to arrange personal interview. Prefers cassette (or VHS videocassette if available) with several songs. SASE. Reports in 1 week.
Music: Mostly rock, pop and dance. Works primarily with rock bands and dance artists. Current acts include Dirinyls (rock), Ten Wedge (dance) and F.O.O.D. (rock/pop).

MAGIC MANAGEMENT AND PRODUCTIONS, 178-49 131st Ave., Jamaica NY 11434. (718)949-0349. General Manager: Bryan P. Sanders. Management firm, booking agency and concert productions firm. Estab. 1987. Represents regional (New York tri-state) individual artists, groups and disc-jockeys; currently handles 12 acts. Receives 20% commission. Reviews material for acts.
How to Contact: Write first and obtain permission to submit. Prefers cassette (or VHS videocassette if available) with minimum of 2 songs and lyric sheet. "Be natural and relaxed. Tape of a song should be no longer than 5-6 minutes in length. Performance length (VHS) no longer than 20 minutes and 4 songs." SASE. Reports in 2½ weeks.
Music: Mostly R&B, "Crossover Club Music" and rap; also "club DJ mixes," gospel and jazz. Works primarily with dance bands, vocalists and disc-jockeys. Current acts include Supreme K and the Wonder Ones (rap/R&B), Kid Quick (disc-jockey/house track mixer) and Nasty Jams (R&B band).
Tips: "Keep in mind that it's not necessarily the size of the company but what that company can do for you that makes the difference."

MAGNUM MUSIC CORPORATION LTD., 8607-128 Avenue, Edmonton Alberta **Canada** T5E 0G3. (403)476-8230. FAX: (403)472-2584 Manager: Bill Maxim. Booking agency, music publisher (Ramblin' Man Music Publishing/PRO, High River Music Publishing/ASCAP) and record company (Magnum Records). Estab. 1984. Represents international individual artists, groups and songwriters; currently handles 4 acts. Reviews material for acts.
How to Contact: Write first and obtain permission to submit. Prefers cassette with 3-4 songs. Does not return unsolicited material. Reports in 1 month.
Music: Mostly country and gospel. Works primarily with "artists or groups who are also songwriters." Current acts include Catheryne Greenly (country), Billy Jay (country), Thea Anderson (country) and Cormier Country (country).
Tips: "Prefers finished demos."

MAINE-LY COUNTRY MUSIC, 212 Stillwater Ave., Old Town ME 04468. (207)827-2185. Owner/ Manager: Jeff Simon. Booking agency, music publisher (Maine-ly Music/BMI, Maine-ly Country Music/SESAC) and record company (Maine-ly Country Records). Estab. 1988. Represents international individual artists, groups and songwriters; currently handles 2 acts. Receives 15-25% commission. Reviews material for acts.
How to Contact: Submit demo tape by mail. Unsolicited submissions are OK. Prefers cassette (or VHS videocassette or performance) with 3-5 songs and lyric or lead sheet. SASE. Reports in 6 weeks.
Music: Mostly country-country rock, pop and gospel. Works primarily with country, country rock vocalists and dance bands. Current acts include Jeff Simon (vocalist/songwriter), Maine-ly Country (country-country rock band), Allison Ames (vocalist/songwriter) and George Willette (songwriter).
Tips: "Send demos, bio, picture or videos (VHS format), think positively and be prepared to work."

MAJESTIC PRODUCTIONS, P.O. Box 330-568, Brooklyn NY 11233-0016. (718)919-2013. A&R: Hank Love or Alemo. Management firm and record company (Majestic Control Records). Estab. 1983. Represents international individual artists and groups; currently handles 3 acts. Reviews material for acts.
How to Contact: Submit demo tape by mail—unsolicited submissions are OK. Prefers cassette (or VHS videocassette) with 2 songs. SASE. Reports in 2 months.
Music: Mostly rap, urban, hip-house, R&B and reggae. Current acts include rap groups, solo artists and urban dance groups.

DAVID MALDONADO MANAGEMENT, Suite 806, 568 Broadway, New York NY 10012. (212)925-2828. Vice President, A&R: Juan Toro. Represents individual artists and groups; currently handles 6 acts. Pays 25% commission. Reviews material for acts.
How to Contact: Prefers cassette and lyric sheet. Does not return unsolicited material. Reports in 3 weeks.
Music: Mostly house, dance, salsa, merengue; also pop/rock, light metal and dance/pop. Works primarily with vocalists. Current acts include Ruben Blades (rock), Chrissy I-Eece (pop/dance), Marc Anthony (pop/dance), Menudo (pop rock), Sa-Fire (dance) and Eddie Palmieri (salsa).

ED MALHOIT AGENCY, P.O. Box 2001, Claremont NH 03743. (603)542-9494. Agent: Ed Malhoit. Management firm and booking agency. Represents groups in eastern US; currently handles 5 acts. Receives 10-20% commission. Reviews material for acts.
How to Contact: Write first. Prefers cassette (or VHS videocassette of performance) with minimum 5 songs. SASE. Reports in 1 month.
Music: Rock, show, dance and bar bands. Current acts include 8084, Al Alessi Band, Fox, The Branches and The Broadcast, (all rock concert/club acts.)

RICK MARTIN PRODUCTIONS, 125 Fieldpoint Road, Greenwich CT 06830. (203)661-1615. President: Rick Martin. Personal manager and independent producer. "Office of Secretary of the National Conference of Personal Managers." Represents groups, artists/songwriters, actresses/vocalists and comedians/vocalists. Currently handles 6 acts. Receives 15-25% commission. "Occasionally, we are hired as consultants, production assistants or producers of recording projects." Reviews material for acts.
How to Contact: Prefers cassette (or VHS videocassette) with 2-4 songs. "Don't worry about an expensive presentation to personal managers or producers; they'll make it professional if they get involved." Artists should enclose a photo. SASE. "We prefer serious individuals who represent themselves professionally."
Music: Mostly top 40, rock and dance; also easy listening and pop. Produces rock dance groups, female vocalists, songwriters and actress/vocalists (pop). Current acts include Babe (all female revue — top 40), Marisa Mercedes (vocalist/pianist/songwriter), Sabel (actress/vocalist), Robert Gordon (artist/songwriter), Robert and Steven Capellan and Festible (Caribbean Revue).
Tips: "Don't spend a lot of money on recordings, but be prepared to have some financial backing if attempting to be an artist. Depend on yourself for everything including, most importantly, creativity. Present material in the simplest way."

MASTER TALENT, 245 Maple Ave. W., Vienna VA 22180. (703)281-2800. Owner/Agent: Steve Forssell. Booking agency. Estab. 1989. Represents local and regional (mid-Atlantic) individual artists and groups; currently handles 4 acts. Receives 10-20% commission.
How to Contact: Write or call first and obtain permission to submit. Prefers cassette (or VHS/Beta videocassette) with 4+ songs and lyric or lead sheet. SASE. Reports in 2 weeks.
Music: Mostly hard rock/metal, progressive/alternative and R&B/dance; also variety/covers. Works primarily with hard rock groups. Current acts include Fraidy Cat (pop metal), Silence (thrash metal), Danny Blitz (power pop), Blues Saraceno (guitar rock) and Randy Covek (bass instrumental rock).
Tips: "Submit only best work when it's *ready*. We're looking for professionally managed groups/artists with good publicist/promotion. Product in market is a plus."

*MCI MUSIC GROUP, Suite 830, 10 Universal Plaza, Universal CA 91608. (818)506-8533. Director: Max Diamond. Management firm, music publisher (Kellijant and Pollyann Music/ASCAP, Jankki Songs, Branmar Songs/BMI and Lonnvaness Music/SESAC) and record company (PPL, Bouview, Credence Records). Estab. 1979. Represents local, regional and international individual artists, groups and songwriters; currently handles 15 acts. Receives 25% commission. Reviews material for acts.
How to Contact: Write first and obtain permission to submit. Prefers cassette (or videocassette of performance) with no more than 4 songs and lyric or lead sheets. SASE. Reports in 1 month.
Music: Mostly R&B, pop and dance. Current acts include I.B. Fynne, Lejenz, D.M. Groove and Phuntaine.

*MEDIA PROMOTION ENTERPRISES, 423 6th Ave., Huntington WV 25701. (304)697-4222. Management firm and booking agency. Represents individual artists, groups and songwriters; currently handles 3 acts. Receives 15-20% commission; multinight 15%. Reviews material for acts.
How to Contact: Submit demo tape by mail (prefers live videocassette), "the simpler, the better." Does not return unsolicited material. "Wait for us to contact you." Reports in 1 month.
Music: Mostly MOR, country, pop and R&B. Works primarily with name entertainers, show groups, dance bands, and variety shows. Current acts include Allen Stotler (pianist/composer), Phillip Swann (songwriter/singer/keyboardist) and Michelle Rowe (songwriter/singer).

Tips: "Submit your tunes to major labels while working dates for us."

ALEX MELLON MANAGEMENT, P.O. Box 614, New Kensington PA 15068. (412)335-5152. President: Alex Mellon. Estab. 1978. Represents individual artists, groups and songwriters; currently handles 2 acts. Receives 20% commission. Reviews material for acts.
How to Contact: Prefers cassette or videocassette with 3-4 songs. "Video is almost a must. Everyone I deal with wants to 'see' the act." Does not return unsolicited material. Reports in 3 weeks.
Music: Mostly pop, rock and country. Works primarily with pop acts and songwriters. Current acts include Shilly Shally (pop act) and Stan Xidas (producer/songwriter).

*JOSEPH C. MESSINA, CARTOON RECORDS, 424 Mamaroneck Avenue, Mamaroneck NY 10543. (914)381-2565. Attorney/Manager. Represents artists, groups, songwriters, movie directors and screen writers; currently handles 3 acts. Receives negotiable commission
How To Contact: Prefers cassette with 1-2 songs and lead sheet. Does not return unsolicited material.
Music: Works primarily with male and female vocal/dance. Current acts include Andrea (top 40 dance) and Blue Clocks Green (performance artist).

*M-5 MANAGEMENT, INC., 23 SE 4th St., Minneapolis MN 55414. (612)331-3222. President: Micah McFarlane. Management firm. Estab. 1988. Represents Midwest groups; currently handles 2 acts. Receives 15% commission. Reviews material for acts.
How to Contact: Write or call first and obtain permission to submit. Prefers cassette or VHS video-cassette with 3 songs and lyric sheet. SASE. Reports in 1 month.
Music: Mostly pop, reggae and rock; also R&B and gospel. Works primarily with pop and reggae groups. Current acts include Ipso Facto (rock/reggae) and Julitta McFarlane (R&B/reggae).
Tips: "Make sure songs are complete in structure."

THE GILBERT MILLER AGENCY, INC., Suite 243, 21243 Ventura Blvd., Woodland Hills CA 91364. (818)377-5900. Agent: Jeff Miller. Booking agency. Represents musical and variety/novelty acts; currently handles 4 bands. Receives 15% commission. Reviews material for acts.
How to Contact: Prefers record, CD or cassette on a record label, 8x10 photo. "MTV-quality videos accepted. Will only call if song or group is accepted. Accepted groups will be notified in 2 weeks. No kits will be returned."
Music: Mostly rock. Works primarily with heavy metal hard rock, new wave, nostalgia rock and new age groups. Current acts include Eric Burdon and Robby Krieger (classic rock), Retaliation—starring Ansley Dunbar and Greg Wright (hard rock), Midnight Voyeur (hard rock), Terriff (heavy metal) and Perfect Stranger (new wave).

MKM MUSIC PRODUCTIONS LTD., Suite 503, 556 Laurier Avenue West, Ottowa, Ontario K1R 7X2 Canada. (613)234-5419. President: Michael Mitchell. Management firm. SOCAN (PROCAN and CAPAC). Estab.1982. Represents individual Canadian artists. Currently handles 3 acts. Receives 20% commission. Review material for acts.
How to Contact: Submit demo tape by mail. Unsolicited submissions are OK. Prefers cassette with 3 songs and lyric sheet. SASE. Reports in 3 weeks.
Music: Folk and pop. Works with concert folk groups. "Always interested in new, well written original material."

MOMENTUM MANAGEMENT, 4859-D Jackson St., Riverside CA 92503. (714)351-6967. Professional Manager: Sterling Pounds. Management firm. Estab. 1988. Represents local groups; currently handles 3 acts. Receives 20% commission. Reviews material for acts. Specializes in professional development.
How to Contact: Prefers cassette or 7½ ips reel-to-reel (or VHS videocassette of performance) with 3-4 songs and lyric sheets. Videocassettes should be "only professional productions. Please, no home videos." May submit albums, EP, 12" singles, etc. SASE. Retains all material for future reference.
Music: Mostly rock, pop and modern rock; also anything unique. Works primarily with local bands (mostly new talent). Current acts include Big Feel (pop/rock), The Remnant (pop/rock) and Undeniable Faith (dance/rock).
Tips: "Honesty works best. Artists shouldn't submit unless they are ready to hear the truth about their work."

Market conditions are constantly changing! If you're still using this book and it is 1993 or later, buy the newest edition of Songwriter's Market at your favorite bookstore or order directly from Writer's Digest Books.

*MORSE ENTERTAINMENT GROUP, INC., P.O. Box 6980, Beverly Hills CA 90212. (213)276-9261. Contacts: Adam Sandler, Mark Adams, Eric Ross, Cathy Gooden. Management firm and record company (Litigous Records). Estab. 1982. Represents local, regional and international individual artists, groups and songwriters; currently handles 6 acts. Receives 15% commission. Reviews material for acts.
How to Contact: Submit demo tape by mail. Unsolicited submissions are OK. Prefers cassette with 3-5 songs and lyric sheet. SASE. Reports in 2 weeks.
Music: Mostly rock and pop. Works primarily with solo artists, rock acts, and groups and artists who are hyphenates; i.e. singer-songwriter-producer. Current acts include Aviators (rock band) and Kilowatt (rock band).
Tips: "Send us your best stuff—don't ask us to hear through a lousy mix or unfinished demos—put your best foot forward."

MOZART MIDNIGHT PRODUCTIONS, Suite 613, 410 S. Michigan Ave., Chicago IL 60605. (312)477-6644. President: Don Kaufman. Management firm. Estab. 1982. Represents international individual artists, groups and songwriters; currently handles 8 acts. Receives 20-25% commission. Reviews material for acts.
How to Contact: Submit demo tape by mail. Unsolicited submissions are OK. Prefers cassette with 3-10 songs and lyric sheet. Does not return unsolicited material. Reports in 1 month.
Music: Mostly dance-pop, light rock and R&B; also metal, ballads and rap. Works primarily with singer/songwriters. Current acts include Kevin Irving (lead singer of Club Nouveau), Darksyde (rap group) and Tribal Opera (progressive rock group).

*MUSIC MANAGEMENT ASSOCIATES, A Sound Column Company, Suite 258, 27 Music Square E., Nashville TN 37203. (615)244-4331. President: Ron Simpson. Estab. 1991. Management company, affiliated with Sound Column Productions. Represents individual artists, bands and songwriters. "Our specialty is helping our clients take the "significant next step," i.e. market focus, material selection, demo recordings, image/photos, contacting industry on artist's behalf, etc. Various fee structures include commission, project bid, hourly rate. We can sometimes secure third party financing to develope unique, exciting artists."
How to Contact: Unsolicited submissions are OK. Should include cassette, VHS video (optional), photos. No returned materials or correspondence without SASE and sufficient postage.
Music: All styles except metal, rap. Demos for Osborn Sisters (now signed to RCA/Nashville); artist development projects for actress/contemporary folk artist Emily Pearson (L.A.), pop/dance artist Shawn Keliiliki (Hawaii). Career direction for Kevin Giddins & Lita Little, (R&B artists from Utah); songplugging for Rob Honey, Nashville (song placed on Arista album).

MUSIC, MARKETING & PROMOTIONS, INC., P.O. Box 22, South Holland IL 60473. (219)365-2516. President: Michael Haines. Management firm. Estab. 1987. Represents international individual artists, groups and songwriters; currently handles 3 acts. Receives 15-20% commission. Reviews material for acts.
How to Contact: Write or call first and obtain permission to submit. Prefers cassette (VHS videocassette if available) with 3-4 songs and lyric sheet. SASE. Reports in 3 weeks.
Music: Mostly rock, country and pop; also R&B. Works primarily with pop/rock bands, solo artists and songwriters. Current acts include John Kontol (singer/songwriter), Rick Anthony (country songwriter) and Face of Luxury (pop/rock band).
Tips: "Send clear demos. We're most interested in the song, not the production, but it must be audible."

MUSIC STAR AGENCY, INC. (INTERNATIONAL HEADQUARTERS), 106 Main St., Binghamton NY 13905. (607)724-4304 and (607)772-0857. Attn: Talent Coordinator. Booking agency with 92 international offices. Represents US and Canadian artists "to be marketed worldwide primarily in hotels, top 40/rock clubs, military installations, conventions, fairs, colleges and concert venues. Currently handles more than 1,000 acts. Receives 20% commission. Reviews material for acts. Submits material to buyers, recording companies, production companies and managers.
How to Contact: Prefers cassette (or VHS videocassette if available) with 1-4 songs "that most represent your act, along with current promo package. In preparing videos, quality audio and video must be maintained throughout the tape. Adequate lighting and professional audio and video engineers will help. Keep the clips short and visually exciting."
Music: Mostly top 40 lounge, top 40 country, top 40 rock and oldies. Works primarily with top 40 touring hotel acts from solo entertainers to show bands. Current acts include Boxtops, Beatlemania, Jay & The Techniques and Vogues (top 40 show bands).

Tips: "Professional quality promotional materials (photos, tape, songlist, equipment list) are essential to securing good engagements for any act. A business-like approach to the music business is also essential."

MUSKRAT PRODUCTIONS, INC., 44 N. Central Ave., Elmsford NY 10523. (914)592-3144. Contact: Bruce McNichols. Estab. 1970. Represents individuals and groups; currently represents 15 acts. Deals with artists in the New York City area. Reviews material for acts.
How to Contact: Write first. Prefers cassette (or short videocassette of performance) with 3 songs minimum. SASE. Reports "only if interested."
Music: "We specialize in old-time jazz, dixieland and banjo music and shows;" also old time, nostalgia, country and jazz. Works primarily with dixieland, banjo/sing-along groups to play parties, Mexican mariachi bands and specialty acts for theme parties, dances, shows and conventions. Current acts include Smith Street Society Jazz Band (dixieland jazz), Your Father's Mustache (banjo sing-along), Roaring 20s Revue (show and dance band) and Harry Hepcat and the Boogie Woogie Band (50s rock revival).

FRANK NANOIA PRODUCTIONS AND MANAGEMENT, 1999 N. Sycamore Ave., Los Angeles CA 90068. (213)874-8725. President: Frank Nanoia. Management and production firm. Represents artists, groups and songwriters. Produces TV specials and concerts. Currently handles 15 acts. Receives 15-25% commission. Reviews material for acts.
How to Contact: Prefers 7½, 15 ips reel-to-reel or cassette (or videocassette of live performance, if available) with 3-5 songs and lyric and lead sheets. "Professional quality please. Check sound quality as well." Does not return unsolicited material. Reports "only if material is above average. No phone calls please."
Music: Mostly R&B and dance, also top 40/pop, jazz fusion, country, easy listening, MOR, gospel and soul. Works primarily with soloists, Latin jazz and R&B groups. Current acts include Marc Allen Trujillo (vocalist/songwriter); Paramour (R&B show group), and Gilberto Duron (recoring artist). Current productions include "The Golden Eagle Awards," The Caribbean Musical Festival and "The Joffrey Ballet/CSU Awards."

*NATIONAL ENTERTAINMENT, INC., Suite 6, 5366 N., Northwest Hwy., Chicago IL 60630. (312)545-8222. FAX: (312)545-3714. President/General Manager: Roger Connelly. Management firm and booking agency. Estab. 1989. Represents local, regional and international individual artists, groups and songwriters; currently handles 100 acts. Receives 15% commission. Reviews material for acts.
How to Contact: Write or call first and obtain permission to submit. Prefers cassette (or VHS videocassette if available) with 1 song and lyric sheet. SASE. Reports in 2 weeks.
Music: Mostly pop, rock and R&B. Works primarily with dance bands, singers and singer/songwriters. Current acts include Dave Pisciotto (guitarist/songwriter), Dynasty (8 piece dance band) and Ivory (5 pc. dance band).
Tips: "Your promotional package is our only representation of your talent. Be prepared to take the necessary steps to organize your materials into a professional presentation."

NELSON MANAGEMENT, Francisco de Rojas, 9, Madrid 28010 **Spain**. Phone: (1)445 12 07. Director: Nelson Hernán Muñoz. Management firm, booking agency and music publisher. Estab. 1980. Represents individual artists, groups and songwriters; currently handles 20 acts. Receives 20% commission. Reviews material for acts.
How to Contact: Write first and obtain permission to submit or to arrange personal interview. Prefers cassette (or VHS/PAL videocassette if available) with 5 songs and lyric or lead sheets. Does not return unsolicited material.
Music: Mostly jazz, fusion and ethnic music. Works primarily with show bands, vocalists, musicians and songwriters. Current acts include Dissidenten (ethno music), Carles Benavent (jazz-fusion) and Pedro Iturralde (jazz).
Tips: "Send us professional samples of your work with the conditions of the type of deal you are looking for."

*NELSON ROAD MANAGEMENT, 138 Nelson Rd., Sth. Melb., Vic. 3205 **Australia**. Phone: (613)6991000. A&R Manager: Andrea Steinfeld. Management firm and music publisher (Ideal Music P/L). Estab. 1981. Represents local, regional and international individual artists, groups and songwriters; currently handles 6 acts. Receives 20% commission. Reviews material for acts.
How to Contact: Submit demo tape by mail. Unsolicited submissions are OK. Prefers cassette (or PAL, VHS videocassette if available) with no more than 5 songs and lyric sheet). Does not return unsolicited material. Reports in 1 month.

Music: Mostly rock, pop and R&B; also hard rock, dance and rap. Works primarily with pop/rock bands and solo artists. Current acts include Mighty Big Crime (pop/rap duo), Brian Mannix (pop/rock solo), and The Prostitutes (dance/rock act).
Tips: "Have good material with commercial potential. Be polite, patient and persistent."

NEW ARTIST'S PRODUCTIONS, 131 Connecticut Ave., N. Bay Shore NY 11706. Professional Department: Jeannie G. Walker. Management firm, record company and music publisher. Estab. 1984. Represents individual artists, groups and songwriters; currently handles 45-60 acts. Receives 20% commission. Reviews material for acts.
How to Contact: Prefers cassette (or professionally prepared videocassette) and lyric sheet; prefers professional videos. SASE. Reports in 8 weeks.
Music: Mostly pop, country and easy listening; also rock, gospel and blues. Works primarily with vocalists and dance bands. Current acts include Rory Bennett (night club act), Cherokee (vocalist & dance band), and Anjel (vocalist).
Tips: "New Artist's Productions will listen to all newcomers in the music field. We will evaluate and give an honest opinion of their songs and help them produce, arrange or market the songs we feel show potential."

*NEW AUDIENCE PRODUCTIONS, INC., 155 West 72nd St., New York NY 10027. (212)595-5272. President: Julius Lukin; Vice President: Eric Lardsman; Director of Artist Relations: Bobby Weiser. Management firm. Estab. 1971. Represents local, regional and international individual artists, groups and songwriters; currently handles 2 acts. Reviews material for acts.
How to Contact: Write first and obtain permission to submit. Prefers cassette (or VHS videocassette if available) with an unspecified number of songs and lyric sheet. Does not return unsolicited material. Reports in 3 weeks.
Music: Mostly rock, pop and jazz; also R&B.

NEW STARS ENTERTAINMENT AGENCY, "Foxhollow," West End, Nailsea Bristol BS19 2DB **United Kingdom**. Proprietor: David Rees. Management firm and booking agency. Estab. 1983. Represents individual artists, groups, songwriters, comedians and specialty acts—all types. Currently handles over 200 acts. Receives 15% commission. Reviews material for acts.
How to Contact: "Songwriters write and ask for type of material we are presently seeking." Prefers cassette with 3 songs and lyric sheet. SAE and IRC. Reports in 1 month.
Music: Mostly MOR, pop, 60s style, country and rock. Works primarily with vocal guitarists/keyboards, pop groups, pub/club acts, guitar or keyboard duos. Current acts include Legend (duo), Ocean (four-piece group), Brotherhood of Man and Chris Holland.
Tips: "Our business is mainly at venues wanting artists who perform well-known covers. Original material can be introduced during an evening as a feature, and this is often an easy way of getting people to accept it, rather than the 'take it or leave it' attitude."

NORTHSTAR MANAGEMENT INC., 33532 Five Mile Rd., Livonia MI 48154. (313)427-6010. President: Angel Gomez. Management firm. Estab. 1979. Represents local and international individual artists, groups and songwriters; currently handles 4 acts. Receives 10-25% commission. Reviews material for acts.
How to Contact: Submit demo tape by mail. Unsolicited submissions are OK. Prefers cassette (or videocassette of performance) with 3-5 songs. SASE. Reports in 4 weeks.
Music: Mostly rock, pop and top 40; also metal. Works primarily with individual artists, groups (bar bands) and songwriters. Current acts include Think Pink (new music), Billy the Kid (rock), Controversy (Top-40) and Hunter Brucks (rock).
Tips: "Think about what you're sending. Are you proud? If so, send it!"

*NOVEAU TALENT, 1006 S. Marshall, Midland TX 79701. (915)682-6333. Producer/Manager: Mel Hinojos. Management firm, booking agency and an independent songwriter/producer. New company. Represents local, regional and international individual artists, groups, songwriters and musicians. Reviews material for acts.
How to Contact: Submit demo tape by mail. Unsolicited submissions are OK. Prefers cassette with 2-4 songs and lyric or lead sheets (if possible). Does not return unsolicited material. Reports in 2 weeks.
Music: Mostly pop, R&B and soul; also new styles. Works primarily with vocalists and bands.
Tips: "Don't quit. An artist/songwriter is as much a business diplomat as he/she is an entertainer."

*CRAIG NOWAG'S NATIONAL ATTRACTIONS, 6037 Haddington Drive, Memphis TN 38119-7423. (901)767-1990. Owner/President: Craig Nowag. Booking agency. Estab. 1958. Represents local, regional and international individual artists and groups; currently handles 37 acts. Receives 15-25% commission.

How to Contact: Submit demo tape by mail. Unsolicited submissions are OK. Prefers cassette (or VHS videocassette if available) with 3-5 songs. Does not return unsolicited material. Reports in 5 weeks.
Music: Mostly R&B, pop and blues; also pop/rock, crossover country and re-makes. Works primarily with oldies record acts, dance bands, blues bands, rock groups, R&B dance bands and nostalgia groups. Current acts include Andy Childs (pop), Johnny Tillotson and The Famous Unknowns.
Tips: "If the buying public won't buy your song, live act or record you have no saleability, and no agent or manager can do anything for you."

N2D, P.O. Box 121682, Nashville TN 37212-1682. Contact: Douglas Casmus. Management firm and publisher (Breezeway Publishing Companies). Represents artists, groups, songwriters and comedians; currently handles 2 acts. Reviews material for acts.
How to Contact: Prefers cassette with 2 songs and lyric sheet. Does not return material. Reports only if interested.
Music: Country, rock and comedy. Current acts include David Murphy and Johnny Cobb (rock). "We've had songs recorded by Julio Iglesias, Ray Charles, John Denver, John Conlee, Dobie Gray and more."
Tips: "Looking for great songs—any format. Also open to crazy and novelty material."

OAK STREET MUSIC, 301-140 Bannatyne Ave., Winnipeg, Manitoba R3B 3C5 **Canada**. Phone: (204)957-0085. FAX: (204)943-3588. CEO: Gilles Paquin. Record label and music publisher. Estab. 1987. Roster includes performers, songwriters and musicians; currently handles 12 acts. Sister company, Paquin Entertainment Group, heads up the artist management division.
How to Contact: Unsolicited material accepted. Prefers cassette (or VHS videocassette if available) with maximum 4 songs and lyric or lead sheet. "Something which shows the artist's capabilities—doesn't need to be fancy. Be *factual*." SASE please.
Music: Primarily a family entertainment label, with interest also in the pop/rock genres. Current acts include Fred Penner (children's entertainer), Al Simmons (singer/actor/comic) and Norman Foote (singer/songwriter, puppeteer).

*OB-1 ENTERTAINMENT, P.O. Box 22552, Nashville TN 37202. (615)672-0307. Partner-in-charge: Jim O'Baid. Management firm and artist development. Estab. 1990. Represents local, regional and international individual artists, groups and songwriters; currently handles 2 acts. Receives 10-20% commission. Reviews material for acts.
How to Contact: Submit demo tape by mail. Unsolicited submissions are OK. Prefers cassette (or VHS videocassette if available) with 3 songs. Does not return unsolicited material. Reports in 3 months.
Music: Mostly country, pop and R&B; also rock. Works primarily with singer/songwriters and groups. Current acts include Jeannie Cruz (singer/songwriter) and Casey Rockefeller (singer/songwriter).
Tips: "Keep your ego in place. Be able to accept criticism."

THE OFFICE, INC., Suite 44G, 322 W 57th, New York NY 10019. President: John Luongo. Management firm, music publisher (ASCAP/BMI) and production company. Estab. 1983. Represents local, regional and international individual artists, groups, songwriters and producer/engineers. Currently handles 6 acts. Receives 25% commission. Reviews material for acts.
How to Contact: Write or call first and obtain permission to submit. Prefers cassette (or VHS videocassette if available) with 2 songs and lyric sheets. Does not return unsolicited material. Reports in 4 weeks.
Music: Mostly hard rock/pop, R&B and CHR/top 40; also dance. Works primarily with groups—female vocalists; solo R&B, male or female. Current acts include Joy Winter (female/dance), Traci Blue (female rock) and Oliver Who? (R&B male vocalist on Zoo/BMG).
Tips: "Do your homework before you submit."

*OLDIES-BUT-GOODIES SPECIALTY!, #252, 1840 South Gaffey St., San Pedro Peninsula CA 90731. (213)514-0920. President: R. Perez. Management firm, promoter, music publisher (ASCAP, BMI) and record company (Scrapbook Records). Estab. 1980. Represents local and regional individual artists, groups and songwriters. Receives 15-20% commission. Reviews material for acts.
How to Contact: Prefers cassette with an unlimited number of songs and lyric and lead sheets. Reports in 2 weeks.
Music: Mostly '50 and '60s oldies but goodies, R&B/blues and rockabilly; also doo-wop/rock-n-roll, '50s and '60s instrumentals (surf-rock sounds) and standards/pop/vintage nostalgia. Works primarily with vocalists, instrumentalists, combos, arrangers, producers, writers and studio engineers. Current acts include Johnny and The Hurricanes, Dick Dale and The Del-Tones, The Ventures and Duane Eddy and The Rebels.

Tips: "No ego hassles. Maintain professional integrity."

ON THE LEVEL MUSIC!, 807 South Xanthus Pl., Tulsa OK 74104-3620. President: Fred Gage. Management firm and booking agency. Estab. 1971. Represents individual artists, groups and songwriters; currently handles 12 acts. Receives 15-25% commission. Reviews material for acts.
How to Contact: Write first for permission to submit. Prefers cassette (or VHS videocassette if available) with 4 songs and lyric or lead sheets. For video: "Full length not needed, short clips only." SASE. Reports in 1 month.
Music: Mostly rock, pop and gospel. Works primarily with rock groups ("arena size to bar bands"). Current acts include Second Chapter of Acts (Christian rock), Wendy Talbot (folk), Disciple (rock), Jamie Norathomas (folk/rock), Terry Talbot (folk/rock), Toymakers Dream (Broadway type) and Tayra Antolick (show rock).
Tips: "Be great not just good and be hungry to make it."

*ON TOUR PRODUCTIONS, 4600 Iris St., Rockville MD 20853. (301)946-9093. President A&R: Dana Sharpe. Management firm, booking agency and promotion agency. Estab. 1989. Represents national individual artists and groups; currently handles 25 acts. Receives 15% commission. Reviews material for acts.
How to Contact: Submit demo tape by mail. Unsolicited submissions are OK. Prefers cassette or VHS videocassette with 3 songs and lyric sheet. SASE. Reports in 6 weeks.
Music: Mostly rock, progressive and metal; also any rock styles and punk/hardcore. Current acts include Skin and Bones (rock), Quade (top 40 rock) and Mark Phillips (acoustic guitar/writer).
Tips: "Be brief but to the point. Long-winded demo packs and full EP cassettes are a pain. What I need is a tape, photo, history or bio (once again, be brief), song list (include covers) and employment history (in music)."

OPEN DOOR MANAGEMENT, Suite 365, 15327 Sunset Blvd., Pacific Palisades CA 90272. (213)459-2559. President: Bill Traut. Associate: Carol Neu. Management firm and production company (Open Door Management and Bill Traut Productions). Represents artists, groups and songwriters; currently handles 8 acts. Receives 20% commission. "We are sometimes paid $240/hour as consultants, and we also package with the artist on a 50/50 basis from time to time." Reviews material for acts.
How to Contact: Prefers cassette with 1-4 songs (or videocassette with 2-3 songs). SASE "with enough postage." Reports in 3 months.
Music: Mostly new A/C, jazz, New Age and acoustic singer/songwriters. Artists include Eliza Gilkyson (new A/C singer/songwriter, Gold Castle Records); Steve Kujala (classical/jazz/fusion flute, Sonic Edge Records); and Oregon (jazz, New Age group, Epic Records); The Greene String Quartet (classical, jazz, pop group, Virgin classics); Ross Traut/SteveRodby (jazz/new A/C, Columbia Records); and Tony Williams (jazz, Blue Note Records).
Tips: "Quality is important to us, both of the music and of the presentation. Send a current photo and your credits along with your demos."

OPERATION MUSIC ENTERPRISES, 1400 E. Court St., Ottumwa IA 52501. (515)682-8283. President: Nada C. Jones. Management firm and booking agency. Represents artists, groups and songwriters; currently handles 4 acts. Receives 15% commission. Reviews material for acts.
How to Contact: Prefers cassette (or VHS videocassette if available) and lyric sheet. "Keep material simple. Groups—use *only group* members—don't add extras. Artists should include references. SASE. Reports in 2 months.
Music: Mostly country; also blues. Works primarily with vocalists and show and dance groups. Current acts include Reesa Kay Jones (country vocalist and recording artist), John Richards Show, Country Class, Prairie Fire and Larry Gillaspie, the Rocky Mountain White Water Band and White River Country (country/bluegrass).

ORACLE ENTERTAINMENT, #1109, 225 Lafayette St., New York NY 10012. (212)925-9599. President: George Gilbert. Vice President: Walter Winnick. Management firm. Estab. 1988. Represents local, regional or international individual artists, groups and songwriters; currently handles 3 acts. Receives 20% commission. Reviews material for acts.
How to Contact: Submit demo tape by mail. Unsolicited submissions are OK. Prefers cassette (or VHS or 3/4" videocassette if available) with any number of songs. SASE. Reports in several weeks (depending on how busy we are at that time).
Music: Mostly rock, pop and metal. Works primarily with national rock bands. Current acts include Meat Loaf, O-Positive and Marchello (all rock bands).
Tips: "Submit as much (and as big a variety of) music as possible."

OREGON MUSICAL ARTISTS, P.O. Box 122, Yamhill OR 97148. (503)662-3309. Contact: Michael D. LeClair. Management firm and production agency. Estab. 1982. Represents artists, groups and songwriters; currently handles 3 acts. Receives 10-25% commission. Reviews material for acts.
How to Contact: Prefers cassette with 3-10 songs and lyric sheet (or videocassette if available). Does not return unsolicited material. Reports in 1 month.
Music: Mostly top 40/pop and R&B; also blues, church/religous, country, dance, easy listening, gospel, jazz, MOR, progressive, hard and mellow rock and soul. Works primarily with writers and bar bands "with excellent vocalists." Current acts include The Hoyt Brothers (easy country ballads), Lee Garrett (songwriter) and Boomer Band (50's bar band).

ORIGINAL PROJECTS UNLIMITED, INC., 36 West 3rd Ave., Denver CO 80223. (303)722-9653. President: Lauri Day-Workman. Management firm (Orignal Projects Unlimited, Inc.). Estab. 1986. Represents international groups and producers/engineers; handles 3 acts. Receives 15-20% commission.
How to Contact: Submit demo tape by mail. Unsolicited submissions are OK. Prefers cassette with 3-4 songs, lyric sheet and photo/promotional/package. SASE. Reports in 4-6 weeks.
Music: Mostly rock, metal and pop; also alternative. Works primarily with rock and heavy metal bands; producers/engineers. Current acts include Strange Parade (rock/band), Dogs of Pleasure (rock/band) and Geoffrey Workman (producer/engineer).
Tips: "Must be original, hardworking and professional. Mostly interested in bands that promote themselves, believe in themselves and have some knowledge of the music business. Must be marketable."

***ORPHEUS ENTERTAINMENT,** P.O. Box 647, Orange NJ 07051. (201)375-5671. President: Chuck Brownley. Contact: A&R Department. Management firm and production company. Estab. 1978. Represents music and variety artists, producers and songwriters; currently handles 5 acts. Receives up to 20% commission. Reviews material for acts. Produces live concerts and sound and video recordings.
How to Contact: Query by mail. Prefers cassette (or videocassette) with 1-3 songs and lead sheet. Does not return material.
Music: Mostly pop; also jazz, comedy, MOR, progressive, R&B, rock, soul, top 40 and fusion. Works primarily with original recording and concert artists. Current acts include Suburban Dog and Elko Band.

***OVERLAND PRODUCTIONS,** 1775 Broadway, New York NY 10019. (212)489-4820. Director of Publishing: Andrea Starr. Management firm, music publisher, record company (Radioactive) and record producer (Overland Production Co.). Represents local, regional and international individual artists, groups and songwriters; currently handles 10 acts. Reviews material for acts.
How to Contact: Write or call first and obtain permission to submit. Prefers cassette (or VHS videocassette if available) with 3-5 songs and lyric sheet. Does not return unsolicited submissions. Reports in 6 weeks.
Music: Mostly rock, pop and R&B; also modern music and dance. Interested in "innovative, intelligent, progressive-rockin." Current acts include David Byrne, Dee-Lite, Ramones, Debbie Harry, Talking Heads, The Toll, B.A.D., Tom Tom Club.
Tips: "Submit 3-5 of best songs—neatly labeled with pix, press bio and video (if available). Listing of any upcoming gigs."

***PALMETTO PRODUCTIONS,** P.O. Box 1376, Pickens SC 29671. (803)855-7065. Owner/President: Brian E. Raines. Management firm, booking agency, music publisher (Brian Raines Music/ASCAP, Brian Song Music/BMI) and record company (Palmetto Records, Rosada Records). Estab. 1985. Represents Southeast regional artists, local individual artists, groups and songwriters; currently handles 4 acts. Receives 20-25% commission. Reviews material for acts.
How to Contact: Submit demo tape by mail. Unsolicited submissions are OK. Prefers cassette (or VHS videocassette if available) with 1 song and lyric sheet. Does not return unsolicited material. Reports in 1 month.
Music: Mostly country, gospel and novelty. Works primarily with artists who already have some regional airplay or recorded material. Current acts include Brian Raines (country vocalist), Country Earl (country vocalist) and Jim Hubbard (gospel vocalist).
Tips: "Send material with photo of artist and/or writer. Send 1 song on a demo, prefer studio demo. Be professional, and don't send a letter stating how big of a hit song you know you have."

***PAQUIN ENTERTAINMENT GROUP,** 108-93 Lombard Ave., Winnipeg MB R3B 3B1 **Canada**. (204)917-9200. Artist Relations: Richard Mills. Management firm and booking agency. Estab. 1984. Represents local, regional and international individual artists; currently handles 3 acts. Reviews material for acts.

How to Contact: Write or call first and obtain permission to submit. Prefers cassette or VHS video-cassette with 3 songs and lyric sheet. Does not return unsolicited material. Reports in 3 weeks.
Music: Mostly children's music, folk music and comedy; also New Age and classical. Works primarily with family performers. Current acts include Fred Penner (family entertainer/songwriter), Norman Foote (entertainer/songwriter) and Al Simmons (entertainer/songwriter).

PARADISE PRODUCTIONS, Box 29367, Honolulu HI 96820. (808)924-3301. General Manager: Kathy Koran. Management firm and booking agency. Estab. 1971. Represents artists, groups and songwriters. Currently handles 25 acts. Receives minimum 15% commission. Reviews material for acts.
How to Contact: Prefers cassette (or VHS videocassette if available) with minimum 4 songs and lyric sheet. SASE. Reports in 1 week.
Music: Mostly rock, top 40/pop, soul, easy listening and Las Vegas style show groups; also dance-oriented, jazz, MOR, progressive, R&B and light rock. Works primarily with Las Vegas show groups, dance bands, vocalists and high energy rock concert groups. Current acts include Rod Young (Las Vegas show band), Triple X (concert rock group), Bobby Hutton (soul/pop show group) and Alexander Butterfield (soul/show/pop group).
Tips: "Top notch polished material is what we need."

JACKIE PAUL MANAGEMENT AND CONSULTANT FIRM, 559 Wanamaker Rd., Jenkintown PA 19046. (215)884-3308. FAX: (215)884-1083. President: Jackie Paul. Management firm (Terrance Moore Music, Inc./BMI). Estab. 1985. Represents local and national artists, groups, producers and musicians. Currently handles 2 acts. Receives 15-35% commission. Reviews material for acts.
How to Contact: Call first and obtain permission to submit. Prefers cassette (or VHS videocassette if available) with 1-3 songs and lyric or lead sheets. "It's not mandatory but if possible, I would prefer a videocassette. A video simply helps get the song across visually. Do the best to help portray the image you represent, with whatever resources possible." SASE. Reports in 2-4 weeks.
Music: Mostly rap, pop and R&B/dance. Works primarily with vocalists (all original acts). Current acts include Blue Eagle (pop singer/songwriter, drummer/producer) and Terrance T'Luv (R&B-dance singer/songwriter/producer).

PERFORMANCE GROUP, P.O. Box 40825, Washington DC 20016. (301)320-4137. President: Dennis Oppenheimer. Management firm. Estab. 1984. Represents local, regional and international individual artists, groups and songwriters; currently handles 6 acts. Receives 20% commission. Reviews material for acts.
How to Contact: Submit demo tape by mail. "Performance videos preferred." Unsolicited submissions are OK. Prefers cassette with 3-5 songs. SASE. Reports in 2 weeks.
Music: Mostly rock, pop and dance. Works primarily with vocalists and original bands. Current acts include Renaissance, Judy Bats, Niagara, Patricia Kaas, Shadowman and East is East.
Tips: "Include bio and photo."

***PERFORMERS OF THE WORLD**, #215, 14011 Ventura Blvd., Sherman Oaks CA 91423. (818)995-2495. President: Terry Rindal. Booking agency. Estab. 1989. Represents local, regional and international individual artists and groups; currently handles 45 acts.
How to Contact: Submit demo tape by mail. Unsolicited submissions are OK. Prefers cassette (or VHS videocassette if available) with several songs and lyric sheet. Does not return unsolicited material. Reports in 3 weeks. "Send SASE or portrait for reply."
Music: Mostly world music, jazz and R&B; also folk and pop. Current acts include David Wilcox (folk singer/songwriter), Jon Hendricks (jazz singer), Eliza Gilkyson (singer/songwriter), Zachary Richard (cajun rocker) and Hugh Masekela (South African trumpeter).

PAUL PETERSON CREATIVE MANAGEMENT, #309, 9005 Cynthia, Los Angeles CA 90069. (213)273-7255. Contact: Paul Peterson. Management firm. Represents artists and groups from the Midwest and West Coast; currently handles 4 acts. Receives 20% commission. Reviews material for acts.
How to Contact: Prefers cassette (or ¼″ or VHS videocassette if available) with 2-4 songs and lyric sheet. SASE. Reports in 3 weeks.
Music: Mostly pop/rock and rock; also jazz and alternative rock. Works with rock bands doing original material. Current acts include Man About Town (pop/rock band), Guido Toledo (alternative rock), Young and Restless (pop/rock) and Brian Savage (jazz/New Age).

PHOENIX TALENT, LTD., #1847, 332 South Michigan, Chicago IL 60604. (312)786-2024. President: Lou Johnson. Management firm and booking agency (AF of M, AFTRA and SAG). Estab. 1986. Represents local, regional or international individual artists, groups and songwriters; currently handles 5 acts. Receives 10-15% commission. Reviews material for acts.

How to Contact: Submit demo tape by mail—unsolicited submissions are OK. Prefers cassette with 3 songs and lead sheets. SASE. Reports in 4 weeks.

Music: Mostly R&B, pop and rap; also gospel and jazz. Works primarily with singer/songwriters who have producer capabilities (R&B/dance). Current acts include Stanley Turrentine (sax), Peter Black and Darryl Pandy (singer).

Tips: "Your material should always be studio quality and practically finished, with the fullest sound possible. Have a flair for what's happening now but still retain your individuality."

*PLATINUM EARS LTD., 285 Chestnut St., West Hempstead NY 11552. (516)489-0738. President: Mike Siskind. Management firm, music publisher (Siskatune Music Publishing Co./BMI) and record company (Storehouse Records). Estab. 1988. Represents local, regional and international individual artists, groups and songwriters; currently handles 3 acts. Receives 15-20% commission. Reviews material for acts.

How to Contact: Submit demo tape by mail. Unsolicited submissions are OK. Prefers cassette (or VHS videocassette if available) with 5-8 songs and lyric sheet. Reports in 3 months.

Music: Mostly rock, pop and R&B; also blues, world beat and jazz. Works primarily with bands (primarily rock of some type). Current acts include Van Gogh's Ear (rock) and Michael Ellis (songwriter).

Tips: "Be professional and don't second guess decisions. As students of the business of music, we attempt to place you with reputable people. If a deal seems too good to be true, many times it is."

PLATINUM GOLD MUSIC, #1200, 9200 Sunset Blvd., Los Angeles CA 90069. Managers: Steve Cohen/David Cook. Management firm and music publisher. ASCAP. Estab. 1978. Represents local or regional (East or West coasts) individual artists, groups and songwriters; currently handles 3-4 acts. Receives 15-20% commission. Reviews material for acts.

How to Contact: Write or call first and obtain permission to submit. Prefers cassette (or VHS videocassette if available) with 3 songs and lyric sheets. Does not return unsolicited material.

Music: Mostly interested in contemporary R&B, dance/pop, hip hop/rap; also pop rock, hard rock and pop. Works most often with vocalists. Current acts include Troop (R&B vocal group) and Def Jef (rap/hip hop).

Tips: "No ballads. We do not look for potential; be prepared and professional before coming to us—and ready to relocate to West Coast if necessary."

*POSSIBILITIES UNLIMITED, INC., 2146 Champions Way, N. Lauderdale FL 33068. (305)721-7342. Owner: Patricia M. Hudson. Booking artists in overseas markets. (Japan, Singapore, England, Canada). Currently handles 25 acts. Receives 15-20% commission. Reviews material for acts. Does marketing (shopping) of tapes and artists to record companies and publishers, etc.

How to Contact: Prefers cassette with lyric sheet (VHS videocassette for performing artists). SASE. Reports in 1 month.

Music: Mostly R&B, top 40 for performance; all types for songwriters.

Tips: "Only want professional demos and/or promotional packages."

POWER STAR MANAGEMENT, #618, 6981 N. Park Dr., Pennsauken NJ 08109. (609)486-1480. President: Brian Kushner. Management firm (Power Star Management). Estab. 1981. Represents international individual artists and groups; currently handles 4 acts. Receives 20% commission. Reviews material for acts.

How to Contact: Submit demo tape by mail. Unsolicited submissions are OK. Prefers cassette (or VHS videocassette if available) with 4 songs and lyric sheet. SASE. Reports in 3 weeks.

Music: Mostly pop/dance, rock and R&B. Current acts include Britny Fox, Alisha, Tuff and Mariah.

PPK AG, Wiesliacher 21, Zurich CH-8053 **Switzerland**. Phone: (01)383 77 55. FAX: (01)383 77 60. Director: Fritz Portner. Management firm and music publisher (PPK Publishing). Represents individual artists, songwriters and producers; currently handles 3 acts. Receives 20-30% commission. Reviews material for acts.

How to Contact: Prefers cassette with 1-5 songs and lyric sheet. SAE and IRC. Reports in 5 weeks.

Music: Mostly country and R&B. Works primarily with vocalists and country bands. Current acts include John Brack (country), Angelika Milster (musical) and Chet & Ray (boogie).

PREMIER ARTISTS, 9 Dundas Ln., Albert Park, Victoria 3206 **Australia**. (03)699-9555. FAX: (03)695-7819. Booking agency. Estab. 1975. Represents groups; currently handles 100 acts. Receives 10% commission. Reviews material for acts.

How to Contact: Prefers cassette (or VHS videocassette of live performance, if available) with 2 or 3 songs. Does not return unsolicited material. Reports in 2 weeks.
Music: Mostly rock and pop. Works primarily with bar bands. Current acts include John Farnham, Jimmy Barnes, Boom Crash Opera, The Angels and Crowded House.

PROCESS TALENT MANAGEMENT, 439 Wiley Ave., Franklin PA 16323. (814)432-4633. Contact: Norman Kelly. Management firm. Estab. 1970. Represents artists and groups; currently handles 4-8 acts. Receives 10-15% commission. Reviews material for acts.
How to Contact: Write or call first and obtain permission to submit. Prefers 7½ ips reel-to-reel, cassette or 8-track cartridge with 2-6 songs. "Send your best songs and performances with photo, audiocassette and SASE. Reports in 2 weeks.
Music: Mostly country; also bluegrass, gospel and MOR. Works primarily with vocalists, self-contained country shows and bar bands. Current acts include Junie Low, Debbie Sue and Bob Stamper.

PROPAS MANAGEMENT CORPORATION, 1407 Mount Pleasant Rd., Toronto, Ontario M4N 2T9 **Canada.** Manager: Steve Propas. Management firm and record company (Spy Records). Estab. 1984. Represents mostly Canadian individual artists, groups and songwriters. Currently handles 6 acts. Receives 20% commission. Reviews material for acts.
How to Contact: Submit demo tape by mail. Unsolicited submissions are OK. Prefers cassette with at least 4 songs and lyric sheets. Does not return unsolicited material. Reports in 2 months.
Music: Mostly rock and A/C. Works primarily with vocalists and bands. Current acts include Dan Hill, Lee Aaron, Frank Marino and Haywire.

*R.V.O. (ROBERT VERKAIK ORGANIZATION), Singel 402, Amsterdam 1016 AK **Netherlands.** Phone: (20)6254258. Manager: Robert Verkaik/Robert van Kleef/Marcél Albers. Management firm, booking agency and music publisher. Estab. 1986. Represents local, regional and international individual artists, groups, songwriters, recording studios in Europe and production companies; currently handles 8 acts. Reviews material for acts.
How to Contact: Submit demo tape by mail only. Unsolicited submissions are OK. Prefers cassette (or VHS videocassette if available) with 3 songs and lyric sheet. SASE. Reports in 4 weeks.
Music: Mostly rock, pop and dance. Works primarily with groups and producers. Current acts include The Pilgrims, Tambourine and Easy Money.

*RAINBOW COLLECTION LTD., 4501 Spring Creek Rd., Bonita Springs FL 33923. (615)320-1177. Executive Producer: Richard (Dick) O'Bitts. Management firm, record company (Happy Man Records) and music publisher (Rocker Music and Happy Man Music). Represents individual artists, groups, songwriters and producers; currently handles 5 acts. Reviews material for acts.
How to Contact: Prefers cassette (or VHS videocassette of live performance, if available) with 4 songs and lyric sheet. SASE. Reports in 1 month.
Music: Mostly country, pop and rock. Works primarily with writer/artists and groups of all kinds. Current acts include Ashley Cleveland, Chris Lenny, Holly Ronick, Tommy Cash, Miracle 7 and Colt Gipson (traditional country).

THE RAINBOW COLLECTION, LTD., P.O. Box 300, Solebury PA 18963. (215)862-0849. President: Herb Gart. Management, production and publishing firm. Represents artists, groups and songwriters; currently handles 10 acts. Receives 20% commission. Reviews material for acts. Signs songwriters.
How to Contact: Prefers cassette (or VHS videocassette) with 3 songs. "Be true to the intent of the song, and don't hide the performer. Simple and straightforward preferred." Does not return unsolicited material. Reports in 6 weeks.
Music: Mostly rock, pop, heavy metal, R&B, rap, country and dance-oriented. Works "almost exclusively with strong songwriters whether they are solo artists or bands." Current acts include Between the Sheets, Funhouse, Michael Purington, Mike Angelo & The Idols and Marc Berger Band.
Tips: "Don't necessarily worry about current trends in music. Just do what you do to the best of your ability. With our company the song is the thing even if production-wise it's in its infant stages. If you feel you have a great and unique talent, contact us."

"How to Use Your Songwriter's Market" (at the front of this book) contains comments and suggestions to help you understand and use the information in these listings.

THE RECORD COMPANY OF THE SOUTH (RCS), 5220 Essen Ln., Baton Rouge LA 70809. (504)766-3233. President: Cyril E. Vetter. General Manager: John Palazzoto. Music publisher and record company. Estab. 1978. Represents artists, groups and songwriters; currently handles 3 acts. Receives 15-20% commission. Reviews material for acts.
How to Contact: "Not accepting submissions at this time."
Music: Country, R&B, rock, soul and top 40/pop. Works primarily with artists, bands and songwriters. Current acts include Irma Thomas (top 40/pop and R&B), Luther Kent (top 40/pop and R&B) and Butch Hornsby (country).

*WALT REEDER PRODUCTIONS, INC., P.O. Box 27641, Philadelphia PA 19150. (215)276-9936. Vice President: Walt Reeder, Jr. Management firm. Estab. 1984. Represents local, regional and international individual artists and groups; currently handles 15 acts. Receives 25% commission. Reviews material for acts.
How to Contact: Submit demo tape by mail. Unsolicited submissions are OK. Prefers cassette (or VHS videocassette if available). SASE. Reports in 3 weeks.
Music: Mostly R&B and pop; also hip-hop. Works primarily with show bands. Current acts include Jean Carne (R&B jazz singer), Billy Paul (R&B singer) and Mary Davis (R&B singer).

*RICHARD REITER PRODUCTIONS, P.O. Box 43135, Upper Montclair NJ 07043. (201)875-2935. President: Richard Reiter. Management firm, booking agency, music publisher (Marchael Music/ASCAP) and record company (City Pigeon Records). Estab. 1974. Represents local individual artists, groups and songwriters; currently handles 6 acts. Receives 15-20% commission. Reviews material for acts.
How to Contact: Write first and obtain permission to submit. Prefers cassette with 3-6 songs and lyric sheet. SASE.
Music: Mostly jazz, R&B and pop. Works primarily with instrumental jazz groups/artists, vocalists of jazz/swing. Current acts include Crossing Point (fusion), Lou Caimano (jazz sax) and Tricia Slafta (swing jazz vocalist).

*REM MANAGEMENT, 9112 Fireside Dr., Indianapolis IN 46250. President: Bob McCutcheon. Management firm. Estab. 1987. Represents local, regional and international individual artists and groups; currently handles 2 acts. Receives 20% commission. Reviews material for acts.
How to Contact: Write or call first to arrange personal interview. Prefers cassette with 3 songs. SASE. Reports in 1 month.
Music: Mostly hard rock and R&B.

*RENERI INTERNATIONAL PRODUCTIONS, P.O. Box 32, Emerson NJ 07630. (201)265-1043. Contact: Ray Reneri. Management firm. Estab. 1966. Represents local, regional and international individual artists and groups; currently handles 15-25 acts. Reviews material for acts.
How to Contact: Submit demo tape by mail. Unsolicited submissions are OK. Prefers cassette (or VHS videocassette if available) with 3-5 songs. Include photo and bio sheet. SASE. Reports in 2 weeks.
Music: Mostly rock, pop, R&B and C&W. Works primarily with vocalists and bands.

*REVEL MANAGEMENT, #106, 9015 Owensmouth, Canoga Park CA 91304. (818)341-7825. V.P. of Development: Gary Revel, Jr. Management firm, booking agency, music publisher (Jongleur Music/ASCAP, BMI) record company (Top's Records) and Revel Pictures (develops motion pictures). Estab. 1980. Represents local, regional and international individual artists, groups, songwriters and screenplay writers; currently handles 23 acts. Reviews material for acts.
How to Contact: Write first and obtain permission to submit. Prefers cassette (or VHS videocassette if available). Does not return unsolicited material.
Music: Deals with all genres of entertainment. Current acts include Todd Taylor (banjo man/artist), Chuck Adams (jazz-R&B and country songwriter/performer) and Cary Solomon (screenplay writer).

 The asterisk before a listing indicates that the listing is new in this edition. New markets are often the most receptive to unsolicited submissions.

JOEY RICCA, JR.'S ENTERTAINMENT AGENCY, 408 S. Main St., Milltown NJ 08850. (201)287-1230. Owner/President: Joseph Frank Ricca, Jr. Management firm and booking agency. Estab. 1985. Represents individual artists, groups and songwriters; currently handles 75-100 acts. Receives 10-15% commission. Reviews material for acts.

How to Contact: Write or call to arrange personal interview. "We prefer that all material be copyrighted and that a letter be sent right before submitting material, but neither of these is essential." Cassette (or videocassette if available) with 3-4 songs and lyric or lead sheets. Does not return unsolicited material. Reports in 6-8 weeks.

Music: Mostly love songs/ballads, songs for big band vocalists, and soft jazz/Latin; also good commercial material. Works with show bands, dance bands and bar bands. Current acts include Maria Angela, Donny "Z," Anthony Paccone, One Trak Mind and Diamond.

Tips: "Good lyrics and strong musical arrangements are essential if one of our vocalists are to select a song they would like to sing. No matter what others may think of your work submit the songs you like best that you wrote. I look for good love songs, ballads and Broadway play type compositions. No metal please."

RIOHCAT MUSIC, P.O. Box 764, Hendersonville TN 37077-0764. (615)824-1435. Contact: Robert Kayne. Management firm, booking agency, record company (Avita Records) and music publisher (Riohcat Music/BMI). Estab. 1975. Represents individual artists and groups; currently handles 4 acts. Receives 20% commission. Reviews material for acts.

How to Contact: Prefers cassette and lead sheet. Does not return unsolicited material. Reports in 6 weeks.

Music: Mostly contemporary jazz and fusion. Works primarily with jazz ensembles. Current acts include Jerry Tachoir Quartet, Marlene Tachoir and Jerry Tachoir/Van Manakas Duo.

Tips: "Be organized, neat and professional."

A.F. RISAVY, INC., 1312 Vandalia, Collinsville IL 62234. (618)345-6700. Divisions include Artco Enterprises, Golden Eagle Records, Swing City Music and Swing City Sound. Contact: Art Risavy. Management firm and booking agency. Estab. 1960. Represents artists, groups and songwriters; currently handles 50 acts. Receives 10% commission. Reviews material for acts.

How to Contact: Write first and obtain permission to submit or to arrange personal interview. Prefers 7½ ips reel-to-reel or cassette (or VHS videocassette if available) with 2-6 songs and lyric sheet. SASE. Reports in 2 weeks.

Music: Mostly rock, country, MOR and top 40. Current acts include Street Corner Symphony, Philthy McNasty, Sammy and the Snow Monkeys, The Blast, Bedrock, Billy-Peek, Jules Blatner, Sgt. Karter, Sneakers, Seen, Catch and Inside Out.

Tips: Artists should be "well-dressed, polished and ambitious. VHS videotapes are very helpful."

RNJ PRODUCTIONS, INC., 11514 Calvert St., North Hollywood CA 91606. (818)762-6105. President: Rein Neggo, Jr. Management firm. Estab. 1974. Represents individual artists; currently handles 8-10 acts. Receives 10-25% commission. Reviews material for acts.

How to Contact: Prefers cassette with 3 songs and lead sheet. SASE. Reports in 1 month.

Music: Mostly A/C, country, pop and folk. Works primarily with vocalists and concert artists. Current acts include Glenn Yarbrough, Arizona Smoke Review, Limeliters, Bill Zorn, Jon Benns and The Kingston Trio.

ROCHESTER TALENT UNLIMITED, INC., 346 Ridge Rd. E, Rochester NY 14621. (716)342-4650. President: Thomas DiPoala. Management firm and booking agency. Estab. 1967. Represents groups in New York state; currently handles 15-20 acts. Receives 15-30% commission. Reviews material for acts.

How to Contact: Query by mail or submit demo tape. Prefers cassette with 3-6 songs; "any artist or band looking for representation should submit a demo video with 3-6 songs featuring an honest representation of the range of their material. We also need promotional material, photos, song lists, letters of recommendation and news clippings." SASE. Reports in 2 weeks.

Music: Mostly top 40/pop, funk and country; also dance, MOR, R&B, rock and soul. Works primarily with show bands, dance bands (high energy to MOR), top 40/light rock bar bands and vocalists. Current acts include The Trend (show/dance band), Centrestage (high energy Top 40) and Streetplayer (top 40/pop band).

Tips: "We need a good cassettes, videos and professional photos. We are always on the lookout for good quality acts that we might manage. We now provide the service of working with any entertainer (vocalist or band), on a fee basis, to provide them with a complete package of audio tape and or video, photo session and any necessary other print promotional materials. The promotional package may be used or presented to recording companies, agencies and management."

ROCK-A-BILLY ARTIST AGENCY, P.O. Box 1622, Hendersonville TN 37077. (615)822-1044. A&R Director: S.D. Neal. Management firm, booking agency and record company. Estab. 1974. Represents artists and groups; currently handles 20 acts. Receives 15% commission. Reviews material for acts.
How to Contact: Prefers cassette (or VHS videocassette if available) with 2-6 songs and lyric sheet. SASE. Reports in 3 weeks.
Music: Mostly R&B, rock and country; also all other types including rockabilly. Works primarily with vocalists. Current acts include Dixie Dee, Rhythm Rockers, Rufus Thomas, Richie Derwald, Mickey Finn Band and Greg Paul.

ROCKVILLE MUSIC MANAGEMENT, Suite 200, 100 Merrick Rd., Rockville Centre NY 11570. (516)536-8341. Executive Director: James Citkovic. Management firm. Estab. 1989. Represents international individual artists, groups, songwriters and producers; currently handles 6 acts. Receives 20% commission. Reviews material for acts.
How to Contact: Submit demo tape by mail. Unsolicited submissions are OK. Prefers cassette (or VHS videocassette of performance) with 1-4 songs and lyric sheet. "Make sure videocassettes are visually clear, and that they are recorded in the SP speed." SASE. Reports in 4-5 weeks.
Music: Mostly rock, pop and alternative dance; also R&B. Current acts are Drew Miles (Nu Music/1990 pop rock), Naked Angels (power pop/rock dance) and Fighter Town (commercial rock).
Tips: "We want quality artists with originality, vision and distinctive lead vocal; imaginative lyrics, memorable hooks and melodies; and artists that project a positive image with their music, look and lyrics."

JAY B. ROSS & ASSOCIATES P.C., 838-40 W. Grand Ave., Chicago IL 60622. (312)243-7876. President: Jay B. Ross. Management firm and law firm. Estab. 1968. Represents local, regional or international artists, groups and songwriters; currently handles 10 acts. Receives 15-25% commission. Reviews material for acts.
How to Contact: Prefers cassette (or videocassette if available) with 3 songs. Does not return submissions without SASE. Reports 2-6 weeks.
Music: Mostly R&B, urban dance and industrial (rock and dance); also rock/pop, heavy metal and gospel/blues. Works primarily with vocalists. Current acts include Sugar Blue, Gene "Duke of Earl" Chandler, Industrial Dance Force, 4 P.M. (Pale Males) RAP and Daughters of the Blues.
Tips: "Submit finished demos if possible, put your best song first."

*JEFFREY ROSS MUSIC, #203, 219 1st Ave. S., Seattle WA 98104. (206)343-5225. Contact: Jeffrey Ross. Management firm and music publisher (High-tech Music/BMI). Estab. 1978. Represents local, regional and international individual artists, groups and songwriters; currently handles 5 acts. Receives 15-20% commission. Reviews material for acts.
How to Contact: Write or call first and obtain permission to submit. Prefers cassette with 5 songs and lyric sheet. SASE. Reports in 2 months.
Music: Mostly pop/dance, jazz and R&B; also rock and alternative. Works primarily with vocalists and instrumentalists. Current acts include Skywalk (jazz rock), Cami McManus (dance alternative) and Laura Love (folk funk).
Tips: "We are artist development-oriented and appreciate true talent."

*CHARLES R. ROTHSCHILD PRODUCTIONS INC., 330 East 48th Street, New York NY 10017. (212)421-0592. President: Charles R. Rothschild. Booking agency. Estab. 1971. Represents local, regional and international individual artists, groups and songwriters; currently handles 10 acts. Receives 15-25% commission. Reviews material for acts.
How to Contact: Submit demo tape by mail. Unsolicited submissions are OK. Prefers cassette (or VHS videocassette if available) with 1 song and lyric and lead sheet. SASE. Reports in 3 months.
Music: Mostly rock, pop and folk; also country and jazz. Current acts include Judy Collins (pop singer/song writer), Leo Kottke (guitarist/composer) and Emmylou Harris (country songwriter).

RUSTRON MUSIC PRODUCTIONS, Send all artist song submissions to: 1156 Park Lane, West Palm Beach FL 33417. (407)686-1354. Main Office: 33 Whittier, Hartsdale, NY 10530. ("Main office does not review new material—only South Florida Branch office does.") Artists' Consultants: Rusty Gordon and Davilyn Whims. Composition Management: Ron Caruso. Management firm, booking agency, music publisher (Rustron Music Publishers/BMI and Whimsong Publishing/ASCAP) and record producer (Rustron Music Productions). Estab. 1970. Represents individuals, groups and songwriters; currently handles 15 acts. Receives 10-25% commission for management and/or booking only. Reviews material for acts.

How to Contact: "Call for interview or submit by mail." Prefers cassette with 3-6 songs and lyric or lead sheet. SASE. Reports in 1-3 months.
Music: Blues (country and rock), country (rock, blues, progressive), easy listening (ballads), R&B, folk/rock (contemporary/topical), MOR (pop style), rock (folk/pop), top 40/pop and salsa/disco; also New Age and New Age folk fusion. Current acts include Marian Joy Ring (folk/jazz fusion), Sue Massek of The Reel World String Band (contemporary folk/country), Circle & Star (contemporary folk), Robin Plitt (historical/contemporary folk), Relative Viewpoint (socio-cultural folk) and Helen Hooke (rock/pop/fusion).

SALT WORKS MUSIC, INC., 21 Fleetwood Ave., Jackson OH 45640-1806. (614)286-3420. (Branch: 4901 Yorkshire Rd., Nashville TN 37204). President: R.J. Elliot. Vice President: M.A. Morgan. Management firm and music publisher (Sojourner Music/BMI and Salt Creek Music/ASCAP). Estab. 1986. Currently handles 9 acts. Reviews material for acts.
How to Contact: "Requests and tapes should be sent to our Jackson, Ohio office." Prefers cassette or 7½ ips reel-to-reel with 3-4 songs and demo and lyric sheet. "We will not return tape unless postage paid envelope is provided." Reports in 3 weeks.
Music: Mostly country, country rock and gospel/religious; also pop and MOR. Works primarily with country group acts. Current acts include Mike Morgan (vocalist/songwriter) and Walt Cook and Carl Angel (vocalists).

*SA'MALL MANAGEMENT, Suite 830, 10 Universal City Plaza, Universal City CA 91608. (818)506-8533. Manager: Nikki Ray. Management firm. Estab. 1990. Represents local, regional and international individual artists, groups and songwriters; currently handles 9 acts. Receives 25% commission. Reviews material for acts.
How to Contact: Write first and obtain permission to submit. Prefers cassette with 2 songs and lyric and lead sheet. SASE. Reports in 4-6 weeks.
Music: All types. Current acts include The Band AKA, I.B. Fynne and Phuntaine.
Tips: "Be professional, say no to drugs and become educated in the business of music."

SANDCASTLE PRODUCTIONS, 236 Sebert Road, Forest Gate, London E7 ONP **England.** Phone (081)534-8500. Senior Partner: Simon Law. Management firm, music publisher (Sea Dream Music/PRS, Scarf Music Publishing and Really Free Music/PRS) and record company (Plankton Records, Embryo Arts/Belgium and Gutta/Sweden) and record producers. Estab. 1980. Represents individual artists, groups and songwriters; currently handles 10 acts. Receives 10% commission. Reviews material for acts.
How to Contact: Prefers cassette with 3 songs and lyric sheet. SAE and IRC. Reports in 6 weeks.
Music: Mostly funk/rock, blues, rock and gospel. Works primarily with bands or artists with a Christian bias to their material. Current acts include Fresh Claim (funk rock), Medals (jazz/rock) and Trevor Speaks (folk).
Tips: "Have a commitment to communication of something real and honest in 'live' work."

SHAPIRO & COMPANY, C.P.A. (A Professional Corporation), Suite 620, 9255 Sunset Blvd., Los Angeles CA 90069. (213)278-2303. Certified Public Accountant: Charles H. Shapiro. Business management firm. Estab. 1979. Represents individual recording artists, groups and songwriters. Commission varies.
How to Contact: Write or call first to arrange personal interview.
Music: Mostly rock and pop. Works primarily with recording artists as business manager.
Tips: "We assist songwriters with deals including administration of publishing."

MICKEY SHERMAN ARTIST MANAGEMENT & DEVELOPMENT, P.O. Box 20814, Oklahoma City OK 73156. (405)755-0315. President: Mickey Sherman. Management firm. Estab. 1974. Represents individual artists and songwriters; currently handles 6 acts. Receives 10-15% commission. Reviews material for acts.
How to Contact: Prefers cassette (or VHS videocassette of live performance, if available) with 3 songs and lyric sheet or lead sheet. "Keep videos simple. Use good lighting." Does not return unsolicited material. Reports in 6 weeks.
Music: Mostly blues, pop and country; also R&B, rock and easy listening. Works primarily with vocalists and showbands. Current acts include Janjo (singer/harmonica), Benny Kubiak (fiddler) and Charley Shaw (vocalist).

SHOE STRING BOOKING AGENCY, 696 The Queensway, Toronto Ontario M8Y 1K9 **Canada.** (416)255-5166. Contact: Armin Darmstadt. Management firm and booking agency. Represents local artists; currently handles 10 acts. Receives 15% commission. Reviews material for acts.

How to Contact: Write first and obtain permission to submit. Prefers cassette (or VHS videocassette if available) with 2-4 songs and lyric sheet. Does not return unsolicited material. Reports in 3 weeks.
Music: Mostly dance, rock, R&B/pop and country/rock. Works primarily with vocalists, bar bands and dance bands. Current acts include SAB, Gigalo, Pulsations and Bitchin'.

*PHILL SHUTE MANAGEMENT PTY. LTD., P.O. Box 273, Duluicm Hill NSW 2203 **Australia**. Phone: (02)5692152. Managing Director: Phill Shute. Management firm, booking agency and record company (Big Rock Records). Estab. 1979. Represents local individual artists and groups; currently handles 3 acts. Receives 25% commission. Reviews material for acts. Charges fee for reviewing material.
How to Contact: Submit demo tape by mail. Unsolicited submissions are OK. Prefers cassette with 4 songs and lyric sheet. Reports in 2 months.
Music: Mostly rock, pop and R&B; also country rock. Works primarily with rock bands, pop vocalists and blues acts (band and vocalists). Current acts include Chris Turner (blues/guitarist/vocalist), Collage (pop/rock band) and Big Rock Band (rock'n'roll).
Tips: "Make all submissions well organized (e.g. bio, photo and experience of the act). List areas in which the act would like to work, complete details for contact."

SIDARTHA ENTERPRISES, LTD., P.O. Box 1414, East Lansing MI 48823. (517)655-4618. President: Thomas R. Brunner. Management firm and booking agency. Estab. 1968. Represents artists and groups; currently handles 2 acts. Receives 15-20% commission. Reviews material for acts.
How to Contact: "Always make phone contact first." Prefers cassette (or videocassette) with at least 4 songs and lyric sheet. SASE. Reports in 1 month.
Music: Rock and top 40/pop. Works primarily with bar bands and recording acts. Current acts include Sheer Threat (rock) and Rumble (rock).

SILVER CREEK PARTNERSHIP, P.O. Box 33, Pope Valley CA 94567. (707)965-2277. Managing Partner: Carla L. Forrest. Management firm and music publisher (Ohana Music Productions/ASCAP). Estab. 1988. Represents local and regional (Northern California) artists, groups and songwriters; currently handles 2 acts. Receives 10% commission.
How to Contact: Submit demo tape by mail. Unsolicited submissions are OK. Prefers cassette with 3-4 songs and lyric and lead sheet. SASE. Reports in 3-4 weeks.
Music: Mostly country, country rock. Works primarily with vocalists/musicians. Current acts include Silver Creek and Kimo Forrest.
Tips: "Demos should be uncluttered with vocals upfront. Strong melody and 'hook.' "

SIMMONS MANAGEMENT CO., P.O. Box 18711, Raleigh NC 27619. (919)851-8321. FAX: (919)851-8441. President: Harry Simmons. Management firm. Represents producers, artists, groups and songwriters; currently handles 10 acts and 4 producers. Receives 15-20% commission. Reviews material for acts.
How to Contact: Prefers cassette (or VHS videocassette of performance) with 3-6 songs and lyric sheet; also submit promotional material, photos and clippings. "Videocassette does not have to be professional. Any information helps." SASE. Reports in 6 weeks.
Music: Mostly modern pop; also modern rock, new wave, rock, metal, R&B and top 40/pop. Works primarily with "original music recording acts or those that aspire to be." Current acts include Don Dixon (producer, songwriter and recording artist), Marti Jones (recording artist), The Woods (recording artists, songwriters), Heidi Rodewald/Danielle Faye (performers/songwriters), and Rev. Billy C. Wirtz (recording artist), Jim Brock (recording artist) and Steve Haigler (producer).
Tips: "We are interested in strong songs; style is not so important."

T. SKORMAN PRODUCTIONS, INC., 4700 L.B. McLeod Rd., Orlando FL 32811. (305)843-4300. President: Ted Skorman. Management firm and booking agency. Estab. 1983. Represents groups; currently handles 40 acts. Receives 10-25% commission. Reviews material for acts.
How to Contact: "Phone for permission to send tape." Prefers cassette with 3 songs (or videocassette of no more than 15 minutes). "Live performance—no trick shots or editing tricks. We want to be able to view act as if we were there for a live show." Does not return unsolicited material. Reports in 1 month.
Music: Mostly top 40 and dance; also rock, MOR and pop. Works primarily with high-energy dance acts, recording acts, and top 40 bands. Current acts include Jadi (dance/country), Ravyn and The End (pop/rock), Virgie and Right on Cue (R&B), Tim Mikus (rock) and Gibralter (R&B).
Tips: "We have many pop recording acts, and are looking for commercial material for their next albums."

SKYLINE MUSIC CORP., P.O. Box 31, Lancaster NH 03584. (608)586-7171. FAX: (603)586-7078. President: Bruce Houghton. Management firm (Skyline Management), booking agency (Skyline Music Agency), record company (Adventure Records) and music publisher (Campfire Music and Skyline Music). Estab. 1984. Represents 15 individual artists and groups. Currently handles 15 acts. Receives 10-15% commission. Reviews material for acts.
How to Contact: Prefers cassette (or videocassette if available) with 3 songs. "Keep it short and sweet." Does not return unsolicited material.
Music: Mostly rock and folk; also pop and dance. Works primarily with concert rock attractions and dance bands. Current acts include Foghat (rock), The Outlaws (rock), Toy Caldwell (rock), Rick Danko, Badfinger, New Riders of the Purple Sage and Revelation.

DAN SMITH AGENCY, P.O. Box 3634, Shawnee Mission KS 66203. (913)648-3906. Contact: Dan Smith. Management firm and booking agency. Estab. 1979. Represents artists, groups and songwriters in the Midwest; currently handles 5 acts. Receives 10% commission. Reviews material for acts.
How to Contact: Prefers cassette with 3-5 songs and lyric sheet (or VHS videocassette if available) "Make sound quality clear and mixed well." SASE. Reports in 1 month.
Music: Mostly country rock, top 40, progressive and R&B; also bluegrass, blues, country, dance-oriented, folk, jazz, MOR and soul. Works primarily with dance, bar and concert bands. Current acts include Riverrock (country rock), Crossroads (country rock), Dixie Cadillacs (country rock), Blackwater (country rock) and La Rose (R&B, MOR, soul).
Tips: "Have complete promo package—bio, photo (glossy), song list, credits, etc."

*SOUND ADVISORS LTD., 400 West Lancaster Ave., Devon PA 19333. (215)975-9212. President: Greg Mizii. Vice Presidents: Steven Bernstein and Howard Scott III. Secretary/Treasurer: Bernard M. Resnick Esq. Management firm and booking agency. Represents individuals, groups, songwriters and performers. Reviews material for acts. Covers all aspects of the business—from legal advice and management to production and promotion. Handles clients worldwide; 5-7 new acts/year. "Negotiated contracts that have resulted in the sale of over 35 million records, tapes and CDs."
How to Contact: Write or call (9-5 PM EST) first to obtain permission to submit. Prefers cassette tapes, CDs and records with resume and picture. Does not accept or return unsolicited material. Reports ASAP. Prefers written request with SASE over calling when seeking permission to submit.
Music: Rock, pop, R&B, rap, reggae, blues, metal, jazz, gospel, contemporary Christian and Christian rock. Booked artists for shows from Bobby Rydell to Sweet Sensations. Does yearly talent search to find great artists.
Tips: "If you get permission to submit a tape—follow our directions and realize that we care about making a great performer top in his field. We are a company that handles more than managing and booking. We can get you recorded, published and offer legal council if you are very good."

SOUND '86 TALENT MANAGEMENT, P.O. Box 222, Black Hawk SD 57718. (605)343-3941. Management firm. Estab. 1974. Represents 10 artists and groups. Receives 5-10% commission. Reviews material for acts.
How to Contact: Query by mail or submit demo tape. Prefers cassette (or VHS videocassette-professional) with 3-8 songs and lyric sheet. SASE. Reports in 1 month.
Music: Mostly rock (all types); also bluegrass, country, dance, easy listening and top 40/pop. Works primarily with single artists. Current artists include Danny Wayne (songwriter), Road House (blues), Johnny Thunder Band, Jack Jenson and Black Hills Country Band.

SOUTHERN NIGHTS INC., 2707 No. Andrews Ave., Ft. Lauderdale FL 33311. (305)563-4000. President: Dick Barten. Management firm and booking agency. Estab. 1976. Represents local and regional individual artists and groups; currently handles 35 acts. Receives 15-20% commission. Reviews material for acts.
How to Contact: Write or call first and obtain permission to submit. Prefers cassette (or VHS videocassette if available) with minimum of 4 songs and lyric or lead sheets. "Keep videos simple—we are not interested in special effects on original material." SASE. Reports in 2 weeks.
Music: Mostly top 40/pop and rock. Works primarily with current top 40, high energy show and dance groups. Current acts include F/X (top 40 rock show), US#1 (touring top 40/dance act), Donna Allen (soul), Ruby Baker & Future and Starlight (top 40).
Tips: "Be prepared; send complete package of promo material and be ready to audition."

SP TALENT ASSOCIATES, Box 475184, Garland TX 75047. Talent Coordinator: Richard Park. Management firm and booking agency. Represents individual artists and groups; currently handles 7 acts. Receives negotiable commission. Reviews material for acts.

How to Contact: Prefers VHS videocassette with several songs. SASE. Reports back as soon as possible.
Music: Mostly rock, nostalgia rock, country; also specialty acts and folk/blues. Works primarily with vocalists and self-contained groups. Current acts include Joe Hardin Brown (C&W), Rock It! (nostalgia) and Renewal (rock group).
Tips: "Appearance and professionalism are *musts*!"

SPIDER ENTERTAINMENT CO., 5 Portsmouth Towne, Southfield MI 48075. (313)559-8230. President: Arnie Tencer. Vice President: Joel Zuckerman. Management firm. Estab. 1977. Represents artists, groups and songwriters; currently handles 2 acts. Receives minimum 20% commission. Reviews material for acts.
Affiliates: Forever Endeavor Music, Inc.
How to Contact: Prefers cassette (or videocassette if available) with 3 songs. Does not return unsolicited material. Reports only if interested.
Music: Mostly rock and roll, contemporary pop; also top/40 pop. Works primarily with "rock bands with good songs and great live shows." Current acts include Gus Papas (rock singer and writer-guitarist) and Legal Tender (high energy "Detroit" rock band).
Tips: Artists "must have commercially viable material."

STAR ARTIST MANAGEMENT INC., 17580 Frazho, Roseville MI 48066. (313)778-6404. President: Ron Geddish. Chairman: Joe Sgroi. Executive VP: Tony Pasqualone. Director of Canadian Operations: Brian Courtis. Director of West Coast Operations: S.D. Ashley. Director of East Coast Operations: Nat Weiss. Management firm (business and personal). Estab. 1972. Represents solo rock performers and rock groups. Receives 5% (business management), 15-20% (personal management). Reviews material for acts.
How to Contact: Prefers cassette (or videocassette if available) with 2 songs. SASE. Reports in 3 weeks.
Music: Rock and alternative/college. Works primarily with alternative music and rock groups. Current acts include Elvis Hitler (Hollywood/Restless Records), His Name is Alive (4AD Records) and The Look (A&M/Canada).

STARCREST PRODUCTIONS, INC., 209 Circle Hills Dr., Grand Forks ND 58201. (701)772-6831. President: George J. Hastings. Management firm and booking agency. Estab. 1970. Represents artists, groups and songwriters; currently handles 8 acts. Receives negotiable commission. Reviews material for acts. Receives 15% commission.
How to Contact: Query by mail. Prefers 7½ ips reel-to-reel or cassette with 2-10 songs with lyric and lead sheet. SASE. Reports in 1 month.
Music: Mostly country/gospel. Works primarily with vocalists and dance bands. Current acts include Mary Joyce (country/gospel), Swinging Doors (country/country rock), The Pioneers (country/country rock group), The Teddy Bears (dance, show band), George Hastings (songwriter) and Bob Angel (country songwriter).

STARSTRUCK PRODUCTIONS, 3057 Main Street, Buffalo NY 14214. (716)835-7625. FAX: (716)835-7701. General Manager: Tom McGill. Management firm and booking agency. Represents 24 groups. Receives 15-20% commission. Reviews material for acts.
How to Contact: Prefers cassette (or VHS videocassette if available) with 4-6 songs and lyric sheet. Please send current press kit with photo. Does not return unsolicited material.
Music: Mostly rock, pop, top 40. Works primarily with rock groups. Current acts include Only Humen (top 40 recording group, EMQ America Records), The Tweeds (rock/recording), Big Wheelie and The Hubcaps (nostalgia/touring act), Lady Five (rock), Silent Scream (rock) and Wright of Way (rock).
Tips: "Approach your career realistically. Overnight success stories are few and far between. Write solid, commercial material and be persistent."

*BILL STEIN ASSOCIATES INC., P.O. Box 1516, Champaign IL 61820. Artists Manager: Bill Stein. Management firm and booking agency. Estab. 1983. Represents artists and groups; currently handles 6 acts. Receives 10-15% commission. Reviews material for acts.
How to Contact: Prefers cassette (or Beta videocassette of live performance, if available) with 3-6 songs and promotional material. "Send complete promo package including video and audio tapes, pictures, references, song and equipment lists." SASE. Reports in 1 month.
Music: Mostly pop rock, country and nostalgia; also dance, R&B, progressive and soul. Works primarily with bar bands, dance bands and concert groups. Current acts include Gator Alley (country), Kick in the Pants (nostalgia), High Sierra (country rock), Greater Decatur R&B Revue (nostalgia), Pink Flamingoes (nostalgia), Nix86 (rock) and 950 Band/Ken Carlyle Band (C&W).

*RONALD STEIN PRODUCTIONS, Box 12194, Dallas TX 75225. (214)369-3800. President: Ronald Stein. Management firm, booking agent, music publisher (Westhaven Publishing), record company (Request Records) and talent agency (Star Images). Estab. 1985. Represents local, regional and international groups and individual artists; currently handles over 200 acts. Receives varying commission. Reviews material for acts.
How to Contact: Submit demo tape by mail. Unsolicited submissions are accepted only if copyrighted. Prefers cassette (or VHS videocassette if available) with at least 3 songs. SASE. Reports in 1 month.
Music: All styles, but mostly pop and MOR. Works with groups and individual artists. Current acts include Fact Four (dance band), Lisa Waggoner (singer) and Paul Lister (pianist).

*STINNETTE ENTERTAINMENT AGENCY, P.O. Box 86384, Portland OR 97286-0384. (503)235-5988. President: Tom Stinnette. Booking agency. Estab. 1973. Represents artists and groups in Northwest, Alaska and Canada; currently handles over 50 acts. Receives 10-15% commission. Reviews material for acts.
How to Contact: Prefers cassette with 5-10 songs (or videocassette of performance from artist; 10 minutes maximum; short clips of each song; use good lighting). Does not return unsolicited material. Give references from appearances.
Music: Mostly top 40/rock; also top 40 country/rock, dance-oriented, MOR, 50s and country rock and pop. Works primarily with show, dance and variety bands.
Tips: "Be well rehearsed and have a good press kit, including 8x10 pictures. Good stage presence is of vital importance—be energetic. Nothing is less exciting than a 'deadpan' band."

AL STRATEN ENTERPRISES, 10303 Hickory Valley, Ft. Wayne IN 46835. President: Allan Straten. Management firm, booking agency, music publisher (Hickory Valley Music/ASCAP and Straten's Songs/BMI) and record company (Yellow Jacket Records). Represents individual artists and songwriters; currently handles 6 acts. Receives 10-20% commission. Reviews material for acts.
How to Contact: Prefers cassette with a maximum of 6 songs and lyric sheet. SASE. Reports in 1 month.
Music: Mostly traditional and contemporary country—no rock. Works primarily with vocalists and writers. Current acts include April (country vocalist), Mike Vernanglia (country/MOR/singer/songwriter), Roy Allan (vocalist/writer) and Sylvia Grogg (writer).

*STRICTLY BUSINESS MUSIC MANAGEMENT, 691 ½ N. 13th St., Philadelphia PA 19123. (215)765-1382. President: Le Roy Rowe. Management firm and booking agency. Estab. 1989. Represents local, regional and international individual artists, groups, songwriters and producers; currently handles 10 acts. Receives 20-25% commission. Reviews material for acts.
How to Contact: Call first and obtain permission to submit. Prefers cassette or VHS videocassette with 3-5 songs and lyric sheet. Does not return unsolicited material. Reports in 3 weeks.
Music: Mostly R&B, pop and rock, and rap; also gospel. Current acts include Averi (songwriter), Rapture (vocalists/artist) and Rob (producer/songwriter).

SUNSET PRODUCTIONS, 117 W. 8th, Hays KS 67601. (913)625-9634. President: Mark Meckel. Management firm, booking agency and music publisher. Estab. 1974. Represents local, regional and international individual artists, groups and songwriters; currently handles 15 acts. Receives 15-20% commission. Reviews material for acts.
How to Contact: Submit demo tape by mail. Unsolicited submissions are OK. Prefers cassette with 3 songs and lyric sheet. Does not return unsolicited material.
Music: Mostly rock, country and pop. Works primarily with bands on college circuit and in bars statewide. Current acts include The Heat (rock band), Jimmy Dee Band ('50s rock'n'roll) and Mark Selby (rock/folk singer, songwriter).
Tips: "Be willing to work with the producer. Take criticism in a constructive manner, be open to making changes."

THE T.S.J. PRODUCTIONS INC., 422 Pierce St. NE, Minneapolis MN 55413-2514. (612)331-8580. Vice President/Artist Manager: Katherine J. Lange. Management firm and booking agency. Estab. 1974. Represents artists, groups and songwriters; currently handles 1 international act. Receives 10-15% commission. Reviews material for acts.
How to Contact: Call or write first before sending package. Prefers "cassette tapes only for music audio (inquire before sending video), with 2-6 songs and lyric sheet." SASE. Reports in 2 weeks.
Music: Mostly country rock, symphonic rock, easy listening and MOR; also blues, country, folk, jazz, progressive, R&B and top 40/pop. Currently represents Thomas St. James (songwriter/vocalist).
Tips: "We will view anyone that fits into our areas of music. However, keep in mind we work only with national and international markets. We handle those starting out as well as professionals, but all must be marketed on a professional level, if we work with you."

*THE TALENT CONNECTION, P.O. Box 2121, Valley Cottage NY 10989. (914)268-4113. Producer/ Manager: Martin Hoberman. Management firm, booking agency and film/video production company. Represents individual artists and groups; currently handles approximately 25 acts. Receives 10-20% commission. Reviews material for acts.
How to Contact: Prefers cassette (or VHS videocassette if available) with 3-5 songs. SASE. Reports in 2 months.
Music: Mostly pop, rock and R&B. Works primarily with rock, top 40, R&B, and oldies acts. Current acts include Paul Whistler and the Wheels (R&B group), John Valby, McCambridge, Moshe Ariel Dance Co., Alive N' Kickin, Boys in the Attic, Ben Robinson and Hits.

*TAS MUSIC CO./DAVE TASSE ENTERTAINMENT, Route Z, Lake Geneva WI 53147-9731. Contact: David Tasse. Booking agency, record company and music publisher. Represents artists, groups and songwriters; currently handles 50 acts. Receives 10-20% commission. Reviews material for acts.
How to Contact: Prefers cassette with 2-4 songs and lyric sheet. Include performance videocassette if available. SASE. Reports in 3 weeks.
Music: Mostly pop and jazz; also dance, MOR, rock, soul and top 40. Works primarily with show and dance bands. Current acts include Geneva Band (pop), Highlights (country) and Major Hamberlin (jazz).

TBM ENTERTAINMENT, (formerly Tim Brack Management), 1st Floor, 677 Passaic Ave., Nutley NJ 07110. (201)667-3010. Vice President A&R: Tony Kee. Management firm. Estab. 1988. Represents international individual artists, groups, songwriters, producers and engineers. Receives 10-20% commission. Reviews material for acts.
How to Contact: Unsolicited submissions are OK. Prefers cassette (or VHS videocassette if available) with 3 songs and lyric or lead sheet. Does not return unsolicited material. Reports in 1 month.
Music: All forms of contemporary music, including rap and metal. Works primarily with writers and performers. Current acts include Immaculate Fools (folk based acoustic rock band), Strawberry Zots, Kid Rock and Skull.
Tips: "Always wait to submit material until it is in the best 'form' you feel is representative *fully* of either songs or a band. We need to see and hear potential, not finished masters. I need something that has achieved substantial development. We don't have time to put into developing bedroom demos."

TEXAS MUSIC MASTERS, (formerly Cedar Hill Studios), Rt. 14 Box 1039, Tyler TX 75707. (903)566-5653. Vice President: Lonnie Wright. Management firm, music publisher (Boggy Depot/BMI) and record company (OL, New Act, Juke Box, Quazar). Estab. 1967. Represents international individual artists, groups and songwriters; currently handles 5 acts. Receives 20% commission. Reviews material for acts.
How to Contact: Submit demo tape by mail. Prefers cassette with 3 songs. SASE.
Music: Mostly country, gospel and blues. Works primarily with vocalists, writers and dance bands. Current acts include Touch of Country (band), Pat Murphy (singer), Marcy Carr (singer) and Beau Dean (writer/singer).
Tips: "Be professional with demos."

3L PRODUCTIONS, 3578 Silverplains Dr., Mississauga, Ontario L4X 2P4 **Canada**. (416)625-2165 or (416)238-2901. Manager: Gino Latini. Management firm and music publisher (Caras ITAA/CIRPA). Estab. 1985. Represents local and regional (Ontario) individual artist and groups; currently handles 5 acts. Receives 10-15% commission. Reviews material for acts.
How to Contact: Call first to arrange personal interview. Prefers cassette (or VHS videocassette) with 3 songs and lyric sheet. SASE and IRC. Reports in 1 month.
Music: Mostly rock, pop and R&B. Works primarily with dance band with good vocals, bar bands and recording bands. Current acts include Ten Seconds Over Tokyo (rock/pop), Tribal Son (new music), Champions (classic rock) and Power Circus (pop/rock).
Tips: "Be willing to work hard and be patient until the right break comes along."

*TIMELESS PRODUCTIONS, 206-207 West Hastings, Vancouver BC V6B 1H7 **Canada**. (604)681-3029. FAX: (604)683-5357. President: Larry Gillstrom. Management firm, booking agency and record company (Magestic Records). Estab. 1984. Represents local, North American and international individual artists, groups and songwriters; currently handles over 80 acts. Receives 5-25% commission. Reviews material for acts.
How to Contact: Submit demo tape by mail. Unsolicited submissions are OK. "Wait at least 30 days before following up." Prefers cassette or VHS videocassette with 3 songs and lyric sheet. SASE. Reports in 3 months.

Music: Mostly hard rock, mainstream pop and alternative rock; also New Age and hard core/metal. Works primarily with vocalists, self-contained rock bands and writers. Current acts include Young Gun (rock band), Kick Axe (rock band) and Lions Gate (rock band).

TIP TOP ATTRACTIONS/KAM MANAGEMENT, P.O. Box 1384, Mobile AL 36633. (205)432-7827. President: Kirke Weinacker. Management firm, booking agency and music publisher. Estab. 1985. Represents local, regional and international individual artists, groups and songwriters; currently handles 5 acts. Receives 10-20% commission. Reviews material for acts.
How to Contact: Submit demo tape by mail. Unsolicited submissions OK. Prefers cassette (or VHS videocassette if available) with 3-5 songs. SASE. Reports in 2 weeks.
Music: Mostly rock, R&B and pop. Works primarily with soloists and bands. Current acts include Mike Lawson (single), Tip Tops (show band) and Tribute (variety band).

A TOTAL ACTING EXPERIENCE, Suite 206, Dept. Rhymes-1, 14621 Titus St., Panorama City CA 91402. Agent: Dan A. Bellacicco. Talent agency. Estab. 1984. Represents vocalists, lyricists, composers and groups; currently handles 27 acts. Uses the services of in-house talent for scoring of motion pictures, television, videos, musicals, jingles, TV commercials and material for major recording artists. Receives 10% commission. Reviews material for acts. Agency License: TA-0698.
How to Contact: Prefers cassette (or VHS videocassette if available) with 3-5 songs and lyric or lead sheets. Please include a revealing "self talk" at the end of your tape. "Singers or groups who write their own material must submit a VHS videocassette with photo and resume." SASE. Reports in 6-12 weeks only if interested.
Music: Mostly top 40/pop, jazz, blues, country, R&B, dance and MOR; also "theme songs for new films, TV shows and special projects."
Tips: "No calls please. We will respond via your SASE. Your business skills must be strong. Please use a new tape and keep vocals up front. We welcome young, sincere talent who can give total commitment, and most important, *loyalty*, for a long-term relationship. We are seeking female vocalists (a la Streisand or Whitney Houston) who can write their own material, for a major label recording contract. Your song's story line must be as refreshing as the words you skillfully employ in preparing to build your well-balanced, orchestrated, climactic last note! Try to eliminate old, worn-out, dull, trite rhymes. A new way to write/compose or sing an old song/tune will qualify your originality and professional standing."

*TREND RECORDS, P.O. Box 201, Smyrna GA 30081. (404)432-2454. President: Tom Hodges. Music publisher (Mimic Music/BMI, Boam/ASCAP) and record company (Trend Recording, Stepping Stone, Trend Setter, Proud Eagle Records, British Overseas Airways Music, Kennesaw Records). Estab. 1965. Represents local, regional and international individual artists, groups and songwriters. Currently handles 20 acts. Receives 15% commission. Reviews material for acts.
How to Contact: Submit demo tape by mail. Unsolicited submissions are OK. Prefers cassette (or videocassette if available) with 10-12 songs and lyric sheets. SASE. Reports in 3 weeks.
Music: Mostly country, gospel and R&B; also jazz, pop and MOR. Works primarily with vocalists. Current acts include Marlon Frizzell (country), JoAnn Johnson (country) and Ginny Peters (country/MOR).

TRYCLOPS LTD., 115 New Barn Lane, Cheltenham, Glouchestershire GL52 3LQ **England**. Phone: 0242-234045. Director: Ian Beard. Booking agency and concert promotional company. Estab. 1971. Represents individual artists and groups; currently handles 20 acts. Receives 10-15% commission. Reviews material for acts.
How to Contact: Write or call first and obtain permission to submit. Prefers cassette (or VHS videocassette of live performance). Does not return unsolicited material. Reports in 4 weeks "if tracks are good standard."
Music: Mostly rock, contemporary folk, pop; also R&B and jazz. Works with very wide range of artists/acts from singer/songwriters to trios and jazz bands. No artists solely represented. Current acts include singer/songwriters Johnny Coppin, Steve Ashley and Dave Cartwright.

*TWIN CITY TALENT, P.O. Box 18508, Minneapolis MN 55418. (612)789-7225. President: Marty Essen. Management firm and booking agency. Estab. 1987. Represents local, regional and international individual artists, groups and songwriters; currently handles 12 acts. Receives 15-20% commission. Reviews material for acts.
How to Contact: Submit demo tape by mail. Unsolicited submissions are OK. Prefers cassette (or VHS videocassette if available) with any number of songs. "Just a rough home video is fine. A video is nice, but not necessary." SASE. Reports in 2 weeks.

Music: Mostly pop, rock and country; also R&B, metal and dance. Works primarily with original artists/bands, cover bands. Current acts include William Ellwood (New Age on Narada/MCA Records), Scott Moore (original dance/rock) and Mary Ott (singer/songwriter).
Tips: "Dedication and professionalism are a must. This is an all or nothing business—success will only be seen by artists that have total committment to their craft."

UMBRELLA ARTISTS MANAGEMENT, INC., P.O. Box 8385, 2612 Erie Ave., Cincinnati OH 45208. (513)871-1500. FAX: (513)871-1510. President: Stan Hertzman. Management firm. Represents artists, groups and songwriters; currently handles 5 acts.
How to Contact: Prefers cassette with 3 songs and lyric sheet. SASE. Reports in 1 month.
Music: Progressive, rock and top 40/pop. Works with contemporary/progressive pop/rock artists and writers. Current acts include The Raisins (modern band), Prizoner (rock band) and Adrian Belew (artist/producer/songwriter/arranger whose credits include Frank Zappa, David Bowie, Talking Heads, Tom Tom Club, Cyndi Lauper, Laurie Anderson, Paul Simon, The Bears and Mike Oldfield).

UNITED ENTERTAINMENT, 4024 State Line, Kansas City KS 66103. Agency Manager: Joel Hornbostel. Operations Manager: Dave Maygers. Management firm, booking agency, music publisher (United Entertainment Music/BMI) and record company (Stress Records). Estab. 1972. Represents local, regional and international individual artists, groups and songwriters; currently handles 25 acts. Receives 15% commission. Reviews material for acts.
How to Contact: Write first and obtain permission to submit. Prefers cassette (or VHS videocassette if available) with 3-5 songs and lyric sheets. SASE. Songlist.
Music: Mostly rock, pop and country; also gospel, blues and R&B. Works primarily with rock bands. Current acts include The Hollow Men, The Bon Ton (soul accordian band), The Songs of Rex, London Drive, Spike Blake, That Statue Moved and Sing Sing.

VAN DYKE ENTERPRISES, P.O. Box 275, Hanover PA 17331. (717)632-4075. Manager: Steve Eck. Management firm, booking agency and record company (Aria Records). Estab. 1983. Represents local, regional and international individual artists; currently handles 4 acts. Receives 10% commission. Reviews material for acts.
How to Contact: Submit demo tape by mail. Unsolicited submissions are OK. Prefers cassette (or videocassette of live performance if available) with 4 songs and lyric sheet. Reports in 3 weeks.
Music: Mostly country, country rock, pop and rock. Works primarily with dance bands and bar bands. Current act includes Bruce Van Dyke (country), Freedom Express (variety) and Don Barns & Debbie Williams (country/variety).
Tips: "We are looking for clean country ballads and up-tempo country songs."

*HANS VAN POL MANAGEMENT, P.O. Box 9010, Amsterdam HOL 1006AA **Netherlands**. Phone: (31)20618-3109. FAX: (31)20689-2751. Managing Director: Hans Van Pol. Management firm and booking agency. Estab. 1984. Represents regional (Holland/Belgium) individual artists and groups; currently handles 5 acts. Receives 20-25% commission. Reviews material for acts.
How to Contact: Call first and obtain permission to submit. Prefers cassette or VHS videocassette with 3 songs and lyric sheets. SASE. Reports in 1 month.
Music: Mostly dance: rap/swing beat/hip house/R&B/soul/c.a.r. Current acts include Tony Scott (dance/rap), Roxy D, Zhype (swingbeat singer), Girlstreet (girlgroup, dance) and Roxanna (singer/songwriter).

RICHARD VARRASSO MANAGEMENT, P.O. Box 387, Fremont CA 94537. (415)792-8910. Management firm. Represents local, regional or international individual artists, groups and songwriters; currently handles several acts. Receives 20% commission or hourly rate. Reviews material for acts.
How to Contact: Submit demo tape by mail. Prefers cassette. Does not return material. Reports in 3 months.
Music: Mostly rock. Works primarily with concert headliners and singers. Current acts include Greg Kihn, Jimmy Lyon, Chaz Ross, Rattleshake and Susan Steele.

VELVETT RECORDING COMPANY, 517 W. 57th St., Los Angeles CA 90037. (213)753-7893. Manager: Aaron Johnson. Management firm and record company. Represents artists, groups and songwriters; currently handles 5 acts. Reviews material for acts.
How to Contact: Prefers cassette with 2-3 songs and lead sheet. SASE.
Music: Mostly blues and gospel; also church/religious, R&B, rock, soul and top 40/pop. Works primarily with show and dance bands and vocalists. Current acts include Arlene Bell (soul/top 40/pop artist) and Chick Willis (blues artist).

VOKES BOOKING AGENCY, Box 12, New Kensington PA 15068-0012. (412)335-2775. President: Howard Vokes. Represents individual traditional country and bluegrass artists. Books name acts in on special occasions. For special occasions books nationally known acts from Grand Ole Op'ry, Jamboree U.S.A., Appalachian Jubliee, etc. Receives 10-20% commission.
How to Contact: New artists send 45 rpm record, cassette or LP. Reports back within a week.
Music: Traditional country, bluegrass, old time and gospel; definitely no rock or country rock. "We work mostly with traditional country bands and bluegrass groups that play various bars, hotels, clubs, high schools, malls, fairs, lounges, or fundraising projects." Current acts include Howard Vokes & His Country Boys (country), Mel Anderson, A.J. Jenkins, Bunnie Mills, Morgan Ruppe, Bobby Yates, Wayne Copley, Shawn Lee, Luke Gordon and Norman Wade.

BEN WAGES AGENCY, 2513 Denny Ave., Pascagoula MS 39567. (601)769-7104. FAX: (601)769-8590. Owner: B. Wages. Management firm and booking agency. Estab. 1978. Represents local, regional and international individual artists, groups and songwriters; currently handles 200 acts. Receives 10-15% commission. Reviews material for acts.
How to Contact: Submit demo tape by mail. Unsolicited submissions are OK. Prefers cassette (or VHS videocassette of live performance, if available). SASE. Reports in 4 weeks.
Music: Mostly country/nostalgia and rock. Works primarily with name acts, dance bands and bar bands. Current acts include Percy Sledge, Ace Cannon and John Fred and the Playboys.

LOUIS WALSH MANAGEMENT/BOOKING AGENCY, 1, The Elms, Grove House, Milltown Road, Dublin 6 **Ireland.** Phone: 619212 or 697025. Management firm and booking agency. Represents individual artists, groups and songwriters; currently handles 10-12 acts. Receives 10% commission. Reviews material for acts.
How to Contact: Prefers cassette (or VHS videocassette of performance) with 2 songs and lyric or lead sheet. Reports in 3 weeks.
Music: Mostly pop, rock and country. Works primarily with pop singers, rock bands, dance bands and country and western. Currrent acts include Johnny Logan (singer/songwriter), Linda Martin (pop female singer), Dickie Rock (male vocalist), Jump the Gun (pop/rock), Shaun O'Farrell (country singer) and Brush Shiels (rock singer).

WESTWOOD ENTERTAINMENT GROUP, Suite 330, 1115 Inman Avenue, Edison NJ 08820-1132. (908)548-6700. FAX: (908)548-6748. President: Victor Kaplij. Director of A&R: Kevin McCabe. Artist management agency (Westunes Music/ASCAP). Estab. 1985. Represents regional artists and groups; currently handles 1 act. Receives 15% commission. Reviews material for acts.
How to Contact: Prefers cassette with 3 songs and lyric sheet. SASE. Reports in 6 weeks.
Music: Mostly rock; also pop. Works primarily with singer/songwriters, show bands and rock groups. Current acts include The Pressures of Time (rock) and Groud Zero (rock).
Tips: "Present a professional promotional/press package with 3 song limit."

SHANE WILDER ARTISTS' MANAGEMENT, P.O. Box 3503, Hollywood CA 90078. (818)508-1433. President: Shane Wilder. Management firm, music publisher (Shane Wilder Music/BMI) and record producer (Shane Wilder Productions). Represents artists and groups; currently handles 10-12 acts. Receives 15% commission. Reviews material for acts.
How to Contact: Prefers cassette (or videocassette of performance if available) with 4-10 songs and lyric sheet. SASE. Reports in 1 month.
Music: Country. Works primarily with single artists and groups. Current acts include Mike Franklin (country recording artist), Teresa O'Dell (country artist), Denise Myatt, Craig Reynolds (songwriter), Wynn Hammons (country artist), Jane Tyler (actress), Melanie Ray (country singer and actress) and Jacklyn Palmer (film actress).
Tips: "Make sure your work is highly commercial. We are looking for strong female country songs for major artists. Material should be available for publishing with Shane Wilder Music/BMI. We do not accept any songs for publishing with a reversion clause."

*WINDFALL TALENT, 920 N. Fairview, Lansing MI 48912. (517)372-0200. President: Don Middlebrook. Management firm and booking agency. Estab. 1982. Represents local, regional and international individual artists, groups and songwriters; currently handles 50 acts. Receives 10-20% commission. Reviews material for acts.
How to Contact: Call first and obtain permission to submit. Prefers cassette (or VHS videocassette if available) with 3 songs and lyric sheet. SASE. Reports in 1 month.
Music: Mostly pop, country and rock; also R&B and rap. Works primarily with groups and vocalists/soloists. Current acts include Huntunes (progressive rock) and Jeff LaDuke (pop songwriter).

*WINGATE, 6920-214 Koll Center Pkwy., Pleasanton CA 94566. (415)846-6194. Manager: Pam Hanna. Management firm, booking agency, music publisher (Parchment Harbor Music/BMI, Hugo First Publishing/ASCAP), record company (Wingate Records) and fan club management. Estab. 1989. Represents local, regional and international individual artists, groups and songwriters; currently handles 8 acts. Receives 10-15% commission. Reviews material for acts.
How to Contact: Write first and obtain permission to submit. Prefers cassette (or VHS videocassette of live performance if available) with 2 songs and lyric sheet, with photo and biosheet. "Artists—We'd rather have 10 minutes of a great performance than 30-60 of a mediocre one. Extend yourself—give more than you thought you ever could in the way of performing." SASE. Reports in 2 weeks.
Music: Mostly pop, country crossover and rock; also R&B and gospel. Works primarily with "vocalists/ bands capable of club and stage performances, as well as aspiring recording artists." Current acts include Robyn Banx (6-piece country/rock band/songwriters), Kayla Moore & Southern Tradition (lead female country vocalist and 4-piece band), Bob Eggert (singer/songwriter, traditional country) and Julissa Lynn.
Tips: "Be prepared emotionally, physically, spiritually to handle success. Listen! We might be saying something! There's a fine line between confidence and arrogance . . . don't cross it."

WOLFTRACKS MANAGEMENT, P.O. Box 10205, Rockville MD 20895. (301)942-5420. Director: David J. Galinsky. Management firm. Estab. 1986. Represents local, regional and international individual artists and groups; currently handles 5 acts. Receives 15-20% commission. Reviews material for acts.
How to Contact: Submit demo tape by mail. Unsolicited submissions are OK. Prefers cassette (or videocassette if available) with 4 songs and lyric sheet. Does not return unsolicited material. Reports in 2-3 weeks.
Music: Mostly original hard rock, pop/dance and progressive. Current acts include Rob Wolf (guitarist/songwriter/singer), The Correctones (world soul) and Dean Ray (alternative rock).
Tips: "Hard work and talent will pay off."

RICHARD WOOD ARTIST MANAGEMENT, 69 North Randall Ave., Staten Island NY 10301. (718)981-0641. Contact: Richard Wood. Management firm. Estab. 1974. Represents musical groups; currently handles 2 acts. Receives 10-15% commission. Reviews material for acts.
How to Contact: Prefers cassette and lead sheet. SASE.
Music: Mostly dance, R&B and top 40/pop; also MOR. Works primarily with "high energy" show bands, bar bands and dance bands.
Tips: "Please be versatile and able to make changes in material to suit the type of acts I book. Most of the material I receive only deals with love as a theme. Try to write to other subjects that are contemporary, such as honesty, politics and peace in the world. Pay special attention to lyrics—try to go beyond the basics and paint pictures with the words."

*WORLD WIDE MANAGEMENT, P.O. Box 599, Yorktown Heights NY 10598. (914)245-1156. Director: Mr. Steve Rosenfeld. Management firm and music publisher (Neighborhood Music/ASCAP). Estab. 1971. Represents artists, groups, songwriters and actors; currently handles 4 acts. Receives 20% commission. Reviews material for acts.
How to Contact: Write or call first and obtain permission to submit or to arrange personal interview. Prefers cassette (or videocassete of performance) with 3-4 songs. SASE. Reports in 2 months.
Music: Mostly contemporary pop, folk, folk/rock and New Age; also A/C, rock, jazz, bluegrass, blues, country and R&B. Works primarily with self-contained bands and vocalists. Current acts include Scarlet Rivera, Bill Popp & The Tapes, Liz Irons and Tommy Eyre.

DOUGLAS A. YEAGER PRODUCTIONS, INC., 300 W. 55th St., New York NY 10019. (212)245-0240. President: Doug Yeager. Management firm and music publisher (Aixoise Music Co./ASCAP). Estab. 1971. Represents local, regional or national individual artists, groups and songwriters; currently handles 5 acts. Receives 10-25% commission. Reviews material for acts.
How to Contact: Prefers cassette with 4 songs and lyric sheets. SASE. Reports in 2 months.
Music: Mostly R&B ballads, R&B dance and pop ballads; also folk/pop, folk/political and gospel pop/ rock. Works primarily with vocalists (pop/R&B/folk-rock). Currents acts include Richie Havens, Cliff Eberhardt (folk/rock), Michelle Pleeter (pop/R&B) and Josh White, Jr. (pop/gospel).
Tips: "Do not send songs that are less commercial (accessible) than what is being played today on commercial radio."

*ZANE MANAGEMENT, INC., 6th Fl., The Bellevue, Broad and Walnut Sts., Philadelphia PA 19102. (215)790-1155. FAX: (215)790-0509. President: Lloyd Zane Remick. Entertainment/sports consultants and managers. Represents artists, songwriters, producers and athletes; currently handles 5 acts. Receives variable commission.

How to Contact: Prefers cassette and lyric sheet. SASE. Reports in 1 month.
Music: Dance, easy listening, folk, jazz (fusion), MOR, rock (hard and country), soul and top 40/pop. Current acts include Bunny Sigler (disco/funk), Pieces of a Dream (consultant), Grover Washington, Jr. (management), Phyllis Nelson (management) and Sister Sledge.

ZAR MANAGEMENT, Dreilinden Str. 42, St. Gallen CH 9011 **Switzerland.** Holder: Victor Waldburger. Management firm, music publisher (Zar Musikveriag), record label and record producer. Estab. 1980. Represents individual artists, groups, songwriters and producers; currently handles 5 acts. Reviews material for acts. Receives 20% commission.
How to Contact: Write or call to submit or to arrange a personal interview. Prefers cassette (or European VHS videocassette). Reports only if interested.
Music: Mostly pop, dance, hard rock, heavy metal. Current acts include Taboo, Sultan and Kaboko.

ZEE TALENT AGENCY, 3095 Sinclair St., Winnipeg, Manitoba R2P 1Y6 **Canada.** (204)338-7094. President/Agent: Linda Zagozewski. Agent: Duncan Wilson. Booking agency. Estab. 1980. Represents groups; currently handles 22 acts. Receives 10-15% commission. Reviews material for acts.
How to Contact: Write first and obtain permission to submit. Prefers cassette (or videocassette of performance). "Submit song list of originals and/or covers, picture and equipment list." SAE and IRC. Reports in 2 weeks.
Music: Mostly rock, top 40 and country/rock; also contemporary, variety and show music. Current acts include Musiqa (variety), Maclean & Maclean (comedy team) and Eagle Feather (country rock).

Managers and Booking Agents/'91-'92 Changes

The following markets appeared in the 1991 edition of *Songwriter's Market* but are absent from the 1992 edition. Most of these companies failed to respond to our request for an update of their listing. Others are not listed for a variety of reasons, which is indicated in parentheses following the company name. For example, they may have gone out of business, or they may have requested deletion from the 1992 edition because they are backlogged with material.

The Act Agency
Act "1" Entertainment
AGF Entertainment Ltd. (asked to be deleted)
All Star Talent Agency
Allegiance Entertainment Corp., Inc. (moved; left no forwarding address)
Michael Allen Entertainment Development
American Concert
Americom
Amethyst Group Ltd. (later response)
Amuse America, Inc.
Angelwood Inc.
Animal Crackers Entertainment
Ancient Springs Music (late response)
David Anthony Promotions
April Productions (late response)
Vic Arkilic
Backstage Productions International
Bandstand (International) Entertainment Agency
Bill Batzkall Productions, Inc. (asked to be deleted)
Barry Bergman Management (asked to be deleted)
Big House Management Pty. Ltd.
Big J Productions (late re-

sponse)
Blank & Blank
Blue Ox Talent Agency
Blue Ridge Booking
Bodo Music
Boggy Depot Music (late response)
Boomtown Music (moved; left no forwarding address)
Bill Boyd Productions
Brock & Associates (asked to be deleted)
Al Bunetta Management
Cactus Industries Music Inc.
Cahn-Man
C&S Talent, Inc. (late response)
Ernie Cash Management/Vision Music Group Inc.
CFB Productions
Chardon Booking and Management
Circuit Rider Talent & Management (late response)
Citi Muzik (moved; left no forwarding address)
City Lights Management, Inc.
Class Act Talent (out of business)
Clayton Productions
C.M. Management
Cocos Island Records, Inc.
Concept 2000 Inc. (late response)
Creative Talent, Inc.

The Current Entertainment Corporation
Current Records/Management (late response)
D.S.M. Producers (late response)
D&M Entertainment Agency
Darkhorse Entertainment (late response)
Peter Dean Management
Phyllis Dumont Agency (asked to be deleted)
E.Z. Money Productions
Steve Eck Entertainment
Edge Entertainment, Inc. (late response)
Encore Talent, Inc.
Entertainment International USA (late response)
Eschenbach Editions
Events Unlimited
Falk & Morrow Talent/Earza Music (late response)
Far West Entertainment (late response)
Fat City Artists (late response)
Finkelstein Management Company Ltd.
Foursquare Management Co.
Foxworthy Music Inc. (late response)
Frost & Frost Entertainment
Gaira Productions
Bob Gallion Productions (late response)

Jo-Ann Geffen & Associates (asked to be deleted)
Godwin Music Group (asked to be deleted)
Lindy Goetz Management
Golden Bull Productions
Greif-Garris Management
Joseph Gunches Management
Hale Enterprises
Lynn Harkins & Associates
Ken Hatley & Associates, Inc.
Glenn Henry Entertainment Agency (late response)
Adam Hurdle Associates, Inc.
Illuminati Group (late response)
In Tunes (asked to be deleted)
Laura John Music
Dusty Jones Management Co. (late response)
Butch Kelly Production
Kinsella
Bob Knight Agency
Howard Knight Entertainment Group (asked to be deleted)
S.V. Kyles & Associates
Las Vegas Entertainment Services (asked to be deleted)
Overton Lee Management
Legion Artists
Life Music Ministries, Inc.
Logan-Gregory and Associates
Tommy Loomas
Richard Lutz Entertainment (late response)
McFadden Artist Corp. (late response)
M&M Talent Agency Inc.

Mainstage Management International (late response)
Makoul Productions (late response)
Management VII
Phil Mayo & Company
MC Promotions & Public Relations
Mean Green Management (Artist Management)
Menes Law Corp. (late response)
Greg Menza & Assoc. (late response)
Metropolitan Talent Authority
Mid-East Entertainment Inc.
Midnight Life Associates
Moonstone Music Ltd.
Moore Entertainment Group
Dale Morris and Associates
Morris & Bradley Management (late response)
Nash Angeles Inc.
Nashville International Entertainment Group (asked to be deleted)
The New Music Times, Inc.
Newall Artists Agency
Nutmeg Management
Out of the Blue Management
Parasol Publications (U.K.)
Pentachord/Pentarch Music
Phil's Entertainment Agency Ltd. (late response)
Placer Publishing (late response)
Podesoir International Management (late response)
Pro Talent Consultants (late response)
Rocken Davie Productions
Red Giant Records/Publishing (late response)
Samuel Roggers & Assoc.
Rusch Entertainment Agency
William Seip Management, Inc.
Select Artists Associates (late response)
770 Music Inc.
Shankman De Blasio, Inc.
Show Time Talent Agency
Showtime Productions
Brad Simon Organization (late response)
Singermanagement, Inc.
Sopro, Inc.
Southern Concerts
Stubblefield Associates
Talent Attractions
Talent Master
TSMB Productions (late response)
V.J.D. Management
Valex Talent Agency (late response)
Victory Artists
Vision Management
Vision Music Group (late response)
Alan Whitehead & Associates Ltd.
World Class Talent (asked to be deleted)
World Wide Media

Remember: Don't "shotgun" your demo tapes. Submit only to companies interested in the type of music you write. For more submission hints, refer to The Business of Songwriting on page 21.

Advertising, AV and Commercial Music Firms

The music for a commercial or audiovisual presentation is secondary to the picture (for TV, film or video) or the message being conveyed. Commercial music must enhance the product; it must get the consumer's attention, move him in some way and, finally, motivate him—all without overpowering the message or product it accompanies. Songwriters in this area are usually strong composers, arrangers and, sometimes, producers.

Commercial music and jingle writing can be a lucrative field for the composer/songwriter who is energetic, has a gift for strong hook melodies, and is able to write in many different styles. The problem is, there are many writers and few jobs—it's a very competitive field. A writer in this field must be quick, good and must usually write on spec when needed.

Advertising agencies

Ad agencies work on assignment as their clients' needs arise. They work closely with their clients on radio and TV broadcast campaigns. Through consultation and input from the creative staff, ad agencies seek jingles and music to stimulate the consumer to identify with a product or service.

When contacting ad agencies, keep in mind they are searching for music that can capture and then hold an audience's attention. Most jingles are quick, with a strong, memorable hook line that the listener will easily identify with. Remember, though, that when an agency is listening to a demo, they are not necessarily looking for a finished product so much as for an indication of creativity and diversity. Most composers put together a reel of excerpts of work from previous projects, or short pieces of music which show they can write in a variety of styles.

Audiovisual firms

Audiovisual firms create a variety of products. Their services may range from creating film and video shows for sales meetings (and other corporate gatherings) and educational markets, to making motion pictures and TV shows. With the increase of home video use, how-to videos are a big market now for audiovisual firms, as are spoken word educational videos.

Like advertising firms, AV firms usually work on specification, so audiovisual producers looking for new songwriters search for those with versatile, well-rounded approaches. The key to submitting demos to these firms is to demonstrate your versatility in writing specialized background music and themes. Listings for companies will tell what facet(s) of the audiovisual field they are involved in and what types of clients they serve.

Commercial music houses and music libraries

Commercial music houses are companies which are contracted (either by an advertising agency or the advertiser himself) to compose custom jingles. Since they are neither an ad agency or an audiovisual firm, their main concern is music. And they use a lot of it—some composed by inhouse songwriters and some contributed by outside writers.

Music libraries are a bit different in that their music is not custom composed for a specific client. They provide a collection of instrumental music in many different styles that, for an annual fee or on a per use basis, the customer can use however he chooses (most often in audiovisual and multi-media applications).

When searching for a commercial music house or music library, they will be indicated in the listings as such by bold typeface.

Most of the companies listed in this section pay by the job, but there may be some situations where the company asks you to sign a contract that will specify royalty payments. If this happens, be sure you research the contract thoroughly, and that you know exactly what is expected of you and how much you'll be paid.

Sometimes, depending upon the particular job and the company, a composer/songwriter will be asked to sell one-time rights or all rights. One time rights entail using your material for one presentation only. All rights means that the buyer can use your work any way he chooses for as long as he likes. Again, be sure you know exactly what you're giving up, and how the company may use your music in the future.

Writing jingles and composing themes on assignment are not easy. All of the aforementioned specialty fields are highly competitive and demanding. You must be sure to make a good impression on the individuals at these companies by finding an inventive way of calling attention to your music. Still, the bottom line is good music.

For additional names and addresses of advertising agencies who may use jingles and/or commercial music, refer to the *Standard Directory of Advertising Agencies* (National Register Publishing Co.). For a list of audiovisual firms, check out the latest edition of *Audiovisual Marketplace* (published by R.R. Bowker).

*THE AD AGENCY, P.O. Box 2316, Sausalito CA 94965. Creative Director: Michael Carden. Advertising agency and **jingle/commercial music production house**. Clients include business, industry and retail. Estab. 1971. Uses the services of independent songwriter/composers and lyricists for jingles for public relations/promotions/publicity and commercials for radio and TV. Commissions 20 composers and 15 lyricists/year.
How to Contact: Query with resume of credits. Prefers cassette with 5-8 songs and lyric sheet. SASE, but prefers to keep materials on file. Reports in 2 weeks.
Music: Uses variety of musical styles for commercials, promotion, TV, video presentations.
Tips: "Our clients and our needs change frequently."

THE AD TEAM, 15251 NE 18th Ave., N. Miami Beach FL 33162. (305)949-8326. Vice President: Zevin Auerbach. Advertising agency. Clients include automobile dealerships, radio stations, TV stations, retail. Seeking background music for commercials and jingles. Uses the services of independent songwriters for jingles for commercials. Commissions 4-6 songwriters. Pays by the job.
How to Contact: Submit demo tape of previously aired work. Prefers cassette. SASE.
Music: Uses all styles of music for all kinds of assignments. Most assignments include writing jingles for radio and television campaigns.

*ADVANCE ADVERTISING AGENCY, 606 E. Belmont, Fresno CA 93701. Manager: Martin Nissen. Advertising agency. Clients include manufacturers, retailers, marketers, financial institutions. Estab. 1950. Uses the services of music houses and lyricists for commercials for radio and TV. Buys all rights.
How to Contact: Submit demo tape of previous work. Prefers cassette with any number of songs. SASE, but prefers to keep materials on file. Include business card. Reports in 3 weeks.
Music: Uses easy listening, up-tempo, Dixieland, C&W for commercials.
Tips: "Consider our local market."

ALEXIS MUSIC INC. (ASCAP), MARVELLE MUSIC CO. (BMI), Box 532, Malibu CA 90265. (213)463-5998. President: Lee Magid. Music publishing and production. Clients include all types—record companies and advertising agencies. Estab. 1960. Uses the services of music houses, independent songwriters and producers for scoring of recordings, background music for film or video or theatre, jingles for commericials, commercials for radio and TV and manufacturers, events, conventions, etc. Commissions 5 composers and 5 lyricists/year. Pays by the job or by royalty. Buys all rights, publishing.
How to Contact: Submit demo tape of previous work or tape demonstrating composition skills or query with resume of credits. Prefers cassette (or VHS videocassette) with 3 pieces and lyric sheets. "If interested, we will contact you." SASE; keeps material on file only if needed. Include phone number and address on tape. Reports in 6 weeks.

Music: Uses R&B, gospel, jazz, Latin, Afro-Cuban, country; anything of substance.
Tips: "Send me a good demo, that can be understood so that we can judge. Send only one cassette."

*AMERICAN MEDIA CONCEPTS, INC., 31 E. 32nd St., New York NY 10016. (212)481-8484. Contact: Creative Director. Advertising agency. Clients include regional retail businesses. Estab. 1982. Uses the services of music houses for jingles and commercials for radio and TV. Commissions 1-3 composers and 1-3 lyricists/year. Pays by the job. Buys all rights.
How to Contact: Submit demo tape of previous work. Prefers cassette. "No phone calls." Does not return unsolicited material; prefers to keep on file. Reports "on as-needed basis."
Music: Uses up-tempo for commercials—humorous lyrics preferred.
Tips: "Enclose letter with demo tape."

ANDERSON COMMUNICATIONS, 2245 Godbyrd, Atlanta GA 30349. (404)766-8000. President: Al Anderson. Producer: Vanessa Vaughn. Advertising agency and syndication operation. Estab. 1971. Clients include major corporations, institutions and media. Uses the services of music houses for scoring and jingles for TV and radio commercials and background music for TV and radio programs. Commissions 5-6 songwriters or composers and 6-7 lyricists/year. Pays by the job. Buys all rights.
How to Contact: Call first and obtain permission to submit. Prefers cassette. SASE, but prefers to keep material on file. Reports in 2 weeks or "when we have projects requiring their services."
Music: Uses a variety of music for music beds for commercials and jingles for nationally syndicated radio programs and commercials targeted at the black consumer market.
Tips: "Be sure that the composition plays well in a 60 second format."

ANGEL FILMS COMPANY, Rt. One, Box 69, New Franklin MO 65274-9998. (314)698-3900. President: Arlene Hulse. Motion picture and record production company (Angel One Records). Estab. 1980. Uses the services of independent songwriters/composers, lyricists and in-house agency for scoring and background music for feature films, music videos, cartoons, television productions and records. Commissions 12-20 composers and 12-20 lyricists/year. Payment depends upon budget; each project has a different pay scale. Buys all rights.
How to Contact: Submit demo tape of previous work or tape demonstrating composition skills; submit manuscript showing music scoring skills; query with resume of credits; or write to arrange personal interview. Prefers cassette (or VHS videocassette) with 3 pieces and lyric and lead sheet. "Do not send originals." SASE, but prefers to keep material on file. Reports in 3 weeks.
Music: Uses basically MOR, but will use anything (except C&W and religious) for record production, film, television and cartoon scores.
Tips: "We prefer middle of the road music, but are open to all types. We use a lot of background music in our work, plus we have our own record label, Angel One, that is looking for music to record. Don't copy other work. Just be yourself and do the best that you can. That is all that we can ask."

APON PUBLISHING COMPANY, INC., Box 3082 Steinway St., Long Island City NY 11103. (718)721-5599. Manager: Don Zeemann. Jingle/**commercial music production house, music sound effect library** and background music. Clients include background music companies, motion picture companies and advertising agencies. Estab. 1957. Uses the services of own special suppliers for background music for every use of the industries, jingles for advertising agencies and commercials for radio and TV. Payment is negotiated. Buys all rights.
How to Contact: Send demo cassette with background music, no voices. Prefers cassette with 2-5 pieces. SASE, but prefers to keep material on file. Reports in 2 months. No certified or registered mail accepted.
Music: Uses only background music, no synthesizer life instruments.

ATLANTIC FILM AND VIDEO, 171 Park Lane, Massapequa NY 11758. (516)798-4106. Sound Designer: Michael Canzoneri. Motion picture production company. Clients include industrial/commercial. Estab. 1986. Uses the services of independent songwriters for background music for movies and commercials for TV. Commissions 1 composer and 1 lyricist/year. Pays $200-250/job. Buys one-time rights.
How to Contact: Submit demo tape of previous work or query with resume of credits. Prefers cassette or 7½ ips reel-to-reel. "Please specify what role you had in creating the music: composer, performer, etc." SASE, but prefers to keep material on file. Reports in 6 weeks.

Listings of companies within this section which are either commercial music production houses or music libraries will have that information printed in boldface type.

Music: Uses jazz—modern, classical for films.
Tips: "Have patience and good songs."

*AUTHENTIC MARKETING, 25 W. Fairview Ave., Dover NJ 07801. (201)366-9326. Director: Dan Kassell. Advertising agency. Estab. 1986. Uses the services of music houses, independent songwriters/composers, lyricists and arrangers for video scripts. Commissions 5 composers and 5 lyricists/year. Pays 1-50% royalty. Buys one-time rights.
How to Contact: Query with resume of credits. Prefers cassette (or VHS videocassette). Does not return unsolicited material. Reports in 6 weeks.
Music: Uses jazz for background music for videoscripts.

AVID PRODUCTIONS, 235 E. 3rd Ave., San Mateo CA 94401. (415)347-3417. Producer: Chris Craig. Music sound effect library, scoring service, **jingle/commercial music production house** and video productions. Clients include corporate clients/independent producer. Estab. 1984. Uses the services of independent songwriters/composers for scoring of video production, corporate identity themes and jingles for video production. Commissions 1-2 composers/year. Pays $100-500/job. Rights negotiable.
How to Contact: Write or call first to arrange a personal interview. Prefers cassette (or VHS/¾" videocassette) with 2 songs. Prefers to keep material on file. Reports in 4 weeks.
Music: Uses up-tempo, high-tech sounds for training tapes/corporate ID pieces.

BALL COMMUNICATIONS, INC., 1101 N. Fulton Ave., Evansville IN 47710. (812)428-2300. President/Creative Director: Martin A. Ball. Audiovisual and television production and meeting production firm. Estab. 1960. Clients include Fortune 500 firms. Uses the services of lyricists and independent songwriters/composers for jingles, background music and theme songs. Commissions 4 songwriters and 4 lyricists/year. Pays $1,500-2,500/job. Buys all rights.
How to Contact: Prefers cassette, 7½ ips reel-to-reel (or ½" videocassette). Does not return unsolicited material; prefers to keep on file. Responds by letter or telephone. SASE. Reports in 1 month.
Music: All types. Uses theme songs/jingles.

TED BARKUS COMPANY, INC., 1512 Spruce St., Philadelphia PA 19102. (215)545-0616. President: Allen E. Barkus. Advertising agency. Uses the services of independent songwriters and music houses for jingles and background music for commercials. Commissions 1-3 songwriters/year. Pays by the job. Buys all rights.
How to Contact: Call to arrange personal interview or write to obtain permission to submit. Prefers cassette (or VHS videocassette) with 3-5 pieces. SASE, but prefers to keep material on file "when the style matches our objectives."
Music: Uses various styles of music depending upon client needs for "positioning concepts with musical beds, doughnut for inserted copy."
Tips: "Learn as much as possible about the product and who the consumer will be before starting a project. Understand that the commercial also has to work with the print and television media in terms of everything else the client is doing."

*AUGUSTUS BARNETT ADVERTISING/DESIGN, 632 St. Helens Ave., Tacoma WA 98402. (206)627-8508. President/Creative Director: Augustus Barnett. Advertising agency/design firm. Clients include food and service, business to business and retail advertisers. Estab. 1981. Uses the services of independent songwriters/composers for scoring of and background music for corporate video work, and commercials for radio. Commissions 1-2 composers and 0-1 lyricist/year. Buys all rights; one-time rights or for multiple use.
How to Contact: Query with resume of credits; write first to arrange personal interview. Prefers cassette. Does not return unsolicited material; prefers to keep on file. Reports in 4 months.
Music: Uses up-tempo, pop and jazz for educational films and slide presentations.

*BASSET & BECKER ADVERTISING, P.O. Box 2825, Columbus GA 31902. (404)327-0763. Production Manager: John Drew. Advertising agency. Clients include medical/healthcare, banking, auto dealers, industrial, family recreation/sporting goods, business to business advertisers. Estab. 1972. Uses the

The asterisk before a listing indicates that the listing is new in this edition. New markets are often the most receptive to unsolicited submissions.

services of music houses and independent songwriters/composers for scoring of and background music for TV spots and AV presentations, jingles for TV spots, AV presentations and radio, and commercials for radio and TV. Commissions 2 composers/year. "Prefers to work with engineer/producer, not directly with composer." Pays by the job. Buys all rights.

How to Contact: Submit demo tape of previous work. Prefers cassette, 7.5/15 ips reel-to-reel, or ¾ or VHS videocassette. Does not return unsolicited material; prefers to keep on file.

*BAXTER, GURIAN & MAZZEI, INC., 8501 Wilshire Blvd., Beverly Hills CA 90211. (213)657-5050. Contact: Steven C. Sperber. Advertising agency. Clients include healthcare, pharmaceutical and consumer businesses. Estab. 1969. Uses the services of music houses for background music for videos, jingles for radio and television spots and commercial for radio and TV. Commissions 1 composer and 1 lyricist/year. Pays $15-20K/job. Buys all rights.

How to Contact: Prefers cassette. "Be patient." Does not return unsolicited material; prefers to keep on file.

Music: "Open to all" styles of music for radio and TV jingles and soundtracks.

NORMAN BEERGER PRODUCTIONS, 3217 S. Arville St., Las Vegas NV 89102. (702)876-2328. Owner: Norman Beerger. Audiovisual firm and wilderness video producer/distributor. Estab. 1984. Clients include Reader's Digest, National Wildlife Federation, consumers, audio/video/book catalogs and retail. Uses the services of music houses and independent songwriters/composers for background music for wilderness exploration videos. Commissions 6 composers/year. Pays 1¢/minute/cassette royalty. Buys non-exclusive rights.

How to Contact: Submit demo tape of previous work. Prefers cassette (or ½" VHS videocassette). SASE, but prefers to keep material on file. Reports in 1 month.

Music: Uses new age, contemporary, synthesizer music for educational films.

Tips: "Submit demo tape. It will be returned."

THE BLACKWOOD AGENCY, INC., Suite 100, 2187 Jolly Rd., Okemos MI 48864. (517)349-6770. Production Manager: Christine Gaffe. Advertising agency. Estab. 1979. Clients include financial and package goods firms. Uses services of music houses for scoring of commercials and training films, background music for slide productions, jingles for clients and commercials for radio and TV. Commissions 3 composers/year. Pays by the job. Buys all rights.

How to Contact: Submit demo tape of previous work. Prefers cassette (or ¾" videocassette) with 6-10 songs. SASE, but prefers to keep material on file.

Tips: "Give us good demo work."

BLAIR/ERIC MOWER & ASSOCIATES, 96 College Ave., Rochester NY 14607. (716)473-0440. President/Chief Creative Officer: John R. Brown. Advertising agency. Member of AFTRA, SAG, ASCAP. Serves consumer and business-to-business clients. Uses independent songwriters, lyricists and music houses for jingles. Commissions 12 songwriters and 4 lyricists/year. Pays $5,000-40,000/job.

How to Contact: Query. Prefers cassette with 3-5 songs. SASE.

Music: "We're seriously interested in hearing from good production sources. We have some of the world's best lyricists and songwriters working for us, but we're always ready to listen to fresh, new ideas."

BLATTNER/BRUNNER INC., 814 Penn Ave., Pittsburgh PA 15222. (412)263-2979. Broadcast Production Coordinator: Traci Trainor. Clients include retail/consumer; service; high-tech/industrial. Estab. 1975. Uses the services of music houses and independent songwriters/composers for scoring of commercials and videos, background music for TV and radio spots, jingles for TV and radio spots and commercials for radio, TV. Commissions 2-3 composers/year. Pays by the job. Buys all rights or one-time rights, depending on the job.

How to Contact: Submit demo tape of previous work demonstrating composition skills. Write first to arrange personal interview. Prefers cassette (or VHS or ¾" videocassette) with 5-10 songs. SASE but prefers to keep submitted materials on file.

Music: Uses up-beat, "unique-sounding music that stands out" for commercials and industrial video.

Tips: "We're always interested in hearing new pieces."

BRADLEY COMMUNICATIONS, Suite 200, 1840 S. Bragaw, Anchorage AK 99508. (907)276-6353. Copywriter: Katie Hickey. Advertising/public relations agency. Clients include tourism and development. Estab. 1968. Uses the services of music houses for background music for informative videos, telecommunications, and jingles and commercials for radio/TV. Pays by the job. Buys one-time rights.

How to Contact: Submit demo tape of previous work which demonstrates composition skills. Cassette, VHS or ¾" videocassette. SASE, but prefers to keep materials on file. Reports back "when need arises."

Music: Uses up-tempo and emotional music.

BRAUNCO VIDEO, INC., Box 236, Warren IN 46792. (219)375-3148. Producer: Magley Tocsin. Video production company. Estab. 1988. Clients include industrial manufacturing, service companies, factories, United Way agencies, entertainers, songwriters, etc. Uses the services of independent songwriters/ composers and house studio bands for jingles and background music for corporate video presentations. Commissions composers. Pays by the job. Buys all rights.
How to Contact: Submit demo tape of previous work or write to arrange personal interview. Prefers cassette or 15 ips reel-to-reel (or ¼″ videocassette) with many pieces. "We have no use for lyric or vocals." Does not return unsolicited material.
Music: Uses up-tempo, heavy metal, R&B with a bit of jazz influence and soft music for promotional corporate demos.
Tips: "Believe in yourself."

BROACH AND CO., Box 1139, Greensboro NC 27402. (919)373-0752. Creative Director: Allen Broach. Advertising agency. Clients include furniture, banking, and consumer goods firms. Estab. 1982. Uses the services of music houses and independent songwriters/lyricists for scoring, background music for commercials and videos, jingles for commercials and commercials for radio and TV. Commissions 1-5 composers and up to 3 lyricists/year. Buys all rights or one-time rights.
How to Contact: Submit demo tape of previous work or tape demonstrating compositional skills. Prefers cassette with 6-10 songs and lead sheet. Does not return unsolicited submissions; prefers to keep submitted material on file.

BROADCAST VIDEO, INC., 20377 N.E. 15th Ct., Miami FL 33179. (305)653-7440. Senior Audio Engineer: Scott Pringle. Film/video post production house. Clients include advertising agencies, film/video producers. Audio department established 1988. Uses the services of music houses, independent songwriters/composers and music libraries for scoring and background music for commercials, documentaries and corporate presentations; jingles for commercials; and commercials for radio and TV. Pays by the job. Rights negotiated with client.
How to Contact: Query with resume of credits or write first to arrange personal interview. Prefers cassette or 7.5 or 15 ips reel-to-reel (or any videocassette). SASE, but prefers to keep material on file. Reports in 1 month.
Music: "We use music for commercials the most, but use songwriters most often for lengthier programs—corporate, documentaries, etc."

BUTWIN & ASSOCIATES, INC., 8700 Westmoreland Ln., Minneapolis MN 55426. (612)546-0203. President: Ron Butwin. Clients include corporate and retail. Estab. 1977. Uses the services of music houses, lyricists and independent songwriters/composers for scoring, background music, jingles and commercials for radio, TV. Commissions 3-5 composers and 1-3 lyricists/year. Pays varying amount/ job. Buys all rights and one-time rights.
How to Contact: Submit demo tape of previous work. Write first to arrange personal interview. Prefers cassette, ¼″ videocassette. "We are only interested in high-quality professional work." SASE, but prefers to keep material on file.
Music: Uses easy listening, up-tempo, pop and jazz for slide presentations and commercials.

CALDWELL VAN RIPER, 1314 N. Meridian, Indianapolis IN 46202. (317)632-6501. Vice President/ Executive Producer: Sherry Boyle. Advertising agency and public relations firm. Serves industrial, financial and consumer/trade clients. Uses jingles and background music for commercials. Commissions 25 pieces/year.
How to Contact: Submit demo tape of previously aired work or submit tape showing jingle/composition skills. Prefers standard audio cassette. SASE. Reports "as soon as possible."

CALF AUDIO, 157 Gray Rd., Ithaca NY 14850. (607)272-8964. President: Haines B. Cole. Vice President: J. Todd Hutchinson. Producer/Engineer: Alfred B. Grunwell. Assistant Engineer: Margaret T. Baker. Professional audio analysis and design; 24-track recording studio; audiovisual firm and **music/ sound effects library**. Estab. 1977. Uses the services of music houses and independent songwriters/ composers for background music, jingles and radio and TV commercials and audiovisual presentations. Pays by the job. Buys all rights.
How to Contact: Submit demo tape of previous work; write to arrange personal interview. Prefers cassette or 15 ips reel-to-reel with 3-5 pieces. Send "full documentation." Does not return unsolicited material; prefers to keep on file. Reports in 3 weeks.
Music: Uses contemporary pop for educational films, slide presentations and commercials.
Tips: "Assimilate but don't duplicate works from the past. Take direction well."

CANARY PRODUCTIONS, Box 202, Bryn Mawr PA 19010. (215)825-1254. President: Andy Mark. **Music library**. Estab. 1984. Uses the services of music houses and independent songwriters for background music for AV use, jingles for all purposes, and commercials for radio. Commissions 10 composers/year. Pays $500-1,000 for 10 cuts of full length music, or on consignment per composition. "No songs, please!"
How to Contact: Prefers cassette with 5-10 pieces. SASE. Reports in 2 weeks.
Music: All styles, but concentrates on industrial. "We pay cash for produced tracks of all styles and lengths. Production value is imperative. No scratch tracks accepted."

CANTRAX RECORDERS, 2119 Fidler Ave., Long Beach CA 90815. (213)498-6492. Owner: Richard Cannata. Recording studio. Clients include anyone needing recording services (i.e. industrial, radio, commercial). Estab. 1980. Uses the services of independent songwriters/composers and lyricists for scoring of jingles, soundtracks, background music for slide shows and films, jingles for radio, commercials for radio and music demos and music videos. Commissions 10 composers/year. Pays by the job. Buys all rights.
How to Contact: Submit demo tape of previous work demonstrating composition skills. Prefers cassette or 7½/15 ips reel-to-reel (or VHS videocassette) with lyric sheets. "Indicate noise reduction if used. We prefer reel to reel." SASE, but prefers to keep material on file. Reports in 2 weeks.
Music: Uses jazz, New Age, rock, easy listening and classical for slide shows, jingles and soundtracks.
Tips: "Send a 7½/15 ips reel for us to audition; you must have a serious, professional attitude."

CAPITOL PRODUCTION MUSIC, #78, 6922 Hollywood Blvd., Hollywood CA 90028. (213)461-2701. Managing Director: Ole Georg. Scoring service, **jingle/commercial music production house, music sound effect library**. Clients include broadcast, corporate/industrial, theatrical, production/post-production houses. Uses the services of independent songwriters/composers for 35-70 minutes of music beds for CD library. Commissions 6 composers/year. Pays by the job. Buys all rights.
How to Contact: Submit demo tape of previous work demonstrating composition skills. Query with resume of credits. Prefers cassette with 5 songs. Does not return unsolicited material but prefers to keep on file. "No report unless we have interest."
Music: Uses hot pop, "big acoustic" corporate industrial, atmospheric.
Tips: "Material most likely to be considered is that with heavy dynamics and strong edit-points."

CHANNEL ONE VIDEO TAPE INC., 3341 NW 82nd Ave., Miami FL 33122. (305)592-1764. General Manager: Jay P. Van Dyke. Video production house, **music library**. Estab. 1969. Clients include commercial, industrial, medical and network programs. Uses music library for commercials for TV and industrials, medical, programs. Pays by the job or "yearly fee." Buys all rights.
How to Contact: Submit demo tape of previous work. Prefers 7½ ips reel-to-reel. Does not return unsolicited material; prefers to keep on file. Reports if interested.
Music: Uses all styles of music for all kinds of assignments.

CHAPMAN RECORDING STUDIOS, 228 W. 5th, Kansas City MO 64105. (816)842-6854. Contact: Chuck Chapman. Custom music and production. Estab. 1973. Clients include video producers, music producers, musicians and corporations. Uses the services of independent songwriters/composers and arrangers for background music for video productions; jingles for radio, TV, corporations; and commercials for radio and TV. Commissions 4 composers and 4 lyricists/year. Buys all rights.
How to Contact: Call to arrange submission of tape demo. Prefers cassette. SASE, but prefers to keep material on file. Reports in 2 months.
Music: Uses all styles, all types for record releases, video productions, and TV and radio productions; and up-tempo and pop for educational films, slide presentations and commercials.

CHASE/EHRENBERG & ROSENE, INC., 211 E. Ontario, Chicago IL 60611. (312)943-3737. Executive Vice President: John Rosene. Advertising agency. Clients include retailers and national manufacturers. Estab. 1942. Uses the services of music houses, independent songwriters/composers and needle drop for scoring of commercials and commercials for radio, TV. Commissions 1 or 2 composers/year. Pays by the job. Buys all rights.
How to Contact: Submit demp tape of previous work demonstrating composition skills. Write or call first to arrange personal interview. Prefers cassette. Does not return unsolicited material but prefers to keep on file.
Music: Uses up tempo, rock, pop for commercials.

CHIAT/DAY/MOJO ADVERTISING, 320 Hampton Dr., Venice CA 90291. (213)314-5000. President/Executive Director: Lee Clow. Chief Creative Officer: Steve Rabosky. Serves health care, packaged food, home loan, automotive, electronics and motorcycle clients. Uses background music in commercials. Commissions 1 piece/year. Pays by the job.

How to Contact: Submit demo tape of previously aired work. Prefers 7½ ips reel-to-reel. SASE. Reports "as soon as possible."

CINEVUE, P.O. Box 428, Bostwick FL 32007. (904)325-5254. Director/Producer: Steve Postal. Motion picture production company. Estab. 1955. Serves all types of film distributors. Use the services of independent songwriters and lyricists for scoring of and background music for movies and commercials. Commissions 10 composers, and 5 lyricists/year. Pays by the job. Buys all rights or one-time rights.
How to Contact: Query with resume of credits or write to arrange personal interview. Prefers cassette or reel-to-reel with 10 pieces and lyric or lead sheet. SASE, but prefers to keep material on file. "Send good audio-cassette, then call me in a week."
Music: Uses all styles of music for features (educational films and slide presentations).

CLEARVUE, INC., 6465 N. Avondale, Chicago IL 60631. (312)775-9433. President: William T. Ryan. Vice President: Matt Newman. Audiovisual firm. Serves the educational market. Estab. 1969. "We only produce core curriculum and enrichment videos for pre-primary through high school students." Uses the services of independent songwriters. Commissions 3 songwriters or composers/year. Pays by the job.
Music: "We are seeking original video proposal and finished product focusing on the teaching of music skills."
Tips: "Look at our catalog—fill in the missing pieces."

COAKLEY HEAGERTY, 1155 N. 1st St., San Jose CA 95112. (408)275-9400. Creative Director: Susan Rivera. Advertising agency. Estab. 1966. Clients include consumer, business to business and high tech firms. Uses the services of music houses for background music for commercials and jingles. Commissions 15-20 songwriters/year. Pays by the job. Buys all rights.
How to Contact: Submit demo tape of previously aired work. Prefers cassette or 7½ ips reel-to-reel with 8-10 pieces. Does not return unsolicited material; prefers to keep material on file. Reports in 2 weeks.
Music: All kinds of music for jingles and music beds.
Tips: "Send a tape with current samples of commercials only with a price list and whether or not you'll do spec work."

*COMMUNICATIONS CONCEPTS INC., P.O. Box 661, Cape Canaveral FL 32920. (407)783-5230. Manager: Jim Lewis. Audiovisual firm. Clients include resorts, developments medical and high tech industries. Uses the services of music houses, independent songwriters, lyricists and music libraries and services for scoring of TV shows and AV presentations, background music for AV programs and marketing presentations, jingles for commercials and AV programs, and commercials for radio and TV. Commissions 2-3 composers/year and 1-2 lyricists/year. Pays $50-5,000/job. Buys all rights or one-time rights.
How to Contact: Prefers cassette. Does not return unsolicited material; prefers to keep on file.
Music: Corporate, contemporary and commercial.

COMMUNICATIONS FOR LEARNING, 395 Massachusetts Ave., Arlington MA 02174. (617)641-2350. Executive Producer/Director: Jonathan L. Barkan. Audiovisual and design firm. Clients include multinationals, industry, government, institutions, local, national and international nonprofits. Uses services of music houses and independent songwriters/composers for scoring and background music for audiovisual and video soundtracks. Commissions 1-2 composers/year. Pays $2,000-3,000/job. Buys one-time rights.
How to Contact: Submit demo tape of previous work or tape demonstrating composition skills. Prefers cassette or 7½ or 15 ips reel-to-reel (or ½" or ¾" videocassette). SASE, but prefers to keep material on file. "For each job we consider our entire collection." Reports in 2 months.
Music: Uses all styles of music for all sorts of assignments.
Tips: "Please don't call. Just send good material and when we're interested, we'll be in touch."

CONTINENTAL PRODUCTIONS, Box 1219, Great Falls MT 59405. (406)761-8816. Production Sales/Marketing: Duke Brekhus. Video production house. Clients include advertising agencies, business, industry and government. Uses the services of independent songwriters/composers for TV commercials and non broadcast programs and jingles for TV commercials. Commissions 1-6 composers/year. Pays $85-500/job. Buys all rights or one-time rights.
How to Contact: Write or call first and obtain permission to submit. Prefers cassette (or ½" VHS videocassette). SASE, but prefers to keep on file. Reports in 2 weeks.
Music: Uses contemporary music beds and custom jingles for TV and non-broadcast video.
Tips: "Songwriters need to build a working relationship by providing quality product in short order at a good price."

T. COOKE PRODUCTIONS, INC., 955 Gardenview Off-Pkwy., St. Louis MO 63141. (314)997-3200. President: Thomas Cooke. Audiovisual firm and motion picture production company. Clients include Fortune 500 industrial/consumer products companies. Uses services of independent songwriters/composers, lyricists and music houses for scoring of industrial video/film, background music for A/V programs. Commissions 4-6 composers/year. Pays $3,000-6,000/job. Buys all rights.
How to Contact: Submit demo tape of previous work or query with resume of credits. Prefers cassette with 6 songs. SASE, but prefers to keep material on file.
Music: Uses music to sell, hype, motivate for slide presentations, corporate image videos, and live industrial stage shows.

CORPORATE COMMUNICATIONS INC., Main St., P.O. Box 854, N. Conway NH 03860. (603)356-7011. President: Kimberly Beals. Advertising agency. Estab. 1983. Uses the services of music houses, independent songwriters/composers for background music, jingles and commercials for radio/video. Commissions 2 or more composers/year. Pays by the job. Buys all rights or one-time rights.
How to Contact: Submit demo tape of previous work demonstrating composition skills and manuscript showing scoring skills. Query with resume of credits. Prefers cassette (or ½" videocassette) with 5 songs. Does not return unsolicited material; prefers to keep on file. Reports in 1-2 weeks.
Music: Uses varying styles of music for varying assignments.

COVENANT PRODUCTIONS—ANDERSON UNIVERSITY, 1100 E. 5th St., Anderson IN 46012. (317)641-4345. Operation Director: Scott Fritz. Teleproduction house. Clients include corporate/industrial; some religious; some broadcast. Estab. 1985. Uses the services of music houses, independent songwriters/composers for scoring of TV programs/productions, background music for TV programs/productions and commercials for radio, TV. Commissions 5 composers/year. Pays by minute of used music $10-100/minute. Buys all rights, one-time rights.
How to Contact: Submit demo tape of previous or tape demonstrating composition skills. Prefers cassette or 15 ips reel-to-reel (or ¾" Betacam or VHS videocassette, if scored) with 3-5 songs. SASE, but prefers to keep material on file. Reports in 2 weeks.
Music: Uses music beds—easy listening, jazz, up-tempo for commercials and documentaries.
Tips: "Avoid a 'generic' sound."

CREATIVE ASSOCIATES, 626 Bloomfield Ave., Verona NJ 07044. (201)857-3444. Production Coordinator: Susan Graham. Audiovisual firm. Clients include commercial, industrial firms. Estab. 1975. Uses the services of music houses and independent songwriters/composers for scoring of video programs, background music for press tours and jingles for new products. Pays $300-5,000 + /job. Buys all or one-time rights.
How to Contact: Submit demo tape of previous work demonstrating composition skills or query with resume of credits. Prefers cassette or ½" or ¾" VHS videocassette. Prefers to keep material on file.
Music: Uses all styles for many different assignments.

CREATIVE AUDIO PRODUCTIONS, 326 Santa Isabel Blvd., Laguna Vista, Port Isabel TX 78578. (512)943-6278. Owner: Ben McCampbell. **Jingle/commercial music production house.** Serves ad agencies, broadcast stations (TV and radio), video/film production houses and advertisers. Uses the services of lyricists for jingles for commercials and commercials for radio and TV. Commissions 1 composer and 2 lyricists/year. Fees negotiable. Buys one-time rights.
How to Contact: Submit demo tape of previous work. Prefers cassette with 3-5 songs. Does not return unsolicited material; prefers to keep on file. Reports in 1 month.
Music: Uses pop, up-tempo, reggae for commercials.

CREATIVE HOUSE ADVERTISING, INC., Suite 301, 30777 Northwestern Hwy., Farmington Hills MI 48334. (313)737-7077. Executive Vice President/Creative Director: Robert G. Washburn. Advertising agency and graphics studio. Serves commercial, retail, consumer, industrial, medical and financial clients. Uses the services of songwriters and lyricists for jingles, background music for radio and TV commercials and corporate sales meeting films and videos. Commissions 3-4 songwriters/year. Pays $50-100/hour or $1,500-5,000/job depending on job involvement. Buys all rights.
How to Contact: Query with resume of credits or submit tape demo showing jingle/composition skills. Submit cassette (or ¾" videocassette) with 6-12 songs. SASE, but would prefer to keep material on file. "When an appropriate job comes up associated with the talents/ability of the songwriters/musicians, then they will be contacted."
Music: "The type of music we need depends on clients. The range is multi; contemporary, disco, rock, MOR and traditional."

CREATIVE SUPPORT SERVICES, 1950 Riverside Dr., Los Angeles CA 90039. (213)666-7968. Contact: Michael M. Fuller. **Music/sound effects library**. Clients include audiovisual production houses. Estab. 1978. Uses the services of independent songwriters and musicians for background music for audiovisuals and commercials for radio. Commissions 3-5 songwriters and 1-2 lyricists/year. Pays by the job or by royalty. Buys exclusive distribution rights.

How to Contact: Write or call first. Prefers cassette ("chrome or metal only") or 7½ ips reel-to-reel with 3 or more pieces. Does not return unsolicited material; prefers to keep on file. "Will call if interested."

Music: Uses "industrial music predominantly, but all other kinds or types to a lesser degree."

Tips: "Target your market. Lower your monetary expectations. Remember the risks that have to be incurred to buy someone's music."

CRESWELL, MUNSELL, FULTZ & ZIRBEL, Box 2879, Cedar Rapids IA 52406. (319)395-6500. Executive Producer: Terry Taylor. Advertising agency. Serves agricultural, consumer and industrial clients. Uses songwriters and music houses for jingles and background music in commercials and multi-image soundtracks. Commissions 7-8 songwriters for 15 pieces/year. Pays by the job. Buys rights on talent residuals.

How to Contact: Submit demo tape of previously aired work. Prefers 7 or 15 ips reel-to-reel or cassette with 7-8 songs maximum. Does not return unsolicited material. Reports "when we want figures on a job."

Music: All types. Likes to hear a good range of music material. Will listen to anything from "small groups to full orchestration."

Tips: "Create unique, recognizable melodies."

CROSS KEYS ADVERTISING, 329 S. Main St., Doylestown PA 18901. President: Laura T. Barnes. Advertising agency. Clients include retail, industrial and commercial. Estab. 1981. Use the services of music houses and independent songwriters/composers for background music, jingles and commercials for radio and TV. Commissions 3-4 composers/year. Pays by the job. Buys all rights.

How to Contact: Submit demo tape of previous work. Prefers cassette. Does not return unsolicited materials; prefers to keep on file.

Music: Uses all styles for commercials.

R.J. DALE ADVERTISING INC., #2204, 500 N. Michigan Ave., Chicago IL 60611. (312)644-2316. Executive Vice President: William Stewart. Advertising agency. Clients include H&BA Manufacturers, retail bank, lottery, food, distilled spirits manufacturers. Estab. 1979. Uses the services of music houses and independent songwriters/composers for background music for sales meetings and commercials for radio and TV. Commissions 5 composers/year. Pays by the job. Buys all rights or two-year rights.

How to Contact: Submit demo tape of previous work showing range of ability. Prefers cassette (or ¾" U-matic videocassette). SASE, but prefers to keep material on file.

Music: Uses pop, jazz, fusion and R&B for commercials.

dbF A MEDIA COMPANY, P.O. Box 2458, Waldorf MD 20604. (301)843-7110. President: Randy Runyon. Advertising agency, audiovisual firm and audio and video production company. Clients include business and industry. Estab. 1981. Uses the services of music houses, independent songwriters/composers and lyricists for background music for industrial videos, jingles for radio and TV and commercials for radio and TV. Commissions 5-12 composers and 5-12 lyricists/year. Pays by the job. Buys all rights.

How to Contact: Submit demo tape of previous work. Query with resume of credits. Prefers cassette or 7½ IPS reel-to-reel (or VHS videocassette) with 5-8 songs and lead sheet. SASE, but prefers to keep material on file. Reports in 6 weeks.

Music: Uses up-tempo contemporary for industrial videos, slide presentations and commercials.

Tips: "Keep us up to date with your current projects."

DELTA DESIGN GROUP, INC., 409 Washington Ave., Greenville MS 38701. (601)335-6148. President: Noel Workman. Advertising agency. Serves industrial, health care, agricultural and retail commercial clients. Uses the services of songwriters for jingles. Commissions 3-6 pieces/year. Pays $500-2,500/job. Buys "rights which vary geographically according to client. Some are all rights; others are rights for a specified market only. Buy out only. No annual licensing."

How to Contact: Submit demo tape showing jingle/composition skills. Prefers 7½ ips reel-to-reel with 3-6 songs. "Include typed sequence of cuts on tape on the outside of the reel box." SASE. Reports "when services are needed."

Music: Needs "30- and 60-second jingles for agricultural, health care, auto dealers and chambers of commerce."

DISK PRODUCTIONS, 1100 Perkins Rd., Baton Rouge LA 70802. (504)343-5438. Director: Joey Decker. **Jingle/production house.** Estab. 1982. Clients include advertising agencies, slide production houses and film companies. Uses independent songwriters/composers and lyricists for scoring of TV spots and films and jingles for radio and TV. Commissions 7 songwriters/composers and 7 lyricists/year. Pays by the job. Buys all rights.

How to Contact: Prefers cassette or 7½ ips reel-to-reel (or ½″ videocassette) and lead sheet. Does not return unsolicited material; prefers to keep on file. Reports "immediately if material looks promising."

Music: Needs all types of music for jingles, music beds or background music for TV and radio, etc.

Tips: "Advertising techniques change with time. Don't be locked in a certain style of writing. Give me music that I can't get from pay needle-drop."

*DRGM, 50 Washington St., Reno NV 89503. (702)786-4900. Also Suite A, 2275 Renaissance Dr., Bldg. 3, Las Vegas NV 89119. (702)736-0065. Vice President/Creative Services: Randy Snow. Creative Director/Reno: Ron Cooney. Creative Director/Las Vegas: Michael Mayes. Advertising agency. Clients include tourism, hotel-casino, retail, financial and healthcare. Estab. 1970. Uses the services of music houses for scoring of television/radio, background music for television/radio, jingles for TV/radio and commercials for radio and TV. Commissions 4-5 composers/year. Pays by the job. Buys all rights.

How to Contact: Submit demo tape of previous work. Prefers cassette (or ¾″ videocassette). SASE, but prefers to keep material on file. Reports in 2 weeks.

Music: Uses contemporary and up-tempo for jingles and commercials.

Tips: "Send me a reel—be aware that clients in Nevada do not understand things like big budgets, royalty payments, etc."

DSM PRODUCERS ENT PUBLISHING COMPANY, Ste. 803, 161 W. 54th St., New York NY 10019. (212)245-0006. Vice President, National Sales Director: Doris Kaufman. Scoring service, **jingle/commercial music production house** and original stock library called "All American Composers Library" record producers. Clients include networks, corporate, advertising firms, film and video, book publishers (music only). Estab. 1979. Uses the services of independent songwriters/composers and "all signed composers who we represent" for scoring of film, industrial films, major films—all categories; background music for film, audio cassettes, instore video—all catagories; jingles for advertising agencies and commercials for radio and TV. Commissions 10 composers and 1 lyricist/year. Pays royalty.

How to Contact: Submit tape demonstrating composition skills. Prefers cassette (or VHS videocassette) with 2 songs and lyric or lead sheet. "Keep the vocals up in the mix—use a large enough return envelope to put in a standard business reply letter." SASE. Reports in 6 weeks.

Music: Needs dance, new age, country and rock for adventure films and sports programs.

ROY EATON MUSIC INC., 595 Main St., Roosevelt Island NY 10044. (212)980-9046. President: Roy Eaton. Jingle/**commercial music production house**. Clients include advertising agencies, TV and radio stations and film producers. Estab. 1982. Uses the services of independent songwriters/composers and lyricists and scoring of TV commercials and films, background music for TV programs, jingles for advertising agencies and commercials for radio and TV. Commissions 10 composers and 1 lyricist/year. Pays $50-3,000/job. Buys all rights.

How to Contact: Submit demo tape of previous work. Prefers cassette with 3-5 pieces. Does not return unsolicted material; prefers to keep on file. Reports in 2 months.

Music: Uses jazz fusion, new age and rock/pop for commercials and films.

EFFECTIVE LEARNING SYSTEMS, INC., 5221 Industrial Blvd., Edina MN 55435. (612)893-1680. Director of Marketing: James W. Griswold. Audio cassette publishers. Clients include general public. Estab. 1972. Uses the services of music houses and independent songwriters/composers for background music for self-help audio cassettes (foreground also). Commissions 1 or 2 composers/year. Pays by the job. Buys unlimited useage, exclusive rights for self-help tapes.

How to Contact: Submit demo tape of previous work. Prefers cassette with at least 4 pieces. "Include fee requirements with sample." SASE. Reports in 4 weeks.

Music: Uses many styles, if good quality, but emphasis on new age/relaxation styles for self-help audio cassettes background; subliminal audio cassettes foreground.

Tips: "Only send professional-sounding demo with realistic fee requirements. Listen to "Love Tapes®" series for examples of acceptable music to date."

THE EFX COMPANY, 2300 S. 9th St., 136A, Arlington VA 22204. (703)486-2303. President: W. P. Fowler. Audiovisual firm. Clients include corporate and commercial video production, graphics and animation. Estab. 1982. Uses the services of independent songwriters/composers for scoring of instructional films, background music for corporate and commercial videos, jingles for TV/in house corporate videos and commercials for TV. Commissions 20 composers/year. Pays by the job or depending upon instruments/studio. Buys rights depending upon assignment.

How to Contact: Submit demo tape of previous work and tape demonstrating composition skills. Prefers cassette (or VHS or ¾ videocassette) with 3-5 pieces and lyric sheets. SASE. Reports in 3 weeks.
Music: Uses contemporary instrumentals, top 40/pop, AOR and MOR for educational films and commercials.

ELITE VIDEO PRODUCTIONS, 1612 East 14th St., Brooklyn NY 11229. (718)627-0499. President: Kalman Zeines. Video production company. Clients include educational and industrial. Estab. 1978. Uses the services of music houses, lyricists and independent songwriters/composers for background music for narration and commercials for TV. Commissions 2 lyricists and 5 composers/year. Pays $500-2,500/job. Buys all rights.
How to Contact: Submit demo tape of previous work. Prefers cassette. "Call first." Does not return unsolicited material; prefers to keep materials on file. Reports back in 2 weeks. Assignments include work on educational films.

ENSEMBLE PRODUCTIONS, P.O. Box 2332, Auburn AL 36831. (205)826-3045. Owner: Barry J. McConatha. Audiovisual firm and video production/post production. Clients include corporate, governmental and educational. Estab. 1984. Uses services of music houses and independent songwriters/composers for scoring of documentary productions, background music for corporate public relations and training videos, jingles for public service announcements, and for montage effects with A/V and video. Commissions 0-5 composers/year. Pays $100-1,000/job or $25/hour, depending upon project. Buys all rights and one-time rights.
How to Contact: Submit demo tape of previous work. Submit demo tape demonstrating composition skills. "Needs are sporadic, write first if submission to be returned." Prefers cassette or 7½/15 IPS reel-to-reel (or VHS videocassette) with 3-5 songs. "Most needs are upbeat industrial sound but occasional mood setting music also. Inquire for details." Does not return unsolicited material; prefers to keep on file. Reports in 3-5 weeks "if solicited."
Music: Uses up-beat, industrial, new age, and mood for training film. PR, education and multi-media.
Tips: "Stay away from disco sound!"

ENTERTAINMENT PRODUCTIONS, INC., #744, 2210 Wilshire Blvd., Santa Monica CA 90403. (213)456-3143. President: Edward Coe. Motion picture and television production company. Estab. 1972. Clients include motion picture and TV distributors. Uses the services of music houses and songwriters for scores, production numbers, background and theme music for films and TV and jingles for promotion of films. Commissions/year vary. Pays by the job or by royalty. Buys all rights.
How to Contact: Query with resume of credits. Demo should show flexibility of composition skills. "Demo records/tapes sent at own risk—returned if SASE included." Reports by letter in 1 month, "but only if SASE is included."
Tips: "Have resume on file. Develop self-contained capability."

RICHARD R. FALK ASSOC., 1472 Broadway, New York NY 10036. (212)221-0043. President: Richard Falk. Public Relations. Clients include national theatrical, corporate and stars. Estab. 1940. Uses the services of lyricists for promotions. Commissions 2-3 composers and 2-3 lyricists/year. Pays $100/job. Buys one-time rights.
How to Contact: Send a simple flyer on some past credits, nothing too involved. SASE. "If accompanied by SASE, replies immediately."

FANCY FREE MUSIC, 300 Hempstead Turnpike West Hempstead NY 11552. Creative Director: Joe Orlando. Scoring service, **jingle/commercial music production house** and **music sound effect library**. Clients include advertising agencies, A/V houses, film editors and independent producers. Estab. 1979. Uses the services of independent songwriters/composers and lyricists and music programmers for scoring of commercials, A/V programs, background music for slide shows, jingles for radio and TV and commercials for radio and TV. Commissions 4 composers and 1 lyricist/year. Pays $100-750/job. Buys all rights.
How to Contact: Submit demo tape of previous work or write or call to arrange personal interview. Prefers cassette or 7½ ips reel-to-reel with 4-6 songs and lyric sheets. SASE for return. Prefers to keep material on file. Reports in 4 weeks.
Music: Uses classical, pop, R&B, jazz and MOR for A/V films, slide shows, TV/radio commercials and songs.
Tips: "Make your demo tape as contemporary as possible. Innovative sounds, strong hooks, tight lyrics."

FILM AMERICA, INC., Ste. 209, 77 Peachtree Rd. NE, Atlanta GA 30305. (404)261-3718. President: Avrum Fine. Motion picture editing house. Clients include advertising agencies, corporate audiovisual producers and film/tape producers. Uses the services of music houses and independent songwriters

for scoring of industrial films/TV spots; lyricists for jingles for TV spots, commercials for TV and theater trailers. Commissions 3 composers and 3 lyricists/year. Pays by the job. Buys all rights.
How to Contact: Submit demo tape of previous work. Prefers cassette (or VHS videocassette). Does not return unsolicited material; prefers to keep on file. Reports in 4 weeks.
Music: "All contemporary idioms."

FINE ART PRODUCTIONS, 67 Maple St., Newburgh NY 12550. (914)561-5866. Producer/Researcher: Richard Suraci. Advertising agency, audiovisual firm, scoring service, jingle/**commercial music production house,** motion picture production company and **music sound effect library.** Clients include corporate, industrial, motion, broadcast firms. Estab. 1987. Uses services of music houses, independent songwriters/composers and lyricists for scoring, background music and jingles for various projects and commercials for radio and TV. Commissions 1-10 songwriters or composers and 1-10 lyricists/year. Pays by the job, by royalty or by the hour. Buys all rights or one-time rights.
How to Contact: Submit demo tape of previous work or tape demonstrating composition skills, submit manuscript showing music scoring skills, query with resume of credits or write to arrange personal interview. Prefers cassette (or ½", ¾", or 1" videocassette) with as many songs as possible and lyric or lead sheets. SASE, but prefers to keep material on file. Reports ASAP.
Music: Uses all types of music for all types of assignments.

GARY FITZGERALD MUSIC PRODUCTIONS, Suite B29, 37-75 63rd St., Woodside NY 11377. (718)446-3857. Producer: Gary Fitzgerald. Scoring service, **commercial music production house and music/sound effects library.** "We service the advertising and record community." Estab. 1987. Uses the services of independent songwriters, vocalists, lyricists and voice-over talent for scoring of TV, radio and industrials; background music for movies; jingles for TV, radio and industrials; and commercials for radio and TV. Commissions 4-5 composers and 2 lyricists/year. Pays per project. Rights purchased depends on project.
How to Contact: Submit demo tape of previous work or tape demonstrating composition skills. Prefers cassette. Does not return unsolicited material; prefers to keep on file. "A follow-up call must follow submission."
Music: Uses all styles of music.
Tips: "Always submit what you feel is your strongest work. Be persistent."

FOREMOST FILMS AND VIDEO, INC., 7 Regency Dr., Holliston MA 01746. (508)429-8046. President: David Fox. Video production company. Estab. 1983. Serves consumer and corporate/industrial clients. Uses the services of independent songwriters and music houses for corporate and industrial videos. Commissions 1-2 composers and 1-2 lyricists/year. Buys all rights.
How to Contact: Submit demo tape of previous work. Prefers cassette, CD or 7½ ips reel-to-reel (or ½" or ¾" videocassette) with 2-3 pieces and lyric or lead sheet. SASE. Reports within weeks.
Music: Styles of music used and kinds of assignments depend on specific jobs.
Tips: "Be patient, the market fluctuates so much for video production. Call every few months just to keep in touch. This keeps your name fresh in my mind."

FREDRICK, LEE & LLOYD, 235 Elizabeth St., Landisville PA 17538. (717)898-6092. Vice President: Dusty Rees. Jingle/**commercial music production house.** Clients include advertising agencies. Estab. 1976. Uses the services of independent songwriters/composers and staff writers for jingles. Commissions 2 composers/year. Pays $650/job. Buys all rights.
How to Contact: Submit tape demonstrating composition skills. Prefers cassette or 7½ ips reel-to-reel with 5 jingles. "Submissions may be samples of published work or original material." Does not return unsolicited material. Reports in 2 weeks.
Music: Uses pop, rock, country and MOR.
Tips: "The more completely orchestrated the demos are, the better."

FREED & ASSOCIATES, Mill Centre, 3000 Chestnut Ave., Baltimore MD 21211. (301)243-1421. Senior Writer/Broadcast Producer: Jeff Grutkowski. Advertising agency. Clients incluse a variety of retail and non-retail businesses. Estab. 1960. Uses the services of music houses and independent songwriters/composers for background music for television commercials, jingles for TV/radio commercials and commercials for radio and TV. Commissions 4-5 composers and 2-4 lyricists/year. Pays $2,000-10,000/job. Buys all rights or one-time rights, depending on the project.
How to Contact: Submit demo tape of previous work. Prefers cassette (or ½" or ¾" videocassette). Does not return unsolicited material; prefers to keep on file. Reports in 1 month.
Music: Uses varying styles for commercials and corporate videos.

PAUL FRENCH AND PARTNERS, 503 Gabbettville Rd., LaGrange GA 30240. (404)882-5581. Contact: Ms. Gene Ballard. Audiovisual firm. Uses the services of music houses and songwriters for musical scores in films and original songs for themes; lyricists for writing lyrics for themes. Commissions 20 composers and 20 lyricists/year. Pays minimum $500/job. Buys all rights.
How to Contact: Submit demo tape of previous work. Prefers reel-to-reel with 3-8 songs. SASE. Reports in 2 weeks.

FRENCH & ROGERS, INC., 5455 Corporate Dr., Troy MI 48098. (313)641-0010. Producer: David Morningstar. Advertising agency. Clients include industrial firms. Estab. 1966. Uses the services of independent songwriters/composers for scoring of video tape productions. Commissions 1 composer/year. Pays negotiated rate by the job. Buys all rights.
How to Contact: Submit demo tape of previous work. Prefers cassette with 3 or more songs. Does not return unsolicited material; prefers to keep material on file.
Music: Uses up-tempo, jazz for trade show tapes and product demonstrations.

FRONTLINE VIDEO, INC., 243 12th St., Del Mar CA 92014. (619)481-5566. Production Manager: Alicia Reed. Television and video production company. Clients include sports programming in surfing, skiing, skateboarding, boardsailing; medical patient education; and various industrial clients. Estab. 1983. Uses the services of independent songwriters/ composers for background music for sports programming and industrial clients; intros, extros. Commissions 5 composers/year. Pays by the composition $35-150 per cut.
How to Contact: Submit demo tape of previous work. Prefers cassette. Does not return unsolicited material, but prefers to keep material on file. "We contact artists on an 'as needed' basis when we're ready to use one of their pieces or styles."
Music: Uses up-tempo, jazzy, rock. "We buy works that come to us for national and international TV programming."
Tips: "Background music for surfing and other sports is our biggest area of need. Current-sounding, driving pieces in rock or jazzy styles are appropriate. We don't have time to respond to every submission, but if your tape is here at the right time and we like it, we'll contact you."

*FURMAN FILMS, INC., Box 1769, Venice CA 90294-1769. (213)306-2700. Producers: Will Furman/Norma Doane. Motion picture production company. Clients include business, industry and education. Uses services of music houses and songwriters for "occasional use for original music and lyrics for motion pictures and background/theme music; rarely use lyricists." Payment varies according to budget. Buys all rights.
How to Contact: Query with resume of credits or submit demo tape of previous work. Prefers cassette with 5-10 songs. Does not return unsolicited material; "kept on file for reference."

GARDINER—A MARKETING COMPANY, Box 30, Salt Lake City UT 84110. (801)364-5600. Vice President/Creative Director: Gordon A. Johnson. Advertising agency. Estab. 1949. Clients include medical, high tech, financial, retail and industrial firms. Uses independent songwriters and music houses for jingles and background music. Commissions 1-3 songwriters/composers per year. Pays $5,000/job average. Buys all rights; "unlimited buyout per market."
How to Contact: Accepts "demo tapes of established music houses only." Prefers cassette or 7½ ips reel-to-reel (or ¾" or VHS videocassette) with 5 or more pieces. SASE, but prefers to keep material on file. Reports if needed.
Music: Mostly MOR, novelty, uptempo contemporary—all styles of music for jingles and scoring for TV commercials.
Tips: "We prefer full cuts of music. Don't think of it as a 'jingle' but more as a 'song.' Lyrics need to be clear."

JAN GARDNER AND ASSOCIATES, Suite 229, 3340 Poplar, Memphis TN 38111. (901)452-7328. Production Director: Danny Umfress. Advertising agency. Serves hospitals, healthcare providers; also automotive, financial and retail businesses. Uses services of songwriters, lyricists and music houses for jingles, commercial and A/V presentations. Commissions 2 songwriters and 2 lyricists/year. Pays by the job, $500-5,000. Buys all rights.
How to Contact: Submit demo tape of previous work. Prefers 7½ ips reel-to-reel or cassette with 3-12 songs. SASE, but prefers to keep material on file.
Music: "We have a wide range of clients and needs."
Tips: "Submit your demo and be willing to spec for bidding."

GEER DUBOIS ADVERTISING INC., 114 Fifth Ave., New York NY 10011. (212)741-1900 ex. 277. Executive Producer: Paul Mavis. Advertising agency. Clients include national, regional and local advertisers. Estab. 1935. Uses the services of music houses and independent songwriters/composers for scoring of TV and radio commercials, background music, jingles and commercials for radio and TV. Commissions 25 composers/year. Pays $750-3,000/job. Buys all rights.

How to Contact: Submit demo tape of previous work; query with resume of credits; write to arrange personal interview or contact Laura Hatton at the above address. Prefers cassette (or ¾″ videocassette). "Keep it short with brief samples of your work." SASE, but prefers to keep material on file. "Unless there's a specific job, I don't have the time to report back on submissions."

Music: Uses all styles—depending on the commercial—for commercials only.

Tips: "Send a cassette or ¾″ videotape with 8-10 samples of your best work with a short letter telling us who you are."

GILLESPIE ADVERTISING, INC., International Corporate Center, P.O. Box 3333, Princeton NJ 08543. (609)799-6000. Associate Creative Director: Bill Spink. Advertising agency. Clients include NBA basketball team, national yogurt franchise chain, shopping malls, several banks, a swimwear company, a chain of drug stores plus several industrial and business to business accounts. Estab. 1974. Uses the services of music houses and independent songwriters/composers for scoring of TV spots and sales videos, jingles for radio & TV and commercials for radio and TV. Commissions 4 composers/year. Pay varies by the job.

How to Contact: Submit demo tape of previous work. Write or call first to arrange personal interview. Prefers cassette (or ½″ videocassette) with 5-10 songs. Does not return unsolicited material; prefers to keep on file.

Music: Uses all types for commercials and videos.

Tips: "Never underestimate the power of your demo!"

GLYN/NET, INC., 12 Floor, 155 W. 23rd St., New York NY 10011. (212)691-9300. Vice President Production: Dawn Salvatore. Motion picture and video production company. Clients include major corporations. Uses the services of music houses, independent songwriters and lyricists for scoring of and background music for films and TV shows. Commissions 2-3 composers/year. Pays by the job. Buys all rights or one-time rights.

How to Contact: Prefers cassette (or ¾″ videocassette). Does not return unsolicited material. Reports in 3 weeks.

Music: All types.

DENNIS R. GREEN AND ASSOCIATES, INC., Suite 110, 29355 Northwestern Hwy., Southfield MI 48034. (313)352-0700. President: Dennis R. Green. Advertising agency. Estab. 1973. Clients include retail and industrial firms. Uses the services of music houses for jingles for radio and television and commercials for radio and TV. Commissions 6 composers/year. Pays $1500-2500/job. Buys all rights.

How to Contact: Submit a demo tape of previous work or query with resume of credits. Prefers cassette or 7.5 ips reel to reel (or VHS videocassette) with 6-10 songs. SASE, but prefers to keep submitted material on file. Reports back in two weeks.

Music: All kinds, depending on clients' needs.

Tips: "Send a demo reel and keep in touch."

*GREINKE, EIERS AND ASSOCIATES, Suite 332, 2466 N. Oakland, Milwaukee WI 53211-4345. (414)962-9810. FAX: (414)964-7479. Staff: Arthur Greinke, Patrick Eiers, Lora Nigro. Advertising agency and public relations/music artist management and media relations. Clients include small business, original music groups, special events. Estab. 1984. Uses the services of independent songwriters/composers, lyricists and music groups, original rock bands and artists for scoring of video news releases, other video projects, jingles for small firms and special events and commercials for radio and TV. Commissions 4-6 composers and 4-6 lyricists/year. Paid by a personal contract.

How to Contact: Query with resume of credits. Prefers compact disc or cassette (or DAT tape or VHS videocassette) with any number of songs and lyric sheet. "We will contact only when job is open—but will keep submissions on file." Does not return unsolicited material.

Music: Uses original rock, pop, heavy rock for recording groups, commercials, video projects.

Tips: "Be creative and original, well organized, lots of energy. Remember: *No Rules!*—strong hooks!!"

GRS, INC., 13300 Broad St., Pataskala OH 43062. (614)927-9566. Manager: S.S. Andrews. Teleproduction facility. Estab. 1969. Varied clients. Uses the services of music houses and independent songwriters/composers for jingles and background music. Pays by the job. Buys all rights.

How to Contact: Submit demo tape of previous work. Prefers cassette. Does not return unsolicited material; prefers to keep on file.

Music: All styles for commercials.

Tips: "Follow our instructions exactly."

HEPWORTH ADVERTISING CO., 3403 McKinney Ave., Dallas TX 75204. (214)526-7785. President: S.W. Hepworth. Advertising agency. Estab. 1952. Serves financial, industrial and food clients. Uses services of songwriters for jingles. Pays by the job. Buys all rights.
How to Contact: Call first and obtain permission to submit or submit demo tape of previously aired work. Prefers cassette. SASE. Reports as need arises.

HEYWOOD FORMATICS & SYNDICATION, 1103 Colonial Blvd., Canton OH 44714. (216)456-2592. Owner: Max Heywood. Advertising agency and consultant. Clients include radio, television, restaurants/lounges. Uses the services of music houses and record companies and writers for background music for video presentation and industrial, and commercials for radio and TV. Payment varies per project.
How to Contact: Submit demo tape of previous work. Prefers cassette or 7½ or 15 ips reel-to-reel (or VHS/Beta videocassette). SASE.
Music: Uses pop, easy listening and CHR for educational films, slide presentations and commercials.

HILLMANN & CARR INC., 2121 Wisconsin Ave. NW, Washington DC 20007. (202)342-0001. President: Alfred Hillmann. Vice President/Treasurer: Ms. Michal Carr. Audiovisual firm and motion picture production company. Estab. 1975. Clients include corporate, government, associations and museums. Uses the services of music houses and independent songwriters/composers for scoring of films, video productions, PSA's and commercials for radio and TV. Commissions 2-3 composers/year. Payment negotiable.
How to Contact: Query with resume of credits, or submit demo tape of previous work or tape demonstrating composition skills, or write to arrange personal interview. Prefers cassette or 7½ ips reel-to-reel (or ¾″ VHS or Beta videocassette) with 5-10 pieces. Does not return unsolicited material; prefers to keep on file only when interested. Reports in 1 month. SASE.
Music: Uses contemporary, classical, up-tempo and thematic music for documentary film and video productions, multi-media exposition productions, public service announcements.

*THE HITCHINS COMPANY, 22756 Hartland St., Canoga Park CA 91307. (818)715-0510. President: W.E. Hitchins. Advertising agency. Estab. 1985. Uses the services of independent songwriters/composers for jingles and commercial for radio and TV. Commissions 1-2 composers and 1-2 lyricists/year. Will negotiate pay. Buys all rights.
How to Contact: Query with resume of credits. Prefers cassette or VHS videocassette. "Check first to see if we have a job." Does not return unsolicited material; prefers to keep on file.
Music: Uses variety of musical styles for commercials.

*HODGES ASSOCIATES, INC., P.O. Box 53805, 912 Hay St., Fayetteville NC 28305. (919)483-8489. President/Production Manager: Chuck Smith. Advertising agency. Clients include industrial, retail and consumer ("We handle a full array of clientel."). Estab. 1974. Uses the services of music houses and independent songwriters/composers for background music for industrial films and slide presentations, and commercials for radio and TV. Commissions 1-2 composers/year. Pays by the job. Buys all rights.
How to Contact: Submit demo tape of previous work. Prefers cassette. Does not return unsolicited material; prefers to keep on file. Reports in 2-3 months.
Music: Uses all styles for industrial videos, slide presentations and TV commercials.

*HODGES MEDIA GROUP, P.O. Box 51483, Palo Alto CA 94303. (415)856-7442. Contact: Ed Hodges. Advertising agency and **music sound effect library**. Clients include sportswear, automotive. Estab. 1987. Uses the services of music houses for backgroung music for industrial videos and commercials for radio and TV. Commissions 3 composers/year. Pays $300-500/job. Buys all rights.
How to Contact: Submit demo tape of previous work. Prefers cassette (or VHS, −f8″ videocassette). Does not return unsolicited material; prefers to keep materials on file. Reports in 3 weeks.
Music: Uses metal, drums and bass line.

HOME, INC., 731 Harrison Ave., Boston MA 02118. (617)266-1386. Director: Alan Michel. Audiovisual firm and video production company. Clients include cable television, nonprofit organizations, pilot programs, entertainment companies and industrial. Uses the services of music houses and independent

Listings of companies within this section which are either commercial music production houses or music libraries will have that information printed in boldface type.

songwriters/composers for background music for videos and TV commercials. Commissions 2-5 songwriters/year. Pays $50-300/job. Buys all rights or one-time rights.
How to Contact: Query with resume of credits, or submit demo tape of previous work. Prefers cassette with 6 pieces. SASE, but prefers to keep material on file. Reports as projects require.
Music: Mostly synthesizer. Uses all styles of music for educational videos.
Tips: "Plan to develop a working relationship for the long term."

INTERMEDIA, 2720 Turner St., Victoria B.C. V8T 4V1 **Canada**. (604)389-2800. Fax: (604)389-2801. President: A.W. (Tony) Reynolds. Motion picture production company. Clients include industrial, educational, broadcast and theatrical. Estab. 1980. Uses the services of independent songwriters/composers for scoring of TV shows and films, jingles for commercials and commercials for radio and TV. Commissions 2-3 composers/year. Pays by the job. Buys all, one-time or varying rights.
How to Contact: Submit demo tape of previous work. Prefers cassette. SASE, but prefers to keep material on file. Reports in 2 weeks.
Music: Uses up-tempo, pop, jazz and classical for theatrical films, educational films and commercials.
Tips: "Be professional and competitive—current standards are very high."

INTERNATIONAL MEDIA SERVICES, INC., 718 Sherman Ave., Plainfield NJ 07060. (201)756-4060. President: Stuart Allen. Audiovisual firm, motion picture and television production company. Clients include schools, businesses, advertising and entertainment industry. Uses the services of music houses, songwriters/composers and lyricists for scoring of corporate and broadcast programs, background music for television and film, jingles for cable TV and broadcast spots, and commercials for radio and TV. Commissions 30 composers and 25 lyricists/year. Pays "per contract or license." Buys all rights or one-time rights.
How to Contact: Query with resume of credits or arrange personal interview. 'We accept no unsolicited material, contact required first." Prefers 7½ ips reel-to-reel, cassette (or ¾" videocassette) with 4-10 songs. SASE.
Tips: "Stay with professional and high quality material. Be persistent. Have a good broadcast quality demo. Follow-up periodically."

INTERNATIONAL MOTION PICTURES LTD., Box 30260, Bakersfield CA 93385-1260. Producer: Judge A. Robertson. Audiovisual firm, scoring service and motion picture production company. Services include original songs and themes for multi-image and motion picture. Uses the services of independent songwriters/composers for the scoring of soundtracks and commercials for radio and TV. Commissions 3 composers/year. Pays by the job. Buys all rights.
How to Contact: Write first and obtain permission to submit. Prefers cassette, reel-to-reel (or videocassette) with 2 pieces. Does not return unsolicited material; prefers to keep on file. Response time varies.
Music: Uses all styles of music for motion pictures, etc.

IZEN ENTERPRISES, INC., 26 Abby Dr., E. Northport NY 11731. (516)368-0615. President: Ray Izen. Video services. Clients are various. Estab. 1980. Uses the services of music houses, independent songwriters/composers and lyricists for scoring of customized songs and background music. Commissions 2 composers and 2 lyricists/year. Pay is open. Buys all rights.
How to Contact: Submit demo tape of previous work. Prefers cassette or VHS videocassette. SASE, but prefers to keep material on file.

THE JAYME ORGANIZATION, 25825 Science Park Dr., Cleveland OH 44122. (216)831-0110. Sr. Art Director: Debbie Klonk. Advertising agency. Uses the services of songwriters and lyricists for jingles and background music. Pays by the job. Buys all rights.
How to Contact: Query first; submit demo tape of previous work. Prefers cassette with 4-8 songs. SASE. Responds by phone as needs arise.
Music: Jingles.

K&R'S RECORDING STUDIOS, 28533 Greenfield, Southfield MI 48076. (313)557-8276. Contact: Ken Glaza. Scoring service and jingle/**commercial music production house**. Clients include commercial, industrial firms. Services include sound for pictures (music, dialogue). Uses the services of independent songwriters/composers for scoring, background music, jingles, commercials for radio and TV, etc. Commissions 2 composers/month. Pays by the job, royalty or hour. Buys all rights.
How to Contact: Write or call first to arrange personal interview. Prefers cassette (or ¾" or VHS videocassette) with 5-7 pieces minimum. "Show me what you can do in 5 to 7 minutes." SASE. Reports in 1 week.
Music: "Be able to compose with the producer present."

KAUFMANN ADVERTISING ASSOCIATES, INC., 1626 Frederica Rd., St. Simons Island GA 31522. (912)638-8678. President: Harry Kaufmann. Advertising agency. Clients include resorts. Estab. 1964. Uses the services of independent songwriters/composers and lyricists for scoring of videos, background music for videos, radio, TV, jingles for radio and commercials for radio and TV. Commissions 0-2 composers and 0-2 lyricists/year. Pays by the job.

KELLIHER/SAMETS, 130 S. Willard St., Burlington VT 05401. (802)862-8261. Associate C.D. Andrew Yavelow. Marketing communications firm. Clients include consumer, business-to-business, trade, public service; local, regional, national. Estab. 1977. Uses the services of music houses and independent songwriters/composers for scoring of commercials, background music for commercials, jingles for commercial, commercials for radio and TV. Commissions 6 composers/year. Pays $100-2,000/ job. Buys all rights.
How to Contact: Submit demo of previous work. Submit tape demonstrating composition skills. "Do not call." Prefers cassette (or VHS videocassette) with lead sheet. Does not return unsolicited material; prefers to keep on file. "Will call if needed."
Music: Uses many types, including folk, New Age, jazz, classical, blues, funk, be-bop, swing, gospel, impressionist and expressionist.
Tips: "No interest in 'over produced' sound; looking for creativity and toe-tapping; ability to convey *mood*; *no* show-biz."

KEN-DEL PRODUCTIONS INC., First State Production Center, 1500 First State Blvd., Wilmington DE 19804-3596. (302)999-1164. Estab. 1950. A&R Director: Shirley Kay. General Manager: Ed Kennedy. Clients include publishers, industrial firms and advertising agencies. Uses services of songwriters for slides, film scores and title music. Pays by the job. Buys all rights.
How to Contact: Submit demo of previous work. Will accept audio or video tapes. "We prefer to keep tapes on file for possible future use." Reports in 1 month.

KEY PRODUCTIONS, INC., P.O. Box 2684, Gravois Station, St. Louis MO 63116. President: John E. Schroeder. Audiovisual firm. Estab. 1964. Clients include church groups, publishers, civic organizations. Uses services of songwriters for stage and educational TV musical dramas, background music for filmstrips, some speculative collaboration for submission to publishers and regional theatrical productions. Commissions 1 songwriter/year. Pays $50 minimum/job or by 10% minimum royalty. Buys one-time rights or all rights.
How to Contact: Query with resume of credits or submit demo tape showing flexibility of composition skills. "Suggest prior fee scales." Prefers cassette with 3-8 pieces. SASE. Reports in 1 month.
Music: "We almost always use religious material, some contemporary Biblical opera, some gospel, a few pop songs, jazz, blues, folk-rock and occasionally soul."
Tips: "Enclose typed lyrics in sequence with the demo cassette recording."

KIMBO EDUCATIONAL UNITED SOUND ARTS, INC., 10 N. 3rd Ave., Box 477, Long Branch NJ 07740. (201)229-4949. Producers: James Kimble or Amy Laufer. Audiovisual firm and manufacturer of educational material: records, cassettes and teacher manuals and guides. Clients include schools and stores selling teachers' supplies. Uses the services of music houses, songwriters and educators for original songs for special education, early childhood, music classes, physical education and pre-school children; lyricists for lyrics to describe children's activities centering on development of motor skills, language, fitness or related educational skills. Commissions 5-7 pieces and 5-7 lyricists/year. Pays by the job or royalty. Buys all rights.
How to Contact: Submit demo tape of previous work, tape demonstrating composition skills, manuscript showing music scoring skills or lead sheet with lyrics. Prefers cassette with 1-12 songs. "Upon receipt of a demo tape and/or written material, each property is previewed by our production staff. The same chances exist for any individual if the material is of high quality and we feel it meets the educational goals we are seeking." Reports in 2 months. Free catalog available.
Music: "Contemporary sounds with limited instrumentation so as not to appear too sophisticated nor distracting for the young or special populations. Lyrics should be noncomplex and repetitive."

SID KLEINER MUSIC ENTERPRISES, 10188 Winter View Dr., Naples FL 33942. (813)566-7701 and (813)566-7702. Managing Director: Sid Kleiner. Audiovisual firm. Serves the music industry and various small industries. Uses the services of music houses, songwriters and inhouse writers for background music; lyricists for special material. Commissions 5-10 composers and 2-3 lyricists/year. Pays $25 minimum/job. Buys all rights.

How to Contact: Query with resume of credits or submit demo tape of previously aired work. Prefers cassette with 1-4 songs. SASE. Reports in 5 weeks.
Music: "We generally need soft background music, with some special lyrics to fit a particular project. Uses catchy, contemporary, special assignments for commercial/industrial accounts. We also assign country, pop, mystical and metaphysical. Submit samples—give us your very best demos, your best prices and we'll try our best to use your services."

KTVU RETAIL SERVICES, Box 22222, Oakland CA 94623. (415)874-0228. TV station and retail Marketing Director: Richard Hartwig. Retail TV commercial production firm. Estab. 1974. Clients include local, regional and national retailers. Uses the services of music houses, independent songwriters/ composers, lyricists and music libraries for commercials for radio and TV. Commissions 50 composers and 4 lyricists/year. Pays by the job. Buys all rights.
How to Contact: Submit demo tape of previous work. Prefers cassette or 7½ ips reel-to-reel with 6 pieces. SASE, but prefers to keep material on file.
Music: All styles for TV and radio commercials.

LA BOV AND BEYOND MUSIC PRODUCTION, Box 5533, Ft. Wayne IN 46895. (219)420-5533. Creative Director: Cheryl Franks. President: Barry La Bov. Scoring service and **commercial music production house.** Clients include advertising agencies, film production houses and A/V firms. Uses the services of independent songwriters/composers and lyricists for scoring and background music for films, TV and audiovisual projects; jingles and commercials for radio and TV. Commissions 4-10 composers and 2-5 lyricists/year.
How to Contact: Submit demo tape of previous work, tape showing composition skills or manuscript showing music scoring skills. Prefers cassette, 7½ or 15 ips reel-to-reel (or VHS videocassette) with 5-10 pieces. SASE, but prefers to keep material on file. Reports in 3 weeks. "We will call when tape has been received and evaluated."
Music: Uses all styles of music for all kinds of assignments from commercials to songs. "We look for positive, eager writers who strive to create unique, outstanding music."
Tips: "Try new approaches and work to keep a fresh sound. Be innovative, conceptually strong, and positive."

LANE AUDIO PRODUCTIONS, INC., 1507 Wesley, Springdale AR 72764. President: Richard Eby. Jingle/**commercial music production house** and general recording studio. Clients include corporate clients (J.B. Hunt, IBM), local agencies and businesses (jingles). Estab. 1988. Uses the services of independent songwriters/composers, lyricists and voice talent (singing and spoken), musicians for background music for various projects, jingles for local businesses and commercials for radio and TV. Commissions 4-8 composers and 2-4 lyricists/year. Pays $75-400/job or 20-50% royalty. Buys all rights, one-time rights and percentage of rights.
How to Contact: Submit demo tape of previous work. Submit tape demonstrating composition skills. Prefers cassette or 7.5 or 15 IPS reel-to-reel with 3-5 songs and lyric sheet. "Most useful to us right now is easy listening instrumental but we will listen to anything." Does not return unsolicited material; prefers to keep on file. Reports in 2 weeks.
Music: Uses all types for commercials, production music on training tapes, etc.

LANGE PRODUCTIONS, 7661 Curson Terrace, Hollywood CA 90046. (213)874-4730. Production Coordinator: Darlene Hall. Medical video production company. Clients include doctors, hospitals, corporations. Estab. 1987. Uses services of independent songwriters/composers for scoring and background music for medical videos. Commissions 6 composers/year. Pays by the job, $300-700. Buys all rights.
How to Contact: Submit demo tape of previous work. SAE, but prefers cassette. Prefers to keep materials on file. Reports in 3 weeks.

LAPRIORE VIDEOGRAPHY, 86 Allston Ave., Worcester MA 01604. (508)755-9010. Owner: Peter Lapriore. Video production company. Clients include business, educational and sports. Estab. 1985. Uses the services of music houses and independent songwriters/composers and music houses for background music for industrial productions and commercials for TV. "We also own a music library." Commissions 2 composers/year. Pays $500-1,000/job. Buys all rights, one-time rights and limited use rights.
How to Contact: Submit demo tape of previous work demonstrating composition skills. Prefers cassette or VHS videocassette with 5 songs and lyric sheet. Does not return material, but prefers to keep material on file. Reports in 2 weeks.
Music: Uses medium, up-tempo, jazz and classical for marketing, educational films and commercials.

LEDFORD PRODUCTIONS, INC., Box 7363, Furnitureland Station, High Point NC 27264-7363. (919)431-1107. President: Hank Ledford. Audiovisual firm and advertising firm. Clients include banks, manufacturers of heavy duty equipment and luxury items and Fortune 500 companies. Uses music

houses for background music for video/slide shows and radio commercials. Commissions 25 pieces or songs/year. Pays by the job. Buys all rights or one-time rights.
How to Contact: Submit demo tape of previous work. Prefers cassette (or ¾″ VHS videocassette). Does not return unsolicited material; prefers to keep on file.
Music: Uses music for videos, slide presentation-industrial/product introductions.

*AL PAUL LEFTON CO., 71 Vanderbilt Ave., New York NY 10169. (212)867-5100. Director of Broadcast: Joe Africano. Advertising agency. Serves financial, industrial and consumer products clients. Uses the services of music houses for jingles and background music for commercials. Commissions 8-10 songwriters or composers/year. Pays by the job. Buys all rights.
How to Contact: Submit demo tape of previously aired work. Prefers cassette with 5 songs minimum. SASE. Reports in 3 weeks.

S.R. LEON COMPANY, INC., 132 South St., Oyster Bay NY 11731. (516)922-0031. Creative Director: Max Firetog. Advertising agency. Serves industrial, drug, automotive and dairy product clients. Uses jingles and background music for commercials. Commissions vary. Rights purchased are limited to use of music for commercials.
How to Contact: Submit demo tape of previously aired work. Prefers cassette. No length restrictions on demo.
Music: Uses all types.

LEWIS, GILMAN & KYNETTE, INC., 200 South Broad St., Philadelphia PA 19102. (215)790-4100. Broadcast Business Manager: Valencia Tursi. Advertising agency. Serves industrial and consumer clients. Uses music houses for jingles and background music in commercials. Pays creative fee asked by music houses.
How to Contact: Submit demo tape of previously aired work. "You must send in previously published work. We do not use original material." Prefers cassette. Will return with SASE if requested, but prefers to keep on file.
Music: All types.

LOTT WALKER ADVERTISING, 2648 Ridgewood Rd., Jackson MS 39216. (601)981-9810. Art Director: John C. Abbate. Advertising agency. Clients include financial, healthcare and telecommunications. Estab. 1976. Uses the services of music houses and independent songwriters/composers for jingles for commercials for radio and TV. Commissions 1-2 composers and 1-2 lyricists/year. Pays by the job. Buys all rights and one-time rights.
How to Contact: Submit demo tape of previous work. Prefers cassette. "Let us know your rates." Does not return unsolicited material; prefers to keep on file.
Music: Uses all types of music for all kinds of assignments.

WALTER P. LUEDKE & ASSOCIATES, INC., Suite One, Eastmoor Bldg., 4223 E. State St., Rockford IL 61108. (815)398-4207. Secretary: Joan Luedke. Advertising agency. Estab. 1959. Uses the services of independent songwriters/composers and lyricists for background music for clients, jingles for clients and commercials for radio and TV. Commissions 1-2 composers and 1-2 lyricists/year. Pays by the job. Buys all rights.
How to Contact: Write first to arrange personal interview. Prefers cassette. "Our need is infrequent, best just let us know who you are." SASE, but prefers to keep material on file. Reports in 1 week.
Music: Uses various styles.

LUNA TECH, INC., 148 Moon Dr., Owens Cross Roads AL 35763. (205)725-4224. Chief Designer: Norman A. Plaisted. Fireworks company. Clients include theme parks, municipalities and industrial show producers. Estab. 1969. Uses music houses, independent songwriters and client music departments for scoring of music for fireworks displays. Commissions 1-2 composers/year. Pays $500-3,000/job. Buys all rights or one-time rights.
How to Contact: Query with resume of credits or submit demo tape of previous work. Prefers cassette (or VHS videocassette) with 1-5 pieces. Does not return unsolicited material; prefers to keep on file. Reports in 1 month; will call if interested.
Music: "Music for fireworks choreography: dynamic, jubilant, heraldic, bombastic, original."
Tips: "Send us a demo tape showing your composition skills and tailored as much as possible toward our needs."

*LYONS PRESENTATIONS, 715 Orange St., Wilmington DE 19899. (302)654-6146. Audio Producer: Gary Hill. Audiovisual firm. Clients include mostly large corporations: Dupont, ICI, Alco Standard. Estab. 1954. Uses the services of independent songwriters/composers and lyricists for scoring of multi-image, film and video. Commissions 8-12 composers/year. Pays by the job. Buys all rights.

How to Contact: Submit demo tape of previous work. Prefers cassette, 15 IPS reel-to-reel, (or VHS or ¾" videocassette) with 3-4 songs. "No phone calls please, unless composers are in local area." SASE, but prefers to keep submitted materials on file.
Music: Usually uses up-tempo motivational pieces for multi-image, video or film for corporate use.
Tips: "Pays close attention to the type of music that is used for TV spots for large companies, like AT&T."

MCCAFFREY AND MCCALL ADVERTISING, 8888 Keystone Crossing, Indianapolis IN 46240. (317)574-3900. V.P./Associate Creative Director: William Mick. Advertising agency. Serves consumer electronics, technical eucation, retail and commercial developers. Estab. 1984. Uses the services of music houses for scoring, background music and jingles for radio and TV commercials. Commissions 3 composers/year; 1 lyricist/year. Pays $3,000-5,000/job. Buys all rights.
How to Contact: Submit demo tape of previous work and write to arrange personal interview. Prefers cassette (or ¾" videocassette) with 6 songs. SASE, but prefers to keep submitted materials on file.
Music: High-energy pop, sound-alikes and electronic for commercials.
Tips: "Keep in touch, but don't be a pest about it."

McCANN-ERICKSON WORLDWIDE, Suite 1900, 1360 Post Oak Blvd., Houston TX 77056. (713)965-0303. Creative Director: Jesse Caesar. Advertising agency. Serves all types of clients. Uses services of songwriters for jingles and background music in commercials. Commissions 10 songwriters/year. Pays production cost and registrated creative fee. Arrangement fee and creative fee depend on size of client and size of market. "If song is for a big market, a big fee is paid; if for a small market, a small fee is paid." Buys all rights.
How to Contact: Submit demo tape of previously aired work. Prefers 7½ ips reel-to-reel. "There is no minimum or maximum length for tapes. Tapes may be of a variety of work or a specialization. We are very open on tape content; agency does own lyrics." SASE, but prefers to keep material on file. Responds by phone when need arises.
Music: All types.

McDONALD DAVIS & ASSOC., 250 W. Coventry Ct., Milwaukee WI 53217. (414)228-1990. Senior Vice President/Creative Director: Steve Preston. Advertising agency. Uses music houses for background music for commercials. Commissions 15 composers and producers/year. Pays $1,000-3,000/job. Buys all rights.
How to Contact: Write to arrange personal interview or submit demo tape of previously aired work or tape demonstrating composition skills. Prefers cassette (or ¾" videocassette) with 10 pieces and resume of credits. Does not return unsolicited material; prefers to keep on file. "We report in 1 week on solicited material."
Music: Uses all styles of music for post-scoring television commercials.

LEE MAGID INC., (Alexis Music Inc., Marvelle Music Co.) P.O. Box 532, Malibu CA 90265. (213)463-5998. President: Lee Magid. Audiovisual firm, scoring service and motion picture production company. Clients include record labels, producers, networks, video/film companies, television, and commercial sequences. Uses the services of songwriters, lyricists and composer/arrangers for scoring, themes and background music for films and videos, jingles and commercials for radio and TV. Commissions 8-10 lyricists/year. Buys all rights. Pays by the job or by royalty.
How to Contact: Send resume of credits or submit tape demonstrating composition skills. Prefers cassette (or videocassette) with maximum 3 songs (or 3 minutes). "I would make direct contact with songwriter/composer and designate preference and style." Reports in 1 month.
Music: Mostly R&B, jazz and gospel; also country, pop and rock. Vocals and/or instrumental.
Tips: "Use your instincts. Write songs for visual and musical memory effect. Try to become an innovator. Think ahead."

MALLOF, ABRUZINO & NASH MARKETING, 477 E. Butterfield Rd., Lombard IL 60148. (708)964-7722. President: Ed Mallof. Advertising agency. Estab. 1980. Works primarily with auto dealer jingles. Uses music houses for jingles. Commissions 5-6 songwriters/year. Pays by the job. Buys all rights.

The asterisk before a listing indicates that the listing is new in this edition. New markets are often the most receptive to unsolicited submissions.

How to Contact: Submit demo tape of previous work. Prefers cassette with 4-12 songs. SASE; but prefers to keep material on file. Reports "when we feel a need for their style."
Tips: "Submit good driving music with clever lyrics."

MANN ADVERTISING, P.O. 466 Hanover St., Box 3818, Manchester NH 03105. (603)625-5403. Broadcast Producer: Terrence Toland. Advertising agency. Clients include retail/industrial/hi-tech. Estab. 1974. Uses the services of independent songwriters and music houses for background music for industrial videos and commercials for radio and TV. Commissions 7-10 songwriters/year. Pays $3,000-7,000/job. Buys all rights and one-time rights.
How to Contact: Submit demo tape of previous work. Prefers cassette (or VHS videocassette) with 3-7 songs. SASE, but prefers to keep material on file. Reports in 2 weeks.
Music: Uses up tempo, easy listening, jazz for commercials, slide shows, industrial videos.
Tips: "Present clean clear work—make it your best work *only*."

THE MARKETING CONNECTION, 7000 Lake Ellenor, Orlando FL 32809. (407)855-4321. Vice President, Sales: Leon Lebeau. Audiovisual firm. Uses services of music houses, independent songwriters/composers, lyricists and recording studios for scoring of A/V sound tracks and videos, walk-in music for shows, jingles for videos (non-commercial) and sound effects. Commissions 2-3 composers and 1-2 lyricists/year. Pays by the job, $30-50/hour or local studio rates. Buys all rights or one-time rights.
How to Contact: Submit demo tape of previous work; call first to arrange personal interview. Prefers cassette (or ¾″ or ½″ videocassette) or 7½ ips reel-to-reel. "New material only." SASE, but prefers to keep material on file. Reports in several weeks.
Music: Uses up-tempo, pop and jazz for educational and training films and slide presentations.

MASTER MANAGEMENT MUSIC, #242, 1626 W. Wilcox St., Los Angeles CA 90028. (213)871-8054, ex. 516. President/CEO: George Van Heel. Advertising agency, jingle/commercial music production house, promotion/production company and music publishing company (BMI). Estab. 1987. Uses the services of music houses, independent songwriters/composers and lyricists for scoring, background music and jingles for campaigns and commercials for radio/TV. Commissions 1 composer/year; 1 lyricist/year. Pays $5,000/job. Buys all rights.
How to Contact: Write first to arrange personal interview. "No personal deliveries; by appointment only!" Prefers cassette or VHS videocassette with 3 songs and lyric and lead sheets. "All songs must be patriotic." Does not return unsolicited submissions; prefers to keep materials on file. Reports in 2 months.
Music: Pop/rock style for campaigns, educational and music videos.

MAXWELL ADVERTISING INC., 444 W. Michigan, Kalamazoo MI 49007. (616)382-4060. Creative Director: Jess Maxwell. Advertising agency. Uses the services of lyricists and music houses for jingles and background music for commercials. Commissions 2-4 lyricists/year. Pays $4,000-20,000/job. Buys all rights or one-time rights.
How to Contact: Submit demo tape of previously aired work or tape demonstrating composition skills. Prefers cassette (or VHS videocassette). No returns; prefers to keep material on file.
Music: Uses various styles of music for jingles and music beds.

MEDIA CONSULTANTS, P.O. Box 130, Sikeston MO 63801. (314)472-1116. Owner: Richard Wrather. Advertising agency. Clients are varied. Estab. 1979. Uses the services of music houses, independent songwriters/composers and lyricists for scoring of and background music for jingles, industrial video and commercials for radio and TV. Commissions 10-15 composers and 10-15 lyricists/year. Pays varying amount/job. Buys all rights.
How to Contact: Submit a demo tape of previous work. Submit tape demonstrating composition skills. Prefers cassette (or ½″ or ¾″ videocassette). Does not return unsolicited material; prefers to keep on file.
Music: Uses all styles of music for varied assignments.

MEDIA PRODUCTIONS, 2095 N. Andrews Ext., Pompano Beach FL 33069. (305)979-6467. President: Jim Haney. Motion picture, TV and post-production company. Clients include advertising agency and commercial production company. Uses the services of music houses and independent songwriters/composers for TV commercials. Commissions 2 composers and 2 lyricists/year. Pays $200-2,000/job. Buys all rights.
How to Contact: Submit tape demonstrating composition skills or manuscript showing music scoring skills. Prefers 7½ ips reel-to-reel (or ¾″ videocassette) with 4-8 songs and lyric sheet. SASE, but prefers to keep material on file. Reports in 2 months.
Music: Uses up-tempo and pop music for commercials.

*MID-OCEAN RECORDING STUDIO, 1578 Erin St., Winnepeg Namitoba R3E 2T1 **Canada.** Producer/ Engineer: Dave Zeglinski. Jingle/**commercial music production house**. Clients include retail/corporate. Estab. 1980. Uses the services of independent songwriters/composers and producers for jingles for commercials for radio and TV. Commissions 3-5 composers/year. Pays $300-500/job. Buys all rights.
How to Contact: Submit demo tape of previous work. Prefers cassette with 1 or 2 songs. Does not return unsolicited material; prefers to keep submitted material on file. Reports in 1 month.
Music: Uses easy listening, up-tempo, pop for commercials.

JON MILLER PRODUCTION STUDIOS, 7249 Airport Rd., Bath PA 18014. (215)837-7550. Executive Producer: Jon Miller. Audiovisual firm, jingle/**commercial music production house** and video production company. Clients include industrial, commercial, institutional and special interest. Estab. 1970. Uses the services of music houses, independent songwriters/composers and lyricists for scoring of themes and background music for audio and video production and live presentations. Commissions 5-15 composers and 2-5 lyricists/year. Pays by the job. Buys all rights or one-time rights.
How to Contact: Submit demo tape of previous work. Query with resume of credits and references. Prefers cassette with 7 songs and lyric or lead sheets. Does not return unsolicited material; prefers to keep on file. Reports in 2-3 weeks.
Music: Uses up tempo and title music, introduction music for industrial marketing and training videos.
Tips: "Provide professional product on time and within budget. Keep communication open."

MITCHELL & ASSOCIATES, 7830 Old George Town Rd., Bethesda MD 20814. (301)986-1772. President: Ronald Mitchell. Advertising agency. Serves food, high-tech, transportation, financial, real estate, automotive and retail clients. Uses independent songwriters, lyricists and music houses for background music for commercials, jingles and post-TV scores for commercials. Commissions 3-5 songwriters and 3-5 lyricists/year. Pays $3,000-10,000/job. Buys all rights.
How to Contact: Submit demo tape of previously aired work. Prefers cassette or 7½ ips reel-to-reel. Does not return unsolicited material; prefers to keep on file.
Music: "Depends upon client, audience, etc."

MONTEREY BAY PRODUCTION GROUP, Suite 204, 563 Arthur Rd., Watsonville CA 95076. (408)722-3132. Owner/Manager: Denise V. Collins. Video production services. Clients include industrial business and broadcast. Estab. 1985. Uses the services of independent songwriters/composers for scoring of promotional, educational and commercial videos. Commissions 3-10 composers/year. Pays by the job.
How to Contact: Submit demo tape of previous work. Query with resume of credits. Prefers cassette (or VHS videocassette) with 5 songs. Prefers to keep material on file. Reports in 1 month.
Music: Uses all types for promotional, training and commercial.

*MORRIS MEDIA, #105, 2730 Monterey, Torrance CA 90503. (213)533-4800. Acquisitions Manager: Roger Casas. TV/video production company. Estab. 1984. Uses the services of music houses, independent songwriters/composers and lyricists for jingles for radio and TV commercials. Commissions 5 composers and 2 lyricists/year. Pays by the job or by the hour. Buys all rights.
How to Contact: Query with resume of credits "Write first with short sample of work." Does not return unsolicited material; prefers to keep submitted material on file. Reports in 2 weeks.
Music: Uses classical, pop, rock and jazz for music video/TV.
Tips: "Persist with good material, as we are very busy!"

MOTIVATION MEDIA, INC., 1245 Milwaukee Ave., Glenview IL 60025. (708)297-4740. Production Manager: Glen Peterson. Audiovisual firm, video, motion picture production company and business meeting planner. Estab. 1969. Clients include business and industry. Uses the services of songwriters and composers "mostly for business meetings and multi-image production"; lyricists for writing lyrics for business meeting themes, audience motivation songs and promotional music for new product introduction. Commissions 3-5 composers/year. Payment varies. Buys one-time rights.
How to Contact: Query with resume of credits; or submit demo tape of previous work. Prefers cassette with 5-7 songs. Responds when the need arises.
Music: Uses "up-beat contemporary music that motivates an audience of sales people."
Tips: "Keep in touch—let us know what new and exciting assignments you have undertaken."

MTC PRODUCTION CENTER, (formerly American Video Factory), 4150 Glencoe Ave., Marina Del Rey CA 90292. (213)823-8622. Music Composer: Emilio Kauderer. Scoring service and jingle/**commercial music production house**. Clients include advertising, corporate, entertainment and other businesses. Uses the services of independent songwriters/composers for background music for commercials, feature films, industrials, jingles and commercials for radio and TV. Commissions 5 composers and 5 lyricists/year. Pays by the job. Buys all rights.

How to Contact: Write or call first to arrange personal interview. Prefers cassette. SASE. Prefers to keep submitted materials on file. Reports in 2 weeks.
Music: Uses jazz, classical, new age, pop and up-tempo.

MULTI IMAGE PRODUCTIONS, 8849 Complex Dr., San Diego CA 92123. (619)560-8383. Sound Editor/Engineer: Jim Lawrence. Audiovisual firm and motion picture production company. Serves business, corporate, industrial, commercial, military and cultural clients. Uses music houses, independent songwriters/composers/arrangers and lyricists for scoring of industrials, corporate films and videos; background music for AV, film, video and live shows; and jingles and commercials for radio and TV. Commissions 2-10 composers and 2-5 lyricists/year. Pays $500+/job. Buys all rights.
How to Contact: Query with resume of credits or write to obtain permission to submit. Prefers 7½ or 15 ips reel-to-reel with 2-5 pieces. Does not return unsolicited material; prefers to keep on file. Reports in 6 weeks.
Music: Uses "comtemporary, pop, specialty, regional, ethnic, national and international" styles of music for background "scores written against script describing locales, action, etc. We try to stay clear of stereotypical 'canned' music and prefer a more commercial and dramatic (film-like) approach."
Tips: "We have established an ongoing relationship with a local music production/scoring house with whom songwriters would be in competition for every project; but an ability to score clean, full, broad, contemporary commercial and often 'film score' type music, in a variety of styles would be a benefit."

MUSIC LANE PRODUCTIONS, Box 3829, Austin TX 78764. (512)447-3988. Owner: Wayne Gathright. Music recording, production and jingle/commercial music production house. Estab. 1980. Serves bands, songwriters and commercial clients. Uses the services of music houses and independent songwriters/composers for jingles and commercials for radio and TV. Pays by the job. Buys one-time rights.
How to Contact: Submit demo tape of previous work or tape demonstrating composition skills; or query with resume of credits. Prefers cassette. Does not return unsolicited material; prefers to keep on file. Reports in 6 weeks.
Music: Uses all styles.

MUSIC MASTERS, 2322 Marconi Ave., St. Louis MO 63110. (314)773-1480. Producer: Greg Trampe. **Commercial music production house** and **music/sound effect library.** Estab. 1976. Clients include multi-image and film producers, advertising agencies and large corporations. Uses the services of independent songwriters/composers and lyricists for background music for multi-image and film, jingles and commercials for radio and TV. Commissions 6 composers and 2 lyricists/year. Pays $100-2,000/job. Buys all rights.
How to Contact: Query with resume of credits or write and obtain permission to submit. Prefers cassette or 7½ or 15 ips reel-to-reel (or Beta or VHS videocassette) with 3-6 pieces. SASE, but prefers to keep material on file. Reports in 1 month.
Music: "We use all types of music for slide presentations (sales & motivational)."
Tips: "Resume should have at least 3 or 4 major credits of works completed within the past year. A good quality demo is a must."

MYERS & ASSOCIATES, Suite 203, 3727 SE Ocean Blvd., Stuart FL 34996. (407)287-1990. Senior Vice President: Doris McLaughlin. Advertising agency. Estab. 1973. Serves financial, real estate, consumer products and hotel clients. Uses music houses for background music for commercials and jingles. Commissions 2-3 songwriters/year and 2-3 lyricists/year. Pays by the job. Buys all rights.
How to Contact: Submit demo tape of previously aired work. Prefers cassette. Does not return unsolicited material; prefers to keep on file.
Music: Uses "various styles of music for jingles, music beds and complete packages depending on clients' needs."

FRANK C. NAHSER, INC., 18th Floor, 10 S. Riverside Plaza, Chicago IL 60606. (312)845-5000. Contact: Bob Fugate. Advertising agency. Serves insurance, telecommunications, toys, bicycles, hotels, and other clients. Uses the services of independent songwriters/composers, lyricists and music houses for scoring of television commercials, background music for commercials for radio and TV and music for industrial/sales presentations and meetings. Commissions 6-10 songwriters and 4 lyricists/year. Pays $5,000-15,000 for finished production or varying royalty. Buys one-time rights.
How to Contact: Submit demo tape of previous work. Prefers cassette. Does not return unsolicited material; prefers to keep on file. "No phone calls, please. When a cassette is submitted we listen to it for reference when a project comes up. We ignore most cassettes that lack sensitivity toward string and woodwind arrangements unless we know it's from a lyricist."
Music: "We mostly use scores for commercials, not jingles. The age of the full sing jingle in national TV spots is quickly coming to an end. Young songwriters should be aware of the difference and have the expertise to score, not just write songs."

Tips: "The writing speaks for itself. If you know composition, theory and arrangement it quickly becomes evident. Electronic instruments are great tools; however, they are no substitute for total musicianship. Learn to read, write, arrange and produce music and, with this book's help, market your music. Be flexible enough to work along with an agency. We like to write and produce as much as you do."

NATIONAL TELEPRODUCTIONS, INC., P.O. Box 1804, W. Palm Beach FL 33402. (407)689-9271. Producer: Robert Peterson. Motion picture and television production company. "70% of our work is programming for national television release; the balance is corporate and international business." Estab. 1975. Uses music houses and independent songwriters/composers for scoring of background music for television programming, documentaries and corporate/industrial presentations and commercials for TV. Commissions 11-15 composers/year. Pays variable rate/job. Rights purchased vary by project.
How to Contact: Submit demo tape of previous work. Prefers cassette. SASE, but prefers to keep submitted material on file. Only reports back if the individual is being considered for an assignment.
Tips: "Keep your sample tape current!"

NEW & UNIQUE VIDEOS, 2336 Sumac Dr., San Diego CA 92105. (619)282-6126. Contact: Pat Mooney. Production and worldwide distribution of special interest videotapes to varied markets. Estab. 1981. Uses the services of independent songwriters for background music in videos. Commissions 2-3 composers/year. Pays by the job, by royalty or by the hour. Buys all rights.
How to Contact: Query with resume of credits. Prefers cassette. Does not return unsolicited material; prefers to keep on file.
Music: Uses up-tempo, easy listening and jazz for educational film and action/adventure, nature and love stories.
Tips: "Let go of the ego and let the music from the far edges of your imagination spill out. That's the kind of sound we like in our videos."

NOBLE ARNOLD & ASSOCIATES, Suite 202 N, 1501 Woodfield Rd., Schaumburg IL 60173. (708)605-8808. Creative Director: John Perkins. Advertising agency. Clients include communication and health care firms. Estab. 1970. Uses the services of independent songwriters/composers for jingles. Commissions 1 composer and 1 lyricist/year. Pays by the job. Buys all rights.
How to Contact: Submit demo tape of previous work. Prefers cassette. Does not return unsolicited material. Reports in 4 weeks.

NORTHLICH STOLLEY LAWARRE, INC., 200 West Fourth St., Cincinnati OH 45202. (513)421-8840. Broadcast Producer: Judy Merz. Advertising agency. Clients include banks, hospitals, P&G, Cintas, Queen City Metro, Dayton Power and Light, Mead Paper. Estab. 1949. Uses the services of independent songwriters and music houses for jingles and background music for commercials. Commissions 3-5 composers/year. Pays by the job. Rights purchased varies.
How to Contact: Submit demo tape of previous work, tape demonstrating composition skills or query with resume of credits. Prefers cassette. SASE, but prefers to keep materials on file.
Music: Uses all kinds for commercials.

*NORTON RUBBLE & MERTZ, INC. ADVERTISING, 2R, 112 N. Green, Chicago IL 60607. (312)942-1405. President: Sue Gehrke. Advertising agency. Clients include consumer products, retail, business to business. Estab. 1987. Uses the services of music houses and independent songwriters/composers for jingles for radio/TV commercials. Commissions 2 composers/year. Pays by the job.
How to Contact: Submit tape demonstrating composition skills; query with resume of credits. Prefers cassette. Does not return unsolicited material; prefers to keep material on file. Reports in 4 weeks.
Music: Uses up-tempo and pop for commercials.

NOTCH/BRADLEY, 801 Vine, Chattanooga TN 37403. (615)756-8647. Creative Director: Doug Cook. Advertising agency. Clients include healthcare, tourism, et. al. Estab. 1984. Uses the services of independent songwriters/composers and lyricists for commercials for radio and TV. Commissions 10 composers and 5 lyricists/year. Pays $1,000-1,500/job. Buys all rights.
How to Contact: Submit demo tape of previous work. Prefers cassette (or ½" videocassette) with 5-7 songs. Does not return unsolicited material; prefers to keep on file. Reports in 2-4 weeks.
Music: Uses mood pieces—relaxed to high drama—primarily for commercials.
Tips: "We're open to different approaches, avoid generic stuff."

OMNI COMMUNICATIONS, 655 W. Carmel Dr., Carmel IN 46032-2669. (317)844-6664. President: W. H. Long. Television production and audiovisual firm. Estab. 1978. Serves industrial, commercial and educational clients. Uses the services of music houses and songwriters for scoring of films and

television productions; background music for voice overs; lyricists for original music and themes. Commissions varying number of composers and lyricists/year. Pays by the job. Buys all rights.
How to Contact: Query with resume of credits. Prefers reel-to-reel, cassette (or videocassette). Does not return unsolicited material. Reports in 2 weeks.
Music: Varies with each and every project; from classical, contemporary to commercial industrial.
Tips: "Submit good demo tape with examples of your range."

ON-Q PRODUCTIONS, INC., 618 Gutierrez St., Santa Barbara CA 93103. (805)963-1331. President: Vincent Quaranta. Audiovisual firm. Clients include corporate accounts/sales conventions. Uses the services of music houses, independent songwriters/composers and lyricists for scoring of and background music for media productions and TV commercials. Commissions 1-5 composers and 1-5 lyricists/year. Pays by the job. Buys all rights or one-time rights.
How to Contact: Submit demo tape of previous work. Prefers cassette or 15 ips reel-to-reel (or VHS videocassete). SASE, but prefers to keep material on file. Reports in 1 month.
Music: Uses up-tempo music for slide and video presentations.

OVERCASH & MOORE, INC., Suite 805, 3100 Smoketree Ct., Raleigh NC 27609. (919)872-0050. Creative Director: Jim Moore. Broadcast Producer: Jerry Stifelman. Advertising agency. Clients include retail and business-to-business. Uses services of music houses and independent songwriters/composers for background music for videos and training films and commercials for radio and TV. Commissions 4-5 composers/year. Pays by the job. Buys all rights.
How to Contact: Submit demo tape of previous work. Prefers cassette (or VHS videocassette) with 4-5 pieces. Does not return unsolicited material; prefers to keep on file. Reports in 2 months.
Music: Uses popular, jazz and classical for commercials and videos.
Tips: "Send memorable lyrics, hummable tunes. No clichés."

OWENS POLLICK AND ASSOCIATES, (formerly Pollick and Associates), 3003 N. Central, Phoenix AZ 85012. (602)230-7557. Broadcast Producer: Susan Reed. Advertising agency. Clients include health care, automotive aftermarket and newspapers. Estab. 1986. Uses the services of music houses for scoring of commercials for radio/TV. Commissions 4-10 composers/year; 4-10 lyricists/year. Pays $2,000/job. Buys all rights.
How to Contact: Submit demo tape of previous work. Prefers cassette or ¾" videocassette. Does not return unsolicited material; prefers to keep materials on file.
Music: Up-tempo, jazz and classical for commercials.

PAISANO PUBLICATIONS/EASYRIDERS HOME VIDEO, Box 3000, Agoura Hills CA 91364. (818)889-8740. Producer/Director: Rick Schmidlin. Home video and TV productions. Clients include consumer/motorcycle enthusiasts. Estab. 1971. Uses the services of music houses, independent songwriters/composers and pre-recorded bands for scoring of video and TV, background music for video and TV, jingles for radio spots and commercials for radio and TV. Commissions 2-3 composers/year. Pays $100/minute of usage. Buys all rights.
How to Contact: Write first to arrange personal interview. Prefers cassette (or VHS/¾" videocassette). SASE, but prefers to keep material on file. Reports in 1-2 months.
Music: Uses rock/country/contemporary.
Tips: "Harley riders a plus."

PHD VIDEO, 143 Hickory Hill Cir., Osterville MA 02655. (508)428-7198. Acquisitions: Violet Atkins. Motion picture production company. Clients include business and industry, production and post-production video houses and ad agencies. Estab. 1985. Uses the services of music houses, independent songwriters/composers and lyricists for scoring and background music for commercials, home video and motion pictures and jingles for TV commercials. Commissions 10-12 composers and 10-12 lyricists/year. Pay is negotiable. Buys all rights preferably or one-time rights in certain circumstances.
How to Contact: Submit demo tape of previous work. Prefers cassette (or VHS videocassette). SASE but prefers to keep material on file. Reports in 2-4 weeks.
Music: Uses up-tempo and pop for commercials, motion pictures and TV shows.
Tips: "Be persistent. Constantly send updates of new work. Update files 1-2 times per year if possible. We hire approximately 25% new composers per year. Prefer to use composers/lyricists with 2/3 years track record."

PHILADELPHIA MUSIC WORKS, INC., Box 947, Bryn Mawr PA 19010. (215)825-5656. President: Andy Mark. Jingle producers/**music library producers**. Uses independent songwriters and music houses for background music for commercials and jingles. Commissions 20 songwriters/year. Pays $200/job. Buys all rights.

How to Contact: Call first and obtain permission to submit. Prefers cassette. "We are looking for quality jingle tracks already produced, as well as instrumental pieces between 2 and 3 minutes in length for use in AV music library." Does not return unsolicited material. Reports in 4 weeks.
Music: All types.
Tips: Looking for "knowledge of the jingle business and what works as background music for audiovisual presentations, such as slide shows, video training films, etc."

PHOTO COMMUNICATION SERVICES, INC., 6410 Knapp NE, Ada MI 49301. (616)676-1499; 676-1454. President: Lynn Jackson. Audiovisual firm and motion picture production company. Serves commercial, industrial and nonprofit clients. Uses services of music houses, independent songwriters, and lyricists for jingles and scoring of and background music for multi-image, film and video. Negotiates pay. Buys all rights or one-time rights.
How to Contact: Submit demo tape of previous work, tape demonstrating composition skills or query with resume of credits. Prefers cassette or 15 ips reel-to-reel (or VHS videocassette). Does not return unsolicited material; prefers to keep on file. Reports in 6 weeks.
Music: Uses mostly industrial/commercial themes.

PHOTO COMMUNICATIONS CORP., 815 Greenwood Ave., Jenkintown PA 19046. (215)572-5900. Vice President-Sales and Marketing: Ken Raichle. Audiovisual production company. Estab. 1970. Serves corporate, industrial, educational, business-to-business and pharmaceutical clients. Uses services of music houses, independent songwriters/composers and lyricists for scoring and background music for videos and multi-image programs. Commissions 1-2 composers and 1-2 lyricists/year. Pays by the job. Buys all rights or one-time rights; other rights sometimes.
How to Contact: Submit demo tape of previous work demonstrating composition skills or query with resume of credits. Prefers cassette with 4-5 pieces and lyric sheet. Sometimes returns unsolicited material with SASE; prefers to keep material on file.
Music: Uses up-tempo, dramatic, pop, classical, MOR, new age and electronic music for educational films, slide presentations, videos, corporate overviews, etc.
Tips: "Be flexible, creative and versatile."

MICHAEL POLLACK PRODUCTIONS, P.O. Box 551, Bearsville NY 11727. (914)679-8743. President: Michael Pollack. Jingle/**commercial music production house** and record production. Clients include recording artists/industry music needs. Estab. 1978. Uses the services of independent songwriters/composers for background music for film. Commissions 6-10 composers and 3-5 lyricists/year. Pays by royalty. Buys one-time rights.
How to Contact: Submit demo tape of previous work or write or call first to arrange personal interview. Prefers cassette. SASE, but prefers to keep material on file. Reports in 3 weeks.
Music: Uses new wave and rock for slide presentations and commercials.

POP INTERNATIONAL CORPORATION, P.O. Box 527, Closter NJ 07624. (201)768-2199. Producers: Arnold De Pasquale and Peter DeCaro. Motion picture production company. Estab. 1973. Clients include "political campaigns, commercial spots, business and industry concerns as a production service; feature films and documentaries as producers." Uses services of music houses and songwriters for "mood purposes only on documentary films. However, Pop International Productions does conceptualize major theatrical and/or album musical projects." Commissions commercial and soundtrack pieces for entertainment specials. Commissions 2-3 composers/year. Pays by the job; or by royalty. Rights are negotiable.
How to Contact: Submit demo tape of previously aired work. Prefers cassette with 2-4 songs. "We review tapes on file, speak with agents and/or referrals, then interview writer. Once committee approves, we work *very* closely in pre-production." SASE. Reports in 3 weeks.
Music: Uses "mood music for documentaries, occasionally jingles for spots or promotional films or theme music/songs for dramatic projects (the latter by assignment only from producers or agencies). Some material is strictly mood, as in documentary work; some is informative as in promotional; some is motivating as in commercial; some is entertaining as in theatrical/TV."
Tips: "Be persistent and very patient. Try to get an agent, use demos and build a reputation for working very closely with scriptwriters/producers/directors."

PPI (PETER PAN INDUSTRIES), PARADE VIDEO, CURRENT RECORDS, COMPOSE RECORDS, 88 St. Frances St., Newark NJ 07105. (201)344-4214. Product Manager: Marianne Eggleston. Video, record label, publishing. Clients include songwriters, music and video. Estab. 1928. Uses the services of music houses, independent songwriters/composers, lyricists, produces video and music for scoring, background music, jingles and commercials for radio and TV. Commissions 100's of composers and lyricists/year. Pays by the job, royalty and per agreement. Rights negotiable.

Close-up

Andy Mark
Philadelphia Music Works, Inc.
Bryn Mawr, Pennsylvania

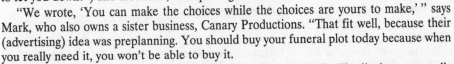

The client asked for a new radio jingle to advertise something people don't buy every day: cemetery plots. Green patches of Midwestern grass in the Ozark Memorial Park in Joplin, Missouri, to be specific.

Composing a tasteful, effective jingle for Joplin's future dead presented quite a challenge to Andy Mark, owner of Philadelphia Music Works, Inc., and his staff. How, he wondered, could they produce a jingle without resorting to corny lines ("We're the last ones to let you down!") and mournful, baroque organ music?

"We wrote, 'You can make the choices while the choices are yours to make,'" says Mark, who also owns a sister business, Canary Productions. "That fit well, because their (advertising) idea was preplanning. You should buy your funeral plot today because when you really need it, you won't be able to buy it.

"And the music we used was almost churchlike — a lot of bells. The jingle was actually very nice. They loved it."

Mark likes to call his jingle-writing business "the king of the small market." And glancing at his current job board, that's obvious. He's producing radio jingles for two hospitals, a car-stereo store, a kitchen designer, a mall and a car dealer in Greenville, South Carolina. Over the years, he has also produced jingles for a few larger companies, such as Burlington carpeting and home furnishings and Armstrong floor coverings, and he's especially proud of the jingle he's done for the '92 Republican National Convention.

"We have two studios and three experienced writers on the staff (including himself), but we still buy from outside sources," says Mark. "We probably get an average of one submission a day, sometimes more. And we find maybe one in 10 that's usable."

In his business, Mark says he's only interested in buying instrumental tracks, not lyrics. "They can be any length and any style, but they have to be good," he says. "We're not looking for junk. We buy to fill in where we have a lot of jingles on the air, or library stuff, to switch our sound a little bit."

Often, though, Mark says he receives submissions that simply aren't suitable. Why? Too many contributors, he says, mistakenly think that good, marketable music always comes out of a good, well-equipped studio, but that's not always the case.

"Our slogan is, 'It's the carpenter, not the tools,'" he explains. "Unfortunately, just because you have a great MIDI (musical instrument digital interface) setup, doesn't mean you know how to write music. You can have the greatest studio in the world, but not know how to work it."

Another mistake contributors make is not understanding that the jingle business is not so much music as it is advertising. And to sell a product effectively, jingle writers must concentrate on writing music that sticks in people's minds long after the jingle is off the air.

"People tend to lose sight of this," Mark says. "You've only got 60 seconds to develop this thing. You can't have a 40-second introduction before you get into it. You've got to sell at the beginning; you've got to sell at the end. You let the announcer do the selling in the middle. If you can't remember the jingle you heard later on, you've got problems. At least the client has got problems."

Mark, who produces 300-350 jingles a year, says his payment rates for an instrumental jingle track are $50-500 at Philadelphia Music Works. At Canary Productions his rate for a library track is "rarely over $100."

"It's a one-time purchase, and we have to own all rights," says Mark. "It's OK if a guy sold it somewhere else maybe one time; we can sort of block out that market. But if a guy has sold a jingle 20 times around the country—which is the way we operate, by the way— invariably somebody is going to get in trouble, and it's probably going to be him, because we will require that he deliver the music to us free and clear. If we happen to sell it close to the market where he sold it, he's in trouble."

Mark encourages composers who submit material for his consideration to include ample return postage affixed to a padded bag. He's impressed with professional packaging, too.

"You can almost tell by the packaging if something is going to be good," he says. "It didn't used to be that way. If you see something come in a slick package, more often than not, it's going to be better than stuff that comes in with a handwritten label on it. We're looking for professionalism all the way through."

— Tyler Cox

How to Contact: Submit demo tape and manuscript showing previous work, composition and scoring skills. Query with resume of credits. Prefers cassete or ½ or ¾ videocassette with 3 songs and lyric sheet. Also include a picture and bio of the artist. SASE. Prefers to keep material on file "if we like it for possible reference when we're looking for new materials."
Music: Uses all musical styles including childrens and health and fitness.
Tips: "Make sure presentation is professionally put together. Names and addresses on all packages and materials."

PREMIER VIDEO, FILM AND RECORDING CORP., 3033 Locust St., St. Louis MO 63103. (314)531-3555. President: Wilson Dalzell. Secretary/Treasurer: Grace Dalzell. Audiovisual firm, album producer and motion picture production company. Estab. 1931. Uses the services of songwriters for jingles and scoring and original background music and lyrics to reinforce scripts. Commissions 6-10 pieces and 5-10 lyricists/year. Pays by the job or by royalty. Buys all rights and "occasionally one-time rights with composer retaining title."
How to Contact: Query with resume of credits. Prefers 7½ or 15 ips reel-to-reel or cassette with any number of songs. SASE. Reports "as soon as possible with a short note using self-addressed envelope enclosed with submitted work informing talent they are on file for future reference."
Music: "As we serve every area of human development, all musical art forms are occasionally used."
Tips: "A limited need for music makes freelance writers a necessity. Be flexible. Have a simple, precise portfolio. Be sure your resume is direct, to-the-point and includes an honest review of past efforts. Be patient."

PREMIUM COMMUNICATIONS OF AMERICA, 36A Mauchly, Irvine CA 92718. (714)727-3203. President: Robert Eissfeldt. Audiovisual firm. Clients include medical, insurance, finance, automotive and industrial firms. Estab. 1973. Uses the services of music houses, independent songwriters and lyricists for background music for multi-media shows, commercials for TV and industrial video productions. Commissions 3 composers and 2 lyricists/year. Pays by the job. Buys all rights or one-time rights.
How to Contact: Prefers cassette. SASE, but prefers to keep material on file.
Music: All types.

PRICE WEBER MARKETING COMMUNICATIONS, INC., P.O. Box 99337, Louisville KY 40223. (502)499-9220. Producer/Director: Kelly McKnight. Advertising agency and audiovisual firm. Estab. 1967. Clients include Fortune 500, consumer durables, light/heavy industrials and package goods. Uses services of music houses, and independent songwriters/composer for scoring, background music and jingles for industrial and corporate image films and commercials for radio and TV. Commissions 6-8 composers/year. Pays by the job ($500-2,000). Buys all rights or one-time rights.

How to Contact: Submit demo tape of previous work demonstrating composition skills. Prefers cassette with 10 pieces. "Enclose data sheet on budgets per selection on demo tape." Does not return unsolicited material; prefers to keep on file. "We report back only if we use it."
Music: Uses easy listening, up-tempo, pop, jazz and classical for corporate image industrials and commercials.
Tips: "Keep us updated on new works or special accomplishments. Work with tight budgets of $500-2,000. Show me what you're best at—show me costs."

PRO/CREATIVES, 25 W. Burda Place, Spring Valley NY 10977. President: David Rapp. Advertising and promotion agency. Serves consumer products and services, sports and miscellaneous clients. Uses background music in TV and radio commercials. Payment negotiable.
How to Contact: Query with resume of credits. SASE.

PROFESSIONAL MEDIA SERVICES, Suite 205, 18530 Beach Blvd., Huntington Beach CA 92648. (714)964-0542. Owner: Roy Moosa. Advertising production firm. Clients include "corporate promos and TV commercials." Estab. 1982. Uses the services of independent songwriters for scoring of commercials, corporate presentations, background music for training tapes, jingles for TV and commercials for radio and TV. Commissions 2 composers/year. Pays by the job. Buys all rights.
How to Contact: Query with resume of credits. Prefers cassette or reel-to-reel (or videocassette). Does not return unsolicited material; prefers to keep on file. Reports "as needed."
Music: "Upbeat background" music.
Tips: "Keep a video resume of your work."

*PUBLICIS, INC., 4 West 58th St., New York NY 10019. (212)980-8550. Creative Director: Nick LaMicela. Group Creative Director: Glen Jacobs. Advertising agency. Clients include retailers of cosmetics, beauty aids and fragrances; also retailers of cellular telephones and FAX machines. Estab. 1931. Uses the services of music houses for background music for test spots and commercials for radio and TV. Commissions 2 composers/year. "Rights purchased depends on job."
How to Contact: Submit demo tape of previous work. Prefers cassette or ¾" videocassette. Does not return unsolicited material; prefers to keep on file.
Music: Uses music for commercials.

PULLIN PRODUCTIONS LTD., 822 5th Ave. SW, Calgary, Alberta T2P 0N3 **Canada**. (403)234-7885. Production Manager: Chris Pullin. Clients include business and industry. Uses the services of music houses, songwriters and lyricists for "original songs and themes for multi-image, motion picture and multi-media." Commissions 4 composers and 2 lyricists/year. Pays minimum $500/job. Buys all rights.
How to Contact: Submit demo tape (or videocassette) of previous work. Prefers reel-to-reel with 4-10 songs but "any format is OK." Does not return unsolicited material. "Contact is made only if interested."
Music: Looking for "strong themes for any number of instruments/vocals (single instrument to full orchestra). Requirements for each job are very carefully specified."

QUALLY & COMPANY INC., Huron Plaza, #2502, 30 East Huron, Chicago IL 60611. (312)944-0237. President/Creative Director: Robert Qually. Advertising agency. Uses the services of music houses, independent songwriters/composers and lyricists for scoring, background music and jingles for radio and TV commercials. Commissions 2-4 composers and 2-4 lyricists/year. Pays by the job, by royalty sometimes. Buys various rights depending on deal.
How to Contact: Submit demo tape of previous work or query with resume of credits. Prefers cassette (or ¾" Beta videocassette). Prefers to keep material on file.
Music: Uses all kinds of music for commericals.

BILL QUINN PRODUCTIONS, 710 Cookman Ave., Asbury Park NJ 07712. (201)775-0500. Production Manager: Bill Newman. Audiovisual firm and motion picture production company. Estab. 1983. Clients include corporate, advertisers on cable and network TV and production companies. Uses the services of independent songwriters/composers and music houses for scoring of original productions and industrial films, background music for client accounts, commercials for radio and TV and video/film production. Commissions 15-20 composers/year. Pays by the job or approximately $25/hour. Buys one-time rights or all rights.
How to Contact: Submit demo tape of previous work or query with resume of credits. Call first to arrange personal interview. Prefers cassette. Will return unsolicited material accompanied by an SASE, but prefers to keep on file. "We respond by phone whenever we find music that fits a particular need."

Music: "We don't use one type of music more than another because our client list is rather lengthy and extremely varied. We use rock, pop, MOR, C&W, etc. Most often we commission music for TV and radio commercials. Interested in doing business with people in the New York and New Jersey area."

Tips: "Be flexible, able to work quickly and possess a working knowledge of all types of music."

RAMPION VISUAL PRODUCTIONS, 316 Stuart St., Boston MA 02116. (617)574-9601. Director/Camera: Steven V. Tringali. Motion picture production company. Estab. 1982. Clients include educational, independent producers, corporate clients and TV producers. Uses the services of independent songwriters/composers for jingles, background music and scoring to longer form programming. Commissions 4-6 composers/year. Pays by the job. Buys all rights.

How to Contact: Submit demo tape of previous work or query with resume of credits. Prefers cassette with variety of pieces. SASE. Does not return unsolicited material; prefers to keep material on file. Reports in 4 weeks.

Music: Uses all styles for corporate, educational and original programming.

REED PRODUCTIONS, INC., Box 977, Warsaw IN 46580. (219)267-4199. President: Howard Reed. Audiovisual firm and motion picture production company. Serves medical-industrial clients. Uses the services of music houses, independent songwriters/composers and lyricists for background music for audiovisual and video and commercials for TV. Commissions 1 composer and 1 lyricist/year. Pays $100-500/job. Buys all rights or one-time rights.

How to Contact: Submit demo tape of previous work. Prefers cassette (or VHS videocassette). SASE. Reports in 3 weeks.

Music: Uses traditional music for industrial, medical, audiovisual and video projects.

RESPONSE GRAPHICS, (formerly Herod Advertising, Inc.), Ste. 130, S-620 Old Bullard Rd., Tyler TX 75703. (903)593-2362. President: Bill Bell. Advertising agency, audiovisual firm and music sound effect library. Clients include full service, banks, retail, industrial and music industry. Estab. 1954. Uses the services of music houses for background music for commercials, audiovisual presentations, jingles for commercials and commercials for radio and TV. Commissions 4-5 composers/year. Pays by the job. Buys shared rights.

How to Contact: Submit demo tape of previous work. Prefers cassette or 7½ or 15 ips reel-to-reel with 3-4 songs and lyric sheet. SASE, but prefers to keep material on file. Reports in 2-3 weeks.

Music: Uses modern contemporary and country western for films, commercials and audiovisual.

Tips: "Send demo tapes of previous or new work."

RHYTHMS PRODUCTIONS, P.O. Box 34485, Los Angeles CA 90034. A&R Department: R.S. White. Children's records, cassettes and videos. Clients include educational and childrens' markets. Estab. 1955. Uses the services of independent songwriters/composers for children's concept albums. Commissions 1-2 composers/year. Pays by royalty. Buys all rights.

How to Contact: Submit tape demonstrating composition skills. Prefers cassette. SASE. Reports in 2 months.

Music: Uses cassettes with educational content, activity or storybook and cassette.

Tips: "We buy completed master tapes."

*RIGHT TRACKS PRODUCTIONS LTD., 226 B. Portage Ave., Saskatoon SK S7H 0Y0 **Canada**. (306)933-4949. Producer/Studio Manager: Lyndon Smith. Scoring service and jingle/commercial music production house. Clients include ad agencies, corporations, film and video producers. Estab. 1986. Uses the services of independent songwriters/composers, lyricists, singers, session players, programmers, and arrangers for scoring of film and broadcast television, jingles for radio and TV, commercials for radion and TV, and AV soundtracks. Commissions 5 composers and 5 lyricists/year. Pays by the job, by royalty, or per hour. Buys all rights.

How to Contact: Submit demo tape of previous work; query with resume of credits. Prefers cassette or 7½/15 ips reel-to-reel. Does not return material; prefers to keep on file.

Music: "Depends on job/target market."

RTG PUBLISHING, INC., 130 E. 6th St., Cincinnati OH 45202. President: John Henry. Music Publisher. Clients include network television (U.S.), foreign television, and syndicated television producers. Uses services of MIDI composers to supply background and feature music. Currently seeking produced, unpublished, original songs for placement on one of several TV programs. Writers paid performance royalties through BMI/ASCAP and applicable synchronization fees.

How to Contact: Composers should submit resume and demo cassette of appropriate material (i.e. examples of television background scoring only). Songwriters should send no more than three songs on one cassette. SASE. Do not call.

Music: Song should be pop or adult contemporary. No country, heavy metal, or rap.
Tips: "We're currently looking for good pop music."

RUFFCUT RECORDING, 6472 Seven Mile, South Lyon MI 48178. (313)486-0505. Production Manager: J.D. Dudick. Jingle/**commercial production house.** Clients include advertising agencies and industrial accounts. Estab. 1990. Uses the services of independent songwriters/composers for background music for industrial films, jingles for local and national accounts and commercials for radio and TV. Commissions 4-5 composers and 1-2 lyricists/year. Pays by the job ($100-2,500) or by royalty (10-20%). Buys one-time rights.
How to Contact: Submit tape demonstrating composition skills. Prefers cassette with 3-5 songs and lyric sheets. Does not return unsolicited material; keeps material on file. Reports in 2-4 weeks.
Music: "All styles that are creative and unique" for commercials/radio, film presentations.
Tips: "Don't worry about the production; keep it catchy with a melody you will hum to."

CHUCK RUHR ADVERTISING, 1221 Nicollett Mall, Minneapolis MN 55403. (612)332-4565. Creative Director: Bill Johnson. Advertising agency. Serves consumer and industrial clients; client list available on request. Uses the services of songwriters and music houses for jingles and background music. Commissions 4-5 songwriters and 1-2 lyricists/year. Pays by the job. Initial fee negotiated, after that pays union scales. Pays residuals for subsequent use of material. Rights purchased are negotiable.
How to Contact: Submit demo tape of previous work. Prefers cassette. Reports "when needed."
Music: Uses background music and "originals befitting the message."
Tips: "Be original and be flexible. Study the best examples."

CHARLES RYAN ASSOCIATES, P.O. Box 2464, Charleston WV 25329. (304)342-0161. Vice President/Account Services: Tad Walden. Advertising agency. Clients in a variety of areas. Uses the services of music houses for scoring, background music, jingles and commercials for radio and TV. Commissions 2-3 songwriters/composers/year. Pays by the job. Buys all rights.
How to Contact: Submit demo tape of previous work or tape demonstrating composition skills; query with resume of credits; or write to arrange personal interview. Prefers cassette with 15-20 songs. SASE, but prefers to keep on file.
Music: Uses easy listening, pop, jazz and classical music for educational films, slide presentations and commercials.
Tips: "The first 2 songs/samples on demo tape better be good or we'll listen no further."

S.A. PRODUCTIONS, INC., 330 W. 58th St., New York NY 10019. (212)765-2669. President: Stan Applebaum. Scoring service, **commercial music production house** and **music/sound effect library.** Clients include motion picture production companies and advertising agencies, Broadway, music publishing and industrials. Estab. 1968. Uses the services of independent composers for scoring, background music, and composers/lyricists for jingles for national radio and TV commercials and industrials. Pays by the job. Buys all rights, one-time rights or negotiates rights purchased.
How to Contact: Query with resume of credits, or submit demo tape of previous work or tape demonstrating composition skills or manuscript showing music scoring skills, or write to arrange personal interview. Prefers cassette or 15 or 7½ ips reel-to-reel with 5-10 pieces. SASE, but prefers to keep material on file. Reports in 1 month.
Music: Uses all styles of music for various kinds of assignments.
Tips: "Be original with interesting harmonic and melodic development, and lyrics that are inventive and interesting."

*PATRICK WILLIAM SALVO, 8686 W. Olympic Blvd., Los Angeles CA 90035. (213)659-1792. Founder: Patrick William Salvo. Advertising agency and public relations, management. Clients include entertainment business, film, television, advertising radio. Estab. 1980. Uses the services of music houses, independent songwriters/composers and lyricists for jingles and background music for radio and TV commercials.
How to Contact: Write or call first to arrange personal interview. Prefers cassette (or VHS videocassette). Does not return unsolicited material; prefers to keep submitted material on file.
Music: Interested in all styles of music.

Listings of companies within this section which are either commercial music production houses or music libraries will have that information printed in boldface type.

SCHEMBRI VISION, 2156 Story Ave., Bronx NY 10473. (212)863-2986. Manager: Sal Schembri, Jr. Jingle/**commercial music production house.** Advertising agency. Serves retail and industrial clients. Uses the services of independent songwriters/composers for background music and jingles for TV commercials. Pays $250/job. Buys one-time rights.
How to Contact: Submit demo tape of previous work. SASE. Reports in 3 weeks.
Music: Uses easy listening and rap music for commercials.

SCHOENBACK ADVERTISING, INC., 1111 Park Ave., Baltimore MD 21201. (301)728-5566. Contact: Sarah Kelly. Advertising agency. Uses music houses for jingles, background music for TV commercials/ films/tapes, and radio commercials. Commissions 5-10 composers/year. Pays by the job. Buys all rights or one-time rights.
How to Contact: Submit demo tape of previously aired work. Prefers cassette or reel-to-reel (or ¾" VHS videocassete). Does not return unsolicited material.
Music: Mostly advertising jingles.

WILSON SCOTT ASSOCIATES, INC., 425 S. Fairfax, Los Angeles CA 90036. (213)934-6150. Creative Directors: Brien Scott and Michael Wilson. Advertising agency. "We are a full service ad agency." Estab. 1986. Uses the services of music houses, independent songwriters/composers for background music, jingles and commercials for radio and TV. Commissions 2 composers and 1 lyricist/year. Pays by the job or by the hour. Buys all rights or one-time rights.
How to Contact: Submit demo tape of previous work or tape demonstrating composition skills or write first to arrange personal interview. Prefers cassette (or ¾" videocassette) with 1-8 songs. SASE, but prefers to keep material on file.
Music: Uses music for commercials.

TAMARA SCOTT PRODUCTIONS, 19062 Two Bar Rd., Boulder Creek CA 95006. Production Manager: Tamara Scott. Audiovisual firm, scoring service, motion picture production company and **music/ sound effects library.** Clients include industrial firms. Uses the services of music houses, independent songwriters, lyricists and musicians for background music and scoring of film; jingles and commercials for radio and TV; and multi-image productions. Commissions 10-20 composers and 10-20 lyricists/ year. Pays $150-1,000/job, $35/hour or by royalty. Buys all rights or one-time rights.
How to Contact: Submit tape demonstrating composition skills. Prefers cassette or reel-to-reel (or videocassette). Does not return unsolicited material; prefers to keep on file. Reports "as needed."
Music: Positive, motivational, inspirational music.

SEASIDE PRODUCTIONS, P.O. Box 93, Sea Isle City NJ 08243. Producer: Gregory C. Guarini. Scoring service and jingle/**commercial music production house.** Clients are mostly businesses and bands in Delaware Valley. Estab. 1987. Uses the services of independent songwriters/composers and lyricists for "management and publishing." Commissions 12 composers and lyricists/year. Pays by the job or by royalty. Rights purchased "depend on situation."
How to Contact: Query with resume of credits, submit tape demonstrating composition skills or write to arrange personal interview. Prefers cassette (or VHS videocassette) with 4 songs and lyric or lead sheet. SASE, but prefers to keep material on file. Reports in 2 weeks.
Music: Uses rock and soul for all types of assignments.

SEATTLE MOTION PICTURE SERVICE, 4717 Aurora N., Seattle WA 98013. Manager: Dick Pappas. Audiovisual firm, motion picture production company and music/sound effect library. Estab. 1962. Uses original music for scoring of films, background music for tapes and productions, jingles and commercials for radio and TV. Pays by the job, by royalty or per hour. Buys all rights or one-time rights.
How to Contact: Write or call first and obtain permission to submit. Accepts cassette or reel-to-reel (or videocassette). Does not return unsolicited material; prefers to keep on file. Reports in 3 weeks.
Music: Uses up-tempo and classical music for all kinds of assignments.

***SHAFFER SHAFFER SHAFFER, INC.,** 1070 Hanna Bldg., Cleveland OH 44115. (216)566-1188. President: Harry Gard Shaffer, Jr. Advertising agency. Clients include consumer and retail. Uses services of songwriters, lyricists and music houses for jingles and background music. Commissions 6 songwriters/year. Pays $2,000-15,000/job. Buys all rights.
How to Contact: Query with resume of credits. Prefers 7½ ips reel-to-reel with 6-12 songs. Prefers to keep material on file. Responds as needs arise.

SILVER BURDETT & GINN, CN 018, 250 James St., Morristown NJ 07960. (201)285-8002. Music Editor: Donald Scafuri. Publisher of textbooks and records for kindergarten through 8th grade. Estab. 1864. "Our books and records are sold directly to schools and are evaluated and chosen for use according

to the adoption procedures of a particular school district." Uses the services of music houses, songwriters and lyricists for original songs for children K-8; lyricists for translating foreign lyrics into a singable English version and "writing original lyrics to a folk tune or a melody composed by someone else." Commissions 0-20 lyricists and 0-20 pieces/year. Pays $55-75 for lyrics and arrangements; up to $400 for original compositions (reprint rights plus statutory record royalty). Buys one-time rights for educational use.
How to Contact: Submit lead sheets of previous work. Prefers cassette. SASE. Reports in 1 month. Free catalog available.
Music: "We seek virtually any kind of song that is suitable both in words and music for children to sing. We are particularly interested in songs that are contemporary pop or folk-like in style. We are also interested in choral compositions for upper grades."
Tips: "Become acquainted with teachers and students in elementary or junior high classrooms. Find out what music they are presently using and what they would like to use."

SINGER ADVERTISING & MARKETING, INC., 1035 Delaware Ave., Buffalo NY 14209. (716)884-8885. Senior Vice President: Marilyn Singer. Advertising agency. Clients include health care, professional football, travel service and industrial. Estab. 1969. Uses the services of music houses for background music for slide presentations, industrial videos, jingles for health care and professional football and commercials for radio and TV. Commissions 1-2 composer and 3-4 lyricists/year. Pay varies.
How to Contact: Submit demo tape of previous work. Prefers cassette or 15 ips reel-to-reel or ½" videocassette. SASE. Reports in weeks.
Music: Uses up tempo pop and New Age jazz for commercial jingles and slide presentations.
Tips: "Study our client list and their current work and then submit."

ROBERT SOLOMON AND ASSOCIATES ADVERTISING, Suite 1000, 505 N. Woodward, Bloomfield Hills MI 48013. (313)540-0660. Copywriter/Producer: Jackie Purtan. Advertising agency. Clients include "food service accounts, convenience stores, retail accounts and small service businesses." Uses independent songwriters, lyricists and music houses for jingles and special presentations. Commissions 1-10 songwriters and 1-10 lyricists/year. Pays by the job. Buys all rights.
How to Contact: Submit demo tape of previously aired work. Prefers cassette or 7½ ips reel-to-reel with 1-5 pieces and lyric or lead sheets. "Submissions must be up-to-date and up to industry standards." Does not return unsolicited material; prefers to keep on file.
Music: "MOR, pop or rock jingles describing specific products or services."
Tips: "Please make sure all information presented is CURRENT!"

SONIC IMAGES PRODUCTIONS, INC., 4590 MacArthur Blvd. NW, Washington DC 20007. (202)333-1063. Vice President/Director of Video Services: Jolie Barbiere. Audiovisual firm, scoring services, **commercial music production house**, motion picture production company, **music/sound effect library**, CD-I/interactive multimedia development. Clients include independent producers, government, entertainment, associations, etc. Uses the services of music houses, independent songwriters/composers and lyricists for scoring of video and film productions; background music for art/experimental films and videos; jingles, public service announcements and radio and TV commercials. Commissions 2-4 composers and 1-2 lyricists/year. Pay varies. Buys all rights.
How to Contact: Submit demo tape of previous work or tape demonstrating composition skills. Prefers cassette (or ¾" VHS or Beta videocassette). "Include a resume." Does not return unsolicited material; prefers to keep on file. Reports if interested.
Music: Uses all commercial and classical styles of music for all kinds of assignments.
Tips: "We look for a clean professional product. Our clients demand it!"

SORIN PRODUCTIONS, INC., Freehold Executive Center, 4400 Route 9 S., Freehold NJ 07728. President: David Sorin. Audiovisual firm. Serves corporate and industrial clients. Uses services of music houses and independent songwriters/composers for background music for industrials. Commissions 1-3 composers and 1-3 lyricists/year. Pays by the job. Buys all rights.
How to Contact: Query with resume of credits. "No submissions with initial contact." Does not return unsolicited material; prefers to keep solicited materials on file. Reports in 1 month.
Music: Uses up-tempo and pop for audio, video and slides.

SOTER ASSOCIATES INC., 209 North 400 W., Provo UT 84601. (801)375-6200. President N. Gregory Soter. Advertising agency. Clients include financial, health care, municipal, computer hardware and software. Estab. 1970. Uses services of music houses, independent songwriters/composers and lyricists for background music for audiovisual presentations and jingles for radio and TV commercials. Commissions 1 composer, 1 lyricist/year. Pays by the job. Buys all rights.
How to Contact: Submit tape demonstrating previous work and composition skills. Prefers cassette or VHS videocassette. Does not return unsolicited submissions; prefers to keep materials on file.

SOUND*LIGHT PRODUCTIONS, 1915 Webster, Birmingham MI 48009. (313)642-3502. Producer: Terry Luke. Audiovisual firm. Estab. 1974. Clients include corporations, industrial, motivational, new age, churches and educational institutions. Uses the services of music houses and independent songwriters/composers for jingles, background music for TV commercials, slide presentations and training videos. Commissions 3-10 songwriters and 2-3 lyricists/year. Pays $40-3,000/job or $4-65/hour. Buys all rights or one-time rights.
How to Contact: Write or call first and obtain permission to submit; submit demo tape of previous work. Prefers cassette (or VHS videocassette). SASE, but prefers to keep material on file. Reports in 3 weeks.
Music: Uses up-tempo, rock, spiritual, easy listening and inspirational for slide presentations, training videos and artistic video-MTV.
Tips: "Be creative and upbeat."

*SOUND ADVISORS LTD., 400 West Lancaster Ave., Devon PA 19333. (215)975-9212. President: Greg Mizii. Vice President: Howard Scott III. Secretary/Treasurer: Bernard M. Resnick. Director: Steven Bernskin. Industrial and consumer jingles. Background music for AV projects and movies. Negotiated contracts with major film companies, publishers and recording companies throughout the world. Covers all aspects of the business—from law and management to producing and promotion. Recording producers on staff.
How to Contact: Write or call first to obtain permission to submit. Does not accept or return unsolicited material. Submit demo tape of previously aired work and resume of credits. Prefers cassette or videocassette (Beta/VHS). Reports ASAP. We prefer you to write us and send SASE prior to submission.
Music: All styles for use as jingles and commercial scores. Target styles are rock, pop, rap, R&B, metal, gospel and jazz.
Tips: "Timing is critical—depending on projects."

SOUND CITY PRODUCTIONS, INC., Suite C, 911 18th Ave. S., Nashville TN 37212. (615)321-5955. President: Gary D. Caudel. Motion picture and video production company. Serves entertainment industry and general clients. Uses the services of independent songwriters/composers for jingles for TV commercials and songs. Pays 10% royalty and expenses; payment varies. Rights purchased vary.
How to Contact: Query with resume of credits. Prefers cassette (or VHS, 8mm or ¾" videocassette) with 2-4 pieces and typed lyric or lead sheet. SASE, but prefers to keep material on file.
Music: Uses all types of music for television programs, experimental video art, movies and videos.

SOUND WRITERS PUBLICATIONS, INC., 223-225 Washington St., Newark NJ 07102. (201)642-5132. Producer/Engineer: Kevin Ford. Advertising agency, audiovisual firm and jingle/commercial music production house. Clients include major labels and large corporations. Estab. 1980. Uses the services of independent songwriters/composers and lyricists for scoring of jingles and TV commercials. Most writing, producing and engineering done in-house. Buys all rights and one-time rights.
How to Contact: Submit demo tape of previous work. Prefers cassette or ¾" videocassette. "We have a no return policy on all material." Prefers to keep material on file. Reports back in 4 weeks.
Music: Uses all types of music for commercials, training tapes and music videos.
Tips: "We don't like big egos."

*SOUVENIRS OF HAWAII, 2290 Alahao Pl., Honolulu HI 96819. (808)847-4608. President: Donald P. McDiarmid III. Audiovisual firm, **commercial music production house** and **music/sound effect library**. Clients include resort retail gift shops. Buys all rights or one-time rights.
How to Contact: Submit demo tape of previous work. Prefers cassette. SASE.
Music: Uses Hawaiian music for Hawaiian videos, and phonograph records, etc.

SPARTRONIX VIDEOSERVICES, 476 Lancaster Pike, Frazer PA 19355. (215)647-2800. President: Dick Spahr. Audiovisual firm and video production/post production house. Estab. 1965. Clients include primarily industrial and corporate accounts. Uses the services of music houses and independent songwriters/composers for scoring of sales, point of purchase displays, industrial and corporate training programs (videos). Commissions 6 composers/year. Negotiates pay. Buys all or one-time rights, depending on project.
How to Contact: Submit demo tape of previous work. Prefers cassette (or ¾" or VHS videocassette). Will keep material on file. Reports in 1 month after interest shown by clients.
Music: Uses up-tempo, bright, hi-tech synth music for corporate and industrial, sales and training, and annual report videos.

SPECTRUM SOUND STUDIOS, INC., 1634 SW Alder, Portland OR 97205. (503)248-0248. Director of Music Operations: Rick Waritz. Jingle/**commercial music production house, music sound effect library** and broadcast production. Estab. 1973. Clients include advertising agencies, corporations and music businesses. Uses the services of independent songwriters/composers for scoring of in-house corporate video, jingles for commercial production and commercials for radio and TV. Commissions 8 composers and 2 lyricists/year. Pays by the job. Rights are up to client.
How to Contact: Submit demo tape of previous work or query with resume of credits. Prefers cassette or 15 ips reel-to-reel (or ¾″ videocassette). SASE. Reports in 1 month.
Music: Uses all styles of music for all kinds of assignments.

SPIVACK ADVERTISING, INC., 7 Church Lane, Baltimore MD 21208. (301)484-9510. President: Irvin Spivack. Advertising agency. Clients include retail, financial and business-to-business. Estab. 1979. Uses the services of music houses for jingles for commercials for radio. Pay is negotiable.
How to Contact: Submit demo tape of previous work. Prefers cassette. Does not return unsolicited material.
Music: Generally up-tempo, but it really depends on clients.

EDGAR S. SPIZEL ADVERTISING, INC., 1782 Pacific Ave., San Francisco CA 94109. (415)474-5735. President: Edgar S. Spizel. Advertising agency, public relations firm and TV/radio production firm. Estab. 1950. Clients include public transportation, developers, retail, sports, auto and broadcast businesses. Uses the services of independent songwriters for background music in commercials. Buys all rights.
How to Contact: Query. Prefers cassette with 3-5 songs. Does not return unsolicited material.
Tips: "Stay in touch. While we seldom use music, when we do we don't like to scrounge. We like to have a selection at our fingertips."

STAN & LOU, INC., #155, 3013 Fountainview, Houston TX 77057. (713)977-5000. Creative Director: Lou Congelio. Advertising agency. Clients include all aspects business's and retail outlets. Estab. 1988. Uses the services of music houses for scoring of video productions, background music for video productions, jingles for radio and TV commercials. Pay thru music house. Buys all rights and one-time rights.
How to Contact: Submit demo tape of previous work. Write first to arrange personal interview. Prefers cassette. SASE, but prefers to keep material on file.
Music: Uses all types music for all types assignments.

STARWEST PRODUCTIONS, INC., Studio A, 4910 Fox St., Denver CO 80216. (303)295-2222. President: Steven Pettit. Audiovisual firm and jingle **commercial music production house.** Clients include Fortune 500 companies to mom and pop shops. Estab. 1979. Uses the services of music houses and independent songwriters/composers for commercials for radio and TV. Commissions 2 composers and 2 lyricists/year. Pays $2,000/job. Buys all rights and rights with royalties.
How to Contact: Submit demo tape of previous work or query with resume of credits. Prefers 7½ ips reel-to-reel with 5-10 songs. SASE, but prefers to keep material on file. Reports in 1 month.
Music: Uses up-tempo music for slide presentations and live performances.
Tips: "Make my foot tap."

STATION BREAK PRODUCTIONS, Suite 1, 40 Glen St., Glen Cove NY 11542. (516)759-7005. Producer: Stephen Meyers. Advertising agency and jingle/**commercial music production house.** Clients include ad agencies, retail businesses, hotels, restaurants, corporate and special projects. Estab. 1985. Uses the services of independent songwriters/composers and singers, and MIDI composers with performer voice overs for commercials for radio and TV. Commissions 2 composers and 1 lyricist/year. Pays by the job. Buys all rights.
How to Contact: Submit demo tape of previous work or write to arrange personal interview. Prefers cassette with 4 pieces. Does not return unsolicited material; prefers to keep material on file. Reports in 1 month.
Music: Uses pop, classical and dance for industrial and commercials.
Tips: "Send your best work to date. Start with your strongest style."

STONE & ADLER, 1 E. Wacker Dr., Chicago IL 60601. Accounts: Ellen Best. Advertising agency and direct marketing firm. Estab. 1966. Serves industrial, consumer and financial clients. Uses music houses for background music in commercials. Commissions 1-2 pieces/year. Pays according to budget. Usually buys one-time rights.
How to Contact: Submit demo tape of previously aired work. Prefers reel-to-reel or cassette. Returns material if requested with SASE, but prefers to keep tape on file.
Music: All types. "Be versatile, cost-effective."

*STRATEGIC PROMOTIONS, INC., Suite 250, 2602 McKinney, Dallas TX 75204. (214)871-1016. Account Coordinator: Rebecca Anderson-Douglas. Advertising agency, marketing. Clients include fast food, retail food, food service, beverage, beer. Estab. 1978. Uses the services of music houses and independent songwriters/composers for scoring of music tracks for TV commercials and background music for TV & radio commercials. Commissions 2-3 composers/year. Pays by the job.
How to Contact: Submit demo tape of previous work. Submit tape demonstrating composition skills. Prefers cassette (or ¾" videocassette) with 4-5 songs. "No phone calls please. Does not return unsolicited material; prefers to keep submitted materials on file.
Music: Uses all types of music for industrial videos, slide presentations and commercials.
Tips: "Submit your favorite and personal best work."

STRAUCHEN ASSOCIATES, INC., 3388 Erie Ave., Cincinnati OH 45208. (513)871-5353. President: Stephen H. Strauchen. Advertising agency. Clients include financial, food, business-to-business and insurance. Estab. 1981. Uses the services of music houses and independent songwriters/composers for scoring of commercial jingles and sales films and background music for radio, TV and audiovisual presentations. Commissions 3-4 composers/year; 1 lyricist/year. Pays $500-1,000/job or $20-30/hour. Buys all rights.
How to Contact: Submit demo tape of previous work. Prefers cassette, 7½ ips reel-to-reel or VHS videocassette. SASE, but prefers to keep materials on file.
Music: Easy listening, up-tempo, pop and jazz.
Tips: "Be specific regarding rates, use rights, etc."

SULLIVAN & FINDSEN ADVERTISING, 2165 Gilbert Ave., Cincinnati OH 45206. (513)281-2700. Director of Broadcast Production: Kirby Sullivan. Advertising agency. Clients include consumer and business-to-business firms. Uses the services of music houses, independent songwriters/composers and lyricists for scoring, background music, jingles and commercials for radio and TV. Commissions 3 composers and 3 lyricists/year. Pays by the job. Buys all rights.
How to Contact: Submit demo tape of previous work. Prefers cassette. Does not return unsolicited material; prefers to keep material on file. "We report back when we need some work."
Music: Uses all styles for commercials.

TALCO PRODUCTIONS, 279 E. 44th St., New York NY 10017. (212)697-4015. President: Al Lawrence. Audiovisual firm, TV and motion picture production company. Clients include corporate, nonprofit and educational organizations. Uses the services of music houses and independent songwriters/composers and lyricists for scoring and background music for film and TV, and radio. Commissions 2-3 composers and 0-3 lyricists/year. Pays by the job. Buys all rights.
How to Contact: Query with resume of credits. Do not send unsolicited submissions. SASE for reply. "Do not submit demo unless request is made!"
Music: Uses easy listening, up-tempo, pop, jazz, classical, adult contemporary and rock for educational films and documentaries.

TEEMAN/SLEPPIN ENTERPRISES INC., 147 W. 26 St., New York NY 10001. (212)243-7836. President: Bob Teeman. Vice President: Stu Sleppin. Management, motion picture and music video production company. Clients include artists, film companies, TV stations and corporate sponsors. Uses the services of independent songwriters/composers and lyricists for scoring of TV shows and films and original songs. Commissions 3 composers and 3 lyricists/year. Pays by the job. Rights negotiable.
How to Contact: Submit demo tape of previous work or write to arrange personal interview. Prefers cassette (or VHS or ¾" videocassette). SASE, but prefers to keep material on file. Reports in 2 months.
Music: Uses pop and dance for original songs tied into a film or campaign.

TELECINE SERVICES & PRODUCTION LTD., 23 Seapoint Ave., Blackrock, Co. Dublin **Ireland**. Phone: 353 1 2808744. FAX: 353 1 808679. Director: Anabella Nolan. Audiovisual firm and video production house. Estab. 1977. Clients include advertising and commercial business. Uses the services of songwriters and music houses for original songs for TV commercials and audiovisual and video programs; lyricists for writing lyrics for commercials and conference themes. Commissions 5 songwriters/composers and 3 lyricists for 20 pieces/year. Pays $5,000/job. Buys all rights or rights within one country.
How to Contact: Query with resume of credits or submit tape demonstrating composition skills. Prefers 15 ips reel-to-reel or cassette with 3-10 songs. SAE and IRC. Reports in 1 month.
Tips: "Understand our marketing needs; know the difference between European and U.S. tastes."

TEXAS AFFILIATED PUBLISHING COMPANY, "STREETPEOPLES WEEKLY NEWS", P.O. Box 270942, Dallas TX 75227-0942. (214)941-7796. Contact: Editor. Advertising agency and newspaper publisher. Clients are corporate and retail. Estab. 1977. Uses the services of independent songwriters/composers, lyricists and music houses for commercials for radio and TV. Pays negotiable amount. Buys all rights and one-time rights.

How to Contact: Write first to arrange personal interview. "No phone calls please. Send *no* originals, include SASE for returns. Our current project is about the problems of the 'homeless.' Persons writing songs about this may want to send for a copy of 'Streetpeoples Weekly News' to get an idea of what's involved. Send $2 to cover handling/postage." Prefers to keep materials on file. Reports in 3 weeks.

Music: Uses easy listening, up-tempo for commercials. "We're interested in many types/styles according to job need of our clients. Also need music production for intros on radio talk shows."

TOP OF THE MOUNTAIN PUBLISHING/POWELL PRODUCTIONS, Suite 123, 11701 S. Belcher Rd., Largo FL 34643. (813)530-0110. FAX: (813)536-3681. Administrator: Dr. Tag Powell. Publisher of books, audio-cassettes and seminars (producer). Clients include domestic and foreign distributors of books and audiocassettes. Estab. 1980. Uses independent songwriters/composers for background music for subliminal audiocassettes and New Age type music audiocassettes. Pays by the job. Buys all rights.

How to Contact: Submit demo tape of previous work. Prefers cassette with 5-7 songs. Does not return material. Prefers to keep submitted materials on file. "Responds when the need arises."

Music: Uses New Age instrumental.

Tips: "Call first to let us know you are submitting material."

TPS VIDEO SVC., Box 1233, Edison NJ 08818. (201)287-3626. President: R.S. Burkt. Audiovisual firm, motion picture production company and **music/sound effects library**. Clients include AT&T, IBM and Xerox (industrial firms). Uses the services of independent composers and arrangers for scoring of industrials, background music and jingles for radio and TV commercials. Does not buy songs. Commissions 20-100 composers/year. Pays by the job. Buys all rights or one-time rights.

How to Contact: Submit demo tape of previous work demonstrating composition skills. Prefers cassette. SASE for response. Reports in 3 weeks.

Music: Considers all types of music for advertising.

TRAYNOR, BREEHL & GLAZEN ADVERTISING, 1250 Old River Rd., Cleveland OH 44113. (216)241-7200. FAX: (216)241-4126. Creative Director: Alan Glazen. Advertising agency. Clients include consumer, retail. Estab. 1972. Uses the services of music houses, independent songwriters/composers and arrangers for jingles for radio/TV spots and commercials for radio and TV. Commissions 6-10 composers/year. Pays $1,500-6,000/job. Buys all rights.

How to Contact: Submit demo tape of previous work. Prefers cassette (or ¾ videocassette) with 5-7 songs. Does not return unsolicited material; prefers to keep on file.

Music: Uses pop, jazz, classical and esoterica for commercials.

Tips: "Put your best foot forward. Lead off with a song you are willing to be judged on."

*TRF PRODUCTION MUSIC LIBRARIES, 40 E. 49th St., New York NY 10017. (212)753-3234. President: Michael Nurko. **Music/sound effect libraries.** Estab. 1931. Uses services of independent composers for jingles, background and theme music for all media including films, slide presentations, radio and television commercials. Pays 50% royalty.

How to Contact: Submit demo tape of new compositions. Prefers cassette with 3-7 pieces.

Music: Primarily interested in instrumental music for assignments in all media.

TRI VIDEO TELEPRODUCTION, P.O. Box 8822, Incline Village NV 89450. (702)323-6868. Director: Jon Paul Davidson. Documentary and corporate television production firm. Clients include corporate accounts, primarily in health care and telecommunications. Estab. 1978. Uses the services of music houses and independent songwriters/composers for scoring of logo soundbeds and intro/conclusions and background music for transitions and presentations. Commissions 0-1 composers/year. Pays $500-2,000/job. Buys all rights and/or one-time rights.

How to Contact: Query with resume of credits. Prefers cassette with 1-3 pieces. SASE, but prefers to keep material on file. "We do not report back. We will use on-file tapes to demo to clients when making selection. If your work is what client likes and is appropriate, we will contact you."

Music: Uses easy, up-tempo and classical for educational and industrial.

Tips: "The corporate market is quite varied. Needs are of every type. Just keep in touch. We do lots of custom work rather than volume, so number of projects is small each year."

TULLY-MENARD, INC., 2207 S. Dale Mabry, Tampa FL 33629. (813)253-0447. Broadcast Producer: Robert A. Ackroyd. Advertising agency. Estab. 1960. Clients include a fast food restaurant, supermarket, theme park, retailers, manufacturers, car dealer. Uses the services of songwriters and music houses for TV and radio commercials, jingles, background music and film and AV soundtracks. Com-

missions 1-2 songwriters/composers per year. Payment negotiable, "dependent on project, budget and needs." Buys all rights.
How to Contact: Write or call for permission to submit demo tape of previous work. Prefers cassette or 7½ ips reel-to-reel with 5-8 songs. SASE, but prefers to keep material on file. "We research our file at the onset of need to determine candidates and parameters, then obtain bids and demos."
Music: "Broadcast and off-line; jingles and music tracks. Institutional jingles for a wide variety of clients."
Tips: "Stay current with today's sound, but be different—give it your own personality. Listen carefully to the parameters we give you, and if you don't quite grasp what we're looking for, ask! Provide the same package services as major music houses but with more originality and ingenuity."

TULLYVISION STUDIOS, 465 Main St., Tullytown PA 19007. (215)946-7444. Producer: Michelle A. Powell. Audiovisual firm. Clients include corporate/industrial. Estab. 1983. Uses the services of music houses and independent songwriters/composers for marketing, training and corporate image video-tapes. Commissions 3 composers/year. Pays $500/job. Buys all rights or one-time rights.
How to Contact: Submit demo tape of previous work. Query with resume of credits. Prefers cassette or ¾" VHS videocassette with 3 songs. SASE, but prefers to keep submitted materials on file. Reports in 3 weeks.
Music: Uses up-tempo and pop for educational films and slide presentations.

27TH DIMENSION INC., Box 1149, Okeechobee FL 34973-1149. (800)634-0091. President: John St. John. Scoring service, jingle/**commercial music production house** and **music sound effect library**. Clients include A/V producers, video houses, recording studios and radio and TV stations. Estab. 1986. Uses the services of independent songwriters/composers for scoring of library material and commercials for radio and TV. Commissions 10 composers/year. Pays $100-1,000/job; publishing (performance fees). "We buy the right to use in our library exclusively." Buys all rights except writer's publishing. Writer gets all performance fees (ASCAP or BMI).
How to Contact: Submit tape demonstrating composition skills or call. Prefers cassette. "Call before sending." Does not return unsolicited material; prefers to keep on file. SASE. Reports in 1 week.
Music: Uses industrial, pop jazz, sports, contemporary and New Age for music library.
Tips: "Follow style instructions carefully."

*UMBRELLA MEDIA, 11314 NE 26th Av., Vancouver WA 98686. (206)690-3833. President: Sid Brown. Advertising agency and audiovisual firm. Clients include high tech, educational and human services organizations. Estab. 1975. Uses the services of independent songwriters/composers and lyricists for scoring of TV productions, corporate videos and commercials for TV. Commissions 2 composers and 4 lyricists/year. Pays $50-500/job or 10% royalty.
How to Contact: Submit demo tape of previous work. Query with resume of credits. Prefers cassette, 7½ IPS reel-to-reel (or VHS videocassette) with no more than 10 songs and lyric sheet. SASE, but prefers to keep submitted material on file. Reports in 1 month.
Music: Uses classic, New Age, rock, folk, jazz for educational, corporate, documentary, videos and slide shows.

VIDEO I-D, INC., 105 Muller Rd., Washington IL 61571. (309)444-4323. Manager, Marketing Services: Gwen Wagner. Post production/teleproductions. Clients include industrial and business. Estab. 1978. Uses the services of professional library music for video production pieces and commercials. Buys all rights.
How to Contact: Submit demo tape of previous work. Prefers cassette or VHS videocassette with 5 songs and lyric sheet. SASE, but prefers to keep submitted materials on file. Reports in 3 weeks.
Music: "Musical styles depend upon client preference."

VINEBERG COMMUNICATIONS, Suite B-800, 61-20 Grand Central Pkwy., Forest Hills NY 11375. (718)760-0333. President: Neil Vineberg. Jingle/commercial music production house. Clients include TV/film producers. Estab. 1986. Uses the services of independent songwriters/composers and lyricists for background music for TV/film, corporate videos/film and commercials for radio and TV. Commissions 5 composers and 2 lyricists/year. Pays by the job. Buys all rights and one-time rights.
How to Contact: Submit demo tape of previous work. Submit tape demonstrating composition skills. Query with resume of credits. Write first to arrange personal interview. Prefers cassette (or VHS videocassette) with 4 songs and lead sheet (if possible). "No calls. Write only." SASE, but prefers to keep material on file. Reports in 1 month.
Music: Uses all types except classical.

VIP VIDEO, Film House, 143 Hickory Hill Cir., Osterville MA 02655. (508)428-7198. President: Jeffrey H. Aikman. Audio visual firm. Clients include business, industry and television stations. Estab. 1983. Uses the services of music houses, independent songwriters/composers and lyricists for scoring of

multi-image productions, background music for videotapes and motion pictures and jingles for TV commercials. Commissions 15-20 composers and 15-20 lyricists/year. Pays by the job, amounts vary depending on the length and complexity of each project. Buys all rights, preferable but can handle one-time rights for special projects.
How to Contact: Submit demo tape of previous work. Prefers cassette with 1-2 songs. SASE but prefers to keep material on file unless specifically stated. Reports in 3 weeks.
Music: Uses easy listening, pop and up-tempo for feature films, TV series, TV pilots and background for videotapes. Currently working or scoring series of 26 feature length silent films. If project is successful, this series will be added to at the rate of 13 per year.

VISION FILM GROUP, INC., 72 Princess St. 2nd Fl., Winnipeg, Manitoba R3B 1K2 **Canada.** (204)942-6215. President: Al Rosenberg. Audiovisual firm, motion picture and music video production company. Estab. 1985. Clients include industrial and entertainment firms. Uses the services of music houses, independent songwriters/composers and lyricists for background music for audiovisual and videos, and TV commercials. Commissions 3-5 composers and 2-4 lyricists/year. Pays $100-500/job. Buys all rights or one-time rights.
How to Contact: Submit demo tape of previous work, or tape demonstrating composition skills. Prefers cassette (or Beta videocassette). Does not return unsolicited material; prefers to keep on file. Reports in 2 weeks.
Music: Uses rock, contemporary, new age, up-tempo, unpublished music for videos, marketing programs, audiovisual presentations and commercials.
Tips: "Currently looking for fresh material for a rock musical for TV and video—as well as touring."

BEN WAGES AGENCY, 2513 Denny Ave., Pascagoula MS 39567. (601)769-7104. FAX: (601)769-8590. Owner/President: Ben Wages. Advertising agency, management firm, booking agency and record company (Sea Coast Recording). Estab. 1978. Uses the services of independent songwriters. Pays by the job, by royalty or per hour. Buys all rights or one-time rights. Depends on particular situation.
How to Contact: Write or call to arrange personal interview or submit demo tape of previously aired work. Prefers cassette (or VHS videocassette). SASE, but prefers to keep material on file. Reports in 4 weeks.
Music: "Country is predominantly used. Assignments are most often commercial jingles."
Tips: "Be as professional as possible when submitting material and be thorough. Neatness is always a plus. Would advise sending copyrighted material only. Include as much info as possible."

WEBER, COHN & RILEY, 444 N. Michigan Ave., Chicago IL 60611. (312)527-4260. Executive Creative Director: C. Welch. Advertising agency. Serves real estate, business, financial and food clients. Estab. 1960. Uses music houses for jingles and background music for commercials. Commissions 2 songwriters and 2 lyricists/year. Pays $500 minimum/job. Buys all rights or one-time rights, "open to negotiation."
How to Contact: Write a letter of introduction to creative director. SASE. "We listen to and keep a file of all submissions, but generally do not reply unless we have a specific job in mind." Songwriters may follow up with a phone call for response.
Music: "We use music for a variety of products and services. We expect highly original, tight arrangements that contribute to the overall concept of the commercial. We do not work with songwriters who have little or no previous experience scoring and recording commercials."
Tips: "Don't aim too high to start. Establish credentials and get experience on small local work, then go after bigger accounts. Don't oversell when making contacts or claim the ability to produce any kind of 'sound.' Producers only believe what they hear on sample reels. Produce a sample reel that's professional and responsive to today's needs. Present a work that is creative and meets our strategies and budget requirements."

WESTERN PUBLISHING COMPANY, INC., 1220 Mound Ave., Racine WI 53404. (414)633-2431. Manager, Youth Electronics: Virginia Clapper. Children's publisher. Distributes entertainment products through mass market channels. Estab. 1907. Uses the services of music houses, independent songwriters/composers and lyricists for scoring of and background music for songs, short films and storytelling audio cassettes. Commissions 2-3 composers and 4-5 lyricists/year. Pays by the job. Buys all rights. Work for hire arrangement preferred.
How to Contact: Submit demo tape of previous work. Wirte first to arrange personal interview. Prefers cassette (or VHS videocassette) with 2-6 songs and lead sheets. SASE, but prefers to keep submitted materials on file. Reports in 6 weeks.
Music: Uses children's songs for film scores; book and tape audio productions.
Tips: "Expect to be employed on a work for hire basis, allowing straight buy-out of all rights."

WESTON WOODS STUDIOS, 389 Newtown Turnpike, Weston CT 06883. Production Manager: Paul R. Gagne. Audiovisual firm, motion picture production company. Estab. 1955. "We produce films and audio visual products based on children's picture books." Clients include educational/institutional market and home market video. Uses services of independent composers and copyists for scoring of short films and filmstrip soundtracks. Commissions 3-5 composers/year. Pays by the job, $600-3500. Buys all rights.

How to Contact: Submit demo tape of previous work, tape demonstrating composition scores or query with resume of credits. Write to arrange personal interview. Prefers cassette. "Write only; we cannot accept telephone queries." Does not return unsolicited material. Prefers to keep material on file.

Music: Uses serious non-commercial scoring for acoustic instruments (synth OK) in classical, folk, or ethnic styles for educational films and filmstrips of children's stories; no driving rhythm tracks; no songs, please—especially "kiddie songs."

WHITE PRODUCTION ARCHIVES, INC., 12233 South Pulaski Drive, Alsip IL 60658. (708)385-8535. President: Matthew White. Motion picture production company. Produces home video entertainment programs. Estab. 1987. Uses the services of independent songwriters/composers for scoring of offbeat documentaries; videogame tapes. Commissions 5 composers/year. Pays by the job. Buys all rights.

How to Contact: Submit demo tape of previous work. Prefers cassette. Does not return unsolicited material. Prefers to keep submitted materials on file.

Music: Uses material for home videos.

SANDY WILBUR MUSIC, INC., 48 E. 43rd St., 7th Floor, New York NY 10017. (212)949-1190. Jingle/ **commercial music production house**. Clients include advertising agencies, film producers and corporate clients. Uses the services of singers, arrangers, players (primarily MIDI keyboards) for scoring of TV and film, and jingles and commercials for radio and TV. Commissions 2 composers and 2 lyricists/ year. Pays by the hour "depending upon what the job is." Buys all rights.

How to Contact: Call first for permission to submit. Prefers cassette (or VHS videocassette) with 3 pieces limit. Does not return unsolicited material; prefers to keep on file. Reports in 1 month.

Music: Uses R&B, rock, jazz, pop, top 40 for commercials, educational films, etc.

Tips: "We're primarily interested in singers, arrangers, players and programmers, but if a songwriter has one or more of these skills, I will listen. This is a competitive business. Apply only if you believe you are different or better than what's out there. Be patient—if I feel you are right for the company, I'll get back to you."

WINMILL ENTERTAINMENT, 813 N. Cordove St., Burbank CA 91505-2924. (818)954-0065. Director/ Music Videos: Chip Miller. Motion picture and music video production company. Clients include record labels, network/cable TV, MTV and motion picture studios. Estab. 1987. Uses the services of music houses, lyricists and independent songwriters/composers for scoring of motion pictures, background music for motion pictures, commercials for TV and music videos for special accounts (i.e. fashion etc.). Commissions 3-12 composers and 1-3 lyricists/year. Pay commensurate with film budget allocation. Rights bought depends on project.

How to Contact: Query with resume of credits. SASE. Report back depends on project deadline and needs.

Music: Music depends upon the project.

EVANS WYATT ADVERTISING, 5151 Flynn Parkway, Corpus Christi TX 78411. (512)854-1661. Owner: E. Wyatt. Advertising agency. Clients are general/all types. Estab. 1975. Uses the services of music houses and independent songwriters/composers for background music for soundtracks, jingles for advertising and commercials for radio and TV. Commissions 8-10 composers/year. Pays by the job. Buys all rights.

How to Contact: Submit demo tape of previous work. Submit tape demonstrating composition skills. Query with resume of credits. Write first to arrange personal interview. Prefers cassette. SASE, but prefers to keep material on file. Reports in 2 months.

Music: Uses all types for commercials plus videos mostly.

Tips: "Make it *easy* to judge your work! Be sure you've got the talent you claim and present it clearly. If we don't like your pitch immediately, chances are we won't like your work."

YARDIS CORPORATION, 9138 West Chester Pike, Upper Darby PA 19082. (215)789-2200. Chairman: Ray Rosenberg. Advertising agency. Clients include travel, financial, car dealers, tour operators. Estab. 1946. Uses the services of music houses and independent songwriters/composers for background music for video presentations, jingles for various spots and commercials for radio and TV. Payment depends on circmstances. Rights purchased depends on circumstances.

How to Contact: "Call; go from there." Prefers cassette (or VHS videocassette). Does not return unsolicited material; prefers to keep material on file.

Music: Uses various styles for various assignments.

GREG YOUNGMAN MUSIC, P.O. Box 381, Santa Ynez CA 93460. (805)688-1136. Advertising agency/ audio production. Serves all types of clients. Local, regional and national levels. Uses the services of independent composers/copywriters for commercials, jingles and audiovisual projects. Commissions 12-20 composers/year. Pays $500-10,000/project. Buys all rights.
How to Contact: Submit demo tape of previously aired work. Prefers cassette, R-DAT or reel-to-reel. Prefers to keep tape on file. Reports in one month.
Music: Uses all types for radio commercials, film cues.
Tips: "We're looking for something we've never heard before. A sound that's fresh and innovative."

ZM SQUARED, 903 Edgewood Lane, P.O. Box 2030, Cinnaminson NJ 08077. (609)786-0612. Estab. 1971. Clients include colleges, schools, businesses and audiovisual producers. Uses the services of songwriters "for themes for our no-needledrop music library, background for audiovisual presentations and jingles. We prefer to work with composer/arranger/performer and use primarily background music." Commissions 2-5 composers/year. Pays 10-35% royalty. Buys all rights.
How to Contact: Submit demo tape of previous work. Prefers cassette with 4-6 songs. SASE. Reports in 3 weeks. Free catalog available.
Music: "We require a variety of background music—educational and industrial for general use with audiovisual programs."
Tips: "Know what we want and be able to produce what you write."

Advertising, AV, and Commercial Music Houses/ '91-'92 Changes

The following markets appeared in the 1991 edition of *Songwriter's Market* but are absent from the 1992 edition. Most of these companies failed to respond to our request for an update of their listing. Others are not listed for a variety of reasons, which is indicated in parentheses following the company name. For example, they may have gone out of business, or they may have requested deletion from the 1992 edition because they are backlogged with material.

Ad Hoc Marketing Reseources, Inc.
Air Sound/Plum Productions (asked to be deleted)
Ancora Productions
Angle Films
Nicolas Astor-Grouf Enterprises
Audio-Visual Associates
Barron Hillman & Mellnick, Inc.
The Berkshire Group (asked to be deleted)
Burkhardt & Christy Advertising, Inc.
Caedmon (asked to be deleted)
Capital Associated Industries, Inc. (asked to be deleted)
Center One Video Productions Inc. (asked to be deleted)
Centra Advertising Company
CGI Advertising (moved; left no forwarding address)
Classic Video Inc.
Communiplex Services Inc.
Connelly & Co. Inc.
Corporate Design Associates
Creative Sound Studios (asked to be deleted)
Creston Associates, Ltd. (asked

to be deleted)
DD&B Studios Inc.
De Wolfe Music Library (asked to be deleted)
Decker, Decker and Freas Inc. (asked to be deleted)
Charles Edelstein Advertising, Inc. (asked to be deleted)
Educational Insights
Don Elliott Productions (asked to be deleted)
ETV
Ferguson & Associates Advertising
Film Classic Exchange
Flynn/Wright, Inc. (asked to be deleted)
Focused Audio (asked to be deleted)
A Gentle Wind (asked to be deleted)
Goodman Associate (asked to be deleted)
Green Advertects, Inc. (asked to be deleted)
Herb Gross & Co.
Innovative Video Associates (asked to be deleted)
Jasen, Navarro & Foster
Lane & Johnson

Christopher Lardas Advertising (asked to be deleted)
Madden & Goodrum
Media Group Television (asked to be deleted)
Arthur Meriwether Inc.
Metrotape Producer Services Inc.
Montemayor Y Asociados (asked to be deleted)
Mystic Oak Records
Henry Nason Productions
New Age Sight & Sound (moved; left no forwarding address)
Ken Schmidt Co. Inc. (asked to be deleted)
Sittason-Co. Inc.
Solo Sports Video
Christopher Thomas/Muller Jordan Weiss (moved; left no forwarding address)
United Entertainment Productions
USAV Communications Group (asked to be deleted)
Video Arts
VTI Communications for Business (asked to be deleted)

Play Producers and Publishers

When writing plays or musicals for theater, today's playwrights should keep it simple. Theaters which produce original shows normally have limited funds and facilities, and they require plays with uncomplicated sets and small casts. Theater directors and producers (even those on Broadway) are always searching for material that they can perform unpretentiously and inexpensively.

And even though Broadway may be your ultimate goal, remember that the smaller regional dinner theaters, children's theaters and college and high school drama departments offer reachable, viable outlets for your work. Don't sell yourself short by ruling out everything except the big time. Your work needs exposure first, and these groups provide an excellent starting block.

Listed in this section are many playhouses and publishers devoted to developing new plays and musicals. They receive hundreds of submissions from playwrights and composers/songwriters each year, but only the very best are chosen for actual production and/or publication. In such a competitive climate, there are several things you can do to to broaden your knowledge of the field and improve the chances of your work being selected.

First, learn as much as possible about theater: its history, what's already been produced and current trends. Research your specialty genre by attending (and reading) plays and musicals, reading theater magazines and discussing related topics with people in your theater group (it's important to join one). All this will help you become a more versatile writer and composer.

And, while keeping set and cast restrictions in mind, remember the importance of expandability. Keeping it simple doesn't mean you should create a two-character, bare-stage play. Instead, provide flexibility and give the piece room for embellishments that seem natural to the work, but which are not essential in the actual production. A musical should be an outline, not a blueprint, which is followed by contributions by the director, choreographer, producer and all involved. In short, it is always beneficial to create a musical that may be further developed, not one that has to be condensed.

Another thing to remember is that works in musical theater are most commonly the products of collaboration. And because of the nature of the musical (the meshing of music and script into a single, unified work), this type of theater is more difficult to successfully develop and produce. Although collaboration is not an absolute for a good musical, the best of musical theater has been written by the combination of playwright and composer.

How does one go about finding a suitable partner? Check the drama departments at local colleges—scan the bulletin boards, talk to professors and maybe even take a few classes. Also join a local theater group. Among the actors and directors you make contact with, there will certainly be a playwright who is also looking for a collaborator.

The following listings provide information you will need to submit to the theater, producer and/or play publisher that's right for you. Research your markets to determine which groups are most apt to find interest in your musical. And then, follow submission instructions meticulously.

THE ACTING COMPANY, P.O. Box 898, Times Sq. Station, New York NY 10108. (212)564-3510. Play producer. Estab. 1972. Produces 2-3 plays/year. "Have done musicals in the past. We are a national touring company playing universities and booking houses." Pays by royalty or negotiated fee/commission. Submit through agent only. SASE. Reports in 12 weeks.

Musical Theater: "We would consider a wide variety of styles—although we remain a young, classical ensemble. Most of our classical plays make use of a lot of incidental music. Our company consists of 17 actors. All productions must be able to tour easily. We have no resident musicians. Taped sound is essential. Actors tend to remain active touring members for 2-3 seasons. Turnover is considerable. Musical ability of the company tends to vary widely from season to season. We would avoid shows which require sophisticated musical abilities and/or training."

ALLEGHENY HIGHLANDS REGIONAL THEATRE, 526 West Ogle St., Ebensburg PA 15931. (814)472-4333. Artistic Director: Mark Hirschfield. Play producer. Estab. 1974. Produces 7 plays and 2 musicals (1 new musical) every other year. "Rural audience, many elderly, many families; we have 2 spaces—a 200 seat arena (4 shows) and a 600 seat proscenium (3- shows)." Pays $75-150/performance. Query with synopsis, character breakdown and set description. SASE. Reports in 3 months.
Musical Theater: "Small cast, full-length musicals, preferably orchestrated for no more than 6 musicians. Anything set in Pennsylvania about Pennsylvanians is of particular interest. Also interested in musicals for children, either one-act or full-length. Roles for children are a plus. We have difficulty finding men to audition. Few mens roles are a plus. No more than 19-20 including chorus, no more than 2-3 settings. We had original music scored for scene changes and intermission music for *She Stoops To Conquer*. Perhaps some underscoring for a mystery would be fun."
Productions: *Oklahoma!*, by Rodgers & Hammerstein; *Cabaret*, by Kander & Ebb; and *George M*, by George M. Cohan.

THE ALPHA THEATRE PROJECT, INC., P.O. Box 2218, 720 South Hamilton, Saginaw MI 48605. (517)790-1005. Executive Producer: Lee-Perry Belleau. Play producer. Estab. 1981. Produces 10 plays and 6 musicals (1-2 new musicals)/year. "We produce mainly for young audiences, although we do produce a 3 show season of musicals and plays for general audiences as well." Pays $15-75/ performance royalty or $500-2,000 by outright purchase.
How to Contact: Query first. Does not return unsolicited material. Reports in 6 months.
Musical Theater: Children's musicals, 40-50 minutes in length with 3-5 characters (for touring); adult full-length musicals and revues for our mainstage stock season, 4-6 characters. Also very interested in topics dealing with social concerns of children (abuse, divorce, drugs, war, etc.). Small casts of 5 or less for mainstage (general audiences); casts of 3 or less for touring theater for youth. No religious material. Would consider original music for use in a play being developed.
Productions: *Unraveling Your Mitten*, by Paul Langford (Michigan History); *Gershwin and Gershwin*, by staff (music of Gershwin); and *Free Beer and Bowling*, by staff (music of '60's).
Tips: "It takes time to develop a project then schedule it for performance. In other words, don't expect to be produced overnight!"

AMAS MUSICAL THEATRE INC., 1 E. 104th St., New York NY 10029. (212)369-8000. Managing Director: Jeffrey Solis. Founder/Artistic Director: Rosetta Lenoire. Produces 3 original musicals/year. Presents 2 children's theater productions and one summer tour. "AMAS is a multi-racial theater, dedicated to bring all people—regardless of race, creed, color or religion—together through the performing arts." Does not pay for manuscripts but "provides a top quality New York showcase with a good record of commercial pick-ups." Submit script with cassette tape of score (or partial score) with SASE.
Musical Theater: Musicals only. "All works to be performed by multi-racial casts. Musical biographies especially welcome. Cast size should be under 13 if possible, including doubling. Because of physical space, set requirements should be relatively simple. We do not want to see material with explicit sex or violence or very strong language. Prefer themes of love, joy and togetherness."
Productions: *Bubbling Brown Sugar*; *Bingo*, by Hy Gilbert, George Fischoff and Ossie Davis (Negro baseball leagues); *Dazy*, by Phillip Rose; *Hot Sake*; *Prime Time*, by Johnny Brandon; and *Step Into My World*, by Miki Grant.
Tips: "A good melody line is important, ideally one that children and adults can hum and sing. Lyrics should tell a story; avoid repetition."

AMELIA MAGAZINE, 329 "E" St., Bakersfield CA 93304. (805)323-4064. Editor: Frederick A. Raborg, Jr. Play publisher. Estab. 1983. Publish 1 play/year. General audience; one-act plays published in *Amelia Magazine*. Best play submitted is the winner of the annual Frank McClure One-Act Play Award. Submit complete manuscript and score per contest rules by postmark deadline of May 15. SASE. Reports in 6-8 weeks. "We would consider publishing musical scores if submitted in clean, camera-ready copy—also single songs. Payment same as for poetry—$25 plus copies."

AMERICAN LIVING, History Theater, Box 2677, Hollywood CA 90078. (213)876-2202. President and Artistic Director: Dorene Ludwig. Play producer. Estab. 1975. Produces 2-5 plays/year. All over U.S., but mostly Southern California—conventions, schools, museums, universities, libraries, etc. Pays by royalty.

How to Contact: Query first. SASE. Reports in 6 months.

Musical Theater: "We use only primary source, historically accurate material: in music — *Songs of the Civil War* or *Songs of the Labor Movement*, etc. — presented as a program rather than play would be the only use I could foresee. We need music historians more than composers."

Tips: "Do not send fictionalized historical material. We use primary source material only."

AMERICAN STAGE FESTIVAL, P.O. Box 225, Milford NH 03055. (603)673-4005. Associate Producing Director: Austin Tichenor. Regional theater. Estab. 1974. Produces 15 plays and 2 musicals (1 new musical)/year. Receives 50 submissions/year. 500 seat theater, Broadway-sized stage, summertime audience. Pays 4-7% royalty.

How to Contact: Submit query letter with synopsis. Reports immediately.

Musical Theater: "We are interested in musicals that tell a story, in which songs make a dramatic contribution. Particularly interested in a return to popular song formats, used dramatically, not nostalgically." Cast and musicians should not total more than 15. Musicals should use traditional song forms.

Productions: *Peg O' My Heart*, by David Heneker (musical comedy); *The Last of the Souhegans*, by Andrew Howard (musical comedy); and *Feathertop*, by Skip Kennon (musical comedy).

Tips: "Be willing to learn from your audience."

ARAN PRESS, 1320 S. Third St., Louisville KY 40208. (502)636-0115. Editor/Publisher: Tom Eagan. Play publisher. Estab. 1983. Publishes 40-50 plays, 1-2 musicals and 1-2 new musicals/year. Professional, college/university, community, summer stock and dinner theater audience. Pays 50% royalty or book royalty 10%. Query first. SASE. Reports in 2 weeks.

Musical Theater: "The musical should include a small cast, simple set for professional, community, college, university, summer stock and dinner theater production."

Productions: *Comedy of History*, by Dick W. Zylstra (musical history); *The Big Dollar*, by Herschel Steinhardt (real estate business); and *Caribbean Blue*, by Jonathan Lowe (tropical island revolution).

ARKANSAS REPERTORY THEATRE, 601 Main, P.O. Box 110, Little Rock AR 72203. (501)378-0445. Contact: Brad Mooy. Play producer. Estab. 1976. Produces 9 plays and 2 musicals (1 new musical)/year. Receives 10 submissions/month. "We perform in a 354-seat house." Pays 5-10% royalty or $75-150 per performance.

How to Contact: Query with cover letter, 10-page synopsis and cassette. SASE. Reports in 3 months.

Musical Theater: "Small casts are preferred. We like issue-oriented pieces (comedy and drama) and prefer shows to run 1:45 to 2 hours maximum. Simple is better; small is better, but we would consider more complex shows. We aren't interested in children's pieces, puppet shows or mime. We always like to receive a tape of the music with the book."

Productions: *Homefires*, by Jack Heifner; *Laughing Wild*, by Christopher Durang; and *Evita*, by Andrew Lloyd Webber.

ARKANSAS STATE UNIVERSITY-BEEBE CAMPUS, P.O. Box H, Beebe AR 72012. (501)882-6452. Director of Theater: L.R. Chudomelka. Play producer. Produces 5 plays (1 musical)/year. Receives 5 submissions/year. Plays are performed in a "600 seat theater (proscenium) in a city of 4,000, 30 miles from metropolitan area of more than 200,000." Pays by royalty. Submit complete manuscript and score. SASE. Reports in 2 weeks.

Musical Theater: "Material should be within the ability of traditional community college with traditional and non-traditional students: simple dancing, innovative and traditional, not over-sophisticated (somewhat family oriented). Variety of music styles and balanced major role shows — no 'star' shows. Flexible cast size, props, staging, etc. We do not want extremes, unnecessary profanity or 'operatic' material."

Productions: *Little Mary Sunshine*, by Besoyan (lampoon of old-time operetta); *Guys and Dolls*, by Loesser, Swerling, Burrows (love, marriage, temperence); and *Working*, adaptation by Schwartz and Faso (occupation).

Tips: "Music should be singable and vary in style. Songs should be an intricate part of the show and not just put in for spectacle. Major roles should be balanced between 4 or 5 characters, rather than one-character shows with chorus."

ASOLO THEATRE COMPANY, 5555 N. Tamiami Trail, Sarasota FL 34243. (813)351-9010. Contact: Literary Manager. Play producer. Produces 8 plays (1 musical)/year. Plays are performed at the Asolo Mainstage (500-seat proscenium house) or by the Asolo Touring Theater (6-member company touring the Southeast). Pays 5% minimum royalty. "We no longer accept unsolicited manuscripts or tapes. Inquiries should be made in the form of a letter, a one-page synopsis, and a self-addressed, stamped postcard." SASE.

Musical Theater: "We want small non-chorus musicals only. They should be full-length, any subject, with not over 10 in the cast. There are no restrictions on production demands; however, musicals with excessive scenic requirements may be difficult to consider."

Productions: *Nunsense*, by Dan Goggin; *Berlin to Broadway*, with Kurt Weill; *Side by Side*, by Sondheim; and *70 Girls 70*, by Kander and Ebb.

*BAILIWICK REPERTORY, 3212 N. Broadway, Chicago IL 60657. (312)883-1091. Executive Director: David Zak. Play producer. Estab. 1982. Produces 5 mainstage, 5 one-act plays and 1-2 new musicals/ year. "We do Chicago productions of new works on adaptations that are politically or thematically intriguing and relevent. We also do an annual director's festival which produces 50-75 new short works each year." Pays 5-8% royalty. "Send SASE (business size) first to receive manuscript submission guidelines. Material returned if appropriate SASE attached."

Musical Theater: "We want innovative, dangerous, exciting and issue-oriented material."

Productions: *Wild Honey*, by Chekha/Frayn; *Animal Farm* (musical), by Orwell/Hall/Peaslee/Mitchell; *Nebraska*, by Logan; *Blues in the Night* (musical); and *Songs of the Season* (musical).

Tips: "Be creative. Be patient. Be persistant. Make me believe in your dream."

BAKER'S PLAYS, 100 Chauncy St., Boston MA 02111. (617)482-1280. Editor: John B. Welch. Play publisher. Estab. 1845. Publishes 15-22 plays and 3-5 new musicals/year. Plays are used by children's theaters, junior and senior high schools, colleges and community theaters. Pays 20-70% royalty. Submit complete manuscript, score and cassette tape of songs. Receives 50-75 submissions/year. SASE. Reports in 3 months.

Musical Theater: "Seeking musicals for teen production and children's theater production. We prefer large cast, contemporary musicals which are easy to stage and produce. Plot your shows strongly, keep your scenery and staging simple, your musical numbers and choreography easily explained and blocked out. Originality and style are up to the author. We want innovative and tuneful shows but no X-rated material. We are very interested in the new writer and believe that, with revision and editorial help, he can achieve success in writing original musicals for the non-professional market." Would consider original music for use in a play being developed or in a pre-existing play.

Publications: *The High School That Dripped Gooseflesh*, by Tim Kelly, Ole Kittleson and Arne Christianson (rock'n roll high school horror spoof); and *I Won't Take a Bath*, by Judith Martin and Donald Ashwander (what it's *really* like being a kid); and *Joseph*, by Earl Reimer and Marshall Laurence (the Biblical Joseph story).

BERKSHIRE PUBLIC THEATRE, P.O. Box 860, 30 Union St., Pittsfield MA 01202. (413)445-4631. Artistic Director: Frank Bessell. Play producer. Estab. 1976. Produces 9 plays (2 musicals)/year. "Plays are performed in a 285-seat proscenium thrust theatre for a general audience of all ages with wide-ranging tastes." Pays negotiable royalty or negotiable amount per performance. Query first. SASE. Reports in 6 weeks.

Musical Theater: Seeking musicals with "no more than 3 acts (2½ hours). We look for fresh musicals with something to say. Our company has a flexible vocal range. Cast size must be 2-50, with a small orchestra." Would also consider original music "for a play being developed and possibly for existing works."

Productions: *Good Time Rock & Roll* and *The Musical Beach Party*, by Tommy De Frantz (surfing R&R); *Hollywood Primitive*, by Frank Bessell (love, innocence and discovery); and *Lysistrata*, by Alice Spatz (modern adaptation of the Greek).

Tips: "We are a small company. Patience is a must. Be yourself—open, honest. Experience is not necessary but is helpful. We don't have a lot of money but we are long on nurturing artists! We are developing shows with commercial prospects to go beyond the Berkshires, i.e., a series of rock music revues is now in its fifth year."

BRISTOL RIVERSIDE THEATRE, P.O. Box 1250, Bristol PA 19007. (215)785-6664. Artistic Director: Susan D. Atkinson. Play producer. Estab. 1986. Produce 5 plays, 2 musicals/year (1 new musical every 2 years). "New 302-seat proscenium Equity theater with audience of all ages from small towns and metropolitan area." Pays by royalty 6-8%. Submit complete manuscript, score and tape of songs. SASE. Reports in 6 months.

Musical Theater: "No strictly children's musicals. All other types with small to medium casts and within reasonable artictic tastes. Prefer one-set; limited funds rectrict. Does not wish to see anything catering to prurient interests."

Productions: *The Robber Bridegroom*, by Alfred Uhry/R. Waldman (E. Welty novella - 1790s Mississippi delta); *A Day in Hollywood/A Night*, by Frank Lazarus/D. Vosburgh (1930s Hollywood); and *Sally Blane, World's Greatest Girl Detective*, by David Levy/Leslie Eberhard (spoof of teen detective genre).

Tips: "He or she should be willing to work with small staff, open to artistic suggestion, and aware of the limitations of newly developing theaters."

CALIFORNIA MUSIC THEATRE, #400M, 2500 E. Colorado, Pasadena CA 91107. (818)792-0776. Artistic Director: Gary Davis. Play producer. Estab. 1986. Produces 4 musicals (1 new musical)/year. "Plays produced at Pasadena Civic Auditorium. Proscenium-3,000 seats. Base of 13,000 subscribers/average of 25,000 per production." Pays by royalty. Submit complete manuscript, score and tape of songs. SASE. Reports in 3 months.
Musical Theater: "Our audience is rather conservative."
Productions: *Babes in Toyland*, by Toby Bluth (new adaptation); *Strike Up the Band*, by Gershwin/Kaufman; *Sayonara*, by Lance, Fischoff and Gilbert (Michener novel); and *Drood*, by Rupert Holmes.
Tips: "Please understand that we place great importance on lyrics. If it doesn't read well, we do not pursue the piece beyond the initial reading."

WILLIAM CAREY COLLEGE DINNER THEATRE, William Carey College, Hattiesburg MS 39401. (601)582-6218. Managing Director: O.L. Quave. Play producer. Produces 2 plays (2 musicals)/year. "Our dinner theater operates only in summer and plays to family audiences." Payment negotiable. Submit complete manuscript and score. SASE. Reports as soon as possible.
Musical Theater: "Plays should be simply-staged, have small casts (8-10 maximum), and be suitable for family viewing; two hours maximum length. Score should require piano only, or piano, synthesizer."
Productions: *Ernest in Love*; *Rodgers and Hart: A Musical Celebration*; and *Side by Side*, by Sondheim.

CENTENARY COLLEGE, THEATRE DEPARTMENT, Shreveport LA 71134-1188. (318)869-5011. Chairman: Robert R. Buseick. Play producer. Produces 6 plays (1-2 new musicals)/year. Plays are presented in a 350-seat playhouse to college and community audiences. Submit manuscript and score. SASE. Reports in 1 month.
Productions: *Man of La Mancha*; *Nunsense*; *Chicago*; *Broadway Bound*; *Into the Woods*; *A Little Shop of Horrors*; and *Jerry's Girls*, by Todd Sweeney.

CIRCA' 21 DINNER PLAYHOUSE, P.O. Box 3784, Rock Island IL 61204-3784. (309)786-2667. Producer: Dennis Hitchcock. Play producer. Estab. 1977. Produces 1-2 plays, 4-5 musicals (1 new musical)/year. Receives 2 submissions/month. Plays produced for a general audience. Two children's works per year, concurrent with major productions. Pays by royalty. Query with synopsis, character breakdown and set description or submit complete manuscript, score and tape of songs. SASE. Reports in 8 weeks.
Musical Theater: "For children's musicals we prefer 2-act, 1½ hour limit with cast of no more than 10, piano and percussion accompaniment, and limited scenic requirements. Folk or fairy tale themes. Works that do not condescend to a young audience yet are appropriate for entire family. We're also seeking full-length, small cast musicals suitable for a broad audience." Would also consider original music for use in a play being developed.
Productions: *Singin in the Rain*, by Betty Comden and Adolph Green; *7 Brides for 7 Brothers*, by Lawrence Kasha and David Landay; *Pump Boys and Dinettes* and *Snow White Goes West*, by Jim Eiler.
Tips: "Small, upbeat, tourable musicals (like *Pump Boys*) and bright musically-sharp children's productions (like those produced by Prince Street Players) work best. Keep an open mind. Stretch to encompass a musical variety—different keys, rhythms, musical ideas and textures."

CIRCLE IN THE SQUARE THEATRE, 1633 Broadway, New York NY 10019. (212)307-2700. Literary Advisor: Nancy Bosco. Play producer. Estab. 1951. Produces 3 plays/year; occasionally produces a musical. Pays by royalty. Query with a letter, 1-page synopsis and script sample (10 pages). Reports in 6 months.
Musical Theater: "We are looking for original material with small cast and orchestra requirements. We're not interested in traditional musical comedies." Will consider original music for use in a play being developed or in a pre-existing play at the option of the director.
Production: *Pal Joey*.

CITIARTS/THEATRE CONCORD, 1950 Parkside Dr., Concord CA 94519. (415)671-3065. Artistic Director: Richard H. Elliott. Play producer. Estab. 1973. Produces 8 plays and 4 musicals (0-4 new musicals)/year. "CitiArts/Theatre Concord is the resident theater in the 203-seat Willows Theatre, a proscenium stage, in Concord, located in suburban San Francisco." Pays 5-12% royalty, or terms negotiated.
How to Contact: Submit complete manuscript and score. SASE. Reports in 2 months.
Musical Theater: "Full-length musicals addressing contemporary themes or issues, small to mid-size cast (maximum 15 characters) with maximum 15 instruments. Topics which appeal to an educated suburban and liberal urban audience are best. Maximum 15 cast members, 15 musicians, prefer unit set (we have no fly loft or wing space)." "We often commission original scores for straight plays. Composer should send resume and recorded example of work with scores if possible."

Productions: *Six Women with Brain Death*, by Mark Houston (women's issues); *A . . . My Name is Alice*, by Various (women's issues); *Little Me*, by Cy Coleman and Neil Simon; and *God Bless You, Mr. Rosewater*, by Ashman and Menken.
Tips: "Be prepared and believe in your material."

CITY THEATRE, 315 S. Bellefield Ave., Pittsburgh PA 15213. (412)624-5041. Resident Dramaturg: Scott Cummings. Play producer. Estab. 1974. Produces 5 plays/year. "Plays are performed in an intimate 117 seat Thrust-Stage Theatre to an adventurous subscriber base." Query with synopsis, character breakdown and set description. Does not return unsolicited material. Reports in 2-3 weeks for query; 3-4 months for script.
Musical Theater: "We want sophisticated plays with music. We prefer a small cast with no more than 10 (including musicians) and single set because we have thrust stage capabilities only. We don't want traditional, large cast musical comedies."
Productions: *Painting It Red*, by Steven Dietz (modern romance); *Lovers and Keeper*, by Irene Fornes (failed romance); and *Maybe I'm Doing It Wrong*, by Randy Newman (musical review).

CLEVELAND PUBLIC THEATRE, 6415 Detroit Ave., Cleveland OH 44102. (216)631-2727. Director of Playwright Development: Linda Eisenstein. Play producer. Estab. 1983. Produces 6 plays plus 12 staged readings; much performance art, 1-2 musicals and 1 new musical/year. "We are a progressive urban loft theater (80-150 seats) with audiences that are adult and sophisticated—mix of yuppies, artists, radicals and punks." Pays $25-100 per performance. Query with synopsis, character breakdown (sample song tape optional) or submit complete ms, score and tape of songs. SASE. Reports in 3-6 months.
Musical Theater: "We seek progressive, political, alternative and outrageous musicals. Also music for our performance art and sound festivals—cutting edge experimental. Don't expect a realistic set— we do mostly 3-quarter and arena, with no fly space. We don't want to see fluff or traditional Broadway fare, would-be Broadway fare or traditional children's plays." "A writer must think weird; don't watch TV." "We use several local composers (Cleveland) to write our 'incidental' music."
Production: *Star Wares: The Next Generation*, by James Levin and Linda Eisenstein (political satirical rock opera); *The Rocky Horror Show*, by Richard O'Brien (transvestite horror spoof); *Chickalena & the End of the World*, by Caroline Van Ausdal (abstract children's folk opera) and *Ripped Van Winkle* by San Francisco Mime Troupe (political satire—touring).
Tips: "If you live in the area, come and work as a volunteer in our Festival of New Plays or other artist outreach. We are particularly committed to local artists."

*CONTEMPORARY DRAMA SERVICE, 885 Elkton Dr., Colorado Springs CO 80907. (719)594-4422. Executive Editor: Arthur Zapel. Associate Editor: Rhonda Wray. Play publisher. Estab. 1979. Publishes 40-50 plays and 4-6 new musicals/year. "We publish for young children and teens in mainstream Christian churches and for teens and college level in the secular market. Our musicals are performed in churches, schools and colleges." Pays 10% royalty (for music books), 50% royalty for performance and "sometimes we pay royalty up to buy-out fee for minor works."
How to Contact: Query first. SASE.
Musical Theater: "For churches we publish musical programs for little children and teens to perform at Easter, Christmas or some special occasion. Our school musicals are for teens to perform as class plays or special entertainments. Cast size may vary from 5-25 depending on use. We prefer more parts for girls than boys. Music must be written in the vocal range of teens. Staging should be relatively simple but may vary as needed. We are not interested in elementary school material. Elementary level is OK for church music but not public school elementary. Music must have full piano accompaniment and be professionally scored for camera-ready publication."
Productions: *A Christmas Carol*, by Larry Nestor (Christmas musical); *Pinnochio*, by Schuman, Nestor, Crowder (children's theater); and *Would You Believe a Stable?*, by Vigilant and Castle (church Christmas musical).
Tips: "Send us a cassette recording of your work."

 The asterisk before a listing indicates that the listing is new in this edition. New markets are often the most receptive to unsolicited submissions.

*THE COTERIE, 2450 Grand Ave., Kansas City MO 64108. (816)474-6785. Artistic Director: Jeff Church. Play producer. Estab. 1979. Produces 7-8 plays/year. Plays produced at Hallmark's Crown Center in downtown Kansas City in The Coterie's resident theater (capacity 240). A typical performance run is one month in length. "We retain some rights on commissioned plays. Writers are paid a royalty for their work per performance or flat fee."
How to Contact: Query with synopsis, character breakdown and set description; or submit complete manuscript and score. We will consider musicals with smaller orchestration needs (3-5 pieces), or a taped score. SASE. Reports in 2-4 months.
Musical Theater: "Types of plays we produce: pieces which are universal in appeal; plays for all ages. They may be original or adaptations of classic or contemporary literature. Limitations: Typically not more than 12 in a cast—prefer 5-9 in size. No fly space or wing space. Material we want/do not want to see: No couch plays. Prefer plays by seasoned writers who have established reputations. Groundbreaking, and exciting scripts from the youth theater field welcome. It's perfectly fine if your musical is a little off center."
Productions: *Animal Farm*, by Sir Peter Hall; *The Wind in the Willows*, (adapted), by Doug Post; and *The Ugly Duckling*, by Pamela Sterling, music by Chris Limber.
Tips: "Make certain your submitted musical to us is very theatrical and not cinematic. Writers need to see how far the field of youth and family theater has come—the interesting new areas we're going—before sending us your query or manuscript. We LIKE young protagonists in our plays, but make sure they're not romanticized or stereotyped good-and-bad like the children's theater playwrights of yesterday would have them."

CREATIVE THEATRE, 102 Witherspoon St., Princeton NJ 08540. (609)924-3489. Artistic Director: Eloise Bruce. Play producer. Estab. 1969. Produces 5 plays, all with music (1 new musical)/year. "Plays are performed for young audiences grades K-6. The plays are always audience participation and done in schools (45 minute format)." Pays a fee for writing and production and royalty for two seasons. Then per performance royalty fee. Query first or query with synopsis, character breakdown and set description. SASE. Reports in 1 month.
Musical Theater: "Audience participation plays, 45 minutes in length, 4-6 performers, usually presentational style. Topics can range from original plots to adaptations of folk and fairytales. Staging is usually in the round with audience of no more than 300/seating on the floor. No lighting and usually piano accompaniment. Actor is focus with strong but very lean set and costume design." Does not wish to see plays without audience participation. "We are not doing as many "heavy musicals," but are looking for light plays with less music."
Productions: *The Legend of Sleepy Hollow*, adaptation by Bernice Bronson (ghost story); *America Before Columbus (ABC)*, by Joseph Robinette; and *The Island of Yakimyim Bamboo*, by Fred Rohan Vargas.
Tips: "Develop child centered work which encourages the imaginations of the audience and is centered in child play."

CREEDE REPERTORY THEATRE, P.O. Box 269, Creede CO 81130. (719)658-2541. Producing/Artistic Director: Richard Baxter. Play producer. Estab. 1966. Produces 6 plays and 1 musical/year. Performs in 187-seat proscenium theatre; audience is primarily tourist base from Texas, Oklahoma, New Mexico and Colorado. Pays 7% royalty. Query first. SASE. Reports in 1 year.
Musical Theater: "We prefer historical western material with cast no larger than 11. Staging must be flexible as space is limited."
Productions: *Baby Doe Tabor*, by Kenton Kersting (Colorado history); *A Frog in His Throat*, by Feydeau, adapted by Eric Conger, (French farce); and *Tommyknockers*, by Eric Engdahl, Mark Houston and Chris Thompson (mining).
Tips: "Songwriter must have the ability to accept criticism and must be flexible."

DEPARTMENT OF THEATRE, MICHIGAN STATE UNIVERSITY, East Lansing MI 48824-1120. (517)353-5169. Producer/Director: Dr. Jon Baisch. Produces 7-10 plays and 4-6 musicals (1-2 new musicals), 4-6 large scale and small revue musicals/year. Payment negotiable. "Our audiences are students, faculty, and members of the Lansing community. We use 8 theatres, ranging from 100 to 2,500 seats, including proscenium, platform, arena, and cabaret theatre types. We stage everything from large-scale productions with orchestra and large casts to small-cast, intimate shows and cabaret entertainment. We seek both adult and children's shows, all types for a variety of audiences. We often use original music composed by faculty or students in MSU's School of Music. They are available to us for the whole term of rehearsal and production." Performance rights negotiable. Query with synopsis and production specifications. SASE. Reports in 1 month.
Musical Theater: "We are interested in all types of new musicals. However, we are espcially interested in small cast revues and book shows for cabaret and summer theatre productions, and unusual material for our small arena and studio theatres."

Productions: *A Chorus Line* and *Brigadoon*.

THE DRAMATIC PUBLISHING COMPANY, 311 Washington St., Woodstock IL 60098. (815)338-7170. Music Editor: Dana Smith. Play publisher. Publishes 35 plays (3-5 musicals)/year. Estab. 1885. Plays used by community theaters, high schools, colleges, stock and professional theaters, churches and camps. Pays standard royalty. Submit complete manuscript, score and tape of songs. SASE. Reports in 5 months.
Musical Theater: Seeking "children's musicals not over 1¼ hours, and adult musicals with 2 act format. No adaptations for which the rights to use the original work have not been cleared. If directed toward high school market, large casts with many female roles are preferred. For professional, stock and community theater small casts are better. Cost of producing a play is always a factor to consider in regard to costumes, scenery and special effects." Would also consider original music for use in a pre-existng play "if we or the composer hold the rights to the non-musical work."
Publications: *Ginger*, book, lyrics by Ronald Alexander, music by Diane Leslie (musical comedy); *Charlotte's Web*, (E.B. White's Story) book by Joseph Robinette, music and lyrics by Charles Strouse; and *Cotton Patch Gospel*, music lyrics score by Harry Chapin, book by Tomkey and Russell Tveyz (contemporary retelling of books of Matthew and John).

EAST WEST PLAYERS (EWP), 4424 Santa Monica Blvd., Los Angeles CA 90029. (213)660-0366. Artistic Director: Nobu McCarthy; Dramaturg: Dick Dotterer. Professional Equity company, established 1965, performing under the Equity 99-seat theater plan for all audiences. Presents one (1) mainstage musical per season, 4-6 productions a year. Receives 4-6 submissions/year. Also has play reading series and writer's laboratory for selected projects, including musicals. Submit complete ms (book & lyrics) and tape of songs. If enough interest generated will ask to see complete score. No ms or tape returned without SASE. Submit to ATTN: Dramaturg. Reports in 6 months. Dramatists Guild approved contract offered, percentage of box office gross against set per performance fee.
Musical Theater: "We are interested in musicals dealing with Asian-American themes and experiences and focus, Asian stories and musicals using non-traditional casting; musicals that are melodious, highly theatrical and imaginative theater pieces. Our acting company is 98% Asian-Pacific/Asian-American, so the majority of important roles should by playable by Asian actors. A cast of 15 to 18 is the largest we can handle readily, and we would prefer smaller casts. We are also establishing a youth theater program, and would be interested in well-written, small cast musicals for that as well. Nothing 'cute,' however. We have used original musical scores for plays originated here or for production revivals of established plays, and we are always open to doing so. All of our productions have music and/or sound effects involved. The demands of the production dictate the uses of music and sound."
Productions: *Company*, by Sondheim/Furth (contemporary relationships); *A Chorus Line*, by Kirkwood/Dante/Hamlisch/Kelban (contemporary show business); *Canton Jazz Club*, by Magwili/Dang/Wang/Iwataki (original musical, Chinatown nightspot, 1943 Los Angeles).
Tips: "East West Players was founded by a group of Asian-American actors weary of playing stereotypes in theater and film. Writers should bear this in mind. It would help if the writers would find out the types of productions we do before they submit."

ECCENTRIC CIRCLES THEATRE, #4N, 400 W. 43rd St., New York NY 10036. (212)564-3798. Artistic Director: Rosemary Hopkins. Play producer. Estab. 1978. Produces 3 plays and 1 new musical/year. "Plays and musicals are preformed at a designated theatre rented by ECT. Audience is generally all ages, and from New York." Query with synopsis, character breakdown and set description. SASE. Reports in 6 weeks. "We have a small set and small cast. We are open to all topics and styles including children's musicals. We don't want puppet shows."
Productions: *Natural Causes*, by Lilian Lieblich (new comedy).
Tips: "Be open for comments and changes and adapt to a small budget and small theatre situation."

ELDRIDGE PUBLISHING CO., INC., P.O. Box 216, Franklin OH 45005. (513)746-6531. Editor: Nancy S. Vorhis. Play publisher. Estab. 1906. Publishes 20 plays and 2-3 musicals/year. Seeking "large cast musicals which appeal to students. We like variety and originality in the music, easy staging and costuming. We serve the school and church market, 6th grade through 12th; also Christmas and Easter musicals for churches." Would also consider original music for use in a play being developed; "music that could make an ordinary play extraordinary." Pays 35% royalty, $150-500 for outright purchase or 10% copy sales. Submit tape with manuscript if at all possible. SASE. Reports in 3 months.
Productions: *It's A Howl*, by Tim Kelly, with music by Larry Nestor ("about a school for young werewolves"); *I Am A Star*, by Billy St. John, with music by Wendell Jimerson ("Hijinks at the high school as students try to get a part in a film that will be made there"); *Dogs!*, by Hamlett/Simpson (homeless dogs); *6 Myths of Christmas*, by Linda Pou (animals at the manger); and *Spring Is Not So Far*, by Allen/Elizabeth Snair (children rescue spring).

Tips: "We prefer musicals be test produced. Have your church youth group or your child's class perform it, if possible. That way you'll work out any bugs before we even see it."

THE EMPTY SPACE THEATRE, P.O. Box 1748, Seattle WA 98111-1748. (206)587-3737. Artistic Director: Kurt Beattie. Play producer. Estab. 1974. Produces 5 plays and varying number of new musicals/year. "We have a subscription audience, mainly composed of professionals. We produce in our own theatre." Pays by royalty. Query with synopsis, character breakdown and set description. SASE. Reports in 4 months.
Musical Theater: "We want broadly comic, satirical or political pieces and all musical idioms, from classical to whatever is the current end of the musical spectrum. We have no limitations, though we rarely produce more than one large cast show per year. We don't want old-fashioned show biz yawners, or yuppie angst. We regularly employ composers/sound designers."
Productions: *Reckless*, by Craig Lucas; *Virtus* by Gregg Loughridge; and *Jar The Floor*, by Cheryl West.
Tips: "Avoid musical-comedy formulae."

ENCORE PERFORMANCE PUBLISHING, P.O. Box 692, Orem UT 84057. (801)225-0605. Editor: Michael C. Perry. Play publisher. Estab. 1979. Publishes 5-12 plays (including musicals)/year. "We are interested in plays which emphasize strong family values and play to all ages of audience." Pays by royalty; 50% performance, 10% book. Query with synopsis, character breakdown and set description then submit complete manuscript, score and tape of songs. SASE. Reports in 6 weeks to 3 months.
Musical Theater: Musicals of all types for all audiences. Can be original or adapted. "We tend to favor shows with at least an equal male/female cast." Do not wish to see works that can be termed offensive or vulgar. However, experimental theater forms are also of interest.
Productions: *Children of the Universe*, by Paul Morse (child self-worth); *Let It Ring!*, by Margaret Smoot, K. Newell Dayley and Michael McLean (patriotic musical); and *Gammer Gurtons Needle*, by Vern Adix (1 hour version of classic).
Tips: "Always write with an audience in mind."

GEOF ENGLISH, PRODUCER, Saddleback College, 28000 Marguerite Pkwy., Mission Viejo CA 92692. (714)582-4763. Performing Arts Director: Geofrey English. Play producer for musical theater. Produces 9 musicals (six new musicals)/year. Community audience of mostly senior citizens. Pays by royalty and performance. Submit complete manuscript, score and tape of songs. SASE. Reports in 2 months.
Musical Theater: Looking for mainly family musicals. Have no limitations am open to options. It is important that music must be sent along with scripts. Best not to call. Just send materials.
Productions: *Mrs. Warren's Profession*, by George Bernard Shaw; *Night Must Fall*, by Emlyn Williams; and *Shooting Stars*, by Molly Newman.
Tips: "Submit materials in a timely manner—usually at least one year in advance."

ENSEMBLE THEATRE OF CINCINNATI, 1127 Vine St., Cincinnati OH 45210. (513)421-3556. Artistic Director: David A. White III. Play producer. Estab. 1986. Produces 6 plays (3 new musicals in 5 years)/year. "We are dedicated to the development of new works. We produce a 6 show season in a beautifully renovated 130-seat 3/4 thrust theater." Pays $600-1,000 outright purchase.
How to Contact: Submit complete manuscript, score and tape of songs. SASE. Reports in 2 months.
Musical Theater: Adult-oriented, risk-taking, simple set, cast of 6-10, with a simple orchestration. Material should be submitted in September or October for consideration for upcoming season.
Productions: *Taming of the Shrew*, by William Shakespeare; *Sleeping Beauty*, and *There's a Ringing in My Ears*, by Kate Dahlgren, Norma Jenks, Mah Wehner and Joe M. McDonough.

THE FIREHOUSE THEATRE, 11 and Jackson, Omaha NE 68102. (402)346-6009. Artistic Director: Dick Mueller. Play producer. Estab. 1972. Producer 6 plays and 1-2 musicals/year. Receives 10-20 submissions/year. General audience. Pays royalty. Query with synopsis, character breakdown and set description. Submit complete ms, score and tape of songs. SASE.
Musical Theater: General interest. "We are a small house of 289 seats. Budget is what limits the scale of production."
Productions: *Best Little Whorehouse In Texas*, by Larry King and *Pump Boys & Dinnettes* by Jim Wann.

FLORIDA STUDIO THEATRE, 1241 N. Palm Ave., Sarasota FL 34236. (813)366-9017. Director of New Play Development: Carolyn Michal. Play producer. Produces 2 plays and 2 musicals/year. "Florida Studio Theatre is a professional, non-profit theatre. It seats 165 and has limited technical abilities. The audience is generally comprised of well-educated people over 50 years of age. FST subscribers expect innovative, contemporary theatre." Pays by royalty. "Workshop productions receive $200 hono-

rarium." Query with synopsis, character breakdown and set description. SASE. Reports in 2 months on queries, 7 months on manuscripts.
Musical Theater: "FST is looking for smaller cast musicals and cabaret musicals. We prefers innovative or off-beat shows. The stage is small. There is no pit. In the past we have had a 3 person musical combo. Send letter of inquiry first with SASE. A tape included with the script and score is helpful." Would also consider original music for use in pre-existing play. "Two of the straight plays we are putting on in the future will have original music underscoring."

*THE FREELANCE PRESS, Box 548, Dover MA 02030. (508)785-1260. Managing Editor: David Downing. Play publisher (but is affiliated with a play producer). Estab. 1985. Publishes 20 plays/year; 19 musicals (3 new musicals)/year. "Pieces are primarily for elementary to high school children; large casts (approximately 30); plays are produced by schools and children's theaters." Pays 10% of purchase price of script or score, 90% of collected royalty. Submit complete manuscript and score. SASE. Reports in 6 months.
Musical Theater: "We publish previously produced musicals and plays for children in the primary grades through high school. Plays are for large casts (approximately 30 actors and speaking parts) and run between 45 minutes to 1 hour and 15 minutes. Subject matter should be contemporary issues (sibling rivalry, friendship, etc.) or adaptations of classic literature for children (*Alice in Wonderland*, *Treasure Island*, etc.). We do not accept any plays written for adults to perform for children."
Productions: *Monopoly*, by T. Dewey/Megan (3 high school students live out the board game); *No Zone*, by T. Dewey/Campion (environmental fantasy about effects of global warming); *The Pied Piper*, P. Houghton/Hutchins (adaptation of Browning poem).
Tips: "We enjoy receiving material that does not condescend to children. They are capable of understanding many current issues, playing complex characters, acting imaginative and unconventional material, and singing difficult music."

SAMUEL FRENCH, INC., 45 W. 25th St., New York NY 10010. (212)206-8990. Editor: Lawrence Harbison. Play publisher. Estab. 1830. Publishes 90-100 plays and 5-6 new musicals/year. Receives 100 new mu;sical submissions per year. Amateur and professional theaters. Pays 80% of amateur royalties; 90% of professional royalties. Query first, then submit complete ms and tape of songs. SASE. Reports in 6 weeks to 8 months.
Musical Theater: "We publish primarily successful musicals from the NYC stage." Don't submit large-cast, big "Broadway" musicals—which haven't been done on Broadway.
Productions: *Starmites*, by Keating and Ross; *Me and My Girl*, by various; and *Mail*, by Colker and Rupert.

THE WILL GEER THEATRICUM BOTANICUM, P.O. Box 1222, Topanga CA 90290. (213)455-2322. Artistic Director: Ellen Geer. Play producer. Produces 4 plays, 1-2 new musicals/year. Plays are performed in "large outdoor amphitheater with 60'x 25' wooden stage. Rustic setting." Pays by royalty or per performance. Query with synopsis, tape, character breakdown and set description. SASE. Submit scripts from September through December.
Musical Theater: Seeking social or biographical works, children's works, full length musicals with cast of up to 10 equity actors (the rest non-equity). Requires "low budget set and costumes. We emphasize paying performers." Would also consider original music for use in a play being developed. Does not wish to see "anything promoting avarice, greed, violence or apathy."
Productions: *Worker's U.S.A.*, a compilation work (labor unions).
Tips: "Reach us with idea and show enthusiasm for theater."

GEORGE STREET PLAYHOUSE, 9 Livingston Ave., New Brunswick NJ 08901. (908)846-2895. Associate Artistic Director: Wendy Liscow. Producing Director: Gregory Hurst. Produces 7 plays, including 1 musical and 1-2 new musicals/year. Receives 100 submissions/month. "We are a 367-seat thrust theater and 100-seat black box, working under a LORT C-contract with a 5,500 subscriber base." Fees vary. "Each situation is handled individually." Query with synopsis, character breakdown and set description. SASE. Reports in 2 months.
Musical Theater: Seeking musical adaptations. "We are interested in a variety of themes and formats. We aren't seeking to limit the things we read."
Productions: *Sarah and Abraham*, by Marsha Norman; *Camping with Henry and Tom*, by Mark St. Germain; and *Sing A Christmas Song*, by Peter Udell and Garry Sherman (musical).

GREAT AMERICAN CHILDREN'S THEATRE COMPANY, 304 E. Florida, Milwaukee WI 53204. (414)276-4230. Managing Director: Annie Jurczyk. Producer: Teri Mitze. Play producer. Estab. 1976. Produces 1 or 2 plays/musical/year. Has done new musicals in the past. Audience is school age children. Pays a negotiable royalty. Query with synopsis, character breakdown and set description. Does not return unsolicited material. Reports as quickly as possible, "depending on our workload."

Musical Theater: Children's musicals. Average cast size is 13. No adult productions. "We have used original music as background for our plays."
Productions: *Charlie & the Chocolate Factory*, by Roald Dahl (children's story); *Charlotte's Web*, by Joseph Robinette (children's story); and *Cinderella*, by Moses Goldberg (children's story).
Tips: "Persevere! Although we don't use a lot of musicals, we will consider one that is of excellent quality."

HERITAGE ARTISTS AT THE MUSIC HALL, Box 586, Cohoes NY 12047. (518)235-7909. Executive Director: Joseph McConnell. Artistic Director: David Holdgrivey. Musical and play producer. Estab. 1982. Produces 6 musicals (1-3 new musicals)/year. "We perform a subscription series of small and/ or principal musicals in the 250-300 seat Cohoes Music Hall." Pays negotiable royalty per performance. Submit synopsis, character breakdown and tape. SASE. Reports in 8 weeks.
Musical Theater: Seeking "adult themes, plays with music, review/cabaret shows and children's musicals." Requires "smaller casts." "Regular season runs from mid-October to June. This is a *professional* company (Equity, SSDC, AFM)."
Productions: *Romance, Romance*, by Harman and Herrmann; *Jacques Brel*, by Blau and Shuman; *No Way to Treat a Lady*, by Douglas J. Cohen; and *Beehive*, by Larry Gallagher.

HEUER PUBLISHING CO./ART CRAFT PUBLISHING CO., Box 248, Cedar Rapids IA 52406. (319)364-6311. Publisher: C. Emmett McMullen. Play publisher. Estab. 1928. "We sell exclusively to junior and senior high school groups throughout the U.S. and Canada; individually, some church and related groups." Pays by royalty or by outright purchase. Query with synopsis, character breakdown and set description. SASE. Reports in 2 months.
Musical Theater: "We prefer comedies with a large number of characters. All material must be suitable for high school production and be within the scope of high school actors. We do not publish individual music. All music should be within the play material."

HIP POCKET THEATRE, 1627 Fairmount Ave., Ft. Worth TX 76104-4237. (817)927-2833. Producer: Diane Simons. Play producer. Produces 10 plays/year (including new musicals). Estab. 1977. "Our audience is an eclectic mix of Ft. Worth/Dallas area residents with multi levels of incomes and backgrounds. Payment varies according to type of script, reputation of playwright, etc." Query with synopsis, character breakdown and set description; "please include tape if possible." Reports in 1 month.
Musical Theater: "We are not interested in cabaret revues, but rather in full-length pieces that can be for adults and/or children. We tend to produce more fanciful, whimsical musicals (something not likely to be found anywhere else), but would also consider political pieces. Basically, we're open for anything fresh and well-written. We require no more than 15 in a cast, and a staging would have to adapt to an outdoor environmental thrust stage." Would also consider original music for use in a play being developed.
Productions: *R. Crumb Comix*, by Robert Crumb (underground cartoons and comic strips from the 60's and 70's); *Molemo!*, by Johnny Simons and Douglas Balentine (autobiographical memory journey); and *Shazam!*, by Johnny Simons and Douglas Balentine (original musical serialization of the Captain Marvel stories).
Tips: "Think creative, complex thoughts and musical visions that can be transformed into reality by creative, visionary musicians in theaters that rarely have the huge Broadway dollar. Cast size must be kept to a minimum (no more than 15)."

*HORIZON THEATRE CO., P.O. Box 5376, Station E, Atlanta GA 30307. (404)584-7450. Co-Artistic Director: Lisa Adler. Play producer. Estab. 1983. Produces 4 plays and 1 musical/year. "Our audience is comprised mostly of young professionals looking for contemporary comedy with a little social commentary. Our theater features a 160-200 seat facility with flexible stage." Query with synopsis, character breakdown, set description and resume. SASE. Reports in 1-2 years.
Musical Theater: "We prefer musicals that have a significant book and a lot of wit (particularly satire). Our casts are restricted to 10 actors. We prefer plays with equal number of male and female roles, or more female than male roles. We have a limited number of musicians available. No musical revues and no dinner theater fluff. One type of play we are currently seeking is a country musical with women's themes. We generally contract with a musician or sound designer to provide sound for each play we produce. If interested send resume, references, tape with music or sound design samples."
Productions: *Angry Housewives*, by A.M. Collins and Chad Henry; *The Secret Rapture*, by David Hare; and *Eastern Standard*, by Richard Greenberg.
Tips: "Have patience and use subtle persistence. Work with other theater artists to get a good grasp of the form."

JEWISH REPERTORY THEATRE, 344 E. 14th St., New York NY 10003. (212)674-7200. Director: Ron Avni. Associate Director: Edward M. Cohen. Play producer. Estab. 1974. Produces 5 plays and 1-2 new musicals/year. Pays 6% royalty. Submit complete manuscript, score and tape of songs. SASE. Reports in 4 weeks.
Musical Theater: Seeking "musicals in English relating to the Jewish experience. No more than 8 characters. We do commission background scores for straight plays."
Productions: *Kumi—Leml* (musical farce); *The Special* (musical comedy); and *The Shop on Main Street* (musical drama).

THE LAMB'S THEATRE CO., 130 W. 44th St., New York NY 10036. (212)997-0210. Literary Manager: Carlotta Scarmack. Play producer. Estab. 1984. Produces 2-3 plays, 1 musical (1 new musical)/year. Receives 5-10 submissions/month. Plays are performed for "the off-Broadway theater audience, also group sales including school programs from New York public high schools and colleges in the area." Pays by royalty. Query with synopsis, character breakdowns and set description. SASE. Reports in 6 months.
Musical Theater: "We are looking for full length musicals that are entertaining, but moving, and deal with serious issues as well as comic situations. No one-act plays. Large-cast epics are out. Both our spaces are intimate theaters, one an 85-seat black box space and one a 385-seat proscenium. Material with explicit sex and nudity and plays which require large amounts of obscene language are not appropriate for this theater. We require a small orchestra in a musical."
Productions: *Johnny Pye & The Foolkiller*, by R. Courts/M. St. Germain (original musical based on Stephen V. Benet short story); *The Gifts of the Magi*, by R. Courts/M. St. Germain (original musical based on O. Henry short stories).

*LILLENAS DRAMA RESOURCES, P.O. Box 419527, Kansas City MO 64141. (816)931-1900. Editor/ Consultant: Paul M. Miller. Play publisher. Estab. 1912. Publishes 10 collections (2 full-length) and 4 program collections, 3 musicals (3 new musicals)/year. "Our plays and musicals are performed by churches, Christian schools, and independent theater organizations that perform 'religious' plays." Pays 10% royalty, by outright purchase ($5 per page for program material only), or $10-25/performance (selected).
How to Contact: Submit complete ms and score or, preferably, submit complete ms, score and tape of songs. SASE. Reports in 3 months.
Productions: *You Can Get There From Here*, by Lawrence & Andrea Enscoe (Youth issues plays); *Journey to the Center of the Stage*, by Martha Bolton (monologues); and *Pew Prompters*, by Lawrence & Andrea Enscoe (short sketches for church use).
Tips: "Remember that religious theater comes in all genres: do not become historically biblical; take truth and couch in terms that are understandable to contemporary audiences in and out of the church. Keep 'simplicity' as a key word in your writing; cast sizes, number of scenes/acts, costume and set requirements will affect the acceptance of your work by the publisher and the market."

LOS ANGELES DESIGNERS' THEATRE, P.O. Box 1883, Studio City CA 91614-0883. (818)769-9000 or (213)650-9600. Artistic Director: Richard Niederberg. Play producer. Estab. 1970. Produces 20-25 plays, 8-10 new musicals/year. Plays are produced at several locations, primarily Studio City, California. Pays by royalty. Submit complete manuscript, score and tape of songs, character breakdown and set descriptions. Video tape submissions are also accepted. SASE. Reports in 3 months but faster if cassette of show is included with script.
Musical Theater: "We seek out controversial material. Street language OK, nudity is fine, religious themes, social themes, political themes are encouraged. Our audience is very 'jaded' as it consists of TV, motion picture and music publisher executives who have 'seen it all.' " Does not wish to see bland, "safe" material. We like first productions. "In the cover letter state in great detail the proposed involvement of the songwriter, other than as a writer (i.e. director, actor, singer, publicist, designer, etc.). Also, state if there are any liens on the material or if anything has been promised."
Productions: *Offenbach in the Underworld*, by Frederick Grab (biography with can-can); *Is Nudity Required*, by Stephen Oakley (comedy); and *Wonderful World of Waiver?* (backstage musical). Also *Vine Street*, by H.D. Parkin III (street musical with film/video elements); *All Coked Out* by S. Oakley and M Guestello (musical tragedy on drug use); *Rainbows' End* by Margaret Keifer (songwriters struggle/musical); and *Hostages* (political musical).
Tips: "Send me a script and a cassette, and be obsessed with your desire to see your show be a success."

*C. EMMETT MCMULLEN, Heuer Publishing Co., Box 248, Cedar Rapids IA 52406. (319)364-6311. Editor: C. Emmett McMullen. Play publisher. Estab. 1928. Produces 10-15 plays/year. Plays and musicals are geared toward church groups and junior and senior high schools. Pays by royalty or by outright purchase. Submit complete manuscript and score. SASE. Reports in 2 months.

Musical Theater: "Seeking material for high school productions. All writing within the scope of high school groups. No works with X-rated material or questionable taboos. Simplified staging and props. Currently seeking material with larger casts, preferably with more women than male roles."
Productions: *Robin Hood*, by Dan Neidermyer; *Invisible Boy*, by Robert Frankel; and *Murder At Coppersmith Inn*, by Dan Neidermyer.
Tips: "We are interested in working with new writers. Writers need to consider that many plays are presented in small — often not well-established stages."

DON AND PAT MACPHERSON PRODUCTIONS, 461 Parkway, Gatlinburg TN 37738. (615)436-4039. Co-owners/producers: Don MacPherson and Pat MacPherson. Play producer. Estab. 1977. Produces 2 musicals/year. Plays are performed at Sweet Fanny Adams Theatre, Gatlinburg, Tennessee to tourist audience. Pays $100-200/week. Query with synopsis, character breakdown and set description. SASE. Reports in 1 month.
Musical Theater: Produce musicals that are funny, fast — in fact, silly; musical farces. Theater is 1890 style so shows should fit that period. Have done many westerns. Cast size limited to 7 or 8 with 2 musicians. Stage very small. Use old-time backdrops forsets. Shows should be no longer than 90 minutes. Does not wish to see shows that would not fit 1890s style — unless it had a country theme.
Productions: *Phantom of the Opry*, by Don & Pat MacPherson/J. Lovensheimer (spoof of *Phanton of the Opera*); *Life & Times of Billy Kincaid*, by MacPherson/Lovensheimer (western); *Not Quite Snow White*, by MacPherson/Lovensheimer (fairytale); and *Not Quite Frankenstein*, by Don and Pat MacPherson.
Tips: "See a production at Sweet Fanny Adams."

MAGNIFICENT MOORPARK MELODRAMA AND VAUDEVILLE CO., 45 E. High St., Moorpark CA 93021. (805)529-1212. Producer: Linda Bredemann. Play producer. Estab. 1982. Produces 7 new musicals/year. "Our audience is family and church groups, ages 2 to 90." Pays by royalty, outright purchase or per performance. Submit complete manuscript, score and tape of songs. SASE. Reports in 12 months.
Musical Theater: "We want plays set in any era, but must have a villain to boo — hero to cheer — heroine to ahh. Each act should run no more than 1 hour with a 2 act maximum. We want family-oriented comedies only. Cast should be no more than 20. We have a small stage (30×30). We don't want obscene, vulgar or off-color material. We want up beat music — can be popular songs or old time."
Productions: *Robin Hood*, by Tim Kelly; *Cinderella Meets the Wolfman*, by Tim Kelly (fairy tale); and *Sourdough*, by Dexter Fisch (Western).
Tips: "Have fun. Make the characters memorable, lovable and believable. Make the music tuneful and something to hum later."

MANHATTAN THEATRE CLUB, 453 W. 16th St., New York NY 10011. (212)645-5590. Director of Script Department: Kate Loewald. Artistic Associate: Michael Bush. Play producer. Estab. 1971. Produces 8 plays and sometimes 1 musical/year. Plays are performed at the Manhattan Theatre Club before varied audiences. Pays negotiated fee. Query with synopsis, "5-10 page libretto and lyric sample." SASE. Reports in 6 months.
Musical Theater: "Small cast, original work. *No* historical drama, verse drama or children's plays." Will consider original music for use in a play being developed or in a pre-existing play.
Productions: *Real Life Funnies*, by Alan Menken and Howard Ashman (topical New York City); *Livin' Dolls*, by Scott Wittman and Marc Shaiman; *Ain't Misbehavin'*, by Fats Waller and Richard Maltby; *On the Swing Shift*, by Michael Dansicker and Sarah Schlesinger; *Urban Blight*, by Richard Maltby, Jr., David Shire and others; and *1-2-3-4-5*, by Maury Yeston and Larry Gelbart.

MERIWETHER PUBLISHING, LTD. (CONTEMPORARY DRAMA SERVICE), 885 Elkton Dr., Colorado Springs CO 80907. (303)594-4422. Editor/President: Arthur Zapel. Play publisher. Estab. 1968. Publishes 40 plays and 5-10 musicals (5 new musicals)/year. Receives 40 musical play submissions/year. "We publish musicals for church school elementary, middle grade and teens. We also publish musicals for high school secular use. Our musicals are performed in churches or high schools." Pays 10% royalty or by negotiated sale from royalties. "Sometimes we pay a royalty to a limited maximum." Query with synopsis, character breakdown and set description or submit script with cassette tape of songs. SASE. Reports in 2 months.
Musical Theater: "We are always looking for good church/school musicals for children. We prefer a length of 15-20 minutes, though occasionally we will publish a 3-act musical adaptation of a classic with large casts and sets. We like informal styles, with a touch of humor, that allow many children and/or adults to participate. We like musicals that imitate Broadway shows or have some name appeal based on the Classics. Box office appeal is more critical than message — at least for teenage and adult level fare. Musical scripts with piano accompaniments only. We especially welcome short, simple

musicals for elementary and teenage, church use during the holidays of Christmas and Easter. We would like to know of arrangers and copyists."

Productions: *Bicycles Built For Two*, by Peg Kehret and Art Wiggins (comedy); *The Velveteen Rabbit*, by Larry Nestor and Gary Peterson (children's show); and *Would You Believe . . . A Stable?*, by Michael C. Vigilant and Gerald V. Castle (Christmas).

Tips: "Keep the music manageable for unprofessional performers. Keep music book costs to a minimum in terms of arrangements and copy or engraving expenses. Keep length under 45 minutes. 15-20 minutes preferred. We will look only at materials that are neatly presented and of professional quality. Anything not completely developed is returned immediately. If the musician can provide a camera-ready music score we are more inclined to publish the work. The competition with Broadway name musicals is great. New musicals must have competitive appeal."

MILWAUKEE REPERTORY THEATER, 108 E. Wells St., Milwaukee WI 53202. (414)224-1761. Artistic Assistant: Norma Saldivar. Play producer. Estab. 1954. Produces 17 plays and 5 cabaret shows/year. "The space is a 106 seat cabaret with a very small playing area (8x28)." Pays by royalty. Send script and/or cassette. SASE. Reports in 3-4 months.

Musical Theater: "Cast size must be limited to 3 singers/performers with minimum movement. Suitable for cabaret. Must appeal to a broad adult audience and should not run longer than 1 hour. We also seek to explore a multi-cultural diversity of material."

Productions: *A Little Tom Foolery*, by Tom Lehrer (political satire); *Jukejointjammin*, by R. Meiksins & B. Roberts (1930s jazz); and *A Gershwin Serenade*, by Larry Deckel (musical retrospective).

*MIXED BLOOD THEATRE CO., 1501 S. 4th St., Minneapolis MN 55454. (612)338-0937. Script Czar: David Kunz. Play producer. Estab. 1976. Produces 5-8 plays and perhaps (1 new musical)/year. "We have a 200-seat theater in a converted firehouse. The audience spans the socio-economic spectrum." Pays 7-10% royalty. Submit complete manuscript, score and tape of songs. SASE.

Musical Theater: "We want full-length, non-children works with a message. Always query first. Never send unsolicited script or tape."

Productions: *Buenavista*, by Bernardo Solano; *Liquid Skin*, by Douglas Anderson (transsexual); and *Boys Next Door*, Tom Griffin (retarded adults).

MUSICAL THEATRE WORKS, INC., 440 Lafayette St., New York NY 10003. (212)677-0040. Business Manager: Todd Rinehart. Produces new musicals exclusively. Estab. 1983. 14 productions have transferred to Broadway, off-Broadway and regional theater. Produces 3-4 new musicals and 12-16 readings each season. Productions and readings are held at the Theatre at Saint Peter's Church, Citicorp Center. No payment for productions.Submit complete script, cassette tape of songs and SASE. Reply in 2-4 months.

Musical Theater: "We are seeking full-length book/avant-garde musicals which have never been produced. Fourteen cast maximum. Full, but modest productions in 164-seat modern off-Broadway theater for metropolitan NYC audience. Only completed projects will be considered."

Productions: *Whatnot*, by Howard Crabtee and Mark Waldrop (won 1990 Richard Rodgers Award); *Love in Two Countries*, by Sheldon Harnick and Tom Shepard (operetta); *Collette Collage*, by Tom Jones and Harvey Schmidt (on the life of French writer Collette); and *The Next to Last Revue*, by Martin Sharnin (skits about life in NYC).

MUSIC-THEATRE GROUP INC., 735 Washington St., New York NY 10014. (212)924-3108. Managing Director: Diane Wondisford. Music-theater production company. Produces 6 music-theater pieces/year. Plays are performed "off-broadway in New York City; for summer audiences in Stockbridge, MA." Pays negotiable royalty or fees. Query with synopsis, character breakdown, set description and tape of music. SASE.

Musical Theater: "We don't actually seek developed properties, but examples of people's work as an indication of their talent in the event that we might want to suggest them for a future collaboration. The music must be a driving element in the work. We generally work with not more than 10-12 in cast and a small band of 4-5."

Productions: *Cinderella/Cendrillon*, based on the opera by Jules Massenet; and *Juan Darien*, by Julie Taymor and Elliot Goldenthal.

NATIONAL MUSIC THEATER CONFERENCE, O'Neill Theater Center, 234 West 44th St., #901, New York NY 10036. (212)382-2790. Artistic Director: Paulette Haupt. "The Conference develops new music theater works." Estab. 1978. Develops 3-4 musicals each summer. 8-10 professional songwriters/musicians participate in each event. Participants include songwriters, composers, opera/musical theater and lyricists/librettists. "The O'Neill Theater Center is in Waterford, Connecticut. The audiences for the staged readings of works-in-progress are a combination of local residents, New York and regional theater professionals. Participants are selected by artistic director and selection panel of professionals." Pays a stipend, room and board, and all costs of the workshops are covered. Query first. SASE. Response within 4 months. Entry Fee $10.

Musical Theater: "The Conference is interested in all forms of music theater. Staged readings are presented with script in hand, minimal props, piano only. There are no cast limitations. We don't accept works which have been previously produced by a professional company."

Productions: *Captains Courageous*, by Frederick Freyer and Patrick Cook; *Il Musico*, by Larry Grossman and Ian Strasfogel; *Swamp Gas* and *Shallow Feelings*, by Jack Erick Williams and Randy Buck.

NATIONAL MUSIC THEATER NETWORK, INC., Third Floor, 1460 Broadway, New York NY 10036. (212)382-0984. President: Timothy Jerome. Service to evaluate new musical works and publish a catalogue of recommended works to play producers. "Our catalogue of recommended works is targeted to approximately 7,000 regional theaters and musical producers interested in presenting new works. Our 'sampler' series concerts feature excerpts from recommended works for the NYC area. In 1991-92 we will present 20 concerts featuring recommended works. Producers contact us for creators' works. We contact creators and creators contact producers." Receives 5 submissions/month. Submit complete manuscript, score and tape of songs. Writers are required to "fill out our submission form plus $30 fee." SASE. Reports in 6 months.

Musical Theater: "We accept all styles. Take the time to present your materials neatly. We accept only *completed* musicals and operas, i.e. script/score/tape."

Tips: "Use us as a resource to help you market your work."

THE NEW CONSERVATORY CHILDREN'S THEATRE COMPANY & SCHOOL, 25 Van Ness, San Francisco CA 94102. (415)861-4914. Executive Director: Ed Decker. Play producer. Estab. 1981. Produces about 5 plays and 1 or 2 musicals (1 new musical)/year. Audience includes families and community groups; children ages 14-19. "Performance spaces are 50-150 seat theater, but we also tour some shows. Pays $25-35 per performance. If we commission, playwright receives a commission for the initial run and royalties thereafter; otherwise playwright just gets royalties."

How to Contact: Query with synopsis, character breakdown and set description. SASE. Reports in 3 months.

Musical Theater: "We seek innovative and preferably socially relevant musicals for children and families, with relatively small cast (stage is small), in which all roles can be played by children. We have a small stage, thus cannot accommodate plays casting more than 10 or 12 people, and prefer relatively simple set requirements. Children cast are in the 9-19 age range. We do not want mushy, cute material. Fantasy is fine, as is something like Sendak & King's *Really Rosie*, but nothing gooey. We are very interested in using original music for new or existing plays. Songwriters should submit a resume and perhaps a tape to let us know what they do."

Productions: *Consensus*, by Dylan Russell (American family); *Get Real!*, by Doug Holsclaw (AIDS education, age 9-12); *Kegger*, by Megan Terry (teen alcohol use).

Tips: "Be flexible, able to revise and open to suggestions!"

NEW THEATRE, P.O. Box 650696, Miami FL 33265. (305)595-4260. Executive Artistic Director: Rafael de Acha. Play producer. Estab. 1986. Produces 10 plays and 2 musicals (2 new musicals)/year. Audience is mixed urban South Florida, with median age of 35, mostly upper-class white and Hispanic. Pays by royalty. Query with synopsis, character breakdown and set description. SASE. Reports in 3 months.

Musical Theater: "Specifically small, revue-style musicals, such as *Brecht on Brecht*; *Side by Side*; *Oh, Coward*, etc. Also interested in experimental work along the lines of *Three Postcards*, etc. We perform in a 70-seat black box theater, with modest production values." Would consider original music for use in a play being developed, but "that kind of work requires the composer to be involved very heavily. We often use incidental music specially composed for a play and have also commissioned original works."

Productions: *Feiffer's People*, by Jules Feiffer (satire); *Dear Liar*, by Jerome Kilty (biographical play); *Spoon River Anthology*, by Edgar Lee Masters (play with music) and *You are Here*, by Susan Westfall and Bernard Harding.

Tips: "Keep lines of communication open."

NEW VIC SUPPER THEATRE, 755 S. Saginaw, Flint MI 48502. (313)235-8866. Executive/Artistic Director: Patricia Victor. Play producer. Estab. 1981. Produces 8-10 plays and 2-3 musicals/year. Audience is a wide range of dinner theater patrons from old to young. Half of the audience is generated by group sales. Perform on small proscenium with thrust. Query with synopsis, character breakdown and set description. SASE. Reports in six months.

Musical Theater: "We will look at most any style or topic of musical; 20-25 is top end of cast size. Staging is detailed but limited because of smaller stage. We will try and accommodate most shows." Will consider adding original music to an already existing show. Last season added original music to a production of Moliere's *The Miser*.

Productions: *1940s Radio Hour*, by Walton Jones; *Joseph and the Amazing Technicolor Dreamcoat*, by Andrew Lloyd Weber & Tim Rice; and *Olymus On My Mind*, by Barry Harmon & Grant Sturale.
Tips: "We have a pretty strong following that has built up with us in our eight years of existence. They are an older audience primarily, but getting younger all the time. Excessive swearing and strong sexual content should be avoided."

NEW YORK STATE THEATRE INSTITUTE, PAC 266, 1400 Washington Ave., Albany NY 12222. (518)442-5399. Literary Manager: James Farrell. Play producer. Produces approximately 5 plays (2 new musicals)/year. Plays performed for student audiences grades K-12, family audiences and adult audiences. Two theaters: main theater seats 950 with full stage, studio theater seats 450 with smaller stage. Pay negotiable. Submit complete manuscript and tape of songs. SASE. Response in 3-4 months.
Musical Theater: Looking for "intelligent and well-written book with substance, a score that enhances and supplements the book and is musically well-crafted and theatrical. Length: up to 2 hours. Could be play with music, musical comedy, musical drama. Excellence and substance in material is essential. Cast could be up to 12; orchestra size up to 8."
Productions: *Pied Piper*, by Adrian Mitchell/Dominic Muldowney (musical adaptation of the classic tale); *The Snow Queen*, by Adrian Mitchell/Richard Peaslee (musical adaptation of the Andersen fairy tale).
Tips: "There is a great need for musicals that are well-written with intelligence and substance which are suitable for family audiences."

NEW YORK THEATRE WORKSHOP, 18th Floor, 220 W. 42 St., New York NY 10036. (212)302-7737. Artistic Director: James C. Nicola. Play producer. Produces 4 mainstage plays and approximately 50 readings/year. "Plays are performed in the Perry Street Theatre, Greenwich Village. Audiences include: subscription/single ticket buyers from New York area, theater professionals, and special interest groups. Pays by artistic fees, approximately $5,400 total annually." Query with synopsis, character breakdown and set description. SASE. Reports in 3 months.
Musical Theater: "As with our non-musicals, we seek musicals of intelligence and social consciousness that challenge our perceptions of the world and the events which shape our lives. We favor plays that possess a strong voice, distinctive and innovative use of language and visual imagery. Integration of text and music is particularly of interest. Musicals which require full orchestrations would generally be too big for us. We prefer 'musical theater pieces' rather than straightforward 'musicals' per-se. We often use original music for straight plays that we produce. This music may be employed as pre-show, post-show or interlude music. If the existing piece lends itself, music may also be incorporated within the play itself. Large casts (12 or more) are generally prohibitive and require soliciting of additional funds. Design elements for our productions are of the highest quality possible with our limited funds— approximately budgets of $10,000 are allotted for our productions."
Productions: *The Waves*, adopted from Virginia Woolf's novel. Music and lyrics by David Bucknam. Text and direction by Lisa Peterson; and *My Children! My Africa*, by Athol Fugard.
Tips: "Submit a synopsis which captures the heart of your piece; inject your piece with a strong voice and intent and try to surprise and excite us."

NEXT ACT THEATRE, (formerly Theatre Tesseract), P.O. Box 394, Milwaukee WI 53201. (414)278-7740. Artistic Director: Jonathan Smoots. Estab. 1984. 4 productions/year, of which 1 is a musical. Playwrights paid by royalty (5-8%). "Performance spaces vary greatly but generally seat 349. We have 1,000 season subscribers and single ticket buyers of every age range and walk of life." Pays $30-50 per performance. Submit complete manuscript, score and tape of songs with at least one professional letter of recommendation. SASE.
Musical Theater: "We produce Broadway and off-Broadway style material, preferring slightly controversial or cutting edge material (i.e. *March of the Falsettos*). We have never produced a work that has not been successful in some other theatrical center. We are very limited financially and rarely stage shows with more than 6 in the cast. Props, sets and costumes should be minimal. We have no interest in children's theater, mime shows, puppet shows, etc. We have never yet used original music for our plays. We may consider it, but there would be little if any money available for this purpose."
Productions: *Billy Bishop Goes to War*, by John Gray/Eric Peterson (World War I flying ace); *A . . . My Name is Alice*, by various writers (women's themes); and *Damn Tango*, by Helena Dynerman (European translation of 17 tangos with cast of 17 singer/dancers).

NORTH CAROLINA BLACK REPERTORY COMPANY, 610 Coliseum Dr., Winston-Salem NC 27106. (919)723-2266. Executive/Artistic Director: Larry Leon Hamlin. Play producer. Estab. 1979. Produces 4 plays and 2 musicals (1 new musical)/year. "Musicals are produced primarily for a Black audience but should also appeal to the general public. Performance in a 540 seat proscenium theater." Pays by royalty, by outright purchase or per performance. Query with synopsis, character breakdown and set description. Tape recording of songs should also be included. SASE. Reports in 4 months.

Musical Theater: "Full length musicals are desired, even musicals for children. As well as being entertaining, musicals should support improving the quality of life for all humanity, offering solutions or alternatives to problems. The company prefers a cast of no larger than 15, but is not limited to that number." Will consider original music for a play in development or pre-existing play that would be used to set mood or enhance dramatic moments.

Productions: *Celebration: African Odyssey* and *Night Voices*, by Ricardo Pitts-Wiley (friendship); and *Don't Bother Me, I Can't Cope*, by Micki Grant (humanity).

Tips: "Constant communication is important. Keep the Director aware of your career progress."

NORTHSIDE THEATRE COMPANY OF SAN JOSE, 848 E. William St., San Jose CA 95116. (408)288-7820. Artistic Director: Richard T. Orlando. Play producer. Estab. 1979. Produces 6 plays and an occasional musical/year. "Family entertainment, plays are performed at the Olinder Theatre." Pays by royalty. Query with synopsis, character breakdown and set description. SASE. Reports in 3 weeks.

Musical Theater: "Classic family plays (with a twist or different concept)." Cast size: 10-15. Sets: Unit in concept with simple additions. Staging: proscenium with thrust. Small 90 seat theater fully equipped. "We are interested in new ideas and approaches. Production should have social relevancy." Will consider using original music for already existing plays. "Example: the underscoring of a Shakespeare piece."

Productions: *A Christmas Carol*, by Charles Dickens (seasonal); *After the Rain*, by John Bowen (future civilization); and *Voices from the High School*, by Peter Dee (youth and their lives).

Tips: "Be aggressive, sell your idea and be able to work within the budget and limitations that the artistic director is confined to."

ODYSSEY THEATRE EMSEMBLE, 2055 S.Sepulveda Blvd., Los Angeles CA 90025. (213)477-2055. Literary Manager: Jan Lewis. Play producer. Estab. 1969. Produces 9 plays, 1 musical and 1-2 new musicals/year. Receives 3-4 submissions/month. "Our audience is predominantly over 35, upper middle-class, audience interested in eclectic brand of theater which is challenging and experimental." Pays by royalty (percentage to be negotiated). Query with synopsis, character breakdown and set description. Query should include resume(s) of artist(s) and tape of music. SASE. "Unsolicited material is not read or screened at all." Reports on query in 2 weeks; manuscript in 6 months.

Musical Theater: "We want nontraditional forms and provocative, unusual, challenging subject matter. We are not looking for Broadway-style musicals. Comedies should be highly stylized or highly farcical. Works should be full-length only and not requiring a complete orchestra (small band preferred.) Political material and satire are great for us. We're seeking interesting musical concepts and approaches. The more traditional Broadway-style musicals will generally not be done by the Odyssey. If we have a work in development that needs music, original music will often be used. In such a case, the writer and composer would work together during the development phase. In the case of a pre-existing play, the concept would originate with the director who would select the composer."

Productions: *Symmes' Hole*, by Randolph Dreyfuss (search for the center of the earth); *Spring Awakening*, by Frank Wedekind (sexual awakening in youth); *McCarthy*, by Jeff Goldsmith (Senator Joe McCarthy); *Struggling Truths* (the Chinese invasion of Tibet); and *It's A Girl* (a capella musical for 5 pregnant women).

Tips: "Stretch your work beyond the ordinary. Look for compelling themes or the enduring questions of human existence. If it's a comedy, go for broke, go all the way, be as inventive as you can be."

OFF CENTER THEATRE, 1501 Broadway, New York NY 10036. (212)768-3277. Producer: Abigail McGrath. Play producer. Estab. 1968. Produces varying number of plays and new musicals/year. The plays are performed "off-Broadway." Pays percentage of box office receipts after initial expenses have been recouped. Submit complete manuscript, score and tape of songs. SASE. Reports in 1 month.

Musical Theater: Socially relevant. Not for children/young audiences. Issue oriented, small cast.

Productions: *Just for Fun—The Music of Jerome Kern* (revue); *Biting the Apple*, by Tony McGrath and Stanley Seidman (revue); and *Hello, This Is Barbara, I'm Not in Right Now . . .*, by Barbara Schottenfeld (singles in New York City).

Tips: "Must be in New York City area for a length of time to work on a piece during readings and/or workshop—without guarantee of production."

OLD GLOBE THEATRE, P.O. Box 2171, San Diego CA 92112. (619)231-1941. Literary Manager: Mark Hofflund. Artistic Director: Jack O'Brien. Produces 12 or 13 plays/year, of which a varying number are musicals. "This is a regional theater with three spaces: 600-seat proscenium, 225-seat arena and large outdoor summer stage. We serve a national audience base of over 260,000." Query with synopsis and letter of introduction, or submit through agent or professional affiliation. No unsolicited material please. Reports in 6 months. Receives 100 submissions/year.

Musical Theater: "We look for skill first, subject matter second. No prescribed limitations, though creators should appreciate the virtues of economy as well as the uses of extravagance. Musicals have been produced on all three of our stages."

Productions: *Into The Woods*, by Stephen Sondheim and James Lapine; *Kiss Me Kate*; *A . . . My Name is Alice*; *Suds*; *Pump Boys and Dinettes*; *Marry Me a Little*; *White Linen*, by Stephen Metcalfe; and the premiere of *Heartbeats*, by Amanda McBroom.

OMAHA MAGIC THEATRE, 1417 Farnam St., Omaha NE 68102. (402)346-1227. Artistic Director: Jo Ann Schmidman. Play producer. Estab. 1968. Produces 8 performance events with music/year. "Plays are produced in our Omaha facility and on tour throughout the midwest. Our audience is a cross-section of the community." Pays standard royalty or commissions. Query with synopsis, character breakdown and set description. SASE. Reports in 3 months.

Musical Theater: "We want the most avant of the avant garde—plays that never get written, or if written are buried deep in a chest because the writer feels there are not production possibilities in this nation's theaters. Plays must push form and/or content to new dimensions. The clarity of the playwright's voice must be strong and fresh. We don't want standard musical plays, naturalism, or realism. We should consider original music as sound structure and for lyrics."

Productions: *Body Leaks*, by Megan Terry, Jo Ann Schmidman and Sora Kimberlain (self-censorship); *Sound Fields/Sound Minds*, Megan Terry, Jo Ann Schmidman and Sora Schmidman (prime kinetic sounts); and *Headlights*, Megan Terry (literacy in America).

THE OPEN EYE: NEW STAGINGS, 270 W. 89th St., New York NY 10024. (212)769-4143. Artistic Director: Amie Brockway. Play producer. Estab. 1972. Produces 9 one-acts, 5-6 full length or new stagings for youth; varying number of new musicals. "Plays are performed in a well-designed and pleasant theater seating 115 people." Pays on a fee basis or by commission. "We are pleased to accept unsolicited play manuscripts under the following conditions: 1) The script must be clean (no pencil marks, magic markers, paste overs, etc.); 2) It must be bound; 3) A self-addressed stamped envelope must be enclosed for each manuscript's return. Also keep in mind: the best time for submission is from April through July. We receive many scripts, and reading takes time. Please allow 3-6 months for a response. Please do not send synopses of your plays. Instead, please consider carefully whether you think your play is something New Stagings should read, and if it is, send the complete script."

Musical Theater: "New Stagings is committed to innovative collaboration and excellence in performance of both classic and new material, presenting the finest of professional talents—established artists and relative newcomers alike. We produce plays which invite us as artists and audience to take a fresh look at ourselves and the world of which we are a part. We seek to involve the performers and the audience in the live theater experience. And we are making a concerted effort to reach new audiences, young and old, and of all ethnic backgrounds. New Stagings for Youth is a not-for-profit professional theater company whose aim is to develop new theater audiences by producing plays for children and young people. New Stagings Lab offers opportunities to performing artists (directors, playwrights, actors, dancers, musicians) to develop new theater pieces through a program of rehearsed readings and workshops. Our stage is roughly 20' x 25' which limits the size of the set, cast and other related details and also, we do not have the height for a fly system. We seldom do political or propaganda related plays. We frequently use music to enhance a script, as well as performing plays with music in them, and also musicals. We believe in using various forms of art (music, movement) in most of our productions."

Productions: *Eagle or Sun*, by Sabina Berman (The Mexican Conquest); *A Woman Called Truch*, by Sandra Acher (Life of Sojourner Truth); and *A Place Beyond the Clouds*, by Sandra Biano (Myths and Stories of Flying).

Tips: "Come see our work."

OZARK ACTORS THEATRE, P.O. Box K, Rolla MO 65401. (314)364-9523. Artistic Director: F. Reed Brown. Play roducer. Estab. 1987. Produces 3 plays and 1 musical/year. South-central Missouri is a rural (primarily agricultural) area. O.A.T. is located in Rolla, which houses the Univesity of Missouri-Rolla. Pays by royalty. Query with snyopsis, character breakdown and set description. SASE. Reports in 2-3 months.

Musical Theatre: "Virtually any subject is desired. We look for shows/musicals that will fit into a summer stock season. Musicaltheatre. No opera." Primarily small casts (not to exceed 15). Relatively small (unit) sets. Without major technical requirements. "O.A.T. does not wish to produce material which might be viewed controversial. Such as strong sexual, racial or political views. No strong language." Will consider original music for work already in progress. "We produced an original work entitled *Voices* with writings by Van Gogh, Thoreau, Emily Dickenson, Ann Frank and Helen Keller. The score composer is Alan Johnson."

Productions: *Voices*, compiled by Fred Brown, music by Alan Johnson (life, death, criticism); *I Do! I Do!*, by Schmidt/Jones (marriage); and *The Boys Next Door* by Tom Griffin (the mentally handicapped).

PAPER MILL PLAYHOUSE, Brookside Dr., Milburn NJ 07041. (201)379-3636. Contact: Angelo Del Rossi. Play producer. Produces 2 plays and 4 musicals (1 new musical)/year. "Audience based on 40,000 subscribers; plays performed in 1,192-seat proscenium theatre." Pays negotiable royalty or will option play under Dramatist Guild. "A synopsis of book plus tape of songs should be submitted first. Scores not necessary. Letter of introduction should accompany each submitted synopsis." SASE. Letter in 2 weeks, response in 6 months.

Musical Theater: Seeking "traditional Broadway sized musicals—either original or adaptations. One act plays are not considered. Developing works can be submitted to our musical workshop series. No cast size limitations—minimum of 5 characters usually to maximum size of 40-45." No nudity, profanity, etc.

Productions: *Me and My Girl*; *Greasepaint*; *Lend Me a Tenner*; *To Kill a Mockingbird* and *A Chorus Line*.

Tips: "New musicals are sought for our Musical Theatre Project development program, which includes a series of staged readings and laboratory (workshop)."

PENNSYLVANIA STAGE COMPANY, 837 Linden St., Allentown PA 18101. (215)434-8570. Production Manager: Peter Wrenn-Meleck. Play producer. Estab. 1979. Produces 7 plays (1 new musical)/season "when feasible." "We are a LORT D theatre with a subscriber base of approximately 6,000 people. Plays are performed at the Pennsylvania Stage Company in the J.I. Rodale Theatre." Payment is negotiated on an individual basis. Query with synopsis, character breakdown, set description and a tape of the music. "Please do not send script first." SASE. Reports in 2 months.

Musical Theater: "We are interested in full-length musicals which reflect the social, historical and political fabric of America. We have no special requirements for format, structure or musical involvement. We ask that once submission of a musical has been requested, that it be bound, legibly typed and include SASE. Cast limit of 10, but we prefer cast limit of 8. One set or unit set. Ours is a 274—seat house, there is no fly area, and a 23-foot proscenium opening."

Productions: *Just So*, by Mark St. Germain (based on Rudyard Kipling's *Just So Stories*); *Shim Sham*, by Johnny Brandon and Eric Blau (Buddy Bradley, an American tap and jazz choreographer); *Feathertop*, by Bruce Peyton and Skip Kennon (Nathaniel Hawthorne short story); *Song of Myself*, by Gayle Stahlhuth, Gregory Hurst and Arthur Harris.

Tips: "Consider the importance of what the musical has to say. Book and lyrics should have equal weight—lyrics should further the plot rather than arrest it."

PIONEER DRAMA SERVICE, P.O. Box 22555, Denver CO 80222. (303)759-4297. Play publisher. Estab. 1963. "Plays are performed by junior high and high school drama departments, church youth groups, college and university theaters, semi-professional and professional children's theaters, parks and recreation departments." Query with synopsis, character breakdown and set description. SASE. "No unsolicited manuscripts." Reports in 6 weeks. Playwrights paid by royalty (10% sales) or by outright purchase ($200-500).

Musical Theater: "We seek full length children's musicals, high school musicals and one act children's musicals to be performed by children, secondary school students, and/or adults. As alway, we are seeking musicals easy to perform, simple sets, many female roles and very few solos. Must be appropriate for educational market. Developing a new area, we are actively seeking musicals to be produced by elementary schools—20 to 30 minutes in length, with 2 to 3 songs and large choruses. We are not interested in profanity, themes with exclusively adult interest, sex, drinking, smoking, etc. Several of our full-length plays are being converted to musicals. We edit them, decide where to insert music and then contact with someone to write the music and lyrics."

Productions: Published *Tied to the Tracks*, by Tim Kelly, Arne Christiansen and Ole Kittleson (musical melodrama); *Little Luncheonette of Terror*, by Tim Kelly, Bill Francoeur and Steve Fendrical (musical comedy); and *The Magical Pied Piper*, by Richard and Pauline Kelvin (children's musical).

Tips: "If one has a musical to publish, send letter of inquiry with plot synopsis, number of male and female characters, number of sets or set changes, approximate duration and production history. Also send complete music score and tape, if possible."

PLAYERS PRESS, INC., P.O. Box 1132, Studio City CA 91614. (818)789-4980. Associate Editor: Marjorie Clapper. Vice President: Robert W. Gordon. Play publisher. Estab. 1965. Publishes 20-30 plays, 8-10 musicals and 1-3 new musicals/year. Plays are used primarily by general audience and children. Pays royalty or negotiable outright purchase. Submit complete manuscript, score and tape of songs. SASE. Reports in 3-5 months.

Musical Theater: "We will consider all submitted works. Presently musicals for adults and high schools are in demand. When cast size can be flexible (describe how it can be done in your work) it sells better."

Publications: *The Deerstalker*, by Doug Flack (Sherlock Holmes-musical); *Rapunzel N the Witch*, by William-Alan Landes (children's musical); and *Sunnyside Junior High*, by Rick Woyiwoda (musical for teen audience).
Tips: "When submitting, it is best to send a clean, clear sounding tape with music. We do not publish a play or musical which has not been produced."

PLAYHOUSE ON THE SQUARE, 51 S. Cooper, Memphis TN 38104. (901)725-0776. Executive Producer: Jackie Nichols. Play producer. Produces 12 plays (4 musicals)/year. Plays are produced in a 260-seat proscenium resident theater. Pays $500 for outright purchase. Submit complete manuscript and score. SASE. Reports in 4 months.
Musical Theater: Seeking "any subject matter – adult and children's material. Small cast preferred. Stage is 26' deep by 43' wide with no fly system." Would also consider original music for use in a play being developed.
Productions: *Gypsy*, by Stein and Laurents; *The Spider Web*, by Agatha Christie (mystery); and *A Midsummer Night's Dream*, by William Shakespeare.

PLAYWRIGHTS HORIZONS, 416 West 42nd St., New York NY 10036. (212)564-1235. Director: Ira Weitzman. Literary Manager/Musical Theater Program Director. Play producer. Estab. 1971. Produces about 6 plays and 2 new musicals/year. "A general New York City audience." Pays by fee/royalty. Send script and tape (not necessarily complete). SASE. Reports in 6 months.
Musical Theater: "No revivals or children's shows; otherwise we're flexible. We can't do a Broadway-size show. We generally develop work from scratch; we're open to proposals for shows, and ideas from bookwriters or songwriters. We have frequently commissioned underscoring and incidental music."
Productions: *Lucky Stiff*, by Lynn Ahrens/Stephen Flaherty (musical comedy); *The Heidi Chronicles*, by Wendy Wasserstein (play); and *Driving Miss Daisy*, by Alferd Uhry (play).

PUERTO RICAN TRAVELING THEATRE, 141 W. 94th St., New York, NY 10025. (212)354-1293. Producer: Miriam Colon Valle. Play Producer. Estab. 1967. Publishes 4 plays and 1 new musical/year. Primarily an Hispanic audience. Playwrights are paid by stipend.
How to Contact: Submit complete manuscript and tape of songs. SASE. Reports in 6 months.
Musical Theater: "Small cast musicals that will appeal to Hispanic audience. Musicals are bilingual; we work in Spanish and English. We need simple sets and props and a cast of about 8, no more. Musicals are generally performed outdoors and last for an hour to an hour and 15 minutes."
Productions: *Chinese Charades*, by Manuel Perralras, Sergio Garcia and Saul Spangenberg (domestic musical); *El Jardin*, by Carlos Morton, Sergio Garcia (Biblical musical); and *Lady With A View*, by Eduardo Ivan Lopez and Fernando Rivas (Statue of Libery musical).
Tips: "Deal with some aspect of the contemporary Hispanic experience in this country."

THE REPERTORY THEATRE OF ST. LOUIS, 130 Edgar Rd., St. Louis MO 63119. (314)968-7340. Associate Artistic Director: Susan Gregg. Play producer. Estab. 1966. Produces 9 plays and 1 or 2 musicals/year. "Mainstream regional theater audience. We produce all our work at the Loretto Hilton Theatre." Query with synopsis, character breakdown and set description. Does not return unsolicited material. Reports in 8 months.
Musical Theater: "We want plays with a small cast and simple setting. No children's shows or foul language. After a letter of inquiry we would prefer script and demo tape."
Productions: *The Merry Wives of Windsor Texas*, by John Haber, Shakespeare (the Shakespearean play gone crooked).

*RICHARD ROSE – AMERICAN STAGE FESTIVAL, Box 225, Milford NH 03055. (603)673-4005. Managing Director: Richard Rose. Play producer. Estab. 1975. Produces 5 mainstage plays, 10 children's, and 1-2 musicals/year. Plays are produced in 500 seat proscenium stage for a general audience. Pays 8-10% royalty or outright purchase of $2,000. Submit complete manuscript, score and tape of songs. SASE.
Musical Theater: "We seek stories about interesting people in compelling situations. Besides our adult audience we have an active children's theater. We will not do a large chorus musical if cast size is over 18. We use original music in plays on a regular basis, as incidental music, pre-show and between acts, or as moments in and of themselves."

"How to Use Your Songwriter's Market" (at the front of this book) contains comments and suggestions to help you understand and use the information in these listings.

Productions: *Rhymes with Evil*, by Charles Traeger (psych thriller); *Peg O' My Heart*, by David Heneker (romantic musical); *Sullivan And Gilbert*, by Ken Ludwig (comic musical); *Starmites*, by Barry Keating (rock/comic book fantasy); and *The Last of the Souhegans*, by Andrew Howard.
Tips: "Write about characters. Understand the reasons why characters break into song. Submit legible script and listenable cassette. And please keep writing!"

SALOME: A JOURNAL FOR THE PERFORMING ARTS, 5548 N. Sawyer, Chicago IL 60625. (312)539-5745. Editor: Effie Mihopoulos. Play publisher and magazine publisher. Estab. 1975. Plays and individual songs are published in the magazine. Pays by a copy of the magazine. Query with synopsis, character breakdown and set description, or submit complete ms, score and tape of songs. SASE. Reports in 1 month.
Musical Theater: Seeks eclectic plays and music. "Good quality is the only criterion." Published *Jean Le Baptiste*, by Kirby Olson (2 characters interacting in a bar).

SEATTLE GROUP THEATRE, 3940 BrooklynAve. NE, Seattle WA 98105. (206)685-4969. Producing Director: Paul O'Connell. Estab. 1978. Produces 6 plays and 1-2 musicals (1 new musical)/year. 200 seat intimate theater; 10' ceiling limit; 35' wide modified thrust; 3 piece band. Pays 6-8% royalty. Query with synopsis, character breakdown and set description. Does not return unsolicited material.
Musical Theater: "Multicultural themes; relevant social issues, (race relations, cultural differences, war, poverty, women's issues, homosexuality, physically challenged, developmentally disabled). Address the issues that our mission focuses on." Past musicals include *A-My Name is Alice*, *Rap Master Ronnie*, *Jacques Brel is Alive*, *Stealing*, *Voices of Christmas*. Cast size of 10 maximum.
Productions: *It's a Girl*, by Tom Burrows; *Fraternity*, by Jeff Stetson and *Latins Anonymous*, by Armando Lomina, Diane Rodriguez, Luisa Leschin and Rick Najera.

*SECOND STAGE THEATRE, P.O. Box 1807, Ansonia Station, New York NY 10023. (212)787-8302. Literary Manager: Erin Sanders. Play producer. Estab. 1979. Produces 4 plays and 1 musical (1 new musical)/year. Receives 30 submissions/year. Plays are performed in a small, 108 seat off-Broadway House." Pays variable royalty. Query with synopsis, character breakdown and set description. SASE. Reports in 4 months.
Musical Theater: "We are looking for innovative, unconventional musicals that deal with sociopolitical themes."
Productions: *In a Pig's Valise*, by Eric Overmyer and Kid Creole (spoof on 40's film noir); *Bolto Days*, by Jonathan Laison (New York angst); and *The Good Times Are Killing Me*, by Lynda Barry (a play with music).
Tips: "Query with synopsis character break-down and set description. Invite to concert readings in New York area."

*SOUND ADVISORS LTD., 400 West Lancaster Ave., Devon PA 19333. (215)975-9212. President: Greg Mizii. Vice President: Howard Scott III. Secretary/Treasurer: Bernard M. Resnick, Esq. Senior Vice President and Director: Steven Bernstein. Produces 1 play/36 musicals. Offers legal council for musicals. Write or call first to obtain permission to submit. Does not accept or return unsolicited material. Reports ASAP. "We prefer writing to us (with SASE) over calling when asking permission to submit."
Musical Theater: Interested in plays with music and songs. Seeking music that has a positive message.
Productions: *In-Out-Throughout, The Quantum Leap.*
Tips: "If you have a great song in your musical let us know about it. We have negotiated recording and publishing contracts with major labels throughout the world. You may have written the next '*Memories.*' Our main interests are the songs in the musical."

SOUTH WESTERN COLLEGE, 900 Otay Lakes Rd., Chula Vista CA 92010. (619)421-6700. Artistic Director: W. Virchis. Play, mime and performance art work producer. Estab. 1964. Produces 6 plays and 2 musicals (1 new musical)/year. Query with synopsis. SASE. Reports in 3 weeks.
Productions: *Evita* (world college premiere); *Wiz* (black musical); *Jesus Christ Superstar* (rock opera); *Pancho Diablo* (Chicano); *Nine* (musical); *Leader of the Pack* (musical); *Laguna*, by Vic Bemeil; *Plymouth Rock*, by Scott Busath; *Nightshriek* (world premier, rock musical based on MacBeth); and *Fantasma* (world premiere), by Edward Gallardu and Mark Allen Trujillo.

STAGE ONE, 425 W. Market St., Louisville KY 40202. (502)589-5946. Producing Director: Moses Goldberg. Play producer. Estab. 1946. Produces 8-10 plays and 0-2 musicals (0-2 new musicals)/year. Receives 100 submissions/year. "Young people ages 5-18." Pays 3-6% royalty, $1,500-3,000 outright purchase or $25-75 per performance. Submit complete manuscript and tape of songs. SASE. Reports in 4 months.

Musical Theater: "We seek stageworthy and respectful dramatizations of the classic tales of childhood, both ancient and modern. Ideally, the plays are relevant to young people and their families, as well as related to school curriculum. Cast is rarely more than 12."

Productions: *Bridge to Terabitha*, by Paterson/Toland/Leibman (contemporary novel); *Little Red Ride Hood*, by Goldberg/Cornett (fairytale); and *Tale of Two Cities*, by Kesselmann (French Revolution).

Tips: "Stage One accepts unsolicited manuscripts that meet our artistic objectives. Please do not send plot summaries or reviews. Include author's resume, if desired. In the case of musicals, a cassette tape is preferred. Cast size is not a factor, although, in practice, Stage One rarely employs casts of over 12. Scripts will be returned in approximately 3-4 months, if SASE is included. No materials can be returned without the inclusion of a SASE. Due to the volume of plays received, it is not possible to provide written evaluations."

SYRACUSE TALENT COMPANY, INC., 100 Southfield Dr., Fayetteville NY 13066. (315)637-3733. Producing Director: Christine Lightcap. Play producer. Produces approximately 3 plays and 7 musicals/year. Performs mainstage at Civic Center, in Syracuse, New York and Central New York dinner theatres including (4) productions (3 musicals, 1 non-musical) in July and August at 3 Rivers Inn. "We want comedies, musicals, not too heavy." Pays royalty or per/performance. Submit complete manuscript, score and tape of songs. SASE. Reports in 2 weeks.

Musical Theater: Seeking an "entertaining comedy with unit set for dinner theatre or unit set with insets for Civic Center. Dinner theatre cast size 2-10; Civic Center 20 or less. No fly space. No heavy material." Musical requirements: dinner theatre and Civic Center: piano, drums and bass, to 8 pieces. Would consider original music for use in a play being developed or for use in a pre-existing play with permission.

Productions: (July-August '88) *Annie, Get Your Gun*; *West Side Story*; *Mousetrap* and *Grease*.

TADA!, 120 West 28th St., New York NY 10001. (212)627-1732. Artistic Directors: Janine Nina Trevens and James Learned. Play producer. Estab. 1984. Produces 3 staged musicals and 3-4 new musicals/year. Receives 50 outside submissions/year. "TADA! is a company producing works performed by children ages 6-17 for family audiences in New York City. Performances run approximately 30-35 performances. Pays by royalty or negotiable commission. Query with synopsis and character breakdown or submit complete manuscript, score and tape of songs. SASE. Reports in 2-3 months.

Musical Theater: "We do not produce plays as full productions. At this point, we do staged readings of plays."

Productions: *The Gift of Winter*, by David Evans (composer), Faye Greenberg (lyricist) and Michael Slade (book) (A town's unhappiness with the bleakness of the season leads them on a journey to lodge a complaint with Winter); *Sleepover*, by Jim Beloff (composer/lyricist) and Philip Freedman (book) (adventures at a sleepover party become especially fun once the boys crash the party).

Tips: "When writing for children don't condescend. The subject matter should be appropriate but the music/treatment can still be complex and interesting."

*THE TEN-MINUTE MUSICALS PROJECT, Box 461194, West Hollywood CA 90046. (213)656-8751. Producer: Michael Koppy. Play producer. Estab. 1987. All pieces are new musicals. Pays 6-7% royalty, $250 award upon selection. Submit complete manuscript, score and tape of songs. SASE. Reports in 2 months after annual deadline.

Musical Theater: Seeks complete short stage musicals of between 8 and 15 minutes in length. Maximum cast: 9. "No parodies—original music only."

Productions: *The Furnished Room*, by Saragail Katzman (the O. Henry story); *An Open Window*, by Enid Futterman and Sara Ackerman (the Saki story); and *Pulp*, by David Spencer and Bruce Peyton (an original detective mystery).

Tips: "Start with a *solid* story—either an adaptation or an original idea—but with a solid beginning, middle and end (probably with a plot twist at the climax)."

THEATRE FOR YOUNG AMERICA, 7204 W. 80th St., Overland Park KS 66204. (913)648-4604. Artistic Director: Gene Mackey. Play producer. Estab. 1977. Produces 8 plays (1-2 new musicals)/year. For children, preschool to high school. Pays $15-70/performance. Query with synopsis. SASE. Reports in 1 month.

Musical Theater: 1-1½ hour productions with small cast oriented to children and high-school youths. "A clear, strong, compelling story is important; a well known title is very important."

Productions: *Androcles and the Lion*, by Aurand Harris and Glen Mack; *Little Lulu*, by Chad Henry (musical for young audience); *The Hare and the Tortoise*, by Cheryl Benge and Gene Mackey (adapted from Aesop's fable); *Tom Sawyer*, by Michael Dansicker and Sarah Marie Schlesinger (adapted from Mark Twain's novel); and *Chicken Little*, by Gene Mackey (book) and Chery Benge (music); among many other productions.

THEATRE OFF PARK, 224 Waverly Pl., New York NY 10014. (212)627-2556. Artistic Director: Albert Harris. Play producer. Estab. 1974. Produces 2-3 plays, variable number of musicals (1 new musical)/year. "We reach a broad audience of primarily middle-income, multi-ethnic and -racial patrons. Our audiences include many seniors and other Manhattanites from all walks of life." Pays by fee, approximately $1,500/work. Query with synopsis, character breakdown and set description. SASE. Reports in 6 months.
Musical Theater: "We desire to produce new musicals of many styles and lengths which give light to a diversity of social issues and lifestyles. We also encourage adaptations or revivals of rarely produced or never performed works of recognized authors. Cast limit is 8. We simply require originality and sophistication in style and presentation. Some projects envisioned would require an original incidental score."
Productions: *I Could Go On Lip-Synching!*, by John Epperson/Justin Ross (fictional biography of a rising performer); *Mademoiselle Colombe*, by Albert Harris from Jean Anonilh (musical-Paris 1890s); *Stardust The Mitchell Parish Musical*, by Albert Harris/Lyrics by Mitchell Parish/Music by Duke Ellington, Glenn Miller, Hoagy Carmichael, etc. (revue); and *A Quiet End*, by Robin Swados.
Tips: "Find a showcase for your work in New York which we may attend or secure the services of a New York agent who is familiar with our work and will submit for you."

THEATRE THREE, P.O. Box 512, Port Jefferson NY 11777. (516)928-9202. Associate Artistic Director: Jerry Friedman. Theater. Estab. 1969. Produces 16 plays and 4 musicals/year. Main stream Long Island audience. Plays produced in our Victorian theater on Main Street in Port Jefferson. Contracts are negotiated on per play basis.
How to Contact: Query with synopsis, character breakdown and set description. SASE. Reports in 3 months.
Musical Theater: Open to many types. Children's musicals as well. No puppet shows. Single sets, smaller casts more desirable.
Productions: *La Cage Aux Folles*; *Singin' in the Rain*; and *Follies*.

THEATRE WEST VIRGINIA, P.O. Box 1799, Beckley WV 25802. (800)666-9142. General Manager: Johanna Young. Play producer. Estab. 1955. Produces 7-9 plays and 2-3 musicals/year. "Audience varies from main stream summer stock to educational tours to dinner theater." Pays 5% royalty or $25 per performance. Query with synopsis, character breakdown and set description; should include cassette tape. SASE. Reports in 2 months.
Musical Theater: "Theatre West Virginia is a year-round performing arts organization that presents a variety of productions including community performances such as dinner theater, *The Nutcracker* and statewide educational programs on primary, elementary and secondary levels. This is in addition to our summer, outdoor dramas of *Hatfields & McCoys* and *Honey in the Rock*, now in their 29th year." Anything suitable for secondary school tours and/or dinner theater type shows. No more than 7 in cast. Play should be able to be accompanied by piano/synthesizer.
Productions: *Thomas Jefferson Still Survives*, by Nancy Moss (historical); *Frogsong*, by Jean Battlo (literary/historical); *Guys & Dolls*, by Frank Loesser; *Grease* (currently in production), by Jim Jacobs and Warren Casey; and *Murder at the Howard Johnsons*, by Ron Clark/Sam Bobrick (comedy).

THEATREVIRGINIA, 2800 Grove Ave., Richmond VA 23221-2466. (804)367-0840. Artistic Director: William Gregg. Play producer. Estab. 1955. Produces 5-9 plays (2-5 musicals)/year. "Plays are performed in a 500-seat LORT-C house for the Richmond-area community." Payment subject to negotiation. "Please submit synopsis, sample of dialogue and sample of music (on cassette) along with a self-addressed, stamped letter-size envelope. If material seems to be of interest to us, we will reply with a solicitation for a complete manuscript and cassette. Response time for synopses is 4 weeks; response time for scripts once solicited is 5 months."
Musical Theater: "We do not deal in one-acts or in children's material. We would like to see full length, adult musicals. There are no official limitations. We would be unlikely to use original music as incidental/underscoring for existing plays, but there is potential for adapting existing plays into musicals."
Productions: *West Memphis Mojo*, by Martin Jones; *Sweeney Todd*, by Stephen Sondheim; and *South Pacific*, by Rodgers and Hammerstein.
Tips: "Read plays. Study structure. Study character. Learn how to concisely articulate the nature of your work. A beginning musical playwright, wishing to work for our company should begin by writing a wonderful, theatrically viable piece of musical theatre. Then he should send us the material requested in our listing, and wait patiently."

THEATREWORKS, 1305 Middlefield Rd., Palo Alto CA 94301. (415)323-8311. Literary Manager: Leslie Martinson. Play producer. Estab. 1970. Produces 12 plays and 5 musicals (2 new musicals)/year. Theatrically-educated suburban area bordering Stanford University 30 miles from San Francisco and

San Jose—3 mainstages and 2 second stage performance spaces. Pays per contract.
How to Contact: Submit complete manuscript, score or sample songs and tape of songs; synopses and character breakdowns helpful. SASE. Reports in 4-6 months.
Musical Theater: "We use original songs and music in many of our classics productions, for instance specially composed music ws used in our production of the *The Tempest* for Ariels song, the pagent song, the storm and the music of theisles. We are looking both for full-scale large musicals and smaller chamber pieces. We also use original music and songs in non-musical plays. No ancient Roman, ancient Greek or biblical settings please!"
Productions: 1989-1991 productions include: *Go Down Garvey* (world premiere); *Galileo* (2nd production in residence); *Into the Woods*; *Big River*; *Oliver, Candide*; *The Tempest* (with original songs); *The Miser* (with original songs), *No Way to Treat a Lady* (composer in residence); *Rags*; *Peter Pan* and *Lady Day at Emerson's Bar and Grill*.
Tips: "Write a great musical. We wish there were more specific 'formula,' but that's about it. If it's really terrific, we're interested."

THEATREWORKS/USA, 890 Biway, New York NY 10003. (212)677-5959. Literary Manager: Barbara Pasternack. Play producer. Produces 10-13 plays, all are musicals (3-4 new musicals)/year. Audience consists of children and families. Pays 6% royalty and aggregate of $1500 commission-advance against future royalties.
How to Contact: Query with synopsis, character breakdown and sample scene and song. SASE. Reports in 6 months.
Musical Theater: "One hour long, 5-6 adult actors, highly portable, good musical theater structure; adaptations of children's literature, historical or biographical musicals, issues, fairy tales—all must have something to say. We demand a certain level of literary sophistication. No kiddy shows, no camp, no fractured fables, no shows written for school or camp groups to perform. Approach your material, not as a writer writing for kids, but as a writer addressing any universal audience. You have one hour to entertain, say something, make them care—don't preach, condescend. Don't forget an antagonist. Don't waste the audience's time. We always use original music—but most of the time a project team comes complete with a composer in tow."
Productions: *The Velveteen Rabbit*, by James Still and Jimmy Roberts (picture book); *Jekyll and Hyde*, book and lyrics by David Crane and Marta Kaufmann, music by Michael Sklopf; *Harold and the Purple Crayon*, music by Jon Ehrlich, lyrics by Robin Pogrebin and Jon Ehrlich, book by Jane Shepard; *Columbus*, by Jonathan Bolt, music by Doug Cohen, lyrics by Thomas Toce; *Class Clown*, book by Thomas West, music by Kim Oles, lyrics by Alison Hubbard; *Heidi*, book and music by David Evans, book and lyrics by Sarah Schlessinger.
Tips: "Write a good show! Make sure the topic is something we can market! Come see our work to find out our style."

*13TH STREET REPERTORY COMPANY, 50 W. 13th St., New York NY 10011. (212)675-6677. Dramaturg: Ken Terrell. Play producer. Estab. 1974. Produces 6 plays/year including 2 new musicals. Receives 16 submissions/month. Audience comes from New York and surrounding area. Children's theater performs at 50 W. 13th in NYC. "We do not pay. The value to the playwright is having a New York production. We are off off-Broadway." Query first. SASE. Reports in 12 months.
Musical Theater: Children's musicals and original musical shows. Small cast with limited musicians. Stagings are struck after each performance. Would consider original music for "pre-show music or incidental music."
Productions: *The Shoemaker and the Elves*, by Michael McGovern (a version of the fairytale); *Cole Porter Revue*, (Cole Porter Music); and *I-Land—a Play With Music*, by Sonia Pilcer (monologues about life in Manhattan).

UNIVERSITY OF ALABAMA NEW PLAYWRIGHTS' PROGRAM, P.O. Box 870239, Tuscaloosa AL 35487-0239. (205)348-5283. Director/Dramaturg: Dr. Paul Castagno. Play producer. Estab. 1982. Produces 8-10 plays and 1 musical/year; 1 new musical every other year. Receives 2 submissions/month. University audience. Pays by arrangement. Submit complete ms, score and tape of songs. SASE. Reports ASAT—usually 1-2 months.
Musical Theater: Any style or subject is acceptable, except children's or puppet plays. Jazz or "New Age" musicals.
Productions: *Gospel According to Esther*, by John Erlancer. No limitations—just solid lyrics and melodic line. Drama with music, musical theater workshops, one-act musicals and chamber musicals.
Tips: "Take your demos seriously—use a recording studio—and get *singers* to showcase your work."

*THE UNUSUAL CABARET, 14½ Mt. Desert St., Bar Harbor ME 04609. (207)288-3306. Artistic Director: Gina Kaufmann. Play producer. Estab. 1990. Produces 4 plays and 4 new musicals/year. Educated adult audiences. 50 seat cabaret. "A casual, festive atmosphere." Pays by royalty (10% of Box). Submit complete manuscript, score and tape of songs. SASE. Reports in 2 months.

Musical Theater: "We produce solely musical or cabaret scripts—45 minutes to 1¼ hours in length. Stylistically or topically unique scripts are encouraged. We strive for as diverse a season as possible within our technical limitations. Our maximum cast size is 8, but cast sizes of 4 or fewer are necessary for half of our productions. Our technical capabilities are minimal. Audience participation is possible because of the cabaret setting. We encourage musical *plays* as well as more traditional musicals. Piano is the only instrument *consistantly* used. We consider adaptations if the written material is being used in an original way in conjunciton with the music."

Productions: *Escape From Eldorado*, by Jeff Goode (wacky spices and a dancing germ); *Dead Poets*, by Jon Price (Emily Dickinson, Walt Whitman and Edgar Allen Poe); *The Beggar's Opera* (adaptation), by John Gray/adaptation: Gina Kaufmann (economic and social structure of society).

Tips: "New musical scripts which interest us must have something 'unusual' about them, either in the ideas, the style, the plot, the structure or the characters."

WALNUT STREET THEATRE COMPANY, 825 Walnut St., Philadelphia PA 19107. (215)574-3584. Literary Manager: Alexa Kelly. Play producer. Estab. 1982. Produces 8 plays and 2 musicals (1 new musical)/year. Plays produced on a mainstage with seating for 1,052 to a family audience; and in studio theatres with seating for 79-99 to adult audiences. Pays by royalty or outright purchase. Query with synopsis, character breakdown, set description, and ten pages. SASE. Reports in 5 months.

Musical Theater: "Adult Musicals. Plays are for a subscription audience that comes to the theatre to be entertained. We seek musicals with lyrical non-operatic scores and a solid book as well as revues. We are looking for a small musical for springtime and one for a family audience at Christmas time. We would like to remain open on structure and subject matter and would expect a tape with the script. Cast size: around 30 equity members (10 for smaller musical); preferably one set with variations." Would consider original music for incidental music and/or underscore. This would be at each director's discretion.

Productions: *Shirley Valentine*, by Willy Russell; *Jesus Christ Superstar*, by Jim Rice and Andrew Lloyd Webber; and *Rumors*, by Neil Simon.

Tips: "Our budget allows very little development time in-house, so the project must be in a state of near-completion before we would consider it."

WASHINGTON JEWISH THEATRE, 6125 Montrose Rd., Rockville MD 20852. (301)881-0100. Artistic Director: Laurie Wagner. Play producer. Estab. 1984. Produces 3-5 plays/year; 50% of productions are musicals (1-2 new musicals)/year. "We are looking for new plays that have some type of Jewish theme. These themes may include biographical plays, plays with Jewish characters in leading roles, World War II plays, etc." Pays by royalty.

How to Contact: Submit complete manuscript, score and tape of songs. SASE.

Musical Theater: "We like musicals with simple sets and few characters. We have no restrictions on style, but topics must in some way conform to the concept of Jewish theater. Our usual running time is 120 minutes including intermission."

Productions: *Adam*, by Joshua Sobel; *The Sunshine Boys*, by Neil Simon ; *Esther*, by Elizabeth Suedos; and *Cabaret*, by Kander and Ebb.

WATERLOO COMMUNITY PLAYHOUSE, Box 433, Waterloo IA 50704. (319)235-0367. Managing Director: Charles Stilwill. Play producer. Estab. 1917. Produces 12 plays (1-2 musicals)/year. "Our audience prefers solid, wholesome entertainment, nothing risque or with strong language. We perform in Hope Martin Theatre, a 368-seat house." Pays $15-150/performance. Submit complete manuscript, score and cassette tape of songs. SASE.

Musical Theater: "Casts may vary from as few as 6 people to 54. We are producing children's theater as well. We're *especially* interested in new adaptations of classic children stories."

Productions: *Oklahoma*, *Little House On The Prairie*, by Patricia Stilwill and Ken Ostercamp; *Camelot*; *You're A Good Man Charlie Brown*; *West Side Story*; and *Fiddler*.

Tips: Looking for "new adaptations of classical children's stories or a good Christmas show."

WEST COAST ENSEMBLE, P.O. Box 38728, Los Angeles CA 90038. (213)871-8673. Artistic Director: Les Hanson. Play producer. Estab. 1982. Produces 6-9 plays and 1 new musical/year. Receives 75 submissions/year. "Our audience is a wide variety of Southern Californians. Plays will be produced in one of our two theaters on Hollywood Boulevard." Pays by royalty or $35-50 per performance. Submit complete manuscript, score and tape of songs. SASE. Reports in 6 months.

Musical Theater: "There are no limitations on subject matter or style. Cast size should be no more than 12 and sets should be simple. If music is required we would commission a composer, music would be used as a bridge between scenes or to underscore certain scenes in the play."

Productions: *Nice People*, by Tony Tanner (modern relationships); *The Club*, by Eve Merriam (the inequity of gender); and *Coming of Age* (original musical), by Tony Tanner (growing older and staying young).
Tips: "Submit work in good form and be patient. We look for musicals with a strong book and an engaging score with a variety of styles."

JENNY WILEY THEATRE, Box 22, Prestonsburg KY 41653-0022. (606)886-9274. General Manager: Tedi Vaughn. Play producer (Jenny Wiley Drama Association, Inc./JWDA). Produces 3 musicals plus 1 new musical/year. Plays are performed for "tourist audience, middle-income (20-25,000 average attendance in summer) in Jenny Wiley State Resort Park Amphitheatre." Pays outright purchase of $4,000-6,000, by royalty or per performance. "Additional payment in ensuing years of performance is variable." Query. SASE. Reports in 3 weeks.
Musical Theater: Seeking "family oriented shows not exceeding 2 hours performance time. The works should not call for more than 20 in the ensemble. Twentieth century setting works best, but historical works with music are strongly considered. Musicals should deal with Appalachia or Kentucky historical figures. Shows are produced outdoors—beware of flashy spectacle at outset of show (while it's still daylight). It must be, at its basis, family entertainment." Would also consider original music for use in play being developed "either as performance music (score and vocal), as part of a musical theater production, or as background (underscoring)."
Productions: *Jenny Wiley Story*, by Daniel A. Stein (historical with music); *Joseph & the Amazing Technicolor Dreamcoat*; *How To Succeed in Business Without Really Trying*; and *Grease*.
Tips: "Present a scenario/synopsis for consideration. If we are interested, we will give aid in developing it (and funding it if it falls under our funding resource availabilities). We would like to develop quality works with appropriate music that deal with historical themes or Appalachian tales. At present we need music for the Jenny Wiley Story. We want exciting original music based on colonial period music or adaptations of music of that period."

WILMA THEATER, 2030 Sansom St., Philadelphia PA 19103. (215)963-0249. Artistic Producing Director: Jiri Zizka; Artistic Producing Director: Blanka Zizka. Play producer. Produces 4-5 plays (1-2 musicals)/year. Plays are performed for a "sophisticated, adventurous, off-beat and demanding audience," in a 100-seat theater. Pays 6-8% of gross income. Submit synopsis, score and tape of songs. SASE. Reports in 10 weeks.
Musical Theater: Seeks "innovative staging, universal issues, political implications and inventive, witty approach to subject. We emphasize ensemble style, group choreography, actors and musicians overlapping, with new, inventive approach to staging. Do not exceed 4-5 musicians, cast of 12, (ideally under 8), or stage space of 30x20." Also interested in plays with music and songs.
Productions: *Hairy Ape*, by O'Neil (search for self-identity); *The Mystery of Irma Zep* by Charles Ludlum; *Incommunicado*, by Tom Dulak; *Marat/Sade* (basic questions of human existence); and *Three Guys Naked From the Waist Down* (worship of success).

*WISDOM BRIDGE THEATRE, 1559 W. Howard St., Chicago IL 60626. (312)743-0486. Producing Director: Jeffrey Ortmann. Play producer. Estab. 1974. Produces 4 plays and 1 musical/year. Plays performed in a 200-seat professional, off-loop theater. Pays 5-8% royalty. Submit through agent only. Does not return unsolicited material. Reports in 2 months.
Musical Theater: "Adult audience, not youth or children's theater. Musical should be well-written, average 2 hours in length. This is a smaller theater, so cast size should be limited." Considers original music for use in plays being developed or for use on existing plays.
Productions: *Forever Plaid*, by Stuart Ross (50s and 60s); and *Lady Day*, by Lanie Robertson (Billy Holiday).

*WOMEN'S PROJECT AND PRODUCTIONS, JULIA MILES, ART DIRECTOR, 220 W. 42nd, 18th Floor, New York NY. (212)382-2750. Literary Manager: Victoria Abrash. Estab. 1978. Produces 3 plays and 1 new musical/year. Pays by outright purchase. Submit through agent only. SASE. Reports in 6 months. "Adult audience. Plays by women only."
Musical Theater: "We usually prefer a small to medium cast of 3-6. We don't want plays by male playwrights. We produce few musicals and produce only women playwrights."
Productions: *A . . . My Name is Alice*, conceived by Joan Micklin Silver and Julianne Boyd (satire of women's issues); *Ladies*, by Eve Ensler (homelessness); and *O Pioneers!*, by Darrah Cloud (adapted) from Willa Cather's novel.
Tips: "Resist sending early drafts of work."

WOOLLY MAMMOTH THEATRE CO., 1401 Church St., Washington DC 20005. (202)393-3939. Literary Manager: Greg Tillman. Play producer. Estab. 1978. Produces 3-4 plays/year. Submit complete manuscript and score and tape of songs. SASE. Reports in 8 weeks.

Musical Theater: "We do unusual works. We have done one musical, the *Rocky Horror Show* (very successful). 8-10 in cast. We do not wish to see one-acts. Be professional in presentation."
Productions: *The Day Room, Luna Vista, The Sound Man* and *The Rocky Horror Show.*
Tips: "Just keep writing! Too many people expect to make it writing one or two plays. I don't think a writer is up to speed until the fifth or sixth work!"

WORCESTER FOOTHILLS THEATRE CO., 074 Worcester Center, Worcester MA 01608. (508)754-3314. Literary Manager: Greg DeJarnett. Play producer. Estab. 1974. Produces 7 plays and 1 or 2 musicals (indefinite new musicals)/year. Receives 10 submissions/month. "General audience, multi-generational. Plays are produced at Worcester Foothills Theatre, a 349-seat Proscenium stage. Pays by negotiable royalty. Query with synopsis, character breakdown and set description. SASE. "Reports back in 4 weeks for synopsis, 3-4 months for scripts."
Musical Theater: "Full length preferred, one-acts considered. Any style or topic. No gratuitous sex, violence or language. Generally a cast of 8-10 and a single set but these are not rigid restrictions."
Productions: *Ain't Misbehavin*, by Richard Moltby and Murray Horowitz (Fat's Waller music); *A Day in Hollywood*, by Dick Vosburgh and Frank Lazarus; and *Little Shop of Horrors*, by Howard Ashman/Alan Menken.

Play Producers/'91-'92 Changes

The following markets appeared in the 1991 edition of *Songwriter's Market* but are absent from the 1992 edition. Most of these companies failed to respond to our request for an update of their listing. Others are not listed for a variety of reasons, which is indicated in parentheses following the company name. For example, they may have gone out of business, or they may have requested deletion from the 1992 edition because they are backlogged with material.

Arena Players Repertory Theatre (asked to be deleted)
Charlottetown Festival
The Cast Theatre
David J. Cogan
Creative Productions, Inc.
Deep Ellum Theatre Group/

Underman Theatre (asked to be deleted)
Delaware Theatre Company
Steve Dobbins Productions
Green Mountain Guild
Kawartha Festival
Jan McArt's Cabaret Theatre

New Tuners Theatre
New Voices: A Writer's Theatre
Round House Theatre
Shenandoah Playwrites Retreat
Theatre-in-the-Schools, Inc.

Fine Arts

The fine arts market is very different from the other markets in this book. The song selection and marketing concerns that weigh on the minds of pop music industry professionals in New York, Los Angeles and Nashville really don't apply to the markets in this section. These markets are for composers of "classical," "serious" or "fine arts" music who do not wish to make "songs" out of their works, but want exposure for their concert music.

All of the groups listed in this section have indicated an interest in hearing new music. From small community groups to major symphony orchestras, they are open to new talent and feel their audiences are progressive enough to support original concert music. While most of these companies usually are unable to pay much (if any), it is a special occasion for a composer to have his work performed by an established orchestra or chorus in a hall filled with interested listeners. Plus, one performance may lead to others by different groups.

Bear in mind financial and artistic concerns as you submit material. Fine arts groups have extremely high standards. Don't hurt your chances by sending anything but your best compositions. Be professional when you contact the music directors, and keep in mind the audience they are selecting music for. Always follow their submission instructions diligently.

AFTER DINNER OPERA CO., INC., 23 Stuyvesant St., New York NY 10003. (212)477-6212. Executive Director: Dr. Richard Flusser. Opera Company. Estab. 1949. Members are professionals. Performs 30 concerts/year, including 4 new works. Concert hall "varies from 200 to 900 seats." Pays $0-500/performance. "Send SASE with postage, or materials cannot be returned. Do not send your only copy. Mail to: Dr. Richard Flusser (H140), After Dinner Opera Co., Inc., Queensborough Community College, 222-05 56th Ave., Bayside, NY 11364-1497. We report to all submissions in May of every year."
Music: "Seeks piano vocal scores with indications of instruments from 2-17, chamber size operas from 10 minutes long to 2 hours; no more than 10 singers. Especially interested in 3 character operas under one hour in length. Also interested in operas for children. No gospel or heavy metal rock." Performances: H.H. Beach's *Cabildo* (one act opera), William Grant Still's *Troubled Island* (opera) and Seymour Barab's *Fair Means or Foul* (children's opera).
Tips: "Start with an interesting, singable libretto. Make sure that you have the rights to the libretto."

THE AMERICAN BOYCHOIR, Lambert Dr., Princeton NJ 08540. (609)924-5858. Music Director: James H. Litton. Professional Boychoir. Estab. 1937. Members are highly skilled children. Performs 150 concerts/year, including 15-20 new works. Commissions 1-2 composers or new works/year. Performs community concerts and for local concert associations, church concert series and other bookings. Pays by commission. Query first. SASE. Reports in 6 months.
Music: "Dramatic works for boys voices (age 10-14); 15 to 20 minutes short opera to be staged and performed throughout the USA." Choral pieces, either in unison, SSA, SA or SSAA division; unaccompanied and with piano or organ; occasional chamber orchestra accompaniment. Pieces are usually sung by 26 to 50 boys. Composers must know boychoir sonority.
Performances: Ned Porem's *Who Has Seen The Wind* (song cycle for boys' voices); Daniel Pinkham's *Angels are Everywhere* (song cycle for boys' voices); and Milton Babbitt's *Glosses* (motet for boys' voices).

*ARIZONA THEATRE COMPANY, P.O. Box 1631, Tucson AZ 85702. Artistic Director: Gary Gisselman. Professional regional theater company. Members are professionsls. Performs 6 productions/year, including 1 new work. Audience is middle and upper-middle class, well-educated, aged 35-64. "We are a two-city operation based in Tucson, where we perform in a 603-seat newly renovated, historic

building, which also has a 100-seat flexible seating cabaret space. Our facility in Phoenix, the Herberger Theater Center, is a 712-seat, proscenium stage." Pays 4-10% royalty. Query first. Reports in 5 months.
Music: Musicals or musical theater pieces. 15-16 performers maximum including chorus. Instrumental scores should not involve full orchestra. No classical or operatic.
Performances: Barbara Damashek's *Quilters* (musical theater piece); Sondheim/Bernstein's *Candide* (musical); and Anita Ruth/American composer's *Dreamers of the Day* (musical theater piece).
Tips: "As a regional theater, we cannot afford to produce extravagant works. Plot line and suitability of music to further the plot is an essential consideration."

*ASHEVILLE SYMPHONY ORCHESTRA, P.O. Box 2852, Asheville NC 28802. (704)254-7046. Music Director: Robert Hart Baker. Symphony orchestra, chamber ensemble, and youth orchestra. Performs 20 concerts/year, including 2 new works. Members are professionals. Commissions 1 composer or new work/year. Concerts performed in Thomas Wolfe Auditorium, which seats 2,400. Subscription audience size is approximately 1,900. Pays by outright purchase (up to $1,000 when commissioning) or via ASCAP or BMI. Submit complete score and tape of pieces. SASE. Reports in 10 weeks.
Music: Seeks "classical, pops orchestrations, full modern orchestral works, concertos and chamber music. Winds in triplicate maximum; not too many extreme high ranges or exotic time signatures/ notation. Do not send unaccompanied choral works or songs for voice and piano only."
Performances: Douglas Ovens' *Play Us A Tune* (cycle for mezzo and orchestra); Howard Hanger's *For Barbara* (for jazz ensemble and orchestra); and Robert Hart Baker's *Fantasie* (arrangement of Chopin work for orchestra).

*AUGSBURG CHOIR (AUGSBURG COLLEGE), 731 21st Ave. S., Minneapolis MN 55454. Director of Choral Activities: Thomas D. Rossin. Vocal ensemble (SATB choir). Members are amateurs. Performs 30 concerts/year, including 5-10 new works. Commissions 1-2 composers or new works/year. Receives 10 submissions/year. Concerts are performed in churches, concert halls, schools. Pays by outright purchase. Submit complete score. SASE. Reports in 1 month.
Music: Seeking "sacred choral pieces, no more than 5-7 minutes long, to be sung a capella or with obligato instrument. Can contain vocal solos. We have 50-60 members in our choir. We do not want secular, jazz or pop songs."
Performances: Donald Busarow's *Hymne* and Leland Sateren's *Laudate* and Stephen Paulus' *Peace*.

*AUREUS QUARTET, 22 Lois Ave., Demarest NJ 07627-2220. (201)767-8704. Artistic Director: James J. Seiler. Vocal ensemble (a cappela ensemble). Estab. 1979. Members are professionals. Performs 35-40 concerts/year, including 3 new works. Pays $150-1,500 for outright purchase. Query first. SASE. Reports in 1 month.
Music: "We perform anything from pop to classic—mixed repertoire so anything goes. Some pieces can be scored for orchestras as we do pops concerts. Up to now, we've only worked with a quartet. Could be expanded if the right piece came along. Level of difficulty—no piece has ever been to hard." Does not wish to see electronic or sacred pieces. "Electronic pieces would be hard to program. Sacred pieces not performed much. Classical/jazz arrangements of old standards are great!"
Tips: "We perform for a very diverse audience—luscious, four part writing that can showcase well-trained voices is a must. Also, clever arrangements of old hits from '20s through '50s are sure bets. (Some pieces could take optional accompaniment.)"

BALTIMORE OPERA COMPANY, INC., 527 N. Charles St., Baltimore MD 21201. (301)727-0592. Artistic Administrator: James Harp. Opera company. Estab. 1950. Members are professionals. Performs 16 concerts/year. Receives 10 outside submissions/year. "The opera audience is becoming increasingly diverse. Our performances are given in the 3,000-seat Lyric Opera House." Pays by outright purchase. Submit complete score and tapes of piece(s). Reports in 1-2 months.
Music: "Our new General Director, Mr. Michael Harrison, is very much interested in presenting new works. These works would be anything from Grand Opera with a large cast to chamber works suitable for school and concert performances. We would be interested in perusing all music written for an operatic audience."
Performances: Bizet's *Carmen*, Verdi's *Un Ballo in Maschera*, Puccini's *Madama Butterfly* and Verdi's *Don Carlo*.
Tips: "Opera is the most expensive art form to produce. Given the current economic outlook, opera companies cannot be too avant garde in their selection of repertoire. The modern operatic composer must give evidence of a fertile and illuminating imagination, while also keeping in mind that opera companies have to sell tickets."

BILLINGS SYMPHONY, 104 N. Broadway, Billings MT 59101. (406)252-3610. Music Director: Dr. Uri Barnea. Symphony orchestra, orchestra and chorale. Estab. 1950. Members are professionals and amateurs. Performs 10 concerts/year, including 5-8 new works. Audience: mostly adults. Hall: Alberta

Bair Theater (capacity 1,418). Pays by royalty or outright purchase. Query first. SASE. Reports in 4 months.

Music: Any style. Traditional notation preferred.

Performances: Ellen Taaffe Zwilich's *Images* (two pianos and orchestra), Allen Vizzutti's *Snow Scenes* (trumpet and orchestra) and Graham Whettam's *An English Suite* (orchestra).

Tips: "Write *good* music. Make sure score and parts are legible and ready for use (rehearsal numbers, other instructions, etc.)."

THE BOSTON MUSICA VIVA, Suite 203, 295 Huntington Ave., Boston MA 02115-4401. Manager: David Chambless Worters. Chamber music ensemble. Estab. 1969. Members are professionals. Performs 12-20 concerts/year, including 6-10 new works. Commissions 3-5 composers or new works/year. "We perform our subscription series in a hall that seats 300, and our audience comes from Boston, Cambridge and surrounding areas. Frequent tours have taken the ensemble across the U.S. and the world." Pays by commission. Submit complete score and tapes of piece(s). Does not return unsolicited material. Reports in months.

Music: "We are looking for works for: flute, clarinet, percussion, piano, violin, viola and cello plus vocalist (or any combination thereof). Made for no more than 10 performers. We're looking for exciting avant garde music. We don't particularly want to see anything on the pop side."

Performances: HK Gruber's *Cello Concerto in One Movement* (chamber concerto); Paul Earls' *Eliotime* (chamber work); and Kathryn Alexander's *Song of Songs* (song cycle).

BRECKENRIDGE MUSIC INSTITUTE, P.O. Box 1254, Breckenridge CO 80424. (303)453-9142. Executive Director: Pamela G. Miller. Chamber orchestra with ensembles: brass, woodwind and string quartets and a vocal quartet. Estab. 1980. Members are professionals. Performs more than 30 concerts/year, including several new works. Commissions 1 composer or new work/year. "We perform our main season in a tent—we are in a resort area, so our audiences are a mix of local citizens and visitors." Chamber orchestra concerts: 300-400 people; chamber ensemble recitals: 85-150 people; choral/orchestra concert: 450 people. "Our contracts include remarks, notes and commissioned work." Query first. Does not return unsolicited material. Usually reports in several months, but depends on the time of year the work is submitted.

Music: "Typically, we try to premiere an orchestral piece each year and highlight the composer's other work during a 4-5 day composer-in-residence program. We need *chamber* orchestra or ensemble music only—nothing for more instrumentation." Doesn't want to see "pops."

Performances: Evan Copley's *Symphony No. 8* (world premiere); Cecil Effinger's *Capriccio for Chamber Orchestra* (world premiere); William Schmidt's *Miniatures for Chamber Orchestra* (premiere).

BREMERTON SYMPHONY ASSOCIATION INC., 535B 6th St., P.O. Box 996, Bremerton WA 98310. (206)373-1722. Contact: Music Director. Sympony orchestra. Estab. 1942. Members are amateurs. Performs 8 concerts/year, including a varying number of new works. The audience is half seniors, half adult. 1,200-seat hall in Bremerton High School; excellent acoustics. Query first.

Music: "Should be good for competent community orchestras."

*BREVARD SYMPHONY ORCHESTRA, INC., P.O. Box 361965, Melbourne FL 32936-1965. (407)242-2024. General Manager: Alan D. Jordan. Symphony orchestra. Estab. 1954. Members are professionals and amateurs. Performs 15-20 concerts/year. "King Center for the Performing Arts, Melbourne, FL: 1,842 seats; Fine Arts Auditorium, Cocoa, FL: 599 seats; Astronaut High School Auditorium, Titusville, FL: 399 seats." Pay negotiable "(VERY limited funding)." Submit complete score and tapes of piece(s). SASE. Reports in 2 months.

Music: "Submit orchestral works with and without soloists, full symphonic orchestration, 5-45 minutes in length, contemporary and popular styles as well as serious compositions." "No non-orchestral materials. Our community is fairly conservative and inexperienced in contemporary music, so a subtle, gradual introduction would be appropriate."

Performances: Dvorak's *Cello Concerto in B Minor, Op. 104*; Shostakovich's *Festive Overture, Op. 96*; *The Messiah*; Mozart's *Symphony No. 38 in D*; Persichetti's *Serenade No. 5, Op. 43*; Griffes' *Poem for Flute and Orchestra*; and Schumann's *Symphony No. 3 in E♭, Op. 97 "Rhenish."*

Tips: "Remember the audience that we are trying to introduce and educate."

CABRILLO MUSIC FESTIVAL, 9053 Soquel Dr., Aptos CA 95003. (408)662-2701. Executive Director: Tom Fredericks. Contemporary/classical music festival. Estab. 1963. Members are professionals. Performs 12 concerts/year. "Our audience consists of people interested in contemporary classical music. We perform in a variety of halls including churches, theaters and outdoor concert sites." Commissioning of new works for a fee. Query first. Submit complete score and tapes of piece(s). SASE. Reports in 2 months.

Performances: Lou Harrison's *Grand Duo* (World Premiere, chamber music for violin and piano); Chinary Ung's *Inner Voices* (West Coast Premiere, full orchestra); and Gordon Mumma's *Than Particle* (percussion and computer).
Tips: "Scores should be sent to Cabrillo Composers Project, % Larry Duckles, 16 Gibbs Ct., Irvine CA 92715. All scores should be sent priority mail. California composers who wish to submit orchestral scores for reading during the 1991 Festival should do so by 12/31/91. Composers must be able to verify that they have been residents of CA for at least one year."

CANADIAN CHILDREN'S OPERA CHORUS, #215, 227 Front St. E., Toronto **Canada** M5A 1E8. (416)366-0467. Manager: Suzanne Bradshaw. Children's vocal ensemble. Estab. 1968. Members are amateurs. Performs 2-3 concerts/year. Performs choral Christmas concert in a church with candlelight; spring opera production often at Harbourfront, Toronto. Pays by outright purchase; "CCOC applies to Ontario Arts Council or the Canada Council for commission fees." Query first. SAE and IRC.
Music: "Operas of approximately 1 hour in length representing quality composers. In addition, the portability of a production is important; minimal sets and accompaniment. CCOC prefers to engage Canadian composers whose standards are known to be high. Being a nonprofit organization with funding difficulties, we prefer piano accompaniments or just a few instruments."
Performances: Derek Holman's *Sir Christëmas* (20-minute choral suite with 5 instruments); Harry Somers' *A Midwinter Night's Dream* (1-hour opera); and Gian Carlo Menotti's *Chip and His Dog* (30-minute opera), all commissioned by CCOC.

CANADIAN OPERA COMPANY, 227 Front St. E, Toronto ON M5A 1E8 **Canada.** (416)363-6671. Artistic Planning Coordinator: Sandra J. Gavinchuk. Opera company. Estab. 1950. Members are professionals. 60 performances, including a minimum of 1 new work/year. Commissions maximum of 3 composers or new works/year. "New works are done in the Texaco Opera Theatre, which seats approximately 400." Pays by contract. Submit complete score and tapes of piece(s). SASE.
Music: Vocal works, preferably operatic in nature. 6 singers, 1½ hour in duration and 12 orchestral players. "Do not submit works which are not for voice. Ask for requirements for the Composers In Residence program."
Performances: John Oliver's *Guacamayo's Old Song and Dance* (opera/music theater); A. Berg's *Lulu*; and Harry Somer's *Mario and the Magician*.
Tips: "We have a Composers-In-Residence program which is open to Canadian composers or landed immigrants 40 years of age or under."

CAPITAL UNIVERSITY CONSERVATORY OF MUSIC OPERA/MUSICAL THEATRE, 2199 E. Main St., Columbus OH 43209-2394. (614)236-6122. Director, Opera/Musical Theatre: William Florescu. College opera/musical theater program. Estab. 1970. Members are students. Performs 2 concerts/year, including 1-2 new works. Commissions 1 composer or new work/year. Receives 3-4 outside submissions/year. "The audience is basically a community arts audience and family and friends of performers. Mees Hall Auditorium (cap. 1,100) is where we perform big, standard works. The Toledo Room (cap. 255) is where we perform chamber and experimental works. Both of these halls are to be upgraded and renovated in the next year-and-a-half." Pays by royalty or $50-150 per performance. Submit complete score and tapes of piece(s). SASE. Reports in 3-4 weeks.
Music: "I am seeking music theater pieces, particularly of a 'chamber' nature. I am open to a wide variety of musical styles, although the music should be singable for undergraduates; piano or small ensemble accompaniment. Ideally, pieces should be for 4-6 performers, most of whom will be able to tackle a wide variety of musical styles. Ideal length for works should be 15 minutes to 45 minutes. I am not particularly interested in 'rock' pieces, although if they work theatrically, I would certainly consider them."
Performances: Chris Becker's (a Capital student) *Satie* (music theater piece); Gustav Holst's *The Wandering Scholar* (chamber opera); and Milton Granger's *The Proposal* (chamber opera).
Tips: "If a composer is interested in writing for the situation we have here at Capital, I would suggest he or she either write or call me to *specifically* discuss a project. This will help both sides bring the performance about."

CARSON CITY CHAMBER ORCHESTRA, P.O. Box 2001, Carson City NV 89702-2001 or 191 Heidi Circle, Carson City NV 89701-6532. (702)883-4154. Conductor: David C. Bugli. Amateur community orchestra. Estab. 1984. Members are amateurs. Performs 5 concerts, including 1 new work/year. Receives 3 outside submissions/year. "Most concerts are performed for about 250 listeners in the Carson City Community Center Auditorium, which seats 840. However, the mid-December concerts have

Listings of companies in countries other than the U.S. have the name of the country in boldface type.

audiences as large as 700. We have no provisions for paying composers at this time but may later." Query first. Reports in 2 months.

Music: "We want classical, pop orchestrations, orchestrations of early music for modern orchestras, concertos for violin or piano, holiday music for chorus and orchestra (children's choirs available), music by women, music for brass choir. Most performers are amateurs, but there are a few professionals who perform with us. Available winds and percussion: 2 flutes and flute/piccolo, 2 oboes (E.H. double), 3 clarinets in B flat, 1 bass clarinet, 2 bassoons, 3 horns, 4 trumpets, 3 trombones, 1 tuba, timpani, and some percussion. Strings: 10-12-3-5-2. Avoid rhythmic complexity (except in pops); no 12-tone music that lacks melodic appeal. Composers should contact us first. Each concert has a different emphasis. Note: Associated choral group, Carson Chamber Singers, performs several times a year with the orchestra and independently."

Performances: David Bugli's *State of Metamorphosis* (overture). Premieres to date include an overture and arrangements of Christmas and popular tunes.

Tips: "It is better to write several short movements well than to write long, unimaginative pieces, especially when starting out. Be willing to revise after submitting the work, even if it was premiered elsewhere."

CARSON-DOMINQUEZ HILLS SYMPHONY, % Music Dept. California State University, Dominquez Hills, Carson CA 90747. (213)516-3947. Music Director: David Champion. Symphony orchestra. Estab. 1973. Members are professionals and amateurs. Performs 4-5 concerts/year, including 2-3 new works. Concerts performed in University Theatre (485 seats), Community Center (1000 seats) and an annual July 4th "Pops" Concert in Olympic Velodrome (10,000 attendance). Pays $100-200 for outright purchase or $25-200/performance. Query first, then submit complete score and tape of pieces. SASE.

Music: "Especially interested in women composers or ethnic minorities." Seeks arrangements for July 4th concert and annual children's concerts. 60-65 performers maximum. Does not wish to see "highly esoteric contemporary music or music which requires numerous unusual instruments."

Performances: Zwillich's *Symphony No. 1*.

CASCADE SYMPHONY ORCHESTRA, 9630 214th Pl. S.W., Edmonds WA 98020. (206)778-6934. Director/Conductor: Robert Anderson. Manager: Ed Aliverti. Symphony orchestra. Estab. 1962. Members are professionals and amateurs. Performs 4-5 concerts/year, including 2-3 new works. "Audience is knowledgeable with a variety of backgrounds and interests—excellent cross-section. Perform in a rather old auditorium seating 950." Submit complete score and tapes of pieces. SASE. Reports in 6 weeks.

Music: "Music should be suitable for symphony orchestra. Nothing over 20 minutes."

Performances: Paul Creston's *Dance Overture* (various dance rhythms); and Daniel Barry's *Sound Scapes* (Premiere based on ostenatos).

CENTER FOR CONTEMPORARY OPERA, Box 1350, Gracie Station, New York NY 10028-0100. (212)870-2010. Director: Richard Marshall. Opera. Estab. 1982. Members are professionals. Performs 3 operas/year; all are new works. 247-seat theater. Pays royalties. Submit complete score and tapes of pieces. SASE.

Music: "Looking for full-length operas. Limited orchestras and choruses. Orchestra—not over 25."

Performances: Sullivan's *Dream Play* (opera); Britten's *The Prodigal Son* (opera) and Beeson's *My Heart is in the Highlands* (stage premiere, opera).

CHAMBER MUSIC IN YELLOW SPRINGS, INC., P.O. Box 448, Yellow Springs OH 45387. (513)767-1458. President: Bruce Bradtmiller. Chamber music presenting organization. Estab. 1983. Members are volunteer staff. Performs 5 concerts/year. "Have commissioned a composer once in 1989. The audience is very enthusiastic and quite knowledgeable in chamber music. The hall is a church, seating 280 with excellent acoustics." Pays $5,000 for outright purchase. Query first.

Music: "We are interested in innovative chamber music; however the composer should approach us with an ensemble identified. We are a chamber music presenting organization. We rarely present groups with more than 6 performers." Does not wish to see popular music.

Performances: Rick Sowash's *Anecdotes and Reflections* (instrumental, chamber work, violin, cello, piano, clarinet).

Tips: "We book primarily on the quality of ensemble. A composer should make an arrangement with a top-notch group and approach us through the ensemble's agent."

CHORUS OF WESTERLY, 22 High St., Westerly RI 02891. (401)596-8664. Music Director: George Kent. Community chorus. Estab. 1959. Members are professionals and amateurs. Performs 12 concerts/year including 1-2 new works. "4 'major works' concerts/year and 2 'pops' concerts/year. Summer pops reaches audiences of 28,000." Pays by outright purchase. Submit complete score and tapes of pieces. Reports in 3 weeks.

Music: "We normally employ a full orchestra from Boston. Major works desired—although 'good' pops charts considered."
Performances: Brahm's *Requiem* and Holst's *Choral Symphony*.

CINNABAR OPERA THEATER, 3333 Petaluma Blvd. N., Petaluora CA 94952. (707)763-8920. Artistic Director: Marvin Klebe. Opera company. Estab. 1974. Members are professionals. Performs 35 concerts/year, including 2 new works. "Audience is ⅓ local, ⅓ Sonoma county, ⅓ greater San Francisco Bay area; theater is converted mission revival schoolhouse seating 99-150; no orchestra pit." Pays by arrangement with composer. Query first. SASE.
Music: "Our musical taste can best be described as eclectic. We produce full-length and one-act works; small orchestrations are preferred. Small casts are preferred. We are interested in works appropriate for opera singers who are also actors."

CITY SUMMER OPERA, Box A-44, 50 Phelan Ave., San Francisco CA 94112. (415)239-3132. Music Department: Madeline Mueller. Opera company. Estab. 1987. Members are professionals and amateurs. Performs 8 concerts/year, including 1 new work. Concert hall seats 300. Chamber orchestra of 30 performers or less. Pays by royalty. Submit complete score and tape of pieces. SASE. Reports in 3 months.
Music: "Contemporary operas suitable for young singers (some young professionals) and a chorus of amateurs. Level of difficulty must be appropriate for young voices and not too complicated musically. Must have large cast (65 approximately). Prefer text in English. Angular lines, difficult harmonies not appropriate. Dramatic works preferred—with interesting story or 'message.' Must be interesting musically but not too complex for our students."
Performances: Zigron's *Sweeney Agonistes* (chamber opera); Virgil Thomson's *Mother of Us All* (opera); and Kurtweill's *Mahogany* (opera).

THE CLEVELAND PLAY HOUSE, P.O. Box 1989, Cleveland OH 44106. (216)795-7000. Literary Manager: Roger T. Danforth. Professional theater. Estab. 1915. Pays by royalty. Agent submission only. Reports in 4 months.
Music: Seeks only musical theater.
Tips: "Find agent to submit."

*COLORADO CHILDREN'S CHORALE, Suite 1020, 910 15th St., Denver CO 80202. (303)892-5600. Artistic Director: Duain Wolfe. Vocal ensemble and highly trained children's chorus (also adult symphony chorus). Estab. 1974. Members are professionals and amateurs. Performs 100-110 concerts/year, including 3-5 new works. Commissions 1-3 composers or new works/year. Receives 3-4 outside submissions/month. "Our audiences' ages range from 5-80. We give school performances and tour (national, international). We give subscription concerts and sing with orchestras (symphonic and chamber). Halls: schools to symphony halls to arenas to outdoor theaters." Pays $100-500 outright purchase (more for extended works). Submit complete score and tapes of piece(s). Does not return unsolicited material. Reports in 2 months.
Music: "We want short pieces (3-5 minutes): novelty, folk arrangement, serious; longer works 5-20: serious; staged operas/musicals 30-45 minutes: piano accompaniment or small ensemble; or possible full orchestration if work is suitable for symphony concert. We are most interested in SA, SSA, SSAA. We look for a variety of difficulty ranges and encourage very challenging music for SSA-SSAA choruses (32 singer, unchanged voices). We don't want rock, charts without written accompaniments or texts that are inappropriate for children. We are accessible to all audiences. We like some of our repertoire to reflect a sense of humor, others to have a message. We're very interested in well crafted music that has a special mark of distinction."
Performances: Henry Milliconi's *The Midnight Ride of Paul Revere* (contemporary; Randall Thompson's *The Place of the Blest* (sacred, medieval text); and Sherman and Sherman's *Tom Sawyer*).
Tips: "Submit score and tape with good cover letter, resume and record of performance. Wait at least 3 weeks before a follow-up call or letter."

COMMUNITY FINE ARTS CENTER, 400 C St., Rock Springs WY 82901. (307)362-6212. Director: Allen Keeney. Orchestras. Estab. 1946. Members are amateurs and professionals. Performs 3-5 concerts/year. "We lean toward orchestras for more classical orientated people. Performances are held in the Rock Springs High School Auditorium with seating capacity of 800 seats." Pays $5,000-12,500/performance. Query first. Does not return unsolicited material. Reports in 1 month.
Music: "We prefer blues and symphony arrangements. No rock."
Performances: Charles Dickens' *Christmas Carol* (musical theater); and Ballet West's *Giselle* (ballet).

CONCORDIA: A CHAMBER SYMPHONY, 21st Floor, 330 Seventh Ave., New York NY 10001. (212)967-1290. Manager: Emilya Cachapero. Symphony orchestra. Estab. 1984. Members are professionals. Performs 5 concerts/year, including 5-6 new works. Commissions 2-3 composers or new works/

year. Receives 35-40 outside submissions/year. "Lincoln Center, Alice Tully Hall. Audiences between 28 and 50 years, mostly." Pays contest winner's prize and copying. Query first. SASE. Reports in 4 months.

Music: "Seeks jazz-influenced works for chamber symphony, 6-9 minutes, 2,2,2,2/2,2,1,0/strings percussion; piano (if needed).

Performances: Jon Deak's *The Legend of Spuyten Duyvil*; Laura Karpman's *Switching Stations* (jazz fusion); Michael Daugherty's *Snap*; and Jeffrey Hass's *City Life* (jazz scored for chamber orchestra).

CONNECTICUT CHORAL ARTISTS, 90 Main St., New Britain CT 06051. (203)224-7500. Artistic Director: Richard Coffey. Professional concert choir. Estab. 1974. Members are professionals. Performs 10-15 concerts/year, including 2-3 new works. "Mixed audience in terms of age and background; performs in various halls and churches in the region." Payment "depends upon underwriting we can obtain for the project." Submit complete score and tapes of pieces. SASE. Reports in 6 months.

Music: Seeking "works for mixed chorus of 36 singers; unaccompanied or with keyboard and/or small instrumental ensemble; text sacred or secular/any langauge; prefers suites or cyclical works, total time not exceeding 15 minutes. Performance spaces and budgets prohibit large instrumental ensembles. Works suited for 750-seat halls are preferable. Substantial organ or piano parts acceptable. Scores should be very legible in every way. Though not a requirement, we find that works with sacred texts get wider coverge."

Performances: Bernstein's *Missa Brevis (*1988 regional premiere; based upon his *The Lark)*; Frank Martin's *Mass for Double Chorus (*1928 (regional premiere); Villa-Lobos' *Magdalena (*1948 performed 1987 revival at Lincoln Center and recorded for CBS).

Tips: "Use conventional notation and be sure manuscript is legible in every way. Recognize and respect the vocal range of each vocal part. Work should have an identifiable *rhythmic* structure."

DENVER CHAMBER ORCHESTRA, #1360, 1616 Glenarm Pl., Denver CO 80202. (303)825-4911. Executive Director: Barbara Kelly. 40 piece chamber orchestra. Estab. 1968. Members are professionals. Performs 35 concerts/year, including 1 new work. Commissions 1 composer or new work/year. "Perform in a 500-seat auditorium in an arts complex and at The Paramount Theatre in Denver which seats 2,000. Usually pay the composer's air fare and room and board for the performance; sometimes an additional small stipend." Query first. SASE. Reports in 2 weeks.

Music: Seeks "pieces orchestrated for 35-40 instruments. No pop, symphonic."

Performances: Edward Smaldone and Otto Luening's *Dialogue*.

Tips: "Submit a query, which we will submit to our music director, Joan Falletta."

DIABLO VALLEY PHILHARMONIC, 321 Golf Club Rd., Pleasant Hill CA 94523. (415)685-1230, Ext. 454. Conductor: Fredric Johnson. Symphony orchestra. Estab. 1974. Members are both professionals and amateurs. Performs 5 concerts/year, including 2 new works. Sometimes commissions 1 composer or new work/year. "We perform in a 400-seat hall to a California audience. They'll go for anything new or unique if we don't overload them (i.e. quantity)." Pays through ASCAP. Submit complete score or complete score and tapes of piece(s). SASE.

Music: "Music must be for full romantic orchestra, without extra parts (harp, piano, English horn, Kazoo)—it's too expensive. Pieces should be of reasonable difficulty for about 65 musicians."

Performances: Marilyn Shufro's *Ciudades: Toledo y Seville* (orchestra); Earle Browne's *Modules* (orchestra); and Aaveneinen's *Rain* (suite for accordian/strings).

Tips: "Our orchestra is formed at the beginning of the season; it's tough to get the good musician in mid-season, so please avoid extra or exotic instruments."

EASTERN NEW MEXICO UNIVERSITY, Station 16, Portales NM 88130. (505)562-2736. Director of Orchestral Activities: Robert Radmer. Symphony orchestra, small college-level orchestra with possible choral collaboration. Estab. 1934. Members are students (with some faculty). Performs 6 concerts/year, including up to 2 new works. Receives 10 submissions/year. "Our audiences are members of a college community and small town. We perform in a beautiful, acoustically fine 240-seat hall with a pipe organ." Query first, submit complete score and tapes of piece(s), submit complete score or submit through agent only. SASE. Reports in 2 months.

Music: "Pieces should be 12-15 minutes; winds by 2, full brass. Work shouldn't be technically difficult. Organ, harpsicord, piano(s) are available. We are a small college orchestra; normal instrumentation is represented but technical level uneven throughout orchestra. We have faculty available to do special solo work. We like to see choral-orchestral combinations and writing at different technical levels within each family, i.e., 1st clarinet might be significantly more difficult than 2nd clarinet."

Performances: Sclater's *Intro to the Orchestra* (kids' concert); Bach's *Cantata No. 150* (classical); and Sibelius' *Finlandia* (classical).

Tips: "I would like to see a choral/orchestral score in modern idiom for vocal solo(s), a chamber choir and large chorus used in concertino/ripeno fashion, with full brass and percussion, featuring first chair players."

*EL TEATRO CAMPESINO, P.O. Box 1240, San Juan Bautista CA 95045. (408)623-2444. Music Director: David Silva. Theater company. Members are professionals and amateurs. Performs 2 concerts/year including 2 new works. Commissions 0-1 composer or new work/year. "Our audiences are varied—non-traditional and multi-cultural. We perform in our own theater as well as area theaters and other performing arts spaces (indoor and outdoor)." Pays $50-750 for outright purchase. Query first. SASE. Reports in 1 month.
Music: "We are interested in cultural and multi-cultural music in all styles and lengths. We are especially interested in blends of cultural/contemporary and indigenous music."
Performances: *La Vizgen Del Tepeyac* (cultural); *The Rose of the Rancho* (Old California); and *Zoot-Suit* (1940s).

EUROPEAN COMMUNITY CHAMBER ORCHESTRA, 2, Five Bells, Offwell, Devon EX14 95B **United Kingdom**. Phone: (44)404 83 701. General Manager: Ambrose Miller. Chamber orchestra. Members are professionals. Performs 70 concerts/year, including 5-10 new works. Commissions 2 composers or new works/year. Performs regular tours of Europe, Americas and Asia, including major venues. Pays $500/performance. Query first. SAE and IRC. Reports in 3 months.
Music: Seeking compositions for strings, 2 oboes and 2 horns with a duration of about 10 minutes.
Performances: Patricia Saunders' *Four Pieces* (strings); Celedonio Romero's *Concierto Malaga* (guitar and chamber orchestra); and Jane O'Leary's *The Petals Fall* (strings, oboes and horns).
Tips: "Write something short and not too difficult, so it is easy to program."

FAIRFAX SYMPHONY ORCHESTRA, P.O. Box 1300, Annandale VA 22003. (703)642-7200. Composer-in-Residence: Daniel E. Gawthrop. Symphony orchestra. Estab. 1957. Members are professionals. Performs 50 concerts/year, including 2 new works. Receives 12 submissions/year. "We perform at two halls: George Mason University's Concert Hall which seats 1939; and The Kennedy Center Concert Hall which seats 2759." Pays by commission. Query first. SASE. Reports in 2-3 months.
Music: "All styles appropriate to symphony orchestra (106 players) or chamber orchestra (50 players). Do not want pop music."
Performances: Ellen Taafe Zwilich's *Cello Symphony*; David Stock's *Symphony in One Movement*; Michael Colgrass's *As Quiet As . . .*; Daniel E. Gawthrop's *Merlin's Vision*; and Nicholas Maw's *Spring Music*.

*FINE ARTS STRINGS, 14507 Trading Post Dr., Sun City West AZ 85375. (602)584-6989. Musical Director & Conductor: Walter F. Moeck. String orchestra (27 members). Members are professionals and amateurs. Performs 6 concerts/year. "Concert Hall at the Scottsdale Jr. College. Other various halls in and around Phoenix and Scottsdale, Arizona." Query first. SASE.
Music: "The 'Fine Arts' Orchestra is a string orchestra. We perform Mozart, Bach, Corelli and modern music for string orchestra. We have 27 performers in the orchestra. We perform rather difficult music. Example—Poulencs' *Organ Concerto*. We look for good musical substance for strings. Good rhythmic and melodic qualities."
Performances: Bach's *Brandenburg No. 3* (Baroque); Nielsen's *Suite for Strings* (modern romantic); and Mozart's *Adagio & Fugue* (classic).
Tips: "Write practical for the instruments and know their limitations and in a manner that shows off the instruments' best qualities."

*THE FLORIDA ORCHESTRA, Suite 512, 1211 N. Westshore Blvd., Tampa FL 33607. (813)286-1170. General Manager: Alan Hopper. Symphony orchestra. Estab. 1968. Members are professionals. Performs 150 concerts/year, including 2 new works. Audiences are "young professionals to established community business people. We perform in three halls of high artistic quality." Average seating is 2,000 per hall. Submit complete score and tapes of piece(s). SASE. Reports in months.
Music: "We want high quality popular programming for pops, park and youth concerts; 5-15 minutes in length utilizing full orchestra. We don't want electric instruments. We like nostalgia, pops or light classical arrangement."
Performances: Joan Tower's *Island Rhythms* (contemporary symphonic); Harbison's *Remembering Gatsby* (contemporary symphonic); and St. Saens' *Carnival of the Animals* (light classical).
Tips: "Make it marketable within the context of a symphony orchestra that is trying to appeal to a wide audience."

FLORIDA SPACE COAST PHILHARMONIC, INC., P.O. Box 3344, Cocoa FL 32924 or 2150 Lake Dr., Cocoa FL 32926. (407)632-7445. General Manager: Alyce Christ. Artistic Director and Conductor: Maria Tunicka. Philharmonic orchestra and chamber music ensemble. Estab. 1986. Members are professionals. Performs 7-14 concerts/year. Concerts are performed for "average audience—they like familiar works and pops. Concert halls range from 600 to 2,000 seats." Pays 10% royalty (rental); outright purchase of $2,000; $50-600/performance; or by private arrangement. Query first; submit complete score and tape of piece(s). SASE. Reports ASAP; "our conductor tours frequently thus we have to keep material until she has a chance to see and hear it."

Music: Seeks "pops and serious music for full symphony orchestra, but not an overly large orchestra with unusual instrumentation. We use about 60 musicians because of hall limitations. Works should be medium difficulty—not too easy and not too difficult—and not more than 10 minutes long." Does not wish to see avante-garde music.

Performances: Marta Ptaszynska's *Marimba Concerto* (marimba solo).

Tips: "If we would commission a work it would be to feature the space theme in our area."

GRAND TETON MUSIC FESTIVAL, P.O. Box 490, Teton Village WY 83025. (307)733-3050. Music Director: Ling Tung. Symphony orchestra and chamber music ensemble. Estab. 1962. Members are professionals. Performs 45 concerts/year. Commissions 1-3 new works/year. "Concerts are aimed at people interested in wide variety of classical music. Concert hall is an enclosed, all-wood structure seating approximately 700." Pays weekly honorarium plus travel expenses. Query first. Does not return unsolicited material. Reports in 6 months.

Music: "For the most part, the Festival performs standard repertoire. New music is usually restricted to small ensembles (less than 10 players), although occasionally, if a noted composer is involved, the orchestra will perform a large scale work. Generally less than 10 players, no restriction on difficulty. No musical theater or opera."

Performances: Joan Tower's *Petroushskates* (quintet: flute, clarinet, violin, cello and piano); John Harbison's *Woodwind Quintet*; George Crumb's *Gnomic Variations* (solo piano).

GREAT FALLS SYMPHONY ASSOCIATION, Box 1078, Great Falls MT 59403. (406)453-4102. Music Director and Conductor: Gordon J. Johnson. Symphony orchestra and chamber music ensemble. Estab. 1959. Members are professionals and amateurs. Performs 7 concerts (2 youth concerts)/year, including 2-3 new works. "Our audience is conservative. Newer music is welcome; however, it might be more successful if it were programatic." Plays in Civic Center Auditorium seating 1,850. Negotiable payment. Submit complete score and tapes of pieces. SASE.

Music: "Compositions should be for full orchestra. Should be composed ideomatically for instruments avoiding extended techniques. Duration 10-20 minutes. Avoid diverse instruments such as alto flute, Wagner tuben, saxophones, etc. Our orchestra carries 65 members, most of whom are talented amateurs. We have a resident string quartet that serves as principals. Would enjoy seeing a piece for quartet solo and orchestra. Send letter with clean score and tape (optional). We will reply within a few weeks."

Peformances: Bernstein's *Chichester Psalms* (choral and orchestra); Hadkinson's *Boogie, Tango and Grand Tarantella* (bass solo); and Milhand's *Le Boef Sur le Toit* (orchestral).

Tips: "Music for orchestra and chorus is welcome. Cross cues will be helpful in places. Work should not require an undue amount of rehearsal time (remember that a concerto and symphony are probably on the program as well)."

GREATER NASHVILLE ARTS FOUNDATION, 111 Fourth Ave. S., Nashville TN 37201. (615)259-6374. Program Coordinator: Chuck Bedwell. Community arts organization. Estab. 1982. Performs 52 concerts/year "in art galleries and shopping malls; places where we can reach the general public of Nashville, which is our constituency, as we are affiliated with the Metropolitan Nashville Arts Commission." Pays union scale or better per performance. Query first. Does not return unsolicited material. Reports in 2 months.

Music: "We program performances of all kinds of music, from classical to country, jazz to rock."

Tips: "Work should have a multi-level appeal."

*THE GRINNELL ORCHESTRA, Dept. of Music, Grinnell College, Grinnell IA 50112. (515)269-3064. Assistant Professor of Music: Jonathan Knight. Chamber orchestra. Members are amateurs and college students. Performs 4-5 concerts/year. "Our audience includes students, faculty and staff of the college, members of the community of Grinnell and nearby towns; performances in Herrick Chapel, seating capacity about 700." Composers are not paid. Submit complete score and tapes of piece(s). SASE. Reports in 2-3 months.

Music: "We can perform scores for chamber-size orchestras: about 20 strings, pairs of woodwinds and brass, harp and keyboard instruments. Please avoid exotic percussion. I would consider any length or style, as long as the difficulty of the work did not exceed the ability of the group, which may be characterized as a fairly good undergraduate ensemble, but not as capable as a conservatory orchestra. No 'pops' music."

Performances: Schubert's *Symphony No. 6*; Lou Harrison's *Seven Pastorales*; and Charles Ives's *The Gong on the Hook and Ladder*.

Tips: "Composers may submit completed works to me, with or without tapes, for consideration. As the relative strengths of my orchestra change from year to year due to normal student turnover, it is difficult to give specific tips other than those above regarding size and difficulty of scores."

GULF COAST SYMPHONY, Box 4303, Biloxi MS 30535. (205)666-9554. Music Director: Andrew Harper. Symphony orchestra. Estab. 1962. Members are professionals and amateurs. Performs 4 concerts/year, including 2 new works. Commissions variable number of composers or new works/year. Saenger Theater in Biloxi seats about 900. Children's Concert and Pops Concert in Biloxi Coliseum seats 2,700. Query first. Submit complete score and tapes of piece(s). "We do not return unsolicited submissions." Reports in 6 months.
Music: Classical, pops, children's pieces. Winds triplicate. Be careful of exposed writing for 2nd violin and viola. Do not wish to see unaccompanied choral pieces, vocal solo or aria with piano accompaniment. Pieces should contain melodic interest. For children's pieces, a narrator or involvement of audience.
Performances: M. Rot's *Overture* (orchestral); L. Zanirelli's *Lexicon of Beasties* (children's concert); and R. Peck's *The Thrill of the Orchestra* (children/youth concert).

*HASTINGS SYMPHONY ORCHESTRA, Fuhr Hall, 9th & Ash, Hastings NE 68901. (402)463-2402. Conductor/Music Director: Dr. James Johnson. Symphony orchestra. Estab. 1926. Members are professionals and amateurs. Performs 6-8 concerts/year, including 1 new work. "Audience consists of conservative residents of mid-Nebraska who haven't heard most of the classics." Concert Hall: Masonic Temple Auditorium (950). Pays commission or rental. Submit complete score and tapes of piece(s). Does not return unsolicited material. Reports in 2 months.
Music: "We are looking for all types of music within the range of an accomplished community orchestra. Write first and follow with a phone call."
Performances: Bernstein's *Candide Overture*; Richard Wilson's *Silhouette (1988)*; and Menotti's *Doublebass Concerto (1983)*.
Tips: "Think about the size, ability and budgetary limits. Confer with our music director about audience taste. Think of music with special ties to locality."

HIGH DESERT SYMPHONY ORCHESTRA, P.O. Box 1255, Victorville CA 92392. (619)247-6966. Music Director: K.C. Manji. Symphony orchestra. Estab. 1969. Members are both amateurs and professionals. Performs 15 concerts/year, including 2 new works/year. Plays in a 500 seat auditorium. Community-based audience; middle class incomes. "Composers usually not paid." Submit complete score and tapes of piece(s). SASE. Reports back in 2 months.
Music: "Style: American nationalistic; length: up to 30 minutes. Level of difficulty must be intermediate/advanced, depending on amount of rehearsal time. Right now I would appreciate anything that would stress ensemble blending and be fairly tonal in color. This is an orchestra in the process of rebuilding and going forward. Submit pieces 5-15 minutes in length, classical size orchestration (2,2,2,2,2,2,0,0) or small ensembles."
Performances: Villa-Lobos' *Fantasia for Sax* (concerto); Stravinsky's *8 Instrument Miniatures* (small ensemble); and J. Berger's *Overture for Strings* (string orchestra).
Tips: "Make the works accessible in difficulty, i.e., rhythm and instrumentation."

THE PAUL HILL CHORALE (AND) THE WASHINGTON SINGERS, 5630 Connecticut Ave., NW, Washington DC 20015. (202)364-4321. Music Director: Paul Hill. Vocal ensemble. Estab. 1967. Members are professionals and amateurs. Performs 8-10 concerts/year, including 2-3 new works. Commissions one new composer or work every 2-3 years. "Audience covers a wide range of ages and economic levels drawn from the greater Washington, DC metropolitan area. Kennedy Center Concert Hall seats 2,700." Pays by outright purchase. Submit complete score and tapes of pieces. SASE. Reports in 2 months.
Music: Seeks new works for: 1)large chorus and symphony orchestras; 2)chamber choir and small ensemble.
Performances: Argento's *Peter Quince at the Clavier*; Rorem's *An American Oratorio*; and Luboff's *A Choral Extravaganza*.
Tips: "We are always looking for music that is high quality and accessible to Washington audiences."

HOUSTON YOUTH SYMPHONY & BALLET, P.O. Box 56104, Houston TX 77256. (713)621-2411. Orchestra Operations Manager: Jesse P. Johnson. Symphony orchestra. Estab. 1947. Members are students. Performs 6 concerts/year. "Performs in Jones Hall: 3,000 seat concert hall; Cullen Performance Hall: 1,000 seat concert hall for general audiences." Query first. SASE. Reports in 2 months.
Music: Uses string orchestra music suitable for players age 7-14. "Full orchestra music suitable for 14-23 players."
Performances: Dzubay's *Ascension* (brass/percussion); and Turner's *Opening Night* (symphony).

HUNTSVILLE YOUTH ORCHESTRA, P.O. Box 7223, Huntsville AL 35801. (205)880-0622. Music Director: Frederick R. Mayer. Chamber music ensemble and youth orchestra. Estab. 1961. Members are students. Performs 4-10 concerts/year, including 0-2 new works. Commissions 0-1 composers or new works/year. Receives 10 submissions/year. Audience is mainly family adults of performers, students, musicians and music educators. Perform at Von Braun Civic Center Concert Hall; 2,200 seats. "Acoustically excellent." Payment individually arranged. Submit complete score and tapes of piece(s) or send representative works, score and tape. "We prefer to keep copies of scores and tapes on file." Reports in 3 weeks initially; 6 months for final decision.

Music: No longer than 3-15 min; Instrumentation: 3-2(1)-2(1)-2, 4331, Perc (3) pno, strings. "Works possessing good rhythmic motion and drive; with dramatically contrasting sections. Areas of tonal centricity helpful. Good parts for all (when possible) and great parts for a few in typically strong instruments. NYSMA Grade 2-3 and 4-6. Must have strong audience appeal on single listening."

Performances: Les Fillmer's *Finale from "Quodlibet"* (full orchestra); and Joann Forman's *Ballet in Progress* (full orchestra).

Tips: "Beautiful sounds that have something to say. Excitement, contrast; challenging, worthwhile parts for young players."

IDAHO STATE—CIVIC SYMPHONY, P.O. Box 8099, Pocatello ID 83209. (208)236-3479. Music Director/Conductor: Dr. Thom Ritter George. Symphony orchestra. Estab. 1934. Members are professionals and amateurs. Performs 12 concerts/year, including 4 new works. "Audience varied, ranges from highly musically educated to little background in music; in general, prefer music with which they have some familiarity. The symphony performs in Goranson Hall, on the campus of Idaho State University—seats 444, good acoustics. We consider works by composers scoring for full orchestra. The majority of our activities are oriented to the classical music audience." Pays by outright purchase or per performance. Query first. Does not return unsolicited material

Performances: Griffes' *Poem for Flute and Orchestra*; Edouard Lalo's *Symphonie Espagnole*; and Sibelius' *Symphony No. 2 in D Major, OP. 43*.

Tips: "Write a work which is structurally sound and score idiomatically for the symphony orchestra."

INTER SCHOOL ORCHESTRAS OF NEW YORK, 125 E. 87 St., New York NY 10128. (212)410-9823. Conductor: Jonathan Strasser. Youth orchestra. Estab. 1972. Members are amateurs. Performs 12-15 concerts/year. "Varied churches to major halls like Carnegie or Alice Tully. Varied audiences." Pays for outright purchase. Does not return unsolicited material.

Music: Orchestra of 70 (advanced) of 30 strings, horns and trumpets; intermediate group of 70; 3 beginner orchestras with 20-30 each. Cheval works or works with huge orchestration. "Composers should realize that players are 18 and younger so works should not be outrageously complicated or difficult."

Performances: Gordon Jacob's *Concerto for Trombone* (full orchestra); Carl Kudik's *Gerald McBoing Boing* (narrated work with violas, celli, winds [single] 2 trumpets and 23 percussion instruments); and Samuel Baker's *Adagio for Strings*.

Tips: "Remember that we are an educational, music making organization seeking to give the youngsters in our orchestras the best learning and performing experiences possible. We wish to stretch their experience but not present them with impossibilities."

ISRAEL SINFONIETTA BEER SHEVA, 12 Derech Hameschachrerim, P.O. Box 6080, Beer Sheva 84 299 **Israel**. Phone: (57)31616. Managing Director: Mr. Moshe Shemma. Chamber orchestra. Members are professionals. Performs 120 concerts/year, including 5 new works. Commissions 1 new composer or new work/year. "Our Beer Sheva audience is a serious but rather conservative one. Concerts are performed in a small hall seating 400 people. In other locations, throughout Israel, audiences are more broad-minded; halls seat 600-800 people." Pays by agreement. Query first; "it is wise to check before sending score to ensure that orchestration is suitable for our orchestra." SAE and IRC. Reports in 3 months.

Music: Seeking pieces with "orchestration: 7/6/5/5/2; 2/2/2/2 2/2/0/0 and percussion. No limitation on difficulty."

Performances: John Downey's *Discourse for Oboe, Strings and Harpsicord*; Tzvi Avni's *Meditations on a Drama*; and André Hajdu's *Piano Concerto*.

JACKSON SYMPHONY ORCHESTRA, P.O. Box 3429, Jackson TN 38303. (901)427-6440. Executive Director: Dr. Carol L. Quin. Symphony orchestra. Estab. 1961. Members are professionals. Performs more than 60 concerts/year, including 1 new work. Commissions 1 composer or new work/year. "The audience is a conservative group with an average age of 50. The hall seats 2,000. Four concerts on the season are 'classical,' three are 'Cabaret' with table seating and dinner." Composer is paid by prize for composition competition. Query first. SASE.

Music: "Music should be melodic, not complicated. No more than 60 performers. Do not send strange requests for instrumentation."

Tips: "Write a letter about the piece—send instrumentation list and description with length."

JOHNSON CITY SYMPHONY ORCHESTRA, P.O. Box 533, Johnson City TN 37604. (615)926-8742. Symphony orchestra. Estab. 1969. Members are professionals and amateurs. Performs 7 concerts/year, including 1 new work. Commissions 1 composer or new work/year. Pays $1,500 outright purchase. Query first. Does not return unsolicited material. Reports in 1 month.
Music: "We have done 3 minute pieces for strings, brass or winds; up to 45 minute pieces for full orchestras. We can perform pieces of moderate difficulty—strings 10-10-6-4-3, 2 oboes max, 1 English horn max, 3 trombones, 1 tuba. Preference has been given to Tennessee residents or composers with a strong connection to Tennessee."
Performances: Lewis Songer's *MacRae Meadow* (brass piece, 3 min.); Martin Herman's *Up a Tree* (storyteller and orchestra); and Alan Murchie's *Daen for Brass and Woodwinds*.
Tips: "Music should not be too atonal. Should be something with market interest and have local color."

KENTUCKY OPERA, 631 S. Fifth St., Louisville KY 40202. (502)584-4500. Opera. Estab. 1952. Members are professionals. Performs 22 concerts/year. Performs at Whitney Hall, The Kentucky Center for the Arts, seating is 2,400; Bomhard Theater, The Kentucky Center for the Arts, 620; Macauley Theater, 1,400. Pays by royalty, outright purchase or per performance. Submit complete score and tapes of piece(s). SASE. Reports in 6 months.
Music: Seeks opera—1 to 3 acts with orchestrations. No limitations.
Performances: Daniel Dutton's *The Stone Man* (1 act opera); Philip Glass' *The Fall of the House of Usher* (2 act opera).

KITCHENER-WATERLOO CHAMBER ORCHESTRA, Box 937, Waterloo ON N2J 4C3 **Canada**. (519)744-3828. Music Director: Graham Coles. Chamber Orchestra. Estab. 1985. Members are professionals and amateurs. Performs 8 concerts/year, including some new works. "We perform at St. John's Lutheran Church (seats 500), Humanities Theatre, University of Waterloo (seats 1,200). We perform mainly baroque and classical repertoire, so that any contemporary works must not be too dissonant, long or far fetched." Pays by music rental and performing rights fees only. Submit complete score. "It's best to query first so that we can outline what not to send. Include: complete CV—list of works, performances, sample reviews." SASE. Reports in 4 weeks.
Music: "Musical style must be accessible to our audience and players (3 rehearsals). Length should be under 20 minutes. Maximum orchestration 2/2/2/2 2/2/0/0 Timp/1 Percussion Harpsichord/organ String 4/4/3/3/1. We have limited rehearsal time, so keep technique close to that of Bach-Beethoven. We also play chamber ensemble works—octets, etc. We do not want choral or solo works."
Performances: John Weinzweig's *Divertimento I* (flute and strings); Peter Jona Korn's *4 Pieces for Strings* (string orch.); and Graham Coles *Variations on a Mozart Rondo* (string orch.).
Tips: "If you want a first-rate performance, keep the technical difficulties minimal."

L.A. SOLO REPERTORY ORCHESTRA, 7242 Louise Ave., Van Nuys CA 91406. (818)342-8400. Music Director: James Swift. Symphony orchestra. Estab. 1968. Members are professionals and amateurs. Performs 6 concerts/year, including 7 new works. Commissions 1 composer or new work/year. "General audience. Hall of Liberty: 1,400 seats, Van Nuys Jr. High School auditorium: 800 seats." Pay is negotiated. Submit complete score and tapes of pieces. SASE. Reports in 6 weeks.
Music: "20th century symphonic, particularly with solo instruments. Many composers extend development to point of boredom, so we reserve right to cut or perform single movements. Use of odd instruments or greatly extended sections tends to inhibit performance. No hard rock—even when intended for large orchestra."
Performances: Mario Bruno's *Voyage and Discovery* (3 mvt Columbus Quincentenary Premiere); and Shigeru Hirisawa's *Concerto for Violin* (3 mvt Premiere).
Tips: "Tapes are nice, but a good score is essential. Edit the work! Keep the moderately sophisticated audience in mind. Compose for audience enjoyment if you want your work repeated."

LAKESIDE SUMMER SYMPHONY, 236 Walnut Ave., Lakeside OH 43440. (419)798-4461. Contact: G. Keith Addy. Conductor: Robert L. Cronquist. Symphony orchestra. Members are professionals. Performs 8 concerts/year. Perform "Chautauqua-type programs with an audience of all ages (2-102). Hoover Auditorium is a 3,000-seat auditorium." Query first. SASE.
Music: Seeking "classical compositions for symphony composed of 50-55 musicians. The work needs to have substance and be a challenge to our symphony members. No modern jazz, popular music or hard rock."
Performances: Richard's Nanes' *Prelude, Canon & Fugue* (classical).

LAMARCA AMERICAN VARIETY SINGERS AND IMAGE, 2424 W. Sepulveda Blvd., Torrance CA 90501. (213)325-8708. Director/Manager: Priscilla LaMarca. Vocal ensembles. Estab. 1979. Members are professionals and amateurs. Performs 20 concerts/year, including 3-10 new works. Commissions 2 composers or new works/year. Performs at major hotels, conventions, community theaters, fundraising events, cable television, community fairs and Disneyland. Submit complete score and tapes of pieces. SASE. Reports in 2 months.

Music: "Seeks 3-10 or 15 minute medleys; a variety of musical styles from Broadway—pop styles to humorous specialty songs. Top 40 dance music, Linda Ronstadt-style to Whitney Houston. Light rock and patriotic themes. Also interested in music for children. No heavy metal or anything not suitable for family audiences."

Performances: Perform at Disneyland, Stouffers Hotel, on cable TV, at celebrity benefits and at patriotic events.

Tips: "Make sure the lyrics fit the accents of the music.[Be-caúse, not Bé-cause]. Make sure there is continuity of the song's meaning throughout. Keep the beat about 120-140 bpm. and no lengthy instrumental interludes."

*LEHIGH VALLEY CHAMBER ORCHESTRA, Box 2641, Lehigh Valley PA 18001. (215)770-9666. Music Director: Donald Spieth. Symphony orchestra. Estab. 1979. Performs 35 concerts/year, including 1-2 new works. Members are professionals. Commissions 1-2 composers or new works/year. Orchestra has "1,000 subscribers for Friday/Saturday pairs of concerts. Also offers youth programs, pops, etc." Pays by outright purchase for commissioned work. Submit complete score and tape of pieces. Reports in 2 months.

Music: "Original compositions for chamber orchestra instrumentation: 2/2/2/2-2/2/1/0 percussion, strings (7/6/4/4/2); amateur of no interest. A composer should not write specifically for us without an agreement."

Performances: Libby Larsen's *Cold, Silent Snow* (flute and harp concerto); James Brown's *Symphony for Chamber Orchestra* (symphony in 3 movements); and Larry Lipkis's *Capprizio* (15 minute, one movement work).

Tips: "Send a sample type and score of a work(s) written for the requested medium."

LINCOLN YOUTH SYMPHONY ORCHESTRA, P.O. Box 82889, Lincoln NE 68501. (402)436-1631. Music Director: Dr. Brian Moore. Youth orchestra. Estab. 1956. Members are amateurs. Performs 3 concerts/year. "The audience is made up of parents, friends, University teachers and teachers from other schools and a general audience." Pays by outright purchase. Query first. SASE. Reports in 2 weeks.

Music: "Needs orchestral compositions of moderate difficulty—new music/contemporary styles are welcomed. Orchestra is full winds and strings."

Performances: Schubert's *Unfinished*; Percy Grainger's *Walking Song* (winds only); and Shastakovich's *Cello Concerto* (solo).

Tips: "Call and talk to us first."

LITHOPOLIS AREA FINE ARTS ASSOCIATION, 3825 Cedar Hill Rd., Canal Winchester OH 43110. (614)837-8925. Series Director: Virginia E. Heffner. Performing Arts Series. Estab. 1973. Members are professionals and amateurs. Performs 5-6 concerts/year, including 1 or 2 new works. "Our audience consists of couples and families 35-65 in age. Our hall is acoustically excellent and seats 400. It was designed as a lecture-recital hall in 1925." Composers "may apply for Ohio Arts Council Grant under the New Works category." Pays 1-2% royalty, $66/performance. Query first. SASE. Reports in 4 weeks.

Music: "We prefer that a composer is also the performer and works in conjunction with another artist, so that they could be one of the performers on our series. Piece should be musically pleasant and not too dissonant. It should be scored for small vocal or instrumental ensemble. Dance ensembles have difficulty with 15' high 15' deep and 27' wide stage. We do not want avant-garde or obscene dance routines. No ballet (space problem). We're interested in something historical—national, or Ohio emphasis would be nice. Small ensembles or solo format is fine."

Tips: "Personally talk to me first and then I can show you our performance hall. Through ORACLE, we might be able to block-book you. We can't financially commission a work—only as it's performed by an artist on our series."

THE LOUISVILLE ORCHESTRA, 609 W. Main St., Louisville KY 40202. (502)587-8681. Music Director: Lawrence Leighton Smith. Symphony orchestra. Estab. 1937. Members are professionals. Performs 100 concerts/year, including 6 new works. Commissions 2 composers or new works/year. MasterWorks classical subscription concerts are performed in the 2,400-seat Whitney Hall of the Kentucky Center for the Arts. "Our audience varies in age from University students to seniors and comes from the areas surrounding Louisville in Kentucky and Indiana." Pays by commission. Submit complete score and tapes of piece(s). Does not return unsolicited material. Reports in months. Planning done year in advance of performance.

Music: "All styles appropriate to symphony orchestras. No chamber works, pop music or lead sheets." Orchestration for standard symphony orchestra. No pop music/pop vocal/New Age. Enclose a tape of performance or keyboard realization.

THE LYRIC OPERA OF DALLAS, Suite 818, 8111 Preston Rd., Dallas TX 75225. (214)368-2183. Artistic Director: John Burrows. Music theater company. Estab. 1982. Members are professionals. Performs 3-4 concerts/year, including 3 new works in 6 years. "The Majestic Theatre in downtown Dallas is a beautifully restored Victorian building, seating 1,500. There are excellent stage facilities and a good orchestra pit." Query first or submit complete score and tapes of piece(s). SASE. Reports in 3 weeks; 2 months if submitted between April and August.
Music: "We want stageworks for not in excess of 35 onstage performers, and 30 orchestra musicians. The only other limitation is that all performances are in English. We don't want works demanding exceptional scenic demands or very large forces. The Lyric Opera of Dallas is known for performing a high proportion of comedic material, and has no tradition of presenting esoteric works."
Performances: Robert Rodriguez *The Ransom of Red Chief* (one-act opera); Leonard Bernstein *Candide* (comic operetta, SW premier of opera version); and Alan Strachan/Benny Green's *Cole* (revue of life and compositions of Cole Porter).

MANITOBA CHAMBER ORCHESTRA, 202-1317A Portage Ave., Winnipeg Manitoba R3G OV3 **Canada.** (204)783-7377. General Manager: Rita Manzies. Chamber orchestra. Estab. 1972. Members are professionals. Performs 10 concerts/year, including 2 new works. "Audiences are generally professionals—also many young people. We perform two series—one in a church (seats 1,000) and the other in a hotel (seats 250). Candlelight concerts in the hotel are more casual." Pays by commission. Query first. SASE.
Music: Seeks "music for string orchestra and one solo instrument. Limitations: 22 strings; no pop music."
Performances: Chan Ka Nin's *Treasured Pastun Leisure Pleasure* (orchestral); and Jerome Summers' *Caprice* (strings and wind).

*MELODIOUS ACCORD, INC., #9D, 801 West End Ave., New York NY 10025. (212)663-1165. Composition Search: Kenneth Nafziger. Vocal ensemble. Estab. 1984. Members are professionals. Performs 3 concerts/year, including 4 new works. Commissions 3 composers or new works/year. "Audience is mostly urban professionals and choral music lovers. We perform in a church." Pays by fee. "We sponsor a biennial composition search. Information is sent to various magazines that composers read and the deadline for material is March 31. Composers inquire, we send more information, then they submit score and tape." SASE. Reports in 2 months.
Music: "Submit melodic choral music for 16 voice professional ensemble, a cappella, or with a few instruments accompanying. 15-20 minutes in length. No non-melodic, non-singable music or music with electronic accompaniment." Apply through composition search.
Performances: Alice Parker's *Listen Lord* (spiritual for solo contralto/chorus/bass and drum accompaniment); Bern Herbolsheimer's *Te Deum* (chorus with piano 4-hands accompaniment); and Carol Barnett's *Epigrams, Epitaphs* (chorus with piano 4-hands accompaniment).
Tips: "Write melodic, singable, enjoyable music that respects the poetry."

MILWAUKEE YOUTH SYMPHONY ORCHESTRA, 929 N. Water St., Milwaukee WI 53202. (414)272-8540. Music Coordinator: Susan Chandler. Youth orchestra. We also have a Junior Wind Ensemble. Estab. 1956. Members are students. Performs 10-12 concerts/year, including 1-2 new works. "Our groups perform in Uihlein Hall at the Performing Arts Center in Milwaukee. The audiences usually consist of parents, music teachers and other interested community members. We usually are reviewed in either the Milwaukee Journal or Sentinel." Query first. SASE.
Tips: "Be sure you realize you are working with students and not professional musicians. The music needs to be technically on a level students can handle."

The asterisk before a listing indicates that the listing is new in this edition. New markets are often the most receptive to unsolicited submissions.

*THE MIRECOURT TRIO, #11M, 3832 Quail Pl., Waterloo IA 50701. (319)273-6073. Contact: Terry King. Chamber music ensemble; violin, cello, piano. Estab. 1973. Members are professionals. Performs 30-80 concerts/year, including 2 new works. Commissions 2 composers or new works/year. Concerts are performed for a "general chamber music audience of 100-1,500. Pays by outright purchase $1,000-3,000 or recording subsidy. Query first. SASE.
Music: Seeks "music of short to moderate duration (5-20 minutes) that entertains, yet is not derivative or cliched. Orchestration should be basically piano, violin, cello, occasionally adding soprano and/or clarinet. We do not wish to see academic or experimental works."
Performances: Lou Harrison's *Trio*; John Cooper's *Parameter*; and Vincent Persichetti's *Parable*.
Tips: "Submit works that engage the audience or relate to them, works that reward the players as well."

MISSOURI SYMPHONY SOCIETY, P.O. Box 1121, Columbia MO 65205. (314)875-0600. Artistic Director and Conductor: Hugo Vianello. Symphony orchestra, chamber music ensemble, youth orchestra and pops orchestra. Estab. 1970. Members are professionals. Performs 23 concerts/year, including up to 8 new works. Commissions one composer or new work/year. Receives 10-15 outside submissions/ year. "Our home base is a 1,200-seat renovated 1928 movie palace and vaudeville stage. Our home audience is well-educated, including professionals from Columbia's five hospitals and three institutions of higher education. Our touring program reaches a broad audience, including rural Missourians and prison inmates." Pays through ASCAP and BMI. Submit complete score (and if available, tapes of pieces). SASE. Reports in 8 weeks.
Music: "We want good orchestral (chamber) music of any length — 2222/2200/timp/strings/piano. There are no limitations on difficulty."
Performances: Marshall Fine's *Missouriana* (world premiere, chamber orchestra); Norman Dello Joio's *New York Profiles* (chamber orchestra); Richard Nanes' *Symphony for Strings*; and Charles Hoag's *When the Yellow Dream Leaves Fell* (world premiere).

MOHAWK TRAIL CONCERTS, P.O. Box 843, Greefield MA 01302. (413)774-3690. Managing Director: Diane Brano. Chamber music presenter. Estab. 1970. Members are professionals. Performs approximately 10 concerts/year, including 2-3 new works. "Audience ranges from farmers to professors, children to elders. Concerts are performed in churches and town halls around rural Franklin County, Massachusetts." Pays by performance. Query first. Does not return unsolicited material. Reports in months.
Music: "We want chamber music, generally not longer than 30 minutes. We are open to a variety of styles and orchestrations for a maximum of 8 performers. We don't want popular, rock or theater music."
Performances: Michael Cohen's *Fantasia for Flute Piano and Strings* (chamber); William Bolcom's *Nes Songs* (piano/voice duo); and Arnold Black's *Laments & Dances* (string quartet and guitar duo).
Tips: "We are looking for artistic excellence, a committment to quality performances of new music, and music that is accessible to a fairly conservative (musically) audience."

MUSIC THEATRE OF ARIZONA, 918 S. Park, Tempe AZ 85281. (602)829-0008. Artistic Director: Ron Newcomer. Music theater production company. Members are professionals and amateurs. Performs 3-7 productions/year, including 1-2 new works. "Performs in three venues: 3,000 seat concert hall (Grady Garmage on ASU's campus) a 7,000 seat concert hall (Sundome) and an 800 seat theater (Herberger) where new works are performed." Pays by royalty (varies). Submit complete score and tapes of pieces. SASE. Reports in 3 months.
Music: "New musical theater works, preferably small casts — any style, from country to jazz, pop, etc. Small casts up to 15 preferred due to Lort contract demands. No hard rock or material you would consider inappropriate for general public. Suggestive material is fine, vulgar is another thing. Stick to *musical theater* format."
Performances: Rodgers & Hammerstein's *The King & I* (musical); Maltby & Shine's *Starting Here Starting Now* (musical revue); Charles Strouse's *Annie* (musical); and Nancy Loeds' *Scrooge: A Musical Ghost Story* (premiere musical).
Tips: "Be flexible and willing to share and blend with the creative effort, without giving up your initial intent. Share and compromise instead of becoming stubborn or closed to any new idea or thought."

MUSIC TODAY, 129 W. 67th St., New York NY 10023. (212)362-8060. Director: Andrew Berger. Chamber music ensemble. Estab. 1980. Members are professionals. Performs 3 concerts/year, including 3-5 new works. Commissions 1-2 composers or new works/year. "We perform in Merkin Concert Hall, seating 450 people. We are trying to attract a large, diverse audience of serious music listeners. Pays by royalty and commissioning grants where available. Query first by mail, please, with resume and letter." SASE. Reports in 3 months.

Music: "Seeks works for conductor and chamber ensemble of varied instrumentation from 6 to 22 players. We are particularly interested in crossover and semi-theatrical pieces. We are not interested in pop music per se."

Performances: Xavier Rodriguez's *Tango* (chamber with vocal soloist); Larry Bell's *Piano Concerto*; and Christopher Rouse's *Rotae Passionis* (chamber with clarinet solo).

Tips: "Write good music. We are especially interested in considering scores from women and minorities although decisions are made strictly according to the quality of the work."

NASHVILLE OPERA ASSOCIATION, 1900 Belmont Blvd., Nashville TN 37212. (615)292-5710. General Director: Kyle Ridout. Opera company. Estab. 1981. Members are professionals and amateurs. Performs 7 concerts/year. "Tennessee Performing Arts Center (Jackson Hall) has 2,400 seats and Tennessee Performing Arts Center (Polk Theatre) has 1,100 seats." Pays by outright purchase. Submit complete score and tapes of pieces. SASE. Reports in 1 month.

Music: Seeks opera and music theater pieces, sometimes accept one-acts."

Performances: Donizetti's *Lucia di Lammermoor*; Sullivan's *The Mikado*; and Verdi's *Il Travatore* (opera).

Tips: "Be willing to work through the score by subjecting the work to readings/workshop."

NATIONAL ASSOCIATION OF COMPOSERS/USA, Nacusa P.O. Box 49652, Los Angeles CA 90049. (213)541-8213. President: Marshall Bialosky. Chamber music ensemble and composers' service organization. Estab. 1932. Members are professionals. Performs 5-9 concerts/year—all new works. Receives 20-30 outside submissions/year. Usually performed at universities in Los Angeles and at a mid-town church in New York City. Paid by ASCAP or BMI (NACUSA does not pay composers). Must join the organization to receive services. SASE. Reports in 3 months.

Music: Popular chamber music for five or fewer players; usually in the 5 to 20 minute range. "Level of difficulty is not a problem; number of performers is solely for financial reasons. We deal in serious, contemporary concert hall music."

Performances: Howard Quilling's *Sonata #1 for Violin and Piano*; David Soley's *Labertino for Solo Flute* and Byong-kon Kim's *Four Short Pieces for Piano*.

NEBRASKA CHAMBER ORCHESTRA, 749 NBC Center, Lincoln NE 68508. (402)477-0366. General Manager: Peggy Chesen. Chamber orchestra. Estab. 1976. Members are professionals. Performs 6 concerts/year, including 6 new works. "We perform in two halls; one seats 850 and the other seats 2,250. Our audience is primarily 30 years or older in age, a minimum of a Bachelor's Degree in education and a minimum income of $25,000. Our audience comes from metropolitan Lincoln and surrounding areas." Pay by individual arrangements. Query first. SASE.

Music: "We want all styles appropriate to a chamber orchestra and accessible for the Nebraska audience. Lengths can vary but prefer approximately 30 minute pieces. NCO standard instrumentation: 2-2-2-2 2-2 timpani, strings (65442). No excessively difficult works due to limited rehearsal time."

Performances: Loris Tjeknavorian's *Concerto for Guitar and Orchestra, "Zareh" Op. 39* (concerto); Russell Peck's *Amber Waves for Brass Quartet and Orchestra* (miniature classical symphony); and Michael Torke's *Ash (1988)*.

NEW YORK CITY OPERA EDUCATION DEPARTMENT, New York State Theater, Lincoln Center, New York NY 10023. (212)870-5635. Administrative Director: Nancy Kelly. "The company produces a total of 110 educational programs/year and one fully staged children's opera each season for elementary, junior high and high school students. Different introductory programs cover opera, operetta, musical comedy and other forms of music theater. The programs are performed in the schools by professional singers with piano accompaniment. Schools must pay a set fee per performance. Query first.

Music: "We look for operas that are appropriate in subject matter for school-age children and theatrical enough to hold the students' attention. Works should be no longer than 1 hour in length in order to fit into class schedules. The limitations of school stages dictate minimal scenic and technical requirements. The total performing ensemble (singers and musicians) should not exceed 9."

Performances: *Opera Adventure, American Patchwork, On Broadway!*; and a newly commissioned opera, *East of the Sun, West of the Moon* by Robert Dennis and Stephen Phillip Policoff.

THE NEW YORK CONCERT SINGERS, 401 East 80th St., New York NY 10021. (212)879-4412. Music Director/Conductor: Judith Clurman. Chorus. Estab. 1988. Performs 2-3 concerts/year, including new works. Commissions 1 composer or new work/year. "Audience is mixture of young and old classical music 'lovers.' Chorus performs primarily at Menkin Concert Hall, NYC." Pays at completion of work. Query first or send score and tape with biographical data. SASE.

Close-up

Bruce Ferden
General Music Director
City of Aachen, Germany

According to Bruce Ferden, the outlook is sunny for young composers seeking performance opportunities for their symphonic works. Ferden should know. Prior to his recent appointment as General Music Director for the City of Aachen, Germany (the first American to hold the post), Ferden spent nearly ten years city-hopping from Lincoln, Nebraska to Spokane, Washington. He served as music director for both the Nebraska Chamber Orchestra and the Spokane Symphony Orchestra, getting firsthand knowledge about the mood of American audiences.

Ferden has had a personal hand in this change of climate. Much of his tenure at these regional orchestras was spent furthering support of living composers—stretching his audiences to receive new works and taking the music to the community through outdoor park concerts, run-out performances and radio broadcasts of the Spokane Symphony's regular subscription concerts. And according to Ferden, this rebirth of audience interest in new symphonic and operatic works is not limited to Lincoln and Spokane.

"I think there are more opportunities for young composers today than there have been in the past in America," he says. "There is just far more commissioning going on. There is a greater awareness of the importance of encouraging future Beethovens and Brahms—or Coplands and Bernsteins, to keep it in America."

Ferden says the nationwide establishment of commissioning projects and awards over the past ten years has encouraged music directors to incorporate more new works into their programming—to take chances with and give chances to new composers.

Ferden's efforts toward more innovative programming have earned recognition from the American Society of Composers, Authors and Publishers (ASCAP) three times—the Regional Award for Adventuresome Programming of Contemporary Music was awarded to the Spokane Symphony in 1989, and to the Nebraska Chamber Orchestra in 1987 and 1990.

A return to more lyrical, tonal composition has helped music directors ease their audiences into accepting new works, Ferden says. "I think we went as far as we could in alienating audiences with music that had shock value, or noise, or all kinds of different effects, or pieces in which the piano was ripped apart or burned on stage. There has been a real return to lyricism, to tonality, and I think that's good." The bottom line is, a composer has to write what's in his heart, but who cares if he writes all this music and it's never performed? Music at its fundamental basis is a communicative art. And if people are leaving the concert hall (mid-performance), you've got to say 'Gee, what happened?' And that has happened a lot in the 20th century. But I see a lot of composers writing music now that is liked on first hearing. I don't think one has to lower one's standards and become crassly commercial to write a piece that a general audience likes."

While audiences are receptive and performance opportunities are multiplying, the supply of quality new works still exceeds the ability of music directors to program them. To better their odds in a still-competitive field, Ferden recommends that composers get performance tapes and go easy on the quantity of submissions.

Ferden, a pianist who studied at Moorhead State College, the University of Miami, the University of Southern California and the Julliard School, recalls his early days: "When I was going to school, I would do anything I could to get players together to let me practice (conducting). One isn't given an orchestra to practice on. I was a pianist, so I would offer to accompany their recitals if they'd come and play a few rehearsals. And I think that's the main thing a new composer needs to do—to hear the music played by live performers and get their reactions. If that means you have to beg, borrow or hire the players to do it and conduct it yourself, do it. Get some tapes of the music so we can hear it."

Ferden says once the composer has his tapes, he needs to be selective about those he chooses to include in a submission packet. "One has to draw a balance between being too pushy and too assertive but yet getting the material out to the music directors who choose these works. One thing I don't like is when (composers) send just bundles and bundles of material. One or two reviews are fine—you don't have to send twenty-five. And a tape— not two tapes or three tapes—just one tape to give us a flavor of the piece. If someone likes it, they'll bite on it. They'll come to the composer and ask for more."

Ferden says it never hurts the composer to understand the orchestra he writes for. "It's been very helpful to us to have composers hear what the Spokane Symphony sounds like and then write a piece for us. If they know the orchestra I think (composers) can write a piece that is better suited to it."

Changes to the piece, while not inevitable, are something every new composer should be prepared for. "The truth of the matter is, music is a living, breathing art," Ferden says. "Every time it's performed it's going to be different—a different hall, a different group of performers—Mozart and Beethoven were changing things all the time. Mozart would add arias for different singers and different performers."

Many times Ferden handpicks for programming a submission that shows promise and represents an opportunity for learning for the composer and the orchestra. "Sometimes I'll choose a young composer who may not be technically totally advanced or in command of his material, but I hear something in the writing that is showing potential. You know, Verdi wrote quite a few before he wrote *La Traviata*. So I don't expect to get a fully blown masterpiece from every young composer."

—Anne M. Bowling

Music: Seeks music "for small professional ensemble, with or without solo parts, a cappella or small instrumental ensemble. Not for large orchestra and chorus (at this stage in the group's development). Looking for pieces ranging for 7-20 minutes."
Performances: Ned Rorem's *Homer: Three Scenes from the Eliad* (30 minutes/chorus/soloist/8 instruments); Richard Hundley's *Ball* (12 minutes/chorus/soloists from chorus/4 hand PN.); and Leonard Bernstein's *Missa Brevis* (15 minutes/chorus/2 percussionsists).
Tips: "When choosing a piece for a program I study both the text and music. Both are important."

NORFOLK CHAMBER MUSIC FESTIVAL/YALE SUMMER SCHOOL OF MUSIC, 96 Wall St., New Haven CT 06520. (203)432-1966. Summer music festival. Estab. 1941. Members are international faculty/artists plus students who are near professional. Performs 12 concerts, 14 recitals/year, including 3-6 new works. Commissions 0-1 composer or new work/year. The 1,100-seat Music Shed (built in 1906 by architect Eric K. Rossiter) is lined with California redwood, with a peaked cathedral, which creates wonderful acoustics." Pays a commission fee (set fee). Submit complete score and tapes of piece(s). SAE. Reports in 1 month.
Music: "Chamber music of combinations, particularly for strings, woodwinds, brass and piano. There are 1-2 chamber orchestra concerts per season which include the students and feature the festival artists. Other than this, orchestra is not a medium featured, rather, chamber ensembles are the focus."
Performances: Joan Panetti's *Fanfare* (trumpet quartet premiere); Martin Bresnick's *String Quartet #4*; and Jacob Druckman's *Incenters* (13 players).

NORTH ARKANSAS SYMPHONY ORCHESTRA, P.O. Box 1243, Fayetteville AR 72702. (501)521-4166. Music Director: Carlton Woods. Symphony orchestra, chamber music ensemble, youth orchestra and community chorus. Estab. 1954. Members are professionals and amateurs. Performs 20 concerts/year, including 1-2 new works. "General audiences—currently perform in churches and schools in six area cities." Pays $500 or more/performance. Query first. SASE.
Music: Seeks "audience pleasers—rather short (10-15 minutes); and full orchestra pieces for subscription (classical) concerts. Orchestra is 60-70 members."
Performances: Robert Mueller's *Deep Earth Passing*; and Will Gay Bottje's *Sounds from the West Shore*.

OLD STOUGHTON MUSICAL SOCIETY, P.O. Box 794, Stoughton MA 02072. (617)344-5993. President: Joseph M. Klements. Music Director: Raymond Fahrner. Community chorus. Estab. 1786. Members are amateurs. Performs 2 concerts/year. "Audience is general public." Query first. Does not return unsolicited material. Reports in 6 weeks.
Music: Seeks "choral compositions by American (preferably New England) composers. We have an extensive collection of materials from early American singing schools but have broadened repertoire to early and modern American composers. Chorus size less than 40, with 1-20 accompanists. Level of difficulty should be geared to accomplished amateurs."
Performances: E.A. Jones' *Easter Oratorio*; Everett Titcomb's *Christmas Story* (cantata); and Leo Sowerby's (anthems).

OPERA IN THE SCHOOLS, 4015 Spotswood Trail, San Antonio TX 78230. (512)699-8791. Director: Evelyn Troxler. Opera company: children's operas. Members are professionals. Performs 200 concerts/year, including 1 new work. Commissions 1 composer/year. "Operas are performed for children, grades kindergarten through 8. We perform in auditoriums, classrooms, gymnasiums, etc." Pays $40/performance. Submit complete score. SASE. Reports in 1 month.
Music: Seeking "operas for young audiences with a good bit of dialogue, not to exceed 30 minutes. 4-5 soloists, no chorus. Accompaniment suitable for piano, synthesizer, flute, clarinet and percussion (any or all of them). No more than 5 singers and 5 in the orchestra. Any level of difficulty. Special emphasis should be on story lines (comedy especially). Must be good theater as well as good music. Story must be full of adventure, not scary but fun; lines need to have comedy, music must be tuneful."
Performances: Rea's *The Wizard's Ring* and *The Enchanted Flute* (children's pieces); and Englebert Humperdinck's *Hansel and Gretel* (30 minute version).
Tips: "Find a good libretto, one which permits a lot of imagination in the staging."

OPERA ON THE GO, 184-61 Radnor Rd., Jamaica Estates NY 11432. (718)380-0665. Artistic Director: Jodi Rose. American opera chamber ensemble. Estab. 1985. Members are professionals. Performs about 30 operas/year; all new works. "We perform primarily in schools and community theaters. We perform only American contemporary opera. It must be lyrical in sound and quality as we perform for children as well as adults. We prefer pieces written for children based on fairy tales needing 4 to 6 singers." Pays $20 per performance. Query first then submit complete score and tapes of piece(s). SASE. Reports if requested within weeks on submissions; if unsolicited, about 2-3 months.
Music: Need works in all age groups including adults. For older ages the pieces can be up to 60 minutes. Rarely use orchestra. "Keep the music as short as possible since we do a prelude (talked) and postlude involving the children's active participation and performance. If it is totally atonal it will never work in the schools we perform in."
Performances: Edith Hemenway's *Goldilocks and the 3 Bears* (opera for N-3 grade); Mark Bucci's *Sweet Betsy From Pike* (opera for 6 grade-adult); and Seymour Barub's *Fair Means or Foul* (opera for grades 3-8).
Tips: "Be flexible. Through working with children we know what works best with different ages. If this means editing music to guarantee its' performance, don't get offended or stubborn."

ORANGE COUNTY OPERA, INC., P.O. Box 1470, Sunset Beach CA 90742. (213)592-2017. Artistic Director: Christopher Webb. Educational opera company. Estab. 1976. Members are professionals. Performs "300 concerts of one opera per year." Receives 4-5 outside submissions/year. "We are an educational opera company that performs in schools in Los Angeles and Orange Counties. We perform at the schools with an average audience of 300 per performance. We are interested in 30 minute operas." Payment open to negotiation. Query first. SASE. Reports in 2 months.
Music: "We want lyrical opera in English. We have done 30 minute versions of *Hansel and Gretel*, *Daughter of the Regiment*, *Act I—Tales of Hoffman*. We want to show off opera as another art form kids do not see or hear often. We want piano accompaniment and lively, humorous music and story. The maximum number of performers should be 5 plus accompanist. Singers are professional level. We don't want avant-garde, atonal music. We want very singable music. Our goal is to entertain with

excellent voices, story and music. We would like a show with both male and female singers, fast-paced; perhaps queries about specific ideas we could address better."

Performances: Mollicone's *The Starbird* (one act opera); Humperdinck's *Hansel & Gretel* (opera); and Rossini's *Barber of Seville* (opera).

Tips: "Show opera to be a wonderful visual and aural experience. Excite the kids—make them want to see and hear more. We would love to have a new work for our company and introduce young audiences to modern opera. We want a story line that will appeal to those audiences and create an interest in opera and musical theater/live theater."

PENSACOLA CIVIC BAND, 1000 College Blvd., Pensacola FL 32504. (904)484-1800. Director: Don Snowden. Community band. Estab. 1971. Members are professionals and amateurs. Performs 6 concerts/year. "Our audience varies in age and we play in a 300 seat auditorium." Query first. SASE.

Music: Popular medleys of Broadway shows and other familiar popular music. Standard instrumentation. No limit on difficulty.

*PERRY COUNTY COUNCIL OF THE ARTS, P.O. Box 354, Newport PA 17074. (717)567-7023. Executive Director: Carol O. Vracarich. Arts organization presenting various programs. Estab. 1978. Members are professionals and amateurs and anyone who pays membership dues. Performs 5-7 concerts/year. "Performances are presented outdoors at a local state park or in a 500-seat high school auditorium. Outdoor area seats up to 5,000." Pays $50-2,000 per performance. Submit complete tapes (or videocassette if available) and background info on composer/performer. Does not return unsolicited material.

Music: "We present a wide variety of programs, hence we are open to all types of music (folk, rock, classical, blues, jazz, ethnic). Most programs are 1-2 hours in length and must be suitable as family entertainment."

*PFL MANAGEMENT, 2424 W. Sepulveda Blvd., Torrance CA 90501. (213)325-8708. Personal Manager: Priscilla LaMarca. Vocal ensemble (all American, Broadway, jazz, light rock, pop, variety, suitable for ages 12-18 group and 20-40 year old group). Soloists available to demo pop, rock, blues (R&B), country music. They also need songs for shows and record demos. Estab. 1978. Members are professionals and amateurs. Performs 20-30 concerts/year, including 10 new works. No commission or budget. Will accept music to showcase. "We perform at private parties, conventions, amusement parks, clubs—indoors and out." Submit complete score and tapes of piece(s). Background desired without soloist if selected. Include this on side B. SASE. Reports in 2 weeks.

Music: "We want up-beat tempos, strong rhythms with variety between sections, 3- minute songs, theme medleys—5-10 minutes. We don't want sex, drugs, profanity. Young love is OK. Songs about dreams, aspirations, gratitude, farewells, positive thoughts desired. Country tunes may have heartache, but up-beat preferred. Stage show format, short introductions, sharp endings, variety in sections and instrumentations that motivate interesting choreography appeal to us."

Performances: John Reed's *Life Saver* (teen pop); Mark Brymer's *Be A Champion* (rock-spirited); and David Martin's *When I Fall In Love* (R&B).

*PHILADELPHIA COLLEGE OF BIBLE, 200 Manor Ave., Langhorne PA 19047-2992. (215)752-5800. Associate Professor: Dale Donovan Shepfer. Symphony orchestra and concert band. Estab. 1980. Members are professionals and amateurs. Performs 6 concerts/year, including 4 new works which must be privately funded in part. "Our audience is predominately classical and sacred music lovers. Hall seats 700. Acoustics are good in the hall." One-time payment, variable. Query first. SASE. Reports in 4 weeks.

Music: "We want non-avante garde, tonal, accessible, challenging and beautiful but playable music in a 6-hour rehearsal format over a four-week span. Of some meaningful religious or spiritual perspective. Orchestral or with chorus or soloists."

Performances: Ronald Alan Matthews' *Antiphonal Fanfare* (6 trumpets and orchestra); Paul Jones' *Spirit of God Descend Upon My Heart* (hymn arrangement with chorus); Kyle Smith's *Sing a Joyful Song* (cantata/orchestra); and David Long's *In Remembrance*.

Tips: "We want something breathtakingly thrilling, uplifting, neo-romanticist, spotlighting sections, superb principals and including some grand tutti climaxes."

PHOENIX SYMPHONY ORCHESTRA, 3707 N. 7th St., Phoenix AZ 85014. (602)277-7291. Music Director: James Sedares. Symphony orchestra. Estab. 1947. Members are professionals. Performs 130 concerts/year, including 15 new works. Commissions 2 composers or new works/year. "Various halls, primarily Phoenix Symphony Hall, Grady Gammage Center on Arizona State University campus (designed by Frank Lloyd Wright), and Scottsdale Center for the Arts. Patrons of all ages." Pays by outright purchase, per performance or commission. "Fee depends upon size and duration." Query first. SASE. Reports in 3 months.

Music: Seeks "serious orchestra works, pops, children's works, chamber orchestra. No theater pieces for concert (except children's)."
Performances: Palus' *Trumpet Concerto*; De Mars' *Two World* Overture.
Tips: "Manuscript should be extremely neat. Score professional in appearance. Include duration and tape (cassette) if available."

PICCOLO OPERA COMPANY, 18662 Fairfield Ave., Detroit MI 48221. (313)861-6930. Executive Director: Marjorie Gordon. Opera company. Estab. 1962. Members are professionals. Performs 5-50 concerts/year, including 1 new work. Commissions 1 composer or new work/year. Receives 3 or more outside submissions/year. Concerts are performed for a mixed audience of children and adults. Pays by royalty or outright purchase. Query or submit complete score and tapes of pieces. Does not return unsolicited material.
Music: "Musical theater pieces, lasting about one hour, for adults to perform for adults and/or youngsters. Peformers are mature singers with experience. The cast should have few performers (up to 10), no chorus or ballet, accompanied by piano or orchestra. Skeletal scenery. All in English."
Performances: Humperdinck's *Hansel & Gretel* (opera); Barab's *Little Red Riding Hood* (opera); Gilbert & Sullivan's *Festival of Highlights* (concert); and Mozart's *Cosi Fan Tutte* (opera).

PLYMOUTH MUSIC SERIES OF MINNESOTA, 1900 Nicollet Ave., Minneapolis MN 55403. (612)870-0943. Managing Director: Jeanne Patterson. Choral orchestral performing society. Estab. 1969. Members are professionals and amateurs. Performs 5 concerts, including 1-2 new works. Audience is generally all ages from late 20s. Comes from entire Twin Cities metro area. "We perform in Ordway Music Theatre, Orchestra Hall, Cathedrals in both Minneapolis and St. Paul." Pays commission fee. Query first. SASE. Reports in months.
Music: All styles appropriate to a choral/orchestral society except pop or rock. "Text used is of special concern. If the work is over ½ hour, the use of soloists is preferred."
Performances: Peter Schickele's *Oedipus Tex* (fully-staged opera); Libby Larsen's *Coming Forth Into Day* (dramatic 1-hour work for narrator, baritone and soprano soloist, chorus and orchestra); and Aaron Copland's *The Tender Land* (semi-staged opera).
Tips: "Be patient. We have a very small staff and are constantly behind in reviewing scores. Tapes are very helpful."

PRO ARTE CHAMBER ORCHESTRA OF BOSTON, #187, 105 Charles St., Boston MA 02114. (617)661-7067. Symphony orchestra. Estab. 1978. Members are professionals. Performs 8 concerts/year, including 4 new works. Commissions 2 composers or new works/year. "We have an average audience of about 700, approximately 340 subscription seats, age range attending is from 17 to 75, the average is 47, income categories in the middle to lower middle income range. Hall seats 1250, small stage, on university campus." Paid only if grant or individual support can be found. Query first. SASE. Reports in 6 months.
Music: "Styles range from baroque to modern, but original; some jazz, some minimilist, open to suggestions. Length of no longer than 15 minutes. Orchestration size of 2222 2200 tmp + 1 perc. (moderate on percussion equipment capacity). Strings 7.6.4.3.2. Level of difficulty not a problem, forces to be utilized must be strictly enforced as stated above."
Performances: Linda Bouchard's *Fanorev* (short, minimilistic); Jay A. Gach's *I Ponentino* (medium length, somewhat dissonant); and Jan Swafford's *Chamber Sinfonietta* (concertino/ripieno utilized medium length, jazzy).
Tips: "Resonable forces without lots of percussion, medium length, not too dissonant, no sound equipment, interesting individual style."

QUEENS OPERA, 313 Bay 14th St., Brooklyn NY 11214. (718)256-6045. General Director: Joe Messina. Opera company. Estab. 1961. Members are professionals. Performs in 9 concerts/year, including 1 new work. SASE. Reports in 1 month.
Music: "Operatic scores and songs, small orchestra."
Performances: Rossini's *Il Barbiere di Siviglia*; Verdi's *Il Trovatore* and *La Traviata*; and Owen's *Tom Sawyer*.

THE RIDGEFIELD YOUTH ORCHESTRA, 700 N. Salem Rd., Ridgefield CT 06877. (203)438-4273. Music Director, Conductor: Dr. Charles Spire. Youth orchestra. Estab. 1971. Members are students. Performs 6 concerts/year, including 3 new works. Audience is the general public, parents and students. Concert hall has 1,000 seats. Pays $400 for outright purchase. Query first. SASE. Reports in 2 weeks.
Music: Modern, serious, light. Level 6-difficult. 100 performers including standard symphony plus saxaphone. "Composer should involve soloists from all sections of the orchestra."
Performances: Dvorak's *Symphony No. 9* (serious); *Music Man Symphonic Impressions* (light); and Curten's *The Phantom of the Opera* (light).

SALT LAKE SYMPHONIC CHOIR, P.O. Box 45, Salt Lake City UT 84110. (801)466-8701. Manager: Richard Taggart. Professional touring choir. Estab. 1949. Members are professionals and amateurs. Performs 4-15 concerts/year, including 1-3 new works. Commissions 1-3 new works or composers year. "We tour throughout U.S. and Canada for community concert series, colleges and universities. Pay is negotiable. Query first. Does not return unsolicited material. Reports in 3 months.
Music: Seeking "4- to 8-part choral pieces for a 100-voice choir—from Bach to rock."

SAN DIEGO SYMPHONY ORCHESTRA, 1245 7th Ave., San Diego CA 92101. (619)699-4200. Artistic Administrator: Bert Harclerode. Symphony orchestra. Estab. 1927. Members are professionals. Performs 85 concerts/year including 100 new works. Copley Symphony Hall: 2,255-seat downtown facility (renovated Fox movie theater) used October-May; 4,000-seat outdoor facility with combination cabaret table and gallery seating used from June-September. Pays through ASCAP or BMI. Submit complete score and tapes of pieces. SASE.
Music: "Orchestral music desired. 85-piece symphony orchestra. No chamber orchestra/music."
Performances: Joseph Schwantner's *Long Before the Winde* (Praeludium for orchestra).
Tips: "Submit works and tapes; information is then given to Executive Director, then to Music Director for consideration."

SARASOTA OPERA ASSOCIATION, 61 N. Pineapple Ave., Sarasota FL 34236. (813)366-8450. Artistic Director: Victor De Renzi. Opera company. Estab. 1959. Members are professionals. Performs 22 opera performances/year. Commissions 1 new work/year maximum. "Our main season of four productions is for a community audience. The opera house has 1,033 seats. We also do children's operas in schools, which may occasionally include original works." Pays royalty (whatever dictated by publisher). Submit complete score and tapes of piece(s). SASE. Reports in 3-4 months.
Music: "For mainstage productions, we use only standard repertoire. However, for the Youth Opera, we use contemporary children's operas. We prefer approximately 45 minutes long, piano accompaniment and few characters, (e.g., 3-4, including a pianist) so as to be able to tour. We want things that are lyrical and singable. Nothing extremely atonal. An emphasis on whimsical material that is appropriate for children is preferred."
Performances: Barab's *The Toy Shop* (children's opera); Davies' *Cinderella* (children's opera); Breedon's *The Frog Prince* (children's opera); and Barab's *Little Red Riding Hood* (children's opera).
Tips: "Be a good grantwriter!"

SAULT STE. MARIE SYMPHONY ORCHESTRA, 801 Prospect, Sault Ste. Marie MI 49783. (906)635-2265. Music Director: Dr. John Wilkinson. Symphony orchestra. Estab. 1972. Members are professionals and amateurs. Performs 5 full orchestra concerts/year, 25-30 other. "Our audience is conservative. Our performance hall seats 964." Query first. SASE. Reports in 2 months.
Music: "We have traditional orchestra size 2222/4231/2, plus strings. String 88552. We want pieces of length (5-15 minutes) in approachable styles. We have 45-50 performers. Pieces should be of moderate difficulty (or less!). Engage the listener; make it playable."
Performances: Ridout-Quesnel's *Colas et Colinette* (light overture); S. Glick's *Elegy* (elegy); and J. Weinzweig's *The Red Ear of Corn* (ballet suite).

SEAWAY CHORALE AND ORCHESTRA, INC., 2450 Middlefield Rd., Trenton MI 48183. (313)676-2400. Conductor, Executive Director: David M. Ward. Auditioned chorus and orchestra. Estab. 1975. Members are professionals and amateurs. Performs 5 major concerts/year, including 4 new works/year. Commissions 0-2 composers or new works/year. "We perform in halls, some church settings and high school auditoriums—large stage with orchestra pit. Our audience is ecumenically, financially, racially, socially, musically, multi-generation and a cross section of our area." Pays by negotiation. Query first by telephone or mail. SASE. Reports in 8 weeks.
Music: "We want 3-minute ballads for orchestra and chorus (for subscription concerts); sacred music, either accompanied or a cappella; Christmas music for chorus and orchestra. We have three performing groups: Voices of the Young—4th through 8th grades (40 members); Youth Sings—9th through 12th grades (a show choir, 24 members); Chorale—adults (70 members). Charismatic Christian music is not high on our priority list. Country music runs a close second. Our major concerts which draw large audiences utilize light selections such as show music, popular songs and music from movies. We present two concerts each year which we call Choral Masterpieces. These concerts include music from master composers of the past as well as contemporary. Our choral masterpieces concerts require Biblical or secular thoughts that are well-conceived musically."
Tips: "Music for adult chorale and orchestra—Christmas or general. Also music for children's chorus with orchestral accompaniment. Find an arts agency which will underwrite a high percentage of the cost of works which you might consider sending us for perusal. We are a nonprofit organization."

SHAW FESTIVAL THEATRE, Box 774, Niagara-on-the Lake, Ontario L0S 1J0 **Canada**. Director of Music: Christopher Donison. Theater company. Estab. 1962. Members are professionals. Commissions 1-5 composers or new works/year. "We have the stages and draw our audience from everywhere in the world, with an obvious emphasis on the New York/Ontario area." Payment is negotiable. Contact by query first and submit complete score and tapes of piece(s). Does not return unsolicited material.
Music: "Intelligent, sophisticated, widely-based, innovative and yet pragmatic, both electronic and conventionally scored."
Performances: Murray Shaffer's *Patria* (opera) and Christopher Donison's *Peter Pan* (theater score).

THE SINGERS FORUM, 31 West 21st St., New York NY 10010. (212)366-0541. Administrator: Denise Galon. Vocal school and presenting organization. Estab. 1978. Members are professionals and amateurs. Performs more than 50 concerts/year, including 4 new works. Commissions 2 composers or new works/year. 99 and 75 seat performance space with varied audience. Pay through donations from patrons. Query first. SASE. Reports in 6 weeks.
Music: "All popular music, art songs, full musicals, small operas with minimal orchestration. No rock. I'm always looking for works to fit our current voices. Mainly new operas and musicals."
Performances: Bernstein's *A Bernstein Valentine* (musical tribute); J.A. Zimmerman's *Concert of Contradiction* (new works); and Lerner & Lowe's *My Fair Lady* (musical theater).
Tips: "Think of the voice."

SINGING BOYS OF PENNSYLVANIA, P.O. Box 206, Wind Gap PA 18091. (215)759-6002. Director: K. Bernard Schade, Ed. D. Vocal ensemble. Estab. 1970. Members are professional children. Performs 120 concerts/year, including 2-3 new works. Commissions 1-2 composers or new works/year. "We attract general audiences: family, senior citizens, churches, concert associations, university concert series and schools." Pays by outright purchase $500-750. Query first. SASE.
Music: "We want music for commercials, music for voices in the SSA or SSAA ranges sacred works or arrangements of American folk music with accompaniment. Our range of voices are from G below middle C to A (13th above middle C). Reading ability of choir is good but works which require a lot of work with little possibility of more than one performance are of little value. We don't want popular songs which are not arranged for SSA or SSAA choir. We sing very few popular songs except for special events. We perform music by composers who are well-known composers and do works by living composers, but ones who are writing in traditional choral forms. Works of music which have a full orchestral score are of interest. The orchestration should be fairly light, so as not to cover the voices. Works for Christmas have more value than some other, since we perform with orchestras on an annual basis."
Performances: Arwel Hughes' *Paul Revere* (choral work with piano and percussion); *Appalachian Suite* (choral work with piano accompaniment, arr. by Schade); and Arthur Harris' *Christmas* (choral work with piano or orchestral).
Tips: "Come to hear the group sing in person!"

SOUTHWESTERN COLLEGE/WINFIELD COMMUNITY ORCHESTRA, 100 College, Winfield KS 67156. (316)221-4150, ext. 300. Conductor: Diane S. Mathie. Symphony orchestra and chamber music ensemble. Members are students and amateurs. Performs 3 concerts/year. Concerts performed for a well-educated audience in Richardson auditorium (seats 700). Pays per performance. Query first. SASE. Reports in 1 month.
Music: "We seek bright, short-overture type works, approximately 5-7 minutes."
Performances: Bizet's *Carmen Suite #1*; Brahms', *Hungarian Dance #5 and 6*; and LeVelle's *Mansfield Overture* (composed by senior composition major).
Tips: "In order to compose for our group, one must learn the strengths and weaknesses of each member of the orchestra. We consist of amateur musicians and 30% college student musicians."

SUSQUEHANNA SYMPHONY ORCHESTRA, P.O. Box 485, Forest Hill MD 21050. (301)838-6465. Music Director: Sheldon Bair. Symphony orchestra. Estab. 1978. Members are amateurs. Performs 5 concerts/year, including 2 new works. "We perform in 2 halls. One is more intimate, 953 seats, mediocre acoustics; the other is larger (999 seats) with fine acoustics. Our audience encompasses all ages." Composers are normally not commissioned, just ASCAP or BMI royalties. Query first or submit complete score. SASE. Reports in 4 months.
Music: "We desire works for large orchestra any length, in a 'conservative 20th century' style. Seek fine, tonal music for chamber or large orchestra (large orchestra is preferable). We are a community orchestra, so the music must be within our grasp. Violin I to 7th position by step only; Violin II—stay within 3rd position, English horn and harp are OK. We don't want avant-garde music."
Performances: Hutt's *Graphic Variations* (short character work); Unger's *Variations for Orchestra* (tonal variations); and Palmer's *Symphony #2* (neo-classic).

TORONTO MENDELSSOHN CHOIR, 60 Simcoe St., Toronto, Ontario M5J 2H5 **Canada.** Phone: (416)598-0422. Manager: Michael Ridout. Vocal ensemble. Members are professionals and amateurs. Performs 30 concerts/year including 1-3 new works. "Most performances take place in Roy Thomson Hall. The audience is reasonably sophisticated, musically knowledgeable but with moderately conservative tastes." Pays by royalty or by direct commission (does not result in ownership of the work). Submit complete score and tapes of pieces. SASE.
Music: All works must suit a large choir (180 voices) and standard orchestral forces or with some other not-too-exotic accompaniment. Length should be restricted to no longer than ½ of a nocturnal concert. The choir sings at a very professional level and can sight-read almost anything. "Works should fit naturally with the repertoire of a large choir which performs the standard choral orchestral repertoire."
Performances: Mahler's *Symphony #8*; (choral-orchestral); Honneger's *King David* (choral-orchestral and narrator); and Orff's *Carmina Burana* (choral-orchestral).

UNIVERSITY OF HOUSTON OPERA THEATRE, School of Music, Houston TX 77204-4893. (713)749-4370 or 749-1116. Director of Opera: Buck Ross. Opera/music theater program. Members are professionals, amateurs and students. Performs 3-4 concerts/year, including 1 new work. Performs in a proscenium theater which seats 1,100. Pit seats approximately 40 players. Audience covers wide spectrum, from first time opera-goers to very sophisticated." Pays by royalty. Submit complete score and tapes of piece(s). SASE. Reports in weeks.
Music: "We seek music that is feasible for high graduate level student singers. Chamber orchestras are very useful. No more than 2½ hours. We don't want serial pieces, aleatoric or children's operas."
Performances: Mozart's *La Finta Giardiniera* (opera); Mary Carol Warwick's *Twins* (opera); and Kurt Weill's *The Tsar Has His Photograph Taken* (opera).

UNIVERSITY OF SOUTHERN MISSISSIPPI SYMPHONY ORCHESTRA, Box 5081, Hattiesburg MS 39406. (601)266-5687. Music Director: Jay Dean. Symphony orchestra. Estab. 1922. Members are college students. Performs 8 concerts/year including 2 new works. Commissions 1 composer or new work/year. Payment negotiable. Submit complete score or score and tapes of piece(s). SASE. Reports in 2 months.
Music: All serious symphonic music. Should be suitable for university level players.

UTAH ARTS FESTIVAL, 168 W 500 N., Salt Lake City UT 84103. (801)322-2428. Assistant Director: Robyn Nelson. Annual 5 day arts festival. Estab. 1977. "We present 50-52 performances of music and dance/year. We have an outdoor festival with a week long attendance of 80,000 with 3 stages, seating 1,500-5,000." Pays per performance. Query first. SASE. Reports in 3 weeks.
Music: "We support new music along the lines of Morton Subotnick, John Zorn, Steve Reich, etc. We present everything from traditional folk/acoustic, reggae, blues, jazz and new music. We aren't looking for rock & roll, rap, heavy metal or New Age."
Performances: By Daniel Lentz & Group, Phillip Glass, Michael Brecker, Morton Subotnick and Anthony Davis.
Tips: "Contact us with tape and press materials."

VALLEY YOUTH ORCHESTRA ASSOCIATION, 18111 Nordhoff St. – MUSC, Northridge CA 91330. (818)885-3074. Music Director: H. Wesley Kenney. Symphony orchestra, youth orchestra and chamber orchestra. Estab. 1970. Performs 3 concerts/year, including 3-5 new works. Receives 4-5 outside submissions/year. Commissions 1-2 composers or new works/year. Members are amateurs and students. "Audience is comprised of parents of members, many senior citizens, other students and professional people. Halls are either Reseda High School (seats about 1,350) or a campus theater (seats 400 with large stage)." Pays outright purchase of $100-200/performance, or negotiated amount. Submit complete score (full score only) and tape of pieces. SASE. Reports in 3 weeks.
Music: "We are seeking pieces of approximately 10-12 minutes in length written for full symphony orchestra, with brass sections of 2-3 horns, 3 trumpets, 1-3 trombones for the Junior Orchestra and full brass for the Senior. We will consider pieces for solo instrument or voice and orchestra. Style is less a concern than accessibility, and there should be something about the piece that will teach them something useful. For the Youth Orchestra, accessibility is often extremely important. If the group can understand the piece within the first rehearsal, they will work harder to perform their best because they enjoy it. But don't make the piece without challenge, or they will become bored with it before it can be perfected."
Performances: Debussey's *Prelude Afternoon of a Fawn* (senior orchestra); Mozart's *Jupiter Symphony* (chamber orchestra); and Copland's *Letter From Home* (junior orchestra).
Tips: "Learn the limitations of the instruments, and rudiments of orchestral balance. In addition, be very specific with what sound is desired. A dot tells a lot, but never enough."

VEREINIGTE BÜHNEN/OPERNHAUS, Kaiser Josef Platz 10, Graz 8010 **Austria**. Phone: 0316/826451. Operndramaturgie: Dr. Monica Pirklbauer, Johannes Frankfurter. Opera house. Members are professionals. Performs 8 operas/year, including 1 new work. Operas are performed in our opera house with 1271 seats, both season tickets and open performances; or in schauspielhaus, young audience." Submit complete score and tapes of pieces. SAE and IRC.
Music: "We would primarily like to find something for our studio, some kind of chamber opera for an orchestra of 10 members maximum and between 1 and 6 singers. Operas for children, any modern operas."
Performances: Otto M. Zykan's *Der Auszälreim* (opera, written 1986) and Friedrich Cerha's *Der Rattenfänger* (opera, written in 1987).

VIRGINIA BEACH ORCHESTRAL ASSOCIATION, #285, 780 Lynnhaven Pkwy., Virginia Beach VA 23452. (804)468-7677. Director Operations/Artistic Consultant: J.L. Kreger. Pops orchestra. Estab. 1983. Members are professionals. Performs 42 concerts/year, including 7 new works. Commissions 4-6 composers or new works/year. "We perform in a hall that seats 972. Our audience varies and comes from metropolitan Virginia Beach and surrounding areas." Pays by outright purchase. Query first. SASE.
Music: "We want styles appropriate to pops orchestra, 8-12 minutes in length. 2222 4331 T 2P harp (optional), keyboard (optional). No limit on difficulty."
Performances: Kreger's *Visions* (ballet); Fluck's *Tribute to Tommy* (orchestra) and *Autumn Leaves* (piano & orchestra).
Tips: "Be open for suggestions!"

WARMINSTER SYMPHONY ORCHESTRA, 524 W. Pine St., Trevose PA 19047. (215)355-7421. Music Director/Conductor: Gil Guglielmi, D.M.A. Community symphony orchestra. Estab. 1966. 12 "pros" and amateurs. Performs 4 concerts/year, including perhaps 1 new work. "We *try* to commission one composer or new work/year." Audience is blue collar and upper middle-class. The concert hall is a local junior high school with a seating capacity of 710. "We operate on a small budget. Composers are not paid, or paid very little (negotiable)." Composer should contact Dr. Guglielmi. Does not return unsolicited material. Reports in months.
Music: Romantic style. Length: 10 minutes to a full symphony. Orchestration: full orchestra with no sound effects, synthesizers, computers, etc. "We play from Mozart to Tschaikovsky." "Performers: we have a maximum of about 60 players. Level of difficulty: medium advanced—one grade above a good high school orchestra. We rehearse 2 hours a week so that anything written should take about 20 minutes a week rehearsal time to allow rehearsal time for the remaining selections. Our musicians and our audiences are middle-of-the-road." "The composer should write in *his* style and not try to contrive a piece for us. The orchestra has a full string section, 4 horns, 3 clarinets, 3 flutes, 2 bassons, 3 trumpets, 2 oboe, 1 English horn, 3 trombones, 1 tuba, 1 harp and a full percussion section."
Performances: Al Maene's *Perla Bella* (mini symphony); and David Finke's *The Wailing Wall* (tone poem).
Tips: "Do not expect the Philadelphia Orchestra. My musicians are primarily lay-people who are dedicated to the performance of good music. What they lack in expertise they more than make up or in practice, work and dedication."

WAYNE CHAMBER ORCHESTRA, 300 Pompton Rd., Wayne NJ 07470. (201)595-2694. Managing Director: Sheri Newberger. Chamber orchestra. Estab. 1986. Members are professionals. Performs 4 concerts/year. Receives 2-3 outside submissions/year. Regional audience from North Jersey area. Attractive and modern concert hall seating 960 patrons. Query with bio first. SASE.
Music: "We are looking for new American music for a 40-piece orchestra. Our only method of funding would be by grant so music may have to tie in with a theme. Although we have not yet performed new works, we hope to in the future."
Performances: Victor Herbert's *Fall of a Nation*; Paul Creston's *Partita for Flute, Violin and Strings*; and Zwilich's *Prologue and Variations*, all orchestral works.

WHEATON SYMPHONY ORCHESTRA, 1600 E. Roosevelt, Wheaton IL 60187. (708)668-8585. Manager: Donald C. Mattison. Symphony orchestra. Estab. 1959. Members are professionals and amateurs. Performs 3 concerts/year, including 1 new work. Composers are paid $100-200/performance. Query first. SASE. Reports in 2 months.
Music: "This is a *good* amateur orchestra that wants pieces in a traditional idiom. No avant garde, 12-tone or atonal material. Pieces should be 20 minutes or less and must be prepared in 3 rehearsals. Instrumentation is woodwinds in 3s, full brass 4-3-3-1, percussion, etc."
Performances: Jerry Bilik's *Aspects of Man* (4-section suite); Walton's *Variations on a Theme of Hindeminth's*; and Augusta Read Thomas' *A Crystal Planet*.

*THE WILLIAMSBURG SYMPHONIA, Box 400, Williamsburg VA 23187. (804)229-9857. Artistic Director: M.E. Andersen. Chamber orchestra. Estab. 1984. Members are professionals. Performs 7 concerts/year, including 2 new works. Commissions 1 composer/year. "Our audience is made up of members of Williamsburg and surrounding communities and Virginia Peninsula—Norfolk to Richmond. We use the public library auditorium, Colonial Williamsburg facilities, or the Phi Beta Kappa Hall at the College of Willam and Mary." Query first. SASE. Reports in 2 months.
Music: "We want traditional music for chamber orchestrations."

ZION CHAMBER ORCHESTRA, Dowie Memorial Drive, Zion IL 60099. (312)872-4803. Music Director: Timothy C. Allen. Chamber orchestra. Members are professionals and amateurs. Performs 12 concerts/year, including occasional new works. Audience is "low-middle class—middle class mostly. 522-seat auditorium, modern, effective acoustically, but a little dry for music." Submit complete score and tape of pieces. Does not return unsolicited material.
Music: "Instrumentation for chamber group—full complement of brass, winds, strings. Not interested in dissonance at this time. Prefers medium level difficulty."
Performances: D. Dickering's *Our Inurement* (serial. . .anti-abortion); A. Koetz's *Sweet Hour of Prayer* (sacred, traditional); and Mendelsohn, Bach, Mozart, Brahms, Ives, Prokofiev, etc.

Fine Arts/'91-'92 Changes

The following markets appeared in the 1991 edition of *Songwriter's Market* but are absent from the 1992 edition. Most of these companies failed to respond to our request for an update of their listing. Others are not listed for a variety of reasons, which is indicated in parentheses following the company name. For example, they may have gone out of business, or they may have requested deletion from the 1992 edition because they are backlogged with material.

Arlington Symphony (asked to be deleted)
Ashland Symphony Orchestra
Bronx Arts Ensemble
Chicago Chamber Orchestra
Cockpit In Court
Commonwealth Opera, Inc.
Dallas Chamber Orchestra
Denver Young Artists Orchestra
Fundacion Teatro Del Libertador
Hautbois Productions

Helsinki Philharmonic Orchestra
Ithaca Opera Association
Knox-Galesberg Symphony
Lexington Philharmonic Society
Lithopolis Area Fine Arts Association
Marshall University Symphony Orchestra

Moravian Philharmonic Olomouc
Music Programs: Los Angeles County Museum of Art (asked to be deleted)
National Sinfonietta (asked to be deleted)
The Northshore Symphonette
Operaworks
Oregon Symphony

Resources

Organizations

by Mark Garvey

Like anyone else, a songwriter occasionally needs encouragement, constructive criticism, solid instruction—and friends. Unlike a lot of other people, however, songwriters have a place to go where they are almost guaranteed to find all those things and more—the songwriter organization.

Those of you who have not yet joined such an organization know the frustrations and doubts facing the lone songwriter: Are my songs any good? What are my strengths and weaknesses? How should I pitch my songs? How can I meet the people I need to meet to get my career moving? How can I better understand the business side of the music industry? Those of you who are lucky enough to belong to a songwriters' group already can testify to the help, education and friendship to be found there.

A songwriter organization can be a lighthouse to those adrift in a tempest of self-doubt and inexperience. The president of the Austin Songwriters Group, Steve Christopher, says, "Songwriters are typically individualists, but the benefits of affiliating [with a group such as ASG] are access to educational opportunities, publishing opportunities and marketing opportunities for their music. The writer can use a songwriting organization as a sounding board." Typical of such groups around the country, the Austin Songwriters Group offers its members monthly meetings, educational programs and a newsletter. They also sponsor workshops and seminars throughout the year, critique sessions, collaborating and showcase opportunities and recording studio discounts.

The Austin Songwriters Group is just one of many similar "local" organizations in cities across the country. From Maine to Washington state, songwriters have banded together in their communities to provide support, education and constructive criticism to one another. Most such organizations are strictly local; they are not organized under the umbrella of a national parent organization. Others are actually branches or chapters of large national groups. NSAI, the Nashville Songwriters Association International, is an example of an organization that's based in a music center but which has branch chapters, called "workshops," in various cities throughout the country. Each local NSAI workshop operates autonomously as a local songwriting group, but they have the connection to Nashville that membership in the parent organization provides. As a result, the workshop groups are able to pull speakers and panelists from Nashville to address their groups, or group members can themselves travel to Nashville and make use of the contacts provided by NSAI.

Dan Kimpel, advertising director for LASS (Los Angeles Songwriters Showcase), says deciding whether to join a strictly local songwriting group or one with a hub office in a major music center is a matter of your personal needs. "In a strictly local organization in a smaller city, you've got the emotional support that you might not find in a national, big city-based organization—the support for the 'artistic' side of being a songwriter. What the bigger organizations can give is a dose of reality; they are for those who are ready to learn

---

Mark Garvey, *former editor of* Songwriter's Market, *is now an Acquisitions and Development Editor for Writer's Digest Books. He specializes in music related titles.*

about the business side of being a songwriter." And membership in a national organization can be a way to make those all-important personal connections so vital to success in the music business. "None of us—as writers, songwriters, artists—live in a vacuum," Dan says. "These organizations can help because success is definitely a matter of who you know and who knows you."

The 20-year-old LASS boasts a membership that stretches far beyond the Los Angeles city limits. They have members all across the country and as far away as Europe, India and Japan. One of the biggest draws for LASS members is their weekly showcase, which offers members from all over the world the chance to have their songs heard, evaluated and possibly "picked up" by producers, publishers and record company executives. Members can mail in their demos for the weekly showcase, so being land-locked somewhere in middle America no longer stands in the way of getting your demos heard by the right people.

NAS (the National Academy of Songwriters) is another organization that offers members information, education, and critiques on a national basis. Their newspaper, "Song-Talk," contains incisive interviews with some of today's top songwriters and articles on the craft of songwriting. They offer mail-in song critique services, weekly song evaluation workshops, songwriting workshops, and monthly seminars featuring discussions with some of the top figures working in the music business today.

Another national organization, the Songwriters Guild of America, has been highly effective as a lobbying group working in the best interests of the songwriters. SGA also offers education and collaboration opportunities for its members. SGA has drafted a Popular Songwriter's Contract which offers very good protection for songwriters entering into a relationship with a publisher. SGA will review free of charge any contract which is offered to any of its members.

The type of songwriter organization you choose to join depends on what you hope to get out of it. As Dan Kimpel indicates, the strictly local organization can become a friendly, supportive group that can give you the encouragement you need to press on with your career. Membership in one of the national organizations can give you access to music business executives and other songwriters—the kinds of contacts you might have a hard time cultivating on your own. Perhaps the best way to go—if you can afford it—is to maintain memberships in two organizations at once, one local and one national.

*ACADEMY OF COUNTRY MUSIC, #923, 6255 Sunset Blvd., Hollywood CA 90028. (213)462-2351. Membership: David Young. Estab. 1964. Serves producers, artists, songwriters, talent buyers and others involved with the country music industry. Eligibility for professional members is limited to those individuals who derive some portion of their income directly from country music. Each member is classified by one of the following categories: artist/entertainer, club operator/employee, musician/ trend leader, DJ. Manager/booking agent, composer, music publisher, promotion, publications, radio, TV/motion picture, record company, or affiliated (general). The purpose of ACM is to promote and enhance the image of country music. "The Academy is involved year round in activities important to the country music community. Some of these activities include charity fund raisers, participation in country music seminars, talent contests, artist showcases, assistance to producers in placing country music on television and in motion pictures and backing legislation that benefits the interests of the country music community. The ACM is governed by directors and run by officers elected annually." Also offers a newsletter. Applications are accepted throughout the year. Membership is $40/year.

AKRON SONGWRITERS WORKSHOP, 625 Hillsdale Ave., Akron OH 44303. (216)836-8065. Director: Glenn Peterhansen. Estab. 1986. Serves songwriters and musicians. "Members are from 14 to 85 years old. Interests go from rap to 40's big band. All levels of writers, performers, hobbyists to full time pros. Members are interested in learning more about the music business and improving their writing and performing skills. We promote, encourage and educate the writing, recording and performaning artists of our area. We offer a chance to meet other writers/musicians and exchange ideas and information about the music industry." Offers performance opportunities, field trips, newsletter, workshops and critique sessions with local/regional writers. Applications accepted year-round. "No dues at this time. A normal admission ($2-5) is charged for some events. Some workshops are $20-25."

Tips: "We have a mailing list of some 1,500 local artists/writers and an active membership of only 75 at any one time. We encourage anyone to join our monthly meetings or showcases and take a step toward being a better writer. We are also working on an outlet for local video air play and developing a radio show 'The Band Next Door' for the fall of 1990."

AMERICAN COUNCIL FOR THE ARTS, 3rd Floor, 1285 Avenue of the Americas, New York NY 10019. (212)245-4510. Contact: Membership Department "We are the leading private national nonprofit organization that serves all the arts." Members are state, regional and community arts agencies, arts centers, performing arts organizations, museums, libraries, parks and recreation departments, professional arts managers and artists and individuals interested in supporting the arts. Services include advocacy for the arts at the federal, state and local levels; arts management training conferences and seminars; *Vantage Point* magazine, featuring articles about major issues facing the arts today; *ACA Up Date*, a monthly up-to-the-minute news bulletin; ACA Books (publisher and distributor of books on the arts); a research library of 10,000 books and documents; and reference and information services. Memberships include individual membership (from $35-100) and institutional membership (from $150-250), depending on services and benefits desired.

AMERICAN FEDERATION OF MUSICIANS (AFM), Suite 600, 1501 Broadway, New York NY 10036. (212)869-1330. Membership available to all qualified musicians and vocalists in the United States and Canada. "The American Federation of Musicians of the United States and Canada is the largest entertainment union in the world and exists solely for the advancement of live music and the benefit of its 250,000 members. In addition to enhancing employment opportunities for members, the AFM aids members in negotiating contracts; enforces employers' observance of working conditions and wage scales; processes traveling members' claims at no cost to members; protects musicians from unfavorable legislation at the federal, state and local levels; negotiates pension, welfare and retirement benefits; offers instrument insurance to members; offers free job referral service to members who are seeking employment with traveling groups; and keeps membership informed of happenings in the business through its publication, *International Musician*. Members also receive numerous benefits provided by each local chapter. Initiation fees and local dues vary; a small percentage of work dues are contributed by members. Write for further information or contact AFM local nearest you."

AMERICAN LISZT SOCIETY, 210 Devonshire Dr., Rochester NY 14625. (716)586-9922. Membership Secretary: Reginald Gerig, 1328 Naperville Rd., Wheaton IL 60187. Estab. 1964. Serves musicians and those interested in music. Members may be any age and have interests in any area of music. Main purpose is to promote "annual music festivals in the US and abroad, residencies at universities, publications and international exchanges." Offers instruction, lectures, performance opportunities, newsletters and festivals. "Members have the opportunity to play recitals, lecture, give lecture-recitals, or publish articles in the society's journal *JALS*." Membership fees vary. "The Festivals are presented at universities, centers for the arts, Library of Congress and colleges in different states every year. The ALS has 3 chapters which present additional programs. They are in Florida, Massachusetts and Connecticut. The Journal of ALS (*JALS*) is listed in the New Groves and is acclaimed internationally. The ALS Archives are kept at the Library of Congress. The ALS is a nonprofit organization."

AMERICAN MUSIC CENTER, INC., Suite 1001, 30 W. 26th St., New York NY 10010-2011. (212)366-5260. Executive Director: Nancy Clarke. Estab. 1939. For composers and performers. Members are American composers, performers, critics, publishers and others interested in contemporary concert music and jazz. Offers newsletter, circulating library of contemporary music scores and advice on opportunities for composers and new music performers; disseminates information on American music. Purpose is to encourage the recognition and performance of contemporary American music. Members receive the twice-yearly *AMC Newsletter*, professional monthly "Opportunity Updates," eligibility for group health insurance and the right to vote in AMC elections.

AMERICAN MUSICIANS UNION INC., 8 Tobin Ct., Dumont NJ 07628. (201)384-5378. President and Treasurer: Ben Intorre. Estab. 1948. Serves musicians and vocalists of all age groups, all ethnic groups, music from gay 90's to contemporary, ballroom music, banquets, weddings, rock, disco, western, Latin, standards, etc. "We assist musicians in their efforts to perform and serve the public. We offer membership in a union, life insurance, meetings and union publication. "Applicant must be a musician, vocalist or manager. Disc-jockeys are not eligible." Offers newsletter and performance opportunities. Applications accepted year-round. Annual dues $27; $10 initiation. Services include life insurance ($2,000 to age 65, reduced insurance to age 70) and advertisements in *Quarternote* are usually free to members. "We have locals in the U.S., in New Jersey, Minnesota, Michigan, etc."

AMERICAN SOCIETY OF COMPOSERS, AUTHORS AND PUBLISHERS (ASCAP), 1 Lincoln Plaza, New York NY 10023. (212)595-3050. Director of Membership: Paul S. Adler. Membership Department Staff: Wanda LeBron, Jonathon Love, Debbie Rose, Lisa Schmidt and Marcy Drexler. Members are songwriters, composers, lyricists and music publishers. Applicants must "have at least one song copyrighted for associate membership; have at least one song commercially available as sheet music, available on rental, commercially recorded, or performed in media licensed by the Society (e.g., performed in a nightclub or radio station) for full membership. ASCAP is a membership-owned, performing right licensing organization that licenses its members' nondramatic musical compositions for public performance and distributes the fees collected from such licensing to its members based on a scientific random sample survey of performances." Primary value is "as a clearinghouse, giving users a practical and economical bulk licensing system and its members a vehicle through which the many thousands of users can be licensed and the members paid royalties for the use of their material. All monies collected are distributed after deducting only the Society's cost of doing business."

Tips: "The Society sponsors a series of writers' workshops in Los Angeles, Nashville and New York open to members and nonmembers. Grants to composers available to members and nonmembers. Contact the membership department in New York or the following branch offices: 6430 Sunset Blvd., Los Angeles CA 90028; 2 Music Square W., Nashville TN 37203; 52 Haymarket, London SW1Y4RP, **England.**"

AMERICAN WOMEN COMPOSERS, INC., Suite 409, 1690 36th St. NW, Washington DC 20007. (202)342-8179. President: Judith Shattin. Estab. 1976. Serves songwriters and musicians. Members are women and men who wish to further compositions written by American women: composers, performers and musicologists. We have a national membership with large concentrations in New York, California, Massachusetts, Illinois and Washington DC metropolitan areas. There are currently two chapters: Midwest (in Chicago) and New England (in Massachusetts). Eligibility requirements are to pay dues and complete application form. "Since we are a support organization, we do not limit ourselves to just professionals. We promote compositions by American women through our concerts and publications and circulating library. The primary value in this organization for a songwriter is free publicity. If songs are performed we mention in our newsletters; music placed in our library is circulated; newsletters provide information on competitions, grants and opportunities for composers in all musical media." Offers library, newsletter, performance opportunities and contact with others interested in women's music. Applications accepted year-round. Annual dues: composer/songwriter, $30; other professionals, $30; senior citizens/students, $15; Associate Members, $20.

ARIZONA SONGWRITERS ASSOCIATION, Box 678, Phoenix AZ 85019. (602)973-1988. Membership Director: Joanne Sherwood. Serves songwriters and musicians. "Membership is open to anyone wanting to learn the craft and business of songwriting. Our members are people of all ages (17-75 years) with interest in all kinds of music (country, rock, R&B, top 40, novelty, jingles). In addition to songwriters, members are studio owners, lyricists and working bands doing original material. We offer educational and promotional activities, and teach the business of songwriting from A-Z. Members have the chance to meet professionals and get first-hand advice and critiques on their songs on a monthly basis." Offers competitions, instruction, lectures, newsletter, performance opportunities, social outings and workshops. Open mike night on the first Tuesday of each month. "We offer a yearly seminar with panels and critique sessions made up of Los Angeles and Nashville professionals from all walks of the business. ASA gets invitations to co-sponsor song contests, perform at public events, do radio and TV spots and have special performance weeks featuring the best of our songwriter/performers. We're getting good press for our meetings and activities. Several members have had cuts from songs picked up at meetings. Local and national airplay received by several members." Applications accepted year-round. Annual dues are $25 per year.

ARTS MIDWEST/REGIONAL JAZZ PROGRAM, Suite 310, 528 Hennepin Ave., Minneapolis MN 55403. (612)341-0755. Senior Program Director: Janis Lane-Ewart. Estab. 1985. Serves composers, musicians, dancers, actors and visual artists. "Arts Midwest is a nonprofit arts organization which fosters and promotes the development of the arts in the Midwest. We are a resource for musicians, songwriters and other artists in the region which includes the states of Illinois, Indiana, Iowa, Michigan, Minnesota, North Dakota, Ohio, South Dakota and Wisconsin. Arts Midwest generates opportunities for artists and arts organizations, extending, enriching and complementing the programs and services of the member state arts agencies. The Jazz Program is but one of the programs of Arts Midwest. The Jazz Program produces technical assistance workshops, conferences and seminars; publishes a quarterly jazz newsletter (free); maintains a data base for the regional jazz community; and publishes a series of technical assistance how-to booklets. Other programs include the Performing Arts Touring Program, the Visual Arts Program, Services Program, and computer services." Applications are accepted throughout the year; however, "there are specific deadline periods for several of our funding programs, including the Performing Arts Touring Program, Meet the Composer, Visual Arts Fellowships, etc." Offers members competitions, lectures, performance opportunities, fellowships, workshops, touring programs and newsletter.

ATLANTA SONGWRITERS ASSOCIATION, INC., 3121 Maple Dr., Atlanta GA 30305. (404)266-2666. Contact: Membership Chairman. Estab. 1979. Serves songwriters, musicians and music industry professionals. Songwriters of all styles of music; music industry professionals who support songwriters. Membership open to any geographic location. Current members throughout Southeast. "We are an educational and service organization." Offers competitions, field trips, newsletter, performance opportunities, social outings, workshops and sells books on songwriting. Applications accepted year-round. Membership fee is regular, $35; deluxe, $50; corporate, $100.

*AUSTIN MUSIC INDUSTRY COUNCIL, P.O. Box 1967, Austin TX 78767. (512)288-1044. President: Martin Theophilus. Estab. 1983. "Serves all persons who are actively engaged in any music industry related business. Plus anyone who participates or supports the Austin Music Industry. (Board member must be in the business of music.)" Main purpose is to support and increase the success of the Austin Music Industry—through public relations, education, seminars and information. "Primary value for a songwriter is the opportunity to know significant business persons and be aware of opportunities in the music industry." Offers instruction, newsletter, performance opportunities, social outings and workshops. Applications accepted year-round. Membership fee is $20/year.

*AUSTIN SONGWRITERS GROUP, P.O. Box 2578, Austin TX 78768. (512)442-TUNE. President: Steve Christopher. Estab. 1986. Nonprofit. Serves songwriters, musicians, producers, engineers and others in the music business. Members include beginning songwriters to published professionals; no age restrictions. All are welcome for membership. "Purpose is to educate songwriters in the areas of lyric development, musical structure, general songwriting skills, publishing, marketing and related music business activities. ASG also provides a networking forum for members to interact with other songwriters and industry professionals." Produces the annual Austin Songwriters *EXPO*, an annual statewide song contest, competitions, field trips, instruction, lectures, library, newsletter, performance opportunities and workshops. Applications accepted year-round. Membership fee is $35/year.

CALIFORNIA COUNTRY MUSIC ASSOCIATION, P.O. Box 6116, Fullerton CA 92631. (714)992-CCMA. Executive Director: Gary Murray. Serves songwriters, musicians and country music fans and business. "Our members are of all ages, from the very young to the very old. They come from a wide variety of vocations, talents and professions. Their common interest is country music. A preferred geographic location would be the state of California, although a member may live out of state. All musicians, artists, and songwriters are eligible to compete in our chapter and statewide award shows, as long they have not charted on a major chart list in the last two years. The main purpose of this organization is to support, sponsor, organize, inform, and promote all facets of country music and entertainment. Our organization works together with the aspiring artist. We recognize, support and award their talents throughout the state and within our chapters. This organization cooperates with and supports country music radio stations, country music publications, charitable organizations, and the country music industry. We are a non-profit organization and our motto is 'God, country and country music.' Country music people are our number one concern." Offers competitions, instruction, lectures, newsletter, performance opportunities, social outings, workshops, showcases and award shows. Applications accepted year-round. Membership fee is $20/year.

CANADA COUNCIL/COUNSEIL DES ARTS DU CANADA, P.O. Box 1047, Ottowa, Ontario K1P 5V8 **Canada**. (613)598-4365/6. Information Officer: Lise Rochon. Estab. 1957. A federal organization serving songwriters and musicians. "Individual artists must be Canadian citizens or permanent residents of Canada, and must have completed basic training and/or have the recognition as professionals within their fields. The Canada Council's objectives are to foster and promote the arts in Canada by offering financial assistance to professional Canadian artists and arts organizations. The Canada Council offers grants to professional musicians to pursue their own personal and creative development." Applications are not accepted throughout the year. "There are specific deadline dates for the various programs we administer." Call or write for more details.

CANADIAN COUNTRY MUSIC ASSOCIATION, Suite 507, 3100 Steeles Avenue West, Concord, Ontario L4K 3R1 **Canada**. (416)739-5014. Executive Director: Sheila Hamilton. Estab. 1976. Members are songwriters, musicians, producers, radio station personnel, managers, booking agents and others. Offers newsletter, workshops, performance opportunities and annual awards. "Through our newsletters and conventions we offer a means of meeting and associating with artists and others in the industry. During our workshops or seminars (Country Music Week), we include a songwriters' seminar. The CCMA is a Federally chartered, nonprofit organization, dedicated to the promotion and development of Canadian country music throughout Canada and the world and to providing a unity of purpose for the Canadian country music industry. We are now involved with the Music Copyright Action Group and the main objective of the group is to get the government of Canada to revise the copyright act.

We are similar to the CMA in the United States, with approximately 1,000 members (some from the US)." Send for application.

*CINCINNATI COMPOSERS' GUILD, P.O. Box 20166, Cincinnati OH 45220. President: John McDaniel. Estab. 1978. Serves composers, primarily of contemporary music—students and established professionals. Membership is also open to composers and noncomposer supporters of new music. Provides professional services/performance opportunities for contemporary composers. Offers competitions, lectures, newsletter, performance opportunities and workshops. Applications accepted year-round (with annual call for scores). Membership fee is $25/year; $15 associate (non-composer); $15/year for full-time students. The CCG presents an annual concert series of 5 or 6 concerts featuring music by CCG Members. The CCG is a nonprofit organization.

COMPOSERS, ARRANGERS AND SONGWRITERS OF KANSAS, 117 W. 8th St., Hays KS 67601. (913)625-9634. Administrator: Mark Meckel. Serves songwriters, musicians, arrangers and lyricists. Membership open to "anyone desiring information on the business of songwriting, copyrights or marketing—from professional musicians to housewives. Our purpose is to help members get songs placed with publishing and record companies." No eligibility requirements other than "a desire for a career in the music industry." Applications accepted year-round.

COMPOSERS GUILD, Box 586, 40 N. 100 West, Farmington UT 84025. (801)451-2275. President: Ruth Gatrell. For composers and songwriters. "We are a nonprofit organization working to help the composer/songwriter. Each year we sponsor classes, workshops, seminars, showcases/concerts and a composition contest, with cash prizes and winning numbers eligible for performance at the Composers Guild Spectacular. A songwriter benefits from joining Composers Guild through lower contest and seminar/class fees, (contest entries for members are $5—non-members are $15); through seminars, workshops and classes, most of which are taped for those who cannot attend; the challenge to write new music for the contest and concerts—we have an 'Americana' and a 'New Sounds for Christmas' concert each year in addition to the 'Spectacular,' featuring contest winners; through association with others with similar interests and from news from the field, as made available to the Guild. Categories for our contest are: orchestra/band; children's arrangments; choral; instrumental; jazz/New Age; keyboard; pop; vocal solo; and young composers (must not have turned 19 before August 31)."

COMPUTER MUSIC ASSOCIATION, 2040 Polk, San Francisco CA 94109. (817)566-2235. President: Larry Austin. Estab. 1978. Serves songwriters, musicians and computer music specialists. Membership includes a broad spectrum of composers, scientists, educators and hobbyists. The function of this organization is "to serve the interests of computer music practitioners and sponsor annual computer music conferences." Primary value in this organization is "music technology information." Offers lectures, performance opportunities, workshops and newsletters to members. Applications are accepted throughout the year. Membership fee is $50/year (individual); $15/year (student); $150/year (nonprofit organization); and $100/year (sustaining).

CONNECTICUT SONGWRITERS ASSOCIATION, Box 1292, Glastonbury CT 06033. (203)659-8992. Executive Director: Don Donegan. "We are an educational, nonprofit organization dedicated to improving the art and craft of original music. Founded in 1979 by Don Donegan, CSA has grown to become one of the best known songwriter's associations in the country. Membership in the CSA gives you 16-24 seminars/workshops per year at 5 locations throughout Connecticut. Noted professionals deal with all aspects of the craft and business of music including lyric writing, music theory, music technology, arrangement and production, legal and business aspects, performance techniques, song analysis and recording techniques. CSA also offers showcases and concerts which are open to the public and designed to give artists a venue for performing their original material for an attentive, listening audience. CSA benefits have helped United Cerebral Palsy, Muscular Dystrophy, group homes, Hospice, world hunger, libraries, nature centers, community centers and more. CSA shows encompass ballads to bluegrass and Back to rock."

COUNTRY MUSIC FOUNDATION LIBRARY & MEDIA CENTER, 4 Music Square E., Nashville TN 37203. (615)256-1639. Estab. 1964. Serves country music researchers. "We have no membership program. We are a research library, open by appointment to someone with serious research needs in country music (past hits, lyrics, biographies, etc.). We also offer research services to those who cannot come in person—$50 per hour, plus cost of copies and postage." Offers library. "Library hours for country music researchers are now limited to 10 a.m. to 5 p.m., Monday through Thursday, closed holidays."

COUNTRY MUSIC SHOWCASE INTERNATIONAL, INC., Box 368, Carlisle IA 50047. (515)989-3676 or 989-3748. President: Harold L. Luick. Vice President: Barbara A. Lancaster. "We are a nonprofit, educational performing arts organization for songwriters, recording artists and entertainers. The organization showcases songwriters at different seminars and workshops held at the request of its members in many different states across the nation. It also showcases recording artists/entertainer members at many Fair Association showcases held across the United States. When a person becomes a member they receive a membership card, newsletters, an educational information packet (about songwriting/entertainment business), a question and answer service by mail or phone, a song evaluation and critique service, info on who's looking for song material, songwriters who are willing to collaborate, and songwriting contests." Supporting Songwriter membership donation and Supporting Recording Artist/Entertainer membership donation are $20.00 per year; Supporting Band, Group or music related business membership donation is $100 per year. For free information, brochure or membership application send SASE to the above address.

DALLAS SONGWRITERS ASSOCIATION, 2932 Dyer St., Dallas TX 75205. (214)691-5318. President: Barbara McMillen. Estab. 1988. Serves songwriters and lyricists of Dallas/Ft. Worth metroplex. Members are adults ages 18-65, Dallas/Ft. Worth area songwriters/lyricists who are 18 years and older who are or aspire to be professionals. Purpose is to provide songwriters an opportunity to meet other songwriters, share information, find co-writers and support each other through group discussions at monthly meetings. To provide songwriters an opportunity to have their songs heard and critiqued by peers and professionals by playing cassettes and providing an open mike at monthly meetings and by offering quarterly contests judged by publishers. To provide songwriters opportunities to meet other music business professionals by inviting guest speakers to monthly meetings. To provide songwriters opportunities to learn more about the craft of songwriting and the business of music by presenting mini-workshops at each monthly meeting. "We offer a chance for the songwriter to learn from peers and industry professionals and an opportunity to belong to a supportive group environment to encourage the individual to continue his/her songwriting endeavors." Offers competitions, field trips, instruction, lectures, library, newsletter, performance opportunities, social outings and workshops. Applications accepted year-round. Membership fee is $25.

THE DRAMATISTS GUILD, INC., 234 W. 44th St., New York NY 10036. (212)398-9366. Membership includes over 7,000 playwrights, composers, lyricists and librettists nationwide. "As the professional association of playwrights, composers and lyricists, the Guild protects the rights of all theater writers, and improves the conditions under which they work. Additionally, the Guild encourages and nurtures the work of dramatists in the U.S. through its program of seminars and workshops. To be a member of The Dramatists Guild, you must have completed a dramatic work (a one-act or full-length play or component part- book, music or lyrics- of a musical) whether produced or not. The Guild offers many services and activities, including use of the Guild's contracts and a royalty collection service; The Hotline, a nationwide toll-free phone number for business or contract problems; an annual marketing directory with up-to-date information on grants, agents, producers, playwriting contests, conferences and workshops; two publications (*The Dramatists Guild Quarterly* and *The Dramatists Guild Newsletter*); access to group health insurance and access to Guild's newsroom."

FEDERATION INTERNATIONAL DES ORGANISATIONS DE FESTIVALS (F.I.D.O.F.), #105, 4230 Stansbury Ave., Sherman Oaks CA 91423. (818)789-7569. FAX: (818)784-9141. Secretary General: Prof. Armando Moreno. Estab. 1967. Serves songwriters, musicians, festival and events managers and organizers. Members are of all ages, from 62 countries around the world. "We coordinate dates of festivals, and coordinate the interests of all involved with festivals and cultural events (artists, songwriters, record, TV, video, publishing and other companies from around the world, as well as the press)." Offers competitions, field trips, instruction, lectures, library, newsletter, performance opportunities, social outings, workshops, annual meetings on international and national levels, exhibition opportunities, etc. Applications accepted year-round. Annual membership fee is $200.

*THE FOLK ALLIANCE, P.O. Box 5010, Chapel Hill NC 27514. (919)542-3957. Contact: Art Menius. Estab. 1989. Serves songwriters, musicians and folk music and dance organizations. Members are organizations and individuals involved in traditional and contemporary folk music and dance in the USA and Canada. Members must be active in the field of folk music (singers/songwriters in any genre—blues, bluegrass, celtic, latino, old-time, etc.). Also must reside in USA or Canada. The Folk Alliance serves members through education, advocacy, field development, professional development, networking and showcases. Offers newsletter, performance opportunities, social outings and workshops. Applications accepted year-round. Membership fee is $25/year/individual (voting); $75-350/year for organizational.
Tips: The Folk Alliance hosts its annual conference in late January/early February at different locations in the USA and Canada.

FORT BEND SONGWRITERS ASSOCIATION, 7010 FM 762, Richmond TX 77469. 713-563-9070. Info line: 713-CONCERT (Access Code FBSA). Coordinator: Dave Davidson. Estab. 1989. Serves "any person, amateur or professional, interested in songwriting or music. Our members write pop, rock, country, rockabilly, gospel, R&B; children's music and musical plays." Open to all, regardless of geographic location or professional status. The FBSA provides its membership with help to perfect their songwriting crafts by conducting workshops, seminars, publishing a monthly newsletter and holding songwriting and vocal performance competitions and showcases. The FBSA provides instruction for beginning writers and pubilshing and artist tips for the more accomplished writer." Offers competitions, field trips, instruction, lectures, newsletter, performance opportunities, workshops, mail-in critiques and collaboration opportunities. Applications accepted year-round. Full membership: $40; Associate Membership: $25. For more information send SASE.

*GOSPEL MUSIC ASSOCIATION, P.O. Box 23201, Nashville TN 37202. (615)242-0303. Membership Coordinator: Laura Harbison. Estab. 1964. Serves songwriters, musicians and anyone directly involved in or who supports gospel music. Professional members include advertising agencies, musicians, agents/managers, composers, retailers, music publishers, print media, broadcast media, and other members of the recording industry. Associate members include supporters of gospel music and those whose involvement in the industry does not provide them with income. The primary purpose of the GMA is to promote the industry of Gospel and Christian music, and provide professional development series for industry members. Offers library, newsletter, performance opportunities and workshops. Applications accepted year-round. Membership fee is $50/year (professional); and $25/year (associate).

THE GUILD OF INTERNATIONAL SONGWRITERS & COMPOSERS, (formerly The Society of International Songwriters and Composers), Sovereign House, 12 Trewartha Rd., Praa Sands, Penzance, Cornwall TR20 9ST **England**. Phone: (0736)762826. FAX: (0736)763328. Secretary: C.A. Jones. Serves songwriters, musicians, record companies, music publishers, etc. "Our members are amateur and professional songwriters and composers, musicians, publishers, independent record publishers, studio owners and producers. Membership is open to all persons throughout the world of any age and ability, from amateur to professional. The society gives advice and services relating to the music industry. A free magazine is available upon request with an SAE or 3x IRC's. We provide contact information for artists, record companies, music publishers, industry organizations; free copyright service; *Songwriting & Composing Magazine*; and many additional free services." Applications accepted year-round. Annual dues are £18 in the U.K.; £20 in E.E.C. countries; £25 overseas. (Subscriptions in pounds sterling only).

THE HYMN SOCIETY IN THE UNITED STATES AND CANADA, P.O. Box 30854, Texas Christian University, Fort Worth TX 76129. (817)921-7608. Executive Director: W. Thomas Smith. Estab. 1922. Serves hymn text and tune writers. "Our members are church musicians, clergy, hymn writers and institutional libraries. The main purpose is to promote hymn singing, sponsor hymn writing, and foster hymnological research. Members will acquire skills in writing congregational hymns." Offers competitions, lectures, library, newsletters, performance opportunites, workshops and annual conferences. Applications accepted year-round. Membership fee and annual dues: $30.

INDIANAPOLIS SONGWRITERS, P.O. Box 44724, Indianapolis IN 46244-0724. (317)257-9200. Secretary: Liz Efroymson. Estab. 1983. Purpose is "to create an affiliation of serious-minded songwriters, promote the artistic value of the musical composition, the business of music and recognition for the songwriter and his craft." Sponsors quarterly newsletter, monthly meetings, periodic showcases and periodic seminars and workshops. "The monthly critiques are helpful for improving songwriting skills. The meetings offer opportunities to share information concerning publishing demos, etc. In addition, it provides the opportunity for members to meet co-writers." Membership fee of $20 per year.

INTERNATIONAL BLUEGRASS MUSIC ASSOCIATION (IBMA), 326 St. Elizabeth St., Owensboro KY 42301. (502)684-9025. Executive Director: Dan Hays; Director of Membership Services and Public Relations: Art Menius. Estab. 1985. Serves songwriters, musicians and professionals in bluegrass music. "IBMA is a trade association composed of people and organizations involved professionally and semi-professionally in the bluegrass music industry, including performers, agents, songwriters, music publishers, promoters, print and broadcast media, local associations, recording manufacturers and distributors. Voting members must be currently or formerly involved in the bluegrass industry as full or part-time professionals. A songwriter attempting to become professionally involved in our field would be eligible. We promote the bluegrass music industry and unity within it. IBMA publishes bimonthly *International Bluegrass*, holds an annual trade show/convention during September in Owensboro, represents our field outside the bluegrass music community, and compiles and disseminates databases of bluegrass related resources and organizations. The primary value in this organization for a songwriter is having current information about the bluegrass music field and contacts with other songwriters, publishers, musicians, and record companies." Offers social outings, workshops, liability insurance, rental car discounts, consultation and databases of record companies, radio stations, press, organizations and gigs. Applications accepted year-round. Membership fee for a non-voting patron

$15/year; for an individual voting professional $35/year; for an organizational voting professional $100/year.

*INTERNATIONAL FEDERATION OF PHONOGRAM/VIDEOGRAM PRODUCERS, 54 Regent St., London WIR 5PJ **England**. Phone: (01)434-3521. Press/Information Officer: Mark Kingston. Serves international record industry. Membership is made up of record companies throughout the world. "We administer to the needs of the record industry, monitoring changes in technology, copyright laws, etc." Offers newsletter. Applications accepted year-round.

INTERNATIONAL LEAGUE OF WOMEN COMPOSERS, Box 670, Southshore Rd., Pt. Peninsula, Three Mile Bay NY 13693. (315)649-5086. Chairperson: Elizabeth Hayden Pizer. Estab. 1975. Serves (women) composers of serious concert music. "Members are women composers and professional musicians, music libraries, institutions and organizations. Full composer membership is open to any woman composer whose seriousness of intent has been demonstrated in one or more of the following ways: (1) by any single degree in composition (if the degree is not recent, some evidence of recent activity should be offered); (2) by holding a current teaching position at the college level, (3) by having had a serious work published; (4) by having had a work performed at a recognized symposium or by professional musicans; or (5) by submitting two compositions to the Executive Board for review, exhibiting competence in scoring for chamber ensemble. Admission is governed neither by stylistic nor regional bias; however, primarily educational music is not considered sufficient. The ILWC is devoted to creating and expanding opportunities for, and documenting information about, women composers of serious music. This organization will help composers stay informed of various career/performance opportunties; plus, allow them to participate in projects spear-headed by ILWC." Offers competitions, newsletter and performance opportunities. Applications accepted year-round. Annual dues are $25 for individuals; $15 for students/senior citizens; $35 for institutions/organizations.

INTERNATIONAL SONGWRITERS ASSOCIATION LTD., 37b New Cavendish St., London WI **England**. Phone: (01)486 5353. Membership Department: Anna M. Sinden. Serves songwriters and music publishers. "The ISA headquarters is in Limerick City, Ireland, and from there it provides its members with assessment services, copyright services, legal and other advisory services and an investigations service, plus the magazine for one yearly fee. Our members are songwriters in more than 50 countries worldwide, of all ages. There are no qualifications, but applicants under 18 are not accepted. We provide information and assistance to professional or semi-professional songwriters. Our publication, *Songwriter*, which was founded in 1967, features detailed exclusive interviews with songwriters and music publishers, as well as directory information of value to writers." Offers competitions, instruction, library and newsletter. Applications accepted year-round. Membership fee for European writers is £13.90; for non-European writers, it is US $20.

KANSAS SONGWRITERS ASSOCIATION, 117 W. 8th, Hays KS 67601. (913)625-9634. President: Mark Meckel. Serves songwriters and musicians. "The purpose of our organization is to help songwriters get songs recorded/published." Offers library for members. No membership fee.

KERRVILLE MUSIC FOUNDATION INC., P.O. Box 1466, Kerrville TX 78029-1466. (512)257-3600. Executive Director: Rod Kennedy. The Kerrville Music Foundation was "founded in 1975 for the promotion and preservation of both traditional and new American music and has awarded more than $25,000 to musicians over the last 15 years through open competitions designed to encourage excellence in songwriting. Six new folk award winners are annually invited to share 20 minutes of their songs at the Kerrville folk festival with one selected to perform on the main stage the next year." Opportunities include: The Emerging Songwriters Competition at the NAPA Valley Folk Festival— Oct. 12th (award winners on Oct. 13th); the Rising Stars Songwriters Competition at Columbia River Folk Festival in Spokane, WA—July 20 (award winners on July 21); and The New Folk Concerts for Emerging Songwriters at the Kerrville Folk Festival.

KEYBOARD TEACHERS ASSOCIATION INTERNATIONAL, INC., 361 Pin Oak Lane, Westbury NY 11590. (516)333-3236. President: Dr. Albert DeVito. Estab. 1963. Serves musicians and music dealers/keyboards. "Our members are music teachers, music dealers, music publishers, especially keyboard/piano/organ. Active members must be teachers. We also have Friend Members who are not teachers. The main purpose of this organization is to keep keyboard teachers informed of what is happening in their field, students evaluation, teacher certification, etc. The primary value in this organization for a songwriter is being in contact with keyboard players, publishers and dealers." Offers evaluations of students, instruction, newsletter and workshops. Applications accepted year-round. Membership fee is $25. "Each student in auditions receives a certificate according to grade level. It is a great experience for them with the encouragement given."

THE LAMBDA PERFORMING ARTS GUILD OF AMERICA®, P.O. Box 14131, Denver CO 80214. Director: Sharon Smith-Fliesher Soria. Estab. 1987. "Serving musicians, vocalists, songwriters, all formats. Operated by lesbians. We are a nonprofit organization. No salaries are paid. "We offer referrals to publishers, recording companies, agents, managers and producers. We have reorganized and introduced a telecom artist promotion, 24 hours a day, 7 days a week. Service limited to a first come, first serve basis, scheduling artists' copyrighted songs weekly. Agents, managers, publishers and producers avoid the middle-man distribution of works by simply calling in and listening to the weekly artists. Artists may schedule their works by first calling the telecom number, deciding if it is indeed for their needs, and sending their tape for approval. A check or money order must accompany the tape at a rate determined for associate membership with a guaranteed play run of three weekly plays. Additional scheduling is at a per rate basis, per week. Scheduling is dependent on a space available basis, we also rotate artists with no additional fee. We will not accept material that is obscene, discriminatory in nature, and a running time exceeding 03:30 min. in duration. 02:30 will be played over the telecom system. Tapes must be sent to us one song per cassette. We also offer a Lambda Songbank® for lyric filing and registration."

THE LAS VEGAS SONGWRITERS ASSOCIATION, P.O. Box 42683, Las Vegas NV 89116-0683. (702)459-9107. President: Betty Kay Miller. Estab. 1980. "We are an educational, nonprofit organization dedicated to improving the art and craft of the songwriter. We offer quarterly newsletters, monthly general information meetings, workshops three times a month and seminars held quarterly with professionals in the music business. Dues are $20 per year." Members must be at least 18 years of age.

THE LOS ANGELES SONGWRITERS SHOWCASE (LASS), Box 93759, Hollywood CA 90093. (213)654-1665. Co-Directors: Len H. Chandler, Jr. and John Braheny. General Manager: Stephanie Perom. "The Los Angeles Songwriters Showcase (LASS), is a nonprofit service organization for songwriters, founded in 1971 and sponsored by Broadcast Music, Inc. (BMI). LASS also provides counseling and conducts classes and seminars. At our weekly Showcase, we feature Cassette Roulette, in which a different publisher every week critiques songs submitted on cassette that night; and Pitch-A-Thon, in which a different producer or record company executive every week screens songs for his/her current recording projects and/or acts for their labels. The Showcase takes place every Tuesday night in front of an audience of songwriters and the music industry guests; there is no prescreening necessary. LASS also produces an annual Songwriters Expo in October." General membership: $120/year. Professional membership: $150/year. Included in both "general" and "professional" membership benefits are: priorities to have tapes listened to first at Pitch-A-Thon sessions; discounts on numerous items such as blank tapes, books, demo production services, tapes of Songwriters Expo sessions and other seminars; discounts on admission to the weekly showcase; career counseling (in person or by phone) and a subscription to the LASS 'Musepaper," a magazine for songwriters (also available to non-members for $19 bulk rate/$29 first class). Professional membership is available to general members by invitation or audition only and features special private pitch-a-thon sessions and referrals.
Tips: "Members may submit tapes to the weekly cassette roulette and pitch-a-thon sessions from anywhere in the world and be sent the recorded comments of the industry guests for that week. Most of the record companies, publishers and producers will not accept unsolicited material so our Wednesday night showcase is the best way to get your material heard industry professionals."

LOUISIANA SONGWRITERS ASSOCIATION, P.O. Box 80425, Baton Rouge LA 70898-0425. (504)924-0804. Vice President, Membership: Janice Calvert. President: Butch Reine. Serves songwriters. "LSA is a support group of songwriters who are interested in helping each other and sharing their abilities. Our membership is not limited to age, music style, ethnic group or musical ability. We have members in their teens, as well as retired persons in our group. LSA was organized to educate and promote songwriting in Louisiana and help develop a market for our writers in Louisiana. We do have members outside of Louisiana, however. LSA has a membership of over 200. Have completed first songwriting contest, Louisiana Hot Sounds—Country Edition. We plan to continue the contest on an annual basis, adding categories as we go along. If you are interested in songwriting you qualify to belong to LSA. Many of us are unable to relocate to major music centers due to responsibilities to jobs and families. Through songwriting organizations like LSA, we are able to work together as a group to establish a line of communication with industry professionals while developing economically a music center in our area of the country. Members must be interested in music and in developing ideas into a marketable format that can compete with other writers. However, if the writer is only interested in expressing himself/herself, that's very important too." Offers competitions, lectures, library, newsletter, performance opportunities, workshops, discounts on various music related books and magazines, and discounts on studio time. General membership dues are $20/year. "Our fiscal year runs June 1-May 31."

LOUISVILLE AREA SONGWRITERS' COOPERATIVE, P.O. Box 16, Pewee Valley KY 40056. President: Paul M. Moffett. Estab. 1986. Serves songwriters and musicians of all ages, races and all musical genres. "The Louisville Area Songwriters' Cooperative is a nonprofit corporation dedicated to the development and promotion of songwriting. Membership is open to any person in the Louisville area (and beyond) who is interested in songwriting. We offer a songwriter showcase on the first Saturday of each month, an open stage on Mondays at the *Rudyard Kipling*, a series of tapes of songs by members of the cooperative, meetings, speakers, the LASC newsletter, a songwriting contest, referral for collaboration, promotion and song plugging to local, regional and national recording artists and occasional bookings for performing members." Applications accepted year-round. Dues are $20/year.

MEMPHIS SONGWRITERS' ASSOCIATION, 1857 Capri St., Memphis TN 38117. (901)763-1957. President: Juanita Tullos. Estab. 1973. Serves songwriters, musicians and singers. Age limit: 18 years and up. No specific location requirement. Must be interested in music and have the desire to learn the basics of commercial songwriting. "We instruct the potential songwriters on how to structure their songs and correctly use lyrics, commercially. We critique their material. We help them obtain copyrights, give them a chance to expose their material to the right people, such as publishers and A&R people. We hold monthly workshops, instructing members in the Commercial Music Techniques of songwriting. We have an annual Songwriters Showcase where their material is performed live for people in the publishing and recording professions and the general public. We have an annual Shindig, for bands and musicians and an annual seminar." Offers competitions, instruction, lectures, newsletter, performance opportunities and workshops. Applications accepted year-round. Annual dues: $25. **Tips:** "Our association was founded in 1973. We have a charter, by laws and a board of directors (8). All directors are professionals in the music field. We are a nonprofit organization. No salaries are paid. Our directors donate their services to our association. We have a president, vice president, secretary, treasurer, music instructor and consultant, production manager, assistant production manager and executive director.

*MID ATLANTIC ARTS FOUNDATION, Suite 2A, 11 East Chase St., Baltimore MD 21202. (301)539-6656. Estab. 1979. Serves songwriters, musicians and arts constituents in the region: DE, DC, MD, NJ, NY, PA, VA, WV, USVI. Members can be anyone interested in the arts. They must be located in our region. The main purpose of this organization is to promote the sharing of arts resources among member states. Members have access to grant programs, such as the performing arts touring program, and information services (through which songwriters can reach other musicians, presenters, etc.)." Offers workshops and funding. The deadline for the Touring Program is February 28, 1992.

*MIDWESTERN SONGWRITERS ASSOCIATION, 91 N. Terrace Ave., Columbus OH 43204. (614)274-2169. Vice President: Al Von Hoose. Estab. 1978. Serves songwriters. All interested songwriters are eligible—either amateur or professional residing in the midwestern region of U.S.A. Main purpose is the education of songwriters in the basics of their craft. Offers competitions, instruction, lectures, library, newsletter, social outings and workshops. Applications accepted year-round. Membership fee is $20 per year, pro-rated at $5 per calendar quarter (March, June, September, December). "We do not refer songwriters to publishers nor artists—we are strictly an educational organization."

*MILWAUKEE MUSICIANS COOPERATIVE, P.O. Box 659, Milwaukee WI 53215. (414)384-6596. Staff Coordinator: A.L. Williams. Estab. 1981. Serves songwriters, musicians and community groups. Serves ages 25 and upward. All members are interested in songwriting, performing and community service. "Our main requirement for membership is that a person write original songs. All of our performing members must write original music. We have a subcategory of membership for supporting members who are simply supporters of original music. We encourage the writing of music and promote the performance of original music in the area. We offer friendly ears, serving primarily to encourage songwriters." Offers competitions, performance opportunities, social outings and workshops. Applications accepted year-round. "There is no monetary fee or membership cash dues, but members must put forth effort on behalf of the organization. At this point in time, the Milwaukee Musicians Cooperative is mostly a folk music organization. Although we accept and work with other kinds of music, we are primarily folk performers and songwriters. We provide entertainment to nursing homes and other community groups and we run contests to promote songwriting. Our annual Talent Hunt provides the winner with a slot to perform at Summerfest—a major music festival."

MISSOURI SONGWRITERS ASSOCIATION, INC., 693 Green Forest Dr., Fenton MO 63026. (314)343-6661. President: John G. Nolan, Jr. Serves songwriters and musicians. No eligibility requirements. "The MSA (a non-profit organization founded in 1979) is a tremendously valuable resource for songwriting and music business information outside of the major music capitals. Only with the emphasis on education can the understanding of craft and the utilization of skill be fully realized and in turn become the foundation for the ultimate success of MSA members. Songwriters gain support from their fellow members when they join the MSA, and the organization provides 'strength in numbers' when approaching music industry professionals." As a means toward its goals the organization offers: "(1) an extremely informative newsletter; (2) Annual Songwriting Contest; prizes include: album and cassette release of winners, publishing contract, free musical merchandise and equipment, free recording studio time, plaque or certificate; (3) Annual St. Louis Original Music Celebration featuring live performances, recognition, showcase, radio simulcast, videotape for later broadcast and awards presentation; (4) seminars on such diverse topics as creativity, copyright law, brainstorming, publishing, recording the demo, craft and technique, songwriting business, collaborating, etc.; (5) workshops including song evaluation, establishing a relationship with publishers, hit song evaluations, the writer versus the writer/artist, the marriage of collaborators, the business side of songwriting, lyric craft, etc; (6) services such as collaborators referral, publisher contacts, consultation, recording discounts, musicians referral, library, etc. The Missouri Songwriters Association belongs to its members and what a member puts into the organization is returned dynamically in terms of information, education, recognition, support, camaraderie, contacts, tips, confidence, career development, friendships and professional growth." Applications accepted year-round. Tax deductible dues are $50/year.

*MUSICIANS FOR SOCIAL RESPONSIBILITY, INC., Suite 301, 142 Monroe Center, Grand Rapids MI 49503. (616)242-6868. President: Mark Stephens. Estab. 1991. Serves songwriters, musicians and concerned citizens. "Our members are musicians, singers, songwriters and corporations in the recording industry. They represent all age groups and come from all over the world. No eligibility requirements. The main purpose of our organization is to lead the way today for a better tomorrow. The prime value of this organization is to offer inspiration to its members." Offers competitions, field trips, instruction, newsletter, performance opportunities and workshops. Applications accepted year-round. Membership fee is $35/year (individuals or bands); $75/year (corporations); $15/year (students in college or high school).

MUSICIANS NATIONAL HOT LINE ASSOCIATION, 277 East 6100 South, Salt Lake City UT 84107. (801)268-2000. Estab. 1980. Serves songwriters and musicians. "Members are musicians and those involved in related musical occupations. Our goal is to help musicians find bands to join, to help bands find musicians and gigs, and to help songwriters find work in a band or group." Offers newsletter (free advertising for members) and computer search file. Applications accepted year-round. Membership fee is $20/year.
Tips: "The Musicians National Hot Line Association is a nonprofit organization dedicated to helping musicians. Those interested in more detailed information may call (1-801-268-2000) or write (Musicians National Hot Line Association, PO Box 57733, Salt Lake City, UT 84157) for a free brochure."

NASHVILLE SONGWRITERS ASSOCIATION, INTERNATIONAL (NSAI), Suite 200, 1025 16th Ave. S, Nashville TN 37212. (615)321-5004. Executive Director: Pat Huber. Serves both professional and beginning songwriters. Members in all states and several foreign countries. "Our purpose is to gain recognition for the songwriter, to serve any purpose toward this recognition and to pursue this on a worldwide basis." Applicants may apply for 2 memberships; "active membership is having had at least one song published with an affiliate of BMI, ASCAP or SESAC. An associate membership is for the yet-to-be-published writer and others interested in the songwriter." Offers information, instruction, lectures, newsletter, seminars, symposiums, workshops, showcases, performance opportunities, songwriter concerts (in various parts of the U.S.) and awards. Applications accepted year-round. Annual dues $55; lifetime $500.

NATIONAL ACADEMY OF POPULAR MUSIC—SONGWRITERS' HALL OF FAME, 8th Floor, 875 3rd Ave., New York NY 10022. (212)319-1444. Managing Director: Christina Malone. Projects Director: Bob Leone. Estab. 1969. The main purpose of the organization is to honor great songwriters and support a Hall of Fame museum. Activities include: songwriting workshops, music industry panels and songwriter showcases. Offers newsletter. "Informally, our projects director helps members to network with each other. For example, publisher/members looking for material are put in touch with writer/members; collaborations are arranged. Nowhere else on the East Coast can a writer learn more about the craft of songwriting, the business of songwriting and the world of songwriting, in general. And nowhere are there more opportunities to meet with all types of music industry professionals. Our activities are available to all of our members, so networking is inevitable." Membership is open to everyone, but consists primarily of songwriters, publishers and other music industry professionals who are eligible to vote in annual inductee election. Annual awards dinner. Applications accepted year-round. Membership fee is $25/year.

NATIONAL ACADEMY OF SONGWRITERS (NAS), Suite 780, 6381 Hollywood Blvd., Hollywood CA 90028. (213)463-7178. Executive Director: Dan Kirkpatrick. A nonprofit organization dedicated to the education and protection of songwriters. Estab. 1973. Offers group legal discount; toll free hotline; *SongTalk* newspaper with songwriter interviews, collaborators network and tipsheet; plus Los Angeles based *SongTalk* seminar series featuring top names in songwriting, song evaluation workshops, song screening sessions, open mics and more. "We offer services to all songwriter members from street-level to superstar: substantial discount on books and tapes, song evaluation through the mail, health insurance program, and SongPitch service for qualifying members. Our services provide education in the craft and opportunities to market songs. The Academy is also active in addressing political issues affecting the profession. We produce the TV show *Salute to the American Songwriter*. Memberships: General—$75; Professional—$120; Gold—$200."

*NATIONAL ASSOCIATION OF COLLEGE BROADCASTERS (NACB), Box 1955-Brown University, Providence RI 02912. (401)863-2225. Association Director: Carolyne Allen. Estab. 1988. Serves musicians, college radio and TV stations, broadcast/communications departments and others interested in the college media market. Members also include students, faculty members, record companies and manufacturers who want to tap into the college media market. Any songwriter/musician may join under Associate Member status. The primary benefits of membership in NACB are the music reviews in every issue of our magazine (which features major label, independent and unsigned acts in equal proportion). It reaches the stations most likely to play new music (audio and video). Also, several music programs on the satellite network give national exposure to new music—free. Offers conferences, instruction, lectures, newsletter, performance opportunities, workshops, magazine subscription, satellite network, station handbook, radio station ratings, consulting hotline, legal advice and more. Applications accepted year-round. Membership fee is $25/year. "Our 'Guide Wire Radio' show on U-NET radio has brought national fame to several unsigned musicians. Also, low-cost advertising in our magazine lets your expose your music to all 2,000 U.S. college radio and TV stations—more than any other publication."

THE NATIONAL ASSOCIATION OF COMPOSERS/USA, Box 49652, Barrington Station, Los Angeles CA 90049. (213)541-8213. President: Marshall Bialosky. Estab. 1932. Serves songwriters, musicians and classical composers. "We are of most value to the concert hall composer. Members are serious music composers of all ages and from all parts of the country, who have a real interest in composing, performing, and listening to modern concert hall music. The main purpose of our organization is to perform, publish, broadcast and write news about composers of serious concert hall music—mostly chamber and solo pieces. Composers may achieve national notice of their work through our newsletter and concerts, and the fairly rare feeling of supporting a non-commercial music enterprise dedicated to raising the musical and social position of the serious composer." Offers competitions, lectures, performance opportunities, library and newsletter. Applications accepted throughout the year. $15 membership fee; $35 for Los Angeles and New York chapter members.
Tips: "99% of the money earned in music is earned, or so it seems, by popular songwriters who might feel they owe the art of music something, and this is one way they might help support that art. It's a chance to foster fraternal solidarity with their less prosperous, but wonderfully interesting classical colleagues at a time when the very existence of serious art seems to be questioned by the general populace."

NATIONAL ASSOCIATION OF SCHOOLS OF MUSIC, 11250 Roger Bacon Dr., Reston VA 22090. (703)437-0700. Executive Director: Samuel Hope. Assistant Director: Karen P. Moynahan. Estab. 1924. Serves songwriters, musicians and anyone interested in music in higher education. Individual Membership in NASM is open to everyone. The major responsibilities of the National Association of Schools of Music are the accreditation of post-secondary educational programs in music. In addition, NASM publishes books and reports, holds an annual meeting and other forums and provides information to the general public about educational programs in music. Offers a newsletter. Applications accepted year-round.

NEW ENGLAND SONGWRITERS/MUSICIANS ASSOCIATION, 2 Roland Kimball Road, Freeport, MA 04032. (207)865-1128. Director: Peter C. Knickles. "Our organization serves all ages and all types of music. We focus primarily on the business of songwriting and overall, the music business. We have done various co-promotions of seminars with BMI in the past and may continue to do so in the future. Membership is free. Call to be on our mailing list and receive our free quarterly newsletter."

NEW JERSERY AND PENNSYLVANIA SONGWRITERS ASSOC., 226 E. Lawnside Ave., Westmont NJ 08108. (609)858-3849. President and Founder: Bruce M. Weissberg. Estab. 1985. Serves songwriters and musicians. Members are all ages 16-80, representing all types of music, from central NJ to Wildwood, NJ to Philadelphia area. Must be serious about songwriting. Provides networking, information center and promotional center for workshops and guest speakers. "Primary value is that it enables musicians to network with other songwriters in the area." Offers lectures, library, newsletter, performance opportunities and workshops. Applications accepted year-round. $25/year (single), $35/year (band), $15/year out of Philadelphia, NJ areas. "Our group is always interested in new ideas, new interested guest speakers and a true professional type of atmosphere."

*NORTH CAROLINA COMPOSERS' ALLIANCE (NCAA), P.O. Box 11163 Bethabara Station, Winston-Salem NC 27116-1163. (919)929-1578. Treasurer: Mark Oldham. Estab. 1984. Serves songwriters, musicians and composers (instrumental). Members include adult composers of classical, folk, jazz and other styles of music. Should be North Carolina resident. "The main purpose of this organization is to encourage and support composers to write and present original compositions of their individual musical styles. The primary values in this organization are performance opportunities with recordings and feedback on the compositions; and composer-related information on the opportunities in the field (i.e. workshops, commissions, competitions). Offers a directory of NC composers, newsletters and concerts." Applications accepted year-round. Membership fee is $25/year.

NORTHERN CALIFORNIA SONGWRITERS ASSOCIATION, Suite 211, 855 Oak Grove Ave., Menlo Park CA 94025. (415)327-8296. Executive Director: Ian Crombie. Serves songwriters and musicians. Estab. 1979. "Our 1,200 members are lyricists and composers from ages 16-80, from beginners to professional songwriters. Our purpose is to provide the education and opportunities that will support our writers in creating and marketing outstanding songs. NCSA provides support and direction through local networking and input from Los Angeles and Nashville music industry leaders, as well as valuable marketing opportunities. We offer opportunities and education for songwriters. Most songwriters need some form of collaboration, and by being a member they are exposed to other writers, ideas, critiquing, etc." No eligibility requirements. Offers annual Northern California Songwriting Conference, monthly visits from major publishers, songwriting classes, seminars conducted by hit songwriters ("we sell audio tapes of our seminars—list of tapes available on request"), a monthly newsletter, monthly performance opportunities and workshops. Applications accepted year-round. Dues: $50/year.
Tips: "NCSA's functions draw local talent and nationally recognized names together. This is of a tremendous value to writers outside a major music center. We are developing a strong songwriting community in Northern California. We serve the San Jose, Monterey Bay, East Bay and San Francisco area and we have the support of some outstanding writers and publishers from both Los Angeles and Nashville. They provide us with invaluable direction and inspiration."

OHIO SONGWRITERS ASSOCIATION, 3682 W. 136th St., Cleveland OH 44111. (216)941-6126. (216)731-SONG. President: Jim Wunderle. Serves songwriters, musicians and related craftspeople (lyricists, arrangers, sound engineers, producers, vocalists, etc.). "Members of the OSA encompass young adults to senior citizens, at all ranges of musical and theoretical advancement, from professionals to amateurs who have written their first song and don't know what to do next. Prospective members are required to submit cassette tape with samples of their material, up to 3 pieces." Purpose is "to preserve and promote the creation of original music through education and opportunity." Services include marketing and copyright assistance, recording time, professional arrangement, lead sheets, career consultation, independent record production, music lessons, printing/artwork/logo designs, legal counsel with staff music attorneys, secretarial services, copyist, engineering/studio musicians/vocalists, practice space rental, collaboration pool, musicians referral service, band/musicians engagement listings, competitions, lectures, library, newsletter, performance opportunities, educational/video tape rental library, numerous books on songwriting and the music industry at 15% discount to members; educational/audio cassettes on songwriting in the music industry; OSA has weekly classes in songwriting and monthly seminars on the art and craft of songwriting in the music business; (professional members may open an account with OSA and make monthly payments, interest-free, on their recording projects. Members are eligible for substantial discounts on studio time at Sessions, Inc., 16-track state of the art recording studio offering digital mixdowns. Applications accepted year-round. Annual membership fee is $40.
Tips: "The main goal of OSA is to help songwriters get their 'creative ideas' to the market place. OSA seminars have included nationally known songwriters, representatives of ASCAP and BMI, professional studio engineers, music industry professionals with proven track records, presenting invaluable information to amateur and professional songwriters. OSA has its own independent label, Hall of Fame of Records, Tapes and Compact Discs, and their own publishing company, Tower City Publishing".

OPERA AMERICA, Ste. 520, 777 14th St. NW, Washington DC 20005. (202)347-2800. Estab. 1954. Members are songwriters, musicians and opera/music theater producers. "Opera America maintains an extensive library of reference books and domestic and foreign music periodicals, and the most comprehensive operatic archive and music theater in the United States. Opera America draws on these unique resources to supply information to its members." Offers conferences. Publishes directories of opera/music theater companies in the US and Canada. Publishes directory of opera and musical premiere's world-wide and US. Applications accepted year-round. Membership fee is on a sliding scale. Please contact for more information.

*OZARK SONGWRITERS ASSOCIATION, INC., P.O. Box 1483, Branson MO 65616. Secretary: Betty Hickory. Estab. 1987. Serves songwriters. Membership composed of lyricists, music writers, composers, novices, professionals from all walks of life. "Main purposes are: 1)Assist songwriters in all ways to perfect the craft; 2)Provide opportunities for songwriters to get songs into the market. Offers competitions, instruction, lectures, library, newsletter, performance opportunities, social outings workshops and access to: 1)Discount studio demo recording time; 2)Professional song "pitch sheet." Our location in Branson, Mo. gives us the opportunity to come in contact with more leads on where and how to "pitch" your songs. Applications accepted year-round. "Applicants must submit lyric sheet from one song they wrote." Membership fee is $30/year for writer members; $100/year for associate members (supporting business people); and corporations or patrols—over $100/year.

PACIFIC NORTHWEST SONGWRITERS ASSOCIATION, Box 98564, Seattle WA 98198. (206)824-1568. "We're a nonprofit association, and have served the songwriters of the Puget Sound area since 1977. Our focus is on professional songwriting for today's commercial markets. We hold monthly workshops and publish a quarterly newsletter. Our workshops are a great place to meet other writers, find collaborators, critique each other's songs and share news and encouragement. Our members get immediate contact with hundreds of the biggest national artists, producers, publishers and record companies. Members also get free legal advice from our staff attorney. All this for only $25 per year. We welcome new members. If you have any questions, just give us a call."

PACIFIC SONGWRITERS ASSOCIATION, Box 15453, 349 W. Georgia, Vancouver, BC V6B 5B2 **Canada.** (604)872-SONG. Estab. 1983. Serves songwriters. All ages, from teens to retired people; writers of music, lyrics and both; also industry people interested in understanding the craft of songwriting. "To inform and promote songwriting and songwriters in the Pacific area; our main activity is a monthly song evaluation session called The Song Works, and 6 times/year we publish the magazine *Hook Line & Singer.* "Songwriting can be a very introverted process. P.S.A. encourages the sharing of frustrations, challenges, information, successes and opens the door to collaborations." Offers access to professional panels for song evaluation and information; opportunity to meet other writers and industry people; a resource place for information. Offers local business discounts to membership card holders (such as specified studios and instrument retailers)." Offers lectures and workshops. Applications accepted year-round. Renewals are based on your 12-month anniversary. $40/year, includes subscription to *Hook Line & Singer.* Subscription only $10.

PENNSYLVANIA ASSOCIATION OF SONGWRITERS, COMPOSERS, P.O. Box 4311, Allentown PA 18105. (215)433-6787. President: John Havassy. Estab. 1979. Serves songwriters and musicians. "Teens to 40's, mostly rock and new music. Open to anyone interested in finding a better, easier, faster way to further needs of songwriters. We offer a venue for original music performances." Applications accepted year-round. Dues are $10 yearly. "Any performing songwriters should send tape and bio and other promotional materials for consideration for bookings. Our organization runs the Airport Music Hall in Allentown."

PITTSBURGH SONGWRITERS ASSOCIATION, 408 Greenside Ave., Canonsburg PA 15317. (412)745-9497. President: Frank J. DeGennaro. Estab. 1983. Serves songwriters. "Any age group is welcome. Current members are from mid-20s to mid-50s. All musical styles and interests are welcome. Country and pop predominate the current group; some instrumental, dance, rock and R&B also. Composers and lyricists in group. Our organization wants to serve as a source of quality material for publishers and other industry professionals. We assist members in developing their songs and getting their works published. Also, we provide a support group for area songwriters, network of contacts and collaboration opportunities. We offer field trips, instruction, lectures, library and social outings. Annual dues are $25. We have no initiation fee."

*PLATINUM MUSIC NETWORK, INC., 390 Ocean Ave., Long Branch NJ 07740. (908)222-6842. President: Steve Zuckerman. Estab. 1988. Serves songwriters, musicians, artists from recording artist to novice. "Main purpose is to provide information—who is in need of material; networking opportunities." Offers lectures, performance opportunities, instruction, newsletter and workshops. Applications accepted year-round. Membership fee: $89. "Our track record speaks for itself."

POP RECORD RESEARCH, 17 Piping Rock Dr., Ossining NY 10562. Director: Gary Theroux. Estab. 1962. Serves songwriters, musicians, writers, researchers and media. "We maintain archives of materials relating to music, TV and film, with special emphasis on recorded music (the hits and hitmakers 1877-present): bios, photos, reviews, interviews, discographies, chart data, clippings, films, videos, etc." Offers library and clearinghouse for accurate promotion/publicity to biographers, writers, reviewers, the media. Offers programming, annotation and photo source for reissues or retrospective album collections on any artist (singers, songwriters, musicians, etc.), also music consultation services for film or television projects. "There is no charge to include publicity, promotional or biographical materials in our archives. Artists, writers, composers, performers, producers, labels and publicists are always invited to add or keep us on their publicity/promotion mailing list with career data, updates, new releases and reissues of recorded performances, etc. Fees are assessed only for reference use by researchers, writers, biographers, reviewers, etc. Songwriters and composers (or their publicists) should keep or put us on their publicity mailing lists to ensure that the information we supply others on their careers, accomplishments, etc. is accurate and up-to-date."

*PORTLAND MUSIC ASSOCIATION, P.O. Box 6723, Portland OR 97228. (503)223-9681. President: Craig Mayther. Serves songwriters, musicians, booking agents and club owners. Members are all ages—amateur and professional musicians, music industry businesses, technical support, personnel, music lovers and songwriters. "Main purpose is in the development and advancement of music and related business opportunities within our metro area and to the international music industry." Benefits include networking opportunities, educational seminars, contests, new talent showcase, local music awards and Musicians' Ball. Offers songwriter contest, lectures, newsletters, performance opportunities, social outings, workshops and songwriter/musician referral. Annual dues: General $15; band $25; business $35; association $50; corporate $100.

RECORDING INDUSTRY ASSOCIATION OF AMERICA, Suite 200, 1020 19th St., NW Washington DC 20036. Director, Member Services: John H. Ganoe. Estab. 1952. Serves recording companies. RIAA membership is corporate. Members include U.S.-based manufacturers of sound recordings. "Membership in RIAA is not open to individuals. RIAA has extensive programs on behalf of our industry in the areas of government relations, public relations and anti-piracy enforcement. RIAA also coordinates industry market research and is the certifying body for gold and platinum records. We will provide, upon request, samples of RIAA publications, including our industry sourcebook, newsletter and annual statistical overview. Dues are corporate, and computed in confidence by an outside auditing firm."

ROCKY MOUNTAIN MUSIC ASSOCIATION, Suite 210 Union Station, 1701 Wynkwop St., Denver CO 80202. (303)355-7426. Executive Director: Daria Castiglione. Serves songwriters and others in the music community. Estab. 1986. Membership: 400 and growing. "Our membership ranges from age 18 to 79. Requirements are only that members demonstrate a keen interest in songwriting, music composition and/or performance. One purpose of this organization is to provide an outlet for songwriters in all genres, and to become an 'umbrella' for a Rocky Mountain music industry. We strive to aid our songwriting members in learning the craft of writing songs, and developing contacts within the music industry. We provide discounts at various recording studios, music stores and performances, and a songwriter's and musician's network. We endeavor to provide musicians and songwriter's with exposure that they would otherwise not have an opportunity to experience within this region." Offers lectures, performance opportunities, library, musical directory, social outings, publications, newsletter and workshops. Applications taken year-round for annual May membership dues. 2 major events/year: Music Explosion, Music Awards Celebration and All Star Jam Music Fest, which showcases talent to major record labels. "We also offer 4 specialized technical workshops and have monthly meetings at 7:00 p.m. on first Monday of each month at the Days Inn, 1150 E.Colfax."
Tips: "A songwriter should belong to our organization so that trips to Nashville, New York or Los Angeles become unneccessary. There is a definite Rocky Mountain sound that deserves to be heard."

SAN FRANCISCO FOLK MUSIC CLUB, 885 Clayton, San Francisco CA 94117. (415)661-2217. Serves songwriters, musicians and anyone who enjoys folk music. "Our members range from age 2 to 80. The only requirement is that members enjoy, appreciate and be interested in sharing folk music. As a focal point for the San Francisco Bay Area folk music community, the SFFMC provides opportunities for people to get together to share folk music, and the newsletter *The Folknik* disseminates information. We publish 2 songs an issue (6 times a year) in our newsletter, our meetings provide an opportunity to share new songs, and at our camp-outs there are almost always songwriter workshops." Offers library, newsletter, informal performance opportunities, annual free folk festival, social outings and workshops. Applications accepted year-round. Membership fee is $5/year.

SANTA BARBARA SONGWRITERS' GUILD, Box 3216, Santa Barbara CA 93130. (805)964-2350. President: Mike Crolius. Estab. 1983. "The Guild helps to open doors to music industry professionals which otherwise, would be closed to them. We are a nonprofit organization for aspiring songwriters, performers, those interested in the music industry, and anyone interested in original music. Our members are able to meet other songwriters, to learn more about the craft of songwriting, to get their songs heard, and to network. The Guild sponsors monthly cassette tape presentations called Songsearches to L.A. publishers, with drawings held for studio time and gift certificates. We also sponsor monthly workshops, classes and lectures on music in film and TV, studio recording, music business contracts and copyright law, record production, song marketing, music composition, lyric writing and vocal techniques, in addition to publishing a directory of local music services and organizations. Discounts available to members include the following: blank tapes, books that deal with a wide range of pertinent music industry information, studio time at local recording studios, equipment and supplies at local music stores." Membership is $35/year.

SESAC INC., 156 W. 56th St., New York NY 10019. (212)586-3450; 55 Music Square E., Nashville TN 37203. (615)320-0055 President and Chief Executive Officer: Vincent Candilora. Vice President: Dianne Petty, Nashville. Serves writers and publishers in all types of music who have their works performed by radio, television, nightclubs, cable TV, etc. Purpose of organization is to collect and distribute performance royalties to all active affiliates. "Prospective affiliates are requested to present a demo tape of their works which is reviewed by our Screening Committee." For possible affiliation, call Nashville or New York for appointment.

*SNOWBELT SONGWRITERS' GUILD, INC., #15, 329 Maple St., Oswego NY 13126. (315)343-8693. President and Founder: Carolyn A. Gunther. Estab. 1985. Serves songwriters, musicians, and "anyone interested in the creative and business aspects of songwriting. We have members from many counties in New York State. Individual members are from 14 to 68 years of age and write EL, MOR, rock, R&B, bluegrass, C&W, folk, gospel and others that defy categorization. We come from all walks of life but share a love for songwriting. We serve beginning, intermediate and advanced writers. Types of memberships available: Active Membership: open to persons who have been or are presently involved with the actual composition of music and/or lyrics. An active member may hold office, vote and be on the board of directors. Dues are $25 per year. Associate Membership: open to persons interested in learning the craft of songwriting and/or assisting in guild activities. Friend/Patron dues are $10/year. Patron/Friend Membership: open to persons interested in contributing their resources to Guild Development. Among the requirements are an interest in songwriting as a serious art form, and the desire to become involved in it through the sharing of songs and ideas with peers and the community. We support the individual songwriter in his endeavor to have songs published, recorded and performed. We provide technical assistance with copywriting, locating publishers and songwriter advocacy. The primary benefits of membership for the songwriter are: 1) education through meetings, workshops and seminars; 2) the opportunity to share material and receive feedback from peers; 3) collaboration opportunities; 4) technical assistance in the business aspects of the craft; and 5) contact with other songwriting associations, professional organizations, and music industry professionals. Each of us individually pursues our craft and career dictated by choice. In our quest, we gather valuable experience and education." Offers instruction, performance opportunities, social outings, workshops and songwriter advocacy. Applications accepted year-round. Dues are $25/year.

SOCIETY FOR THE PRESERVATION AND ENCOURAGEMENT OF BARBER SHOP QUARTET SINGING IN AMERICA, INC. (S.P.E.B.S.Q.S.A., INC.), 6315 Third Ave., Kenosha WI 53143-5199. (414)656-8440. Membership Manager: Ron Rockwell. Estab. 1938. Serves songwriters, musicians and world's largest all male singing organization. "Members are from teenage to elderly. All are interested in vocal harmony (4 singing, barbershop style). The main purpose of this organization is to perpetuate and preserve the musical art form known as Barbershop Harmony. We are always looking for new songs that will adapt to barbershop harmonization and style." Offers competitions, instruction, lectures, library, newsletter, performance opportunities, social outings and workshops. "A week-long 'Harmony College' is presented each year, open to over 700 men. Instruction in all areas of music: vocal techniques, arranging, songwriting, show production, chorus directing, etc. A 'Young Men In Harmony' program is offered, especially designed to appeal to young high school boys. Approved by MENC and ACDA. Our publishing program, which at present offers over 600 songs, is arranged in the barbershop style. The Society offers the opportunity for songwriters to have their music arranged and published. We maintain a library of over 600,000 pieces of sheet music—most of which is turn of the century to the mid-late 20s." Applications accepted year-round. Membership is usually in local chapters with dues about $70 annually. A chapter-at-large membership, The Frank H. Thorne Chapter, is available at $70 annually.

SOCIETY OF COMPOSERS, AUTHORS AND MUSIC PUBISHERS OF CANADA (SOCAN), Head Office: 41 Valleybrook Dr., Don Mills, Ontario M3B 2S6 **Canada**. (416)445-8700. FAX: (416)445-7108. Chief Executive Officer: Jan Matejcek. (415)445-8700. Chief Operating Officer: Michael Rock (416)445-8700. In March, 1990, CAPAC and PROCAN merged to form a single, new Canadian performing rights society. The purpose of the society is to collect music user license fees and distribute performance royalties to composers, authors and music publishers. The SOCAN catalogue is licensed by ASCAP and BMI in the United States.

SONGWRITERS & LYRICISTS CLUB, %Robert Makinson, Box 023304, Brooklyn NY 11202-0066. Director: Robert Makinson. Estab. 1984. Serves songwriters and lyricists. Currently has 75 members. Gives information regarding songwriting: creation of songs, reality of market, collaboration, disc jockeys and other contacts. Only requirement is ability to write lyrics or melodies. Beginners are welcome. The primary benefits of membership for the songwriter are opportunities to collaborate and assistance with creative aspects and marketing of songs through publications and advice. Offers newsletter and assistance with lead sheets and demos. Applications accepted year-round. Dues are $24/year, remit to Robert Makinson. Write with SASE for more information. "Plan and achieve realistic goals. If you have a great song, we'll make every effort to help promote it."

SONGWRITER'S AND POET'S CRITIQUE, 2804 Kingston Ave., Grove City OH 43123. (614)875-5352. President: Patricia A. Adcock. Estab. 1985. Serves songwriters, musicians, poets, lyricists and performers. "We provide information, encouragement and help with the critiquing, networking and pairing of collaborators." Offers field trips, instruction, lectures, library, performance opportunities, social outings, workshops and critiquing sessions. Applications accepted year-round. Annual dues are $12. "We're a talented and diverse group; some of our members are published and recorded writers, and we invite all songwriters, musicians and poets in the Columbus area to visit and share their creativity."

SONGWRITERS ASSOCIATION OF WASHINGTON, Suite 632, 1377 K St. NW, Washington DC 20005. (301)654-8434. President: Marcy Freiberg. Estab. 1979. "S.A.W. is a nonprofit organization committed to providing its members with the means to improve their songwriting skills, learn more about the music business and gain exposure in the industry. S.A.W. sponsors various events to achieve this goal, such as workshops, seminars, meetings, showcases and the mid-Atlantic song contest. S.A.W. publishes *S.A.W. Notes*, a bi-monthly newsletter containing vital information on changes in the business markets for demos, free classifieds to members and upcoming events around the country. For more information regarding membership write or call.

THE SONGWRITERS GUILD OF AMERICA, Suite 306, 276 Fifth Ave., New York NY 10001. (212)686-6820. West Coast: Ste. 317, 6430 Sunset Blvd., Hollywood CA 90028. (213)462-1108. Nashville: United Artists Tower, 50 Music Square West, Nashville TN 37203. (615)329-1782. Founded as the Songwriters' Protective Association in 1931, name changed to American Guild of Authors and Composers in 1958, and expanded to AGAC/The Songwriters Guild in 1982. Effective 1985, the organizational name is The Songwriters Guild of America. "The Songwriters Guild of America is the nation's largest, oldest, most respected and most experienced songwriters' association devoted exclusively to providing songwriters with the services, activities and protection they need to succeed in the business of music." President: George David Weiss. Executive Director: Lewis M. Bachman. National Projects Director: George Wurzbach. West Coast Regional Director: Aaron Meza. Nashville Regional Director: Kathy Hyland. "A full member must be a published songwriter. An associate member is any unpublished songwriter with a desire to learn more about the business and craft of songwriting. The third class of membership comprises estates of deceased writers. The Guild contract is conceded to be the best available in the industry, having the greatest number of built-in protections for the songwriter. The Guild's Royalty Collection Plan makes certain that prompt and accurate payments are made to writers. The ongoing Audit Program makes periodic checks of publishers' books. For the self-publisher, the Catalogue Administration Program (CAP) relieves a writer of the paperwork of publishing for a fee lower than the prevailing industry rates. The Copyright Renewal Service informs members a year in advance of a song's renewal date. Other services include workshops in New York and Los Angeles, free Ask-A-Pro rap sessions with industry pros (see Workshops), critique sessions, collaborator service and newsletters. In addition, the Guild reviews your songwriter contract on request (Guild or otherwise); fights to strengthen songwriters' rights and to increase writers' royalties by supporting legislation which directly affects copyright; offers a group medical and life insurance plan; issues news bulletins with essential information for songwriters; provides a songwriter collaboration service for younger writers; financially evaluates catalogues of copyrights in connection with possible sale and estate planning; operates an estates administration service; and maintains a nonprofit educational foundation (The Songwriters Guild Foundation)."

SONGWRITERS OF OKLAHOMA, 211 W. Waterloo Rd., Edmond OK 73034. (405)348-6534. President: Harvey Derrick. Estab. 1983. Serves songwriters and musicians, professional writers, amateur writers, college and university faculty, musicians, poets and others from labor force as well as retired individuals. Age range is from 18 to 90. "Must be interested in writing and composing and have a desire to help others in any way possible. We have members from coast to coast. We offer workshops, critique sessions, contests, civic benefits, education of members on copyright, contracts, publishers, demos, record companys, etc., as well as a sounding board of peers, education, camaraderie and sharing of knowledge." Offers competitions, field trips, instruction, lectures, library, newsletter, per-

WOULD YOU USE THE SAME CALENDAR YEAR AFTER YEAR?

Of course not! If you scheduled your appointments using last year's calendar, you'd risk missing important meetings and deadlines, so you keep up-to-date with a new calendar each year. Just like your calendar, *Songwriter's Market®* changes every year, too. Many of the buyers move or get promoted, rates of pay increase, and even record companies' needs change from the previous year. You can't afford to use an out-of-date book to plan your marketing efforts!

So save yourself the frustration of getting your work returned in the mail, stamped MOVED: ADDRESS UNKNOWN. And of NOT submitting your work to new listings because you don't know they exist. **Make sure you have the most current marketing information by ordering *1993 Songwriter's Market* today.** All you have to do is complete the attached post card and return it with your payment or charge card information. Order now, and there's one thing that won't change from your *1992 Songwriter's Market* - the price! That's right, we'll send you the 1993 edition for just $19.95. *1993 Songwriter's Market* will be published and ready for shipment in September 1992.

Let an old acquaintance be forgot, and toast the new edition of *Songwriter's Market*. Order today!

(See other side for more books for songwriters)

- -

To order, drop this postpaid card in the mail.

☐ Yes! I want the most current edition of *Songwriter's Market®*. Please send me the 1993 edition at the 1992 price - $19.95.* (NOTE: *1993 Songwriter's Market* will be ready for shipment in September 1992.) #10275

*Plus postage & handling: $3.00 for one book, $1.00 for each additional book. Ohio residents add $5^{1}/_{2}\%$ sales tax. Also send me the following books:

____ (#10219) Songwriters on Songwriting, $17.95*, paper (available NOW)
____ (#10220) The Songwriter's Workshop, $24.95*, paper (available NOW)
____ (#10234) The Songwriter's & Musician's Guide to Nashville, $18.95*, paper (available NOW)

☐ Payment enclosed (Slip this card and your payment into an envelope)
☐ Please charge my: ☐ Visa ☐ MasterCard

Account # _____ Exp. Date _____

Signature _____ Phone ( ) _____

Name _____

Address _____

City _____ State _____ Zip _____

(This offer expires May 31, 1993)

Credit Card Orders Call Toll-Free 1-800-289-0963

1507 Dana Avenue
Cincinnati, OH 45207

6046

MORE BOOKS FOR SONGWRITERS!

formance opportunities, social outings and workshops. Applications accepted year-round. Membership fee is $15/year.

SONGWRITERS OF WISCONSIN, P.O. Box 874, Neenah WI 54957-0874. (414)725-1609. Director: Tony Ansems. Estab. 1983. Serves songwriters. "Membership is open to songwriters writing all styles of music. Residency in Wisconsin is recommended but not required. Members are encouraged to bring tapes and lyric sheets of their songs to the meetings, but it is not required. We are striving to improve the craft of songwriting in Wisconsin. Living in Wisconsin, a songwriter would be close to any of the workshops and showcases offered each month at different towns. The primary value of membership for a songwriter is in sharing ideas with other songwriters, being critiqued and helping other songwriters." Offers competitions, field trips, instruction, lectures, newsletter, performance opportunities, social outings, workshops and critique sessions. Applications accepted year-round. $7.50 subscription fee for newsletter.

*SOUTHERN SONGWRITERS GUILD, INC., P.O. Box 6817, Shreveport LA 71136-6817. Public Relations Officer: Tommy Cassel. Estab. 1983. Serves songwriters, musicians and students. Members are multi-race, amateur/professional, all ages, with an interest in the entertainment business. Open membership. Purpose is to provide education in entertainment business and to provide scholarships. Offers competitions, instruction, lectures, newsletter, performance opportunities, social outings and workshops. Applications accepted year-round. Annual dues: $30 member, $100 organization, $500 or more Benefactor.

SOUTHWEST VIRGINIA SONGWRITERS ASSOCIATION, P.O. Box 698, Salem VA 24153. (703)389-1525. President: Sidney V. Crosswhite. Vice President: Robert W. Arrington. Estab. 1982. Nonprofit, tax exempt organization which sponsors monthly newsletter, mail-in critique service for out-of-town members at no charge, and monthly meetings featuring song critiques, guest speakers and workshops. Also offers library, field trips and social outings. Purpose is "to increase, broaden and expand the knowledge of each member and to support, better and further the progress and success of each member in songwriting and related fields of endeavor through meetings, workshops, correspondence and any other educational means available." Must submit application and be approved by Board of Directors. One-time initiation fee is $15. Dues are $12/year. "Every *serious* songwriter should belong to a local and a national organization. It's important to be around other songwriters on a regular basis."

THE TENNESSEE SONGWRITERS ASSOCIATION, Box 2664, Hendersonville TN 37077. (615)824-4555. Executive Director: Jim Sylvis. Serves songwriters. "Our membership is open to all ages and consists of both novice and experienced professional songwriters. The only requirement for membership is a serious interest in the craft and the business of songwriting. Most of our members are local, but we also accept out-of-state memberships. Our main purpose and functon is to educate and assist the songwriter, both in the art/craft of songwriting and in the business of songwriting. In addition to education, we also provide an opportunity for camaraderie, support and encouragement, as well a chance to meet co-writers. Our members often will play on each others' demo sessions. We also critique each others' material and offer suggestions for improvement, if needed. We offer the following to our members: 'Pro-Rap'—once a month a key person from the music industry addresses our membership on their field of specialty. They may be writers, publishers, producers and sometimes even the recording artists themselves. 'Pitch-A-Pro'—once a month we schedule a publisher, producer or artist who is currently looking for material, to come to our meeting and listen to songs pitched by our members. Annual Awards Dinner—honoring the most accomplished of our TSA membership during the past year. Tips—letting our members know who is recording and how to get their songs to the right people. Other activities—a TSA summer picnic, parties throughout the year, and opportunities to participate in music industry-related charitable events, such as the annual Children's Christmas Caravan benefit, which the TSA proudly supports." Applications accepted year-round. Membership runs for one year from the date you join. Membership fee is $25/year.

TEXAS MUSIC ASSOCIATION, Box 2547, Austin TX 78705. (512)447-2744. Secretary/Treasurer: Steve Hudson. Estab. 1981. Local chapters in Austin, Dallas, San Antonio and Houston. Serves songwriters, musicians and all music industry professionals. Voting members must have significant professional involvement in the music industry; non-voting (associate) membership is open to everyone who supports Texas music. The TMA is the principal trade association for the Texas music industry, offering educational and professional development programs, newsletters, awards programs and lobbying for the industry's interests. Networking with professionals working in other fields of the music business (such as publishers, managers, agents, publicists, studio personnel, etc.) Offers lectures, newsletter, workshops, group health and equipment insurance, credit union, discount long distance phone service. Applications accepted year-round. General membership (voting) $50/yr. Company membership (voting) $150/yr. (All full-time employees qualify for benefits.) Associate membership (nonvoting) $25/yr. "TMA members are also eligible for discounted registration fees at the annual South By Southwest Music and Media Conference in Austin. Songwriters can benefit from TMA membership by taking advantage of our many member services, our networking opportunities and our educational and professional development programs."

TEXAS SONGWRITERS ASSOCIATION, P.O. Box 1344, Shepherd TX 77371. (713)592-8886. Executive Director: Linda Ledbetter. Director Emeritus: Shirley Horton Hutchins. Estab. 1986. Serves songwriters. "Our members are people of all ages, interested in all categories of music—any person interested in songwriting, whether professional or pre-professional, who will support the goals of TSA. Our organization assists those interested in songwriting through educational and informational programs and workshops and offers career guidance throughout all stages of individual development. We provide guidance and encouragement in all aspects of songwriting, from craft techniques to business and industry preparation." Offers instruction, lectures, newsletter, performance opportunities, social outings and workshops. Applications accepted year-round. General membership fee is $40; annual dues are $40.
Tips: "The informed songwriter stands a better chance of succeeding in the highly complex field of songwriting. TSA workshops inform writers, both on craft and business."

THEATRICAL ENTERTAINMENT OF ACTORS & MUSICIANS, Box 30260, Bakersfield CA 93385. President: Judge A. Robertson. "Our purpose is to advance, educate, encourage, protect and promote overlooked creative talent. We help you help yourself to become a professionally paid artist by producing the creative aspects of songwriters, actors, and artists, and by providing performance opportunities. We notify publishers that demo tapes have been pre-screened by T.E.A.M. Our media showcase is in coproduction with Superstar Productions, Element Records, International Motion Pictures, Ltd., and Element Movie and Music (BMI)." Applications accepted year-round; one-time $55 fee and annual membership fee of $25.

*TRIAD SONGWRITER'S ASSOCIATION, Box 24095, Winston-Salem NC 27104-4095. (919)765-8306. President: Ceedi Leffler. Estab. 1985. Serves songwriters and musicians. "Our membership is a broad-based group of musicians/lyricists interested in writing, workshops, performing and critiques. Triad Songwriters' Association is designed to provide a forum for all local musicians and songwriters to perform, learn and network. Secondarily, to form associations with other national and local organizations dedicated to the same primary purpose. Offers competitions, instruction, lectures, library, newsletter, performance opportunities and workshops. Applications accepted year-round. Membership fee is $20. Annual dues are $15.

TULSA SONGWRITERS ASSOCIATION, INC., P.O. Box 254, Tulsa OK 74101-0254. (918)660-2035. President: Bryan Huling. Estab. 1983. Serves songwriters and musicians. Members are age 18-65 and have interests in all types of music. Main purpose of the organization is "to create a forum to educate, develop, improve, discover and encourage songwriting in the Tulsa area." Offers competitions, lectures, performance opportunities, field trips, social outings, instruction, newsletter and workshops. Applications accepted year-round. Dues are $30/year.
Tips: "We hold a monthly 'Writer's Night' open to the public for performance of original songs to expose the many talented writers in Tulsa."

UNITED SONGWRITER'S ASSOCIATION, 6429 Leavenworth Rd., Kansas City KS 66104. (913)788-7716. President: Victor J. Stoway. Vice President: Steven D. Caldwell. Treasurer: Rodney Brock. Estab. 1987. Serves songwriters and musicians. "Members run the full spectrum of ages, with interest in every aspect of the music business. We help songwriters achieve the recognition they deserve; combining the talents of the members makes this possible. Members may also make contact with people in the music business. Copyright information, collaborating information, songwriting tips and the lowest prices on demo fees and cassette tapes are some of the benefits the members derive. We also have a song catalog, song critique workshops, open door invitation to two of Kansas City's record companies, and a 20-40% discount at some of the local music stores. USA is a non-profit association. The plans are in the works for USA to perform for charity fund-raising benefits. We would like for USA to be known as a friend to all the songwriters of the world." Offers field trips, instruction, lectures, library, newsletter (bi-monthly), performance opportunities, social outings and workshops (bi-monthly). Membership fee is $15/year.

UTAH SONGWRITERS ASSOCIATION, P.O. Box 71325, Salt Lake City UT 84107. (801)596-3058 or (801)964-1227. Estab. 1985. Serves songwriters and musicians. Interest lies mainly in country and folk music, along with pop, bluegrass and contemporary music. Writers are interested in learning how to get their music published. We offer monthly workshops for the songwriters in our area, monthly showcases where writers can perform original material for the public, an annual seminar where writers can meet and talk with major publishers and producers, and an annual songwriting contest. Our goal is to help educate the songwriters in this area and to let them know there is a support group willing to listen to their music and offer advice." Annual events sponsored by Utah Songwriters Association include: Intermountain Songwriters Seminar (May or June) and Intermountain Songwriting Competition (Oct. 15 through Dec. 31 of each year). Winner of the songwriting competition wins money or a free trip to Nashville to attend the Nashville Songwriters Association Spring Symposium in March or a trip to L.A. to attend the Songwriters Workshop in October. The trip is funded by entry fees of $10 for first song, $5 for each additional song. Membership dues are $25.

*VERMONT SONGWRITERS ASSOCIATION, RD 2 Box 277, Underhill VT 05489. (802)899-3787. President: Bobby Hackney. Estab. 1991. "Membership open to anyone desiring a career in songwriting, or anyone who seeks a supportive group to encourage co-writing, meeting other songwriters, or to continue their songwriting endeavors." Purpose is to give songwriters an opportunity to meet industry professionals at monthly meetings and seminars, to have their works critiqued by peers and to help songwriters learn more about the craft and the complete business of songwriting." Offers competitions, instruction, lectures, library, newsletter, performance opportunities, workshops. Applications accepted year-round. Membership fee is $30/year.
Tips: "We are a nonprofit association dedicated to creating opportunities for songwriters. Even though our office address in in Underhill, Vermont, our primary place of business is in Burlington, Vermont, where monthly meetings and seminars are held."

*VICTORY MUSIC, P.O. Box 7515, Bonney Lake WA 98390. (206)863-6617. Estab. 1969. Serves songwriters, audiences and specifically local acoustic musicians of all music styles. Victory Music provides places to play, showcases, opportunities to read about the business and other songwriters, referrals and seminars. Produced 4 albums of NW songwriters. Offers library, newsletter, performance opportunities and workshops. Applications accepted year-round. Membership fee is $20/year (single); $50/year business; $28/year couple; $178 lifetime.

*THE VIRGINIA ORGANIZATION OF COMPOSERS AND LYRICISTS, P.O. Box 34606, Richmond VA 23234. (804)733-5908. Chairman/Membership Committee: Colin Campbell. Estab. 1986. Serves songwriters. Members range in age from 20-70 years old, and come from all fields of music—gospel, rock, country and R&B. All songwriters are welcome to join. The main purpose of VOCAL is to educate and provide opportunities for songwriters to learn whatever they need to know about the business of songwriting. Offers competitions, instruction, lectures, newsletter, performance opportunities, social outings and workshops. Applications accepted year-round. Membership fee is $15.
Tips: "VOCAL is a complete nonprofit organization established solely for the purpose of advancing the talents, knowledge, skills and abilities of its membership."

VOLUNTEER LAWYERS FOR THE ARTS, 3rd Floor, 1285 Avenue of the Americas, New York NY 10019. (212)977-9270. Estab. 1969. Serves songwriters, musicians and all performing, visual, literary and fine arts artists and groups. Offers legal assistance and representation to eligible individual artists and arts organizations who cannot afford private counsel. Also sells publications on arts-related issues. In addition, there are affiliates nationwide who assist local arts organizations and artists. Offers conferences, lectures, seminars and workshops.

*WASHINGTON AREA MUSIC ASSOCIATION, 1690 36th St., N.W., Washington DC 20007. (202)337-2227. Membership Chairman: B.J. Cohen. Estab. 1985. Serves songwriters, musicians and performers, managers, club owners, entertainment lawyers; "all those with an interest in the Washington music scene." Members must be Washington area residents. The organization is designed to promote the Washington music scene and increase its visibility. Its primary value to members is its seminars and networking opportunities. Offers lectures, newsletter, performance opportunities and workshops. Applications accepted year-round. Annual dues are $25.

WHITEWATER VALLEY SONGWRITERS AND MUSICIANS ASSN., (formerly NSAI-WVSM Songwriters Association), RR #4, Box 112, Liberty IN 47353. (317)458-6152. Founder: Ann Hofer. Serves songwriters and musicians. Estab. 1981. "Our members are songwriters of all ages. Some are interested in all aspects of the music business and others just songwriting. We have artists, musicians, lyricists and melody writers. Our purpose is to assist our members with finding co-writers, keep them informed on publishers accepting material, help them make demo contacts, provide list of record companies, and to educate them on the ever-changing music and songwriting business. We are available to assist the songwriter in any way we can; we are dedicated to his/her needs. We believe that believing in yourself is the beginning of your dream coming true, and we want to encourage songwriters to do just that: believe in themselves." Offers competitions, instruction, lectures, library, performance opportunities, social outings and song critique sessions. For more information call Ann at (317)458-6152.

*WICHITA SONGWRITERS GROUP, 2450 Somerset, Wichita KS 64204. (316)838-6079. Contact: David Kinion. Estab. 1988. Serves songwriters. Members include teenagers to retired people from the community. Members must live close enough to be present at meetings. Main purpose is to provide a sense of community for songwriters while helping them write better songs. Wichita Songwriters Group provides instruction, common support and a songwriter's network for placement of songs. Offers field trips, instruction, lectures, library, performance opportunities and workshops. Applications accepted year-round. Fee of $1 per meeting.
Tips: WSG meets on the first Monday of each month (except holidays) at 7:30 pm at Miller Music, 4235 West Central, Wichita, KS.

WYOMING COUNTRY MUSIC FOUNDATION, 1645 Sussex Road, Kaycee WY 82639. (307)738-2303 or 684-7305. President and Founder: Helen D. Ullery. Estab. 1983. Festival Coordinator: Mike Kuzara, Box 7224, Sheridan WY 82801. (307)672-0529. Serves songwriters and musicians. Members include "youth, amateurs, professionals, pioneers, country and gospel/country songwriters, musicians and vocalists. No eligibility requirements. Our purpose is to promote country music and country music performers, showcase talent, educate members, and coordinate our annual festival each summer." Offers competitions, lectures, performance opportunities, social outings, newsletter, workshops and annual songwriters contest. "Our songwriter contest is held each spring. Contest deadline is April 15, 1992. Entry is $10/song; 50% of entry fees goes back as prizes to winners. Entrants can not have been in top 50 in charts in the last 10 years. Final review is done in Nashville." Membership fee is $25; festival registration is $15. For membership application and a copy of contest rules send SASE to WCMF address above.

Workshops

Conferences and workshops provide a means for songwriters to have songs evaluated, hear suggestions for further improvement, and receive feedback and motivation from industry experts. In the past few years, major regional music conferences have gained a lot of attention, and are an excellent place to make valuable industry contacts.

Usually, major workhops and events occur in the music hubs: New York, Los Angeles and Nashville. But there are organizations that offer travelling workshops on just about every songwriting topic imaginable – from lyric writing and marketing strategy to contract negotiating. More and more small and mid-size cities with strong songwriter organizations are running their own workshops as well, drawing on resources from within their own groups or importing professionals from the music centers.

Whatever your needs are, there is a workshop for you. There are programs for pop songwriters and performers, musical theater enthusiasts, jazz musicians and much more. The following list includes national and local workshops, with a brief description of what each offers. For more information, write to the sponsoring organization.

*ANNUAL NATIONAL CONFERENCE OF COLLEGE BROADCASTERS & REGIONAL CONFERENCES OF COLLEGE BROADCASTERS, Box 1955-Brown University, Providence RI 02912. (401)863-2225. Association Director: Carolyne Allen. Estab. 1988. "The purpose of these conferences is to bring top media leaders together with students from college broadcasting to learn and share ideas. Several sessions on music licensing, record company relations and alternative/new music programming trends are typically included. We conduct the NACB 'Top Station Search' (not open to songwriters). We also have a comprehensive awards/competitions listing every month in *College Broadcaster* magazine, many of which relate to musicians. The Annual Conference (November) and Regional Conferences (Spring) last 1-3 days at various host college campuses around the U.S. Participants include artists, producers, TV/radio program directors, amateur and professional songwriters, bands, composers and record label reps. Participants are selected through submission of demo tapes and leads from college broadcasting stations. For information about dates and participation, call Carolyne Allen at (401)863-2225. Closing date for application is September/October for the National Conference and one month prior to each regional conference. There is a $50 registration fee. Lunches, receptions and refreshments throughout day are included. A discount hotel package is available to attendees."

*APPEL FARM ARTS AND MUSIC FESTIVAL, P.O. Box 888, Elmer NJ 08318. (609)358-2472. Artistic Director: Sean Timmons. Estab. Festival: 1989; Series 1970. "Our annual open air festival is the highlight of our year round Performing Arts Series which was established to bring high quality arts programs to the people of South Jersey. Festival includes acoustic and folk music, blues, etc." Programs for songwriters and musicians include performance opportunities as part of Festival and Performing Arts Series. Programs for musical playwrights also include performance opportunities as part of Performing Arts Series. Festival is a one-day event held in June, and Performing Arts Series is held year-round. Both are held at the Appel Farm Arts and Music Center, a 176-acre farm in Southern New Jersey. Up to 20 songwriters/musicians participate in each event. Participants are songwriters, individual vocalists, bands, ensembles, vocal groups, composers, individual instrumentalists and dance/mime/movement. Participants are selected by demo tape submissions. Applicants should send a press packet, demonstration tape and biographical information. Application materials accepted year round. Faculty opportunities are available as part of residential Summer Arts Program for children, July/August.

APPLE HILL SUMMER CHAMBER MUSIC FESTIVAL, Apple Hill Center for Chamber Music, P.O.Box 217, E. Sullivan NH 03445. (603)847-3371. Student Recruitment and Special Projects Coordinator: Harriet Feinberg. "Apple Hill welcomes 45-50 students of all ages and abilities to each of 5 summer music sessions for coaching by the Apple Hill Chamber Players and distinguished guest faculty artists and opportunities to perform chamber music of all periods. Musicians may choose from 5 short sessions (10 days each), in which participants are assigned to 2 or 3 ensembles coached daily for up to 1½ hours. Programs are offered June-August. 55 musicians participate in each workshop. Participants are amateur and professional individual instrumentalists, singers and ensembles. Participants are selected by demo tape submissions. Send for application. Suggested application deadline: May 1st. There is a $25 application fee. Total cost for the short sessions: $835 (after May 1st $860). Programs take place on a 70-acre New England farm. Includes the Louise Shonk Kelly Concert Barn, home of countless rehearsals, student performances and festival concerts; general meeting place and dining hall/bathroom facilities; rehearsal barn; faculty and student cabins; tennis courts."

BMI-LEHMAN ENGEL MUSICAL THEATRE WORKSHOP, 320 W. 57th St., New York NY 10019. (212)586-2000. Director of Musical Theatre: Norma Grossman. Estab. 1961. "BMI is a music licensing company, which collects royalties for affiliated writers. We have departments to help writers in jazz, concert, Latin and pop writing." Offers programs "to musical theater composers, librettists and lyricists. The BMI-Lehman Engel Musical Theatre Workshops were formed in an effort to refresh and stimulate professional writers, as well as to encourage and develop new creative talent for the musical theater." Offers 250 musical theater workshops and 100 jazz workshops/year. Each workshop meets one afternoon a week for two hours at BMI, New York. Participants are professional songwriters, composers, playwrights and librettists, solo instrumentalists and opera/musical theater writers. "BMI-Lehman Engel Musical Theatre Workshop Showcase presents the best of the workshop to producers, agents, record and publishing company execs, press people and agents for possible option and production." Applicants should call for application. Tape of 3 compositions required with application. Librettists should submit excerpts from works published, produced or in progress. No entry fee.

BROADWAY TOMORROW PREVIEWS, % Broadway Tomorrow Musical Theatre, Suite 53, 191 Claremont Ave., New York NY 10027. Artistic Director: Elyse Curtis. Estab. 1983. Purpose is the enrichment of American theater by nurturing *new musicals*. Offers series in which composers living in New York City area present scores of their new musicals in concert. 2-3 composers/librettists/lyricists of same musical and 1 musical director/pianist participate. Participants are professional singers, composers and opera/musical theater writers. Submission by recommendation of past participants only. Submission is by audio cassette of music, script if completed, synopsis, cast breakdown, resume, reviews, if any, acknowledgement postcard and SASE. Participants selected by screening of submissions. Programs are presented in fall and spring with possibility of full production of works presented in concert. No entry fee.

CHICAGO JAZZ FESTIVAL, City of Chicago, Mayor's Office of Special Events, City Hall Rm. 703, 121 N. LaSalle St., Chicago IL 60602. (312)744-3315. Coordinator: Penny Tyler. Estab. 1979. "World's largest free outdoor jazz festival. Presents jazz in all of it's forms, free to the public." Festival takes place the 4 days of Labor Day weekend at Petrillo Band Shell, Grant Park. 200 songwriters/musicians participate. Participants are professional jazz vocalists, bands, ensembles, vocal groups, composers, individual instrumentalists and orchestras. Participants are selected by audition (tape, not live). Send tape and bio with photo for consideration. Individuals or groups are hired by Festival.

COMPOSERS' INSTITUTE, The Festival at Sandpoint, P.O. Box 695, Sandpoint ID 83864. (208)265-4554. Executive Director: Timothy Hunt. Estab. 1989. Programs offered summer only (July 24-August 17), last 3 weeks each (staggered) and take place at Schweitzer Mountain Resort (Sandpoint). 98 songwriters/musicians participate. Participants are professional individual vocalists, bands, ensembles, composers and individual instrumentalists. Participants are selected by demo tape and resume submissions. Send for application. Closing dates for application are April 15-May 15. Registration fee: $25. Costs are all-inclusive and include room and board. Prices range from $1,000-1,400. Housing at Overniter Lodge at Schweitzer Mountain Resort. Meals at the Saint Bernard Restaurant, also at Schweitzer.

***DOULOS TRAINING SCHOOLS,** P.O. Box 60341, Nashville TN 37206. Toll free: 1-800-235-1944. Estab. 1987. "Doulos Training Schools is a fully dedicated training center for Christian communicators, especially singers and songwriters. Separate 5 day schools for both performers and songwriters are held in Nashville every quarter in January, April, July and October (approximately 25-50 amateur and professional participants/session). The schools offer in-depth career development information to help both beginning and advanced songwriters, singers, bands, vocal groups, composers and ensembles get and stay on track. Each session is taught by recording artist and songwriter Russ Hollingsworth, and involves other major recording artists and songwriters from the Christian Music community. Past guests have included Steve Green, Steve Camp, Scott Wesley Brown, Kim Boyce and many more. Call or write for complete tuition information and description of curriculum. Entry fee ranges $675-875.

***FOLK ALLIANCE ANNUAL CONFERENCE,** P.O. Box 5010, Chapel Hill NC 27514. (919)542-3997. Contact: Art Menius. Estab. 1989. Conference/workshop topics change each year. Subjects covered at 1991 conference include "Survival on the Road," "Career Management" and "Grants for Folk Artists." Conference takes place late January/early February and lasts 4 days and take place at a different location each year. 150 amateur and professional musicians participate. Artist showcase participants are songwriters, individual vocalists, bands, ensembles, vocal groups and individual instrumentalists. Participants are selected by demo tape submission. Applicants should send 4 demo tapes and 4 copies of promotional material to "Showcase Committee" at above address. Closing date for application is August 31. Charges $50 on acceptance. Additional costs vary from year to year. For 1991 the cost is $85 in advance, which covers two meals, a dance, workshops and our showcase. Performers' housing is separate for the event, which is usually held in Convention hotel.

GRAND TETON MUSIC FESTIVAL, P.O. Box 490, Teton Village WY 83025. (307)733-3050. Music Director: Ling Tung. Estab. 1962. "Purpose is to present a wide variety of classical music over a seven week summer season. The Festival engages a resident company of approximately 130 professional musicians to perform orchestral music, chamber music and contemporary music." Offered in Teton Village, Wyoming. 130 musicians participate. Participants are professional composers and individual instrumentalists. Participants are selected by audition in person, performers selected by invitation, submit demonstation tape and referral. Auditions are held December-April in Philadelphia (where the music director lives during the winter). Contact Ling Tung, 2373 Terwood Dr., Huntingdon Valley, PA 19006. Closing date for application is April 30. Festival musicians are housed in condominiums. Rehearsals and concerts take place in the Festival's 700-seat concert hall. "The Festival presents a weekly series of concerts devoted to contemporary music, each one centered around a specific composer who is invited to take part, either as performer, commentator or both. All inquiries from musicians and composers should be directed to the music director."

*GREAT SMOKIES SONG CHASE & PERFORMING ARTISTS WORKSHOPS, P.O. Box 7, Swannanow NC 28778. Director: Billy Edd Wheeler. Estab. 1988. "Offers seminars in lyric and melody writing, publishing, studio work, collaboration—almost all aspects of the creative and business side of music. This year's Performing category, aimed at songwriters and others who want to improve their voices, stage presence and performing abilities, will be directed by Ewel Cornett, founder of Actors Theatre of Louisville. For a brochure or further info contact Billy Edd Wheeler at the phone number/address above." Program offered annually.

GROVE SCHOOL OF MUSIC, 14539 Sylvan St., Van Nuys CA 91411. (818)904-9400. Contact: Jerry Gates or John Cheas. Workshops are offered for guitarists, bassists, synthesists, recording engineers, drummers, keyboardists, vocalists and brass and reed players. "The Grove School of Music offers a wide range of workshops at various proficiency levels; music and MIDI classes, film and video programs, harmony and ear training classes, professional instrumentals program, and demo and master production workshops. Our instructors are all working, well-respected professionals in the caliber of Doug Thiele, Jack Smalley and John D'Andrea. Details on classes, instructors and procedure are available through the admissions office in brochure form. Four 10-week terms/calendar year. Average class size is 15. Classes range from $150-250, covering five to ten 2-hour sessions. Some classes require texts or materials that are not included in the tuition fee. Complete classroom facilities. GSM offers year long, full-time programs for arrangers/composers, vocalists, players, recording engineers and synthesizer programmers. The school also offers the Composition and Musicianship Program (COMP) for a student wishing a primary career as a songwriter. The course includes instruction in record producing, the record industry and publishing. Students can obtain in-depth experience in all styles of song composition and learn concepts about the lyrical and compositional aspects of songwriting. Many of our students have won song contests, accepted positions at major publishing companies or trade magazines and have had songs recorded by such artists as the Jefferson Starship. Applicants must be interviewed for placement prior to enrolling. Certain classes require auditions. Request current catalog by mail or telephone."

GUELPH SPRING FESTIVAL, Edward Johnson Music Foundation, P.O. Box 1718, Guelph, Ontario N1H 6Z9 **Canada**. (519)821-3210. Artistic Director: Simon Streatfeild. Estab. 1968. "We are basically a 3-4 week festival of the performing arts, with an emphasis on professional performers. We strive to bring together the best international and Canadian talent, to promote emerging Canadian talent and new music. We promote opera, chamber music, choral music and some jazz. We regularly commission new works. In addition to concerts, the Edward Johnson Music Competition is for student musicians from Wellington County and Waterloo Region. A national vocal competition is held every 5 years for Canadian singers. Cash scholarships and awards are given." Festival lasts for 3-4 weeks in May. Participants are professional composers, vocalists, instrumentalists, bands, orchestras, choirs, ensembles, opera/musical theater writers and vocal groups. Participants are selected by the artistic director. Applicants should express interest by letter.

KERRVILLE FOLK FESTIVAL, Kerrville Festivals, Inc., P.O. Box 1466, Kerrville TX 78029. (512)257-3600. Founder/President: Rod Kennedy. Sponsors songwriters school and new folk concert competition. Programs held in late spring and late summer. Spring festival lasts 18 days and is held outdoors at Quiet Valley Ranch. Around 110 acts participate. Performers are professional instrumentalists, songwriters and bands. Participants selected by auditioning in person or submitting demo tape, by invitation only. Send cassette, promotional material and list of upcoming appearances. "Songwriter schools are $100 and include breakfast, instructors, camping on ranch and concert. Rustic facilities — no electrical hookups. Food available at reasonable cost."

*MANCHESTER MUSIC FESTIVAL, 93 Franklin Ave., Yonkers NY 10705. (914)965-5533. Director: Michael Rudiakov. Estab. 1974. "Music students from 16 years and up take part in instruction on their instrument, chamber music and chamber orchestra. We give scholarships to those who need and deserve them." Festival features 5 faculty concerts and 5 student concerts and takes place in Manchester, VT from July 1-August 11. Participants are professional and amateur ensembles and composers. Participants are selected by auditions. Contact by mail or phone. Tuition $800. Registration fee $35.

*MUSIC BUSINESS SEMINARS, LTD., 2 Roland Kimball Rd., Freeport ME 04032. (800)448-3621 and (207)865-1128. Director: Peter C. Knickles. "Now in its fifth year MBS, Ltd., presents 'Doing Music & Nothing Else: The Music Business Seminar.' The program is a weekend long, classroom style, multimedia educational experience that is presented in 16 major cities each year. Seminar is for all ages, all styles of music, bands and soloists, who are pursuing a career in original music songwriting, recording and performing. Learn how to establish goals, attract a songwriting or recording contract, book profitable gigs, raise capital and much, much more. Aftercare opportunities include toll free counseling with the instructor, A&R Tip Sheet/Showcase program and 2 free directories (A&R and T-100). Seminar is also available on 8 audio tapes with workbook. This is the only music seminar in US with a money back guarantee. Call for free cassette tape entitled 'Your First Record Deal,' 2-year complimentary quarterly journal subscription and seminar brochure."

MUSICAL THEATRE WORKS, INC., 440 Lafayette St., New York NY 10003. (212)677-0040. Literary Manager: Mike Teele. Estab. 1983. "We develop and produce new works for the musical theater: informal readings, staged readings and full productions of new musicals." Functions year-round. Participants are amateur and professional composers and songwriters and opera/musical theater writers. Participants are selected through a critique/evaluation of each musical by the Literary Manager and his staff. To contact, send complete script, cassette and SASE to the above address.

NATIONAL ACADEMY OF SONGWRITERS (NAS), Suite 780, 6381 Hollywood Blvd., Hollywood CA 90028. (213)463-7178. Staff Members: Dan Kirkpatrick and Steve Schalchlin. Estab. 1972. "Offers programs for songwriters including Publishers' Evaluation Workshops and SONGTALK seminar series, featuring top names in songwriting, lyric writing, demo production and more." Attendance: up to 30/workshop. Participants are amateur and professional songwriters, singers, bands and composers. Length: 2-4 hours/workshop. Membership is $75/year, professionals $120/year; Gold membership $200/year. Call hotline for application: 1-800-826-7287. "NAS is a nonprofit membership organization dedicated to the protection and education of songwriters. NAS also provides a bimonthly newsletter containing tipsheet (*Open Ears*) and collaborators' network."

*NATIONAL MUSIC THEATER CONFERENCE, 234 West 44th St., New York NY 10036. (212)382-2790. Artistic Director: Paulette Haupt. Estab. 1978. Sponsored by the Eugene O'Neill Theater Center. 8-10 songwriters/musicians participate in each event. Participants are professional composers, opera/musical theater writers, lyricists, playwrights in collaboration with composers. "The Conference offers composers, lyricists and book writers the opportunity to develop new music theater works of all forms during a 2-5 week residency at the O'Neill Theater Center. Some works are given publicly staged readings; others are developed in private readings during the conference with artistic staff and dramaturgs. All works selected are developed over at least a 2-3 month period. A professional company of approximately 20 singer/actors provides the writers with daily musical and dramatic readings during the Conference period. Staged works are read with script in hand, with minimal lighting and no physical properties, to allow flexibility for day-to-day rewrites. The Conference is held in August of each year. Participants are selected by Artistic Director and a panel of theater professionals. Composers and writers selected receive room, board and a stipend." Charges entry fee of $10. Send SASE for application.

NORFOLK CHAMBER MUSIC FESTIVAL/YALE SUMMER SCHOOL, 96 Wall St., New Haven CT 06520. (203)432-1966. Director: Joan Panetti. Manager: Sharon D. Moore. Estab. 1941. The Norfolk Festival/School offers training and performances, including a 2-week seminar in June specializing in a particular ensemble medium, followed by a 6-week intensive chamber music session. The Festival/

School is geared towards the standard chamber music ensembles; string quartets, woodwind quintets, brass quintets and ensembles, including piano. Each student receives an Ellen Battell Stoeckel scholarship, which covers all costs except for administrative fees (covers room, board, faculty, music, etc.) Offered in summer only—mid-June through mid-August. 65-80 songwriters/musicians participate. Participants are young professionals, ensembles and individual instrumentalists and are selected by audition in person. Submit demonstration tape for consideration. Auditions are held in New Haven, CT—early to mid-March each year; Rochester, NY; Oberlin, OH; Chicago, IL; San Francisco, CA. Send for application or call (203)432-1966. Closing date for application is early to mid-February (some exceptions may apply). Application fee $25. 2-week session runs $280 and 6-week session runs approximately $600 (covers administrative fees). Students are housed in the town of Norfolk with host families in groups of 1 to 3 per home. The festival takes place on the beautiful 70-acre Ellen Battell Stoeckel Estate which includes the 1,100-seat Music Shed, various barns and cabins for practice and coachings.

OCTOBER FEST OF CHAMBER MUSIC, Mohonk Mountain House, Lake Mohonk, New Paltz NY 12561. (914)255-4500. Manager of Programs and Evening Entertainment: Michelle E. DuBois. In 1976, the Octoberfest program was started at the Mohonk Mountain House. "Purpose: Octoberfest is a theme program which offers amateurs and professionals the chance to play in a relaxed, beautiful atmosphere." Octoberfest is lead by Alice Smiley and is offered annually. 100 musicians participate. Participants are amateur and professional individual instrumentalists and orchestras. Submit demonstration tape and résumé. Call and request an Octoberfest brochure. Closing date for application is a month before or until all positions are filled. Fee $20. The hotel rates include 3 meals a day and use of the hiking trails. Taxes and service charge are added. Hotel resort located in the Shawangunk Mountains of the Hudson Valley on a lake with hiking, tennis, golf, cross-country skiing, skating, horseback riding, etc. Located 7 miles off the NYS Thruway, exit 18. 90 miles from NYC.

THE OTTAWA INTERNATIONAL JAZZ FESTIVAL, P.O. Box 3104, Station D, Ottawa, Ontario K1P 6H7 **Canada**. (613)594-3580. Managing Director: Karen Dalzell. Estab. 1981. The Festival features 10 days of jazz music (and some blues) on primarily outdoor stages. It is a celebration of jazz designed to introduce new audiences, and to promote lesser known artists. Everyday beginning at noon and running until 3 a.m., we run a number of series, each with an emphasis on a scene (e.g. local, national, international) or an approach (duo, solo, piano, etc.). 13 different series run daily so that all jazz approaches are covered in the festival." 400-500 professional vocalists, instrumentalists, bands, ensembles and vocal groups participate in each event. Performers are selected by demo tape submissions. "Programming committee reviews all submissions. Send us a letter of proposal along with any recorded material, bio, reviews, etc. All proposals should be in the Festival office by early April for consideration, as the Festival is always in late July. The 1991 edition will mark the eleventh anniversary of the Festival. Dates are July 12 to 21st." No entry fee.

*PLATINUM MIDATLANTIC MUSIC CONFERENCE, Platinum Music Network, Inc., 390 Ocean Ave., Long Branch NJ 07740. (908)222-6842. President/Coordinator: Steven Zuckerman. Estab. 1989. Purpose is to educate songwriters by networking them with major industry executives. Offers seminars with major A&R people for songwriters, musicians, playwrights or other artists related to the music industry. Offers programs year-round, every 6 weeks. Workshops held in New Jersey and New York City. More than 400 songwriters/musicians participate in each workshop. Participants are amateur and professional songwriters, composers, individual vocalists, individual instrumentalists, bands, vocal groups and record label executives. Send for application. $50 per workshop. "Endorsed by record industry professionals."

SONGCRAFT SEMINARS, 441 East 20th Street, New York NY 10010. (212)674-1143. Estab. 1986. Year-round classes for composers and lyricists conducted by teacher/consultant Sheila Davis, author of *The Craft of Lyric Writing* and *Successful Lyric Writing*. "The teaching method, grounded in fundamental principles, incorporates whole-brain writing techniques. The objective: To express your unique voice. All courses emphasize craftsmanship and teach principles that apply to every musical idiom—pop, theater, or cabaret. For details on starting dates, fees and location of classes, write or call for current listing."
Successful Lyric Writing: A 3-Saturday Course. Three 6-hour classes on the fundamental principles of writing words for and to music. Required text: *Successful Lyric Writing*. Held 3 times a year at The New School. Limited to 12.
Successful Songwriting A one-day seminar/workshop/critique designed for composers as well as lyricists. Topics covered include: music forms, melody writing, plot development, guidelines on figurative language and whole-brain writing. Attendees receive "Keynotes on Successful Songwriting," a digest of seminar theory. Held at colleges and songwriting associations around the country.

Song by Song by Sondheim: A one-day seminar focused on the elements of fine craftsmanship exemplified in the words and music of Stephen Sondheim, America's pre-eminent theater writer. Significant songs are played and analyzed from the standpoint of form, meter, rhyme, literary devices, and thematic development. Attendees are helped to apply these elements to their own writing. Held in April and November at The New School.

Whole-Brain Creativity: A five-week workshop that puts you in touch with your thinking/writing style through an understanding of split hemispheric specialization. While having fun doing exercises to access each quadrant of the brain, you'll acquire new tools for increased creativity and successful songwriting. Limited to 10.

Successful Lyric Writing Consultation Course: This course, an outgrowth of the instructor's book, covers the same theory and assignments as The Basics Course. Participants receive critiques of their work by the book's author via 1-hour phone sessions.

SONGWRITER SEMINARS AND WORKSHOPS, 928 Broadway, New York NY 10010. (212)505-7332. President: Ted Lehrman. Vice President: Libby Bush. Estab. 1975. Offers programs for songwriters: introduction to pop songwriting; advanced workshop; and at-home songwriter workshop. Cycles begin in September and February. Approximately 10 in each songwriter workshop; participants are songwriters/composers, singers and bands. Each cycle lasts 8 weeks. "Our programs stress the craft and business realities of *today's* pop music industry. We guide our members in the writing of the hit single song (both lyrics and music) for those recording artists who are open to outside material. We also share with them our considerable experience and expertise in the marketing of commercial pop music product. Our instructors, Ted Lehrman and Libby Bush, both members of ASCAP, have had between them more than 80 songs recorded and commercially released here and abroad. They continue to be highly active in writing and placing pop songs for publication. Industry guests (record producers, record company, A&R people, publishers) frequently attend workshop sessions." Workshops: Pop Songwriting—Preparing for the Marketplace; Advanced Songwriter Seminar and Workshop—Ready for the Marketplace. Cost of 8 week workshops: $175-185. Cost of at-home songwriter workshop: $25/lyric; $35/song. Private song and career consultation sessions: $45/hour. Top 40 single stressed. Collaboration opportunities available. No housing provided. Interviews/auditions held for songwriters and singer/songwriters to determine which workshop would be most helpful. Call for free brochure and/or to set up interview.

THE SONGWRITERS ADVOCATE (TSA), 47 Maplehurst Rd., Rochester NY 14617. (716)266-0679. Director: Jerry Englerth. "TSA is a nonprofit educational organization that is striving to fulfill the needs of the songwriter. We offer opportunities for songwriters which include song evaluation workshops to help songwriters receive an objective critique of their craft. TSA evaluates tapes and lyric sheets via the mail. We do not measure success on a monetary scale, ever. It is the craft of songwriting that is the primary objective. If a songwriter can arm himself with knowledge about the craft and the business, it will increase his confidence and effectiveness in all his dealings. However, we feel that the songwriter should be willing to pay for professional help that will ultimately improve his craft and attitude." Membership dues are $10/year. Must be member to receive discounts or services provided.

THE SONGWRITERS GUILD OF AMERICA, New York Office: 276 Fifth Ave., New York NY 10001. (212)686-6820. National Projects Director: George Wurzbach. Los Angeles Office: Ste. 317, 6430 Sunset Blvd., Hollywood CA 90028. (213)462-1108. Estab. 1931.

Ask-A-Pro: "2-hour bi-weekly music business forum to which all writers are welcome. It features industry professionals—publishers, producers, A&R people, record company executives, entertainment lawyers, artists—fielding questions from new songwriters." Offered year-round, except during summer. Charge: free to members, $2 for nonmembers.

Song Critique: "New York's oldest ongoing song critique. Guild songwriters are invited to either perform their song live or present a cassette demo for feedback. A Guild moderator is on hand to direct comments. Non-members may attend and offer comments. Free to members, $2 charge for non-members.

The Practical Songwriter: This is a 10 week nuts and bolts seminar dealing with song re-writing, demo production, industry networking, song marketing, contracts and publishing. Sessions are highlighted by visits from industry professionals. Instructor is songwriter/musician George Wurzbach. Fee: $130 for SGA members, $175 for non-members.

Pro-Shop: For each of 6 sessions an active publisher, producer or A&R person is invited to personally screen material from professional Guild writers. Participation is limited to 10 writers. Audition of material is required. Coordinator is producer/musician/award winning singer, Ann Johns Ruckert. Fee: $75 (SGA members only).

Writing For The Nashville Market: An important 4 session workshop for any writer considering writing for the expanding market of country/pop music. Developed to give writers a realistic approach to breaking into this market. Instructor is hit songwriter, author of *How To Pitch and Promote Your*

Songs (Writer's Digest Books), Fred Koller. Fee; $60 for SGA members, $80 for non-members.
Other Courses And Workshops Will Include: Music Theory for Songwriters, Pop Music Workshop, Understanding MIDI, Lyric Writing, Saturday Afternoon Live (one day, selected topics) and Artist/Songwriter Career Development. Other workshops presented in Nashville (615)329-1782 and Los Angeles (213)462-1108.

THE SONGWRITERS GUILD OF AMERICA, Suite 317, 6430 Sunset Blvd., Hollywood CA 90028. (213)462-1108. West Coast Director: B. Aaron Meza. Estab. 1931.
ASK-A-PRO: "2-hour music business rap session to which all writers are welcome, held on the first Tuesday of each month at 7:00 pm. Features industry professionals fielding questions from songwriters." Each session lasts 2 hours. Free to all Guild members, $2 for non-members. Reservations necessary. Phone for more information.
Jack Segal's Songwriters Guild Supershop "Creating Your Career Song, Your Market Breakthrough": This very successful workshop focuses on working a song through to perfection, including title, idea, re-writes and pitching your songs. Please call for more information regarding this very informative workshop. Dates to be announced.
Song Critique Sessions: Held on the last Tuesday of the month at 7:00 pm, SGA members are given the opportunity to present their songs and receive constructive feedback from industry professionals and peers. There is a limit on the number of songs critiqued, and reservations are required. Call the SGA office for more information.
Supershop: SGA professional writers explore the marketing aspects of songwriting. Over 7 sessions, the group meets with music industry professionals. Supershop is a unique experience in networking.

SUMMER LIGHTS FESTIVAL, Greater Nashville Arts Foundation, 111 Fourth Ave. S., Nashville TN 37201. (615)259-6374. Program Coordinator: Chuck Bedwell. Estab. 1981. Goal is to present the arts of Nashville to the world. Featured music is the music of Nashville: jazz, bluegrass, country, rock and gospel. Nashville Songwriters Association International always has a featured segment of the festival. Offers programs year-round. GNAF presents music programs all year; festival lasts 4 days. Approximately 2,000 songwriters/musicians participate in festival. Participants are amateur and professional individual vocalists, bands, ensembles, vocal groups, composers, individual instrumentalists, orchestras and opera/musical theater writers. Performers selected by invitation only. Take name and number and present before Programming Committee, which issues invites. Performers work outside on stages and in the street of the city; those from out of town stay in hotels and motels.

UTAH ARTS FESTIVAL, Utah Arts Festival Foundation, Inc., 168 W 500 N, Salt Lake City UT 84103. (801)322-2428. Assistant Director: Robyn Nelson. Estab. 1977. "We promote the arts in Utah—visual, performing and literary. All types of music are presented—emphasis on new music." Programs offered summer only. Performances last 5 days and take place at Triad Center, downtown Salt Lake City during the third week in June. Participants are amateur and professional songwriters, individual vocalists, bands, ensembles, vocal groups, composers, individual instrumentalists and orchestras. Participants are selected by demo tape submissions. Send for application. Closing date for application is February. Musicians and performers are paid. Artists stay in local hotels. Festival will negotiate with national artists.

Contests and Awards

Contests may not seem to be a major song "market" in the normal sense, but a songwriter should still approach a contest entry just as he would a music publisher or record company: with care, thorough research and professionalism. Appropriate marketing techniques shouldn't be disregarded. Remember, you're still selling yourself and your work—and you always want both presented in the best light possible.

Participation in songwriting or musical contests is a great way to gain exposure for your music. Although a small entry fee is usually required, winners stand to gain cash prizes, musical merchandise and sometimes a recording deal. Additionally, even if you don't win, valuable contacts can be made. Some contests are judged by music publishers and other music industry professionals, so your music will at least reach the ears of a few important people. The bottom line is, even if you don't win, there is a chance that a beneficial business relationship could result from entering.

Not all songwriting contests are legitimate, so be sure to do proper research to ensure that you're not wasting your time and money. Based on the information given to us, we have confidence in the contests listed in this edition of *Songwriter's Market*. But, if you are considering entering an unlisted contest from another source, there are a few things to be aware of. After obtaining the appropriate entry forms and contest rules, be sure you understand the contest stipulations . . . BEFORE signing your name or sending an entry fee. If a publishing contract is involved as a prize, do not sign away your songwriter's publishing rights. If you do, you're endangering possible future royalties from the song. This is clearly not in the songwriter's best interest. In evaluating any contest, you must weigh what you stand to gain against what you are giving up. If the entry fee is exorbitant, be particularly wary. And if you must give up any of your rights as a songwriter (copyright, publishing), it's almost always a good idea to stay away.

Contests listed in this section encompass all types of music at all levels of competition. Read each listing carefully and contact the sponsoring organization if the contest interests you. And, once again, when you receive the contest information, read the rules carefully and be sure you understand them before entering.

*AMERICAN MUSICAL THEATRE FESTIVAL/NATIONAL CONTEST FOR NEW AMERICAN MUSICALS, % California Music Theatre, #400M, 2500 E. Colorado Blvd., Pasadena CA 91107. (818)792-0776. President: Mikel Pippr. For songwriters, composers and musical playwrights. Annual award.
Purpose: The National Contest for New American Musicals is designed to give creators of new musicals a forum for further creative work and exposure to musical theatre professionals.
Requirements: Entries must be full length, previously unproduced musicals with commercial potential. Deadline: December 30. Send for application. Samples of work required with application. Initial submissions must include 2 songs, 2 scenes and a synopsis with application and a $15 fee.
Awards: The winning entrant receives a $2,000 grand prize and a possible workshop or production. Award is good for the year. Applications are judged by a panel from the New York-based National Music Theatre Network and Dramaturgs.

ARTISTS' FELLOWSHIPS, New York Foundation for the Arts, Suite 600, Beekman St., New York NY 10038. (212)233-3900. For composers. Annual award. Estab. 1985.
Purpose: "Artists' Fellowships are $7,000 grants awarded by the New York Foundation for the Arts to individual originating artists. The Foundation is committed to supporting artists from all over New York State at all stages of their professional careers. Fellows may use the grant according to their own needs; it should not be confused with project support."

Requirements: Must be 18 years of age or older; resident in New York State for 2 years prior to application; and cannot be enrolled in any graduate or undergraduate degree program. Deadline: October 18, 1991. Samples of work are required with application. 1 or 2 original compositions on separate audiotapes and at least 2 copies of corresponding scores or fully harmonized lead sheets.
Awards: All Artists' Fellowships awards are for $7,000. Payment of $6,500 upon verification of NY State residency, and remainder upon completion of a mutually agreed upon public service activity. Nonrenewable. "Fellowships are awarded on the basis of the quality of work submitted and the evolving professional accomplishments of the applicant. Applications are reviewed by a panel of 5 composers representing the aesthetic, ethnic, sexual and geographic diversity within New York State. The panelists change each year and review all allowable material submitted."

BALTIMORE OPERA COMPETITION FOR AMERICAN OPERATIC ARTISTS, 101 W. Read St., Baltimore MD 21201. (301)727-0592. Competition Coordinator: James Harp. For performing artists. Annual award.
Purpose: "Prizes are awarded to talented operatic artists in order to further their development in the study of languages, voice and acting."
Requirements: Singers must be between the ages of 20 and 35, inclusive, and must be citizens of the United States. They must present two letters of recommendation from recognized musical authorities." Deadline: May 18. Send for application. Singers must audition in person.
Awards: 1st Prize: $10,000; 2nd Prize $8,000; 3rd Prize $5,000; Steber Award $2,500; Puccini Award $2,000; Janowski Award $1,000; Collinge Memorial Award $1,000; $150 stipends to all semifinalists. Prize may be renewed upon audition. Singers are judged by a panel of internationally recognized judges eminent in the field of opera.
Tips: "The purpose of the competition is to encourage young operatic talent on the verge of a career. Singers must demonstrate potential in singing, fluency in languages and histrionic capability."

THE BUNTING INSTITUTE OF RADCLIFFE COLLEGE FELLOWSHIP PROGRAM, 34 Concord Ave., Cambridge MA 02138. (617)495-8212. Contact: Fellowship Coordinator. For songwriters, composers, performing artists and musical playwrights, among others. Annual award. Estab. 1960.
Purpose: Fellowship program is designed to support women who wish to pursue independent study in the creative arts and performing arts, as well as other scholarly fields.
Requirements: Ph.D. or equivalent professional experience. Deadline: October 1. Send for application. Samples of work required with application. "Send 1 or 2 samples of recent compositions or performances on a single cassette tape; supply written scores when appropriate."
Awards: The Bunting Fellowship Program: $20,500 for a one-year appointment. Applications are judged "on the significance and quality of the project proposal and on the difference the fellowship might make in the applicant's career."

BUSH ARTIST FELLOWSHIPS, E-900 First National Bank Bldg., 332 Minnesota St., St. Paul MN 55101. (612)227-5222. Director, Bush Artist Fellowships: Sally Dixon. Estab. 1976. For composers, playwrights, screenwriters, visual artists, writers and choreographers. Annual award. Applications in music composition, scriptwork (including playwriting & screenwriting), film, video, multi-media, performance art and choreography are accepted in alternate years.
Purpose: "To provide uninterrupted time (6-18 months) for artist to pursue their creative development—do their own work."
Requirements: Applicant must be a Minnesota, North Dakota or South Dakota or western Wisconsin resident for 12 of preceeding 36 months, 25 years or older, not a student. Deadline: October-November. Send for application. Samples of work on cassette required with application. "Music composition applications will not be taken again until the fall of 1992. Applications will be taken in the fall of 1991 in the following areas: fiction, creative non-fiction, poetry, choreography, film, video, multimedia, performance art, painting, photography, drawing, printmaking, artists books and sculpture."
Awards: Bush Artist Fellowships: $26,000 stipend and $7,000 additional for production and travel. Award is good for 6-18 months. "5 years after completion of preceeding fellowship, one may apply again." Applications are judged by peer review panels.

CINTAS FELLOWSHIP, I.I.E 809 UN Plaza, New York NY 10017. (212)984-5564. Program Officer: Vanessa Palmer. For songwriters, composers and musical playwrights. Annual award. Estab. 1964.
Purpose: "Fellowships awarded to persons of Cuban citizenship or lineage for achievement in music composition (architecture, painting, sculpture, printmaking, photography and literature); students wishing to pursue academic programs are not eligible, nor are performing artists. Applicants must be creative artists of Cuban descent who have completed their academic and technical training." Deadline: March 1. Send for application. Samples of work required with application. "Send complete score and a cassette tape. Compositions submitted must be serious classical works. Popular songs and ballads will not be accepted."

Awards: Cintas Fellowship: $10,000 per grantee. Fellowship is good for 12 months. Applicant may apply no more than twice. Selection committee reviews applications.

COLUMBIA ENTERTAINMENT COMPANY'S NATIONAL CHILDREN'S PLAYWRITING CONTEST, 309 Parkade Blvd., Columbia MO 65202. (314)874-5628. Chairperson, CEC Contest: Betsy Phillips. For musical playwrights. Annual award.
Purpose: "We are looking for top-notch scripts for theater school use, to challenge and expand the talents of our students, ages 10-15. We want good plays with large casts (20-30 characters) suitable for use with our theater school students. Full production of the winning script will be done by the students. A portion of travel expenses, room and board offered to winner for production of show."
Requirements: "Must be large cast plays, original story lines and cannot have been previously published. Please write for complete rules." Deadline: June 30. Send for application; then send scripts to address above. Full-length play, neatly typed. No name on title page, but name, address and name of play on a 3×5″ index card. Cassette tape of musical numbers required."
Awards: $250 first prize and partial travel expenses to see play produced. Second place winner gets no prize money but receives production of the play by the theater school plus partial travel expenses. This is a one-time cash award, given after any revisions required are completed. "The judging committee is taken from members of Columbia Entertainment Company's Executive and Advisory boards. At least eight members, with at least three readings of all entries, and winning entries being read by entire committee. We are looking for plays that will work with our theater school students."
Tips: "Remember the play we are looking for will be performed by 10-15 year old students with normal talents—difficult vocal ranges, a lot of expert dancing and so forth will eliminate the play. We especially like plays that deal with current day problems and concerns. However, if the play is good enough, any suitable subject matter is fine. It should be fun for the audience to watch."

COMPOSERS GUILD, 40 N. 100 W., Box 586, Farmington UT 84025. (801)451-2275. President: Ruth Gatrell. For composers and songwriters. "We are a nonprofit organization working to help the composer/songwriter. Each year we sponsor classes, workshops, seminars, showcases/concerts, and a composition contest, with winning numbers eligible for performance in Composers Guild Spectacular." Estab. 1963.
Requirements: "Annual dues of $25 entitles members to reduced entry fee for contest ($5 members, $15 non-members), and classes, seminars, activities, critiques, musical showcases, and the opportunity to associate with other composers and learn from them." Annual composition contest deadline: August 31. Send for application. Scores and/or cassettes for entry are acceptable.
Awards: $1,900 distributed among 8 categories: keyboard, popular, choral, vocal solo, arrangements, instrumental, jazz and children's music. The best-of-the-show (can be from any music category) is awarded $500. "Applicants judged by professional, usually head of university music department or firmly established producer of performed music."
Tips: "Be as professional as possible—clear, neat manuscript. Have music taped on cassette. Sloppy manuscripts will not be accepted by Composers Guild. Do not send only copy of score or tape."

DELIUS COMPOSITION CONTEST, Jacksonville University, Jacksonville FL 32211. (904)744-3950, Ext. 3370. Chairman: William McNeiland. For composers. Annual award.
Requirements: Send for application.
Awards: First Prize: $500. Three Best-of-Category Prizes: $100 each.

DIVERSE VISIONS REGIONAL GRANTS PROGRAM, Intermedia Arts, 425 Ontario SE, Minneapolis MN 55414. (612)627-4444. Director of Artist Programs: Al Kosters. For composers, performing artists and artists in all disciplines and genres. Annual award.
Purpose: "Intermedia Arts encourages artists to investigate diverse issues/concerns in their work while challenging traditional, conventional and widely accepted contemporary approaches when creating, producing and presenting that work. *Diverse Visions,* formerly the Grants Program for Interdisciplinary Artists, is a regional grants program administered by Intermedia Arts which was developed to respond to those artists who attempting to explore new definitions of, or the boundaries between cultures, art disciplines and/or traditions in their work."
Requirements: Grants are available to artists working individually or collaboratively for personally-conceived productions. Only noncommercial projects over which the applicant has creative control and responsibility will be considered. Applicants must be a resident of Iowa, Kansas, Minnesota, Nebraska, North Dakota, South Dakota or Wisconsin, and must have physically resided in one of these states for at least 12 of the 24 months preceding the application deadline, and intend to remain a resident in that state during the grant period. Students who will be attending school full-time during the grant period are not eligible. Projects associated with degree programs will not be considered. Deadline: Spring, 1992 (TBA). Send for application. Applications received by the deadline are reviewed by staff for eligibility and completeness. Late or incomplete applications will not be considered.

To apply, all written materials must by typed. Do not reduce the size, staple or bind application materials. Do not submit additional pages and/or support materials that are not listed as required or optional. Place your name in the top righthand corner of each page of submitted material. The application form, a one-page projected description, a current resume and work samples. All applications must be submitted on appropriate grant form. Write *Diverse Visions* for more information.

Awards: 2 year period from date of award. "Extensions granted—but no additional money available."
Tips: "Submit quality work samples (of previous work) and be certain to respond with *all* that is required."

*ECKHARDT-GRAMATTÉ NATIONAL MUSIC COMPETITION FOR THE PERFORMANCE OF CANADIAN MUSIC, Queen Elizabeth II Music Bldg., Room 2-11, 270 - 18th St., Brandon Manitoba R7A 6A9 **Canada**. (204)728-8212. Administrative Officer: Mrs. Debbie Bjornsson. For performing artists. Annual competition alternating each year between voice, piano, and strings.
Purpose: To encourage young musicians to perform the works of modern (especially but not exclusively Canadian) composers.
Requirements: Must be citizens of Canada or resident in Canada for 2 years, under 30 years for piano and strings, and under 35 for voice. Deadline: October. Send for application. Samples are not required.
Awards: 1st Prize: $2,500 and national recital tour. 2nd Prize: $1,500. 3rd Prize: $1,000. Best performance of imposed piece: $500. Preliminaries: Tape recordings are forwarded to jurors to mark. The tapes are numbered, not named. Semi-finalists: Attend competition in May where 4 jurors listen and compare. Finalists: Same as semi-finals.

*ENTERTAINMENT SERVICES, INC. ANNUAL SONGWRITER'S CONTEST, 27 Music Square East, Nashville TN 37203. (615)244-7171. Contact: Hannah Onassis. For songwriters of country music. Annual award. Deadline for entry is May 1st.
Requirements: Submit 1 country song in demo form on cassette with lyric sheet per entry. A song is defined as words and music. Contestant may submit more than one song but each song entry must be accompanied by entry fee. Writer must be affiliated with BMI as a songwriter or be willing to join BMI if his/her song is the winning entry. Song must be an unpublished work and a song that has not received radio air play before or during contest. Contestant must enclose a SASE with entry for acknowledgement of entry. Entry fee is $15 per entry. Entries will be judged on lyric , tune and commercial value by Entertainment Services staff to determine 10 finalists. ("Please, no uncopyrighted material for your protection"). The 10 finalists' demos will be copied as well as the lyric sheet and will be judged for 2nd and 1st runner's up and the winner by notable Nashville producers, publishers and other Nashville music industry professionals.
Awards: Winner will receive $100 cash award; the winning entry will be published by a Nashville, BMI publishing company and will be actively pitched to major recording artists through their various contact personnel at major label recording studios throughout the Nashville Music Row area; a trophy for display and certificate for framing to commemorate the winning; an 11″ × 14″ photo of songwriter will be displayed at the Entertainment Services, Inc. booth at the forthcoming Fan Fair, also stating the writer's name and title of winning song.

FORT BEND SONGWRITERS ASSOC. SONGWRITING AND LYRIC WRITING CONTEST, P.O. Box 117, Richmond TX 77469. Executive Director: Terry Miller. For songwriters and lyricists; "amateurs only." Annual award.
Purpose: Objective is to promote the growth of songwriting by providing an arena of competition for amateur writers and lyricists.
Requirements: Applicants must be of amateur status, must not have ever received royalties from ASCAP, BMI or SESAC, and must not have ever been or currently be signed to a *national* record label. Deadline: April 30. Send for application. Samples of work required with application. "One song on a cassette with neatly printed or typed copy of the lyrics. Label lyric sheet and tape with name of song, songwriter, address and phone number. Cue tape before sending."
Awards: Songwriting category: Grand prize is $100 plus recording time and/or merchandise from sponsor as made available. Judged by impartial personnel from the music industry.
Tips: "Read 'The Craft of Lyric Writing' by Sheila Davis and 'The Craft and Business of Songwriting' by John Braheny, and have your songs critiqued by other writers and performers. While simple demo tapes are allowed, studio demos will probably get the most attention and have the best chance of winning. Each year the FBSA will try to have publishers, agents and record company people act as judges in our contest. This contest may be your foot in the door to a new career. Therefore, be honest with yourself. Send only your *best* material. Don't accept the opinion of friends and relatives, try to

participate in some songwriters group that will give you a valid critique of your entry before you enter."

FULBRIGHT SCHOLAR PROGRAM, COUNCIL FOR INTERNATIONAL EXCHANGE OF SCHOLARS, Suite 5M, 3007 Tilden Dr., NW, Washington DC 20008-3009. (202)686-7877. Estab. 1946. Director, Academic & University Liaison: Steven A. Blodgett. For songwriters, composers, performing artists, musical playwrights and scholars/artists in all disciplines. Annual award in composition.
Requirements: "U.S. citizenship at time of application; M.F.A., Ph.D. or equivalent professional qualifications; for lecturing awards, university teaching experience." Application materials for the competition become available in March each year, for grants to be taken up 1½ years later. Application deadlines: June 15 – Australia, USSR, Latin America, except lecturing awards to Mexico, Venezuela, and the Caribbean. August 15 – Africa, Asia, Western Europe, East Europe, the Middle East and lecturing awards to Mexico, Venezuela, and the Caribbean. Send for application. Samples of work are required with application. Applicant should refer to checklist in application packet.
Awards: "Benefits vary by country, but generally include round-trip travel for the grantee and for most full academic-year awards, one dependent; stipend in U.S. dollars and/or local currency; in many countries, tuition allowance for school age children; and book and baggage allowance. Grant duration ranges from 2 months-1 academic year. Applications undergo a two-stage peer review by CIES advisory committees; first by subject matter specialists and then by an interdisciplinary group of geographic area specialists. After nomination, applications are sent to the J. William Fulbright Scholarship Board and the host countries for final review."
Tips: "The Applicant's Handbook, which is included in the application packet, provides suggestions on preparing a competitive application, as well as in-depth information about the review committee structure, etc."

HARVEY GAUL COMPOSITION CONTEST, The Pittsburgh New Music Ensemble, Inc., Duquesne University School of Music, Pittsburgh PA 15282. (412)261-0554. Conductor/Executive Director: David Stock/Eva Tumiel-Kozak. For composers. Biennial.
Purpose: Objective is to encourage composition of new music. Winning piece to be premiered by the PNME.
Requirements: "Must be unpublished and unperformed compositions – new works scored for 6 to 16 instruments drawn from the following: flute, oboe, 2 clarinets, bassoon, horn, trumpet, trombone, tuba, 2 violins, cello, bass, 2 percussion, piano, harp, electronic tape." Deadline: April 30. Send for application. Samples of work are required with application. "Real name must not appear on score – must be signed with a 'nom de plume'." Entry fee: $10.
Awards: Harvey Gaul Composition Contest: $1,500.

HEMPHILL-WELLS SORANTIN YOUNG ARTIST AWARD, P.O. Box 5922, San Angelo TX 76902. (915)658-5877. For performing artists. Annual award. Estab. 1959.
Purpose: "There are 3 divisions of competition: Vocal, Instrumental and Piano. All candidates will be judged by the highest artistic standards, in regard to technical proficiency, musicianship, rhythm, selection of repertoire and stage presence. Objective: to further the career of the young artist."
Requirements: Piano/instrumental: not reached their 28th birthday by competition. Vocal: not reached their 31st birthday by competition. All contestants will perform all repertoire from memory. Deadline: October 25. Send for application. Judged on performance contest weekend.
Awards: A winner and runner-up will be declared in each division. The division winner will receive a cash award of $500; the runner-up will receive $250. An overall winner will be selected to appear with the San Angelo Symphony Orchestra on February 1, 1992, and will receive an additional $1,500 cash award. $500 to be paid at time of selection and $1,000 on February 1, 1992. Title held as winner of that year. Printed on all future information. Contest held every year. Can only win once. No limit on number of times you may enter. This is a competition for the young artist; highest priority will be placed on artistry, communication and stage presence.

*HENRICO THEATRE COMPANY ONE-ACT PLAYWRITING COMPETITION, P.O. Box 27032, Richmond VA 23273. (804)672-5100. Cultural Arts Coordinator: J. Larkin Brown. For musical playwrights. Annual award.

Market conditions are constantly changing! If you're still using this book and it is 1993 or later, buy the newest edition of Songwriter's Market at your favorite bookstore or order directly from Writer's Digest Books.

Purpose: Original one-act musicals for a community theater organization.
Requirements: "Only one-act plays or musicals will be considered. The manuscript should be a one-act original (not an adaptation), unpublished, and unproduced, free of royalty and copyright restrictions. Scripts with smaller casts and simpler sets may be given preference. Controversial themes should be avoided. Standard play script form should be used. All plays will be judged anonymously, therefore, there should be two title pages; the first must contain the plays title and the author's complete address and telephone number. The second title page must contain only the play's title. The playwright must submit two excellent quality copies. Receipt of all scripts will be acknowledged by mail. Scripts will be returned if a stamped, self-addressed envelope is included. No scripts will be returned after the winner is announced. The HTC does not assume responsibility for loss, damage or return of scripts. All reasonable care will be taken." Deadline September 15. Send for application first.
Awards: 1st prize $250.

INTERMOUNTAIN SONGWRITING COMPETITION, P.O. Box 71325, Salt Lake City UT 84107. (801)292-1609 or (801)964-1227. Contest Directors: C. Boone-Smith and Jerri Ashurst. Estab. 1987. For songwriters. Annual award by Utah Songwriters Association.
Purpose: First place winner receives an all-expense paid trip to Nashville, Tennessee to attend Nashville Songwriters Association International Spring Symposium in March or to the LASS Expo in Los Angeles in October.
Requirements: All amateur songwriters may enter. Deadline: December 31. Send for application to enter. Send cassette tape and lyric sheet. SASE. "Or by phone—leave return address on answering machine." Entry fee: $10 for first song, $5 each additional song.
Awards: First prize is a trip to Nashville, approximate value of $750.
Tips: "Submit a well-written song on a quality demo tape. Studio demos are not required but they usually get the most attention. Lyric sheets should be typed or legibly hand written. Noisy cassettes should be avoided. Radio deejays are among the judges, so they listen for commerciality. We look for songs that say something important,and songs with a good hook."

*INTERNATIONAL SOCIETY OF DRAMATISTS, Box 1310, Miami FL 33153. (305)531-1530. Estab. 1987. President: Andrew Delaplaine. For composers, musical playwrights and librettists.
Purpose: To "reward excellence in the area of musical theater writing."
Adriatic Award: "Scripts may be unproduced or produced previously, but only *one* previous professional production is permitted. Staged readings, workshops, etc., are not counted against an entry." Deadline: November 1. Applicants should submit script with cassette tape of songs. $250 award granted annually.
Lincoln Memorial One-Act Contest: Open to "unproduced one-act music theater work in any style, musical, opera, etc." Deadline: January 15. Applicants should submit script with cassette tape of songs. $50 award granted annually.
Perkins Playwriting Contest: Open to "unproduced musical or music theater work, full-length, any style or subject." Deadline: December 6. Applicants should submit script with cassette tape of songs. $100 award granted annually.
Senior Award: Applicant "must be currently enrolled in college or university (graduate or undergraduate)." Open to "musical theater work in any style, any length, and any dramatic medium." Deadline: May 1. Applicants should submit script with cassette tape of songs. $100 award granted annually.
Tips: "Always be sure to have the best quality recording possible. Include as much information as possible about the piece. Send a synopses and resume."

KENNEDY CENTER FRIEDHEIM AWARDS, Kennedy Center for the Performing Arts, Washington DC 20566. (202)416-8062. Estab. 1978. For American composers. Annual award. For symphonic instrumental compositions in even-numbered years; for instrumental compositions for 1-13 instruments (chamber music) in odd-numbered years.
Purpose: Annual award for new music by an American. "Our goal is to bring high level public recognition and honor to contemporary American composers."
Requirements: Requirements for application: American citizenship or permanent residency status; composition must have had American premiere performance within 2 year period, July 1-June 30 in year of composition. May not include voices unless used as an instrument-must be without words. Deadline: July 15th. Send or call for application. 3 tapes and 1 score with application plus $20 fee.
Awards: 1st prize: $5,000; 2nd prize: $2,500; 3rd prize: $1,000; 4th prize: $500. Applications are judged by a 3-person jury: 1) each receives copy of taped performance; 2) jury gathers to listen collectively to all compositions and examine score. They then nominate 10 semi-finalists; 3) jury members individually study scores (of 10) with tape; 4) these works are performed for final ranking. Prizes awarded at the conclusion of performance. This year's concert date: November 10 at 3 p.m. in the Terrace Theater of the Kennedy Center. Admission is free to the public, but tickets are required.

Tips: "Get a top quality recording by a fine chamber group if possible."

KATE NEAL KINLEY MEMORIAL FELLOWSHIP, College of Fine & Applied Arts, 110 Architecture Bldg., 608 E. Lorado Taft Dr., Champaign IL 61820. (217)333-1661. Contact: Dean—College of Fine & Applied Arts. For graduates of College of Fine & Applied Arts of the U of I or to graduates of similar institutions of equal educational standing whose major studies have been in art, architecture or music. Annual award.
Purpose: "Award $6,500 is to be used toward defraying the expenses of advanced study of the Fine Arts in America or abroad."
Requirements: "Submit an application with purpose, 3 letters of reference, copies of transcripts and examples of work." Deadline: March 15. Send for application or call. "Slides, musical compositions, tapes, films, essays or publications which the applicant wishes to exhibit as evidence of artistic ability or attainment are required. Applicants in musical performance may audition in person."
Awards: Judged by "high attainment in the applicant's major field of study as witnessed by academic marks and quality of work submitted or performed; high attainment in related cultural fields as witnessed by academic marks; the character, merit and suitability of the program proposed by the applicant; excellence of personality, seriousness of purpose and good moral character. Also preference will be given to applicants who have not reached their twenty-fifth birthday." "You need a Bachelors in Fine Arts, Architecture or Music. Also, 3 substantiating letters from competent scholars under whom the candidate may have studied and who are capable of speaking of the candidate's fitness must be mailed separately to the committee."

MARIMOLIN COMPOSITION CONTEST, 44 Lorraine St., Roslindale MA 02131. (617)325-6477. For composers. Annual award.
Purpose: To encourage the creation of works for the combination of marimba and violin, or violin and marimba with tape accompaniment.
Requirements: Open to all composers. $20 entry fee. Deadline: July 1. Send for application. A completed new work for violin and marimba. 2 scores, or 1 score and parts. "Winners announced by August 1. Prize of $600 awarded to up to 3 composers."
Awards: "Up to 3 winners will be selected. A total of $600 will be awarded at the judges discretion. The winning work(s) will be premiered during the following season. Works are judged anonymously by Marimolin, and the opinion of a reputable composer is sought in the final selection."

MID-SOUTH PLAYWRIGHTS CONTEST, 51 S. Cooper, Memphis TN 38104. (901)725-0776. Executive Director: Jackie Nichols. For musical playwrights. Annual award. Estab. 1983.
Requirements: Send script, tape, SASE. "Playwrights from the South will be given preference." Open to full-length, unproduced plays. Musicals must be fully arranged for the piano when received. Deadline: April 1.
Awards: Grants may be renewed. Applications judged by 3 readers.

MIXED BLOOD VERSUS AMERICA PLAYWRITING CONTEST, 1501 S. 4th St., Minneapolis MN 55454. (612)338-0937. Script Czar: Dave Kunz. For musical playwrights. Annual award. Estab. 1983.
Purpose: To encourage emerging playwrights (musical playwrights).
Requirements: "Send previously unproduced play (musical) resume, cover letter stipulating contest entry." Deadline March 15. Send SASE for copy of contest guidelines. Samples are not required.
Awards: Winner: $2,000 and full-production of winning play/musical. Review/reading by local theater professionals.
Tips: "Professionalism is always a plus. Surprise us."

MONTREAL INTERNATIONAL MUSIC COMPETITION/COUNCOURS INTERNATIONAL DE MUSI-QUE DE MONTRÉAL, Place des Arts, Montréal, Quebec H2X 1Z9 **Canada.** (514)285-4380. FAX: (514)285-4266. General Director: Mme. Monique Marcil, C.M. Estab. 1963.
Purpose: "The Montreal International Music Competition, operating on a 4-year cycle, is devoted to violin, piano and voice. The schedule for the coming years will be as follows: 1992 - piano; 1993 - voice; 1995 - violin (1994 being a recess year). Award estab. 1963.
Requirements: "Musicians in the violin and piano competitions must be 16 to 30 years old; in the voice competition, musicians must be 20 to 35 years old. Rules and regulations are available one year prior to each competition. Artists interested in receiving information write to the Secretary's Office of the Montreal International Music Competition, Place des Arts, 1501 Jeanne-Mance Street, Montréal (Québec) Canada H2X 1Z9." Registration fee: $35 (Canadian). Deadline: February 1, each year.
Awards: 9 prizes totalling $36,900 (Canadian); 2 additional prizes of $700 each; concerts.

MUSEUM IN THE COMMUNITY COMPOSER'S AWARD FOR STRING QUARTET, P.O. Box 251, Scott Depot WV 25560. (304)757-2509. Contest Administrator: Trish Fisher. For composers. Biennial.

Purpose: The Composer's Competition is to promote the writing of new works for string quartet (2 violins, viola and cello).

Requirements: Work must not have won any previous awards nor have been published, publicly performed or used commercially. Requires 3 copies of the original score, clearly legible and bound. Title to appear at the top of each composition, but the composer's name must not appear. Entry forms must be filled out and a SASE of the proper size enclosed for return of entry. Enclose $25 entry fee (non-refundable). Send for application.

Awards: Museum in the Community Composer's Award First place: $2,500. Up to 3 honorable mentions will be awarded at the discretion of the judges." Jurors will be 3 nationally known musicologists. Winning composer will be awarded $2,500 prize and a premiere concert of the composition by the Montclaire String Quartet at the Teays Valley School for the Arts. Transportation to the premiere from anywhere in the continental United States will be provided by the Museum.

NACUSA YOUNG COMPOSERS' COMPETITION, NACUSA, Box 49652 Barrington Station, Los Angeles CA 90049. (213)541-8213. President, NACUSA: Marshall Bialosky. For NACUSA members 18-30 years of age. Annual award.

Purpose: Goal is "to encourage the writing and performance of new American concert hall music."

Requirements: Must have NACUSA membership and meet age restrictions. Samples are not required. Write for information.

Awards: Judged by a committee of composers.

NATIONAL MUSIC THEATER NETWORK, INC., 3rd Floor, 1360 Broadway, New York NY 10036. (212)382-0984. President: Timothy Jerome.

Purpose: "The objective of the award is to seek out the future creators of musicals/operas for Regional/Broadway development, as well as to focus attention via the award on the materials available today, that otherwise might not be visible. The goal of the incentive grant monies that are part of the award is to encourage a producer to take on the work and bring it to full presentation. A $30 evaluation fee and a completed musical theater or opera work, with book and score is required, as well as a completed submission form, provided by the Network." Send for application. Submit completed works.

Awards: Gala staged readings of the best new musical and opera.

NATIONAL YOUNG ARTIST COMPETITION, Midland-Odessa Symphony & Chorale, Inc., P.O. Box 60658, Midland TX 79711. (915)563-0921. For student musicians under 26 years (30 yrs.—voice) who are not launched on a professional career under management. Annual competition the last Friday and Saturday of January in 1993.

Purpose: To encourage and promote young musicians' careers.

Requirements: Applicant must be a student musician under age 26 studying with music teacher, completed application forms, $25 entry, 5×7 glossy portrait-type photo (for publicity). Application deadline: December 30. Send for application. Samples are not required.

Awards: Lara Hoggard performance medallion. Up to $10,000 distributed among finalists and performing winners. Up to four winners perform with Midland-Odessa Symphony & Chorale, Inc., at regular classical subscription concerts. Contestants are judged by a panel of five judges.

Tips: Categories are for: piano, winds, strings and voice. Includes all categories but voice in secondary division. At least one of performing winners is from secondary division.

NEW FOLK CONCERTS FOR EMERGING SONGWRITERS, Box 1466, Kerrville TX 78029. (512)257-3600. Attn: Kerriville Festivals Office. For songwriters and composers. Annual award.

Purpose: "Our objective is to provide an outlet for unknown songwriters to be heard."

Requirements: Songwriter enters 2 previously unpublished songs on same side of cassette tape—$6 entry fee per tape; more than one tape may be entered; 6-8 minutes total for 2 songs. No written application necessary; no lyric sheets or press material needed. Deadline: April 15th. Call or write for detailed information.

Awards: New Folk Award Winner. 40 writers invited to sing the 2 songs entered during The Kerrville Folk Festival. 6 writers are chosen as award winners. Each of the 6 receives a cash award of $150 and performs at a winner's concert during the Kerrville Folk Festival. Initial round of entries judged by the Festival Producer. 40 semifinalists judged by panel of 3 performer/songwriters.

Tips: "Keep in mind that the quality of the original song is more important than the singer, group or presentation of the song on the entry tape. Persons interested should contact our office for printed information."

NEW MUSIC FOR YOUNG EMSEMBLES, Suite 9E, 12 W. 72nd St., New York NY 10023. (212)601-0085. Executive Director: Clair Rosengarten. For composers. Annual award.

Purpose: "To create a repertory of contemporary chamber music of intermediate difficulty, to make the music of living composers more accessible and to interest a new and ever-increasing advance in the music of today."

Requirements: American citizenship or resident of the US. Deadline: varies; send for application. Samples of work are required with application form. Samples should be copies of the original work.

Award: $750 first prize. Applications are judges by a "panel of professional composers."

*OMAHA SYMPHONY GUILD NEW MUSIC COMPETITION, 310 Aquila Court, Omaha NE 68102. (402)342-3836. Contact: Chairman, New Music Competition. For composers with an annual award. Estab. 1976.

Purpose: "The objective of the competition is to promote new music scored for chamber orchestra."

Requirements: "Follow competition guidelines including orchestration and length of composition." Deadline: usually May 15. Send for application or call (402)342-3836. Each fall new guidelines and application forms are printed. Scores are due by May 15.

Awards: "Monetary award is $2,000. Winner has an optional premiere performance by the Omaha Symphony Chamber Orchestra. Applications are screened by Omaha Symphony music director. Finalists are judged by a national panel of judges."

Tips: "This is an annual competition and each year has a new Symphony Guild chairman; all requests for extra information sent to the Omaha Symphony office will be forwarded. Also, 1,700-1,800 application information brochures are sent to colleges, universities and music publications each Fall."

*OPERA-MUSICAL THEATER PROGRAM, National Endowment for the Arts, 1100 Pennsylvania Ave. NW, Washington DC 20506. (202)682-5447. Estab. 1979. Contact: Program Director or Assistant Director, Opera-Musical Theater Program. For composers, performing artists and/or musical playwrights working with producing organizations, or who are themselves producers. "The Opera-Musical Theater Program assists all forms of music theater generally involving voice, from experimental musical theater to operetta, from ethnic musical theater to classic musical comedy, from grand opera to still-developing forms. Grants are awarded to support professional opera-musical theater organizations that produce works of high artistic quality and of national or regional significance; regional touring; the creation, development, rehearsal, and production of new American works and/or the support of seldom-produced works; independent producers, artist-producers, and artistic associates; projects which contribute significantly to the development and future of the art; and national and regional service organizations."

Requirements: "Eligibility requirements and deadline dates vary from category to category. Applicants should send for application guidelines. Samples of work are required with application. The grant is good up to one-year, then applicants/grantees must reapply. Upon receipt of the Opera-Musical Theater Program Guidelines, applicants must carefully review the sections labeled 'We Fund' and 'We Do Not Fund.' Applicants must then consult the general instructions for application procedures for their category. These instructions list what supporting material is required with the application. Applicants are advised not to send supporting materials separately from the applications. If an applicant has any questions or needs help in completing the application forms or other required materials, they should contact the Opera-Musical Theater Program staff. Late applications are returned. Incomplete applications are not likely to be funded. After the Opera-Musical Theater Program staff has checked the application for completeness, the appropriate Opera-Musical Theater Program Advisory Panel, a rotating committee of experts in the field, reviews them. Following panel review, the National Council on the Arts makes recommendations to the Chairman of the Arts Endowment for final decision."

Awards: Grants are awarded in two categories and may range from $5,000-145,000 for organizations; $5,000-45,000 for individuals as producers.

Tips: "Call a program specialist after carefully reading the Guidelines to determine eligibility."

*PAINTER MUSIC TOP TALENT SEARCH, P.O. Box 111717, Nashville TN 37222-1717. (615)776-5188. President: Richard Allan Painter.

Purpose: To discover and develop outstanding talent for a sustained and successful musical career.

Requirements: Send SASE for free entry forms and information. Entry forms are available during July and August. All entrees are due by the end of September and final results are announced with prizes awarded in October. Samples of work on cassette and lyric sheet (properly labeled) are required for entry with completed entry form and entry fee of $25 with SASE. All inquiries must be by mail with SASE. No phone calls, please. Entering or winning the Painter Music Top Talent Search does not tie up and does not give PMTTS any publishing or promotional rights to your work or material.

Awards: Prizes in 1990 totaled over $7,000. There are 3 top divisions: Top Female Talent, Top Male Talent and Top Group Talent. Judging is done by active music industry professionals.
Tips: "Read and follow the instructions on the entry form. This will help you make your best first impression. The PMTTS exists to help you. When you do things right the first time, you will help others to help you."

PULITZER PRIZE IN MUSIC, 702 Journalism, Columbia University, New York NY 10027. (212)854-3841. Administrator: Robert C. Christopher. For composers and musical playwrights. Annual award.
Requirements: "The piece must have its American premiere between March 15 and March 14 of year it is submitted for consideration." Deadline: March 14. Samples of work are required with application and $20 entry fee. "Send tape and score."
Awards: "1 award: $3,000. Applications are judged first by a nominating jury, then by the Pulitzer Prize Board."

THE QUINTO MAGANINI AWARD IN COMPOSITION, % Norwalk Symphony Society, Inc., P.O. Box 550, Norwalk CT 06852. (203)454-2011. Contact: Dr. Richard Epstein. For composers.
Requirements: The competition is open to all American composers. Entries should be submitted anonymously, with Social Security Number as identity and appropriate return envelope and return postage. In an accompanying sealed envelope, composer should give name, address, social security number, and brief resume. The composition is to be scored for standard symphonic orchestra, and should not exceed 15 minutes in length; no soloists or concerti. Write for more information.
Awards: The recipient will receive a cash award ($2,500) and will have the composition performed in world premiere by the Norwalk Symphony Orchestra under the direction of Jesse Levine, Musical Director, during the 1990-91 season.

RICHARD RODGERS PRODUCTION AWARD, American Academy and Institute of Arts and Letters, 633 W. 155th St., New York NY 10032. (212)368-5900. Assistant to the Executive Director: Betsey Feeley. Estab. 1978. "The Richard Rodgers Production Award subsidizes a production by a nonprofit theater group in New York City of a work by composers and writers who are not already established in the field of musical theater. Development grants for staged readings may be given in lieu of the Production Award or in addition to it. The award is only for musicals—songs by themselves are not eligible. The authors must be citizens or permanent residents of the United States." (Guidelines for this award may be obtained by sending a SASE to above address.)

ROME PRIZE FELLOWSHIP, 41 East 65th St., New York NY 10021. (212)517-4200. Contact: Fellowships Coordinator. For composers. Annual award.
Purpose: "A center for artistic creation and for independent study and advanced research in the humanities, the academy provides living and working space for artists and scholars atthe Academy's ten-building, eleven-acre campus in Rome."
Requirements: "U.S. citizens only may apply. B.A. required in field of musical composition." Deadline: Nov. 15. Send or call for application. Samples of work are required with application. Tapes and scores.
Awards: "Rome Prize Fellowships—2 available in musical composition: $7,000 stipend, $500 European travel, $800 travel allowance, room, board, studio. One year in Rome. Judged by independent juries of professionals in the field."
Tips: "Write a good proposal explaining why a year in Rome would be invaluable to your development as a composer. Explain what you would do in Rome."

LOIS AND RICHARD ROSENTHAL NEW PLAY PRIZE, % Cincinnati Playhouse, P.O. Box 6537, Cincinnati OH 45206. (513)421-5440. Contact: Literary Manager. Annual award.
Purpose: The Rosenthal Prize was established to encourage the production of new work in the theater and to give playwrights the opportunity to see their work through all stages of production.
Requirements: A work of any style or scale constituting a full evening of theater, musicals, collaborations or adaptations. Must not have received a full-scale professional production and must be unpublished at time of submission. Deadline: Jan. 15, 1992. Samples of work are required with application. Format should be complete, neatly typed, securely bound script.
Awards: Lois and Richard Rosenthal New Play Prize—$1,500 stipend, residency expenses and appropriate royalties. The prize is awarded by May; production of the show in winter or spring of following season. Each submission is read and evaluated by a member of the Playhouse Literary staff; finalists are judged by Artistic Director.
Tips: "Follow submission guidelines carefully, make sure script is securely bound. Works of timely interest and a theatrical nature are encouraged. Works with previous readings or workshop productions are helpful. No submissions accepted before October 15, 1991."

SANTA FE SYMPHONY COMMISSIONING PROGRAM, P.O. Box 9692, Santa Fe NM 87504-9692. (505)983-3530. General Manager: Lynn Case. For composers. Annual award.
Purpose: Work to be commissioned for premiere during season either for orchestra chorus or chamber music or any combination of above. Submit scores and/or tapes of other classically-oriented works for chamber, chorus and/or orchestra.
Requirements: Submit resume, other scores and tapes. "Send legible scores and cassette tapes."
Awards: Judged by panel of composers/musicians, including Music Director.

SONGWRITERS ASSOCIATION OF WASHINGTON MID-ATLANTIC SONG CONTEST, Suite 632, 1377 K St. NW, Washington DC 20005. (301)654-3434. Contact: Director. Estab. 1982. Gives awards to songwriters and/or composers annually. "Contest is designed to afford *amateurs* the opportunity of receiving awards/exposure/feedback of critical nature in an environment of peer competition. Applicants must send for application; rules and regulations explained—amateur status is most important requirement. Samples of work are required with application: cassette, entry form and 3 copies of lyrics.
Awards: "Awards usually include free recording time, merchandise (for category winner) and cash and air fare (for grand prize winner). Awards vary from year to year." Awards must be used within one calendar year. "Applications are judged by a panel of 3 judges per category, for 4 levels, to determine top winners in each category and to arrive at the grand prize winner. Reduced entry fees are offered for SAW members. Membership also entitles one to a newsletter and reduced rates for special events/seminars."

THE JULIUS STULBERG AUDITIONS, INC., P.O. Box 107, Kalamazoo MI 49005. (616)375-2808. Business Manager: Mrs. Zoe Forsleff. For performing artists. Annual award.
Purpose: "To encourage continued excellence in musical education and accomplishment for young string players studying violin, viola, cello and string bass."
Requirements: Must be 19 year of age of younger. There is a $30 application fee. Deadline: 1/11/92. Send for application. Prefers cassette tape, not to exceed 10 minutes in length. "Music on tape must be from standard concerton repertoire, and accompanied."
Awards: 1st place: $3,000 and solo performance with Kalamazoo Junior Symphony; 2nd place: $1,500 and recital performance with Fontana Concert Society; 3rd place: $1,000.
Tips: The cassette tapes are screened by a local panel of judges, from which 12 finalists are selected to compete in live competition. An outstanding panel of three judges are engaged to choose the winners. The 1990 judges were Sir Yehudi Menuhin, Maestro Catherine Comet and internationally-known violist, Csaba Erdelyi. The 1991 live competition will be February 29, 1992.

TALENT SEARCH AMERICA, 273 Chippewa Dr., Columbia SC 29210-6508. For songwriters, composers, poets and lyricists. Awards given quarterly.
Purpose: "To discover and award new songwriters and lyricists." Deadlines are February 1, May 2, August 3, and November 4. Send SASE for entry forms and information. Samples of work on cassette and lyric sheet are required for entry *with entry form*. "All inquiries must be by mail. No phone calls, please. Many entrants have gained contracts and other interests with many music and creative writing companies. Winners lists are sent to winners only. Talent Search America is co-sponsored by selected companies in the music and creative writing businesses. Talent Search America is a national nonprofit contest partnership. Entrant information will not be returned or disclosed without written permission from winning entrants. Proper postage must be sent to gain entry forms. Entrants from around the world are welcome. All inquiries must include *firstclass postage* for *each entry form* desired. Non-published/unpublished lyrics and music accepted."
Awards: 6 awards given every quarter: 3 for songwriters, 3 for lyricists (cash awards and award certificates). Entries are judged on creativity, commercial appeal and originality.

MARVIN TAYLOR PLAYWRITING AWARD, P.O. Box 3030, Sonora CA 95370. (209)532-3120. Estab. 1980. For musical playwrights.
Purpose: To encourage new voices in American theater.
Requirements: Mail script with SASE. "We accept phone calls or written inquiry." No application form or fee. Submissions must be full-length, typewritten. SASE if manuscript is to be returned. Prefers cassette to written score with original submissions. No more than 2 prior productions of script. Deadline: May 15.
Awards: Marvin Taylor Playwriting Award: $500 and full staging. Applications are judged by a committee of the theater's artistic staff.

***THE TEN-MINUTE MUSICALS PROJECT**, P.O. Box 461194, West Hollywood CA 90046. (213)656-8751. Producer: Michael Koppy. For songwriters, composers, musical playwrights. Annual award.
Purpose: "We are building a full-length stage musical comprised of complete short musicals, each of which play for between 8-14 minutes. Award is $250 for each work chosen for development towards inclusion in the project, plus a share of royalties when produced."

Requirements: Deadline: October 1st, annually. Send for application or call (213)656-8751. Application should be accompanied by a script, cassette and lead sheets.

Awards: $250 for each work selected. "Works should have complete stories, with a definite beginning, middle and end."

SIGVALD THOMPSON COMPOSITION AWARD COMPETITION, Fargo-Moorhead Symphony Orchestra, P.O. Box 1753, Fargo ND 58107-1753. (218)233-8397. Executive Director: Mark D. Madson. For "American citizens." Biennial award.

Purpose: "To select an orchestral composition by an American composer to be premiered by the Fargo-Moorhead Symphony. The objective of this award is to stimulate and encourage the writing and performance of works by American composers."

Requirements: "Manuscript must be of medium length. Only manuscripts written or completed during the past 2 years and which have not been performed publicly will be considered. Scoring should be for standard symphonic or chamber orchestra instrumentation and should not include soloist." Deadline:September 30, of even-numbered years. Send manuscript with composer's name, address, telephone number and date of composition on cover sheet. Samples are not required.

Awards: Sigvald Thompson Composition Award Competition-one award of $2,500 will be made, plus the premiere performance of the winning entry by the Fargo-Moorhead Symphony Orchestra. "Compositions will be screened by a local panel, and the finalists will be submitted to national judges for review and recommendation."

Tips: "Only manuscripts written or completed during the past 2 years and which have not been performed publicly will be considered. Date of composition must be included on cover sheet."

VOCAL SONGWRITER'S CONTEST, P.O. Box 34606, Richmond VA 23234. (804)733-5908 and (804)541-3333. President: Robert (Cham) Laughlin. For songwriters and composers. Annual award.

Purpose: "To recognize good songs and lyrics as well as the writers of same."

Requirements: "Original songs, lyrics, compositions only." Deadline: March 31. Send for application. Samples of work are required with application. "Send cassette tape for songs; lyrics should be typed or neatly printed."

Award: Grand prize $100. 1st, 2nd and 3rd place entries in each category receive certificates.

Tips: "Prepare your song correctly for entry into the contest."

WYOMING COUNTRY MUSIC FOUNDATION ANNUAL SONGWRITING CONTEST, 1645 Sussex Road, Kaycee WY 82639. (307)738-2303 or 836-2939. Estab. 1983. Executive and Promotional Director: Helen Ullery or Floyd Haynes. For songwriters, composers and performers. Annual award.

Purpose: "To promote and encourage upcoming talent both in songwriting and the performing arts."

Requirements: Applicants can be from any geographical area. Deadline: April 15. Send for application (include SASE). Samples are not required. Annual membership fee: $25; entry fee per song: $10. For gospel song entries and information, contact Helen D. Ullery, Sussex Rt., Kaycee, WY 82639; for country songs and information, contact Floyd Haynes, P.O. Box 132, Guensey, WY 82214.

Awards: "Top 10 country and Top 5 gospel songs are sent to Nashville for review; 50% of entry fees go back to the top winners. Contestants cannot have been in the top 50 in national charts in the last 10 years."

*YOUNG COMPOSERS AWARDS, % NGCSA, Suite 32, 40 North Van Brunt St., Box 8018, Englewood NJ 07631. (201)871-3337. Executive Director: Lolita Mayadas. For songwriters, composers, those who submit works that are vocal, instrumental, operatic, or for dance or lyric stage. Open to students age 13-18. Annual award.

Purpose: "To encourage young students to write music, so that the art of composition—with no restrictions as to the category of music in which the works are written—will once again occupy the place in the center of music education where it belongs. It takes tons of ore to extract one ounce of gold: by focusing on the inventiveness of many students, the Awards may lead to the discovery of genuine creative talents—that is the eventual goal."

Requirements: "Applicants must be enrolled in a public or private secondary school, in a recognized musical institution, or be engaged in the private study of music with an established teacher. No compositions will be considered without certification by the applicant's teacher. Each applicant may submit only one work. Deadline: April 1. Send for application. Samples of work are required with application. Four photocopies of the work must by submitted and, if available, a cassette recording. All manuscripts must be in legible form and may be submitted on usual score paper or reduced under a generally accepted process. The composer's name must not appear on the composition submitted. The composition must be marked with a pseudonym on the manuscript as well as on the optional accompanying cassette recording."

Awards: Herbert Zipper Prizes: First Prize, $1,000; Second Prize, $750; Third Prize, $500; Fourth Prize, $250. "Announcement of the Awards are made no later than May 15 each year. In the event that no entry is found to be worthy of the $1,000 Prize, the jury may award one or both of the other Prizes or none at all. NGCSA appoints an independent jury to review all entries submitted. The jury consists of not less than three qualified judges."
Tips: "Paramount would be neatness and legibility of the manuscript submitted. The application must be complete in all respects."

YWCA STUDIO CLUB COMPETITION, 610 Lexington Ave., New York NY 10022. (212)735-9763. Auditions Coordinator: Mrs. Cora Ette Brown Caldwell. For young opera singers age 17-35. Annual award.
Purpose: First prize $1,500; second prize $1,000, awarded to the winner from the final competition.
Requirements: Write or call for application; "you must sing opera, one song must be in English, one aria or an art song. We have auditions from September through March. The annual competition is always in May.

*ANNA ZORNIO MEMORIAL CHILDREN'S THEATER PLAYWRITING AWARD, Dept. of Theater and Dance, Univ. of NH, Durham NH 03824-3538. Annual award.
Purpose: Playwriting contest for new plays and musicals, with an award of up to $250 to a winning playwright(s), and a guaranteed production by the UNH Theater For Youth Program. The Award will be administered by the Directors of the UNH Theater Resources For Youth Program. This faculty will reserve the right to withhold the Award if, in their opinion, no plays merit the Award. Production of the prize-winning script will be scheduled by the UNH Theater Resources for Youth Program during the 1991-92 academic year.
Requirements: The contest is open to all playwrights in the United States and Canada. The contest is for new plays, with a maximum length of 60 minutes, suitable for young audiences. Plays submitted must not have been: previously published; previously produced by a professional Equity company; a previously produced winner of an award or prize in another playwriting contest; and must not be under contract for publication before UNH's announcement of the award winner. Playwrights may submit more than one play, but not more than three. Deadline: May 1. Send for rules of entry for a complete list of requirements.
Awards: Anna Zornio Award-$250 and production of the play/musicals.

Publications of Interest

Staying in touch with the music industry is imperative for your success—in both a creative and business sense. There is a publication aimed at just about every type of musician, songwriter and music fan. These publications can enlighten and excite you and provide information essential to helping you become a more well-rounded, educated and, ultimately, a satisfied and successful songwriter.

Books

For a complete list of Writer's Digest music titles, turn to the back of this book.

HOW TO OPEN DOORS IN THE MUSIC INDUSTRY—THE INDEPENDENT WAY, by Frank Fara/Patty Parker. Autumn Gold Publishing; distributed by Starfield Press, Suite 114, 10603 N. Hayden Rd., Scottsdale AZ 85260. 110 pages. $8.95; $10 mail order. Ground rules for successful songwriting."

THE MUSIC BUSINESS HANDBOOK, by Jojo St. Mitchell. Amethyst Press, 273 Chippewa Dr. Columbia SC 29210-6508. $16.95 paperback. "A brief overview of the music business for the new-comer with over 100 contacts in the music business."

MUSIC DIRECTORY CANADA '90, Edited by Richard Allen and Andy Charron. CM Books, 3284 Yonge St., Toronto, Ontario M4N 3M7 **Canada.** (416)485-1049. FAX: (416)485-8924. 700 pages. $26.95. Over 3,000 listings of record companies, music publishers and recording studios.

SOME STRAIGHT TALK ABOUT THE MUSIC BUSINESS, 2nd edition, by Mona Coxson. 3284 Yonge St., Toronto, Ontario M4N 3M7 **Canada.** (416)485-1049. FAX: (416)485-8924. 207 pages. $19.95. "The book's 16 chapters show the musician how to reach goals and avoid pitfalls."

SONGWRITERS CREATIVE MATRIX, by Carl E. Bolte, Jr. Holly Productions, 800 Greenway Terrace, Kansas City MO 64113. (816)444-8884. 25-page workbook. $11.50. A unique matrix/guideline for composers/lyricists including examples, instructions and 25 blank forms.

THE SONGWRITER'S DEMO MANUAL AND SUCCESS GUIDE, by George Williams. Box 935, Dayton, Nevada 89403. (702)246-5409. Music Business Books. 200 pages. $12.95. A practical guide to selling songs and landing a record contract.

THE SONGWRITER'S GUIDE TO CHORDS AND PROGRESSIONS, by Joseph R. Lilore. Lionhead Publishing, Box 1272, Dept. WD, Clifton NJ 07012. 80-page method/instruction book. $10.95.

SUCCESSFUL SONGWRITING, by Carl E. Bolte, Jr. Holly Productions, 800 Greenway Terrace, Kansas City MO 64113. 206 pages. $11.50 paperback.

SUCCESSFUL SONGWRITING AND MARKETING, by Glenn Ray and David Leary. Greater Songs Publications, P.O. Box 38, Toowong, Brisbane, QLD **Australia** 4066. (011)61-7-870-7078. FAX: (011)617-870-5127. 220 pages. US $24.95 hardback. "Covers all aspects of songwriting."

Periodicals

ASCAP IN ACTION, published by ASCAP—American Society of Composers, Authors & Publishers, One Lincoln Plaza, New York NY 10023. (212)621-6322. Quarterly (semi-annual) magazine; 44 pages. Features news about ASCAP members, events sponsored by the Society and articles on songwriters.

AWC NEWS/FORUM, American Women Composers, Inc., Suite 409, 1690 36th St. NW, Washington, DC 20007. (202)342-8179. Semi-annual; 20 pages. Subscription $13.50. Contains articles of interest to women, notices of performances of women composers and composition competition info.

BUZZ MAGAZINE, P.O. Box 3111, Albany NY 12203. (518)489-0658. Monthly; 32 pages; Subscription price: $6 for 6 issues. Music magazine. College radio focus.

CANADIAN MUSICIAN, 3284 Yonge St., Toronto, Ontario M4N 3M7 **Canada**. (416)485-8284. Published 6 times per year; 70 pages; $19/year. "We provide musicians and music makers with in-depth, inside information that they can put to use in furthering their musical endeavors."

CLOSE UP MAGAZINE, Country Music Association, One Music Circle South, Nashville TN 37203. (615)244-2840. Monthly; 28-32 pages. Subscription $12. Tips for songwriters on what kind of materials country music industry professionals want.

COUNTRY MUSIC MAGAZINE, Silver Eagle Publishers, Suite 1, 329 Riverside Ave., Westport CT 06880. (203)222-5800. Bi-monthly; 72 pages. Subscription price: $13.98. Focuses on current performers, their professional and personal lives and the industry which sustains them.

COUNTRY MUSIC NEWS, (97594 Canada Ltd.), Box 7323, Vanier Term., Ottawa ON K1L 8E4 **Canada**. (613)745-6006. FAX: (613)745-0576. Monthly; 36 pages (tabloid size). Subscription price: $20 (Canada), $32 (US). Covers the country music scene in Canada as well as many extra columns on bluegrass, gospel, fiddle and 50's music.

GAVIN REPORT, 140 Second St., San Francisco CA 94105. (415)495-1990. Weekly; 60 pages. Subscription price: $250/year. Music/radio trade journal/; includes research of airplay on 1,200 radio stations, intelligent artist interviews and other related articles.

INDIE BULLET, Country Music Magazine, P.O. Box 7468, San Antonio TX 78207. (512)736-1804. Subscription price: $80/year bulk or $100/year for 1st class. Features a top 50 independent label chart.

LIVING BLUES, Center for the Study of Southern Culture, University of Mississippi, University MS 38677. (601)232-5574. Bimonthly; 64 pages. Subscription price: $18/year. "Everything you want to know about America's musical legacy to the world—the blues."

THE MAGIC OF SONGWRITING, BI-MONTHLY, 5832 S. 2000 W., Roy UT 84067. (801)825-9637. Bi-monthly; 4-6 pages. Subscription price: $11.98 yearly. "For the beginner. Written to inspire creativity."

MUSIC BUSINESS DIRECTORY, P.O. Box 120675, Nashville TN 37212. (615)255-1068. Bi-annual; 96 pages. Subscription price: $13.95. "A Complete Guide To The Nashville Music Industry."

THE MUSIC REVIEW, 46 Robin Rd., Poughkeepsie NY 12601. General Manager: Rick Carbone. Bi-monthly; 10-30 pages. $15/year. Reviews country and gospel singles by independent artists.

MUSIC ROW MAGAZINE, Published by Music Row Publications, Inc. 1231 17th Ave. S., Nashville TN 37212. (615)321-3617. Published 23 times a year; 28 pages. Price: $50/year. Nashville tip sheet.

PROBE AND CANADIAN COMPOSER, Society of Composers, Authors and Music Publishers of Canada (SOCAN), 41 Valleybrook Dr., Don Mills, Ontario M3B 2S6 **Canada**. (416)445-8700. Published through the SOCAN public relations department.

SONG PLACEMENT GUIDE, 4376 Stewart Ave., Los Angeles CA 90066-6134. (213)285-3661. Monthly newsletter; 2 pages; $6 introductory, $65/year. Los Angeles tipsheet for music publishers/songwriters.

SOUND CHOICE MAGAZINE, Audio Evolution Network, P.O. Box 1251, Ojai CA 93023. (805)646-6814. Quarterly; 96 pages. Subscription price: $10/year. Sample copy $3 ppd. "We review more than 800 independently produced and marketed recordings per issue."

WASHINGTON INTERNATIONAL ARTS LETTER, Allied Business Consultants, Inc., P.O. Box 12010, Des Moines IA 50312. (515)255-5577. Magazine published 10 times/year; 6-8 pages. Concentrates on discovering sources of funding for the arts. Songwriters and composers can get grants for their work through our information."

Glossary

A&R Director. Record company executive in charge of the Artists and Repertoire Department who is responsible for finding and developing new artists and matching songs with artists.

A/C. Adult contemporary music.

ACM. Academy of Country Music.

Advance. Money paid to the songwriter or recording artist before regular royalty payment begins. Sometimes called "up front" money, advances are deducted from royalties.

AFM. American Federation of Musicians. A union for musicians and arrangers.

AFTRA. American Federation of Television and Radio Artists. A union for performers.

AIMP. Association of Independent Music Publishers.

Air play. The radio broadcast of a recording.

AOR. Album-Oriented Rock. A radio format which primarily plays selections from rock albums as opposed to hit singles.

Arrangement. An adaptation of a composition for a performance or recording, with consideration for the melody, harmony, instrumentation, tempo, style, etc.

ASCAP. American Society of Composers, Authors and Publishers. A performing rights organization.

A-side. The side of a single which is considered to have "hit" potential and is promoted as such by the record company.

Assignment. Transfer of rights of a song from writer to publisher.

Audiovisual. Refers to presentations which use audio backup for visual material.

Bed. Prerecorded music used as background material in commercials.

Beta. ½″ videocassette format. The Beta System uses a smaller cassette than that used with the VHS system.

BMA. Black Music Association.

BMI. Broadcast Music, Inc. A performing rights organization.

B-side. The flip side of a single promoted by a record company. Sometimes the B-side contains the same song as the A-side so there will be no confusion as to which song should receive airplay.

Booking agent. Person who solicits work and schedules performances for entertainers.

Business manager. Person who handles the financial aspects of artistic careers.

b/w. Backed with. Usually refers to the B-side of a single.

C&W. Country and western.

CARAS. Canadian Academy of Recording Arts and Sciences. An association of individuals involved in the Canadian music and recording industry.

Catalog. The collected songs of one writer, or all songs handled by one publisher.

CD. Compact Disc (see below).

Chart. The written arrangement of a song.

Charts. The weekly trade magazines' lists of the best selling records.

CHR. Comtemporary Hit Radio. Top 40 pop music.

CIRPA. Canadian Independent Record Producers Association.

CMA. Country Music Association.

CMPA. Church Music Publishers Association.

CMRRA. Canadian Musical Reproduction Rights Association. A mechanical rights agency.

Collaborator. Person who works with another in a creative endeavor.

Compact disc. A small disc (about 4.7 inches in diameter) holding digitally encoded music that is read by a laser beam in a CD player.

Co-publish. Two or more parties own publishing rights to the same song.

Copyright. The exclusive legal right giving the creator of a work the power to control the publishing, reproduction and selling of the work.

Cover record. A new version of a previously recorded song.

CRIA. Canadian Recording Industry Association.

Crossover. A song that becomes popular in two or more musical categories (i.e. country and pop).

Cut. Any finished recording; a selection from an LP. Also to record.

DAT. Digital Audio Tape. A professional and consumer audio cassette format for recording and playing back digitally-encoded material. DAT cassettes are approximately one-third smaller than conventional audio cassettes.

Demo. A recording of a song submitted as a demonstration of writer's or artist's skills.

Distributor. Marketing agent responsible for getting records from manufacturers to retailers.

Donut. A jingle with singing at the beginning and end and instrumental background in the middle. Ad copy is recorded over the middle section.

Engineer. A specially trained individual who operates all recording studio equipment.

EP. Extended play record (usually 12″) containing more selections than a standard single, but fewer than a standard LP.

Evergreen. Any song that remains popular year after year.

Exploit. To seek legitimate uses of a song for income.

Folio. A softcover collection of printed music prepared for sale.

GMA. Gospel Music Association.

Harry Fox Agency. Organization that collects mechanical royalties.

Hip-hop. A dance oriented musical style derived from a combination of disco, rap and R&B.

Hit. A song or record that achieves top 40 status.

Hook. A memorable "catch" phrase or melody line which is repeated in a song.

IMU. International Musicians Union.

Indie. An independent record label.

ips. Inches per second; a speed designation for tape recording.

IRC. International reply coupon, necessary for the return of materials sent out of the country. Available at most post offices.

Jingle. Usually a short verse set to music designed as a commercial message.

Label. Record company, or the "brand" name of the records it produces.

LASS. Los Angeles Songwriters Showcase.

Lead sheet. Written version (melody, chord symbols and lyric) of a song.

Leader. Plastic (non-recordable) tape at the beginning and between songs for ease in selection.

LP. Designation for long-playing record played at 33⅓ rpm.

Lyric sheet. A typed or written copy of a song's lyrics.

Market. A potential song or music buyer; also a demographic division of the record-buying public.

Master. Edited and mixed tape used in the production of records; a very high-quality recording; the best or original copy of a recording from which copies are made.

Maxi-single. The cassette equivalent of a 12″ single. Also called Maxi-cassettes or Maxi-plays. (See 12″ Single.)

Mechanical right. The right to profit from the physical reproduction of a song.

Mechanical royalty. Money earned from record, tape and CD sales.

MIDI. Musical instrument digital interface. Universal standard interface which allows musical instruments to communicate with each other and computers.

Mix. To blend a multi-track recording into the desired balance of sound.

MOR. Middle of the road. Easy-listening popular music.

Ms. Manuscript.

Music jobber. A wholesale distributor of printed music.

Music publisher. A company that evaluates songs for commercial potential, finds artists to record them, finds other uses (such as TV or film) for the songs, collects income generated by the songs and protects copyrights from infringement.

NAIRD. National Association of Independent Record Distributors.

NARAS. National Academy of Recording Arts and Sciences.

NARM. National Association of Record Merchandisers.

NAS. National Academy of Songwriters, formerly Songwriters Resources and Services (SRS).

Needle-drop. Use of a prerecorded cut from a stock music house in an audiovisual soundtrack.

NMPA. National Music Publishers Association.

NSAI. Nashville Songwriters Association International.

One-off. A deal between songwriter and publisher which includes only one song or project at a time. No future involvement is implicated. Many times a single song contract accompanies a one-off deal.

One-stop. A wholesale distributor of records (and sometimes videocassettes, blank tapes and record accessories), representing several manufacturers to record stores, retailers and jukebox operators.

Overdub. To record an additional part (vocal or instrumental) onto a basic multi-track recording. To sweeten.

Payola. Dishonest payment to broadcasters in exchange for airplay.

Performing rights. A specific right granted by US copyright law that protects a composition from being publicly performed without the owner's permission.

Performing rights organization. An organization that collects income from the public performance of songs written by its members and then proportionally distributes this income to the individual copyright holder based on the number of performances of each song.

Personal manager. A person who represents artists, in numerous and varying ways, to develop and enhance their careers. Personal managers may negotiate contracts, hire and dismiss other agencies and personnel relating to the artist's career, screen offers and consult with prospective employers, review possible material, help with artist promotions and perform many services.

Piracy. The unauthorized reproduction and selling of printed or recorded music.

Pitch. To attempt to sell a song by audition; the sales talk.

Playlist. List of songs that a radio station will play.

Plug. A favorable mention, broadcast or performance of a song; to pitch a song.

Points. A negotiable percentage paid to producers and artists for records sold.

Producer. Person who supervises every aspect of recording a song or album.

Product. Records, CDs and tapes available for sale.

Production company. Company that specializes in producing jingle packages for advertising agencies. May also refer to companies that specialize in audiovisual programs.

Professional manager. Member of a music publisher's staff who screens submitted material and tries to get the company's catalog of songs recorded.

Program director. Radio station employee who screens records and develops a playlist of songs that station will broadcast.

PRS. Performing Rights Society of England.

PSA. Public Service Announcement: a free broadcast "advertisement" for a nonprofit service organization.

Public domain. Any composition with an expired, lapsed or invalid copyright.

Publish. To reproduce music in a saleable form and distribute to the public by sale or other transfer of ownership (rent, lease or lending).

Purchase license. Fee paid for music used from a stock music library.

Query. A letter of inquiry to a potential song buyer soliciting his interest.

R&B. Rhythm and blues.

Rack jobber. A wholesaler of records, tapes and accessories to retailers and mass-merchandisers not primarily in the record business (e.g. department stores).

Rate. The percentage of royalty as specified by contract.

Release. Any record issued by a record company.

Residuals. In advertising or television, payments to singers and musicians for subsequent use of a performance.

RIAA. Recording Industry Associations of America.

Royalty. Percentage of money earned from the sale of records or use of a song.

RPM. Revolutions per minute. Refers to phonograph turntable speed.

SAE. Self-addressed envelope (with no postage attached).

SASE. Self-addressed stamped envelope.

Self-contained. A band or recording act that writes all their own material.

SESAC. A performing rights organization.

SFX. Sound effects.

Shop. To pitch songs to a number of companies or publishers.

Single. 45 rpm record with only one song per side. A 12″ single refers to a long version of one song on a 12″ disc, usually used for dance music.

SOCAN. Society of Composers, Authors and Music Publishers of Canada. A performing rights organization formed in 1990 by the merger of CAPAC and PROCAN.

Solicited. Songs or materials that have been requested.

Song plugger. A songwriter representative whose main responsibility is promoting uncut songs to music publishers, record companies, artists and producers.

Song shark. Person who deals with songwriters deceptively for his own profit.

The Songwriters Guild of America. Organization for songwriters, formerly called AGAC.

Soundtrack. The audio, including music and narration, of a film, videotape or audiovisual program.

Split publishing. To divide publishing rights between two or more publishers.

Standard. A song popular year after year; an evergreen.

Statutory royalty rate. The maximum payment for mechanical rights guaranteed by law that a record company may pay the songwriter and his publisher for each record or tape sold.

Subpublishing. Certain rights granted by a US publisher to a foreign publisher in exchange for promoting the US catalog in his territory.

Synchronization. Technique of timing a musical soundtrack to action on film or video.

Synchronization rights. Rights to use a composition in film or video.

Take. Either an attempt to record a vocal or instrumental part, or an acceptable recording of a performance.

Top 40. The first forty songs on the pop music charts at any given time. Also refers to a style of music which emulates that heard on the current top 40.

Track. Divisions of a recording tape (e.g., 24-track tape) that can be individually recorded in the studio, then mixed into a finished master.

Trades. Publications that cover the music industry.

12″ Single. A twelve inch record containing one or more remixes of a song, originally intended for dance club play.

U/C. Urban contemporary music.

Unsolicited. Songs or materials that were not requested and are not expected.

VHS. ½″ videocassette format. The VHS system uses a larger cassette than that used with the Beta system.

Work. To pitch or shop a song.

Index

Can't find a listing? Check the end of each market section for the '91-'92 Changes lists. These lists include any market listings from the 1991 edition which were either not verified or deleted in this edition.

Can't find a listing? Check the end of each market section for the '91-'92 Changes lists. These lists include any market listings from the 1991 edition which were either not verified or deleted in this edition.

Can't find a listing? Check the end of each market section for the '91-'92 Changes lists. These lists include any market listings from the 1991 edition which were either not verified or deleted in this edition.

Can't find a listing? Check the end of each market section for the '91-'92 Changes lists. These lists include any market listings from the 1991 edition which were either not verified or deleted in this edition.

Can't find a listing? Check the end of each market section for the '91-'92 Changes lists. These lists include any market listings from the 1991 edition which were either not verified or deleted in this edition.

Can't find a listing? Check the end of each market section for the '91-'92 Changes lists. These lists include any market listings from the 1991 edition which were either not verified or deleted in this edition.

Can't find a listing? Check the end of each market section for the '91-'92 Changes lists. These lists include any market listings from the 1991 edition which were either not verified or deleted in this edition.

Can't find a listing? Check the end of each market section for the '91-'92 Changes lists. These lists include any market listings from the 1991 edition which were either not verified or deleted in this edition.

OTHER BOOKS TO HELP YOU MAKE
MONEY AND THE MOST OF
YOUR MUSIC TALENT

The Songwriter's & Musician's Guide to Nashville, by Sherry Bond 208 pages/$18.95, paperback

Songwriters on Songwriting, edited by Paul Zollo 208 pages/$17.95, paperback

The Songwriter's Workshop, edited by Harvey Rachlin 96 pages + 2 cassettes/$24.95, paperback

Singing for a Living, by Marta Woodhull 160 pages/$18.95, paper

Jingles: How to Write, Produce, & Sell Commercial Music, by Al Stone 144 pages/$18.95, paperback

Music Publishing: A Songwriter's Guide, by Randy Poe 144 pages/$18.95, paperback

Making Money Making Music (No Matter Where You Live), by James Dearing 192 pages/ $17.95, paperback

Beginning Songwriter's Answer Book, by Paul Zollo 128 pages/$16.95, paperback

Playing for Pay: How To Be A Working Musician, by James Gibson 160 pages/$17.95, paperback

You Can Write Great Lyrics, by Pamela Phillips Oland 192 pages/$8.99, paperback

Protecting Your Songs & Yourself, by Kent J. Klavens 112 pages/$7.99, paperback

Gigging: The Musician's Underground Touring Directory, by Michael Dorf & Robert Appel 224 pages/$3.99, paperback

The Craft & Business of Songwriting, by John Braheny 322 pages/$19.95, hardcover

The Craft of Lyric Writing, by Sheila Davis 350 pages/$19.95, hardcover

Successful Lyric Writing: A Step-by-Step Course & Workbook, by Sheila Davis 292 pages/ $18.95, paperback

Getting Noticed: A Musician's Guide to Publicity & Self-Promotion, by James Gibson 240 pages/$12.95, paperback

The Songwriter's Guide to Making Great Demos, by Harvey Rachlin 192 pages/$12.95, paperback

Writing Music for Hit Songs, by Jai Josefs 256 pages/$8.99, hardcover

Making It in the New Music Business, (Revised & Updated!) by James Riordan 384 pages/ $22.95

The Songwriter's Guide to Collaboration, by Walter Carter 178 pages/$5.25, paperback

How to Pitch & Promote Your Songs, by Fred Koller 144 pages/$5.25, paperback

88 Songwriting Wrongs and How to Right Them, by Pat and Pete Luboff 144 pages/paperback (available in February, 1992)

A complete catalog of all Writer's Digest Books is available FREE by writing to the address shown below. To order books directly from the publisher, include $3.00 postage and handling for one book, $1.00 for each additional book. Ohio residents add 5½% sales tax. Allow 30 days for delivery.

Writer's Digest Books
1507 Dana Avenue
Cincinnati, Ohio 45207

Credit card orders call TOLL-FREE
1-800-289-0963

Prices subject to change without notice